Caldera OpenLinux

David Skoll

SAMS

Unleashed

Caldera OpenLinux Unleashed

Copyright ©2000 by Sams Publishing

All rights reserved. No part of this book shall be reproduced, stored in a retrieval system, or transmitted by any means, electronic, mechanical, photocopying, recording, or otherwise, without written permission from the publisher. No patent liability is assumed with respect to the use of the information contained herein. Although every precaution has been taken in the preparation of this book, the publisher and author assume no responsibility for errors or omissions. Neither is any liability assumed for damages resulting from the use of the information contained herein.

International Standard Book Number: 0-672-31761-3

Library of Congress Catalog Card Number: 99-64106

Printed in the United States of America

First Printing: December 1999

01   00   99   4   3   2   1

Trademarks

All terms mentioned in this book that are known to be trademarks or service marks have been appropriately capitalized. Sams Publishing cannot attest to the accuracy of this information. Use of a term in this book should not be regarded as affecting the validity of any trademark or service mark.

Warning and Disclaimer

Every effort has been made to make this book as complete and as accurate as possible, but no warranty or fitness is implied. The information provided is on an "as is" basis. The authors and the publisher shall have neither liability nor responsibility to any person or entity with respect to any loss or damages arising from the information contained in this book or from the use of the CD or programs accompanying it.

ASSOCIATE PUBLISHER
Michael Stephens

EXECUTIVE EDITOR
Don Roche

DEVELOPMENT EDITOR
Jim O'Shea

MANAGING EDITOR
Charlotte Clapp

TECHNICAL EDITORS
Gert-Jan Hagenaars
Carl Constantine
Steve Epstien

TEAM COORDINATOR
Pamalee Nelson

MEDIA DEVELOPER
Dan Scherf

INTERIOR DESIGN
Gary Adair

COVER DESIGN
Aren Howell

COPY WRITER
Eric Borgert

PRODUCTION
Lisa England
Dan Harris
Brad Lenser

Contents at a Glance

Introduction 1

Part 1 Essential OpenLinux 5

1 Introduction to Caldera OpenLinux 7
2 Basic Linux Concepts and Commands 23
3 Using the Shell 55
4 Using X Window System 79
5 Exploring KDE 111
6 Using Text Editors 135

Part 2 System Administration 169

7 Software Management with RPM 171
8 Setting Up File Systems 185
9 Printing 209
10 OpenLinux Administration Tools 231
11 Setting Up TCP/IP Networking 267
12 Setting Up DNS—The Domain Name System 293
13 Configuring PPP 307
14 Configuring NIS—The Network Information System 325
15 Configuring NFS—The Network File System 339
16 Configuring SAMBA 349
17 NetWare Integration 367
18 Configuring Apache 395
19 Mail Services 419
20 Internet News 459
21 IP Firewalling and Masquerading 474
22 Running Proxies 507
23 Performing Backup and Restore 529
24 Securing Linux 549

Part 3 Linux Applications 575

- 25 Using Productivity Software 577
- 26 Setting up Database Servers 593
- 27 Using Image Manipulation Tools 615
- 28 Typesetting Documents 649
- 29 Setting up Sound and Multimedia 671

Part 4 Programming, Automation, and Kernel Compilation 707

- 30 Shell and Awk Programming Essentials 709
- 31 Configuring and Building the Kernel 735

Part 5 Development Environment 753

- 32 Perl Essentials 755
- 33 Tcl/Tk Essentials 781
- 34 Python Essentials 807
- 35 C and C++ Essentials 857
- 36 Using GNU Development Tools 899

Part 6 Appendixes 921

- A Useful Unix Commands 923
- B Installing Caldera OpenLinux 965
- C Bibiliography 1001
- D RPM 1005
- Index 1021

Contents

Introduction 1
    Who Is This Book's Intended Audience? 1
    What Do You Need to Know Prior to Reading This Book? 2
    What Will You Learn from This Book? 2
    What Software Will You Need? 2
    How This Book Is Organized 2
    Conventions Used in This Book 4

PART I Essential OpenLinux   5

1 Introduction to Caldera OpenLinux   7
    What Is Linux? 8
        The History of UNIX 8
        The UNIX Philosophy 11
        Linux Distributions 13
    Why Linux? 14
        Free Software 14
        UNIX Compatibility 15
        Reliability and Performance 15
        Support of Open Standards 15
    Linux Features 16
        Complete Memory Protection 16
        Virtual Memory 16
        Full Multiuser Features 16
        Support for Multiprocessing 16
        Best-of-Breed TCP/IP Networking 17
        Interoperability with Windows and Macintosh 17
        Internet Server Software 17
        Top-Notch Development Tools 17
        Modular Kernel 17
    Caldera OpenLinux 18
    Sources of Linux Information 19
        The Linux Documentation Project 19
        Portal Sites 19
        Newsgroups 19
    Hardware Requirements 20
    Going Ahead with Linux 21

2 Basic Linux Concepts and Commands 23

- Logging In and Out 24
  - Logging In 24
  - Logging Out 25
  - Changing Your Password 25
- Why Learn the Command-line Interface? 26
- The Linux File System 26
  - Pathnames 27
  - Changing the Working Directory 27
  - Creating Directories 28
  - Removing Directories 28
  - Listing Directories 29
  - File Permissions 30
  - Symbolic Links 31
  - Mount Points 32
- The Layout of the File System 32
- Shells 35
  - I/O Redirection 36
  - Discarding Output 37
- Basic UNIX Commands 37
  - List Files: `ls` 38
  - Change Directory: `cd` 38
  - Rename or Move a File: `mv` 38
  - Remove Files: `rm` 39
  - Make Directories: `mkdir` 40
  - Remove Directories: `rmdir` 40
  - See the Contents of Files: `cat` 41
  - Page Through a File: `more` 42
- UNIX Manual Pages: `man` 42
  - Parts of a Manual Page 43
  - Manual Sections 43
  - Reading a Manual Page 45
- Virtual Consoles 46
- Typing Shortcuts 47
  - Filename Completion 47
  - Command Editing 48
- Configuration Files 49
  - `bash` Configuration Files 49
  - `tcsh` Configuration Files 50
- Processes 50
  - Listing Processes 50
  - Killing Processes 51

Common Problems 53
    The Terminal Is Frozen 53
    I Type and All I Get Is "?" 53
    The Shell Prompt Changed and the Shell Ignores Me 54
Summary 54

3 Using the Shell 55

bash 56
Shell History 57
    I/O Redirection 60
    Pipes 62
    Background Processes and Job Control 62
    Shell Syntax 63
    Filename Completion 65
    Wildcard Expansions and Path Expansions 66
Shell Variables 68
    bash Configuration Files 70
tcsh 72
    Comparing tcsh and bash 72
    tcsh Command Summary 72
    Command History 73
    tcsh Command Completion 75
    tcsh Variables 76
    tcsh Configuration Files 76
Summary 7

4 Using the X Window System 79

The History of X 80
Essential X Concepts 80
    The Client/Server Nature of X 80
    The Display 81
    Window Managers 82
    The Pointer and the Selection 84
    Events 85
    Focus 85
    Resources 85
Configuring XFree86 88
    Identifying Your Video Hardware 89
    Running XF86Setup 89
    Running xf86config 92
    Editing the Configuration File 93
Colors 97

Fonts 98
    X Logical Font Descriptions 99
    Looking at Fonts 100
    Scalable Fonts 101
Starting X 101
Some X Clients 102
    Standard X Client Options 102
    xterm 103
    xclock 105
    xload 105
    xcalc 106
    xbiff 106
    xman 107
    xeyes 107
    xvidtune 108
    xset 108
Summary 110

5 Exploring KDE   111

The Desktop 113
    The Window Manager 113
    The Panel 116
    The Desktop Menu 120
The KDE File Manager 121
    Selecting Files 122
    Views 122
    The Desktop Directory 123
    URLs 123
    Bookmarks 123
    Mime Types 124
    Drag and Drop 124
The KDE Control Center 124
    Applications 125
    Desktop 126
    Information 127
    Input Devices 127
    Keys 127
    Network 127
    Sound 128
    Windows 128

	Some KDE Applications	128
	The KDE Package Manager	128
	The KDE Task Manager	130
	The KDE Image Viewer	131
	Summary	133
6	**Text Editors 135**	
	vi	136
	A Little History	137
	Editing Modes	138
	Running vi	138
	Saving Files and Quitting vi	140
	Moving Around in a File	142
	Editing the File	149
	XEmacs	155
	Starting XEmacs	157
	Opening and Creating Files	158
	Saving Files and Exiting XEmacs	160
	Closing a File Without Exiting XEmacs	161
	Updating the Buffer When the File Has Changed on Disk	161
	Editing a Buffer	161
	Editing Modes	163
	Working with Multiple Windows	165
	Getting More Information	166
	Summary	166

PART II System Administration 169

7	**Software Management with RPM 171**	
	Installing New Packages	172
	Package and File Dependencies	174
	Package and File Conflicts	176
	Checking for Potential Problems First	177
	Uninstalling Packages	177
	Package and File Dependencies	178
	Checking for Potential Problems First	179
	Upgrading Installed Packages	179
	Getting Information About Packages	180
	Package Selection Options	181
	Information Selection Options	182
	Summary	184

8 Setting Up File Systems 185

- Devices 186
  - Device Names 186
  - Naming Partitions 187
  - The Kernel's View of Device Names 187
- Partitions 188
  - Partition Tables 189
  - Cylinders, Heads, and Sectors..189
  - Creating and Deleting Partitions 190
- File Systems 191
  - Types of File Systems 192
  - Creating a File System 193
- Mounting a File System 193
  - Mounting a File System Manually 194
  - Mounting a File System Automatically..195
- Checking a File System 197
  - Invoking `fsck` 197
- Accounting and Quotas..198
- File Permissions 198
  - Symbolic Permissions 199
  - SUID, SGID, and Sticky Bits 200
  - Numeric Permissions..202
  - The `umask` 203
- File Ownership 204
- Swap Space 204
  - Creating a Swap Partition 205
  - Creating a Swap File 205
  - Formatting a Swap Area 206
  - Enabling a Swap Area 207
  - Disabling a Swap Area 208
- Summary 208

9 Printing 209

- Local Printing from Caldera..210
  - How Does Caldera Locate My Printer? 210
  - Printer Selection (or the Default If Only One Is Available) 211
  - Printing That First Page...211
- Tools and Locations Used in Printing 216
- Understanding the Printing Process 219
- Using COAS to "Administrate" Your Printer 220
- Setting Up and Using a Remote Printer 222
  - Printing That First Page over the Network 224

Contents

Formatted Printing	225
Using Your Printer with Other Applications	226
Useful Print Capability Enhancing Programs (and Where to Find Them)	229
Some Secrets of the Guru (Junior Division)	229
Summary	230

10 OpenLinux Administration Tools 231

File System Organization	232
Essentials of `/bin` and `/sbin`	232
Configuration Files in `/etc`	233
`/home`	235
`/mnt`	235
`/tmp` and `/var`	236
`/usr`	237
Console Administration Tools	238
User Management	238
Programs for User Management	239
Services	241
Task Scheduling	243
Kernel Administration with `/proc`	244
Caldera Open Administration System	247
COAStool	247
The COAS Menu	248
Network Information Service	249
Resolver	250
Peripherals	251
Mouse	252
Printer	253
System	256
Kernel	263
Software	264
Summary	265

11 Setting Up TCP/IP Networking 267

Networking Fundamentals	268
Important Definitions	268
TCP/IP	269
IP Addresses	269
TCP	271
UDP	272
DNS	272
Routing	272

	Network Devices	274
	Network Device Names	274
	Configuring TCP/IP Networking	275
	Configuring an Interface: `ifconfig`	275
	Setting Up Routes	279
	Caldera's Networking Setup	283
	Overall Network Setup	283
	Interface Configuration	284
	Starting and Stopping Networking	285
	Adding Interfaces	285
	Name Service	287
	Resolver Configuration	288
	Useful Diagnostic Programs	288
	`ping`	288
	`traceroute`	289
	DHCP	290
	Setting Up a DHCP Client	290
	Setting Up a DHCP Server	290
	Summary	292
12	**Setting Up DNS—The Domain Name System 293**	
	DNS Fundamentals	294
	Root Servers	294
	Anatomy of a Query	295
	DNS Record Types	296
	DNS Configuration	297
	Options	297
	Zones	298
	DNS Database Files	299
	Master Zone Files	299
	Reverse Lookup Files	302
	Cache Hint Files	303
	Using `nslookup`	304
	Summary	306
13	**Configuring PPP 307**	
	PPP Background	308
	Serial Port Configuration	309
	Serial Hardware	309
	Running `pppd`	310
	Setting Up a Connection with `chat`	312
	IP Configuration Options	314
	PPP Authentication	314

Restoring Files with tar and cpio 539
Compressed Backups...541
Performing Backups with BRU-2000..542
File Selection 544
Backup Definitions 545
Backup Options 545
Running the Backup 546
Scheduling Backup Definitions..546
Restoring Files with BRU-PE 547
Summary 548

24 Securing Linux 549

Computer Security Basics 550
Hackers and Crackers 550
Risk Assessment 551
Physical Security 551
Employee Security 551
Network Security 552
Data Loss 552
The UNIX Security Model 553
The root Account 553
SUID and SGID Programs 553
Device Files 555
Common Attacks 555
Buffer Overrun 555
Network Sniffing 556
Social Engineering 556
Password Guessing 557
Denial of Service Attacks 557
Preventing Attacks 558
Firewalls 558
SUID/SGID Programs 560
Monitoring, Detection, and Logging 560
System Logs 561
Monitoring Files 562
What to Do When Faced with Intrusion 564
Controlling Access to Services 565
TCP Wrappers 565
Access Control 566
Access Control Options 567
Other Programs 567
Keeping Your System Up-to-Date 568

Caldera OpenLinux Unleashed

   Security Tools 569
    nmap 569
    SAINT 569
    Crack 569
    Trinux 569
    Open Security Solutions 570
   Privacy 570
    PGP 570
    Virtual Private Networks 571
   Summary 572

PART III Linux Applications 575

25 Using Productivity Software 577
   Using WordPerfect 578
    Installation 578
    Getting Started 578
    File Management 579
    Formatting Documents 580
    Advanced Features 585
   Using StarOffice 586
    Installation 586
    Getting Started 586
    Components of the Desktop 586
    Customizing Your Workspace 588
    Working with StarOffice 588
    Events 589
   Summary 592

26 MySQL Essentials 593
   What Is MySQL? 594
   Installing MySQL 595
    Getting MySQL 595
    Installing the Files 596
    Testing the Installation 599
   MySQL Administration 600
    Setting the `root` Password 600
    The Privilege System 600
    Setting Up Your First MySQL Privileges 602
    `tables_priv` and `columns_priv` 605
   Managing Databases with MySQL 606
    MySQL Basics 606
    Useful MySQL Features 610
   Summary 613

27 Using Image Manipulation Tools 615

xv 616
   Using the Menus 617
   Loading an Image File..621
   Saving an Image to a File 623
Image Magick 624
   `animate` 624
   `combine` 626
   `convert` 627
   `display` 628
   `identify` 630
   `import` 631
   `mogrify` 633
   `montage` 634
   Finding More Information About Image Magick 636
The GIMP 636
   Running the GIMP for the First Time...............................637
   The Toolbar 639
   Opening an Image File 640
   Creating a New Image..641
   The Pop-up Menus 643
   Saving an Image to a File 643
   Using Script-Fu Scripts 645
   Installing a New Script-Fu Script 646
   Installing a New Plug-In 646
   Finding More Information..646
Summary..647

28 Typesetting Documents 649

Creating a Typeset Document..651
Typesetting Entry Tools 654
   Creating a LaTeX Input File 654
Utilities Used with Typesetting 662
   Viewing Utilities for Use with Typesetting.....................662
   `xdvi` 662
   Converting Utilities for Use with Typesetting.................665
   WEB—Literate Programming...667
   Exporting Utilities for Use with Typesetting 668
Exotica (or Really Fancy Typesetting) 669
   Typesetting Music 669
   Typesetting Plots 669
Summary..670

29 Setting Up Sound and Multimedia 671

- Introduction 672
- Getting Sound 672
- Linux Kernel Sound 673
  - Initial Manual Configuration 676
  - Automatically Loading Modules 676
  - ISA PnP Cards 676
  - The Final PnP Step—Making Your PnP Settings Permanent 679
- OSS—Open Sound System 679
  - OSS Download and Installation 680
  - OSS Configuration Tips and Industry News 681
  - Configuring SoftOSS 682
- ALSA—The Advanced Linux Sound Architecture 683
  - Installing ALSA 684
  - Testing ALSA 685
  - Making ALSA Load on Startup 687
- Audio Data Manipulation and Conversion 687
- Extracting Digital Audio Data 689
  - Technical Details 690
  - cdparanoia 691
- MPEG 1 Layer 3 Encoding 692
  - MP3—Use and Misuse 692
  - MP3 Archiving 693
  - bladeenc 694
- Lossless Audio Encoding Using shorten 695
  - shorten—Where to Get It 695
  - shorten—How to Use It 695
- SoundTracker Modules 697
  - libmikmod 697
  - Testing libmikmod 698
- Introduction to MIDI 700
  - General MIDI System 701
  - MIDI Instruments—FM Versus Wavetable Synthesis 701
- Software MIDI Synthesis 702
  - SoftOSS 703
  - Kmidi 703
  - TiMidity++ 703
  - Installing Patch Files for TiMidity++ and OSS 704
- Where to Go from Here 705

Part IV Programming, Automation, and Kernel Compilation 707

30 Shell and awk Programming 709

Shell Programming with bash 710
bash Variables 711
Environment Variables 712
Shell Scripts 713
Conditional Constructs 714
    The if Statement 714
    The case Statement 715
Looping Constructs 716
    The while and until Statements 717
    The for Statement 719
Built-In Shell Variables and Positional Parameters 719
Functions 720
Going Further with Shell Programming 721
awk Scripting 722
    awk Patterns 722
    Records and Fields 723
Invoking awk 723
    Changing the Field Separator 725
    Assigning Variable Values 725
Built-in awk Variables 725
Arrays 726
awk Expressions 728
Control Statements 729
    The if Statement 730
    The while Statement 730
    The do Statement 730
    The for Statement 730
    The break and continue Statements 731
    The delete Statement 731
    The exit Statement 731
I/O Statements 731
Built-in Functions 732
User-defined Functions 733
Going Further with awk 734
Summary 734

31 Configuring and Building the Kernel 735

Why Rebuild the Kernel? 736
Modules Versus Integrated Drivers 736
Building a Kernel 737

Configuring the Kernel 737
    Code Maturity Level Options 741
    Processor Types and Features 741
    Loadable Module Support 741
    General Setup 742
    Plug and Play Support 742
    Block Devices 742
    Networking Options 743
    SCSI Support 744
    SCSI Low-Level Drivers 744
    Network Device Support 744
    Amateur Radio Support 744
    IrDA Subsystem Support 745
    Infrared Port Device Drivers 745
    ISDN Subsystem 745
    Old CD-ROM Drivers 745
    Character Devices 745
    Mice 746
    Video for Linux 746
    Joystick Support 746
    Ftape 746
    File Systems 746
    Network File Systems 747
    Partition Types 747
    Native Language Support 747
    Console Drivers 747
    Sound 748
    Universal Serial Bus 748
    Kernel Hacking 748
Compiling the Kernel 748
    Make Dependencies 749
    Build the Kernel 749
    Build Modules 749
    Install Modules 749
    Install the Kernel 749
Summary 751

Part V Development Environment 753

32 Perl Programming 755

- A Simple Perl Program 756
- Perl Variables and Data Structures 758
  - Perl Variable Types 758
  - Special Variables 759
- Operators..760
  - Comparison Operators..760
  - Compound Operators..761
  - Arithmetic Operators 761
  - Other Operators 762
  - Special String Constants 763
- Conditional Statements: `if/else` and `unless` 763
  - `if`..764
  - `unless` 765
- Looping...765
  - `for` 766
  - `foreach` 766
  - `while` 767
  - `until` 767
  - `last` and `next` 767
  - `do...while` and `do...until` 767
- Regular Expressions 767
- Access to the Shell 768
- Switches 770
- Modules and CPAN 773
- Code Examples..774
  - Sending Mail 774
  - Purging Logs 775
  - Posting to Usenet..776
  - One-Liners...776
  - Command-Line Processing 778
- Perl-Related Tools..778
- For More Information 778
  - Books...778
  - Usenet 779
  - WWW 779
  - Other 780
- Summary 780

33 Introduction to Tcl/Tk 781

- Quick Example 782
- "Hello, World" in Tk 783
- Tcl Syntax and Concepts 784
  - Variable Substitution 784
  - Command Substitution 785
  - Backslash Substitution 786
  - Quoting 786
  - Comments 787
- Variables 787
  - Arrays 788
- Expressions 789
  - Numbers 789
  - Operators 789
  - Built-in Functions 791
- Lists 791
  - Extracting List Elements 791
  - Creating Lists 791
  - Manipulating Lists 792
  - Lists and Commands 793
- Control Structures 794
  - if 794
  - while 794
  - for 795
  - foreach 795
  - break and continue 796
  - switch 796
  - source 796
  - eval 797
- Procedures 797
  - proc 797
  - Local and Global Variables 798
  - Arguments 798
- Tk 799
  - Widgets 802
- Tcl Extensions 805
- Going Further 805
- Summary 806

34 Introduction to Python 807

- Introduction 808
  - `pullpush` 808
  - Running `pullpush` 808
  - What Is Python? 809
  - Benefits 809
  - Getting Up to Speed 810
- Fundamentals 811
  - Numeric Objects Overview 812
  - String and String Conversion Overview 813
  - Writing Python Scripts 814
- The Power of Python 816
  - List Processing Power 816
  - List Processing Operators 818
- More Sequence Types 818
  - Mutability of Strings 819
  - Mutability of Lists 819
  - The `del` Statement 820
  - The Value `None` 820
  - Sorting Lists 821
  - Tuples 821
- Dictionaries 821
- Comparisons and Looping Constructs 823
  - Comparisons 823
  - Looping Constructs 826
  - Loop Control Statements 828
- Functions and Namespaces 828
  - Function Descriptions 828
  - Return Values 829
  - Introduction to Namespaces 830
  - Namespace Confusion—global to the Rescue 830
- Input and Output 831
  - Input 831
  - Output 833
  - OS Module, Functions, and Methods 833
- Exceptions 835
  - `try...except` 835
  - `try...finally` 836
  - Lots of Exceptions 837
- The Real World: Example Code 837
  - Example: Graphical Directory Listing 837
  - Python Power Tool: Embedded Python 839

Using Embedded Python to Insert a Timestamp into
    HTML Code 843
Object-Oriented Programming 845
    Intro to OOP—How to Not Get Confused 845
    Class Definitions 847
    Special Method Demo—Talkative Objects 848
Standard Modules Overview 849
    `sys` Module 849
    `types` Module 850
    `string` Module 851
    `math` Module 852
    `time` Module 852
    `shutil` Module 854
    `commands` Module...854
Where to Go from Here 855
    `http://www.python.org` 855
    Continuing Education 856
Summary 856

35 Introduction to C and C++ 857

A History of C 858
"Hello, World" in C 859
    Comments 860
    Include a Header 860
    Main Function 861
Data Types 861
Declaring Variables 862
    Variable Scope 863
    Variable Storage Class 863
Statements 866
    Declarations 866
    Definitions 867
    Expression Statements 867
    The `if` Statement 870
    The `switch` Statement 871
    The `while` Statement 871
    The `do` Statement 874
    The `for` Statement 874
    The `return` Statement 875
Functions 876
Arrays, Structures, and Pointers 877
    Arrays 877
    Structures 879
    Pointers 881

The C Preprocessor	885
Include	886
Define	886
Conditional Compilation	887
More C	888
C++	888
Classes	890
Member Functions	892
Main Program	892
Inheritance	892
Virtual Functions	893
Multiple Inheritance	894
Operator and Function Overloading	894
More C++	896
Summary	897

36 Using GNU Development Tools 899

Terminology	900
The GNU C Compiler	901
Invoking gcc	901
gcc Compilation Options	902
gcc Path and Linking Options	903
Compiling C++ Programs	904
GNU Make	904
Makefiles	904
make Variables	907
Implicit Rules	909
Common make Command-Line Options	910
Building Third-Party Packages	911
Going Further with make	912
The GNU Debugger	912
Post-Mortem Debugging	914
Attaching to a Running Process	916
The Data Display Debugger	918
Going Further with ddd	919
Summary	920

PART VI Appendixes 921

A Useful Linux Commands 575

Online Documentation	924
man and apropos	924
info	925
The /usr/doc Hierarchy	927

Managing Files 929
    Copying Files: cp 929
    Finding Files: find 930
    Making Links: ln 936
Examining Files 937
    Identifying a File: file 937
    Looking at Part of a File: head and tail 938
    Comparing Files: cmp and diff 939
Regular Expressions 941
    Atoms 942
    Quantifiers 942
    Concatenation 943
    Alternation 943
    Meta-Characters 943
    Grouping 944
Text Manipulation 944
    Search for Text in a File: grep 944
    Altering Text Streams: sed 946
    Update a File: patch 949
Compressing and Archiving Files 950
    Compressing and Uncompressing Files 950
    Archiving Files: tar 951
Informational Commands 954
    The Name of the Computer 954
    Who Am I? 954
    How Long Since the Last Reboot? 955
    Who Is Logged On? 955
    Free Memory 956
Disk Space 957
    Free Space 957
    Used Space 958
Process Management 959
    Signaling Processes: kill 959
    Monitoring Processes: top 960
Starting and Stopping the System 961
    Shut Down with Warning: shutdown 962
    Halt or Reboot Now 962
    Three-Fingered Salute 962
Miscellaneous Commands 963
    Printing a Calendar 963
    Getting or Setting the System Date 963

B Installing Caldera OpenLinux 965

Introduction 966
Installing Caldera OpenLinux 966
Installing Caldera OpenLinux Using LIZARD 966
    Starting the LIZARD Install Process 967
Installing Caldera OpenLinux Using LISA 973
    Creating Disks for LISA 973
    Using LISA 974
    Configuring Extra Hardware in LISA 975
    The LISA Kernel Module Manager 975
    Partitioning Under LISA 976
    Selecting LISA Install Method 976
    Installing Packages Under LISA 977
    Enabling/Disabling Services in LISA 978
Introduction to Partitions 978
    Primary Partitions 979
    Extended Partitions 979
Getting Up to Speed with Partitions 980
Advanced Partitioning—Solutions for Optimal Performance 983
    Organizing to Reduce Fragmentation 983
    Organizing to Facilitate Backups 983
    Organizing for Performance 983
    Optimizing for Reliability 985
Partitioning Tutorial 1—Moving Home 986
Partitioning Tutorial 2—Using Symlinks 989
Linux Software RAID 990
Implementing Software RAID 992
    Patching the Kernel 993
    Installing RAIDTools 994
Configuring a RAID 0 Volume 994
Configuring a Linear Volume 996
Configuring a RAID 1 Volume 997
Summary 999

C Bibliography 1001

D RPM Listing 1005

Index 1021

About the Lead Author

David F. Skoll is a long-time user of UNIX and free software, and an ardent advocate of Linux, a synthesis of the two. He has designed several large UNIX software projects for use in areas as diverse as integrated circuit design, integrated circuit reverse engineering, image processing and calendar management. David is the founder of Roaring Penguin Software Inc., a Linux consulting company specializing in network setup, network security and application development. He also writes a monthly Linux column and the occasional inflammatory op-ed piece.

About the Contributing Authors

Residing in Albuquerque, New Mexico, **Daniel Robbins** is the Chief Architect of Enoch GNU/Linux, as well as a Stampede GNU/Linux Developer. Daniel has been involved with computers in some fashion since second grade, when he was first exposed to the Logo programming language as well as a potentially dangerous dose of Pac Man. This probably explains why he has since served as a Lead Graphic Artist at SONY Electronic Publishing/Psygnosis, and is currently developing a high-performance multithreaded application server for one of those hot Internet-based startup companies you hear about on the news. When he is not in front of a computer, Daniel enjoys spending time with his wife, Mary, who is expecting a child this spring. Daniel has taken up extreme mountain biking and secretly hopes that it will physically and mentally prepare him for fatherhood.

Carl B. Constantine lives in beautiful Victoria, British Columbia, Canada and works as a technical writer for Metrowerks, makers of the CodeWarrior development environment for Mac OS, Windows, and Linux. When not working, Carl enjoys spending time with his wife, Terry, and three kids (Rebekah - 4, Emily - 2, and Matthew - 2 months), programming, cryptography, computer graphics, chess, and playing Descent 2. Carl is also an active member of his local Linux Users Group (VLUG - Victoria Linux Users Group)

Gert-Jan Hagenaars graduated at the University of Technology Eindhoven the Netherlands in Mathematics. He started looking for alternative operating systems and platforms in 1984 when he wrote his first relational database from scratch in BASIC. In 1991 an upstart Operating System seemed to have some potential at version 0.99 patchlevel 11, and the rest is history. He has taught Linux at an evening course at Algonquin College in Ottawa and he has trained system administrators and programmers wherever he has worked. He has been a senior system administrator of over 80 servers running anything from HP-UX, SunOS and Solaris, BSDI, IRIX, NetBSD, FreeBSD to Linux. Some people say that he has looked after NT servers as well, but that has never been proven. He can generally be found on the OCLUG mailing list where he has a habit of answering unconventional questions with scripts and programs, and everything else with "RTFM" or "buy a book and read it".

Glenda R. Snodgrass is lead consultant and managing partner of The Net Effect, LLC, a consulting firm in Mobile, Alabama. She has spent most of the past four years instructing local area businesses in commercial uses of the Internet, conducting numerous beginner- and intermediate-level seminars and workshops, and consulting with and training employees of local industries on intranet development. Glenda is an avid Linux enthusiast with extensive background in database design and management. She holds a B.A. from the University of South Alabama in Mobile, and a Masters from Universitde Paris I-on-Sorbonne in Paris, France. When not in front of the computer, Glenda can be found on trails across the Southeast, riding endurance on her Arabian gelding Lakota with her Dobie, Bailey, for company.

Mitch Adair has been working with Linux since 1995. He has served as systems and network administrator for various governmental agencies, non-profit organizations, and commercial enterprises, using Linux systems wherever possible and promoting its use. In his current position as network security consultant and software developer for The Net Effect, LLC he gets to use Linux in a variety of ways nearly every day. What little time he's not with his computers, he spends riding his Arabian gelding Embers, cycling, cooking and occasionally playing very bad rugby.

David Schwering is Chairman (Emeritus) of American Communication & Computation, Inc. and is a practitioner of the black arts of computing. He has been practicing in the area of computer systems infrastructure and security since the late '60s. His clients include many US Government Agencies as well as the governments of Jamaica and the Former Soviet Union. He has addressed the American Society for Industrial Security, the Public Relations Society of America, and the Annual Surveillance Conference several times. When not traveling internationally on business he spends time working on Kha0s (The secure Linux kernel) and working on device drivers for both UNIX (AIX, SCO, Solaris) and Linux. While still under 50 and always in blue jeans and a corporate tee shirt he uses his spare time to work as a Director of International Digital Maintenance, Ltd. and as a Director of The Internet Growth Fund (A mutual fund investing in the Internet) - Symbol: FND on the American Stock Exchange. He has been working with Linux for over 6 years and has many articles and publications to his credit. Comments, Criticisms, and Questions related to this book can be addressed to him at calderaunleashed@qhq.com.

Lyle R. Taylor received his Bachelor of Arts degree in Computer Science from Utah State University in Logan, Utah, where he still resides. For the past three years, he has been working as an independent software engineer developing database and graphics applets and applications in Java, C++ and Perl under Linux and Windows. He has been a UNIX and Linux enthusiast since he was first introduced to UNIX on an old DEC machine in the early days of his college career. His joy was full when he later discovered that he could run Linux on his own PC at home and have pretty much everything he liked about the DEC, Sun and Hewlett-Packard workstations at the university (except the expensive software). He now uses Linux as the glue to hold together a home network made up of Macintoshes, Linux and Windows machines and as his primary development platform.

Daniel Solin is a Linux enthusiast from the northern parts of Europe. Ludvika, Sweden to be more precise. He first got in touch with Linux in 1994, and has been a devoted fan ever since. Currently, Daniel is running a Linux consulting business. He has always been interested in software development and has been teaching C/C++ the last six months. When Daniel is not staring at his monitor (and not someone else's either), he likes to spend time with his girlfriend Linda, watch a good movie, play soccer, or tease his dog, Hjalmar (in a very friendly way though). Daniel can be reached at daniel@solin.org.

Dedication

To Norine, Elizabeth and Gillian.

Acknowledgments

I would like to thank the staff at Macmillan Computer Publishing for their professionalism in helping to put together this book. In particular, I would like to thank Don Roche and Jim O'Shea, my editors, for starting the project and keeping it going. I'd also like to thank my technical reviewers, Gert-Jan Hagenaars, Steve Epstien and Carl Constantine, who greatly improved the book, and my co-authors who put in a lot of work to complete the book. Thanks, too, to Gary Lawrence Murphy of TeleDynamics for introducing me to Macmillan. Finally, I'd like to thank my wife, Norine, and daughters, Elizabeth and Gillian, for gracefully accepting the long working hours that writing a book entails.

Tell Us What You Think!

As the reader of this book, *you* are our most important critic and commentator. We value your opinion and want to know what we're doing right, what we could do better, what areas you'd like to see us publish in, and any other words of wisdom you're willing to pass our way.

You can fax, email, or write me directly to let me know what you did or didn't like about this book—as well as what we can do to make our books stronger.

Please note that I cannot help you with technical problems related to the topic of this book, and that due to the high volume of mail I receive, I might not be able to reply to every message.

When you write, please be sure to include this book's title and author as well as your name and phone or fax number. I will carefully review your comments and share them with the author and editors who worked on the book.

Fax: 317-581-4770

Email: mstephens@mcp.com

Mail: Michael Stephens
Associate Publisher
Sams Publishing
201 West 103rd Street
Indianapolis, IN 46290 USA

Introduction

This book is a comprehensive guide to the use and administration of Linux. Although it is tailored to the OpenLinux distribution developed by Caldera Systems, Inc., the vast majority of the material is relevant for any Linux distribution. Quite a lot of information is applicable to UNIX systems in general.

This book covers a lot of ground. Linux is a sophisticated and powerful system, with both a rapid pace of development and a long UNIX heritage. The rapid development ensures that Linux is exciting and at the cutting edge; the UNIX heritage ensures that most of the information in this book will be relevant and accurate for years to come.

Even a book as large as this cannot cover every aspect of Linux in detail. Instead, I explain the basic concepts behind the various topics and flesh out some of the details with descriptions and examples. It is much better to understand the basic concepts and know where to look for details than to be presented with a checklist of point-and-click operations. When things go wrong, you're much better off with a deep understanding of the fundamentals than a hodge-podge of recipes.

However, that approach means many times I refer you to online Linux documentation for details. I urge you to read the excellent online manual and info pages; they are authoritative and exhaustive in their coverage. This book provides you with the background you need to understand and appreciate the online documentation. Install Linux and experiment with it. You can memorize by reading, but you can understand only by doing.

Many graphical tools exist to control various aspects of Linux administration, such as networking setup, domain name service setup and user administration. Although I encourage you to examine and use these tools, I discuss system administration from a traditional UNIX command-line perspective. This gives you a deeper understanding of the issues involved and an appreciation for both the usefulness and limitations of the graphical configuration tools. The initial learning effort is well worth it.

Who Is This Book's Intended Audience?

This book is intended for anyone who wants to set up and administer a Linux system. Whether you are setting up a personal workstation, a multiuser server, or a large farm of Linux Web servers, the fundamentals of Linux and UNIX use and administration remain the same. This book helps you get the most out of your Linux system.

What Do You Need to Know Prior to Reading This Book?

I do not assume you have any UNIX or Linux experience—this book explains UNIX fundamentals even for people who have never seen UNIX before. I do, however, assume that you have some experience with another operating system, such as Windows or Mac OS. Furthermore, I assume that you have a passing knowledge of PC hardware and hardware terminology.

What Will You Learn from This Book?

After reading this book, you will know how to use and administer a Linux system. You will understand fundamental UNIX concepts and know the "UNIX philosophy"—the underlying design principles behind a UNIX system. You will also know how to configure and administer TCP/IP networking and various network services such as electronic mail, news, Web service, file sharing, and so on. Most important, you will know where to look for the nitty-gritty details that are too numerous to be covered directly in this book. Knowing your way around a Linux system is immensely satisfying; this book will make you confident that you can find your way around the system.

What Software Will You Need?

This book assumes that you have installed Caldera OpenLinux, either version 2.2 or 2.3. (Version 2.3 is mostly a bug-fix release; it is very similar to 2.2.) Although you can use other Linux distributions, the locations of files and the software packages included with the distribution might differ slightly from Caldera OpenLinux. If you are new to Linux, it is best to use Caldera OpenLinux so the book accurately reflects your system.

How This Book Is Organized

This book is divided into the following parts:

Part I: The Basics

This part introduces fundamental Linux and UNIX concepts. It covers the history of Linux, basic Linux concepts and commands, the UNIX shell (your main interface to a Linux system), the X Window system, and KDE (OpenLinux's graphical user interface). The final chapter covers text editors—almost every piece of system administration in Linux is accomplished by editing a text file, so you should learn a Linux text editor as early as possible.

The chapters in this book are organized in a logical progression for learning Linux. However, before you proceed to Part II, you should read Appendix A, "Useful UNIX Commands." Appendix A contains much information that will be useful in later parts.

Part II: System Administration

This part teaches you how to perform basic system administration. You will learn how to manage software packages with the RPM package manager, how to set up file systems, and how to set up the printing system. You'll also learn how to manage user accounts, remote logins, and regularly scheduled tasks.

Several chapters describe Linux networking, from the basics of TCP/IP networking through setting up PPP dial-up networking and various network services such as the Network File System, file and print sharing for Windows clients, Web and e-mail configuration, and firewall configuration. You'll also learn the importance of backing up your system, as well as how to perform backups and restores. Finally, the part concludes with a chapter on security, which you must read if you intend to put a Linux server on the Internet.

Part III: Linux Applications

This part covers the many Linux applications available. The first chapter describes productivity suites such as office suites and word processors. The remaining chapters cover database servers, graphics and image-processing tools, typesetting tools, and sound and multimedia applications.

Part IV: Programming, Automation, and Kernel Compilation

Part IV introduces you to shell and awk programming. The shell and awk are tools that can greatly ease the burden of system administration by automating many steps. Scripting is one of the most powerful aspects of UNIX, and these tools can save you many hours of tedium.

Chapter 31, "Configuring and Building the Kernel," describes how to recompile a new Linux kernel. You might want to do this to exclude certain features from the kernel (to save memory) or if a new kernel that fixes important bugs is released.

Part V: Development Environment

Part V describes the many programming and application development tools available on Linux. The first three chapters cover Perl, Tcl/Tk, and Python, three interpreted languages. These languages are excellent for rapid application development, prototyping, and quick scripts to automate tedious tasks. Tcl/Tk enables you to build full-featured graphical programs without worrying about the intricacies of the X Window System.

The last two chapters briefly cover C and C++ development and the GNU compiler tools. If you are familiar with C or C++ programming in other environments, these chapters will teach you how to develop under Linux.

Part VI: Appendixes

Appendix A is a list of useful UNIX commands. You should know them before you attempt to administer a Linux system. Appendix B describes how to install Caldera OpenLinux. Appendix C is an annotated bibliography—you'll soon learn that understanding Linux requires a lot of reading.

Conventions Used in This Book

The following typographic conventions are used in this book:

- Code lines, commands, statements, variables, and any text you type or see onscreen appears in a `mono` typeface. **`Bold mono`** typeface is often used to represent the user's input.
- Placeholders in syntax descriptions appear in an *`italic mono`* typeface. Replace the placeholder with the actual filename, parameter, or whatever element it represents.
- *Italics* highlight technical terms when they're being defined.
- The ➥ icon is used before a line of code that is really a continuation of the preceding line. Sometimes a line of code is too long to fit as a single line on the page. If you see ➥ before a line of code, remember that it's part of the line immediately above it.
- The book also contains Notes, Tips, and Cautions to help you spot important or useful information more quickly. Some of these are helpful shortcuts to help you work more efficiently.

Essential OpenLinux

PART
I

IN THIS PART

1 Introduction to Caldera OpenLinux *7*
2 Basic Linux Concepts and Commands *23*
3 Using the Shell *55*
4 Using X Window System *79*
5 Exploring KDE *111*
6 Text Editors *135*

Introduction to Caldera OpenLinux

CHAPTER 1

IN THIS CHAPTER

- What Is Linux? *8*
- Why Linux? *14*
- Linux Features *16*
- Caldera OpenLinux *18*
- Sources of Linux Information *19*
- Hardware Requirements *20*
- Going Ahead with Linux *21*

What Is Linux?

Linux is a robust UNIX-like network operating system, which has taken the computing community by storm. This book will teach you how to get the most out of your Caldera OpenLinux system. It will also give you enough background to feel confident with any version of Linux and indeed most brands of UNIX.

Before starting the technical discussion, it is worthwhile to review the history of Linux. Linux is part of a strong UNIX tradition that dates back almost 30 years. Much of this rich and colorful history has influenced Linux design decisions, so being aware of it will help you understand the philosophy behind Linux and the approaches taken to implementing various pieces of functionality.

The History of UNIX
Birth

In the late 1960s, AT&T's Bell Telephone Labs was working on a time-sharing computer system known as Multics. Prior to Multics, most computer systems operated in batch mode. Users would submit jobs to a queue and come back the next day to see what had happened. Multics, on the other hand, allowed users to sit in front of terminals and interact with the system. Each user was given a time slice of computing time. This allowed real-time interaction with the computer and a much faster realization and correction of errors.

Multics was a very ambitious project—too ambitious, in fact—and became unmanageable. Although its users appreciated the time-sharing concept, the project was unsustainable.

In 1969, Ken Thomson and Dennis Ritchie began implementing an operating system on a DEC PDP-7. It borrowed some good ideas from Multics but was a much smaller system. In 1970, Brian Kernighan dubbed it "UNIX" as a sarcastic play on the word "Multics." Thus began the operating system we know today, as well as the tradition of word-play in the naming of UNIX commands and functions.

Originally, UNIX (like most operating systems of the day) was written in assembly language (a very low-level language specifying each microprocessor instruction). By 1973, after creating the language B (derived from an earlier language called BCPL), Brian Kernighan and Dennis Ritchie invented a language called C, and the UNIX kernel was rewritten in C. (The *kernel* is the core of an operating system; it controls memory allocation, process scheduling, resource management, and hardware drivers.) Writing an operating system in a high-level language was a major innovation and a huge contributor to the proliferation of UNIX—a system written in C is orders of magnitudes easier to port to new architectures than one written in assembly language.

Adolescence

In 1973, Thomson and Ritchie presented a paper on UNIX at the Symposium for Operating System Principles, and interest in the system was phenomenal. At the time, AT&T was under antitrust investigation and was barred from entering the computer market. However, AT&T lawyers approved the release of UNIX to universities under the conditions that there would be no promotion, no guaranteed bug fixes, and no support.

Universities eagerly adopted the system. Because of AT&T's release policies, UNIX users had to band together to support each other. This led to a long-standing UNIX tradition of sharing and collaborating. UNIX users are loyal to the system as much because of the values instilled by UNIX's history as because of the system's technical merits.

In 1975, Ken Thomson returned to the University of California at Berkeley and brought UNIX with him. Two graduate students, Bill Joy and Chuck Haley, began working on the system, with Joy authoring the Vi full-screen text editor. Out of the work at Berkeley, the Berkeley System Distribution (BSD) version of UNIX was created.

In 1979, AT&T realized it had a valuable product and changed the licensing terms of UNIX. Its source code could no longer be used by universities in operating systems courses. UNIX was suddenly a business product, not a community good to be shared freely. This period also marked the end of hobbyist computing and the free sharing of software and the beginning of the serious PC software market.

Adulthood

Until the early 1980s, UNIX was derided as a rogue operating system mostly used by college students, not a serious environment for work. Large computer companies had their own proprietary (and incompatible) systems, and users of these systems were locked in.

However, in the 1980s, a new class of computer began encroaching on the minicomputer's territory: The scientific workstation offered lots of processing power in a small box on a worker's desk. The first workstations used proprietary operating systems, but a start-up known as Sun Microsystems took the radical approach of offering UNIX workstations. Within a few years, other vendors like Silicon Graphics, Hewlett-Packard, and even IBM and DEC offered UNIX workstations. UNIX wiped out proprietary competition in the workstation market and destroyed the minicomputer market. UNIX was set to explode.

Midlife Crisis

Unfortunately, UNIX had begun to splinter. Each manufacturer offered slightly different versions of UNIX with minor incompatibilities. Although the incompatibilities really were minor, managers who may not have understood computers saw a confusing mess when they looked at UNIX. Some vendors offered UNIX with a BSD heritage, whereas others were derived from AT&T's "official" System V UNIX.

In the late 1980s and early 1990s, the computing power of PCs began to approach that of UNIX workstations. Although PCs were saddled with DOS and early versions of Windows, they quickly became a standard for business computing. Before the UNIX vendors could react, their "next big market" had been swallowed whole by Microsoft and the personal computer.

UNIX vendors formed alliances to combat this threat, but the alliances were shaky at best and simply wasted energy. All the while Windows' market share was increasing. Windows even began to threaten UNIX's supremacy in the scientific and server market.

Maturity

During this period, members of the UNIX community had become unhappy with AT&T's licensing terms and had begun several projects to produce a less-restrictive version of UNIX.

P. J. Plaugher's Idris project and Andrew Tanenbaum's Minix were aimed at replacing the UNIX kernel. BSD developers began replacing all AT&T code in their system with code written from scratch.

At the same time, another group took a different approach. In 1983, Richard Stallman founded the Free Software Foundation and began the GNU Project. (GNU is a self-referencing acronym that stands for GNU's Not UNIX.) Rather than starting with the kernel, GNU began writing free replacements for the system utilities such as compilers, editors, and utility commands. After years of effort, GNU versions of practically every UNIX system program existed. The GNU software was of such high quality that even users of commercial UNIX systems routinely replaced the vendor utilities with the GNU utilities.

By the mid-1990s, the splinters in UNIX had largely been repaired. Standards such as those developed by the IEEE's (Institute of Electrical and Electronic Engineers) POSIX committees and the ANSI/ISO committees largely unified the various flavors of UNIX.

However, Microsoft had by then grown into the world's largest software company and was aggressively pursuing UNIX's market with its new Windows NT operating system. Microsoft owned the desktop and was targeting the server room, promising a uniform interface and a universal de facto standard. UNIX's future was in question.

Microsoft had overlooked one critical development: the Internet.

Microsoft was totally unprepared for the explosion in popularity of the Internet. Suddenly, everyone wanted to be on the Internet, and UNIX ruled the Internet. The native networking protocol of UNIX is TCP/IP, and it had been used for years to power the Internet. Microsoft fought back hard, but UNIX had gained a reprieve.

Children of UNIX

Linus Torvalds was a computer-science major at Helsinki University in Finland. He had been exposed to UNIX in university and wanted to run it at home on his PC. He bought Andrew Tanenbaum's Minix but was frustrated by its limitations. He began working on his own kernel and released it in 1991 on the Internet under the GNU General Public License. He quickly got feedback from programmers around the world. The kernel grew and became more useful; it was joined with the GNU UNIX utilities. Suddenly, a complete UNIX replacement was born.

Programmers around the world who were frustrated with their unreliable and slow Windows systems simply downloaded Linux and turned their PC into a UNIX workstation. Because of Linux's licensing terms, it swept into corporations and homes, at first clandestinely and later openly. Linux precipitated a surge of interest in UNIX and other free UNIX-like systems. A generation of students was exposed to the values of UNIX: cooperation, sharing, technical excellence, and distrust of proprietary systems. The enduring legacy bequeathed by Thomson and Ritchie has been accepted by a new generation.

The UNIX Philosophy

Let's pause at this point to look at the UNIX philosophy. By this I mean the technical philosophy—the reason UNIX works the way it does.

Organization Around Software Tools

The original UNIX developers had a clear vision for software development:

- Write programs that do one thing and do it well.
- Make these programs fit together seamlessly.

This philosophy has succeeded beyond their wildest expectations. UNIX remains one of the smallest and simplest general-purpose operating systems in existence. UNIX tools written in the 1970s are still used to good effect today.

Let me illustrate this philosophy with a concrete example. I am writing this book using a UNIX text editor. The text editor does one thing: It lets me edit text files. It doesn't do typesetting or graphics or spell-checking or cross-referencing. I use separate programs for each of those things, but because they all work together smoothly, the process is quite painless. If I suddenly discover a better spell-checker, I don't have to throw out my editor, typesetter, or graphics tool. I simply replace the spell-checker.

Unfortunately, most PC software doesn't work this way. Microsoft Word, for example, is a text editor, graphics editor, typesetter, spell-checker, and even programming environment. This makes it rather large and unwieldy. Furthermore, you are forced to use all the components of Word together. If you like Word's editor and typesetter, but not its spell-checker, there's very little you can do about it. Word is monolithic.

Multiuser Capability

UNIX was designed to be multiuser from the ground up. It cleanly separates different users' setups from each other. UNIX supports multiple interactive sessions. Every UNIX file is associated with a user. This clean design remains elusive even under Windows NT, which stores a lot of systemwide configuration data and does not allow multiple interactive sessions without third-party add-ons. For example, under stock NT Server and Workstation, it is not possible for two users to run interactive sessions on the same NT machine at the same time.

Configurability

UNIX is highly configurable. UNIX was written by programmers for programmers, and programmers generally have strong ideas about their ideal environment. For this reason, there are several shells (command interpreters) available for UNIX, as well as a multitude of graphical user interfaces and desktops. Some see this as a weakness of UNIX, but I see it as a strength. All these features are configurable on a per-user basis. You can set up your system exactly as you like it, not as it is dictated by the manufacturer.

The critics of UNIX configurability point out the lack of standardization of graphical user interfaces. They claim that more tightly controlled systems provide a more consistent interface. This is true, but it's questionable whether consistency is a worthier goal than customization. I believe a computer user should force the user interface to conform to her tastes rather than change work habits to conform to the user interface.

Simplicity and Uniformity

UNIX does not make unnecessary distinctions. For example, there is no difference in UNIX between a binary file and a text file. A file is a file. Many UNIX applications save their data in human-readable format, which makes debugging and crash-recovery much easier.

UNIX does not distinguish between local and remote file systems. Applications and users are entirely ignorant of whether the file they're editing resides on their local hard disk or on a disk 20 miles away (unless they take pains to find out).

Under the X Window system, UNIX blurs the distinctions between local and remote processes. As I type this text, I have two windows on my screen. One is running on my personal computer, and another is running on a computer two floors down. I can't tell which is which without doing some investigating.

The X Window System is a networked graphics system. It allows programs to run on one machine and have their interfaces presented on another. The system is described in Chapter 4.

Linux Distributions

As Linux became more and more successful, several organizations developed Linux distributions. A distribution is a convenient prepackaged Linux installation that includes the kernel, utilities, and application programs. It is far simpler to install and use a distribution than to gather source code from all over the Internet, compile it, and install it by hand.

Some Linux distributions, such as Debian, have strong free-software traditions and are noncommercial. Most, however, are distributed by for-profit companies. These companies take different approaches to commercializing Linux.

Red Hat Software, for example, adds no proprietary enhancements to the system. All their code is freely redistributable. They rely on a strong brand-name image for their business model.

Caldera, on the other hand, includes some proprietary enhancements to Linux that make it very easy to install and administer. They also have strategic partnerships with several commercial software vendors and value-added resellers. Caldera OpenLinux ships with personal versions of WordPerfect, Star Office, and BRU (a backup utility). Caldera also offers support and training.

Most Linux distributions include a package-management system. This program and database keep track of installed software and make sure that there are no version conflicts or missing dependencies. Package managers make it very easy to upgrade your system.

Both Caldera and Red Hat use the RPM package-management system, which has become a de facto standard in the Linux world.

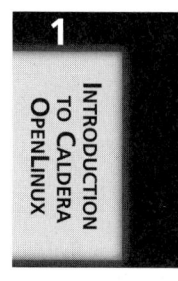

Why Linux?

Why should you use Linux? What advantages does it offer? In this section, I hope to show you some compelling advantages of Linux over other systems.

Linux has a strong UNIX heritage that (in my opinion) is enough to recommend it as a good operating system. Linux is also freely available with source code, which again is a strong recommendation. Finally, Linux is very stable and flexible. This section will expand on these points.

Free Software

The Linux kernel is licensed under the GNU General Public License. Most system utilities are from the GNU project. In recognition of this heritage, some people refer to Linux systems as GNU/Linux systems.

The fact that Linux is built around free software has been critical to its success. Software developed by programmers in their spare time and without pay has proven to be more robust and flexible than commercial software—a startlingly counterintuitive result.

However, deeper reflection reveals no inconsistency. Free software has the following advantages over proprietary software:

- Because source code is available, thousands of people inspect the software. Bugs are caught and fixed quickly.
- End users can customize free software to their hearts' content. Users with specialized needs (who are ignored by commercial software vendors because they form only a niche market) can customize Linux exactly as they see fit.
- Free software does not include superfluous features. If someone adds a useless feature, anyone else can remove it.
- Free software prevents reinvention of the wheel. By sharing code and ideas, you can save yourself a lot of work.
- Free software is inherently more secure than proprietary software. You have complete control. You can audit the code (or hire someone to do it) and fix security problems. You can verify the robustness of security algorithms. There is no "security by obscurity."
- Free software is inexpensive. You can copy it as much as you like.

UNIX Compatibility

Another reason to choose Linux is because of its UNIX compatibility. At the user level, Linux is very similar to UNIX. If you know UNIX, you know most of Linux.

At the programming level, most applications can be ported between Linux and UNIX with very little effort. Linux was deliberately designed to be UNIX-compatible to take advantage of the large body of UNIX software available.

Linux will interoperate exceedingly well with other UNIX machines. It uses standard UNIX services like RPC (Remote Procedure Call) and NFS (Network File System). It will also interoperate with Windows machines (via the Samba suite) and Macintoshes (with AppleTalk support).

Linux inherits UNIX's strong flexibility and customizability, making it suitable for a wide range of applications, in traditional server and desktop applications as well as unusual applications such as embedded systems.

Reliability and Performance

Yet another reason to choose Linux is its reliability and performance. Linux machines routinely stay up for months at a time. Linux provides full memory protection and isolation of tasks from the kernel and each other. That is, misbehaving or badly written programs can only crash themselves. They cannot bring down the operating system or crash other programs. Linux is a very robust system.

Linux is very small and makes efficient use of your hardware. You can quite comfortably set up Linux on an old 486 machine and use it as a firewall or Web server. Linux can breathe new life into old machines, saving you a lot of money.

Support of Open Standards

Linux is a completely open system. It adheres to open standards like the various POSIX standards and the Internet Engineering Task Force standards for TCP/IP. By avoiding proprietary APIs (Application Programming Interfaces) and protocols, you lessen your dependence on a single supplier. You can choose from a number of Linux providers based on the service and value you get. With proprietary systems, once you commit, you have no choice but to continue with the original system provider, even if you become unhappy with the level of service.

Linux Features

This section gives a brief overview of the outstanding technical features of Linux. These features provide much of the flexibility and stability of Linux. They are what make Linux so popular in critical server applications.

Complete Memory Protection

As mentioned previously, Linux offers complete memory protection for all processes. Each process runs in its own virtual address space and cannot damage the address space of other processes or the kernel. A crashing process almost never brings down the system.

Virtual Memory

Linux can extend the size of physical memory by using part of a disk drive as swap space. This allows you to run more programs at once than will fit into physical memory. This happens invisibly and without the programs' knowledge. They simply assume they have exclusive access to a large memory space, and the Linux kernel manages the memory for them.

> **Note**
>
> Although this capability is referred to as swapping and the disk space as swap space, Linux's mechanism for using disk space as virtual memory is more correctly referred to as paging.

Full Multiuser Features

Linux is inherently multiuuser. Each process and file is associated with a user. Using "telnet" or the X Window system, your Linux machine can run multiple interactive sessions simultaneously. You can also start jobs in the background and let them continue even after you log out.

Linux offers complete file protection to prevent users from damaging or (if you choose) accessing each other's files. Important system files are protected from casual users.

Support for Multiprocessing

If you are lucky enough to have a computer with more than one CPU, Linux can take advantage of multiple processors. The recent 2.2-series kernels greatly improve Linux's handling of multiple CPUs when compared to the 2.0 series.

Best-of-Breed TCP/IP Networking

Linux's TCP/IP networking code is among the most advanced available. It offers full support for current TCP/IP protocols and includes experimental support for IPv6, the next-generation Internet protocol.

In addition to standard TCP/IP support, the Linux kernel includes IP firewalling code, IP masquerading (which lets you hide an entire network behind a dial-up link), IP quality-of-service controls, and many security features. These features rival similar features found in high-end routing equipment sold by companies like Cisco and Nortel.

Finally, because Linux uses resources quite sparingly, very low-end PCs can be used as routers and firewalls. I set up a Linux router and firewall on a second-hand Intel 386 machine that cost $200—less than the cost of an NT Server license.

Interoperability with Windows and Macintosh

With the Samba suite, Linux can act as a file and print server for Windows clients. It can also be a client for an NT file and print server. Linux includes an AppleTalk module, which allows it to be a file and print server for Macintosh clients.

Internet Server Software

Apache, the world's most popular Web server, runs on Linux. Linux also includes an ftp server, an email transfer agent, and POP and IMAP mail servers. You can obtain an LDAP server for Linux for free on the Internet.

Top-Notch Development Tools

Linux includes the GNU C, C++, Objective-C, and FORTRAN compilers, which are widely recognized as top-notch professional tools, used to develop everything from high-end Linux systems to embedded systems and video game consoles.

In addition, Linux includes a plethora of scripting languages like Perl, Tcl/Tk, Python, and many lesser-known ones. There are also a Linux port of Sun's Java Development Kit and several Java Virtual Machine implementations.

Combined with powerful editors like Emacs and Vi, and professional debuggers like Gdb and Ddd, Linux provides an unparalleled development environment.

Modular Kernel

The Linux kernel allows hardware drivers (and other modules) to be loaded and unloaded at runtime. This maximizes efficient use of memory—you don't need to load drivers for hardware you seldom use.

Most drivers can be compiled either as an integral part of the kernel or as a loadable module. Hardware that must be configured before the kernel can access it (such as plug-and-play cards) must have modular drivers.

Caldera OpenLinux

Caldera OpenLinux is a Linux distribution sold by Caldera Systems, Inc., of Provo, Utah. The version discussed in this book is OpenLinux 2.2, which includes a kernel of the modern 2.2 series. Caldera OpenLinux is a complete Linux distribution with hundreds of free software packages as well as some commercial software. The following commercial software is included with Caldera OpenLinux:

- WordPerfect 8 for Linux from Corel. Note that the version included with OpenLinux is the "download" version for personal use only.
- The StarOffice 5.0 office suite. Again, this version is for personal use only.
- The BRU backup and restore utility.
- Netscape Navigator, Communicator, and Composer.
- Power Quest Partition Magic (Caldera Systems Edition). This version does not recognize hard drives larger than 8 GB; you must purchase the full 4.0 version to handle larger drives.
- Power Quest Boot Magic. The Power Quest software eases the management of dual-boot systems.

Caldera OpenLinux also includes the following proprietary components:

- The Lizard graphical installation program
- The Lisa system administration tool
- Netware Linux Client
- OpenLinux Windows tools

Caldera's differentiating features are its excellent graphical installation tool and its carefully chosen mix of packages, which, combined with the K Desktop Environment (KDE), make it an excellent choice for a desktop PC or personal workstation. Although most Linux vendors have concentrated on the server market, Caldera OpenLinux is a strong product aimed squarely at the desktop user.

Unfortunately, the license terms of Lizard and Lisa may prevent you from installing Caldera OpenLinux on more than one computer unless you purchase additional licenses. You may download the "Lite" version of the system, which does not include these components.

Sources of Linux Information

There are many valuable online sources of Linux information. Because Linux is developed and distributed over the Internet, much of its documentation is too. To get the most out of your Linux system, you should get connected to the Internet.

The Linux Documentation Project

The Linux Documentation Project (LDP) is an online repository of thousands of pages of Linux documentation. It contains invaluable tips for setting up, configuring, and running Linux. The Linux Documentation Project has its own domain at `http://www.linux-doc.org`, and its home page is `http://metalab.unc.edu/LDP`. I refer to documents in the Linux Documentation Project many times in this book.

Many of the most useful pieces of Linux documentation are called the Linux HOWTOs. These are short documents detailing how to accomplish a particular task or understand a particular aspect of Linux. When in doubt, please check the Linux HOWTO index at `http://metalab.unc.edu/LDP/index.html#howto`.

Portal Sites

The following Web sites are good places to start looking for Linux information. They have links to many other more specialized sites:

- `http://www.linux.com` A sophisticated portal site
- `http://www.kernelnotes.org` A kernel-related sites with many good documentation links
- `http://www.freshmeat.net` The latest Linux application software announcements
- `http://www.linuxtoday.com` Linux-related news headlines

Newsgroups

`comp.os.linux.announce` is a moderated newsgroup for Linux-related announcements.

`comp.os.linux.answers` is a moderated newsgroup for periodic postings such as FAQ lists and HOWTO documents.

`comp.os.linux.hardware` is devoted to hardware-related questions. If you're having problems with a piece of hardware, you can post it here.

`comp.os.linux.networking` deals with everything related to Linux networking, including discussions of protocols and possibly some hardware issues.

`comp.os.linux.x` is devoted to running X Windows (specifically, XFree86) on Linux. There are other newsgroups devoted to X (but not Linux) that may contain valuable information.

Before posting a question to a newsgroup, read through `comp.os.linux.answers` and browse the Linux Documentation Project. Check older news articles first to see if someone has asked your question already. Chances are your question has been asked and answered before.

Hardware Requirements

By now, you're probably eager to try Linux. Although Linux has been ported to many processor architectures, most people run it on (and Caldera only supports) Intel x86 machines.

Because Linux is developed by volunteers, and because most hardware manufacturers do not write Linux drivers for their hardware, you must take care when buying hardware intended for a Linux system.

For the most up-to-date listing of Linux-supported hardware, check the Linux Hardware-HOWTO at `http://metalab.unc.edu/LDP/HOWTO/Hardware-HOWTO.html`.

Please remember: When you set up Linux, it's important to know all the details of your hardware. If you are buying new hardware for a Linux system, get a written guarantee that you can return or exchange it if it won't work with Linux. Although most hardware works fine, it is better to protect yourself.

Hardware Component	Notes
Motherboard	Most PCI, VLB, EISA, and ISA motherboards are fine.
Microprocessor (Intel family)	80386 or higher. Non-Intel x86 clones from AMD and Cyrix work too.
Video Cards	All video cards work well in text mode. See the Hardware-HOWTO for details on graphics mode.
I/O Controllers	All standard serial/parallel/joystick combo cards are supported.
Network Adapters	All modern Ethernet cards (PCI and ISA) are supported. See the Hardware-HOWTO for recommendations.

Hardware Component	Notes
Sound Cards	Many popular cards are supported, but sound is somewhat of a problem area. Check the Hardware-HOWTO and Sound-HOWTO for details.
Tape Drives	All SCSI drives are supported. Some IDE and "Floppy-Tape" drives are supported, as are some parallel-port tape drives.
CD-ROM Drives and Writers	All SCSI and ATAPI CD-ROM drives are supported. Many SCSI CD writers and some IDE writers are supported.
Removable Drives	Zip, Jaz, and SyQuest SCSI drives are supported, as are parallel-port ZIP drives.
Mice	All serial and PS/2 mice work. Get a three-button mouse if possible; most graphical Linux programs assume a three-button mouse.
Modems	All external modems work. Internal modems work if they appear as serial ports. "WinModems" *do not* work and should be avoided at all costs.
Printers	All parallel-port and serial-port printers work. PostScript and Hewlett-Packard PCL printers are well supported. "WinPrinters" do not work and should be avoided.
Scanners	Many SCSI scanners are supported by the SANE project (http://www.mostang.com/sane). Some parallel-port scanners are supported, but not many and not well.

Going Ahead with Linux

You're now ready to begin your Linux journey. If you already know UNIX, Linux will seem familiar and friendly. If you are new to UNIX, Linux may seem strange and mysterious at first. Persevere. As you get to know the system, you will appreciate its elegance and power.

Linux is a system with a long history and a legacy of sharing and cooperation. Linux belongs to everyone; it is a heritage bequeathed to us by the visionaries of the free software movement. I hope you enjoy discovering Linux.

Basic Linux Concepts and Commands

CHAPTER 2

IN THIS CHAPTER

- Logging In and Out *24*
- Why Learn the Command-line Interface? *26*
- The Linux File System *26*
- The Layout of the File System *32*
- Shells *35*
- Basic UNIX Commands *37*
- UNIX Manual Pages: man *42*
- Virtual Consoles *46*
- Typing Shortcuts *47*
- Configuration Files *49*
- Processes *50*
- Common Problems *53*

Linux is a multiuser system, so it seems a little more complex at first than other operating systems you may be used to. To use Linux effectively, you have to understand how to log in and out of the system, how the Linux file system is organized, and how the command-line interface works. After you've mastered these basics, you'll be ready to explore some of the more interesting and powerful aspects of the system.

Logging In and Out

As mentioned in the "Full Multiuser Features" section, Linux is a fully multiuser system. Before you can use the system, you need to provide it with your identity and password.

If you've installed Caldera OpenLinux as described in Appendix B, you should have created at least two accounts.

The first account, usually called *root*, is the account of the "superuser." This user is all-powerful; almost all permission and sanity checks are skipped for root on the assumption that root knows what he is doing. For this reason, you should never log in as root unless you are performing system maintenance. Even then, it's better to log in as yourself and switch to root with the su command as required.

The second account you created should have been your own personal account. You should log in and work using this account.

Logging In

If you configured X Windows and the K Desktop Environment to run, you'll see a graphical dialog box prompting you to log in. Enter your login name and password, and click on Go.

If you do not have X Windows running, your computer will be in text mode, and you'll be prompted for your login. Type your login name and press Enter. Then enter your password. Nothing will be echoed as you type your password. (You may be accustomed to systems that display an asterisk as you type each character of your password. Linux does not do this.)

> **Note**
>
> Almost everything in Linux is case-sensitive. Make sure that you type your login name and password in the correct case, usually lowercase.

If you are in a graphical desktop environment, click on the terminal icon to open a text terminal. (See Figure 2.1.)

FIGURE 2.1
Terminal Icon

A terminal window will open. It will contain a prompt that looks something like this:

```
[dave@machine dave]$
```

Your prompt will look slightly different because it is based on your user name, machine name, and working directory. In the examples in this book, we will show the shell prompt like this:

```
$.
```

If you log in as root, the dollar sign ($) in the prompt will be replaced with a pound sign (#) to remind you that you are root. Be extra vigilant when operating as root because a mistake can wipe out your system.

Logging Out

To log out of KDE, click on the logout icon to close your KDE session. (See Figure 2.2.)

FIGURE 2.2
KDE Logout Icon

If you are not in graphics mode or simply wish to log out of the terminal you opened (but not KDE as a whole), type **exit** in the terminal:

```
$ exit
```

Changing Your Password

It is important to keep your password secret. A strong password is the first and best line of defense against an attack on your Linux system.

If you ever need to change your password, follow this procedure.

1. Open a terminal window by clicking on the terminal icon as described earlier.
2. Enter the command: **passwd**
3. Enter your old password when prompted.

4. Enter your new password when prompted.
5. Reenter your new password as confirmation.

Why Learn the Command-line Interface?

If you installed Caldera OpenLinux, you probably have the KDE desktop interface up and running. This is a friendly, modern graphical desktop that lets you accomplish most tasks with simple mouse clicks and menu choices. KDE is fully described in Chapter 5; however, if you've used Windows or Mac OS, you will find it quite intuitive. By all means, go ahead and explore KDE.

However, you should come back to this chapter. KDE makes using Linux easy, but to be a power user—to unleash your system—you must know UNIX basics. Although the command-line interface is not as glamorous as a graphical interface, it is still the most powerful means for interacting with a UNIX system. Many everyday tasks can still be completed more quickly using the command-line interface than using a graphical interface.

Furthermore, graphical interfaces come and go, but the command line is forever. UNIX and Linux systems offer KDE, GNOME, CDE, and a myriad of lesser-known graphical interfaces. But the command-line shells are very similar to each other. So, you can move from Linux to different UNIXes with ease if you know UNIX commands.

The Linux File System

Understanding file system concepts is central to understanding Linux and UNIX. The Linux file system is a hierarchical system of files and directories, similar to Windows or the Macintosh. However, the Linux file system has a few differences compared to those systems:

- Linux has no concept of "drive letters." The entire Linux file system starts at the root directory, called /.
- Linux uses the slash character (/) to separate components of a pathname rather than backslash (\) or colon (:).

A directory or file is specified as a slash-separated list of its components, like this: /home/dfs/book.tex. Such a list is often referred to as a path or pathname.

UNIX places no restrictions on where files and subdirectories reside, but conventions have developed over the years, and almost all UNIX systems have a fairly standard directory layout. That is, most UNIX systems by convention store programs and configuration files in certain standard directories, described in "The Layout of the File System" section.

Pathnames

Let's look at the basic syntax of pathnames. A path consists of slash-separated components. A path can be either relative or absolute. A *relative path* is interpreted relative to the current working directory. An *absolute path* is interpreted starting from the root directory or the basic starting point of the hierarchical file system.

A relative path does not begin with a slash. For example, all these paths are relative:

- junk
- junkdir/subdir/foo.txt
- ..
- ../../foo
- .

They are all interpreted relative to the current directory. The special name . refers to the current directory, and the special name .. refers to the parent of the current directory.

So the relative path ../../foo refers to the file foo in the parent directory of the parent directory of the current directory.

An absolute path begins with a slash. Absolute paths specify the path starting from the root of the file system. All these paths are absolute:

- /etc/passwd
- /tmp/..
- /home/dave
- /

Note that the tricky path /tmp/.. is simply a synonym for the root directory (/).

Changing the Working Directory

Every process in Linux has an associated *working directory*. This is the directory from which relative pathnames are interpreted. If you create a file without specifying a directory, it is created in the working directory. When you first log in, your working directory is a directory called your *home directory*. Home directories are usually subdirectories of

/home. If your login name is dave, your home directory is probably /home/dave.

To see which directory you are in, type **pwd** (Print Working Directory) in a terminal window:

```
$ pwd
/home/dave
```

To change your working directory, use the cd command. Type this:

```
$ cd /usr/bin
$ pwd
/usr/bin
```

Your working directory is now /usr/bin.

To return to your home directory, type a plain cd command like the following example:

```
$ cd
$ pwd
/home/dave
```

Creating Directories

It is not a good idea to keep all kinds of files directly in your home directory. It will quickly become cluttered and unmanageable. It is better to create subdirectories under your home directory to organize your files.

Switch to your home directory and type this command:

```
$ mkdir test
```

The mkdir command creates a directory called test. Change to the newly created directory:

```
$ cd test
$ pwd
/home/dave/test
```

Removing Directories

If you're still in the test directory, change back to your home directory by typing this:

```
$ cd ..
```

Remember that the special name .. refers to the parent of the current directory.

To remove the test directory, type this:

```
$ rmdir test
```

The directory is gone. You can verify this by trying to change directories into it:

```
$ cd test
bash: test: No such file or directory
```

> **Note**
>
> We'll explain what bash means in the "Shells" section, later in this chapter.

Listing Directories

You're not expected to remember all the files and directories contained in a directory. The `ls` command lists the contents of a directory. If you run `ls` from your home directory, you'll see something like this:

```
$ ls
Desktop
```

`ls`, like almost all UNIX commands, accepts command-line options that change its behavior. An option begins with a dash (-) usually followed by a letter. Type this:

```
$ cd
$ ls -a
.               .bash_logout    .gcalrc    .login    .tcshrc
..              .bashrc         .inputrc   .logout   .wmrc
.Xauthority     .config         .kde       .profile  Desktop
.bash_history   .cshrc          .kderc     .seyon
```

You see a cornucopia of files. Files whose names begin with a period (.) are called hidden files and are not displayed by `ls` unless you use the -a option.

Hidden files are usually used for configuration data or user options. You don't usually want to know about these files, so they're not displayed. However, they are just regular files, and you can look at them with `ls -a`, edit them, rename them, and so on.

> **Note**
>
> Most UNIX programs store customization information in files in your home directory. The names of these files usually start with a period so that normal `ls` listings are not cluttered with dozens of configuration filenames. This, in fact, is the whole reason behind the hidden file concept.

The file named . refers to the current directory, whereas .. refers to the parent of the current directory.

The `ls` command has another option, `-l` for long. Its output looks something like Figure 2.3.

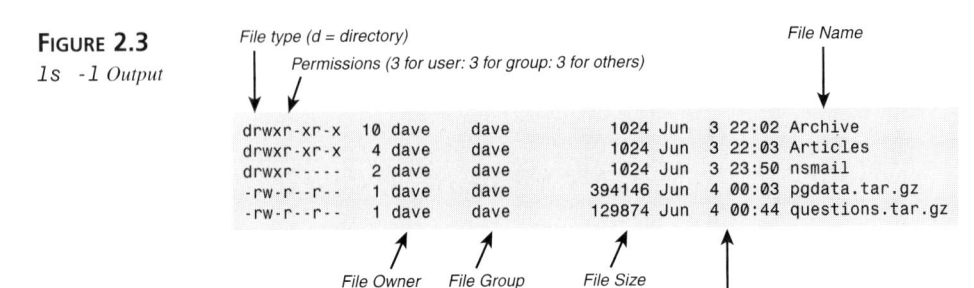

FIGURE 2.3
`ls -l` *Output*

```
                  File type (d = directory)                                   File Name
                  │
                  │  Permissions (3 for user: 3 for group: 3 for others)
                  ▼  ▼                                                         ▼
              drwxr-xr-x  10 dave      dave       1024 Jun  3 22:02 Archive
              drwxr-xr-x   4 dave      dave       1024 Jun  3 22:03 Articles
              drwxr-----   2 dave      dave       1024 Jun  3 23:50 nsmail
              -rw-r--r--   1 dave      dave     394146 Jun  4 00:03 pgdata.tar.gz
              -rw-r--r--   1 dave      dave     129874 Jun  4 00:44 questions.tar.gz
                             ▲          ▲          ▲
                        File Owner  File Group  File Size
                                                           Date of Last Modification
```

File Permissions

Each file in Linux is associated with an owner and a group. Caldera OpenLinux follows the custom of putting each user in her own group. (The reason for this will become clear in Chapter 8.)

Linux allows you to assign different permissions to the file's owner, members of the file's group, and everyone else. A typical listing of permissions in `ls -l` output looks like this:

`drwxr-xr-x`

The first d indicates that the file is a directory. Plain files have a dash in the first position. The next three letters (rwx) indicate that the directory's owner has read, write, and execute permission. The second group of three letters (r-x) indicates that members of the directory's group have read and execute permission. The final group of three letters (r-x) indicates that everyone else has read and execute permission.

How are these permissions interpreted? For ordinary files, it's quite simple:

- If you have read permission for a file, you can look at the contents of the file.
- If you have write permission for a file, you can alter the contents of the file.
- If you have execute permission for a file, you can execute the file as a program.

> **Note**
>
> Note that UNIX does not recognize executables by looking for special filenames ending in .COM or .EXE. Instead, it recognizes executables by looking at the permission settings.

For directories, the permissions are interpreted as follows:

- If you have read permission for a directory, you can list the contents of the directory.
- If you have write permission for a directory, you can create new files in the directory, rename existing files, and delete files.

> **Note**
>
> You do not need to have write permission for a file to delete it. You only need write permission for the directory containing the file.

- If you have execute permission for a directory, you can make the directory your current working directory (with cd).

> **Note**
>
> This is not the whole story of file permissions. But it's enough to keep you going for now. Chapter 8 has the rest of the details.

Symbolic Links

UNIX symbolic links are similar in some ways to shortcuts in Windows, except that they are understood because they are part of the file system code in the kernel rather than an add-on "feature" only understood by some parts of the system.

A symbolic link lets you refer to a file by another name. Let's say that you have a file in your home directory called report-v.1. You sometimes want to refer to it by the simple name report.

To create a symbolic link for our file, report-v.1, type:

```
$ ln -s report-v.1 report
$ ls -l
lrwxrwxrwx 1 dave dave 10 Jun 7 15:44 report -> report-v.1
-rw-rw-r- 1 dave dave 28 Jun 7 15:43 report-v.1
```

Note the listing for report. The initial l indicates that the file is a symbolic link. The permissions on the link itself are irrelevant; the permissions on the file pointed to by the link are what count. Note how ls shows that report "points to" report-v.1.

Symbolic links break the strict hierarchical structure of the UNIX file system, but they are very useful. After you've used UNIX for a while, you'll appreciate the flexibility offered by symbolic links.

> **Note**
>
> If there are symbolic links, are there nonsymbolic links? Yes, the UNIX file system has the concept of a hard link, which is created without the -s option to ln. Don't try to use them yet, however. Always use -s with ln.

Mount Points

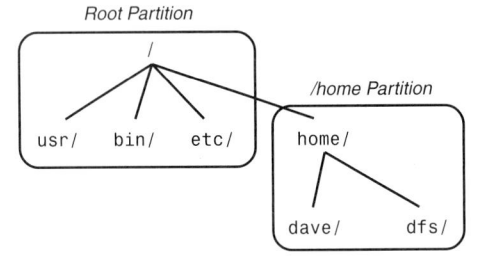

If Linux has no concept of a drive letter, how do you use more than one drive? The answer is that Linux allows you to insert an entire disk partition's hierarchy at any point in the directory tree. (The commands for doing this are be covered in Chapter 8.)

The root directory / is special. It is mounted when Linux starts. That is, the root directory on a disk partition becomes the root directory of the entire Linux tree.

Other partitions may be mounted under the root directory. On my system, I keep all the /home directories on a separate partition. (See Figure 2.4.) When you change directories from / to /home, the disk partition changes. All this is hidden; however, Linux keeps track of the mount points for you.

FIGURE 2.4
Mount Points

You can have many mount points, and some of them can refer to different disks or even to remote disks. As far as most applications are concerned, however, the Linux file system is a simple single-rooted tree. You usually don't worry about what is mounted where.

The Layout of the File System

Even though the Linux kernel does not impose any particular layout for the file system, most Linux installations more or less adhere to the Linux Filesystem Standard, which specifies which directories should exist and what should be in them. This section gives a brief overview of important directories in the Linux file system.

/ The root directory is the starting point of the file system. Typically, this directory contains only subdirectories, although some systems (including Caldera OpenLinux) put a file called vmlinuz in the root directory. vmlinuz is the linux kernel loaded at boot time.

/bin This directory contains critical program files that are needed early in the boot process or may be useful for system recovery if a disk goes bad.

/sbin Like /bin, this directory contains critical programs needed early in the boot process. Programs in /sbin, however, are intended for system administration and maintenance purposes and are not meant to be used by casual users. To be honest, the division between /bin and /sbin is somewhat arbitrary.

/lib This directory contains critical shared libraries. These correspond to dynamic link libraries in Windows. They contain libraries of code that are shared by many programs and hence only need to be loaded into memory once.

/lib/modules This directory tree containssubdirectories contain configuration information that applies to the machine as a whole. You'll find things like the password file (the list of users), the host name, startup and shutdown scripts, and mail transfer agent configuration files in /etc.

/tmp This directory is for temporary files. Anyone can create files here, but they are deleted each time the system is rebooted.

/home This directory usually contains users' home directories.

/boot This directory contains files related to the boot loader. It includes such esoterica as master boot records. Some Linux setups place bootable Linux kernel files in /boot.

> **Note**
>
> A *boot loader* is a small program that is loaded off the hard disk when the computer first boots. It is responsible for loading the rest of the operating system. The PC architecture uses *master boot records* to inform the BIOS (the built-in ROM software) which parts of the disk contain boot loaders.

/proc This directory is quite unusual: Files and directories in it do not correspond to real files. Rather, they let you get at (and in some cases set) internal kernel parameters. For example, the file /proc/cpuinfo contains information about your CPU. Type

```
$ cat /proc/cpuinfo
```

to see this rather interesting information, which contains, among other things, the type of processor and its clock speed.

/opt   Optional (usually large) software packages on Caldera OpenLinux, Netscape, WordPerfect, StarOffice, and KDE are put into /opt.

/dev   This directory contains special device files. These are not real files but rather special entries in the file system that correspond to device drivers for actual hardware.

> **Note**
>
> Device files are covered in Chapter 8.

/usr   This is a large hierarchy all to itself. Most of your Linux system files live in this directory.

/usr/bin   Most executable files live here.

/usr/sbin   Additional system-administrator programs stay in this directory.

/usr/lib   This directory contains more shared libraries. In addition, many programs put private information or executables here.

> **Note**
>
> Why mirror /bin, /lib, and /sbin under /usr? Traditionally, UNIX systems used a rather small disk partition as the root partition and mounted a larger partition under /usr. There seems to be a law that large things fail more often than small things, so having a small root partition increases the chances of having a salvageable system in the event of a disk crash. The root partition should contain just enough software to get the system up and running and check or repair the /usr partition.

/usr/X11R6   This rather large directory tree contains everything related to the X Window System.

/usr/dict   This directory contains /usr/dict/words, a list of English words used by spell-checking programs.

/usr/man   Most system manual pages (see the "UNIX Manual Pages: man section") live here.

/usr/src   Source code can be found in this directory. In particular, /usr/src/linux contains the source code for the Linux kernel.

/usr/share   Similar to /usr/lib, this directory is meant as a repository for architecture-independent information. Thus, even though /usr/lib will often contain shared libraries and programs for a particular processor architecture, /usr/share contains text files and other files that work on any processor architecture.

/usr/local   This directory is meant for local installation of software, but you can put whatever you like here.

/usr/doc   This directory is reserved for documentation. It usually contains text files but could house almost anything. Linux HOWTO's and Linux Documentation Project books go here.

This list is not exhaustive, but it should give you a feeling for how the file system is organized. For a more complete description and the rationale behind the organization, consult the Linux Filesystem Standard in the Linux Documentation Project.

Shells

When you type commands at a command prompt, you are not interacting directly with the Linux kernel. Rather, a program called a shell is interpreting your commands.

In the great UNIX tradition of customization, you can choose from several shells. These shells include:

sh   The original UNIX shell, known as the Bourne Shell (after its author). It is hardly ever used on Linux because it is fairly primitive.

bash   The default shell on most Linux systems, including Caldera OpenLinux. It offers sophisticated interactive features like command-line editing and filename completion, both of which make working at a command-line interface a pleasure compared to a graphical user interface.

> **Note**
>
> bash stands for the Bourne Again Shell, illustrating another time-honored UNIX tradition—bad puns.

csh   The C shell developed at Berkeley. For interactive use, it's fairly similar to sh, but it has a different programming syntax.

tcsh   An enhanced version of csh with command-line editing and completion.

There are other lesser-used shells like zsh and ksh, which you can investigate if you don't like any of the standard ones.

More advanced features of the shell are covered in Chapter 3, "Using the Shell"; this section simply serves as an introduction.

I/O Redirection

Now that you've seen and created directories, it is time to work with files. Let's create our first file. Change to your home directory and type this:

```
$ cat
```

Now type some text.

```
Help, I am stuck in a UNIX system.
Help, I am stuck in a UNIX system.
Stop it!
Stop it!
```

That gets boring quickly. Press Ctrl-D; that is, hold down the Ctrl key and type **D**.

The `cat` command doesn't seem like a cat; it seems like a parrot. The `cat` command as used here is an example of a filter. It reads from the *standard input stream* and writes to the *standard output stream*.

The standard input stream is normally your keyboard, and the standard output is normally the terminal window. So `cat` reads lines from the keyboard and prints them to your terminal. It does this until you press Ctrl-D, which is the terminal end-of-file character. When a program is reading from the keyboard, Ctrl-D indicates the end of the input. When `cat` sees the end of input, it exits.

> Ctrl-D is normally the terminal end-of-file character, but like most aspects of UNIX, you can configure it to be something else. Keep in mind, however, that practically every Linux system in existence is set up to use Ctrl-D as the end-of-file character.

Although standard input normally comes from the keyboard and standard output normally goes to the terminal, you can redirect either stream. For example, type this:

```
$ cat > myfile
```

Now type some text.

```
Help, I am stuck in a UNIX system.
Stop it!
```

And press Ctrl-D. Note that your input was not echoed. Type **ls**, and you should see a file named `myfile`. The > symbol redirected the output of `cat` to `myfile`.

If you can redirect standard output, surely you can redirect standard input. Here's how:

```
$ cat < myfile
Help, I am stuck in a UNIX system.
Stop it!
```

The `<` symbol takes input from `myfile` instead of the keyboard. You can combine redirections like this:

```
$ cat < myfile > yourfile
```

This copies `myfile` to `yourfile`.

Discarding Output

The special file `/dev/null` is used for <$/dev/null file>discarding output. Anything you send to `/dev/null` is simply consumed and discarded. If you try to read from `/dev/null`, it returns an immediate end-of-file.

The following command does nothing but waste CPU cycles:

```
$ cat < myfile > /dev/null
```

This may seem pretty useless, but there are times when you want to run commands but don't want to see their output. You can easily achieve this by redirecting the output to `/dev/null`.

Basic UNIX Commands

Now that you've had a taste of UNIX files and directories, it is time to look at UNIX commands in more detail. There are many UNIX commands, but most of them have the same structure, which looks like this:

```
command options arguments
```

The `command` is the name of the command. The `options` are special character sequences that alter the behavior of the command in some way. Options usually begin with a dash. We've already seen options at work (see the "Listing Directories" section) when we looked at the `-a` option for `ls`.

The `arguments` are other pieces of information supplied to the command. For many commands, the arguments are filenames.

For example, consider the line: `ls -a /home/jim`. The command `ls` is followed by the option `-a` and the argument `/home/jim`.

List Files: ls

We've already seen the `ls` command at work. Let's look at more aspects of the command.

- If you want to list a particular file or directory, you can supply the file or directory name as an argument. For example:

  ```
  $ ls -l /etc/hosts /etc/passwd
  -rw-r--r-- 1 root root 1419 Jun 8 21:03 /etc/hosts
  -rw-r--r-- 1 root root 1807 Jun 7 11:53 /etc/passwd
  ```

  Note that the `-l` option asks for a "long listing" and the two arguments `/etc/hosts` and `/etc/passwd` specify the files we want listed.

- If you want a recursive listing of a directory, use the `-R` option. For example, `ls -R /` will list every file and directory in your Linux system. This will take a long time and produce copious output. To stop the listing, press Ctrl-C, which is the standard interrupt character.

Change Directory: cd

We've also seen `cd` at work. With an argument, it changes to the specified directory. Without an argument, it changes to your home directory.

If your shell is `bash` (which it probably is if you're using a standard Caldera setup), the `cd` command has one additional enhancement: Typing **cd -** changes you to the previous directory (that is, the one before the previous `cd` command).

You can use `cd -` to alternate between two directories without having to type (or remember) the pathnames. This can be very handy.

Special Name for Home Directory

Most modern shells allow you to give a special name to your home directory. The name ~ (tilde) refers to your home directory. If your home directory is `/home/dave`, then the file `/home/dave/work.txt` can also be referred to as `~/work.txt`.

Rename or Move a File: mv

To rename a file, use the `mv` command. This command has quite a few options and different modes of behavior:

- To simply rename a file, use `mv` *oldname* *newname*. But beware: If *newname* already exists, it will be deleted before the renaming.

> **Warning**
>
> UNIX assumes that you know what you are doing. Therefore, almost no commands ask for verification before doing something dangerous. This is another good reason not to work as root unless absolutely necessary.

- To move file to another directory, use mv *file directory*. The target directory must already exist.
- To move and rename a file, use mv *oldname directory/newname*.
- You can move entire directories by using a directory name as the first argument to mv.
- You can move whole sets of files into a directory by using mv like this:

    ```
    $ mv file1 file2 ...fileN directory
    ```
- If you would like mv to ask for confirmation before overwriting a file, use the -i option:

    ```
    $ mv -i file preciousName
    ```

    If preciousName already exists, mv will prompt for confirmation.

Remove Files: rm

The rm command removes files.

- To remove a file, simply type rm *filename*. You can remove many files by supplying a list of filenames.

> **Warning**
>
> You will not be prompted for confirmation. Under Linux, it is practically impossible to "undelete" a file. Once a file is gone, it's gone. Be careful.

- To have rm prompt for confirmation, use the -i option:

    ```
    $ rm -i junk trash precious temp
    ```

    You will be prompted for each file that is about to be deleted.
- To remove entire directory trees recursively, use the -r option:

    ```
    $ rm -r junkdir
    ```

> **Warning**
>
> Recursive removal is very dangerous. Pause for breath and examine the command line before pressing Enter.

- `rm` will sometimes prompt you even if you don't supply the `-i` option. (For example, it prompts if you try to remove a file to which you don't have write permission. Even though it is legal to remove the file if you have write permission in the directory containing it, `rm` views this situation as unusual and prompts.) If you want `rm` to forge ahead no questions asked and without printing any error messages, use the `-f` option:

    ```
    $ rm -r -f ireallymeanit
    ```

Make Directories: `mkdir`

The UNIX file system is organized around hierarchical directories. The `mkdir` command creates these directories. Use it as follows:

- To create a directory, use `mkdir` *directory*. The parent directory must exist. For example, if you wish to create the directory `/home/dave/Projects/calendar`, the directory `/home/dave/Projects` must already exist.
- However, if you would like `mkdir` to make parent directories if necessary, use the `-p` option:

    ```
    $ mkdir -p /home/dave/a/very/deep/subdirectory
    ```

- You can make a number of directories at once, like this:

    ```
    $ mkdir dir1 dir2 dir2 dir4 dir5
    ```

Remove Directories: `rmdir`

The command `rmdir` removes directories. However, it will only remove a directory if it is empty. You're more likely to use `rm -r` to remove a whole directory tree.

- To remove a directory, use:

    ```
    $ rmdir directory
    ```

- You can remove many directories at a time:

    ```
    $ rmdir dir1 dir2 dir3
    ```

- If you have a subtree of otherwise-empty directories, you can use the `-p` option:

    ```
    $ rmdir -p a/b/c
    ```

which is equivalent to

```
$ rmdir -p a/b/c
$ rmdir -p a/b
$ rmdir -p a
```

See the Contents of Files: cat

Let's look at cat in more detail. In the "I/O Redirection" section, we saw cat operating as a simple filter. In fact, cat is a far more complicated animal.

Arguments to cat

cat can take arguments. Each argument is treated as a filename; each is opened in turn and the contents sent to standard output. For example,

```
$ cat file1 file2 file3
```

sends the contents of file1, file2, and file3 in turn to standard output.

> This explains the origin of the name *cat*: It stands for *concatenate*. (Even if it turns out that this derivation is not really true, it's a nice rationalization.)

Numbering Lines

The -n option causes cat to number lines as it prints them. Here's an example:

```
$ cat > tmpfile
A line

Another line
Ctrl-D
$ cat -n tmpfile
1  A line
2
3  Another line
```

If you don't want blank lines numbered, use the -b option:

```
$ cat -b -n tmpfile
1  A line

2  Another line
```

The blank line is still displayed; it's just not numbered.

Squeezing Blank Lines

If you have files with many blank lines interspersed between lines of text, use the -s option to "squeeze" multiple blank lines into single blank lines.

Page Through a File: more

The more command lets you view a file in manageable chunks. Whereas cat sends its (possibly voluminous) output to standard output without pausing, more is more civilized—after each screenful of output, it pauses to let you read the information.

> **Note**
>
> MS-DOS and Windows have a *more* command, but the UNIX version is far more capable.

To page through a file, use

```
$ more filename
```

Try it on an example: Try more /etc/zshrc.

After the first screenful of information, the computer will display something like:

```
-More-(14%)
```

in reverse-video.

- Press Enter to advance by a single line.
- Press the spacebar to advance by a screenful.
- Press **b** to go back by a screenful.
- Press **?** to get a help screen. This shows the available commands.

Although more is the traditional UNIX pager, the far more powerful less program is a better choice for paging through files. It has many advanced features and may be quicker than more. You use less just like more:

```
$ less filename
```

UNIX Manual Pages: man

The command for accessing on-line UNIX documentation is man.

man is both one of the most useful and one of the least useful UNIX commands available. If you are fairly familiar with UNIX, man is very useful: The UNIX manual pages are the definitive description of UNIX commands, system calls, file formats, and library functions. However, if you are just starting out with UNIX, the manual pages can be very intimidating. For an example, try this command:

```
$ man ls
```

You will see (paged through more) a huge piece of documentation, which mentions such esoterica as "POSIX options," "GNU options," and "-1abcdfgiklmnopqrstuxABCD FGLNQRSUX." Who would have thought that our friend ls could be so complicated?

Parts of a Manual Page

To understand a manual page (often called a man page), let's first look at the structure of a man page. A man page is divided into sections; typical sections are

> NAME   The name of the command with a one-line description of its purpose
>
> SYNOPSIS   A brief illustration of how to invoke the command, a list of options and a list of arguments
>
> DESCRIPTION   A long description of the function of the command
>
> OPTIONS   An exhaustive description of the commands' options and their meanings
>
> ENVIRONMENT   Any special environment variables used by the command

> **Note**
>
> Environment variables will be described in Chapter 3.

> FILES   Any particular files used or referenced by the command
>
> AUTHOR   The author of the command
>
> CONFORMING TO   Standards to which the command conforms
>
> BUGS   Known problems or inelegances
>
> SEE ALSO   A list of related man pages

Not all man pages have all these sections, and some man pages have additional sections, but these sections are the most common.

Manual Sections

By ancient UNIX tradition, the entire set of manual pages is divided into sections. These sections are usually (but not always) named by a single digit or letter. The most commonly agreed-upon sections are

1. User commands. The usual UNIX commands like `ls` and `cat`.
2. System calls. Procedures that invoke code in the UNIX kernel. They are of concern to UNIX programmers.
3. Subroutines. Library functions that may not involve a system call such as Standard C functions. Section 3 is mostly of interest to programmers.
4. Devices. Documentation of the kernel's interface between hardware devices and user programs. This section is definitely only of interest to programmers and system administrators.
5. File formats. Format and meaning of editing text files. Most UNIX programs are configured by editing text files. This information is of interest to system administrators and casual users—Section 5 will tell you how to configure various programs according to your preferences.
6. Games. This section does not officially exist, because we all know that UNIX is meant for serious work.
7. Miscellaneous. Man pages that couldn't be otherwise classified.
8. System Administration. Commands that only system administrators should use but that every casual user reads about and tries.

These manual section numbers are fairly standardized but are by no means universal. For example, many installations feature sections *n* for "new" pages and *l* for "local" pages. Others feature even more sections. Unfortunately, the choice of which section to place a page in differs from system to system.

Often, you'll see a reference to a man page written as `command(section)`. For example, the `ls` man page is often referred to as `ls(1)`. You can specify a particular section to man by typing

```
$ man section entry
```

Try these commands:

```
$ man 1 chown
$ man 2 chown
```

As you see, `chown` is both a user command and a system call. The pages are distinguished by calling one `chown(1)` and the other `chown(2)`.

> **Note**
>
> Please note: The man section entry syntax works on Linux, but other UNIX versions use a different syntax. On Solaris, for example, you specify the section as `man -s section entry`.

Most sections have a page called *intro*, which may or may not contain useful information about the section. On Caldera OpenLinux, for example, intro(1) is terse and unhelpful, but intro(3) is quite useful.

> **Note**
>
> You know by now that to see intro(3) you must type `man 3 intro`.

Reading a Manual Page

Let's go through the ls(1) man page. After you know how to decipher that, you'll be confident enough to use man like a pro, and no UNIX command will intimidate you.

Name

The name section is fairly straightforward. It lists ls, dir, and vdir as commands that "list directory contents."

Synopsis

The synopsis line reads:

```
ls [options] [file...]
```

This means that ls is optionally followed by options (the square brackets indicate optional items) possibly followed by one or more filenames (square brackets indicate that they're optional; the ellipsis indicates possible repetition).

The next line reads:

```
POSIX options: [-CFRacdilqrtu1]
```

As mentioned in Chapter 1, POSIX, a committee of the IEEE, is standardizing UNIX-like operating systems. The POSIX options are likely to work on virtually all UNIX systems.

The next line, GNU options, indicates those options specific to the GNU version of ls. These options are likely to work on any Linux system and will work on other UNIX systems that use the GNU ls but are not standardized by POSIX.

Note that GNU programs usually have two forms for their options: short and long forms. For example, considering ls, the option -a causes all files, even those that start with a period (.), to be listed. With GNU ls, you can also use the equivalent long option -all. The GNU long options always start with two dashes and are designed to be readable. The POSIX short options always start with one dash and are designed to be easy to type. You can pick whichever style you prefer or even mix-and-match them.

Description

The description section is noted for its insistence on completeness and accuracy, not for helping beginners along. However, if you persevere, you'll appreciate having access to all the information rather than having "advanced" information hidden from you for the sake of softening the learning process.

Environment

This section lists the environment variables that `ls` cares about. It is primarily used for fine-tuning its behavior or altering the language of messages to other than English.

Bugs

This section lists odd behavior of `ls`. It so happens that the only `ls` bugs reported are for other UNIX systems, not for Linux. Linux `ls` is therefore bug-free…

Conforming To

GNU `ls` conforms to POSIX standard 1003.2.

See Also

We are told to look at `dircolors(1)`. This tells us how to set up `ls` to display its output in color if the terminal supports that. This lets us see directories in blue, compressed files in red, and so on.

Virtual Consoles

Even if you don't have a graphical interface, Linux lets you run several terminal sessions at once from the console. Imagine an array of seven or eight computers side by side. Linux lets you switch among these virtual computers by pressing Ctrl+Alt+Fn. For example, Ctrl+Alt+F1 switches you to the first virtual console.

Each virtual console can contain a full terminal session or even the whole KDE desktop environment. Try switching consoles, logging in at various places, and seeing what happens.

Virtual consoles are extremely useful. Even if you do not run the X Window System, virtual consoles allow you to have multiple interactive login sessions. This can be handy for performing administrative tasks or killing misbehaving programs. On slow systems, you might not want to run X, and virtual consoles give you the convenience of multiple terminals.

> **Note**
>
> Under the standard Caldera setup, KDE runs in virtual console 8. There's nothing useful in virtual console 7, but virtual consoles 1–6 offer full login sessions. If you're in a text-mode virtual console, you can use Alt+F*n* to switch consoles. In an X Window session, you need to use Ctrl+Alt+F*n*. It's easier to use Ctrl+Alt+F*n* everywhere because it doesn't hurt in a text-mode console.

Typing Shortcuts

The problem with a command-line interface is that it involves a lot of typing, and people tend to minimize the amount of typing they do. This means that they name files with names like `frpt9899` rather than `fiscal-report-1998-99.txt`. Graphical interfaces reduce the problem because files are often selected from a graphical dialog, eliminating the need to type their names.

Filename Completion

With modern shells, there is no excuse for taking typing shortcuts. Let's create four files named `a-long-filename`, `b-long-filename`, `b-long-again`, and `c-what-i-mean`. Create an empty test directory and change to it. Then type:

```
$ cat < /dev/null > a-long-filename
$ cat < /dev/null > b-long-filename
$ cat < /dev/null > b-long-again
$ cat < /dev/null > c-what-i-mean
```

(Recall our discussion concerning `/dev/null` in the "Discarding Output" section.)

Now, let's say we want to use `cat` to filter `a-long-filename`. At the command prompt, type **cat a** and then press Tab. The shell fills in the whole filename `a-long-filename` for you.

How did this work? The shell examined the partial command line and determined that you were looking for a file whose name began with *a*. It scanned the directory, found the only possible file that would match, and completed the name for you.

What if you start with **cat b** and then press Tab? In this case, the shell fills in as far as `b-long-`, and the terminal beeps. The shell knows you're looking for a file starting with *b*, but there is more than one possibility. It completes up to the longest common stem and then beeps.

If you press Tab a second time, the shell lists the possibilities. You can complete the filename yourself, or type enough characters to disambiguate the choice and then press Tab again.

> **Tip**
>
> The second Tab trick works for bash. If your shell is tcsh, you need to press Ctrl+D to get a listing of the possibilities. If your shell is csh or sh, you do not have completion at all. tcsh has a very elaborate completion mechanism and is described in Chapter 3.

If a completed filename is a directory, the shell is clever enough to add a trailing slash to it. You can even keep going, completing your way all the way down a long directory path. On my Caldera OpenLinux system, I can get to the 38-character file /usr/share/sendmail/cf/ostype/linux.m4 with just 15 keystrokes:

```
$ /u Tab sh Tab se Tab c Tab o Tab l Tab
```

Command Editing

The shell lets you edit commands as you type them.

- Use the left and right arrow keys to move back and forth in the command line.
- Type characters to insert them where the cursor is.
- While you're editing a command, press Ctrl+D to delete the character under the cursor.

> **Note**
>
> Don't press Ctrl+D if you just have a shell prompt and no command yet. Ctrl+D is the terminal end-of-file character, and pressing it first thing after a shell prompt may log you out!

- Press up or down arrow to move to the previous or next command in the command history. Note that moving around in the command history discards any edits you may have made to the current command.
- Press Ctrl+A to move to the beginning of the command.
- Press Ctrl+E to move to the end of the command.

- Press Ctrl+K to delete all characters from the cursor's position to the end of the command.

> **Note**
>
> As always, the keystrokes described here are completely configurable. The settings described are merely the defaults for the bash and tcsh shells.

Configuration Files

Most UNIX programs are configurable. They read their configuration information from configuration files, which are usually plain text files. You can look at configuration files for now, but don't edit them. The meanings of the configuration files are explained in the chapters that describe the programs that use them.

Configuration files may be grouped into two broad categories:

- Systemwide configuration files apply to every user and are usually stored in the directory /etc or one of its subdirectories.
- Per-user configuration files are stored in each user's home directory. They are usually hidden files: They are named starting with a period, so they don't appear in normal ls listings.

bash Configuration Files

bash uses several systemwide and per-user configuration files. If your shell is a login shell (which it usually is), bash starts like this:

- If /etc/profile exists, the shell reads it and executes commands found there. This is called sourcing the file.
- If ~/.bash_profile exists, it is sourced. Otherwise, if ~/.bash_login exists, it is sourced. Otherwise, if ~/.profile exists, it is sourced.

  When you exit from a login bash shell, it sources ~/.bash_logout if it exists.

  If bash is not a login shell (if, for example, you type **bash** at the shell prompt), then it simply sources ~/.bashrc if it exists.

> **Note**
>
> bash has command-line options that alter this behavior. For more details, see the man page bash(1).

tcsh Configuration Files

tcsh has a more complicated startup sequence. A login *tcsh* sources the following files if they exist:

- /etc/csh.cshrc
- /etc/csh.login
- ~/.tcshrc or, if not found, ~/.cshrc
- ~/.history
- ~/.login
- ~/.cshdirs

Non-login shells only read /etc/csh.cshrc and ~/.tcshrc or ~/.cshrc.

Chapter 3 describes the contents of these text files in detail. You can use any text editor (such as the simple KDE text editor) to edit the files.

You might want to look at some of these files with more to get a feeling for the types of things that can be configured. Don't expect to understand too much at this point, however.

Processes

Every running program on a UNIX system is called a process. Each process is identified by a small integer called the process ID or pid for short. You should understand how UNIX processes work. Often, you need to find out the process ID of a runaway program to terminate it. If the system is busy, you need to find out which processes are running and hogging the computer.

Listing Processes

To see the processes on your Linux system, type this:

$ **ps**

The output will probably look something (but not exactly) like this:

```
  PID TTY          TIME CMD
  889 ttyp0    00:00:00 bash
  903 ttyp0    00:01:48 emacs
 1088 ttyp0    00:00:00 ps
```

The PID column lists the process IDs. The TTY column specifies the terminal associated with the command. The TIME column specifies how much CPU time the command has consumed. Finally, the CMD column is the name of the command that is running.

ps has a slew of command-line options. The `-u` option formats the output in a user-oriented fashion. The output produced by the `-u` option provides information about which user is running which processes. This lets you assign blame if someone is taking up all your memory or CPU time.

```
$ ps -u
USER  PID %CPU %MEM   VSZ  RSS TTY   STAT START  TIME COMMAND
dfs   889  0.0  0.8  1860 1036 ttyp0 S    09:07  0:00 bash
dfs   903  2.3  7.0 11488 9060 ttyp0 S    09:09  1:51 emacs ch2.tex
```

The new columns have the following meanings:

- USER The user running the process.
- %CPU The percentage of CPU time used by the process.
- %MEM The percentage of physical memory used by the process.
- VSZ   The size of the process's virtual memory space.
- RSS   The "resident set size" of the process. This is the amount of physical memory currently consumed.
- STAT The process status, which is usually R (runnable), S (sleeping), or T (stopped). There are other status codes. See ps(1) for details.
- START When the process was started.

ps usually shows you only your processes; to see all processes, use the `-a` option. To see processes not associated with any terminal, use the `-x` option. Try this to get a feeling for what's running on your system:

```
$ ps -aux
```

Wow. There's a lot going on behind the scenes. (See Figure 2.5.)

Killing Processes

Usually, you look at the process listing just before you're about to kill a process. For example, let's say you have an `ls` process that seems to be hung up—it refuses to stop.

You can open another terminal window if you're using KDE, or you can switch to another virtual console if you're not and use ps to get the pid of the ls process. Armed with that number, type this:

```
$ kill pid
```

This should terminate the process.

> **Note**
>
> It does this by sending it a "terminate signal."

Essential OpenLinux

PART I

FIGURE 2.5
Output of `ps -aux`

USER	PID	%CPU	%MEM	VSZ	RSS	TTY	STAT	START	TIME	COMMAND
root	1	0.3	0.3	1104	476	?	S	12:42	0:04	init [5]
root	2	0.0	0.0	0	0	?	SW	12:42	0:00	[kflushd]
root	3	0.0	0.0	0	0	?	SW	12:42	0:00	[kpiod]
root	4	0.0	0.0	0	0	?	SW	12:42	0:00	[kswapd]
root	161	0.0	0.2	1072	300	?	S	12:42	0:00	update (bdflush)
root	576	0.0	0.4	1284	572	?	S	12:43	0:00	syslogd
root	579	0.0	0.5	1384	728	?	S	12:43	0:00	klogd -k /boot/Sy
root	592	0.0	0.7	1664	932	?	S	12:43	0:00	named
root	598	0.0	0.4	1252	532	?	S	12:43	0:00	inetd
bin	600	0.0	0.3	1108	392	?	S	12:43	0:00	rpc.portmap
daemon	634	0.0	0.6	1700	824	?	S	12:43	0:00	lpd START_IDLE
root	641	0.0	0.4	1248	600	?	S	12:43	0:00	cron
root	649	0.0	0.5	1444	744	?	S	12:43	0:00	mountd
root	651	0.0	0.5	1460	752	?	S	12:43	0:00	nfsd
daemon	657	0.0	0.4	1228	516	?	S	12:43	0:00	atd
root	663	0.0	0.8	1916	1076	?	S	12:43	0:00	sendmail: accepti
root	674	0.0	0.3	1092	396	?	S	12:43	0:00	rpc.rstatd
postgres	698	0.0	0.8	5640	1116	?	S	12:43	0:00	/usr/local/pgsql/
root	718	0.0	0.7	2280	1000	?	S	12:43	0:00	httpd -f /etc/htt
nobody	722	0.0	0.7	2292	1000	?	S	12:43	0:00	httpd -f /etc/htt
nobody	723	0.0	0.7	2292	1000	?	S	12:43	0:00	httpd -f /etc/htt
root	732	0.0	0.6	1924	812	?	S	12:43	0:00	smbd -D
root	734	0.0	0.6	1504	800	?	S	12:43	0:00	nmbd -D
root	827	0.0	0.2	1076	376	tty1	S	12:43	0:00	/sbin/getty tty1
root	828	0.0	0.2	1076	376	tty2	S	12:43	0:00	/sbin/getty tty2
root	829	0.0	0.2	1076	376	tty3	S	12:43	0:00	/sbin/getty tty3
root	830	0.0	0.2	1076	376	tty4	S	12:43	0:00	/sbin/getty tty4
root	831	0.0	0.2	1076	376	tty5	S	12:43	0:00	/sbin/getty tty5
root	832	0.0	0.2	1076	376	tty6	S	12:43	0:00	/sbin/getty tty6
root	833	0.0	0.4	1280	584	?	S	12:43	0:00	/usr/sbin/mgetty
root	834	0.0	1.7	5444	2252	?	S	12:43	0:00	/opt/kde/bin/kdm
root	836	0.9	4.8	17096	6184	?	S	12:43	0:11	/usr/X11R6/bin/X
root	840	0.0	3.1	6364	4036	?	S	12:43	0:00	-:0
dfs	853	0.0	3.2	6156	4112	?	S	12:43	0:00	kwm
dfs	864	0.0	2.7	6120	3544	?	S	12:43	0:00	/opt/kde/bin/kbgn
dfs	880	0.0	2.6	6820	3376	?	RN	12:43	0:00	/opt/kde/bin/kpip
dfs	888	0.0	3.4	7660	4372	?	S	12:43	0:00	kfm
dfs	889	0.0	2.0	5788	2600	?	S	12:43	0:00	kaudioserver
dfs	890	0.0	2.5	5584	3220	?	S	12:43	0:00	kwmsound
dfs	891	0.0	2.6	5664	3432	?	S	12:43	0:00	krootwm
dfs	892	0.0	3.1	6120	4080	?	S	12:43	0:00	kpanel
dfs	895	0.0	1.9	5816	2484	?	S	12:43	0:00	maudio -media 4
dfs	908	0.0	2.7	5632	3508	?	S	12:43	0:00	/usr/opt/kde/bin/
root	910	0.0	1.4	3252	1888	?	S	12:43	0:00	xterm
dfs	911	0.0	0.8	1864	1036	ttyp0	S	12:43	0:00	bash
dfs	925	1.4	21.2	40336	27224	ttyp0	S	12:44	0:16	/opt/Office50/bin
dfs	943	0.0	21.2	40336	27224	ttyp0	S	12:44	0:00	/opt/Office50/bin
dfs	944	0.0	21.2	40336	27224	ttyp0	S	12:44	0:00	/opt/Office50/bin
dfs	945	0.0	21.2	40336	27224	ttyp0	S	12:44	0:00	/opt/Office50/bin
dfs	946	0.0	21.2	40336	27224	ttyp0	S	12:44	0:00	/opt/Office50/bin
dfs	947	0.0	21.2	40336	27224	ttyp0	S	12:44	0:00	/opt/Office50/bin
dfs	962	0.0	0.6	2576	896	ttyp0	R	13:03	0:00	ps -aux

Some processes refuse to die even if killed. For stubborn processes like those, use this:

```
$ kill -9 pid
```

> This sends the victim process a "kill" signal, which is the UNIX equivalent of a nuclear bomb. Nothing should be able to survive a "kill" signal. For readability, you can use `kill -KILL` instead of `kill -9`.

Common Problems

Here are some common problems that new UNIX users sometimes encounter. They relate to problems when you type at the terminal, not problems associated with setting up Linux or using a graphical interface.

The Terminal Is Frozen

Sometimes, you'll be typing happily and suddenly the terminal will stop responding. Nothing you type appears; the shell is likewise silent.

In all likelihood, you accidentally pressed Ctrl+S. To unfreeze the terminal, press Ctrl+Q. But beware: Everything you typed has been queued, so you may be greeted with a lot of output, error messages, and unfriendly beeping.

> Why on earth does the terminal behave this way? Back in the Mesozoic era of computing, terminals used a software flow-control protocol called XON/XOFF. If the computer was sending data too quickly, the terminal sent an XOFF character to tell it to stop for a while. When the terminal was ready for more, it sent XON. You may have guessed that XOFF corresponds to Ctrl+S and XON to Ctrl+Q.

I Type and All I Get Is "?"

If the computer gets into a mode in which it seems to ignore everything you type, responding with a simple question mark (?), then you probably accidentally invoked the ed text editor. This is an ancient (though quite powerful) line-oriented text editor. To get out of it, just press Ctrl+D.

> **Note**
>
> Ctrl+C won't get you out of ed; it intercepts the interrupt key.

The Shell Prompt Changed and the Shell Ignores Me

If the shell prompt changes to > and the shell seems to consume your input without reacting, you probably accidentally typed an unmatched quote character. Quote characters, as is explained in Chapter 3, have special meaning to the shell, and it wants them to be matched.

To get out of this situation, simply press Ctrl+C.

Summary

In this chapter, you learned how to log in and out of Linux and how to change your password with passwd. You learned the basic structure of the file system and the commands for creating and removing directories. You learned about file permissions and symbolic links.

Next, you learned how most UNIX commands are structured and some of the common commands for manipulating files. You learned the most important UNIX command, man, for reading online manual pages. You learned about advanced features like switching virtual consoles and filename completion. Finally, you learned how to examine which processes are running and how to terminate runaway processes.

Using the Shell

CHAPTER 3

IN THIS CHAPTER

- bash *56*
- Shell History *57*
- Shell Variables *68*
- tcsh *72*

The shell is your most basic, and in many ways most flexible, interface to the system. You can access every imaginable nook and cranny of your system with a few keystrokes. The power one wields with a shell can be wonderfully useful and entertaining. What is elegant simplicity to some, though, is indecipherable gibberish to others, and it is this interaction with the command line, probably more than anything else, that has won UNIX its reputation for difficulty. That said, UNIX isn't as difficult as you may fear.

The one thing UNIX shells reward most is thoughtfulness. It is a well-worn saying that UNIX gives you enough rope to hang yourself (sometimes several times over), so it pays to think about what you want to accomplish and think about how you are going to accomplish it. One would hardly expect that asking a user to think is the worst sin an Operating System can commit, yet it certainly isn't fashionable.

You *will* need to interact with the shell. If you start slowly and work at it some, you will come to appreciate it, probably more than any other part of the system.

There are many different shells around. People have different tastes in how they want to interact with the system, and from this have grown a wide assortment of shells. OpenLinux includes the following:

```
/bin/bash (and possibly bash2, depending on how you installed)
/bin/sh (symbolic link to /bin/bash)
/bin/tcsh
/bin/csh (symbolic link to /bin/tcsh)
/bin/zsh
```

There are a number of other shells around if you don't like those choices. Largely all shells break down into three categories based on the command syntax they use: those based on `sh` (the Bourne shell), those based on `csh` (the C shell), and those based on `ksh` (the Korn shell). Because the Korn shell is not represented in OpenLinux (although many of its features are), we will look at the two shells representative of their class that OpenLinux does provide: `bash`, a Bourne-type shell, and `tcsh`, a C-type shell.

bash

`bash`—the Bourne Again Shell—is based loosely on the traditions of the first real command interpreter in UNIX, the Bourne Shell. The purpose was to provide a solid shell for the GNU system, of course, and ultimately POSIX Shell conformance. (POSIX is the IEEE Portable Operating System Interface—a series of standards that define basic interfaces and functionalities for an operating system. Systems that attain POSIX conformance should, theoretically, be able to run programs for the same code base.)

As in most GNU projects, however, simply providing a working program turned out not to be enough. Either by design or simply because of the needs of each person working on it, the `bash` shell has grown to be a very full-featured shell. It proudly "stole" all the best features it could from the other shells around (notably `sh`, `csh`, and `ksh`) and then added many unique features of its own. `bash` is the de facto standard shell on all major Linux distributions. Many UNIX users and system administrators won't last five minutes with `/bin/sh` before installing `bash`, and a plethora of the other GNU tools, on whatever box they happen to be on.

> **Caution**
>
> The `bash` shell is, without a doubt, the most popular and commonly used shell for Linux. Caldera OpenLinux allows you to choose the initial default shell for users during installation. If you want to try a different shell after install, you must use the `chsh` command after logging in to change shells. When changing shells, the `chsh` command will ask for your password and the location and name of the new shell. The new shell will become your default shell, but only if its name is in the list of acceptable system shells in `/etc/shells`. Make sure the shell is installed and listed in your system's `/etc/shells` file, or you won't be able to log in!

Shell History

`bash` has a very useful feature called command history. It is one of the features borrowed from the C shell. Command history keeps track of the last commands you have used (the number kept is configurable). Using this, you can view the commands and, more important, reuse them. This is wonderful when you must do many repetitive tasks; you can let the history feature type for you.

The number of options for using history can be quite staggering (as are most options in `bash`). A few options you will use daily and come to rely on; some you will only be reminded of when you rediscover them in the documentation or this book. Probably the most used of all isn't exactly a command, but rather a use of the cursor keys. In `bash` (assuming a normal 101- or 104-key keyboard), the up arrow will scroll through the previous commands, which you can edit using the left- and right-arrow keys and then execute by pressing Enter. The down-arrow key will scroll back down through your history to the current command line. Also, as indicated earlier, the number of items in your command history is configurable. The `bash` environment variable HISTSIZE controls the number of commands that are remembered. `bash` also stores your history in a file pointed to by the environment variable HISTFILE (the default value is `/your/home/.bash_history`), and the number of commands kept in HISTFILE is controlled by the environment variable HISTFILESIZE. The point of this is that if you log out, then log back in, you can still retrieve commands from your last session. You can examine all this command history data using the shell command history, which gives a numbered list of all the commands you have executed (up to HISTSIZE). history [n] will show the last n commands.

The following commands are likely to be used frequently, too. They are what bash refers to as event designators. Basically that means that they reference a particular event or command line in the history. Be aware that the whole of the previous command will be executed (barring substitution).

!	This, the "bang" character, tells bash you want to use a previous command in the history list.
!!	This tells bash to execute the previous command again (that is, the very last command entered will be executed again). This could also be written !-1.
!string	Execute the most recent command starting with string.

Example 3.1

```
$ ls /
auto/   bru/   home/    lib/          net/    root/   usr/
bin/    dev/   initrd/  lost+found/   opt/    sbin/   var/
boot/   etc/   install/ mnt/          proc/   tmp/    vmlinuz

$ !ls
auto/   bru/   home/    lib/          net/    root/   usr/
bin/    dev/   initrd/  lost+found/   opt/    sbin/   var/
boot/   etc/   install/ mnt/          proc/   tmp/    vmlinuz
```

!n	Execute the command line numbered n (that is, if there are 500 lines in your history, you could say !400 and execute the 400th command). This is very useful in combination with the history command.
!-n	Execute the current command line minus n (that is, -1 is the immediately preceding command, -2 is the one preceding that, and so on).
!?string[?]	Execute the previous instance of the command containing string (note the difference between !string and !?string—the latter will execute a command that contains string anywhere within the command. !string only repeats commands that begin with string.)
^string1^string2^	This is a substitution command. It repeats the last command, replacing string1 with string2.

Example 3.2

```
$ ls /
auto/   bru/   home/     lib/          net/    root/   usr/
bin/    dev/   initrd/   lost+found/   opt/    sbin/   var/
boot/   etc/   install/  mnt/          proc/   tmp/    vmlinuz

$ ^/^/mnt^
ls /mnt
cdrom/   fd0/   fd1/   floppy/   floppy2/
```

```
You can see where "/" was replaced with "/mnt".
```

Next are the commands bash calls word designators (that is, they act on words or elements of a command line). These are denoted by a colon (:) between the ! and the word designator. The most useful of these include:

0   This means execute the 0 word; it denotes the actual program name itself. For example:

Example 3.3

```
$ ls /
auto/   bru/   home/     lib/          net/    root/   usr/
bin/    dev/   initrd/   lost+found/   opt/    sbin/   var/
boot/   etc/   install/  mnt/          proc/   tmp/    vmlinuz

$ !:0
ls
Desktop/   geekcode-1.1.tar.gz   src/              tmp/
Mail/      nsmail/               test/             updates/
book@      pinfo-0.5.6.tar.gz    tkinfo-2.5.tar.gz
```

As you can see, the execution of !:0 executed ls with no arguments—it executed the 0th word, the command itself, only.

^   This means the first word, not the command itself, but its argument.

Example 3.4

```
$ ls /
auto/   bru/   home/     lib/          net/    root/   usr/
bin/    dev/   initrd/   lost+found/   opt/    sbin/   var/
boot/   etc/   install/  mnt/          proc/   tmp/    vmlinuz

$ cd !:^
cd /
$ pwd
/
$
```

And of course everybody's favorite:

s/old/new/   (substitute new in place of old).

Example 3.5

```
$ ls /usr
X11R6/  dict/    games/       include/ java/ libexec/  man/       sbin/ src/
bin/    doc/     i386-linux/  info/    lib/  local/    openwin/   share/

$ !:s/usr/var/
ls /var
adm/  catman/  lib/ lock/  log/   nis/  run/spool/ state/  tmp/
```

I/O Redirection

Data presented to or produced by UNIX shells is separated into one of three categories—stdin, stdout, or stderr. These data can be directed by using the > and < characters to a file or command you want to manipulate or store the data in.

- stdin   Standard input is the input a command receives and is represented by <.
- stdout Standard output is the output a command produces and is represented by >. (It is technically the first file descriptor, so it can also be represented by 1> or 1 see the following discussion.)
- stderr Standard error is the output a command produces on error and is represented by >. (It is the second file descriptor.)

Example 3.6   stdout to a File

```
$ command > file
$ command 1> file
$ command >| file    [This is a clobber redirection]
```

In this example, you can see stdout at work. The output of command is directed to file. The significance of the >| in the third line is that it will "clobber" the file. In other words, the shell will not check whether you had intended to destroy an already existing file; it will just write to it. (This normally only matters if you had previously set the noclobber shell variable.)

Example 3.7   Appending stdout

```
$ command >> file
```

This shows appending stdout to a file. If file already exists and contains data you want to keep, you can add the output of command to file by appending with >>.

Example 3.8   Redirecting stdin

```
$ command < file
```

Here you can see `stdin` being directed from `file` to `command`. Note that this isn't always needed and that some programs won't even work with it. This is support for some programs that don't take the fairly standardized:

```
$ command file
```

to mean use `file` as standard input for `command`; they require you to be explicit about it. Many other programs will accept either syntax for their input.

Example 3.9 Reducing `stderr`

```
$ command 2> file.err
```

This shows the redirection of any errors produced by `command` to `file.err`. In fact, any output of `command` that goes to `stderr` will be redirected; it is, however, most often error information that is sent to `stderr`. Regular output of `command`—stdout—will still be displayed directly to your screen.

Example 3.10 Redirecting `stderr` *and* `stdout`

```
$ command > file 2>&1
$ command >& file
$ command &> file
```

These show the several different ways to get both `stderr` and `stdout` directed to a file. Note that the first example is the most generically useful because nearly any Bourne-type shell will understand it. The second example is borrowed from C-shell syntax, whereas the final is a pure `bash`-ism.

Example 3.11a

```
$ command << EOF
text content
you can put $VARIABLES here, too
EOF
```

Example 3.11b

```
$ command <<- EOF > file
[TAB]text
[TAB]text
EOF
```

These are "here documents"—incredibly useful little constructs, particularly in shell programs. Basically, `command` gets fed the content of the "text content" until the keyword EOF is reached (the keyword is set in the first line to the right of the << and can be anything). Example 3.11b shows the <<- construct, which does the same as the first except that it also strips off any [TAB] characters at the beginning of the text.

Pipes

It is also possible to direct the output of one command to form the input of another command. This is accomplished using the pipe ¦ character. A group of commands linked by pipes is called a pipeline. This is extremely useful. You can take a number of simple, single-purpose programs and string them together in a way that outputs precisely what you want or need. This is one of the cornerstones of UNIX philosophy—simple tools that do a single job well can be combined in nearly infinite ways to do whatever you can imagine.

Example 3.12   Simple Pipeline

```
command1 ¦ command2
```

This shows a simple command pipeline—`command1` sends its output to `command2` for processing.

Example 3.13   Redirection Plus Piping

```
command1 < file ¦ command2 2> file.err ¦ command3
```

This example is more complicated because it shows redirection and piping combined. `command1` takes its input from `file` and pipes its output to `command2`, which redirects its `stderr` to `file.err` and pipes its `stdout` to `command3`.

Background Processes and Job Control

`bash` has the capability of running programs in the background; in other words, you can start a program and have it run "out of sight" while you continue to work in the same running `bash` process. `bash` can also control these running processes: it can stop and resume them, and it can take processes running in the foreground and move them to the background. The ability to change the state of running programs is called job control.

Job control commands are frequently used when someone wants to run a command in the background, but started it in the foreground by accident, or when the command started in the foreground is running much longer than the user had anticipated. When a command starts in the foreground, it locks the user out of further interaction with the shell until it is completed. This is why most nontrivial, noninteractive jobs are started in the background.

Example 3.14 shows how to start a program running in the background. When you type the command followed by an ampersand (`&`), the process will run in the background. The line after `./job-cntrl &` in this example gives some important information from the shell. The `[1]` is the program's job number, a unique number for the shell starting from 1. The `3510` is the Process ID (pid) of the program, which identifies the process across the entire system. Either of these numbers can be used to interact with the program through `bash`. As you can see, the pid is used to kill the running program.

Example 3.14

```
$ ./job-cntrl &
[1] 3510
$ kill 3510
$
[1]+  Terminated              ./job-cntrl
```

The jobs command is a `bash` command that is used to examine all the programs `bash` is currently executing. To suspend a process running in the foreground, press Ctrl+z (denoted by ^Z in the examples). After the foreground process is suspended, you can then manipulate it using the commands `bg` (background the command) and `fg` (return the command to the foreground). You can also refer to the command by its job number by placing a % sign in front of its job number. All this is shown in Example 3.15.

Example 3.15

```
$ ./job-cntrl
^Z
[1]+  Stopped                 ./job-cntrl
$ bg
[1]+ ./job-cntrl &
$ jobs
[1]+  Running                 ./job-contrl &
$ kill %1
[1]+  Terminated              ./job-contrl
```

Here `job-cntrl` is started, suspended with Ctrl+z, and backgrounded with `bg`. Then the jobs running are examined, and the job is killed using its job number (`kill %1`).

Shell Syntax

Because `bash` is a Bourne-style shell, it shares a largely common syntax with `sh` and other Bourne-type shells. The way you address commands, arguments, values, and program shell scripts is one of the major distinguishing features among the major shell types. Bourne syntax is visually different from C shell and from Korn shell (although the differences with Korn shell are somewhat less obvious). The major linguistic constructs needed to work and program within `bash` follow.

Linux supports long filenames (up to 255 characters) and has for quite a long time now. It also supports spaces in names—files, variables, and the like. People don't often use spaces, but it is important and useful to know how. It is, however, necessary to quote or escape spaces and some other special characters in order to get `bash` to recognize them. You quote them by enclosing them in single (') or double (") quotes or by using the escape character—the backslash (\). The characters that need special attention are the <space>, dollar-sign ($), back-tick (`), and quoting characters (", ', and \).

Quoting a character in single quotes ('x') preserves all characters within the single quotes. It saves spaces, but it also removes the special meaning of characters (for example, if you had assigned a value to X, the $X in single quotes will no longer have that value—it will be a literal *dollar-sign X*).

Quoting a character in double quotes ("x") preserves spaces as well as the special meaning of the characters. This means that you can use "$X" and still have it expand to the meaning of the variable X.

Quoting using the escape character (\) can preserve spaces (that is, x\ x means x<space>x), and it can also remove the special quality of the characters. If used preceding a special character (say ", $, or another \), the backslash removes the quality of the special character (for example, \$X means just dollar sign-X, not the value of variable X). Used inside double quotes, it is particularly useful for embedding a double quote within double quotes.

Example 3.16

You want to have the following in double quotes:

`"some text "with quoted parts" and the end."`

Normally the first " would match the " before "`with`" and you wouldn't end up with what you wanted. To avoid this, type:

`"some text \"with quoted parts\" and the end."`

`bash` also has a way of allowing you to denote a sequence of commands and have commands execute conditionally off other commands. This is useful for quick automation of tasks or in shell programming.

Commands separated by a semicolon are run sequentially:

`$ command ; command`

When the first command is complete, the second command will run. This feature is useful in ordering how you want things to go before starting. You will not have to wait around for something to stop so that you can type in the next thing for the shell to do.

Commands separated by && are run conditionally based on the exit status of the first command:

`$ command && command`

If the first command runs correctly, then the second command will run. If the first command fails, the second command won't run.

Commands separated by ¦¦ are run conditionally, opposite the logic of &&:

```
$ command ¦¦ command
```

If the first command fails, the second command will run; if the first command runs successfully, then the second won't run at all.

bash also allows you to group commands together:

```
$ { x ; y ; }
```

This command grouping will run all commands in curly braces ({ }), and the exit value will be the value of the last command run—success or failure.

The following command grouping runs all the commands in a subshell:

```
$ ( x ; y ; )
```

This means current shell variables and environment don't affect the commands inside the subshell. The exit status of the grouping is the exit status of the last command run.

Filename Completion

Filename completion is typically known by its more common name—"the greatest thing since sliced bread." If you can't type, or even if you can but don't find it exactly thrilling, you will love this feature—a lot. Basically, bash scans the directory and files you are working with, determines what you are trying to type, and finishes typing it for you—with a little bit of help from you, of course.

Let's take an example. Assume that the current working directory contains the following files and subdirectories:

```
News/  bin/  games/     mail/  samplefile  test/
```

If you want to change directories from the current working directory to the test subdirectory, you would normally enter the command:

```
$ cd test
```

Although this will work, bash allows you to accomplish the same thing in a more efficient manner. Because test is the only item in the directory that begins with the letter *t*, bash can figure out what you wanted when you type:

```
$ cd t[TAB]
```

After you type **t**, bash knows that you can only be referring to the `test` subdirectory and will thus complete the directory name *test* after you press the Tab key. bash then finishes the command for you and displays it on the screen. When you press Enter, the command line will be executed just as if you had typed the complete file name yourself.

For short commands like this, you might not see much value in having the shell complete the command for you. You might even be slowed down slightly on a command line as short as this. After you get used to this function, however, and as the commands you type in get longer, you will wonder how you ever lived without it.

So what happens if more than one file in the directory begins with the letter *t*? It would seem that this would cause a problem if you wanted to use command-line completion. Let's see what happens when you have the following directory contents:

```
News/  bin/  mail/  samplefile  test/  tools/  working/
```

Now you have two subdirectories in the current directory that begins with *t*. If you still want to change directories into the test subdirectory, how do you get bash to complete the subdirectory name for you? If you type **cd t[TAB]**, bash will not know which subdirectory you want to change to because **t** alone is not sufficient to distinguish `test/` from `tools/`. If all you type is **cd t[TAB]**, bash will beep at you, to let you know it doesn't know what you want. You can then add letters to the command line until what you want is clear. In this case, you would only need to type one more letter before bash could complete the command. Typing **e[TAB]** gives you:

```
$ cd test
```

If you had wanted to change into the `tools` subdirectory, you would only have had to type:

```
$ cd to[TAB]
```

Whenever you press the Tab key while typing a command, bash will try to complete the command for you. If it can't, it will fill in as much as it can and then beep, notifying you that it needs more information. All you need do is enter the next letter and press the Tab key; as soon as the partial word is unique, bash will finish the typing for you.

Wildcard Expansions and Path Expansions

bash can take shorthand notations (wildcards) and expand them into complete words and commands for you. This is another of bash's typing aids—it allows you to type in a few short letters that it will expand into a multitude of commands and arguments.

Basic wildcards are of the following types:

*	matches any character and any number of characters
?	matches any single character
[...]	matches any single character contained within the brackets

The * wildcard is likely used most often because it has the broadest meaning and can be used at both the beginning and end of words. For example, *t* will expand to absolutely any word that contains a *t* anywhere within it. It is for this reason that * can be both useful and somewhat dangerous, for it can expand beyond what you anticipate. As always, it is important to consider the ultimate consequence of what you type.

A general use of the * wildcard is to include all things of a particular type as an argument to your commands. For example, you have the following files in a directory:

work.txt   work1.txt   work2.txt   work3.txt   sched.txt

and you want to print all these text files. You could do so by using the following command:

$ lpr *.txt

All the files with the .txt extension would be printed.

The ? wildcard is much more restrictive than the * wildcard. It matches exactly one single character. Again, taking the preceding directory as an example, if you typed the following:

$ lpr work?.txt

only work1.txt, work2.txt, and work3.txt would be printed. Note that work.txt would *not* be printed. If there is no character for ? to match, then it is considered not a match and is excluded.

The [...] wildcard allows you to specify certain characters or ranges of characters to match. To print the files work1.txt, work2.txt, and work3.txt using the [...] wildcard you could enter the following:

$ lpr work[123].txt

Using a command to specify a range of characters, you would enter:

$ lpr work[1-3].txt

You can also use the [...] wildcard to *not* match certain characters or ranges. This is accomplished by making the first character inside the [ ] a ! or ^ character. For example:

$ lpr work[!12].txt

would only print work3.txt. Again, it doesn't match the lack of a character where it is trying to match, so work.txt does not print.

Shell Variables

One of the most important things in shell, particularly in programming, is assigning values to variables. Shell variables can have numeric or string (text) values; they are not typed (that is, in Example 3.17, X is an integer and Y is a string, but the reverse would work equally well).

Example 3.17

Let's say that you have two variables, X and Y. To set the value of X as the number 72 and the value of Y as "hello", type:

```
$ X=72
$ echo $X
72

$ Y="hello"
$ echo $Y
hello
```

The echo function confirms that each variable ($X and $Y) has the value we just assigned it. (Note that variables are assigned with just the variable name, whereas assigned variables are later referred to with a preceding $.)

Variables can also be assigned the output of a command, as shown here:

```
$ X=`date`
echo $X
Wed Sep 1 13:23:03 CDT 1999
```

Variables can also be compared with each other for value. This can be based on textual or arithmetic value. For example:

```
$ X=hello
$ Y=goodbye
$ [ $X = $Y ] && echo "hi"
$
$ [ $X != $Y ] && echo "bye"
bye
```

Variables can also be "exported" so that subshells will inherit their value. You will see this mostly in the configuration files that bash uses to set up its initial working environment. For example:

```
$ LESS="-M"
$ export LESS
```

This will assign the value -M to the LESS environment variable, both in the current environment and in any subshells that are run (starting another shell from this one or running a shell program inside the current shell).

bash starts up with a number of variables initialized. Many of these are important in determining how the shell functions. A description of the most useful of these variables follows:

EDITOR	The default editor program.
HISTFILE	The file used to store the command history.
HISTSIZE	The number of commands bash will hold in memory.
HOME	The current user's HOME directory.
MAIL	The path to the user's mail folder.
MAILCHECK	The interval in seconds to check $MAIL for the arrival of new mail. When new mail arrives, the user is notified.
OLDPWD	The previous working directory (the one current before the current directory was entered).
PAGER	Default program to run when presented with multiple pages of output by a program that reads this variable.
PATH	The search path that bash uses when looking for executable files (multiple paths can be listed in a single value, each separated by a colon).
PS1	The first-level prompt that is displayed on the command line. It can be set to anything, including the following special values:
\!	Displays the history number of the command.
\#	Displays the command number of the current command.
\$	Displays a $ in the prompt unless the user is root. In that case, it displays a # prompt.
\\	Displays a backslash.
\d	Displays the current date.
\h	Displays the hostname of the computer on which the shell is running.
\n	Displays a newline character.
\nnn	Displays the character that corresponds to the octal value of the number nnn.
\s	Displays the name of the shell that is running.
\t	Displays the current time.
\u	Displays the current user.
\W	Displays the base name of the current working directory.
\w	Displays the full path of the current working directory.
PWD	The current working directory.

SECONDS   The number of seconds that have elapsed since the current bash session was started.

TERM   The type of terminal the current shell is running on. (This must be accurate for a correct display.)

bash Configuration Files

As with most shells, bash looks at a number of configuration files upon startup to set initial values and environment variables. Which files get looked at (sourced) and in which order depends on how the shell was started and to some extent on the distribution running it. (OpenLinux, for example, has a somewhat more complex sequence of startup files than bash would normally use.)

The normal sequence for a login shell (one started from a login prompt or a bash started with the -login option) is as follows:

/etc/profile   bash and Bourne-type shells source this file first. It contains systemwide default values for all Bourne shells.

~/.bash_profile   bash then tries to source this bash and user-specific file.

~/.bash_login   bash then tries to source this bash and user-specific file.

~/.profile   Finally bash tries to source this Bourne-type and user-specific file.

~/.bash_logout   On exit, it tries to source this file (which 99% of the time only contains the clear command to clear the screen).

In OpenLinux, this process is a bit more complicated. The files ~/.bash_profile and ~/.bash_login don't exist (in the distribution install). When you log in to OpenLinux, things go like this:

/etc/profile

bash initially sources this.

~/.profile

bash then sources this. It is intended to hold user-specific settings for any Bourne-type shell. This then pulls in the next file:

~/.bashrc

This is normally used to hold bash and user-specific settings. The OpenLinux distribution, however, intends for this file to hold per-user variables set by the installation. (.bashrc-private serves the same purpose in OpenLinux that .bashrc normally would.) This then pulls in the next file:

/etc/config.d/shells/bashrc

This is the systemwide initialization file for interactive shells (this file is unique to OpenLinux and so is only the case for OpenLinux), which sources:

`~/.bashrc-private`

This file is also unique to OpenLinux and is intended to hold settings for a particular user that would be held in `~/.bashrc` on other systems. After this one is done, control is returned to:

`~/.profile`

which pulls in ...

`/etc/config.d/shells/profile`

This holds systemwide defaults for any Bourne-type login shells (this file, too, is unique to OpenLinux):

`~/.profile-private`

Finally this file is sourced. It is intended to hold user-specific settings for any Bourne-type shell. This again is a pure OpenLinux-ism. In fact, the file doesn't actually exist in the default OpenLinux install (but if it did it would get sourced).

`~/.bash_logout`

On exit, this file is sourced (which in OpenLinux only contains the command to clear the screen).

Also, interactive shells can source a `~/.inputrc file`, if available (not by default in OpenLinux), to get key bindings.

For an interactive but not login shell (`bash` without the `-login` option) only the file `~/.bashrc` is sourced (by `bash` itself). Of course, in OpenLinux `~/.bashrc` pulls in `/etc/config.d/shells/bashrc` and `~/.bashrc-private`.

Noninteractive shells (generally shells started for or from a program) will source the file pointed to by the `BASH_ENV` variable and then the `ENV` variable, if either of those exists.

Also, if `bash` is invoked as `sh` (that is, if it is started up as `/bin/sh` and not `/bin/bash`) it only sources `/etc/profile` and `~/.profile` (but you have already seen what all those files bring in under OpenLinux).

Basically, configuring `bash` in OpenLinux boils down to looking at all the preceding files to see what they do. This exercise provides an excellent education in how shell variables and commands work.

You should, however, only need to make changes to `~/.bashrc-private` to get the shell configured the way you want it.

tcsh

`tcsh` is a modified version of the C shell (`csh`). It is fully backward-compatible with `csh` but contains many new features that make user interaction much easier. The biggest improvements over the `csh` are in the areas of command-line editing and history navigation. You will find that `tcsh` and `bash` have much in common, with each shell offering a few "special features" responsible for its uniqueness. A bit of experimentation and familiarity with your own working style will help you determine which of these shells is more comfortable and useful for you.

Comparing tcsh and bash

The C shell was originally developed by Bill Joy (of Sun fame) while working on BSD UNIX. Basically it was written to approximate C-language syntax in a shell (hence the name) because many programmers found Bourne syntax unpleasant. As it turned out, early versions of `csh` had some flaws that would pop up most spectacularly and frequently in programming, so, ironically, the shell grew more popular among everyday users as a login shell, while many professionals continued writing programs in `sh`.

Many of the useful features in `bash` are present in `tcsh` and even work the same way (for example, command completion, wildcards, and input/output redirection). Other features, like command history, are similar without being identical. `tcsh` also offers features not available in `bash`, such as spelling correction.

tcsh Command Summary

A brief list of some of the most useful `tcsh` commands follows:

- `alias`   Used to set and display aliases, command nicknames that can be set by the user.
- `bg`   Background command. Used to force a suspended process to continue running in the background.
- `bindkey`   Allows users to change the editing actions that are associated with a key sequence.
- `cd`   Allows users to change the current working directory to the directory specified.
- `exit`   Allows the users to terminate the shell.
- `fg`   Foreground command. Used to force a suspended process to continue running in the foreground.
- `history`   Allows users to display and modify the contents of the history list and the history file.

- `kill` Allows users to terminate another process.
- `logout` Allows users to terminate a login shell.
- `set` Used to set the value of tcsh variables.
- `source` Used to read and execute the contents of a file.
- `unalias` Used to remove aliases that have been defined using the `alias` command.

Further details and sample usage of these commands may be found in the `tcsh` man page. At the prompt, type:

`man tcsh`

Command History

The `tcsh` shell provides a mechanism for accessing the command history that is similar to that in `bash`. The shell remembers the last history commands that have been entered into the shell (where history is a user-definable `tcsh` variable).

`tcsh` stores the text of the last history commands in a history list. When you log in to your account, the history list is initialized from a history file. The default filename for this history file is `.history`, but you can change it using the `histfile` tcsh variable. This file is located in your `home` directory. (Notice that the file begins with a period. This means that the file is a hidden file and will appear in a directory listing only if you use the `-a` or `-A` options of the `ls` command.)

> **Note**
>
> In order for the history list to be saved in the history file, you must make sure that the `savehist` variable is set to the number of commands that you want to be saved.

The simplest way to use the history list is to use the up- and down-arrow keys to scroll through the commands that were entered earlier. Pressing the up-arrow key will cause the last command entered to appear on the command line. Pressing the up-arrow key again will put the command before that on the command line, and so on. If you move up in the command buffer past the command that you wanted, you can move down the history list one command at a time by pressing the down-arrow key.

The command that is on the command line can be edited. You can use the left- and right-arrow keys to move along the command line, and you can insert text at any point. You can also delete text from the command line by using the Backspace or Delete keys. Most users should find these simple editing commands sufficient, but, for those who do not, `tcsh` also supports a wide range of equivalent emacs and vi editing commands.

Another method of using the history file is to display and edit the history list using a number of other editing commands that `tcsh` provides. The history command can be invoked by any one of three different methods.

First, the history list may be displayed to the screen as follows:

```
history [-hr] [n]
```

- The n option is used to specify the number of commands to display. If the n option is not used, the `history` command will display the entire history list.
- The -h option causes `history` to remove the command numbers and timestamps that are usually present in the output of the `history` command.
- The -r option tells history to display the commands in reverse order, starting with the most recent command.

Second, the contents of the history file or the history list may be modified as follows:

```
history -S | -L | -M [filename]
```

- The -S option writes the history list to a file.
- The -L option appends a history file to the current history list.
- The -M option merges the contents of the history file with the current history list and sorts the resulting list by the timestamp contained with each command.

> **Note**
> All the options for the second form of the `history` command use the filename option as the name of the history file. If no filename is specified, the `history` command will use the value of the `histfile` variable. If the `histfile` variable isn't set, it will use the ~/.history (home directory) file.

Third, the current history list may be cleared with this command:

```
history -c
```

In addition to the `history` command and its options, `tcsh` also contains many history navigation and editing commands. The following commands are used to navigate through the history list:

- `!n`: Reexecutes the command with the history number of n.
- `! -n` Reexecutes the command that is n commands from the end of the history list.
- `!!` Reexecutes the last command that was entered.
- `!c` Reexecutes the last command in the history list that begins with the letter *c*.
- `!?c?` Reexecutes the last command in the history list that contains the letter *c*.

The history editing commands allow you to replace words and letters in previously entered commands, as well as to add words to the ends of previously entered commands. More information on these editing commands can be found by referring to the `tcsh` man page.

`tcsh` Command Completion

Just like `bash`, `tcsh` command-line completion may be invoked by pressing the Tab key at any point while typing a command.

When you press the Tab key, `tcsh` tries to complete the command by matching what has been typed with any file in the directory to which the command is referring. For example, assume that you typed the following command and then pressed the Tab key:

`emacs hello`

Here, `tcsh` will try to match the letters in `hello` with any file (or subdirectory) in the current directory. If there is a simple file in the current directory that begins with the letters *hello*, `tcsh` fills in the rest of the filename for you. Now assume that you typed the following command and then pressed the Tab key:

emacs /usr/bin/hello

In this case, `tcsh` would try to match the letters *hello* with any file in the `/usr/bin/` directory. From these examples, you can see that you must give `tcsh` something to go on before asking it to complete the command for you.

Here is another example of using command-line completion. Assume that the directory you are currently in contains these files:

```
News/   bin/   mail/    sample.txt    testfile    ttd.txt
```

If you want to print the `sample.txt` file, you could type the following command:

lpr sample.txt

Using command-line completion, you could get away with typing the following command and then pressing the Tab key:

lpr s

At this point, tcsh attempts to complete the command and finds that the only file that can possibly match what was typed so far is the `sample.txt` file. tcsh would then complete the command by putting the following text on the command line:

```
lpr sample.txt
```

You can now either confirm that this is the intended command by pressing the Enter key, or you can edit the command if it isn't what you intended.

tcsh Variables

Following are some of the most useful tcsh variables:

- `autocorrect`   If this is set, tcsh will automatically try to correct command-line spelling errors.
- `histfile`   The name of the file that is used to store the command history.
- `history`   The size of the history list.
- `home`   The user's home directory.
- `path`   The search path that tcsh uses when looking for executable programs.
- `prompt`   The first-level prompt that is displayed on the command line.
- `prompt2`   The second-level prompt that is displayed when a `for`, `for each`, or `while` loop is expecting input.
- `prompt3`   The third-level prompt that is displayed when tcsh has attempted to correct a spelling error in a command.
- `savehist`   This variable must be set to the number of history commands that you want to save, if you want tcsh to save the history list when you log out.
- `watch`   Contains a list of user terminal pairs to watch for logins and logouts.

These variables are used to customize tcsh for each user and are explored in the section on configuration files.

tcsh Configuration Files

Many of the tcsh variables may be used at the command line to change the way tcsh operates for a single session. For the changes to apply to all future sessions, however, they must be saved to a file that is executed each time you start tcsh.

Several initialization files are important to tcsh. The commands in these files are executed when you first log in.

For a login to a standard installation of tcsh, configuration files would be sourced in this order:

/etc/csh.chsrc	The commands in this file are executed each time a copy of the tcsh program is run. Examples of the types of commands that usually appear in this file are aliases and variable declarations.
/etc/csh.login	Normally, to change any of the settings found in csh.login, you would copy it to your home directory as ~/.login and make the changes you want there.
~/tcshrc or ~/.cshrc	tcsh next sources any copy of the .cshrc file in your home directory.
~/.history	The history file is brought in next.
~/.login	Your personal login file in your home directory (if you have created one) follows.
~/.cshdirs	Finally, tcsh checks your home directory for this file, which loads the directory stack.

For a normal non-login shell, startup would occur as follows:

/etc/csh.cshrc   -> ~/.tcshrc (or ~/.cshrc)

In OpenLinux, however, the tcsh startup process is considerably more complex. The file

/etc/csh.cshrc

is sourced first, followed by

~/.tcshrc

which pulls in

/etc/config.d/shells/csh.cshrc

This additional layer of configuration is unique to OpenLinux, which then sources:

~/.tcshrc-all

The individual user's tcsh defaults; however, if this file is not available:

~/.cshrc-all

Then the individual user's tcsh defaults, followed by:

~/.tcshrc-interactive

The individual user's tcsh interactive shell defaults or, if this file is not available,

~/.cshrc-interactive

The individual user's tcsh interactive shell defaults, followed by

~/.history

for the user's command history, and then by

`~/.login`

for the individual user's generic login settings. It pulls in

`/etc/config.d/shells/csh.login`

for the system login defaults. Finally,

`~/.login-private`

which is the individual user's `tcsh` login settings.

Summary

In this chapter, we studied the basic configuration and usage of two popular shells, `bash` and `tcsh`. The commands detailed in this chapter will get you started working in a shell.

Either of these two shells is admirably suited for everyday use of your OpenLinux system, and your choice between the two will depend on your individual preference and usage patterns.

Using the X Window System

CHAPTER 4

IN THIS CHAPTER

- The History of X *80*
- Essential X Concepts *80*
- Configuring XFree86 *88*
- Colors *97*
- Fonts *98*
- Starting X *101*
- Some X Clients *102*

The X Window system is a networked graphics system, which is the infrastructure underlying most graphical user interfaces on Linux (and indeed most UNIX systems).

The History of X

The X Window system was first released in 1984 by the Massachusetts Institute of Technology. The first release of the current version, version 11, was released in September 1987. The most up-to-date version of X is version 11 release 6, often referred to as X11R6. (Actually, the truly latest and greatest is release 6.4, or X11R6.4.)

X was developed by MIT's Project Athena and Digital Equipment Corporation with contributions from many other organizations and companies. Control of X passed in 1988 to the X Consortium, composed of practically all large workstation and software vendors. On December 31, 1996, all rights to the X Window system were assigned to the Open Software Foundation, which became the Open Group. On May 17, 1999, the Open Group formed a subsidiary called X.Org, which is now officially in charge of X development.

X is released under a very liberal license that not only allows free copying and use of the software but also allows it to be incorporated into commercial products with no license fee.

On Linux, the most popular X implementation is the XFree86 implementation provided by the XFree86 Project, Inc. This is a not-for-profit organization that releases X implementations for common PC video cards. The XFree86 implementation runs mostly on Intel processors, but it has been ported to all the processor architectures supported by Linux. In addition, XFree86 is the standard X server for other free UNIXes such as FreeBSD.

Essential X Concepts

X has a number of interesting design concepts that differ from other graphical systems such as Microsoft Windows or MacOS. To fully appreciate the power of X, you must understand these differences.

The Client/Server Nature of X

The X Window system is a client/server system. The X server controls the display on the terminal where you work. X clients send requests to the X server to draw windows, draw lines, render text, and so on. The X server sends replies back the to the clients and also sends them events such as mouse motion, mouse button clicks, and key presses.

The X server is simply an ordinary Linux program. The Linux kernel knows nothing about graphics or windows; all of that is taken care of by the X server. This arrangement has an very important consequence: If, for some reason, the X server has a bug in it, which that locks it up or causes it to crash, you can usually just kill it and your Linux system will be remain perfectly functional.

A very powerful feature of X is that the server accepts connections from clients on the local machine or over the network. X supports a number of networking protocols, including TCP/IP, the standard Internet protocol. This means that clients can run on any machine connected to the server machine (even across the Internet) and have their windows appear seamlessly on the display. With X, the difference between local and remote programs is blurred.

This feature of X leads to the introduction of *X terminals*, which are simply terminals with a built-in X server and no other software. Users log in and run all their programs remotely on a (presumably powerful) central computer. The advent of cheap and powerful personal computers has rendered X servers almost irrelevant, but the powerful remote access possibilities offered by X are still very useful.

For example, suppose you have a number of servers locked away in a server room. There's really no point in equipping each one with a keyboard and monitor, because no one ever sits in front of them. With X, you can remotely open windows on the servers and control them from your workstation, using graphical administration tools with ease.

The client/server nature of X is sometimes confusing because the server runs on the local workstation, whereas the client may run elsewhere. To reiterate:

- The X server controls the video card and performs all the drawing operations. It runs on the local workstation.
- X clients are application programs that ask the server to perform drawing operations for them. X clients can run on the local workstation or on remote machines.

The Display

Each X server manages a display. A display refers to a keyboard, mouse, and one or more screens. (Although the X system supports multiheaded displays, the current XFree86 implementation does not. The next major release of Xfree86 (release 4.0) promises support for multiheaded displays.)

Each screen has a name that that looks something like this:

```
machine:dispNum.screenNum
```

The *machine* is the name of the machine on which the X server is running. It might be blank if the server is running on the local machine.

The *dispNum* is a number specifying the display number.

> **Background Material**
>
> It is possible to have more than one display on a given machine. For example, under Linux, you can run two completely separate X servers in different virtual consoles. One would be display 0 and the other display 1.

The *screenNum* is the screen number. A multiheaded display can have more than one machine.

On my network, I'm running a terminal on the machine *shevy* and the X server on *shishi*. The display for the client on *shevy* is called *shishi:0.0*. You can specify the display when you start an X client with the `-display` option, but usually you set the `DISPLAY` environment variable to the display's name. The startup process for X automatically sets the variable correctly for local clients.

Window Managers

Another design feature of X is that it provides mechanism, not policy. That is, the core X system provides a mechanism for drawing windows, rendering text, and handling mouse and keyboard events. It does not specify how windows should look, what a particular mouse click should do, or which keystrokes do what. For example, X does not specify which keystrokes open or close windows, minimize them, and so on.

The policy or look-and-feel of the interface is left up to the window manager. The window manager is an ordinary X client that with has special powers. It draws decorative frames around windows, draws any required buttons, and provides means for users to resize, move, open, and close windows.

Figure 4.1 illustrates the X architecture. The figure shows an X server running on the local workstation. There are two local X clients connected to the server, as well as a window manager. In addition, there is a remote X client is connected from another machine.

FIGURE 4.1
X Window system architecture.

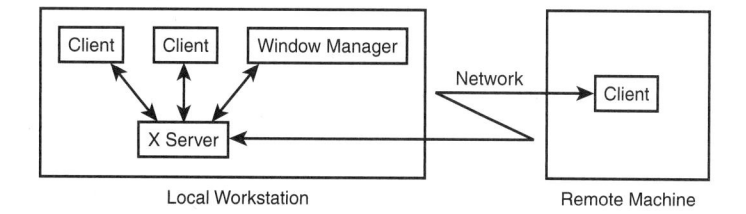

> **Background Material**
>
> In principle, the window manager could be run remotely, but it is usually run on the same machine as the X server for performance reasons.

The separation of duties between the X server and the window manager has meant that you can try many different user interfaces. Consequently, because you can vary the look and feel simply by changing window managers without altering the core X system, it is easy to experiment with different interfaces and make customize them.

> **Background Material**
>
> This is, in fact, one of the most criticized aspects of X: Because of a lack of standardization, X programs tend to have small but annoying differences in which keys are used for what operations, which mouse buttons bring up open menus, and so on.

In the commercial UNIX world, after a number of years of battles and disagreement, the Motif user interface was chosen as the standard. The Common Desktop Environment (CDE) is the standard commercial UNIX desktop.

Unfortunately, Motif and CDE are not free or open-source. For this reason, they have not found much favor on Linux, although Linux implementations are available.

For a while, Linux continued along with using many different graphical user interfaces. Eventually, two large projects emerged, promising a standardized desktop for Linux: the K Desktop Environment (KDE) and the GNU Network Object Model Environment (GNOME). Caldera chose to use KDE as the standard desktop environment for OpenLinux KDE is covered fully in Chapter 5.

KDE includes its own window manager called kwm. This window manager draws the KDE window borders and implements the KDE desktop look and feel. If you choose not to use KDE but still want to use X, the only other window manager supplied with OpenLinux is the truly ancient twm, which makes Linux look like a creaky old system from the early 1980s. I recommend sticking with KDE unless you have a slow computer or limited memory, in which case KDE may place too much stress on your system.

The Pointer and the Selection

The mouse cursor is referred to as the pointer. Mouse buttons are typically not referred to as left, middle, and right. Rather, they are called button 1, button 2, and button 3. For a right-handed person, buttons 1, 2, and 3 are the left, middle, and right button, respectively. However, they can be reversed for a left-handed person.

The X server maintains a property called the selection. This can contain selected text that is cut from one application and pasted into another.

For most text-based applications, you manipulate the selection as follows:

1. While holding down button 1, drag the mouse pointer over the text you wish want to select.
2. To extend the selection, move the mouse pointer to the location at which you want the selection to end and press button 3. This implicitly copies the text to the selection.

   Normally, the selection grows in character-sized increments. If you double-click button 1 prior to dragging or extending the selection, it will grow in word-sized increments. Triple-clicking yields a selection which that grows in line-sized increments.
3. To paste the selection, press button 2.

> **Note**
>
> There is no explicit Copy or Cut action. The mere action of making a selection performs an implicit copy so you can paste immediately after creating the selection.

X does not mandate the behavior of mouse buttons with respect to the selection, but (thankfully) making and extending the selection are two of the GUI operations on which almost all X clients agree.

Events

All X programs are *event driven*. The X server monitors the mouse and keyboard and sends events to clients. Table 4.1 lists some common events.

TABLE 4.1 X Window Events

Event	Meaning
`ButtonPress`	A mouse button was pressed.
`ButtonRelease`	A mouse button was released.
`KeyPress`	A key was pressed.
`KeyRelease`	A key was released.
`Motion`	The mouse pointer was moved.
`Enter`	The pointer entered a window.
`Leave`	The pointer left a window.

There are many more events, and events in general are mostly of interest to X programmers. However, the manual pages of some programs discuss binding actions to events, so it's worth having an idea of what X events are all about.

Focus

Under X, keyboard events are sent to one window at any given instant. The window that receives the keyboard events is said to have the keyboard *focus*.

There are two basic policies for setting the input focus:

- *Click-to-type*   The last window in which a mouse button was clicked has the focus, and it keeps the focus until a mouse button is clicked in another window.
- *Focus-follows-mouse*   Whichever window contains the mouse pointer has the focus.

Choose whichever scheme you like better (do this with the KDE Control Center), but be aware that the window manager can set the focus policy only for top-level windows. Applications may require you to click within particular graphical elements to set focus even if you have selected focus-follows-mouse for top-level windows.

Resources

X, like most UNIX programs, is customizable—incredibly, unbelievably, confusingly customizable. Many of the things you can customize are customized with X resources.

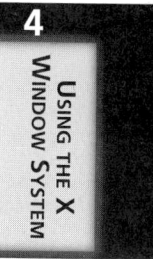

> **Background Material**
>
> Actually, KDE uses customization files in your home directory for most of its customization work, so you don't need to play with X resources much if you use KDE applications. However, there are still many useful non-KDE X applications that use resources for customization.

X resources are simply key-value pairs that are stored by the X server and that X clients can query or set. Use the xrdb command to manipulate the X resource database. For example, to get a listing of all current X resources, use:

```
$ xrdb -q
XTerm*background: Black
XTerm*foreground: Wheat1
Emacs.background: Black
Emacs.foreground: Wheat1
```

These resources specify that I like my xterm background to be Black and the foreground Wheat1. The same preferences apply to emacs. (xterm is a terminal emulator and emacs is a text editor; they will be discussed in later sections.)

The value component of a resource specification is straightforward: In these examples, the values are simply color names.

However, the syntax of the key component is slightly complicated. The specification of the key looks like this:

component...component...resourceName

Each *component* can be either an instance name or a class name. By convention, instance names begin with a lowercase letters, and class names begin with an uppercase letters.

For example, the emacs shown in the preceding example is a class name. There are two variations of the emacs text editor, GNU emacs and Xemacs. Both are very similar, however, and both are of class emacs. The resources therefore apply to both programs. Application designers pick the instance names and class names when they create programs. You have to read the documentation for the program to discover the instance and class names.

To differentiate between emacs and Xemacs, you could set resources like this:

```
emacs.foreground: wheat1
xemacs.foreground: red
```

That would make GNU emacs use wheat1 for the foreground and Xemacs use red.

X applications usually consist of hierarchical collections of windows. Consider the hypothetical CD player application illustrated in Figure 4.2.

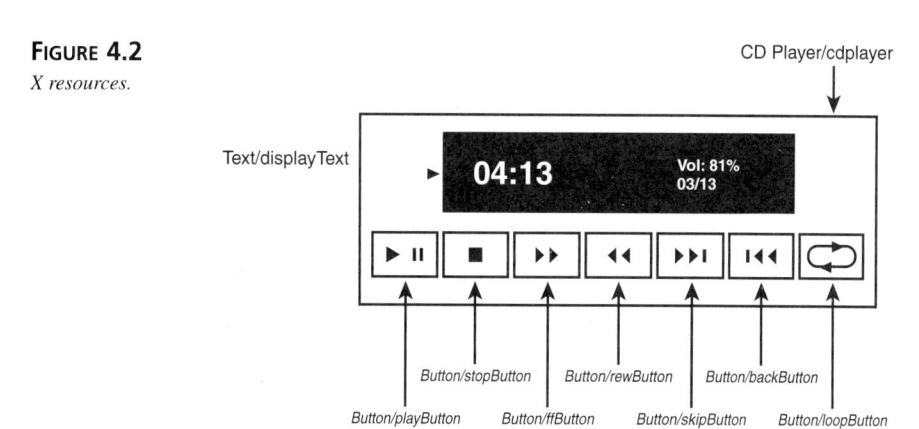

FIGURE 4.2
X resources.

CD Player/cdplayer

Text/displayText

Button/stopButton   Button/rewButton   Button/backButton
Button/playButton   Button/ffButton   Button/skipButton   Button/loopButton

In the figure, each window is shown with its class name followed by a slash followed by the instance name. For example, all of the buttons are of class Button, but each button has its own instance name.

Here are some examples of X resources:

```
! Set the background of everything to yellow
CDPlayer*background: yellow
! But make the buttons green
CDPlayer*Button.background: green
! And make the "loop" button red
CDPlayer*loopButton.background: red
```

Consider the first resource, which sets the background to yellow. The class name of the application CDPlayer is followed by an asterisk and the resource name background. The asterisk stands for any number of levels of hierarchy. So it sets the background for the application as a whole, for nested windows, for subnested windows, and so on.

The second resource sets the background for any window of class Button, no matter where it is in the window hierarchy. The third command sets the background for the specific window loopButton (wherever it appears in the hierarchy).

The precise syntax for X resources is documented in the X(1) man page in the section "Resources."

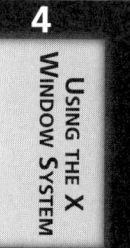

Note that each application defines its own window (or widget) hierarchy and class names. Although applications built with the same widget toolkit (a library for building graphical interfaces) are likely to have consistent class names for their windows, X itself does not impose a standard for window class names. (Remember, it provides mechanism, not policy.)

Use the xrdb program to set resources. The easiest way to set resources is to create a file (usually called .Xresources in your home directory) specifying the resources you wish to set. The file looks something like this:

```
! A comment line -- begins with exclamation mark.
XTerm*background: white
Ghostview*arguments: -dNOPLATFONTS
XTerm*font: 10x20
```

You simply list the resources followed by a colon and the value. You can continue long lines with the backslash character (\).

Remember that you need to read the manual page for each application to discover which resources it uses or expects.

After you've created the resource file, load it into the X server with this command:

```
$ xrdb -merge $HOME/.Xresources
```

This adds the resources specified in the file to the X resource database. xrdb has a number of options:

- xrdb -query   Queries the X resource database and prints the results to standard output.
- xrdb -merge *filename*   Merges resources from a file into the database.
- xrdb -load *filename*   Replaces the resources in the database with the resources in the file.

xrdb has a number of more advanced (and less used) options for processing resource files; see xrdb(1) for more details.

Configuring XFree86

Historically, configuring the X server has been one of the most difficult tasks under Linux. However, modern XFree86 servers support a wide range of video cards, and the PCI bus makes identifying hardware easier. Most likely, when you installed Caldera OpenLinux, the installation program correctly configured the X server. If it didn't, or if you wish to reconfigure the X server for some reason (adding a new video card, perhaps), this section will explains how to do it.

Identifying Your Video Hardware

If you don't know the details of your video hardware, the `SuperProbe` program might be able to probe for the information. To run it, become root and type:

```
# SuperProbe
```

You might want to redirect the output to a file:

```
# SuperProbe > probe.log 2>&1
```

The output from `SuperProbe`, if it successfully identifies your video hardware, will be something like this:

```
First video: Super-VGA
        Chipset: Matrox G200 AGP (PCI Probed)
        RAMDAC:  Matrox G200 built-in DAC w/clock
```

> **Warning**
>
> `SuperProbe` can hang your system if you have strange hardware. Make sure that you run it from text mode (not from within an X server) and that you don't have any vital unsaved work.

`SuperProbe` has several options, but most assume that you have quite intimate knowledge of video cards and your hardware. One generally useful option is `-verbose`, which makes `SuperProbe` print details as it probes for various video cards.

Running XF86Setup

The `XF86Setup` program is a tool for configuring XFree86. You can run it either in text mode or in an X window. If you're setting up X for the first time, you have no choice but to use the text-mode version. If you want to adjust the setup, you can use the graphical version.

To invoke `XF86Setup`, become root and type:

```
# XF86Setup
```

If you are running under X, you are asked whether or not you wish want to adjust the current setup. If you answer yes, a graphical configuration tool appears.

The graphical tool has six main buttons, entitled Mouse, Keyboard, Card, Monitor, Modeselection, and Other.

Configuring Your Mouse

To set up your mouse, click on the Mouse button. If your mouse is not yet working (a reasonable situation), press Tab to highlight the Mouse button and then press the spacebar or Enter. Alternatively, press Alt-M to go directly to the Mouse Configuration menu.

Select your mouse protocol from the choices. You probably have a PS/2 mouse or a serial mouse. Most serial mice use the Microsoft protocol.

Select the mouse device from the list offered. If you have a two-button mouse, enable `Emulate3Buttons`. This mode emulates a third mouse button when you press both mouse buttons together.

Press A to apply changes and check whether the pointer moves around properly. Keep trying different settings until it does.

Configuring Your Keyboard

Click on the Keyboard button to set up your keyboard. There's usually not much to do here; in the vast majority of cases, selecting the generic 101-key PC keyboard with the U.S. English layout works fine.

Additional options let you place the Control key next to the A key. If you're used to working on Sun workstations, this move can save your sanity.

Configuring Your Video Card

Click on Card to configure your video card.

If you are lucky, your video card will be listed in the card list and you can simply select it. (If you do not get a card list, but instead are presented with a window full of options and questions, click Card List to get the card list.)

If you do not see your card, you must click on Detailed Setup to enter various parameters yourself.

First, you must know which server to pick for your video card. Sometimes, it is obvious; the Mach64 server supports Mach64 cards. Other times, it is not so obvious. If you don't know which server to pick, just pick one and read the README file. (The Read README File button opens the file for the currently selected server.) If you cannot find the README file, look in the directory `/usr/X11R6/lib/X11/doc`. A number of README files might help.

In general, if a server name matches your card or chipset's name, use it. Otherwise, try the SVGA server, which supports many cards and chipsets. As a last resort, you can use the VGA16 server, which provides only 640 by 480 resolution at 16 colors.

The Chipset option lets you specify your graphics chipset. Pull down the list and choose the chipset that matches your card. If nothing matches or you are unsure, leave the chipset entry blank. Do the same for RamDac and ClockChip.

If you know how much video memory your graphics card has, select the appropriate amount from the list of options.

Configuring Your Monitor

Click on Monitor to configure your monitor.

Monitors are usually easier to configure than a graphics card. The X server needs to know the horizontal and vertical frequency ranges accepted by the monitor. These are usually indicated at the back of the monitor's manual in a section entitled "Specifications." If your monitor does not have a manual, choose a generic monitor from the list provided.

> **Warning**
>
> Do not exceed the horizontal sync range specified in your monitor's manual. Doing so can seriously damage the monitor.

Configuring the Graphics Mode

After you've configured the video card and monitor, click on Modeselection to choose a graphics mode. From a list of resolutions, choose the mode you want to use. You should also pick a default color depth; this specifies how many bits of video memory are occupied by each pixel. A depth of 8 allows up to 256 different colors on the screen at a time. A depth of 16 allows 65,536 different colors, and 24 or 32 allows 16,777,216 colors. Choose the best mode and color depth that your hardware will support.

Configuring X Server Behavior

Click on Other to configure some other aspects of X behavior.

- *Allow server to be killed with hotkey sequence* Allows you to kill the X server by pressing Ctrl+Alt+Backspace. Choosing this option is generally a good idea because it gives you an escape hatch if your X configuration is wrong. For secure applications or Internet kiosks, you should disable this option. Otherwise, leave it on.
- *Allow video mode switching* If you selected more than one resolution when configuring the graphics mode, you can switch between them with Ctrl+Alt++ (the plus sign) and Ctrl+Alt+– (the minus sign) where the plus and minus are the keys on the numeric keypad.
- *Don't trap signals* Never enable this. It is for programmers who wish to debug the X server.
- *Allow video mode changes from other hosts* If this option is enabled, remote X clients are allowed to change the server's video mode.
- *Allows changes to keyboard and mouse settings from other hosts* If this option is enabled, remote X clients are allowed to change the keyboard and mouse settings.

The default values for the X server behavior are probably fine; you shouldn't have to change them.

Running `xf86config`

If you do not start `XF86Setup` under X, it attempts to run the VGA16 X server to give you a graphical interface. If this fails, you must use the nongraphical program `xf86config`:

```
# xf86config
```

`xf86config` is the text-mode analog to `XF86Setup`. It asks you questions about your hardware, and you type the answers. `xf86config` runs through the following items:

- *Mouse configuration* This area is similar to that in `XF86Setup`. Just type the correct answers.
- *Keyboard configuration* Say "y" to "Do you want to use XKB?" Then, select your keyboard from the list.
- *Monitor configuration* This area is similar to that in `XF86Setup`. However, you are asked to enter identification strings to identify your monitor. The monitor model and manufacturer are usually good choices.

- *Card configuration*   Answer "y" to "Do you want to look at the card database?" and select your card from the list. If it is not found, you are asked questions similar to `XF86Setup`'s option settings. Based on your card, `xf86config` will choose the appropriate X server.
- `xf86config` will ask if whether you want to set up a symbolic link to the appropriate X server set up. Answer "y."
- Enter your video card's memory size and identifier strings. (The identifier strings are similar to those in the monitor configuration section.)
- `xf86config` will ask whether or not it should probe for your video card's clock settings. Answering "y" is usually safe.
- Select graphics modes just as with `XF86Setup`.
- `xf86config` will ask whether or not it should save the configuration file in `/etc/XF86Config`. Answer "y" if you are sure you will not overwrite an existing configuration file. Otherwise, answer "n." Keep answering "n" until you are asked to supply a filename. This lets you examine the setup file without overwriting an existing one.

Editing the Configuration File

Under Caldera OpenLinux, the configuration file for XFree86 is `/etc/XF86Config`. This is a text file that you can edit with a text editor. The file format is documented in the manual page `XF86Config(5)`, but we'll I cover the main sections here.

> **Note**
>
> The file is heavily commented; you should look at it while reading this section. Otherwise, you will find the instructions hard to understand.

Files Section

The first section, identified by the "Files" heading, specifies the locations of various files used by the X server.

- `RgbPath`   Specifies the location of the RGB database. This is simply a text file containing hundreds of color names (such as red, papaya whip, and royal blue) along with the red, green, and blue intensities that correspond to the color.

- `FontPath` Specifies where the X server should look for font files. X can render both bitmap and scalable (Type 1) fonts. You can provide multiple `FontPath` specifications; they are searched in order.

  If you have both bitmap and scalable versions of the same font, you should put the bitmap version directory ahead of the scalable version directory, and append `:unscaled` to the bitmap version directory. This causes the X server to use the bitmap font if an exact size match is found and resort to the slower rendering of the scalable font if no exact match is found.

- `ModulePath` Specifies the location of dynamically loadable modules that add extra features to the X server. These modules include extensions to X as well as modules for unusual input devices such as touch screens and graphics tablets. The default value is probably fine.

Module Section

The "Module" section specifies which dynamic objects to load into the X server. If you have a Summagraphics graphics tablet, for example, you probably want to put `Load "xf86Summa.so"` in this section. If you don't have exotic hardware, leave the section alone.

ServerFlags Section

The "ServerFlags" section specifies certain aspects of the X server's behavior. Most of the flags are well commented in `/etc/XF86Config`. The only flags that you are likely to want to change are:

- `DontZoom` This flag prevents video-mode switching with Ctrl-Alt-+ (the plus sign) or Ctrl+Alt+– (the minus sign).
- `DontZap` This flag prevents you from killing the X server with Ctrl+Alt+Backspace.

Keyboard Section

The section identified by the "Keyboard" heading controls the keyboard configuration:

- `Protocol` Should always be set to "Standard" under Linux.
- `AutoRepeat` *delay rate* Specifies the auto-repeat behavior of the keyboard. After an initial delay of *delay* milliseconds, keys repeat at a rate of *rate* times per second.

Additional settings in this section let you fine-tune the control of your keyboard; see `XF86Config(5)` for details.

Pointer Section

The section identified by the "Pointer" heading controls the mouse configuration:

- `Protocol`   Specifies the mouse protocol. It is most likely either PS/2 or Microsoft, but check the manual page for additional possibilities if neither of those works.
- `Device`   Specifies the mouse device file. Usually, the file `/dev/mouse` is a symbolic link to the real mouse device, and it is the appropriate entry. (Device files are discussed in detail in Chapter 8.)
- `Emulate3Buttons`   Tells the server to emulate a middle mouse button when both left and right mouse buttons are pressed. Use it if you have a two-button mouse.
- `ChordMiddle`   Required for some mysterious reason by some Logitech mouse (or so I am told; I have never encountered a mouse that requires it).

As usual, many more esoteric settings are available, and as usual I refer you to `XF86Config(5)` for more details.

Monitor Section

The section identified by the "Monitor" heading specifies your monitor to the X server. Any number of monitor sections can be present. (This feature could be useful if you switch monitors often; you can store both definitions in the configuration file and make a simple change to select the currently connected monitor.)

Each monitor section has the following entries:

- `Identifier`   A unique identifier for your monitor. Something like `AcerView 99c` might be a good choice.
- `VendorName`   The name of your monitor's vendor—for example, `Acer`.
- `ModelName`   The model of your monitor vendor—for example, `99c`.
- `HorizSync`   Specifies the horizontal sync range of your monitor. It can be specified as a list of discrete values such as `31.5, 35.2` or a list of ranges like such as `16-26, 31-60`. The units are in kilohertz.
- `VertRefresh`   Specifies the vertical refresh range of your monitor in hertz. Like `HorizSync`, it can be specified as a list of discrete values or a list of ranges.
- `ModeLine`   Specifies low-level video timings. You really don't want to edit mode lines; use the defaults. Editing mode lines requires a fairly deep understanding of video hardware; look at `/usr/X11R6/lib/X11/doc/VideoModes.doc` for all the gory details.

Device Section

The section identified by the "Device" heading specifies graphics card settings to the X server.

> **Background Material**
>
> Why is it called Device and not Card or GraphicsCard? We'll never know. It's one of those design decisions that are preserved forever, like bugs preserved in amber.

The device section contains the following entries:

- `Identifier`   An identifier that uniquely identifies your graphics card. Something like `Matrox Millennium G200` might be appropriate.
- `VendorName`   The name of your video card's vendor—for example, `Matrox`.
- `BoardName`   The model of your video card—for example, `Millennium G200`.

Additional optional entries such as `Chipset`, `VideoRam`, and some card-specific entries let you tune your card's configuration. Consult `XF86Config(5)` for details.

Screen Section

The section identified by the "Screen" heading specifies which graphics card and monitor combination to use for each X server. The entries in this section are:

- `Driver`   Specifies which X server should use the screen configuration. Possible values are:
    - `Accel`   All the accelerated X servers use settings in this section. Essentially, all the card-specific X servers such as `XF86_Mach32` and `XF86_S3V` fall into this category.
    - `Mono`   The non-VGA monochrome X server uses settings in this section.
    - `SVGA`   The `XF86_SVGA` SuperVGA X server uses settings in this section.
    - `VGA2` and `VGA16`   These settings are used by the VGA drivers in the two-bit and four-bit servers in `XF86_VGA16`.

You only need to supply entries for video cards you actually have. Most likely, you'll need only the `VGA16` and either `Accel` or `SVGA`; these types cover the majority of modern video cards.

- `DefaultColorDepth` *bpp*   Specifies the default color depth of the screen.
- `Device`   Specifies which video card to use. This should match the `Identifier` entry from one of the device sections.
- `Monitor`   Specifies which monitor to use. This should match the `Identifier` entry from one of the monitor sections.

Within the screen section, there are a number of subsections called "Display." Each display subsection has the following entries:

- `Depth` *bpp*   The color depth for which the subsection applies. This lets you configure different resolutions for different color depths. (For example, your video card might have enough memory to run at 1280 by 1024 with 8 bits per pixel, but only at 1024 by 768 at 16 bits per pixel.
- `Virtual` *x y*   Specifies the "virtual" resolution of the screen. For example, if your monitor is capable only of 1024 by 768, but your video card can do 1280 by 1024, you could specify a mode of 1024 by 768 for the monitor, but a virtual size of 1280 by 1024. This creates a screen larger than your monitor. As you move the mouse pointer to one edge of the screen, the entire screen scrolls. The scrolling is done in hardware and is fast and impressive, but is usually too distracting to use in practice.
- `Modes` *modeName...*   Specifies a list of resolutions to use. You can cycle through the list with Ctrl+Alt++ (plus) and Ctrl+Alt+– (minus).

Consult `XF86Config(5)` for more configuration options in the screen section and device subsection. There is a nicely commented sample `XF86Config` file in `/usr/lib/X11/XF86Config.eg`.

Colors

You can specify colors may be specified to X programs using one of two methods:

- *By name*   Type **xcolorsel** at the shell prompt to see a list of all the named colors known to the X server.
- *By red-green-blue value*   Such a color is specified as:

  `#RRGGBB`

  The `RR` are two hexadecimal digits specifying the value of the red component from 00 to FF. Likewise, the `GG` and `BB` are two hexadecimal digits each specifying the values of the green and blue components.

> **Note**
>
> Hexadecimal numbers are numbers expressed in base 16. The digits 0 through 9 have their usual meaning, and the "digits" A through F represent 10 through 15. To convert a two-digit hexadecimal number to decimal, multiply the first digit by 16 and add the second digit. For example, the hexadecimal number A6 is 10*16 + 6 or 166. Commonly seen numbers in color specifications are 00 (0), FF (255) and 80 (128).

Here are some examples:

#FF0000	Fully saturated red
#FF00FF	Fully saturated magenta
#008000	A dark green
#000000	Black
#FFFFFF	White

In xcolorsel, you can set the display format to 8-bit scaled RGB (using the Display Format pull-down menu) to see the color values in a format similar to the hexadecimal scheme illustrated here.

> **Background Material**
>
> There are other ways to specify colors, but the two described here are the most common. See X(1) for more details.

Fonts

XFree86 comes with a large collection of fonts. It also comes with a rather unwieldy (but powerful) mechanism for naming fonts.

X servers can render a variety of font types: PCF and BDF fonts are bitmap fonts used only by the X Window system. Type 1 fonts are scalable PostScript fonts, and Speedo fonts are another kind of scalable font. Currently, X does not support TrueType scalable fonts, although the next release of Xfree86 will support them.

X Logical Font Descriptions

In X, a font's name contains 14 (!) parts. The 14 parts are listed in Table 4.2.

TABLE 4.2 Fields in an X Logical Font Description

Field	Meaning
Foundry	The organization that created the font. Examples are `adobe` and `bitstream`.
Family	The general font family, such as `courier` or `times`.
Weight	The weight of the font. Examples are `bold` or `medium`.
Slant	The slant of the font. Examples are `i` for italic, `o` for oblique, and `r` for upright.
Set Width	The "compactness" of the font. It is usually `normal` but may be `condensed` or `semicondensed`.
Additional Style	Additional style parameters. This is hardly ever used. The only example I could find was a Lucida font that specified `sans` in this field.
Pixel Size	Specifies the size of the font in pixels.
Point Size	Specifies the size of the font in tenths of a point. You should usually specify point size and not pixel size; the X server will calculate the correct pixel size to use.
X Resolution	The horizontal resolution of the font in dots per inch. Used only for bitmap fonts.
Y Resolution	The vertical resolution of the font in dots per inch. Used only for bitmap fonts.
Spacing	The spacing scheme used by the font. Can be `p` for proportional, `m` for monospaced, or `c` for constant spacing.
Average Width	The average width (in tenths of a pixel) of all characters in the font.
Registry	The authority responsible for determining the encoding scheme of the font. For example, all fonts encoded according to the ISO 8859 standard have a registry of `iso8859`.
Encoding	The particular encoding scheme. Western European characters are encoded using the `iso8859-1` scheme, whereas Hebrew characters are encoded using `iso8859-8`.

For example, a rather attractive 24-pixel upright Courier font may be specified as:

-adobe-courier-bold-r-normal--24-240-75-75-m-50-iso8859-1

The font name begins with a dash, followed by a dash-separated list of the 14 fields described in Table 4.2.

This is certainly an awkward way to specify fonts! Fortunately, most of the fields can be wildcarded, leaving it up to the server to pick a matching font. You can get a 24-pixel upright Courier font just by specifying the family, weight, slant, and size, like this:

-*-courier-bold-r-*--24-*

If more than one font matches a wildcarded specification, the first one found is used. In general, you should explicitly specify the font family, weight, slant, and either point or pixel size. These fields are usually large enough to yield the font you want.

Many X clients allow you to specify the font name on the command line using the -fn option. If you use wildcard font names, be sure to quote them to avoid shell expansion.

For example, to start an xterm session using the Courier font described earlier, use:

```
$ xterm -fn '-*-courier-bold-r-*-24-*'
```

Looking at Fonts

The xfontsel program lets you view available fonts. To start it, type:

```
$ xfontsel
```

Use the pull-down menus to fill in the various font name fields. The indicator in the top right-hand corner of the window tells how many fonts match the remaining wildcarded fields.

You can get a listing of the fonts available on your system with xlsfonts. This command produces a huge amount of output, so you might want to send its output to a file or pipe it through more:

```
$ xlsfonts | more
```

You can limit the output of xlsfonts by providing an -fn option followed by a wildcard pattern. Remember to quote the pattern to prevent the shell from trying to expand it. This example lists all Courier fonts on the system:

```
$ xlsfonts -fn '*-courier-*' | more
```

Scalable Fonts

Scalable fonts are a fairly recent addition to X. They are named by using 0 for the pixel size, point size, x and y resolution, and average width. Note that only Type 1 and Speedo fonts are scalable; scaling bitmap fonts produces poor results.

> **Background Material**
>
> The technical term for using "magical" values in the XLFD is *kludge*. It overloads the meaning of fields in the XLFD in a questionable and nonintuitive manner.

When you use `xlsfonts`, you might see some proportional fonts such as:

```
-bitstream-courier-medium-r-normal--0-0-0-0-m-0-iso8859-1
```

You can view the font in a specific size by specifying a particular size. This gives an xterm with 48-pixel-high letters:

```
$ xterm -fn \
'-bitstream-courier-medium-r-*-*-48-*-*-*-*-*-*-*'
```

Starting X

If you successfully installed KDE as part of your installation, X Windows probably starts automatically when you boot the computer. The program which that manages the login session is called `kdm`. It is covered in the Chapter 5.

If X does not start automatically (because you couldn't configure it or you prefer booting into text mode), you can start X from the shell prompt with the `startx` command. The simplest way to invoke `startx` is:

```
$ startx
```

This starts an X server and executes the shell script `$HOME/.xinitrc`. Usually, you place commands to start various X clients and a window manager in `$HOME/.xinitrc`. If this file does not exist, the file `/etc/X11/xinit/xinitrc` is run instead. This starts a clock and a few `xterm` terminal windows, which is probably not what you want.

If you want to start KDE, you can use this command:

```
$ kde
```

This is similar to startx, but looks for $HOME/.kdeinitrc or /etc/X11/xinit/kdeinitrc. These should contain commands to start KDE correctly. Take a look at /etc/X11/xinit/kdeinitrc to see what it does.

With either startx or kde, you can specify X server options by preceding them with a double dash. For example, to start KDE in 8-bit-per-pixel mode, use:

```
$ kde -- -bpp 8
```

For a list of options accepted by the X server, see XFree86(1).

Some X Clients

This section covers some of the more popular X clients. Note that many of the X clients have equivalent KDE programs. Which you choose to use is a matter of taste. The KDE programs offer a more consistent look and feel, but if you move to a different UNIX system, you are more likely to find the standard X clients than their KDE counterparts.

Standard X Client Options

Most X clients accept the following standard options. They are called the standard X toolkit command-line options.

- -display *dpyname*   Specifies the display of the X server to connect to. If it's not supplied, the client uses the value of the DISPLAY environment variable.
- -fn *font*   Specifies the font to use.
- -fg *color*   Specifies the foreground color.
- -bd *color*   Specifies the border color.
- -bg *color*   Specifies the background color.
- -title *string*   Requests the window manager to display *string* in the window's title bar.
- -name *name*   Uses *name* as the application name when looking up resources in the resource database.
- -geometry *w*x*h*+*x*+*y*   Asks the window manager to make the window *w* by *h* units in size at an offset of *x* and *y*.

    For most applications, the *w* and *h* units are pixels, but for some (such as editors and terminal emulators), they are characters.

The *x* and *y* offsets specify where to place the window. If *x* is a number preceded by +, the left edge of the window is placed *x* pixels from the left edge of the screen. If it is a number preceded by -, the right edge of the window is placed *x* pixels from the right edge of the screen.

If *y* is a number preceded by +, the top edge of the window is placed *y* pixels from the top edge of the screen. If it is a number preceded by -, the bottom edge of the window is placed *y* pixels from the bottom edge of the screen.

- `-iconic`   Indicates that the window should start up "iconified" rather than open.

xterm

`xterm` is a terminal emulator for the X Window system. It is testament to (some would say indictment of) UNIX's command-line heritage that one of the most popular graphical applications is a terminal emulator. To start an `xterm` session, simply type:

```
$ xterm &
```

It's usually convenient to put the command in the background so you get your original shell prompt back.

An `xterm` emulates a VT-102 terminal, which was a popular serial terminal used on multiuser systems in times gone by.

`xterm` is pretty simple without too many flashy features. However, it does offer some features above what the original VT-102 offered.

Font Selection

To change the `xterm`'s font, press Ctrl and click mouse button 3. You are given a choice of several font sizes, ranging from unreadable to huge. Pick the one you want.

VT Options

VT options are options that control various aspects of the terminal's behavior. For example, you can enable a scrollbar on the left-hand side of the terminal, turn on reverse video, or switch between abrupt and smooth scrolling.

To change the VT options, press Ctrl and mouse button 2. A menu of various options appears, allowing you to change aspects of the terminal's behavior. Most times, you'll leave the settings alone.

Main Options

To change the main options, press Ctrl and mouse button 1. Another menu of various options appears, allowing you to change aspects of the terminal's behavior. The most important settings are:

- *Secure Keyboard*   Use this option to "grab" the keyboard in a secure manner. If you are running X in an insecure manner, it is possible for others to "snoop" in on your X session. xterm offers a simple-minded way to secure the keyboard in a way which that prevents snooping. The details are provided in the "Security" section of xterm(1).
- *Allow SendEvents*   Use this option to allow other programs to send fake key and button events to your xterm. Normally, this is a large security hole, so don't activate this option!

See xterm(1) for more details about the available options.

The ScrollbarNavigation

To one side of the xterm window, you should see a scroll bar. You can move the slider with button 2 to move through the last few dozen lines that have scrolled off the window. You can also use Shift+PgUp and Shift+PgDn to move around in page-size chunks. (If you don't see a scroll bar, enable it by selecting it from the VT Options menu.) The Shift+PgUp and Shift+PgDn keys work even if the scroll bar is turned off.

An Interesting xterm Trick

The VT-102 xterm emulator recognizes certain escape sequences or sequences of special characters. If you use the bash shell, you can put this in your .bashrc file:

```
if [ $TERM = "xterm" ] ; then
        PS1='\[\033]2;\u@\h:\w\007\033]1;\w\007\]\!:\u@\h(\W)\$ '
fi
```

This magical incantation sets the primary prompt of bash so that the title bar of the xterm window is set to something like this:

```
user@host:current_directory
```

If you have several xterm windows open at once, this trick is handy—it lets you keep track of the current working directory of the shell in each xterm.

xclock

What graphical display is complete without an analog clock? To finish off your X desktop, add `xclock` (see Figure 4.3).

FIGURE 4.3
xclock.

`xclock` accepts all the standard X toolkit command-line options as well as the following:

- `-analog`   Indicates that an analog clock is desired. This is the default.
- `-digital`   Yields a boring digital clock.
- `-chime`   Causes the clock to "chime" once on the half hour and twice on the hour. Because the clock's chime is simply the computer's speaker beeping, it's not too impressive.
- `-hands color`   Sets the color of the hands.
- `-update seconds`   Specifies how often in seconds to update the clock display. The default is 60; any value of 30 or less causes a second hand to be shown.

xload

The `xload` program shows a graphical display of the system load average. The load average is a measure of how many processes are ready to run at a given instant, averaged over time. A busy system will have a higher load average than an idle one. The xload display isn't very useful, but it's nice to see how busy your computer is.

xload accepts the standard X toolkit command-line options as well as the following:

- -highlight *color*   Specifies the color of the scale lines.
- -jumpscroll *n*   Causes the display to advance by *n* pixels when the graph fills the window. The default is half the window size.
- -label *string*   The label to place in the window.
- -update *seconds*   Specifies how often to update the display by sampling the load average.

xcalc

The command xcalc pops up a handy little scientific calculator. (See Figure 4.4.) If you are a fan of old Hewlett-Packard RPN calculators, you can start xcalc with the -rpn flag.

FIGURE 4.4
xcalc.

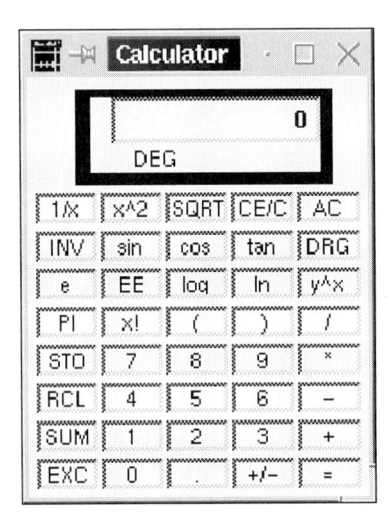

xbiff

The xbiff command monitors your UNIX mail folder. Normally, it displays a picture of a mailbox with the flag down (see Figure 4.5). When you receive mail, the flag goes up and the computer beeps.

FIGURE 4.5
xbiff.

xman

The xman command gives you a simple point-and-click interface to UNIX manual pages.

> **Note**
> The KDE help browser is superior; you'll probably want to use it rather than xman whenever you can.

xman pops up a small window with three buttons. Click on Manual Page to bring up the manual page window. (Curiously enough, this initial window contains the xman manual page.) Choose a section from the Sections menu, and then click on an entry to bring up a man page.

Alternatively, you can type Ctrl+S and type the name of the man page you're looking for.

xeyes

The xeyes command lets you perform vital system management functions. Figure 4.6 shows what I mean.

FIGURE 4.6
xeyes.

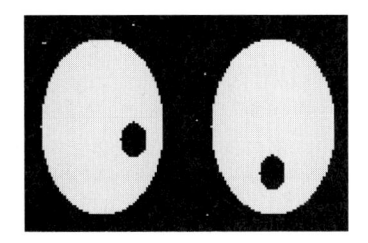

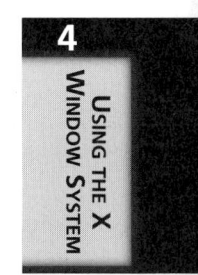

xvidtune

The `xvidtune` command lets you tune the video mode. This is useful if (for example) the display is not centered nicely on your screen, and you're unlucky enough to have one of those annoying monitors that rely on Windows drivers rather than front-panel buttons to change their display settings.

> **Note**
>
> `xvidtune` is specific to XFree86; it does not work with (and is not supplied by) other X servers.

To run `xvidtune`, simply type:

```
$ xvidtune
```

After reading and agreeing to the panel entitled "WARNING WARNING WARNING…," you can play with the video modes.

- To have all your changes applied immediately as you make them, enable Auto. Otherwise, click on Apply to let the changes you made take effect.
- Click on Left, Right, Wider, or Narrower to alter the horizontal settings.
- Click on Up, Down, Shorter, or Taller to alter the vertical settings.
- Click on Restore to restore the original settings.
- Click on Next or Prev to cycle through the available list of resolutions for which the X server was configured.
- Click on Show to print a mode line for the current settings to standard output. This mode line is suitable for inclusion in the `/etc/XF86Config` configuration file.
- Click on Quit to exit from `xvidtune`.

xset

The `xset` command lets you set up various aspects of your X server. It controls many different things, so this section contains several subsections.

Bell Volume

To control the bell (the beep emitted by the computer speaker), use `xset` like this:

```
$ xset b off # Disable bell
$ xset b vol pitch duration
```

For the second form of `xset`, use these arguments:

- *vol*   A number from 0 to 100, specifying silence to maximum volume.
- *pitch*   The pitch of the beep in hertz. Most computers are capable of a limited range of pitches; experiment.
- *duration*   The duration in milliseconds.

Key Click

Use `xset` like this to control key click:

```
$ xset c off # Disable key click
$ xset c vol # Turn on key -click
```

vol is a number from 0 to 100. If your hardware supports it, turning on key click causes the computer speaker to click each time you press a key. You'll probably find this very annoying after a while.

DPMS

DPMS (Display Power Management System) lets X power down your monitor after a period of inactivity. To control it, use `xset` like this:

```
$ xset dpms off # Disable DPMS
$ xset dpms standby suspend off
```

In the second form of `xset`, use these arguments:

- *standby*   Specifies how long to wait in seconds before placing the monitor in "standby" mode.
- *suspend*   Specifies how long to wait in seconds before placing the monitor in "suspend" mode.
- *off*   Specifies how long to wait in seconds before switching the monitor off.

> **Note**
>
> Not all monitors obey the power-saving signals. "Green" power-saving monitors are the most likely to obey them.

Font Path

You can change the X server's font path at runtime. You may wish to do this if you add new font directories and wish to test the fonts.

- To restore the font path to the default specified in the configuration file, use `xset fp default`.
- To remove a directory from the font path, use `xset fp- dir`.
- To prepend a directory to the font path, use `xset +fp dir`.
- To append a directory to the font path, use `xset fp+ dir`.
- To force the server to update its list of fonts (in case extra font files have been added to existing font directories), use `xset fp rehash`.

Mouse Acceleration

The X server "accelerates" the mouse pointer when you move the mouse quickly. This results in a more natural feel. You control the acceleration like this:

- To set the acceleration to the default, use `xset m default`.
- To specify the acceleration, use `xset m n/d t`.

    This works as follows: If the mouse moves more than *t* pixels between samples, the pointer is accelerated by *n/d*. For example:

    ```
    $ xset m 3/2 4
    ```

    This example causes the mouse pointer to move 1.5 (3/2) times as fast as normal when you make large movements. To see the mouse pointer really fly, try:

    ```
    $ xset m 8/1 4
    ```

    Now, that's acceleration!

Summary

In this chapter, you learned the history of the X Window system and some essential X concepts. We covered configuration of the Xfree86 X server. You learned how to specify fonts and colors to X applications, how to start an X session and how to run some common X clients. We discussed the standard X toolkit command-line options. Finally, you learned how to tune the X server video settings with `xvidtune` and how to alter many X server settings (normally specified in the configuration file) with `xset`.

// CHAPTER 5

Exploring KDE

IN THIS CHAPTER

- The Desktop *113*
- The KDE File Manager *121*
- The KDE Control Center *124*
- Some KDE Applications *128*

The K Desktop Environment (KDE) is the standard graphical environment shipped with Caldera OpenLinux. As mentioned in Chapter 4, X does not impose any particular look and feel or behavior on graphical objects. Higher-level programs like the window manager and various programming libraries are obliged to impose a consistent look and feel.

KDE consists of a number of components that implement the graphical environment. The KDE window manager (kwm) provides standard window decorations. These decorations include the three "minimize-maximize-close" buttons on the right-hand side of each window frame, the resize handles on each window, and the pull-down menus on the left-hand side of each window frame.

The second important component is the KDE file manager (kfm) provides a graphical file-system navigation tool. It also cooperates with the window manager so that you can create icons on the background window. These icons provide handy shortcuts for launching programs or browsing commonly used directories.

The third important component is the KDE panel (kpanel), which draws a bar on one edge of the screen. This bar contains the K menu (similar to Microsoft Windows' Start menu) for launching programs. It also contains buttons for locking the screen, logging out, switching virtual desktops, and launching programs. You can customize the panel so that commonly used programs are available with a single mouse click.

Figure 5.1 illustrates a typical KDE desktop. The panel is visible at the bottom of the screen. Several icons near the upper left provide quick buttons for launching programs. You can see the window decorations placed by kwm on each window.

FIGURE 5.1
Typical KDE desktop.

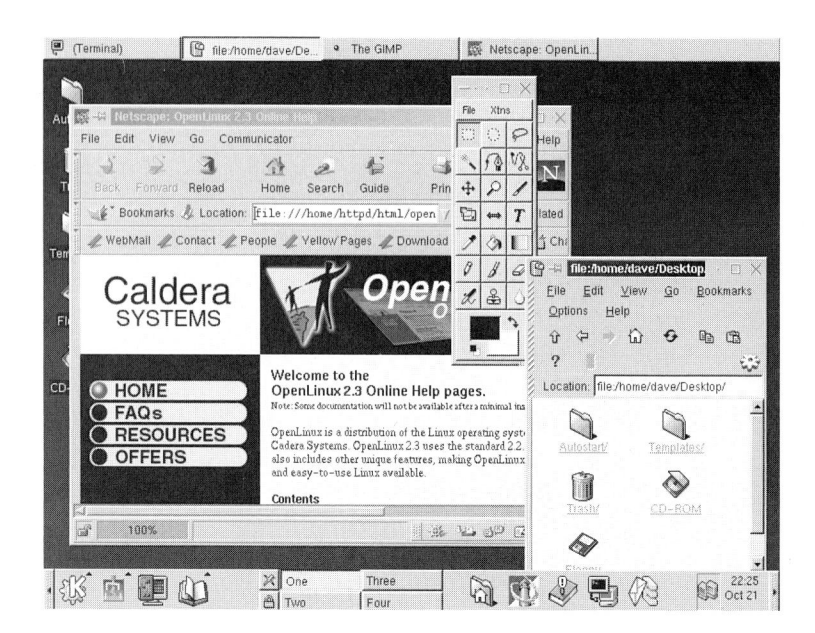

KDE also provides a consistent framework for interapplication communication. You can drag objects from one KDE application and drop it on another. For example, you can drag a file icon from the KDE file manager and drop it on another KDE program's window. The second program will react to the drop and open the file.

In addition to the uniform look, all KDE applications share a uniform feel. That is, every application responds in the same way to certain standard keystrokes. All KDE applications with a File menu, for example, terminate when you press Ctrl+Q, and they open a File Open dialog box when you press Ctrl+O.

Given the anarchic nature of Linux development, however, and the general freedom-of-choice attitude that prevails in UNIX circles, there will always be many useful non-KDE graphical programs. The GNOME desktop, for example, is an alternative to KDE based on completely different software libraries. And there are still many programs using the Motif libraries or other X libraries. Luckily, the GNOME and KDE developers are talking, so there is hope that GNOME and KDE programs will respect each others' drag-and-drop protocols. But a solidly uniform graphical interface like Microsoft Windows or Mac OS is not likely to happen soon. You might as well get used to (and enjoy) the diversity of X programs.

In this chapter, we will cover the basic setup of the KDE desktop and go over basic window operations. Next, we will discuss three important KDE applications—the window manager, the panel, and the file manager. These three applications provide most of the desktop functionality and behavior. Finally, we will cover three sample KDE applications. Although there are dozens of KDE applications, we will examine only these three because they demonstrate typical KDE application behavior. A full discussion of all KDE applications would fill an entire book.

The Desktop

This section provides an overview of the KDE desktop. We will look at how the window buttons work, how to use the panel, and how to create icons. These are basic requirements for navigating KDE. Fortunately, they are quite easy to master, especially if you have used Microsoft Windows. The KDE designers consciously took ideas from Windows to make an interface familiar to many computer users.

The Window Manager

The KDE window manager kwm places decorative frames and buttons around windows. These decorations are illustrated in Figure 5.2. (Although the objects drawn by the window manager are called decorations in standard X Window System terminology, they are both functional and decorative.)

FIGURE 5.2
KDE window manager decorations.

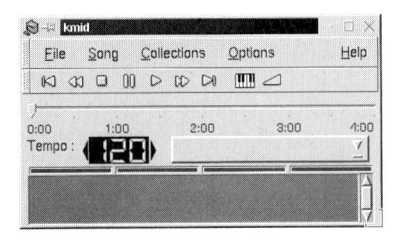

Before describing the operation of kwm, let's look at a few terms:

- The mouse buttons are numbered. If you are right handed, button 1 is the left mouse button, button 2 is the middle mouse button, and button 3 is the right mouse button. If you are left handed, you can reverse the interpretation of the buttons. If your mouse has only two buttons, you should configure X to interpret pressing both buttons as a middle-button press.
- A widget is a graphical object like a button, a scrollbar, or a pull-down menu.
- Clicking a widget means moving the mouse pointer over the widget and pressing and releasing button 1.
- Double-clicking a mouse button means pressing and releasing the button twice in succession without significantly moving the mouse pointer.
- Dragging a widget means moving the mouse pointer over the widget, pressing button 1 and moving the mouse while continuing to press button 1.
- Dropping a widget means releasing button 1 after having dragged the widget to its destination.

Window Buttons

Now that the terms are out of the way, let's examine the kwm window decorations.

To make a window occupy the entire screen, click the maximize button. The window expands the fill the screen. Note also that the maximize button changes from a raised square to a sunken square. If you click the maximize button again, the window shrinks back to its original size.

To temporarily remove a window from the screen, click the minimize button. The window disappears from the screen. However, a thin bar along one edge of the screen called the taskbar contains a button for each window on the desktop. When you minimize a window, its taskbar button continues to exist. You can restore the window to its original size by clicking its button on the taskbar.

By default, KDE animates the shrinking of a window. This provides a convenient visual cue that lets you locate the window's taskbar button.

To permanently close a window, click the close button. If the window is the main window of an application, the application will terminate. If it is just one of several open application dialog boxes, usually just the window will disappear. However, various applications may respond in different ways to the close button—you need to experiment.

The menu button provides a pull-down menu of window operations. To see the menu, click the menu button. Applications can add extra entries to the window menu; however, all applications have the following entries:

- *Maximize*   Corresponds to the maximize button. If a window is already maximized, the menu entry reads Restore.
- *Iconify*   Corresponds to the minimize button.
- *Move*   Allows you to move the window by moving the mouse pointer. Click button 1 when the window is where you want it.
- *Resize*   Allows you to resize the window. As you move the mouse pointer, an outline of the window shows its new size. When it is the size you want, click button 1 to make the size change take effect.
- *Sticky*   Makes a window "sticky." KDE supports virtual desktops. Imagine that the actual KDE desktop is much larger than your monitor is. A virtual desktop is a monitor-sized window inserted into this larger desktop. KDE allows you to switch between virtual desktops by clicking buttons on the panel. A sticky window "sticks" to the monitor and is always visible, even if you change virtual desktops. Normal windows disappear when you switch away from their virtual desktop. (All this is discussed in more detail in the section entitled "The Panel" later in this chapter.)

  The little push-pin button next to the menu button toggles a window between sticky and normal. When a window is sticky, the pin changes position so the window looks pinned to the screen.
- *To Desktop...*   Allows you to move a window to a different virtual desktop. You select which desktop you want from a submenu.
- *Close*   Corresponds to the close button.

Window Title Bars

If you have many windows on the screen, they will probably overlap. To raise a window, click mouse button 1 in the window's title bar. The window will move in front of all other windows. You can also achieve this by holding down the Alt key and clicking button 2 anywhere in the window.

To lower a window, click button 2 in the window's title bar. The window will move behind all other windows. In addition, pressing Alt+button 2 anywhere in the window moves the window behind other windows if it is currently in front of all other windows.

Essential OpenLinux

PART I

To shade a window, double-click button 1 in the window's title bar. The window disappears, leaving only the title bar. Double-click once more in the title bar to restore the window.

To move a window, drag the window's title bar. The window follows the mouse pointer as you drag it. You can also move a window by holding down Alt and dragging anywhere in the window with button 1.

> **Note**
> These mouse clicks are the defaults for KDE. You can configure KDE to react to mouse clicks any way you prefer. The section entitled "KDE Control Center" describes how to configure KDE.

Resizing a Window

To resize a window, move the mouse pointer to the very edge or corner of the window frame. This can be quite tricky and takes a bit of practice. After the pointer is in the right place, it changes to a bar with an arrow. The direction of the arrow shows the direction in which the window will be resized. For example, if you move near the top left-hand corner of the window frame, the mouse pointer changes to a resize pointer that looks like this: ⌐

With the resize cursor, drag the corner or edge of the window to resize it. An outline illustrates how the final window will look. After you have resized the window to the desired size, release the mouse button and the window will resize.

You can also resize a window by holding down the Alt key and dragging anywhere in the window with button 3.

The Panel

The panel is a bar that appears on one side of the screen. It provides a convenient central place for launching applications. A typical panel is shown in Figure 5.3.

FIGURE 5.3
The KDE panel.

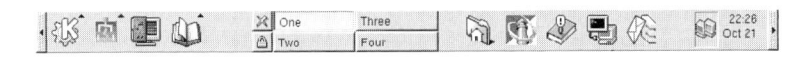

Hiding the Panel

The two textured bars on each end of the panel contain little arrows. Click either of the two bars to shrink the panel. The panel shrinks down to a tiny bar on one side of the screen. Click on the tiny bar to make the panel reappear.

Note that when you shrink the panel, the K button, a window list button, and a disk navigator button appear in a tiny box in the top left-hand corner of the screen. These select buttons give you access to the most common panel functions without having to re-expand the entire panel bar.

The Application Starter

The official title of the K button is the Application Starter, but we will refer to it simply as the K button. Clicking it brings up the KDE application menu shown in Figure 5.4.

FIGURE 5.4
KDE application menu.

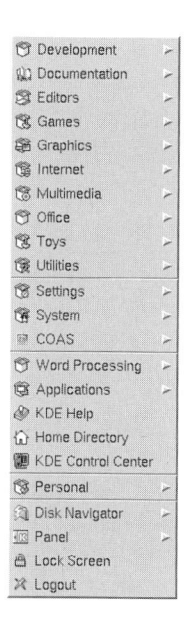

With the KDE application menu, you can launch most KDE applications without typing a command line. The first group of entries on the menu is a list of categories (Development, Documentation, Editors, Games, Graphics, Internet, Multimedia, Office, Toys, and Utilities). Clicking these entries brings up a submenu of application programs. The organization of programs into general categories makes the menu tidier and helps you navigate the contents of your disk.

The second group of entries (Settings, System, and COAS) brings up programs related to desktop configuration and system administration. Settings lets you customize KDE itself, changing its appearance and behavior to suit your taste. System provides access to various system configuration and information tools. Feel free to experiment with some of these tools; they are too numerous to be covered in this chapter. COAS provides access to the Caldera Open Administration System, a graphical configuration system for Linux. The administration tools are covered in Chapter 10.

The next group of entries (Word Processing, Applications, KDE Help, Home Directory, and KDE Control Center) includes other applications that (for some unknown reason) are not categorized in the first group. The most important menu entry in this group is KDE Help, which launches the KDE help browser. The KDE help browser includes help for most KDE programs, as well as being a one-stop browser for system man and information pages. The separation of documentation into traditional manual pages, GNU-style information pages, and KDE HTML pages is unfortunate. The KDE help browser mitigates this by providing access to all these resources from one application. Use KDE Help. You'll like it.

The Home Directory entry opens a file manager at your home directory. The file manager will be described later in this chapter in the section entitled "The KDE File Manager."

KDE Control Center starts an application that lets you customize the look and feel of KDE. It is described in the next section, "The KDE Control Center."

The Personal menu brings up a menu of personal and non-KDE applications. You can customize this menu; it is described in more detail in the section entitled "Customizing the Panel" later in this chapter.

The Disk Navigator menu presents the entire Linux file system as a series of cascading menus. You can walk through your home directory, your CD-ROM, or the root directory simply by passing from menu to menu. The disk navigator also remembers recent files and applications you have used and presents them in a Recent section.

Lock Screen and Logout do exactly what they say they do. The screen locker is password-protected with your UNIX password. The Logout entry terminates your KDE session. However, the KDE window manager saves the state of your desktop so that the next time you start KDE, the same applications are opened at the same locations as when you logged out.

Customizing the Panel

From the K menu, select Panel to customize the panel. The panel customization menu (Figure 5.5) pops up.

FIGURE 5.5
Panel customization menu.

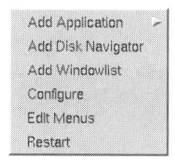

```
Add Application
Add Disk Navigator
Add Windowlist
Configure
Edit Menus
Restart
```

Clicking the Add Application entry opens a cascaded menu of all available KDE applications. When you select an application, its icon is added directly to the panel. You can then launch the application by clicking the icon in the panel. This is a great time-saver for frequently used applications.

The Add Disk Navigator and Add Windowlist entries add special buttons to the panel. The disk navigator button lets you access the disk navigator directly from the panel without going through the K menu. The window list button adds to the panel a special button that lists all windows on the desktop. Selecting a window opens it (if it is minimized) and brings it in front of other windows.

The Configure entry lets you configure the panel. You can control its location (top, bottom, left or right) and size. You can also control the location of the taskbar (recall that the taskbar is a small bar that holds a button for each active window).

From the Configure entry, you can also set the number of virtual desktops and other aspects of the panel's behavior. For more details, consult the KDE help entry for the panel application.

The Edit Menus entry lets you edit the K menu. Selecting it starts a special menu-editing application as well as the help screen for the menu editor. The menu editor is fairly easy to use, and the help documentation is reasonable. However, one thing that may not be obvious is that the K menu is divided into a system-wide standard part and a per-user part. You can edit your per-user part, but only root can edit the system-wide menu.

The Restart entry restarts the panel. Although you can customize the panel using KDE applications, you can also customize it by editing text files. Section 4 of the KDE Help entry *The K Panel Handbook* describes how to edit the files. Selecting Restart causes the panel to reread its configuration from the text files.

On the panel, you can move any button by dragging it while holding mouse button 2. If you click button 3 over an icon, a pop-up menu will appear. This menu will let you move or remove an icon, or edit its properties. The properties you can edit are

- *General properties*   The file name of the icon.
- *Permissions*   UNIX permissions of the target of the icon.
- *Execute*   Program to execute and how to run it. You can also select a new image for the icon by clicking the icon button on the Execute tab.

    The panel can swallow X Window programs. This means that the programs appear right in the panel rather than in their own window. For details of how to do this, see Section 3 of the KDE Panel help page.

- *Application*   The human-readable name of the application that the button will launch. Whatever you place in the Comment field in this panel appears as pop-up help balloons when the mouse pointer hesitates over the button.

Virtual Desktops

Near the center of the panel are buttons for switching virtual desktops. KDE divides your workspace into as many as eight (four by default) virtual desktops. Think of these as extra work areas that can hold additional windows. By clicking the virtual desktop buttons on the panel, you can switch to a different desktop. You can arrange your work so that, for example, your Web browser is on one desktop, your email client is on another desktop, and your text editor is on a third. This lets you make efficient use of screen space.

One nice touch is the integration of the virtual desktop scheme with the taskbar. If you press a button on the taskbar that belongs to a window in a different virtual desktop, KDE automatically changes to the desktop containing the window. This makes it even more convenient to arrange your work in multiple virtual desktops.

The Desktop Menu

Pressing button 3 over the desktop background brings up the desktop menu (Figure 5.6).

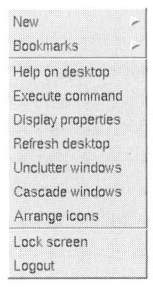

The desktop menu entries are described in Table 5.1.

FIGURE 5.6

Desktop menu.

TABLE 5.1 Desktop Menu Entries

Entry	Meaning
New	Brings up a submenu that allows you to create new files, folders, URLs, application icons, and so forth.
Bookmarks	Brings up a submenu that displays any bookmarks you have created with the file manager. The menu also has an entry for editing existing bookmarks.
Help on desktop	Brings up the KDE help browser.
Execute command	Prompts you to type a command and then executes it. You can press Alt+F2 as a shortcut. This entry is useful for typing commands if you don't have a shell window open.
Display properties	Brings up the KDE display property editor, which allows you to change the background, colors, fonts, style, and screen saver.
Refresh desktop	Causes all windows to redisplay their contents (in case a buggy program disturbed the display).
Unclutter windows	Moves windows so that the maximum amount of each window is visible.
Cascade windows	Moves windows so that they occupy as little of the desktop as possible.
Arrange icons	Arranges desktop icons neatly.
Lock screen	Locks the screen with a password-protected screen saver.
Log out	Terminates the KDE session.

The KDE File Manager

The KDE file manager, `kfm`, is a file manager and Web browser in one. You can use it to navigate your file system and browse the Web. The file manager is also responsible for the desktop icons, which provide convenient shortcuts to commonly used files and applications.

To start the file manager, click the home directory icon on the panel. (See Figure 5.3.) The KDE file manager starts. (See Figure 5.7.)

To open a file or folder, click it once with button 1.

> **Note**
>
> Most KDE programs require only a single click to perform an action. Unlike most GUIs (including Microsoft Windows), KDE programs require a double-click to open a file or launch an application. Single-click activation is the way most Web browsers work, but it takes some getting used to in a file manager.

FIGURE 5.7
KDE file manager.

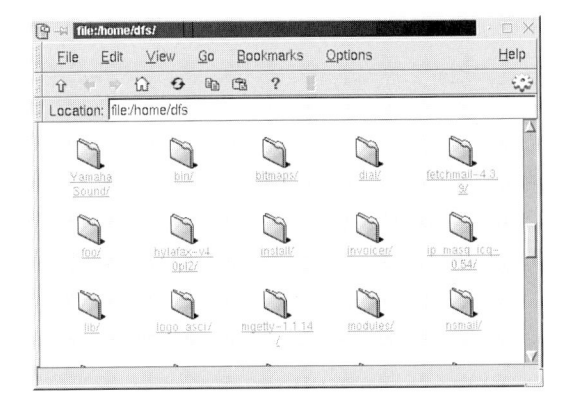

Use the file manager's toolbar to perform the following operations:

- To change to the parent directory of the current directory, click Up.
- To go back to the last directory (retrace your steps), click Back.
- To undo the last Back step, click Next.
- To change to your home directory, click Home.
- To refresh the current display, click Refresh.

Click the question mark button to bring up the KDE file manager's help page. This page explains additional features of the file manager.

Selecting Files

Normally, clicking a file opens it. If you just want to select a file to perform some operation on it (like deleting it), you have a couple of options:

- To select a single file and perform an operation on it, click the file with button 3. A menu will pop up. From this menu, you can delete the file, move it to the trash, or edit its properties. Within the property editor, you can change the file's name, permissions, and icon.
- To select several files, hold the Control key down and click button 1 on each file. If you wish to deselect a selected file, hold down Control and click again. After you have selected the files, you can open a menu with button 3 and operate on all the files.

Views

The View menu lets you alter the appearance of files in the file manager. The normal view is called Icon View and displays files and directories as little icons. The other kinds of views are:

- *Text View*   A display similar to the output of the `ls -l` command.
- *Long View*   Similar to Text View, but with small icons on the left-hand side of the listing.
- *Short View*   A display similar to the output of the `ls` command, but with small icons to the left of each file name.

In addition, the Show Tree option turns on a tree-like display of the directory structure starting from the file system root, your home directory, and your Desktop directory.

The Desktop Directory

Any files deposited in the Desktop directory under your home directory appear as icons on the desktop surface itself. You can create these icons in a number of ways:

- Using the KDE file manager, simply create a directory or file in Desktop. It will appear as an icon.
- Drag a file or directory from the KDE file manager onto the desktop background. A small menu with the Copy, Move, and Link options will appear. The Copy operation will copy the file or directory from its source location into the Desktop directory. The Move operation will move the file or directory into the Desktop directory (and remove it from its original location). Finally, the Link operation will place a symbolic link to the file in *Desktop*. This will appear as an icon with a little arrow, denoting a shortcut.

URLs

Not only is the KDE file manager a handy tool for navigating your file system, but it is also a full Web browser. In the Location text entry box, just type a URL like `http://www.roaringpenguin.com` to open a Web page. You can also open FTP URLs and use the file manager as an FTP client.

Anything you can view with the file manager can be made into a desktop icon. You can even drag links from a Web page and drop them on the desktop. This will create an icon that, when clicked, will take you instantly to the URL.

Bookmarks

The KDE file manager Bookmarks menu allows you to add the current location to your set of bookmarks. Bookmarks are links to often-visited files and URLs. They let you organize your browsing and work exactly as bookmarks in Web browsers do. Any bookmarks you create with the file manager are available from the button 3 pop-up menu on the desktop background.

Mime Types

The KDE file manager can automatically open many different types of files with the correct application. For example, it knows to open GIF and JPEG images with the KDE image viewer. The rules mapping file types to applications are stored in the Mime Types folder. You can edit the Mime Types folder by selecting Edit:Mime Types from the file manager menu.

Mime types are named as a general category followed by a slash and a specific instance. For example, GIF images are of type image/gif, whereas JPEG images are of type image/jpeg. HTML documents are of type text/html.

Each general category has a directory in the Mime Types folder, and within each category are files specifying how to open each file type. Click on one of these files to edit the type.

For example, the image/gif Mime type's properties specify that the KDE image viewer should be used to open files of this type. Click the various Mime types to look at (and edit) their properties. For more information on adding and editing Mime types, see Section 3.2 of the KDE file manager online manual.

Drag and Drop

Most KDE programs let you drag files from one window and drop them on another. For example, start the KDE text editor by selecting Editors:Text Editor from the K menu. Open a KDE file manager window and change to the /etc directory. Drag the file magic from the file manager onto the text editor window. As you release the file, the text editor opens the file and displays its contents.

Similarly, if you drag a file from the file manager onto the Printer Queue application, KDE will print the file. (The Printer Queue application is available from the K menu under System:Printer Queue.)

The KDE Control Center

The KDE Control Center controls all aspects of the KDE user interface. Launch it by clicking the control center icon on the panel (Figure 5.3). The KDE Control Center window is shown in Figure 5.8.

The KDE Control Center contains many configuration modules, and more may be added as KDE evolves. I will give a brief overview of the modules; for more details, see the KDE online help or experiment with the configuration modules. Most modules are quite intuitive.

FIGURE 5.8
The KDE Control Center.

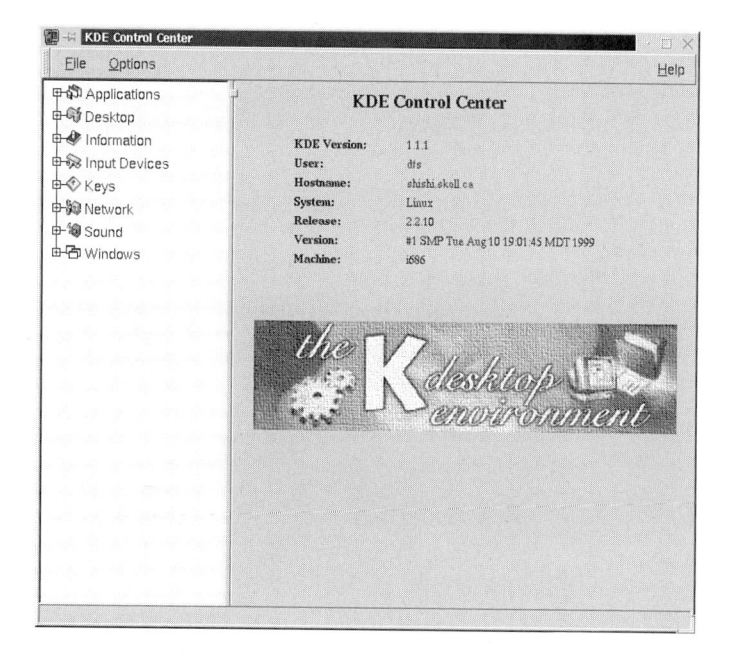

Applications

The applications category lets you change the behavior of important KDE programs: the login manager, the file manager, the Web browser, and the panel.

The login manager is the graphical login screen that greets you when the system is waiting for you to log on. Note that only root can modify the login manager's behavior.

You can alter the login manager's appearance, such as the background image, the sign-on logo and the text fonts. You can also ask the login manager not to display a list of users. By default, the login manager displays a list of users, making it easier for you to log in: You simply click on your user name. However, revealing the names of all users on a system is a security risk, and I recommend turning off this display.

The file manager's configuration module lets you select fonts and colors for the file manager display. You can also select the default terminal program and text editor.

The Web browser's configuration module lets you configure the Web browser. If you use a proxy server, you can fill in the proxy information here. You can also configure how the Web browser handles cookies.

> **Note**
>
> Cookies are bits of information sent from Web servers that allow them to track your Web visits across sessions. Some people consider them a violation of privacy, but I don't see much harm in accepting cookies.

The panel's configuration module lets you configure where the panel and taskbar are placed on the screen, the size of the panel, and whether or not the panel and taskbar "auto-hide" when they are not being used. You can also change the number of virtual desktops from the default four to two, four, six, or eight.

Desktop

The desktop category lets you alter the overall appearance of the desktop. You can alter the background of the desktop, making it a solid color, a color gradient, or a wallpaper image.

The Borders entry lets you set up active desktop borders. These make KDE automatically switch desktops if you "push" on the edge of a desktop with the mouse pointer. You can also set up snap zones so that windows snap neatly against the edge of the screen and against each other. Play around to see what the settings do.

The Colors and Fonts entries let you change the colors and fonts used by KDE to decorate windows. KDE-aware applications obey the color and font settings you choose here, but non-KDE X programs may choose their own color scheme and fonts.

The Desktop Icons entry lets you control how desktop icons are placed. You can specify the horizontal and vertical spacing grids and the text colors. You can also have transparent icon labels, which look quite nice.

If you have installed the *kdetheme** packages from the `contrib` directory on the main CD-ROM, the Theme Manager entry will let you select a KDE theme. These themes drastically alter the appearance of KDE, letting you make it look as boring as Windows 98 or as exciting as a high-tech arcade game. KDE themes are another fun productivity destroyer.

The Language entry allows you to select the default language for applications. If you are multilingual, you can select up to three languages. Because some applications are not translated into all languages, you can select more than one language to give an application a fighting chance of picking a language you understand.

The Screensaver entry lets you set up the KDE screen saver, including the delay before it kicks in, the cool graphics it displays, and whether or not it is password protected.

Finally, the Style entry lets you choose whether or not KDE widgets should be drawn in Windows 95 or Motif style. The Theme Manager entry makes the Style entry obsolete if you installed KDE themes.

Information

The Information category displays information about many aspects of your Linux system. This information includes which devices have kernel drivers; which DMA channels, I/O ports, and interrupts are in use; memory usage; file system partitions; PCI bus devices; processor information; SCSI information, and more. Most of this information is accessible via the /proc file system, but the KDE Control Center presents it in a more attractive and understandable format.

Input Devices

The Input Devices category lets you configure your keyboard and mouse. If you have a non-English keyboard, the International Keyboard entry lets you select from about four-dozen different international keyboard layouts. The Keyboard entry lets you control other aspects of the keyboard, such as key repeat and key click volume. (Note that not all computers support keyboard click—thankfully.)

The Mouse entry lets you control mouse acceleration and button mapping. If you are left-handed, you may wish to make the right mouse button behave as button 1.

> **Note**
>
> Mouse acceleration refers to a software speedup of mouse motion when you move the mouse quickly. This speedup makes large motions more efficient while maintaining precision for small motions.

Keys

The Keys category lets you modify KDE's keyboard shortcuts. The Global Keys entry edits global keys that operate at the desktop level (such as keys to switch virtual desktops), whereas the Standard Keys entry edits standard per-application keys, such as the cut and paste shortcuts.

Network

The Network category is rather sparse, containing only a Talk Configuration entry. This lets KDE react to the UNIX talk program by playing a sound and opening a terminal window. To use this feature, you have to run the `ktalkd` daemon. However, the default Caldera OpenLinux setup does not use the `ktalkd` daemon. If you are interested in setting it up, see the online help by pressing Help on the Talk Configuration module.

Sound

The Sound category lets you control system sounds. The Bell entry lets you set the volume, pitch, and duration of the system beep. Note that not all systems can change the volume or pitch of the beep.

The System Sounds entry lets you associate sounds with various events like opening or closing a window, logging out, and so forth. Whenever you perform an action with a matching sound, the KDE window manager plays the sound. This is fun at first, but it quickly becomes annoying.

Windows

Finally, the Windows category lets you alter the behavior of KDE windows. You can change things like which buttons appear in the window title bar and which keys walk through the list of windows.

This category also lets you change how windows react to mouse clicks. For example, if you want button 2 in the title bar to raise a window instead of button 1, you can configure it to be so.

There are many configuration options in this category, but they are all self-explanatory. Spend a happy few minutes poking around and seeing how you can configure your system.

Some KDE Applications

Now that I have covered the basics of KDE itself, let's look at some KDE applications. KDE applications are normal X Window applications that understand the KDE conventions and follow the KDE user interface guidelines. This means that KDE applications can exchange data using drag and drop, they have a consistent user-interface with similar shortcut keys, and they all have a uniform appearance.

The KDE Package Manager

The KDE package manager is a graphical front end for the RPM software package management system. (RPM is described in detail in Chapter 7.)

To start the KDE package manager, type **kpackage** at the shell prompt. Alternatively, click on an `.rpm` file from the file manager. The kpackage window appears (Figure 5.9).

FIGURE 5.9

The KDE package manager.

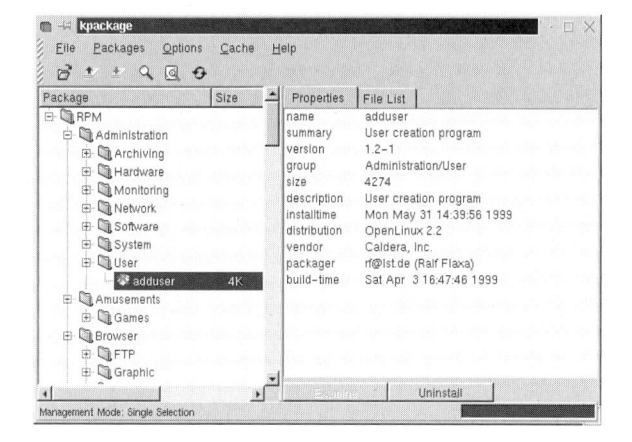

kpackage arranges all installed packages into a hierarchy. You can view the hierarchy in the left-hand window pane. Click the arrows to expand or collapse a subtree.

After you traverse the hierarchy down to an actual package, click the package to view its properties. These properties include the package name, version, summary, size, and description. Click the File List tab to get a list of all files owned by the package.

If you click Uninstall while examining a package, the package will be removed from the system.

If you open an .rpm file (using File:Open or dragging a file from the file manager), kpackage gives you the option of installing the package. It lists the package properties and all the files that the package will install. Click Install to install the package.

> **Note**
>
> You have to be root to install a package. If you are running as a nonroot user and click on an .rpm file in the file manager, you will be prompted for the root password so you can run kpackage as root. If you do not want to run kpackage as root, but merely wish to examine an RPM, start kpackage from the command line and use File:Open to open the RPM, or drag it from the file manager.

Using the menu entry File:Open URL, you can even open an HTTP or FTP URL pointing to an RPM package and install it from kpackage. This lets you easily update your system over the Internet.

The KDE package manager has many more features for manipulating software packages; see the KDE package manager's help pages for more information.

The KDE Task Manager

The KDE Task Manager is a graphical version of the ps command as well as a nice display of system load. To start the KDE Task Manager, select System:Task Manager from the K menu or type **ktop** at a shell prompt. The Task Manager opens showing a list of processes (Figure 5.10).

FIGURE 5.10
The KDE Task Manager (processes list).

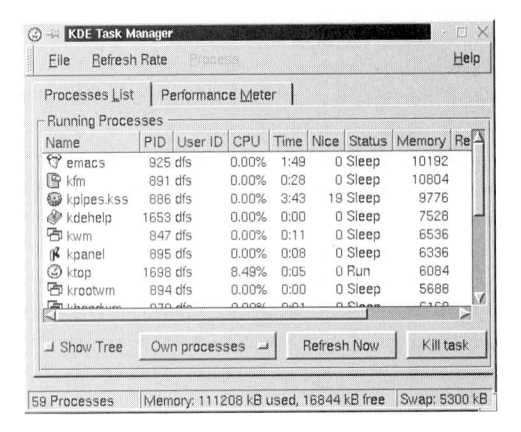

From this window, you can perform the following operations:

- Activate Show Tree to turn on a tree-oriented process display. This reveals processes' parents and children.
- Select one of Own Processes, User Processes, System Processes, or All Processes to control which processes are displayed.
- Highlight a process by clicking it. You can then kill it by clicking Kill Task. You can perform other manipulations on a selected process by pulling down the Process menu. This lets you alter the process's priority or send it a signal other than KILL.
- Click a table heading to sort processes by that heading. For example, you can sort processes by memory usage by clicking on the Memory heading. Note that this sorting does not work properly in tree mode because the parent-child relationships override the sorting criteria.

The Performance Meter tab displays CPU usage and memory usage statistics for your computer. As shown in Figure 5.11, the display is organized as a pair of strip charts, which are updated every second or so.

FIGURE 5.11
The KDE Task Manager (performance meter).

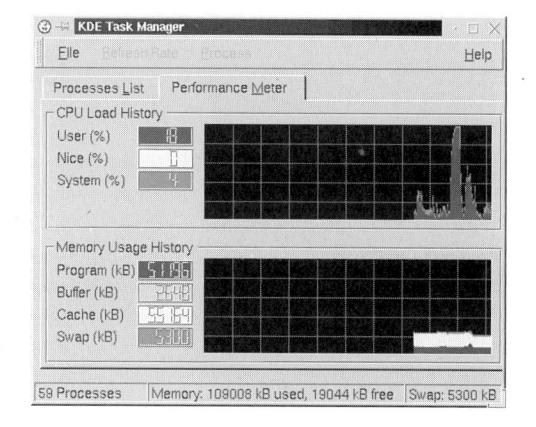

The CPU load history panel breaks CPU usage into three categories:

- *User* The percentage of CPU time spent executing user code (in other words, actual application code).
- *Nice* The percentage of CPU time used by "niced" processes (that is, processes running at lower-than-normal priority).
- *System* The percentage of CPU time used to execute system calls. This is time spent executing inside the kernel.

The memory usage history panel breaks memory usage into four categories:

- *Program* Memory used by applications.
- *Buffer* Memory used by kernel buffers for internal purposes.
- *Cache* Memory used by the kernel to cache file system accesses. The kernel caches these accesses to improve performance. If applications require additional memory, the kernel shrinks the file system cache as required.
- *Swap* Space consumed by memory pages that have been written out to disk. If the system runs low on memory, it swaps some pages out to disk. This practice allows the system to run more processes than will fit in memory at a time; however, too much swapping will slow down the system and might render it practically unusable.

The KDE Image Viewer

The KDE image viewer allows you to view GIF, JPEG, TIFF, PNG, and other images. Unfortunately, it is (as of KDE version 1.1.1) very poorly documented, so the online help is useless.

To start the KDE image viewer, type **kview** at a shell prompt or click an image in the KDE file manager. Alternatively select Graphics:Image Viewer from the K menu. The image viewer window with an image in it is shown in Figure 5.12.

FIGURE 5.12
The KDE image viewer.

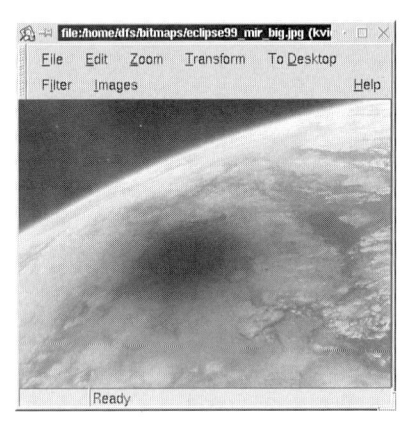

To view an image, open it with File:Open or drag the image file from the file manager. When you have the image in memory, you can manipulate it with some simple image-processing operations.

To change the image size, select an entry from the Zoom menu. You can shrink or enlarge the image. To fit the image in the window exactly, select Zoom:Max/aspect. This makes the image as large as possible while still fitting it into the window and maintaining the original aspect ratio.

The Transform menu lets you rotate and mirror the image. You can rotate clockwise or counterclockwise and mirror horizontally or vertically.

The To Desktop menu lets you put the image on the desktop. The various entries in the menu control how the image is tiled on the desktop. Note that if you have configured KDE to use a wallpaper image, the image placed by kview will be lost when you switch virtual desktops.

The Filter menu lets you perform simple filtering on the image. To alter the brightness of the image, select Intensity:Brightness and enter a number. Numbers larger than 100 brighten the image, and numbers smaller than 100 darken it.

To alter the gamma response of the image, select Intensity:Gamma Correct and enter a gamma value. Values larger than 1 tend to brighten the image and enhance the distinction of features in dark areas of the image, while reducing detail in bright areas. Values less than 1 do exactly the opposite—the image is darkened and detail in dark areas is suppressed.

To convert a color image to a grayscale image, select Filter:Grayscale. Finally, Filter:Smooth smoothes an image. There is no documentation on how the smoothing is done, but it appears to be with a linear blurring filter. This filter replaces each pixel with the average of the nine pixels surrounding and including the original pixel.

You can open many image files with kview, either by supplying file names on the command line or by dragging the images onto the viewer window. The Images menu lets you manipulate the list of images known to kview. You can even start a slideshow mode that displays images in succession. If the various images are frames of a movie, you can use kview as a primitive movie viewer.

Summary

This chapter presented an overview of the K Desktop Environment. You learned how the desktop is laid out and how to perform fundamental operations like opening, closing, moving, and resizing windows. You learned about the three most important KDE applications—the window manager, which provides window buttons and decorations; the panel, which supplies the K menu, various application launching buttons, and the taskbar; and the KDE file manager, which lets you navigate the file system and browse the Internet.

Next, you learned about the KDE Control Center, which lets you customize all aspects of KDE. Finally, we covered three sample KDE applications: the KDE package manager, the KDE Task Manager, and the KDE image viewer. These three applications illustrated how KDE applications operate. I encourage you to explore the K menu and discover the many other KDE applications.

Text Editors

CHAPTER 6

IN THIS CHAPTER

- vi   *136*
- XEmacs   *155*

Caldera OpenLinux comes with a few different text editors that are good for accomplishing different tasks. In this chapter, we will discuss two of them: *vi* (pronounced vee-eye) and *XEmacs* (pronounced ex-ee-max).

Both vi and XEmacs are common editors and have a rich heritage, but vi is *the* de facto standard editor included with all UNIX implementations. When using other versions of UNIX, if nothing else in life is sure, you are pretty much guaranteed that vi will always be there for you.

Neither vi nor XEmacs behaves quite like most modern text editors. vi was written in a different era, before the GUI became commonplace, and XEmacs was originally based on Emacs, a more recent editor than vi, but still developed to run in a terminal window or on the console. This does not mean that they should be retired and left behind. Given that vi is essentially omnipresent, it is a good idea, and definitely to your advantage, to learn at least the basics. Also, if you ever have to rescue your system from a crash and edit configuration files from the command line (don't worry, your time will come), when you boot up with a rescue diskette, vi will probably be the only editor you will have available to work with.

Although XEmacs may behave a little differently than you are used to, it is a very powerful editor and one of the best freely available for use under Linux or UNIX.

vi

If you're new to Linux and UNIX, vi will be a bit of a shocker for you. Even though a plethora of text editors are available, many of which are new ones with graphical user interfaces, vi is one of the most common and widely used, or at least the most widely available.

The reason vi will be a bit of a shocker is because it doesn't work like you would expect a modern editor to work, and it is nothing like nearly any Windows or other modern editor with a GUI. vi is a text-based editor designed to be run in a terminal window or from the console. It was also designed in a different world and based on a different paradigm than what we have become accustomed to today. This makes it appear weird and difficult to use.

But fear not! You will be able to get by without using vi most of the time, if you want. Nevertheless, it can be extremely handy, and even essential, at times. It is very convenient for moving through a text file, searching for and substituting text, and performing quick edits. It is also an excellent editor for programming (many old programmers swear by it!). I use it mostly for making quick changes to things like configuration files (which you'll probably see plenty of in your life with Linux). I find that it's often much easier and quicker to simply type vi */the/file/I/want/to/edit* and do what I want, than to work through the menus until I find the editor I want, wait for it to start, and then work through the file dialog until I find the file I want to edit.

There are also times when vi will be the only choice available to you. One such time is if you need to boot your system from a rescue diskette and make changes to configuration files to fix something. In a case like that, the creators of the rescue diskette probably will have included only vi.

As mentioned before, you can live a happy and productive life without using vi, but if you do know the basics of vi, you'll be able to use it when you get in a pinch. Note, however, that you will only learn how to use it effectively by actually using it. As you read through the discussion, try things out. Use the commands. Even if you don't want to use it all the time, practicing a bit will help you get the feel for things and save you a lot of frustration later.

A Little History

Before getting into how to use vi, let's look at where it came from. That will help you to understand why it works differently than most modern editors.

It's interesting to note that when vi was written, it was pretty much the culmination of everything that had come before. It was top of the line, cutting-edge technology. This is because vi was written back when we were just recovering from the teletype terminal—something akin to a typewriter attached to a computer that ate reams of paper tape for breakfast.

There was no easy way to edit a file at a teletype terminal. About all you could do was print a line, enter commands to a line editor telling it to make any required changes, and then print it again to see if you got it right. Because you were viewing all the output on a printed page, there was no cursor to move around. Consequently, you had to specify the words you wanted changed along with what to change them to. For example, if you accidentally typed *hte* instead of *the*, you would fix it with a command like this:

```
:substitute/hte/the/
```

After the teletype came the CRT. However, the first CRTs only allowed you to edit the current line, so you weren't a whole lot better off, aside from the fact that you could finally edit the line directly. The next generation of CRTs fixed that problem by allowing the cursor to move around the whole screen, paving the way for the screen editor. Then vi was born. vi is a screen editor; however, it also includes many of the features of the older command and line editors. In that way, people who were accustomed to the older editors could still feel at home and continue to live happy and productive lives.

Editing Modes

vi runs in one of two editing modes: *command mode* and *input mode*. When vi is in command mode, it is ready to accept and act on commands. Any keystrokes are interpreted as commands and will not appear in the text. The commands do certain editing functions, move you around in the file, and switch vi to input mode. Most commands are a single keystroke, but some are a combination of two or more keys. When you press a key for a command, in most cases vi will simply execute the command without echoing the key you typed to the screen. There are, of course, exceptions, and we will get to those later.

Bill Joy (the father of vi) tried to use mnemonics when creating the command set for vi. For example, *i* stands for insert. He also tried to use characters that suggested meaning. For example, the right curly brace (}) moves you to the end of a paragraph, and the left curly brace ({) moves you to the beginning of a paragraph. Part of learning vi is learning to think vi. Pretty soon, you learn to think "backward" and associate it with the letter *b*, instead of thinking something like "left" and getting something totally different. It all comes quickly with use.

When vi is in input mode, it interprets keystrokes as text to be placed in the file. Everything you type shows up on the screen and the changes are made to your file, as you would expect. You get out of input mode and go back to command mode by pressing the Esc key.

In general, during an editing session, you will switch often between command and input mode. It is very important to always know what mode you are in. It is very easy to start typing text, thinking that you are in input mode, only to find out that you were in command mode and that vi made changes to your file that you didn't want. Of course, there are ways to undo those changes, so don't panic when it happens to you.

Running vi

To create a new file using vi, you simply type **vi** on the command line followed by the name you want for your new file. Figure 6.1 shows a screen shot of vi running in a terminal window with a new, empty file called `newFile`. The cursor is the block in the upper-left corner, and all the tildes (~) represent empty lines, or rather, lines beyond the end of the file. That is to say, if you had a file with only six lines in it, there is nothing to display after the six lines, so vi prints tildes to let you know that there is nothing after the six lines. The bottom line is used as a type of status line and is where you type in certain editing commands. By default, vi starts up in command mode.

FIGURE 6.1

Screen shot of vi running in a terminal window ready to edit the new file newFile.

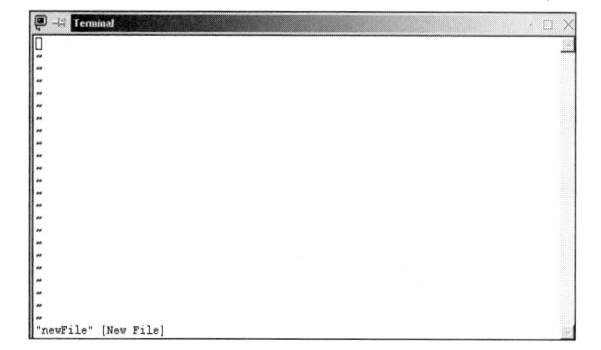

> **Tip**
>
> vi doesn't actually create a new file until you save it. So if you were to exit vi without typing any text, or without saving any text that you had typed in, the file would not be created. You'll do this a lot when you mistype the name of an existing file you want to edit, and vi comes up thinking you want to create a new file.

Similarly, to edit an already existing file, you just put the name of the file on the command line:

```
$ vi anExistingFile
```

vi then loads the file into a buffer and displays it. If you simply type a simple file name without any slashes (/), vi will look for or create the file in the current directory. If you want to edit a file in a different directory, then you need to include the path to the file. Figure 6.2 shows how vi looks just after opening the file /etc/printcap.

FIGURE 6.2

Screen shot of vi just after opening the file /etc/printcap.

Saving Files and Quitting vi

There are numerous ways to save your file and quit vi. Some commands allow you to do both actions together, whereas others allow you to combine the two actions. Table 6.1 lists some of the most common of these methods.

TABLE 6.1   Commands for Saving Files and Quitting vi

Command	Mnemonic	Description
:w	Write	Saves the file
:w!	Write	Forces vi to save the file
:w *newName*	Write	Saves the file as *newName*
ZZ	—	Saves the file and quits
:wq	Write/quit	Saves the file and quits
:q	Quit	Exits vi
:q!	Quit	Exits vi without saving changes

> **Note**
>
> vi must be in command mode to use any of the commands listed in Table 6.1. If it is not, press the Esc key to switch to command mode.

The commands that start with a colon (:) are ex commands. ex is an old line editor, and vi is a superset of ex, so all valid ex commands are also valid in vi. When you type the colon, the cursor goes to the lower-left corner of the screen and displays the command you type. The command will not be executed until you press the Enter key. This is true of all ex commands. vi commands are executed as soon as you press the key(s) for that command and are not displayed on the screen. So, for example, :w will only be executed after you press the Enter key, but ZZ will be executed as soon as you press the second Z.

The exclamation point (!) tells vi that you really want it to do what you are telling it to do. For these commands, you will use the exclamation point in two cases. You will need to use :w! if the permissions for the file are set so that you do not have write permission. Normally, if you don't have write permission, and you try to execute :w without the exclamation point, vi will tell you that it can't write to the file and leave it at that. The exclamation point tells it to try to write to the file anyway. Note, however, that this will only work if you are the owner of the file. If you don't own the file, you will not be able to write to it no matter how many exclamation points you add to the command! You will use :q! when you want to exit vi after having made changes that you don't want to save. If you have made changes and try to quit using only :q, vi will tell you that there are unsaved changes and will *not* quit.

vi also allows you to save portions of a file by specifying the line numbers of the first and last lines of the range that you want to save. It saves everything between the two lines specified including those lines. You do this using the following command:

```
:first_line, last_linew newName
```

Where *first_line* and *last_line* are line numbers or special characters that can be used to specify certain lines. For example a period (.) signifies the current line (that is, the line the cursor is on), and a dollar sign ($) signifies the last line of the file. *newName* is the name of the file to save to. Note the w on the end of *last_line* in the command. That is not a typo. It is the write command.

> **Tip**
>
> - To find out what line you are on along with some other information, press Ctrl+G.
> - To go to a specific line, use the :line_number command. For example, :25 will take you to line 25 in the file.
> - To have vi display line numbers on the left side of the screen, use the :set number command. You can turn them off again using the :set nonumber command.

Table 6.2 lists a few examples of saving part of a file.

TABLE 6.2 Examples of Saving Part of a File

Command	Action
:25,50w newFile	Saves lines 25 through 50 to the file newFile.
:.,50w newFile	Saves everything from the current line through line 50 to the file newFile.
:1,.w newFile	Saves everything from the beginning of the file to the current line to the file newFile.
:50,$w newFile	Saves everything from line 50 to the end of the file to the file newFile.

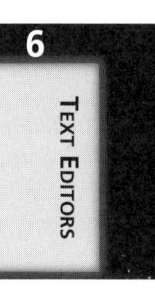

If you don't want to save the selected part to a new file, you can save it to the current file, but you need to change the command slightly. Instead of specifying a file name at the end of the command, add an exclamation point after the w. This tells vi that you really do want to save only the selected part of the file, throwing away the rest. For example, to save only lines 10 through 100 of a file, you would use the following command:

`:10,100w!`

If you fail to add the exclamation point, vi won't save the file, but will tell you to use it in order to save only part of the file.

Moving Around in a File

vi has many commands to help you move around in a file. The number of different commands to move around may seem like overkill at first, but they can be very useful and make editing much easier and quicker if you learn them.

The easiest and most basic way to move around is to simply use the arrow keys and the Page Up and Page Down keys. These work as you would expect most of the time. Note, however, that you cannot move beyond the end of a line, and the cursor does not wrap around to the next line when you try. For example, if the cursor is at the end of the line, and you press the right-arrow key, vi will just beep at you (as if you should know better).

> **Note**
>
> You can move around using the arrow, Page Up, and Page Down keys in both command and input mode. However, all other movement commands can only be used in command mode.

> **Note**
>
> The version of vi that comes with OpenLinux is actually an enhanced version with many more features than the generic vi. For the most part, we will be talking about features that can be found in nearly any version of vi, but you may find that some other version of vi doesn't have a feature you are used to using or behaves slightly differently. For example, many versions of vi don't let you use the arrow, Page Up, and Page Down keys. For this reason, you should still learn the normal commands for basic cursor movement.

When you can't use the arrow keys to move around, or you want to move around more quickly, use vi commands. In general, you can move around more quickly and more easily using vi commands than using the arrow keys because vi commands allow you to move in jumps to specific types of locations instead of just one character or line at a time. For example, w moves you to the beginning of the next word, and } moves you to the end of the current paragraph. Table 6.3 summarizes most of the movement commands for vi. Each command is then briefly described in the following sections.

TABLE 6.3 vi Movement Commands

Command	Mnemonic	Moves...
h	—	Cursor left one space.
j	—	Cursor down one space.
k	—	Cursor up one space.
l	—	Cursor right one space.
w	Word	Cursor to the beginning of the next word.
W	Word	Cursor to the beginning of the next word ignoring symbols and punctuation marks.
e	End	Cursor to the end of the current word (or the next word if the cursor is in a blank area or at the end of a word).
E	End	Cursor to the end of the current word ignoring symbols and punctuation marks (or the next word if the cursor is in a blank area or at the end of a word).
b	Backward	Cursor to the beginning of the current word (or previous word if the cursor is in a blank area or at the beginning of a word).
B	Backward	Cursor to the beginning of the current word ignoring symbols and punctuation marks (or the previous word if the cursor is in a blank area or at the beginning of a word).
0 (zero)	—	Cursor to the beginning of the line.
^	—	Cursor to the first nonblank character on the line.
Enter key	—	Cursor to the beginning of the next line.
$	—	Cursor to the end of the current line.
+	—	Cursor to the first nonblank character of the next line.
-	—	Cursor to the first nonblank character of the previous line.

continues

TABLE 6.3 continued

Command	Mnemonic	Moves...
(	—	Cursor to the beginning of the current sentence (or previous sentence if the cursor is in a blank area or at the beginning of a sentence).
)	—	Cursor to the end of the current sentence (or the next sentence if the cursor is in a blank area or at the end of a sentence).
{	—	Cursor to the beginning of the current paragraph (or the previous paragraph if the cursor is in a blank area or at the beginning of a paragraph).
}	—	Cursor to the end of the current paragraph (or the next paragraph if the cursor is in a blank area or at the end of a paragraph).
H	Home	Cursor to the first line on the screen.
M	Middle	Cursor to the middle line on the screen.
L	Last	Cursor to the last line on the screen.
nH	—	Cursor to *n* lines below the first line on the screen (will not move past the last line on the screen).
nL	—	Cursor to *n* lines above the last line on the screen (will not move past the top line on the screen).
nG	Go	Cursor to line *n*.
:n	—	Cursor to line *n*.
Ctrl+F	Forward	Forward one screen.
Ctrl+B	Backward	Backward one screen.
Ctrl+D	Down	Forward one-half screen.
Ctrl+U	Up	Backward one-half screen.
Ctrl+E	Expose	Scrolls up one line.
Ctrl+Y	—	Scrolls down one line.

> **Tip**
>
> You can tell vi to repeat a command a given number of times by preceding that command with the number of times you want it to be repeated. For example, if you want to move the cursor forward three words, you type **3w**, effectively repeating the w command three times.

Moving One Space at a Time

To move left or right one space, you use the commands h and l. To move up or down one space, you use the commands j and k. h moves you left one space, whereas l moves you right one space. j moves you down one space, whereas k moves you up one space.

There is no real mnemonic for these keys, but it may help to remember that these movement keys are all located together on the keyboard. The leftmost and rightmost keys move you left and right, and the middle ones move you down and up. Even if you forget whether j moves you down or up, remembering that the key to move you down is in the middle of the group will get you 50% of the way there. Then once you try it, you'll see which direction you go. Then you can go the other way if you need to.

Moving One Word at a Time

Six commands allow you to move one word at a time: w, W, e, E, b, and B. Note that lowercase and uppercase letters are different commands. vi is case sensitive.

These commands use two different definitions of what a word is. The first one defines a word as a consecutive group of letters or symbols. A word boundary occurs when that group ends. This means that *asdf* is considered a word and so is *@#$%*. Note, however, that *asdf@#$%hjkl* is considered three words because the first group of letters ends at the first symbol, and the group of symbols, which is considered a word, ends at the letter *h*. This also means that punctuation marks will be treated as words. So, with the phrase *bye, bye.*, there are effectively four words; *bye* is two of them, and the comma and period count as the other two.

The second definition of a word says that a word is any collection of letters and symbols, and that a word terminates at the next blank character (or the end of the file, if you are at the last word in the file).

The lowercase letters use the first definition, and the uppercase letter use the second definition. w and W move you to the beginning of the next word. e and E move you to the end of the next word (or the current one if the cursor is somewhere in a word besides the end). And b and B move you to the beginning of the previous word (or the current one if the cursor is somewhere in a word besides the beginning).

Moving One Line at a Time

There are two types of line commands—one that moves you to some point at the beginning or the end of the current line and another that moves you to some point at the beginning of the previous or next line. I say some point at the beginning because some commands will move you to the very beginning of the line, whereas others will move you to the first nonblank character on a line. A line is defined as the text between carriage returns. If autowrap is turned off, a line can span several physical lines on the screen. If it is on, then vi will automatically insert carriage returns at 80 characters (generally the edge of the screen). It is turned off by default.

In the first group, we have 0 (zero), which moves you to the beginning of the current line. ^ moves you to the first nonblank character of the current line (that is, it ignores spaces and tabs). And $ moves you to the end of the current line.

In the second group we have the Enter key, which moves you to the beginning of the next line. + moves you to the first nonblank character of the next line, and - moves you to the first nonblank character of the previous line.

Moving One Sentence or Paragraph at a Time

To make things even more convenient for you, vi can even move one sentence or paragraph at a time. This is most convenient when editing English text, or rather, just normal text. vi finds the end of a sentence by looking for a period followed by a blank space, or a blank line if it can't find a period. vi finds the next paragraph by finding the next blank line. So a paragraph is all the text between two blank lines (or before or after a blank line in the cases where it is at the beginning or end of a file).

(moves you to the beginning of the previous sentence (or the current sentence, if the cursor is somewhere in a sentence besides the beginning), and) moves you to the beginning of the next sentence. { moves you to the beginning of the previous paragraph (or current paragraph, if the cursor is somewhere in a paragraph besides the beginning), and } moves you to the beginning of the next paragraph.

Moving Around the Screen

Five commands allow you to conveniently move to common lines on the screen or somewhere relative to the top or bottom line of the screen. H moves the cursor to the beginning of the first line on the screen. M moves the cursor to the middle line on the screen, and L moves the cursor to the last line on the screen. *n*H moves the cursor to the beginning of the line that is *n* lines below the top line. For example, 7H would move the cursor to the beginning of the line 7 lines below the top line. So if the top line were the first line of the file, the cursor would now be at line 8. *n*L moves the cursor to the beginning of the line that is *n* lines above the bottom line, similar to the previous command.

Moving to a Particular Line

You can move to a specific line in a file by using one of the two following commands: *n*G or :*n*, where *n* is the number of the line you want to move to. So to move to line 123, you could type either 123G or :123. Note that the second command needs to be followed by the Enter key because it is an ex command, whereas the first command will be executed as soon as you press the G.

Scrolling the Screen Up or Down

You can scroll the screen (the part of the file you are viewing) up or down in increments of a whole screen, a half screen, or one line at a time. Ctrl+F and Ctrl+B scroll the screen forward and backward one full screen, respectively. Ctrl+D and Ctrl+U scroll forward and backward one-half screen, respectively. And Ctrl+Y and Ctrl+E scroll forward and backward one line, respectively.

Moving by Searching for Text

You can also move around a file by searching for a text pattern. To search forward for a text pattern, you use the following command:

`/pattern`

pattern is the text or alphanumeric pattern you want to search for. The command will appear at the bottom of the screen as you type it. Thus, even though this is not an ex command, you still need to finish it off by pressing the Enter key. Basically, all commands that you type in at the bottom of the screen are completed by pressing the Enter key.

You can search backwards by using this command:

`?pattern`

If you are at the end of the file searching forward, vi will automatically wrap the search around and start searching from the beginning of the file. Likewise, if you are at the beginning of the file searching backward, vi will wrap around to the end of the file and keep searching from there. If no matches are found, vi will say so.

To repeat a search and move on to the next match, you just use / or ? without reentering the text pattern. vi remembers what you searched for before and does the same search again from the current position. You can also use the vi commands n and N, which do the same things as / and ?, respectively. / and n find the next match searching forward, and ? and N find the next match searching backward.

You can also use wildcard characters in your search. For example, the asterisk (*) will match zero or more alphanumeric characters. So, if you wanted to find all the words that start with *th* in a file (I don't know why you would want to do that, but let's pretend that you do), you would use the following command:

`/th*`

That would match words like *the*, *this*, *that*, and *think*. Table 6.4 describes some of the wildcard characters available to you.

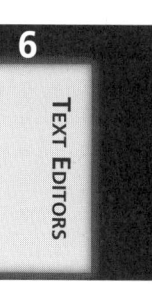

TABLE 6.4 Wildcard Characters Useful in Searches

Wildcard	Represents...
.	Any single character
*	Zero or more characters
[...]	Any character in the brackets (for example, [xyz] would match any one of x, y, or z)
[..-..]	Any character in the range specified (for example, [a-z] would match any single character from a to z).

If you want to find only text patterns at the beginning or end of the line, use the caret (^) and the dollar sign ($) respectively. The caret is placed *before* the text pattern and tells vi to consider something a match only if it starts the line. For example, if you're editing a list of names and phone numbers where the last name is the first thing on a line, and you want to skip to the section of last names that start with a *P*, you could use the following command:

/^P

That would take you to the next line where P is the very first character on the line. Note that as far as this command is concerned, whitespace (spaces and tabs) are considered characters, so if the P had a space in front of it on the line, then it would not be matched.

The dollar sign is placed *after* the text pattern to be matched and tells vi to consider something a match only if it is the *last* thing on the line. For example, let's say you have an international address list where all the information is placed in columns, and the country is listed in the last column. If you wanted to find the next person in Germany, you could use the following command:

/Germany$

You can also combine the caret and the dollar sign to find a line with only the text pattern on it. For example, the following command would search for a line that has only the word *this* on it:

/^this$

So, if you had a file something like this:

this
this & that

The first this would be matched, but the second one would not.

Editing the File

Now that you can move anywhere you want with ease, we can start doing something more interesting—like actually editing a file. There are numerous commands for editing a file—far too many to cover in any real depth in this chapter—so we will discuss only the more common ones you are likely to use.

Keep in mind that many of these commands put vi in input mode, which means that everything you type is inserted (or placed) into the text. When you are ready to use some commands again for other editing tasks or to move around, you will need to put vi back into command mode by pressing the Esc key.

Inserting Text

To insert text, you need to switch to insert mode. Table 6.5 lists some common commands that put vi in insert mode. The main difference between the commands is *where* you start to insert text.

TABLE 6.5 Commands for Switching to Insert Mode

Command	Mnemonic	Description
i	Insert	Inserts text before the cursor.
I	Insert	Inserts text at the beginning of the line.
a	Append	Inserts text after the cursor.
A	Append	Inserts text after the end of the line.
o	Open	Opens a newline below current line and inserts text at the beginning of that line.
O	Open	Opens a newline above the current line and inserts text at the beginning of that line.

The main difference between the i and a commands is simply that i causes text to be inserted just before the current position of the cursor, and a causes text to be inserted just after the current position of the cursor. For example, if the cursor is over the letter t and you use the i command, you could type ca to form the word cat. If you use the a command, you could then type in ar to form the word tar.

You might think, "Well, what's the point? You could just as easily move the cursor just past the t, use the i command and type ar to get tar." This is mostly true. Even though you may be able to do this most of the time, the distinction between these two commands is important in two cases. The first is if you are at the beginning of a line with text on it, and you want to insert text at the beginning. You can only do this with the i (or I) command because the a command will start inserting text just after the first character. Likewise, if you are at the end of a line of text and want to append some text to the line, you must use the a (or A) command because the i command will insert text just before the last character on the line. If you want to place text on an empty line (for example, when you first start adding text to a new file), then it doesn't matter which command you use.

The I and A commands are just there for your convenience. You can accomplish the same results by moving either to the beginning or the end of the line and using the appropriate lowercase command.

The o and O commands insert a new blank line after and before the current line, respectively, and place the cursor at the beginning of the newline ready to insert text. As for the i and a commands, the distinction between the o and O commands becomes important in two cases. First, if you are at the top of the file and want to insert a blank line before the top line, you can only do it with the O command. This will move everything else down and leave a blank newline at the top of the file. Likewise, if you are at the bottom of the file and want to add a blank newline, you can only do it with the o command. (Actually, that's not quite true. You could also use something like A on the last line and press the Enter key, but you can't do that with the O command.)

Changing and Replacing Text

vi has some very useful commands for changing and replacing text. For example, it will let you replace just one word, the next three words, everything up to the end of a sentence, or even everything up to the end of a paragraph. It will also let you replace a single character or overwrite text up to the end of the line. Table 6.6 summarizes some of the possibilities.

TABLE 6.6 Commands for Changing and Replacing Text

Command	Mnemonic	Description
cw	Change/word	Changes text to the end of the word.
c^	Change/—	Changes text to the beginning of the line.
c$	Change/—	Changes text to the end of the line.
c)	Change/—	Changes text to the end of the sentence.
c}	Change/—	Changes text to the end of the paragraph.
3cw	3 times/change/—	Changes the next three words.
r	Replace	Replaces the character under the cursor with the next character typed.
R	Replace	Overwrites the text under the cursor.

> **Tip**
>
> You should see some familiar characters with familiar meanings in the commands listed in Table 6.6. Note that the change command is a multipart command. The c says "I want to change something," and the letter or character that comes after it tells it what you want to change. You can use the c command with all the movement commands to specify what you want to change.

When you use the change command, vi deletes the appropriate amount of text and goes into insert mode, so you can type in the new text. For example, to change a word, place the cursor at the beginning of the word and use the cw command. vi will delete the word at the cursor and go into input mode. You can then type the word you want to replace the old one with. You are not limited to typing in only one word, though. You can type in as much as you want. vi acts as though you had deleted the word yourself and then put it into input mode by using the i command.

You can change part of a word by placing the cursor over the first character of the word that you want to change and using the cw command. vi will delete everything from the cursor up to the end of the word and go into input mode as before. The other change commands behave similarly.

There are times when you will only want to change one character. The easiest way to do this is to use the replace command, r. To replace a character, place the cursor over it, and press r followed by the character you want to replace it with. vi stays in command mode for this command.

The R command puts vi into replace mode, which is essentially the equivalent of overwrite in other text editors and word processors. When you put vi into replace mode, whatever you type replaces the text under the cursor. With the version of vi that comes with OpenLinux, you can even move around with the arrow keys and replace text in different parts of the file without putting vi in command mode first. One thing to note, however, is that pressing the Enter key does not simply take you to the next line, but it will insert a carriage return where the cursor is.

Substituting Text

A powerful feature of vi is its ability to search for and substitute text based on text patterns (the equivalent of find and replace). For example, you can tell it to replace every occurrence of the word *cat* with the word *dog* with one simple command. vi uses the ex substitute (s) command to do this. The simplest form of this command follows:

```
:s/old_text/new_text
```

This will replace the first occurrence of `old_text` on the current line with `new_text`. For example, if you had the line:

```
Our cat fought with the neighbor's cat.
```

and you realized that you don't have a cat, but a dog, you could replace the first instance of *cat* using the following command:

```
:s/cat/dog
```

which would yield the following line:

```
Our dog fought with the neighbor's cat.
```

Now, if you wanted to replace *all* occurrences of the word *cat* with *dog* on the line, you need to add /g (global) to the end of the substitute command as follows:

```
:s/cat/dog/g
```

That would give you the following line:

```
Our dog fought with the neighbor's dog.
```

But wait! It gets better! You can specify a range of lines (or the entire file!) that you want the substitute command to act on. To specify a range of lines, use this command:

```
:first_line,second_line s/old_text/new_text
```

As when saving only part of a file, you can use a period (.) to represent the current line, and the dollar sign ($) to represent the last line in the file. For example, to substitute the first occurrence of *cat* with *dog* on every line from the current line to the end of the file, you could use the following command:

```
:.,$ s/cat/dog
```

To specify the whole file, you use this command:

```
:%s/old_text/new_text
```

As before, without the /g on the end, these commands will only replace the first occurrence of `old_text` on each of the lines specified. In order to replace all occurrences of `old_text`, you need to add /g to the end of the substitute command.

For example, if you were writing an English paper and learned that the teacher would take off points for saying "we was" instead of "we were," you could replace all occurrences of "we was" with "we were" in the file with the following command:

```
:%s/we was/we were/g
```

The ability to make global replacements is a very nice feature; however, you need to be careful because you can get unexpected results otherwise. For example, while you're replacing "we was" with "we were" in your paper, if you had "we washed" in there somewhere, vi would match "we was" with the first part of "we washed" and change it to "we werehed"! There are effective ways around this problem, though. One way is to have vi confirm a substitution before doing it. That way, you can see if it's going to mess something up and tell it not to do the substitution in that case. You tell vi to confirm substitutions by adding c to the end of the command:

:s/*old_text*/*new_text*/c

You can still specify lines and global substitution in conjunction with asking it to confirm substitutions. For example, in order to avoid the problem with "we washed," you could use this command:

:%s/we was/we washed/gc

When it finds a match, vi will then give you a chance to respond. Press y, n, a, or q for yes, no, all, and quit, respectively.

Deleting Text

To delete text, you use the delete command, d. The delete command works much like the change command in that you can use it in combination with all the movement commands to specify what to delete. For example, to delete a sentence, you would place the cursor at the beginning of the sentence and press d. Table 6.7 lists some common delete command combinations. Table 6.8 lists some other common commands for deleting text.

TABLE 6.7 Common Delete/Movement Command Combinations

Command	*Deletes...*
dw	Up to the end of the word (this command will also delete any whitespace after the word)
d0 (zero)	To the beginning of the line
d$	To the end of the line
3dw	The next three words
3dl	The next three letters

TABLE 6.8 Other Common Deletion Commands

Command	Deletes...
x	The character under the cursor
X	The character before the cursor
6x	The next six characters (including the one under the cursor)
dd	The entire current line
4dd	The next four lines (the current one and the three after)
D	Everything from the cursor to the end of the line

Note that dd does not just clear the current line of text, it actually removes the line altogether, moving everything below it up one line.

Cut, Copy, and Paste

vi doesn't have a cut, copy, and paste mechanism like you're probably used to seeing. Instead, whenever you delete something, vi stores that in a buffer, which you can then paste anywhere you want using one of the put commands, p and P. p pastes the deleted (cut) text after the cursor, and P pastes it before the cursor.

For example, if you had two lines that were out of order, you could delete the first one using the dd command, move the cursor to the line below the second one, and then use the P command to place it just after the second line.

To copy text, use the yank command, y. The yank command works in much the same way as the delete command, except that it doesn't change the text in any way. It just places the specified text in a buffer that can be pasted anywhere you want using one of the put commands. As for the delete commands, you can use the yank command with any of the movement commands to specify what to delete. There are a couple of special yank commands that are not combinations of y with a movement command. For example, yy yanks the entire current line into the buffer, and Y yanks everything from the cursor to the end of the line (just like y$). Table 6.9 lists some common yank command combinations.

TABLE 6.9 Common Yank Command Combinations

Command	Yanks...
yw	Up to the end of the word (this command will also yank any whitespace after the word)
y0 (zero)	Everything from the cursor to the beginning of the line

Command	Yanks...
y$	Everything from the cursor to the end of the line
y)	Everything up to the end of the sentence
y}	Everything up to the end of the paragraph
yy	The entire current line
Y	Same as y$

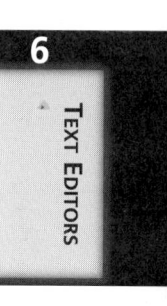

Joining Lines

Occasionally you want to join lines; in other words, you want to bring the text from the line below up to join the current line at the end. In many text editors, you can do this simply by placing the cursor at the end of the upper line and pressing the Delete key. vi doesn't work this way. If you move to the end of a line and try to delete a character using, for example, the x command, you will simply delete the last character on the line. Instead, vi has a special command for joining two lines, J. Place the cursor on the first line, and just press J. That brings the line below up onto the end of the first line.

Undoing and Redoing Commands

vi has two undo commands, both of which act a little differently. One is the u command, which undoes the last command executed. Note that this can really be a lot. For example, if you use the insert command to enter a paragraph and then press the Esc key to go back to command mode, for u to undo the last command means to remove all the text you just typed in (that is, the whole paragraph). You can do multiple undos. Ctrl+R redoes the last command that was undone using the u command. You can do multiple redos.

The other undo command is U, which undoes all edits done on the last line edited. Pressing U again will redo them. Once you start to work on a different line, the U command will only apply to the newline you are editing. You can still go back to another line to make changes using the u command, however.

XEmacs

XEmacs is a powerful, highly configurable editor that can be customized through the use of modules that you can write using the Lisp programming language. You could configure XEmacs to cook your toast for you if you wanted to. XEmacs goes a step or two beyond the older Emacs editor by giving it a graphical user interface and adding many different features and functions, such as syntax highlighting for different types of files. This makes Xemacs very useful for programming and writing shell scripts. XEmacs also comes *Internet ready* with a built-in Web browser as well as email and news clients. Heck! It even has games!

XEmacs is similar to vi in that you can use keyboard commands to move around and edit the text in advanced ways. However, you are generally not required to use most of them. For example, there are commands to move forward and backward one word, sentence, paragraph, or page at a time, but you can also use the arrow keys or just place the cursor where you want with the mouse. It also behaves more like what you would expect of a modern editor in that you don't have to worry about things like it being in input or command mode as you do with vi. You can just click and edit text whenever and wherever you want. For the most part, you won't worry too much about those commands, but if you want to learn about them (they can be handy if you run XEmacs in Emacs emulation mode, for example, on the console), you can go through the learn-as-you-do tutorial for Emacs after starting it by pressing Ctrl+h and then t.

Before we start discussing how to use XEmacs, let's define a few things, so we can keep them straight. First, a *buffer* is a region of memory containing the text you are editing. Second, a *frame* is the window that XEmacs runs in—a window in the traditional Windows and Macintosh sense. Third, a *window* is the editing space of XEmacs within which a buffer is displayed. If you have a second window within your frame, you will see two editing spaces within your traditional window. Figure 6.3 illustrates this.

FIGURE 6.3

Frame and window. The frame is the "window" that XEmacs runs in. The windows are the editing spaces in the frame.

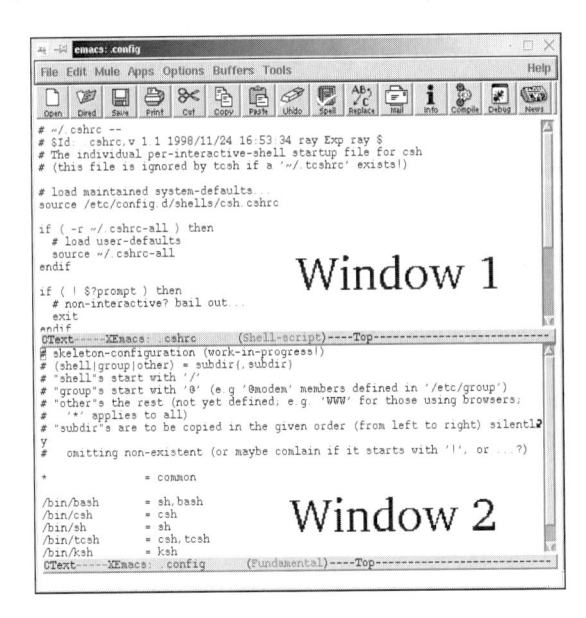

Starting XEmacs

Starting XEmacs from the command line is really easy. Just type **xemacs &** and then press Enter. This starts XEmacs in the background so you can keep using your terminal for other things. Figure 6.4 shows how XEmacs looks when you start it up. If you have a screen smaller than 1024 × 768, you will likely need to resize it, as it will probably start out too tall.

FIGURE 6.4
Screen shot of XEmacs when it first starts up.

You can also bring it up ready to edit a file (new or existing) by simply adding the name of the file to the command line:

```
$ xemacs myFile &
```

From the top to the bottom of the frame, you can see the menu bar, the tool bar, the editing window, the mode line, and the echo line. The menus mostly just provide convenient shortcuts to keyboard commands that you can type in. For many menu items, the keyboard commands are displayed on the right side of the menu item. The tool bar provides shortcuts to even more commonly used commands.

The mode line gives you a description of what's happening in the associated window. From left to right, the mode line contains the following information. First, (ISO8) is the language environment that XEmacs is using. Second, the two spaces tell whether the file has been modified, or if it is read only. When it is not modified and not read only, you only see dashes (—). If it has been modified, you see two asterisks (**). If the buffer is read only, you will see two percent signs (%%). Third, the buffer you are editing. In this case the buffer *scratch* is being edited. This buffer is always there and can be used as a scratch pad, just as it sounds. Fourth, the major and minor modes that XEmacs is operating in given between the parentheses in the form of (major minor). In this case, it is Lisp Interaction. XEmacs can operate in several modes, which will be discussed later. Last is the position in the buffer. If you are viewing the entire contents of the buffer, then All is displayed. If you are viewing the top of the file, Top is displayed. Likewise, if you are viewing the bottom of the file, Bot is displayed. Otherwise, the percentage of the file above the top of the screen is displayed as nn% (for example, 10%).

The echo line is used to print error messages and other info to you. It is also where XEmacs displays the text you type in for commands.

Opening and Creating Files

There are a few different ways to open files in XEmacs, and a few different options as to where they will be opened. XEmacs allows you to edit several files at once. You can have one frame open and view them one at a time by selecting the one you want to view from the Buffers menu, or you can view your files in separate frames or windows or any combination of those.

The easiest way to open a file is to click on the open button in the tool bar. This brings up a dialog window, like the one in Figure 6.5, that allows you to choose the file you want to open. When the dialog window first comes up, all the contents of the current directory are listed. The directories are listed on the left, and all the files are listed on the right. On the bottom is an area where anything you type is displayed.

If you want to use the mouse to move around the directory structure or to select a file, you can click on the directory you want to move to or the file you want to open with the *middle* mouse button (clicking with the left mouse button does not select the file or directory under the mouse as you would expect). You do not need to double-click. Immediately upon clicking on a directory, the file dialog window changes to that directory and lists all its contents. Immediately upon clicking on a file, XEmacs opens the file. By default, the file is displayed in the main frame in the current window.

FIGURE 6.5

Dialog window for opening a file. Directories are displayed on the left and files on the right. The current path is displayed at the bottom of the window, as is any text you type.

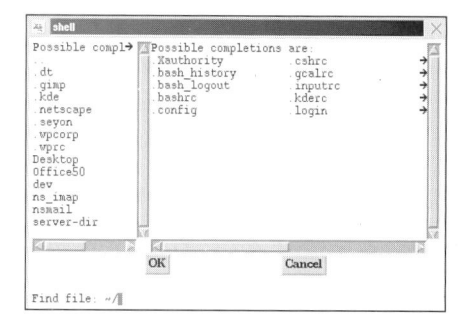

You can also type in the name of the file directly, including the path to it if necessary. Pressing Enter or clicking on the OK button will open the file.

> **Tip**
>
> XEmacs has a feature that can be very useful when you are typing in the name of a file. If you type in only the first character (or as much as you want) and then press the spacebar, XEmacs will complete the name of the file or directory for you. If more than one completion is possible, then it will complete the name as much as possible and then list all the possible completions in the file area on the right. If the completion is a directory, then the file dialog window will change to that directory and list its contents. When you've found the file you want, pressing the Enter key or clicking the OK button will close the dialog window and open the file.

You can also open a file from the file menu. You have three options for opening a file for editing, one for inserting a file into the current buffer, and another for simply viewing a file (i.e., opening it read-only). The first option, Open…, works in the same way as clicking on the open button. The second option, Open in Other Window…, will create a new window within the current frame (similar to Figure 6.3) and open the file in the new window. Open in New Frame… will create a new frame and open the file there. Insert File… will insert the selected file into the current buffer at the position of the cursor. View File… opens a file just for viewing and allows you to page forward and backward using the familiar *more* commands, spacebar and b. Pressing q will close the file.

> **Tip**
>
> If you open a file in a new window (so that two or more windows are visible in the frame), you can go back to using only one window by clicking in the window with the buffer you want to be visible and using the command Ctrl+x 1. That will close all other windows and use all the free space in the frame to display the selected buffer.

To create a new file, you must go through the same process as for opening a file, except that you type in the name for your new file. This creates a new buffer to edit the file in. The actual file is not created, however, until you save it.

> **Note**
>
> When XEmacs is emulating Emacs in a terminal window or on the console, you can open a file or create a new one using the Ctrl+x Ctrl+f command. This allows you to type in the name of the file in the echo line at the bottom of the terminal window or screen.

Saving Files and Exiting XEmacs

To save a file, you simply click on the save button on the tool bar or select Save *Filename* from the file menu, where *Filename* is the name of the current buffer. If you want to save a buffer to a new file, you select Save As… from the file menu. XEmacs then pops up a file dialog box where you can enter the name for the file you want to save to.

To exit XEmacs, simply select Exit… from the file menu, or click on the button to have the window manager close the window, if your window manager is set up to display one. If there are modified buffers that have not been saved, XEmacs will display a dialog box asking if they should be saved. You can also cancel the action at that point and keep working, if you want to.

> **Note**
>
> You can also save files using the Emacs commands Ctrl+x Ctrl+s and Ctrl+x Ctrl+w for save and save as, respectively. You can exit using the command Ctrl+x Ctrl+c.

Closing a File Without Exiting XEmacs

If you are done editing a file and want to close it without exiting XEmacs, select Delete Buffer *Filename* from the file menu. This does not delete the file, only the memory space used to store the file while you were editing it. That file will no longer be listed in the buffers menu.

Updating the Buffer When the File Has Changed on Disk

If a file you are viewing or editing has changed on disk, you can update the buffer so that the most recent version is displayed by choosing Revert Buffer *Filename*. This will reload the file and refresh the buffer.

Editing a Buffer

After a file has been opened into a buffer, or a new buffer has been created for a new file, you can edit the buffer directly in the window. For basic editing, XEmacs behaves pretty much as you would expect. There are a few things to note, however.

In many editors, you can select some text and press the Delete or Backspace key to delete it. XEmacs doesn't work this way. If you select some text with the mouse and press the Delete or Backspace key, XEmacs simply deletes the character before or at the cursor (or after if you have a vertical bar as the cursor), as though the text weren't selected. The Delete key deletes the character after or at the cursor, and the Backspace key deletes the character before the cursor. Likewise, you cannot select some text and start typing expecting that the selected text will be replaced with the new text you are typing. Instead, it will just start inserting the text wherever the cursor is. In general, you will only select text with the mouse in conjunction with the cut and copy actions.

Also, some editors will let you click anywhere and start editing from that point, filling in the line with spaces if necessary. *XEmacs* will not let you do that. If you click at a point after the last character on a line (that can be a whitespace character just like any other character), XEmacs will simply place the cursor at or just after that character. Likewise, if you click beyond the end of the buffer, XEmacs will simply place the cursor at the end of the buffer (that is, after the last character in the buffer).

XEmacs may also behave differently than you expect depending on what mode it is in. Many of the different modes customize certain aspects of XEmacs to make it more convenient to use for a particular purpose. For example, when XEmacs is in C mode, it is customized to help make programming in C easier and quicker. One way it does that is by autoindenting based on the position of braces and whether or not the previous line was finished (that is, constitutes an entire C statement or was continued on another line). To help to reformat a C file that was not nicely indented, XEmacs will properly indent a line based on its surroundings if you place the cursor anywhere on the line and press the Tab key. It does not insert a tab character as would happen in most other programs. This is a nice feature because, to reformat an entire file, all you need to do is start at the top and work your way down pressing the Tab key at each nonempty line. If that seems too long and tedious, you can record a macro that will do it for you, if you want.

Cut, Copy, and Paste

XEmacs has some advanced features for working with text, including copying and moving it. Most of the time, though, you will just simply want to cut, copy, or paste it. The easiest way to do that is to select the text you want to copy or paste and then click on the appropriate button on the tool bar. You can then position the cursor where you want to paste it and click the paste button.

> **Tip**
>
> To quickly copy text, you can simply select it with the mouse like normal and then click where you want to paste it with the middle mouse button. Note that this does not handle the text exactly the same as using the copy button, however. If you select some text, click on the copy button, and then select some other text, clicking on the paste button will paste the first text that you selected, whereas clicking with the middle mouse button will paste the other text that you selected.

Searching for and Substituting Text

XEmacs lets you search forward or backward for text using the Ctrl+s and Ctrl+r, respectively. When you issue the command, the text I-search:, or I-search backward for a reverse search, appears in the echo area. You can then type in the text you want to search for, which will also be displayed in the echo area. XEmacs will immediately start searching for the text you type as you type it, starting at the position of the cursor. It highlights any matches it finds. To search again for the next match, simply issue the command again. XEmacs does not wrap around to the beginning or the end of the file when doing forward or reverse searches. Once either end of the file is reached, the search will fail.

When you have finished searching, you can quit in a few different ways. To quit and return to the original position of the cursor, you can press Ctrl+g. If you want to move to the position of the current match, you can press Enter, or you can click where you want the cursor to be with the left mouse button.

> **Note**
>
> By default, all searches in XEmacs are case insensitive. So, the string "cat" will match "cat", "Cat", and "CAT". You can change this behavior by selecting Case Sensitive Search in the Editing Options item of the options menu.

> **Tip**
>
> If you don't want XEmacs to do an incremental search (that is, search as you type), you can have it search only after you have typed in the whole string by issuing the search command by first pressing Ctrl-s and then typing the search string.
>
> XEmacs will start searching when you press Enter after typing in the search string. The same procedure applies to reverse searches.

To search and replace text, you can use Esc+% (press Esc and then Shift+5 for the %). When you issue the command, `Query replace:` appears in the echo window. You then can type in the text to be replaced and press Enter. The text in the echo area will then change to `Query replace old_text with:`. You then type in the new text and again press Enter. XEmacs then searches forward from the position of the cursor until it finds a match for `old_text`. When it does, it asks you if it should replace it. Pressing y will cause it to be replaced, and n will cause it to be skipped. Pressing ! will cause it to replace all remaining matches without prompting you, whereas pressing q will cause it to stop searching and replacing without replacing the current match.

Editing Modes

One of the best things about XEmacs is that it is *language sensitive*. It has several major and minor modes that customize its operation to better suit the editing of different kinds of text. For example, there are major modes for C, Lisp, Emacs Lisp, English text, and so on. XEmacs can only be in one major mode at a time for any particular buffer. There are many minor modes that provide certain features that you can turn on and off at any time. XEmacs can have several minor modes turned on at the same time.

Major Modes

When you open a file, XEmacs can often tell what kind of file it is by its extension and put itself in the proper mode. For example, if you open the file `main.c`, it will recognize that this is a C language file and put itself in C mode. If it doesn't correctly recognize a file or put itself in the mode you want, you can set the mode manually by pressing Esc+x and then typing the name of the mode you want to switch to. The major mode of the current buffer is listed between parentheses in the mode line. Table 6.10 lists some of the major modes available.

TABLE 6.10 Some XEmacs Major Modes

Mode	Description
fundamental-mode	This is the default mode when you start XEmacs. It has no special features or key bindings.
nroff-mode	This mode is for editing `nroff` files before they are formatted. It redefines some indentation commands.
tex-mode	This mode is for editing LaTeX source files. It adds commands for inserting quotes, braces, and other characters. It will also help nicely format the file for printing.
outline-mode	This mode is for editing outlines. It allows you to make parts of the text invisible so that you can see the overall structure of the document.
c-mode	This mode is for editing C source files. It redefines commands for indentation and performs syntax highlighting—a very useful feature.
c++-mode	This is similar to c-mode but for C++ source files.
lisp-mode	This mode is for editing Lisp source files.
fortran-mode	This mode is for editing Fortran source files. It adds special commands for moving around and indentation.
asm-mode	This mode is for editing assembly source files.

> **Tip**
>
> You can get information about the mode you are in by selecting Mode under the Commands and Keys menu item of the help menu.

Minor Modes

Minor modes provide optional features that you can turn on and off as you like. You can have any number of minor modes active with any major mode. You turn minor modes on and off using the same command as for major modes. If the mode is turned off, then issuing the command will turn it on. Issuing the same command will turn it off again. In short, the command simply toggles the minor mode on and off. Some of the active minor modes are listed next to the major mode on the mode line. Table 6.11 lists some of the minor modes available.

TABLE 6.11 Some XEmacs Minor Modes

Mode	Description
font-lock-mode	This mode displays the text in different colors and fonts depending on the type of the text. You can also toggle this mode under the Syntax Highlighting menu item of the options menu.
auto-fill-mode	This mode enables automatic word wrapping.
overwrite-mode	This mode causes text to be overwritten instead of moved to the right when you type in new text. You can toggle this mode with the Insert button or from the options menu.
auto-save-mode	This option causes the buffer you are working on to be automatically saved periodically. This option is a must if you're not in the habit of saving your work often.
line-number-mode	This mode causes the line number the cursor is on to be continuously displayed in the mode line.
blink-paren	When you place the cursor next to a parenthesis, brace, or bracket, this mode will cause XEmacs to make the matching parenthesis, brace, or bracket flash. This is very useful for determining the bounds of blocks of code in languages like C and practically a necessity for staying sane when editing languages like Lisp. (There is no "–mode" on this mode name.)

Working with Multiple Windows

XEmacs will allow you to work in more than one window within a frame. We have already mentioned that you can open a file into a new window. You can also create new windows and close them whenever you want. Using windows, you can edit several files in a single frame, or you can edit at different locations within the same buffer. For example, you can create a second window and select the same buffer for each window. You can then view one area of a document while editing another. If the same area of the document is visible in both windows, you will see the changes you make in one window happen in the other window as well. Each window has its own mode line and echo area. Table 6.12 lists some commands for working with windows.

TABLE 6.12 Commands for Working with XEmacs Windows

Command	Description
Ctrl+x 0 (zero)	Close the selected window. If the current window is the only window in the frame, then the frame is closed as well, unless it is the only frame open.

continues

TABLE 6.12 continued

Command	Description
Ctrl+x 1 (one)	Close all windows except the selected one.
Ctrl+x 2	Split the current window into two windows, one above the other. Both windows will display the same buffer. The window with the cursor in it is the *selected window*. You can change the buffer of a particular window by selecting the desired buffer from the buffers menu.
Ctrl+3	Split the current window into two windows, one beside the other.

Getting More Information

In this section, we have only covered the basics of using XEmacs. While, in most cases, this should be enough to get you started using it productively, XEmacs is a huge program with many features, and you will benefit from taking the time to look through the user and reference manuals. You can find these and much more information at http://www.xemacs.org/.

Summary

In this chapter, you learned how to do the following things in vi:

- Start and stop it
- Create new files and open existing files
- Save part or all of a file
- Move around efficiently
- Insert, delete, and change text
- Search for and substitute text
- Join two lines together
- Undo commands

You also learned how to do the following things in XEmacs:

- Start and stop it
- Create new files and open and close existing files
- Work with multiple files

- Cut, copy, and paste text
- Search for and replace text
- Change major modes
- Enable and disable minor modes
- Work with multiple windows

System Administration

PART II

IN THIS PART

7 Software Management with RPM *171*

8 Setting Up File Systems *185*

9 Printing *209*

10 OpenLinux Administration Tools *231*

11 Setting Up TCP/IP Networking *267*

12 Setting Up DNS—The Domain Name System *293*

13 Configuring PPP *307*

14 Configuring NIS—The Network Information System *325*

15 Configuring NFS—The Network File System *339*

16 Configuring Samba *349*

17 NetWare Integration *367*

18 Configuring Apache *395*

19 Mail Services *419*

20 Internet News *459*

21 IP Firewalling and Masquerading *477*

22 Running Proxies *507*

23 Performing Backup and Restore *529*

24 Securing Linux *549*

Software Management with RPM

CHAPTER 7

IN THIS CHAPTER

- Installing New Packages   *172*
- Uninstalling Packages   *177*
- Upgrading Installed Packages   *179*
- Getting Information About Packages   *180*

All software that comes with Caldera OpenLinux is stored in RPM packages (often referred to as RPMs). RPM packages are file archives that include extra information about the archives including the package name, a description, the version number of the software, dependencies on other packages and files, as well as other information. The Red Hat Package Manager (*rpm*) is used to install, upgrade, remove, verify, and get information about packages.

Information about each installed package is stored in a database. This information includes a list of files in the package and all information about the package stored with it. *rpm* uses the information in the database to allow you to uninstall a package cleanly or to verify that all the files in a package have not changed or have not turned up missing since it was installed. Of course, you can always install software that you compile or that comes in "tarballs." But you can keep your system cleaner and more organized and make it easier to uninstall something or make other changes if you can find and will use the RPM package you want. Learn to use *rpm*; it is your friend.

rpm has 10 modes of operation, each with its own set of command-line arguments. The different modes are install, uninstall, query, verify, signature check, build, rebuild database, fix permissions, set owners and groups, and show RC. In this chapter, we will discuss only the first three modes, which you are most likely to use.

Installing New Packages

At some point, you will come across a program that you absolutely must have and that either wasn't installed when you installed OpenLinux 2.2 or didn't come with the distribution. Well, you're in luck. Installing new software that comes in RPMs is very easy. You use it with the -i option to put *rpm* in install mode. Here's the general command-line format for installing a package:

```
rpm -i [install-options] <package-file>+
```

<package-file>+ represents one or more filenames of the package(s) to install.

There are three parts to the filename of a package. First is the name of the package. Second is the architecture that the package was put together for. Third is the .rpm extension indicating that the file is an RPM package.

```
<package-name>.<architecture>.rpm
```

For example, the package foo-1.2.i386.rpm is the RPM package foo-1.2 put together for Intel processor–based machines.

> **Note**
>
> You must be logged on as root or the super-user in order to install, upgrade, or remove packages.

So to install the package `foo-1.2.i386.rpm`, enter the following command:

```
# rpm -i foo-1.2.i386.rpm
```

The + at the end of the general command-line format simply means that you can install more than one package at a time simply by placing the name of each package that you want to install at the end of the command. So if you have the packages `foo-1.2.i386.rpm` and `bar-3.4.i386.rpm`, you would use the following command:

```
# rpm -i foo-1.2.i386.rpm bar-3.4.i386.rpm
```

You can also use wildcard characters recognized by the shell to install multiple archives or to save keystrokes by typing as little of the name as possible:

```
# rpm -i foo*
```

> **Note**
>
> Another wonderful way that you can specify a package file is by using an ftp URL. The general format of the URL is:
>
> `ftp://<user>:<password>@hostname/path/to/package.rpm`
>
> `<user>` represents the username that you wish to log in as, and `<password>` represents the password to use. `hostname` is the host to connect to. If you leave out `:<password>`, you will be prompted for a password. If both `<user>` and `<password>` are left out, RPM will use an anonymous ftp. Note that, in this case, you should also leave out the colon (:) and at symbol (@).
>
> For example, let's say you want to install the package `foo-1.2.rpm` on the machine `ftp.foobar.net`. If it were in the directory `/pub/packages` and you could access it using an anonymous ftp, you could access it using the following URL:
>
> `ftp://ftp.foobar.net/pub/packages/foo-1.2.rpm`
>
> If your name is Susan, and it's in your home directory, `/home/susan`, you could access it with this URL:
>
> `ftp://susan@ftp.foobar.net/home/susan/foo-1.2.rpm`
>
> *continues*

In this case, you didn't supply a password, so it will prompt you for one. This is preferred for security reasons (for example, this keeps your password from appearing in your command history). But if you're not worried about that, you can include it in the URL like this:

```
ftp://susan:wright@ftp.foobar.net/home/susan/foo-1.2.rpm
```

You can use ftp URLs when installing, upgrading, or querying a package. RPM uses passive ftp to transfer packages.

Package and File Dependencies

An RPM can contain dependency information stating that certain files or packages are required before the installation can be completed. That means whenever you begin to install a package, *rpm* checks to make sure that any dependencies are met before attempting the installation. If it finds that the package being installed requires a file or package that isn't already installed, it reports an error and exits without installing the package.

> **Note**
>
> *rpm* checks the database only to see if it installed the needed packages or files. It does not check to see if the files actually exist. So, if you installed a package and then deleted one of the files, *rpm* would act as though the file were still there. Likewise, if you compiled a certain library from the sources and installed it manually, unless you had previously installed a package containing the same files, *rpm* would act as though the library weren't there and give you an error, even though the file(s) actually exist(s).

The mere fact that there are dependency errors does not mean that you cannot install a package. You should look at the errors and determine if another package must be installed first. In the case of a library that isn't installed on your system, it is probably best to find an RPM of that library and install it. Then you can try reinstalling the original package. In some cases, though, you will want to install the package as is without making any other changes to your system (that is, without installing any other packages first). You can accomplish this by adding the --nodeps option to the command line, which tells *rpm* to ignore dependency information:

```
# rpm -i --nodeps <package-file>+
```

There are various reasons to want to do this. An example might be a package that contains two versions of a program: one statically linked to Motif and another dynamically linked to it. The package will say that it needs the Motif libraries in order to be installed, but you don't have Motif and don't plan on getting it anytime in the near future. However, because there is a statically linked version of the program in the package, you can just use that one instead. Using the --nodeps option allows you to at least install the package, so that you can then proceed to use the statically linked program.

Let's consider another example where you have a package that requires a library file that you compiled from the sources and installed manually. Because the library file isn't in *rpm*'s database, *rpm* will think that the file doesn't exist and give you a dependency error unless you tell it to ignore dependencies.

I often use this option when installing a large number of interdependent RPMs. For example, the RPMs for KDE are dependent in a way that normally requires you to install them in a certain order. I just place them all in an otherwise empty directory and execute the following command:

```
# rpm -i --nodeps *.rpm
```

This approach saves all the typing necessary to install the packages in the order normally required. It simply installs them in alphabetical order without regard to what else has already been installed.

> **Note**
>
> Although this is an easy way to install a large set of packages, it may not be recommended. Packages can include scripts that are executed before or after the files in the package are installed. If the proper installation of package B depends on the proper installation of package A because of something an install script does, you may run into problems installing them out of order. Although I have not run into problems installing KDE in this way, there is no guarantee that you will not run into problems installing other packages this way. Always proceed with caution before doing something like this. Make sure that you know what you are doing first.

> **Note**
>
> Sometimes you will run into dependency problems because a package requires a version of a library older than what you have installed. If the newer library
>
> *continues*

version is source and binary compatible with the older version, you can often cheat by simply creating a symbolic link to the library you have installed and install the package as is. For example, I have a package that requires `libtermcap.so.2`, which doesn't come with OpenLinux 2.2. It works out that `libncurses.so.4.2` is binary compatible with `libtermcap.so.2` (at least for what I need), so I simply created a symbolic link from `/usr/lib/libtermcap.so.2` to `/lib/libncurses.so.4.2` and ran `ldconfig` to update the dynamic linker.

Package and File Conflicts

When *rpm* checks the database for package and file dependencies, it also checks for conflicts. A conflict arises when you try to install a package that has already been installed, or when a package contains a file that was installed with another package. When *rpm* finds a conflict, it spits out an error message describing the conflict and quits without installing the package. If you want to install a package that has already been installed (that is, over the previous installation), you can tell *rpm* to replace the currently installed package with the one you are now installing using the `--replacepkgs` option:

```
# rpm -i --replacepkgs <package-file>+
```

Here is a situation where you might want to use this option. When you installed your system, it installed a certain version of the C libraries. You decide that you wanted to try to update them to a newer version by compiling the newer version from the sources. So you compile the libraries and replace the original files with the new ones without uninstalling the package they came in. After you do that, you will realize that you messed things up somewhere and decide that you want to put the original ones back. So you find the RPM with the original C libraries and try to reinstall it. *rpm* complains that the package has already been installed and refuses to work with you. You then force it into submission by using the `--replacepkgs` option, which allows you to replace your messed-up files with the originals.

If there are file conflicts and you want *rpm* to replace the file(s) with the file(s) in the package(s) you are trying to install, you use the `--replacefiles` option:

```
# rpm -i --replacefiles <package-file>+
```

The `--force` option is equivalent to specifying both the `--replacefiles` and `--replacepkgs` options:

```
# rpm -i --force <package-file>+
```

> **Note**
>
> Before you use the ==replacefiles option, be sure that replacing the file(s) won't mess anything up. For example, if you have a newer version of a file installed on your system than what comes with the package you are installing, programs that depend on the newer version may stop working. In general, you may not run into problems, but look before crossing the street.

Checking for Potential Problems First

If you want to know if there might be any potential conflicts or problems before attempting to install a particular RPM, you can use the --test option to tell *rpm* not actually to install the RPM, but only to check for and report potential conflicts or problems. This could save you a headache or two.

```
# rpm -i --test <package-file>+
```

Uninstalling Packages

One of the nicest things about *rpm* is its ability to uninstall programs cleanly, easily, and safely. Using one of the traditional methods of installing software, such as from tar archives or even using make with Makefiles configured to install the software, can make uninstalling programs difficult. If you use one of those methods, you generally must hunt down all the files and delete them manually. (I don't think I have ever seen a Makefile with an uninstall target.) This can be a real pain and even very dangerous because you usually need to be root to do it, and it is just too easy to delete the wrong files as root. Additionally, because Linux is as advanced as it is, when it deletes a file, it does a really good job of it—you just can't get it back, no matter how hard you try, plead, beg, or cry.

Although you still need to be careful when uninstalling RPMs, it is generally much safer to uninstall software using *rpm* than to manually delete the files. This is because *rpm* keeps track of all your files so that it knows what files belong to what package and only deletes the appropriate files. It also does dependency checks similar to those done at installation, except that, in this case, it tells you whether other packages need the files in the package you want to uninstall (or the package itself). This information helps prevent you from uninstalling something like the C libraries without knowing that you're going to completely mess up your system by doing so.

For example, if you were to try to uninstall the C libraries (the package glibc-2.1-3) from a full install of OpenLinux 2.2, *rpm* would present you with a list of over 800 dependencies on files in the package. It would also tell you that the development package (the package `glibc-devel-2.1-3`) depends on the `glibc-2.1-3` package. That's a pretty good indication that you probably don't want to remove the package unless you know what you're doing!

To uninstall an RPM, use *rpm* with the -e option (for erase) to put *rpm* in uninstall mode:

```
# rpm -e [uninstall-options] <package-name>+
```

Note that <package-name> is not the same as <package-file> when using *rpm* in install mode. It is, however, related. In general, if you install a package from the file `foo-1.2.i386.rpm`, the package will be entered into the *rpm* database as `foo-1.2`, or as package `foo` version 1.2. *rpm* doesn't need the complete package name with the version number to know which package to remove. The package name alone (`foo`) is sufficient. So, to remove the package `foo-1.2`, you would enter:

```
# rpm -e foo-1.2
```

or

```
# rpm -e foo
```

The second command will work if you have only one version of the `foo` package installed. However, if you also have `foo` version 1.35 installed, *rpm* will find both of them and not know which one to remove, so it will complain and exit. You will then need to decide which one you want to remove, or to tell *rpm* to remove all versions of the `foo` package using the --allmatches option. So to remove only version 1.2, you would enter:

```
# rpm -e foo-1.2
```

But if you want to remove both versions, you would enter:

```
# rpm -e --allmatches foo
```

Package and File Dependencies

As noted in the "Package and File Conflicts" section, packages can have many interdependencies. *rpm* checks them to see if any packages are dependent on the package or files in the package you are removing. If it detects any, it will issue an error message and exit without removing the package. If you know that removing the package will not cause any problems despite the reported dependencies, you can tell *rpm* to remove the package without checking them first. Use the --nodeps option as you did when installing an RPM:

```
# rpm -e --nodeps <package-name>+
```

This might happen when you remove a set of related packages out of order. For example, many library packages also come with "development" packages. The library package just contains the compiled library files necessary for running programs, whereas the development packages contain the necessary header files and the like to allow you to compile programs that use the libraries. In general, if you try to remove the library package before the development package, *rpm* will tell you that the library package is needed by the development package. You can avoid the conflict either by uninstalling the files in the proper order (that is, the development package before the library package) or by using the --nodeps option.

Recall that *rpm* doesn't actually check to see if the files in the database are on the system. Consequently, if you intend to replace a package with software that you compile yourself, you can generally ignore the dependency errors. For example, if you have the Xpm library installed as an RPM but plan to compile the latest version and replace the one currently installed, you can safely uninstall the Xpm RPM despite error messages stating that it is needed by certain other packages. You can do this because, in the end, a valid Xpm library will still be on the system. Note, however, that if you later try to install a package that requires the Xpm library, *rpm* will give you an error message stating that there are failed dependencies because it thinks that the Xpm library isn't installed. This is not a problem because you know the library is actually there.

Checking for Potential Problems First

You can have *rpm* check for potential problems without actually attempting to uninstall any packages. You do this, as before, using the --test option:

```
# rpm -e --test <package-name>+
```

Just for fun (and to see what some of the different errors look like), execute the following command:

```
# rpm -e --test glibc-2.1 2>&1 | more
```

This will give you a screen full of error messages about dependencies. Pressing the spacebar will let you advance through the list one screen full at a time. When you think you've seen enough, press q.

Upgrading Installed Packages

The time will come when a new version of software comes out that you absolutely must have. You already have the older version installed and have just downloaded RPMs for the newer version. What's the best way to upgrade your packages? Use the upgrade mode of *rpm*. The upgrade mode is not listed at the beginning of the chapter because it is really just a special case of the install mode. When you use the upgrade mode, *rpm* uninstalls the old package(s) before installing the new one(s). The -U option puts *rpm* in upgrade mode:

```
# rpm -U [install-options] <package-file>+
```

All command-line options that work in install mode also work in upgrade mode, and all the problems that you can encounter when installing an RPM for the first time or when uninstalling an RPM can also show up when upgrading an RPM. This is because, before *rpm* uninstalls the older package, it installs the newer package. So everything that was said in the "Installing New Packages" section and the "Uninstalling Packages" section applies equally well to this section.

One thing to note, however, is that, when upgrading certain packages, you may get dependency errors because *rpm* wants to uninstall the old package before installing the new one. Because other packages need the old package, *rpm* won't uninstall it, so the upgrade will fail. In most cases like that, you will need to use the --nodeps option to tell *rpm* to ignore dependencies. A common example of this is library files. For example, if you want to upgrade the C libraries to the latest and greatest version, you will need to specify the --nodeps option so that *rpm* can remove the older version. This is not a problem because the upgraded version will replace all the files that other packages depend on, keeping everything working as smoothly as before.

> **Note**
>
> When you are upgrading a package, you normally assume that the package you are trying to install is newer than the package you already installed. *rpm* works off this assumption and complains and exits if it finds that the "newer" package is actually older than the "older" package. If you really want to "upgrade" to an older package, you can force *rpm* into submission by using the --oldpackage option, which tells *rpm* to allow a newer package to be replaced with an older one:
>
> ```
> # rpm -U --oldpackage <package-file>+
> ```

Getting Information About Packages

One of the great and useful things about *rpm* is your ability to get information about installed or uninstalled RPMs. You can get several different types of information, such as what packages are installed, the files in a package, a description of a package, what other packages depend on a package, and what packages a certain package depends on.

Because the RPM database does not change when making queries, you do not need to be logged in as root or the super-user in order to use *rpm* to get information about a package. To get information about a package, use *rpm* in query mode. The -q option puts *rpm* in query mode:

```
$ rpm -q [query-options]
```

There are two subsets of `query-options` for specifying a query: one for package selection and the other to select the information desired.

Package Selection Options

The package selection options are used to specify which package(s) will be queried. The easiest and most direct way of specifying a single package is simply to give its name:

```
$ rpm -q foo
```

Or, if you want to be more specific, you can also include the version number:

```
$ rpm -q foo-1.2
```

Now, a simple query like this won't get you much. It will simply print out the full package name for the package, including any extra version information. For example, if this were the package `foo`, version 1.2, release 3, *rpm* would print out:

```
foo-1.2-3
```

You start getting interesting information when you combine a package selection option with an information selection option. The -a option tells *rpm* to query all installed packages.

```
$ rpm -q -a
```

By itself, this isn't much more interesting than directly specifying a single package name because it will list only all the installed packages. However, this option combined with a command such as `grep` can be very useful. For example, I have created an alias called `rpmgrep` that takes the output of the preceding command and pipes it to `grep`. Using the `bash` shell, the alias is specified like this:

```
$ alias rpmgrep='rpm -q -a | grep'
```

I then use this alias followed by a regular expression recognized by `grep`. I use this when I'm looking for a particular package to get information about or uninstall, but I don't know its exact name. For example, the command

```
$ rpmgrep kde
```

lists all installed packages that contain `kde` in their name, or, in my case, this:

```
kdebase-opengl-1.1.1-1
kdesupport-devel-static-1.1.1-1
kdesupport-devel-1.1.1-1
kdeapps-1.1-6
kdegames-1.1.1-1
kdedoc-990211-1
kdegraphics-1.1.1-1
kdetoys-1.1.1-1
kdelibs-devel-1.1.1-1
kdesupport-1.1.1-1
kdelibs-1.1.1-1
kdestart-1.1-14
kdethemes-2.0.0-1
kdelibs-doc-1.1.1-1
kdenetwork-1.1.1-1
kdebase-1.1.1-1
kdemultimedia-1.1.1-1
kdeutils-1.1.1-1
```

It just happens that all the installed packages that contain kde in their names start with kde. However, if I had a package called packdemon, or anything with kde anywhere else in the name, it would also show up in the list.

If you know a file in the package you want to query, you can tell *rpm* to query the package that owns the file. You specify the filename with the -f option:

```
$ rpm -q -f file-name
```

Note, however, that *file-name* must include the full path to it. For example, if I want to know which package the file libX11.so belongs to, I would use the following command:

```
$ rpm -q -f /usr/X11R6/lib/libX11.so
XFree86-devel-3.3.3.1-3
```

This tells me that it belongs to the package XFree86-devel-3.3.3.1-3.

You can also get information about an RPM that hasn't been installed by using the -p option:

```
$ rpm -q -p package-file
```

Information Selection Options

You use the information selection options in combination with the package selection options to get information about specific packages. To get basic information about a package, including its name, version number, and a description, use the -i option:

```
$ rpm -q -i package-selection-option
```

It doesn't matter if the *package-selection-option* comes after the -i option or before it. For example, to view information about the glibc package, you would use the following command (and get the following output):

```
$ rpm -q -i glibc
Name        : glibc                         Vendor: Caldera, Inc.
Version     : 2.1                     Distribution: OpenLinux 2.2
Release     : 3                         Build Host: knob.calderasystems.com
Install Date: Mon May 24 09:08:32 1999   Build Date: Sat Apr  3 21:07:18 1999
Size        : 2528618                   Source RPM: glibc-2.1-3.src.rpm
Group       : System/Library
Copyright   : LGPL
Packager    : duwe@caldera.de (Torsten Duwe)
URL         : http://www.gnu.org/software/libc/
Summary     : Standard shared libraries for programs.
Description :
Contains the standard libraries that are used by multiple programs on
the system. In order to save disk space and memory, as well as to ease
upgrades, common system code is kept in one place and shared between
programs. This package contains the most important sets of shared
libraries, the standard C library and the standard math library. Without
these, a Linux system will not function.
```

You can view a complete list of files in the package using the -l option:

```
$ rpm -q -l package-selection-option
```

If you want to get more specific, you can list only documentation files using the -d option or configuration files using the -c option:

```
$ rpm -q -d package-selection-option
```

or

```
$ rpm -q -c package-selection-option
```

For example, let's say that you want to see if there is any documentation that came in the package that the file /usr/X11R6/lib/libXpm.so came from. You can get a list of all documentation files installed with the package by issuing the following command:

```
$ rpm -q -d -f /usr/X11R6/lib/libXpm.so
```

This tells *rpm* to query the package that the file /usr/X11R6/lib/libXpm.so belongs to and list all documentation files. This command produces the following output:

```
$ rpm -q -d -f /usr/X11R6/lib/libXpm.so
/usr/X11R6/man/man1/sxpm.1x.gz
/usr/doc/xpm-devel-4.11/xpm.PS.gz
```

From the output, we learn from that there is a man page for the command `sxpm` and a PostScript document in the directory `/usr/doc/xpm-devel-4.11` that we can view in a program such as `ghostview` or `kghostview` (the KDE version of `ghostview`).

We learned earlier that you could use the `--test` option in install or uninstall mode to check for potential problems like dependency conflicts. We can also use the `-R` option to list what packages or files a package depends on:

```
$ rpm -q -R package-selection-option
```

Whether it lists packages or files (or both) will depend on how the dependencies were set up by the package creator. For example, listing dependencies for the `xpm-devel` package lists only files, whereas the listing for `kdebase` lists both packages and files.

Summary

In this chapter, we learned about the Red Hat Package Manager (*rpm*), a powerful software package manager. *rpm* allows you to bundle up software into RPM files (packages) that are easily installed, uninstalled, and upgraded. It makes software management much easier than it would otherwise be using other traditional methods of software packaging such as `tar` files. It does this by maintaining a database containing information about each installed package including the files in the package, a description of the package, and any dependencies that the package has on other packages. Using this information, *rpm* safely installs and uninstalls all the files in a package without your needing to worry about what or where they are. It also helps keep you from uninstalling packages that are needed for the proper operation of other packages or from installing packages that conflict with packages already installed. It does this by informing you of any dependencies listed in its database or of potential conflicts before completing the requested action.

We learned about three of *rpm*'s modes of operation (install, uninstall, and query) with the most commonly used options in each of these modes. We learned how to install, uninstall, and upgrade packages, as well as how to query the RPM database or an RPM file for information about a package.

For more information including options not discussed in this chapter and other modes of operation, see the man page (using the command `man rpm`). There is also a Web site dedicated to information about *rpm* at `http://www.rpm.org/`. From there, you can also download a (long) book, *Maximum RPM*, which talks about *rpm* in much greater detail. A PostScript version can be downloaded from `http://www.rpm.org/maximum-rpm.ps.gz`, or you can get a LaTeX version at `http://www.rpm.org/maximum-rpm.tar.gz`.

CHAPTER 8

Setting Up File Systems

IN THIS CHAPTER

- Devices   *186*
- Partitions   *188*
- File Systems   *191*
- Mounting a File System   *193*
- Checking a File System   *197*
- Accounting and Quotas   *198*
- File Permissions   *198*
- File Ownership   *204*
- Swap Space   *204*

You were introduced to the Linux file system in Chapter 2. This chapter describes the various kinds of Linux files and file systems. In this chapter, you'll learn how to set up file systems and manage file permissions. You will also learn how to set up swap space (disk space used to extend physical memory by swapping some data out to disk). These tasks are essential for the installation and maintenance of a Linux system.

Devices

In addition to regular files and directories, the UNIX file system can hold several other types of files. A device file is not a real file; rather, it is a "hook" into a kernel device driver. If a program reads from or writes to a device file, the data are not transferred to or from a disk. Instead, the data are passed to a kernel device driver that communicates directly with a hardware device. Note that reading or writing to a device file may be dangerous—writing the wrong data to a hardware device can lock up your system. For that reason, most device files can be written to only by *root*.

Device files come in two different flavors:

- *Character devices* refer to devices that produce or consume data as a stream of bytes. These include such things as terminals, serial ports, printer ports, and mice.
- *Block devices* refer to devices that organize data into blocks. Almost all block devices are disk drives (hard or floppy).

Device Names

Most device files live in the /dev directory. Certain naming conventions have developed. Note that these naming conventions are Linux-specific; other UNIXes use different device names. Table 8.1 shows how disk drives are named.

TABLE 8.1 Disk Device Names

Device Name	Meaning
/dev/hda	The master drive on the first IDE controller
/dev/hdb	The slave drive on the first IDE controller
/dev/hdc	The master drive on the second IDE controller
/dev/hdd	The slave drive on the second IDE controller
/dev/sda	The first (lowest-LUN) SCSI drive
/dev/sdb	The second SCSI drive
/dev/cdrom	Usually a symbolic link to the "real" CD-ROM device, which is often one of the IDE or SCSI disk devices

Table 8.2 shows how various character devices are named.

TABLE 8.2 Character Devices

Device Name	Meaning
Dev/ttyS0	The first serial port (COM1)
/dev/ttyS1	The second serial port (COM2)
/dev/lp0	The first parallel port
/dev/mouse	Usually a symbolic link to the "real" mouse device, which is often /dev/psaux for a PS/2 mouse or one of the serial ports for a serial mouse.

Naming Partitions

Disk drives can be partitioned. That is, an entire disk drive may be (in fact, usually is) divided into chunks called *partitions*. Under Windows, each partition appears as a different drive letter. Under Linux, it is somewhat different. Each partition can hold a file system that can be mounted somewhere in the directory hierarchy. Under Linux, a partition can also be designated as a swap partition, in which case the space is used for swapping.

Each partition has a name in the /dev directory, which is formed by adding a digit to the end of the base device name. So, for example, /dev/hda1 refers to partition 1 on the master drive of the first IDE controller and /dev/sdb3 refers to partition 3 on the second SCSI drive.

The Kernel's View of Device Names

The Linux kernel and kernel device drivers know nothing about these naming conventions. Within the Linux kernel, a device driver is identified by exactly two pieces of information:

- Whether the device is a block or character device
- The major number of the device

Within a device driver, a particular physical device is recognized by its minor number.

Let's look at a concrete example:

```
$ ls -l /dev/hdb
brw-r---   1 root     operator    3, 64 Apr  3 16:47 /dev/hdb
```

From this code, we can see three points:

- The initial b tells us that this is a block device.
- The 3 after the word `operator` tells us that the major number for this device is 3. All block devices with major number 3 are IDE disk drives; this is hard-coded in the Linux kernel.
- The 64 after the 3 is the minor number. It identifies the particular IDE disk drive.

> **Background Material**
>
> Note the rather restrictive permissions on the device. The permissions on a device file control access to the device driver in exactly the same way regular file permissions control access to a file. You don't want casual users accessing most device files because this would give them power to read file systems, format disk drives, or even crash the system.

Let's look at a character device:

```
$ ls -l /dev/ttyS1
crw-rw-- 1 root uucp 4, 65 Apr 3 16:47 /dev/ttyS1
```

From this example, we see:

- The initial c tells us that this is a character device.
- The 4 after the word `uucp` tells us that the major number for this device is 4. All character devices with major number 4 are serial ports.
- The 65 after the 4 is the minor number. It identifies the particular serial port (COM2: in the Windows world).

> **Background Material**
>
> The assigned device driver numbers are found in `/usr/src/linux/Documentation/devices.txt`.

Partitions

Before you can create file systems, you must partition the disk drive. Partitions divide the space on the disk into separate chunks. Each partition can create a file system. This scheme allows multiple operating systems to coexist on a disk—each system uses different partitions for its own file systems.

Under Linux, you can use either fdisk (a command-line oriented program) or cfdisk (a menu-driven program) to partition disk drives. I recommend cfdisk because it's much simpler—the menu-driven interface is easier to use than the command-line fdisk.

Partition Tables

On the Intel PC architecture, hard disk drives can contain up to four primary partitions and a number of logical partitions, sometimes called secondary or extended partitions.

> **Background Material**
>
> Why is this? This is a sad relic from days of bad design and underestimation. The original partition table left room only for four partitions, a "surely sufficient" number. Logical partitions were added as a workaround ("hack") to extend the partition table.

You can mostly ignore the distinction between primary and logical partitions; Linux doesn't care about them. Some operating systems, however, are picky and demand that their root file systems reside in a primary partition. Read the documentation for those (broken) operating systems. If you are only running Caldera OpenLinux on your system, you don't need to worry about primary versus logical partitions. If you are dual-booting with Windows, for example, make sure your Windows partition is a primary partition.

Cylinders, Heads, and Sectors

A hard disk drive has a number of heads. Inside the disk drive are a number of metal platters with read-write heads on each side of the platter. Most IDE drives have 16 heads.

Each platter contains a number of concentric "tracks," which are accessed by moving the head assembly. Each track on the drive is called a cylinder, which is further divided into sectors, which are arc-shaped sections of the cylinder. Almost all PC IDE drives have 63 sectors per cylinder.

Most IDE hard drives fix the number of heads at 16 and the number of sectors at 63. This leaves the number of cylinders as the parameter that determines drive capacity. Modern hard drives can have thousands of cylinders. Unfortunately, another ancient lapse in judgment resulted in BIOSes that only recognize up to 1023 cylinders, about 504MB with standard head counts and sector sizes. When those BIOSes were designed, 504MB was an unimaginably huge amount of disk space for a PC.

To handle larger IDE drives, the BIOSes lie when confronted with these large disks. They pretend to increase the head count and perform translations between the "fake" head numbers and the real drive geometry. All this is cumbersome and annoying.

Modern BIOSes can handle drives with up to 65,536 cylinders, or about 32GB for standard geometries. These BIOSes must be put into "LBA" mode to enable this.

Here's the bottom line: Before partitioning your disk, you must know the true geometry of the disk. For ide disks, you can get this by looking at /proc/ide/drive/geometry. Here's the output from my system:

```
$ cat /proc/ide/hda/geometry
physical 19885/16/63
logical 1247/255/63
```

This tells me that the real geometry is 19,885 cylinders, 16 heads, and 63 sectors per cylinder. The logical geometry (as lied about by the BIOS) is 1247 cylinders, 255 heads and 63 sectors per cylinder.

SCSI drives can have a wider variety of geometries. Fortunately, they report their geometries consistently, so fdisk and cfdisk don't need help determining the geometry.

Creating and Deleting Partitions

Now that you understand why partitions are needed and how disk drive geometry works, you are ready to partition your disk.

To run cfdisk, type:

```
# cfdisk /dev/device
```

where *device* is a disk device. For example, to partition the first IDE master, use:

```
# cfdisk /dev/hda
```

After you type the cfdisk command, you will be presented with a graphical interface in the terminal window. This interface is implemented in text mode, so it looks like some of the older DOS character-mode interfaces.

Deleting Partitions

To delete a partition, highlight the partition (with up and down arrow) and select Delete (with left and right arrow).

Creating Partitions

To create a partition:

1. Select New.
2. Select Primary or Logical, depending on the type of partition.
3. Type the size (in megabytes) of the partition and press Enter.

Partition Types

Each partition has a flag marking its type. The most common types for a Linux system are Linux Native (also called Linux Ext2) and Linux Swap. Linux native partitions are for normal Linux file systems, whereas Linux swap partitions are for swap space.

To change the type of a partition:

1. Highlight the partition whose type you wish to change. Press the up arrow or down arrow until the right partition is highlighted.
2. Select Type.
3. Enter the code for the type of partition you wish to create.

Writing the Changes

Any changes you make to the partition table are not actually written to disk until you select Write. If you wish to quit without writing the changes, select Quit.

Telling `cfdisk` About Disk Geometry

There is no menu item for setting the disk geometry. Rather, press g to get to the geometry menu. There are items for entering the disk's head, cylinder, and sector parameters.

> **Warning**
>
> Don't do this unless you know what you're doing. Most of the time, it is not necessary to tell `cfdisk` about the disk geometry.

Most modern BIOSes do not require you to change `cfdisk`'s view of disk geometry. If you have an older system, read the Large Disk HOWTO in the mini-HOWTO section of the Linux Documentation Project HOWTO page.

File Systems

A file system is an implementation of a UNIX directory tree. Although the UNIX file system is quite simple, the implementation details required to maintain the structure are fairly complex. A file system must be created on a disk partition before it can become part of the UNIX directory tree. Creating a file system writes all kinds of bookkeeping information to the disk partition, which allows Linux to keep track of files and directories.

> **Warning**
>
> Creating a file system on a disk partition also permanently destroys anything that may have been on the partition previously.

Types of File Systems

Linux supports many different kinds of file systems. From a user's perspective, they all look pretty similar: They all look like hierarchical trees of directories and files. However, the low-level bookkeeping details differ from system to system, as do some of the capabilities. Let's look at some file systems.

- `ISO 9660` The ISO 9660 file system is the standard file system for CD-ROMs. Linux supports the "Rock Ridge Extensions," which allow for long filenames and symbolic links. It also supports Microsoft's "Joliet" extensions.

- `ext2` The `ext2` file system is the standard Linux file system. It features file names up to 255 characters long, symbolic links, normal UNIX permissions and ownerships, and some advanced features.

> **Background Material**
>
> `ext2` stands for second extended because it was the second reimplementation of the Linux file system. There was an `ext` file system, but no one uses it any more.

- `vfat` The `vfat` file system includes the family of Microsoft file systems including `FAT`, `VFAT`, and `FAT32`. Linux can read and write these file systems but must make assumptions to fill in missing information such as UNIX file permissions and ownerships.

Linux supports many other file systems, but these three are probably those you'll care about most.

> **Background Material**
>
> Remote file systems, such as the NFS and SMB shares that are served from another machine, are more properly called volumes. This section covers only file systems on local disk drives.

Creating a File System

To create a file system, simply use the `mkfs` (make file system) command:

```
# mkfs -t ext2 /dev/device
```

For example, to create a file system on the first partition of `/dev/hda`, use:

```
# mkfs -t ext2 /dev/hda1
```

> **Background Material**
>
> Note the *root* prompt, #. You have to be root to create file systems, unless the permissions in your `/dev` directory are horribly wrong.

The `-t ext2` option tells `mkfs` to make an `ext2` file system. For this type of file system, you can supply additional options:

- `-c` causes `mkfs` to check the device for bad blocks before creating the file system. This is probably a good idea; it may prevent problems later on.
- `-v` causes `mkfs` to be more verbose. It prints lots of messages as it works.
- `-q` causes `mkfs` to be very quiet. It prints nothing as it works.

There are many other options; most of them are useful only for Linux developers or extreme tuning of the system. Consult the manual page `mkfs(8)` for details about `mkfs` and `mke2fs(8)` for details about `ext2` file systems.

Mounting a File System

The act of *gluing* a file system into the Linux directory tree is called mounting a file system. The root file system is a special case; it is mounted by the kernel upon system initialization and can never be unmounted. Remaining file systems can be mounted and unmounted while the system is running.

FIGURE 8.1
Mount example.

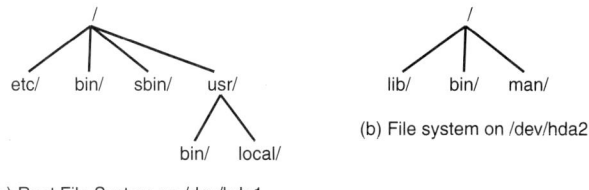

(a) Root File System on /dev/hda1

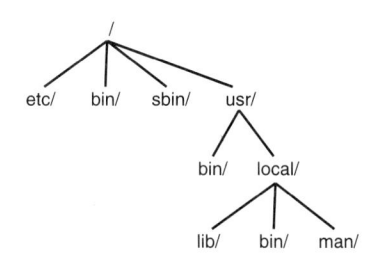

(b) File system on /dev/hda2

(c) Result of mount -t ext2 /dev/hda2 /usr/local

Consider the example in Figure 8.1. The root file system is assumed to be on /dev/hda1 with another file system on /dev/hda2. When this second file system is mounted on /usr/local, its directory hierarchy seamlessly blends into the UNIX hierarchy.

> **Note**
>
> If there are any files or directories under /usr/local in the original root file system, they are hidden as long as the second file system is mounted over them. They become visible again when the second file system is unmounted. Although this is not harmful, files hidden in this way take up disk space even though they are inaccessible. For this reason, it is usual to mount file systems on empty directories.

Mounting a File System Manually

To mount a file system, use the mount command:

```
# mount -t fstype device mount_point
```

Here, *fstype* is the file system type, usually ext2; *device* is the device file containing the file system; and *mount_point* is the location where you want the new file system mounted. For example:

```
# mount -t ext2 /dev/hdb1 /home
```

mounts the file system on `/dev/hdb1` on `/home`.

Note that you usually have to be root to mount and unmount file systems.

Mounting a File System Automatically

It would be a real chore to have to type `mount` commands each time you wanted to mount file systems. The file `/etc/fstab` contains lines describing file systems which should be mounted when the system boots.

Background Material

This file may be named something else on other UNIX systems. On Solaris, for example, it's called `/etc/vfstab`.

Each line of `/etc/fstab` looks something like this:

```
# Comment line -- lines starting with # are ignored
# device  mount_point  type    opts               dump fsck
/dev/hda1 /            ext2    defaults           1    1
/proc     /proc        proc    defaults           0    0
/dev/hdc  /mnt/cdrom   iso9660 ro,nouser,noauto   0    0
```

Each line either is blank, is a comment line (starting with #), or consists of six fields:

- The `device` field specifies the device that is to be mounted.
- The `mount_point` field specifies where the file system is to be mounted. We see that my root file system is held on `/dev/hda1`.

Background Material

This is a chicken-and-egg problem. How do we know that it holds the root file system until we read `/etc/fstab`, which is itself on the root file system? In fact, the kernel uses a different mechanism to mount the root file system; it's included in `/etc/fstab` for the benefit of startup scripts, which check file system integrity.

- The `type` field specifies the file system type. My root file system is `ext2`, the `/proc` pseudo-file system is of type `proc`, and my CD reader usually mounts file systems of type `iso9660`. This type is fed to `mount` via the `-t` option.
- The `opts` field specifies any options to be passed to `mount`. They are given as a comma-separated list with no spaces between items. Most file systems simply have

`defaults` in this field, but the CD-ROM has `ro,nouser,noauto`. The `ro` option means to mount the file system read-only. `nouser` means that we do not want mortal users to mount the system; only root is given the privilege. And `noauto` tells the system not to mount the CD-ROM at startup. (After all, there may be no CD in the drive.)

- The `dump` field is used by the `dump` command, which backs up entire file systems. I don't know anyone who actually uses `dump` to make backups; if you choose to, you can read the man pages `fstab(5)` and `dump(8)` for details.

- The `fsck` field specifies the order in which to check file system integrity upon booting. The root partition should always have a 1 in this field. Other `ext2` partitions should have a 2 in this field. On bootup, the system checks the partitions in the order indicated by this field. File systems that don't need checking, like the CD-ROM or the `/proc` file system, should have a 0 in this field.

Mount Options

Here are some of the most popular `mount` options (as they may appear in the `opts` field of `/etc/fstab`):

- `ro`   This option mounts the file system read-only. Even though it is usually used with read-only hardware like CD-ROMs, other file systems may be mounted read-only for security or efficiency reasons.

- `auto`   This option is on by default and means that the file system should be mounted automatically at startup.

- `noauto`   This option causes the file system not to be mounted automatically at startup.

- `user`   This option allows normal users (not just root) to mount the file system. It's safe to use this for CD-ROM file systems, but you should not normally make file systems user-mountable.

- `nodev`   This option prevents the system from recognizing device files on the mounted file system. If you allow ordinary users to mount file systems, the `nodev` option should be on for security reasons. (The `user` option turns this on by default.)

> **Background Material**
>
> Why is it a security hole to allow device files on user-mounted file systems? A criminal could create a file system with world-writable device files corresponding to your disk partitions, mount this file system, and then have full access to your disks.

- `noexec`   This option prevents the system from recognizing the `execute permission` bits. Useful if you're mounting a file system containing executables for a different CPU architecture.
- `nosuid`   This option prevents recognition of `set-user-id` and `set-group-id` bits. See the discussion under *nodev* for why this might be a good idea.

There are many more mount options, and some file systems have file-system-specific options; consult the `mount(8)` man page for details.

Checking a File System

One day (it will happen to you) you will be faced with a corrupted file system. Most likely, this will be the result of hardware or power failure; Linux itself almost never wrecks a file system.

On bootup, Linux attempts to repair minor problems with file systems. If it cannot, however, you will receive a prominent warning to run `fsck` manually and be dropped into maintenance mode.

To continue in maintenance mode, enter the root password. You will be given a shell prompt.

Invoking `fsck`

To check a file system, use the `fsck` command:

```
# fsck -t fstype device_file
```

For example:

```
# fsck -t ext2 /dev/hdb1
```

> **Warning**
>
> Make sure the device file you are checking is not mounted. Running `fsck` on a mounted file system will corrupt the file system. If the root file system is corrupt, you'll have to boot from a rescue disk and run `fsck` from there.

For `ext2` file systems, you can use the `-p` option, which causes `fsck` to repair the file system without asking any questions:

```
# fsck -t ext2 -p /dev/hdb1
```

Otherwise, you'll be prompted to answer questions. Unless you're an expert file system hacker, answer Y to all of `fsck` questions.

If `fsck` is unable to repair a file system, you're out of luck. You'll need to re-create the file system and restore it from backup.

> **Background Material**
>
> You do make backups, right?

Check the man pages `fsck(8)` and `e2fsck(8)` for all of the gory details about `fsck`.

Accounting and Quotas

Linux allows you to set limits on the amount of disk space consumed by users. However, Caldera OpenLinux does not come with the necessary tools to manage disk quotas. Disk quotas are typically intended for central file servers, and Caldera OpenLinux is targeted at the desktop user. However, you can obtain and install the quota tools from a Linux archive site. You will also have to recompile the kernel for quota support.

File Permissions

Correct file permissions are a critical part of Linux system security. Controlling who can alter sensitive files is important for keeping your system secure and your users' information private. You should make sure files have correct permissions and ownerships.

Every file or directory is associated with two IDs:

- The owner of the file is a single user.
- The group of the file is a group of possibly many users.

Every file or directory has three sets of permissions:

- The owner's permissions specify what the owner can do with the file.
- The group's permissions specify what members of the file's group can do with it.
- The "other" permissions specify what users who are not the owner or members of the file's group can do with it.

Within each set of permissions, three types of permission can be granted:

- Read permission gives permission to read the file or directory.
- Write permission gives permission to write to the file. For a directory, write permission allows creation of new files within the directory or deletion of existing files.
- Execute permission gives permission to execute the file. For a directory, execute permission allows the directory to be made the current directory.

To change the permissions of a file or directory, use the `chmod` command. Note that you must be either the owner or the root to change the permissions of a file or directory. Group members who are not the owners of a file cannot change its permissions.

Symbolic Permissions

`chmod` understands a large number of ways to express file permissions. The easiest way to change permissions is to use symbolic permissions. A symbolic permission looks something like this:

who how what

Here, *who* is a list of letters specifying whose permissions are to be affected:

- u specifies that the permissions of the file's owner (the "user") should be changed.
- g specifies that the permissions of the file's group should be changed.
- o specifies that the permissions for others should be changed.
- a specifies that permissions for all should be changed. a is equivalent to ugo.

how is a single character specifying how the permissions are to be affected:

- + means that the person or persons named by *who* should be granted additional permissions.
- − means that the person or persons named by *who* should have permissions taken away.
- = means that the person or persons named by *who* should be given exactly the specified permissions.

what is a list of letters specifying the permissions:

- r signifies read permission.
- w signifies write permission.
- x signifies execute permission.
- X is like x, but it only turns on execute permission if the file is a directory or one of the `execute permission` bits is already on.

> **Background Material**
>
> There are more possibilities for what; we'll cover them shortly.

The `chmod` command looks like this:

```
$ chmod permissions file...
```

Here are some examples:

```
Give everyone read permission for public.txt
''who'' is a, ''how'' is +, ''what'' is r
$ chmod a+r public.txt
```

```
Remove read and write permission for group and others
''who'' is go, ''how'' is -, ''what'' is rw
$ chmod go-rw private.txt
```

SUID, SGID, and Sticky Bits

In addition to the nine flags controlling read, write, and execute permission for the user, group, and others, each file has three additional permission flags:

The `set-user-id` or `suid` bit controls what happens when the file is executed. If the `suid` bit is set, then when the file is executed, the effective user ID of the process becomes that of the owner of the file rather than the person executing the file.

This mechanism is how UNIX gives certain programs additional permissions. For example, the `passwd` command (which changes your password) requires root privileges to modify the system password file. The executable file `/usr/bin/passwd` is owned by root and has its `suid` bit turned on:

```
$ ls -l /usr/bin/passwd
-r-sr-xr-x 1 root bin 38837 Apr 3 16:49 /usr/bin/passwd
```

Note the `s` in the owner's permission flags. This indicates that the `suid` and `execute` bits are on. If the `suid` bit were on and the `execute` bit off, `ls` would display an `S` instead. (This combination of bits should not occur.)

> **Warning**
>
> Suid programs can give ordinary users extra or even root privileges. Do not turn on the `suid` bit unless you are certain that it is safe to do so.

The `set-group-id` or `sgid` bit is analogous to the `suid` bit—when a file with the `sgid` bit set is executed, the process's effective group becomes that of the file.

For example, the `mail` program needs to be able to write files in the `/var/spool/mail` directory. This directory is owned and writable by group `mail`; the `/bin/mail` program is sgid to group `mail`:

```
$ ls -l /bin/mail
-rwxr-sr-x 1 root mail 70552 Apr 3 16:53 /bin/mail
```

Whenever `/bin/mail` is run, it has the privileges associated with the `mail` group rather than just the privileges of the person running it. For a directory, the `sgid` bit takes on a different meaning: Any files or directories created in a directory with the `sgid` bit set will be given the same group as the directory. Furthermore, any directories created in the directory will have their `sgid` bit set.

This is very useful for group projects. You can create a common project directory and group. Make the directory's group the common project group, and turn on the `sgid` bit. Any files or directories placed in the project directory will belong to the project group, not the group of the person placing them there.

The *sticky bit* modifies the interpretation of directory permissions. Normally, to remove or rename a file, you only need write permission in the file's directory. The file's permissions themselves are irrelevant. This causes problems in shared directories like `/tmp`, which are world-writable. Even though it is necessary to allow anyone to create files in `/tmp`, it is not desirable for one user to be able to delete someone else's file from `/tmp`.

If the sticky bit is set on a directory, then only the owner of a file (or the owner of the directory) may remove the file from the directory. If we look at `/tmp`, we see the sticky bit set:

```
$ ls -ld /tmp
drwxrwxrwt 34 root root 3072 Jun 20 11:38 /tmp
```

The `t` flag signifies the sticky bit. Anyone can write into `/tmp`, but only root or a file's owner can remove the file from `/tmp`. (This example also illustrates the `-d` option of `ls`, which makes `ls` treat directories just like normal files rather than listing their contents.)

> **Background Material**
>
> The sticky bit is so named because in very old versions of UNIX, the sticky bit indicated an often-executed program, and the system kept the program code around in swap space for faster execution the next time it was invoked. Modern virtual memory techniques have made this optimization unnecessary, and the sticky bit has taken on its modern interpretation.

In the chmod command, you control the suid, sgid, and sticky bits like this:

```
$ chmod u+s file  # Turn on suid
$ chmod u-s file  # Turn off suid
$ chmod g+s file  # Turn on sgid
$ chmod g-s file  # Turn off sgid
$ chmod o+t dir   # Turn on sticky
$ chmod o-t dir   # Turn off sticky
```

chmod has a couple of useful options:

- -R causes chmod to recursively change permissions of directories and their contents.
- -v causes chmod to print messages saying exactly what changes it is making. (This option is available with GNU chmod; it is not standard on most UNIX systems.)

See the man page chmod(1) for additional ways to specify symbolic permissions.

Numeric Permissions

Macho UNIX users sometimes use numeric permission descriptions rather than symbolic ones. Each permission flag occupies one bit in the file system. The value of the permission word is often expressed in octal, or base 8.

> **Background Material**
>
> Why does UNIX use base 8? There are three types of permission (read, write, and execute), and each octal digit represents three binary bits; therefore expressing the permission word in base 8 yields very natural values. (This reasoning is natural to UNIX people, anyway.)

Here's how it works. A numeric mode consists of up to four octal digits. For the first digit:

- sticky permission is stored in the least significant bit of the octal digit; it has a value of 1.
- sgid permission is stored in the middle bit of the octal digit; it has a value of 2.
- suid permission is stored in the most significant bit of the octal digit; it has a value of 4.

For the remaining three digits, specifying the user, group, and other permissions, respectively:

- Execute permission is stored in the least significant bit of the octal digit; it has a value of 1.
- Write permission is stored in the middle bit of the octal digit; it has a value of 2.
- Read permission is stored in the most significant bit of the octal digit; it has a value of 4.

To derive the value of the permission word, add up the values for each enabled permission bit.

This cries out for examples. Here are symbolic permissions as listed by `ls` with the corresponding numeric permissions:

- `-rw-r--r--` corresponds to 644. The user has read and write (4+2) permissions, whereas group and other have only read (4) permission. Because the `sgid`, `suid`, and `sticky` bits are not used, the first digit is (implicitly) zero. For clarity, you could write the permission as 0644.
- `-rwxr-xr-x` corresponds to 755. The user has read, write, and execute (4+2+1) permissions, whereas group and other have only read and execute (4+1) permission.
- `-r-sr-xr-x` corresponds to 4555. The `suid` bit (4) is on, and user, group, and other have read and execute (4+1) permissions.
- `-rw-------` corresponds to 600. The user has read and write (4+2) permissions, whereas group and other have no permissions at all.

The umask

Each UNIX process has a special value called the `umask` associated with it. By default, most UNIX programs create ordinary files with permissions 666 and directories with permissions 777. This gives everyone full access to the files or directories, which is probably not desirable.

The `umask` value specifies which permission bits to turn off. To see the value of your `umask`, type:

```
$ umask
002
```

In this example, only write permission for others is turned off. Some common values for `umask` are:

- `002` Turn off write permission for others. This value is safe if each user belongs to his or her own unique group. This is the default for Caldera OpenLinux.
- `022` Turn off write permission for the group and for others. This is commonly used on many UNIX systems.

- 07 Turn off all permissions for others.
- 27 Turn off write permission for the group and all permissions for others.
- 77 Turn off all permission for the group and others. This is used to achieve maximum privacy.

To set the umask, simply specify the value:

```
$ umask 077
```

You can (and should) set the umask early on in your shell's startup file. This ensures that any files created during login are properly protected.

File Ownership

To change the owner or group of a file, use the chown command. You can change just the group with the chgrp command. The commands look like this:

```
# chown [options] user[:group] file...
$ chgrp [options] group file...
```

Only root can change the ownership of a file. The owner of a file can change the file's group to any group of which he or she is a member. Root can change a file's group arbitrarily.

To change a file's owner, simply specify the login name or numeric user ID of the new owner:

```
# chown dave /home/dave/foo.txt
```

If you want to change the owner and group at the same time, separate them with a colon:

```
# chown dave:users /home/dave/foo.txt
```

If you only want to change the group, use chgrp:

```
# chgrp users /home/dave/foo.txt
```

The most commonly used option for chown and chgrp is -R, which causes them to recursively change the owner or group down directory hierarchies. The man pages chown(1) and chgrp(1) discuss other less commonly used options.

Swap Space

Linux can provide processes with more memory than your computer has physical RAM. It does this by paging blocks of memory to a disk file or partition when they are not being used, and paging them back in on demand.

Linux can use either a file or a special disk partition for swap space. A swap file is more convenient—you can create it and activate it when you need it and adjust its size fairly easily. However, a swap file is slower than a swap partition.

A swap partition is faster than a swap file, but you cannot easily change its size or create extra partitions while Linux is running. I recommend creating one swap partition of about twice the size of your computer's physical memory. If you need extra swap space, you can always create one or more swap files temporarily.

Creating a Swap Partition

Creating a swap partition is just like creating any type of partition. Use `fdisk` or `cfdisk` to create the partition and then set its type to Linux Swap.

Creating a Swap File

To create a swap file, you need to create a large file somewhere in the file system. The easiest way to do this is with the `dd` command.

`dd` (according to its man page) "converts and copies a file." It reads block-sized chunks from an input file, possibly performs some kind of conversion on the data, and writes chunks (possibly of different size from the input chunks) to the output file.

For our purposes, we'll just use a standard recipe involving `dd` to create the swap file. To create a swap file of *n* megabytes, use this command:

```
# dd if=/dev/zero of=/swapfile bs=1k count=nk
```

For example, to create a 32MB swap file called /var/swap, use:

```
# dd if=/dev/zero of=/var/swap bs=1k count=32k
```

The `if=/dev/zero` tells `dd` to read from the input file /dev/zero. This is a special device file (similar to /dev/null), which simply returns an endless stream of zero-valued bytes when you read from it.

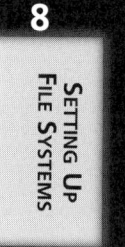

> **Background Material**
>
> Like /dev/null, anything written to /dev/zero is discarded.

The `of=/var/swap` tells `dd` to write to the normal file /var/swap. The `bs=1k` tells `dd` to read and write in 1KB (1024-byte) chunks.

> **Background Material**
>
> You can specify different-sized chunks for input and output with `ibs=` and `obs=`, respectively.

The `count=32k` tells `dd` to read 32KB (that is, $32 \times 1024 = 32{,}768$) blocks. The combination of block size and count yields $32 \times 1024 \times 1024$ bytes, or 32MB.

Because sensitive information may be placed in a swap file when a process is swapped out, you should make sure the swap file is owned by root and is not readable by other users. Do this as follows:

```
# chown root.root /swapfile
# chmod go-rwx /swapfile
```

Formatting a Swap Area

Before you can use a swap file or partition, you must format it. This needs to be done only once, immediately after the swap file or partition is created.

To format a swap partition, use the `mkswap` command:

```
# mkswap /swapfile; sync
# mkswap -c /dev/hdc3
```

In the first example, we use `mkswap` on a swap file. Because a swap file is a normal file in the file system, we use the `sync` command to flush the output to disk. This makes sure that the formatting information is really written to the disk and not just buffered in memory.

In the second, we use it on a swap partition. For swap partitions, supply the name of the device file representing the partition. Also, for the partition, we use the `-c` option, which tells `mkswap` to check for bad disk blocks. Always use `-c` when formatting a swap partition; never use it when formatting a swap file.

> **Background Material**
>
> The method of keeping track of swap space changed between kernel versions 2.0 and 2.2. The "old style" allows an area of swap space to be at most about 128MB, whereas the "new style" allows it to be about 2GB. `mkswap` automatically chooses the appropriate style. (Don't make more swap space than about twice your physical RAM—if you really start using that much virtual memory, the disk paging will slow your system to a crawl.)

Enabling a Swap Area

To enable swapping, use the `swapon` command:

```
# swapon /swapfile
# swapon /dev/hdc3
```

The first example enables swapping on a swap file; the second enables a swap partition.

If you want a swap partition to be activated every time you boot the system, add a line like this to `/etc/fstab`:

```
/dev/hdc3 swap swap defaults 0 0
```

The `swap` in the `mount_point` and *type* partition informs the bootup scripts that `/dev/hdc3` is a swap partition. You can enable swapping on all partitions listed in `/etc/fstab` like this:

```
# swapon -a
```

> **Note**
>
> You cannot change the size of a swap file while it is being used for swap space. You can only do this by disabling swapping on the file, changing its size, rerunning `mkswap`, and re-enabling swapping.

`swapon` has a `-p` option that lets you set the "priority" of a swap space. The option takes an integer argument between 0 and 32767. The higher the number, the higher the priority. Higher-priority swap areas are used in preference to lower-priority ones. If you have both swap partitions and swap files, give the swap partitions a higher priority because they have better performance.

In `/etc/fstab`, you can put a `pri=n` entry in the `opts` field to set the priority of a swap area.

`swapon` has a very useful `-s` option, which displays the status of your swap areas:

```
$ swapon -s

Filename    Type       Size    Used  Priority
/dev/hda4   partition  377520  0     -1
```

Disabling a Swap Area

To disable a swap area, use the `swapoff` command:

```
# swapoff /swapfile
# swapoff /dev/hdc3
```

The first example disables swapping on a swap file, and the second disables a swap partition. You can use `swapoff -a` to disable all swap partitions listed in `/etc/fstab`.

Summary

In this chapter, you have learned how Linux represents device drivers with special device files. You learned how to partition disks and create file systems as well as how to mount a file system in the Linux directory hierarchy. You also learned about file permissions and how to check and set them. Finally, you learned how to create and use swap files.

CHAPTER 9

Printing

IN THIS CHAPTER

- Local Printing from Caldera *210*
- Tools and Locations Used in Printing *216*
- Understanding the Printing Process *219*
- Using COAS to "Administrate" Your Printer *220*
- Setting Up and Using a Remote Printer *222*
- Formatted Printing *225*
- Using Your Printer with Other Applications *226*
- Useful Print Capability Enhancing Programs (and Where to Find Them) *229*
- Some Secrets of the Guru (Junior Division) *229*

Local Printing from Caldera

In this chapter we will explore the options available to print within Caldera. Many print functions are available, and we need to cover a multitude of programs and supporting files. Caldera gives you the option to print from your local machine, from another machine that is connected to a local area network, or even to a printer remotely situated (if it can be addressed over either a WAN or the Internet). All that is required is permission to use the printer, which you supply to yourself for a locally attached printer.

If you have permission to use the printer, the rest is easy. It is, however, just a bit detailed. We will cover the simple case—printing locally to a parallel printer—as well as the complicated case—printing remotely over the Internet to a PostScript printer running off a serial port that is behind a firewall.

Caldera has many utilities that make installing a printer a snap. If you are using a local parallel printer, you should be up and running in about 10 minutes. But just to verify that the hardware works, it is always a good idea to boot from a DOS floppy and attempt to print a file on the printer before getting involved with setting up a Linux printer. Many times I have spent an hour trying to get a printer to work under Linux only to discover that there was a hardware problem or a setup issue that prevented the printer from ever working. This simple DOS test first would have saved all the frustration.

How Does Caldera Locate My Printer?

Caldera, like all other flavors of UNIX, "talks" to all hardware devices through special device files. These device files are merely entries in Linux's file structure that are handled by a "device driver" located in the kernel. If you were to do a listing of the printer device special files on the default install of Caldera, you would see something similar to the following:

```
{command used is #ls -l /dev/lp*}

crw-rw----   1 root     lp        6,   0 Apr  3 16:47 /dev/lp0  (Printer at
address 0x3BC)
crw-rw----   1 root     lp        6,   1 Apr  3 16:47 /dev/lp1  (Printer at
address 0x378)
crw-rw----   1 root     lp        6,   2 Apr  3 16:47 /dev/lp2  (Printer at
address 0x278)
```

It is important for you to know that the c in the first column of the device entries stands for character special device, which tells the operating system not to write data to the file system on the disk, but rather to give any data destined for this printer to the driver in position 6 (major device number in column 32 followed by a comma) for appropriate handling. The number after the comma and before the Month is called the minor device number and tells the driver which printer the data are destined for.

If your printer stops printing, but the system acts like it is printing, check the printer device special files. Often the device entry has been deleted (or you have mistyped the printer name) and the system has put the data in a file rather than hand it to the device driver for output on the device. This will be most evidenced if the number before the date does not have a comma in it.

Serial devices likewise have entries in the /dev directory. Serial devices' entries will be similar to /dev/ttyS? Where the ? is replaced by the serial port number (0, 1, 2, 3, or 4), and these are also character special devices.

Remote printing is accomplished in a slightly different manner so that those printers do not need an entry in the /dev directory.

Printer Selection (or the Default If Only One Is Available)

Printers come in many types and technologies. Almost all will work with Caldera, although you will probably want to use a PostScript printer to be able to print the graphics.

Some printers use proprietary software architectures that require factory-configured driver software. The HP 1000 series printers is an example. Until HP is able to provide software drivers for Linux, these will not work on your system. Other proprietary architectures exist; however, this is the most common series and the most common manufacturer. Drivers will come along, possibly written by the hardware manufacturer or by a guru under the GNU General Public License, but until then, don't bang your head against a doorstop.

Printing That First Page

In order to print, you must first check several things:

- Is the computer turned on?
- Is Caldera OpenLinux installed?
- Is the printer plugged in to the appropriate port?
- Is the printer turned on?

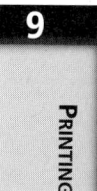

If your printer is plugged into your parallel port (as we will assume here), you should be able to cause output on the printer with the following command:

```
#ls > /dev/lp0
```

If you are not using a laser printer, *something* should print on your printer, or at least the print head should move. If you are printing on a laser printer, you should take the printer offline and eject a page in order to see what you have printed. This is because printing to a laser printer is really just printing to the buffer in the printer itself, until it receives a command to physically print the page. Laser printers cannot print just a line—they must print an entire page as it passes over the laser in a continuous manner.

Most printers eject a page by taking the printer offline (press the Online button and the light will go out) and subsequently pressing a button that is usually labeled "Form Feed."

> **Note**
>
> After you have manually ejected the page, remember to press the Online button so that the light comes on. Otherwise, the printer will just sit there like a doorstop not listening to the computer.

When the Online light is on, the printer is "talking" to the computer (and listening to it). When it is off, it is not listening to the computer and will not receive or process any instructions or print any pages. Leaving the Online light on is the normal situation.

For many printers (and certainly laser printers) you will see lines printed in a step fashion (where each line is printed one line below and to the right of the previous line). A lack of carriage return is probably the cause and should not worry you. We will use a filter to insert the carriage return later.

If your printer sits there like a doorstop and refuses to do anything, then you need to determine what is going on.

First, you must verify that the printer port is enabled and appropriately addressed. If you are using a computer with a BIOS (basic input/output system) that allows you to set which address the onboard parallel port(s) respond to, make sure that the port that the printer is connected to is set to 0x3bc (address for /dev/lp0). If this is handled by switches on a board in the computer, you need to check the switch settings to verify these settings.

Next, you need to verify that the parallel port driver was compiled into the kernel. (The parallel port driver is the software that talks with the hardware parallel port.) To determine whether the parallel port driver was compiled into the kernel (the parallel port driver would be there by default with the distribution kernel but may have been removed by any subsequent kernel rebuilds), you need to perform the following tests.

Enter the following command:

```
#cat /proc/devices | grep lp
```

you should see one and only one line:

```
6 lp
```

This notation indicates that the parallel port is compiled into the kernel and that it is set to Major Device 6. This major device number must agree with the major device number from the `ls -l` command used earlier.

If your printer is still acting like a doorstop, then reverify the port (if you have more than one) your printer is plugged into and check the cable and printer to see if they work on another known working system.

After you are successful (possibly after many tries) in causing output on the printer, the next step is to check (just to make sure) that the line printer daemon (spooler) is working.

Use LISA, not the pretty girl down the street, but The Linux Installation and System Administration program, which is as a part of the Caldera OpenLinux distribution. LISA is covered more fully in Appendix B, but here are some simple guidelines to get you started.

1. For a quick check, enter:

   ```
   #lisa
   ```

2. When the LISA screen comes up, select 3 (System Configuration), 2 (System Configuration), and 6 (Configure daemon/server autostart).
3. Scroll down to view Printer Server (LPD). This probably will be at number 12.
4. Verify that Printer Server (LPD) has an X in the parenthesis indicating autostart when the system boots up. If that X is present, then the spooler (line printer daemon) will start up automatically every time the system is rebooted.

Now that you have configured the spooler to start automatically, you can move on to creating a printer that the spooler can work with. Note that Caldera OpenLinux makes several print spoolers available. For information on these options, refer to the section entitled "Tools and Locations Used in Printing."

Again, we can use LISA to do this (there are other methods, but this is the simplest one to use).

1. Start this procedure again by entering:

   #lisa

2. When the LISA screen comes up, select 3 (System Configuration), 1 (Hardware Configuration), and 6 (Configure Printer).

3. Select a printer driver at the prompt. (See Figure 9.1.)

FIGURE 9.1
The Select Printer Driver dialog box.

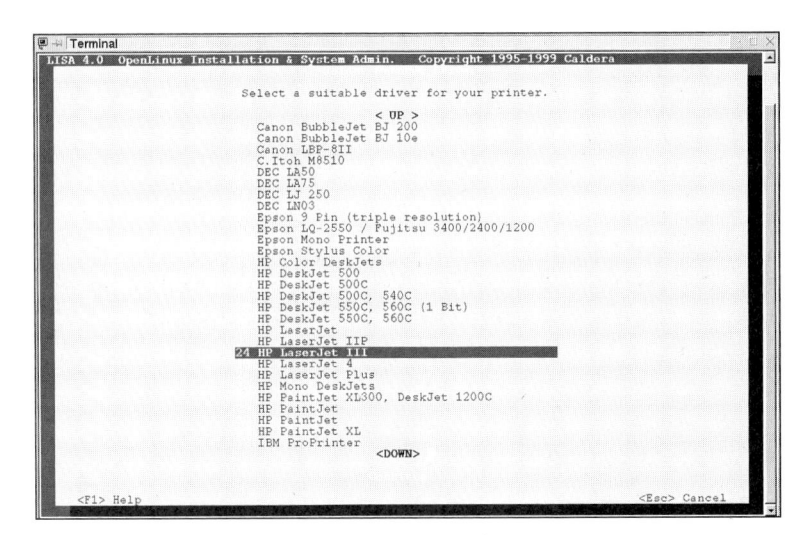

Select the appropriate printer from this list. The "No printer available" selection is generally a poor choice, or you shouldn't be here, but the rest of them are appropriate and useful.

4. Select a printer connection at the prompt. (See Figure 9.2.)

FIGURE 9.2
The LISA Select Printer Driver dialog box.

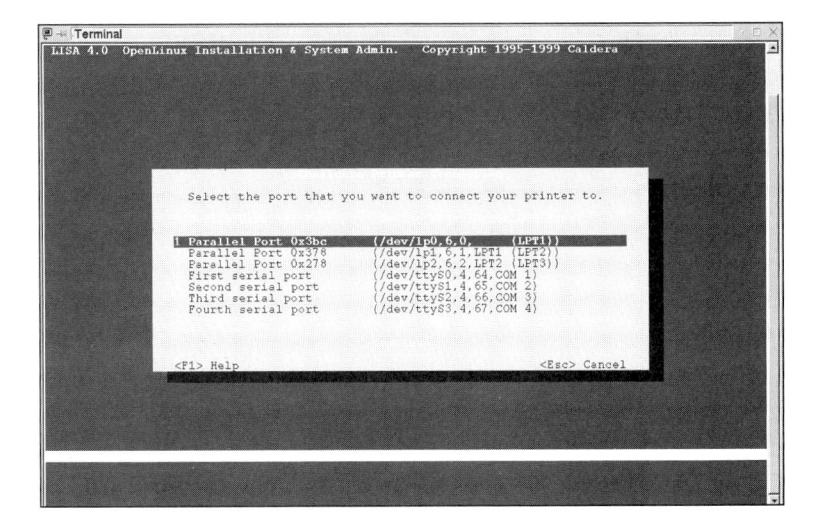

In this dialog box you select the physical port to which your printer is connected. In our example this would be Parallel Port 0x3bc, which is the first physical parallel port and agrees with our earlier selections.

> **Note**
>
> Consistency is very important here. If you lie to the computer about where to find the printer, it will believe you!

5. If you are taken to the dialog box shown in Figure 9.3, select a printer resolution (dots per inch) that is appropriate to your printer.

FIGURE 9.3
The LISA Default Printer Resolution dialog box.

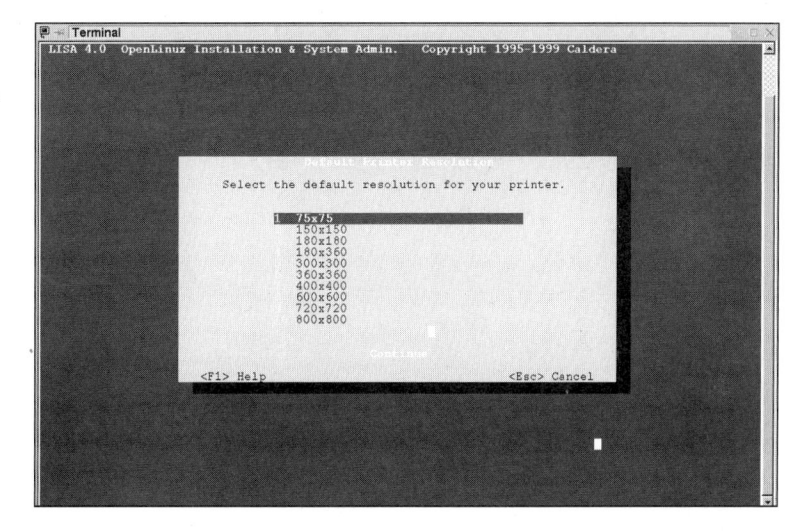

Selecting a resolution that is higher (larger number of dots per inch) than your printer can support will usually cause the printer either to not print or to print garbage. On laser printers, this is often a limitation of the amount of memory in the printer itself (the printer must buffer a complete page image before printing), so reducing the resolution will allow it to print a full page (albeit at a grainy texture) before physically printing the page.

6. If you are taken to the Default Paper Size dialog box (see Figure 9.4), select the appropriate paper size. Most people will want to select 4 Letter, which is 8-1/2" × 11". However many users from the Middle East or Europe will want to select the 2 A4 size, which is more common there.

FIGURE 9.4
The LISA Default Paper Size dialog box.

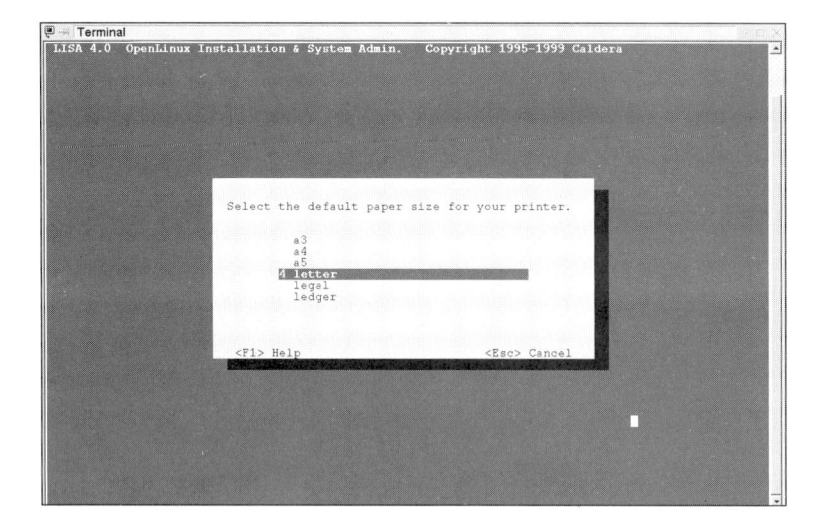

After all required selections are complete, you will be taken back to the Hardware Configuration dialog box and all you need to do to print is to escape backward to the desktop.

So now, as you were promised, you can print the first page. The command that will accomplish this feat of modern marvels is:

```
#lpr /etc/profile (a text file that is always present)
```

Now let's delve a bit more deeply into the details of how the printing subsystem works in Caldera OpenLinux.

Tools and Locations Used in Printing

The first thing to understand is that a program that runs in the background on Caldera OpenLinux handles almost all printing issues. This is the line printer daemon (LPD). Caldera offers three spooler choices. The selection of which spooler process to use was made at installation time. The most common one (and the one we will work with here) is called LRPng.

The LPD script starts the line printer daemon at boot time and can be found in the /etc/rc.d/init.d directory along with other initialization scripts. From the moment this script is executed, the lpd process runs in the background. You can find out the process number and status of this daemon with the following command:

```
#ps -ef ¦ grep lp
```

This will print out one line containing the word `daemon`, the process number, and some other information including current status of the daemon such as `START_IDLE`.

With this process running in the background and waiting for commands, everything happens automatically when you request it.

Some of the commands that talk to the line printer daemon follow.

/usr/sbin/lpd	The actual printer daemon.
/usr/sbin/lpc	The line printer control program.
/usr/sbin/lpraccnt	Listens on TCP for accounting information for the printer.
/usr/bin/lp	Old style print spooler submission program (usually just links to lpr).
/usr/bin/lpq	Line printer queue examination program.
/usr/bin/lpr	New style print spooler submission program.
/usr/bin/lprm	Program to remove jobs from the print queue.
/usr/bin/lpstat	Pprogram to provides information about the current status of the spooler and managed jobs.
/usr/sbin/tunelp	Program that tunes up printer operations.
/usr/bin/pr	Another old style spooler submission program that allows a lot of options including printing starting at a given page and support for printing in columns (even if the file-originating process doesn't support this).
/usr/libexec/LPRng-3.5.3/lpbanner	A simple banner- printing program often used by the spooler.
/usr/libexec/LPRng-3.5.3/lpf	A basic print filter program that at the least adds a carriage return to each line feed in the print data stream.
/usr/lib/coas/scripts/ctrlprinter	Script used by COAS to set printer and spooler parameters.

Some of the files used by the line printer daemon follow.

`/etc/printcap`	File that contains control codes and print definitions for all printers available on your system. If you wish to add another printer or you wish to add features to an existing printer, it will be done in this file. It is best to let LISA and COAS modify this file.
`/etc/rc.d/init.d/lpd`	Shell script that takes care of all issues associated with the starting and stopping of the spooler daemon.
`/etc/sysconfig/daemons/lpd`	Control file for daemon startup.
`/etc/sysconfig/printers`	Directory that contains a file for each printer defined to Caldera OpenLinux. Each of these files (the file name is the same as the printer name) contains control information for the printer, including ghostscript interface information and resolution data.
`/etc/lpd.conf`	Configuration file for the line printer daemon. The Caldera default distribution file contains dozens of options for the line printer daemon, but they are all commented out (# in the first column). If you wish to set any of these options (which are well documented in the file), you need to edit the file and uncomment the options that you want the line printer daemon to observe.
`/etc/lpd.perms`	File that contains permissions definitions for the LPD spooler. Every time a spool or unspool operation is performed, this file is checked to determine if the operation is permissible on this computer and on the requested printer.
`/var/lock/subsys/lpd`	File that contains "lock" information for the spooler. When the printer is actively printing a file, print requests are accepted and sent to a queue directory until the printer is physically able to print the file. Lock files prevent multiple processes from sending print data to the printer simultaneously, thereby causing garbage output.

`/var/spool/lpd`	Directory that contains a subdirectory for each printer defined to Caldera OpenLinux. Each of these subdirectories (the directory name is the same as the printer name) contains a filter definition, a control file, a status file, and a log file for that printer.
`/var/spool/lpd/lpd.lock.*`	Files containing `lpd`'s process number on that computer. Used to check and lock the process.

Finally, some of the device entries used by the line printer daemon follow.

`/dev/lp0`	Character special device for LPR1:
`/dev/lp1`	Character special device for LPR2:
`/dev/lp2`	Character special device for LPR3:

Understanding the Printing Process

If you're mind is foggy from all the information that is being thrown at you about printing, then you may want to skip this section and go on to the next section on using COAS to "administrate" your printer. If, on the other hand, your taste buds have merely been whetted by the preceding information, then this section is for you. This is where we bring it all together.

When lpr receives anything (it could be a file name or data piped into it), it parses the first line of the data to see if you have specified a printer. If you have not specified a printer, lpr will default to the first printer entry in the `/etc/printcap` file. The actual order of priority for selecting the printer can be found by using the command:

`#man lpr`

and looking under the `-P` option.

When lpr has the data and knows where it is going, it stores a copy of the data in a file it creates in the `/var/spool/lpd/`*printer name*`/` directory with a name beginning with df and followed by some host information and a sequence number. In the same directory, it also stores a file that begins with cf and is followed by the rest of the file name—this is the control file.

These files stay in the spool directory until the line printer daemon determines that the printer is not busy and is available (online) at which time it will read from the control file and determine which actions are to be taken prior to copying the data to the printer device.

While these two files are in the spool directory (normally referred to as queued for printing), other programs can query or change the status of the files (and therefore the print job itself). lpq and lpstat can display the status of jobs. lprm can remove a job. lpc can cancel, enable, disable, or hold a job or a printer.

A very important command to verify function of the printers is:

```
#lpc status all
```

This command will give you a quick overview of the printer status for all printers that this computer knows about.

If the printer is not busy and is online, the LPD will search the spool directories (there actually is a method in this madness, but we won't go into it here) for the next highest priority job and then pipe it into this printer's filter (which can be found at /var/spool/lpd/*printer name*/filter—Caldera put it there when you set up the printer) and on to its physical port.

After the LPD copies the entire file through the filter to the physical printer port, it checks for the next highest priority print job. If there is none, it goes to sleep until LPD is called the next time.

Using COAS to "Administrate" Your Printer

COAS (The Caldera Open Administration System) is an X Window-based printer administration tool that will often come in handy.

The COAS Printer Configuration dialog box is depicted in Figure 9.5. To reach this entry screen, click on the COAS icon on the X Window task bar (it is usually third from the left). Then, highlight both Peripherals and Printer and click the mouse. Click OK on the welcome screen that appears.

FIGURE 9.5

The COAS Printer Configuration dialog box.

On the entry screen, the selection bar has only two options Printer and Daemon. The Daemon button allows you to start or stop the printer daemon (which will start or stop the printer). The Printer button allows you to edit, add, or remove a printer. The operating system lists the name and description of all printers that it is aware of.

If you highlight a printer name, click on the Printer button, and select Edit, you will be moved to the Printer Attributes dialog box (see Figure 9.6).

FIGURE 9.6

The COAS Printer Attributes dialog box.

Some of the fields in this dialog box are dimmed out. In COAS, the Name, Uniprint Driver, Remote Host (you are not editing a remote printer after all), and Remote Queue will all be dimmed out for local printers.

You can, however, assign an alternative name that is easier to understand and enter a description of the printer.

The Type field allows you to select the type of printer attached to the port. It is interesting to note that the selection available in the edit dialog box is different from the selection available in the add dialog box (see the discussion in the next section). If, while adding a printer, you do not find a printer selection that is appropriate to your printer, you can enter anything and then come back and edit the printer to select a more appropriate printer driver.

The Resolution field (if not dimmed out) will allow you to select a resolution appropriate to the printer you have selected in the Type field.

The remaining fields are pretty much self explanatory and probably should not be modified by the unwary. Do not be disturbed by the requirement to have a Speed parameter on a parallel printer (as in the example) because it does not appear to affect the speed of parallel printers at all.

After you have made the changes you wish, click on the OK button. You will be moved to a confirmation dialog box that will ask you to confirm the changes, discard the changes, or cancel the edit. After you select the appropriate button, you will be returned to the Printer Configuration dialog box.

Setting Up and Using a Remote Printer

Setting up a remote printer is simple, straightforward, and *detailed*. The details are very important here, a capital letter on another machine must be a capital letter on your machine. Everything must match precisely. If you can ping the other machine, and you cannot print to it, you will probably find that you have mistyped something minor.

You will need at a minimum the following information:

- The hostname of the remote machine hosting the printer.
- The queue name on the remote machine for that printer.

In addition, if you are going to print on a LAN or a WAN, you need to support the LAN/WAN protocol that talks to the remote printer's computer or print server hardware.

After properly setting up a remote printer, you will be able to send print output anywhere that you have permission. All your work on your local computer can (and will be) stopped dead by a remote machine that denies you permission.

Several protocols are commonly used to communicate with remote printer gateways (computers or print servers). Two of the more common are TCP/IP and SMB (Session

Message Block). TCP/IP is the protocol used in many non-Microsoft environment (especially UNIX environments) and SMB has been available in Microsoft environments since 1987. Caldera OpenLinux supports both protocols. However, the installation of the SMB environment requires an additional installation of Samba, which is provided on the Caldera OpenLinux media. Both SMB and Samba are covered more fully in Chapter 16.

The steps for adding a remote printer capability to Caldera are very similar to those for setting up a local printer. The remote printer is included in the local /etc/printcap if you wish to verify any of the parameters.

Although you may use LISA or edit specific files to create a remote printer, COAS may be the simplest method to use.

All of this should be familiar from the section entitled "Using COAS to 'Administrate' your Printer."

1. Select Printer and then Add from the screen in Figure 9.5.
2. Select Generic Remote Printer from the COAS Select Printer Model dialog box shown in Figure 9.7.

FIGURE 9.7
The COAS Select Printer Model dialog box.

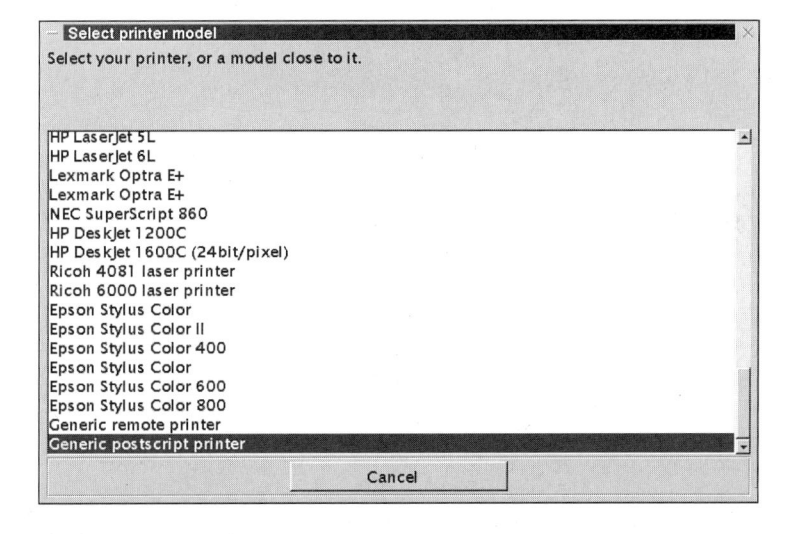

> **Note**
>
> Be very careful. Generic Remote Printer it is near the end of the list and and is followed by Generic PostScript Printer. If you don't select a remote printer, you will set up a local printer, which is not what you are trying to do here.

3. Give the remote printer a name in the COAS Name Printer dialog box show in Figure 9.8. It is a very good idea to give the remote printer a name that both indicates that it is remote and identifies its actual physical location. This is especially true when the "remote" printer is in fact local, but connected over the network.

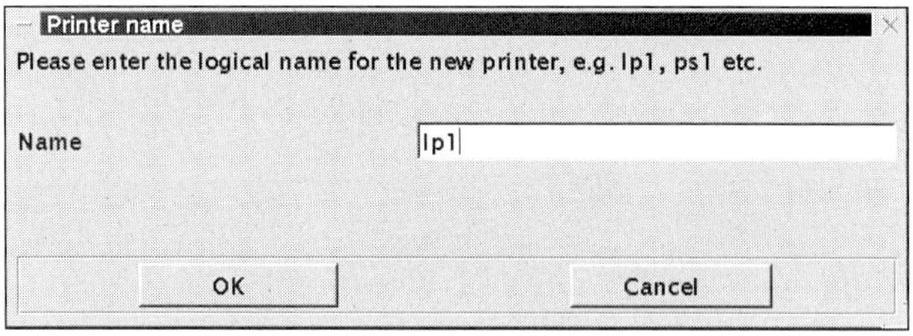

FIGURE 9.8
The COAS Name Printer dialog box.

4. Inform the spooler which remote host controls this printer and what the remote host calls this printer. (See Figure 9.9.)

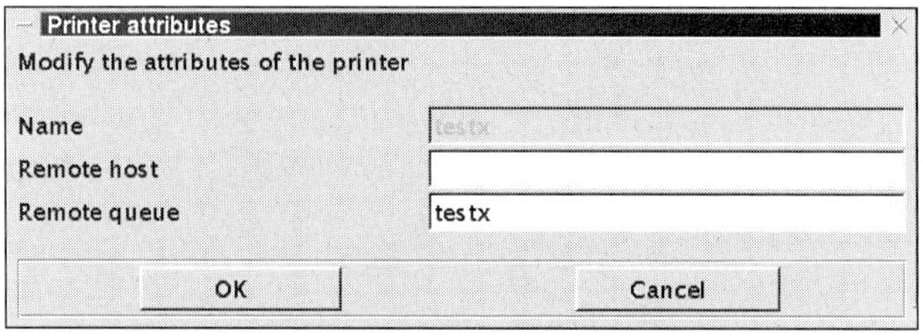

FIGURE 9.9
The COAS Remote Printer Attributes dialog box.

5. Save, Discard, or Cancel this printer entry from the confirmation screen that appears.

Printing That First Page over the Network

We are now ready to print that first page over the network. You can use several methods to accomplish this, depending on the type of network protocol you are using and how your network is connected.

If you are trying to print over a LAN using Samba, you can test the configuration of the Samba mount with the following command:

```
#testprns remotelp
```

whereyou replace *remotelp* with the actual name of the remote printer in your /etc/printcap file.

You should perform several other Samba tests, which are covered in Chapter 16 on Samba. However, if the preceding test works, then your remote printer will probably work also.

To print on a Samba attached printer, enter the following command:

`#smbclient //servername/printername`

You will be prompted for a password on `servername`, which in some instances must be in capital letters. After this you are off and running with a printer available over the network.

If we are trying to print over the network using TCP/IP, entering the following command *should* produce some printout on the remote printer:

`#lpr -PRemotePrinterName /etc/profile`

This will print the file `/etc/profile` (a file that is always present) on the remote printer *RemotePrinterName*.

Formatted Printing

If you are doing just junk printing, everything we have done so far is just fine, but I guess we could save a few trees by limiting the junk printing we do.

The alternative to junk printing is nonjunk printing (also known as formatted printing). Formatted printing is useful when we have a long printout where we need page numbers (ever played 357 pickup?) or headers and footers. Another instance where the ability to add information to each page of a printout would be beneficial is where we wish to have an eyes-only or confidential notice printed on each page of a printout.

If you are using a word processor, this is often very easy. However, you usually don't print out financial records or customer lists with a word processor.

One very effective solution to these issues is the `pr` command. It is found in many versions of UNIX and provides a plethora of options to meet your every need.

For example, the following command:

`# pr -h Public Information -o 20 < pr --help | lpr`

will give you a nicely formatted page with "Public Information" at the top (along with time and date) containing the help list for the `pr` command.

A little explanation is in order. The first part of the command to be executed is `pr --help`, which produces the help list for the `pr` command. This text is piped into the `pr` command at the beginning of the line `pr -h Public Information -o 20`. Not only will it produce formatted output of the input text with a header containing "Public Information" as well as other standard header information, but it will also give you a left margin of 20 spaces (for notes perhaps). The output of this `pr` command is then piped to the `lpr` spooler.

If you think this is more of a typing test than a tree saver, you are probably right. However, if you just add a +356 between the pr and the -h, this command would be:

```
pr +356 -h Public Information -o 20 < longprintout.txt | lpr
```

This command will truly save trees because you will start the printout with the 356th page of `longprintout.txt`. This page will, of course, have the proper header and page number.

Another command that is very useful for formatting text (and saving trees) is the `groff` command. This command is really a front end to the entire `groff` document formatting system and has extensive capabilities especially if you want to format a document for a specific device.

The version of `groff` that is delivered with Caldera supports the following target devices:

- PostScript Printers
- TeX dvi devices
- Several X11 viewers (at 75 and 100 dpi)
- Typewriter-like devices
- Typewriter-like devices using the ISO Latin-1 Character Set
- PCL5 compatible printers

Yet Another formatting command is `troff`. When you require formatting containing fractional point sizes and numeric expressions as might be contained in a physics or mathematics thesis, `troff` is most useful.

Using Your Printer with Other Applications

Caldera OpenLinux comes bundled with WordPerfect 8 for Linux, which is covered along with other word processing packages in Chapter 25. In order to set up the printer to work with WordPerfect, Select the K-Gear icon in the corner, highlight applications, and click on WordPerfect.

On the WordPerfect logo window, select Program and then Printer Control.

In the Printer Control dialog box shown in Figure 9.10, you can administer WordPerfect printers.

FIGURE 9.10
WordPerfect Printer Control dialog box.

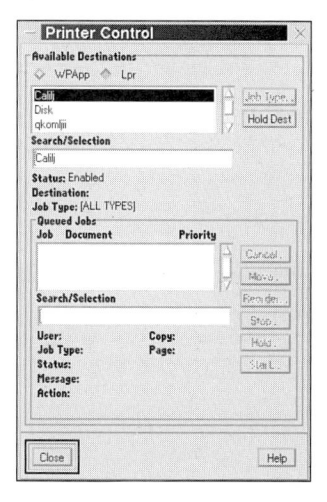

In this dialog box, you can select the destination of any WordPerfect print job and hold that printer so that other applications don't interfere with your printer setup by WordPerfect.

In addition, you can view the current WordPerfect print queue and optionally cancel the print job, move it to another printer, reorder the print jobs, stop a print job, or hold a print job.

You can also check the status of a print job by clicking on the print job and then the Status button.

Caldera OpenLinux also comes bundled with Star Office 5.0. Setting up the printers for this application is handled in the dialog box shown in Figure 9.11.

FIGURE 9.11
The Star Office Printer Installation dialog box.

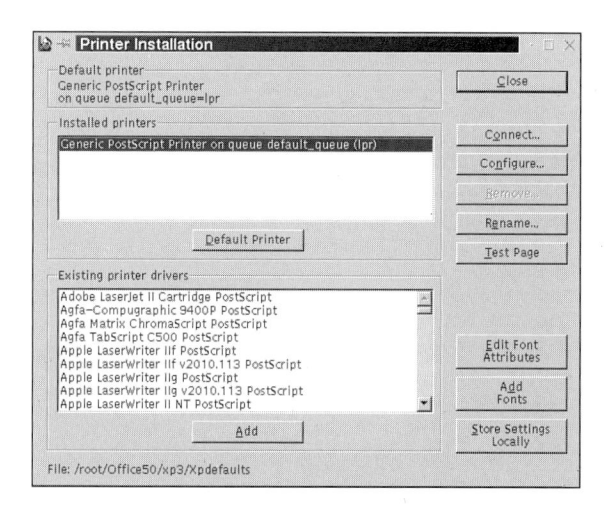

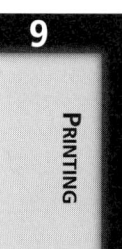

The defaults for this application will work for most printers right out of the box. As you can see, many options that can improve the performance of Star Office are possible. Those of you who wish to use the faxing capabilities of Star Office under Caldera OpenLinux need to explore some of these options.

To start with, if you highlight the printer and click on the Connect button on the Printer Installation dialog box, the Connect dialog box shown in Figure 9.12 will be displayed on your monitor.

FIGURE 9.12
The Star Office Printer Connect dialog box.

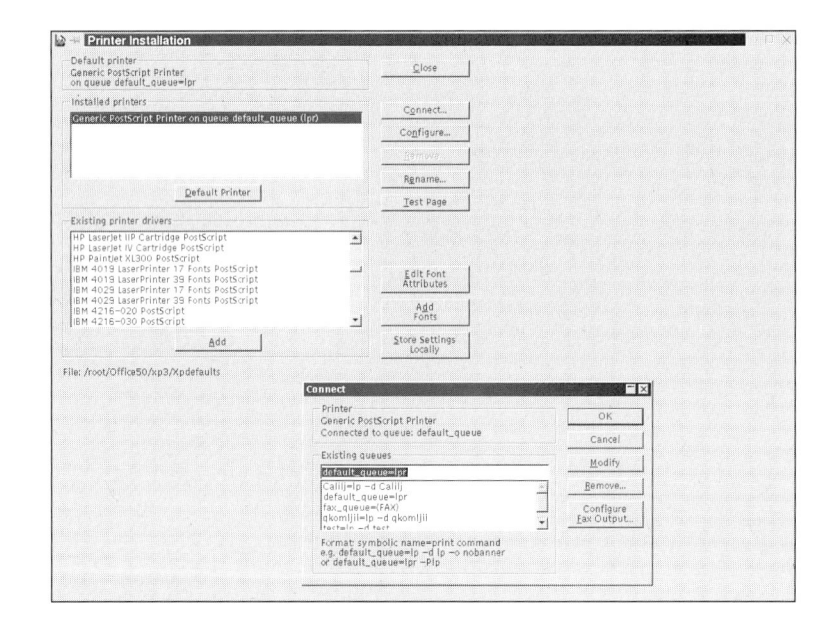

This dialog box allows you to modify or remove printer queues and to configure fax output from Star Office.

If you select Configure fax, you will be taken to an entry box that allows you to select printing to a file or to a pipe and to enter the specific fax command for use by Star Office. The Star Office documentation will provide you with additional information on the specifics of the fax printing options.

Useful Print Capability Enhancing Programs (and Where to Find Them)

One of the most useful printing tools gives you the ability to print multiple pages of your documents on a single sheet of paper (saving trees again). This tool is `mpag`, which is available from:

`http://www.userfriendly.net/linux/RPM/turbolinux/1.2/RPMS/mpage-2.4-1.i386.html`

Note that archives use the `-z` suffix to mean `.Z`; in other words, this file is compressed using `compress` not `gzip`. This command not only speeds up printing considerably but also saves trees.

Another useful program is `nenscript`, which will format an ASCII file, convert it to PostScript, and then allow you to select many options such as print in landscape or portrait mode, with one or two columns, with or without headers. `nenscript` can be found at:

`http://www.im.lcs.mit.edu/magnus/nenscript/`

Some Secrets of the Guru (Junior Division)

When all else fails, sometimes it is useful to check out Grant Taylor's Linux Printing HOWTO Homepage, which can be found at

`http://www.picante.com/~gtaylor/pht/`

Another very good site to visit if you are attempting to print from Linux to a Windows 95 sited printer is:

`http://home1.pacific.net.sg/~harish/linuxprint.html`

And a final site for the guru (Junior Division) that contains most of the packages you would ever want (including the printing packages) is:

`http://www.shopthenet.net/publiclibrary/RPM/Groups.html`

which has all the packages sorted by function.

Summary

Unfortunately for the trees, humans still want to print out just about everything and then they usually file it. Consequently, setting up a printer on Caldera OpenLinux is a necessity.

With the onset of useful PostScript devices and the excellent support for these devices under Caldera OpenLinux, we may have a chance in the future to just keep things on the hard disk and display them on the screen. But today we can't and so we print.

Printing on Caldera is straightforward, even though it has many steps to set it up (all of which it inherited from UNIX) and many options after it is set up.

In this chapter, we set up the hardware for the printer and verified that the kernel driver was installed. We also looked at how to use COAS to work with your printer and LISA to modify the installation. We briefly outlined all the programs and files used by the printing system and discussed adding a remote printer and setting it up. Finally, we explored sources of additional information regarding printing and the print spooler.

CHAPTER 10

OpenLinux Administration Tools

IN THIS CHAPTER

- File System Organization *232*
- Console Administration Tools *238*
- Caldera Open Administration System *247*
- COAStool *247*

This chapter covers the basics of administering an OpenLinux installation. First, we'll look at the system's directory structure, known as the file system, and then we'll explore some command-line tools and the excellent graphic administration tools included in Caldera OpenLinux.

File System Organization

OpenLinux mostly follows the Linux file system standard (FSSTND—complete description available at `http://www.pathname.com/fhs/`) and is thus a well-organized system. One feature of FSSTND is that the root directory (`/`) is very clean and only holds the most essential files. Immediately after installation, your root directory should look something like this:

```
auto/   bru/   home/     lib/          net/    root/   usr/
bin/    dev/   initrd/   lost+found/   opt/    sbin/   var/
boot/   etc/   install/  mnt/          proc/   tmp/    vmlinuz
```

The following sections cover the types of files contained in most of these directories.

Essentials of `/bin` and `/sbin`

Most of the essential programs for using and maintaining OpenLinux are stored in the `/bin` and `/sbin` directories. The *bin* in the names of these directories comes from the fact that executable programs are binary files.

The `/bin` directory holds most of the user programs that are essential to getting the system up and running, such as:

- login
- Shells (`bash`, `tcsh`)
- File manipulation utilities (`cp`, `mv`, `rm`, `ln`, `tar`)
- Editors (`ed`, `vi`)
- File system utilities (`dd`, `df`, `mount`, `umount`, `sync`)
- System utilities (`uname`, `hostname`, `arch`)

In addition to these types of programs, the `/bin` directory also contains GNU utilities such as `gzip` and `gunzip`.

The `/sbin` directory holds essential maintenance or system programs, such as:

- `fsck`
- `fdisk`

- `mkfs`
- `shutdown`
- `lilo`
- `init`

The main difference between the programs stored in `/bin` and `/sbin` is that nearly all the programs in `/sbin` are intended for use by root for system administration and startup; many cannot be executed by regular users. By default, the `/sbin` and `/usr/sbin` directories are not included in a normal user's PATH.

Configuration Files in `/etc`

The `/etc` directory is normally used to store systemwide configuration files required by many programs. Some of the important files in `/etc` are as follows:

- `passwd`
- `shadow`
- `fstab`
- `hosts`
- `inittab`
- `otd`
- `profile`
- `shells`
- `services`
- `lilo.conf`

> **Note**
>
> Manually editing these files is generally not recommended and probably not needed because OpenLinux offers both command-line and graphical tools for administering users.

The first two files in this list, `/etc/passwd` and `/etc/shadow`, are authentication files, which are explained later in this chapter.

The next file on the list, `/etc/fstab`, contains a list of devices the system knows how to mount automatically. This is the file system table. A line from this file looks something like the following:

```
/dev/hda1         /                   ext2        defaults 1 1
```

The first part, /dev/hda1, indicates the device to mount (in this case the first partition of the internal hard drive, hda). The second part, /, indicates where to mount the device. The entry ext2 indicates what type of file system the device contains, and the rest of the entries are mount options. (The default options are specified for this device. There are many other options; see the mount command's man page for details.)

This file contains at least two other entries, one for swap and another for /proc. On many systems, /etc/fstab also contains entries for CD-ROMs, floppy disks, zip disks, and other mountable media. To add, delete, or change mount information, use the Caldera OpenLinux Administration System (COAS) File Systems menu entry (type **coastool** at a command prompt, then choose File Systems from the menu).

The file /etc/hosts contains a list of IP addresses and the corresponding hostnames (and aliases). This list is used to resolve the IP address of a machine when its name is given. A sample entry might look like this:

```
# IP address        the hostname                host alias
206.202.56.3        consider.theneteffect.com   consider www
```

The /etc/inittab, or system initialization table, is another important file under the /etc directory. This text file contains directions for how you normally start Linux.

/etc/motd is the file in which the system administrator puts the message of the day (hence the name motd). Usually it contains information related to the system, such as scheduled downtime or upgrades of software, but it can contain anything. The contents of this file are usually displayed at login.

/etc/profile is the default initialization file for users whose shell is either sh or bash (the default shell for OpenLinux). Mostly it is used for settings variables such as PATH and PS1 (for Bourne shells), along with such things as the default umask. The /etc/profile file is not meant to be used in place of personal initialization files and should be kept small because it is used by scripts as well as users. See Chapter 3 for additional information.

The file /etc/shells also pertains to shells. It is a list of "approved" shells for users. One of its primary uses is to prevent people from accidentally changing their shells to something unusable.

/etc/services contains a list of the services that run on the various ports on the system. The entries will look something like this:

```
telnet          23/tcp
http            80/tcp
```

The first entry is the name of the service, the second entry is the port on which the service runs, and the final entry is the type of service. From the preceding lines you can see that Telnet runs on port 23 and HTTP runs on port 80, which are the standard ports for those services.

The last file on the list is /etc/lilo.conf. This file contains a description of the behavior of the system at boot time, along with a list of all of the bootable images on the system.

Two important subdirectories are also in /etc: X11 and rc.d. The X11 subdirectory of /etc contains the configuration files for the X display managers (such as xdm and kdm), the window managers such as twm, and the font server (xfs). Most window manager packages add their configuration files into a directory located under /etc/X11. An exception to this would be X desktop environments, such as KDE (which puts all its files in /opt/kde/). The X server configuration file is /etc/XF86Config.

The rc.d subdirectory of /etc contains initialization scripts that run when Linux is started or shut down. Some of the scripts contain commands to load modules; others handle general boot behavior.

In addition to the files discussed, many other configuration files are found in the /etc directory.

/home

The /home directory is where all home directories for all users on a system are stored. This includes home directories for actual users (people) and for users such as FTP or HTTPD.

/mnt

By convention, the /mnt directory is the directory under which other file systems, such as DOS, network-mounted NFS file systems, or removable media such as CD-ROMs, floppy disks, zip disks, or Jaz disks, are mounted. Usually the /mnt directory contains a number of subdirectories, each of which is a mount point for a particular device type. Your /mnt directory may look like this:

```
cdrom/     dos/     floppy/     zip/
```

By using subdirectories under /mnt to house all of your mounted media, you keep the / directory clean.

/tmp and /var

The /tmp and /var directories are used to hold temporary files or files with constantly varying content.

The /tmp directory is usually a dumping ground for files that only need to be used briefly and can afford to be deleted at any time. It usually is quite unstructured, but on a multiuser system, most users abide by the convention of creating a personal directory (given the same as their username) in /tmp for storing their temporary files. The most common use of /tmp (other than as a location for throwaway files) is as a starting point for building and installing programs.

The /var directory is a bit more structured than /tmp and usually looks something like this:

```
adm/
catman/
lib/
lock/
log/
nis/
run/
spool/
state/
tmp/
```

Of these directories, the /var/log directory is one with which all users should be familiar, because most of the messages generated by the system are stored in it. Your /var/log may look like this:

```
httpd/
kdm
lastlog
lastlog.01
mail
mail.01.gz
majordomo/
messages
messages.01.gz
news.all
samba.d/
secure
secure.01.gz
spooler
uucp/
vbox/
wtmp
wtmp.01
xferlog
```

Of these files, `messages` is most helpful when attempting to diagnose system problems, as it contains all system messages since the system was first booted.

For example, one helpful way to diagnose problems, such as establishing a Point-to-Point Protocol (PPP) connection, is to use the tail command to continuously display the last few lines of /var/log/messages like this:

```
# tail -f /var/log/messages
```

/usr

By convention, the /usr directory is where most programs and files directly relating to users of the system are stored. It is in some ways a miniversion of the / directory. Your /usr directory might look like this:

```
X11R6/
bin/
dict/
doc/
games/
i386 linux/
include/
info/
java/
lib/
libexec/
local/
man/
openwin/
sbin/
share/
src/
```

The contents of several of these directories are briefly described in the following paragraphs.

The /usr/bin and /usr/sbin directories hold the vast majority of the executables available on a system. The function and type of the executables placed into these directories follow the same general convention as for /bin and /sbin. However, in many cases, unless you are logged in as the root operator, you won't often be able to run commands from the /usr/sbin or /sbin directories, because these programs might act on important system files.

The /usr/opt or /opt directories under Linux are equivalent to the /opt directory in Solaris. Optional software packages are usually installed in /opt; for example, the Star Office Suite and the latest version of WordPerfect for Linux are both stored under the /opt directory.

The /usr/X11 and /usr/X11R6 directories and subdirectories contain nearly all of the X Window–related files, such as man pages, libraries, and executables. OpenLinux systems contain only /usr/X11R6, the sixth revision of the X Window version 11.

The /usr/local directory is the location where local programs, man pages, and libraries are installed. At many sites, most of the directories in /usr are kept the same on every computer, but anything that needs to be installed on a particular machine is placed in /usr/local, thus identifying these files as local files and making maintenance of large numbers of systems easier.

Finally, one of the most useful directories under /usr is /usr/dict, where the local dictionary for the system, called /usr/dict/ words, is stored. Most versions of /usr/dict/ words contain about 45,000 words, but some can be as large as 100,000 words or more. In OpenLinux, the words file is a symbolic link to the file linux.words. The main dictionary for OpenLinux's default spelling checker, ispell, resides under the usr/lib/ispell directory, but you can force ispell to use /usr/dict/words with the -L command-line option.

Console Administration Tools

Linux is remarkably flexible in the ways it can be administered. Even though OpenLinux includes a wealth of capable graphical tools (explained in the next section), it can be administered equally well (and in many instances better) from the command line. Indeed, one of the many superior qualities of UNIX systems is that they can be administered from half a world away in exactly the same manner, and to the same capacity, as if you were sitting right in front of it.

This section on console administration will touch on the tools you'll need to do the basics: add and remove users, schedule jobs, and start and stop system services. Nearly all the same tasks can be accomplished using the COAS graphical tools. If you have the need (for example, for remote administration of your OpenLinux system), or just want to learn the "real" UNIX way of doing things, though, this section should get you well under way.

User Management

One of the main jobs in System Administration, particularly at large sites, turns out to be dealing with user accounts: adding them, deleting them, and changing them. Originally dealing with user accounts was a time-consuming and largely irritating task that had to be done by hand; however, now a number of tools largely automate the procedure.

The files that contain most of the login-related information and control login and account creation follow:

- `/etc/passwd`   This file holds user account information. Login name, user ID (UID), group ID (GID), full name, home directory, and login shell are all here.
- `/etc/shadow`   This file holds the users' encrypted passwords, as well as information about password expiration.
- `/etc/group`   This file holds group information (group ID), group members, and a field for rarely used group passwords.
- `/etc/login.defs`   This file holds default information for the creation of new logins. You can set password expiration, group IDs, default shells, and a range of other options here.
- `/etc/pam.d/`   This directory holds the Pluggable Authentication Module (PAM) configuration information for individual login tools. An entire book could be written about PAM alone because it is quite complex. If you are interested in all the options, look at the documentation in `/usr/doc/libpam-0.66/`. Until you have done that and feel confident that you understand the subject, it is recommended you leave these files alone.
- `/etc/skel/`   This directory holds the default configuration files for the creation of user home directories. These are the initial dot files (so named because they are preceded by a period) that are copied to a new user's home directory.

Programs for User Management

Outlines of the following figures are used for creating, deleting, and configuring user logins:

`/usr/sbin/useradd`   This program adds individual new users and can set various defaults for them on the command line. In the absence of command-line options, it reads defaults from /etc/login.defs. Its options follow:

-u	UID—Set the numeric user ID from the command line.
-g	group—Set the group ID from the command line.
-m	If the user's home directory does not already exist, create it.
-d	home directory—Set user's home directory to value on command line rather than append user's login name to default `<rootdir>` (generally set to `/home` in `/etc/login.defs`).
-s	shell—Set login shell from command line.
-r	rootdir—Set root of home directory (that is, don't put directory in `/home`).

`-e`	expire date—Absolute date the password will expire in day/month/year (dd/mm/yyyy) format.
`-f`	inactive period—Days of inactivity after the password has expired before the account is locked out.
`name`	The login name to use for this account.
`-D`	display default values from `/etc/login.defs`—Requires no login name argument.

`/usr/sbin/userdel` This program removes the specified user from the system authentication files (`/etc/passwd`, `/etc/shadow`, `/etc/group`). In most other versions of UNIX, this program will take a `-r` argument telling it to remove the user's home directory as well. OpenLinux's version does not, so you need to remove the home directory yourself.

`/usr/sbin/usermod` This program will alter the login information for a user. The user must not be logged in or executing programs when you run this command. It takes the following command-line arguments:

`-u`	Change the user's numeric UID.
`-c`	Add comment to the user's `/etc/passwd` entry; this is normally the user's full name.
`-g`	Set user's initial group.
`-G`	Add user to additional groups, specified after the `-G`.
`-d`	home directory—Change the user's home directory to another directory, specified after the `-d`.
`-m`	If this is given along with `-d`, then the current directory of the user will be copied to the new location.
`-e`	expire date—Set the account expiration to expire on this date (mm/dd/yyyy).
`-f`	inactive period—Set period of inactivity before account is locked following expiration of the password.
`-l`	login name—Change the user's login name.
`-s`	Change the user's default shell.
`name`	The login name to make changes to.

`/usr/bin/passwd` Allows you to change a user password. Only root may change another user's password. Normal users are prompted for their current password before being allowed to change it. The program requests the new password and then requires you to correctly retype it before accepting it.

`/usr/bin/chfn` This program changes a user's "finger" information. This is personal information for the user: full name, office, telephone numbers, and the like.

Invoked with a login name, it will interactively request the new information. You can just hit return for any field you do not want to update.

/usr/bin/chsh   This program changes a user's default shell. This will allow you to change a user's shell to any in the /etc/shells file.

Services

UNIX systems largely work on the model of separate, individually configurable programs, each doing a specific job. There is no monolithic master program that is and does everything. It's all spread out and available to change in whatever way you see fit—as long as you're willing to get your hands a little dirty.

Programs that normally start when the system boots, run in the background, and provide some service to the system or system users are generally referred to as *daemons* (pronounced demons). It's a very loose definition; really the only requirement is that the program background itself and run until explicitly stopped. Most of the programs that define how the system operates and what functions it performs fully meet the first definition, however. Largely, though again this is no requirement, these daemons live in /usr/sbin, store their configuration files in /etc, and generally store their process IDs in a file in /var/run.

Take for example syslogd (the system event logger). The daemon itself is /usr/sbin/syslogd, its configuration file is /etc/syslog.conf, and it maintains a PID file /var/run/syslogd.pid.

The process by which an OpenLinux (or any UNIX) system boots and the services it provides are largely controlled by a program called init. In OpenLinux, init lives in /sbin. It is the very first program that the Linux system starts upon boot, and it controls how all other processes start, run, and stop. Basically all UNIX systems work under the assumption that there are different "levels" of system operation and that the processes that run in each level are or can be different. These are called *runlevels*, and there are two main models for defining runlevels: the BSD model and the System V model.

The BSD model is the simpler of the two; it has fewer configuration files and fewer runlevels. The System V model is somewhat more complicated; this is the one OpenLinux and most other Linux distributions use. In the SysV model there are several numbered runlevels, and each runlevel has a specfic meaning to the system. These are the runlevels as used in OpenLinux:

- *runlevel 0*   This is the runlevel a system goes to when it is shut down. It is intended for use when one needs to remove power from a system.
- *runlevel 1*   This is the single-user mode—no networking is set up, and no system daemons are run. This is intended as a system maintenance mode.

- *runlevel 2*   This traditionally means normal multiuser state, except no NFS or other networking services are run. Basically, it is a state where you can access the network, but others can't access your services.
- *runlevel 3*   This is the normal multiuser mode—all system and network services that are configured are started. This is the normal runlevel for systems not running X logins.
- *runlevel 4*   This is an undefined state. OpenLinux treats this exactly as level 3.
- *runlevel 5*   Multiuser plus X Display Manager—all configured system and network services are run. Additionally, the xdm or kdm program is started to allow X logins from the console (and possibly remotely, depending on setup).
- *runlevel 6*   This is the runlevel a system goes to when it is rebooted.
- *runlevel s/S*   This is another name generally for single-user mode.

The /etc/inittab file controls how or whether each of these runlevels is entered. This controls the very early portion of the boot process. It generally tells init to run a few crucial programs; then it tells init what the default runlevel will be. It also holds configuration information for the programs that control the Linux console (gettys). In OpenLinux, your default runlevel is likely to be 5, unless you haven't set up X, in which case it should be 3.

After all the kernel setup is done, init switches into its default runlevel and starts up the daemons that should run there. This process is controlled by files under the /etc/rc.d/ directory. Basically, for every runlevel there is an rcN.d directory, where N is equal to the runlevel number. So all the files in /etc/rc.d/rc3.d/ would be run when the system goes to runlevel 3.

In fact, it's all a bit more complicated than this. (Somehow you just knew that, didn't you?) The actual control files for the daemons reside in /etc/rc.d/init.d/. The files in the various rcN.d directories are actually symbolic links back to the files in /etc/rc.d/init.d/ so that init can be cued on which order to start things and whether to start or stop things at all. Here is an example—the listing of the /etc/rc.d/rc2.d/ directory:

```
K09samba     K40rstatd    K70ntp         S05syslog    S40cron      S99rmnologin
K25gpm       K44dhcpd     K73ipxripd     S05urandom   S41atd       S99skipped
K25httpd     K47rusersd   K79nis-client  S26ipx       S75keytable  S99zap
K30logoutd   K48rwhod     K85inet        S30amd       S98local
K39rwalld    K50mta       S01network     S35lpd       S99bigfs
```

If the command is preceded by a K, the daemon is killed; if it is preceded by an S, the daemon is started. The numbers are used to order things—S30amd is started before S98local, for example.

The really nice thing about the system is the /etc/rc.d/init.d/ directory. If you want to start and stop system services after everything is up and running, you don't have to look around anywhere, you can just do this:

```
$ /etc/rc.d/init.d/ntp stop
```

or

```
$ /etc/rc.d/init.d/ntp start
```

Now if you desire to change what and how things start at system boot, all you have to do is either change the ordering in the /etc/rc.d/rcN.d directories or change an S to a K. The configuration files for the scripts in /etc/rc.d/init.d are stored in /etc/sysconfig/daemons. By altering things in those directories, you can completely change how the system boots by hand.

Of course, you should know that altering those files is a wonderful way of rendering your system completely unbootable until some nice Linux guru comes by to fix it for you. That said, there is a remarkable amount of power and control concentrated among those few programs, so it is certainly good to know how it all works. You'll never become a Linux guru yourself without knowing.

Task Scheduling

One of the conveniences of Linux and UNIX systems is how easy it is to schedule the system to do work when you aren't there. Many tasks are set up by the system to take care of things in the middle of the night when they won't bother you. You can also take advantage of this. Most of this scheduling is done using two programs: crontab and at.

crontab is the user interface to the cron daemon. The cron daemon runs all the time and reads system and user configuration files to determine when it has a job to run. Using crontab, you can schedule programs for crond to run at any time in the future and at regular intervals.

If you just run the crontab program, it will start up an editor for you to write your schedule with. You can also feed it a file directly that already has your schedule in it. You can list your file with the -l option and change your editor with the -e option. Personal crontabs created with the crontab program have the following syntax:

```
[minute]  [hour]   [day of month]  [month]    [day of week]  [command to run]
0-59      0-23     0-31            0-12       0-7
                                   [or name]  [or name]
```

Each of the individual fields can be replaced by an asterisk (*) to mean run on any of these. For the month and day of week fields that accept names, just use the first three letters of the name. So an example of running a command at 5:45 a.m. every Thursday in July would be:

```
45 05 * Jul Thu command_to_run
```

There are also system crontabs in the file /etc/crontab and in the directories under /etc/cron.d/. These system crontabs add a user field—who to run the program as—between day of week and command. So for a command that needs to be run as root from a system crontab, the previous example would become:

```
45 05 * Jul Thu root command_to_run
```

at is a command that is used to run a particular program at one particular point in the future. The at command will not repeat commands indefinitely like cron. The syntax of at is somewhat friendlier than that of crontab; it will accept most time formats, and even "natural language" words for times. The following are some examples:

```
at midnight command_to_run

at 2pm Aug 2 command_to_run

at 11:45am Jan 2 2000 command_to_run
```

The command atq will list the invoking user's jobs and when they are scheduled to run. atrm will remove the specified job number, which you can get by examining the output of an atq command.

Kernel Administration with /proc

/proc is your friend. With the Linux kernels, the pseudofiles in the /proc directory hold a wealth of diagnostic information and a simple means to set runtime parameters.

The most frequently useful /proc diagnostic files are as follows.

ppcpuinfo lists the processor type, speed, and other essential information about the computer hardware:

```
$ cat /proc/cpuinfo
processor    : 0
vendor_id    : GenuineIntel
cpu family   : 6
model        : 1
model name   : Pentium Pro
stepping     : 7
cpu MHz      : 199.436220
```

```
cache size      : 256 KB
fdiv_bug        : no
hlt_bug         : no
sep_bug         : no
f00f_bug        : no
fpu             : yes
fpu_exception   : yes
cpuid level     : 2
wp              : yes
flags           : fpu vme de pse tsc msr pae mce cx8 sep mtrr pge mca cmov
bogomips        : 199.07
```

ioports shows the starting and ending addresses of installed devices:

```
$ cat /proc/ioports
0000-001f : dma1
0020-003f : pic1
0040-005f : timer
0060-006f : keyboard
0070-007f : rtc
0080-008f : dma page reg
00a0-00bf : pic2
00c0-00df : dma2
00f0-00ff : fpu
01f0-01f7 : ide0
02f8-02ff : serial(auto)
0378-037a : parport0
03c0-03df : vga+
03e8-03ef : serial(auto)
03f6-03f6 : ide0
03f8-03ff : serial(auto)
ff80-ff9f : eth0
ffa0-ffa7 : ide0
ffa8-ffaf : ide1
```

interrupts maps IRQ lines to devices:

```
$ cat /proc/interrupts
           CPU0
   0:   50449731        XT-PIC  timer
   1:     594122        XT-PIC  keyboard
   2:          0        XT-PIC  cascade
   4:    1324260        XT-PIC  serial
   8:          1        XT-PIC  rtc
   9:     280466        XT-PIC  eth0
  13:          1        XT-PIC  fpu
  14:     304916        XT-PIC  ide0
 NMI:          0
```

`meminfo` shows memory usage on the system:

```
$ cat /proc/meminfo

            total:     used:     free:  shared: buffers:  cached:
Mem:  64913408  63381504   1531904 46358528  1388544 24969216
Swap: 66056192   7503872  58552320
MemTotal:    63392 kB
MemFree:      1496 kB
MemShared:   45272 kB
Buffers:      1356 kB
Cached:      24384 kB
SwapTotal:   64508 kB
SwapFree:    57180 kB
```

`pci` displays information about all PCI devices on the system:

```
$ cat /proc/pci

PCI devices found:
  Bus  0, device   0, function  0:
    Host bridge: Intel 82441FX Natoma (rev 2).
      Medium devsel.  Fast back-to-back capable.  Master Capable.  Latency=64.
  Bus  0, device   7, function  0:
    ISA bridge: Intel 82371SB PIIX3 ISA (rev 0).
      Medium devsel.  Fast back-to-back capable.  Master Capable.  No bursts.
  Bus  0, device   7, function  1:
    IDE interface: Intel 82371SB PIIX3 IDE (rev 0).
      Medium devsel.  Fast back-to-back capable.  Master Capable.  Latency=64.
      I/O at 0xffa0 [0xffa1].
  Bus  0, device  11, function  0:
    VGA compatible controller: S3 Inc. Vision 968 (rev 0).
      Medium devsel.  IRQ 11.
      Non-prefetchable 32 bit memory at 0xfa000000 [0xfa000000].
  Bus  0, device  17, function  0:
    Ethernet controller: Realtek 8029 (rev 0).
      Medium devsel.  IRQ 9.
      I/O at 0xff80 [0xff81]
```

`parport` contains directories for each parallel port and reports on the devices attached to each port:

```
$ cat /proc/parport/0/hardware

base:   0x378
irq:    none
dma:    none
modes:  SPP
```

Kernel and other low-level runtime parameters can be set through the `/proc/sys` pseudo-files. For example, to set the maximum number of file handles to a higher value, you can include a line in the boot scripts that echoes the new number directly into `/proc/sys/fs/file-max`.

Caldera Open Administration System

The Caldera Open Administration System (COAS) is a group of graphical tools that enable you to set most of the important services and functions of your machine without having to be familiar with all the many files. This is a major step forward in ease-of-use for UNIX. It should be noted that COAS has the ability to run with different graphical "front ends"—it can be run on the console or in X. We will provide screen captures of the X Window System/KDE version of COAS, but the console version is functionally identical.

COAStool

The program that provides the graphical interface for COAS is called COAStool. This program can be started, on console or in X, by simply typing its name. Most COAStool functions need root privilege, although you can certainly look around most of the features as a normal user, just to get a sense of it.

Starting COAStool this way gives access to all the same functions that the COAS menus in KDE do, with the addition of one item. This can be found in:

```
Network Administration -> TCP/IP Network Options
```

This allows for configuration of the basic state of networking on your workstation. Root privilege is required; it is recommended that you not alter the defaults without specific reason.

As shown in Figure 10.1, the available options are:

- *Networking*   This toggle switch (Enabled/Disabled) allows you to select whether you want any networking at all the next time you boot.
- *IP Forwarding*   This toggle switch (Enabled/Disabled) allows you to select whether network traffic will be forwarded between multiple network interfaces. It requires, obviously, that you have more than one network interface (that is, multiple ethernet interfaces, ethernet/ppp interfaces, and the like). Unless you intend for your computer to act as a router or firewall, it is strongly recommended that you leave this set to the default, Disabled.

FIGURE 10.1
Networking Options dialog box.

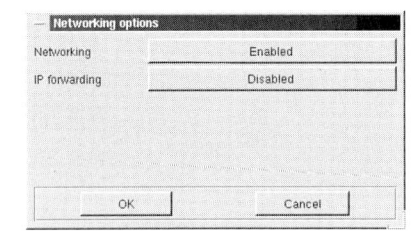

The COAS Menu

The COAS menu is denoted by the COAS menu icon on the KDE toolbar (or the COAS menu item on the KDE main menu). One nice thing about running COAStool from the KDE menu bar is that you can run in X/KDE as a normal user. The COAStool will start up a little program called the COAS su wrapper to get the root password from you, if the program you invoke needs that level of privilege. See Figure 10.2.

FIGURE 10.2
COAS su wrapper dialog box.

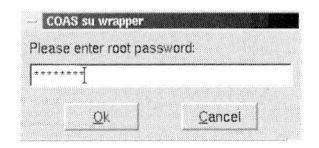

The COAS menus have the following structure:

```
Network ->
    TCP/IP ->
        NIS
        Resolver
    Ethernet Interfaces
Mail Transfer

Peripherals ->
    Keyboard
    Mouse
    Printer

System ->
    Accounts
    Daemons
    File system
    Hostname
    Resources
    Time
Kernel
Software
```

Each of these menu options is explained here.

- *Network*   This menu item opens the configuration dialog boxes and menus that control most of the functions of your workstation on the network.
- *TCP/IP*   These menu items can be used to control your workstation's basic networking functionality.

Network Information Service

Network Information Service (NIS) allows configuration of the NIS domain and options as shown in Figure 10.3. This is a Sun-originated protocol that has found fairly wide acceptance for large UNIX installations. In short, NIS can be used to provide a means for host and user locating and authentication. The specifics and setup can be (and generally are) quite complicated, and the need to configure this would probably apply only if you are trying to integrate your new OpenLinux box into a much larger UNIX population. If that is the case, you can use COAS to configure your box as an NIS client using the following dialog boxes and fields:

FIGURE 10.3

NIS Client/Server Setup dialog box.

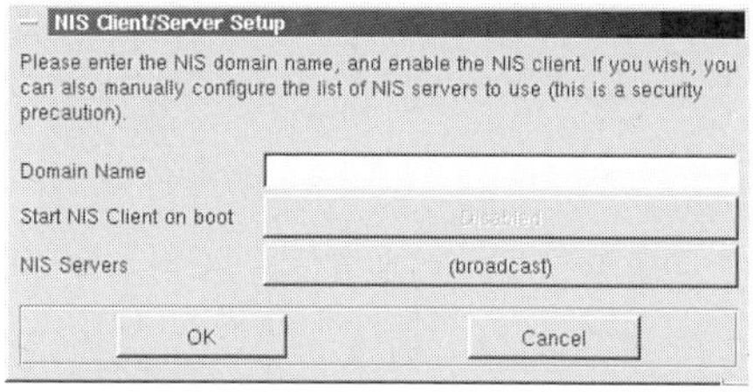

- *Domain Name*   NIS domain that your client box is to be part of. Note that this is probably different from your DNS domain name. If you think you need to enable the NIS configuration, make sure that you have all the correct information for these boxes before you start. Badly misconfiguring NIS on your box will cause grief for your Network Administrator and is likely to have unpleasant consequences on your health.
- *Start NIS Client on Boot*   Allows you to start `ypbind` on your workstation bootup. This allows you to take advantage of NIS services. If the Domain Name box is empty, this toggle box will be grayed out.
- *NIS Servers*   Normally set to broadcast so that it can detect any available NIS servers on the network. Using this dialog box you can manually set up to ten NIS servers that your client workstation will be allowed to bind to. See Figure 10.4.

FIGURE 10.4

NIS Servers dialog box.

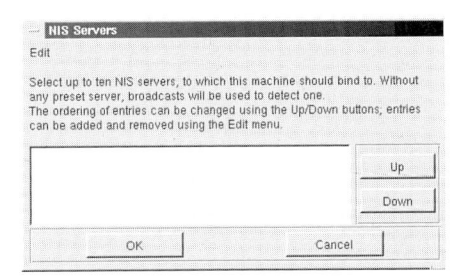

Note that the Resolver and Account dialog boxes (discussed later in this chapter) also can have some interaction with and effect on NIS. The Resolver section can control the order in which hostnames are looked up (NIS can be used to look up hostnames as well as DNS). The Account dialog boxes can enable NIS authentication lookups for usernames. See those sections of the chapter for more information.

Resolver

The Name Resolver Setup dialog box allows you to configure how the resolver library works on your workstation. The resolver converts IP addresses (the dotted quad number notation, such as 10.10.10.1, that computers use to identify other computers in a TCP/IP network) to hostnames and back again. The following fields can be used to configure it and are also shown in Figure 10.5.

FIGURE 10.5

Name Resolver Setup dialog box.

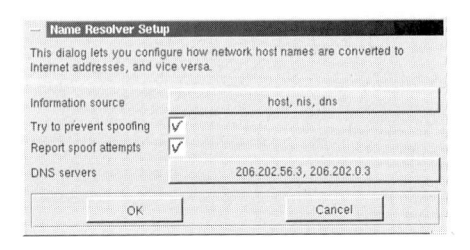

- *Information Source*   Pops up the Search Order dialog box, which is shown in Figure 10.6, when clicked. It allows you to configure the order in which various name resolution sources are queried and even to add or remove resolution sources.
    - `host`—Refers to the `/etc/hosts` file
    - `nis`—Refers to NIS resolution
    - `dns`—Refers to Domain Name Service resolution

FIGURE 10.6
Search Order dialog box.

- *Try to Prevent Spoofing*   Requires the resolver library to do two lookups when trying to determine what name belongs to an IP address. First, it requests the name that belongs to the IP address; then it requests the IP address that goes along with the name it just got back. They match most of the time; when they don't, it could mean that someone is trying to conceal her true identity (or at the least has poorly or wrongly configured his DNS). This technically toggles the `nospoof` option on/off in the /etc/host.conf file.
- *Report Spoof Attempts*   Enables logging of all DNS spoofing attempts to the system log (/var/log/messages by default). This technically toggles the `spoofalert` option on/off in the /etc/host.conf file.
- *DNS Servers*   Pops up the DNS Name Servers dialog box, shown in Figure 10.7, when clicked. Through the Edit menu item you can add, edit, or remove a name server, and you can use the Up and Down buttons to determine in what order the name servers are consulted.

FIGURE 10.7
DNS Name Servers dialog box.

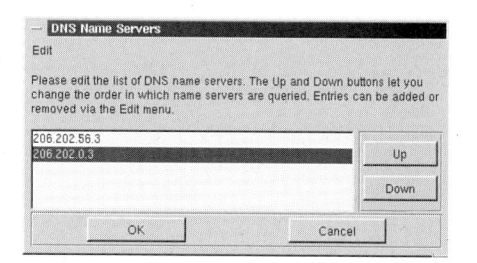

Peripherals
Keyboard
The Keyboard Configuration dialog box allows you to set the important control parameters for your keyboard, as shown in Figure 10.8.

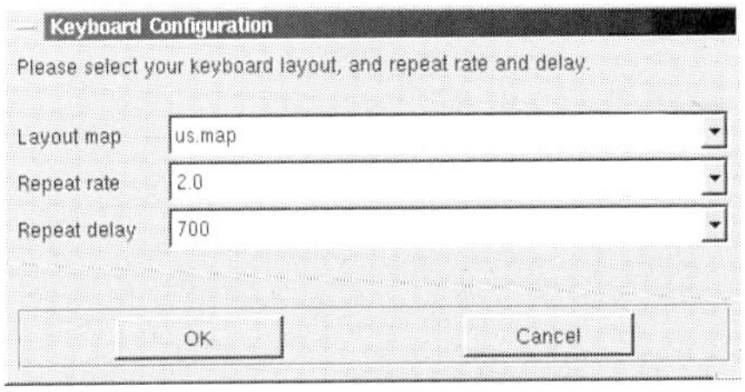

FIGURE 10.8
Keyboard Configuration dialog box.

- *Layout Map*   Enables you to choose between eight different keyboard mappings that match both the keyboard you use and your country of origin. Selections include U.S., French, German, and a number of other European language maps.
- *Repeat Rate*   Allows you to set the number of times a selected key repeats per second. The standard value for the Linux console is 30.0 cps. Adjust to personal taste.
- *Repeat Delay*   Allows you to adjust to your personal taste the milliseconds of delay before a key begins repeating. Standard value for the Linux console is 250 ms.

Mouse

You can configure the GPM program for using the mouse on the console with the GPM Mouse Configuration dialog box shown in Figure 10.9.

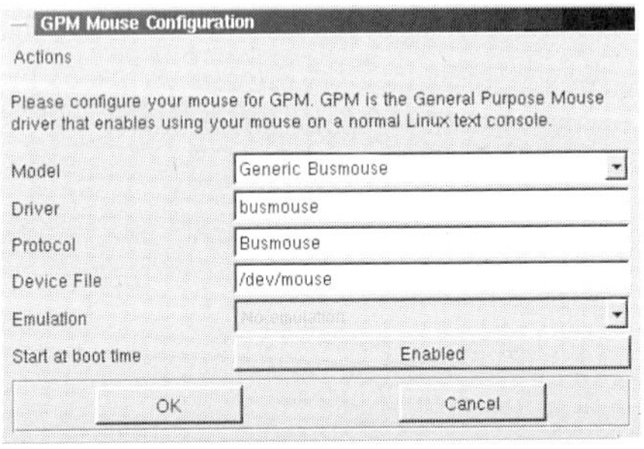

FIGURE 10.9
GPM Mouse Configuration dialog box.

> **Note**
>
> The GPM Mouse Configuration will not configure your mouse running in X. If you've started COAStool from the console, or want to configure GPM while you are still in X, then this is right. If you want to change mouse behavior in X, however, you should not be using this configuration tool—use XF86 setup or the KDE configuration tools instead.

The following options can be set in this dialog box:

- *Model*   Allows you to choose from nearly a dozen different mouse drivers. The most common drivers that are likely to be used are Microsoft Serial Mouse and PS/2 Mouse.
- *Driver*   Allows you to choose the module that will work with the model of mouse you select. It should not be necessary to set this, as it corresponds to the Model you choose. Possible options are serial, busmouse, and PS/2.
- *Protocol*   Indicates the language the mouse speaks. Again, this corresponds to the model you choose, so it should not be necessary to change this setting.
- *Device File*   Indicates which port this mouse is connected to. Normal values are /dev/mouse for MS protocol mouse, and /dev/psaux for PS/2 protocol mouse.
- *Emulation*   Allows you to emulate a three-button mouse by pressing button 1 and button 2 simultaneously to simulate the third button. This option is normally shaded, except when you select MS Serial Mouse.
- *Start at Boot Time*   Allows you to specify whether to start the GPM service at boot time (it must be started for mouse support to work on the console).

Printer

The Printer Configuration dialog box lets you create, edit, and delete new printers, as well as start and stop printing services. As shown in Figure 10.10, there are many options available.

FIGURE 10.10
Printer Configuration dialog box.

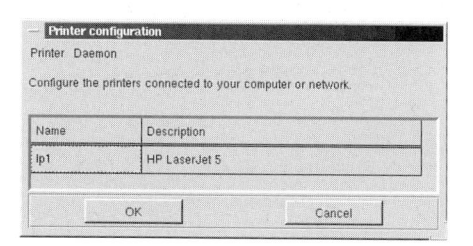

Printer Menu Item	
Edit	Lets you edit the current entry.
Add	Allows you to add a new printer to the system and configure it.
Remove	Allows you to delete the current selection.

Daemon Menu Item	
Start	Allows you to start printer services.
Stop	Allows you to stop printer services.

To add a new printer, select Add from the Printer menu. You are then asked to select your printer model (or a model similar to it), give it a name, and confirm its attributes (paper size, device). The only real thinking you have to do here is in choosing the printer model because the other defaults are generally correct. After the printer attributes are confirmed, you are asked to save the data and then whether to create a *print queue* (this is the intermediary directory where files are held waiting to go to the printer). Answer yes to both questions. The printer daemon will then be restarted, and your printer should work.

If the printer doesn't work as expected, or if you just want to change some of its configuration, select the printer and then choose Edit from the Printer menu. You will be presented with an extended list of printer attributes, as shown in Figure 10.11.

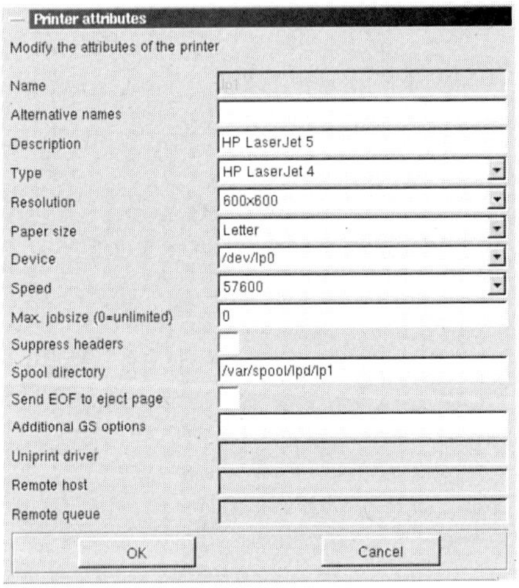

FIGURE 10.11
Printer Attributes dialog box.

- *Name* The printer name is chosen at original setup time and is not configurable.
- *Alternative Names* Lists other names by which the printer may be addressed.
- *Description* Lists the make and model as chosen during the initial setup.
- *Type* The printer type as it relates to Linux printing. This is frequently not the exact name of the printer but rather the class of printer. For example, choosing HP LaserJet III will allow printing to all LaserJet III family printers.

- *Resolution* The standard Horizontal × Vertical resolution you want the output to be. Normal values for Lasers and InkJets are generally 300 × 300 and 600 × 600.
- *Paper Size* Setting is generally Letter for the United States and A4 for Europe.
- *Device* The printer port to which your printer is attached. In UNIX, printers are generally referred to as `lp`-something (`lp` being a leftover from the old days of Line Printers). In Linux the ports are called `lpN`, where `N` is a number starting from 0 (LPT1 = `lp0`). The ports available to you are those autodetected by Linux, so if you only have one printer port you will only have one `lpN` entry from which to choose. There are also serial ports listed for the odd serial printer.
- *Speed* Setting for serial printers.
- *Max Jobsize* Allows you to set the maximum size for allowable print jobs. This is particularly useful for keeping remote printer users from sending huge print jobs to your printer. Sizes are in 1KB blocks.
- *Suppress Headers* Enables you to suppress headers. By default, the printing system will display a banner page or header to separate print jobs, which is useful in a multiuser environment. If you are the only person using the printer, however, it is a waste of paper, so you can check this box to suppress headers.
- *Spool Directory* Indicates the directory in which this printer will hold files waiting to be printed. This is generally set and created at original printer configuration time and should not be changed under normal conditions.
- *Send EOF to Eject Page* If your printer sometimes eats the last page you send, you need to check this option to send an additional end-of-file message to the printer.
- *Additional GS Options* Lists the printer drivers that OpenLinux uses to print with based upon the program GhostScript. This program has a myriad of options, which you can set here. Except under extraordinary conditions (or if you really know what you are doing), you shouldn't need to put anything here.
- *Uniprint Drive* Uniprint is a generic printer driver that allows you to specify an exact printer through assigning specific options. Unless you already know you need this, you probably don't (and unless you select the Uniprint driver from the Type menu, it will be grayed out anyway).
- *Remote Host* Name of the host to which the printer is attached. It is grayed out unless you selected Remote Printer from the Type menu.
- *Remote Queue* Name of the printer on the the remote host. It is grayed out unless you selected Remote Printer from the Type menu.

> **Note**
>
> If you edit the settings for one of your printers, you will need to manually stop and restart the printer service for the changes to take effect. You do this with the Daemon menu. First stop the printer daemon, and then start it. Your changes will then be in effect.

System

The system menus hold all the basic system administration tools.

Accounts

The User Accounts dialog box allows you to add, edit, and delete users from the system as well as to set login policies and defaults. There are a number of menu items, which are shown in Figure 10.12.

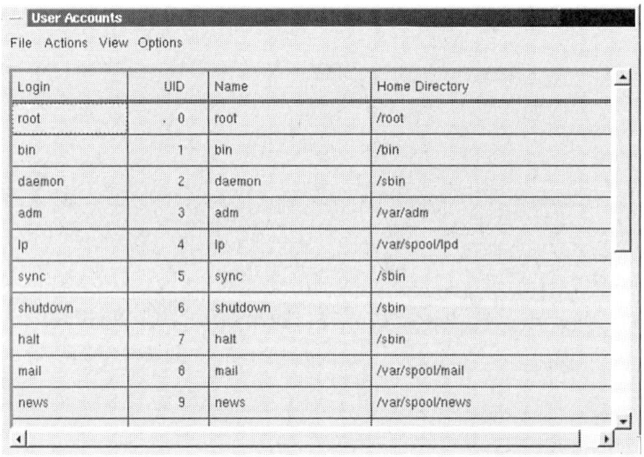

FIGURE 10.12
User Accounts dialog box.

- *File*   Allows you to exit.
- *Actions*   Allows you to Edit, Create, and Delete users.
- *View*   Allows you to view All users (including system accounts) or to limit the display to Regular users (normal users without any system privileges).
- *Options*   Allows you to set preferences, allow shadow passwords, and enable NIS lookups. Choosing Preferences pops up the Edit Preferences dialog box, which is shown in Figure 10.13.

FIGURE 10.13
Edit Preferences dialog box.

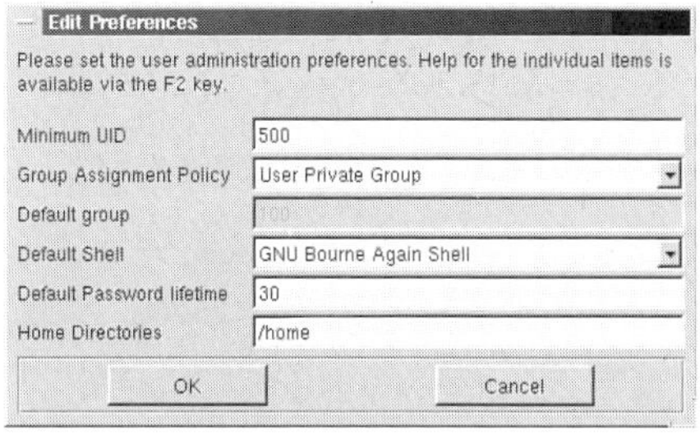

> *Preferences* Allows you to set preferences for creating all new user accounts.
>
> *Minimum UID* Indicates the minimum number that the user ID is allowed to be. All users are generally set to a higher ID (starting at 500 by default) to differentiate them from system accounts.
>
> *Group Assignment Policy* Determines whether every new user also gets his own group or whether they all get put into a single "users" group.
>
> *Default Group* Set to 100 (users) and is grayed out.
>
> *Default Shell* Indicates which shell users will have at first login.
>
> *Default Password Lifetime* Identifies the default period (in days) that passwords will last before users must replace them with new ones.
>
> *Home Directories* Indicates the base directory into which all new home directories will be put.

- *Disable Shadow Passwords* Converts shadow passwords (passwords held in a dedicated, protected file) back to the normal `passwd` format (password data in with user info and available for all to see in an encrypted format). Unless you have very specific reasons for doing this, and know the consequences, it is highly recommended you not disable shadow passwords.
- *Enable NIS Lookups* Turns on NIS user authentication. This isn't needed if you don't use NIS and, in fact, may slow things down and cause other problems. If you don't need it, don't turn it on.

To create a new account with COAS, open the Actions menu and select Create User. Type the new user's login name (the eight-letter name with which the system will identify the user). The Edit User dialog box shown in Figure 10.14 will appear.

FIGURE 10.14
Edit User dialog box.

- *Full Name*   Holds the user's real name.

   UID   User ID—Leave at the default value.

   Group ID   Leave at the default value.
- *Login Shell*   Set to the user's preference (probably GNU Bourne Again Shell).
- *Password*   Allows you to type in the user's password when clicked.
- *Home Directory*   Leave at the default. This is where all the user's personal files go.
- *Disabled*   Allows you to enable or disable a user account. Leave at Enabled on creation (there's not much point in creating a new account and disabling it immediately).
- *Shadow Information*   When clicked, pops up the Password Expiration dialog box (as shown in Figure 10.15), which can be used to set policies on passwords.

FIGURE 10.15
Password Expiration dialog box.

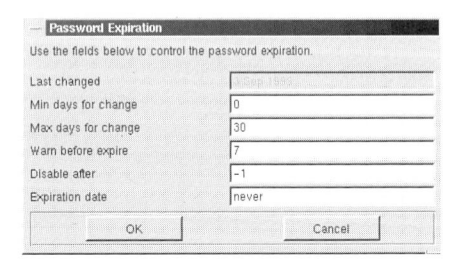

Last Changed   Should be set to current date and shaded.

Min Days for Change   Lists minimum number of days before user is allowed to change password (default of 0 means no minimum).

Max Days for Change   Lists maximum number of days a password is allowed to be used (default is 30 days). After this many days have passed without a password change, the user must change passwords before being allowed to log in.

Warn Before Expire Lists number of days before the password expires. The user will start getting warning messages telling her that her password is about to expire.

Disable After Indicates the number of days of inactivity after the password expires when the account will be disabled. The default setting of –1 means that the account won't actually be disabled.

Expiration Date Allows the administrator to set a particular date on which this account will expire. This date may be expressed in the MM/DD/YY format.

> **Note**
>
> Although there are many options, basically all you should have to do is set the user login name, full name, and perhaps shell and password. All the other defaults should provide a sane starting point.

Daemons

The System Services dialog box allows you to determine which services will be activated on each system bootup. As shown in Figure 10.16, boxes next to each service can be checked or unchecked. Many of the services have short but helpful comments next to each of them.

FIGURE 10.16
System Services dialog box.

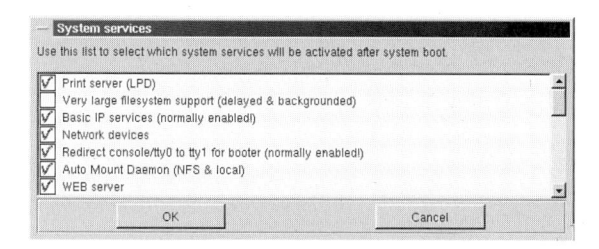

File Systems

The File System dialog box allows you to mount and unmount system devices, get information about devices already mounted or to be mounted, and configure mounts from NFS servers. (See Figure 10.17.)

FIGURE 10.17

File System dialog box.

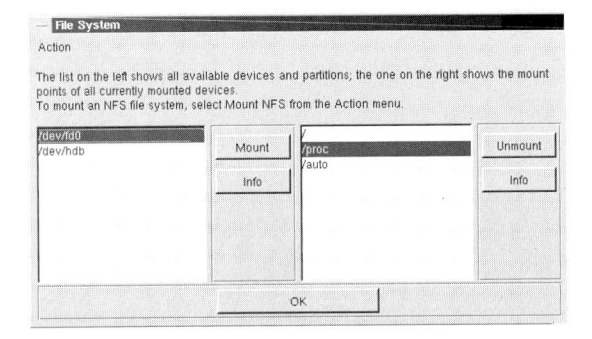

Items in the left pane are devices that are in `/etc/fstab` (the File System table) that aren't currently mounted. You can mount these by clicking on the Mount button to their immediate right.

Items in the right pane are devices that have already been mounted. You can unmount them by clicking on the Unmount button to their right.

Information about both mounted and unmounted devices can be received by highlighting the appropriate entry and clicking on the Info button to its right. This information shows the name of the actual system device (Device), the directory it is or would be mounted on (Directory), the type of file system (FS Type - `ext2`, `msdos`, `nfs`, and the like), and the options set for that mount (Options).

By opening the Action menu, you can add an NFS (Network File System) mount to your system.

The Mount File System dialog box shown in Figure 10.18 presents you with the following options:

FIGURE 10.18

Mount File System dialog box.

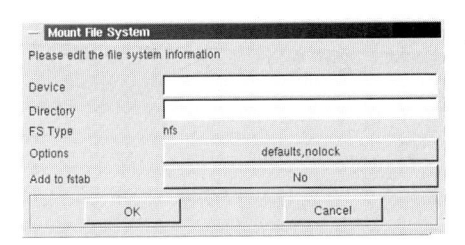

- *Device*   The server:/export pair that characterize NFS mounts.
- *Directory*   The directory you want the server:/export mounted into.
- *FS Type*   Set to nfs and noneditable.

- *Options* Launches the File System Options dialog box when clicked. See Figure 10.19. (These options fall outside the scope of the primer in this chapter. To find out more about this, see Chapter 15 or look at the `nfs(5)` man page.)

FIGURE 10.19
File System Options dialog box.

- *Add to fstab* This toggle switch determines whether you will add this mount to your /etc/fstab file and thereby try to remount this on every boot.

Hostname

The System Hostname dialog box shown in Figure 10.20 allows you to change the hostname of your computer. This should be a fully qualified name if you have a computer on the Internet where "fully qualified" means `hostname.domain.name`.

FIGURE 10.20
System Hostname dialog box.

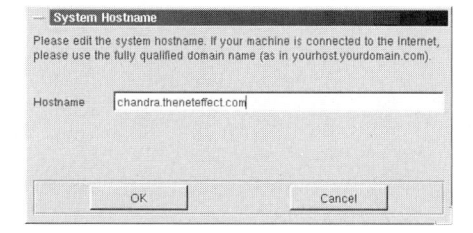

Resources

The Resources utility provides a wealth of useful information about your system, composed of information the kernel tracks during startup and while running.

The System Resource Information dialog box shown in Figure 10.21 initially starts up with all the information available about the system CPU. By selecting the Info menu you can get access to many more pieces of information:

FIGURE 10.21
System Resource Information dialog box.

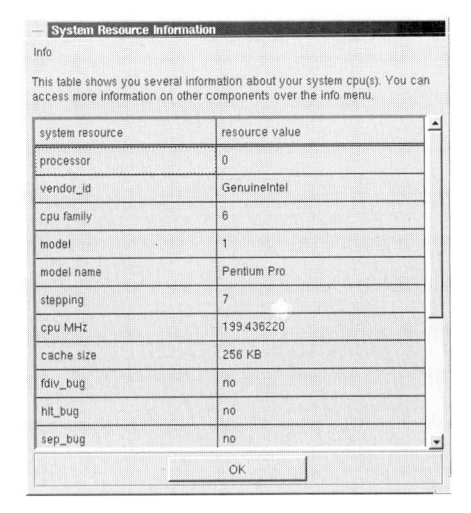

- *Block Devices* Lists the block devices available to the system such as floppies (fd) and harddrives (ide/scsi). Also lists a Major number (number the kernel uses to keep track of its devices).

- *Character Devices* Lists the available character devices such as serial ports (ttyS) and printers (lp). Also lists a Major number.

- *Interrupts* Shows all the interrupts in use on your system, what they belong to, whether they are shared, and the total number of interrupts that have been on the particular interrupt line.

- *System Load Average* Shows the load on the system (number of processes waiting to run) over a 15-minute period, number of currently running processes, total number of processes alive on the system (tasks), and PID of the last process started. (See Figure 10.22.)

FIGURE 10.22
System Load Average dialog box.

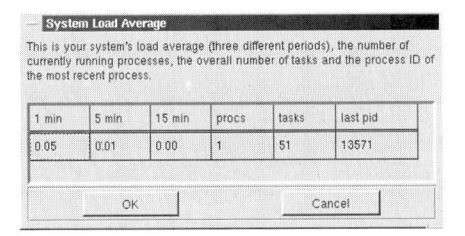

- *IOports* Lists the I/O ports in use on your system. Shows the beginning and ending address for each device and the name of the device that has claimed that port range.

- *DMA* Lists the Direct Memory Access channels in use on your system and what device has claimed each.

Time

As shown in Figure 10.23, the System Time dialog box allows you to manually set current system time and time zone.

- *Current Time* Contains the current time on the system, grayed out
- *Set Current Time* Allows you to set current time
- *Your Time Zone* Allows you to select a new time zone for your computer when clicked

FIGURE 10.23
System Time dialog box.

Kernel

The kernel controls the loading and unloading of crucial kernel modules.

The Kernel Modules dialog box allows you to view which kernel modules are loaded and which are available for loading, load and unload them, and view a little bit of information about each of them.

As shown in Figure 10.24, the left pane of the Kernel Modules dialog box shows the modules available for loading. To load a module, highlight the module and then select the Load button to its immediate right. To get a (very) short description of the module, highlight it and select the Info button to its immediate right.

FIGURE 10.24
Kernel Modules dialog box.

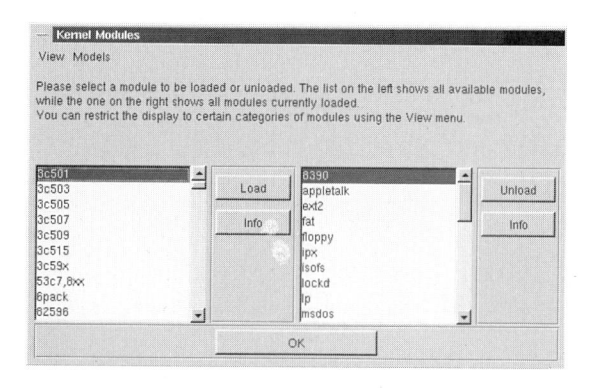

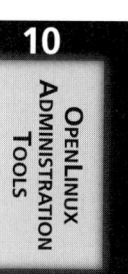

The right pane shows modules that are already loaded. You can either unload these modules or obtain a short description by using the buttons to the immediate right.

The View menu item can be used to restrict or broaden the display of modules in the two panes beneath. By selecting one of the categories in the menu, you can see which modules of only that type are available and currently loaded. Available View options include: All, Arcnet, CDROM, Ethernet, Misc, Network, SCSI, SCSI Host Adapters, Sound, Token Ring, File System, ISDN, and Multimedia.

The Models menu can be used to set specific information for ARCnet, Ethernet, and Token Ring network cards. After you select one of the three categories, you are then asked to select your card by Model or by Driver. A dialog box to set options specific to that driver then appears. As stated earlier, these options vary depending on the card.

Unless you have specific reasons to change the options in the Kernel Module Configuration dialog box shown in Figure 10.25, you should leave them set to their defaults. The modules are remarkably good at setting up the cards properly without any outside assistance.

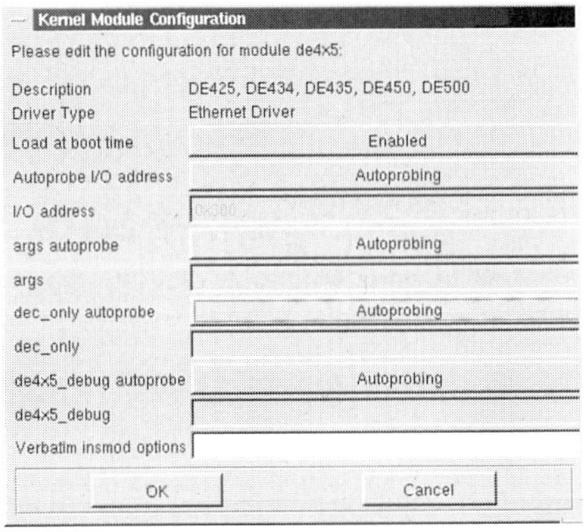

FIGURE 10.25
Kernel Module Configuration dialog box.

Software

The Software item controls the installation and removal of software packages. (*Hint*: Stick with kpackage.)

The Software Selection dialog box shown in Figure 10.26 allows you to catalog the software available on your system and uninstall packages simply by unchecking them.

FIGURE 10.26
Software Selection dialog box.

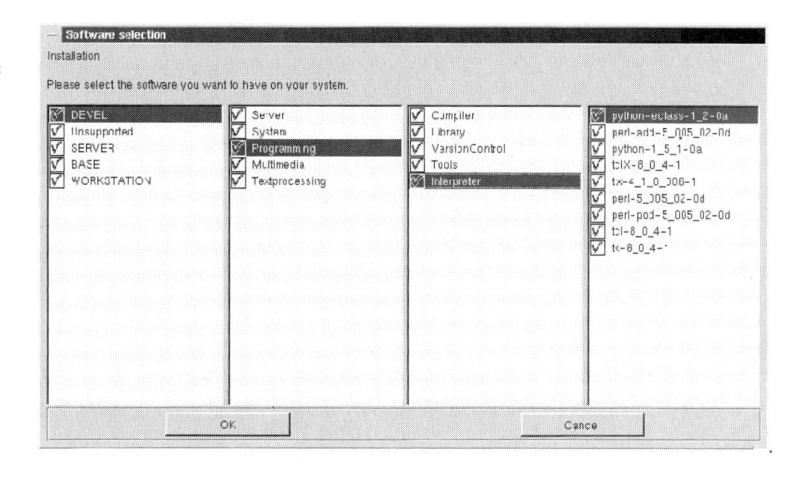

By using the Installation menu, you can also select a source for new packages to install.

This can be your distribution CD or even a server you are attached to through NFS. After the source of new packages (RPMs) is set up, the Software Selection program will provide you with a list of packages you don't have installed (unchecked boxes). All you need do to install additional packages is check the applicable box(es). (See Figure 10.27.)

FIGURE 10.27
Source Selection dialog box.

Summary

In this chapter we explored the basic file system organization of Caldera OpenLinux, as well as the most useful command-line and graphical tools for system administration. With these tools, you can apply the information in the following chapters to customize the configuration and administration of your OpenLinux system for maximum efficiency and ease of use.

Setting Up TCP/IP Networking

CHAPTER 11

IN THIS CHAPTER

- Networking Fundamentals 268
- Network Devices 274
- Configuring TCP/IP Networking 275
- Caldera's Network Setup 283
- Name Service 287
- Useful Diagnostic Programs 288
- DHCP 290

Although it is possible to run a Linux system disconnected from any other machine, almost all Linux installations are networked to other machines, even if this networking is only over a dial-up line for Web browsing.

This chapter describes how to set up TCP/IP networking under Linux. We'll start with background information on TCP/IP itself and then describe the Linux implementation. After reading this chapter, you will be able to network your Linux machine.

Networking Fundamentals

Linux supports a number of network protocols, but the most important by far is TCP/IP. In addition to being the native Linux and UNIX networking protocol, TCP/IP is the protocol used by the Internet.

> **Background Material**
>
> A protocol is an agreed-upon method that computers (or people) use to communicate.

Important Definitions

Several terms appear often in discussions about networking. This chapter defines these terms as follows:

- A *network* is a collection of machines that can communicate directly with one another. For example, all machines on an Ethernet cable make up a network.
- A *host* is a machine on a network.
- An *interface* is a connection between a host and a network. For example, an Ethernet card is an interface, as is the serial port used in a dial-up connection.
- An *internet* is a set of networks connected together. The machines that connect networks together are called *routers*.
- The *Internet* is the worldwide collection of interconnected networks based on the TCP/IP protocol.
- A *packet* is a single unit of information sent across a network. Most computer networks send packets of information rather than a continuous stream of bytes. Packets are also called *datagrams*.
- A *broadcast packet* is a packet intended to be received by every host on a network. A *multicast* packet is intended for a certain set of hosts, and a *unicast* packet is intended for one specific host.

TCP/IP

TCP/IP is actually a family of protocols. These include:

- *IP*, the Internet Protocol. IP is a network protocol whose function is getting packets of data from their source to their destination. IP is an unreliable protocol; it makes its best effort to get packets to their destination, but it does not guarantee delivery.
- *UDP*, the User Datagram Protocol. UDP is a very simple protocol built on top of IP; like IP, UDP does not guarantee delivery of packets.
- *TCP*, the Transmission Control Protocol. TCP is a complex transport protocol that provides a "pipe" between two processes. TCP guarantees that what one computer puts in one end of the pipe comes out without errors on the other end. TCP is built on top of IP, and to make a (virtual) error-free channel on top of IP, it includes a fairly complex arrangement of timers, acknowledgments, and retransmissions.
- *ICMP*, the Internet Control Message Protocol. ICMP (built on IP) is used to controls the operation of the Internet itself. For example, ICMP is used to signal unreachable machines or to suggest better routes for packets to travel.

IP Addresses

Every computer on an IP network is assigned an IP address.

> **Background Material**
>
> Actually, this is not quite true. More accurately stated, every interface has an IP address, and it is possible for a single computer to have more than one interface.

An IP address is a 32-bit number, usually written as four numbers ranging from 0 to 255 separated by periods. For example, an IP address might look like this: `192.168.4.7`.

An IP address is divided into two parts: the network address and the host address. The network address consists of the first part, and the host address is the last part. In general, each machine on a network is a host.

The size of the network and host parts of the address depends on the address class:

- Class A addresses include IP addresses ranging from `0.0.0.0` to `127.255.255.255`. The first 8 bits identify the network, and the last 24 bits identify the host.

- Class B addresses include IP addresses from 128.0.0.0 to 191.255.255.255. The first 16 bits identify the network, and the last 16 bits identify the host.
- Class C addresses include IP addresses from 192.0.0.0 to 223.255.255.255. The first 24 bits identify the network, and the last 8 bits identify the host.
- Class D addresses include IP addresses from 224.0.0.0 to 239.255.255.255. They are used for multicasting (sending data to a number of destinations at once) and are not discussed here.
- Class E addresses range from 240.0.0.0 to 247.255.255.255 and are reserved for future use, as are addresses from 248.0.0.0 to 255.255.255.255.

> **Background Material**
>
> The different classes of addresses have become less important with the advent of classless interdomain routing and subnetting. Subnetting is a further division of the host portion of the address into a subnet and host part.

As an example, The IP address 134.117.9.35 is a class B address with network part 134.117 and host part 9.35. Organizations may can choose to subdivide addresses. For example, the organization assigned the address block 134.117 might assign 134.117.1 as a class C network to one department, 134.117.2 to another department, and so on. Thus, The address 134.117.9.35 represents host number 35 on subnetwork 9 of network 134.117.

If you are setting up a network, you should use the size of the network to decide which class to use. Most small LANs have fewer than 254 hosts, so a class C network is adequate. Large organizations, which may require several interconnected LANs, might require a class B network. Very few organizations require class A networks.

Private Addresses

Normally, IP addresses must be globally unique. They are assigned by a central authority called the Internet Network Information Center (InterNIC). However, certain blocks of addresses are reserved for private use. If you are setting up a network of machines that will not be connected to the Internet, you should use these private addresses. Even if you plan on Internet connectivity, you should use private addresses for internal hosts that you do not want seen from the outside world. The private network addresses are:

- Class A: 10.0.0.0. (All addresses beginning with 10.)
- Class B: 172.16.0.0 through 172.31.0.0. (All addresses beginning with 172.16 through 172.31.)

- Class C: 192.168.0.0 through 192.168.255.0. (All addresses beginning with 192.168.)

> **Background Material**
>
> Linux features IP masquerading, which allows translation between real IP addresses and private IP addresses to take place on a firewall, without either the outside or inside host being aware of it. Always pick private IP addresses for internal networks.

TCP

The Transmission Control Protocol is a transport protocol built on IP. It creates a virtual error-free channel for two processes to communicate.

TCP adds the concept of a port to the addressing scheme. When a TCP connection is made from one host to another, the originating end is associated with an IP address and a 16-bit port number. Similarly, the destination end has an IP address and port number. One analogy is that of a telephone conversation: The telephone numbers correspond to IP addresses and identify the hosts (or houses). Ports are like names of particular people; a given house may might have more than one person who uses the telephone just as a host might have more than one process that uses TCP.

Note that a TCP connection is fully identified by four pieces of information: the source address, source port, destination address, and destination port. It is quite possible (in fact, very common) for different TCP connections to have the same destination address and port. They are distinguished by the source address and port.

The *telnet* program allows you to remotely log in to another machine. It works as follows: On the destination machine, a telnet daemon (a program that runs in the background) "listens" for incoming connections on a "well-known" port number (port 23). The telnet client picks any available port and initiates a connection to port 23 on the destination machine. The telnet daemon responds and lets you log in. You can open another telnet session to the same machine; although both telnet clients talk to destination port 23, they have different source ports, and the destination TCP code keeps track of both connections.

The telnet client picks any available port and initiates a connection to port 23 on the destination machine. The telnet daemon responds and lets you log in.

You can open another telnet session to the same machine; although both telnet clients talk to destination port 23, they have different source ports, and the destination TCP code keeps track of both connections.

TCP is used for many applications that require a reliable virtual connection, including remote login, file transfer, e-mail transfer, Web browsing, and network news transfer.

UDP

The User Datagram Protocol, is a much simpler protocol than TCP. UDP makes a best effort to deliver packets, but it does not guarantee delivery. It also does not guarantee that packets will not be duplicated.

UDP, like TCP, uses 16-bit port numbers to coordinate data between different processes on two machines. UDP ports are entirely separate from TCP ports, however.

UDP is used for applications that can withstand unreliable transfer, such as multimedia broadcasts. (The odd dropped video frame or audio packet doesn't really matter.) UDP is also useful for multicasting (sending data to a number of destinations at once) or where simplicity is essential such as the TFTP protocol for booting diskless clients. (TCP would be rather burdensome to encode into cheap diskless clients.)

DNS

DNS is the domain name system. Remembering numeric IP addresses for machines you wish to connect to is burdensome. The DNS is a giant worldwide distributed database that maps machine names (such as www.foo.ca) to IP addresses. Chapter 12 describes how to set up DNS. For now, you should be aware that IP (and TCP and UDP) know nothing about machine names; they only use IP addresses.

A machine name under DNS has two parts: the hostname and the domain name. For example, the machine www.foo.ca has the hostname www and the domain name foo.ca. A full machine name such as www.foo.ca is called a fully qualified hostname.

Routing

It's fairly easy to understand how IP routes data between machines on the same Ethernet cable (for example). The source machine simply places the packet on the Ethernet, and the destination machine picks it up.

However, packets must move from one network to another. This routing is performed by a router. A router is a machine that is connected to both networks and passes packets from one to the other. Routers have more than one IP address (one for each network they are on).

IP uses the network portion of the IP address to perform routing. Each machine in an IP network has a routing table that specifies how to route packets. For example, packets destined for any machine on the local Ethernet are simply placed on the Ethernet directly. Packets destined for other locations must be sent to a router, which (having more routing knowledge) decides where to send them next.

Consider the networks shown in Figure 11.1. The lines represent network connections, and the circles represent Ethernet networks.

FIGURE 11.1
IP routing.

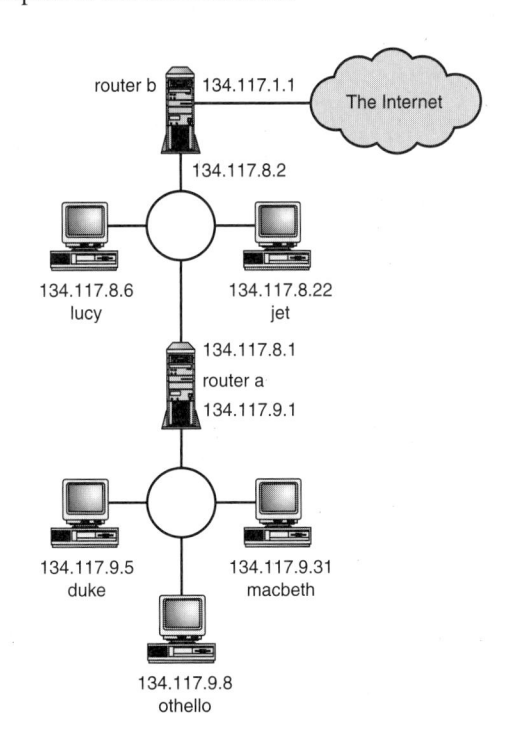

If duke wishes wants to send a packet to macbeth, it simply places the packet on its Ethernet interface, and the packet appears sometime later on macbeth's Ethernet interface.

However, if duke wishes to send a packet to jet, it sends it to the interface 134.117.9.1 on router a. router a examines the destination and determines that the packet should be placed on the outgoing interface 134.117.8.1, from which it reaches jet.

As a final example, if othello wishes to send a packet to some machine on the Internet, it sends the packet to 134.117.9.1. router a examines the destination address and sends the packet to 134.117.8.2, which is router b's interface on the 134.117.8.0 network.

> **Background Material**
>
> IP networks are often named by putting zeros in the host part of the address.

router b in turn examines the destination and sends the packet out to the Internet via the interface 134.117.1.1.

Note that duke, macbeth, and othello simply know to forward packets for any network other than 134.117.9.0 to router a. router a knows about the two networks 134.117.9.0 and 134.117.8.0, but forwards any other packets to router b. In this way, routing knowledge can be distributed and fairly localized.

Network Devices

Linux supports many network interfaces, but the two most common interfaces are Ethernet cards and serial ports. Ethernet cards offer fast inexpensive local area networking. Serial ports are often used with the Point-to-Point Protocol (PPP) to connect a host (or network) to the Internet.

Chapter 13 describes how to set up PPP. In this chapter, however, we concentrate on networking with Ethernet. Let's examine how Linux names and controls network devices.

Network Device Names

Network devices are not special files in the file system like most other devices; rather, they have names that are separate from any file system. That is, the network device names are internal to the kernel and do not correspond to any name in the file system. You need to access network devices with special commands; you cannot use the normal UNIX file-manipulation commands.

We will examine three types of network devices—the loopback interface, Ethernet interfaces, and PPP interfaces.

The Loopback Interface

Every Linux machine that supports TCP/IP networking has a special interface called lo, which is the loopback interface. The loopback interface is implemented entirely in software. Any packet transmitted on the loopback interface is received by the same host.

> **Background Material**
>
> The loopback interface might sound useless, but it is actually very useful. The loopback interface allows programs that require TCP/IP networking to operate on a single host. The loopback interface is also used for forwarding broadcast packets to the transmitting host because most Ethernet cards cannot receive packets that they transmit.

Ethernet Interfaces

Ethernet interfaces are named `eth0`, `eth1`, and so on (depending on how many Ethernet cards your machine has).

Linux supports a wide variety of Ethernet cards, including practically all modern PCI cards. If you have an older ISA card, you might need to set some jumpers to get it to work. If you are unlucky enough to have an ISA plug-and-play card, you need to configure it using the `isapnp` package. For information on setting up Ethernet hardware, see the Ethernet HOWTO (`/usr/doc/HOWTO/Ethernet-HOWTO.gz`). In the same directory is the `Plug-and-Play-HOWTO.gz`, which explains how to set up plug-and-play hardware under Linux.

PPP Interfaces

PPP interfaces are named `ppp0`, `ppp1`, and so on. They are created when a PPP link is brought up and destroyed when it is brought down. (A link is "brought up" when it is activated and "brought down" when it is deactivated.)

Configuring TCP/IP Networking

This section describes how you set up TCP/IP networking on an Ethernet network. We assume that you have your Ethernet card up and running, following the instructions in the Ethernet HOWTO.

Configuring an Interface: `ifconfig`

Use the `ifconfig` command to configure a network interface.

The `ifconfig` command sets up the following information:

- *The interface's IP address.*

- *The interface's network mask.* Remember that each IP address consists of a network part and a host part. The network mask is a 32-bit binary number with ones in the bit positions representing the network part, and zeros in the bit positions representing the host part.

  For example, consider the class C network 192.168.4.0. The first 24 bits are the network part, and the last 8 bits are the host part. The network mask is therefore 255.255.255.0.

  If you subnet the class C network into two more networks, 192.168.4.0 and 192.168.4.128 (leaving seven bits for the host part on each network), the network mask for each subdivided network is 255.255.255.128. (To *subnet* a network, simply choose the appropriate address and mask for each interface.)

  > **Note**
  >
  > Network masks always consist of a run of 1 bits followed by a run of 0 bits.

  The interface uses the network mask to determine whether an IP address is on the same network. For example, 192.168.4.73 is on the same class C network as 192.168.4.222. However, if the networks are subnetted as described earlier, the addresses are on different networks; 192.168.4.73 is on 192.168.4.0 and 192.168.4.222 is on 192.168.4.128.

  Networks are sometimes written as *address/bits* where *address* is the network address and *bits* is the number of bits in the network part. For example, the class C network 192.168.4.0 can be written 192.168.4.0/24, and the subnetted network 192.168.4.0 with seven host bits can be written as 192.168.4.0/25.

  You can also write networks as the *address/mask* like this: as in 192.168.4.0/255.255.255.0 and 192.168.4.128/255.255.255.128.

- *The interface's broadcast address.* This is a special IP address reserved for broadcast packets on the local network. The broadcast address is simply the network address with all 1 bits in the host part. The broadcast address for the network 192.168.4.0/24 is 192.168.4.255, and the broadcast address for 192.168.4.0/25 is 192.168.4.127.

- *Interface flags.* This includes whether the interface is up, whether it can broadcast packets, and so on.

Invoking `ifconfig`

You invoke `ifconfig` in the following manner:

```
$ ifconfig interface [aftype] [options] [address]
```

Here, *interface* is the name of the interface. *aftype* is the address family type, which for this example can be omitted or always supplied as `inet`, meaning the IP address family.

> **Background Material**
>
> Other supported address families are `inet6` for IPv6 (the next-generation IP), `ax25` (amateur packet radio), `ddp` (AppleTalk), `ipx` (Novell IPX), and `netrom` (another amateur packet radio protocol).

If you don't supply any options, `ifconfig` simply displays information about the interface. Let's look at the loopback interface:

```
$ ifconfig lo

lo   Link encap:Local Loopback
     inet addr:127.0.0.1  Mask:255.0.0.0
     UP LOOPBACK RUNNING  MTU:3924  Metric:1
     RX packets:16 errors:0 dropped:0 overruns:0 frame:0
     TX packets:16 errors:0 dropped:0 overruns:0 carrier:0
     collisions:0 txqueuelen:0
```

Now let's examine at the output of `ifconfig`:

- `Link encap:Local Loopback` indicates that this is the local loopback device. Ethernet cards have a link encapsulation of Ethernet.
- `inet addr:127.0.0.1` is the Internet address of the local loopback. The address 127.0.0.1 is a special address that always refers to the local host. The `Mask:255.0.0.0` means that the loopback address is connected to the "network" 127.0.0.0/8. This is a class A pseudo-network; any host on 127.0.0.0/8 simply refers to the local host.
- `UP LOOPBACK RUNNING` indicates that the interface is up, that the `loopback` flag is set, and that it the interface is currently running.
- `MTU:3924` specifies the maximum transmission unit for the interface. Packets larger than 3,924 bytes must be split. The `Metric:1` is used for routing purposes.

- The remaining lines provide information about the interface's usage. The interface has transmitted 16 packets and received 16 packets. The process encountered no errors, dropped packets, or overruns, as expected for a software-only interface.

Before setting up an Ethernet interface, let's look at the output of `ifconfig` for an Ethernet interface to get a feel for the information you need to supply:

```
$ ifconfig eth0
eth0 Link encap:Ethernet  HWaddr 00:60:67:62:31:D4
     inet addr:192.168.2.3  Bcast:192.168.2.255  Mask:255.255.255.0
     UP BROADCAST RUNNING MULTICAST  MTU:1500  Metric:1
     RX packets:19392 errors:0 dropped:0 overruns:0 frame:0
     TX packets:30536 errors:0 dropped:0 overruns:0 carrier:0
     collisions:31 txqueuelen:100
     Interrupt:5 Base address:0x320
```

In this output, we see

- The link encapsulation of is Ethernet, along with the Ethernet hardware address, is `00:60:67:62:31:D4`. Every Ethernet card has a unique 6-byte hardware address.

> **Background Material**
>
> Packets on an Ethernet network are routed using Ethernet addresses as sources and destinations. How are these mapped to IP addresses? The Address Resolution Protocol (ARP) automatically and dynamically maps the Ethernet addresses to IP addresses; you generally don't need to worry about how the networking software finds out which Ethernet address corresponds to which IP address.

- The card's IP address is `192.168.2.3`. The broadcast address for the network it is on is `192.168.2.255`, and the network mask is `255.255.255.0`. These addresses correspond to the class C network `192.168.2.0/24`.
- The interface is up and running, and we you see that it supports both broadcast and multicast packets. The MTU for Ethernet cards is always `1500` because that is the maximum size of a legal Ethernet frame.
- Many thousands of packets have been transmitted and received by the interface. You see a small number of collisions. Ethernet is a broadcast medium; consequently, two Ethernet interfaces might transmit at the same time. When this happens, both frames are garbled, and a collision has occurred.

- As a convenience, `ifconfig` prints the IRQ (5) and I/O port base address (`0x320`) used by the Ethernet card.

Setting Up an Ethernet Interface

To set up an Ethernet connection, you must arm yourself with the following information:

- *The IP address of the interface.* This will be assigned by the LAN administrator. If you are the LAN administrator, pick a private address block and assign an IP address to each interface. You can assign addresses however you like (within your chosen or assigned network block) as long as each interface on the network has a unique address. Also, you cannot assign addresses whose host part is all zeros or all ones; these addresses are network and broadcast addresses, respectively.

- *The network mask.* Get it from the administrator or pick one; you can get away with using a class C (`255.255.255.0`) network for most LANs.

- *The broadcast address.* This is simply the network part followed by a host part of all 1 bits. For a class C network `x.y.z.0/24`, the broadcast address is `x.y.z.255`.

To set up the Ethernet card, use

```
# ifconfig eth0 broadcast bcast_addr C
netmask mask ip_addr
```

Here, `bcast_addr` is the broadcast address, `mask` is the network mask, and `ip_addr` is the IP address of the interface. Note that only root can configure an interface. You can replace The `eth0` can be replaced with `eth1` to set up the second Ethernet card, and so on.

To bring up the interface, use

```
# ifconfig eth0 up
```

This command brings up (activates) the interface and adds a route for the interface's network.

Setting Up Routes

The `route` command sets up the kernel's routing table. The router consults this table each time a packet must be transmitted. The routing table indicates which interface should be used to transmit the packet. For the purposes of illustration, Figure 11.2 shows the topology of my network (how it is connected).

FIGURE 11.2
My local network.

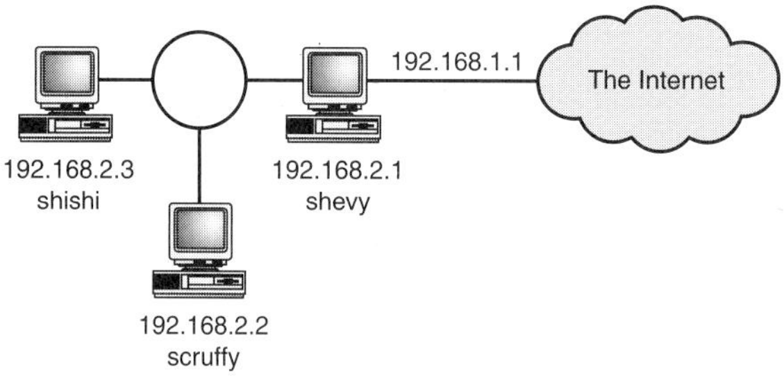

Loopback Route

Let's look at a very simple routing table—the table for a machine with only the a loopback interface:

```
$ route -n

Kernel IP routing table
Destination Gateway Genmask     Flags Metric Ref Use Iface
127.0.0.0   0.0.0.0 255.0.0.0 U     0      0   0   lo
```

Each line in the listing is called a route. Here's what each column means:

- `Destination` specifies the destination host or network.
- `Gateway` is the IP address of a gateway to use. (*Gateway* is an older term for *router*.) If the gateway address is `0.0.0.0`, it means the destination is directly connected to the host, and no gateway is needed.
- `Genmask` is the "generality mask," which specifies the generality of the route. For this route, the genmask is `255.0.0.0`, meaning that only the first eight bits of the destination address need to match the Destination column. Thus, Any packet destined for `127.x.y.z` will use the route. When trying to matching a route for an IP address, the kernel bitwise ANDs the address with the genmask, and then performs the comparison.
- `Flags` lists some flags associated with the route. The most common flags are `U` (the route is up), `H` (the target is a host rather than a network), and `G` (use a gateway). Other flags are possible; consult `route(8)` for more details.
- `Metric` is a measure of the "cost" of the route.
- `Ref` is the count of the number of connections currently using the route.
- `Use` is the number of times the route has been used in a routing lookup.
- `Iface` is the interface to use.

For this example, therefore, all packets with a destination of 127.x.y.z will be routed through lo, the loopback interface.

Local Network Route

The next step up in routing complexity is a route to a local network. My main computer (shishi) is at address 192.168.2.3 and is connected to the network 192.168.2.0/24. Here's the routing table (from route -n):

```
Destination  Gateway   Genmask        Flags Metric Ref Use Iface
192.168.2.0  0.0.0.0   255.255.255.0  U     0      0   0   eth0
127.0.0.0    0.0.0.0   255.0.0.0      U     0      0   0   lo
```

The packets destined for the 127.0.0.0/8 network still use the loopback interface, but packets bound for anywhere on 192.168.2.0/24 (see the genmask!) use eth0, the first (and only) Ethernet card. We know that 192.168.2.0/24 is a local network because the gateway address is 0.0.0.0.

Default Route

Finally, how does shishi communicate with machines not on the local network? The gateway machine shevy has an Internet connection; all nonlocal packets must be forwarded to it. Here's the complete routing table for shishi:

```
Destination  Gateway     Genmask        Flags Metric Ref Use Iface
192.168.2.0  0.0.0.0     255.255.255.0  U     0      0   0   eth0
127.0.0.0    0.0.0.0     255.0.0.0      U     0      0   0   lo
0.0.0.0      192.168.2.1 0.0.0.0        UG    1      0   0   eth0
```

Note some important things about the last route:

- The destination of 0.0.0.0 and genmask of 0.0.0.0 indicate that this is a default route. Any packet that isn't routed on the first two routes will be sent out on the third route.

- The gateway address is 192.168.2.1 (a real gateway machine) and the G flag is set. This indicates that the route is not direct, but must go through a gateway. Also, the metric is set to 1, indicating a more expensive route than the local routes.

Let's look at examples of how packets will be routed using this table:

- A packet from the local host to 192.168.2.2 matches the first entry. It will be sent directly to the destination using the eth0 interface.

- A packet from the local host to 127.0.0.1 matches the second entry. It will be sent through the loopback interface.

- A packet from the local host to 134.117.9.35 matches the third entry (the default route). It will be sent to the gateway 192.168.2.1 through interface eth0. From there, it will (presumably) be forwarded by the gateway through some connection to the Internet.

Adding Routes

In addition to displaying the routing table, the route command is used to add and delete routes. Note that if you have a fairly simple network and you use Caldera's graphical setup tools, routes will be created for you automatically.

Before you attempt to create routes, you should configure all network devices with ifconfig. Also, only root can adjust the routing table.

To add a route, use

```
# route add [-net|-host] target dev
```

If you are adding a route for a particular host, use the -host option. If it's a route for a network, use -net.

The *target* specifies the target of the route. If the target is a host, then it is simply the host's IP address. If the target is a network, then it is the network address followed by a slash and the number of bits in the network part. The *dev* specifies the network interface to use for the route.

Here's an example: To set up the local network route on shishi (the first route in the routing table), use

```
# route add -net 192.168.2.0/24 eth0
```

To add a route for a particular host, use

```
# route add -host 192.168.2.244 eth0
```

> **Background Material**
>
> Of course, this host route is redundant, given the network route.

If you need to add a default route through a gateway, use

```
# route add default gw gateway
```

For example, shishi's default route is set up like this:

```
# route add default gw 192.168.2.1
```

> **Note**
>
> To use a gateway, there must be a route to the gateway machine. In this example, the gateway machine is on the `192.168.2.0/24` network, so it can be reached with the first route.

`route` has many more options for configuring the routing table; see `route(8)` for details.

Deleting Routes

`route` can delete a route. Use

```
# route del [-net|-host] target
```

For example, to delete all routes except the loopback route from `shishi`, use

```
# route del default
# route del -net 192.168.2.0/24
```

Caldera's Networking Setup

Caldera OpenLinux includes a number of networking scripts that greatly ease the configuration of TCP/IP. Be aware that these are simply shell scripts that ultimately use `ifconfig` and `route` to do the real work.

Overall Network Setup

The shell script `/etc/sysconfig/network` contains three variable assignments used by the other networking scripts. It looks something like this:

```
NETWORKING=yes|no
HOSTNAME=hostname
IF_LIST=interface_list
```

For example, `/etc/sysconfig/network` on `shishi` looks like this:

```
NETWORKING=yes
HOSTNAME=shishi.skoll.ca
IF_LIST='lo eth tr sl ppp'
```

The first line indicates that we want to use TCP/IP networking. The second line sets the full hostname of the machine, and the third line lists possible interfaces to attempt to initialize.

> **Background Material**
>
> We've seen the `lo` and `eth` interfaces. The `tr` interfaces are for token-ring networks, `sl` is for SLIP interfaces (an older protocol for running IP over a serial link), and `ppp` are the a Point-to-Point protocol interfaces (discussed in Chapter 13).

Interface Configuration

Each interface has a configuration script called /etc/sysconfig/network-scripts/ifcfg-ifname. For example, interface eth0 has a configuration script /etc/sysconfig/network-scripts/ifcfg-eth0. This script looks something like this:

```
#!/bin/sh
#>>>Device type: ethernet
#>>>Variable declarations:
DEVICE=eth0
IPADDR=192.168.2.3
NETMASK=255.255.255.0
NETWORK=192.168.2.0
BROADCAST=192.168.2.255
GATEWAY=192.168.2.1
ONBOOT=yes
DYNAMIC=
#>>>End variable declarations
REMIP=0.0.0.0
MTU=1500
```

The variables have the following meanings:

- DEVICE is the interface name.
- IPADDR is the IP address of the interface.
- NETMASK is the network mask of the interface.
- NETWORK is the network address of the interface.
- BROADCAST is the broadcast address of the interface.
- GATEWAY is the IP address of a gateway machine. If the network has no gateway, this variable is set to none. The presence of a gateway causes the network scripts to set up a default route using the gateway.
- ONBOOT is either yes or no. If it is yes, the interface upstarts when the computer is booted. This is appropriate for Ethernet interfaces, but might not be appropriate for modem lines.

- `DYNAMIC` is either blank or a dynamic address assignment protocol such as `dhcp` or `bootp`. If `DYNAMIC` is nonblank, the system will dynamically configures the IP address, netmask, and so on. (Dynamic address assignment is covered in the section "DHCP.")
- `REMIP` specifies the remote IP address. This is useful only for point-to-point links; it is meaningless for Ethernet interfaces.
- `MTU` specifies the maximum transmission unit. You can't change it for Ethernet interfaces, but you can adjust it for serial links.

Starting and Stopping Networking

At boot time, the shell script `/etc/rc.d/init.d/network` is executed with the argument `start`. This script performs the following actions:

- It enables or disables IP forwarding according to the setting in `/etc/sysconfig/network`. IP forwarding lets you use your Linux machine as a router. To enable it, put the line `IPFORWARDING=yes` in `/etc/sysconfig/network`.
- It initializes the loopback interface, `lo`.
- For each interface of each type in `IF_LIST` (from `/etc/sysconfig/network`), it runs another shell script called `/sbin/ifup`. This shell script reads the appropriate `ifcfg-interface` file from `/etc/sysconfig/network-scripts` and actually executes the `ifconfig` and `route` commands to bring up~~start~~ the interface.
- If the shell script `/etc/sysconfig/network-scripts/ifcfg-routes` exists, it is executed. You can put `route` commands in this script to set up any special routes you require.

To stop networking (for example, at system shutdown), you invoke the `/etc/rc.d/init.d/network` script is invoked with the argument `stop`, which causes it to bring down~~close~~ the interfaces.

While ~~Although~~ these shell scripts are fairly complex internally, they are quite easy to use. Unfortunately, they are not well documented. You should read through the scripts to understand how they work.

Adding Interfaces

Adding additional interfaces is quite easy. Simply create the appropriate `/etc/sysconfig/network-scripts/ifcfg-interface` script. You can create this ~~it~~ with a text editor or the graphical Caldera Open Administration System panel. To add an interface using COAS, select Network:Ethernet Interfaces from the COAS menu. The window in Figure 11.3 pops up.

FIGURE 11.3
COAS Ethernet Interface Configuration dialog box.

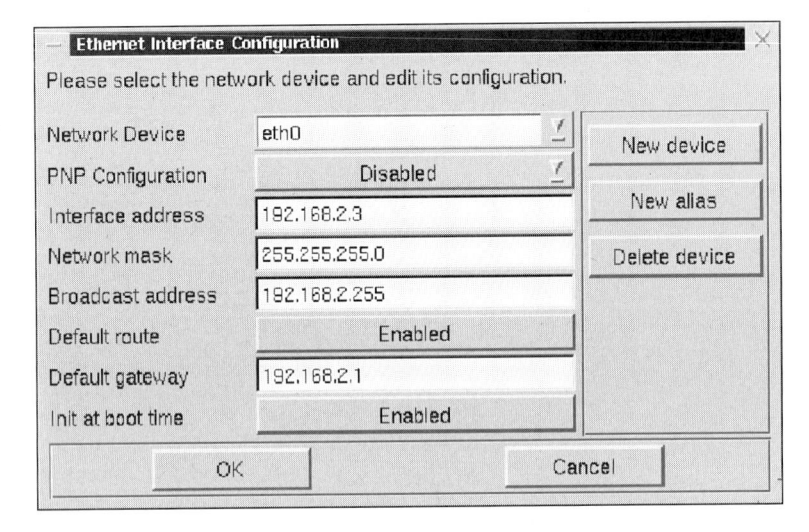

Ethernet Interface Configuration	
Please select the network device and edit its configuration.	

Network Device	eth0
PNP Configuration	Disabled
Interface address	192.168.2.3
Network mask	255.255.255.0
Broadcast address	192.168.2.255
Default route	Enabled
Default gateway	192.168.2.1
Init at boot time	Enabled

[New device] [New alias] [Delete device] [OK] [Cancel]

In this window, simply fill in the fields to create the setup script. The fields are

- *Network Device*   The network device name.
- *PNP Configuration*   This has nothing to do with plug-and-play hardware. Rather, it indicates a protocol for centrally assigning IP addresses, such as DHCP.
- *Interface Address, Network Mask, and Broadcast Address*   The IP address, network mask, and broadcast address of the interface.
- *Default Route*   If this option is enabled, the interface sets up a default route using the interface.
- *Default Gateway*   If you are using the interface for a default route, this field contains the IP address of the gateway.
- *Init at Boot Time*   If this option is enabled, the interface and its routes are initialized at boot time. This is usually appropriate for Ethernet interfaces.

Background Material

The New Alias button lets you create interface aliases. Aliases let you split a single physical interface into multiple logical interfaces, each with its own IP address. This arrangement is useful for virtual Web hosting, for example, where you wish to have a single machine appear to be many different machines. Aliases are nicely described in the online WWW-HOWTO.

Name Service

It is very awkward to always use IP addresses for host and network addresses. Linux supports a number of name services that map names to numbers and vice versa.

The file `/etc/nsswitch.conf` controls which name services are used and in what order. For this section, the lines we are interested in look something like this:

```
hosts:        files nis dns
networks:     nis files dns
```

The first line means that for looking up hostnames or addresses, the system first consults the `files` service. If that fails, the system tries the `nis` service and finally the `dns` service. What do these services mean?

- `files` The `files` service causes a lookup in a simple text file. Exactly which file is used depends on what is being looked up. For host to address mappings, the system consults the `/etc/hosts` file. This is a plain text file. Blank lines and lines beginning with # are ignored; other lines consists of an IP address followed by the "canonical" name of a host followed by the host's "nicknames." For example, here is the `/etc/hosts` file for `shishi`:

  ```
  192.168.2.1    shevy.skoll.ca shevy
  192.168.2.2    scruffy.skoll.ca scruffy
  192.168.2.3    shishi.skoll.ca shishi
  ```

  The fully qualified hostname and the short name follow each address.

> **Background Material**
>
> Comments in `/etc/hosts` urge you not to edit it. Serious Linux users edit it anyway.

- `nis` The `nis` service is a database lookup system designed by Sun Microsystems. It lets you store centralized versions of many lookup files such as `/etc/hosts` and have clients perform lookups on the server.

  NIS (Network Information Service) is intended for use on small networks. It is not intended for Internet-wide lookups. NIS is covered in Chapter 14.

- `dns` The `dns` services refers to the Domain Name System, the Internet-wide distributed database of hostname to address mappings. Chapter 12 covers DNS in detail.

Resolver Configuration

A collection of functions for looking up host addresses resides in the resolver library. It performs file lookups, NIS lookups, and DNS lookups. The DNS lookup part of the resolver library is controlled by the file /etc/resolv.conf. This file looks something like this:

```
domain skoll.ca
nameserver 192.168.2.1
nameserver 192.168.2.22
nameserver 192.168.2.33
```

The domain line specifies the local DNS domain. Unqualified hostnames have this domain appended if a DNS lookup fails.

The nameserver lines specify IP addresses of name servers. These are hosts specially configured to respond to DNS requests. The first line is the primary name server and is normally the only one used. If the primary name server is down, the secondary and remaining name servers are tried in order.

The nsswitch.conf file is documented in info; type **info -n "(libc)NSS Configuration File"** to see the documentation.

Useful Diagnostic Programs

Linux includes two useful diagnostic programs (ping and traceroute) that let you determine whether your computer is successfully networked and whether routes are set up correctly.

ping

The ping program tests connectivity from one host to another.

> **Background Material**
>
> ping is named after sonar echo-locators, which "ping" objects with bursts of sound.

To ping a host, use:

```
$ ping host
```

host can be an IP address or hostname. (If your name service isn't working, you might need to supply an IP address.)

Here's an example running on `shishi`:

```
$ ping shevy
PING shevy.skoll.ca (192.168.2.1): 56 data bytes
64 bytes from 192.168.2.1: icmp_seq=0 ttl=64 time=1.2 ms
64 bytes from 192.168.2.1: icmp_seq=1 ttl=64 time=1.2 ms
Hit interrupt (Ctrl-C)
-- shevy.skoll.ca ping statistics --
2 packets transmitted, 2 packets received, 0% packet loss
round-trip min/avg/max = 1.2/1.2/1.2 ms
```

`ping` works by sending special ICMP echo request datagrams. The system being pinged returns echo reply datagrams. `ping` keeps sending one datagram each second until you press the interrupt key. `ping` then lists a summary of the results.

If you can `ping` another host on your LAN, you're off to a good start in setting up networking.

`ping` has many options; see `ping(8)` for details.

> **Note**
>
> You might be connected to the Internet but be unable to ping a host across the Internet. Many sites block ICMP echo-request datagrams.

traceroute

The `traceroute` program displays the route taken by packets from your host to a destination.

> **Background Material**
>
> Actually, this is not quite true. More accurately stated, `traceroute` displays a plausible route that is probably the route taken, but may might not be. Routes on the Internet can change dynamically.

You use `traceroute` just like `ping`:

```
$ traceroute host
```

Here's an example running on `shishi`:

```
$ traceroute shevy
traceroute to shevy.skoll.ca (192.168.2.1), 30 hops max, 40 byte packets
1 shevy (192.168.2.1) 1.263 ms 1.128 ms 1.123 ms
```

This is not too exciting because the route is direct. A better example is shown in the `traceroute` manual page, `traceroute(8)`.

DHCP

For small networks, it is acceptable to assign fixed IP addresses to each host and configure each host to know its IP address upon startup.

As networks get larger, it becomes difficult to manage hosts and annoying to have to customize each host's setup files for a particular IP address.

DHCP (Dynamic Host Configuration Protocol) is a protocol for dynamically assigning IP addresses to hosts on a network. The basic idea is that on bootup, a client broadcasts a DHCP request. A DHCP server hears the broadcast. It assigns the client an IP address, hostname, network mask, and so on and sends the reply back to the client. The client then finishes configuring its network interfaces with `ifconfig` based on the server's reply.

With DHCP, a client does not own its IP address indefinitely. The server gives it a lease. After the lease expires, the client can no longer use the IP address. Clients are expected to renew their leases before they expire.

Setting Up a DHCP Client

Setting up a DHCP client is easy. Simply set `DYNAMIC=dhcp` in the `/etc/sysconfig/network-scripts/ifcfg-ifname` file, or enable plug and play in the COAS graphical configuration utility.

The program `dhcpcd` contacts the DHCP server and sets up the network configuration. The configuration supplied by a DHCP server includes:

- *The client's IP address, address mask, and broadcast address.* This information is used by `ifconfig`.
- *The IP addresses of routers and DNS servers.* This information is used to set up routes and `/etc/resolv.conf`.
- *The client's hostname and domain name.*

Setting Up a DHCP Server

Setting up a DHCP server is more complex than setting up a DHCP client. First, you have to make sure that the DHCP server is starts on bootup. You can do this from the COAS System:Daemons menu (see Figure 11.4). Enable DHCP and BOOTP boot server.

FIGURE 11.4
COAS System Services dialog box.

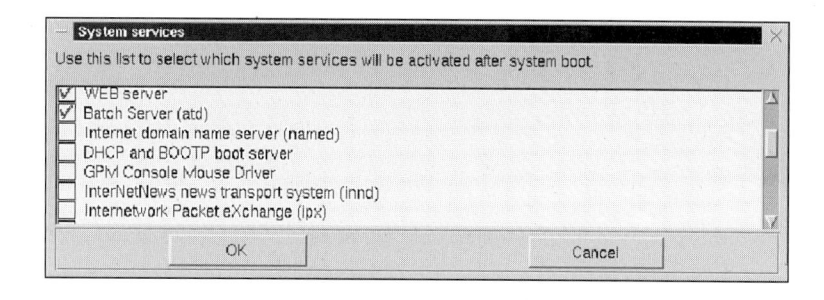

Configuring the DHCP Server

The DHCP server is controlled by a configuration file called /etc/dhcpd.conf.

The DHCP server can assign addresses randomly. That is, it can maintain a pool of available IP addresses and assign clients addresses as they request them. This arrangement is appropriate for machines that are often moved (such as laptops) and that are not servers for other machines. Here is an example /etc/dhcpd.conf file:

```
default-lease-time 600;
max-lease-time 7200;
option subnet-mask 255.255.255.0;
option broadcast-address 192.168.2.255;
option routers 192.168.2.1;
option domain-name-servers 192.168.2.1, 192.168.2.22;
option domain-name "skoll.ca";

subnet 192.168.2.0 netmask 255.255.255.0 {
    range 192.168.2.2 192.168.2.100;
    range 192.168.2.150 192.168.2.200;
}
```

Let's look at the options:

- default-lease-time 600 specifies a 10-minute (600-second) default lease time. This is the default length of time clients can hold on to an IP address before renewing it. If your clients hardly ever change, you can specify long lease times on the order of hours or days. If your network is in a factory that plugs Internet appliances into the network for testing and then ships them, lease times on the order of 5 minutes are appropriate.

- max-lease-time 7200 specifies that no client will be given a lease longer than 2 hours, even if it requests more time.

- subnet-mask and broadcast-address specify the subnet mask and broadcast address that clients should use. ifconfig uses these values.

- `routers 192.168.2.1` specifies the IP address of the router. Clients will add a default route using this address as the gateway.
- The `domain-name-servers` and `domain-name` options set up the resolver configuration.
- The `subnet` section controls configuration for a particular subnet. The DHCP server hands out IP addresses in the ranges `192.168.2.2` through `192.168.2.100` and `192.168.2.150` through `192.168.2.200`. It does not give clients IP addresses outside this range.

Machines with Fixed IP Addresses

Some machines should always be allocatedget a fixed address. For example, a file or Web server should probably be givenget a fixed address. You can add lines like this to `/etc/dhcpd.conf`:

```
host shishi {
   hardware ethernet 00:60:67:62:31:D4;
   fixed-address 192.168.2.3;
}
```

This code lets you assign IP addresses based on the client's Ethernet address. You can mix and match dynamic and static address allocation according to the needs of your network.

This section has just touched the surface of DHCP server configuration. For more details, see `dhcpd.conf(5)` and the DHCP mini-HOWTO in `/usr/doc/HOWTO/other-formats/html/mini/DHCP.html`.

Summary

This chapter covered the fundamentals of TCP/IP networking. You learned how IP addresses identify network interfaces. You learned how to configure Linux network interfaces with `ifconfig` and how to set up IP routing tables with route. We looked at Caldera's organization of the network setup shell scripts. You then learned how to configure name service on a client and how to use `ping` and `traceroute`to perform network diagnostics. Finally, you learned how to set up a DHCP client and server to centralize the administration of IP address assignment.

CHAPTER 12

Setting Up DNS— The Domain Name System

IN THIS CHAPTER

- DNS Fundamentals *294*
- DNS Configuration *297*
- DNS Database Files *299*
- Using `nslookup` *304*

Chapter 11 introduced the Domain Name System and described how to set up a Linux machine as a client for a DNS server. This chapter describes DNS in detail and explains how to set up a DNS server on Linux.

Setting up DNS is fairly simple but requires a lot of attention to detail. By the time you finish this chapter, you should be able to set up a working DNS server. Even if you are only running a small home network, a DNS server on your network can reduce the number of DNS lookups that go out onto the Internet, saving bandwidth on your Internet link.

DNS Fundamentals

DNS is a database system. It answers queries from clients. Identifying the IP address of host *hostname* is the most common query answered by DNS.

DNS is a distributed database. This means that no central server knows the answer to all DNS queries. Instead, various servers around the world are responsible for their local domains. Top-level servers, or root servers, know only which DNS servers to refer a client to for next-level queries.

DNS uses a hierarchical naming scheme for Internet hosts. A host's name is something like `host.subdomain.subdomain.domain`.

There are a number of top-level domains. Some common top-level domains are:

- `.com` Commercial entities. This is the most sought-after top-level domain.
- `.edu` American educational institutions.
- `.org` Noncommercial organizations.
- `.mil` American military institutions.
- `.gov` American government institutions.

In addition, each country has a two-letter national domain, such as `.us` for the United States, `.ca` for Canada, `.fr` for France, and so on. Within each national domain, a national organization decides on the organization of subdomains. For example, Australia mirrors the original top-level domains to yield subdomains such as `.com.au` and `.edu.au`. Other countries use their own delegation scheme. Canada, for example, has some domains based on provinces (`.on.ca` and `.nf.ca`), and "large" organizations are privileged enough to have their own top-level Canadian domains (`.linux.ca` and `.gc.ca`).

Root Servers

A number of well-known *root servers* are the starting points for DNS queries. (A root server is simply a normal DNS server that has information about top-level domains.)

You can obtain the list of root servers via anonymous FTP from `ftp.rs.internic.net` in the file `/domain/named.root`. This list forms the starting point for all DNS queries.

Anatomy of a Query

Let's examine how a DNS query works. Suppose a client on `shishi.roaringpenguin.com` wishes to find the IP address of `www.linux.com`.

First, the resolver on `shishi` sends the query to one of the root servers discussed previously. The root server replies, "I do not have an answer to your query, but the following servers know all about the `.com` domain."

The resolver then queries a `.com` server. It replies "I do not have an answer to your query, but the following servers know all about the `.linux.com` domain."

Finally, the resolver queries a `.linux.com` server. It replies with the correct IP address. This process is illustrated in Figure 12.1.

FIGURE 12.1

DNS query example.

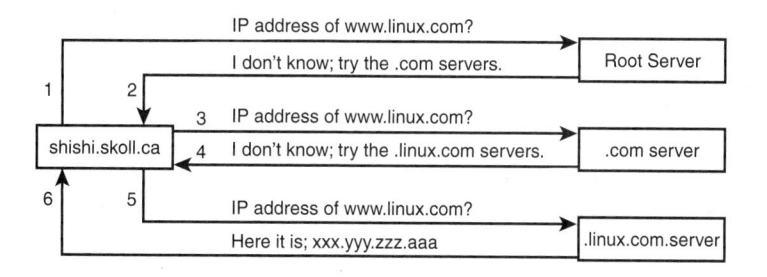

The name servers for `.linux.com` are said to be authoritative because they contain the absolutely authoritative information about machines in the `.linux.com` domain. The same administrators who run the network named by the servers generally run authoritative name servers.

This seems to be an incredibly convoluted and wasteful way to answer a DNS query. For a single host lookup, three queries and responses are sent across the Internet. Surely this would eventually overload the root name servers, which must participate in every DNS query?

In fact, the power of DNS comes from caching. Organizations set up local name servers that perform queries on behalf of clients. The answer to a query is cached on the local name server. The next time the same query is performed, the local name server answers without querying any other name servers.

Thus, for example, if `shishi` were running a local name server, it would quickly build up a cache of answered queries. Eventually, `shishi` would directly answer most queries, with only occasional queries being sent out over the Internet.

Of course, answers to DNS queries cannot be cached forever—if a host's IP changes, the cached results are invalid. For that reason, the authoritative servers for a query specify a "time to live" for the query's answer. If the answer to a query is cached for longer than its time to live, the cached result is invalidated and the authoritative server is queried.

> **Background Material**
>
> This is why when a machine's IP address changes, it may take hours or days for the change to propagate across the worldwide DNS. All the cached entries have to expire.

DNS Record Types

All DNS queries have a type and the answers have a corresponding record type. Each answer is called a resource record or RR for short. Here are some DNS RR types:

- **A** An A-type record contains the IP address of a host. This record type is queried most often.
- **CNAME** A CNAME-type record holds a host's canonical name. For example, many organizations name their Web server www. However, this is usually just a nickname for the real Web server. If your Web server's real name is `bigserver.roaringpenguin.com`, you can create a CNAME record for `www.roaringpenguin.com`, which lists `bigserver.roaringpenguin.com` as the canonical name. If you ever have to move the Web server to a different machine, you need only change the CNAME record.
- **MX** An MX-type record holds the machine used for mail exchange. For example, the machine handling mail for `roaringpenguin.com` might be called `mail.roaringpenguin.com`.
- **NS** An NS-type record lists the name servers used for a domain. For example, the name servers for `roaringpenguin.com` are `pns.storm.ca` and `sns.storm.ca`.
- **PTR** A PTR-type record is used for reverse DNS—that is, given an IP address, find the host name corresponding to the IP address.
- **SOA** An SOA-type record holds the start-of-authority information for a domain. This includes the e-mail address of the person responsible for the DNS domain as well as various time-to-live and timeout values.

There are other DNS record types, but the ones described above are the most common.

DNS Configuration

Under Linux, the `named` program propvides DNS. This program is usually started at boot time by specifying that Internet domain name server (`named`) should be activated. (You can do this using COAS.)

Named reads a configuration file called `/etc/named.conf`, any other files specified by that file, and then listens for DNS queries. `named` is part of the BIND (Berkeley Internet Name Daemon) distribution. In addition to the manual page `named(8)`, you can look at the file `/usr/doc/bind-8.1.1/html/index.html` with a Web browser for more details. (We'll refer to this as the HTML documentation.)

The file `/etc/named.conf` is the master configuration file for `named`.

> **Background Material**
>
> If you have use an old version of `named`, the old `/etc/named.boot` file is no longer used. The new configuration file is in a different format; the program `named-bootconf` will convert a `named.boot` file into a `named.conf` file.

The `named.conf` file has many options; we'll just cover the most frequently used ones here. Read the HTML documentation for all the details.

Options

The `options` statement sets up global options for `named`. There are many options; some of them are as follows:

- `directory`   Specifies the directory for remaining configuration files. `named` uses many auxiliary configuration files; any relative pathnames are assumed to be relative to the directory specified with this option.

- `recursion`   This option can be either `yes` or `no`. If it is `yes` (the default), then the name server does all the work of looking up a name. If it is `no`, then the name server simply refers the client to an authoritative name server if it does not have the information itself. (See Figure 12.1.)

- `forwarders`   This option can be used to forward queries to other name servers. For example, in a large organization, each departmental name server can forward queries to a central name server. The central name server will quickly build up a rich cache of information, greatly reducing the need to perform name queries outside the organization (and presumably over a slow link). The `forwarders` option takes a list of IP addresses.

Here's a sample `options` section from `/etc/named.conf`:

```
options {
        directory "/var/named";
        forwarders { 134.117.9.46; 134.117.9.33; 134.117.1.11; };
};
```

In this example, all the other configuration files are placed in `/var/named`. We forward queries to the three IP addresses named in the second line. (`134.117.9.46` is tried first; then `.33` is tried and finally `.1.11`, if the first two do not respond.)

Zones

The `zone` statement defines a zone. For example, any domain that you administer is a zone. The root domain (called ".") is typically a zone too.

The `zone` statement looks something like this (in its simplest form):

```
zone "zone_name" zone_class {
type zone_type;
file "file_name";
}
```

- *zone_name*   The name of the zone. For example, the zone name might be `roaringpenguin.com`. The zone `.` refers to the root domain.
- *zone_class*   The address family of the zone. For Internet zones, it is always `in`.
- *zone_type*   The zone type. There are four zone types:
    - *Master zone*   Zone for which your name server is authoritative.
    - *Slave zone*   A replica of a master zone. For slave zones, your name server periodically contacts one of a list of master servers to replicate the information. The list of master servers is in a `masters` clause in the `zone` statement; see the HTML documentation for details.
    - *Stub zone*   Similar to a slave zone, but it replicates only the NS records rather than all the master records.
    - *Hint zone*   Specifies the initial set of root name servers. When `named` starts, it uses the root hints to find a root name server (and update its list of root name servers.)

For simple configurations, you will probably only use master and hint zones.

- *file_name*   The file containing the resource records. For master zones, this is the file with the master information. For slave and stub zones, `named` writes a replica of the master information to the file. For hint zones, the file contains a list of root name servers.

Remember that, if you specify a relative path for *file_name*, it will be relative to the directory given in the *directory* option.

DNS Database Files

`named` stores DNS information in files called DNS database files. These files are just plain text files that are read when `named` starts. The master configuration file tells `named` which database file to use for each zone.

Here's the `/etc/named.conf` file on `shishi`:

```
options {
        directory "/var/named";
        forwarders { 134.117.9.46; 134.117.9.33; 134.117.1.11; };
};

zone "roaringpenguin.com" in {
        type master;
        file "master/roaringpenguin.com";
};

zone "." in {
        type hint;
        file "named.cache";
};

zone "127.in-addr.arpa" in {
        type master;
        file "master/127";
};

zone "2.168.192.in-addr.arpa" in {
        type master;
        file "master/192.168.2";
};
```

We've seen the `options` statement before; let's look at the various zones.

Master Zone Files

The first zone is for the domain `roaringpenguin.com`. `shishi` is the master name server for this domain. The resource records are stored in the file `/var/named/master/roaringpenguin.com`. Here are the contents of that file:

```
@ IN SOA shishi.roaringpenguin.com. dfs.roaringpenguin.com. (
                1999060501      ; serial
                10800           ; refresh
                3600            ; retry
```

```
                              604800         ; Expire
                              86400          ; Minimum
                              )
                  IN NS    shishi.roaringpenguin.com.
                  IN MX 10 shevy
                  IN MX 20 mail.isp.example.
localhost  IN A       127.0.0.1
shevy      IN A       192.168.2.1
scruffy    IN A       192.168.2.2
shishi     IN A       192.168.2.3
www        IN CNAME   shevy
```

Each RR is of the form:

`[domain] [ttl] [class] type data`

These parts have the following meaning:

- `domain`   The domain name to which the record applies. If no domain is given, the domain of the previous record is used.
- `ttl`   The time-to-live in seconds of the record. This specifies how long the record is valid; after this time has expired, any cached versions are invalidated and other name servers reload the record from the master server. If the `ttl` is omitted, it defaults to the `minimum` field of the preceding SOA record. (This is described later.)
- `class`   This is the class of the record. For TCP/IP networking, the class is always IN.
- `type`   This is the record type described in the section entitled "DNS Record Types."
- `data`   This is the record's data. The format depends on the record type.

The SOA Record

The SOA record in the example file contains the following parts:

- `@`   The domain of the record. The `@` character is special in that it signifies the "origin" of the file. The origin is simply the domain named in the corresponding zone portion of `/etc/named.conf`. For this example, therefore, the origin is `roaringpenguin.com`.
- `IN`   The class is IN.
- `SOA`   The type is SOA, or Start Of Authority.
- `shishi.roaringpenguin.com.`   The canonical hostname of the primary server for `roaringpenguin.com`.

> **Warning**
>
> Note the trailing dot in:
>
> `shishi.roaringpenguin.com.`
>
> This marks it as an absolute name. If you omit the trailing dot, all names are assumed relative to the file's origin. This would result in something like `shishi.roaringpenguin.com.roaringpenguin.com`, which is clearly wrong.

- `dfs.roaringpenguin.com.` The contact. This is the e-mail address of the domain administrator with the @ sign replaced with a period. Note also the trailing dot marking an absolute name.
- `1999060501` The serial number of the record. Whenever the data for the zone changes, this serial number should be increased. Secondary name servers periodically retrieve the SOA record from the primary name server. If the serial number has increased, they reload all the zone information from the primary server.

  An easy way to generate serial numbers is to use `YYYYMMDDSS` where `YYYY` is the year, `MM` is the month, `DD` is the day, and `SS` is a two-digit change number, allowing up to 100 changes per day.
- `10800` The refresh value in seconds. This specifies how often secondary name servers should synchronize themselves with the primary name server.
- `3600` The retry value in seconds. If a zone refresh fails, this specifies how often secondary servers should retry the refresh.
- `604800` Value that specifies how long secondary servers should keep trying before finally discarding zone information if they can't contact the primary server. (604,800 seconds is one week. This value should normally be quite large.)
- `86400` Value that specifies the default time to live for resource records in the domain. 86,400 seconds is one day. If your network changes very infrequently, you can set this value to be longer, perhaps a week.

The NS Record

The NS record specifies the name server for the domain. In the example, the domain part is omitted, so it defaults to the domain of the previous RR, or `roaringpenguin.com`.

The data portion of the NS record specifies the name server for the domain. It must be the canonical name of the name server. In this example, the name server for `roaringpenguin.com` is:

`shishi.roaringpenguin.com.`

Note the trailing dot in the configuration file to denote an absolute name.

The A Records

The A records map hostnames to IP addresses. Let's consider the entry for shevy. The domain part of the record is specified as shevy, but because there is no trailing dot, the domain is relative. Thus, the true domain for the record is shevy.roaringpenguin.com.

The data portion of the record specifies shevy's IP address, which is 192.168.2.1.

For convenience, we also define a local host entry, although most clients will probably find the entry in their /etc/hosts file rather than consulting DNS.

The MX Records

MX records specify mail exchangers; these machines handle mail for the domain. Each record consists of a preference followed by a hostname. Machines with lower preferences are tried first; if they cannot be contacted, machines with higher preferences are tried next.

In this example, the preferred mail exchanger for roaringpenguin.com is shevy.roaringpenguin.com. If this machine is down, the secondary mail exchanger is mail.isp.example. Note the absolute name for the second example.

The CNAME Record

The CNAME record specifies a "canonical" hostname. In the example shown, we set the canonical name of www.roaringpenguin.com to be shevy.roaringpenguin.com.

Reverse Lookup Files

It's fairly clear how a forward lookup is made: Given a hostname, the resolver queries the DNS server, which eventually returns an IP address. But how are reverse lookups done?

The solution is a clever hack. A pseudo domain in-addr.arpa is defined. To look up an IP address, a search is made in this pseudo domain. The IP address is reversed, in-addr.arpa is appended and a lookup for a PTR record is issued. This scheme allows the existing DNS machinery to be leveraged without adding any programming changes or complexity.

For example, to look up the name of the host with IP address 192.168.2.3, the resolver queries the name 3.2.168.192.in-addr.arpa for a PTR record. Let's look at the last zone in the example /etc/named.conf, the zone 2.168.192.in-addr.arpa:

```
@ IN SOA shishi.roaringpenguin.com. dfs.roaringpenguin.com. (
                  1999060501      ; serial
                  10800           ; refresh
                  3600            ; retry
```

```
                 604800        ; Expire
                 86400         ; Minimum
                 )
   IN NS   shishi.roaringpenguin.com.
1  IN PTR  shevy.roaringpenguin.com.
2  IN PTR  scruffy.roaringpenguin.com.
3  IN PTR  shishi.roaringpenguin.com.
```

The SOA and NS records we've seen before. Note the PTR records. The PTR record with domain 3 (for example) has a relative domain; the actual domain is therefore `3.2.168.192.in-addr.arpa`. The PTR record gives the hostname, which is:

`shishi.roaringpenguin.com.`

Note the trailing dot on the host name signifying an absolute name.

> **Background Material**
>
> This method of performing reverse lookups is quite clever; however, it makes life difficult if you subnet your networks on other than 8-bit boundaries. Delegating the reverse lookup files to subnet administrators is tricky, because reverse lookups rely on breaking up IP addresses at 8-bit boundaries.

The reverse lookup file for the domain `127.in-addr.arpa` contains the same SOA and NS records, but this PTR record:

```
1.0.0   IN      PTR     localhost.
```

This makes the reverse lookup for `1.0.0.127.in-addr.arpa` return `localhost`.

> **Note**
>
> It's a common mistake to set up forward name server records (A, MX, and CNAME) and forget about the reverse lookups (PTR). Many servers will refuse connections if they cannot perform a reverse lookup of your hostname, so you should ensure that both forward- and reverse-lookup databases are up to date.

Cache Hint Files

Let's look at the file `/var/named/named.cache`, which is the hint file for the root zone ".". (It is called a hint file because it lists the root name servers, which are the starting point for any external DNS query.)

```
;       This file is made available by InterNIC
;       registration services
;       under anonymous FTP as
;           file            /domain/named.root
;           on server       FTP.RS.INTERNIC.NET

.                        3600000   IN NS A.ROOT-SERVERS.NET.
A.ROOT-SERVERS.NET.      3600000   A  198.41.0.4
.                        3600000   NS B.ROOT-SERVERS.NET.
B.ROOT-SERVERS.NET.      3600000   A  128.9.0.107
.                        3600000   NS C.ROOT-SERVERS.NET.
C.ROOT-SERVERS.NET.      3600000   A  192.33.4.12
.                        3600000   NS D.ROOT-SERVERS.NET.
D.ROOT-SERVERS.NET.      3600000   A  128.8.10.90
.                        3600000   NS E.ROOT-SERVERS.NET.
E.ROOT-SERVERS.NET.      3600000   A  192.203.230.10
.                        3600000   NS F.ROOT-SERVERS.NET.
F.ROOT-SERVERS.NET.      3600000   A  192.5.5.241
.                        3600000   NS G.ROOT-SERVERS.NET.
G.ROOT-SERVERS.NET.      3600000   A  192.112.36.4
.                        3600000   NS H.ROOT-SERVERS.NET.
H.ROOT-SERVERS.NET.      3600000   A  128.63.2.53
.                        3600000   NS I.ROOT-SERVERS.NET.
I.ROOT-SERVERS.NET.      3600000   A  192.36.148.17
.                        3600000   NS J.ROOT-SERVERS.NET.
J.ROOT-SERVERS.NET.      3600000   A  198.41.0.10
.                        3600000   NS K.ROOT-SERVERS.NET.
K.ROOT-SERVERS.NET.      3600000   A  193.0.14.129
.                        3600000   NS L.ROOT-SERVERS.NET.
L.ROOT-SERVERS.NET.      3600000   A  198.32.64.12
.                        3600000   NS M.ROOT-SERVERS.NET.
M.ROOT-SERVERS.NET.      3600000   A  202.12.27.33
```

This file lists the 13 root name servers for the entire Internet as retrieved from `ftp://ftp.rs.internic.net/domain/named.root`. (We show a slightly edited version of the file.)

When you're setting up a caching name server, you should retrieve the file from the InterNIC server. The version shown here has not changed since August 1997, but there is no guarantee that it will not change in the future. Still, in a pinch, you can probably type the file as shown to get up and running. `named` should update the file automatically (assuming it does manage to contact a root name server).

Using `nslookup`

The program `nslookup` performs DNS queries and can be used to debug problems with DNS setup.

To start `nslookup`, type:

```
$ nslookup
Default Server: shishi.roaringpenguin.com
Address: 192.168.2.3
>
```

The program prints the name and IP address of the name server it is using (this is taken from /etc/resolv.conf and prompts for input.

To look up a hostname's IP address, simply enter the hostname:

```
> scruffy.roaringpenguin.com
Server: shishi.roaringpenguin.com
Address: 192.168.2.3
Name: scruffy.roaringpenguin.com
Address: 192.168.2.2
```

`nslookup` prints the name and address of the machine you queried. (It also prints the server name and IP address; we'll omit those lines from now on.)

If you want to do a reverse lookup, you must first tell `nslookup` that you are interested in PTR records, and then enter the `in-addr.arpa` domain name:

```
> set type=PTR
> 1.2.168.192.in-addr.arpa
1.2.168.192.in-addr.arpa name = shevy.roaringpenguin.com
2.168.192.in-addr.arpa nameserver = shishi.roaringpenguin.com
shishi.roaringpenguin.com internet address = 192.168.2.3
```

`nslookup` prints the name of the machine, as well as the name and IP address of the name server for the `2.168.192.in-addr.arpa` domain.

You can look at the SOA record for a domain with `nslookup`:

```
> set type=SOA
> roaringpenguin.com
roaringpenguin.com
        origin = shishi.roaringpenguin.com
        mail addr = dfs.roaringpenguin.com
        serial = 1999060501
        refresh = 10800 (3H)
        retry = 3600 (1H)
        expire = 604800 (1W)
        minimum ttl = 86400 (1D)
```

The type in the `set type=type` command can be any RR type or the word ANY. The ANY record type returns all records associated with the host or domain name. If you are connected to the Internet, you can do these lookups for any host or domain. This verifies that your name server setup works for domains other than ones for which it is authoritative. In this example, we look up the publisher's information from the author's network:

```
> set type=ANY
> mcp.com
Non-authoritative answer:
mcp.com  nameserver = NS1.IQUEST.NET
mcp.com  nameserver = NS2.IQUEST.NET
mcp.com  nameserver = NS2.mcp.com
Authoritative answers can be found from:
mcp.com  nameserver = NS1.IQUEST.NET
mcp.com  nameserver = NS2.IQUEST.NET
mcp.com  nameserver = NS2.mcp.com
NS1.IQUEST.NET  internet address = 198.70.36.70
NS2.IQUEST.NET  internet address = 198.70.36.95
NS2.mcp.com  internet address = 204.95.224.200
```

To exit from nslookup, type the end-of-file character (normally Ctrl-D).

For more information about nslookup, see the man page nslookup(8).

Summary

In this chapter, you learned how DNS is set up as a worldwide distributed database. You learned how DNS queries are performed and how name server caching is critical for efficient DNS operation. Next, you learned about the various DNS record types, and how to set up the named DNS server on Linux. Finally, you learned how to make interactive DNS queries using nslookup.

CHAPTER 13

Configuring PPP

IN THIS CHAPTER

- PPP Background 308
- Serial Port Configuration 309
- Running pppd 310
- Setting Up a Connection with chat 312
- IP Configuration Options 314
- PPP Authentication 314
- Connecting to an ISP 316
- Setting Up a Dial-In PPP Server 317
- Routing Through PPP Links 319
- Automatically Bringing Up PPP Links 320
- kppp 324

Most people do not have the luxury of a high-speed Internet connection. Instead, they rely on modem connections over telephone lines for Internet access.

PPP (Point-to-Point Protocol) is a protocol for transmitting packets over a serial line. Ethernet is typically used to link computers that are close to each other, and a serial line commonly links far-flung networks. PPP requires inexpensive hardware (a serial port, modem, and telephone line) to provide connectivity between two networks or between a local network and the Internet.

Using PPP, Linux can be used both as a dial-up client and a dial-in server. Linux machines can therefore serve as gateways linking local networks to the Internet or provide remote access service to dial-in users.

PPP Background

PPP is a fairly complex protocol. In addition to handling IP traffic, PPP has provisions for other networking protocols such as Novell's IPX and Appletalk. We'll concentrate on routing IP traffic over a PPP link.

PPP consists of a whole family of protocols. At the lowest level is High-Level Datalink Control (HDLC), which defines the framing for raw PPP packets and provides a checksum. HDLC is an international standard and is analogous to the raw Ethernet frame.

The Link Control Protocol (LCP) sits on top of HDLC. It is responsible for negotiating options relating to the data link itself, such as the MTU and whether or not each side should periodically send echo requests to determine if the link is still up.

For each networking protocol supported on a PPP link, there is a corresponding control protocol. For example, for an IP link, there is the Internet Protocol Control Protocol (IPCP), which negotiates various aspects of the IP link, such as which IP address each side will use.

The Linux implementation of PPP is split into two parts. Within the kernel, the low-level PPP driver handles the HDLC framing and the actual transmission and reception of packets. The `pppd` program (which is an ordinary program—not part of the kernel) handles option negotiation, authentication, and so forth. `pppd` is fairly complex and has many options; we'll discuss the most common ones. After you have read this chapter and understand how PPP works, you should be able to fine-tune `pppd` after reading the manual page `pppd(8)`.

Serial Port Configuration

To use PPP, you must configure the serial ports on your computer. Serial ports in Linux are named /dev/ttyS?. For example, the first serial port (corresponding to DOS's COM1:) is /dev/ttyS0 and the third serial port is /dev/ttyS2.

Serial Hardware

Linux supports standard PC serial port hardware and a number of multiport serial boards for hooking up many modems to a remote access server. In this book, we'll only discuss the standard PC serial hardware.

Standard PC serial ports support the RS-232 serial standard. This is a widely used standard, which specifies the meanings of various signals on the serial port as well as their voltage levels.

A serial link requires at least three wires: a ground wire to act as a voltage reference, a wire for transmitting data, and a wire for receiving data. Because serial ports are relatively slow, additional wires are used for flow control: A modem can ask the computer to stop sending for a while so as not to lose data. Similarly, the computer can ask the modem to stop sending it data. The lines for achieving this are called Clear To Send (CTS) and Ready To Send (RTS). RS-232 hardware flow-control is sometimes called RTS/CTS for this reason.

Modems use additional wires to signify the presence of a carrier. Usually, if the carrier is lost, the computer should hang up the modem and bring down the link.

From the PC side, a serial port has an I/O address and IRQ line. The I/O address is an address used by the computer to send or receive data. The IRQ (Interrupt Request) line is used to alert the computer when data are received.

A special chip on the serial port called the UART converts serial data to parallel data readable by the computer and vice versa. Almost all modern serial ports use the 16550A chip (or a clone thereof). Older computers may use the 16450 chip. The 16550A has a 16-byte buffer that lets it run at much higher speed than a 16450.

Most internal modems emulate a serial port. From the computer's point of view, an internal modem is just another serial port.

> **Warning**
>
> This is not true for WinModems. They use proprietary software drivers to work. If you have a Linux machine, a WinModem makes a handy paperweight—but that's about it.

Configuring Serial Hardware

To view your serial port settings, type:

```
# setserial -bg /dev/ttyS?
/dev/ttyS0 at 0x03f8 (irq = 4) is a 16550A
/dev/ttyS1 at 0x02f8 (irq = 3) is a 16550A
```

In this example, the computer has two serial ports whose IRQ and I/O address lines are as shown.

In all likelihood, Linux will correctly detect and configure at least the first two serial ports, and you won't have to do anything special. If you do need to set up a serial port, use the `setserial` command. This allows you to configure things such as the IRQ line and the I/O address. The manual page `setserial(8)` describes the various settings. There's also an excellent Serial-HOWTO in `/usr/doc/HOWTO`, which explains how to configure serial ports.

Running pppd

For the purpose of illustration, I have created the network in Figure 13.1.

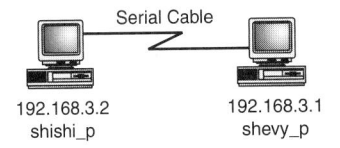

FIGURE 13.1
Example PPP link.

Serial Cable

192.168.3.2
shishi_p

192.168.3.1
shevy_p

To create the network, I simply connected a null modem cable from the serial port on `shishi` to the serial port on `shevy`.

To bring up the link, I run this command on `shevy`:

```
# /usr/sbin/pppd /dev/ttyS0 C
57600 192.168.3.1:192.168.3.2 crtscts
```

Here's an explanation of the arguments to `pppd`:

- /dev/ttyS0   Specifies the serial port to use.
- 57600   Specifies the speed of the port in bits per second.
- 192.168.3.1:192.168.3.2   Specify the local and remote IP addresses. In this case, the local address (shevy_p) is 192.168.3.1 and the remote address is 192.168.3.2.

> **Background Material**
>
> Usually, you do not specify the IP addresses. In most cases, the dial-in server picks IP addresses. If you do specify IP addresses, the remote server can refuse them. We'll discuss this a bit later.

- crtscts   Turns on hardware flow control for the port.

The pppd command performs the following steps:

1. It puts the serial port (/dev/ttyS0) in PPP mode.
2. It negotiates several aspects of the link with the remote end using LCP. Usually, the defaults work fine.
3. It negotiates the local and remote IP addresses using IPCP.
4. It creates a network interface (in this case, ppp0) and sets up a routing table entry. In this case, it simply creates a host route from 192.168.3.1 to 192.168.3.2.

Here is the routing entry on shevy after the PPP link is up:

```
$ route -n
Destination Gateway Genmask         Flags Metric Ref Use Iface
192.168.3.2 0.0.0.0 255.255.255.255 UH    0      0   1   ppp0
```

Note that a host route was created. Here's the interface configuration for ppp0:

```
$ ifconfig ppp0
ppp0 Link encap:Point-to-Point Protocol
     inet addr:192.168.3.1  P-t-P:192.168.3.2  Mask:255.255.255.255
     UP POINTOPOINT RUNNING NOARP MULTICAST  MTU:1500  Metric:1
     RX packets:20 errors:1 dropped:1 overruns:0 frame:0
     TX packets:22 errors:0 dropped:0 overruns:0 carrier:0
     collisions:0 txqueuelen:10
```

Note the link encapsulation of Point-to-Point Protocol. The IP address of the interface is 192.168.3.1 and the IP address of the other end is given by P-t-P as 192.168.3.2. Also, the interface has the POINTOPOINT flag set.

This example is unrealistically simple. The computers were connected by a dedicated cable, IP address negotiation was hard-coded by the client, and no authentication was required. In the real world, you would probably have to dial into an Internet Service Provider (ISP), authenticate yourself, accept IP addresses from the provider, and so on.

Here is the syntax of the pppd command:

```
# pppd [tty_name] [speed] [options]
```

The *tty_name* is simply the name of the serial port device, and the *speed* is the speed in bits per second. Here are some commonly used *options*:

- auth   Requires the remote system to authenticate itself. Dial-in servers usually use this to require clients to authenticate themselves.
- crtscts   Use hardware flow control. Disable this with nocrtscts.
- defaultroute   Add a default route to the system routing table using the remote system as the gateway. The default route is removed when the PPP link is broken. For the typical situation where you dial-in to a service provider, you should specify defaultroute.
- connect program   Run program to set up the serial line. PPP setup is attempted after program exits. This option lets you automatically establish a connection (providing, for example, your login name and password to a service provider) before switching to PPP mode.
- debug   Enables debugging. If set, pppd logs information about control packages to the system logging facility. This information can be directed to a file by setting up the system logger. See syslog.conf(5) for details.
- modem   Informs pppd that the connection is through a modem. This causes pppd to monitor modem status lines and drop the connection if the modem carrier is lost.

All options can be found listed in a file called /etc/ppp/options. The options should appear one per line.

Setting Up a Connection with chat

Many dial-in service providers require a login and password before switching to PPP mode. The chat program automates modem dialing and the login process.

chat uses a special script called a chat script to perform the setup. The chat script simply consists of pairs of strings called expect and send strings. chat waits for an expect string and, if it receives it, sends the corresponding send string.

Here's a sample `chat` script:

```
""         ATZ
OK         "ATDP 555-7634"
ogin:      davey
word:      K3wld00d
```

The first string is `""`, or the empty string. This causes `chat` to skip the first expect part and immediately send the `ATZ`. This is the command to reset the modem.

The modem responds `OK`, and `chat` sends the string `ATDP 555-7634`, causing the modem to dial my Internet Service Provider.

> **Background Material**
>
> Yes, I am one of the last people in North America with a pulse-dial line.

After a while, the remote computer answers and prints `Login:`. `chat` sees this and sends the user name `davey`. Similarly, after the last piece of the `Password:` prompt, it sends the password `K3wld00d` and exits. At this point, the remote computer flips into PPP mode and `pppd` takes over on the local computer.

Actually, this script is not complete. Here is the whole script:

```
ABORT      BUSY
ABORT      "NO CARRIER"
ABORT      VOICE
ABORT      "NO DIALTONE"
ABORT      "NO DIAL TONE"
""         ATZ
OK         "ATDP 555-7634"
ogin:      davey
word:      K3wld00d
```

The special keyword `ABORT` lists strings that should abort the connection. If any of `BUSY`, `"NO CARRIER"`, and the like is received, `chat` exits immediately.

To invoke `chat`, you can either place the entire script on the command line like this:

```
# chat '' ATZ OK 'ATDP 555-7634'...
```

or put the script in a file (for example, `/etc/ppp/chat-script`) and invoke `chat` like this:

```
# chat -f /etc/ppp/chat-script
```

You should always use the second method. Putting the script on the command line may reveal passwords (with the `ps` command). You should make the chat script file readable only by root.

Within a `pppd` invocation, you would use something like this:

```
# pppd /dev/ttyS0 57600 connect 'chat -f /etc/ppp/chat-script'...
```

Note the quotes to make the `chat -f /etc/ppp/chat-script` appear as a single argument to `pppd`.

`chat` has many other options and script commands; see `chat(8)` for details. The most useful command-line option is `-v`. The `-v` command causes `chat` to log everything sent or received from the modem to the system logger. This is very useful for debugging connection problems but could result in passwords being made visible in the system log files. These log files should be readable only by root.

IP Configuration Options

We've already seen that you use `local_addr:remote_addr` on the `pppd` command line to ask for particular IP addresses. However, if you are dialing in to a remote access server, it will most likely assign IP addresses. To use this, supply the `noipdefault` command-line option. The remote server will supply the IP addresses of each end of the link.

Alternatively, you can specify local and remote addresses, but use the `ipcp-accept-local` and `ipcp-accept-remote` options. If the remote machine does not supply addresses, the addresses you supplied will be used. Otherwise, the addresses supplied by the remote machine will be used.

For example, if you use the local and remote addresses 192.168.3.1 and 192.168.3.2, respectively, but are willing to use other addresses if the server insists on it, use:

```
# pppd ... 192.168.3.1:192.168.3.2 ipcp-accept-local ipcp-accept-remote
```

PPP Authentication

If you operate a dial-in remote access server, it is critical to authenticate incoming clients. And if you are dialing in to a server, you may wish to authenticate the server and make sure that you haven't reached the wrong server.

There are two main methods for authentication of a PPP link. The Password Authentication Protocol (PAP) is a simple protocol that works like a normal login. The client sends a user name and password, and the server compares this to its password database. This technique is not secure; eavesdroppers can easily obtain the user name and password.

The Challenge Handshake Authentication Protocol (CHAP) is a more secure protocol. The server sends a randomly generated string (the "challenge") to the client along with the server's hostname. The client looks up a "secret" associated with the server's hostname, combines it with the challenge, encrypts it with a one-way encryption function, and sends the result to the server. The server performs exactly the same computation and compares its answer with the response from the client. If they don't match, the link is taken down.

In addition, CHAP allows either side to challenge the other periodically. This process makes sure that the other side hasn't been replaced by an intruder.

> **Background Material**
>
> PPP is symmetric. In the preceding paragraphs, *server* means the computer requesting authentication, and *client* means the computer that responds by authenticating itself.

By default, pppd does not require authentication, but it will agree to authenticate itself when asked (providing, of course, it knows the proper secrets).

The authentication passwords for PAP and CHAP are called secrets. They are stored in `/etc/ppp/pap-secrets` and `/etc/ppp/chap-secrets`, respectively. These files contain a plain-text password and should be readable only by root.

The PAP Secrets File

If you are using PAP authentication, the PAP secrets file `/etc/ppp/pap-secrets` looks like this example from `shevy`:

```
#user      server     secret      address
davey      other      K3wld00d    192.168.1.1
other      shevy      Doh344      192.168.1.2
```

In this example, when `shevy` connects to the machine `other`, it responds with the user name `davey` and the password `K3wld00d`.

When authenticating itself to another machine, pppd picks a line containing the name of the remote server as the second field and the local user name as the first field. By default, the local user name is the host's name, but this can be changed with the `user` option to pppd. Because pppd has no way of knowing the remote server name, it must be supplied with the `remotename` option:

```
# pppd...remotename other user davey
```

If the `address` column is not blank, it specifies the IP address to assign to the `user` machine.

When checking the authentication of the remote machine, `pppd` uses the local hostname as the server (although the `name` option overrides this) and the user name supplied by the remote system as the user. Thus, for example, if `other` wished to connect to `shevy`, the `pppd` on `shevy` would expect the password `Doh344` and assign the address `192.168.1.2` to `other`.

You can place more than one IP address in the `address` field; the addresses in the `address` field specify a list of acceptable IP addresses. To allow any address, use `*`. You can also use a network address like `192.168.2.0/24`, which allows any address on the class C `192.168.2.0` network.

`pppd` has many more options for dealing with PAP; consult `pppd(8)` for details.

The CHAP Secrets File

The CHAP secrets file `/etc/ppp/chap-secrets` has the same format as the PAP secrets file. For CHAP, however, you do not need to specify the remote computer's name because that information is passed by the remote computer in the CHAP dialog.

If you are unfortunate enough to have to dial into a Windows NT PPP server, you may encounter connection problems. Some Windows NT servers are configured to use a non-standard (of course) Microsoft authentication protocol called MS-CHAP. The `pppd` supplied with Caldera OpenLinux appears to be able to handle this protocol, but I was unable to test it. Read the PPP-HOWTO document for more information. The HOWTO explains how to examine logging information to determine whether MS-CHAP is being used, and how to set up `pppd` to use it.

Connecting to an ISP

To connect your system to an ISP, you need the following pieces of information:

- *The IP address of one (or more) name servers.* These go in `/etc/resolv.conf`.
- *The kind of login dialog the ISP uses.* This is required to write a `chat` script. You may be able to figure this out by dialing in with a terminal emulator program and manually answering the prompts.
- *The kind of authentication the ISP uses.* It may use CHAP, PAP, or no authentication beyond the login chat.

Unfortunately, many ISPs target Windows users as their primary customers, and their customer support staff are not equipped to answer these questions—they know little beyond point and click. If you do not yet have an ISP, shop around for a provider that is Linux-friendly. Some ISPs even offer Linux PPP and chat scripts to their clients.

If you already have an ISP whose customer support staff cannot help you, you need to figure out the settings yourself. If you dial in using Windows, you should be able to get the name server IP addresses from the networking dialogs. A little experimentation should eventually uncover the rest of the information you need.

Setting Up a Dial-In PPP Server

The preceding sections covered dialing out using pppd. This section describes how to set up your Linux machine as a remote access server for dial-in clients.

There are several steps to setting up a dial-in server:

- For each serial port, you must start an mgetty process. The mgetty program listens for activity on a serial port and allows logins.
- You must configure mgetty to recognize PPP Link Control Protocol messages and switch the serial port to PPP mode.
- You must set up the appropriate secrets files for the dial-in users.

The following sections show a simple way to achieve the desired setup.

Starting mgetty

To configure a serial port for logins using mgetty, place a line like this in /etc/inittab:

```
S0:2345:respawn:/usr/sbin/mgetty -s 57600 ttyS0
```

This causes mgetty to listen to serial port /dev/ttyS0 after setting the speed to 57,600 baud. mgetty has many more options. It is part of a larger package called mgetty+sendfax, which allows you to handle fax transmission and reception as well as remote logins and terminals. See mgetty(8) for details.

Configuring mgetty for PPP Operation

The easiest way to set up dial-in accounts is to configure mgetty to recognize PPP LCP messages and switch the serial port to PPP mode automatically.

> **Warning**
>
> If you do this, mgetty will not authenticate incoming calls. You must use CHAP or PAP to authenticate incoming PPP connections in this case.

The file `/etc/mgetty+sendfax/login.config` holds configuration relating to the login process for `mgetty`. To automatically recognize incoming PPP connections, place a line similar to this in the file:

```
/AutoPPP/ - a_ppp /usr/sbin/pppd auth modem require-chap refuse-pap
```

In this example, we require CHAP authentication and refuse to allow or perform PAP authentication. You can change this according to your taste.

The `auth` option makes `pppd` close down the link if the remote computer cannot authenticate itself.

Setting Up the Secrets File

Let's continue this example. Suppose we wish to allow the user `dfs` to dial in. We assign his computer the IP address `192.168.3.1`. Here's the line from `/etc/ppp/chap-secrets`:

```
#client  server                   password  IP addresses
dfs      shishi.roaringpenguin.com k3wld00d  192.168.3.1
```

On the client side, the CHAP secrets file would look something like this:

```
#client  server                   password   IP addresses
dfs      shishi.roaringpenguin.com k3wld00d
```

The client `pppd` will accept the IP address assigned by the server.

Per-Port Options

If you are setting up a dial-in server for a network, you may have several modems attached to the server. In this case, you could create a global `/etc/ppp/options` file that looks something like this:

```
proxyarp
crtscts
modem
```

The `proxyarp` option creates an entry in the systems Address Resolution Protocol table with the IP address of the remote machine. If the dial-in server is on a LAN, this is the simplest way for other machines on the LAN to see the machine that is dialing in. More complex connections will require additional routes to be set up; this will be covered later.

Then, for each port, create a file called `/etc/ppp/options.ttyXX`. For example, if you have two modems (one on `/dev/ttyS0` and the other on `/dev/ttyS1`), you could create these two files:

```
# File: /etc/ppp/options.ttyS0
server_ip:192.168.7.1
```

```
# File: /etc/ppp/options.ttyS1
server_ip:192.168.7.2
```

Here, `server_ip` is the address of the server's PPP interface, and the `192.168.7.x` entries are the IP addresses assigned to the remote machines. In this case, a machine dialing in to `/dev/ttyS0` would be assigned the address `192.168.7.1`, and a machine dialing in to `/dev/ttyS1` would be assigned `192.168.7.2`. Note that you can use valid host names rather than hard-coded IP addresses; this may make the files more readable.

Routing Through PPP Links

In many cases, the routing for a PPP link is simple. Most times, a PPP link connects a machine or LAN to the Internet. In this case, the `defaultroute` option can be used with the `pppd` command to set up a default route through the PPP link. All other machines on the LAN should have default routes with the machine with the PPP link acting as a gateway.

However, sometimes you need to set up nondefault routes for two networks. For example, consider the two networks `192.168.7.0/24` (Network 7) and `192.168.8.0/24` (Network 8), each with their own independent links to the Internet. (See Figure 13.2.) For simplicity, assume that the same machines are used for the PPP links as for the Internet links. This allows other hosts on the two networks to have simple default routes through the gateways.

FIGURE 13.2
Two networks connected via PPP.

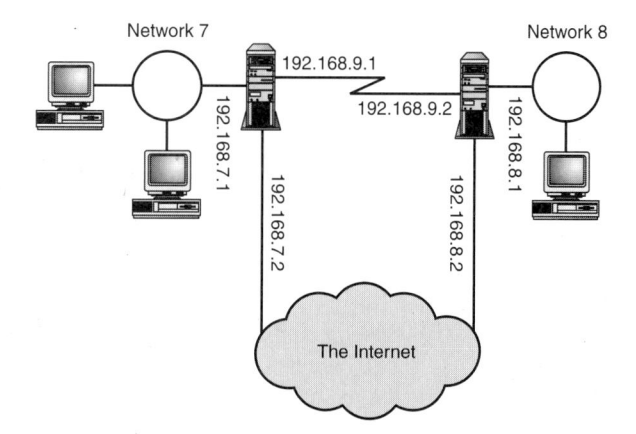

When the PPP link comes up, Gateway 8 must add a route for Network 7 through its PPP interface and vice versa. When the PPP link goes down, the route must be deleted.

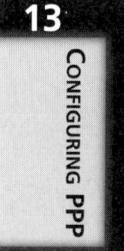

Whenever a PPP link comes up, the script /etc/ppp/ip-up is executed with five arguments:

- The PPP device (for example, ppp0).
- The tty device (for example, /dev/ttyS1).
- The tty speed in bits per second.
- The local IP address.
- The remote IP address.

As an example, suppose Gateway 7's IP address appears as 192.168.9.1 on the other end of Gateway 8's PPP link. Then /etc/ppp/ip-up on Gateway 8 might look like this:

```
if [ "$5" = 192.168.9.1 ] ; then
    # Add the network route for Network 7
    route add -net 192.168.7.0 netmask 255.255.255.0 gw 192.168.9.1
fi
```

Similarly, when the PPP link goes down, the script /etc/ppp/ip-down is executed with the same five arguments. It might look like this:

```
if [ "$5" = 192.168.9.1 ] ; then
    # Delete the network route for Network 7
    route del -net 192.168.7.0
fi
```

A complementary pair of scripts on Gateway 7 would set up routes to Network 8.

Note that we created another network 192.168.9.xxx for the PPP link. This is not strictly necessary, but it keeps both gateways symmetrical.

Automatically Bringing Up PPP Links

If you are dialing in to a PPP server, you normally have to invoke pppd manually to start a PPP connection. The diald program can automate this task; it can bring up PPP links on demand and bring them down after a certain period of inactivity.

diald has many options and can be fairly complex. We'll just illustrate the common case of connecting a local machine or LAN to a PPP server and using the PPP link as the default route.

Configuring `diald`

`diald` reads a configuration file called `/etc/diald.conf`. Consider my local network (Figure 11.2). Here is `/etc/diald.conf` on shevy:

```
mode ppp
connect "/usr/sbin/chat -f /etc/ppp/mychat"
device /dev/ttyS2
speed 38400
modem
lock
crtscts
local 192.168.1.1
remote 192.168.1.2
pppd-options 192.168.1.1:192.168.1.2
defaultroute
include /usr/lib/diald/standard.filter
```

shevy uses a PPP link with a local address of 192.168.1.1 and a remote address of 192.168.1.2 to connect to the Internet. Let's examine each line of `/etc/diald.conf`:

- `mode ppp`   Specifies that we will be using a PPP connection for the link. This should probably always be the case.
- `connect...`   Specifies the connect script. This is exactly the same option as would be given to `pppd`. Note that we specify the full path name of the chat program as `diald` runs with an empty PATH for security reasons.
- `device /dev/ttyS2`   Specifies the serial port of the connection.
- `speed 38400`   Specifies the speed of the serial port.
- `modem`   Specifies that the serial port is connected to a modem and the modem control lines should be respected.
- `lock`   Specifies that `diald` should create a lock file for the port. Many programs that use serial ports create a standard lock file and respect lock files left by other such programs.
- `crtscts`   Turns on hardware flow control.
- `local` and `remote`   Specify the local and remote IP addresses.
- `pppd-options...`   Specifies options to pass to `pppd` when the link is brought up. It seems that you should not need to specify local and remote IP addresses here, but my version of `diald` did not work unless I passed the options to `pppd`.
- `defaultroute`   Tells *diald* to make the new connection the default route.
- `include...`   Includes various rules that determine how long to keep the connection up. Some types of packets (for example, HTTP or FTP packets) should not

keep the connection up for long because they tend to come in solid stretches without much idle time for a given connection. Telnet packets, however, keep the link up longer because there may be a lot of idle time between them on a given connection.

The rules for determining how long to keep a link up can be very finely tuned; see dial(8) for all of the (gory!) details.

To invoke diald in its simplest form, simply create /etc/diald.conf and type:

```
# diald
```

Let's watch diald in action on shevy. First, here is the routing table before invoking diald:

```
Destination Gateway Genmask         Flags Metric Ref Use Iface
192.168.2.0 0.0.0.0 255.255.255.0   U     0      0   25  eth0
127.0.0.0   0.0.0.0 255.0.0.0       U     0      0   2   lo
```

Next, we invoke diald:

```
# diald
# route -n

Destination Gateway Genmask         Flags Metric Ref Use Iface
192.168.1.2 0.0.0.0 255.255.255.255 UH    1      0   0   sl0
192.168.2.0 0.0.0.0 255.255.255.0   U     0      0   26  eth0
127.0.0.0   0.0.0.0 255.0.0.0       U     0      0   2   lo
0.0.0.0     0.0.0.0 0.0.0.0         U     1      0   0   sl0
```

Note the two extra routes: The route to 192.168.1.2 (the other end of the PPP link we wish to establish) and the default route (0.0.0.0) both go through interface sl0. It turns out that sl0 is a "fake" interface; the diald program simply listens to it and intercepts packets sent on the interface.

Background Material

The sl0 device is a Serial Link Internet Protocol (SLIP) device. This is an older, less capable protocol that has largely been displaced by PPP. Nevertheless, to use diald, your kernel must support SLIP. The standard Caldera OpenLinux kernel works fine.

Now let's try to access a host on the Internet:

```
$ telnet www.roaringpenguin.com 80
```

The `telnet` command seems to take a long time, but the modem on `shevy` starts dialing. After a few seconds, the routing table looks like this:

```
Destination Gateway Genmask         Flags Metric Ref Use Iface
192.168.1.2 0.0.0.0 255.255.255.255 UH    0      0   0  ppp1
192.168.1.2 0.0.0.0 255.255.255.255 UH    1      0   0  sl0
192.168.2.0 0.0.0.0 255.255.255.0   U     0      0   28 eth0
127.0.0.0   0.0.0.0 255.0.0.0       U     0      0   2  lo
0.0.0.0     0.0.0.0 0.0.0.0         U     0      0   1  ppp1
0.0.0.0     0.0.0.0 0.0.0.0         U     1      0   13 sl0
```

Note the `ppp1` interface. Now, the default route and the host route to `192.168.1.2` go through it.

> **Background Material**
>
> The `sl0` routes are still present, but they are not used because they have a higher metric than the `ppp1` routes.

After the PPP link is up, `dial d` monitors traffic on it. After a certain amount of idle time, `dial d` shuts the link down and removes the `ppp1` routes from the routing tables.

`dial d` can be used in many more complex situations such as connections with dynamic IP addresses and connections with more complicated routing requirements. There are a number of excellent manual pages; look at `diald(8)`, `diald-examples(5)`, `diald-monitor(5)`, and `diald-control(5)`.

Monitoring `diald`

`diald` comes with a very nice graphical utility called `dctrl` for monitoring and controlling `diald`. In /etc/diald.conf, put the line

fifo /var/run/fifo_name

When `diald` starts, it creates a named pipe in the specified file. The `dctrl` program reads and writes this pipe to monitor `diald`. To invoke `dctrl`, simply type

 # dctrl

A graphical window appears. Figure 13.3 shows the window with all displays turned on (from the Options menu).

FIGURE 13.3
diald Control window.

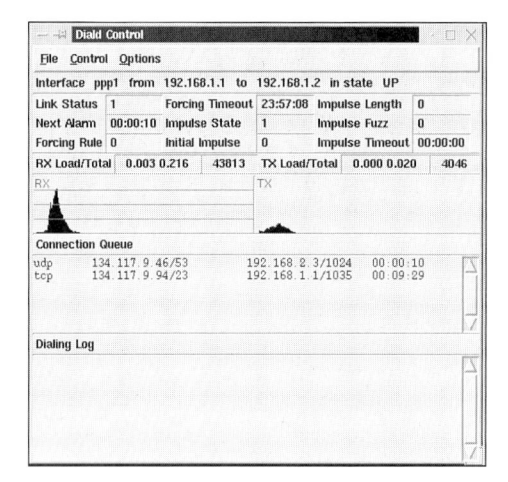

The Interface lines show all lines and their states. The next section shows detailed link status. There are a couple of pretty graphs showing link activity.

From `dctrl`, you can force a link up or down or even force `diald` to exit completely. For this reason, the FIFO should be accessible only by root or someone you trust; see `dctrl(1)` for more details.

kppp

The `kppp` program is a graphical KDE program for dialing out using a PPP link. It has excellent online help and is simply a front-end for `pppd`. Having read this chapter, you should have no problems understanding `kppp` and using it to set up a PPP link.

All the PPP settings are accessible from the Setup button. On the Modem tab, you can press the Terminal button and type directly to your modem. This is handy for debugging `chat` scripts.

Summary

In this chapter, you have learned how serial hardware is named and configured on Linux. You learned how to run `pppd` to bring up a PPP link and how to use `chat` to dial and log in to a remote computer. Next, you learned how PPP uses PAP and CHAP authentication for security, and how to link a personal workstation to an ISP. You then learned more advanced PPP scenarios, such as how to set up a remote access server and how to modify the routing table as a PPP link comes up and go down. Finally, you learned how to create on-demand PPP links with `diald` and how to use the graphical `kppp` application to set up a PPP link.

CHAPTER 14

Configuring NIS—
The Network
Information System

IN THIS CHAPTER

- How NIS Works   *326*
- RPC   *327*
- Setting Up an NIS Server   *329*
- Setting Up an NIS Client   *331*
- Slave Servers   *334*
- NIS Client Tools   *335*

NIS (the Network Information System) is a method for sharing information across a computer network. NIS enables you to log on to any computer in a network (with the same login name and password) by using a shared password database. NIS can also be used to share the `/etc/hosts` information (providing a service analogous to DNS).

By distributing system configuration across a network, all computers appear almost identical. In addition, the master files are centralized, easing the maintenance of configuration information if you need to add or move hosts.

How NIS Works

An NIS server maintains databases of information. NIS clients send requests to the server, which looks up information in its databases and returns the results to the clients.

NIS networks are divided into administrative groupings called NIS domain names. Note that NIS domains have nothing to do with DNS domains; they are simply groups of hosts created for administrative purposes. Having said that, an NIS domain typically corresponds to all the computers on a LAN.

For example, even though all computers in a fairly large organization (Sun Microsystems, say) will all be under the same DNS domain `sun.com`, they will be divided into many NIS domains, each of which corresponds to a local area network.

Originally, NIS was called Yellow Pages, or YP. However, British Telecom holds the trademark to Yellow Pages and forced Sun Microsystems to drop the name. Nevertheless, many NIS-related command names begin with *yp* as a result of the heritage.

NIS Maps

An NIS server maintains its information in databases called NIS maps. The maps are usually generated from normal system configuration files. Table 14.1 lists some typical NIS maps and the corresponding system configuration files.

TABLE 14.1 NIS Maps

System File	Maps
/etc/passwd	passwd.byname, passwd.byuid
/etc/hosts	hosts.byname, hosts.byaddr
/etc/group	group.byname, group.byuid

Note that many configuration files generate two maps. The `passwd.byname` map, for example, supports efficient location of password information given a login name. The `passwd.byuid` supports efficient searching based on the numerical user ID.

Many maps have nicknames because typing long names is unwieldy. A list of nicknames is stored in the file `/var/yp/nicknames`. If you have NIS up and running, you can get a list of nicknames like this:

```
$ ypcat -x
Use "ethers" for map "ethers.byname"
Use "aliases" for map "mail.aliases"
Use "services" for map "services.byname"
Use "protocols" for map "protocols.bynumber"
Use "hosts" for map "hosts.byaddr"
Use "networks" for map "networks.byaddr"
Use "group" for map "group.byname"
Use "passwd" for map "passwd.byname"
```

There may be many other maps used for other purposes. These usually contain specialized information for particular applications. Applications that use NIS should include documentation specifying which maps they use and what the maps contain.

NIS+

NIS consists of a "flat" set of maps with a single namespace. Sun Microsystems has developed a new network information system called NIS+. NIS+ has many more enhancements than NIS, including hierarchical namespace and relations between table entries. NIS+ is considerably more secure and scalable than NIS, but a production version of NIS+ does not yet exist for Linux.

RPC

The NIS server is the first server we've discussed that uses the Remote Procedure Call (RPC) facility developed by Sun Microsystems.

RPC allows clients to invoke remote procedures in server machines. The RPC mechanism includes facilities for accepting arguments from client procedures, transmitting them over the network, invoking the server procedure, and transmitting the answer back to the client.

For administration purposes, you must know how RPC picks port numbers. Normal TCP or UDP servers pick a "well-known" port number. For example, the Telnet server always listens to port 23. All Telnet clients know to contact the server at port 23.

RPC programs do not generally pick fixed port numbers. When an RPC server starts, it picks whichever port the operating system gives it (sometimes called an ephemeral port) and registers this port with another server known as the port mapper. The port mapper is itself an RPC server, but it does listen on a well-known port (port 111).

Every RPC server is assigned a program number and a version. The program number for an NIS server happens to be 100004, and the versions supported by Linux are 1 and 2.

When an RPC client wishes to contact an RPC server, it first contacts the port mapper on the remote machine (at the well-known port, 111). It specifies the program number it is looking for. If such a server is registered with the port mapper, the port mapper replies with the TCP or UDP port on which the RPC server is listening. The client then contacts the RPC server directly.

This means that before you start any RPC services, you must start the /usr/sbin/rpc.portmap program. Fortunately, the default Caldera OpenLinux setup starts the port mapper as part of the basic networking setup.

If you wish to see what RPC servers are running on a host, use the rpcinfo command like this:

```
$ rpcinfo -p hostname
   program vers proto   port
    100000    2   tcp    111  portmapper
    100000    2   udp    111  portmapper
    100005    1   udp    825  mountd
    100005    2   udp    825  mountd
    100005    1   tcp    828  mountd
    100005    2   tcp    828  mountd
    100003    2   udp   2049  nfs
    100003    2   tcp   2049  nfs
    100001    5   udp    851  rstatd
    100001    3   udp    851  rstatd
    100001    2   udp    851  rstatd
    100001    1   udp    851  rstatd
    100009    1   udp    742  yppasswdd
    100004    2   udp    743  ypserv
    100004    1   udp    743  ypserv
    100004    2   tcp    746  ypserv
    100004    1   tcp    746  ypserv
```

For information on a specific server, use the -t option (for TCP servers) or -u option (for UDP servers) like this:

```
$ rpcinfo -t hostname 100004
program 100004 version 1 ready and waiting
program 100004 version 2 ready and waiting
```

For more information, see rpcinfo(8).

Setting Up an NIS Server

A single NIS server can serve information for multiple NIS domains. We cover setting up a server for a single domain; the extension to multiple NIS domains is straightforward.

> **Note**
>
> Although an NIS server can serve multiple domains, it cannot support multiple password files, at least according to the documentation in `/usr/doc/nis-server-2.0/README.server`. Thus, for all practical purposes, it is useless to have a server serving more than one NIS domain.

To set up an NIS server, you must decide on an NIS domain name. For historical reasons, many people choose yp followed by their DNS domain name, as in `yp.roaringpenguin.com`. However, there's no real reason to do this; you could as easily choose `yp.foo` if you wish. At any rate, pick an NIS domain name. Also, decide on a machine to use as an NIS server.

On the NIS server, create a directory called `/etc/nis/domainname`. If you picked `yp.foo` as the domain name, the directory would be `/etc/nis/yp.foo`.

Setting Up Map Sources

In the directory `/etc/nis/yp.foo`, you must set up the source files for all the NIS maps. For example, if you are going to publish the `passwd` and `group` maps, you should place the text files for those maps under `/etc/nis/yp.foo`. If the NIS maps are to contain the same information as the system configuration files on the NIS server (a fairly common setup), just make symbolic links from `/etc/passwd` and `/etc/group` into `/etc/nis/yp.foo`. If you are using shadow passwords, you need to link `/etc/shadow` as well.

> **Warning**
>
> Using NIS with shadow passwords defeats the whole point of shadow passwords. With NIS, anyone can read the password database with a simple `ypcat` command. If you want to use shadow passwords, do not distribute the password files with NIS.

Building Map Databases

To build map databases from the (text file) sources, you need to copy `/etc/nis/.nisupdate.conf.sample` to `/etc/nis/yp.foo/.nisupdate.conf`. That is, copy the sample configuration file into the domain's directory as `.nisupdate.conf`.

> **Warning**
>
> The `.nisupdate.conf` file as distributed with Caldera OpenLinux does not work correctly. Before using it, make the following fixes.

Edit the `.nisupdate.conf` file to correct some errors. Change the rule for `hosts` to read:

```
$rule{"hosts"} =
    "mkdb2 hosts hosts.byname,hosts.byaddr 1,0";
```

Change the rule for `services` to read:

```
$rule{"services"} =
    "mkdb2 services services.byname,services.bynumber n0,n1";
```

Select the maps you wish to distribute by uncommenting (removing the # signs) from the appropriate rules. You will probably want to distribute at least the `passwd`, `group`, and `hosts` maps.

After you have set up `.nisupdate.conf`, run the command:

```
# /etc/nis/nis_update
```

This command performs the following steps:

1. For each subdirectory `dir` of `/etc/nis`, read the `.nisupdate.conf` file in `dir`.
2. For each map in the configuration file, generate a corresponding database in `/var/nis/dir`. These databases are in a form that allows efficient lookup of information.

> **Note**
>
> Actually, `nis_update` updates the binary database only if it does not exist or is older than the corresponding master text file.

Each time you change information in a master text file, you should run `nis_update` to update the NIS maps.

In our example for yp.foo, after running nis_update, there will be a directory called /var/nis/yp.foo, which contains files like these:

```
group.bygid    hosts.byname
group.byname   passwd.byname
hosts.byaddr   passwd.byuid
```

These are the databases used by the NIS server.

Starting the NIS Server

To start the NIS server, execute the following command:

```
# sh /etc/rc.d/init.d/nis-server start
```

To have the NIS server start automatically upon booting, go to the System : Daemons panel of COAS and enable NIS-Network Information Service (server part).

When you start an NIS server, two programs are actually started:

- The program ypserv is the actual NIS server. Its manual page is ypserver(8).
- The program yppasswdd allows users on NIS clients to change their passwords on the NIS server. It is documented in yppasswdd(8). On client machines, users should invoke yppasswd to change their passwords (rather than passwd).

NIS Security

By default, anyone is allowed to request information from the NIS server. This is undesirable because (unless a firewall prevents it) anyone can download your entire password file and crack it at his or her convenience.

Fortunately, the NIS server supports a feature called securenets, which limits who can contact it. In the file /var/nis/securenets, place a list of netmask/network pairs. Only machines on the specified networks can contact the NIS server.

For example, if your local network is 192.168.2.0/255.255.255.0, put this line in /var/nis/securenets:

255.255.255.0   192.168.2.0

Connections from any other hosts will be dropped.

Setting Up an NIS Client

To set up an NIS client, you need to set the NIS domain name and run a program called ypbind. ypbind is responsible for locating an NIS server for the domain.

Traditionally, ypbind finds an NIS server by broadcasting a request on the local network and listening for responses. This is not secure, however: Anyone who has physical access to your network can plug in a Linux laptop and supply an NIS server with fake password entries.

Because broadcasts are insecure, it is usual to specify the NIS server. This is done in the file /etc/nis.conf. If your NIS domain is yp.foo and your NIS server's IP address is 192.168.2.3, put a line like this in /etc/nis.conf:

domain yp.foo server 192.168.2.3

To start ypbind, run this command:

 # sh /etc/rc.d/init.d/nis-client start

This command parses /etc/nis.conf, sets the NIS domain name with the domainname command, and starts ypbind.

The domainname command displays the NIS domain name. Invoke it like this:

$ domainname
yp.foo

If you run with root privileges, you can set the domain name as follows:

 # domainname my.domain.name

The ypbind command creates a file called /var/nis/binding/domain.version. For example, the file might be called /var/nis/binding/yp.foo.2. The Linux C library looks for this file to determine how to connect to the NIS server.

ypbind has many options; they are documented in ypbind(8).

Name Service Switch

The standard Linux runtime library has functions for accessing various pieces of system information. For example, the getpwnam and getpwuid functions obtain password information keyed from the login name or numerical user ID, respectively. In traditional UNIX systems, these functions simply read the /etc/passwd file to obtain the required information.

Modern Linux systems are NIS-aware, meaning that these functions may retrieve information from an NIS server rather than (or in addition to) reading configuration files in /etc.

To determine how the library functions retrieve information, the system consults the file /etc/nsswitch.conf. Each line in /etc/nsswitch.conf looks like this:

database: services

Here, *database* is the name of a database (like `passwd` or `hosts`) and *services* is a list of information sources to be consulted. Each entry in *services* can be one of the following:

- `files` Consult the appropriate system configuration files. For the `passwd` database, for example, the file `/etc/passwd` is consulted.
- `nis` Consult the NIS server.
- `nisplus` Consult an NIS+ server. This may not be available for Linux systems and will be ignored if it is not.
- `dns` Consult the DNS system (used for the `hosts` database).
- `compat` Use a method of access compatible with those old hacks developed before `/etc/nsswitch.conf` was invented. We discuss this soon.

Here is a typical `/etc/nsswitch.conf` file for Caldera OpenLinux:

```
# /etc/nsswitch.conf
#
# Name Service Switch configuration file.
#

passwd:         compat
shadow:         compat
group:          compat

hosts:          files nis dns
networks:       nis files dns

ethers:         nis files
protocols:      nis files
rpc:            nis files
services:       nis files
```

The `passwd`, `shadow`, and `group` databases use the `compat` service. Here's how it works for `passwd`; the operations for `shadow` and `group` are the same.

First, the system reads the password database file in `/etc/passwd`. If it encounters an entry that looks like this:

```
+:x:0:0:::
```

it consults the NIS server. Essentially, this lets you keep the first part of your password database in `/etc/passwd` and the rest of it on the NIS server. Local entries in `/etc/passwd` override entries from the NIS server because the local file is consulted first.

This is indeed a hack. It's much cleaner to remove the "magic" entry from `/etc/passwd` and then use this specification in `/etc/nsswitch.conf`:

passwd: files nis

In the example file, we see that hostname lookups are first attempted with `files`, then with `nis`, and finally with `dns`. What this means is that a hostname is looked up first in /etc/hosts, next on the NIS server, and finally via DNS.

For more information on the name service switch file, consult the following info page:

```
$ info '(libc)Name Service Switch'
```

Name Service Switch Actions

After each service in the services list, you can specify an action. Normally, each service is tried in turn until a lookup succeeds. You can modify this behavior with actions.

Actions are written like this:

`[status=action]`

Here, *action* is either `return` (meaning ignore remaining services and return the looked-up key if it was found) or `continue` (meaning continue trying the lookup with the next service).

status is one of the following:

- `success` The lookup succeeded for the service. The default action is `return`.
- `notfound` The lookup process worked, but the value was not found. The default action is `continue`.
- `unavail` The lookup service is permanently unavailable. The default action is `continue`.
- `tryagain` The lookup service is temporarily unavailable. The default action is `continue`.

For example, consider this entry in /etc/nsswitch.conf:

`services:   nis [NOTFOUND=return] files`

Here, if NIS is up and running but the service is not found, we do not bother looking in the system configuration files. The NIS server presumably has complete information, and if the data are not found on the NIS server, they will not be in the system configuration file.

However, when the network boots, the NIS server might be unavailable. In this case, the status will be `unavail`, and the local configuration file will be used.

Slave Servers

The problem with NIS as described so far is that it introduces a single point of failure on your network. If the NIS server crashes, no one will be able to log into any host on the network. All host lookups using NIS will fail, and the situation will be generally chaotic.

The solution to this problem is to run more than one NIS server. One NIS server is designated as the master server. It holds the original master copies of the maps. A number of slave servers hold copies of the maps, which are periodically updated from the master.

To set up a slave NIS server, set up the machine as a client for the NIS domain. Also, set it up as an NIS server.

Next, copy the NIS maps from `/var/nis/domain` on the master to `/var/nis/domain` on the slave.

The command `ypxfr` is used to update maps on the slave from the master. You should run this command periodically (using `cron`) on the slave servers to synchronize their maps with the master server.

On Caldera OpenLinux, the files `ypxfr_1perday`, `ypxfr_1perhour`, and `ypxfr_2perday` in `/usr/libexec/nis` are sample shell scripts meant to be used by slave servers to update their maps. For example, you could put these lines in `root`'s `crontab` file on a slave server:

```
0 * * * * /usr/libexec/nis/ypxfr_1perhour
15 11,23 * * * /usr/libexec/nis/ypxfr_2perday
30 03 * * * /usr/libexec/nis/ypxfr_1perday
```

This would run `ypxfr_1perhour` every hour on the hour, `ypxfr_2perday` at 11:15 a.m. and 11:15 p.m., and `ypxfr_1perday` every day at 3:30 a.m.

These shell scripts simply invoke `ypxfr` with the names of various maps to transfer. You should edit them to reflect the maps used by your network setup. For more information on `ypxfr`, consult `ypxfr(8)`.

One last detail remains: Clients need to be told of the existence of slave servers. You could put the following line in `/etc/nis.conf`

domain yp.foo broadcast

but this is insecure because it uses broadcasting. Instead, it's better to add a list of slave servers like this:

domain yp.foo server *master_ip_addr*
ypserver *slave1_ip_addr*
ypserver *slave2_ip_addr*

NIS Client Tools

The NIS suite comes with a number of tools for checking the NIS setup. These tools allow you to query or list NIS maps. You can use them to check that your NIS setup is correct or to examine any of the NIS maps.

ypcat

The `ypcat` command lists an NIS map. Run it on a properly setup client like this:

```
$ ypcat map_name
```

For example, you could list the `passwd.byname` map like this:

```
$ ypcat passwd.byname
```

```
root:znj3jf9HJa93j:0:0:root:/root:/bin/bash
gopher:*:13:30:gopher:/usr/lib/gopher-data
bin:*:1:1:bin:/bin
ftp:*:14:50:FTP User:/home/ftp
dfs:943jfrssJd9aa:500:500:David F. Skoll:/home/dfs:/bin/bash
nobody:*:65534:65534:Nobody:/:/bin/false
...
```

The `ypcat` command understands nicknames (discussed previously in the "NIS Maps" section); you can type **ypcat passwd** to list `passwd.byname`.

`ypcat` has a few options that can be found. They are documented in `ypcat(1)`.

ypwhich

Sometimes, you need to know the name of the NIS server. If you have slave servers, you may not know for sure which server a client is using. The `ypwhich` command displays the name of the NIS server being used. You can use it like this:

```
$ ypwhich
shishi.roaringpenguin.com
```

Or, if you want to know the master for a particular map (say, `passwd.byname`), use:

```
$ ypwhich -m passwd.byname
shishi.roaringpenguin.com
```

See `ypwhich(1)` for details.

ypmatch

Although `ypcat` lists the entire contents of an NIS map, the `ypmatch` command lets you look up a particular key in a map without listing the entire map. This is much more efficient than retrieving the entire map and then searching for a particular entry. For example, to look up root's password entry on the NIS server, use:

```
$ ypmatch root passwd.byname
root:znj3jf9HJa93j:0:0:root:/root:/bin/bash
```

`ypmatch` has a few options documented in `ypmatch(1)`.

yppasswd

If you use NIS to distribute the password database, users on client machines should not change their passwords using the usual `passwd` command. Instead, they should invoke yppasswd. This changes the password on the NIS server. To invoke it, use a command something like this:

```
$ yppasswd
Please enter old password: OlDPwd
Please enter new password: k3w1D00d
Please retype new password: k3w1D00d
The NIS password has been changed on shishi.roaringpenguin.com
```

You may wish to rename /usr/bin/passwd to /usr/bin/passwd.local on client machines and make /usr/bin/passwd a symbolic link to /usr/bin/yppasswd. That way, users on NIS clients can use the familiar `passwd` command to change their NIS passwords.

Summary

In this chapter, we learned how NIS information is organized into NIS maps and how NIS servers provide information to clients. We also learned that NIS servers and clients are organized into groups called NIS domains.

We were introduced to Sun RPC, a facility used by many UNIX programs. We learned how to set up an NIS server, build the map databases, and start the server. We then learned how to set up an NIS client and how the Name Service Switch file /etc/nsswitch.conf controls name lookups.

Finally, we learned how to set up slave NIS servers and how to query NIS servers with ypcat, ypwhich, and ypmatch.

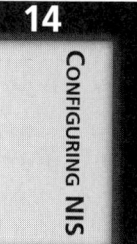

CHAPTER 15

Configuring NFS— The Network File System

IN THIS CHAPTER

- How NFS Works 340
- Configuring an NFS Server 342
- Configuring an NFS Client 344
- The showmount Program 347
- Automounting 347

The Network File System (NFS) is the standard UNIX method for sharing file systems between computers, meaning that NFS enables you to access remote file systems exactly as if they were local. NFS file systems accessed in this way are called NFS volumes.

NFS has a couple of important uses:

- Users' home directories can be kept on a central NFS server and mounted by clients. This allows users to use any of a number of workstations and still have access to their files in the same location in the file system tree. Combined with NIS, NFS allows you to make workstations on a LAN "generic," providing exactly the same login environment to all users.
- Large local software installations can be kept on a central server. This reduces disk space requirements and simplifies software updates.

> **Note**
>
> NFS does have its drawbacks, however. NFS is not secure—anyone who has physical access to your network can intercept and inspect NFS data. Furthermore, it is relatively easy for computer criminals to fool NFS's authentication mechanisms and impersonate another user on your network. For this reason, you should never use NFS to share sensitive information or use it across the Internet. You should set up firewalls to block NFS traffic.

How NFS Works

NFS uses Sun RPC (as discussed in Chapter 14) for client-server communications.

Under Linux, the client side of NFS is built directly into the Linux kernel. However, two normal Linux programs implement the server side.

> **Background Material**
>
> Traditional UNIX systems implement both client and server directly in the kernel. There is a kernel-space NFS server for Linux, but it is still experimental. You should use the user-space programs for now.

NFS is a stateless protocol. This means that the server does not remember anything about file operations; each operation is atomic as far as the server is concerned. For example, suppose you wish to read a 2KB file. You may read one kilobyte first, followed by the second kilobyte. The NFS server does not remember a "file position" or any such thing; it is up to the NFS client to handle all the state.

In the example, the NFS client would do an atomic "read one kilobyte starting at location 0" followed by an atomic "read one kilobyte starting at location 1024."

This design is highly unusual, but it has a number of benefits:

- An NFS server can crash and reboot, and the client won't notice anything wrong. Because the server doesn't store any information about "connections," it can't lose any information if it crashes. (Until the server reboots, however, the client will notice that it is taking a very long time to respond.)
- An NFS server can handle many clients. Because there is no per-client connection or state to maintain, thousands of clients can mount NFS volumes with no impact on the server (unless they all try accessing the volumes at the same time!).

However, the stateless design has a serious drawback: There is no way to lock NFS files because a file lock implies that the server must remember some state. There are a number of ways around this, usually involving special locking daemons, but none of these is available for Caldera OpenLinux. So do not place database files (which often require locking) on an NFS volume.

Mounting an NFS Volume

To mount an NFS volume, the kernel (on the client) contacts a special mount daemon on the server. It passes the path name of the volume to mount. The mount daemon returns a handle, which is a chunk of bytes. The meaning of the handle is irrelevant to the client; presumably, it means something to the server. Whenever the client wishes to refer to the mounted volume, it passes the same handle back to the server.

To refer to a particular file, the client asks the NFS server to perform directory searches (starting with the handle given by the mount daemon). The NFS server returns another handle, which refers to the file. From this point on, the client specifies the handle and the desired operation for all subsequent NFS operations.

The server generates handles in such a way that if the server crashes and restarts, the handles are still valid. This allows clients to keep going as if nothing but a slowdown in the network traffic happened.

> **Background Material**
>
> Actually, things are a little more complicated, but this is conceptually how NFS works.

NFS Permissions

Each NFS transaction uses the user ID and group-ID from the client. For the sake of security and sanity, these IDs must match. This implies that all NFS servers and clients should have the same password file or should all be using the same NIS maps for authentication.

There are provisions for mapping nonmatching client IDs to the appropriate server IDs, but they are far more trouble than they are worth.

Configuring an NFS Server

To set up an NFS server, you need to decide which directory trees to make available to clients and to whom they should be made available. The file /etc/exports contains a list of NFS volumes being exported. As usual, blank lines and lines beginning with # are ignored. Other lines look something like this:

`volume who_and_how...`

In this line, *volume* is the root of the directory tree being exported, and *who_and_how* is a list of clients that might access the tree and how they can access it. Each entry in *who_and_how* looks something like this:

`host(options)`

The *host* part specifies which clients may access the volume. It may be specified in any of the following forms:

- A single host name or IP address.
- A netgroup specified by @group. See netgroup(5) for details about netgroups.
- A hostname with wildcards. The characters * and ? are interpreted the same as shell wildcards. For example, *.roaringpenguin.com would match shevy.roaringpenguin.com and shishi.roaringpenguin.com, but not mach.subdomain.roaringpenguin.com.
- An entire IP network specified as address/netmask (for example, 192.168.2.0/255.255.255.0).

Each host specification can be followed by one or more options. Options are enclosed in parentheses and separated with commas. Do not put spaces in the option lists. Available options are:

- `secure` Requires that mount requests originate from a "reserved" Internet port. UNIX machines limit access to ports below 1024 to root; this option adds a small measure of security by ensuring that requests from UNIX machines come from root-privileged sources. This option is on by default.
- `ro` Allows read-only access to the volume.
- `noaccess` Disallows access to the volume. This seemingly useless option allows you to export a volume but disable access to certain subdirectories within the volume.

> **Background Material**
>
> The `noaccess` level only works on Linux. Most UNIX NFS servers do not allow the `noaccess` level of control.

- `root_squash` Converts access from root on a client to nobody on the server. It actually reduces root's privileges. This option is on by default. It was intended to provide some extra security—anyone who gains root privileges on a client will still be unable to modify sensitive files on the NFS server. In practice, the option doesn't provide that much extra security.
- `no_root_squash` Turns off `root_squash`.

For more options, see `exports(5)`. Most of the remaining options relate to user- and group-ID mapping.

Sample /etc/exports File

Here is a sample `exports` file:

```
/                  shishi(ro) trusted(rw,no_root_squash)
/usr/local         *.roaringpenguin.com(ro)
/pub               (ro,insecure)
/pub/private       (noaccess)
```

Let's look at it line-by-line:

- `shishi` is allowed to mount the root directory read-only. `trusted` can mount it read/write and, in addition, `root` on `trusted` retains root privileges on the server.
- Any machine in `roaringpenguin.com` can mount `/usr/local` read-only.

- Anyone at all can mount /pub read-only, and the mount request need not come from a UNIX reserved port.
- However, no one can look at /pub/private.

Starting an NFS Server

You can start an NFS server at boot time by enabling NFS Server from the COAS System:Daemons dialog box.

To start the NFS server manually, type this command as root:

```
# sh /etc/rc.d/init.d/nfs start
```

To shut down the NFS server, use:

```
# sh /etc/rc.d/init.d/nfs stop
```

The /etc/rc.d/init.d/nfs file is simply a shell script that starts or stops two programs—rpc.mountd (the mount daemon) and rpc.nfsd (the NFS server daemon).

These programs have command-line options that may be useful for debugging or in esoteric situations; see mountd(8) and nfsd(8).

Security Considerations

NFS was never designed for high security. Consider these potential problems:

- NFS does not encrypt data in transit. Anyone who has physical access to your network can watch data going by.
- NFS servers trust the user and group IDs they are presented by the client. If someone can plug his laptop Linux machine into your network, he can impersonate any user and have access to any NFS files that would be accessible to that user. You may want to make all NFS volumes read-only to reduce problems with tampering.
- A compromised NFS client can be used to compromise the NFS server, which in turn can compromise all other clients served by the server. For example, an intruder who gains root privileges on one client can modify binaries on the NFS server and thereby compromise the entire network. Again, this is a strong argument for only using read-only NFS mounts.

Configuring an NFS Client

To configure an NFS client, you need to ensure that the kernel supports NFS-mounted file systems. The standard Caldera OpenLinux kernel offers this support; you shouldn't have to do anything special.

To mount an NFS file system, use the `mount` command like this:

```
# mount -t nfs server:volume mountpt
```

Here, `server` is the name of the NFS server and `volume` is the volume on the server. `mountpt` is a local mount point.

Here is a concrete example. I have a fast CD-ROM drive on `shishi` and would like `shevy` to be able to access the drive.

On `shishi`, there's a line in `/etc/exports` like this:

```
/mnt/cdrom      shevy(ro,no_root_squash)
```

This allows `shevy` to mount `/mnt/cdrom` read-only. To mount the volume on `shevy`, I type:

```
# mount -t nfs shishi:/mnt/cdrom /mnt/shishi-cd
```

After this command has executed, the CD-ROM on `shishi` is available under `/mnt/shishi-cd` on `shevy`.

To unmount the volume, I use the usual `umount` command:

```
# umount /mnt/shishi-cd
```

NFS Mount Options

NFS volumes can have a number of mount options associated with them. These include:

- `rsize=n`   Sets the number of bytes NFS uses when reading from an NFS server. The default is 1024, but throughput may be improved for some servers by specifying 8192.

- `wsize=n`   Sets the number of bytes NFS uses when writing to an NFS server. The default is 1024, but throughput may be improved for some servers by specifying 8192.

- `timeo=n`   Sets the initial retransmission timeout in tenths of a second. NFS has a complex system of back-off if transmissions time out; see `nfs(5)` for more details.

- `retrans=n`   Sets the number of minor timeouts and retransmissions before a major timeout occurs. Depending on other NFS options, a major timeout either causes a message to be printed on the console or the file operation to be aborted.

- `retry=n`   The number of minutes that `mount` will keep trying to mount an NFS file system. The default is 10,000 minutes or about a week.

- `bg` If the first NFS mount attempt times out, `mount` puts itself in the background and keeps trying. If this option is missing, `mount` remains in the foreground and keeps trying to mount the file system.

  You should use this option carefully depending on the file system you are trying to mount. For example, if you are NFS-mounting /usr at boot-time, then in all likelihood the workstation will be unable to proceed until /usr is mounted. Do not use bg in this situation.

  However, if you are NFS-mounting a USENET news directory, it's probably more important to get the workstation up and running than wait for the news server to come alive. You should use the bg option in this case.

- `fg` This option does the opposite of bg (and the default behavior).
- `soft` If an NFS file operation has a major timeout, report an I/O error to the calling program.
- `hard` If an NFS file operation has a major timeout, print a message on the console and keep trying. This is the default.

  The hard and soft options should be used carefully, too. You probably want important volumes hard-mounted because the system cannot continue unless they are mounted. Less important volumes can be soft-mounted. Be aware that soft-mounted file systems can cause data loss because NFS may not report errors immediately (because of network latency and other factors).

> **Background Material**
>
> Hard-mounted NFS file systems have been compared to slow disk drives, and soft-mounted ones have been compared to broken ones.

- `intr` If the volume is hard-mounted, this option allows you to interrupt the NFS file operation with the interrupt key. The default is to disallow this and force you to wait until the NFS server comes back up.

There are several more options for specialized situations; see `nfs(5)` for more details.

NFS Volumes in `/etc/fstab`

You can automatically mount NFS volumes at startup by placing their mount parameters in /etc/fstab. Here's an example:

```
# Filesystem         Mountpoint       Type Options Dump Pass
shishi:/mnt/cdrom    /mnt/shishi-cd   nfs  ro,bg   0    0
```

This option mounts `shishi:/mnt/cdrom` on `/mnt/shishi-cd` read-only. If the initial mount request times out, mount puts itself in the background and keeps trying while the rest of the boot sequence continues.

The showmount Program

The `showmount` command is useful for seeing which NFS volumes have been mounted by clients and which NFS volumes are being exported by a server.

To see the list of file systems exported by a server, type:

```
$ showmount -e server
```

For example:

```
$ showmount -e shishi
Export list for shishi:
/mnt/cdrom *.roaringpenguin.com
```

On the NFS server, you can see a list of hosts mounting file systems from the server:

```
$ showmount
Hosts on shishi.roaringpenguin.com:
scruffy.roaringpenguin.com
shevy.roaringpenguin.com
```

You can get more details with the `-a` option:

```
$ showmount -a
All mount points on shishi.roaringpenguin.com:
scruffy.roaringpenguin.com:/mnt/cdrom
shevy.roaringpenguin.com:/mnt/cdrom
```

This lets you see which hosts are mounting which volumes.

showmount has a few more options; see `showmount(8)` for details.

Automounting

Sometimes it is convenient to distribute users' home directories across many NFS servers. It would be highly annoying to have to always mount all the directories on all the machines when at any given time only one or two are required.

The automounter lets you create automount maps that specify which machine a certain directory resides on. Only when the directory is actually requested (for example, when someone logs in or tries to read a file from a directory) is the mount performed.

Linux supports two types of automounters: The `autofs` file system is built into the kernel and is configured by a utility program called *automount*. Unfortunately, Caldera OpenLinux does not include this package. It is available on most Linux archives, however.

The second automounter is called `am-utils` and does not rely on kernel support. Instead a daemon called `amd` "pretends" to be an NFS server. It intercepts NFS requests and performs any mounts needed to satisfy them.

Unfortunately, `amd` is quite complicated to set up. It comes with a 97-page manual whose contents are beyond the scope of this chapter. You can look at the manual using `info` like this:

```
$ info "(am-utils)Top"
```

Automounting is powerful, but it is often more trouble than it is worth. Unless you have a large network with many NFS servers, it is easier to use normal NFS mounts. In particular, most small networks are organized around a central file server with many clients. In this case, each client can directly mount files from the server without requiring complex automount maps.

Summary

In this chapter, you have learned the basic principles of NFS, including its stateless design. You have learned how to mount NFS file systems and how NFS uses user and group IDs to determine access permissions. Next, you learned how to configure an NFS server by editing `/etc/exports` and how to start and NFS server by invoking `rpc.mountd` and `rpc.nfsd`. You learned some security considerations when setting up NFS servers. Next, you learned how to configure an NFS client and mount NFS volumes. Finally, you learned how to use `showmount` to get information about mounted and available NFS volumes. You were given a brief introduction to automounting and a pointer to the `amd` documentation.

CHAPTER 16

Configuring Samba

IN THIS CHAPTER

- Overview of SMB *350*
- Samba Configuration *351*
- Running Samba *360*
- Debugging a Samba Setup *360*
- Mounting SMB Shares *362*
- Checking Samba's Status *363*
- Web-Based Samba Configuration *364*

Samba is software that allows Linux machines to share disk directories and printers with Windows clients. Samba uses the Server Message Block (SMB) protocol to communicate with Windows clients. This chapter will teach you how to set up a Linux machine to serve as a file and print server for Windows clients. You will also learn how to set up a Linux machine as a client for a Windows file server. These capabilities let you use Linux machines seamlessly in a mixed UNIX/Windows environment. By using Linux as a file and print server, you can save the often considerable cost of an NT license and the associated Windows NT maintenance and upgrade costs.

Overview of SMB

SMB is a protocol originally designed to share resources over a local area network. It was originally a very primitive protocol, running on a proprietary network protocol called NetBIOS. Over the years, as more features were required, SMB became more and more complex until it grew into the complicated and ugly protocol it is today.

Until Samba was available, only Microsoft Windows, OS/2, and a number of proprietary and expensive add-on programs for UNIX machines could implement the SMB protocol. Samba is a free software suite that implements SMB by encapsulating NetBIOS packets over TCP/IP. Microsoft Windows can be configured to do the same and can interoperate with Samba as if Samba were a native Windows NT file and print server.

> **Note**
>
> To use Samba, your Windows clients must have TCP/IP networking enabled and must be configured to use Client for Microsoft Networks and File and Printer Sharing for Microsoft Networks using TCP/IP.

Mapping SMB clients to UNIX poses some difficult problems because of the widely different philosophies of Windows and UNIX. Let's look at some of the areas of difficulty.

UNIX uses user IDs to validate all file-access operations. SMB has a very loose username concept; early SMB protocols had no concept of usernames at all. Samba tries to cope with this by using user-level share security where possible. Windows 95/98 has no concept of user-level security; it permits only share-level security. In user-level security, access is granted based on a user supplying a username and a valid password. In share-level security, each shared resource is given a password, and a person connecting to it need only supply the password. This is clearly a problem for UNIX, which always requires a user ID.

UNIX has a strict and consistent notion of file ownership. Windows 95/98 SMB protocols have no concept whatsoever of file ownership. There is no way, therefore, for a UNIX SMB server to signal to a Windows 95/98 client that permission to access a file is denied because of lack of ownership.

Many SMB clients convert passwords to uppercase before transmitting them. Samba tries to compensate by trying various permutations of passwords. Other SMB clients encrypt passwords before transmitting them. Samba supports encrypted passwords.

SMB provides many types of locks to Windows clients. Samba can simulate most of these locks, but it cannot enforce locking against UNIX programs. That is, if a Windows client locks a file, it will be locked for other Windows clients, but a UNIX process can access the file without difficulty. This can lead to problems if both Windows and UNIX processes update a file at the same time.

Finally, SMB is poorly documented. Although the Samba team did receive some documentation and help from Microsoft, and SMB is an X/Open standard, much of the Samba functionality was implemented by reverse-engineering the protocol. It is a tribute to the Samba team's tenacity that Samba works as well as it does.

Samba Configuration

Samba uses the file /etc/samba.d/smb.conf to hold configuration options. Samba has a huge number of configuration options, all of which are described in the smb.conf(5) manual page. To aid in your understanding of Samba, let's look at a simple configuration file that illustrates some of the common options and then build from there.

The configuration file (as is usual on UNIX) is a plain text file. Blank lines and lines beginning with # or ; are ignored.

The configuration file is divided into a number of sections. The *global* section controls the overall behavior of Samba. Each *share* has its own section that controls parameters related to it. (A share is a shared resource such as a printer or disk directory that the server offers to clients.)

Global Configuration Options

Global options apply to the Samba server as a whole. Here are some global settings. They are edited versions of the sample configuration options in /etc/samba.d/smb.conf.sample supplied with Caldera OpenLinux.

```
# Sample SAMBA file
# The global settings begin with the tag [global]
```

```
[global]

# Workgroup (NT domain name)
workgroup = WORKGROUP

# Server string — equivalent of NT "Description" field
server string = Samba Server on Caldera OpenLinux

# Automatically set up printers from /etc/printcap
load printers = yes

# Caldera uses LPRng printer daemon
printing = lprng

# Cap the size of the log file at 50kB
max log size = 50

# Security mode:  Don't use share-level security!
security = user

# How to fiddle with upper/lowercase matches
password level = 1
username level = 1

# Encrypt passwords? (commented out)
# encrypt passwords = yes
# smb passwd file = /etc/samba.d/smbpasswd
```

The `[global]` tag indicates the start of the global options section. The `workgroup` option specifies a Microsoft domain name. You should set it to your Windows NT domain name. The `server string` option is a comment that appears in the Network Neighborhood browser on a Windows client in Detailed view mode.

The `load printers = yes` option tells Samba to create a shared printer for each printer found in the system `/etc/printcap` file. We will cover Samba printer configuration later in this chapter. UNIX systems have a number of methods for print spooling; the `printing = lprng` tells Samba that the server uses the `LPRng` print spooler.

The `security = user` option tells Samba that all users must authenticate themselves with a username/password pair. This is far more secure than share-level security. In share-level security, a password is associated with the shared resource itself, and any user who can produce that password is granted access. Modern clients (Windows 95/98 and NT) support user-level security, and you should configure Samba to use it.

The `password level` and `username level` options specify how many combinations of upper- and lowercase letters to try when matching usernames and passwords. Some silly clients convert usernames and passwords to uppercase; this is clearly no good for UNIX authentication. A level of 1 means that Samba tries the following possibilities:

- The name as sent.
- The name in all uppercase.
- The name in all lowercase.
- All combinations of one uppercase and the rest lowercase.
- All combinations of one lowercase and the rest uppercase.

The higher this value, the longer a connection attempt may take and the lower security.

Encrypted Passwords

Modern Windows clients can encrypt passwords before sending them over the network. This increases security because a person listening in on your network cannot capture users' passwords.

Samba supports encrypted passwords, but it is mildly painful to set them up. SMB does not use the same encryption algorithm as the UNIX password file, so it needs a separate file to store encrypted passwords. This file is typically /etc/samba.d/smbpasswd.

To set up the file, you must create an entry for each user in your system password file. If you are not using NIS, do it like this (as root):

```
# mksmbpasswd < /etc/passwd > /etc/samba.d/smbpasswd
```

If you are using NIS, run this command instead:

```
# ypcat passwd | mksmbpasswd > /etc/samba.d/smbpasswd
```

These commands set up a file with everyone's password locked. Next, you must set the password for each user who wishes to access shares from a Windows client. Do this as follows (as root):

```
# smbpasswd user
New SMB password: gr9x3wq
Retype new SMB password: gr9x3wq
Password changed for user user
```

Disabling Encrypted Passwords

If your local network is secure or you are using other protocols (like Telnet) that transmit clear-text passwords anyway, you may wish to disable encrypted passwords. This simplifies maintenance of the password file. (You don't need to maintain a separate smbpasswd file.)

You can disable encrypted passwords on Windows clients. The mechanism for doing this varies depending on which version of Windows you are using. For details, see the files `NT4_PlainPassword.reg`, `Win95_PlainPassword.reg`, and `Win98_PlainPassword.reg` in `/usr/doc/samba-2.0.3/docs`. You should also look at the documentation files in `/usr/doc/samba-2.0.3/docs/textdocs`, especially the `ENCRYPTION.txt` file.

File Shares

After the global configuration options come share configurations. Each share section specifies a resource to be shared with Windows clients. Continuing with the sample configuration file, here is a section which that shares the CD-ROM volume:

```
# Make the CD-ROM available to anyone read-only
[cdrom]
    path = /mnt/cdrom
    public = yes
    writable = no
```

The `[cdrom]` section creates a share called `cdrom`. The path specifies which directory is to be shared. Any Windows client accessing the share will see the directory tree rooted at `/mnt/cdrom`.

The `public = yes` option specifies that anyone may access the share without a password. The Samba daemon changes its user ID to nobody when a public connection is made. The `writeable = no` option provides read-only access, which is certainly to be expected for a CD-ROM device.

I have set up the `cdrom` share on `shishi`. From the test Windows machine, the resource is known as `\\shishi\cdrom`. Windows names network resources as two backslashes followed by the server name, another backslash, and the share name.

Samba supports a special kind of share called `[homes]`. Here is an example:

```
[homes]
    valid users = %S
    only user = yes
    user = %S
    writeable = yes
    create mask = 0750
```

The share is special because it creates artificial shares based on the user name. If, for example, user `dfs` connects to a share called `dfs`, Samba first looks for a share named `dfs` in the `smb.conf` file. Not finding one, it checks for the presence of a `homes` share. If this exists, and if `dfs` has an entry in the UNIX password file, the `homes` share is cloned with a default path equal to the user's home directory. In essence, this makes `\\servername\username` map to `username`'s home directory (as long as `username` has an entry in the UNIX password file).

The `valid users` option specifies a list of users who are allowed to connect to the share. We see here the first example of Samba's percent substitution mechanism. In this case, `%S` is replaced by the name of the share. Setting `valid users` to `%S` enforces the convention that the share name must match the username. Various other percent substitutions are documented in `smb.conf(5)`.

The only user and user options cooperate to ensure that only the user named in the `valid users` option can connect to the resource and that the access is made under the user's UNIX user ID.

The home directory is writeable, allowing the user full access to his or her files. The create mask specifies the umask to use for creating files; in this case, the owner will have full access, the group will have read and execute access, and others will have no access.

> **Note**
>
> The default Caldera setup sets the path to `%H/Public`. That is, the share user is mapped to the `Public` directory under the user's home directory. The rationale for this is that all the configuration files look ugly from Windows and that it's better to restrict access to a subdirectory of the home directory. You may choose either mapping.

For the last example of a file share, consider a public directory in which anyone might read and write files. Such a share can be created like this:

```
# A publicly-accessible directory
[public]
    comment = Public directory for sharing files
    path = /var/public
    browseable = yes
    writable = yes
    create mask = 0755
```

In this example, a public share called `public` is created. The path is `/var/public`. The create mask of 0755 means that the owner of a file has full access and that others have read and execute permission.

The UNIX permissions on the `/var/public` directory are important. If you wish to allow anyone to delete anyone else's files, make the permissions on `/var/public` 0777. However, I recommend that you make the permissions 1777. This allows anyone to write into the directory, but the sticky bit (covered in Chapter 8) prohibits people from deleting files that belong to other users.

Because Windows 95/98 has no concept of file ownership, attempting to delete a file owned by another user yields the unhelpful and misleading error message `Cannot delete file: Access is denied. Make sure the disk is not full or write-protected and that the file is not currently in use.` Unfortunately, the only way to see who owns the file is to log on to the UNIX server and run `ls`.

Printer Shares

The load printers and printing options in the global configuration section usually eliminate the need to define separate printer shares. Samba creates the shares automatically by reading the `/etc/printcap` file.

However, Caldera OpenLinux's printing system is too clever for its own good. Caldera makes all printers look like PostScript printers. Windows clients often have their own printer drivers and their own ideas about what a printer should look like. To use a printer from a Windows client, therefore, you should not use the normal UNIX printer definition. You should define a generic printer and install printer drivers on the client machine.

> **Warning**
>
> The Caldera administration system has no way to create a generic local printer. You must edit `/etc/printcap` by hand. You can try selecting PostScript Printer as the printer type. This should disable any filtering, but it's safer to create the entry by editing `/etc/printcap` directly.

For example, I have a Lexmark Optra E+ laser printer. It uses Hewlett-Packard's Printer Control Language (PCL), but Caldera installs a print filter that makes it accept PostScript. (The conversion is done using `ghostscript`.)

The Windows clients have their own Optra E+ drivers and expect to be able to speak PCL to the printer. Here's Caldera's entry for the printer in `/etc/printcap`:

```
lp:\
        :lp=/dev/lp0:\
        :br#57600:\
        :rm=:\
        :rp=:\
        :sd=/var/spool/lpd/lp:\
        :mx#0:\
        :sh:\
        :if=/var/spool/lpd/lp/printfilter:
```

To make the generic version, simply copy everything except the `if` line and change the printer name:

```
generic:\
        :lp=/dev/lp0:\
        :br#57600:\
        :rm=:\
        :rp=:\
        :sd=/var/spool/lpd/generic:\
        :mx#0:\
        :sh:
```

You need to change the printer name and the spool directory (`sd`). Create the directory restart the line printer daemon (as root) like this:

```
# mkdir /var/spool/lpd/generic
# sh /etc/rc.d/init.d/lpd reload
```

From the Windows client, connect to the printer \\server\generic, but choose the correct Windows printer driver (in this case, for the Lexmark Optra E+). Doing this causes Windows to send the correct data to the printer and the Linux server to pass it straight to the printer unmodified. If you hadn't deleted the `if` line, the Linux server would pass the data through the print filter, mangling it beyond repair.

Alternatively, you can pretend to Windows that all printers on the server are generic PostScript printers. (You can select the Apple LaserWriter driver, for example.) You then use the normal Caldera print filters to convert from PostScript to whatever language the printer actually uses. This results in a simpler setup, but makes it impossible to use any special features that may be available in the Windows printer driver for the actual printer.

A PDF Pseudo-Printer

Portable Document Format (PDF) is a popular document format defined by Adobe for electronically distributing documents. Its main feature is that it preserves all formatting, allowing electronic documents to appear exactly like printed ones. It also allows for efficient interchange of vector graphics.

Normally, to create PDF documents from Windows, you need to purchase Adobe's PDF Writer software. However, with a little cooperation from Linux, Samba, `ghostscript`, and a small shell script, you can have a free PDF document creator.

First, set up a printer in the Samba configuration file:

```
[pdfwrite]
   comment = Convert docs to PDF
   public = no
   printable = yes
   path = /tmp
   print command = /usr/local/bin/makePDF %s %u
```

Note that this share has the attribute `printable = yes`. This tells Samba that the share is a printer and not a disk. The path tells Samba where to deposit incoming spool files.

All the magic is in the `print command` option. Every time you print to this share, the shell script `/usr/local/bin/makePDF` is called with two arguments—the name of the incoming spool file (%s) and the name of the user (%u). Let's examine this shell script:

```sh
#!/bin/sh
# Script to convert PostScript into PDF and
# save it in /var/public/pdfs/username

umask 022
INPUTFILE=$1
USER=$2
DIR=/var/public/pdfs/$USER
# Create directory in case it doesn't exist
mkdir -p $DIR

# Generate a unique filename
CTR=1

while [ true ] ; do
        OUTPUTFILE=$DIR/out-$CTR.pdf
        if [ ! -f $OUTPUTFILE ] ; then
                break
        fi
        CTR=`expr $CTR + 1`
done

# Convert the file
ps2pdf -dSAFER $INPUTFILE $OUTPUTFILE

# Remove input file
rm -f $INPUTFILE

exit 0
```

First, the shell script sets the `umask` to `022`, so that any files and directories it creates are not world- or group-writeable.

The variables `INPUTFILE` and `USER` are set from the command-line arguments. The shell script then creates a directory `/var/public/pdfs/user`, where `user` is the name of the user.

Next, the `while` loop generates a unique file name. Finally, the shell script runs the `ps2pdf` program to convert PostScript into PDF and removes the incoming spool file.

A couple of steps remain to complete the setup: Create the directory `/var/public/pdfs` owned by root with permissions 1777. This is a shared directory in which PDF files will be deposited.

Finally, create a network printer on the Windows client. Use the `pdfwrite` share as the network printer, and use the Apple LaserWriter driver. You are now all set!

> **Warning**
>
> Make sure that only users with valid login names can access the PDF printer. Otherwise, users could supply carefully constructed fake usernames that cause Samba to execute arbitrary UNIX commands. Also, make sure to include the `-dSAFER` option on the `ps2pdf` command line.

Print a test page to the printer. If you've set up the public share earlier, a file called `out-1.pdf` will magically appear in the `pdfs\user` folder in the public share. Whatever you print to the network printer will simply be added to this folder in PDF format. Any user can print to the printer and her PDF files will be neatly organized in a folder bearing her name. She doesn't even need to know there's a Linux server behind the scenes.

> **Note**
>
> This example illustrates the extreme flexibility of UNIX. By breaking up tasks into small parts and using shell scripting judiciously, you can achieve very useful results. The shell script shown is not optimal, however—if there are many files in the output directory, it could take a long time to generate output file names. Also, it would be nice if the output file name bore some relationship to the name of the document being printed. Some of this information can be gleaned by examining the PostScript code produced by Windows; it is left as an exercise to improve on the shell script. (Perl is probably more appropriate for a more elaborate script; see Chapter 32, "Perl Programming".)

The PDF conversion by `ghostscript` is not as good as Acrobat's PDF Writer. It can only convert the standard 14 PostScript fonts in vector format; all other fonts are rendered as bitmaps. For this reason, you should edit the PDF printer properties in Windows and select Send TrueType Fonts to Printer According to the Font Substitution Table. Also, stick to the standard PostScript fonts (Times, Courier, and Helvetica/Arial) when you create documents.

Because PDF files are so easy to create, are cross-platform, and do not carry the risk of macro viruses, I urge you to distribute formatted documents as PDF files rather than in proprietary formats like Microsoft Word or WordPerfect format.

Running Samba

A Samba server consists of two daemons: The nmbd daemon provides NetBIOS name service, and the smbd daemon provides actual resource sharing.

To have Samba start automatically when you boot, open the COAS System:Daemons dialog box and enable SMB Server Processes (Samba).

To manually start Samba, run this command as root:

```
# sh /etc/rc.d/init.d/samba start
```

To stop Samba, use:

```
# sh /etc/rc.d/init.d/samba stop
```

If you have changed the configuration file and need to restart Samba, use:

```
# sh /etc/rc.d/init.d/samba restart
```

The script /etc/rc.d/init.d/samba starts or stops the nmbd and smbd programs. These programs have a number of command-line options; see the manual pages nmbd(8) and smbd(8), respectively.

Debugging a Samba Setup

Samba includes a couple of utility programs for debugging your Samba setup. They verify that your configuration file is sane and allow you to connect to SMB servers from the Linux command line.

Verifying the Samba Configuration File

The program smbtestparm parses the Samba configuration file and reports any errors. Here is an example:

```
$ smbtestparm
Load smb config files from /etc/samba.d/smb.conf
Processing section "[homes]"
Processing section "[cdrom]"
Processing section "[printers]"
Processing section "[public]"
Processing section "[pdfwrite]"
Loaded services file OK.
Press enter to see a dump of your service definitions
```

After verifying that all services are correct, smbtestparm prompts you to press Enter. When you do so, it dumps a complete list of global parameters. This includes both the parameters in the configuration file and default values for those not in the configuration file. It then prints a complete list of shares.

The prompt to press Enter is rather annoying because it makes it hard to pipe smbtestparm's output to a file or through more. If you wish to put smbtestparm's output in a file, invoke it with the -s option:

```
$ smbtestparm -s > tempfile
```

Command-Line SMB Client

smbclient is a command-line SMB client program. This lets you connect to SMB shares from a Linux machine, eliminating the need to test your setup from a Windows machine.

The simplest way to connect to a share is as follows:

$ smbclient //*server*/*share*

Here's an example:

```
$ smbclient //shishi/dfs
Added interface ...
Password: k3wld00d
Domain=[WORKGROUP] OS=[Unix] Server=[Samba 2.0.3]
smb: \>
```

The share to which you connect (in this case, //shishi/dfs) is referred to as the remote directory, and the current UNIX working directory is the local directory.

The smb: prompt is an FTP-like prompt. To list the available commands, type help:

```
smb: \> help
ls dir du lcd cd
...
```

Some of the more useful smbclient commands are given in Table 16.1.

TABLE 16.1 smbclient **Commands**

Command	Meaning
ls	List the contents of the current remote directory.
pwd	Show the current remote directory.
rename	Rename a file.
rm	Delete a file.
get	Transfer a file from the remote directory to the local directory.
put	Transfer a file from the local directory to the remote directory.

continues

TABLE 16.1 continued

Command	Meaning
print	Print a local file. Only valid if the share is a printer share.
help	List available commands.
help cmd	Get help about the command cmd.
quit	Log off from the SMB server.

As you see, smbclient is very similar to the command-line FTP client. For details about other commands, type help at the smbclient prompt. For details about invoking smbclient, see the man page smbclient(1).

Backing Up SMB Shares

smbclient has a very useful command called tar. This command creates a tar file of the remote directory. You can use smbclient to back up or restore SMB shares from a Linux machine.

To back up an SMB share, use the c option:

```
smb: \> tar c backup.tar
    5166 (  280.3 kb/s) \SUHDLOG.DAT
   20553 (  386.0 kb/s) \BOOTLOG.TXT
   20553 (  378.7 kb/s) \BOOTLOG.PRV
   93812 (  424.1 kb/s) \COMMAND.COM
   ...
```

smbclient backs up the entire share in backup.tar. The x option is the opposite; it causes smbclient to extract files from the local tar file and place them on the SMB share.

You can invoke smbclient with the -T option to automatically invoke the tar command. This lets you write shell scripts to back up SMB shares from Linux. See smbclient(1) for details.

Mounting SMB Shares

Not only can Linux act as an SMB server, it can also mount SMB file systems. You can put SMB shares in your Linux directory tree, just as you can put NFS volumes in the tree.

To mount an SMB share, use the smbmount command:

```
# smbmount //server/share password -c 'mount mountpt
```

For example, the following command mounts the \\windoze\c share under /mnt/w:

```
# smbmount //windoze/c k3wld00d -c 'mount /mnt/w'
```

You can verify that the mount worked by listing the directory contents:

```
$ ls /mnt/w

AUTOEXEC.BAT    DETLOG.TXT      SETUPLOG.TXT
Acrobat3        DRVSPACE.BIN    SUHDLOG.DAT
BOOTLOG.PRV     IO.SYS          SYSTEM.1ST
BOOTLOG.TXT     MSDOS.—·        WEBSHARE
COMMAND.COM     MSDOS.SYS       WINDOWS
CONFIG.SYS      NETLOG.TXT      dfs
DBLSPACE.BIN    Program Files   logo.sys
DETLOG.OLD      RECYCLED
```

Yes, all the ugly Windows files are there.

Because SMB does not have the concept of users or groups, the `smbmount` command lets you specify the user and group for the mounted share (from UNIX's point of view). The `-u` option specifies the numeric user ID, and the `-g` specifies the numeric group-ID. They default to the user ID and group ID of the person who invoked `smbmount`. You can also specify file and directory permissions as octal numbers with the `-f` and `-d` options. See the `smbmount(8)` and `smbmnt(8)` manual pages for details.

To unmount an SMB share, use the usual `umount` command:

```
# umount /mnt/w
```

Checking Samba's Status

The `smbstatus` command displays a short listing of all currently active shares. Here is an example:

```
$ smbstatus

Samba version 2.0.3
Service    uid   gid   pid    machine
-------------------------------------------
dfs        dfs   dfs   1056   windoze Mon Aug 23 09:02:21 1999
cdrom      dfs   dfs   1056   windoze Mon Aug 23 09:02:21 1999
public     dfs   dfs   1056   windoze Mon Aug 23 09:02:21 1999

No locked files

Share mode memory usage (bytes):
   1048464(99%) free + 56(0%) used + 56(0%) overhead = 1048576(100%) total
```

The `-b` option provides "brief" output:

```
$ smbstatus -b

Samba version 2.0.3
PID     Username    Machine     Time logged in
------------------------------------------------
1056    dfs         windoze     Mon Aug 23 09:02:21 1999
```

Web-Based Samba Configuration

If editing the text `smb.conf` file has depressed you, cheer up: Samba supports web-based configuration file editing via a program called SWAT (Samba Web-based Administration Tool).

To enable SWAT, make sure that the following line appears in `/etc/services`:

```
swat    901/tcp    # Samba Web Administration Tool
```

Next, make sure that the following line appears in `/etc/inetd.conf`:

```
swat stream tcp nowait.400 root /usr/sbin/tcpd swat
```

Finally, and most importantly, put this line in `/etc/hosts.deny`:

```
swat:ALL EXCEPT 127.0.0.1
```

> **Warning**
>
> SWAT requires you to enter the root password in your Web browser. Do not use SWAT over the network; intruders could sniff the root password. The line in `/etc/hosts.deny` ensures that all SWAT sessions are run on the Samba server itself.

Restart `inetd` as follows:

```
# kill -HUP `cat /var/run/inetd.pid`
```

On the Samba server, start a Web browser and open the URL `http://localhost:901`:

```
$ netscape http://localhost:901
```

Enter the root login and password. You will be presented with the wonderful SWAT home page (Figure 16.1).

FIGURE 16.1
SWAT home page.

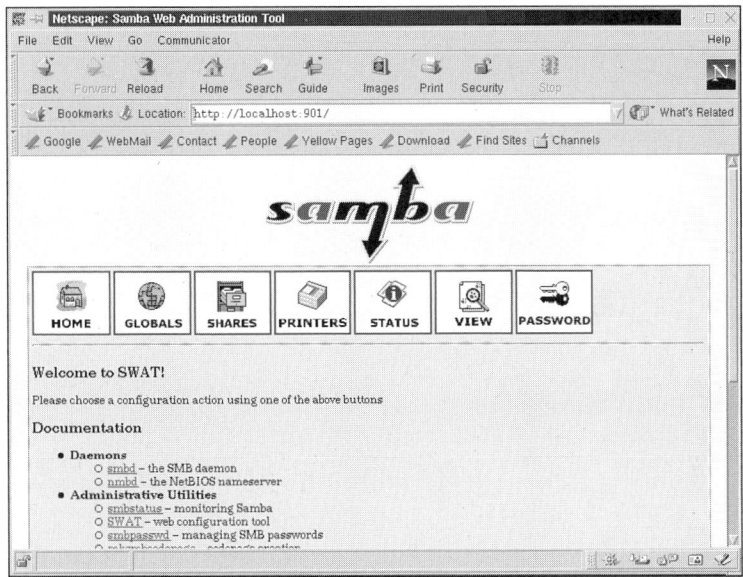

From this home page, all the Samba documentation is instantly accessible. You can click on the Globals, Shares, and Printers icons to configure global variables, disk shares and printer shares, respectively. The Status icon gives a table showing current active Samba connections, and View lists the /etc/samba.d/smb.conf file. Finally, password lets you manage server and client passwords.

As Figure 16.2 shows, SWAT provides an attractive interface for entering data and includes links to help files for each parameter setting. This is invaluable when you are learning Samba.

> **Warning**
>
> If you have hand-edited /etc/samba.d/smb.conf, committing changes with SWAT will discard any comments you may have added. SWAT faithfully preserves the meaning of the configuration file, but it discards comments and notes.
>
> After you have finished configuring Samba with SWAT, exit the Web browser (even if you intend to browse the Web). As long as the same Web browser runs, it caches the root login and password that may allow others to access SWAT if you leave your terminal unattended.

FIGURE 16.2
SWAT global variable configuration.

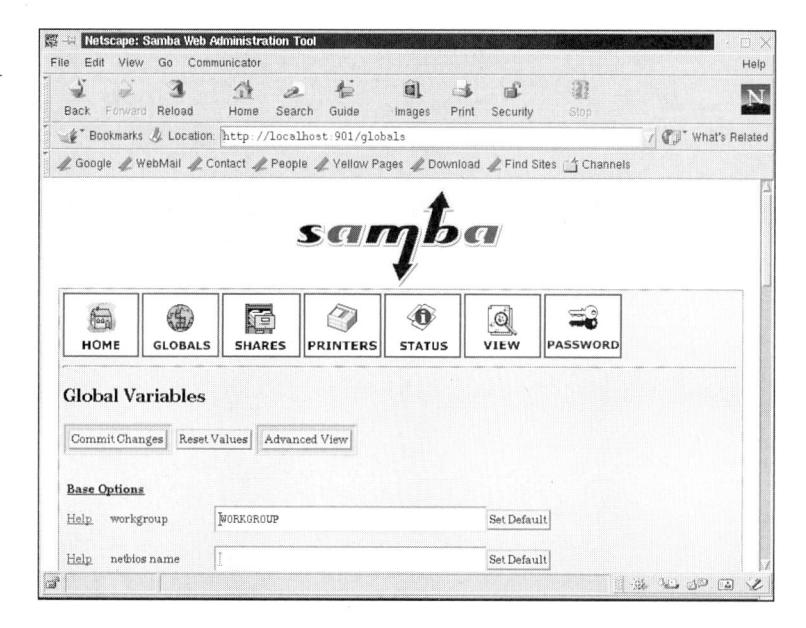

Summary

In this chapter, you learned some of the background of SMB, a protocol widely used by Microsoft Windows to share disk and printer resources. We covered Samba configuration including global options, share options, and printer options. We also developed a special printer that produces PDF documents when used as a Windows printer. Next, you learned how to start and stop Samba and how to use `smbtestparm` and `smbclient` to test your Samba setup. You learned how to mount SMB shares as part of the Linux file system. Finally, you learned about SWAT, the Web-based Samba configuration tool (and probably wondered why I forced you to plow through the text-based configuration procedure).

NetWare Integration

CHAPTER 17

IN THIS CHAPTER

- Introduction to the NetWare Client for Linux   368
- Getting Started with the NetWare Client   368
- Activating and Deactivating the NetWare Client   371
- Using the NetWare Client for Linux   371
- Printing with the NetWare Client   375
- NetWare Administration for Bindery Servers   377
- File Systems and Quotas on Bindery Servers   381
- Administration for Novell Directory Service   383
- Managing Disk Quotas on NDS Servers   391
- File System Trustees on NDS Servers   392

Introduction to the NetWare Client for Linux

The NetWare client component of Caldera OpenLinux lets you seamlessly integrate your Linux installation into your organization's existing NetWare environment. The client provides full functionality for communicating with NetWare 3.*x* and 4.*x* servers. Specifically, it provides the following services:

- Recognition of all NDS trees and bindery servers on the network
- Utilities for logging in and out of NDS trees and bindery servers
- Mounting of all accessible NDS objects and files upon NDS login
- Printing and print queue management utilities
- NetWare broadcast message utilities
- Other utilities for managing user passwords, mount points, and so forth

Getting Started with the NetWare Client

This section will explain how to get started with NetWare. That is, how to install, configure, and perform other basic tasks.

Installing the NetWare Client and Utilities

To install the NetWare client, Internetwork Packet Exchange (IPX) must be either compiled into the kernel or loaded as a module. Load as Module is the default of a Caldera OpenLinux installation, and unless you have changed it, your system should be ready to install the client packages and utilities.

To install the NetWare client, you must execute the following series of commands as user root, with the floppy (which comes with your Caldera OpenLinux distribution) inserted in the floppy drive:

```
mount -t ext2 /dev/fd0 /mnt/floppy
```

```
rpm -ivh /mnt/floppy/nwclient-4.2.0-col22-1.i386.rpm
```

Once installed, the NetWare client automatically starts each time you reboot your system. If you want to start it immediately without rebooting, enter the following command:

```
/etc/rc.d/init.d/nwclient.
```

The Novel Directory Service (NDS) is a great help for organizing large networks. NDS is a database of objects, where each object represents users or resources in a network. Within each object is stored information about the individual user or network resource as well as which relations this objects has to other object in the network. The bindery is a special database; it stores network configuration information on a Novell fileserver. Netware clients query the bindery to get information on available services, users, and routing information.

The Caldera NetWare client provides many NetWare NDS tree and bindery administration utilities. For the NDS tree, these are

- `nwdscreate`   Creates a new NDS object.
- `nwdsattrs`   Lists attributes of an NDS object's class.
- `nwdsvalues`   Lists values of an NDS object's attribute.
- `nwdsmodify`   Modifies values of an NDS object's attribute.
- `nwdsrm`   Removes an NDS object from the tree.
- `nwdsaddtrust`   Gives an NDS object rights to a NetWare directory.
- `nwdsshowtrust`   Displays NDS object rights for NetWare directories.
- `nwdssetspace`   Sets the disk quota for a specific NDS directory.
- `nwdsshowspace`   Shows the disk quota for a specific NDS directory.

And for the bindery server, these are:

- `nwbocreate`   Creates a new NetWare bindery object (user, group, or queue).
- `nwboprops`   Lists the properties of a NetWare bindery object.
- `nwbpcreate`   Creates a new property for a NetWare bindery object.
- `nwbpadd`   Adds a value to a property of a NetWare bindery object.
- `nwbpvalues`   Lists all values of a property of a NetWare bindery object.
- `nwbprm`   Removes a value from a property of a NetWare bindery object.
- `nwborm`   Removes an object from the NetWare bindery.
- `nwboaddtrust`   Gives a NetWare bindery object rights to a NetWare directory.
- `nwboshowtrust`   Displays a bindery object's right-top NetWare directories.
- `nwbosetspace`   Sets a disk quota for a specific NetWare bindery directory.
- `nwboshowspace`   Shows the disk quota for a specific NetWare bindery directory.

To install these NetWare administration utilities, execute the following command, with the floppy inserted and mounted as outlined earlier:

```
rpm -ivh /mnt/floppy/nwutils-static-cl-1.1-17.i386.rpm
```

Once installed, the NetWare administration utilities are immediately available for use, assuming the NetWare client has been installed and started.

Configuring the NetWare Client

When you install the NetWare client for Linux, the client is configured for immediate use. However, you can make changes to the default configuration at any time. To reconfigure the NetWare client, log into the Linux client as user root, and open the /etc/sysconfig/nwclient file with any text editor. Upon opening this file, you will notice that two default options are set: ONBOOT=yes and NWCLIENT_SINGLE_CONNECTION_TABLE=no.

ONBOOT indicates whether the NetWare client starts automatically every time you boot. If the client is active, NetWare servers and trees appear under the /NetWare directory, and all NetWare utilities will function.

By default, each NetWare user has a separate connection table for NetWare resources. This means that if two different users are logged into Linux, each can log in to the same (or multiple) NetWare servers, using different NetWare usernames. In every case, the root user's access is the combined total of all Linux users who have logged in to NetWare systems.

If the parameter NWCLIENT_SINGLE_CONNECTION_TABLE is set to yes, all users share a single connection table. You might find advantages to this, but it can reduce the usefulness of the NetWare client and can also present security issues. For example, if two Linux users want to access the same NetWare server, whoever logs in first will have her name in the connection table. Although the second user can't log in again because that connection already exists for that server, the second user has access to the NetWare server, based on the rights of the first user's login.

> **Note**
>
> Note that after any changes are made, you must shut down and start the client again for any changes to take place.

Setting the NetWare Environment Variables

Many of the utilities provided with the NetWare client for Linux require that you set certain environment variables to obtain information on how to interact with your NetWare systems. If an environment variable isn't set, you must specify it when you execute a command that relies on a given variable. For example, if the print queue and server variables are not set, you must specify them when you print files; otherwise, the system will not allow you to print.

The following are NetWare environment variables:

- `NWCLIENT_PREFERRED_SERVER`—Preferred server when a server option is expected in the syntax.
- `NWCLIENT_PREFERRED_QUEUE`—Preferred print queue to use when the queue option is expected in the syntax.
- `NWCLIENT_PREFERRED_TREE`—Preferred tree when a NDS tree is expected in the syntax.
- `NWCLIENT_DEFAULT_NAME_CONTEXT`—Default context within an NDS directory tree for the username you provide.
- `NWCLIENT_DEFAULT_USER`—Default name to use when logging in to the NetWare server.

Activating and Deactivating the NetWare Client

The NetWare client's default behavior is to start automatically on every boot, so you must deactivate this setting if you do not want to use it. Deactivating the client frees up approximately 500KB of disk space and 1.2MB of RAM. You can safely restart the client in most cases without restarting the system.

To deactivate, issue:

`/etc/rc.d/init.d/nwclient stop`

To activate, issue:

`/etc/rc.d/init.d/nwclient start`

Using the NetWare Client for Linux

Let's look at how to use the NetWare client for Linux. This includes logging in/out, working on a NetWare server and identifying and changing login information.

Logging In

Before you can view or store information in NetWare objects or view directories and files, you must log in (be authenticated) to a bindery server or NDS directory tree. You use the command nwlogin. If not specified on the command line, the environment variables NWCLIENT_PREFERED_TREE and NWCLIENT_PREFERRED_SERVER determine the server or tree that you should be authenticated on. If you do not specify the environment variables and you provide no server or tree on the command line, the program authenticates you on the first discovered NDS tree. If you specify both the tree and server, the tree takes precedence. When logging into a tree, nwlogin authenticates you on the first available server in that tree.

If the requested server is a member of an NDS tree to which you have already been authenticated, nwlogin will authenticate you to the server using NDS Background Authentication. You can specify your username on the command line or in the environment variable NWCLIENT_DEFAULT_USER. If you do not specify a username, nwlogin prompts you for a login, using the Linux login name as the default. For NDS users, the environment variable NWCLIENT_DEFAULT_NAME_CONTEXT is the default NDS context. If the user cannot be located in that context, the server's context is used.

> **Note**
>
> If the NWCLIENT_DEFAULT_USER variable doesn't exist, your Linux login name is used. If the NWCLIENT_DEFAULT_NAME_CONTEXT is also set, you only need to type nwlogin.

After you're authenticated to a server in an NDS directory tree, you can view any files and directories on that server (according to your access rights and privileges). If you try to view NDS objects in a tree that you're not authenticated to or reach files on a volume that your login did not give you rights to use, the corresponding Linux directory under /NetWare appears empty.

To log in to an NDS directory tree if the environment variable (NWCLIENT_DEFAULT_NAME_CONTEXT) is set, enter nwlogin and your NetWare username:

nwlogin hsimpson

To log in to a NDS directory tree if the environment variable is not set, enter nwlogin and your user context:

nwlogin .hsimpson.this.computer.nowhere

To log in to a certain NDS directory tree, you add the name of the tree to your username and the options -t and -u:

```
nwlogin -t tree1 -u .hsimpson.this.computer.nowhere
```

To log in to a certain server in a directory tree, you use the server name with your username and the options -s and -u:

```
nwlogin -s server1 -u .hsimpson.this.computer.nowhere
```

> **Note**
>
> You can also access any other servers in the same NDS directory tree as the server you specify, as long as you possess the required access rights and privileges.

To log in to the nearest NDS directory tree, simply enter the command nwlogin. Enter your username at the prompt. To use the default, simply press Enter; otherwise, enter an alternate login name.

To log in to a NetWare 4.*x* server in bindery emulation mode, enter the following command:

```
nwlogin -s server -b -u username
```

Here's an example:

```
nwlogin -s server1 -b -u .hsimpson.this.computer.nowhere
```

This command forces bindery authentication of an NDS object within the bindery context defined for that server instead of NDS authentication.

In all the preceding examples, you are prompted for your NetWare password after a successful login. After you're logged in to the NetWare server, you have access to the files that reside there as if they were part of your local file system, based on the user rights and privileges of your login. As you browse the NetWare directories, the system automatically finds any NetWare servers on your network.

Working on a NetWare Server

To access the bindery servers on your Network, change directories to /NetWare/bindery. Each server's subdirectory includes filelike objects such as users, groups, and print queues that contain references to volumes or objects on that NetWare bindery server.

To access the NDS directory trees on your network, change directories to /NetWare/NDS. Here, the name of each NDS directory tree is synonymous with the root object in that directory tree. When you change to a NDS directory tree, you see the top-level objects in that tree. You can continue to traverse this directory system through layers of NDS container objects. A leaf object such as a user or group object appears in the directory tree as a file with the object's name.

Although items such as directories and files on NetWare volumes appear to be part of the native file system, the NetWare servers themselves control the security and access to items based on your NetWare access privileges. For example, if you log in as admin to a NDS directory tree, you can use the nwdsmodify utility to change the values of an attribute. If you log out and then log in again as user hsimpson, you might not have sufficient rights to see the values of that attribute even though the rights to those objects have not changed when viewed from the Linux directory listing.

Logging Out

When you no longer need your connection to the NetWare server or directory tree, then for security reasons you should log out. Use the nwlogout command to log out of a NetWare server, an NDS tree, or all NetWare connections. Logging out of an NDS tree includes logging out of all servers in the tree and destroying the credentials created as part of the authentication process to the tree.

To log out of a NetWare server, simply enter the following:

nwlogout -s server

In this case, you are only logged out of the specified server. Any other servers you logged in to are still accessible.

To log out of a NetWare directory tree, use:

nwlogout -t tree

In this case, all servers in the specified tree are inaccessible.

To log out of all connections, simply enter the nwlogout command with the -a switch:

nwlogout -a

Identifying and Changing Login Information

The NetWare utilities provide a wealth of information about your NetWare connection. In fact, simply typing nwwhoami lists all the NDS trees that you're connected to as well as the username used to connect to each tree. Also, the server name and NetWare version for each server in each NDS tree to which your connected is shown, along with the authentication status of the connection to the server (NDS, Bindery, or none). If you connected using Bindery authentication, the username under which you're logged in on that server is also displayed. Finally, the connection numbers for each connection are displayed along with similar connection information for each bindery server that your connected to that isn't part of a NDS tree.

Because of the grace login feature of NetWare servers, even after your password expires, you are still allowed to login a set number of times. This is to allow adequate time to make the change. Because you may be connected to many different NDS trees and NetWare servers, you must specify for which connection you want to change the password. To view your current connections and their properties, use the `nwwhoami` command as explained earlier. To change the password for a NDS tree, use the `nwpasswd` command with the following syntax:

`nwpasswd -t tree -u username`

You use the same command to change the password for a bindery-based server but alter the syntax slightly:

`nwpasswd -s server -u username`

Even after your password expires, NetWare's grace login feature allows you to log in a set number of times, providing adequate time to make the password change. You might be connected to many different NDS trees and NetWare servers, so you must specify which connection the password change affects. View your current connections and their properties with the `nwwhoami` command as explained earlier.

If your are changing a user's password other than your own, and you are not logged in with administrative or equivalent privileges, you will be prompted for the current password. In which case you enter the current password, then enter the new password, and finally re-enter it to confirm.

Printing with the NetWare Client

The NetWare client allows you to print directly to a NetWare print server and also lets you specify how those files should be printed. When you print files in NetWare, they are sent to a print queue. The print queue is a holding area where files from many users are stored; there they wait for their turn to be printed. These files are sometimes also referred to as print jobs. Using the NetWare client, you can print from the command line, and even specify how the file will print. Such options could be the number of copies, and whether or not to automatically insert carriage returns. You use the `nwprint` command to print the specified file(s) on a specific NetWare print queue. The user must already be authenticated to the server or tree associated with the print queue. The server and queue, either directly or indirectly, can be specified directly using the `-s` (or `--server`) and `-q` (or `--queue`) options. They may also be specified indirectly by passing the path of a NetWare bindery queue, using the `-b` (or `--bindery`) option, or the path to a NetWare Directory Services queue or printer object, using the `-n` (or `--nds`) option. If you do not specify any queue or servers, the environment variables `NWCLIENT_PREFERRED_QUEUE` and `NWCLIENT_PREFERRED_SERVER` are used to determine the queue and server to print to. If no filename is specified on the command line, then `stdin` is printed instead.

To print a file if the NetWare environment variables are set, type:

`nwprint filename`

To print a directory list from the command line (if the environment variables are set), switch to the directory you want to list and type:

`ls | nwprint`

Note that with both commands, if the environment variables are not set, you must use the `-q` or `-s` switch to specify either a print queue or a specific server to use. The proper syntax for this is

`nwprint -s server -q queue_file`

One other option for the `nwprint` command is the `-b` switch; this is used to specify a bindery server at the time you print. The syntax is as follows:

`nwprint -b bindery/path/to/print/queue_file`

Here's an example:

`nwprint -b /NetWare/bindery/hsimpson/objects/Q1 somefile.txt`

Use the –n option to send the print job to an NDS server:

`nwprint -n NDS/path/to/print/queue_file`

Your command will resemble this example:

`nwprint -n /NetWare/NDS/tree1/myorg/Q1 somefile.txt`

When the printer doesn't automatically return to the beginning of the next line, your text shows what is known as a stair-stepping effect. Add the `-c` option to the `nwprint` command so the printer will automatically insert carriage returns after each line:

`nwprint -c somefile.txt`

When you change your mind about a print job, you might want to view the print queue and delete it. The NetWare client allows you to do this fairly easily. You use the `nwqstat` command to view the print requests in a queue. `nwqstat` displays the status of a specific

NetWare print queue, optionally limited to job IDs, jobs submitted by certain users, or both. As with `nwprint`, you must be authenticated to the server or tree on which the print queue is located. If you specify job IDs and usernames, only the status of those job IDs and the jobs submitted by those users is displayed. The job ID is the eight-digit hexadecimal job number returned when the print job is launched by `nwprint`. On the command line, job IDs must follow all options, and usernames must follow all job IDs.

To see a list of print jobs in a certain queue, you use `nwqstat` with the following syntax:

```
nwqstat -s server -q queue
```

Here are two different examples of the command in use:

```
nwqstat -s server1 -q bjc4000
nwqstat -n /NetWare/NDS/tree1/myorg/Q1
```

If you want to view the print jobs in a certain queue that were sent by a certain user, the syntax is basically the same, and you just add the username to the end of the command:

```
nwqstat -s server1 -q bjc4000 hsimpson
```

In either of these cases, you'll see a list of print requests:

```
hsimpsonsilver:/a/colors/exam.doc job Active 01e00001
hsimpson C:\BURNS\SAFTEY.WPD job Active 01e02002
hsimpson Donut Order job Active 01e01001
```

To delete one or more print jobs, you use the `nwdelqjob` command. This command removes the specified jobs from the specified NetWare print queue. As with `nwprint` and `nwqstat`, you must already be authenticated to the server or tree on which the print queue is located. You identify the job to be deleted with the job ID. To delete one print job, you type:

```
nwdelqjob -s server -q queue job_number
```

Check out these two examples:

```
nwdelqjob -s server1 -q bjc4000 01e00001
nwdelqjob -n /NetWare/NDS/BURNS/Q1 01e02002
```

NetWare Administration for Bindery Servers

Caldera NetWare for Linux includes utilities for administering a NetWare server from the NetWare client for Linux, including ways to administer bindery and NDS services.

NetWare 3.*x* servers store such essential information as usernames and their group membership in a special database called the bindery. The NetWare client utilities provide a means to administer NetWare 3.*x* servers by creating, viewing, modifying, and deleting objects and their properties in the server's bindery. The utilities include the facilities to administer disk space quotas and file system trustees.

NetWare 3.*x* servers also use bindery objects to represent and hold information about entities such as users, groups of users, print queues, and other application-specific entities. To create new bindery objects, you use the `nwbocreate` command. This command creates an object of the specified type in the bindery of the NetWare server indicated by the NetWare path. You must already be authenticated to the server on which the bindery object is to be located. You must provide the server, object name, and object type; there are no defaults for these objects. If you create an object of type 1 (user), you can also provide the home directory volume and path, where the user's home directory will be created.

To create a new user object on a bindery server, type:

`nwbocreate -s server_name -o object_name -t user_type -H home_directory`

For example, to create a user object named `hsimpson` of type 1 (user) on the bindery server cburns, type:

`nwbocreate -s /NetWare/bindery/cburns -o hsimpson -t 1 -H sys/home`

To create a new group object on the bindery server, type:

`nwbocreate -s server_name -o object_name -t user_type`

For example, to create a group object called `writers` of type 2 (group) on the bindery server cburns, type:

`nwbocreate -s /NetWare/bindery/cburns -o writers -t 2`

Just as the bindery contains objects representing nonfile system resources, each bindery object consists of properties that contain information about the resource it represents. For example, a user object contains information about the groups it is a member of. Bindery objects are stored in the `GROUPS_I'M_IN` property. To create these properties, you use the `nwbpcreate` command. This command creates the property of the specified type in the bindery object whose path is indicated on the NetWare server. You must provide the object name and property name because there are no default values for these arguments. For property type, the default is `ITEM`, for read security, the default is `ANYONE`, and for write security, the default is `ANYONE`. To create a property, type `nwbpcreate` and use the following options:

-o   With the object name to create a new property for the object on a NetWare bindery server; both the object and server are indicated by the NetWare bindery object path. Alternately, if the `NWCLIENT_PREFERRED_SERVER` environment variable is defined, the value can be simply an object name. A NetWare path always begins with `/NetWare/bindery/` followed by the NetWare server's name, then a forward slash, then `objects/`, and then the object's name. After the `NetWare` portion of the path, all names are case insensitive.

-p   With the property's name.

-t   With the property's type. The type can have one of the following values: `SET`, a set of bindery object names, or `ITEM`, a set of 0 or more 128-byte segments of context-specific content.

-r   With the property's read security.

-w   With the property's write security. Both read and write security can each have one of the following values:

- `ANYONE`   Anyone can access the property.
- `LOGGED`   Anyone who is logged in can access the property.
- `OBJECT`   Anyone who is logged in as the object or `SUPERVISOR` equivalent can access the property.
- `SUPERVISOR`   Anyone who is logged in as a `SUPERVISOR` equivalent can access the property.
- `NETWARE`   Only the bindery can access the property.

-h   Help to display information about this utility with examples.

Suppose you want to create a new property named `PIZZA_NUMBER` on the object `hsimpson` of the bindery server `cburns`. `PIZZA_NUMBER` is of property type `ITEM` with read access by anyone and write access by the object `hsimpson` or a supervisor equivalent:

```
nwpcreate -o /NetWare/bindery/cburns/objects/hsimpson
➥-p PIZZA_NUMBER -t ITEM -r ANYONE -w OBJECT
```

To delete a property, you use the `nwbprm` command, which removes a value from a property for the bindery object whose path and NetWare server you provide. If the property is of type `SET`, only the specified value is removed from the property of the object. If the property is an `ITEM` type, the entire property with all its values is removed. You must provide the object path and property name, and if the property is of type `SET`, you must also provide the value. To delete a property, use the `nwbprm` command and the following options:

-o   With the object's name.

-p   With the property's name.

-v   With the value to be removed. Use this option only with a property of type SET. If the property is an ITEM type, the entire property with its all values is removed from the object, so you don't need the -v option.

-h   Display information about this utility with examples.

Here's an example of the nwbprm command with its options:

```
nwbprm -o /NetWare/bindery/cburns/objects/hsimpson -p groups_i\'m_in -v ATG
```

In this example, the reference to the object named ATG is removed from the GROUPS_I'M_IN SET property of the object hsimpson on the bindery server cburns. The next example refers to an ITEM type property:

```
nwbprm -o /NetWare/bindery/cburns/objects/hsimpson -p chocolate
```

Because the CHOCOLATE property is not a SET property in this example, no -v option is necessary to remove it and its existing values from the object hsimpson on the bindery server cburns.

You can display the values of any property of a bindery object, provided that you're authorized to view it. Authorization is based on the value of the property's read security flag. You can add or remove a value from any property of any bindery object you're authorized to modify (based on the property's write security flag). To view a bindery object's property values, you use the nwbpvalues command. You must provide the object and property name because they have no defaults. To view property values, use this syntax:

```
nwbpvalues -o object -p property
```

The next example lists to stdout the values of the bindery property GROUPS_I'M_IN of an object named hsimpson on the authenticated bindery server cburns.

```
nwbpvalues -o /NetWare/bindery/cburns/objects/hsimpson -p groups_i\'m_in
```

Notice that you must precede the apostrophe in the property name with a backslash.

To add a property value, you use the nwbpadd command. You must provide the object path, property name, property type, and value. The syntax is

```
nwbpadd -o object -p property -t type -v value
```

To add a reference to the bindery object named ATG to the GROUPS_I'M_IN property of the user hsimpson on the bindery server cburns, do the following:

```
nwbpadd -o /NetWare/bindery/cburns/objects/hsimpson/
↳-p groups_i\'m_in -t SET -v ATG
```

To add a new string value `Safety Agent 1` to the `CHOCOLATE` property of the user `hsimpson` on the bindery server `cburns`, you type:

```
nwbpadd -o /NetWare/bindery/cburns/objects/hsimpson
➥-p chocolate -t STRING -v "Safety Agent 1"
```

Perhaps you want to add a new 4-byte binary value of 0x0000010b (high-low order, no byte-swapping) to the `REVISION` property of the user `hsimpson` on the bindery server `cburns`:

```
nwbpadd -o /NetWare/bindery/cburns/objects/hsimpson
➥-p revision -t SEGMENT -v "04 00 00 01 0b"
```

File Systems and Quotas on Bindery Servers

You can assign a space quota to each directory on a volume attached to a bindery server. A space quota limits the amount of disk space used by a particular user or application directory. For example, if a user's home directory is limited to 5MB, the user cannot store excessive amounts of information that could make the system unusable for others.

To view the current disk space quota for any directory, you use the `nwboshowspace` command. You must include the `-d` argument with its parameter. The syntax is

```
nwboshowspace -d directory_path
```

To show the disk quota for the directory `/users/hsimpson` on the volume `sys:` of the bindery server `cburns`, you type:

```
nwboshowspace -d /NetWare/bindery/cburns/volumes/sys/users
/hsimpson
```

To set the disk space quota, you use the `nwbsetspace` command. You must provide both the `-d` and `-b` options, each with their parameter. The `blocks` parameter is the limit of space in 4KB blocks. To remove all restrictions on a directory, specify `0` for blocks. To limit disk space to 0 bytes, specify `-1` for blocks. You can limit the directory `/users/hsimpson` on the volume `sys:` of the bindery server `cburns` to approximately 4MB (4,096,000 bytes):

```
nwbosetspace -d /NetWare/bindery/cburns/volumes/sys/users
/hsimpson -b 1000
```

Maybe you decide that you want to remove any space restrictions because he is such a good person:

```
nwbosetspace -d /NetWare/bindery/cburns/volumes/users/hsimpson -b 0
```

If he has been wasting space with noncompany work or materials, you might want to restrict him from saving anything to this directory:

```
nwbosetspace -d /NetWare/bindery/cburns/volumes/users/hsimpson -b -1
```

A file system trustee on a NetWare bindery server is an object (usually a user object) that has been granted a set of access rights to a file or directory on a NetWare volume. As you view trustee assignments, remember that the effective rights a user has (that is, what the user can actually do with a file or directory) can be a combination of the trustee assignments that the user has to a file or directory, trustee assignments to parent directories, and group trustee assignments.

First, locate the bindery object that you want to be the trustee; for example, find the user you want to grant access to and then use the `nwboshowtrust` command to view an object's rights to files and or directories on the server. You must include either the -o or -p option. If you use -o, `nwboshowtrust` displays the trustee rights the object has to any and all directories on the server specified in the bindery object path. If you use -p, you see all the objects that are trustees of the directory.

The rights for the user are displayed as a symbolic rights mask. Rights are enclosed inside square brackets, using standard NetWare rights syntax, containing zero or more of the following values:

- R   Read from file.
- W   Write to file.
- C   Create directory or file.
- E   Erase directory or file.
- M   Modify directory or file.
- F   File scan.
- A   Access control.

If `nwboshowtrust` returns [RWF], the user has read, write, and file scan rights to that directory.

To show the rights for all directories that the bindery object `hsimpson` has on the authenticated server `cburns`, use the following:

```
nwboshowtrust -o /NetWare/bindery/cburns/objects/hsimpson
```

You can also show the rights of all bindery trustees for the directory or file `SYS:/users/hsimpson` on the server `cburns`:

```
nwboshowtrust -p /NetWare/bindery/cburns/volumes/SYS/users
/hsimpson
```

To add an object as a trustee to another file or directory, use the command nwboaddtrust. The new rights you give with this command override any rights that were previously granted explicitly to that object. You must include all three parameters: object, path, and rights mask.

You specify the new rights mask for the user with RIGHTS_MASK, which can be a mnemonic or a hexadecimal byte value. To represent the RIGHTS_MASK as a mnemonic, enclose the mnemonic inside square brackets using zero or more of the values outlined earlier. To represent the RIGHTS_MASK as a hexadecimal byte value, enter the sum of the following hexadecimal values for individual rights:

- 00   No access.
- 01   Read access.
- 02   Write access.
- 04   Open access.
- 08   Create access.
- 10   Delete access.
- 20   Ownership access.
- 40   Search access.
- 80   Modify access.

A total of ff gives all rights.

The syntax is

```
nwboaddtrust -o object -r [rights-mask] -p object_path
```

To give the object hsimpson on the bindery server cburns all rights to the directory /users/hsimpson on the sys volume, do the following:

```
nwboaddtrust -o /NetWare/bindery/cburns/objects/hsimpson
 -r ff -d/NetWare/bindery/cburns/volumes/sys/users/hsimpson
```

You can also use:

```
nwboaddtrust -o /NetWare/bindery/cburns/objects/hsimpson
 -r [RWCEMF] -d /NetWare/bindery/cburns/volumes/sys/users/hsimpson
```

Administration for Novell Directory Service

NetWare 4 servers store such essential information as usernames and their group memberships in a special distributed database. This database is the repository of all the information used by NDS. The Caldera NetWare client provides many utilities to administer an NDS directory so that you can create, view, modify, or delete objects and their attributes. The utilities also provide facilities for administering disk space quotas and file system trustees.

It is possible to create NDS objects under any container object in the NDS tree, including the tree's root. When creating a new NDS object, you must include values for some of its attributes. These mandatory attributes vary from object to object, although most objects don't have a mandatory attribute other than their common name. For example, when you create a user object, you must provide a value for both its common name (the name of the object in the directory tree) and its surname. To create NDS objects, you use the `nwdscreate` command. `nwdscreate` has the following options:

- `-p` The NetWare path to the NDS tree where you want to create a given object. A NetWare path always begins with `/NetWare/NDS/`, followed by the NDS tree name.
- `-o` The type of object you want to create.
- `-t` The NDS object class of the object to be created. You can create the first two types, country and organization, just under the tree's root. Note that objects of type country can contain objects of type organization.

    You can create objects of the following types under any NDS container object other than the tree's root or under objects of type country:

AFP server	Computer
Directory map	External entity
Group	List
Message routing group	NetWare Core Protocol (NCP) server
Organizational role	Organizational unit
Print server	Printer
Profile	Queue
User	Volume

> **Note**
>
> You must enclose object types with embedded spaces in double quotes, such as `"Message routing group"`.

- `-H` The home directory volume object and path in which you want to create a user's home directory. If the object is not of type user, this option is ignored.
- `-h` Displays information about this utility with examples.

If you want to create an NDS object `writers` of type group in the NDS organization `Publishing` on the authenticated tree `Macmillan`, you type:

```
nwdscreate -p /NetWare/NDS/Macmillan/Publishing -o writers -t Group
```

Here's a second example that creates a type user:

```
nwdscreate -p /NetWare/NDS/Macmillan/Publishing
➥-o silenuz -t User -H /NetWare/NDS/Macmillan/Publishing/Server_SYS/users
/silenuz Surname writers
```

This example creates an NDS object named `silenuz` of type user in the NDS organization `Publishing` on the authenticated tree `Macmillan`. Because the attribute `Surname` is required for objects of type user, it is specified along with its value `writers`. This user object is automatically added to the group Everyone in the default context. Because the command also includes a home directory path, the directory `users/silenuz` is created on the volume `Server_SYS`, and the new user object gets full rights to that directory.

Table 17.1 lists command parameters and describes what they do.

TABLE 17.1 Command Parameters

To Set Up This Type of Object	Specify These Parameters
Apple Talk filing protocol server for NetWare AFP NLM.	`-p` *path to NDS object's parent* `-o` *object* `-t` `"AFP Server"`
Computer object; contents may be application-specific.	`-p` *path to NDS object's parent* `-o` *object* `-t` `Computer`
Top-level nationality container for worldwide NDS trees.	`-p` *path to NDS object's parent* `-o` *object* `-t` `Country`
Directory map, which represents "changeable" directory specifications, such as an application indicated within a login script.	`-p` *path to NDS object's parent* `-o` *object* `-t` `"Directory Map"` `"Host Server"` *host server*

continues

TABLE 17.1 continued

To Set Up This Type of Object	Specify These Parameters
MHS-specific placeholder for a nonuser email recipient.	-p *path to NDS object's parent* -o *object* -t "External Entity"
Collection of users who will get equivalent access (a group).	-p *path to NDS object's parent* -o *object* -t Group
MHS-specific equivalent to group that isn't limited to containing users.	-p *path to NDS object's parent* -o *object* -t List
MHS-specific common group of messaging servers.	-p *path to NDS object's parent* -o *object* -t "Message Routing Group"
"Division" level container that can be under a country object.	-p *path to NDS object's parent* -o *object* -t Organization
Generic "role" equivalent of a person (changeable).	-p *path to NDS object's parent* -o *object* -t "Organizational Role"
Workgroup-level container object. This type of container holds other objects.	-p *path to NDS object's parent* -o *object* -t "Organizational Unit"
An object representing a NetWare print server.	-p *path to NDS object's parent* -o *object* -t "Print Server"
An object representing the printer connected to a print server.	-p *path to NDS object's parent* -o *object* -t Printer
An object representing a shared NetWare login script.	-p *path to NDS object's parent* -o *object* -t Profile "Login Script" *login script*

To Set Up This Type of Object	Specify These Parameters
An object representing a queue of a print server.	-p `path to NDS object's parent` -o `object` -t `Queue` `"Queue Directory"` `path to queue directory`
A user who can authenticate to NDS servers.	-p `path to NDS object's parent` -o `object` -t `User` -H `path to user's home directory` `Surname` `user's surname`
An object that represents a volume on an NCP server (with files and directories below).	-p `path to NDS object's parent` -o `object` -t `Volume` `"Host Resource Name"` `host server`

You can remove an NDS object at any time. However, if the object is a container, you must empty it first. To remove NDS objects, use the `nwdsrm` command with the following syntax:

`nwdsrm -o path_to_object`

To remove an object named `silenuz` from the tree named `Macmillan`, you type:

`nwdsrm -o /NetWare/NDS/Macmillan/Publishing/silenuz`

NetWare also allows you to assign various attributes to each object. The attributes for a user can include the user's name, phone number, security access, and so on. The many types of attributes are categorized. First of all, you need to know how to view an object's attributes. Use the `nwdsattrs` command with the following syntax:

`nwdsattrs -o path_to_object -a attribute`

You can list all the attributes of the object `silenuz` under the container object `Publishing` on the NDS tree `Macmillan`:

`nwdsattrs -o /NetWare/NDS/Macmillan/Publishing/silenuz`

To find out about a specific attribute, such as the group membership for `silenuz`, you add the attribute using the `-a` argument:

`nwdsattrs -o /NetWare/NDS/Macmillan/Publishing/silenuz -a "Group Membership"`

If you need to add or modify an attribute's value, use the `nwdsmodify` command. You must include the object's path, attribute, syntax, change, and value. Use this command as follows:

```
nwdsmodify -o path_to_object -a attribute -v value -s syntax -c operation
```

attribute is the attribute of the object you want to change, and *value* is the value being added, modified, or deleted. The delimiter between parts of a multipart value is a colon. The syntax of the attribute to be modified is a mnemonic for the syntax ID used in directory services. The possible syntaxes follow; those with an asterisk have some restrictions on how they are entered and will be discussed in greater detail after the list.

CE string	CI string
PR string	NU string
CI list*	Boolean*
Integer	Octet string*
Telephone number	Fax number*
Network address*	Octet list
Email address*	Path*
Replica pointer	ACL*
P.O. address*	Time stamp*
Class name	Stream*
Counter	Back link*
Time*	Typed name*
Hold*	Interval

Enter CI list values as a series of strings separated by colons (:). An example is a series of language codes for a user object's `Language` attribute, such as `US:DE:UK`.

Boolean values are entered as true or false and are case insensitive.

You can enter octet string values as a string, except when you want to represent the `Login Allowed Time Map` attributes for user objects. In this case and this case only, the value consists of between one and seven ranges of half-hour time blocks (in 24-hour format), separated by colons. Each range has the syntax `DayHHMMHHMM`. An example is `Mon0700-1730:tue0700-1730:fri0700-1730`, which restricts access from 7 a.m. to 5:30 p.m. on Monday, Tuesday, and Friday. Even if you want to grant fully unrestricted access, you must specify seven ranges, one for each day of the week.

Fax number values in NetWare, DOS, and Windows utilities are simple phone numbers. `nwdsmodify` lets you enter only telephone numbers, but by using the NDS specification for the fax number, you can store a series of bits associated with the fax, such as a company logo for the cover page. If you want to store this information, the syntax is `PhoneNumber:NumberOfBits:ByteEncoding`. The `PhoneNumber` field is the fax telephone number, the `NumberOfBits` field is the number of bits in the series of bits that follow, and the `ByteEncoding` field is a series of hexadecimal bytes that contain the series of bits. For example, `435-763-4357":33:DE AD BE EF 80` represents the telephone number 435-763-4357 with 33 bits of associated information. The 33 bits are encoded in the hexadecimal byte encoding `DE AD BE EF 80`.

Enter network address values as `TYPE:ADDRESS`. The type can be IPX, IP, SDLC, TokenRing/Ethernet (TRE), OSI, or AppleTalk (AFP). The format for entering the `ADDRESS` differs depending on the type of protocol. The syntaxes for each protocol are

`IPX:net:node:socket`	(Hexadecimal numbers)
Example:	`IPX:1234abcd:1234abcdef:12ab`
`IP:class:domain:subnet:node`	(Decimal numbers)
Example:	`IP:192.168.1.45`
`SDLC:cua:blockid:puid`	(Hexadecimal numbers)
Example:	`SDLC:12ab:123abc:12345abcde`
`TRE:sap:blockid:puid`	(Hexadecimal numbers)
Example:	`TRE:12ab:123abc:12345abcde`
`OSI:hexaddress`	(Hexadecimal numbers with spaces)
Example:	`OSI:12 34 56 78 9a bc`
`AFP:net:node:socket:object:type:zone`	(Decimal numbers and hexadecimal numbers)
Example:	`AFP:1234:56:78:myObject:aType:aZone`

Email address values are represented by a numeric address type and then the address, separated by a colon. An example is `23:hsimpson@springfield.doh`, representing the address `hsimpson@springfield.doh` and type 23. Novell's MHS provides further encoding of these values for its MHS services so that the address type is a flag that distinguishes between a foreign email alias (1) and a foreign email address (0). The address itself indicates the type of address as text and then the email address itself, separated by an additional colon. `1:SMTP:hsimpson@springfield.doh` represents an SMTP foreign email alias with the address `hsimpson@sprinfield.doh`.

You enter path values as `NAMESPACE:VOLUME:PATH`. The namespace is always a single digit number, such as `0` for a DOS namespace. The `VOLUME` is a distinguished character, and the `PATH` is an absolute path from the volume's root.

ACL values are assigned as `ATTR:SUBJECT:PRIVILEGES`. The `ATTR` is an NDS attribute name to receive the access control, or it can be one of the special values `[All Attribute Rights]`, `[SMS Rights]` (Storage Management System), or `[Entry Rights]`. The `SUBJECT` is either a NetWare path or a distinguished name to the object receiving the access. `PRIVILEGES` is an encoded string that indicates the cumulative privileges given, represented as a sum of symbolic privileges. These symbolic privilege values can differ depending on the type of attribute being assigned. For the attribute `[SMS Rights]`, you can assign the symbolic privileges scan, backup, restore, rename, delete, and admin. For the `[Entry Rights]` attribute, the possible symbolic privileges are browse, add, delete, rename, and supervisor. For all other attributes, including `[All Attribute Rights]`, symbolic privileges are compare, read, write, self, manager, and supervisor. For example, `Group Membership:silenuz.MyOrg:Compare+Read` provides compare and read access to the object's `Group Membership` attribute for the object `silenuz.MyOrg`.

You enter P.O address values as a series of strings separated by colons. An example is `Name:Address:PO Box:City:State:Zip`.

Time stamp values consist of a number of whole seconds and an event ID, separated by a colon. Both of these quantities are long (32-bit) integers. For example, `123:456` represents 123 whole seconds for event ID 456.

Stream values hold long strings, such as login scripts or printer information. You can include several lines by separating them with \n, which represents a newline. For example, `echo this is line 1\n echo this is line two\n echo this is line three` converts into a three-line script with each line beginning with `echo this is line` followed by the line number.

Back link values consist of a remote ID and then an object name, separated by a colon. The remote ID is a long (32-bit) integer quantity. The object name is an NDS distinguished name. `123:silenuz.MyOrg` represents a back link to the object `silenuz.MyOrg`, which has a remote ID of 123.

Time values take the form `YYMMDD:HHMMSS`, where `YY` is the last two digits of the year, `MM` is the numeric month, `DD` is the day of the month, `HH` is the hour of the day in 24-hour format, `MM` is the minute of the hour, and `SS` is the second of the minute. For example, `960514:053100` represents 5:31 a.m. on May 14, 1996.

Typed name values consist of a numeric level, a numeric interval, and then a textual object name, separated by colons. `123:456:silenuz.MyOrg` represents the object `silenuz.MyOrg`, which has a level of 123 and an interval of 456.

Hold values consist of a numeric amount of time and then a textual object name, separated of course by colons. For example, `123:silenuz.MyOrg` represents a hold by `silenuz.MyOrg` for 123 units of time.

Suppose you want to add the string value `"Winner of the 1999 safety award."` to the `Description` attribute of the object named `hsimpson`, which is in the `PowerPlant` organization of the NDS tree named `cburns`. You issue the following `nwdsmodify` command:

```
nwdsmodify -o /NetWare/NDS/cburns/PowerPlant/hsimpson
➥-a Description -v "Winner of the 1999 safety award." -s "CI String" -c a
```

You can also use:

```
nwdsmodify -o /NetWare/NDS/cburns/Engineering/ATG
➥-a Member -v hsimpson.PowerPlant -s "Distinguished Name" -c d
```

In the first case, the distinguished name `hsimpson.PowerPlant` (which could have also been represented /NetWare/NDS/cburns/PowerPlant/hsimpson) is removed from the `Member` attribute of the group named `ATG`, which is in the `Engineering` organization of the NDS tree named `cburns`.

Here's another version of `nwdsmodify` for the example:

```
nwdsmodify -o /NetWare/NDS/Macmillan/Publishing/silenuz -a "Home Directory"
➥-v "0:server1_sys.Publishing:/home/silenuz" -s Path -c a
```

This command adds a new value to the `Home Directory` property of the object `silenuz` in the `Publishing` organization of the `Macmillan` NDS tree. The `Home Directory` property is type `Path`, and that new path value is the directory `/home/silenuz` on the volume whose NDS distinguished name is `server1_sys.Publishing`.

Managing Disk Quotas on NDS Servers

As with bindery servers, you can assign a space quota to each directory on a volume attached to an NDS server. To view the present disk space allocated for a quota, you use `nwdsshowspace`:

```
nwdsshowspace -d path_to_directory_service
```

To change the disk quota or to set it in the first place, you use the `nwdssetspace` command. You must include the `-d` argument along with one of the `-b`, `-k`, or `-m` arguments, each with its own parameter. The syntax is

```
nwdssetspace -d path_to_directory_service
```

At the end, you must add one of the following options:

- `-k` With the number of kilobytes that this directory can use.
- `-m` With the number of megabytes that this directory can use.

- `-b` With the number of 4KB blocks that this directory can use.

To limit the size of the home directory for user `silenuz` to about 50MB of disk space, use `nwdssetspace` as follows:

```
nwdssetspace -d /NetWare/NDS/Macmillan/Publishing/sys/home
/silenuz -m 50
```

File System Trustees on NDS Servers

A file system trustee on a NetWare NDS server is an object (usually a user object) that has been granted a set of access rights to a file or directory on a NetWare volume.

As you view file system trustee assignments, remember that the effective rights for a user can be a combination of the trustee assignments the user has to a file or directory, to parent directories, to parent NDS objects (as limited by any inherited rights filters that might exist), and to security equivalence or group trustee assignment. Because all the possible rights a file or directory can hold are the same in NDS as they are for bindery servers, refer to the section entitled "NetWare Administration for Bindery Servers," earlier in the chapter.

To view an object's rights to files and or directories on the server, use:

```
nwdsshowtrust -o path_to_object
```

To add or change an object as a trustee to another file or directory, use:

```
nwdsaddtrust -o path to object
```

Suppose you want to grant an object called `silenuz` in the `Publishing` organization of the authenticated NDS tree `Macmillan` all rights to the directory `/users/hsimpson` on `workserver`'s old volume. You use `nwdsaddtrust` as follows:

```
nwdsaddtrust -o /NetWare/NDS/Macmillan/Publishing/silenuz -r -ff
-p /NetWare/NDS/Macmillan/workserver_old/users/hsimpson
```

Notice that this example uses the hexadecimal value ff to assign full rights, but it could have used the mnemonic value `[RWCEMF]`.

Summary

The NetWare client brings practical NetWare integration and administrative capabilities to the Linux platform. You can use the utilities to simply log in and access your personal work files on any NDS or bindery server, as well as perform many important administrative functions. If you want to stay up to date with the developments Caldera makes to the client, or you are looking for additional information on how the client functions, I recommend joining the NetWare mailing list at Caldera. Send an email message to `majordomo@lists.calderasystems.com` with `subscribe NetWare` as the body. If you are interested in learning more about how NetWare works, I recommend the book *NetWare Unleashed* by Macmillan Publishing.

CHAPTER 18

Configuring Apache

IN THIS CHAPTER

- What Is Apache? *396*
- Server Installation *397*
- Basic Configuration *398*

This chapter covers the installation, configuration, and administration of the Apache Web server. Apache will serve up Web pages for users who request them, whether internally (an intranet or just you on your own OpenLinux box) or externally (a Web server on the Internet). The Web server installation discussed in this chapter covers only the foundation software; you can also add various modules and configure Apache to run with other third-party software (databases, form processors, and the like) to create sophisticated, dynamic Web sites.

What Is Apache?

Apache is the most widely used Web server on the Internet today, according to the NetCraft survey of Web sites. The name *Apache* appeared during the early development of the software because it was "a patchy" server, made out of patches for the freely available source code of the NCSA HTTPd Web server. For a while after the NCSA HTTPd project was discontinued, a number of people wrote a variety of patches for the code, either to fix bugs or to add desired features. There was a lot of this code floating around, and people were freely sharing it, but it was completely unmanaged. After a while, Bob Behlendorf set up a centralized repository of these patches, and the Apache project was born. The project is still composed of a rather small core group of programmers, but anyone is welcome to submit patches to the group for possible inclusion in the code.

In the last year, interest in the Apache project surged, partially buoyed by the new interest in Open Source. It's also due, in part, to IBM's announcement regarding its plans to devote substantial resources to the project because it made more sense to use an established, proven Web server than to try to write its own. The consequences of this interest include intensified development of an NT version and an accelerated release schedule.

The best places to find out about Apache are the Apache Group's Web site, http://www.apache.org/, and the *Apache Week* Web site, http://www.apacheweek.com/, where you can subscribe to receive *Apache Week* by email to keep up on the latest developments in the project.

> **Tip**
>
> In addition to the extensive online documentation, you will also find the complete documentation for Apache in the /home/httpd/doc/ directory. You can access this documentation by looking at the file home/httpd/apache/doc/index.html on your new OpenLinux system. You can open these URLs with Netscape or Lynx, which can also be installed on your system.

OpenLinux ships with a version of Apache, but its version is likely to be several versions old due to Apache's rapid release schedule. You can obtain the latest version OpenLinux maintains from `ftp://ftp.calderasystems.com/pub/OpenLinux/updates/2.2/current/RPMS/`.

You can also obtain Apache as an RPM file from `http://rufus.w3.org/linux/RPM/`, or you can get the very latest source from the Apache Web site and, in true Linux tradition, build it for yourself.

This chapter covers the Apache version in OpenLinux: version 1.3.4.

Server Installation

You probably already have the Apache server on your computer, if you went through the standard installation. If not, you can install Apache with RPM or by building the source code yourself. You can install the RPM with the command-line `rpm` tool, by typing the following:

`rpm -Uvh apache-VERSION.rpm`

where VERSION is the Apache version number (for example, `apache-1.3.4-4.rpm`).

The Apache RPM installs files in the following directories:

- `/etc/httpd/apache/conf/` This directory contains all the Apache configuration files, which include `access.conf`, `httpd.conf`, and `srm.conf`. See the section on configuration files later in this chapter.

- `/etc/rc.d/` The tree under this directory contains the system startup scripts. The Apache RPM installs a complete set for the Web server. These scripts, which you can use to start and stop the server from the command line, will also automatically start and stop the server when the workstation is halted, started, or rebooted.

- `/home/httpd/` (from *rpm*) *rpm* installs the default server icons (`/home/httpd/apache/icons/`), CGI programs (`/home/httpd/cgi-bin/`), HTML files (`/home/httpd/html/`), HTML manual (`/home/httpd/apache/doc/manual`), and support binaries (`/home/httpd/bin/`) in this location. If you want to keep Web content elsewhere, you can do so by making the appropriate changes in the server configuration files.

- `/usr/doc/` and `/usr/man/` *rpm* contains manual pages and readme files, which are placed in these directories. As is the case for most RPM packages, the readme file and other related documentation are placed in a directory under `/usr/doc`, which is named for the Apache server version.

- `/usr/sbin/` The server executable is placed in this directory (`httpd.apache`).
- `/var/log/httpd/apache/` The server log files are placed in this directory. By default, there are two log files—`access_log` and `error_log`—but you can define any number of custom logs containing a variety of information. See the section on logging later in this chapter.

> **Note**
>
> If you are upgrading to a newer version of Apache, *rpm* will not write over your current configuration files. Instead, it moves your current files and appends the extension `.rpmnew` to them. For example, `srm.conf` becomes `srm.conf.rpmnew`. Don't underestimate the importance of a good backup. Always make a backup before upgrading anything you care about on a server.

Basic Configuration

The instructions for the basic configuration of the Apache Web server included in this section will have your server up and running correctly in a very short time.

Runtime Server Configuration Settings

Traditionally, Apache kept the runtime configurations in three files—`httpd.conf`, `access.conf`, and `srm.conf`—mainly because that's how the config files were written for NCSA and Apache grew out of NCSA. Starting with Apache 1.3.4, as distributed by apache.org, the runtime configurations are stored in just one file—`httpd.conf`. OpenLinux, however, continues to use the older three-part layout.

Apache still recognizes this configuration and works with it. We do not know whether it is a layout they will support indefinitely. If you intend to use only Caldera-distributed versions of Apache, it will be easiest for you to stay with the three-file system. If you intend to use the apache.org versions, you can create a unified `httpd.conf` file by typing:

```
cat srm.conf >> httpd.conf
cat access.conf >> httpd.conf
```

Then make sure that `srm.conf` and `access.conf` are empty.

Apache reads the data from the configuration file(s) when the process is started (or restarted). You can cause the Apache process to reload configuration information while running with commands we will discuss later in this chapter in "The `/etc/rc.d/httpd` Scripts" section.

You perform runtime configuration of your server with configuration directives, which are commands that set some options. You use them to tell the server about the various options that you want to enable, such as the location of files important to the server configuration and operation. Configuration directives follow this syntax:

directive option option...

You specify one directive per line. Some directives only set a value such as a filename, whereas others let you specify various options. Some special directives, called sections, look like HTML tags. Section directives are surrounded by angle brackets, such as <directive>. Sections usually enclose a group of directives that apply only to the directory specified in the section:

```
<Directory somedir/in/your/tree>
  directive option option
  directive option option
</Directory>
```

All sections are closed with a matching section tag that looks like </*directive*>. Note that section tags, like any other directives, are specified one per line.

Editing `httpd.conf`

Most of the default settings in the config files are okay to keep, particularly if you have installed the server in a default location and are not doing anything unusual on your server. In general, if you don't understand what a particular directive is for, you should leave it set to the default value.

Some of the settings that you might want to change follow.

`ServerType`	This directive is mentioned more as a curiosity than anything else. The two server types are `standalone` and `inetd`. You will want this to be `standalone` in almost every imaginable case. Setting the `ServerType` to `inetd` will cause a new server to be spawned to handle every incoming HTTP request. That server will then die off immediately when the request has been served. This is presumably useful for testing configuration changes because the configuration files will be reloaded each time a new server process is spawned. Of course, this is extremely slow because you have the overhead of server startup with every request.
`ServerRoot`	This directive sets the absolute path to your server directory, telling the server where to find all the resources and configuration files. Many of these resources are specified in the

configuration files relative to the `ServerRoot` directory. Your `ServerRoot` directive should be set to `/etc/httpd/apache` by default.

Port
: The `Port` directive indicates which port you want your server to run on. By default, this is set to 80, which is the standard HTTP port number. You may want to run your server on another port, for example, in order to run a test server that you don't want people to find by accident. (Don't confuse this option with real security!)

User and Group
: The `User` and `Group` directives should be set to the user ID (UID) and group ID (GID) that the server will use to process requests. Generally, you will want to leave these settings as the defaults: `nobody` and `nobody`. If you want to use a different UID or GID, you need to be aware that the server will run with the permissions of the user and group defined here. This means that in the event of a security breach, whether on the server or (more likely) on your own CGI programs, those programs will run with the assigned UID. If the server runs as root or some other privileged user, someone can exploit the security holes and do nasty things to your site. If you think in terms of the specified user running a command like `rm -rf /`, you should be convinced that leaving this as nobody and nobody is probably the safest practice.

  Instead of specifying the `User` and `Group` directives using names, you can specify them using the UID and GID numbers. If you use numbers, be sure that the numbers you specify correspond to the user and group you want and that they are preceded by the pound symbol (#).

  Here's how these directives look if specified by name:

  User   nobody

  Group   nobody

  Here's the same specification using UID and GID numbers:

  User   #65534

  Group   #65534

ServerAdmin
: Set this directive to the address of the Web master managing the server. It should be a valid email address or alias, such as `webmaster@your-domain.com`. Setting this value to a valid address is important because this address will be returned to a visitor when a problem occurs on the server.

ServerName
: This directive sets the hostname the server will return. Set it to a fully qualified domain name (fqdn). For example, set it to www.*your-domain*.com rather than simply www. This is particularly important if this machine will be accessible from the Internet rather than just on your local network. You really do not need to set this unless you want a different name returned than the machine's canonical name. If this value is not set, the server will figure out the name by itself and set it to its canonical name. However, you might want the server to return a friendlier address, such as intranet.website.for.your.domain. Whatever you do, ServerName should be a real domain name system (DNS) name for your network. If you are administering your own DNS server, remember to add an alias for your host. If someone else manages the DNS for you, ask that person to set this name for you.

DocumentRoot
: Set this directive to the absolute path of your document tree, which is the top directory from which Apache will serve files. By default, it is set to /home/httpd/html. This directive appears in the srm.conf file in OpenLinux.

UserDir
: This directive defines the directory relative to a local user's home directory where that user can put public HTML documents. It's relative because each user will have his or her own HTML directory. The default setting for this directive is public_html. So, each user will be able to create a directory called public_html under his or her home directory, and HTML documents placed in that directory will be available as http://*servername*/~*username*, where *username* is the username of the particular user. This directive appears in the srm.conf file in OpenLinux.

DirectoryIndex
: This directive indicates which file should be served as the index for a directory, such as which file should be served if the URL http://www.server.com/Directory/ is requested. It is often useful to put a list of files here so that, in the event that index.html (the default value) is not found, another file can be served instead. If you have Windows users uploading files, it would be helpful to add index.htm to this list. The most useful application of this is to have a CGI program run as the default action in a directory. In this case, the directive would look like DirectoryIndex index.html index.cgi. This directive appears in the srm.conf file in OpenLinux.

> **Caution**
>
> Allowing individual users to put Web content on your server poses several important security considerations. If you are operating a Web server on the Internet rather than on a private network, you should read the *WWW Security FAQ* by Lincoln Stein. You can find a copy at http://www.genome.wi.mit.edu/WWW/faqs/www-security-faq.html.

.htaccess Files and Access Restrictions

Almost any directive that appears in the configuration files can appear in an .htaccess file. This file, specified in the AccessFileName directive in srm.conf in OpenLinux, sets configurations on a per-directory basis. As the system administrator, you can specify both the name of this file and which of the server configurations may be overridden by the contents of this file. This is especially useful for sites where there are multiple content providers and you want to control what these people can do with their space.

To limit what .htaccess files can override, you need to use the AllowOverride directive in the access.conf file (in OpenLinux). This can be set globally or per directory. To configure which options are available by default, you need to use the Options directive.

For example, you will see the following in your access.conf file:

```
# Each directory to which Apache has access can be configured with respect
# to which services and features are allowed and/or disabled in that
# directory (and its subdirectories).

# First, we configure the "default" to be a very restrictive set of
# permissions.

<Directory />
Options None
AllowOverride None
</Directory>
```

Options Directives

Options can be None, All, or any combination of Indexes, Includes, FollowSymLinks, ExecCGI, or MultiViews. MultiViews is not included in All and must be specified explicitly. Explanations of these options follow.

None	None of the available options are enabled for this directory.
All	All of the available options, except forMultiViews, are enabled for this directory.

`Indexes`	In the absence of an `index.html` file or another `DirectoryIndex` file, a listing of the files in the directory will be generated as an HTML page for display to the user.
`Includes`	Server Side Includes (SSI) are permitted in this directory. This can also be written as `IncludesNoExec` if you want to allow includes but don't want to allow the `exec` option in these includes. For security reasons, this is usually a good idea in directories over which you do not have complete control, such as `UserDir` directories.
`FollowSymLinks`	This directory allows access to directories that are symbolically linked to a document directory. This is usually a bad idea, and you should not set this globally for the whole server. You might want to set this for individual directories, but only if you have a really good reason to do so. This option is a potential security risk because it allows a Web user to escape from the document directory, and it could potentially allow them access to portions of your file system where you really don't want people poking around.
`ExecCGI`	CGI programs are permitted in this directory, even if it is not a `ScriptAlias`-ed directory.
`MultiViews`	This directory is part of the `mod_negotiation` modules. When the document that the client requests is not found, the server tries to figure out which document best suits the client's requirements. See `http://www.apache.org/docs/mod/mod_negotiation.html` or the same document on your system (should be `/home/httpd/apache/doc/manual/mod/mod_negotiation.html` as long as the apache-docs RPM has been installed).

Note

These directives also affect all subdirectories of the specified directory.

`AllowOverrides` Directives

The `AllowOverrides` directives specify which options `.htaccess` files can override. You can set this directive differently for each directory. For example, you can have different standards about what can be overridden in the main document root and in `UserDir` directories.

This capability is particularly useful for user directories, where the user does not have access to the main server configuration files.

`AllowOverrides` can be set to be `All` or any combination of `Options`, `FileInfo`, `AuthConfig`, and `Limit`. Explanations for these options follow.

`Options`	The `.htaccess` file can add options not listed in the `Options` directive for this directory.
`FileInfo`	The `.htaccess` file can include directives for modifying document type information.
`AuthConfig`	The `.htaccess` file may contain authorization directives.
`Limit`	The `.htaccess` file may contain allow, deny, and order directives.

Virtual Hosting

One of the more popular services to provide with a Web server is to host a virtual domain, also known as a virtual host. This is a complete Web site with its own domain name, as if it were a standalone machine, but it's hosted on the same machine as other Web sites. Apache implements this capability in a simple way with directives in the `httpd.conf` configuration file. There are two ways to host virtual hosts on an Apache server. Either you can have one IP address with multiple CNAMEs, or you can have multiple IP addresses with one name per address. Apache has different sets of directives to handle each of these options.

Address-Based Virtual Hosts

After you have configured your Linux machine with multiple IP addresses, setting up Apache to serve them as different Web sites is quite simple. You need only put a VirtualHost directive in your `httpd.conf` file for each of the addresses that you want to make an independent Web site:

```
<VirtualHost www.virtual.com>
ServerName www.virtual.com
DocumentRoot /home/virtual/public_html
TransferLog /home/virtual/logs/access_log
ErrorLog /home/virtual/logs/error_log
</VirtualHost>
```

You should use the IP address, rather than the hostname, in the `VirtualHost` tag.

You may specify any configuration directives within the `<VirtualHost>` tags. For example, you may want to set AllowOverrides directives differently for virtual hosts than you do for your main server. Any directives that are not specified default to the settings for the main server.

The directives that cannot be set in `VirtualHost` sections are `ServerType`, `StartServers`, `MaxSpareServers`, `MinSpareServers`, `MaxRequestsPerChild`, `BindAddress`, `Listen`, `PidFile`, `TypesConfig`, `ServerRoot`, and `NameVirtualHost`.

Name-Based Virtual Hosts

Name-based virtual hosts allow you to run more than one host on the same IP address. You need to add the additional names to your DNS as CNAMEs of the machine in question. When an HTTP client (browser) requests a document from your server, it sends with the request a variable indicating the server name from which it is requesting the document. Based on this variable, the server determines from which of the virtual hosts it should serve content.

> **Note**
>
> Some older browsers are unable to see name-based virtual hosts because this is a feature of HTTP 1.1, and those older browsers are strictly HTTP 1.0-compliant. However, many other older browsers are partially HTTP 1.1-compliant, and this is one of the parts of HTTP 1.1 that most browsers have supported for a while.

Name-based virtual hosts require just one additional step more than IP-address-based virtual hosts. You first need to indicate which IP address has the multiple DNS names on it. This is done with the `NameVirtualHost` directive.

```
NameVirtualHost 192.168.204.24
```

You then need to have a section for each name on that address, setting the configuration for that name. As with IP-based virtual hosts, you only need to set those configurations that need to be different for the host. You must set the `ServerName` directive because that is the only thing that distinguishes one host from another:

```
<VirtualHost 192.168.204.24>
ServerName bugserver.databeam.com
ServerAlias bugserver
DocumentRoot /home/bugserver/htdocs
ScriptAlias /home/bugserver/cgi-bin
TransferLog /home/bugserver/logs/access_log
</VirtualHost>

<VirtualHost 192.168.204.24>
ServerName pts.databeam.com
ServerAlias pts
DocumentRoot /home/pts/htdocs
ScriptAlias /home/pts/cgi-bin
TransferLog /home/pts/logs/access_log
ErrorLog /home/pts/logs/error_log
</VirtualHost>
```

> **Tip**
>
> If you are hosting Web sites on an Intranet or internal network, there is often a chance that users will use the shortened name of the machine rather than the fully qualified domain name. For example, they might type `http://bugserver/index.html` in their browser location field, rather than `http://bugserver.databeam.com/index.html`. In that case, Apache will not recognize that those two addresses should go to the same virtual host. You could get around this by setting up `VirtualHost` directives for both `bugserver` and `bugserver.databeam.com`, but the easy way around this is to use the `ServerAlias` directive, which lists all valid aliases for the machine:
>
> ```
> ServerAlias bugserver
> ```

> **Caution**
>
> If you plan to run a large number of virtual hosts on your system, you should consider sending all logged information to the standard Apache log files instead of to individual files. The reason is that you may reach your system's file descriptor limit because you would be consuming one file descriptor per log file. The system per process limit is 1024 in Linux 2.2, but may be much lower due to `ulimit` restrictions. Symptoms of this problem include error messages such as "unable to fork()," "no information being written to the log files," or "poor response to HTTP requests."

Logging

Apache provides for logging just about any information you might be interested in from Web accesses. Two standard log files are generated when you run your Apache server—access_log and error_log. All logs except for the `error_log` (by default, this is just the `access_log`) are generated in a format specified by the `CustomLog` and `LogFormat` directives. These directives appear in your `httpd.conf` file.

A new log format can be defined with the `LogFormat` directive:

```
LogFormat "%h %l %u %t \"%r\" %>s %b" common
```

The common log format is a good starting place for creating your own custom log formats. Note that most of the log analysis tools available will assume that you are using the common log format or the combined log format, both of which are defined in the default configuration files.

The following variables are available for `LogFormat` statements:

%b	Bytes sent, excluding HTTP headers.
%f	Filename.
%{VARIABLE}e	The contents of the environment variable VARIABLE.
%h	Remote host. (*Note*: Do not include this variable if you have high traffic because it incurs reverse DNS lookup on every hit.)
%a	Remote IP address.
%{HEADER}i	The contents of HEADER: header line(s) in the request sent to the server.
%l	Remote logname (from `identd`, if supplied).
%{NOTE}n	The contents of the note NOTE from another module.
%{HEADER}o	The contents of HEADER: header line(s) in the reply.
%p	The canonical port of the server serving the request.
%P	The process ID of the child that serviced the request.
%r	First line of request.
%s	The status of the original request for internally redirected requests. For status of the last request, use %>s.
%t	Time, in common log format time format.
%{format}t	The time, in the form given by format, which should be in `strftime(3)` format.
%T	The time taken to serve the request, in seconds.
%u	Remote user from auth; may be bogus if return status (%s) is 401.
%U	The URL path requested.
%v	The canonical Server Name of the server serving the request.

In each variable, you can put a conditional in front of the variable that will determine whether the variable is displayed. If it is not displayed, - will be displayed instead. These conditionals are in the form of a list of numerical return values. For example, %!401u will display the value of REMOTE_USER unless the return code is 401.

You can then specify the location and format of a log file using the `CustomLog` directive:

```
CustomLog /var/log/httpd/apache/access_log common
```

If it is not specified as an absolute path, the location of the log file is assumed to be relative to the `ServerRoot`.

CGI and SSI

The most common way to provide dynamic content on Web sites is with CGI (Common Gateway Interface) programs. The CGI is a specification of communication between server processes (such as programs that generate dynamic documents) and the server itself. Server Side Includes (SSI) allow output from CGI programs, or other programs, to be inserted into existing HTML pages.

CGI

By default, you may put any CGI program in the `ScriptAlias` directory on your server. These programs must be executable by the user as which the server is running. This usually means that you will need to change the mode of the files to 755 so that nobody but the user can execute them.

```
chmod 755 program.cgi
```

In order to execute CGI programs outside of the `ScriptAlias` directory, you will need to enable the `ExecCGI` option for that directory. This is done either in your `access.conf` file or in an `.htaccess` file in the directory.

CGI programs can be written in any language. The most popular languages for CGI programming are Perl and C. Because this book is not intended to be a CGI book, you may want to pick up a good book on CGI programming, such as *CGI Programming with Perl, Second Edition*.

To test whether you have CGI configured correctly, try the following CGI program, written in Perl, which displays the values of the HTTP environment variables.

```perl
#!/usr/bin/perl
print "Content-type: text/html\n\n";
print "<html><head><title>Simple CGI
program</title></head><body>\n";
for (keys %ENV)    {
    print "$_ = $ENV{$_}<br>\n";
}
print "</body></html?\n";
```

If you are going to be writing CGI programs in Perl, you may want to look at the CGI modules that come bundled with Perl.

SSI

Server Side Includes are directives that are written directly into an HTML page, which the server parses when the page is served to the Web client. They can be used to include other files, the output from programs, or environment variables.

The most common way to enable SSI is to indicate that files with a certain filename extension (typically .shtml) are to be parsed by the server when they are served. This is accomplished with the following lines in your srm.conf file:

```
# To use server-parsed HTML files
# AddType text/html .shtml
# AddHandler server-parsed .shtml
```

By uncommenting the AddType and AddHandler lines, you could tell the server to parse all .shtml files for SSI directives.

The less commonly used way of enabling SSI is with the XBitHack directive. XBitHack can be set to a value of on, off, or full and can be set in the server config, per <Directory>, per <VirtualHost> or in .htaccess files. If the XBitHack directive is on, it indicates that all files with the user execute bit set should be parsed for SSI directives. This has two main advantages. One is that you do not need to rename a file and change all links to that file simply because you want to add a little dynamic content to it. The other reason is more cosmetic—users looking at your Web content cannot tell by looking at the filename that you are generating a page dynamically—and so your wizardry is just that tiny bit more impressive. If XBitHack is set to full, Apache also tests the group execute bit. If it is on, it returns a Last-Modified header containing the file's last modified time; otherwise, it doesn't generate a Last-Modified header. Allowing a Last-Modified header to be generated allows the data to be cached.

In addition to these directives, the Options Includes directive must be specified for directories where you want to permit SSI. This may be set in the server access.conf file or in an .htaccess file.

Basic SSI Directives

SSI directives look similar to HTML comment tags. The syntax follows:

```
<!--#element attribute=value attribute=value ... -->
```

The *element* can be one of the following:

- config — This lets you set various configuration options regarding how the document parsing is handled. Because the page is parsed from top to bottom, config directives should appear at the top of the HTML document. Three configurations can be set with this command:

  - errmsg — Allows you to set the error message that is returned to the client if something goes wrong while parsing the document. This is usually [an error occurred while processing this directive], but you can set it to anything with this directive.

    Example: `<!--#config errmsg="[It's broken, dude]" -->`

Sizefmt   Allows you to set the format used to display file sizes. You can set the value to bytes to display the exact file size in bytes, or abbrev to display the size in KB or MB.

Example: `<!--#config sizefmt="bytes" -->`

Timefmt   Allows you to set the format used to display times. The format of the value is the same as is used in the `strftime` function used by C (and Perl) to display dates, shown in the following table.

%%	Percent
%a	Day of the week abbreviation
%A	Day of the week
%b	Month abbreviation
%B	Month
%c	ctime format: Sat Nov 19 21:05:57 1994
%d	Numeric day of the month
%e	DD
%D	MM/DD/YY
%h	Month abbreviation
%H	Hour, 24-hour clock, leading 0s
%I	Hour, 12-hour clock, leading 0s
%j	Day of the year
%k	Hour
%l	Hour, 12-hour clock
%m	Month number, starting with 1
%M	Minute, leading 0s
%n	Newline
%o	Ornate day of month such as 1st, 2nd, or 25th
%p	a.m. or p.m.
%r	Time format: 09:05:57 p.m.
%R	Time format: 21:05
%S	Seconds, leading 0s
%t	Tab
%T	Time format: 21:05:57
%U	Week number; Sunday as first day of week

%w	Numerical day of the week; Sunday = 0
%W	Week number; Monday as first day of week
%x	Date format: 11/19/94
%X	Time format: 21:05:57
%y	Year (two digits)
%Y	Year (four digits)
%Z	Time zone in ASCII, such as PST
echo	Displays any one of the include variables, listed here. Times are displayed in the time format specified by `timefmt`. The variable to be displayed is indicated with the `var` attribute.
DATE_GMT	Current date in Greenwich Mean Time.
DATE_LOCAL	Current date in the local time zone.
DOCUMENT_NAME	The filename (excluding directories) of the document requested by the user.
DOCUMENT_URL	The (%-decoded) URL path of the document requested by the user. Note that in the case of nested include files, this is not the URL for the current document.
LAST_MODIFIED	The last ification date of the document requested by the user.
exec	Executes a shell command or a CGI program, depending on the parameters provided. Valid attributes are `cgi` and `cmd`.
cgi	The URL of a CGI program to be executed. The URL needs to be a local CGI, not one located on another machine. The CGI program is passed the `QUERY_STRING` and `PATH_INFO` that were originally passed to the requested document, so the URL specified cannot contain this information. You should really use `include virtual` instead of this directive.
cmd	A shell command to be executed. The results will be displayed on the HTML page.
fsize	Displays the size of a file specified by either the file or virtual attribute. Size is displayed as specified with the `sizefmt` directive.
file	The path (filesystem path) to a file, either relative to the root if the value starts with / or relative to the current directory if not.
virtual	The relative URL path to a file.
flastmod	Displays the last modified date of a file. The desired file is specified as with the `fsize` directive.

include	Include the contents of a file. The file is specified with the file and virtual attributes, as with `fsize` and `flastmod`. If the file specified is a CGI program and `IncludesNoExec` is not set, the program will be executed and the results displayed. This is to be used in preference to the `exec` directive. You can pass a `QUERY_STRING` with this directive, which you cannot do with the `exec` directive.
printenv	Displays all existing variables. There are no attributes. Example: `<!--#printenv -->`
set	Set the value of a variable. Attributes are var and value. Example: `<!--#set var="animal" value="cow" -->`

> **Note**
>
> All defined CGI environment variables are also allowed as include variables.

> **Note**
>
> In your configuration files (or in .htaccess), you can specify Options IncludesNoExec to disallow the exec directive because this is the least secure of the SSI directives. Be especially cautious when Web users are able to create content (like a guestbook or discussion board) and these options are enabled!

These variables can be used elsewhere with some of the following directives.

Flow Control

Using the variables set with the `set` directive and the various environment variables and `include` variables, you can use a limited flow control syntax to generate a certain amount of dynamic content on server-parsed pages.

The syntax of the `if/else` functions is as follows:

```
<!--#if expr="test_condition" -->
<!--#elif expr="test_condition" -->
<!--#else -->
<!--#endif -->
```

expr can be a string, which is considered true if nonempty, or a variety of comparisons between two strings. Available comparison operators are =, !=, <, <=, >, and >=. If the second string has the format /string/, the strings are compared with regular expressions. Multiple comparisons can be strung together with && (AND) and ¦¦ (OR). Any text appearing between the if/elif/else directives will be displayed on the resulting page.

An example of such a flow structure follows:

```
<!--#set var="agent" value="$HTTP_USER_AGENT" -->
<!--#if expr="$agent = /Mozilla/" -->
Mozilla!
<!--#else -->
Something else!
<!--#endif -->
```

This code will display `Mozilla!` if you are using a browser that passes Mozilla as part of its `USER_AGENT` string, and `Something else!` otherwise.

Starting and Stopping the Server

At this point, you have your Apache server installed and configured the way you want it. It's time to start it up for the first time.

The server, httpd, has a few command-line options you can use to set some defaults specifying where httpd will read its configuration directives. The Apache httpd executable understands the following options:

```
httpd [-d directory] [-f file]
      [-C "directive"] [-c "directive"]
      [-v] [-V] [-h] [-l] [-L] [-S] [-t]
```

The `-d` option overrides the location of the `ServerRoot` directory. It sets the initial value of the `ServerRoot` variable (the directory where the Apache server looks for its files) to whichever path you specify. This default is usually read from the `ServerRoot` directive in `httpd.conf` and is `/etc/httpd/apache` as set up by OpenLinux.

The `-f` flag specifies the location of the main configuration file `httpd.conf`. It reads and executes the configuration commands found in `ConfigurationFile` on startup. If the `ConfigurationFile` is not an absolute path (it doesn't begin with a /), its location is assumed to be relative to the path specified in the `ServerRoot` directive in `httpd.conf`. By default, this value is set to `/etc/httpd/apache/conf/httpd.conf`.

The `-v` option prints the development version of the Apache server and terminates the process.

The `-V` option shows all of the settings that were in effect when the server was compiled.

The `-h` option prints the following usage information for the server:

```
Usage: httpd [-d directory] [-f file]
             [-C "directive"] [-c "directive"]
             [-v] [-V] [-h] [-l] [-L] [-S] [-t]
```

The following options can be used:

- `-D name`   Defines a name for use in `<IfDefinename>` directives.
- `-d directory`   Specifies an alternate `initialServerRoot`.
- `-f file`   Specifies an alternate `ServerConfigFile`.
- `-C "directive"`   Processes directive before reading configuration files.
- `-c "directive"`   Processes directive after reading configuration files.
- `-v`   Shows version number.
- `-V`   Shows compile settings.
- `-h`   Lists available command-line options (this page).
- `-l`   Lists compiled-in modules.
- `-L`   Lists available configuration directives.
- `-S`   Shows parsed settings (currently only `vhost` settings).
- `-t`   Runs syntax test for configuration files only.
- `-l`   Lists those modules that are compiled into your Apache server.
- `-L`   Lists all the configuration directives available with the modules available to you.
- `-S`   Lists the virtual host settings for the server.
- `-t`   Extremely useful option that runs a syntax check on your configuration files. (It's a good idea to run this check before restarting your server after you have changed your configuration files.)

> **Note**
>
> When you start the server manually from the command line, you need to do so as root. There are two main reasons for starting as root:
> - If your standalone server uses the default HTTP port (port 80), only the super-user can bind to Internet ports that are lower than 1025.
> - Only processes owned by root can change their UID and GID as specified by the `User` and `Group` directives. If you start the server under another UID, it will run with the permissions of the user starting the process.

The `/etc/rc.d/httpd` Scripts

OpenLinux uses scripts in the `/etc/rc.d/` directory to control the startup and shutdown of various services, including the Apache Web server. The main script installed for the Apache Web server is `/etc/rc.d/init.d/httpd`. The stock httpd script from OpenLinux is shown in Listing 18.1. If you ever install Apache from source, you may want to make a symlink from `/usr/local/apache/apachectl` to `/etc/rc.d/init.d/httpd`.

> **Note**
>
> `/etc/rc.d/init.d/httpd` is a shell script and is not the same as the Apache server located in `/usr/sbin`. That is, `/usr/sbin/httpd.apache` is the program executable file, and `/etc/rc.d/init.d/httpd` is a shell script that helps control that program.

You can use the following options when executing the httpd script:

- start   The system uses this option to start the Web server during bootup. You, as root, can also use this script to start the server.
- stop   The system uses this option to stop the server gracefully. You should use this script, rather than the `kill` command, to stop the server.

> **Tip**
>
> There are two ways to get Apache to reread its configuration files and incorporate any changes you have made, without having to stop and start Apache using the script. This is accomplished by sending the httpd process signals using the `kill` command.
>
> `# kill -HUP `cat /var/run/httpd.pid``
>
> The preceding will cause the httpd process to drop all connections, kill all child processes, reread its configuration file, and then start new child processes and connections using the new configuration. You would use this if you wanted to stop serving all connections immediately under the old configuration and start under the new.
>
> `# kill -USR1 `cat /var/run/httpd.pid``
>
> The preceding will cause the httpd process to reread its configuration files. It will NOT drop its current connections, however. Child processes will continue to run under the old configuration rules until the connections they are serving terminate. This is the least disruptive way to incorporate configuration changes. On production Web servers, where downtime is not acceptable, it is the best way to restart for anything other than security-related configuration changes.

LISTING 18.1 `/etc/rc.d/init.d/httpd`

```sh
#!/bin/sh
#
# httpd    This shell script takes care of starting and stopping
#   httpd.
#

# Source function library.
. /etc/rc.d/init.d/functions

NAME=httpd
DAEMON=/usr/sbin/$NAME
DAEMON=$DAEMON.$VARIANT

# Source networking configuration.
. /etc/sysconfig/network

# See how we were called.
case "$1" in
 start)
   grep -q nobody /etc/group || echo "nobody::65534:" >> /etc/group
   [ ! -e $LOCK ] || exit 1
   [ -x $DAEMON ] || exit 0
   [ ${NETWORKING} != "no" ] || exit 0

   # Start daemons.
   if [ -f /etc/httpd/$VARIANT/conf/httpd.conf ]; then
     echo -n "Starting $IDENT services ($VARIANT): "
     ssd -S -n $NAME -x $DAEMON -- -f /etc/httpd/$VARIANT/conf/httpd.conf
     touch $LOCK
     echo "."
   elif [ "$PROBABLY" = "goofing" ]; then
     echo "$VARIANT httpd not configured: Skipped!"
   fi
   ;;

 stop)
   [ -f $LOCK ] || exit 0

   # Stop daemons.
   echo -n "Stopping $VARIANT httpd: "
   ssd -K -p /var/run/$NAME.pid -n $NAME

   echo "."
   rm -f $LOCK
   ;;

 *)
```

```
    echo "Usage: httpd {start|stop}"
    exit 1
    ;;
esac

exit 0
```

Summary

You now have the most popular Web server in the world up and running on your computer. Your Apache Web server is ready to serve basic Web pages for multiple domain names and provide dynamic content using CGI and SSI. A number of excellent open-source, low-cost commercial software programs such as PHP and mySQL work with Apache to provide sophisticated, dynamic content to Web sites. Visit the Apache sites mentioned in the Server Installation section of this chapter or see www.devshed.net, www.php.net, or www.mysql.org for more information. You'll find a wide variety of software available to build a powerful and attractive Internet or intranet Web site server.

Mail Services

CHAPTER 19

IN THIS CHAPTER

- The Basics of Email *420*
- Configuring Sendmail *423*
- Setting Up a Mail Hub *454*

The Basics of Email

Electronic mail (email) has become the communication medium of choice for both corporations and individuals. Email is both faster and easier to compose and send than regular first-class mail ("snailmail") or faxes, and its cost is negligible. Because many of the formal rules of business correspondence are suspended in email communications, email is faster to write and faster to read, often creating a comfortable level of communication not possible on letterhead stationery. Because requests sent by email don't demand that you drop everything you are doing to respond right this minute (the way telephone calls do!), it's generally the preferred way to communicate nonurgent messages and requests. Email travels the world in a matter of minutes, enabling international communication to take place quickly and inexpensively in a way not possible before. Additionally, the ability to attach binary files (from word processing documents to CAD drawings) creates a whole new dimension of information exchange.

As of May 1999, 37.4% of the North American (U.S. and Canadian) population was online, or about 101 million people. Many have two or more email addresses, usually a combination of business and personal accounts. The proliferation of free email providers, such as Hotmail and Juno, enables those without individual Internet access to maintain a private email account at public-use access facilities (schools, libraries, multiuser workstations in the office). There is no denying that email usage has exploded: business communications, personal messages, junk mail, autoresponders ("I will be out of the office until…"), professional- and hobbyist-oriented mail lists, and the list goes on.

Providing mail services is a natural purpose for Linux because email was initially developed and matured under UNIX. To provide email access for yourself and anyone else accessing your machine, you need to set up mail server software on your system and acquire Internet access.

In this chapter, you'll learn how to configure your Linux machine to transport email from your system to the Internet for distribution. You'll learn how to configure your OpenLinux machine as a mail server and how to set up mail services for virtual domains/hosts on your system. Several mail server alternatives are available for Linux. We chose to discuss the most popular mail server software available: Sendmail. Almost all Linux distributions, including OpenLinux, provide Sendmail as the standard mail server software.

Mail Agents: MTA, MDA, and MUA

There are three main parts of a Linux email system: Mail Transport Agent (MTA), Mail Delivery Agent (MDA), and Mail User Agent (MUA). For users, electronic mail is usually rather simple: they deal primarily with the MUA, which is the program that allows users to read and send email. It reads incoming messages that have been delivered to the user's mailbox. It also passes outgoing messages to an MTA for sending to the remote recipient. There are many Linux software packages to compose and to read email. For example, pine, elm, MH, Mail, and exmh are some of the most popular mail readers. The Linux system administrator deals primarily with the transport and delivery of electronic mail.

MDA accepts the mail from the server and is responsible for actually delivering mail to a user. MDA usually delivers only one specific type of mail. On a UNIX system, the standard MDA is the program `/bin/mail`. Its responsibility is to deliver email into a user's local mailbox file. OpenLinux uses `mail.local`, a more secure and single-purpose program than `/bin/mail`, as its MDA. Another very popular MDA, which is standard on many recent Linux systems, is procmail. procmail can be used as the local delivery agent, as well as an advanced filter for mail before delivery; OpenLinux uses procmail as a filter.

The MTA is basically a mail router. It takes a message from either an MUA or another MTA. It decides which delivery method it should use based on the information on the mail header. It then passes the message to the appropriate MDA or to another MTA. In short, the MTA handles everything needed to get a mail message from a mail user agent to a mail delivery agent. MTA also interprets aliases and rewrites addresses for other mail delivery agents. It relays mail from other transport agents. Undeliverable mail is queued by the MTA for later transport.

The predominant mail transport agent in the UNIX world (accounting for approximately 70–80% of all Internet email) is Sendmail. There are several differing versions of Sendmail (Berkeley, IDA, Sendmail Inc.), as well as alternative MTAs such as qmail, smail, zmail. This chapter will cover the Berkeley/Sendmail Inc. 8.9 variant as included in OpenLinux.

Simple Mail Transfer Protocol

Sendmail uses the simple mail transfer protocol (SMTP) to transport mail across the Internet between hosts. SMTP is described in RFC821, or the Request for Comments #821, and is a very simple protocol consisting of four-character commands and three-digit reply codes. The protocol is simple enough that one can use it merely by telnetting directly to the SMTP port, 25. This method is most often used as a means of determining what has gone wrong in an SMTP setup. However, telnetting in does not provide the level of functionality or versatility of a standard mail user agent. ESMTP, an extended version of SMTP, is now very widely used.

To see an example of a simple SMTP transaction, which is actually an SMTP server in this case, telnet into a SMTP server as shown in the next section.

SMTP Session

```
$ telnet theneteffect.com 25
Trying 206.202.56.3...
Connected to theneteffect.com.
Escape character is '^]'.
220 consider.theneteffect.com ESMTP Sendmail 8.9.3/8.9.3; Thu, 26 Aug 1999 21:35:42 -0500
helo theneteffect.com
250 consider.theneteffect.com Hello chevaliere.theneteffect.com [206.202.0.252], pleased to meet you
MAIL From: <mitch@theneteffect.com>
250 <mitch@theneteffect.com>... Sender ok
RCPT To: <mitch@acan.net>
250 <mitch@acan.net>... Recipient ok
DATA
354 Enter mail, end with "." on a line by itself
This is a test.
.
250 VAA24159 Message accepted for delivery
QUIT
221 consider.theneteffect.com closing connection
Connection closed by foreign host.
```

In this example, we began by telnetting into an SMTP server and exchanging greetings with the server. We told the SMTP server to send a message from `mitch@theneteffect.com` to `mitch@acan.net`, and the SMTP server verified the two addresses. We then typed the command DATA followed by the text of the message. When the message was complete, we closed the SMTP session by typing QUIT at the prompt. The mail message was queued for sending.

Message Format

The format of email messages is specified in RFC822. An Internet email message consists of a header and a body. The fields of the header are keyword/value pairs separated by a colon. Certain header fields are required by RFC822, and many others are optional and give information about the message.

It is useful to look at the header fields of mail messages to see what kind of information is in the mail message. For example, look at the message sent by the previous SMTP session:

```
Return-Path: <mitch@theneteffect.com>
Received: from consider.theneteffect.com (consider.theneteffect.com [206.202.56.3])
```

```
        by ns1.acan.net (8.9.2/8.9.2) with ESMTP id VAA06337
    for <mitch@acan.net>; Thu, 26 Aug 1999 21:37:44 -0500 (CDT)
Received: from theneteffect.com (chevaliere.theneteffect.com [206.202.0.252])
    by consider.theneteffect.com (8.9.3/8.9.3) with SMTP id VAA24159
    for <mitch@acan.net>; Thu, 26 Aug 1999 21:36:27 -0500

Date: Thu, 26 Aug 1999 21:36:27 -0500From: Mitch Adair
➥<mitch@theneteffect.com>Message-Id:
<199908270236.VAA24159@consider.theneteffect.com>To: undisclosed-
➥recipients:;This is a test.
```

The message headers give basic information like the address of the sender and the recipient and the date and time the message was originally sent, as well as the identity of every server that handled or relayed the message and the date and time each relay was effected. Errors are also reported and can be used to troubleshoot email delivery problems.

Configuring Sendmail

Sendmail is arguably the most difficult subject broached in this book. Fortunately for users of Caldera OpenLinux 2.3, however, an extended lesson in Sendmail is not necessary to set up mail services on your new OpenLinux box. For the sake of thoroughness, we'll briefly discuss the old-fashioned way of configuring Sendmail and then touch on the intermediate "easy" way to configure Sendmail using the M4 macros. If you aren't seriously interested in the subject, however, you can go straight to the section entitled "Configuring with COAS" and make your life a lot simpler.

Normally, Sendmail waits in the background for new messages. When an SMTP connection is made, a child process is invoked to handle the connection. The parent Sendmail process goes back to listening for new SMTP connections.

The Sendmail child process puts the newly arrived message into the mail queue (usually stored in /var/spool/mqueue). If it is immediately deliverable, the message is delivered and deleted from the queue. If it is not immediately deliverable, the message will be left in the queue, and the child Sendmail process will terminate.

Delivery of messages left in the queue will be attempted the next time the queue is processed. The parent Sendmail will usually fork a child process to attempt to deliver anything left in the queue at regular intervals.

File Locations

Over the years, the Sendmail distribution has largely standardized where it puts its files, although there are some variations generally between types of boxen (or multiple workstations or servers) and the various UNIX distributions. OpenLinux has departed somewhat from that loose standard into the world of "vendor configurations." OpenLinux is not the first and surely will not be the last to depart from the vanilla locations. In fact, their system is certainly as logical as any other system, if not more so. Nevertheless, it will help you to know that some things are where you expect them to be, many aren't, and there are several things you won't understand at all if you're new to OpenLinux.

To start with, the "standard" places for Sendmail to keep its files are:

- /etc for the sendmail.cf configuration file, sendmail.cw and aliases files, and assorted hash files for Sendmail's many, many optional features.
- /usr/sbin for the Sendmail binary (or /usr/lib with a symbolic link generally in whichever one the binary actually isn't).
- /usr/lib for the sendmail.hf help-text file.
- /var/log for the sendmail.st statistics file.
- /var/spool/mail for the mailbox files (that's a bit of a Linux-ism but it refers to /var/mail, /usr/mail, /usr/spool/mail—there are lots of places that it can go).
- /var/spool/mqueue for the queue files (mail waiting to be sent or delivered).
- /var/run for the sendmail.pid PID (Process ID) file.
- /usr/bin generally holds all the support files/links: newaliases, praliases, makemap, mailq.

Okay, so that's pretty straightforward and simple—well, maybe not simple, but fairly standard. Of course, if you've been using Suns all these years, you probably think all this stuff is supposed to live in /etc/mail.

OpenLinux has based many of its configuration files around extensibility and configurability, largely by graphical and/or automated tools where possible. This means that configuration can range from absurdly simple, if all you need to do is click a couple of options with the mouse, to somewhat more difficult and complex than normal, if you need to do something by hand.

For starters, OpenLinux supports changing between multiple MTAs to supporting user preference. This is accomplished through the program /usr/sbin/mta-switch. mta-switch can change between Sendmail, qmail, and smail, arranging your configuration files for you after the switch and basically making sure things don't go wrong. Its configuration files and links to programs are spread among the /etc/mta directory, /etc/sysconfig/mta, and /etc/sysconfig/daemon/mta. The contents of the file /etc/sysconfig/mta determines how the sendmail.cf file gets rebuilt by the Caldera Open Administration System (COAS) or mta-switch—that's an important one.

Now Sendmail itself has the important configuration files in the normal place: /etc. That is where sendmail.cf, sendmail.cw, and the aliases are. From this point, you need to look around a bit. sendmail.hf is in /usr/share/sendmail, the program binaries themselves are in /usr/libexec/sendmail, and all of the m4 files for rebuilding your sendmail.cf are in /usr/share/sendmail/cf. If you choose to use smrsh (Sendmail Restricted Shell), then program binaries go in /usr/libexec/sm.bin. Finally, if you need access to sendmail's mailertable feature, the default install puts that in /etc/sendmail.

By listing where all these files are, we certainly don't intend to encourage people to go play around with them, because there is no small potential to wreak havoc by doing so. Additionally, by using the excellent administrative tools OpenLinux provides, it is entirely possible to avoid ever having to see a Sendmail configuration file, while still ending up with a perfectly functioning Internet mail host. Sometimes, however, you really need or just want to see where and what everything is—that is very much in the spirit of Linux. So now you know where to look.

Sendmail Configuration Files

The Sendmail configuration file is /etc/sendmail.cf. It includes directives about general configuration options, such as queue directory and timeout values, definitions for each MDA, including pathnames and options, rulesets for header processing/rewriting, and the "routing table," which determines which MDAs get used for which messages.

The Sendmail configuration file is very cryptic and hard to understand; it always has been. Sendmail was created a long time ago when UNIX machines were very slow and there was no standardized email transfer protocol available. The Sendmail configuration file was deliberately designed to be as flexible and efficient as possible, so that Sendmail could readily read and parse it. No consideration was given to human "user friendliness." Indeed, it's a standard joke that sendmail.cf syntax is closer to the garbage modems display for noise than it is to English. As a result, sendmail.cf is often considered to be one of the greatest puzzles a Linux system administrator will ever face.

From the following printout of the default /etc/sendmail.cf file included in Caldera OpenLinux 2.3, you can get a sense of why many people have dreaded working with Sendmail. It is staggeringly complicated the first time you see it (and becomes only a bit less so after the 100th endeavor) and requires serious, directed study to master. Some configuration options that are both necessary and thankfully fairly straightforward appear at the beginning of the file, but other parts of the file are pretty incomprehensible. That's okay. This printout is included here mostly for familiarization. Read the comments. You may never need to actually modify this file manually, but it will nevertheless help to look it over.

A few of the configuration options to look for are as follows:

`Fw/etc/sendmail.cw`	This option sets the name of the file where you can put your machine's aliases—domain and hostnames for which it will accept mail.
`Dj$w.Foo.COM`	This option sets your machine's fully qualified domain name. Sendmail will normally figure this out for itself, but if you have a need, you can set it here.
`DS`	This option sets the name of your "Smart Relay"—a hub machine that accepts mail from you and figures out what to do with it. This will be discussed in more detail later in the chapter.
`FR-o /etc/mail/relay-domains`	This file contains a list of hosts that will accept and relay mail from your machine.
`O MaxMessageSize=1000000`	This option allows you to set the maximum size of a message you will send or receive. Here it is set to 1MB.

There are many, many other configuration options, as you can see. Many have comments with a brief explanation. It would probably serve you well to look through the comments and familiarize yourself somewhat with the file. There is admittedly little that you will understand after the "REWRITING RULES" section begins. These are the actual rules Sendmail uses to deliver mail. A dedicated book on Sendmail should be used to decipher their meanings.

```
/etc/sendmail.cf
#
# Copyright  1998 Sendmail, Inc.  All rights reserved.
# Copyright  1983, 1995 Eric P. Allman.  All rights reserved.
# Copyright  1988, 1993
#    The Regents of the University of California.  All rights reserved.
#
# By using this file, you agree to the terms and conditions set
# forth in the LICENSE file which can be found at the top level of
# the sendmail distribution.
#
#
```

```
#######################################################################
#######################################################################
#####
#####           SENDMAIL CONFIGURATION FILE
#####
#####   built by root@knob.calderasystems.com on Sat Apr  3 16:20:40 MST 1999
#####   in /usr/share/sendmail/cf/cf
#####   using ../ as configuration include directory
#####
#######################################################################
#######################################################################

#####   @(#)cfhead.m4    8.22 (Berkeley) 5/19/98   #####
#####   @(#)cf.m4        8.29 (Berkeley) 5/19/98   #####

#
# Copyright  1996, 1997 Caldera Inc., Provo
#
#
# This is a generic configuration file for Caldera OpenLinux
#
# Basic ideas taken from Red Hat contrib/sendmail-8.7.5-1.src.rpm.
# Credits go to Marc (whoever built it).
#
#####   $Id: generic-col2.2.mc,v 1.4 1999/02/23 15:36:07 okir Exp $   #####

#####   @(#)linux.m4     8.7 (Berkeley) 5/19/98   #####

#####   @(#)local_lmtp.m4    8.5 (Berkeley) 5/19/98   #####

#####   @(#)redirect.m4     8.10 (Berkeley) 5/19/98   #####

#####   @(#)always_add_domain.m4    8.6 (Berkeley) 5/19/98   #####

#####   @(#)use_cw_file.m4    8.6 (Berkeley) 5/19/98   #####

#####   @(#)mailertable.m4    8.9 (Berkeley) 5/19/98   #####

#####   @(#)proto.m4     8.223 (Berkeley) 6/30/98   #####

# level 8 config file format
V8/Berkeley

# override file safeties - setting this option compromises system security
# need to set this now for the sake of class files
#O DontBlameSendmail=safe
```

```
##################
#   local info   #
##################

Cwlocalhost
# file containing names of hosts for which we receive email
Fw/etc/sendmail.cw

# my official domain name
# ... define this only if sendmail cannot automatically determine your domain
#Dj$w.Foo.COM

CP.

# "Smart" relay host (may be null)
DS

# operators that cannot be in local usernames (i.e., network indicators)
CO @ % !

# a class with just dot (for identifying canonical names)
C..

# a class with just a left bracket (for identifying domain literals)
C[[

# Mailer table (overriding domains)
Kmailertable hash /etc/sendmail/mailertable

# Resolve map (to check if a host exists in check_mail)
Kresolve host -a<OK> -T<TEMP>


# Hosts that will permit relaying ($=R)
FR-o /etc/mail/relay-domains

# who I send unqualified names to (null means deliver locally)
DR

# who gets all local email traffic ($R has precedence for unqualified names)
DH

# dequoting map
Kdequote dequote

# class E: names that should be exposed as from this host, even if we masquerade
# class L: names that should be delivered locally, even if we have a relay
# class M: domains that should be converted to $M
#CL root
CE root
```

```
# who I masquerade as (null for no masquerading) (see also $=M)
DM

# my name for error messages
DnMAILER-DAEMON

CPREDIRECT

# Configuration version number
DZ8.9.1


###############
#    Options   #
###############

# strip message body to 7 bits on input?
O SevenBitInput=False

# 8-bit data handling
O EightBitMode=pass8

# wait for alias file rebuild (default units: minutes)
O AliasWait=10

# location of alias file
O AliasFile=/etc/aliases

# minimum number of free blocks on filesystem
O MinFreeBlocks=100

# maximum message size
#O MaxMessageSize=1000000


# substitution for space (blank) characters
O BlankSub=.

# avoid connecting to "expensive" mailers on initial submission?
O HoldExpensive=False

# checkpoint queue runs after every N successful deliveries
#O CheckpointInterval=10

# default delivery mode
O DeliveryMode=background

# automatically rebuild the alias database?
#O AutoRebuildAliases

# error message header/file
#O ErrorHeader=/etc/sendmail.oE
```

```
# error mode
#O ErrorMode=print

# save Unix-style "From_" lines at top of header?
#O SaveFromLine

# temporary file mode
O TempFileMode=0600

# match recipients against GECOS field?
#O MatchGECOS

# maximum hop count
#O MaxHopCount=17

# location of help file
O HelpFile=/usr/share/sendmail/sendmail.hf

# ignore dots as terminators in incoming messages?
#O IgnoreDots

# name resolver options
#O ResolverOptions=+AAONLY

# deliver MIME-encapsulated error messages?
O SendMimeErrors=True


# Forward file search path
O ForwardPath=$z/.forward.$w:$z/.forward

# open connection cache size
O ConnectionCacheSize=2

# open connection cache timeout
O ConnectionCacheTimeout=5m

# persistent host status directory
#O HostStatusDirectory=.hoststat

# single thread deliveries (requires HostStatusDirectory)?
#O SingleThreadDelivery

# use Errors-To: header?
O UseErrorsTo=False


# log level
O LogLevel=9

# send to me too, even in an alias expansion?
#O MeToo
```

```
# verify RHS in newaliases?
O CheckAliases=False

# default messages to old style headers if no special punctuation?
O OldStyleHeaders=True

# SMTP daemon options
#O DaemonPortOptions=Port=esmtp

# privacy flags
O PrivacyOptions=authwarnings

# who (if anyone) should get extra copies of error messages
#O PostMasterCopy=Postmaster

# slope of queue-only function
#O QueueFactor=600000

# queue directory
O QueueDirectory=/var/spool/mqueue


# timeouts (many of these)
#O Timeout.initial=5m
#O Timeout.connect=5m
#O Timeout.iconnect=5m
#O Timeout.helo=5m
#O Timeout.mail=10m
#O Timeout.rcpt=1h
#O Timeout.datainit=5m
#O Timeout.datablock=1h
#O Timeout.datafinal=1h
#O Timeout.rset=5m
#O Timeout.quit=2m
#O Timeout.misc=2m
#O Timeout.command=1h
#O Timeout.ident=30s
#O Timeout.fileopen=60s
O Timeout.queuereturn=5d
#O Timeout.queuereturn.normal=5d
#O Timeout.queuereturn.urgent=2d
#O Timeout.queuereturn.non-urgent=7d
O Timeout.queuewarn=4h
#O Timeout.queuewarn.normal=4h
#O Timeout.queuewarn.urgent=1h
#O Timeout.queuewarn.non-urgent=12h
#O Timeout.hoststatus=30m

# should we not prune routes in route-addr syntax addresses?
#O DontPruneRoutes

# queue up everything before forking?
```

```
O SuperSafe=True

# status file
O StatusFile=/var/log/sendmail.st

# time zone handling:
#   if undefined, use system default
#   if defined but null, use TZ envariable passed in
#   if defined and nonnull, use that info
#O TimeZoneSpec=


# default UID (can be username or userid:groupid)
#O DefaultUser=mailnull

# list of locations of user database file (null means no lookup)
#O UserDatabaseSpec=/etc/userdb

# fallback MX host
#O FallbackMXhost=fall.back.host.net

# if we are the best MX host for a site, try it directly instead of config err
#O TryNullMXList

# load average at which we just queue messages
#O QueueLA=8

# load average at which we refuse connections
#O RefuseLA=12

# maximum number of children we allow at one time
#O MaxDaemonChildren=12

# maximum number of new connections per second
#O ConnectionRateThrottle=3

# work recipient factor
#O RecipientFactor=30000

# deliver each queued job in a separate process?
#O ForkEachJob


# work class factor
#O ClassFactor=1800

# work time factor
#O RetryFactor=90000

# shall we sort the queue by hostname first?
#O QueueSortOrder=priority

# minimum time in queue before retry
```

```
#O MinQueueAge=30m


# default character set
#O DefaultCharSet=iso-8859-1

# service switch file (ignored on Solaris, Ultrix, OSF/1, others)
#O ServiceSwitchFile=/etc/service.switch

# hosts file (normally /etc/hosts)
#O HostsFile=/etc/hosts

# dialup line delay on connection failure
#O DialDelay=10s

# action to take if there are no recipients in the message
#O NoRecipientAction=add-to-undisclosed

# chrooted environment for writing to files
#O SafeFileEnvironment=/arch

# are colons OK in addresses?
#O ColonOkInAddr

# how many jobs can you process in the queue?
#O MaxQueueRunSize=10000

# shall I avoid expanding CNAMEs (violates protocols)?
#O DontExpandCnames

# SMTP initial login message (old $e macro)
O SmtpGreetingMessage=$j Sendmail $v/$Z; $b

# UNIX initial From header format (old $l macro)
O UnixFromLine=From $g  $d

# From: lines that have embedded newlines are unwrapped onto one line
#O SingleLineFromHeader=False


# Allow HELO SMTP command that does not include a host name
#O AllowBogusHELO=False

# Characters to be quoted in a full name phrase (@,;:\()[] are automatic)
#O MustQuoteChars=.


# delimiter (operator) characters (old $o macro)
O OperatorChars=.:%@!^/[]+

# shall I avoid calling initgroups(3) because of high NIS costs?
#O DontInitGroups

# are group-writable :include: and .forward files (un)trustworthy?
```

```
O UnsafeGroupWrites=True

# where do errors that occur when sending errors get sent?
#O DoubleBounceAddress=postmaster

# what user id do we assume for the majority of the processing?
#O RunAsUser=sendmail

# maximum number of recipients per SMTP envelope
#O MaxRecipientsPerMessage=100

# shall we get local names from our installed interfaces?
#O DontProbeInterfaces

###########################
#   Message precedences   #
###########################

Pfirst-class=0
Pspecial-delivery=100
Plist=-30
Pbulk=-60
Pjunk=-100


######################
#   Trusted users    #
######################

# this is equivalent to setting class "t"
#Ft/etc/sendmail.ct
Troot
Tdaemon
Tuucp


#########################
#   Format of headers   #
#########################

H?P?Return-Path: <$g>
HReceived: $?sfrom $s $.$?_($?s$|from $.$_)
    $.by $j ($v/$Z)$?r with $r$. id $i$?u
    for $u; $|;
    $.$b
H?D?Resent-Date: $a
H?D?Date: $a
H?F?Resent-From: $?x$x <$g>$|$g$.
H?F?From: $?x$x <$g>$|$g$.
H?x?Full-Name: $x
# HPosted-Date: $a
# H?l?Received-Date: $b
H?M?Resent-Message-Id: <$t.$i@$j>
```

H?M?Message-Id: <$t.$i@$j>

###
###
#####
REWRITING RULES
#####
###
###

##
Ruleset 3 -- Name Canonicalization
##
S3

handle null input (translate to <@> special case)
R$@ $@ <@>

strip group: syntax (not inside angle brackets!) and trailing semicolon
R$* $: $1 <@>   mark addresses
R$* < $* > $* <@> $: $1 < $2 > $3   unmark <addr>
R@ $* <@> $: @ $1   unmark @host:...
R$* :: $* <@> $: $1 :: $2   unmark node::addr
R:include: $* <@> $: :include: $1   unmark :include:...
R$* [$* : $*] <@> $: $1 [$2 : $3]   unmark IPv6 addrs
R$* : $* [$*] $: $1 : $2 [$3] <@>   remark if leading colon
R$* : $* <@> $: $2   strip colon if marked
R$* <@> $: $1   unmark
R$* ; $1   strip trailing semi
R$* < $* ; > $1 < $2 >   bogus bracketed semi

null input now results from list:; syntax
R$@ $@ :; <@>

strip angle brackets — note RFC733 heuristic to get innermost item
R$* $: < $1 >   housekeeping <>
R$+ < $* >   < $2 >   strip excess on left
R< $* > $+   < $1 >   strip excess on right
R<> $@ < @ >   MAIL FROM:<> case
R< $+ > $: $1   remove housekeeping <>

make sure <@a,@b,@c:user@d> syntax is easy to parse — undone later
R@ $+ , $+   @ $1 : $2   change all "," to ":"

localize and dispose of route-based addresses
R@ $+ : $+ $@ $>96 < @$1 > : $2   handle <route-addr>

find focus for list syntax
R $+ : $* ; @ $+ $@ $>96 $1 : $2 ; < @ $3 >   list syntax

```
R $+ : $* ;        $@ $1 : $2;          list syntax

# find focus for @ syntax addresses
R$+ @ $+           $: $1 < @ $2 >            focus on domain
R$+ < $+ @ $+ >    $1 $2 < @ $3 >            move gaze right
R$+ < @ $+ >       $@ $>96 $1 < @ $2 >       already canonical

# do some sanity checking
R$* < @ $* : $* > $*    $1 < @ $2 $3 > $4    nix colons in addrs

# convert old-style addresses to a domain-based address
R$- ! $+           $@ $>96 $2 < @ $1 .UUCP >    resolve uucp names
R$+ . $- ! $+      $@ $>96 $3 < @ $1 . $2 >     domain uucps
R$+ ! $+           $@ $>96 $2 < @ $1 .UUCP >    uucp subdomains

# if we have % signs, take the rightmost one
R$* % $*           $1 @ $2              First make them all @s.
R$* @ $* @ $*      $1 % $2 @ $3            Undo all but the last.
R$* @ $*           $@ $>96 $1 < @ $2 >     Insert < > and finish

# else we must be a local name
R$*                $@ $>96 $1



##################################################
###   Ruleset 96 -- bottom half of ruleset 3   ###
##################################################


S96

# handle special cases for local names
R$* < @ localhost > $*          $: $1 < @ $j . > $2     no domain at all
R$* < @ localhost . $m > $*     $: $1 < @ $j . > $2     local domain
R$* < @ localhost . UUCP > $*   $: $1 < @ $j . > $2     .UUCP domain
R$* < @ [ $+ ] > $*             $: $1 < @@ [ $2 ] > $3  mark [a.b.c.d]
R$* < @@ $=w > $*               $: $1 < @ $j . > $3     self-literal
R$* < @@ $+ > $*                $@ $1 < @ $2 > $3       canon IP addr




# if really UUCP, handle it immediately

# try UUCP traffic as a local address
R$* < @ $+ . UUCP > $*       $: $1 < @ $[ $2 $] . UUCP . > $3
R$* < @ $+ . . UUCP . > $*   $@ $1 < @ $2 . > $3

# pass to name server to make hostname canonical
R$* < @ $* $~P > $*          $: $1 < @ $[ $2 $3 $] > $4

# local host aliases and pseudo-domains are always canonical
```

```
R$* < @ $=w > $*        $: $1 < @ $2 . > $3
R$* < @ $j > $*         $: $1 < @ $j . > $2
R$* < @ $=M > $*        $: $1 < @ $2 . > $3
R$* < @ $* $=P > $*     $: $1 < @ $2 $3 . > $4
R$* < @ $* . . > $*     $1 < @ $2 . > $3


####################################################
### Ruleset 4 -- Final Output Post-rewriting   ###
####################################################
S4

R$* <@>                 $@              handle <> and list:;

# strip trailing dot off possibly canonical name
R$* < @ $+ . > $*       $1 < @ $2 > $3

# eliminate internal code — should never get this far!
R$* < @ *LOCAL* > $*    $1 < @ $j > $2

# externalize local domain info
R$* < $+ > $*           $1 $2 $3        defocus
R@ $+ : @ $+ : $+       @ $1 , @ $2 : $3   <route-addr> canonical
R@ $*                   $@ @ $1            ... and exit

# UUCP must always be presented in old form
R$+ @ $- . UUCP         $2!$1           u@h.UUCP => h!u

# delete duplicate local names
R$+ % $=w @ $=w         $1 @ $2         u%host@host => u@host


################################################################
### Ruleset 97 -- recanonicalize and call ruleset zero       ###
###              (used for recursive calls)                  ###
################################################################

S97
R$*             $: $>3 $1
R$*             $@ $>0 $1


#######################################
### Ruleset 0 -- Parse Address      ###
#######################################

S0

R$*             $: $>Parse0 $1     initial parsing
R<@>            $#local $: <@>     special case error msgs
```

```
R$*                 $: $>98 $1         handle local hacks
R$*                 $: $>Parse1 $1     final parsing


#
#   Parse0 -- do initial syntax checking and eliminate local addresses.
#     This should either return with the (possibly modified) input
#     or return with a #error mailer.  It should not return with a
#     #mailer other than the #error mailer.
#

SParse0
R<@>                    $@ <@>           special case error msgs
R$* : $* ; <@>           $#error $@ 5.1.3 $: "List:; syntax illegal for recipient
 addresses"
#R@ <@ $* >           < @ $1 >     catch "@@host" bogosity
R<@ $+>                 $#error $@ 5.1.3 $: "User address required"
R$*             $: <> $1
R<> $* < @ [ $+ ] > $*    $1 < @ [ $2 ] > $3
R<> $* <$* : $* > $*      $#error $@ 5.1.3 $: "Colon illegal in host name part"
R<> $*          $1
R$* < @ . $* > $*    $#error $@ 5.1.2 $: "Invalid host name"
R$* < @ $* .. $* > $*    $#error $@ 5.1.2 $: "Invalid host name"

# now delete the local info -- note $=O to find characters that cause forwarding
R$* < @ > $*        $@ $>Parse0 $>3 $1      user@ => user
R< @ $=w . > : $*   $@ $>Parse0 $>3 $2      @here:... -> ...
R$* - < @ $=w . >      $: $(dequote $1 $) < @ $2 . >    dequote "foo"@here
R< @ $+ >           $#error $@ 5.1.3 $: "User address required"
R$* $=O $* < @ $=w . >    $@ $>Parse0 $>3 $1 $2 $3    ...@here -> ...
R$* -               $: $(dequote $1 $) < @ *LOCAL* >    dequote "foo"
R< @ *LOCAL* >         $#error $@ 5.1.3 $: "User address required"
R$* $=O $* < @ *LOCAL* >
            $@ $>Parse0 $>3 $1 $2 $3    ...@*LOCAL* -> ...
R$* < @ *LOCAL* >   $: $1

#
#  Parse1 -- the bottom half of ruleset 0.
#

SParse1
# handle numeric address spec
R$* < @ [ $+ ] > $*    $: $>98 $1 < @ [ $2 ] > $3    numeric internet spec
R$* < @ [ $+ ] > $*    $#esmtp $@ [$2] $: $1 < @ [$2] > $3    still numeric:
send


# short circuit local delivery so forwarded email works
R$=L < @ $=w . >    $#local $: @ $1       special local names
R$+ < @ $=w . >         $#local $: $1         regular local name


# not local -- try mailer table lookup
```

Mail Services
Chapter 19

```
R$* <@ $+ > $*          $: < $2 > $1 < @ $2 > $3     extract host name
R< $+ . > $*        $: < $1 > $2           strip trailing dot
R< $+ > $*       $: < $(mailertable $1 $) > $2    lookup
R< $~[ : $+ > $*     $>95 < $1 : $2 > $3     check — resolved?
R< $+ > $*       $: $>90 <$1> $2         try domain

# resolve locally connected UUCP links
R$* < @ $=Z . UUCP. > $*     $#uucp-uudom $@ $2 $: $1 < @ $2 .UUCP. > $3
R$* < @ $=Y . UUCP. > $*     $#uucp-new $@ $2 $: $1 < @ $2 .UUCP. > $3
R$* < @ $=U . UUCP. > $*     $#uucp-old $@ $2 $: $1 < @ $2 .UUCP. > $3

# resolve remotely connected UUCP links (if any)

# resolve fake top level domains by forwarding to other hosts


# forward other UUCP traffic straight to UUCP
R$* < @ $+ .UUCP. > $*          $#uucp-old $@ $2 $: $1 < @ $2 .UUCP. > $3
➥user@host.UUCP


# pass names that still have a host to a smarthost (if defined)
R$* < @ $* > $*          $: $>95 < $S > $1 < @ $2 > $3    glue on smarthost name

# deal with other remote names
R$* < @$* > $*         $#esmtp $@ $2 $: $1 < @ $2 > $3     user@host.domain

# handle locally delivered names
R$=L          $#local $: @ $1         special local names
R$+           $#local $: $1        regular local names

######################################################################
###    Ruleset 5 -- special rewriting after aliases have been expanded    ###
######################################################################

S5

# deal with plussed users so aliases work nicely
R$+ + *           $#local $@ $&h $: $1
R$+ + $*          $#local $@ + $2 $: $1 + *

# prepend an empty "forward host" on the front
R$+            $: <> $1



# see if we have a relay or a hub
R< > $+           $: < $H > $1         try hub
R< > $+           $: < $R > $1         try relay
R< > $+           $: < > < $1 $&h >     nope, restore +detail
R< > < $+ + $* > $*       < > < $1 > + $2 $3    find the user part
R< > < $+ > + $*     $#local $@ $2 $: @ $1     strip the extra +
R< > < $+ >       $@ $1         no +detail
```

```
R$+                     $: $1 $&h          add +detail back in
R< local : $* > $*       $: $>95 < local : $1 > $2    no host extension
R< error : $* > $*       $: $>95 < error : $1 > $2    no host extension
R< $- : $+ > $+          $: $>95 < $1 : $2 > $3 < @ $2 >
R< $+ > $+               $@ $>95 < $1 > $2 < @ $1 >


######################################################################
###     Ruleset 90 -- try domain part of mailertable entry       ###
######################################################################

S90
R$* <$- . $+ > $*    $: $1$2 < $(mailertable .$3 $@ $1$2 $@ $2 $) > $4
R$* <$~[ : $+ > $*    $>95 < $2 : $3 > $4      check — resolved?
R$* < . $+ > $*       $@ $>90 $1 . <$2> $3     no — strip & try again
R$* < $* > $*         $: < $(mailertable . $@ $1$2 $) > $3    try "."
R< $~[ : $+ > $*      $>95 < $1 : $2 > $3      "." found?
R< $* > $*            $@ $2                    no mailertable match


######################################################################
###   Ruleset 95 -- canonify mailer:[user@]host syntax to triple ###
######################################################################

S95
R< > $*                  $@ $1          strip off null relay
R< error : $- $+ > $*    $#error $@ $(dequote $1 $) $: $2
R< local : $* > $*       $>CanonLocal < $1 > $2
R< $- : $+ @ $+ > $*<$*>$*    $# $1 $@ $3 $: $2<@$3> use literal user
R< $- : $+ > $*          $# $1 $@ $2 $: $3 try qualified mailer
R< $=w > $*              $@ $2          delete local host
R< $+ > $*               $#relay $@ $1 $: $2 use unqualified mailer


######################################################################
###   Ruleset CanonLocal -- canonify local: syntax               ###
######################################################################

SCanonLocal
# strip trailing dot from any host name that may appear
R< $* > $* < @ $* . >     $: < $1 > $2 < @ $3 >

# handle local: syntax — use old user, either with or without host
R< > $* < @ $* > $*       $#local $@ $1@$2 $: $1
R< > $+                   $#local $@ $1     $: $1


# handle local:user@host syntax — ignore host part
R< $+ @ $+ > $* < @ $* >    $: < $1 > $3 < @ $4 >

# handle local:user syntax
R< $+ > $* <@ $* > $*     $#local $@ $2@$3 $: $1
R< $+ > $*                $#local $@ $2     $: $1


######################################################################
```

```
###################################################################
###   Ruleset 93 -- convert header names to masqueraded form    ###
###################################################################

S93


# special case the users that should be exposed
R$=E < @ *LOCAL* >      $@ $1 < @ $j . >       leave exposed
R$=E < @ $=M . >        $@ $1 < @ $2 . >
R$=E < @ $=w . >        $@ $1 < @ $2 . >


# handle domain-specific masquerading
R$* < @ $=M . > $*       $: $1 < @ $2 . @ $M > $3    convert masqueraded doms
R$* < @ $=w . > $*       $: $1 < @ $2 . @ $M > $3
R$* < @ *LOCAL* > $*     $: $1 < @ $j . @ $M > $2
R$* < @ $+ @ > $*        $: $1 < @ $2 > $3      $M is null
R$* < @ $+ @ $+ > $*     $: $1 < @ $3 . > $4    $M is not null

###################################################################
###   Ruleset 94 -- convert envelope names to masqueraded form  ###
###################################################################

S94
R$* < @ *LOCAL* > $*     $: $1 < @ $j . > $2

###################################################################
###   Ruleset 98 -- local part of ruleset zero (can be null)    ###
###################################################################

S98


# addresses sent to foo@host.REDIRECT will give a 551 error code
R$* < @ $+ .REDIRECT. >         $: $1 < @ $2 . REDIRECT . > < ${opMode} >
R$* < @ $+ .REDIRECT. > <i>     $: $1 < @ $2 . REDIRECT . >
R$* < @ $+ .REDIRECT. > < $- >  $# error $@ 5.1.1 $: "551 User has moved;
➥please try "<$1@$2>



###################################################################
###   ParseRecipient --    Strip off hosts in $=R as well as possibly
###                $* $=m or the access database.
###                Check user portion for host separators.
###
###       Parameters:
###           $1 -- full recipient address
###
###       Returns:
###           parsed, non-local-relaying address
###################################################################
```

```
SParseRecipient
R$*               $: <?> $>Parse0 $>3 $1
R<?> $* < @ $* . >     <?> $1 < @ $2 >     strip trailing dots
R<?> $- < @ $* >    $: <?> $(dequote $1 $) < @ $2 >    dequote local part

# if no $=O character, no host in the user portion, we are done
R<?> $* $=O $* < @ $* >    $: <NO> $1 $2 $3 < @ $4>
R<?> $*            $@ $1

R<NO> $* < @ $* $=R >    $: <RELAY> $1 < @ $2 $3 >
R<RELAY> $* < @ $* >    $@ $>ParseRecipient $1
R<$ -> $*          $@ $2


#####################################################################
### check_relay -- check hostname/address on SMTP startup
#####################################################################

SLocal_check_relay
Scheck_relay
R$*              $: $1 $| $>"Local_check_relay" $1
R$* $| $* $| $#$*     $#$3
R$* $| $* $| $*       $@ $>"Basic_check_relay" $1 $| $2

SBasic_check_relay
# check for deferred delivery mode
R$*              $: < ${deliveryMode} > $1
R< d > $*         $@ deferred
R< $* > $*        $: $2


#####################################################################
### check_mail -- check SMTP `MAIL FROM:' command argument
#####################################################################

SLocal_check_mail
Scheck_mail
R$*              $: $1 $| $>"Local_check_mail" $1
R$* $| $#$*         $#$2
R$* $| $*         $@ $>"Basic_check_mail" $1

SBasic_check_mail
# check for deferred delivery mode
R$*              $: < ${deliveryMode} > $1
R< d > $*         $@ deferred
R< $* > $*        $: $2

R<>              $@ <OK>
R$*              $: <?> $>Parse0 $>3 $1       make domain canonical
R<?> $* < @ $+ . > $*    <?> $1 < @ $2 > $3     strip trailing dots
# handle non-DNS hostnames (*.bitnet, *.decnet, *.uucp, etc)
R<?> $* < $* $=P > $*    $: <OK> $1 < @ $2 $3 > $4
R<?> $* < @ $+ > $*    $: <? $(resolve $2 $: $2 <PERM> $) > $1 < @ $2 > $3
```

```
R<? $* <$-.>> $* < @ $+ > $*
                $: <$2> $3 < @ $4 > $5

# handle case of @localhost on address
R<$+> $* < @localhost >     $: < ? $&{client_name} > <$1> $2 < @localhost >
R<$+> $* < @localhost.$m >
                $: < ? $&{client_name} > <$1> $2 < @localhost.$m >
R<$+> $* < @localhost.UUCP >
                $: < ? $&{client_name} > <$1> $2 < @localhost.UUCP >
R<? $=w> <$+> $*        <?> <$2> $3
R<? $+> <$+> $*         $#error $@ 5.5.4 $: "553 Real domain name required"
R<?> <$+> $*       $: <$1> $2

# handle case of no @domain on address
R<?> $*         $: < ? $&{client_name} > $1
R<?> $*         $@ <OK>         ...local unqualed ok
R<? $+> $*      $#error $@ 5.5.4 $: "553 Domain name required"
                        ...remote is not
# check results
R<?> $*         $@ <OK>
R<OK> $*        $@ <OK>
R<TEMP> $*      $#error $@ 4.1.8 $: "451 Sender domain must resolve"
R<PERM> $*      $#error $@ 5.1.8 $: "501 Sender domain must exist"

######################################################################
###   check_rcpt -- check SMTP `RCPT TO:' command argument
######################################################################

SLocal_check_rcpt
Scheck_rcpt
R$*             $: $1 $| $>"Local_check_rcpt" $1
R$* $| $#$*     $#$2
R$* $| $*       $@ $>"Basic_check_rcpt" $1

SBasic_check_rcpt
# check for deferred delivery mode
R$*             $: < ${deliveryMode} > $1
R< d > $*       $@ deferred
R< $* > $*      $: $2

R$*             $: $>ParseRecipient $1     strip relayable hosts

# anything terminating locally is ok
R$+ < @ $=w >        $@ OK
R$+ < @ $* $=R >     $@ OK

# check for local user (i.e. unqualified address)
R$*             $: <?> $1
R<?> $+ < @ $+ >     $: <REMOTE> $1 < @ $2 >
# local user is ok
R<?> $+         $@ OK
```

```
R<$+> $*          $: $2


# anything originating locally is ok
R$*            $: <?> $&{client_name}
# check if bracketed IP address (forward lookup != reverse lookup)
R<?> [$+]        $: <BAD> [$1]
# pass to name server to make hostname canonical
R<?> $* $~P        $: <?> $[ $1 $2 $]
R<$-> $*         $: $2
R$* .             $1              strip trailing dots
R$@              $@ OK
R$=w             $@ OK
R$* $=R           $@ OK


# check IP address
R$*           $: $&{client_addr}
R$@             $@ OK         originated locally
R0              $@ OK         originated locally
R$=R $*           $@ OK           relayable IP address
R$*             $: [ $1 ]      put brackets around it...
R$=w             $@ OK           ... and see if it is local

# anything else is bogus
R$*           $#error $@ 5.7.1 $: "550 Relaying denied"

#
######################################################################
######################################################################
#####
#####              MAILER DEFINITIONS
#####
######################################################################
######################################################################


###############################################
###   Local and Program Mailer specification   ###
###############################################

#####  @(#)local.m4    8.30 (Berkeley) 6/30/98  #####

Mlocal,        P=/usr/libexec/sendmail/mail.local, F=lsDFMAw5:/|@qSXfmnz9,
S=10/30, R=20/40,
       T=DNS/RFC822/X-Unix,
       A=mail.local -l
Mprog,         P=/bin/sh, F=lsDFMoqeu9, S=10/30, R=20/40, D=$z:/,
       T=X-Unix,
       A=sh -c $u


#
#  Envelope sender rewriting
```

```
#
S10
R<@>              $n              errors to mailer-daemon
R@ <@ $*>         $n              temporarily bypass Sun bogosity
R$+               $: $>50 $1      add local domain if needed
R$*               $: $>94 $1      do masquerading

#
#  Envelope recipient rewriting
#
S20
R$+ < @ $* >      $: $1           strip host part

#
#  Header sender rewriting
#
S30
R<@>              $n              errors to mailer-daemon
R@ <@ $*>         $n              temporarily bypass Sun bogosity
R$+               $: $>50 $1      add local domain if needed
R$*               $: $>93 $1      do masquerading

#
#  Header recipient rewriting
#
S40
R$+               $: $>50 $1      add local domain if needed

#
#  Common code to add local domain name (only if always-add-domain)
#
S50
R$* < @ $* > $*   $@ $1 < @ $2 > $3   already fully qualified
R$+               $@ $1 < @ *LOCAL* > add local qualification

######################################
###    SMTP Mailer specification    ###
######################################

#####  @(#)smtp.m4    8.38 (Berkeley) 5/19/98  #####

Msmtp,      P=[IPC], F=mDFMuX, S=11/31, R=21, E=\r\n, L=990,
        T=DNS/RFC822/SMTP,
        A=IPC $h
Mesmtp,     P=[IPC], F=mDFMuXa, S=11/31, R=21, E=\r\n, L=990,
        T=DNS/RFC822/SMTP,
        A=IPC $h
Msmtp8,     P=[IPC], F=mDFMuX8, S=11/31, R=21, E=\r\n, L=990,
        T=DNS/RFC822/SMTP,
        A=IPC $h
Mrelay,     P=[IPC], F=mDFMuXa8, S=11/31, R=61, E=\r\n, L=2040,
```

```
         T=DNS/RFC822/SMTP,
         A=IPC $h

#
#  envelope sender rewriting
#
S11
R$+             $: $>51 $1         sender/recipient common
R$* :; <@>      $@                 list:; special case
R$*             $: $>61 $1         qualify unqual'ed names
R$+             $: $>94 $1         do masquerading


#
#  envelope recipient rewriting --
#  also header recipient if not masquerading recipients
#
S21
R$+             $: $>51 $1         sender/recipient common
R$+             $: $>61 $1         qualify unqual'ed names


#
#  header sender and masquerading header recipient rewriting
#
S31
R$+             $: $>51 $1         sender/recipient common
R:; <@>         $@                 list:; special case

# do special header rewriting
R$* <@> $*      $@ $1 <@> $2       pass null host through
R< @ $* > $*    $@ < @ $1 > $2       pass route-addr through
R$*             $: $>61 $1         qualify unqual'ed names
R$+             $: $>93 $1         do masquerading


#
#  convert pseudo-domain addresses to real domain addresses
#
S51

# pass <route-addr>s through
R< @ $+ > $*    $@ < @ $1 > $2          resolve <route-addr>


# output fake domains as user%fake@relay

# do UUCP heuristics; note that these are shared with UUCP mailers
R$+ < @ $+ .UUCP. >   $: < $2 ! > $1     convert to UUCP form
R$+ < @ $* > $*       $@ $1 < @ $2 > $3   not UUCP form


# leave these in .UUCP form to avoid further tampering
```

```
R< $&h ! > $- ! $+       $@ $2 < @ $1 .UUCP. >
R< $&h ! > $-.$+ ! $+    $@ $3 < @ $1.$2 >
R< $&h ! > $+            $@ $1 < @ $&h .UUCP. >
R< $+ ! > $+             $: $1 ! $2 < @ $Y >       use UUCP_RELAY
R$+ < @ $+ : $+ >        $@ $1 < @ $3 >            strip mailer: part
R$+ < @ >                $: $1 < @ *LOCAL* >       if no UUCP_RELAY


#
#  common sender and masquerading recipient rewriting
#
S61

R$* < @ $* > $*          $@ $1 < @ $2 > $3         already fully qualified
R$+                      $@ $1 < @ *LOCAL* >       add local qualification


#
#  relay mailer header masquerading recipient rewriting
#
S71

R$+              $: $>61 $1
R$+              $: $>93 $1


######################################
###   UUCP Mailer specification   ###
######################################

#####   @(#)uucp.m4     8.30 (Berkeley) 5/19/98   #####

#
#  There are innumerable variations on the UUCP mailer.  It really
#  is rather absurd.
#

# old UUCP mailer (two names)
Muucp,         P=/usr/bin/uux, F=DFMhuUd, S=12, R=22/42, M=100000,
        T=X-UUCP/X-UUCP/X-Unix,
        A=uux - -r -a$g -gC $h!rmail ($u)
Muucp-old,     P=/usr/bin/uux, F=DFMhuUd, S=12, R=22/42, M=100000,
        T=X-UUCP/X-UUCP/X-Unix,
        A=uux - -r -a$g -gC $h!rmail ($u)


# smart UUCP mailer (handles multiple addresses) (two names)
Msuucp,        P=/usr/bin/uux, F=mDFMhuUd, S=12, R=22/42, M=100000,
        T=X-UUCP/X-UUCP/X-Unix,
        A=uux - -r -a$g -gC $h!rmail ($u)
Muucp-new,     P=/usr/bin/uux, F=mDFMhuUd, S=12, R=22/42, M=100000,
        T=X-UUCP/X-UUCP/X-Unix,
```

```
                A=uux - -r -a$g -gC $h!rmail ($u)


# domain-ized UUCP mailer
Muucp-dom,      P=/usr/bin/uux, F=mDFMhud, S=52/31, R=21, M=100000,
        T=X-UUCP/X-UUCP/X-Unix,
        A=uux - -r -a$g -gC $h!rmail ($u)

# domain-ized UUCP mailer with UUCP-style sender envelope
Muucp-uudom,    P=/usr/bin/uux, F=mDFMhud, S=72/31, R=21, M=100000,
        T=X-UUCP/X-UUCP/X-Unix,
        A=uux - -r -a$g -gC $h!rmail ($u)



#
#   envelope and header sender rewriting
#
S12

# handle error address as a special case
R<@>                    $n      errors to mailer-daemon

# list:; syntax should disappear
R:; <@>                 $@


R$* < @ $* . > $*       $1 < @ $2 > $3     strip trailing dots
R$* < @ $=w >           $1      strip local name
R<@ $- . UUCP > : $+       $1 ! $2         convert to UUCP format
R<@ $+ > : $+           $1 ! $2     convert to UUCP format
R$* < @ $- . UUCP >        $2 ! $1         convert to UUCP format
R$* < @ $+ >            $2 ! $1     convert to UUCP format
R$&h ! $+ ! $+             $@ $1 ! $2     $h!...!user => ...!user
R$&h ! $+              $@ $&h ! $1     $h!user => $h!user
R$+                  $: $U ! $1     prepend our name
R! $+                $: $k ! $1     in case $U undefined


#
#   envelope recipient rewriting
#
S22


# list:; should disappear
R:; <@>                 $@

R$* < @ $* . > $*       $1 < @ $2 > $3     strip trailing dots
R$* < @ $=w >           $1      strip local name
R<@ $- . UUCP > : $+       $1 ! $2         convert to UUCP format
R<@ $+ > : $+           $1 ! $2     convert to UUCP format
R$* < @ $- . UUCP >        $2 ! $1         convert to UUCP format
R$* < @ $+ >            $2 ! $1     convert to UUCP format

#
```

```
# header recipient rewriting
#
S42

# list:; syntax should disappear
R:; <@>                 $@

R$* < @ $* . > $*       $1 < @ $2 > $3    strip trailing dots
R$* < @ $=w >           $1          strip local name
R<@ $- . UUCP > : $+       $1 ! $2          convert to UUCP format
R<@ $+ > : $+           $1 ! $2      convert to UUCP format
R$* < @ $- . UUCP >        $2 ! $1          convert to UUCP format
R$* < @ $+ >            $2 ! $1      convert to UUCP format
R$&h ! $+ ! $+             $@ $1 ! $2    $h!...!user => ...!user
R$&h ! $+               $@ $&h ! $1    $h!user => $h!user
R$+                     $: $U ! $1    prepend our name
R! $+                   $: $k ! $1    in case $U undefined


#
#   envelope sender rewriting for uucp-dom mailer
#
S52

# handle error address as a special case
R<@>                    $n      errors to mailer-daemon

# pass everything to standard SMTP mailer rewriting
R$*                     $@ $>11 $1

#
#   envelope sender rewriting for uucp-uudom mailer
#
S72

# handle error address as a special case
R<@>                    $n      errors to mailer-daemon

# do standard SMTP mailer rewriting
R$*                     $: $>11 $1

R$* < @ $* . > $*       $1 < @ $2 > $3    strip trailing dots
R<@ $- . UUCP > : $+       $@ $1 ! $2    convert to UUCP format
R<@ $+ > : $+           $@ $1 ! $2    convert to UUCP format
R$* < @ $- . UUCP >        $@ $2 ! $1    convert to UUCP format
R$* < @ $+ >            $@ $2 ! $1    convert to UUCP format
```

M4 Configuration File: `Sendmail.mc`

For years, administrators had to struggle with the `sendmail.cf` file by hand to get it to do what they wanted. There was no standard or default way to make changes easily. Eventually, computers became much faster, and SMTP was standardized. So, starting with version 8 of Sendmail, a set of macros for the m4 macro language were written to make it easy to create, modify, and maintain all the common configurations for the `sendmail.cf` file. The file that contains these macros is called an `mc` file.

The `sendmail.mc` for Caldera OpenLinux 2.2 follows. This file is used to generate the gigantic `sendmail.cf` that you just finished looking over. As you can see, it is considerably smaller and somewhat easier to understand (though you certainly wouldn't call it easy). Basically each of the options in the `sendmail.mc` file is tied to a specific set of rules and option lines in the `sendmail.cf` file. So if you set an option in `sendmail.mc`, it will be used to change all that relevant information in the `sendmail.cf`. An excellent reference for each of the options is included in `/usr/share/sendmail/cf/README` if you are interested in working with this by hand.

```
/usr/share/sendmail/cf/cf/generic-col2.2.mc
divert(0)
#
# Copyright  1996, 1997 Caldera Inc., Provo
#
divert(-1)
# THIS SOFTWARE IS PROVIDED BY Caldera AND CONTRIBUTORS ``AS IS'' AND
# ANY EXPRESS OR IMPLIED WARRANTIES, INCLUDING, BUT NOT LIMITED TO, THE
# IMPLIED WARRANTIES OF MERCHANTABILITY AND FITNESS FOR A PARTICULAR PURPOSE
# ARE DISCLAIMED.  IN NO EVENT SHALL Caldera OR CONTRIBUTORS BE LIABLE
# FOR ANY DIRECT, INDIRECT, INCIDENTAL, SPECIAL, EXEMPLARY, OR CONSEQUENTIAL
# DAMAGES (INCLUDING, BUT NOT LIMITED TO, PROCUREMENT OF SUBSTITUTE GOODS
# OR SERVICES; LOSS OF USE, DATA, OR PROFITS; OR BUSINESS INTERRUPTION)
# HOWEVER CAUSED AND ON ANY THEORY OF LIABILITY, WHETHER IN CONTRACT, STRICT
# LIABILITY, OR TORT (INCLUDING NEGLIGENCE OR OTHERWISE) ARISING IN ANY WAY
# OUT OF THE USE OF THIS SOFTWARE, EVEN IF ADVISED OF THE POSSIBILITY OF
# SUCH DAMAGE.

divert(0)dnl
#
# This is a generic configuration file for Caldera OpenLinux 2.2
#
# Basic ideas taken from Red Hat contrib/sendmail-8.7.5-1.src.rpm.
# Credits go to Marc (whoever built it).
#
VERSIONID(`$Id: generic-col2.2.mc,v 1.4 1999/02/23 15:36:07 okir Exp $')
divert(-1)
OSTYPE(`linux')
```

```
undefine(`UUCP_RELAY')
undefine(`BITNET_RELAY')
undefine(`LOCAL_MAILER_PATH')
dnl ############################################################
dnl # Changed Aug/20/1997 --okir
dnl # we now use FEATURE(local_procmail)
dnl define(`LOCAL_MAILER_PATH', `/usr/bin/procmail')
dnl define(`LOCAL_MAILER_FLAGS', `SPfhnu9')
dnl define(`LOCAL_MAILER_ARGS', `procmail -Y -a $h -d $u')
define(`STATUS_FILE', `/var/log/sendmail.st')
define(`HELP_FILE', `/usr/share/sendmail/sendmail.hf')
define(`confUNSAFE_GROUP_WRITES', `True')
dnl ############################################################
dnl # Sendmail comes with a program called smrsh, which restricts
dnl # the programs that can be executed as a result of an alias or
dnl # .forward expansion. Only those commands found in /usr/libexec/sm.bin
dnl # can actually be executed (for details, see smrsh(8)).
dnl #
dnl FEATURE(`smrsh', `/usr/libexec/sm.bin')
dnl ############################################################
dnl # Use mail.local as the local delivery agent
dnl #
FEATURE(local_lmtp, `/usr/libexec/sendmail/mail.local')
dnl ############################################################
dnl # Enable the .REDIRECT feature in alias lookups
dnl #
FEATURE(redirect)
dnl ############################################################
dnl #
dnl #
FEATURE(always_add_domain)
dnl ############################################################
dnl # Let the user specify host aliases in sendmail.cw
dnl #
dnl The following doesn't seem to work..
dnl define(confCW_FILE, `/etc/sendmail/sendmail.cw')
FEATURE(use_cw_file)
dnl ############################################################
dnl # We provide a mailertable to fine-tune routing.
dnl #
FEATURE(mailertable, `hash /etc/sendmail/mailertable')
dnl ############################################################
dnl # Include COL setup
dnl #
ifdef(`COL_FEATURES',,`define(`COL_FEATURES',`/dev/null')')
include(COL_FEATURES)
dnl ############################################################
dnl # Include the following mailers:
dnl #
MAILER(local)
MAILER(smtp)
MAILER(uucp)
```

To use the M4 macros to configure your Sendmail, save the `sendmail.mc` file in the `/usr/share/sendmail/cf/cf` directory first. Then type the following command to generate a `sendmail.cf` file:

```
m4 ../m4/cf.m4 generic-col2.2.mc > sendmail.cf
```

As root, move the `sendmail.cf` file to `/etc`, and make it mode 64. (Remember to back up the existing `sendmail.cf` file first.)

Configuring with COAS

The m4 macro source files offer virtually unlimited configurability. Nearly any way in which you can modify `/etc/sendmail.cf` for your needs can be duplicated using the m4 files. The m4 format is a tremendous improvement over hand-editing the cryptic `sendmail.cf` to make the daemon do our bidding. Still, it isn't exactly what you would call user friendly. Fortunately, Caldera has included with their COAS administration system a tool to configure some of the most generally necessary options in Sendmail.

While in X, start the COAS tool (third icon from left in the KDE desktop) and choose Network:Mail Transfer. A dialog box with the following options will appear.

- *Visible Domain*   This option allows you to change what domain people "see" in the mail you send. If you want your mail to appear to come from a machine or domain different from the one Sendmail is currently running on, you would enter that domain name here. This is frequently used to make sure that people send mail back to <user@domain.com> if the mail is actually originating from <user@host1.domain.com>. Sendmail documentation and configuration files refer to this feature themselves as masquerading, and it is technically the DM option in the `sendmail.cf` file.

- *Mail Relay Host*   This option tells Sendmail to forward all mail it can't deliver locally to a host that is expected to know what to do with it. This situation might occur in an organization with complex mail routing needs where it would be difficult or impossible to configure each workstation to route mail properly to all possible destinations. It might also occur when workstations have a limited view of the network or outside world and can only send mail properly by sending to a mail relay. Sendmail refers to this feature as a "smart" relay host, and it is technically the DS option in the `sendmail.cf` file.

- *Transport Method*   This drop-down box is grayed out if you haven't selected a Mail Relay Host and defaults to SMTP. If you select a Mail Relay Host, you are then given the option of selecting between SMTP and UUCP. Unless you really know what you are doing, you should leave this set to SMTP. UUCP is UNIX to

UNIX Copy Protocol—a protocol used on few and dwindling numbers of hosts these days. UUCP can be very useful in certain situations. However, if you are an Internet-connected host, it's highly unlikely that you'll ever need to bother with anything but SMTP.

- *Relay Is Internet Hub*   This check box option pertains to the Mail Relay Host. It turns off name canonicalization. With this option set, the Sendmail process will no longer look up hostnames in DNS to make sure that they are valid. This takes some burden off the local machine in that it does not need to do DNS lookups for mail it relays. It is also useful if the local machine has limited or no access to DNS. Also, any mail to be sent to hosts local to your domain are sent directly using SMTP, and not to the Mail Relay. The Mail Relay is expected to handle anything else that you send its way.

- *Relay Is Local Hub*   This option sends absolutely everything to the Mail Relay Host, even if the syntax of the address you are sending to would indicate it should be delivered locally. (It is normally the case that a mail sent to `<user>` would be delivered locally, whereas `<user@domain.com>` would be delivered to another host. With Relay Is Local Hub set, even `<user>` will be sent off to the Mail Relay.)

Modifying any of these fields will cause OpenLinux to rebuild your `sendmail.cf` for you with your new features enabled.

Aliases

Aliasing is a method by which mail is redirected to a different email address. Aliases can be redirected to one or more email accounts, a file, a program, or a combination of these. Aliasing is often used to forward mail to a user's preferred mail drop, to filter incoming mail, to allow users to be referred to by more than one address, and to define mailing lists. The aliases file is `/etc/aliases`.

The format of the aliases file, `/etc/aliases`, is

`local-name: recipient1,recipient2,...`

where `local-name` is the address to the alias. The list of comma-separated addresses after the colon all recieve that alias. Lines beginning with whitespace are continuation lines. Lines beginning with a # are comments and ignored. The following are some example aliases from an aliases file:

```
# Support Group
glenda:     grs@theneteffect.com
mitch:      mitch@theneteffect.com
geoffp:     geoff@theneteffect.com
charlotte:  charlott@theneteffect.com
support:    glenda, mitch, geoffp
```

The first three aliases (`glenda`, `mitch`, `geoffp`) are for those users. They simply redirect each user's mail to user@theneteffect.com. So, instead of being delivered locally, mail to each of those users will go to them @theneteffect.com. The fourth alias redirects mail for a username longer than the standard eight letters.

The last alias is a group alias. The group alias does not correspond to an actual user. It is an alias pointing to a group of users. So, an alias can direct mail to more than one address as long as the addresses are separated by commas.

Setting Up a Mail Hub

A mail hub is a central server to handle all email traffic within a local network. Computers on the network route all mail through the hub rather than send it directly to the recipient. The hub rewrites the header of all the outgoing messages so that they appear to come directly from the hub. Received mail is automatically routed to the hub and spooled there. None of the clients receive mail directly.

The primary advantages of a mail hub follow:

- Addressing is simplified. All mail is addressed to one machine.
- All mail is spooled centrally. It is easier to manage.
- Client machines are insulated from the outside world. This adds an extra level of security.
- There is no need to configure mail on each client machine. Any changes in the mail configuration need only be done at the mail hub.
- Client machines are unconcerned with hangs in network routing and do not need to queue messages. They forward mail to the hub, which takes care of everything.

There are, of course, disadvantages:

- The mail hub must know all the users on the network.
- There may be performance problems.
- There may be delays in transport when mail travels through the mail hub.

Configuring a Mail Hub

To configure a mail hub, you must do several things:

- Create the `sendmail.cf` file of the local computers. This will tell Sendmail to route all mail through the hub, a smarthost. It also rewrites addresses so that outgoing mail appears to have come from the hub rather than the client machine.

- Create a DNS MX record for each client machine, redirecting to the hub all mail addressed to the client.
- Change the Sendmail configuration on the hub so that mail addressed to client machines will be deliverable on the hub.

Client Configuration

To configure a client machine on a network using a mail hub, you must do two basic things: (1) configure delivery agents to direct mail to hub and (2) configure rulesets to rewrite sender address to appear to be from the hub. This is accomplished by making a special client `sendmail.cf`. How this is done will vary between versions of `sendmail`. Generating this file by hand can be complex. However, it is also possible to generate this file using m4, as outlined in the section on configuring Sendmail.

Here is the m4 code that would be used to generate a client `sendmail.cf`:

```
include(`../m4/cf.m4')
VERSIONID(`linux for smtp-only setup')dnl
OSTYPE(linux)
MASQUERADE_AS(theneteffect.com)
define(`STATUS_FILE', `/var/log/sendmail.st')
define(`HELP_FILE', `/usr/share/sendmail/sendmail.hf')
FEATURE(always_add_domain)
EXPOSED_USER(root)
EXPOSED_USER(postmaster)
EXPOSED_USER(MAILER_DAEMON)
FEATURE(nullclient, mail.theneteffect.com)
```

Here, `mail.theneteffect.com` would be replaced with the name of the mail hub.

Do the following to generate this file using COAS:

1. Select COAS:Network:Mail Transfer.
2. In the Visible Domain dialog box, enter the domain you are in (for example, `theneteffect.com`).
3. In the Mail Relay Host dialog box, enter the name of your mail hub (for example, `mail.theneteffect.com`).
4. Leave the Transport Method drop-down dialog box set to SMTP.
5. Check the Relay Is Internet Hub check box. (In point of fact, you could leave this option unchecked and only check the Relay Is Local Hub option. Either way will produce the same `sendmail.cf` file. Checking both options clearly establishes what you are doing given that the hub will be both a local and an Internet relay.)
6. Check the Relay Is Local Hub check box.
7. Click OK to confirm your decision.

Generating this in COAS will not provide exactly the same file as the m4 method. It will provide a functional replacement for it, however. Unless you already know you need something particular in the m4 method, you may feel more comfortable using the COAS tool.

DNS Configuration

In order to have mail addressed to client machines automatically delivered to the hub, you must create MX records for each client machine. The MX record for each client machine should point to the mail hub. If name service is administered off-site, you must ask your DNS administrator to make these changes.

The primary file for your DNS zone should contain entries for each client machine. They will look something like this:

```
client_hostname      IN    A     206.202.42.31
```

A new MX record should be added immediately after the A record, pointing to the mail hub:

```
client_hostname      IN    A     206.202.42.31
                     MX    10    mail.theneteffect.com
```

The `10` in the MX record specifies the priority of the mail exchanger; this only comes into play if there is more than one MX record. After the file has been reconfigured, the SOA record must be updated. The nameserver must be told to reload the file by executing `/usr/sbin/ndc reload`.

Hub Configuration

Although MX entries allow mail addressed to a client to be redirected to the hub, this is not sufficient by itself. The email is still addressed to the client, and the hub will attempt to deliver the message to the client and fail. The easiest way is just to add the hostnames of client machines to the class macro w in `sendmail.cf`. Class macro w is a list of names that the hub can go by. If the client machines are on this list, then the hub will receive mail addressed to a client machine as if it were addressed to the hub. For example, if a hub had three clients, with hostnames `foo`, `bar`, and `baz`, do the following:

1. Add the following line to the `sendmail.mc` file created in the client configuration operation:

    `FEATURE(use_cw_file)dnl`

2. Generate the `/etc/sendmail.cf` file from the new `sendmail.mc` file modified to use the `/etc/sendmail.cw` file. Make sure that the following statements are in the `/etc/sendmail.cf` file:

```
# file containing names of hosts for which we receive email
Fw-o /etc/sendmail.cw
```

3. Add the clients foo, bar, and baz to the /etc/sendmail.cw file.
4. Restart Sendmail.

Summary

In this chapter, we learned how to set up and configure the SMTP server and Sendmail and also how to set up a mail hub. The Sendmail configuration file, /etc/sendmail.cf, is overwhelming but can be neatly avoided (if you so choose) by using the m4 macro files, or the easier still COAS administrative tool. We also learned how to set up a central mail server, a mail hub, in a three-step process: (1) configure the client computers to deliver all outgoing mail to the mail hub, which is also a smarthost; (2) configure DNS to deliver all email destined to the client computers from outside to go through the mail hub first; and (3) configure the mail hub itself to accept mail from its clients through the use of class w, /etc/sendmail.cw.

Internet News

IN THIS CHAPTER

- About Usenet News *460*
- Linux and Usenet *461*
- InterNet News Server Software *464*
- The `tin` Newsreader *475*

Usenet newsgroups are a fascinating and informative source of information, entertainment, news, and general chat. Usenet is one of the oldest components of the Internet and was popular long before the World Wide Web came on the scene. Usenet is still the most popular aspect of the Internet in terms of user interaction, offering a dynamic and often controversial forum for discussion on any subject. Though email lists are increasingly popular, particularly among newcomers to the Internet scene, the serious "net nerds" will always need a regular Usenet fix to survive.

In this chapter, you'll learn how to configure your Linux machine to download newsgroups from your Internet connection and how to install and configure tin, a basic Linux newsreader (software used to read postings in a newsgroup). Several alternatives are available for Linux access to newsgroups, but we will look at INN (InterNet News), the most common news server package for Linux, which is included in the OpenLinux distribution package.

About Usenet News

Usenet began in 1979 as a project of Jim Ellis and Tom Truscott. They used older technologies such as UUCP to transfer small bundles of newsgroups to and from local computers. With time, better software emerged to carry these newsgroups over TCP/IP connections, meaning that Usenet was now platform independent. In other words, a user could enter one of the newsgroups via a UNIX, VMS, Windows, Macintosh, mainframe terminal, or terminal emulator. Eventually, specific GUI-based software was developed, and modern Web browsers commonly feature an integrated Usenet reader.

With the move of Usenet to TCP/IP, the method of transferring news was refined and called NNTP, or Network News Transfer Protocol. It is assigned TCP/IP port number 119.

Usenet offers the user a great deal of interactivity and widespread human contact, which are the chief reasons for its long-time popularity. The user has many options, which can be quite involving. The user may read the articles particular to a newsgroup, post her own original message, reply to a message's author by email, or reply to a previous message publicly on that list.

Today's Usenet user should be able to find at least one newsgroup suited to his interests. Newsgroups are arranged into a few master hierarchies that contain thousands of subsidiary groups. The major hierarchies begin with the terms alt.* (alternate or additional groups on a topic already covered), comp.* (computers), rec.* (recreation), sci.* (science), biz.* (business), among others.

Although Usenet was designed as a text-based medium, it is now commonly used for handling almost any type of file, as long as proper methods for converting those files to text (such as UUencoding) are employed. UUencoding allows binary software packages, pictures, music, movies, and data, to be transferred in text form and then UUdecoded by any user. Such UUencoded files are usually enormous compared to simple text files, so it is not uncommon for Usenet feeds to either eliminate those special message types or drastically curtail their availability.

Usenet newsgroups now number well over 100,000 groups dedicated to many different subjects. A full feed of an average day's newsgroup postings takes several gigabytes of disk space and associated transfer time. Obviously, if you are going to access Usenet over anything slower than a T1 (1.544MBps) line, you have to be selective in what you download. An analog modem simply can't download the entire Usenet feed in a reasonable time. Selective access to newsgroups suits most users, however, because nobody can actually read all the postings on Usenet every day!

Linux and Usenet

Providing access to Usenet newsgroups is a natural function of Linux because newsgroups evolved under UNIX. All it takes to provide Usenet newsgroup access for yourself and anyone else on your network is properly configured newsgroup software and Internet access for your system. Almost any connection to the Internet provides some form of news access, whether directly (through your own gateway), through a news forwarding service, or through a third-party access service.

Many Internet Service Providers (ISPs) offer news access to you as part of their basic service: You choose which newsgroups you may be interested in from the complete list of all available newsgroups, and those groups are transferred to your machine for reading. If you want to access a newsgroup you didn't download, a quick connection to your ISP lets you sample the postings.

There are three main ways to download newsgroups onto your Linux system: INN, C News, and NNTPCache. C News was designed for downloading news through UUCP (UNIX to UNIX Copy Protocol) connections. NNTPCache is a good choice for small sites, especially those that do not have the bandwidth to download all the news required. INN, however, is the most widely used. Fortunately, it is included on your OpenLinux distribution CD.

INN is the most flexible and configurable method of downloading entire newsgroups and works especially well on larger sites that have high-speed connections to the Internet or those sites where a lot of news is transferred (for example, large educational institutions).

Rich Salz developed INN to provide a complete Usenet application in one package. One of the attractions of INN is that it doesn't care whether you are using TCP/IP or UUCP to transfer your newsgroups; INN handles both methods equally well. INN handles NNTP for transferring news with the innd server process and provides news reading services (nnrp) as a separate server, nnrpd, which is executed when it detects a connection on the news TCP/IP port (119).

How a Newsfeed Works

Usenet newsgroup postings are sent from machine to machine across the Internet all the time. To send mail from one system to another, Usenet uses a technique called *flooding*. Flooding happens when one machine connects to another and essentially transfers all the postings in the newsgroups as one big block of data. The receiving machine then connects to another machine and repeats the process. In this way, all the postings in the newsgroups are transferred across the entire Internet. This is much better than maintaining a single source of newsgroup information on a server isolated somewhere on the Internet.

Each machine that participates in the flooding has a list of all other machines that can send or receive newsgroup postings. Each connection is called a newsfeed. When you connect to an ISP and download newsgroup postings, you are creating a newsfeed between your machine and the ISP's machine, which in turn has a newsfeed to another machine somewhere on the Internet. By tuning the flooding of subsequent newsfeeds locally, the sheer load and quantity of messages can be drastically reduced or filtered depending on the needs of the clients and the health of the server system. For example, the fourth or fifth flood down the list of NNTP servers may only be a fraction of the size of the initial server's flood.

Newsfeeds are rarely open to anonymous usage, if at all. Some are for reading only, with no posting allowed. Great efforts are undertaken to safeguard newsfeeds from unauthorized access. When a machine is involved in flooding or relaying newsfeeds, it is given a list of machines that are authorized to send and/or receive postings to newsgroups. Unfortunately, a poorly maintained machine can sometimes allow a hole or open port as an unauthorized access point. INN provides tables and configuration files to safeguard against unauthorized access. This feature is discussed later in this chapter.

Posting a message to a newsgroup may seem like a local process to the end user, but a chain of events actually occurs. The new post is relayed over a variety of newsfeed relay machines until the posting is sufficiently widespread to appear everywhere.

When a posting jumps from machine to machine, those visits are catalogued in a message header field called the *path*, so that the message is not repeatedly stored on each previous machine by mistake. As an additional indexing tool to prevent chaotic message relaying and duplication, each separate posting is given its own identification number related to the newsgroup it is intended for.

Server software such as INN operates by trusting the client's software to send a list of its current posts so that messages are not present.

Preventing Duplicate News Postings

When you connect to your ISP and request newsgroup updates, one of two methods is usually used to ensure that you don't get duplicate postings when you use your newsreader. The most common technique is called *ihave/sendme*, which informs the machine at the other end of your newsfeed (such as your ISP's server) which message IDs you already have and which ones are lacking. Then, only the missing postings are transferred to your Linux machine.

The ihave/sendme protocol is excellent for updating a few newsgroups, but starts to bog down dramatically when handling very large volumes of newsgroups. For this reason, a method called *batching* is used to transfer large newsgroup feeds. With batching, everything on one end of the newsfeed is transferred as a block. Your machine then sorts through the download, discarding any duplicates. Batching adds more overhead to your local Linux machine than ihave/sendme, but it involves a lot less messaging between the two ends of the newsfeeds. As is often the case, the choice of update protocol involves choosing the most efficient use of your own resources (bandwidth vs. local processing power).

Pushing and Pulling

Two other terms are used to describe the transfer of newsgroup postings from one machine to another: pushing and pulling. These terms apply especially to smaller systems that don't download the entire newsfeed every day. Your system can download articles from the newsfeed using the ihave/sendme protocol, a technique called *pushing*. Alternatively, your machine can request specific postings or entire newsgroups from the newsfeed based on the date of arrival of the posting, a technique called *pulling*.

Alternative Methods to Downloading Newsgroups

If you don't use Usenet a lot or have limited connection time to the newsfeed, there is an alternative method for downloading Usenet newsgroups. This approach allows you to interact with a news server on a remote network and read the postings on that server rather than download them to your machine. Many ISPs allow you to choose whether to download newsgroups to your machine or to read them on their news server. Obviously, if you are reading on the server, you must be connected all the time, but this might be a better choice if you do not do a lot of Usenet surfing or have limited disk space on your machine. Another alternative is to read news via the web at http://www.deja.com. This is a large Web site that displays postings from nearly all the newsgroups from around the world in a format your Web browser can use. It also offers a very powerful search facility. If you are looking to solve a particular problem, chances are you will find an answer, if you do a search there.

InterNet News Server Software

InterNet News (INN) server software was originally designed for handling news on very large systems with complex connections and configuration problems. INN contains an NNTP component, but it is noticeably faster than NNTP alone when downloading and handling newsgroups. Luckily, INN can be quickly configured for most basic Linux setups. Our setup example is based on an ordinary dial-up connection to an ISP using TCP/IP.

One problem with INN is a lack of good documentation. To date, no one has spent the time to produce a good public-domain how-to file about configuring and maintaining INN on Linux systems, but an INN-FAQ, among other things, is available from the INN homepage at http://www.isc.org/inn.html. You will also find documentation and samples in /usr/doc/inn-2.2.1/ on your OpenLinux system, as well as in the man pages, of course.

INN Hardware and Software Requirements

INN doesn't impose too many hardware requirements; most Linux-capable hardware is sufficient to run INN. If you do download a lot of newsgroup postings, however, slow processors will be affected. Because INN often works in background, your foreground tasks get slower while INN crunches away. This is usually not a problem with Pentium or better CPUs running Caldera OpenLinux. It is safe to suggest that your INN server should carry as much RAM as you can afford, with a great amount of swap space on disk equally as important. Also, a separate partition, or even a separate disk, is highly recommended for the newsfeed spool(s).

Additionally, if you are setting up a news server for many users, it would help to have your INN server not handle any other tasks such as printing, file sharing, or mail services. Although the kernel in Caldera OpenLinux is built for multitasking and is inherently powerful, the disk bottleneck of a multitasked server will cause the greatest speed and efficiency troubles.

Disk space may be a problem if you don't have a lot to spare. Downloading newsgroups can eat up disk space at an alarming rate, even if you download only a few groups a day. Because newsgroup postings are not automatically deleted after you read them, the effect is cumulative. This is especially a problem with newsgroups that contain binary information such as compiled programs or pictures. A typical newsgroup download can range from a few kilobytes to several megabytes. Some of the binary newsgroups get many megabytes daily, all of which accumulate over a week or so to huge amounts of disk space. It is not unusual for a day's complete download of all the newsgroups to take up 4 or 5GB of disk space, so you must be careful about which newsgroups you select to download.

Modems are another issue, and the speed of your modem directly impacts how many newsgroups you can download in a reasonable amount of time. Obviously, the faster your modem is the better. A 56Kbps modem will download much more data in a minute than a 14,400bps modem. That doesn't mean you need to junk your existing slower modems and replace them. The determining factor for your connection is the amount of data you will be transferring. If you download fewer than a dozen nonbinary newsgroups a day, a 14,400bps modem is just fine. When you start downloading megabytes of data a day, as often happens with binary-laden newsgroups, you need a much faster connection to keep the download time to a minimum. Any of today's 56Kbps modems will suit your purposes for typical Usenet downloads of a few dozen nonbinary newsgroups.

When you start downloading large amounts of news, you should look at faster connections. If your goal is to provide INN services at a professional standard, the minimal connection to your batch or flood server should be of the class beyond conventional telephony modems. Commercial or corporate INN servers should at least be using ISDN (128Kbps), T1 (1.544Mbps), or T3 (45Mbps) connection for the news transfer. Fractional use of ISDN and T1 lines are available for a reasonable cost these days (depending on where in the world you live), but the overall expense of the line and routers is usually more than the newsgroup reading is worth to end users. Private users or less official organizations now have an increasingly available choice of home high-speed Internet access via cable-TV modems (2–10Mbps) or ADSL (2–7Mbps), although with lesser technical and business-class support in most cases. As always, a high-quality emergency power supply (UPS) is very desirable, particularly in a commercial setup.

Software requirements for INN are simple: You need INN and a configured connection to a newsfeed source (such as UUCP or TCP/IP to an ISP). INN is supplied with Caldera OpenLinux, and you can also obtain it from the Internet Software Consortium (www.isc.org), which maintains INN.

How INN Works

The main process of an INN server is innd, a daemon that continually listens to TCP/IP port 119 and attaches incoming connections to their proper services. When innd first starts, it opens port 119 and then places the contents of the incoming.conf, actsync.ign, actsync.cfg, and newsfeeds files from /etc/news into RAM for immediate, high-speed accessibility.

The incoming.conf file contains the names of all remote NNTP servers that feed your INN server with floods or batches. The actsync.* files are considered history files, in that they contain one line for each newsgroup that are or were stored on your INN server. Because they are constantly in RAM and can vary widely in size throughout a given period, the importance of having lots of RAM and swap space on an INN server becomes evident.

The active files have an even greater purpose. Because you may not wish to allow your users to have full access privileges to all newsgroups, you can decide on relative states for each newsgroup based on your own criteria. Active files allow a variety of rules for each newsgroup, and constantly see that those rules are in effect until you change them.

TABLE 20.1 Newsgroup Status As Set in Active Files

Status	Meaning
n	Posting to remote groups are allowed.
x	No posting to this group are allowed.
y	Only local postings are allowed.
=alt.*	Locally stored in a folder by that newsgroup name.
m	Post allowed only by moderator of that newsgroup.
j	Posts are sent but are locally junked if received again.

Of all the configuration files for INN, perhaps the most important is /etc/news/control.ctl, which is the master database of all newsgroups. It automatically tells innd how to treat postings to or from each of the denoted newsgroups in its tables. Because there may be over 50,000 newsgroups for the administrator to preside over, wildcards and "blanket" dispositions are easily allowed. This file is typically the most customized of all INN configuration files.

No serving of Internet resources, of any variety, should be performed without proper logging and monitoring of your server. INN is fully capable of keeping logs, and Caldera OpenLinux even puts an entry into your /etc/syslog.conf file specifically for INN. A discussion of the /etc/syslog.conf file is outside the scope of this chapter, but it is sufficient to say that the entries in the /etc/syslog.conf file tell INN where to keep its log files.

In Caldera OpenLinux, all news-related messages that are syslogged go to /var/log/news.all, whereas news-related messages of severity error or higher also go to /var/log/spooler. INN maintains its own log files in /var/log/news.d.

Monitoring your INN server for such topics as disk inode usage, cpu load, and other parameters is facilitated by editing your /etc/news/innwatch.ctl file, which looks like a terrible mess inside but which actually follows a logical format. Just remember that the fields in that file are delimited with a bang (!) symbol. Some knowledge of advanced system administration, awk, and shell syntax is definitely required in manipulating this file. Thus, new users may find monitoring via the /etc/news/innwatch.ctl file somewhat intimidating.

Installing INN

Caldera OpenLinux provides a special directory for all INN configuration files called /etc/news and installs the main INN binaries into /usr/libexec/inn with many compatibility links to standard places like /usr/sbin. This means that running your INN server from the Linux command line or in scripts requires little additional effort other than in properly setting up the /etc/news configuration files. As a bonus, Caldera OpenLinux offers a variety of INN sample templates found in the directory /usr/doc/inn-2.2.1/samples/ for your use and comparison.

After you have committed to making your Caldera OpenLinux machine an INN server, some of the INN binaries will run constantly, but the remainder will be used on an as-needed basis. Because your news-reading clients may not share your particular daily schedule, it is likely that your INN server will need to run 24 hours per day.

To install INN, do the following:

1. Check the /etc/group file for a group called news. If one does not exist, create it. The news login should be the only user in the news group. Providing a dedicated group for INN access enhances system security. This group should exist by default.

2. Check your /etc/passwd file for a user called news. If one does not exist, create the news user. The user news should belong to the group news. The home directory can be anything, and the startup command should be blank or something like /bin/false for security reasons—no one should ever need to actively login as the

news user. The system does not use either of these parameters. The `news` user is created to allow INN to run as a nonroot login for better system security. This account should exist by default. Also make sure that the password field is filled by an asterisk (*). This makes doubly sure that no one can log in interactively as the `news` user.

3. INN often sends mail to the `news` logins, so you might want to create an alias for the usernames `news` and `usenet` to root, postmaster, or whatever other login you want these messages to be sent to. The alias file is kept in `/etc/aliases`. When you add aliases, make sure to run the `/usr/bin/newaliases` command afterward so that the added aliases will take effect.

4. Check to see if INN is already installed on your system by typing:

   `rpm -q inn`

   If you installed INN at setup time, you will see the reply:

   `inn-2.2.1-1`

   If INN is not yet installed on your OpenLinux box, type:

   `rpm -i inn-2.2.1-1.i386.rpm`

   Installing the package should create two files: `/etc/rc.d/init.d/news` and `/usr/libexec/inn/bin/rc.news`. These files will be used by `init` to start news services each time you boot. Once installed, these files are executed automatically during the boot process unless explicitly disabled or removed. If these files are not created, see the following instructions.

   The OpenLinux INN RPM file will install INN and newsgroup support under various directories. All bundled documentation will be installed under `/usr/doc/inn-2.2.1`, and the main INN binaries are in `/usr/libexec/inn/bin`.

5. After the INN package has successfully been installed and you've properly configured the `/etc/news` files, you can start `news` services by typing:

   `/etc/rc.d/init.d/news start`

The INN Startup Files

When the INN RPM is installed, it should automatically install the important INN startup files, `/etc/rc.d/init.d/news` (shown in Listing 20.1) and `/usr/libexec/inn/bin/rc.news` (shown in Listing 20.2).

LISTING 20.1 Contents of `/etc/rc.d/init.d/news`

```
#! /bin/bash

# Source function library (and set vital variables).
```

```
. /etc/rc.d/init.d/functions

# See how we were called.
case "$1" in
 start)
   [ ! e $SVIlock ] ¦¦ exit 1

   SVIemptyConfig /etc/news/inn.conf && {
      echo "$DESCRIPTIVE: not configured! Skipped..."
      exit 2
   }

   echo  n "Starting $IDENT services: "
   SVIrun S I "innd" "!innd" \
   /usr/libexec/inn/bin/rc.news

   echo "."
   touch $SVIlock
   ;;

 stop)
   [ e $SVIlock ] ¦¦ exit 0

   echo  n "Stopping $IDENT services: "
   SVIrun S I "innd." "ctlinnd failed." \
   /usr/libexec/inn/bin/ctlinnd  s  t 30 shutdown System stopped
   test  f /var/run/news/innwatch.pid &&
         kill  1 `cat /var/run/news/innwatch.pid`

   #echo "."
   rm  f $SVIlock
   ;;

 *)
   echo "Usage: $SVIscript {start¦stop}"
   exit 1
   ;;
esac

exit 0
```

As you can see, /etc/rc.d/init.d/news is a relatively standard control file, very similar to all the others in the /etc/rc.d/init.d directory. It starts off by checking to see that all the various networking services are running; then depending on what argument is passed to it (start or stop), it performs the appropriate action. Most of the work is performed in the rc.news file, an example of which is displayed in Listing 20.2.

LISTING 20.2 Contents of /usr/libexec/inn/bin/rc.news

```
##  News boot script.  Runs as "news" user.  Requires inndstart be
##  setuid root.  Run from rc.whatever as:
##      su news -c /path/to/rc.news >/dev/console
##
##  Modified by okir@caldera.de
##  No longer require inndstart to be setuid--it's a tattered bag of fleas.

. /usr/libexec/inn/innshellvars

AZ=ABCDEFGHIJKLMNOPQRSTUVWXYZ
az=abcdefghijklmnopqrstuvwxyz

action=$1
#shift

case $action in
"")
    $0 start-innd "$@"
    exec $0 start-misc "$@";;
start-innd)
    # This runs with root privilege.
    # Make sure you don't trash any news-owned files.

    ##  Pick ${INND} or ${INNDSTART}
    WHAT=${INNDSTART}
    MAIL="${MAILCMD} -s 'Boot-time Usenet warning on `hostname`' ${NEWSMASTER}"

    ##  RFLAG is set below; set INNFLAGS in inn.conf(5)
    RFLAG=""

    ##  Clean shutdown or already running?
    if [ -f ${SERVERPID} ] ; then
        if kill -0 `cat ${SERVERPID}` 2>/dev/null; then
     echo '    INND:  apparently running! Exiting...'
     exit 1
        fi
        echo '    INND:  PID file exists — unclean shutdown! ...'
        RFLAG="-r"
    fi

    if [ ! -f ${PATHDB}/.news.daily ] ; then
        echo 'No .news.daily file; need to run news.daily?' | eval ${MAIL}
    else
        case `find ${PATHDB}/.news.daily -mtime +1 -print 2>/dev/null` in
        "")
    ;;
        *)
    echo 'Old .news.daily file; need to run news.daily?' | eval ${MAIL}
    ;;
```

```
            esac
        fi

        ##  Active file recovery.
        if [ ! -s ${ACTIVE} ] ; then
            if [ -s ${NEWACTIVE} ] ; then
    mv ${NEWACTIVE} ${ACTIVE}
            else
        if [ -s ${OLDACTIVE} ] ; then
            cp -p ${OLDACTIVE} ${ACTIVE}
        else
            echo '  INND:   No active file! Exiting...'
            exit 1
        fi
            fi
            RFLAG="-r"
            # You might want to rebuild the DBZ database, too:
            #cd ${PATHDB} \
            #           && makehistory -r \
            #           && mv history.n.dir history.dir \
            #           && mv history.n.index history.index \
            #           && mv history.n.hash history.hash
        fi

        ##  Remove temporary batchfiles and lock files.
        ( cd ${BATCH} && rm -f bch* )
        ( cd ${LOCKS} && rm -f LOCK* )
        ( cd ${TEMPSOCKDIR} && rm -f ${TEMPSOCK} )
        rm -f ${NEWSCONTROL} ${NNTPCONNECT} ${SERVERPID}

        ##  Start the show.
        eval ${WHAT} ${RFLAG} ${INNFLAGS}
        : ;;

start-misc)
        # This runs with news privilege:

        ##  Set to true or false
        : ${DOINNWATCH:=true}
        DOINNWATCH=`echo ${DOINNWATCH} | tr ${AZ} ${az}`
        if [ -z "${DOINNWATCH}" \
             -o "${DOINNWATCH}" = "on" \
             -o "${DOINNWATCH}" = "true" \
             -o "${DOINNWATCH}" = "yes" ]; then
            DOINNWATCH=true
        else
            DOINNWATCH=false
        fi

        # Gee, looks like lisp, doesn't it?
        ${DOINNWATCH} && {
```

continues

LISTING 20.2 continued

```
            echo "  INND:  Scheduled start of innwatch."
            ( sleep 60 ; ${INNWATCH} ) </dev/null >/dev/null 2>&1 &
        }

        : ${DOCNFSSTAT:=false}
        DOCNFSSTAT=`echo ${DOCNFSSTAT} | tr ${AZ} ${az}`
        if [ -z "${DOCNFSSTAT}" \
            -o "${DOCNFSSTAT}" = "on" \
            -o "${DOCNFSSTAT}" = "true" \
            -o "${DOCNFSSTAT}" = "yes" ]; then
            DOCNFSSTAT=true
        else
            DOCNFSSTAT=false
        fi

        ${DOCNFSSTAT} && {
            echo "Scheduled start of cnfsstat."
            ( sleep 60 ; ${PATHBIN}/cnfsstat -s -l ) &
        }

        RMFILE=${MOST_LOGS}/expire.rm
        for F in ${RMFILE} ${RMFILE}.*; do
            if [ -f $F -a -s $F ] ; then
         echo "  INND:  Removing articles from pre-downtime expire run (${F})."
         (
             echo 'System shut down during expire.' \
                 'Unlinking articles listed in'
             echo ${F}
         ) | eval ${MAIL}
         ${PATHBIN}/expirerm ${F}
            fi
        done &
        : ;;
esac

exit 0
```

This script does numerous housekeeping chores, which includes checking to see that the news.daily script has been run recently (news.daily takes care of things such as article expiration) and actually starting INN.

After the INN package is installed and ready to go, you still need to check the configuration information to make sure that everything will run smoothly when innd connects to the newsfeed.

> **Note**
>
> INN is very particular about its user and group setup and about file permissions in general. As a general rule, don't modify any INN file permissions at all, or you may find the package ceases to work properly.

Configuring INN

Configuring INN can take hours because it is a complex package allowing many newsfeeds at once—but don't panic. For a simple connection to an ISP through TCP/IP or UUCP, you can configure INN in just a few minutes. Most of the work was already done when you installed the package.

Follow these steps to check and configure your INN setup, being careful not to corrupt any files or change permissions as you go:

1. Edit the /etc/news/incoming.conf file. This file lists all the newsfeeds that your system connects to and is read by the INN daemon. Enter the names or IP addresses of the newsfeed machines using the following as an example:

   ```
   peer newsfeed {
             hostname:     news.isp.net
   }
   ```

   Because most systems will have only a single newsfeed, you will only need one peer entry. If your newsfeed requires a password, add another parameter password: with the appropriate password after the colon. There are many other parameters that can be specified on a per newsfeed basis. For a full list, see the man pages.

2. Because you must be concerned with preventing abuse of your system by unknown or unauthorized message posters, INN provides a file called /etc/news/nnrp.access to allow or prohibit a wide range of user activity. Based on the entries to that file, a user's client software will be told whether uploading messages to that particular newsgroup from the client's particular host name or IP address will be allowed. If you allow other machines on your local area network, or machines connecting through a remote access server on your machine, to read news collected by your system, you need to add their names to this file.

   The /etc/news/nnrp.access file is read when the nnrpd daemon starts for each person invoking a newsreader, and follows this syntax:

   name:perms:user:password:newsgroup

name is the address of the machine that you are allowing to read news. (You can use wildcards to allow entire subnets.) *perms* is the permissions and has one of the following values: `Read` (for read-only access), `Post` (to allow posting of messages), or `ReadPost` (for both `Read` and `Post`). The *user* field is used to authenticate a username before it is allowed to post, and *password* accomplishes the same task. To prevent a user from posting messages through your server, leave *user* and *password* as spaces so that they can't be matched.

The *newsgroup* field is a pattern of newsgroup names that can be either read or not read, depending on how you set up the contents. Access to newsgroups uses wildcards, so `comp*` allows access to all newsgroups starting with *comp*, whereas `!sex` disables access to any newsgroups starting with the word *sex*. The default setting in the `nnrp.access` file is to prevent all access. To allow all users in the domain `tpci.com` to read and post news with no authentication required, you add this line to `nnrp.access`:

`*.tpci.com:Read Post:::*`

To open the news system to everyone on your system regardless of domain name, use an asterisk instead of a domain name.

3. The file `inn.conf.sample` should be in your `/etc/news` directory. Copy this file to `inn.conf` and change the line with *organization* in it to:

```
organization:    Your company name
        pathhost:        your FQDN
```

This specifies the default for the organization header for those newsgroup users who use your server.

Of course, if you are setting up INN to get news from your ISP's news server, your ISP would have to set up their end with the newsgroups that you want your users to be able to access. Remember that news takes up a lot of bandwidth, so try to minimize the amount of news you download.

As noted, the innd daemon monitors port 119 for NNTP activity regarding floods and batches, but it also has another function related to a different protocol. The innd daemon also listens for NNRP (Net News Read Protocol) activity coming in from Usenet reader software.

As your server continues efficiently serving Usenet newsgroups, accepting or rejecting posts, filtering unwanted messages or groups, and performing other housekeeping tasks, you must carefully watch the output of the monitoring tools to see how your available disk space is accommodating the load.

If your INN server is showing signs of unacceptably high load (known to be slowing down all machine functions or compromising disk space), an INN administrator will typically take such steps as prohibiting most of the `alt.binaries` groups and setting the article expiration times to a rather short value in the `/etc/news/expire.ctl` file. The sooner you can get them off your server, the sooner replacements can be brought in.

An emergency feature included in `/usr/sbin/ctlinnd` is *throttling*, which can either reduce the transfer capabilities between newsfeed servers during floods or batches or sever all connections! Only with careful monitoring will you know whether throttling your INN server is needed to prevent a possible disk overload or system saturation.

Finally, if for any reason your `/etc/services` file is compromised, your Linux kernel may not understand the mapping of TCP/IP port 119 to NNTP, so it is suggested that you keep that file backed up along with your INN files.

After installing and configuring INN and notifying your ISP that you want to access their NNTP service, you should be able to use INN to download news and access it with a newsreader (assuming that you've granted yourself permission in the `nnrp.access` file). A lot of complexity can be introduced into INN's configuration file, but keeping it simple tends to be the best method. As your experience grows, you can modify the behavior of the newsfeeds.

The `tin` Newsreader

Many newsreaders are available for Linux systems. Your OpenLinux distribution includes `tin`—a simple yet fast and efficient newsreader for Linux. You might not need a newsreader at all if you have Web services on your system. Many Web browsers allow access to newsgroups either in your own news directory or through a connection to an ISP's newsfeed.

The primary advantage of `tin` over earlier newsreaders like the `rn` (read news) package is that `tin` lets you follow threads. A *thread* in a newsgroup is a continuing discussion with one primary subject. Before threaded newsreaders became available, you had to read news in consecutive order from first to last, trying to assemble several different conversations into logical groups as you went. With `tin`, you can start with one thread or subject and read all the postings about that subject and then move on to another subject, regardless of the chronological order in which the postings were made.

Threads are usually handled automatically so that they require no special user interaction, although there is some work performed behind the scenes on your newsfeed. Some newsgroups do not support threading, but most do. If threads are available, you can follow the thread from start to finish, or jump out and change threads at any time.

Installing and Configuring `tin`

The `tin` newsreader is easy to install as a binary package; an RPM is included with Caldera OpenLinux. To see if `tin` is already installed on your system, type:

```
rpm -q tin
```

You should see the reply:

```
tin-1.3ub-4
```

If you do not find a package by that name, you can install the `tin` package from the directory on your CD containing RPM files by issuing the following command:

```
rpm -i tin-1.3ub-4.i386.rpm
```

There really is no special configuration required for `tin` to run. When the binary is available on your system, it will check for the newsgroup information in your news spool and present it to you. If you are running it on a system that does not have news locally, you must set an environment variable telling `tin` where to read news from. If your news server is news.home.com the command sequence to type is:

```
$ NNTPSERVER=news.home.com
$ export NNTPSERVER
$ tin -r
```

You can also set the newserver in a systemwide file called /etc/nntpserver (create this file with the single entry of your nntp server name). In that way, you only need to start the newsreader to read news.

Summary

In this chapter, you learned how Usenet news works and how to install and configure the InterNet News service and the basic Linux newsreader `tin`. Before setting up your INN server, you need to consider the size of newsfeed you wish to serve, the length of time you are willing to house messages, the complexity of maintaining files regarding allowed and disallowed capabilities, and the amount of time you can afford to spend presiding over your INN server. Remember that Usenet is a constantly changing ocean of messages and newsgroups, so administering it is quite dynamic. Because INN is one of the most popular and powerful Usenet news servers today, you can be assured of its capabilities. Remember that you do need a connection available to a newsfeed before you complete and test the INN configuration. Setting up TCP/IP and UUCP connections are explained elsewhere in this book.

CHAPTER 21

IP Firewalling and Masquerading

IN THIS CHAPTER

- The Firewall   478
- Packet Filtering   479
- IP Firewalling Chains   480
- Using ipchains to Configure and Check the Firewall   483
- IP Masquerading   502
- Saving and Restoring the Firewall   504
- Further Reading   505

One of the greatest concerns of our times is computer security, that is, how to protect a computer or network of computers from illegal access by unauthorized people or computers. It has been said that the only secure computer is one that is turned off, completely unhooked, encased in a block of concrete, and buried at least 10 feet under the ground. Although this might make the computer secure, most of us would like to be able to use our computers and still maintain a reasonable level of security. This condition effectively rules out the scenario.

So that we might use our computers safely, many different schemes have been developed to help secure them from unauthorized access. These strategies include such things as password protection, encryption, various authentication protocols, disabling unnecessary services, and firewalls. No single method of protection is sufficient for good security. If you want a really secure computer, you need to use a combination of these and other methods.

In this chapter, we will discuss one method of protection: the firewall—in particular, the filtering firewall. Another type of firewall, the proxy firewall, is discussed in Chapter 22.

The Firewall

The term *firewall* actually comes from the world of cars. It is a wall that separates passengers from the engine. Its purpose is protection—it insulates the passengers from the engine compartment in the case of fire while still enabling access to the engine's controls.

In the world of computers, a firewall is a device or computer that joins two networks and protects them from each other. Usually, it is used to protect a private network from a public one, such as the Internet. The firewall computer (hereafter simply called *firewall*) has access to both networks, and, in general, neither network has access to the other, except through the firewall.

There are basically two types of firewalls—filtering firewalls and proxy firewalls. Filtering firewalls look at each individual IP packet and determine whether to let it through based on a set of rules. Packets can be filtered based on several criteria including their source address, destination address, type of packet, protocol used, and port they originated from or are addressed to. You can also specify different rules based on whether the packet is incoming, outgoing, or being forwarded.

A proxy firewall takes a different approach. A proxy firewall has a proxy server set up for each type of service you want to allow "through" the firewall. A machine that wants to connect to a machine on the other side of the firewall connects to the proxy server instead. Rather than filtering packets, the proxy server connects to the appropriate machine on the other side of the firewall and copies the data through. In this way, a machine on one side of the firewall cannot get direct access to a machine on the other side, whereas with filtering firewalls, it can.

To help illustrate the difference between the two types of firewalls, you could say that a telephone is a type of filtering firewall. With a telephone you communicate directly with the person at the other end, but you can't see each other. Only your voice is transmitted to the other person. A telegram is more like a proxy firewall. You give the information to Western Union; they make a copy of it and give the copy to the other person.

Setting up a firewall can help protect your computer or network from unauthorized access, but a firewall in and of itself is not sufficient. You also need to take other measures to secure your computer or network properly. For example, you can have a great firewall in place, but if you've chosen inadequate passwords for the accounts on your systems, it may still be fairly easy for someone to break in.

Packet Filtering

All traffic over a network is sent in small chunks of data called *packets*. When a large file is sent over a network, it is broken up into smaller, more manageable packets, rather than in one big chunk. This allows for more efficient transmission and control of data from multiple sources. A packet has essentially two parts to it—a header, which says what kind of packet it is, where it's from, and where it's going, and the body, which is a piece of the actual data being sent.

Some protocols have the concept of a connection. Before any packets with actual data are sent, special packets are exchanged to establish a connection. These packets say things like "I want to establish a connection," "ok," and "thanks." After the connection has been established, packets with the real data are sent.

An IP filter looks at the headers of these packets and decides whether to accept them (let them pass through), deny them (discard them as though it never saw them) or reject them sending back a message saying that they were rejected and discarded. Linux has this capability built right into the kernel. The program `ipchains` is used to set up the rules that govern how packets will be filtered.

> **Note**
>
> Even though the kernel source contains the necessary code to do packet filtering, the default kernel that comes with OpenLinux is not configured to use it. In order to do IP filtering and set up a filtering firewall, you must reconfigure, recompile, and reinstall the kernel. If you have never done this or are unsure about the process, read through Chapter 31, which talks about it in detail.

To use the filtering capabilities of the kernel and `ipchains`, the following options must be enabled in the kernel:

- Network firewalls
- IP: firewalling

The following options may also be enabled if desired:

- *IP: Always Defragment*   Recommended, but only necessary if you will use transparent proxy support or IP masquerading.
- *IP: Masquerading*   Necessary if a private network does not have valid IP addresses and is connected to the Internet via the firewall.
- *IP: Transparent Proxy Support*   Useful for redirecting specific traffic to a different port on the firewall.

IP Firewalling Chains

Lists of rules called *firewall chains*, or simply *chains*, are used to determine what to do with a particular packet. Each chain has an associated name, and built-in chains have an associated *policy*. The policy tells the kernel what to do with the packet if none of the rules were matched. User-defined chains do not have a policy.

Each rule can have an associated action or *target* that tells the kernel what to do with the packet if that rule is matched. The target can be another chain of rules to test the packet against, or it can be one of six special targets: ACCEPT, REJECT, DENY, MASQ, REDIRECT, and RETURN. These special targets ultimately control the fate of a packet. You can find a detailed description of them in Table 21.1.

Table 21.1   The Six Special Targets for a Rule

Target	Description
ACCEPT	Allows the packet through.
REJECT	Does not allow the packet through. The packet is discarded, but if it was not an ICMP packet, an ICMP reply is sent back to the source to tell it that the destination was unreachable. For ICMP packets, REJECT is the same as DENY.
DENY	Does not allow the packet through. The packet is simply discarded.

Target	Description
MASQ	Tells the kernel to masquerade the packet. In other words, the kernel makes it appear as though the packet originated at the firewall, effectively hiding the source of the packet behind the firewall. This is necessary if machines behind the firewall don't have valid IP addresses for the Internet. This will be the case for most home and many small office networks. This target is only valid for rules in the forward and user-defined chains. The kernel must be configured for IP masquerading to use this target.
REDIRECT	Tells the kernel to redirect the packet to a local port instead of where it was originally headed. This target can only be used in rules that have TCP or UDP specified as their protocol and is only valid for packets traversing the input and user-defined chains.
RETURN	Tells the kernel to stop traversing the chain and jump to the end. The end result is the same as if no rules were matched in the chain. If the chain being traversed was a built-in chain, then the policy for that chain will be used to determine the fate of the packet.

The packet is tested against each rule in the chain in order from first to last until a rule is matched. If a rule is matched, then the kernel looks at the rule's target to see what to do with the packet. If the target is another user-defined chain of rules, then it tests the packet against each of the rules in that chain until it matches a rule or reaches the end of the chain. Upon reaching the end of the chain, it falls back to the rule in the chain it that just jumped from. When it reaches the end of the possible rules to test against (that is, the end of a built-in chain), the kernel checks the policy for that chain and acts accordingly. The policy can be any one of the first four special targets: ACCEPT, REJECT, DENY, or MASQ.

The kernel has three built-in chains called input, forward, and output. When a packet comes in, the kernel checks it against the rules in the input chain. If it succeeds in passing all the input rules, the kernel then decides where to send it next (this is called *routing*). If the packet is headed for a different machine, the kernel tests it against the forward chain. If it passes there, too, then the kernel tests it against the output chain before actually sending it on to the next machine. Figure 21.1 illustrates the path of a packet through the filter.

FIGURE 21.1

The path of a packet through the filter.

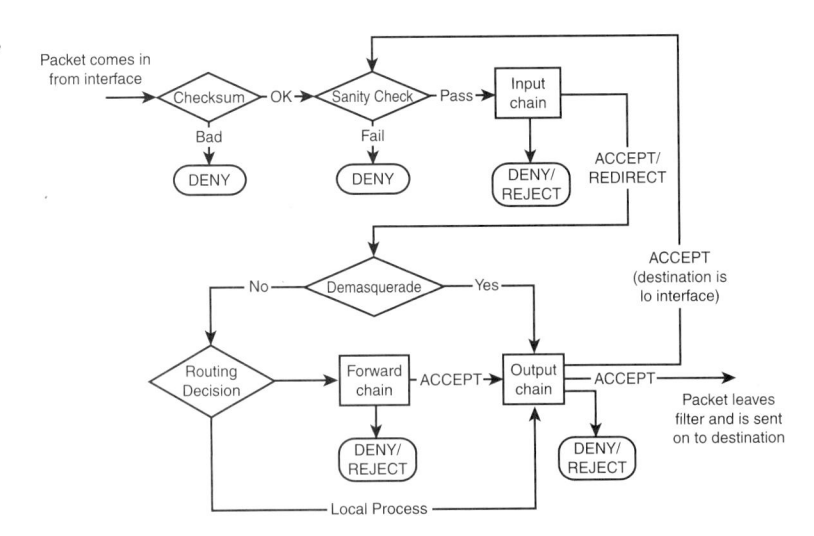

Checksum	Makes sure that the packet hasn't been corrupted in some way. If it has, then it is denied.
Sanity Check	Malformed packets can confuse the rule-checking code, so they are detected and discarded. For clarity, the sanity check is only shown before the input chain in Figure 21.1, but it actually is performed before traversing each firewall chain.
input Chain	The input chain is the first chain that a packet is tested against. Unless the packet is denied or rejected, it is passed on.
Demasquerade	If the packet is a reply to a masqueraded packet, the packet is demasqueraded and passed directly on to the output chain. (*Note*: This applies only if you are using IP masquerading.)
Routing Decision	The destination of the packet is examined to see if it is headed toward a local process or needs to be forwarded to another machine. If the destination is a local process, the packet is sent to the output chain; otherwise, it is sent to the forward chain.

Local Process	A local process can receive packets after the routing decision and send them through the routing decision step on to the `output` chain.
lo Interface	If packets from a local process are sent to another local process, they are sent through the `output` chain with the interface set to 'lo' (usually called the loopback interface) and come back in to the `input` chain with the interface still set to 'lo'.
`forward` Chain	Any packets destined for another machine pass through the `forward` chain.
`output` Chain	The `output` chain is traversed by all packets just before they are sent on.

Using `ipchains` to Configure and Check the Firewall

The program `ipchains` is used to configure the firewall (firewall chains) and view information about it. `ipchains` allows you to work on entire chains or the rules within a chain. It also allows you to define new chains in addition to the three built-in chains. It is generally run from the command line to set things up, and then preferably from a system startup script when the firewall boots.

`ipchains` doesn't store the firewall configuration anywhere, so it is lost when the firewall is shut down. However, it is easy to add `ipchains` commands to system startup scripts that will reconfigure the firewall when it boots up. There are also a few scripts that help simplify the process.

Working on an Entire Chain

Six operations work on entire chains. The first five all have the same syntax:

`ipchains -[LFXNZ] [chain] [options]`

The brackets (`[ ]`) are not part of the command, but signify either optional arguments, or that only one of the arguments within the brackets is used. For example, you may not have any *options* because they are not required. However, you must choose one of `-L`, `-F`, `-X`, `-N`, and `-Z` to perform the corresponding action.

> **Note**
>
> You must be root or the superuser to use `ipchains`.

Listing the Rules in a Chain

You can list the rules in a chain by using the -L option:

ipchains -L [*chain*] [*options*]

For example, with my present setup, I get the following output when I list the contents of the forward chain:

```
# ipchains -L forward
Chain forward (policy ACCEPT):
target     prot opt      source           destination    ports
MASQ       all  ------   192.168.0.0/16   !192.168.0.0/16 n/a
```

This says that the policy for the forward chain is ACCEPT, which means that by default packets that come in and are destined for a different machine are forwarded, or ACCEPTed for forwarding. The second line is just a line of column headers explaining the information on the following lines. Everything after is a list of the rules for the chain. In this case, the chain only has one rule. In short, it says that all packets originating on a local network and destined for anywhere else are to be masqueraded so that they appear to be coming from the firewall machine. If it appears cryptic, don't worry. It will make sense after you read the sections on specifying rules.

If you don't specify a chain, the rules in all chains are listed:

```
# ipchains -L
Chain input (policy ACCEPT):
Chain forward (policy ACCEPT):
target     prot opt      source           destination    ports
MASQ       all  ------   192.168.0.0/16   !192.168.0.0/16 n/a
Chain output (policy ACCEPT):
```

Note that the input and output chains have no rules. By default, the three built-in chains have no rules, and the policy for each is ACCEPT. If all you need is a machine that will route packets freely between two or more networks, you will only need to configure the kernel for firewalling and then enable IP forwarding. In this case, the local network does not have valid IP addresses, so IP masquerading is used for packets leaving the local network. Otherwise, this firewall is simply acting as a router.

Table 21.2 lists some useful options that can be used in conjunction with the -L option.

Table 21.2 Options That Can Be Used with -L Option

Option	Description
-n	Numeric output. Causes IP addresses and ports to be printed out numerically. By default, ipchains tries to print out the host, network, and service names wherever applicable. This can greatly speed up this command because it saves ipchains from having to do reverse DNS lookups.
-v	Verbose. Causes ipchains to list interface addresses, rule options, TOS masks, and packet and byte counters along with the other information given by default. The suffixes K, M, and G are added to the packet and byte counters to signify the one thousand, one million, and one billion multipliers, respectively.
-x	Exact. Causes the exact values of the packet and byte counters to be displayed instead of the rounded numbers using the multipliers K, M, and G. This option is only meaningful when specified along with the -v option.

Deleting All Rules from a Chain

To delete or remove all the rules from a chain leaving it empty, you use the -F (flush) option:

ipchains -F [*chain*]

If no chain is specified, all chains are flushed and left empty. For example, with the simple firewall listed earlier, flushing the forward chain and listing the firewall rules would give the following results:

```
# ipchains -F forward
# ipchains -L
Chain input (policy ACCEPT):
Chain forward (policy ACCEPT):
Chain output (policy ACCEPT):
```

In this case, you could have simply entered ipchains -F to obtain the same result because the other chains were already empty. There's no compelling reason to do that, however, aside from avoiding the few keystrokes needed to type forward.

Deleting a Chain

You can delete a user-defined chain using the -X option:

ipchains -X [*chain*]

Before a chain can be deleted, it must be empty (use the -F option to flush it), and there must be no rules in other chains that refer to it. Any rules that refer to it must either be deleted or replaced by rules with different targets. If no chain is specified, `ipchains` will try to delete all user-defined chains.

> **Note**
>
> The three built-in chains (input, forward, and output) cannot be deleted.

For example, if you wanted to clear the entire firewall setup so that you could start over, you could issue the following two commands, which will flush all chains and then delete all user-defined chains:

```
# ipchains -F
# ipchains -X
```

Creating a New Chain

You can create a new chain of rules (a user-defined chain) using the -N option:

ipchains -N *new_ chain*

new_chain is the name you want for your new chain. You cannot use a name that is already in use. So, right from the outset, you cannot use the names input, forward, and output.

There is no easy way to rename a chain. You will simply have to create a new chain with the new name and set it up like the old chain. Any rules that referred to the old chain must be redefined to refer to the new chain. You can then delete the old chain and forget that it ever existed.

For example, if you wanted to set up a chain for packets coming in off the ppp0 interface, you could create a new chain called ppp0 with the following command:

```
# ipchains -N ppp0
```

You can then place rules that apply only to packets coming from the ppp0 interface in this chain.

Creating the chain and adding rules to it is not sufficient, however, to put the chain in use. The name of the chain is only there for your convenience and is meaningless to the kernel. The kernel does not look at the name and think, "Okay. Packets coming from ppp0 go to the ppp0 chain." You need to set up a rule in one of the built-in chains (or a user-defined chain that can be reached from one of the built-in chains) that has the chain ppp0 as its target. This is easy to do and will be discussed later.

There are several reasons for wanting to define your own chains. One reason is organization. It will be easier to administer and troubleshoot your firewall if you keep it organized. If you group rules together logically, it will be easier for you to trace through the rules and see where things are going wrong. Another reason is efficiency. If you have different interfaces and want to filter packets differently for each interface, creating your own chains with rules for each separate interface can save the kernel the trouble of comparing packets from, say, the eth0 interface against rules for the eth1 interface. If you have a lot of traffic going through your firewall, this can save a lot of CPU cycles.

Zeroing the Packet and Byte Counters

Each rule in a chain has packet and byte counters that count the number of packets that have matched that rule and the sum of the sizes of those packets in bytes. These counters can be viewed using the -L and -v options as described earlier in the section entitled "Listing the Rules in a Chain."

Sometimes it becomes necessary to reset these counters to zero. For example if you want to keep track of traffic on a daily basis for accounting reasons, you could reset them once a day at midnight, so that only traffic for the following day is counted. You reset the counters using the -Z (zero) option:

```
ipchains -Z [chain]
```

If you don't specify a chain, the counters in all chains will be reset.

For example, the following command sequence shows the counters before and after zeroing them in the forward chain (the output is very long, so only the first part of each line is shown):

```
# ipchains -L forward -vn
Chain forward (policy ACCEPT: 6 packets, 432 bytes):
pkts bytes target ...
  97 10723 MASQ ...
# ipchains -Z forward
# ipchains -L forward -vn
Chain forward (policy ACCEPT: 6 packets, 432 bytes):
pkts bytes target ...
   0     0 MASQ ...
```

Note that only the counters for the rules are zeroed. The counts listed after the policy are different and cannot be zeroed.

Setting a Chain's Policy

The sixth command that works on an entire chain allows you to set its policy. It has the following syntax:

```
ipchains -P chain target
```

The policy gives the action to be taken if no rules in the chain were matched. A policy can only be specified for built-in chains and can only be one of the first four special targets: ACCEPT, REJECT, DENY, or MASQ.

For example, if you only want to allow a few certain types of packets to be forwarded through the firewall, it would probably be easiest to make the default policy be DENY or REJECT and then to specify rules for the packets to forward. You would set the policy using the following command:

```
# ipchains forward DENY
```

or

```
# ipchains forward REJECT
```

Working on Individual Rules

Now that you know how to work with entire chains of rules, we can talk about actually working with the rules that make the chains useful. There are five basic actions that can be taken on rules. You can append a rule to the end of a chain, insert a rule at a given position within a chain, replace a given rule, delete a rule at a given position within a chain, and delete the first rule that matches a given specification.

> **Note**
>
> The next four sections only describe the command used to perform the specific action. For the most part, they don't give enough information to actually use the command until you learn how to specify a rule. This will be discussed in the section entitled "Specifying a Rule."

Appending a Rule to the End of a Chain

The easiest way to add a rule to a chain is simply to append it to the end. You do this using the -A option:

```
ipchains -A chain rule-specification [options]
```

Recall, however, that the order of the rules is important. Appending a rule to the end of a chain will make it the last rule examined. If you want to place a rule at a different point in the chain, you must insert it using the insert command.

Inserting a Rule into a Chain

You can insert a rule into a chain at a given position using the insert option, `-I`:

```
ipchains -I chain [position] rule-specification [options]
```

The rules are numbered starting at one (1), so inserting a rule at position one inserts it at the beginning of the chain. Not specifying a position will also insert the rule at the beginning of the chain. If there are n rules, inserting at position n+1 appends the rule to the end of the chain. Attempting to insert at a position greater than n+1 produces an error; it can't be done. There is no easy way to determine what position a rule is in other than listing the rules and counting.

Replacing a Rule

You can replace a rule at a given position in a chain using the replace option, `-R`:

```
ipchains -R chain position rule-specification [options]
```

This changes the *rule-specification* of the rule at position *position* to the given *rule-specification*. It is an error to omit the position or to specify a position that doesn't exist (for example, *n*+1).

Deleting a Rule

There are two ways to delete a rule. You can specify the position of the rule to delete, or you can give a rule specification so that the first rule in the chain that matches that specification is deleted. In both cases, the `-D` option is used. The two different methods have the following syntax:

```
ipchains -D chain position
ipchains -D chain rule-specification
```

Specifying a Rule

Here comes the interesting part — how to specify a rule. Everything else is pretty much useless unless you can specify rules. There are many aspects to specifying a rule, just as there are many different things you can specify about a packet that will match the rule. You can specify things such as the source and destination addresses, the protocol used, and ports. Each aspect will be discussed in a separate section, but keep in mind that they can all be combined to form more complex rules.

Specifying the Source and Destination Address

The `-s` and `-d` options are used to specify the source and destination addresses, respectively. The source and destination address specifications both have the same syntax:

```
-s [!] address[/mask] [!] [port[:port]]
-d [!] address[/mask] [!] [port[:port]]
```

The addresses themselves can be specified in one of five ways. The easiest and most common way to specify a specific address is simply to give its fully qualified domain name (for example, `localhost` or www.gnu.org). The second way is to give the actual IP address (for example, `127.0.0.1` for `localhost` or `209.81.8.252` for www.gnu.org).

The other three ways allow you to specify groups of addresses. If you have a network named `localnet`, you can simply give the network name, similar to giving the domain name of a host. Otherwise, you can use a network address followed by a network mask or a plain number representing the number of 1s on the left side of the network mask. So `192.168.1.0/255.255.255.0` and `192.168.1.0/24` are equivalent and match any address from `192.168.1.1` to `192.168.1.255`.

> **Tip**
>
> You can specify any address with `0/0` (those are zeros). So, `-s 0/0` will match a packet coming from anywhere, and `-d 0/0` will match a packet going anywhere. This usually is not necessary, however, because it is the same as not specifying a source address (or destination address as the case may be).

The exclamation point (`!`) before the address and port inverts the sense of the address. That is to say, `-s 127.0.0.1` would match any packet whose source was `localhost`, and `-s ! 127.0.0.1` would match any packet whose source was *not* `localhost`. The exclamation point can be used with several different rule specification options to negate the sense of the option. This can be very convenient. For example, if the address of your local network is `192.168.1.0` and you want to match all packets destined for *another* network, you could specify the addresses like this: `-s 192.168.1.0 -d ! 192.168.1.0`. This matches any packet originating on your network that is not destined for it.

You can make things more precise by specifying ports or an ICMP type along with the address. You can see a list of the valid ICMP types by executing the command `ipchains -h icmp`. You can specify the port using a service name or a port number. You can also specify a range of ports using the syntax *lower_port:upper_port*. For example, you would specify all ports from 25 to 1023 as `25:1023`. If you omit the lower number, then it will include all ports from 0 to the upper number. If the upper number is omitted, it will include all ports from the lower number to 65535 (the highest port number available). For example, `:1023` includes all ports from 0 through 1023, and `1024:` includes all ports from 1024 through 65535. Simply using a colon (`:`), that is, omitting both the lower and upper numbers, is the same as specifying `0:65535` or not specifying a port.

> **Note**
>
> Ports can only be specified in combination with the TCP, UDP, and ICMP protocols.

> **Note**
>
> It is important to remember that, in general, the source and destination ports are not the same. For example, if you want to limit your local network's access to the Internet by only allowing users to connect to Web servers, you would not do it by allowing only packets whose source and destination port are 80 or www. You would omit the source port (or limit it to ports above 1023) and make the destination port 80. For example, with a local network at 192.168.1.0, you might set up a rule with the following addresses:
>
> -s 192.168.1.0/24 1024: -d ! 192.168.1.0 www
>
> Don't forget that you can only specify ports in conjunction with the TCP, UDP, or ICMP protocols. In this case, you would specify the TCP protocol along with the preceding address specifications.

> **Note**
>
> *Do not* block all ICMP type 3 packets (destination-unreachable). If you do, you will never get Host unreachable or No route to host errors. This is not a serious problem in and of itself, but it means that you will never find out that connections can't be completed because you won't get the message. The messages will just sit and wait until they time out.
>
> More serious, however, is the fact that these packets are used for MTU discovery. MTU discovery tries to figure out the size of the largest packet that can be sent without the packet being fragmented (avoiding fragmentation helps improve performance). It works by sending packets with the Don't Fragment bit set. If it receives a reply saying that fragmentation is needed but the Don't Fragment bit was set (ICMP type fragmentation-needed), it sends smaller and smaller packets until the packet goes through. The fragmentation-needed packet is a type of destination-unreachable packets. If it is blocked, the local host will never reduce the size of the packets it is sending, and network performance will be extremely slow or even stopped.

Specifying a Protocol

You can match packets of a specific protocol by using the `-p` option:

`-p [!] `*`protocol`*

protocol can be a protocol number, `tcp`, `udp`, `icmp`, any protocol listed in the file `/etc/protocols`, or `all`. It is not case sensitive, so `TCP` works just as well as `tcp`. Specifying `0` (zero) as the protocol number is the same as specifying `all`, which means that any protocol will match.

To make the example in the note in the last section complete, you would specify the TCP protocol along with the addresses like this:

`-s 192.168.1.0/24 1024: -d ! 192.168.1.0 www -p tcp`

Specifying an Interface

You can specify the name of an interface to match using the `-i` option:

`-i [!] `*`interface_name`*`[+]`

Running the command `ifconfig` will list all the interfaces that are up. At the very least, you will have the loopback interface, `lo`. The first Ethernet interface will be `eth0`. The second one will be `eth1`, and so on. A modem connection to the Internet will likely be `ppp0`.

The interface for packets traversing the `input` chain is the interface they came in on. For the `forward` and `output` chains, the interface is the interface they will be going out on. So if you want to match packets coming in from a certain interface, you need to do it in the `input` chain. To match packets going out on a certain interface, you can do it in the `forward` or `output` chain.

You can specify interfaces that aren't up or don't exist when the rule is specified. They simply won't be matched until the interface comes up. This is useful for interfaces like `ppp0`, which will only be up when the computer is connected to the Internet via the modem.

The plus sign (+) is a wildcard character. It allows you to match all interfaces with a given name (or part of a name). For example, `ppp+` will match all PPP interfaces, and `et+` will match all Ethernet interfaces as well as any other interface that begins with `et`.

Specifying SYN Packets

It can be useful to allow TCP connections in one direction only, for example, *to* a certain Web server but not *from* the Web server. It won't work to simply block all TCP packets coming from that server, however. Blocking all TCP packets from a machine will keep you from opening a connection to it, and will keep it from sending you any data, which is not quite what you want when connecting to a Web server. The solution is to block TCP SYN packets coming from the Web server. TCP SYN packets (or SYN packets for short) are special packets used to set up TCP connections. If you block SYN packets coming from the Web server, it won't be able to connect to your machine, but you will be able to connect to it. Blocking SYN packets to a machine will keep you from connecting to it.

You specify that a rule is to match SYN packets using the -y option. There are not arguments to this option. However, you can precede it with an exclamation point (!) to reverse its sense. This option can only be used when the protocol is set to TCP.

For example, you match all SYN packets coming from the machine 192.168.2.5 like this:

`-p tcp -s 192.168.2.5 -y`

You would match all TCP packets *except* SYN packets coming from the same machine like this:

`-p tcp -s 192.168.2.5 ! -y`

Handling Fragments

When a packet is too large to be sent across the network in one piece, it is broken up into fragments. These fragments are put together again at the receiving machine to get back the entire packet. This is generally acceptable; however, one side effect of fragmentation is that the header of the original packet is only placed in the first fragment. So rules that look at this information will only be able to find it in the first fragment; hence, the rest of the fragments won't match the rule. The information that will only be placed in the first fragment is the source and destination ports, ICMP type, ICMP code, and the TCP SYN flag.

It is usually OK to let second and later fragments through the firewall because they can't be reassembled at the receiving end if the first fragment is blocked by the firewall. However, there have been bugs that have allowed a machine to be crashed simply by sending fragments.

If your firewall is your network's only connection to the Internet or another network, the easiest and best solution is probably to compile the kernel with IP: Always Defragment enabled. This causes the firewall to assemble all fragments into the original packets before passing them on. This choice effectively eliminates the problem of fragments in the IP firewall chains.

If your firewall is not the only link to an external network, then you should not enable IP: Always Defragment. In that case, you can set up special rules that match second and later fragments using the `-f` option. Preceding the `-f` with an exclamation point (!) will match anything *but* second and later fragments. Recall, however, that rules intended to match fragments cannot look for the information only included in the first fragment.

For example, the following specification will match all second and later fragments coming from the machine `192.168.2.5`:

`-s 192.168.2.5 -f`

Specifying a Target

Each rule can have a target that can be one of the six special targets or a user-defined chain. A rule does not need to have a target, and there are cases where you would not put one. For example, if you simply wanted to keep track of the amount of traffic coming in from the first Ethernet interface, you could place a rule in the `input` chain that matches all packets with their interface set to `eth0`. Otherwise, most rules will have a target. If a rule does not have a target, even if it is matched, the filter will continue testing against the rest of the rules in the chain.

The target tells the filter what to do with the packet. The six built-in targets define special actions to be taken, such as denying a packet or masquerading it. Otherwise, if the target is a user-defined chain, the filter jumps to the beginning of that chain and proceeds to test the packet against the rules there. If it reaches the end of a user-defined chain, it starts where it left off in the previous chain.

For example, if a packet traversing the `input` chain matches rule 2, which has the user-defined chain `ppp` set as its target, the filter will jump to the beginning of the `ppp` chain and start testing against rules there. If any rules are matched there, the appropriate action is taken. If the end of the `ppp` chain is reached, the filter goes back to the `input` chain and starts testing against the rules there, again starting with rule number 3. Upon reaching the end of the `input` chain, the chain policy determines the fate of the packet.

You specify a target using the `-j` (jump) option:

`-j target`

For example, if you only want traffic from the machine `sally` to be forwarded through the firewall, you could set the policy for the `forward` chain to be DENY or REJECT and then add this rule to it:

`-s sally -j ACCEPT`

Or if you wanted to block traffic to the machine john, you could do that with the following rule:

```
-d john -j DENY
```

If you enabled IP: Transparent Proxy Support in your kernel, you can use the REDIRECT target in the `input` chain or user-defined chains. The REDIRECT target redirects packets to the local host (the firewall) at the original destination port or any specified port regardless of where it was headed originally. The syntax for specifying the REDIRECT target can be slightly different than for other targets:

```
-j REDIRECT [port]
```

If the port number is omitted, the packet is redirected to the port specified in the packet (the original port). Specifying 0 (zero) has the same effect as not specifying a port. Otherwise, the packets are all directed to the given port on the firewall.

Rules with Side Effects

In general, rules don't have any side effects other than changing the packet and byte counters and whatever the rule's target does to the packet. There are two options that will change the packet matching a rule in some way. The only one that's useful, though, is the `-t` option. The `-t` option is for modifying the TOS (Type Of Service) field in the IP header and has the following syntax:

```
-t and_mask xor_mask
```

When a packet matches a rule with this option, the TOS field is first bitwise ANDed with the *and_mask* and then bitwise XORed with the *xor_mask*. The *and_mask* and *xor_mask* are specified as 8-bit hexadecimal values.

The TOS field of the header is 4 bits that affect the way packets are treated. The four types of service that they specify are minimum delay, maximum throughput, maximum reliability, and minimum cost. Only one of them can be set at a time. Consequently, any rule that attempts to set two or more bits will be rejected. If there is a possibility of a rule setting more than one bit for certain packets, a warning will be printed to `stdout`, but it can be safely ignored if you know that that type of packets will never reach that rule. Table 21.3 lists the four types of service with the masks used to set them and typical uses for each.

Table 21.3 The TOS Bits and Values

Name	AND Mask	XOR Mask	Typical Uses
Minimum delay	0x01	0x10	FTP or telnet
Maximum throughput	0x01	0x08	ftp-data
Maximum reliability	0x01	0x04	SNMP
Minimum cost	0x01	0x02	NNTP

For example, if you frequently have telnet sessions while downloading data via FTP over a modem, you could set the Minimum Delay TOS bit for all packets going out on ppp0 and destined for the telnet port and the Maximum Throughput bit for packets destined for the ftp-data port. This can help improve throughput for the FTP data while reducing latency in your telnet sessions. You could do that with the following two commands:

```
# ipchains -A output -p tcp -d 0/0 telnet -t 0x01 0x10 -i ppp0
# ipchains -A output -p tco -d 0/0 ftp-data -t 0x01 0x08 -i ppp0
```

Logging Packets

You can log packets that match a rule by specifying the -l option with the rule. This will send some logging information about the matching packet to the system log. In general, you will not want to do this because if many packets match the rule, you will fill your system logs with a lot of data. It can be useful, though, if you want to look for certain exceptional events.

Checking the Firewall

Now that you know everything about specifying rules and building chains, you have set up a magnificent firewall and want to test it. A very nice feature about ipchains is that it allows you to see what will happen to a particular packet that enters the firewall. You specify a packet the same way that you specify rules. In particular, you must specify the source and destination addresses, the protocol, and the interface. If you specify TCP or UDP as the protocol, you must also specify a single (as opposed to a range) source and destination port. If you specify ICMP as the protocol, you must also specify an ICMP type and code. If the protocol is TCP, you can specify that the SYN flag is to be set using the -y option.

You use the `-C` option to check a packet against a chain:

`ipchains -C chain packet-specification`

Whereas the kernel normally starts testing a packet with the `input` chain, `ipchains` allows you to specify any chain to test it against.

For example, to test a TCP SYN packet coming from 192.168.2.1 port 60000 to 192.168.2.2 port www (80) on interface eth0 against the `input` chain, you would use the following command:

```
# ipchains -C input -p tcp -y -i eth0 -s 192.168.2.1 60000 -d 192.168.2.2 www
Packet accepted.
```

In this case, the packet was accepted.

Some Useful Examples

By now, you know most of what you need to know to use `ipchains` effectively to set up a firewall. However, seeing some examples of common and useful things to do with the firewall, and how to do them, may help solidify and clarify things in your mind, if they aren't already.

Protecting a Single Host

A firewall is generally designed to protect a network from another network. However, what if you only have one computer and use that to connect to the Internet via a modem? Don't worry. You're in luck. A simple firewall setup can still help protect you and optimize transfer performance across the PPP connection.

You can use the `input` chain to control what kinds of packets come into your computer. For example, if you don't want anyone to be able to connect to your computer, you can block all SYN packets coming in on the `ppp0` interface.

You can use the `output` chain to optimize certain types of data transfers (you can't really do that in the `input` chain). For example, you can set it up so that `telnet` and `www` packets are set for minimum delay to help keep things responsive. You can also set it up so that FTP transfers put through as much as possible by setting the maximum throughput TOS bit.

To start with, let's define a new chain called `ppp-in`. We'll put all the rules pertaining to the `ppp0` interface (the connection to the Internet via the modem) that we want checked in the `input` chain there.

```
# ipchains -N ppp-in
```

Now, when a packet comes in, it will start with the `input` chain, so you need to put a rule there telling it to jump to the `ppp-in` chain if the packet came from the `ppp0` interface:

```
# ipchains -A input -i ppp0 -j ppp-in
```

Now you can put all the rules about incoming packets there. For example, if you don't want to allow anyone to connect to your machine, you can deny or reject all SYN packets. You would do that with the following command:

```
# ipchains -A ppp-in -p tcp -s 0/0 -y -j REJECT
```

However, simply denying or rejecting them all can cause problems with FTP. There are two types of FTP: active and passive. Passive FTP only makes connections to the FTP server. Active FTP makes a connection to the FTP server for sending commands, but the FTP server makes a connection back to your machine to send back data. This means that if you block all SYN packets, you won't be able to use active FTP because the FTP server won't be able to connect to your machine to send back data. Most Web browsers use passive FTP, however, so you would be okay there if that's all you use for FTPing. Otherwise, you can get around this problem by blocking all SYN packets except those coming from the ftp-data port:

```
# ipchains -A ppp-in -p tcp -s 0/0 ! ftp-data -y -j REJECT
```

This will reject any SYN packet coming from anywhere other than the `ftp-data` port. Now nobody can make a TCP connection to your computer from the Internet unless they do it from the `ftp-data` port. Most likely, only FTP servers will do that.

If you didn't want anyone to ping your computer (possibly subjecting it to the "Ping of Death" attack), you could reject or deny any `echo-request` packets like this:

```
# ipchains -A ppp-in -p icmp -s 0/0 echo-request -j REJECT
```

By default, the policy for the `input` chain will be ACCEPT. In that case, you need to specify everything that you *don't* want to get through. You could also do it the other way around and change the default policy to DENY or REJECT and then specify everything you *do* want to get through. Which way you go depends mostly on what you do or don't want to get through.

To help optimize things a bit, let's create a new chain called `ppp-out` that will go in the `output` chain:

```
# ipchains -N ppp-out
```

All packets destined for the `ppp0` interface must pass through this chain:

```
# ipchains -A output -i ppp0 -j ppp-out
```

You can add rules to help speed up responsiveness with Web traffic and telnet:

```
# ipchains -A ppp-out -p tcp -d 0/0 www -t 0x01 0x10
# ipchains -A ppp-out -p tcp -d 0/0 telnet -t 0x01 0x10
```

And lower the cost of FTP, mail, and news transfers:

```
# ipchains -A ppp-out -p tcp -d 0/0 ftp-data -t 0x01 0x02
# ipchains -A ppp-out -p tcp -d 0/0 pop-3 -t 0x01 0x02
# ipchains -A ppp-out -p tcp -d 0/0 nntp -t 0x01 0x02
```

Protecting a Network with Valid IP Addresses

If you are setting up a firewall on a network that has valid IP addresses (for example, you have applied for and obtained a domain from InterNIC or another appropriate agency), then your local network has effectively become part of the Internet. The key to securing your network will be to decide what types of packets you want to let in and out of your network. If you will have a very lenient policy (that is, not much will be restricted), it may be easiest to simply forward packets by default and then specify which ones you don't want to get through. If you will have a strict policy (that is, not much will get through), then it may be easiest to deny or reject packets by default in the forward chain and then specify which ones you will let through.

You will also need to look at what kinds of machines you will have on your local network and the types of functions they will perform. For example, will they all be Linux boxes, Windows NT or 95 boxes, Macintoshes? What types of vulnerabilities does each of these machines have, and what types of problems could they cause others on the Internet? For example, you wouldn't want someone in your company to be able to perform an IP Spoofing attack. Will you be running mail, Web, or news servers? You need to allow (limited) access to these machines and allow them to have (limited) access to the Internet while protecting them from unauthorized access or malicious attacks.

Depending on your setup, protecting your network can get quite complicated. If you only have a few computers with users connecting to the Web, sending and receiving e-mail, and reading news, you can keep things tight pretty easily and simply. However, if you have different servers behind the firewall, lots of users with different levels of access to various services inside and outside the firewall, and machines you want to protect from access from the outside, your firewall setup will likely be very complicated. In this case, your needs are beyond the scope of this book, and you should consider getting a good book on computer and network security and/or consulting a security professional.

In this case, let's stick with a simple scenario. You have a small home office network with four computers. You have one machine permanently connected to the Internet via a cable modem that hooks up to your first Ethernet interface, `eth0`, and you want to use that machine as a gateway. That is, your three other machines are connected to the gateway/firewall machine via your second Ethernet interface, `eth1`, through a hub, and traffic goes through it to get to or from the Internet. You have paid a few dollars extra so that your ISP will give you four valid IP addresses that you have assigned to your machines. Your ISP handles all your DNS worries for you, but you must set up a mail server and a Web server on the second and third machines (and not the firewall). You use the last machine to work on. The only traffic that needs to get through the firewall is Web and mail traffic to the two servers, and Web and telnet traffic from your work machine. Your hosts are named `gateway`, `mail`, `www`, and `work`. (This is starting to sound like an adventure game—do you want to go forward, left or right?)

First let's create an input chain for `eth0`:

```
# ipchains -N eth0-in
# ipchains -A input -i eth0 -j eth0-in
```

Now, let's say that you don't want to allow anyone to actually connect to your firewall machine from the outside. To avoid that, we can reject all SYN packets coming in on the first Ethernet interface and destined for `gateway`:

```
# ipchains -A eth0-in -p tcp -d gateway -y -j REJECT
```

Note that this does not keep you from connecting to your firewall from one of the machines in your home office because they will be connecting through the *second* Ethernet interface.

We don't want anyone to send any of the computers a Ping of Death, so we simply deny all incoming ping packets from the Internet:

```
# ipchains -A eth0-in -p icmp -s 0/0 echo-request -j DENY
```

The only connections we want to allow to the mail server are SMTP connections to send us mail, so we stop all other connections:

```
# ipchains -A eth0-in -p tcp -d mail ! smtp -y -j REJECT
```

Likewise, we only want Web connections to our Web server:

```
# ipchains -A eth0-in -p tcp -d www ! www -y -j REJECT
```

We want to be able to telnet in to our work machine and use active FTP, so we reject SYN packets unless they are directed to the telnet port or are coming from the ftp-data port. We do this by creating a new chain with three rules: two that allow connections to be made for telnet and active FTP, and a third that rejects all others.

```
# ipchains -N work-connect
# ipchains -A eth0-in -p tcp -d work -y -j work-connect
```

```
# ipchains -A work-connect -p tcp -d work telnet -y -j ACCEPT
# ipchains -A work-connect -p tcp -s 0/0 ftp-data -y -j ACCEPT
# ipchains -A work-connect -j REJECT
```

> **Tip**
>
> User-defined chains can't have policies, but a policy can be easily simulated by simply adding a rule to the end of the chain that matches any packet and jumps to the special target you want for a policy. For example, the last rule above will match any packet and then go to the REJECT target. If one of the first two rules matches, then the "policy rule" will not be reached. Otherwise, the packet will be rejected, as though we had specified REJECT as the chain's policy.

To be on the safe side, we only want our mail server to connect to other mail servers and our DNS server (named nameserver for simplicity):

```
# ipchains -N eth1-in
# ipchains -A input -i eth1 -j eth1-in
# ipchains -N mail-connect
# ipchains -A eth1-in -p tcp -s mail -y -j mail-connect
# ipchains -A mail-connect -p tcp -d nameserver domain -j ACCEPT
# ipchains -A mail-connect -p tcp -d 0/0 smtp ACCEPT
# ipchains -A mail-connect -j REJECT
```

We don't want our Web server connecting to anything except our DNS server:

```
# ipchains -N www-dns-connect
# ipchains -A eth1-in -p tcp -s www -y -j www-dns-connect
# ipchains -A www-dns-connect -p tcp -d nameserver domain -j ACCEPT
# ipchains -A www-dns-connect -j REJECT
```

We'll let our work machine connect to anything it wants.

While this would help protect your machines from unauthorized access, it is really only a start. All we did here was limit who could connect to what and stop the Ping of Death attack. It may also be worthwhile to see what other types of packets you don't want going through your firewall and adding rules for those as well.

> **Note**
>
> Don't forget that even if the forward chain will accept packets by default, you must enable IP forwarding in the kernel before it will forward packets between two or more interfaces. The easiest way to do that is to add the following line to the file /etc/sysconfig/network:
>
> IPFORWARDING=yes

IP Masquerading

It is possible to set up a private network with IP addresses set aside for private use (see Chapter 11 for more information about private IP addresses). These IP addresses are not valid IP addresses for the Internet and cannot be used on the Internet. The problem then is how do you connect your private network with IP addresses that can't be used on the Internet to the Internet? The answer is by using IP masquerading.

IP masquerading occurs when one machine (the firewall machine) has at least two interfaces. One interface is connected to the Internet and has a valid IP address. This can be a modem connection to the Internet through your ISP. The ISP gives you a valid IP address when you log on. The other interface hooks up to your internal network and has an IP address valid for your private network. The firewall is set as the default route or gateway for the other machines on the network, so when they have traffic destined for the Internet, it gets sent to the firewall to be forwarded. The firewall machine then makes a copy of the packet and "masquerades" it by saying that it came from it instead of the actual machine that it came from (hence keeping the private IP address off the Internet). It remembers what packets were masqueraded, so that when it receives a reply, it makes a copy of the returning packet and sends it back to the machine that started the whole thing off. The local machine thinks it's talking to the machine on the Internet, but the machine on the Internet thinks it's talking to the firewall.

This can be useful in several different ways. The most obvious one is that you don't need to get a whole class of IP addresses to set up a private network that you want to have access to the Internet. You don't even need to get a bunch of static IP addresses from your ISP.

For example, I have two local networks using the network addresses `192.168.1.0` and `192.168.2.0`. I only have five machines, but I have two Ethernet cards in the firewall one for machines with 100Mb cards and the other for machines with only 10Mb cards. Using private IP addresses, I can network all the machines together, and using IP masquerading, I can give them all access to the Internet via the firewall machine that just dials in when I need it.

Another reason to do it this way is that, in some ways, your network will be more secure. This is because no outside machine can connect directly to a machine on the private network except the firewall. All the machines behind the firewall are effectively hidden from the Internet while still having access to it. The only way for someone to get into your network is to connect to the firewall first and then go from there. For example, to telnet to an internal machine, a person would first need to telnet to the firewall and then from the firewall to the internal machine.

There is, however, an attack called "IP Spoofing" where a person on the outside sends in packets with doctored source and destination addresses so that it appears that the packet came from inside the network. They can't connect to any machines on the inside (because no packets will come back to them), but they can send packets in that could cause trouble with buggy software. For example, it could send in a whole bunch of SYN packets (called a SYN Flooding attack) making a machine think that someone is trying to set up a whole bunch of connections. This can cripple a machine by using all its resources. Luckily, there are ways to protect against these kinds of attacks. For example, you could add a rule to the input chain that makes sure that no packets coming in off the interface connected to the Internet claim to have IP addresses from the private network. For example, if you are using the network address 192.168.1.0 for your private network and are connecting to the Internet through the ppp0 interface, the following rule would protect your from an IP spoofing attack:

```
# ipchains -A input -i ppp0 -s 192.168.1.0/24 -j DENY
```

There are drawbacks to IP masquerading, however. Because no host from the outside can connect to a host on the inside (the other direction is okay, of course), certain protocols don't work very well. For example, there are two types of FTP: passive and active. With active FTP, the client makes a connection to the server to exchange commands and responses, but the server makes a connection back to the client machine to send the files. With IP masquerading in use, the FTP server won't be able to make a connection with the client machine, unless the user is FTPing from the firewall. Active FTP is the default for most FTP clients (for example, when you run `ftp` from the command line). With passive FTP, however, the client is always the one making the connections, so passive FTP works without any hitches. Most Internet browsers use passive FTP.

People are actively working at trying to fix the problems with IP masquerading, however. For example, there are several kernel modules that you can load that help deal with certain problematic protocols. You can find them in the directory `/lib/modules/2.2.5/ipv4`. They are all the modules with "masq" in their name somewhere. The name of the module generally offers a key to what the module was designed to do. For example, ip_masq_irc is for helping masquerade the Internet Relay Chat protocol.

Setting up your firewall to use IP masquerading is really easy. After you have configured your kernel correctly (see the first part of this chapter—that would be the only hard part), you set up rules in the `forward` chain that have MASQ set as their target for all the packets that you want to masquerade. In my case, it's very simple. Any packets that are from one of the local networks and not destined for a local network are masqueraded.

```
# ipchains -A forward -s 192.168.0.0/16 -d ! 192.168.0.0/16 -j MASQ
```

You can be more selective, of course, and only masquerade certain types of packets.

> **Note**
>
> Just as for forwarding packets with valid IP addresses, in order for IP masquerading to work, you must enable IP forwarding in the kernel.

Saving and Restoring the Firewall

Two utility scripts will save and restore your firewall for you. They can be very handy because the firewall needs to be set up each time the machine boots, and it can be difficult to remember all the commands you used to set up your firewall, so that you can place them in a system startup script.

The `ipchains-save` script allows you to save the firewall setup in a format that can be used by `ipchains-restore` to restore your firewall setup. They have the following syntax:

```
ipchains-save [-v] [chain]
ipchains-restore [-f]
```

`ipchains-save` sends its output to `stdout` and tells you what it's doing on `stderr`, so to save your firewall setup to a file, you redirect `stdout` to a file:

```
# ipchains-save > file_name
```

`ipchains-save` will save the entire firewall setup, unless you specify a chain, in which case it saves only the specified chain. For example, the following command will save the input chain to the file `firewallInput`:

```
# ipchains-save input > firewallInput
```

The `-v` option causes it to print the rules out to `stderr` as it saves them.

`ipchains-restore` takes its input from `stdin`, so you would restore the firewall setup stored in the file myFirewall with the following command:

```
# ipchains-restore < myFirewall
```

If `ipchains-restore` comes across a user-defined chain, it will check first to see if it already exists. If it does, `ipchains-restore` will ask you if the chain should be flushed, replacing it with the setup stored in the file, or skipped, not changing it. If you specify the `-f` option, you will not be prompted; the chain will be flushed and replaced.

Further Reading

For more information on firewalls and TCP/IP networking, see the Firewall HOWTO, the Ipchains HOWTO, the Ethernet HOWTO, and the NET-3 HOWTO. These all come with OpenLinux in the online documentation or can be viewed on the Web at `http://metalab.unc.edu/LDP/`. A few IP masquerading HOWTOs can also be found on the Internet. Finding a good book on computer and network security is also highly recommended.

Summary

In this chapter, you learned about filtering firewalls and how to set them up using `ipchains`. You also learned about IP masquerading and how to set it up using `ipchains`.

Running Proxies

CHAPTER 22

IN THIS CHAPTER

- Understanding Proxy Technology 508
- Proxy Server Software 511
- Putting Proxy Servers to Work 513

Modern network administrators know that connecting a local area network to the Internet or to other high-volume networks used by strangers is a somewhat risky business, with serious security concerns. An additional problem with Internet access is IP address availability: Since every computer accessing the Internet must have its own IP address, the pool of available numbers must be enormous in order to handle all the traffic. Unfortunately, that pool of numbers just isn't available using today's most common numbering scheme, so alternative measures need to be found.

Yet another consideration about Internet access is whether every machine on a local area network has the capability to fend for itself in such a very insecure environment. Since configuring each and every machine for maximum security is a very time-consuming and difficult task, with ongoing preventative maintenance adding to the burden, a better solution must be found.

Small offices and home users also often face the need to operate several local hosts through a single Internet connection. Since most ISPs assign a single IP address, conventional setups forbid several machines from sharing that Internet access in real time.

One solution is a packet-filtering firewall, as covered in the previous chapter. Another option, however, that may prove simpler and more effective in some ways is a proxy server.

There are a few proxy software options available, each with its merits and each with its own configuration requirements. Although they can be quite distinct from each other, they perform essentially the same function: All machines on a local area network that connect to the Internet appear on the Internet as the proxy server (with the proxy's IP address) and not as themselves.

In this chapter, you will learn how to configure your Caldera OpenLinux 2.3 machine as a proxy server, which will allow several local hosts to safely access an Internet connection through it.

Understanding Proxy Technology

In the computer security world there is no small amount of debate as to what constitutes a firewall—its particular and ideal qualities, configurations, and so on. A large part of that debate includes the issue of proxies: to what extent a proxy server is a firewall, and what sorts of firewalls exist without proxies. There are lots of differing opinions on this topic and, as often happens, the discussion has largely taken on religious qualities to its participants. Thankfully, the specifics of that religious warfare are beyond the scope of this discussion.

Suffice it to say that proxies can be used to create a firewall. It is entirely dependent on the end purpose and total setup of the box in question whether any particular proxy server is actually a firewall. Proxies may also be used in combination with other types of firewalls (notably packet-filtering firewalls and their various derivatives—"stateful" or dynamic packet filters). Some people contend that the best firewalls can be made of these combined technologies, which can provide "defense in depth"—multiple layers of security preventing attackers from getting into the internal network.

Proxy servers need not act as firewalling devices at all, however. They can be purely authentication devices, providing the enforcement of networking policy on who can go where and when, without being fully hardened against attack or truly intended to provide that protection for clients and servers on either side of it. They can also be used as caching devices that store the data retrieved from requested sites and serve it in response to subsequent requests from clients instead of going out on the Internet again and wasting precious bandwidth.

In summary, to a large extent the purpose of your proxy and the specifics of how you set it up determine whether it might serve as a firewall. You can use totally inappropriate software to build your proxy and render it insecure and useless as a security device right from the start. It is more likely that you won't pay close enough attention to the details and will end up with a server that could be a firewall but isn't. If you don't plan for your box to be secure, you can be certain it won't be.

> **Note**
>
> It is important to keep in mind that firewalls may include other important features such as logging, intrusion detection systems, encrypting, and tunneling technologies. Again, the distinction is largely a matter of purpose, policy, and setup. Labeling something as a firewall or not a firewall merely on the basis of a particular function ignores the real issues involved.

The nice thing about proxies is that you can turn off routing. With packet filters, you have to route packets between the interfaces. Security professionals always fear that a small mistake in the routing rules or a small failing in the operating system itself will lead to harmful packets getting inside the network. In the worst-case scenario, the routing fails due to a routing/firewalling rule problem or OS failure, and then ALL packets to and from the Internet are allowed, a so-called "fail open" event.

This is practically impossible in a proxy with routing turned off. No packets are passed between interfaces except those accepted on one interface and then re-initiated on the other interface by the proxy. And even that is allowed only by those services for which the proxy is configured. That said, proxy firewall failure can still lead to disastrous results if set up improperly, and the need for a protocol-aware proxy for each service can be too limiting for an organization to work under. This is why many firewalling devices and products are moving to hybrid proxy and filtering designs.

When a machine is set up as a proxy, it is in fact a server that will have one or more machines using it as a proxy client to access the Internet. While the proxy software is installed on the server, it may not be necessary to install proxy software on clients, nor is it necessary to have Internet or external entities treat your network connection in any different way.

Let's consider how a proxy server works in simple terms. First, the proxy server makes a TCP/IP connection to an Internet or external resource on behalf of the client. As far as the other end of the Internet connection is concerned, it is in contact only with the proxy server and knows nothing about the client.

As a result, a client of circuit-level proxies. The main difference between them is the type of traffic they proxy for, or the type of data they work with. SOCKS is an example of a circuit-level proxy, and Squid and the TIS proxies are examples of application proxies. It is important to understand, however, that one of these is not exclusive of the others. It is possible to have one firewall implementing packet-filtering, circuit-level, and application-level proxies.

A circuit-level proxy such as SOCKS is concerned with only its own protocol for authenticating, routing decisions, and so on. It doesn't really care at all about what other protocol is involved. In a sense what SOCKS does is wrap a request for a particular service inside a SOCKS request. The SOCKS request is then evaluated according to the policies of the SOCKS proxy: IP numbers or domain names, usernames and passwords, the interface on which the request arrived, routing rules, and so on. SOCKS is a very generic proxying protocol. Any service that can be wrapped inside a SOCKS request can generally be used by a client.

This has the great advantage of enabling you to allow many different services on your network, while setting policy (which users can utilize which services) in a single place—the SOCKS server. The downside to this is that most software is not SOCKS aware. Therefore, any software package needs to be either rewritten to use the SOCKS service, or some type of "shim" software must be used to wrap the original software's TCP/IP requests in SOCKS requests. Dealing with shim software can sometimes be a painful and brain-wracking experience.

Application proxies actually "understand" the protocol that is being spoken to them, and they then relay the client's request to the intended recipient on the Internet. These proxies not only provide the protection against malicious packets that all proxies do by initiating separate connections, but they also protect against malicious attacks inside the application protocol itself. They do this because they understand the language that the application is speaking, and they know what should be said and when.

For example, say you have a proxy for SMTP. Because the proxy knows about the SMTP protocol, it can stop attacks that use the protocol itself, for example overly long message header lines, attempts to invoke programs from subject lines, and so forth. Indeed, many proxies that are used in security implement a "dumbed-down" version of the protocol they proxy, so that only the specific information they know they can verify will be let through.

For proxy server administrators, a variety of tools and techniques exists to help tune and control such things as content, host and domain accessibility, and logging of all transactions. Further, user authorization (incoming and outgoing) can be tested, and a user's sessions can be documented and logged for use in handling system abuse.

Proxy Server Software

Of the many proxy software packages available today, three in particular stand out: SOCKS, TIS, and Squid. Your choice from among these three proxies will depend on a combination of financial resources, internal network services, and end user needs.

SOCKS

Without question, some of the most popular proxy software is based on the SOCKS protocol. SOCKS stands for "SOCK-et-S," apparently an internal name that has stuck with the protocol. (All programmers seem to enjoy amusing themselves with their program naming.) SOCKS was developed by the NEC Corporation, and NEC provides the reference implementations available at http://www.socks.nec.com. The source is available for download at no cost.

There are two publicly available versions of the protocol: version 4 and version 5. NEC continues to develop version 5 in its implementation, and that is what many current products use. Version 5 is a more advanced version of the protocol that, in addition to SOCKS over TCP, also works with UDP and proxies DNS requests as well. Version 4 proxies only TCP and also requires access to DNS servers inside the firewall to resolve hostnames. Some products, notably versions of Netscape Navigator and Communicator, support only version 4, largely due to licensing issues. Version 5 is the one to go with if you have a choice. You should note that the licensing of NEC's version is not open however, and, while it is a good product, you should be certain you meet its licensing requirements before you use it.

Another well-developed SOCKS v4/v5 product is Dante, developed by Inferno Nettverk in Norway. This is available at http://www.inet.no/dante/. Full source code is available with a BSD-style license. Inferno also packages its source in an RPM-friendly way, so you can build a binary RPM from the tarballs by typing

```
rpm -ta dante-VERSION.tar.gz.
```

There are still several versions of the original NEC reference software for the SOCKS version 4 server. Versions up to 4.2.2 and the 4.3 betas (which implement SOCKS version 4A with DNS resolution like version 5) are publicly available. These can be found on Sunsite, mirrors, and other FTP archives. These are getting on in years, though, and are not being developed any more. If you want more detailed knowledge of the SOCKS protocol, these are good examples, but you may have considerable difficulty building and working with this code.

SOCKS offers the following assets:

- Proxy clients "hidden" behind the server
- "Transparency" to other network systems
- Simple network security policy implementation on one machine
- Flexible filtering and screening of traffic from both directions
- Comparatively easy configuration

TIS

Another strong proxy software package is the TIS (Trusted Information System) Firewall Toolkit. This is available at http://www.tis.com/fwtk/ in source code form and uses a proprietary licensing arrangement instead of the GNU Public License. Registration is mandatory prior to download.

TIS differs from SOCKS in several key areas:

- Configuration is significantly more complex but versatile.
- It rides on top of designated firewalls.
- It is comprised of separate protocol proxies.
- It adds a layer of user interface that may hinder local transparency.
- It is very secure.

Squid

Recently, an Open Source proxy software package called Squid has emerged as a powerful tool for advanced users. Squid, available at http://www.squid-cache.org in source code, is more than a program for handling client Internet transactions, since it also integrates a robust caching technology that vastly improves proxy server performance for large local area networks.

The Squid proxy software program is designed to handle requests for Internet resources that client users want to download, then handle the transaction transparently. Squid then streams the information to the client machine but keeps a copy for itself in a cache—so that if the user seeks the page again, it is read from the local cache at a much higher speed than if the request was sent again across the World Wide Web.

Squid is designed to handle today's chief Internet protocols: HTTP, FTP, WAIS, Secure Socket Layers, and Gopher. As of recently, Squid is not suitable for NNTP, POP, or streaming media such as RealAudio and other UDP-type resources.

While Squid is at its best at caching relatively static Internet resources, it has to update its caches routinely for dynamic sites, so it should be noted that some highly changeable Web sites may not seem particularly faster under a Squid proxy.

Squid's chief qualities are

- Proxy services as with SOCKS
- Caching of Internet resource data for faster local response
- Capability to coexist with TIS's HTTP firewall proxy or SOCKS
- Significantly more complex to configure and implement
- Handles large volumes better than SOCKS

Putting Proxy Servers to Work

The first issue to consider when contemplating the installation of a proxy server system is the nature of the local area network. For home users who wish to have two or more PCs access the Internet through a cable modem or other high-speed residential hookup, installing SOCKS onto a Caldera OpenLinux 2.3 machine is a good choice and requires only a bit of networking background.

For commercial users already employing a firewall, the SOCKS option is available, but it doesn't measure up to TIS or Squid when contemplating processing large numbers of clients or Internet transactions.

Putting SOCKS to Work

SOCKS is an umbrella proxy server that conducts transactions in HTTP, FTP, and other protocols, all under one roof. This is in contrast to TIS, for example, which breaks the protocols up into discrete areas of responsibility, so that it is necessary to configure a proxy service for the World Wide Web, FTP, the ARPA/Berkeley "r" commands (`rlogin`, `rsh`, `rcp`), and other protocols. SOCKS is very easy to set up; there are really only two configuration files to be concerned with after installation. The first is the file `sockd.conf`, which is the "butler at the door" for Internet access.

The `sockd.conf` file contains pass and block lines, each to be customized according to IP address ranges. To bar an IP range from access, the deny line would contain that number range. Similarly, allowing only a certain range of IP addresses is also possible. An additional number can be applied exactly like a netmask to further tune the permit and deny IP ranges.

We will look at the Dante SOCKS package, which is freely available Open Source software and is extremely simple to get running. For the RPM version, simply log in as `root` and type

```
# rpm -ta dante-VERSION.tar.gz
```

Compiling the old-fashioned way is nearly as simple, because it uses autoconfig. Simply untar the package and type

```
# ./configure
# make
# make install
```

The file `/etc/sockd.conf` (in the Dante implementation; it is called `socksd.conf` in the NEC version) configures how the SOCKS server itself runs, who it allows in, and where they can go. An annotated example of a working Dante `sockd.conf` file is shown below. You should note that this is a simple example that will get you a working sockd. It does not use some of the advanced features of SOCKS, such as authentication. You will want to refer to your documentation and man pages for more advanced configurations.

```
# /etc/sockd.conf - Example configuration file for the Dante SOCKS server.

# Log information via syslog
logoutput: syslog
# It can also log to stderr, stdout, or a file (as shown here)
#logoutput: /var/log/sockd.log

# The server can be made to bind to only one address and port - very
# useful in a multihomed (multiple network interfaces) setup.
internal: 192.168.7.1 port = 1080
```

```
# all outgoing connections from the server will use the ipaddress
# 192.168.7.1
external: 192.168.7.1

# Available ways to authenticate, and their order of preference
#method: username none
method: none


###
### PRIVILEGE ASSIGNMENT - IMPORTANT
###

# UserID the server runs under when it needs to perform privileged operations
# (such as binding to privileged sockets, writing to files, etc.)
user.privileged: root

# when running as usual, it will use the unprivileged userid of "socks".
user.notprivileged: socks


###
### MISC OPTIONS
###

# how many seconds can pass from when a client connects til it has
# sent us it's request?  Adjust according to your network performance
# and methods supported.
connecttimeout: 30    # on a lan, this should be enough if method is "none".


###
### RULES SECTION
###

# The actual rules.  There are two kinds and they work at different levels.
#
# The rules prefixed with "client" are checked first and say who is allowed
# and who is not allowed to speak/connect to the server.  I.e the
# ip range containing possibly valid clients.
# It is especially important that these only use ipaddresses, not hostnames,
# for security reasons.
#
# The rules that do not have a "client" prefix are checked later, when the
# client has sent its request and are used to evaluate the actual
# request.
#
# The "to:" in the "client" context gives the address the connection
# is accepted on, i.e the address the socksserver is listening on, or
# just "0.0.0.0/0" for any address the server is listening on.
#
```

```
# The "to:" in the non-"client" context gives the destination of the clients
# socksrequest.
#
# "from:" is the source address in both contexts.


###
### CLIENT RULES
###

# All clients connect from our lan 192.168.7.0/24
client pass {
        from: 192.168.7.0/24 to: 0.0.0.0/0
}

# drop everyone else as soon as we can and log the connect, they are not
# on our net and have no business connecting to us.  This is the default
# but if you give the rule yourself, you can specify details.
client block {
        from: 0.0.0.0/0 to: 0.0.0.0/0
        log: connect error
}


###
### RULES
###

# you probably don't want people connecting to loopback addresses,
# who knows what could happen then.
block {
        from: 0.0.0.0/0 to: 127.0.0.0/8
        log: connect error
}

# If you want to use normal (not PASV) ftp you need this.  Note it does allow
# clients to bind to addresses on your server (for example ftp-data for ftp.)
# You don't need this if all you use are web browsers
pass {
        from: 0.0.0.0/0 to: 0.0.0.0/0
        command: bind bindreply
        log: connect error data iooperation
}

# everyone from our internal network, 192.168.7.0/24 is allowed to use
# tcp and udp for everything else.
pass {
        from: 192.168.7.0/24 to: 0.0.0.0/0
        protocol: tcp udp
}
```

```
# last line, block everyone else.  This is the default but if you provide
# one   yourself you can specify your own logging/actions
block {
        from: 0.0.0.0/0 to: 0.0.0.0/0
        log: connect error
}
```

The second configuration file used by SOCKS is the `socks.conf` file, which is concerned with matching desired IP ranges or addresses to either direct resources, such as those within the local area network, or those on the Internet requiring proxy handling.

By tuning the `socks.conf` file's direct entries, no access beyond the local area network is allowed or required. If an Internet connection is requested, the file's deny entries are consulted and the connection is rejected according to the administrator's specifications. Lastly, if the Internet connection is acceptable, the `socks.conf` file directs the request to the proxy server.

An annotated working example of `socks.conf` follows:

```
# /etc/socks.conf - Configuration file for Dante SOCKS clients.

###
### GLOBAL CONFIGURATION SETTINGS
###

# DNS    hostname resolution

resolveprotocol: udp     # Use UDP to resolve names    default

#resolveprotocol: tcp    # Use TCP to resolve names   set this if your
                         # SOCKS server only supports Version 4.
#resolveprotocol: fake   # No DNS is available, just fake it.


###
### ROUTES
###

# Route going to a local nameserver.  This could improve performance, but
# is commented out, because we don't have a local nameserver.
#route {
#       from: 0.0.0.0/0 to: 192.168.7.1/32 port = domain via: direct
#}

# have a route making all connections to loopback addresses be direct.
route {
        from: 0.0.0.0/0   to: 127.0.0.0/8  via: direct
        command: connect udpassociate # everything but bind, bind confuses us.
}
```

```
# Addresses to the local lan go direct
route {
        from: 0.0.0.0/0 to: 192.168.7.0/24 via: direct
}

# Traffic to the rest of the universe goes out the SOCKS server at
# 192.168.7.1   If you don't have internal DNS setup, you should give
# the server as an IP number.
route {
        from: 0.0.0.0/0 to: 0.0.0.0/0 via: 192.168.7.1 port = 1080
        protocol: tcp udp                      # server supports tcp and udp.
        proxyprotocol: socks_v4 socks_v5 # server supports socks v4 and v5.
        method: none #username              # we are willing to authenticate via
                                            # method "none", not "username".
}
```

For the home user, a SOCKS server may be a good choice for Internet access over one connection, but it has its drawbacks. Client hosts on the inside of a SOCKS proxy server are effectively shut off from the outer world, meaning that such common World Wide Web features as streaming multimedia, chat sessions, or even direct Telnet access may be impossible. It should be noted that SOCKS v5 deals with many of these issues, but the administrator must be aware that trial and error may be required to implement some otherwise common features of a typical single-machine Internet connection.

Putting TIS to Work

If we think of SOCKS as a relatively easy proxy software to setup and configure, TIS's Firewall ToolKit (FWTK) is its snarling pit bull counterpart. TIS requires a great deal of attention to detail and testing. If set up properly, however, it serves as an extremely secure proxy/firewall. The FWTK is well designed, small, and verifiably correct. If you think you have the considerable skill needed to get it compiled and working properly, TIS is likely a good place to begin your ascent to firewall guru.

You should note that FWTK is not an Open Source project, and it has considerable restriction on its use. Part of the license reads as follows:

1. LICENSE.

    TIS grants you a non-exclusive, non-transferable license for the TIS Firewall Toolkit programs (the "FWTK") and its associated documentation, subject to your acceptance of all of the terms and conditions contained in this software license. This license permits you to use, copy, and modify the FWTK solely for the internal, non-commercial, use of your organization. The FWTK, if modified, must carry prominent notices stating that changes have been made, and the dates of any such changes. All rights not expressly granted herein are reserved to TIS.

2. LIMITATIONS ON LICENSE.

   a. You may only use, copy, and modify the FWTK as expressly provided for in this Agreement. You may not redistribute or otherwise make available the FWTK to another person, organization or entity. You must reproduce and include this Agreement, and TIS' copyright notices on any copy and its associated documentation even though said use, as required by this license, is restricted to your internal use only.

   b. The use of the FWTK is limited to your internal, non-commercial use only. Neither the FWTK, in its entirety, nor any part or element of the FWTK, is being licensed to you for use with, or in, any hardware, firmware, software, program or other product (i) which is sold; (ii) for which you receive any revenue; or (iii) which is provided by you (even for free) in conjunction with any commercial activity.

   c. You are prohibited from disclosing to any other person, organization or entity the on-line location of the FWTK source code and/or documentation which will be provided to you following your acceptance of the terms and conditions of this license.

Building, Installing, and Configuring TIS

Once you have the latest FWTK, you have to build it, which requires knowing a good bit about your system. See the diffs to `Makefile.config.linux` and `firewall.h` included below (for V2.1 release of March 2, 1998). A *diff* shows the differences between one file and another—lines from the old file are marked with a minus sign, and lines from the new file are marked with a plus sign.

Move `Makefile.config` to `Makefile.config.bak`, and copy `Makefile.config.linux` to `Makefile.config`. Then make the following changes to `Makefile.config` (change the lines with a – to match the lines with a ¶):

```
# Destination directory for installation of binaries
-DEST=     /usr/local/etc
+DEST=     /usr/local/tis

# Names of any auxiliary libraries your system may require (e.g., -lsocket)
# If you want to link against a resolver library, specify it here.
-AUXLIB=
+AUXLIB= -lresolv -lcrypt

-LDFL= -g -static
+LDFL= -g #-static

# Location of the fwtk sources [For #include by any external tools needing it]
```

```
-FWTKSRCDIR=/u/b/mjr/firewall/fwtk
+FWTKSRCDIR=/usr/local/tis/src

# Location of X libraries for X-gw
-XLIBDIR=/usr/X11/lib
+XLIBDIR=/usr/X11R6/lib

# Location of X include files
-XINCLUDE=/usr/X11/include
+XINCLUDE=/usr/X11R6/include
```

Then in the file firewall.h change as follows:

```
 #ifndef    PERMFILE
-#define    PERMFILE "/usr/local/etc/netperm-table"
+#define    PERMFILE "/usr/local/tis/netperm-table"
 #endif
```

Then save the changes to `firewall.h` and type the following:

```
# make
# make install
```

The most critical file in TIS is the proprietary netperm-table file, which is the "traffic cop" of connections through the TIS protocols over the firewall. Inside this file are such entries as user and group authentication from within the firewall and from without. For this reason, a TIS installation is conducted either by a chief administrator or in conjunction with network security authorities at the local site.

Assuming authentication has been correctly set up, additional features include custom tuning of timeouts to prevent multiple assaults on login sessions from Internet hacking tools such as Satan and Cracker.

While TIS excels at providing secure Telnet and FTP sessions, it should be understood that a proxy service of any sort still effectively shuts off the internal network from the external, so such common Internet features as chat, mail, and streaming multimedia will require much deeper consideration and greater configuration.

An example config for Telnet proxying follows:

in /usr/local/tis/netperm-table:

```
# Netacl Rules
netacl-telnetd: permit-hosts 127.0.0.1 -exec /usr/sbin/telnetd
# if the next line is uncommented, the telnet proxy is available
netacl-telnetd: permit-hosts * -exec /usr/local/tis/tn-gw
# Telnet Gateway Rules
tn-gw:          timeout 3600
tn-gw:          permit-hosts 192.168.7.*
```

Make sure nothing is running on the Telnet port (23) and start upnetacl as follows:

```
# /usr/local/tis/netacl -daemon telnet telnetd
```

Alternatively, the system's /etc/inetd.conf file, which controls the behavior of the "super server" daemon known as inetd (it acts as overseer of many typical Internet protocols on a local UNIX or Linux machine), may be edited to include specific instructions on how the new TIS protocol versions will be handled.

The following is an example of how the line would look in /etc/inetd.conf:

```
telnet  stream  tcp     nowait  root    /usr/local/tis/netacl   telnetd
```

Once this is done, users should be greeted by the following:

```
$ telnet comet
Trying 192.168.7.1...
Connected to comet.theneteffect.com.
Escape character is '^]'.
comet.theneteffect.com telnet proxy (Version V2.1) ready:
tn-gw->
```

At the tn-gw-> prompt, the user can then connect to an outside host by typing connect hostname or c hostname.

The important point is that forwarding is shut off and no services, except of course the FWTK ones you need, are used. This will provide an extremely secure proxy setup.

With TIS, Telnet and FTP sessions are not transparently conducted for end users, but external access points using those protocols are. Thus, a user would open a Telnet session with the TIS Telnet daemon, which would open an acceptable portal through the firewall and allow the external session to piggyback over it. FTP is handled similarly.

Putting Squid to Work

The proxy server known as Squid uses Internet caching to reduce the number of external connections from a local area network, while also speeding up the response to the local clients if the material is within the cache.

Many philosophical issues are at play when implementing any sort of Internet caching. The server is effectively making an external connection on behalf of the local client and conducting all of the transactions as if it was the inner client.

The implication is that the contents of the cache may now contain extremely private or sensitive material, such as credit card numbers, personal data, corporate secrets, and other highly important items. Additionally, legal precedent has yet to be set on whether the caching (copying) of material constitutes copyright infringement.

As mentioned previously, a cache may not even be suitable if the majority of external connections go out to particularly dynamic Internet resources. The benefits of caching in such cases may be meager.

Once you have decided that Squid is for you (and you would certainly be following in the footsteps of many large installations and ISPs if you did so), you have to deal with building and installing it. (It doesn't come with the default OpenLinux). This is another package that uses autoconfig, so it is relatively simple to get going (though there are some advanced options you need to be aware of.)

Before installing Squid, you need to seriously consider how many clients will be using your cache and plan your hardware and installation requirements around that. For 5 to 10 workstations, 64 to 128MB of RAM and a gig of disk space should do well in improving your Web surfing experience. The hardware requirements can grow to tremendous proportions as you add users, however, and putting a lot of people behind a too-small cache is likely to slow down access to the Internet rather than speed it up.

A major part of a caching proxy server system is the configuration and management of large disk quantities, sometimes in the 10- to 20-gigabyte range of space for large local area networks. Without a solid understanding of disk hardware management, the task of setting up Squid could be difficult. The simplest implementation would be an assignment (in `squid.conf`) of all caching to one disk, but this results in the presence of a physical choke point as many users try to access that disk.

For large disk systems, even using RAID, Squid allows assignment of multiple caches across that disk real estate in a wide variety of configuration options.

By default, the software installs to `/usr/local/squid`. If you have a particular place with more space and faster disks, you can set that by invoking `configure` as

```
$ ./configure --prefix="/path/to/squid"
```

Some other `configure` options you might want to set are as follows:

`--enable-gnuregex`	Compiles `GNUregex`, a purportedly superior Regular Expression library for Squid to use.
`--enable-icmp`	Enables ICMP pinging. This feature allows Squid to map other caches and destination sites to determine which cache is the closest from which to retrieve cached data, or whether it should retrieve the URL directly.
`--enable-delay-pools`	Enables delay pools to limit bandwidth usage. This can be used as a type of "traffic shaper"; that is, it can effectively limit the bandwidth of client computers to a pre-determined amount.

`--enable-useragent-log`	Enables logging of User Agent header. This turns on logging of User Agent headers, the HTTP header that identifies the type of Web browser being used.
`--enable-snmp`	Enables SNMP monitoring. Allows you to monitor your cache using the Simple Network Monitoring Protocol.
`--disable-ident-lookups`	This allows you to remove code that performs ident (RFC 931) lookups. This might be extremely useful at sites with predominately Windows clients that don't generally run an identd.

Once you have decided on your options, then you need only to type

```
# make all
# make install
```

Squid will be built and placed where you have specified.

Squid actually has only one configuration filewhich may seem simple but is not. Squid's `squid.conf` file can start out rather basic, but it soon takes on a life of its own on larger installations. For this reason, taking care to make clear comments inside it is highly recommended, and backing it up for safekeeping is critical. Before configuring the `squid.conf` file, a great deal of prior information should be accumulated. Since this file controls incoming and outgoing requests, timeout measures, firewall access information, HTTP port number assignment, and other important values, setting it up should not be done with guesswork. A clear picture of the network and firewall should be hashed out beforehand.

A sample `squid.conf` file will be installed into *prefix*/etc (where *prefix* is the location in which you installed). You MUST configure this file for your site before you start Squid. All of the options are commented out. You should uncomment and change the ones you need to, but no others.

Some of the important options you may have to set are as follows:

`http_port`	This defaults to 3128; another popular port is 8080. This is the port your browsers will have to point to. This line can contain multiple port numbers.

`tcp_incoming_address`
`tcp_outgoing_address`
`udp_incoming_address`
`udp_outgoing_address`
	These set the addresses Squid will bind to when it starts. By default, it will bind to all interfaces, but for security reasons you may want to change these to be specific addresses (for example, in a multi-homed situation).

`cache_peer`	If you intend to have your cache interact with other caches (this is explained later chapter), you need to set this. An example line might be
	
	`#                            proxy   icp`
	`#        hostname  type  port  port options`
	`#`
	`cache_peer parent.foo.net`
	↪`parent  3128  3130  [proxy only]`
	`cache_peer sib1.foo.net`
	↪`sibling 3128  3130  [proxy only]`

`acl QUERY urlpath_`
↪`regex cgi bin \?`
`no_cache deny QUERY`
	These two lines define an ACL (Access Control List) that disallows caching of dynamic content.

`cache_mem`	This is the ideal amount of memory to use for object caching. This is not an upper bound on the total amount of memory that Squid can use. A good number for this is 1/3 to 1/2 of your physical memory for a dedicated Squid cache.
`maximum_object_size`	Largest object that squid will cache.
`cache_dir`	This sets the path to the cache directory, the maximum size to which the cache will grow in that directory, and the number of first and second level directories to create to store the cache, as follows: `[cachedir] [size] [level1] [level2]`
`client_netmask`	Determines the accuracy of IP logging. Set to `255.255.255.255` and the exact IP of the connecting client is logged. Set to `255.255.255.0` and the last octet is set to `0`.
`acl aclname acltype`	This allows you to define Access Control Lists. This can get complicated, but it is extremely important to get right. An example of an ACL defining your internal LAN might be as follows (assuming your LAN is `192.168.7.0/24`): `acl mylan src 192.168.7.0/255.255.255.0`
`http_access`	This allows you to define who can access your cache based on the ACLs you have previously defined. An example `http_access` line that would allow your LAN, defined with the ACL above, to access the cache would be: `http_access allow mylan`
`cache_effective_user` `cache_effective_group`	Set the UID the cache uses after startup. Should be set to `nobody` or another unprivileged user you've set up to run Squid.

`visible_hostname`	Hostname Squid returns for error messages and such.
`logfile_rotate [num]`	Number of logfiles to keep. These can grow quite massive, so be sure you have the space.
`minimum_direct_hops`	If using ICMP pinging, do direct fetches for sites that are no more than this many hops away.
`query_icmp [on/off]`	Whether to use ICMP pinging.

`anonymize_headers`	This allows you to filter out the headers of client browsers that Squid will show to the destination sites. For somewhat sanitized headers you might try
	
	`anonymize_headers deny From Referer Server`
	
	`anonymize_headers deny User Agent WWW-Authenticate Link`

In addition to these (the most important ones), there are only perhaps another hundred or so. You would do well to read through the entire `squid.conf` file (yes, it is quite long) and all the documentation as well. This should get you started with some reasonable defaults, however.

Once you have configured your `squid.conf` file, you then have to initialize the cache directories by typing

`# /usr/local/squid/bin/squid -z`

This will likely take a few minutes. You can then start Squid using the `RunCache` command in `/usr/local/squid/bin`:

`# /usr/local/squid/bin/RunCache &`

Squid is capable of much more than just a local Web cache. It can also take advantage of a native protocol, Internet Cache Protocol (ICP). This is the language that caches use to communicate between each other. They use this to find out what objects a particular cache has and to request cached information (the objects themselves). This is the default inter-cache language used by Squid.

The relationships that Squid caches have to each other determine whether a particular cache is a parent, a child, or a sibling. This is known as a hierarchical caching arrangement. Large caches positioned near high-traffic Internet gateways are parent caches; others, farther away, are children. A sibling is a child cache at the same level as its parent cache. Children caches initially request cache data from siblings, then parents, and then the actual (real) URL destination. Using ICMP round-trip mapping allows Squid to make even more accurate calculations about which sibling, parent, or destination should be tried first.

The configuration difficulties implied by hierarchical caching means that this technique is best administered by a team, not an individual. A drawback to this caching method (sometimes quite significant) is that the time required to actually access the correct resources and deliver them to the client can be noticeably longer than a direct Internet connection, depending on configuration, the state of the Internet, and the parent and sibling caches.

A further permutation of Squid proxy caching is "accelerated caching," in which internal client users are not particularly the focus of attention, but speedier HTTP serving is. By spreading a Web server's resources across Squid's caching system, many typical bottlenecks (disk, virtual memory swapping, file system overhead, and so on) are no longer factors.

If a corporate intranet or an Internet HTTP server is known to have difficulty meeting its demand, strategically placed Squid accelerator proxies can propagate the material more rapidly. Since they are caches and not separate Web servers, they are easily filled with the latest changes to the original site. Careful attention to `squid.conf` settings that describe how to prevent multiple storage of stale data can dramatically improve the network performance of Web servers.

A major benefit of Squid caching of Web servers is security, since external users and connections are not made aware of the original Web server's identity. It is better to have a Squid cache server under fire than the original Web server.

About the only downside of using Squid HTTP accelerators is that important information is now difficult to gather; it is conceivable, however, that a resourceful network administrator could automate the accelerators to report information to a central database.

Configuring an accelerator is merely a matter of telling the local Squid proxy which HTTP port to listen to and cache. This is entered into its `squid.conf` file.

Squid might seem simple when one considers that only a single configuration file is needed but, as noted above, this is very deceiving. Squid is a highly complex tool worthy of a great deal of testing, planning, attention, and configuration.

Summary

Caldera OpenLinux 2.3 users come from a cross section of people with different levels of training, experience, and aptitude. Depending on your needs and comfort level, any of the proxy server packages described in this chapter can provide suitable Internet access for the local area network while also safeguarding local resources.

For the home user wondering how to take greatest advantage of a single Internet connection, SOCKS is an ideal tool. For the firewall user with advanced security concerns or large networks, the TIS tools can be greatly beneficial. Where Web serving or a large pool of users is concerned, a solution using Squid can make dramatic improvements in speed and efficiency, for both internal clients and external Web browsers, depending on the particular Squid configuration.

Above all, comfort with these technologies is the cornerstone to getting the most from them. Fortunately, each of them has a variety of Internet resources for tips, support, FAQs, and other information.

Performing Backup and Restore

CHAPTER 23

IN THIS CHAPTER

- Qualities of a Good Backup *531*
- Selecting a Backup Medium *532*
- Selecting a Backup Tool *533*
- Backup Strategy *535*
- Performing Backups with BRU-2000 *542*

Your data is valuable, made so by both the time it took to create it and its uniqueness. It will cost you time and effort to re-create it. That costs money or, at the very least, personal grief. In some instances, it may not even be possible to re-create your data, for example the results of a poll, or a scientific experiment. Since your data is such an investment of time and effort, appropriate steps should be taken to protect and avoid losing it.

There are basically four reasons why you might lose data:

- Human action
- Hardware failure
- Software bugs
- Natural disaster

Humans are quite unreliable and often make mistakes. Mishaps caused by carelessness, such as an `rm -r` issued in the wrong directory, can lead to the loss of data. Additionally, some human beings are malicious and will purposefully try to destroy data. Even on a system with premium security, data is still at risk.

Although modern hardware tends to be more reliable than its predecessors, it can still break down with seeming spontaneity. The crucial piece of hardware usually used for storing data is the hard drive, and, although newer hard drives are more reliable than older ones, they still fail. After all, the hard drive depends on tiny magnetic fields remaining intact in a world filled with electromagnetic noise.

Modern software tends to be unreliable, and a rock-solid program is an exception instead of the rule. Due to the unreliability of such software, the tool you use to manipulate data may instead destroy that data. Often this is because the software is released before it is ready and contains bugs. These bugs may be fixed later when a patch is issued for the software, but unfortunately both the time you invested in the manipulation of the data and the data itself are gone.

Nature may not be evil, but it can wreak havoc even when being good. Hurricanes, tornadoes, earthquakes, tidal waves, and even a simple thunderstorm all pose a threat to your data.

Backups are a way to protect your investment in critical data. By having several copies of the data, it is less of a problem if one copy is destroyed. With multiple copies, the only loss will be the time it takes for the restoration process, assuming that the backup was successful in storing the data. Therefore, it is important to perform backups properly.

Part of a good backup protocol is to make sure your backups work. For example, you do not want to be faced with an unsuccessful backup if you just lost a hard drive with a

15,000-user database on it. To avoid this, it is recommended that you devise a test strategy to spot-check backups. The easiest way to do this is to perform an actual restore, which should be attempted before the backup is actually needed.

The future is unknown and no one knows what might happen. Perhaps your system goes down in the middle of making a backup, and you've been using only a single backup medium, which might be destroyed as well. This would leave you with nothing of your hard work. Or perhaps while restoring something, you notice you forgot to back up something important, such as the payroll for your division. Maybe your backups all went fine, but your tape drive broke, and they no longer make tape drives to read that kind of tape. As you can see, a proper backup protocol is of crucial importance to the protection of your investment. In fact, when it comes to backups, paranoia can be said to be a conservative disposition.

Because a good backup strategy involves both archives and backups, you should understand the difference between the two. *Backups* are file operations to save your data at regular intervals, either in whole or incrementally. *Archives* are file operations to save your data for long periods of time.

This chapter covers the qualities of a good backup and the process of selecting a backup medium. Some backup tools will be discussed, along with strategies for incremental and full backups.

Qualities of a Good Backup

In the best of all possible worlds, backups would be perfectly reliable, always available, easy to use, and extremely fast. In the real world, however, trade-offs must be made. For example, backups stored offsite are good for disaster recovery but are not always available. In order to choose the proper backup strategy, you must look at the following factors:

- Cost
- Reliability
- Speed
- Availability
- Usability

Cost is important because an inexpensive medium will allow you to have adequate storage space for your data. It is recommended that you have several times more storage space than what you need for data. Thus, many factors need to be considered when calculating the cost, such as initial investment and the cost of media. For example, the cost of a CD-RW drive is approximately three times that of a zip drive, but writeable CDs are about one third the cost of a zip disk.

Reliability is extremely important. A backup medium should be able to hold the data without corruption for many years. The way you use a backup medium affects its reliability. For example, a hard disk is typically very reliable, but if the hard drive is in the same computer that you are backing up, you probably should not consider it to be reliable. If something should happen to the computer, such as a power surge, everything may be wiped out. Of course, if the backups are never successfully written to the backup medium, it does not matter how good the medium is.

Speed is more important or less, depending on the system. If backups can be done without interaction, it doesn't matter that it takes two hours to do a backup, as long as it needs no supervision. On the other hand, if the backup cannot be done when the computer is otherwise idle, speed is an issue. Also, restoration time may be an issue because the time it takes to restore the data can be just as critical as the need to have that data available.

Availability is obviously necessary because you cannot use a backup medium if it is unavailable. Less obvious is the need for the medium to be available in the future and on computers other than your own. Thus, it is important to have both onsite backups for restoring small amounts of files that are lost due to user mishaps and off-site backups for full disaster recovery.

Usability is a large factor in how often backups are made because fast, available, reliable backups are no good if they are not usable. The easier it is to make backups the better; a backup medium should not be difficult to use. This is especially important for restoration. In an emergency, the person who usually performs the backups and restores may be unavailable, and a non-technical person may need to perform the task. Good documentation is an integral part of usability.

Selecting a Backup Medium

Once upon a time, the typical alternatives for a backup medium were floppies, tapes, and hard drive. Today, many other choices of media exist. The following provides a comparison of various media that you might consider using for backup and archival purposes.

Media Type	Cost	Speed	Reliability	Availability	Usability
Floppy Disks	cheap	slow	good	high	Not very usable for large amounts of data

Media Type	Cost	Speed	Reliability	Availability	Usability
CDR	cheap to medium	slow	good	high	Read-only media good for archives
CDRW	medium	slow	good	medium	Read/write media: economical for mid-size systems (each disk usually 500MB)
Iomega zip	medium to expensive	slow	good	high	May be economical for small systems, each zip drive holds 120MB
Flash ROM	very expensive	fast	excellent	low	May be good for small systems, currently limited to 200MB
Tapes	cheap to medium	medium to fast	good	high	Depending on the size, tapes can be a solution for most systems
Removable HDD	expensive	fast	excellent	high	Portable, reliable, and available in sizes of 2GB or more
Hard drives	expensive	fast	excellent	high	Highly usable, but not reliable if used to back up a hard drive in the same computer

Writeable CDs are good for archival purposes, and some formats can be overwritten, allowing for a reusable backup medium. Flopticals have the good qualities of both floppies (they're random access, allowing for quick restoration of a single file) and tapes (they contain a lot of data), but they have not really penetrated the consumer market to any great degree. However, they are usually popular in high-end, large-scale computing operations. More popular removable media are the Iomega Zip and Jaz drives, which come in 120MB Zip and 1 to 2GB Jaz form factors. Though a Zip or Jaz drive is cheaper than a CDR drive, the media itself is quite a bit more expensive than a writeable CD.

Selecting a Backup Tool

There are many tools that can be used to make backups. The traditional tools are *tar* and *cpio*. They are similar and mostly equivalent from a backup point of view, in that both are capable of storing files on tapes and retrieving files from them. Both are capable of using almost any media because the kernel device drivers take care of the low-level device handling.

Because tapes were once the *de facto* standard for backups, throughout the rest of this chapter I will refer to the backup device as a tape. This is just to represent it in a generic way and should be replaced with the device you actually use.

> **Note**
>
> In addition to the tools I will be covering, there is a large number of third-party packages (both freeware and commercial) that can be used for backups. The Linux Software map lists many of the freeware packages.

The following tar command saves all files under /home to the default tape drive:

```
tar -c /home
```

the -c option (--create) tells tar to create a new archive by gathering files from the path that follows, in this case /home.

Although similar to the tar command, cpio has several advantages. First, it packs data more efficiently. Second, it is designed to back up arbitrary sets of files, whereas tar is meant for backing up subdirectories and trees. Third, cpio is designed to span several tapes, skipping over any bad sections on the tape, whereas tar will crash and burn if it tries to write to a bad section. cpio also supports archives in the following formats:

- binary
- old ASCII
- new ASCII
- crc
- HPUX Binary
- HPUX old ASCII
- old tar
- POSIX.1 tar

> **Note**
>
> By default, cpio creates binary format archives for compatibility with older cpio programs. When extracting from archives, cpio automatically recognizes what kind of archive it is reading and can read archives created on machines with different byte-orders.

Backup Strategy

A simple backup scheme is to back up all your data once and then, when a set amount of time has passed, back up everything that has been modified since the previous backup. The first backup is called a *full* backup, and the subsequent ones are *incremental* backups. A full backup is often more work than an incremental because there is more data. Also, restoring a single file from a large archive can be very cumbersome. In most cases, however, restoring from many incremental backups can be much more work than restoring from a single full backup because each incremental backup requires the one before it to be restored first.

Restoration, in turn, can be optimized so that you always back up everything since the previous full backup; that way, backups are a bit more work, but there should never be a need to restore more than one full and one incremental backup. A good backup and recovery strategy identifies when a full backup is necessary and when incremental backups should be performed instead.

> **Note**
>
> If you use your Open Linux system for business, you should definitely have a backup strategy. Creating a formal plan to regularly save critical information is of the utmost importance in preventing any sort of financial loss due to loss of data. Once you devise and implement a backup strategy, be sure you stick to it.

Linux uses the concept of a backup level to distinguish between different kinds of backups. A full backup is designated as a level 0 backup. The other levels indicate the need to back up files that have changed since the preceding level. For example, on Friday you might do a level 0 backup (full) and then on Monday a level 1, which would back up all the files changed since the level 0 backup. On Tuesday night you would perform a level 2 backup, which would back up only those files changed since the level 1 backup. If you had six tapes and wanted to do a backup on every business day (Monday to Friday), you could use tape 1 on Friday for a full backup, tapes 2–5 for incremental backups on Monday through Thursday (level 1, level 2, level 3, and level 4), and then on the next Friday a full backup on tape 6. You would then start doing incremental backups with tapes 2–5 again. You don't want to overwrite tape 1 until you have a second full backup on tape 6. Once you've successfully made a full backup to tape 6, tape 1 can be moved off site, in case something should happen to destroy the building in which the tapes are stored. When it comes time again to make a full backup, you use tape 1 and put tape 6 in its place. This is a very simple strategy, as are the two that follow.

The following table shows a simple backup strategy using only two tapes:

Sunday	Level 0
Monday	Level 1
Tuesday	Level 1
Wednesday	Level 1
Thursday	Level 1
Friday	Level 1
Saturday	Level 1

The advantage to this strategy is that it requires only two sets of media, and restoring the full system requires only that you restore the full backup and the last incremental one. One negative feature of this approach is that the size of the backup will increase throughout the week, perhaps even growing to the point of requiring additional media. The following shows another simple strategy that uses seven tapes:

Monday	Level 0
Tuesday	Level 1
Wednesday	Level 2
Thursday	Level 3
Friday	Level 4
Saturday	Level 5
Sunday	Level 6

The advantage to this strategy is that each backup is relatively fast and small and thus remains easy to manage. However, the disadvantage of this scheme is that it uses seven sets of media and, in order to restore the full system, all seven sets will have to be used.

> **Note**
>
> Backup levels can also be used to keep file system restoration time to a minimum. For example, if you have many incremental backups with growing level numbers, you need to restore all of them in order to rebuild the whole file system. Instead, you can use level numbers that keep down the number of backups needed to restore the file system. To minimize the number of tapes needed for a restore, you could use a smaller level for each incremental tape. However, the time to make the backups increases (each backup copies everything since the previous full backup).

When deciding which backup scheme to employ, you need to know how your file system is being used. In most cases, you will want to back up as much as possible, with files that change often taking precedence over those files that rarely change. Some files, such as software that can be easily re-installed, doesn't necessarily have to be part of the backup. The configuration files for that software should be; otherwise, you would need to configure them all over again. Some directories, such as /tmp and /proc, never need to be backed up, especially /proc because it contains only data that is generated by the kernel automatically. Some gray areas include the news spool, the log files, and many other things in /var. You must decide what you consider important. The obvious targets for backup are user files (/home) and system configuration files (/etc), as well as any other important data scattered about your file system.

Performing Backups with tar and cpio

A full backup can be achieved easily and simply with the following command:

```
tar -c /
```

This will back up the full file system to the default device of /dev/rmt0.

The same result can be achieved using the following:

```
tar --create --file /dev/rmt0 /
```

This example uses the long option names available in GNU tar. The traditional version of tar on most UNIX systems understands only the single character options.

> **Note**
>
> The GNU version of tar included with OpenLinux also has several options useful for file compression and multi-volume backup operations. If you use the -Z option, the archive will be compressed using compress, and if you use the -z option, the archive will be compressed using gzip compression. Also, to perform a multivolume backup or restore, you use the -M option on the command line. For example, to make a compressed multivolume archive of /usr/src on multiple floppies, use the following:
>
> ```
> tar -cMzf /dev/fd0 /usr/src
> ```
>
> The floppies should already be formatted before beginning the backup.

After you've made a backup, you should check it to be sure it was made properly. After all, you don't want to wait until you need the data to find out the backup is corrupt. In order to do this, you will use tar with the --compare (-d, --diff) option:

```
tar -compare -verbose -f /dev/rmt0
```

An incremental backup can be done with tar using the -N (--newer) option. For example, in order to back up all the files that have been modified in /usr/src since July 8, 1999, you would use tar as follows:

```
tar -cN '8 jul 1999' -f /dev/rmt0 /usr/src -v
```

Unfortunately, tar doesn't notice when a file's inode information, such as its permission bits or its name, has changed. This can be worked out using find and comparing the current file system state with lists of files that have been backed up previously.

> **Note**
>
> Many scripts and programs for using find in incremental backups can be found on most Linux FTP sites. One good place to look is at ftp://ftp.sunsite.edu/pub/linux/utils/compression.

Using the find command to make incremental backups takes a bit more work than doing a simple backup, as previously discussed. The find command is capable of finding all files that have changed since a certain date or files that are newer than a specified file. Using this information, it is easy to perform an incremental backup. The following command finds files that have been modified today and backs up those files, using tar to create an archive on /dev/ftape.

```
tar -cf /dev/ftape `find /mtime -1 ! -type d -print`
```

The ! -type d (not equal to type d) says that if the object is a directory not to archive it. This is done because tar follows directories, and you don't want to back up a directory unless everything in it has changed. Of course the Find command can also be used with cpio. The following command performs the same task as the preceding tar command:

```
find / -mtime -1 | cpio -o >/dev/ftape
```

As mentioned, the find command can find files that are newer than a specified file, making it is easy to touch a file after it has been successfully backed up. Then at the next backup, you simply search for files that are newer than the file you touched. To use cpio and find to search for and archive files newer than the file /tmp/backup, use the following:

```
find / -newer /tmp/backup -print | cpio >/dev/rmt0
```

With tar, the same result would be achieved using the following:

```
tar -cf /dev/rmt0 `find / -newer /tmp/backup -print`
```

> **Note**
>
> You will always want to touch the file before you begin the backup process because this will ensure that the next backup will include any files that are altered during the current backup. This means that you have to use a different file for each different backup level you use.

What's on the Tape?

When you have an archived tape, you may not be quite sure what is on it. It may contain older files because corrupted files are sometimes not noticed for a long time. Perhaps it's from an incremental backup, in which case it would have only those files that changed after the backup before it. A perplexing problem, but here's a solution. Both tar and cpio offer a way to create a table of contents (TOC) for the backup. The most convenient time to create a backup's TOC is during the backup process. The following command shows you how to use both tar and cpio to do just that:

```
tar -cv / > /tmp/backup/monday.TOC

find / -print | cpio -ov >/dev/rmt0 2>/tmp/backup/monday.TOC
```

> **Note**
>
> If you are going to create a TOC every time you back up, then this makes an excellent file to use the —newer command with when doing an incremental backup. That way, each day you just touch the TOC from the last backup.

The cpio backup automatically sends the list to stdout; therefore, this command simply captures the output and writes it to a file. The -v (--verbose) option will also list the files to stdout.

Restoring Files with tar and cpio

> **Note**
>
> tar always reads the backup volume sequentially, so for large volumes it is rather slow. You also need to keep in mind that it's not possible to use random access database techniques when using a tape drive or another sequential medium.

Backing up files is a good thing; it's like an insurance policy. But when disaster strikes, you will have to be ready to restore your data. Restoring files is fairly easy with either tar or cpio.

Sometimes before you restore, you may find it prudent to view the contents of the archive to see what exactly it is you need to restore. To do this, you will use tar and cpio with the `--list` (`-t`) option. For example, to view the contents of a tar archive on a floppy, you would use the following command:

```
tar --list --file /dev/fd0
```

To execute the same with cpio, you would use the following:

```
cpio -it < /dev/fd0
```

Now that you know how to check the contents of your archives for specific files, you can proceed to extracting the files you need. In order to extract using tar, you use the `--extract` (`-x`) option. For example, to extract all the files from a tar archive on floppy, keeping all permissions intact, you would use the following command:

```
tar --extract -pvf /dev/fd0
```

To do the same with cpio, you would use the following:

```
cpio -im < /dev/fd0
```

The `-p` option in tar tells it to preserve the file permissions, the `v` option tells it to be verbose (listing all files it's restoring), and the `f` option tells it to look on `/dev/fd0` (remember that the default device for tar is `/dev/rmt0`). The `-m` option in cpio tells it the same thing as the `-p` option in tar, which is to preserve all the file attributes of the original.

> **Note**
>
> When you use cpio to restore directories, remember that cpio uses the `-d` option in order to create sub-directories. With tar, this is done automatically.

Knowing how to restore a whole archive is important, but what if you just have to restore a single corrupted file? Restoring the whole archive would not be economical or practical. Luckily, with both cpio and tar you can extract and restore specific files and directories (which includes their files and sub-directories) by naming the file you want to restore on the command line. For example, say you had `/usr/src` archived on

/mnt/ftape, and you are about to recompile your kernel, but one of the files is corrupt. You need to restore the corrupt file, /usr/src/linux/include/linux/hdreg.h in the example. To do this

```
tar -xpvf /dev/ftape usr/src/linux/include/linux/hdreg.h
```

To do the same with cpio

```
cpio -im `*hdreg.h` < /dev/ftape
```

> **Note**
>
> tar doesn't always handle deleted files properly. If you restore a file system from a full and incremental backups, and you have deleted a file between the two, the deleted file will exist again after the restore. This can be a security problem if the file was deleted because it contained sensitive data that should no longer be available.

Compressed Backups

Backups can be quite space intensive, which may in turn lead to the need to purchase costly additional media. In order to maximize the media space you already have, compression can be used. There are several ways to do this. As mentioned earlier, you can use the -z or -Z option with tar so that tar pipes the whole output through either the gzip or compress program before writing it to the backup medium.

Unfortunately, compressed backups can cause problems because of the way compression works. If a single bit is wrong, all the rest of the compressed data will be unusable. Some backup programs have built-in error correction, but there is no method that can handle a large number of errors. This means that if the backup is compressed using tar with the -z option, a single error can mean the entire backup is lost. because Because backups must be as reliable as possible, this method of compression is not necessarily a good idea.

Another way is to compress each file separately. This means that if the compression fails, one file is lost, but all other files remain unharmed.

Compression takes time, which may make the backup program unable to write data fast enough for a tape drive. This can be avoided by buffering the output, either internally if the backup program supports this or externally using another program. This should be a problem only with older, slower computers.

Performing Backups with BRU-2000

OpenLinux users who purchase the commercial version of COL 2.2 will find that the CD-ROM includes a copy of Enhanced Software Technologies' BRU PE include on the CD-ROM. In fact, if you did the recommended install from either Lisa or Lizard, then it is already installed. BRU-PE is a personal edition of the more robust BRU-2000 commercial edition. Though only a personal edition, it is still a fairly advanced backup and restore utility. In fact, it supports

- Command line or graphical interface for KDE
- Error detection during backup
- Data integrity verification
- Backup and restore of live file systems
- On-line help
- Automatic recognition of compressed files
- Background mode for scheduled backups

The BRU software is actually two programs, the standard BRU for performing backups from the console and the GUI program xbru for use under KDE. BRU-PE uses several files and directories on your Linux system. Much of the graphical interface support is found under /opt/xbru, and the configuration file /etc/brutab is used to configure various backup devices.

As mentioned earlier, if you did the recommended install with either Lisa or Lizard, BRU-PE is already installed. If not, you will have to install it manually. To do so, mount your COL 2.2 CD. Then, as root go to the /OpenLinux/install/RPMS directory on the CD and issue the following command:

```
rpm -ivh BRU*.rpm
```

To do full or incremental backups of your system, you must be logged in as user root. To use the graphical interface version, you can start the program in many ways. You can initiate it by choosing the K menu, Utilities, BRU-PE backup utility, or you can press Alt+F2 and then type **xbru** in the command-line box that appears. At this point the dialog box seen in Figure 23.1 should appear.

FIGURE 23.1
The BRU-2000 program is a commercial backup and restore utility for nearly 20 operating systems, including Linux.

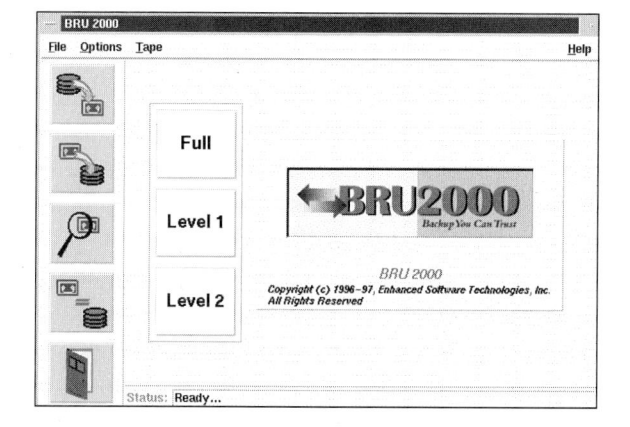

If you choose Backup at this point, the first thing the program will do is check the status of the default backup device. If you have not run BRU-PE before, clicking on the backup button will display a message, as shown in Figure 23.2.

FIGURE 23.2
The status of the default backup device.

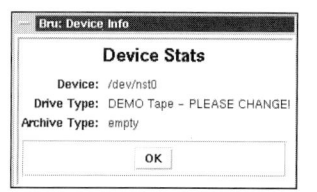

As you can see, the default demo device is not an actual device. So before you can perform any backups using BRU-PE, you will have to set up an actual device that you will be using to store your archives. In order to do so, choose Configure BRU from the File menu, and a new dialog box will appear, as shown in Figure 23.3.

FIGURE 23.3
To configure your backup device for use with BRU-PE, choose the Devices tab from the Configuration dialog box.

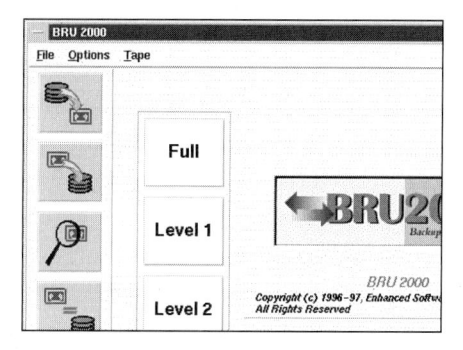

Select the Devices tab, near the top-left corner, and then select the New button. The New Device window will appear, as shown in Figure 23.4. Select a device type from the pull-down menu, and then type the path to the device in the Device Node box. Then click Create.

FIGURE 23.4
The New Device dialog box is used to select a backup device or create a new one.

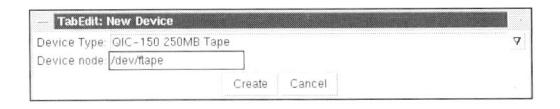

File Selection

Selecting the Backup button or selecting Backup from the File menu will bring up the File Selection interface, as shown in Figure 23.5. The box on the left displays the contents of the current directory with the name of the directory above it. To change directories, you can either change the CD entry or double-click on the directory listings in the left window. The box on the right displays the current files or directories that have been selected for backup.

FIGURE 23.5
Backup File Selection interface for BRU.

You can add files or directories by highlighting them and then clicking the Add button. To add all the files and sub-directories in the current directory, use the Add All button.

> **Note**
>
> You cannot add a directory if a file or directory within that directory is already in the backup list. This would tell BRU to back up those files or directories twice. Therefore, you will have to remove the subdirectories or files before you can add the parent directory.

BRU-PE also provides a search function, accessible by clicking on the Search button. When clicked, this button will bring up a search window, where you can enter a shell-style pattern and optionally turn on recursive searching.

Backup Definitions

Backup definitions enable you to define a set of backup options and selected files or directories for a scheduled backup at some future time or for quick retrieval. The backup interface has both a Save and a Load button for backup definitions. Choosing Save will prompt you for a name for the definition. Save will then store all the relevant information, including the current device selection, backup options such as compression, include/exclude pattern settings, and selected files and directories. After the definition has been saved, you will be prompted to schedule the definition to run at some future time.

Selecting Load will present a dialog box showing all current definitions. After selecting the desired definition, BRU-PE will then set the device and backup options to those stored when the definition was created.

Backup Options

The Backup Options interface can be accessed by selecting either the Options button from the Backup File Selection interface or Backup from the Options menu. The Backup Options interface will then appear, as shown in Figure 23.6.

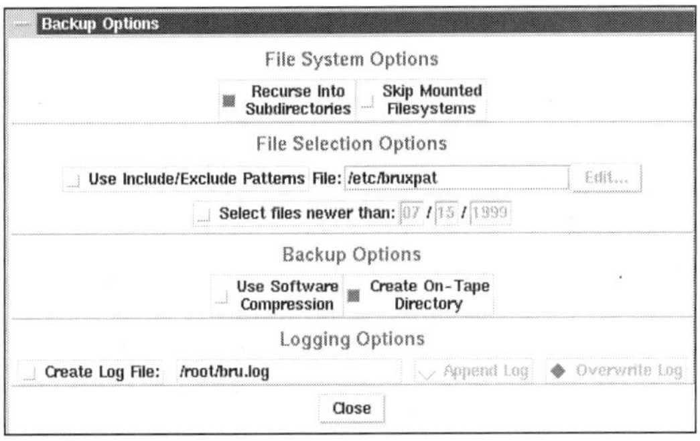

FIGURE 23.6
The Backup Options window for BRU-PE.

As you can see from this window, you can change various settings such as incremental backups, mount point handling, compression settings, and logging options.

There is one option here that I would recommend always checking, and that is Create On-Tape directory. By selecting this for your backups, they will always contain a table of contents that BRU-PE can use to determine quickly what they contain.

To save your settings for future use, select Save Options from the Options menu.

Running the Backup

After you have selected at least one file or directory for backup, click the Continue button. You will then be presented with a couple of dialog boxes for overwriting or appending to tapes and labeling backups.

Then, the Estimate window will appear, showing the number of files to be backed up and the size of the backup in kilobytes and approximately how many volumes the backup will take.

> **Note**
>
> If compression is being used, the volume estimation will not take that into account.

From this point on, the backup can be completed without further intervention, as long as volumes won't have to be changed. Once the estimate is complete, click the Continue button to perform the backup. If no selection is made in 30 seconds, the backup will proceed automatically.

Scheduling Backup Definitions

BRU-PE provides a scheduler for setting up backup definitions to run at future times. The Scheduler interface may be opened through the dialog window that appears after saving a definition or by selecting Scheduler from the File menu. The Scheduler interface is shown in Figure 23.7.

FIGURE 23.7

The Scheduler for BRU-PE allows scheduling full and incremental backups in advance.

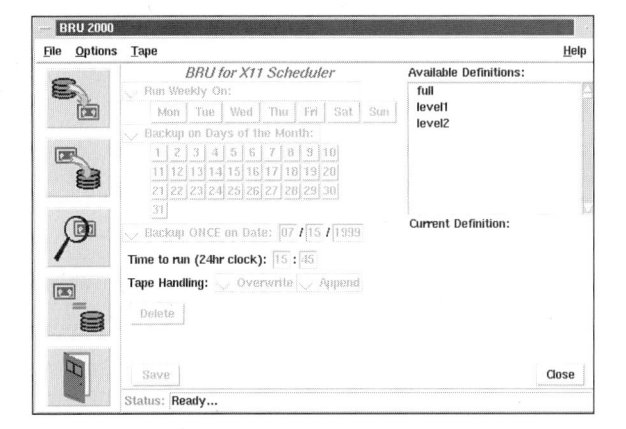

The box on the right shows a list of definitions for the current user. A scheduled definition appears with an * beside it. To schedule a definition, double-click on the definition name.

You may then choose to run the definition in a variety of ways, such as by days of the week, days of the month, or specific dates and times. For example, you may have a definition named Daily that runs each Monday through Thursday at 23:30, performing an incremental backup. Then you could schedule a definition called Weekly to perform a full backup every Friday at 23:30.

> **Note**
>
> You must select Save to store your changes and have them take effect. Selecting a different definition or closing the window will result in any unsaved changes being discarded.

Restoring Files with BRU-PE

Before BRU-PE can allow you to select files to restore, it must retrieve the contents of the archive. If the archive was created with the On-Tape Directory option, this is simply a matter of reading the file list; otherwise, BRU-PE has to scan the entire archive to get the list.

Once the contents of the archive have been retrieved, it will display a listing similar to the one used for selecting files for backup. The box on the right displays the current directory (as it is stored on tape). You can change directories by double-clicking on them.

When you have selected all of the files or directories you want to restore, click on the Restore button.

There are certain Restore options that can be accessed either by clicking on the Options button on the Restore interface or by selecting Restore from the Options menu. Here you can control such features as overwriting files during a restore, restoring a file under a new name, and converting absolute pathnames to relative pathnames.

Summary

A backup is an important way to avoid disaster as a result of lost data. A good backup strategy is important, but being able to restore the files is also important. Remember to always check your backups. It will save you time and grief in the long run.

Securing Linux

CHAPTER 24

IN THIS CHAPTER

- Computer Security Basics 550
- The UNIX Security Model 553
- Common Attacks 555
- Preventing Attacks 558
- Monitoring, Detection, and Logging 560
- Controlling Access to Services 565
- Keeping Your System Up-to-Date 568
- Security Tools 569
- Privacy 570

Computer and network security has become critically important in the last few years. As more and more systems have been attached to the Internet, the opportunities for security problems have skyrocketed.

Linux itself can be set up very securely. Unfortunately, because Linux is a fairly rich system with many network services, there are numerous opportunities for bugs or misconfigurations to cause security problems. In addition, Linux machines often use convenient facilities like remote log-in and NFS file sharing. Once one system is compromised by these facilities, it is relatively easy to compromise others and use them as a base for new attacks.

Computer Security Basics

A computer system is *secure* if it does what you expect it to do. Different people have different definitions of security, but most security models include the following features:

- The system should prevent unauthorized people from accessing confidential information.
- The system should prevent unauthorized modification of information.
- The system should prevent people from denying services to other people (by hogging resources, exploiting bugs, and so on).
- The system should ensure that information is not lost due to accidents, negligence, or disasters.
- The system should keep audit trails so that unauthorized or unapproved use can be tracked down and traced to individual users.

The various aspects of security differ in importance, depending on your goals. For example, a bank probably wants to ensure that no one can modify information and that it won't be lost in case of a disaster. Confidentiality is somewhat less important. Defense agencies, on the other hand, probably place confidentiality at the top of the list.

Hackers and Crackers

The popular press often uses the term *hacker* to refer to a computer criminal. In the Linux world, hackers are simply talented (if obsessed) programmers. Computer criminals are referred to as *crackers*. However, I believe that both of these terms are too euphemistic and hide the criminal nature of those who deliberately breach computer security. I will refer to computer criminals as criminals, vandals, or attackers, depending on their intent.

Make no mistake: Deliberately breaking into a computer system is a crime. It should not be tolerated.

Risk Assessment

Before planning computer security, you need to assess what you're trying to protect. Do you have highly confidential information, the disclosure of which can cause financial harm? Do you have users who depend on continuous access to your computing facilities? Do you have expensive computer equipment? Once you know what you are trying to protect, you'll have a better idea of how to protect it.

Physical Security

One of the most overlooked aspects of computer security is physical security. If you have no connection to the Internet, no modem lines, and an untappable fiber-optic LAN, you may think your network is pretty secure. But if someone can break in to your computer room at night and make off with the server, sophisticated network security tools are useless.

To physically secure your computers, consider the following:

- Place servers with confidential data in lockable rooms with secure walls. Make sure no one can enter server rooms through false ceilings or raised floors.
- Consider removing floppy disk drives from servers and workstations. Password-protect the BIOS so that a criminal cannot change the boot-up sequence and boot from his own device.
- Have computers marked with identifying marks. Use lock-down devices to secure computers to tables or shelves.
- Protect the computers' environment. Use uninterruptible power supplies or surge suppressors to protect computers from power problems. Do not place computers near sprinklers; if possible, use carbon dioxide fire extinguishers in computer rooms. If your building is subject to flooding, place water sensors in server rooms.
- Protect network connections with steel conduits or cable trays.

Essentially, you should consider applying any measures you take to physically protect valuable assets to protecting computer equipment.

Employee Security

Many computer crimes are "inside jobs." That is, they are performed by employees who abuse their computer privileges.

Practically speaking, there is no technological solution to criminal employees. At some point, you have to trust someone. However, there are various measures you can take to reduce the chance of employee computer crime:

- Make sure your employees are compensated appropriately, not overworked, and feel appreciated. Disgruntled employees are far more likely to commit crimes than happy ones.
- Log all access to computer systems securely. For example, all logins could be logged to a printer in a locked room. Only the person who can access the room can modify the log. If you have several redundant logs, it would require collaboration to alter them all.
- Ensure that employees appreciate the need for computer security and understand the cost and consequences of computer crime.
- If an employee leaves or is dismissed, immediately disable all login accounts. Retrieve any pass cards, keys, and so on that have been issued to the employee.
- Make background checks on people you're considering for sensitive positions. Make sure all educational and work experience claims are true. Someone who lies on a resume probably isn't the right person for a position requiring security.

Network Security

Many security breaches are the result of exploitation of bugs in network programs. These security breaches can be made over the Internet, making it extremely difficult to track down the perpetrators. We'll cover these breaches in detail later in the chapter.

Data Loss

It still astounds me that many people and organizations do not have a good backup system in place. From the very beginning, you should plan and implement a backup system. Here are some things to consider:

- If you go to great lengths to protect data but leave backup tapes lying around, you should consider encrypting your backups. Make sure the encryption keys are written down and locked in a safe somewhere in case you forget them!
- Every so often, take backup media off-site to a secure location. If all backups are in one location, a fire could destroy everything.
- Make sure your backup media lasts. Do not use magnetic tapes more than the manufacturer-recommended number of times. Consider using long-lasting media like recordable CDs for archive purposes. (But note that the lifetime of recordable CDs is still not well established.)
- Make sure that you can restore files. Have backup personnel periodically attempt to restore a random file from a backup set to keep their skills up-to-date.

The UNIX Security Model

Linux uses the traditional UNIX security model. Every file and directory has two IDs: the owner ID and the group ID. Every user has a user ID and a number of group IDs. Here is how file access rights are determined:

1. If your effective user ID matches the file owner's ID, you are granted the rights in the user portion of the permission settings.
2. If you belong to the file's group, you are granted the rights in the group portion of the permission settings.
3. Otherwise, you are granted the rights in the "other" portion of the permission settings.

The root Account

Linux has a special account (usually called root) with user ID zero. Most permission checks are suspended for this user ID; a user ID of zero can pretty much do *anything*. UNIX has been roundly criticized for this; its separation of privileges is very coarse. Other systems offer finer-grained authority divisions that greatly reduce the need for a "superuser" account (but don't necessarily eliminate it).

However, root is conceptually simple and (in theory) quite secure. In fact, I believe the simplicity of the UNIX permission model goes a long way to increasing its security.

> **Note**
> There is a draft standard to introduce capabilities to UNIX that would allow a finer-grained division of privileges. Internally, the Linux kernel has provisions for capabilities, but they are not yet fully implemented. Most likely, some kind of capabilities will be in place for the next stable kernel release.

SUID and SGID Programs

Sometimes, a normal user legitimately needs extra privileges. For example, to change your password, you need to be able to modify the /etc/passwd file. Obviously, the extra privileges must be tightly controlled—you should be able to change only your password, not someone else's.

In UNIX and Linux, *SUID* programs allow you to temporarily assume a different user ID. For example, if a program is owned by root and has the `set-uid` flag turned on, then when anyone runs that program, the effective user ID of the process is root.

Similarly, the `set-gid` flag allows anyone to assume an effective group ID that is the group ID of the executable file.

SUID and SGID programs are major sources of security problems in UNIX and Linux. The problem is that these programs are responsible for carefully controlling access to increased privileges. Unfortunately, bugs in SUID and SGID programs often allow criminals to fool the programs into providing uncontrolled access to extra privileges.

Let me repeat: All SUID and SGID security problems are the result of *bugs in user-level programs*. They are *not* a result of inherent insecurity in the SUID and SGID mechanisms themselves.

> **Note**
>
> This was not the case for older versions of UNIX, which had problems in the way they handled SUID programs. All known systemic problems with the SUID mechanism have been corrected.

Older UNIX systems used SUID and SGID programs quite freely. The modern trend is to reduce the number of SUID and SGID programs to the bare minimum. If programs don't absolutely require extra privileges, they should not be given.

You should be aware of all SUID and SGID programs on your system. Another Linux distribution, called Debian Linux, has an excellent shell script called `/usr/sbin/checksecurity` that finds all SUID and SGID programs and alerts you if changes are found since the last scan. You can do something similar with this snippet:

```
#!/bin/sh
cd /var/securitystuff
find / -type f -perm +06000 | sort > setuid.today
if cmp -s setuid.today setuid.yesterday > /dev/null
then
        :
else
        echo "*** Changes found!  Run"
        echo "*** diff -c setuid.today setuid.yesterday"
fi

mv -f setuid.today setuid.yesterday
```

Treat the sudden appearance of a SUID or SGID program with great suspicion.

Note that if you wish to use the shell script above, you have to create the /var/securitystuff directory. It does not exist on standard Caldera OpenLinux systems. You should make the directory owned by root with permissions 700 so that casual users cannot look at the results of the security scan.

Device Files

Device files allow access to the system hardware. Permissions on device files should be set so that casual users cannot access devices inappropriately. For example, the device files corresponding to disk drives should not be readable or writable by casual users; otherwise, they could access the device directly and circumvent all file system permission checks.

Unless you trust an NFS server, you should mount NFS volumes with the nodev and nosuid options, so that device files and SUID/SGID flags are ignored. This reduces the chance of a compromised NFS server compromising your system.

Common Attacks

This section outlines some common attack techniques used by criminals to break into Linux systems.

Buffer Overrun

By far the most common exploit is the *buffer overrun*. The C language, in which Linux and virtually all Linux utilities are written, does not perform runtime array bounds checking. Thus, for example, if you declare an array of size 256 but write to the 257th element, the C runtime library will not detect this.

Unfortunately, many UNIX and Linux programs do not perform checks before writing into arrays. (Since C strings are implemented as arrays of characters, arrays are commonly used in practically all significant C programs.)

Sometimes these arrays are local variables, which are commonly placed on the stack. The stack is a region of memory used to store local variables, return addresses for subroutine calls, and temporary variables. By writing past the end of a local buffer, an attacker can cause data on the stack to be corrupted. By carefully controlling what gets written, the attacker can corrupt the stack data in such a way as to launch the application of his choice.

Now consider a SUID program that can be exploited this way. The attacker can cause the stack to be corrupted such that the shell `/bin/sh` is executed. If the original SUID program ran with root privileges, the attacker is given a shell as root. From there, he can compromise the entire system.

While this sounds very difficult (you have to know a program is vulnerable; you need to know how to supply it with bad data that will corrupt the stack; you need to corrupt the stack in just the right way), advanced UNIX programmers can quite quickly develop an exploit once they suspect a weakness. Furthermore, many computer criminals distribute canned exploits called *scripts* that allow unsophisticated users to launch attacks on vulnerable programs. The great facility with which UNIX automates tasks can unfortunately be used to automate attacks as well.

Network Sniffing

Ethernet is inherently a broadcast medium. Anyone who can plug into your network can monitor all traffic on the ethernet. Attackers can hide a laptop somewhere that monitors and records all ethernet traffic. From this, they can obtain passwords, read confidential information, and compromise your network security.

The Internet is an extreme example of this. You should not transmit anything over the Internet unless you are willing to let anyone see it. Email, in particular, should not be considered a private medium. Encryption tools can help, but sometimes even the fact that you are sending someone email should be confidential, and current encryption tools cannot hide this information.

Social Engineering

Social engineering is a non-technological attack that relies on human interaction. For example, suppose you are a busy system administrator and someone calls you and says, "Hi, this is Bob MacKenzie at extension 4322. I'm working at home today and I've forgotten my password. Could you help me log in?"

Perhaps the caller sounds like Bob, and you know that Bob's extension is 4322, so you comply. If the caller is an attacker who happens to have gleaned information about Bob, you have been a victim of a social engineering attack.

Here are some tips to prevent these kinds of attacks:

- Keep company information such as employee names, office locations, telephone extensions, and login names confidential. The less information an attacker has to begin with, the harder it is to mount a social engineering attack.

- Train employees *never* to accept or give out login or password information over the telephone or via email.
- Train employees *never* to use their internal login names or passwords for outside services (such as Web page logins, personal ISP accounts, and so on).
- Set up formal procedures for dealing with lost passwords and the like. For example, if someone loses his password, the policy might require him to appear in person to ask for a new one.
- Counsel users *never* to run executables they receive via email. These kinds of shenanigans are not common in the UNIX world but, as more Microsoft Windows users migrate to Linux, the potential for this attack increases.

Password Guessing

Strong passwords are your first line of defense against attacks. Train users to pick good passwords. A good password is not a dictionary word, someone's name, telephone number, and so on. As a rule of thumb, a good password should be at least six characters long and contain at least one uppercase letter, one lowercase letter, and one non-letter.

Linux supports password expiration, forcing users to change their passwords periodically. On the COAS User Accounts panel, this appears in the Shadow Information dialog when you create or edit an account.

Password expiration is a delicate issue. On the one hand, forcing users to change passwords every so often limits the length of time a cracked password is valuable. On the other hand, if users have to change passwords too often, they will get annoyed and pick sequences of easy-to-remember passwords.

My recommendation is to train people to use strong passwords and forget about expiration. If you really want expiration, pick a reasonable expiration period (30–90 days) so that users have time to remember passwords without writing them down or constructing sequences of similar passwords.

Denial of Service Attacks

A denial of service attack is one in which the attacker monopolizes system resources so that other users cannot be serviced. Denial of service attacks are the hardest type to prevent, because preventing them may require imposition of arbitrary limits that in themselves may be considered denial of service.

As an example of a denial of service attack, consider a site connected to the Internet with a 64kbps ISDN line. If an attacker on a fast computer with a T3 link sends packets to the small site as fast as he can, the ISDN link will be filled with packets, denying service (or at least greatly degrading it) to the small site.

As another example, if a Web server has a CGI script that is quite resource-intensive and someone sends many requests to the Web server, the CGI script may tie up the processor, denying access to others.

As a final example, consider a bug in a TCP/IP stack that crashes a computer if a certain malformed packet is sent. Although the bug cannot be exploited directly to take control of the computer or obtain confidential information, it can be used to deny service.

Only the last of these examples is a true bug that can be fixed. The first and second examples are very difficult to prevent entirely. Their impact can be reduced only by carefully engineering the network and Web server.

Preventing Attacks

This section describes some ways you can prevent attacks on your Linux machines. If you are connected to the Internet, you should consider these techniques carefully.

Firewalls

A *firewall* can help prevent attacks on a network of computers. A firewall is a gateway that has one interface on an internal LAN and another on the Internet. The firewall has rules that determine whether or not packets are allowed to leave the internal network and travel onto the Internet and vice-versa.

Firewalls have already been covered in an earlier chapter; I will just go over some of the security considerations of firewalls.

Dedicated Machine

A firewall should be a dedicated machine. Do not run anything else on the firewall. For maximum security, observe these principles:

- Do not install unnecessary software on a firewall. In particular, do not install Telnet clients or servers, FTP clients or servers, compilers, Perl, or other development tools. The lack of these tools hinders attackers who may break into the firewall.

- Do not run any Internet services on the firewall. That means no sendmail, no FTP or Web server, not even the `daytime`, `echo`, or `discard` services. To turn off services, edit `/etc/inetd.conf` to turn everything off. Better yet, do not even run `inetd`. To turn off non-inetd–controlled services, remove their startup scripts from the appropriate `/etc/rc.d/rc?.d` directory.

- Use non-routable (private) addresses for machines on the local network. Drop all packets coming from the Internet destined for (or claiming to come from) non-routable addresses. Use masquerading to allow internal machines to access the Internet.
- Have all firewall rules log hits. The log should be done on the firewall machine as well as on a logging host on the internal network.

For the ultimate in firewall security, you could set up a firewall something like this:

- Use a machine with no hard drive.
- Create a write-protected bootable Linux floppy that contains the kernel and a minimal file system.
- When the firewall boots from the floppy, it should create a RAM disk and use that as a `root` partition. Once the system has booted, configured all interfaces and set up the firewall rules, delete the `sh`, `route`, and `ifconfig` binaries. (In fact, delete all system binaries—they are not needed once the system is up and running.) Because the binaries are in a RAM disk, the bootable floppy is unaffected.

The beauty of this setup is that the lack of even `sh` makes it very difficult for an attacker to take control of the firewall. Even if he does somehow manage to get a shell, the attacker cannot permanently modify the firewall setup (which is on a write-protected floppy).

The mechanics of this kind of firewall setup are a bit involved; a starting point is the "Initial RAMDisk" article in `/usr/src/linux/Documentation/initrd.txt`. Of course, you need a second machine for testing purposes until you have the setup just right.

A Firewall Is Not a Panacea

A firewall prevents certain packets from the Internet from entering your LAN and certain packets from your LAN from entering the Internet. That is all. If you are running a Web browser with an exploitable buffer overrun from behind your firewall, the firewall cannot prevent a buffer overrun attack. For this reason, you need to practice deep security. Make all of your LAN workstations secure enough that you'd feel confident putting them on the Internet even without a firewall. Then put in a firewall anyway.

Each LAN machine (if it is running Linux) should have its own firewall rules to reject packets from outside machines. For example, no outside machine should attempt to access any UNIX services on internal machines, so all packets not coming from the local network destined for ports below 1024 should be blocked.

In particular, internal machines should not trust the firewall. The firewall will be the first machine compromised by an attacker; internal machines should not allow connections originating from the firewall machine.

Although it may be overkill, you can use the TCP Wrappers facility as well as firewall rules to restrict access to TCP services. For an overview of the facility, see manual pages `hosts_access(5)`. On modern computers, the overhead introduced by multiple levels of access control is acceptable.

SUID/SGID Programs

Get a list of every SUID or SGID program on your system and make sure you understand why it needs to be SUID or SGID. In many cases, such programs can run quite well without special privileges. If you are unhappy with a SUID program, remove it or turn off the SUID bit.

For example, on my system, the file `/usr/bin/xmonisdn` is installed in SUID `root`. Since this command is for monitoring the ISDN subsystem and I do not have any ISDN hardware, it is better to remove the program (or at least turn off the SUID bit) than leave it around for a potential exploit.

Keeping Up-to-Date

You should periodically check your vendor's Web site for security updates. Security problems and fixes happen with startling frequency; if you are serious about security, you'll try to keep on top of them. An excellent resource is the BUGTRAQ list at `http://www.securityfocus.com`. This is a full-disclosure list (it will tell you exactly how to exploit bugs). Since computer criminals most likely read the list, you'd better read it too, to stay ahead (or at least abreast) of them.

Be careful, however: Usually it's a good idea to update software when new versions are released, but sometimes new versions introduce new bugs or security holes.

Unless you know for certain that a release fixes a critical security problem, I would evaluate each upgrade and wait before updating. The brave souls who upgrade first will report their experiences soon enough if new security bugs are found.

Monitoring, Detection, and Logging

Monitoring and logging tools are essential parts of overall security. They can alert you to attack attempts before an attacker gains entry to your system. They can also help you trace attackers who compromise your system (providing logs are set up so that attackers cannot destroy them).

System Logs

Most logging on Linux is done with the *syslog* facility. A file called /etc/syslog.conf controls how and where information is logged. This information was covered earlier; for more details, see syslog.conf(5) and syslogd(8).

For maximum security, you should log messages to the local host and to a central logging host. For ultimate security, pass the log output to a line printer. It is much easier for an attacker who has gained root access to delete disk files than to destroy pieces of paper in a locked room hundreds of miles away.

Log Analysis

System logs typically contain quite a bit of information, most of which is boring and routine. This is dangerous, because it can cause you to skip over log entries that should alert you to problems.

There are several log analysis tools available, but (unfortunately) none is included with Caldera OpenLinux 2.3.

One of my favorite log analysis tools is *swatch*, available from ftp://ftp.stanford.edu/general/security-tools/swatch. This is a Perl script that lets you specify which log entries you are *not* interested in (using regular expressions). The tool scans the log files, discards uninteresting messages, and mails you the rest.

Specifying uninteresting messages is safer than specifying which messages you want, because an unanticipated message type might crop up and be discarded.

You should run swatch on your log files daily and spend 5–10 minutes reading the output every day.

Typical Signs of Attacks

What log entries might indicate attack attempts? Look for these entries and treat them as suspicious:

- Many failed login attempts. These could indicate password cracking attempts. However, do not overreact—a legitimate user may have forgotten her password.
- Many failed (or successful!) su attempts. Again, a few failed attempts might be accidental (typing du instead of su, for example).
- Accesses to many different network services. If something is connecting to your mail agent, FTP server, Web server, or Telnet client often and in quick succession, your machine is likely being *port scanned*. In this process, an attacker tries connecting to many different ports on your machine to determine which services are running. Some

attack scripts even read banners returned by the various service daemons, determine which security holes they contain (if any), and automatically compromise them.

- Any strange or persistent failure messages. These could be caused by hardware or software problems—or by an attacker probing your setup.

Please note that the system logger itself can be used in a denial of service attack. The system log daemon `syslogd` has an option (`-r`) that lets it receive logging messages over the network. An attacker can send thousands of spurious logging messages to the system logger, filling the disk space on the logging machine. You should normally disable the `-r` option or use firewalling rules to control which machines can send logging messages to the logging daemon.

Monitoring Files

If an attacker gains control of your system, he typically modifies some files to leave a backdoor for later access. You can prevent such actions by making it hard to modify files, or you can detect them by using monitoring tools.

Prevention of File Modification

The only sure way to prevent file modification is to mount files from a read-only device such as a CD-ROM. Note that mounting a normal hard disk as read-only is *not* secure, because an attacker who gains root access can easily remount the disk as read-write.

> **Note**
>
> You may be able to make hardware modifications that render the disk drive truly read-only. A simple switch on the write line of the disk cable could do the trick. However, I am unaware of any disk hardware that actually implements this. If you are handy with a soldering iron and brave enough, you could cut the write line on your disk cable and insert a switch. But don't do this unless you absolutely know what you are doing.

Mounting large parts of the file system as read-only is tricky, but it can be done. In principle, the root partition should be mountable as read-only. The only directory trees that actually need write access are

- `/var`   Contains runtime modifiable data
- `/tmp`   Contains temporary files
- `/home`   Contains users' home directories

You can place these three trees on a hard disk and the rest of the system on read-only media.

Detecting File Modification

For most people, however, it is impractical to set up large parts of the system as read-only. You may have a legitimate need to modify files in /etc, for example, and not want the hassle of burning a new CD or playing with hardware switches. In that case, file modification detection is the next best thing to prevention.

The Tripwire package by Gene Spafford and others can be used to check whether files have been modified. Tripwire works by keeping a database of modification times for files and directories. It also keeps a number of *hash values* for files.

A hash value is a number computed by processing the contents of a file. The idea of the hash function is that a given file will always yield the same hash value, but a different file is highly unlikely to yield the same hash value. Furthermore, the hash function is designed to make it extremely difficult to modify a file in order to give a specific hash value. This makes it difficult for an attacker to modify a file but arrange for it to have the same hash value as the unmodified file.

Tripwire is available via FTP from ftp://coast.cs.purdue.edu/pub/COAST/Tripwire. Note that this FTP site contains only an old version of Tripwire in source form. This source must be massaged slightly to compile under Linux.

If you are unwilling to edit C source files to compile Tripwire, commercial versions are available from Tripwire Security at http://www.tripwiresecurity.com.

Tripwire has a number of different hash functions; you can use all of them for added security. For details, download or purchase Tripwire.

Most Linux distributions (including Caldera OpenLinux) include a program called *md5sum* that performs similar (but weaker) checks. The md5sum program checks only the contents of files, not their permissions or modification times. However, it is better than nothing.

To create a signature list for a number of files, invoke md5sum like this:

```
$ md5sum file...
```

For example, to check all the files in /sbin and place the checksums in a file called CKSUMS, use this command:

```
# md5sum /sbin/* > CKSUMS
```

The md5sum command must be run as root because some files in /sbin are readable only by root.

The file CKSUMS should be kept in a safe place, preferably on a write-protected floppy disk.

To verify that the files' checksums have not changed, invoke md5sum with the -c option:

```
$ md5sum -c CKSUMS
```

With the -c option, md5sum reads the list of files from CKSUMS and verifies each one. If all goes well, you should see a whole list of filenames, followed by OK.

If a file has been modified, you'll see something like this:

```
$ md5sum -c CKSUMS
...
sbin/udosctl: OK
/sbin/umssetup: OK
/sbin/umssync: FAILED
/sbin/update: OK
md5sum: WARNING: 1 of 87 computed checksums did NOT match
```

This indicates that the file /sbin/umssync has been modified.

For more information on md5sum, see md5sum(1) or the md5sum info page.

What to Do When Faced with Intrusion

If you suspect that your system has been compromised, it is important to remain calm. If you suspect that system executables have been modified, realize that you can trust *nothing* on your system. You should bring the system down and reboot with a rescue floppy built from a distribution CD. Mount the file systems and copy all log files to a safe place. Then format all partitions and reinstall the operating system from the distribution medium. Recover home directories from backup tapes, but treat any executables in home directories as suspect. In extreme cases, you may have to examine all files in home directories for tampering.

If you catch an intruder in the act, you can monitor his actions with commands like ps, who and w. Try to gather as much information as possible to trace the intruder. If the intruder has entered over the network, you can also run tcpdump as root to dump every network packet sent to or from the intruder into a file. This lets you reconstruct his entire session.

Once you feel you have collected enough information, shut down the intruder's connection. You can try to talk to him using talk or write to verify his intentions but, if they are malicious, the intruder may decide to cause the maximum amount of damage once he knows he has been discovered.

Controlling Access to Services

UNIX services (or *daemons*) are a frequent source of security problems. Attackers can connect to services and often easily determine which version of the program is running. Armed with knowledge of version-specific bugs, attackers can exploit these bugs to gain access to your machine.

An obvious security enhancement is to limit access to services. Machines that provide services to the outside world (such as Web, mail, and FTP servers) should be on their own network and separated from your internal network via a firewall. These machines should be treated by your internal machines as external, even though they are under your administrative control.

On your internal network, you should restrict access to services only to those computers that really need them. Even machines that provide services to the outside world should limit the services they provide only to absolutely necessary services.

TCP Wrappers

The TCP Wrappers suite by Wietse Venema provides a flexible and convenient mechanism for controlling access to services. The suite consists of two components: a stand-alone program called tcpd and a library called `libwrap.a` that can be linked with other programs.

Most Internet services are started by the inetd daemon, which reads a configuration file called `/etc/inetd.conf`. On Caldera OpenLinux, this file is already set up to make use of the TCP Wrappers suite. Let's look at a sample `inetd.conf` line:

```
telnet  stream  tcp  nowait  root  /usr/sbin/tcpd  in.telnetd
```

This line specifies that incoming connections for the Telnet service should run the program `/usr/sbin/tcpd` with the argument `in.telnetd`.

What happens is that tcpd checks whether or not access is allowed and, if so, runs the program `in.telnetd`, which is the actual Telnet server. The `inetd.conf` file is set up so that almost all services are protected with tcpd.

> **Note**
>
> The only unprotected services are the trivial internal services such as `echo`, `discard`, and so forth. You should disable these services unless you have a good reason for enabling them.

Access Control

tcpd controls access to services using the language described in the manual pages `hosts_access(5)` and `hosts_options(5)`. tcpd normally uses two access files, `/etc/hosts.allow` and `/etc/hosts.deny`, but you can place all of the access control information in a single file for ease of maintenance.

For example, suppose you want to allow access to services only for hosts in `local.domain`, but not for any other hosts. Place these lines in `/etc/hosts.allow`:

```
ALL: .local.domain: ALLOW
ALL: ALL: DENY
```

The first match always determines whether or not access is granted. In this case, any host in `local.domain` (note the leading period in the pattern) will be allowed access to all services. All other hosts will be denied access.

Each line in `/etc/hosts.allow` looks something like this:

```
daemon_list : client_list : option : option ...
```

`daemon_list` is a list of services. For services in `/etc/inetd.conf`, use the name of the daemon program. For example, for Telnet service, the service name is `in.telnetd`, because that is the argument to the tcpd program. You can list several daemons, separated by blanks.

In addition, the EXCEPT operator can be used in daemon and client lists. For example, to deny access to all services except FTP, use

```
ALL EXCEPT ftp: ALL: DENY
```

`client_list` is a space-separated list of client machines. Each entry in the list can take one of the following forms:

- A string that begins with . (period). A hostname matches if the last components of its fully qualified domain name match the string.
- A string that ends with . (period). A hostname matches if the first portion of its IP address matches the string. For example, `192.168.` matches any machine whose IP address begins with `192.168`.
- An expression of the form *n.n.n.n/m.m.m.m*, which is interpreted as a network/netmask pair. For example, `192.168.4.0/255.255.255.128` matches addresses from `192.168.4.0` through `192.168.4.127`.

In addition, you can use special keywords to match hosts:

- ALL matches any host (and any daemon in `daemon_list`).

- UNKNOWN matches a host whose name is unknown (has no entry in the DNS). Be careful with this, because DNS can experience transient failures.
- KNOWN matches a host whose name is known.
- PARANOID matches a host whose name does not match its address. This could indicate a spoofing attempt. By default, tcpd drops such requests even before consulting the access tables; you need to rebuild it from the source if you want to allow such requests.

Access Control Options

The options portion of the tcpd configuration line can contain the following:

- ALLOW allows access to the specified service.
- DENY denies access to the specified service.
- spawn executes a command after performing certain expansions described in hosts_access(5). For example
  ```
  spawn (/usr/sbin/safe_finger \
  -l @%h | /usr/ucb/mail root) &
  ```
  runs the command safe_finger with the connecting hostname as the argument and mails the result to root. This may provide some information as to who is trying to connect to the service. (Or it may provide useless information from an attacker who has control over the remote system.)
- twist replaces the current process with the specified shell command. Standard input, output, and errors are connected to the client process. For example, suppose you want to deny access to FTP to clients in bad.domain. You could use this:
  ```
  in.ftpd : .bad.domain : \
  twist /bin/echo 421 No bad people allowed
  ```

The TCP Wrappers suite has many more options; see hosts_access(5) and hosts_options(5) for more details.

Services that are not started from inetd can take advantage of the TCP Wrappers library, but they must be written and configured to do so. In particular, sendmail can make use of TCP wrappers, but the default sendmail binary supplied with Caldera OpenLinux 2.3 has not been configured to take advantage of this. You have to rebuild it from source if you want this capability.

Other Programs

Other programs such as sendmail, in.ftpd, and the Apache Web server httpd have their own access control configuration files. You should use them and configure them appropriately.

Finally, you can enable IP firewalling even on workstations to filter access to services. While multiple access control facilities are redundant and use up processing power, on modern computers the speed penalty is unnoticeable, and the extra layers of control add protection.

> **Note**
>
> If you use multiple layers of access control, be sure to test them separately. Otherwise, you may think that all the configuration files are correct when in fact the first layer is protecting all the remaining layers. (Some tools for testing your system's security are described later in this chapter in the section "Security Tools.")

Keeping Your System Up-to-Date

It is very important to keep your system up-to-date. When security flaws are discovered, fixes or workarounds are usually supplied very quickly. Programs that typically need watching include

- The Linux kernel itself. Bugs are occasionally found in the Linux TCP/IP stack or other subsystems that could cause denial of service problems.
- The Apache Web server
- The in.ftpd FTP server
- The sendmail mail transfer agent
- Any other program that offers network services or is installed SUID or SGID

Places you should look for security problems and software updates include

- The BUGTRAQ list at http://www.securityfocus.com.
- CERT (Computer Emergency Response Team) at http://www.cert.org. See the "CERT Advisories" section.
- CIAC (Computer Incident Advisory Capability) at http://ciac.llnl.gov.
- Caldera's security advisories page at http://www.calderasystems.com/news/security.

In general, keeping your system up-to-date is as simple as obtaining and installing new RPMs. Make sure you verify them and check the signatures before installing them.

In some cases, you may have to rebuild from source or patch source files. You should become comfortable with this process so that you can do it quickly if an emergency arises.

Security Tools

Several useful tools allow *port-scanning* to detect which services are exported by remote computers. Attackers will often use these tools as a prelude to a computer crime; you should use these same tools to scan your own computers and verify that scans cause log entries to be produced.

> **Warning**
> Do not scan a remote computer without the permission of the system administrator. The very act of scanning may be viewed as a hostile act.

We will list the tools available here, but we won't describe their operation or setup. You should download the tools and read the included documentation for setup information.

nmap

The nmap program is a sophisticated port scanner that can scan for TCP and UDP services. It can use special tricks to try to dodge firewalls and avoid target machines from logging connection attempts. It can also usually identify target operating systems, based on their responses to malformed TCP packets. The nmap Web page is at `http://www.insecure.org/nmap/index.html`.

SAINT

SAINT is another scanning tool similar to nmap, but it can perform different kinds of probes. SAINT's home page is `http://www.wwdsi.com/saint/index.html`.

Crack

Crack is a program for cracking UNIX passwords. You can use it to ensure that your users pick strong passwords. Crack's home page is at
`http://www.users.dircon.co.uk/crypto`.

Trinux

Trinux is a floppy-based Linux distribution with many security tools included. Its home page is `http://www.trinux.org`.

Open Security Solutions

The open security solutions page at http://www.opensec.net contains links to over 100 security tools for cryptography and authentication, host security checking, network mapping, intrusion detection, logging and monitoring, and more. This is a treasure chest for security information.

Privacy

Internet email and other forms of information exchange suffer from the following problems:

- Lack of privacy   Information can be intercepted and read as it moves from source to destination.
- Lack of authentication   It is trivial to create fake email messages that appear to come from someone else. It is somewhat harder but nevertheless quite possible to modify messages in transit or fake other kinds of information flow.

The Internet is not private. You should assume that others can read anything you send over the Internet and perhaps even modify it. Even internal corporate email is not likely to be private. Most companies have policies that allow them to read all email to or from an employee, as well as any files owned by that employee.

The only practical method to achieve some degree of privacy and authentication is to use *encryption* to encode information and *digital signatures* to authenticate it.

> **Note**
>
> But even this does not give complete protection. These techniques cannot hide the fact that communication took place. For example, a mail message from julia@mycompany.com to recruiting@competitor.com might cause trouble for Julia even if the contents are encrypted.

PGP

The most popular encryption and authentication tool is PGP, or Pretty Good Privacy. You can get commercial versions from http://www.pgp.com or download a free (for non-commercial use) version from http://web.mit.edu/network/pgp.html. Note that, because of U.S. export restrictions, these packages are available only to residents of the U.S. and Canada.

Another authentication and encryption tool is GNU Privacy Guard, available from http://www.gnupg.org. Since this tool was written outside the U.S. and its FTP servers are in Europe, anyone can obtain and use the tool. It follows the OpenPGP format as described in RFC 2440.

> **Warning**
>
> Unfortunately, GNU Privacy Guard is *not* compatible with PGP version 2, because it does not use the RSA or IDEA algorithm. These algorithms are patented and hence cannot be used in free software. This is yet another example of software patents restricting the use of free software and an illustration of why software patents are a bad idea.

Public Key Cryptography

PGP and GNU Privacy Guard provide facilities for encrypting and authenticating email messages and files. They use *public key cryptography* for this purpose. In public key cryptography, a pair of keys is generated. The *private key* should be kept secret. Disclosure of the private key is a serious breach of security. The *public key* corresponding to the private key should be published far and wide.

To encrypt a message so that only a specific recipient can decrypt it, you encrypt the message with that person's *public* key. The message can be decrypted only by someone who knows the person's *private* key. The security of public key encryption relies on the assumption that it is very difficult to deduce a private key given a public key. This difficulty has not been conclusively proven but is believed by most cryptographic experts to be true.

To authenticate a message, you encrypt it (or a hash calculated from it) with your private key. Anyone who knows your public key can decrypt it and verify that it came from you. No one else can create a message that can be decrypted with your public key, because to do so requires knowledge of your private key.

PGP and GNU Privacy Guard are fairly complex and have many options. You should download the tools and read the documentation that comes with them. GNU Privacy Guard has some facilities for interoperability with PGP, but the patent and export problems are thorny.

Virtual Private Networks

A virtual private network is a network that includes the Internet as one or more of its links (see Figure 24.1).

FIGURE 24.1

A virtual private network.

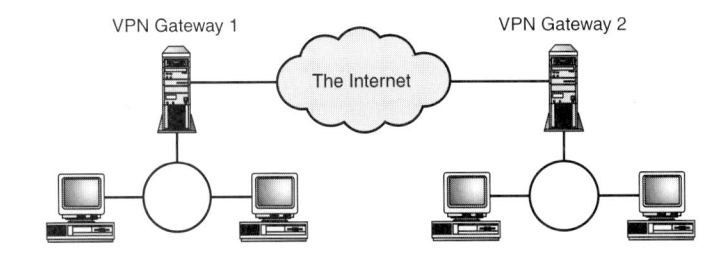

In a virtual private network, all traffic across the Internet is encrypted by the transmitting gateway and decrypted by the receiving gateway. For example, to the hosts on the left part of the network in Figure 24.1, the hosts on the right part may appear simply as local hosts on the local network. The two gateways take care of encrypting the traffic that crosses the Internet.

The IP Secure (IPSec) standard specifies protocols for building virtual private networks across the Internet. A free VPN implementation for Linux is FreeS/WAN, whose home page is http://www.xs4all.nl/ freeswan/. Since the software was developed outside the U.S., it is freely exportable.

FreeS/WAN lets you set up two Linux machines to act as VPN gateways. It includes several encryption algorithms and supports public key encryption and standards for key exchange.

Unfortunately, FreeS/WAN requires modifications to the Linux kernel and (as of this writing) works reliably only with kernels in the 2.0 series. Setting it up is beyond the scope of this book; download the package and read the excellent documentation included with it if you are interested in setting up a VPN.

Another VPN option is PoPToP, which provides a virtual private network compatible with Microsoft's PPTP setup. PoPToP does not require kernel modifications. Its home page is http://www.moretonbay.com/vpn/pptp.html.

There may be other tools available; check the "Tunneling" section on http://www.opensec.net.

Summary

In this chapter, you have learned computer security basics, including a useful definition of a secure computer. You learned about the various components of security, including physical security, personnel security, and network security.

Next, you learned the UNIX security module, which provides unlimited permissions to the `root` account. You learned about common attacks on UNIX programs, including buffer overruns, network sniffing, social engineering, password guessing, and denial of service attacks.

After learning about attacks, you learned how to prevent them by using firewalls and limiting the use of SUID/SGID programs. You also learned how and what to monitor to detect intruders and how to control access to network services using the TCP Wrappers package.

Next, you learned about the importance of keeping your system up-to-date and were given some resources for learning about security problems and fixes.

Finally, you learned how to ensure a modicum of privacy over the Internet and how to obtain software to set up secure virtual private networks.

Linux Applications

PART III

IN THIS PART

25 Using Productivity Software *577*

26 MySQL Essentials *593*

27 Using Image Manipulation Tools *615*

28 Typesetting Documents *649*

29 Setting up Sound and Multimedia *671*

Using Productivity Software

IN THIS CHAPTER

- Using WordPerfect 578
- Using StarOffice 585

Caldera Open Linux 2.3 ships with many productivity packages—in fact, there are too many to cover in a single chapter. Just to get you started, we'll take a look at two of them: WordPerfect, long considered the premier word processing package worldwide; and StarOffice, which combines word processing with spreadsheet, presentation, email, and other software into a first-class office suite.

After getting your feet wet with these two, you really should take the time to investigate some of the many other productivity software packages available, such as Plan and Korganizer (scheduling), Kaddressbook (contacts), and The Gimp (graphics). Variety is the spice of life, and it is definitely one of the many advantages to Linux computing.

Using WordPerfect

WordPerfect, in its many incarnations and ownerships, has set the standard for word processing worldwide for more than a decade. Over the last few years, it has evolved into a virtual office suite all by itself, incorporating graphics manipulation and spreadsheet functions directly into document processing, while advanced layout features enable the production of handsome, professional-looking presentations.

Installation

If you performed a recommended install using Lisa, or recommended plus commercial using Lizard, the main portion of WordPerfect is already installed. If not, mount your Caldera OpenLinux 2.3 CD-ROM, switch to the /OpenLinux/install/RPMS, and install using the following command:

```
rpm -ivh WordPerfect-8.0-7.i386.rpm
```

After the main portion of the install has finished, WordPerfect must be set up for individual use. You must log in as the user you are setting up for, and then run /usr/bin/xwp. At this point, you will be prompted for a serial number, which can be obtained by registering your software at
http://venus.corel.com/nasapps/wp8linuxreg/register.html.

Getting Started

While Corel WordPerfect 8 for Linux functions essentially the same as WordPerfect 8 for Windows, you will nevertheless notice an immediate difference when you first launch the Linux version: WordPerfect begins by opening a small program box that contains all your setup options (display, document locations, quick format, and so on) and also controls WordPerfect. From here, you can open multiple WordPerfect windows (referred to as *WPwindows* in this chapter) containing new or existing documents. Here you will also find a list of the most recently-opened documents (your current task list).

Be careful with those WPwindows, though! They operate somewhat differently than you might expect. When you choose Open or New from the File menu in a WPwindow, you are telling WordPerfect to open another document in this window, thus closing the document you have on your screen. In other words, the File menu options of a WPwindow are replacement functions and will not open an additional WPwindow. This is one of those things you'll learn after the fourth or fifth time you accidentally close the document on which you're working.

The other primary difference that experienced WordPerfect users will notice lies in the shortcut keys. Many of the shortcuts used in Windows versions of WordPerfect can have unexpected results in the X Windows environment, so some have been eliminated and others have been changed. It is wise to use the menu options until you become accustomed to the new shortcuts.

File Management

To open an existing file, choose Open from the File menu of a WPwindow, or choose Open Window from the Program menu in the Program box (referred to in this chapter as simply *Program*).

To create a new document from scratch, choose New from the File menu of a WPwindow, or choose New Window from Program.

Remember that the work you do in a WPwindow is not permanently stored until you save it as a file. Use File, Save to save your work from time to time to prevent its loss in the event of a system failure.

> **Tip**
>
> WordPerfect for Linux has the same automated backup function that other versions of WordPerfect use. From Program, choose Preferences, Files to set the location of your temporary backup files and the frequency of automated backups. This doesn't take the place of using File, Save every so often to preserve your work, but it does serve as an additional safeguard.

To save a file for the first time, choose Save from the File menu. Then place the cursor in the Filename/Current Selection text box, and type the new filename. Remember to check the path where you are saving the file. You can change directories by navigating in the Directory List section on the right. Finally click OK, and the file will be saved.

> **Tip**
>
> Remember that Linux supports long filenames, which can be very handy but only up to a point. If your filenames are too detailed, you'll still find yourself reading line after line of directory listings, trying to determine which file you're after. Develop abbreviations for certain document types (ltr for letter, env for envelope, lab for labels, and so on) that make searching easy, and utilize a good directory structure to organize your files just as you would in a filing cabinet.

To save the current document under a new name (if you're editing a form you want to preserve or aren't certain you want this new version to be "The Version"), choose File, Save As and proceed as if you're saving a new file. Double-check that filename and path before clicking OK.

To save a file in a different file format, choose File, Save As and make a selection from the Save Options/File Format dropdown box. Specify a filename and path (you can use the current filename to replace the existing file or type in a new name to preserve the old format), and then choose OK to save the file under a new name and format.

Remember, use File, Save to save successive updates on an open document under the same filename, and use File, Save As to save the open document under a new name.

Formatting Documents

Happily, page formatting is essentially the same in WordPerfect 8 for Linux as in other versions of WordPerfect and many other popular word processing programs. The following basics will get you started, and a bit of experimentation with various menu options will help you perfect your technique.

Page Setup

Choose Format, Page for most of your basic page setup options: size and layout of page, numbering, and so on. Headers and Footers, however, are under the Insert menu.

Use Format, Margins to change the whitespace between the text and the edge of a printed page. The default settings for margins are 1 inch on all sides of the page.

To change your margins, move your cursor to the paragraph (for side margins) or page (for top or bottom margins) where you want to make a change, or select (with your mouse) the paragraphs for which you want to change the left or right margins, and choose File, Page Setup, Margins or choose Format, Margins. Next, specify new settings for Left, Right, Top, or Bottom margins and then click OK to activate the new settings.

Justification

Use Justification to align text on the page, either right, left, center, or between both the left and right margins.

To use a different justification, place your cursor at the desired location, choose Justification from the Format menu, and then select the justification type you want. As you begin to type, the text will have the new justification applied.

To change justification on existing text, select the paragraphs you want to justify or move your cursor somewhere in the paragraph you want to change the justification. Choose Justification from the Format menu, and then choose the justification type you want. The paragraph(s) will then be formatted with the justification you chose.

> **Note**
>
> If you choose to use the second option, the change will affect the entire paragraph and any subsequent text.

Tabs

Use Tab Set to determine where the insertion point stops when you press Tab or Back Tab (Shift+Tab). To alter the tab set, place your cursor in the paragraph where you want the new tab settings to take effect. Choose Format, Line, Tab Set. To clear a single existing tab setting, specify the setting in the Position text box, and then choose Clear. To delete all current tab settings, choose Clear All.

To set new tabs, you must first decide how you want to measure tabs: from the Left Margin (Relative) or from the Left Edge of Paper (Absolute). Select a tab type from the Type options menu. Table 25.1 shows the options available.

TABLE 25.1 Tab Set Options

Option	Description
Left	Text you type moves to the right of the Tab.
Center	Text you type centers itself around the Tab.
Right	Text you type moves backward to the left of the Tab.
Decimal	Text you type before you insert the align character (usually a decimal point) moves to the left of the tab. Text you type after the align character moves to the right of the tab. The decimals stay aligned.

continues

TABLE 25.1 continued

Option	Description
Dot leader	A row of dots is inserted in your text when you press Tab. Dot leaders are inserted from the insertion point to the next tab setting. You can insert dot leaders with a left, right, center, or decimal tab.

Next, specify a tab setting in the Position text box, and then click the Set button. If you just click OK without first clicking the Set button, your new tab isn't set. For multiple tabs on a set spacing pattern, specify the beginning tab setting in the Position text box, select Repeat Every, and then specify the distance you want between tabs. To clear all your manually-set tabs and return to WordPerfect's default tab settings, click Default. Finally, click OK to have the new tab settings take effect.

Line Spacing

Use Line Spacing to specify the spacing between lines of text.

To change the line spacing, place your cursor anywhere in the paragraph where you want the spacing change to begin, or select any amount of text in the paragraphs you want to reformat.

Choose Format, Line, Spacing and specify the line spacing you want to use in your document. Lastly, click OK to have these changes take effect.

> **Tip**
>
> The line height is the distance from the top of one line to the top of the next line. Corel WordPerfect determines line spacing by multiplying the current line height by the value you specify. Different fonts will have varying line heights, and you can adjust these even further with the Format, Make It Fit option box settings.

Fonts

Use Font to change the basic typeface in which your document is printed. The font in any document consists of three elements: the font face (such as Times Roman or Courier), the font style (such as Bold or Italic), and the font size (such as 10cpi or 10pt).

> **Note**
>
> With font sizes measured in cpi or characters per inch (also known as "pitch" in ancient typists' parlance, or "monospaced" fonts), each character takes up a specific amount of space on your page, regardless of whether it is narrow (ones and exclamation points) or wide (Ms and zeroes). This can be useful when manually spacing text that should be aligned a certain way without the use of tabs, indents, tables, or other formatting codes that may not properly translate into different document formats.
>
> Font sizes measured in pt or points, however, are known as proportionally-spaced fonts. In other words, each character takes up an amount of space on your page proportionate to its size and shape.

> **Tip**
>
> It is generally thought that the human eye reads "point" fonts more easily than "pitch" fonts, which is good to know when you're formatting an important business proposal or term paper.
>
> You can generally fit more text on a page with a point font because of the more efficient spacing system, which may or may not work in your favor, depending on the project.
>
> Use the options in Format, Typesetting to further adjust character placement and spacing.

To change the font for an entire document, place your cursor at the top of the first page and choose Format, Font. To change a font from this point forward, place your cursor wherever you want the change to take effect. You can also select text with your mouse (from a single character to whole paragraphs) and use the Font options to apply changes only to the selected text. Special text formatting features, such as strikeout and double-underline, are also available in the Font options box.

Page Numbering

Use Page Numbering to select the type of page numbers you want and place them in specific locations on the printed page. You can also insert a page, secondary, chapter, or volume number anywhere in the text of your document.

To number pages, place your cursor at the top of the page where you want numbering to begin. Choose Format, Page, Page Numbering, Numbering. Select a location for the page numbers from the Position options menu and click OK.

To insert formatted page numbers in text, place your cursor where you want the formatted page number to appear. Choose Format, Page, Page Numbering, Numbering, and then choose Options to display the Page Numbering Options dialog box. Choose from the available options, check the Insert Format and Accompanying Text at Insertion Point box, and click OK.

To insert only the page number (no special formatting) in text, place the insertion point where you want the number to appear and choose Format, Page, Page Numbering, Insert Page Number, Page Number.

Centering Pages

Use Center Page to center text between the top and bottom margins (the title page of a proposal or script, for example).

If you want to turn centering on or off for a single page, place your cursor on that page; for multiple pages, place your cursor on the first page of the section. Choose Format, Page, Center. Select an option to indicate which pages you want to center (or to turn off centering), and then click OK to have the changes take effect.

Remember that Center Page is used only for vertical alignment; to center text on the page left-to-right, use the justification function.

Advanced Features

Corel WordPerfect 8 for Linux offers many advanced features that effectively place this software between the categories of word processing and desktop publishing. A brief overview of a few of these features is included to entice you into exploring the possibilities of WordPerfect on your own.

Inserting Graphics

Everyone knows that simple graphic images, when not overdone, can liven up an otherwise very dull document. WordPerfect makes it easy to insert clipart, custom graphics such as logos, or graphs and such generated by third-party software. Choose Insert, Graphics, From File to insert a ready-to-go graphic image already saved to disk. WordPerfect creates a little box with your image inside. You can use the mouse to drag the box to different positions on the page and drag the box margins to resize it. For more precision, right-click the image box to view the entire menu of image box options, including figure number and captions.

If your printer can't produce good prints of graphics or you can't use images for some other reason, try creating text boxes (Insert, Text Box) with various borders and fill to set off quotations or special points of interest. You can also use graphical lines and other shapes (Insert, Shape) to separate sections. Finally, you can simply insert individual interesting characters (Insert, Symbol) like stars, arrows, pointing fingers, and so on to bring attention to particular points or section headings.

Outlines/Bulleted Lists

Many varieties of ordered and unordered lists are possible in WordPerfect. Choose Insert, Bullets & Numbering to create bulleted lists, numbered lists, numbered paragraphs, and various outline formats. A bit of experimentation with these functions can turn pages of mindless prose into eye-catching, logical arguments in support of your position—in appearance, at least.

Custom Configuration

For the advanced user, there are many advanced features in WordPerfect 8 that can be customized or even turned off. Under Program, you will find a Preferences menu with configuration settings for nearly all available options in WordPerfect. Some features you will want to use every day, some only occasionally, and some never. A bit of experimentation with these configuration settings will enable you to customize your copy of WordPerfect 8 for maximum efficiency.

In addition to word processing and basic desktop publishing features, WordPerfect also offers HTML editing, basic graphics manipulation with its Draw program (Insert, Graphics, Draw Picture), and limited spreadsheet capabilities with its tables functions (Insert, Table). For a full-fledged office suite, however, you should take a look at StarOffice.

Using StarOffice

StarOffice is a full-featured office suite with software applications to handle word processing, spreadsheets, graphics, presentations, address book, and scheduling, in addition to Internet functions (email, news, FTP and web browsing).

StarOffice is arguably the first truly integrated office suite in that launching StarOffice provides you with a complete workspace, known as the StarOffice Desktop, that integrates all StarOffice functions in a single presentation with multiple toolbars and navigation features. Documents of all types, from Web pages in Africa to graphics on your marketing department's server and the grocery list on your local hard drive—all are readily available with a click of the mouse on the Star Desktop.

Installation

If you performed a Recommended install using Lisa or Recommended Plus Commercial using Lizard, the main portion of StarOffice is already installed. If not, mount your Caldera OpenLinux 2.3 CD-ROM, switch to the `/OpenLinux/install/RPMS`, and type

```
rpm -ivh StarOffice-5.0_01_506L-2.i386.rpm
```

After the main portion of the install has finished, StarOffice must be set up for individual use. You must log in as the user you are setting up for, and then run `/opt/Office50/bin/setup`. At this point, you will be prompted for a media key, which can be found on the inside cover of your OpenLinux 2.3 *Getting Started Guide*.

Getting Started

The Star Desktop can be a bit daunting at first glance, but it doesn't take long (just start clicking) to get a handle on it. Essentially the Star Desktop incorporates all the typical elements of a GUI (graphical user interface) environment into a single workspace, much like the Windows 95/98 OS desktop. It takes a bit of mind-bending to adjust your thinking because you expect a certain specificity of function when you launch a software program, but repeated use will quickly endear you to this integrated approach to document management.

> **Tip**
>
> As a new StarOffice user, you might want to activate the Extended Tips. When you rest the mouse pointer on a screen element for a moment, a short description of the element will be displayed. Extended Tips can be toggled by choosing it from the Help menu.

Components of the Desktop

The StarOffice desktop incorporates many elements, which range from truly useful to simply functional and some that are just plain "kewl." This section briefly outlines the main elements used in basic navigation of the suite.

Bars

The Star Desktop includes a variety of toolbars, including the following:

- *Title Bar*—Contains the title of the present active document within StarOffice
- *Menu Bar*—Contains various menus ordered according to their basic functions

- *Function Bar (just beneath the menu bar)*—Contains icons for important commands and functions that you can use when working on your documents
- *Task Bar*—Contains icons for various desktops, all open tasks and creating new ones

> **Tip**
>
> The menu bar, as well as the toolbars and status bar, can be changed to suit your needs. To do so, choose Tools, Configure. You can also alter the appearance of icons in the various toolbars through Tools, Options, General, View.

Additional toolbars include the Object Bar, Main Toolbar, and Option Bar. You can read about all these in the excellent online documentation included in StarOffice by choosing Help from any window.

On the left end of the Function Bar, the URL field indicates the location of the active document. By typing a file location in this box, you can open a document stored anywhere accessible by your system, whether locally or on the Internet. StarOffice will determine the file type and open it using the appropriate software (Web browser, spreadsheet, word processing, and so on).

Windows

The main window of StarOffice contains all elements of the desktop, including many sub-windows. Windows can be full- or partial-screen views and are moveable (just drag them around with your mouse). Inside windows are icons relating to specific software functions or shortcuts to individual documents. You can drag and drop icons from and among various windows and toolbars, depending on individual needs.

In StarOffice, like most programs, it is the active document that is displayed in the foreground. The active window accepts keyboard input and can be a directory view or a document. To switch between open documents, choose the appropriate icon from the Task Bar or use the Windows menu.

Menus in StarOffice are context-sensitive—the visible menus will constantly change according to active window and open tasks. Menu items are ordered according to purpose (cut, copy, and paste are all under the Edit menu). Functions not available to you at a particular time will be grayed out.

Explorer and Beamer

These two functions form the basis for Star's file management system. The Explorer is used to browse folders/directories, while the Beamer displays the contents of the current folder highlighted in the Explorer. Double-clicking a document in the Beamer window will open that document in the appropriate application (word processing, spreadsheet, and so on).

For example, the Star Address Book is a database in dBase format, which is integrated into StarOffice. Under Address Book, Tables in the Explorer, double-click Address, and a database table with a few sample address records will be displayed in the Beamer.

Explorer also allows you to delete files or simply remove them to the Recycle Bin, where they will be stored until you empty the bin.

> **Tip**
>
> At any time while working with StarOffice, the Explorer can be opened using Shift+Ctrl+E, and the Beamer can be opened with Shift+Ctrl+B.

Customizing Your Workspace

StarOffice offers many ways to customize your workspace. You can create multiple desktops (for example, you might want one desktop for business affairs and a separate one for private matters). You can customize each desktop by layout and theme (colors, backgrounds, and so on).

Workspace customization features are found under Tools, Options, General. Here you can create additional desktops (Paths), or change the "look and feel" of your Desktop (View) to emulate a GUI with which you are more comfortable (Mac, OS/2, or X Windows).

Also under the View tab, you can change the scale for the display (useful if you have trouble reading the small fonts in menus and dialogs boxes that are the default for the StarOffice Desktop) as well as options for mouse positioning and showing the contents of windows while they are moved.

Working with StarOffice

With the advent of the GUI, radical differences in software operation essentially ended. "If you've seen one, you've seen them all" is an adage that may be readily applied to most contemporary software applications. For this reason, we will only briefly overview the basic steps to perform various functions under StarOffice and encourage you to experiment on your own or purchase a book written specifically for in-depth coverage of this productivity package. *Sams Teach Yourself StarOffice 5 for Linux* is a good choice.

Documents

Documents—whether word processing, spreadsheets, or presentations—are the most common file types used in StarOffice. Each time you create a new document or open an existing one, StarOffice launches the appropriate application to handle that document type.

Creating New Documents

Creating new documents in StarOffice is almost too easy. Simply click the Start button (lower-left corner of your desktop) and choose the appropriate document category from the list.

If you want to use a different format than the default template, select File, New, From Template. StarOffice displays a template selection dialog box where you can choose a template on which to base a new document. There are many useful document templates included in StarOffice.

Opening Documents

There are many ways to open documents in StarOffice, depending on where you are and which windows are open. You can use the Explorer and Beamer to identify files and then double-click the filename, choose File, Open from any window, use the Start button; or type the document name and path in the URL window on the Function Bar.

Creating Templates

The easiest way to create a new template is through the use of Autopilot. When you use Autopilot to create a template, that template can then be accessed in the same way as the default templates. Generally speaking, you will only have to fill in the information in Autopilot once and then use it as a basis for creating new documents.

For example, to create a Fax Cover Sheet template, choose File, Autopilot, Fax. The Autopilot walks you through a series of dialog boxes in which you can choose various options, such as inserting a company logo, and basic information on sender and recipient. Finally, click Create and a new fax template is added to the template list.

Events

Star Scheduler makes it easy to plan appointments and tasks. To activate Star Scheduler, double-click the Events folder on your desktop. In the default setting, an overview of appointments for the current date appears. To the right, a monthly calendar and task list are displayed. Use the icons in the Object Bar or the commands in the View menu to view your appointments, tasks, or the calendar.

A colored bar at the left of the event area marks the hours corresponding to the event or appointment, giving you a quick overview of free and occupied time for the day. The colors vary according to settings under the context menu for the Event Overview window. Your Scheduler can be customized to show various layout formats, filters, and styles.

Creating New Appointments

Creating a new appointment is easy with your mouse. In the Event Overview, click the beginning time and drag your mouse pointer to the ending time. Now type some text to define the appointment. Appointment duly noted. Click somewhere else with your mouse to exit the text input mode or simply press Enter.

For an all-day event with no specific beginning or ending time, put your cursor on the top of the Event Overview of the Day and simply type text as if you were creating an appointment.

Modifying Appointments

To change the time(s) of an appointment, simply drag the appointment to the new time(s). To copy an appointment, drag it to the new time while holding down the Ctrl key. A plus sign (+) next to the mouse pointer indicates that the appointment will be copied when you release the mouse button.

To delete an appointment, right-click the appointment to open the Context menu, and then choose Delete.

Email

StarOffice supports POP3, IMAP, and VIM. To set up your StarOffice email software for an existing email account, begin by choosing New, Folder under Explorer and name it something like `mail`. In this mail folder, you must create an email account and an outbox. Right-click n the new `mail` folder, choose New, and choose the type of account you are setting up. Click the General tab and fill in the name you want to use for this entry—perhaps `inbox`. Click each tab in succession and fill in the required information.

> **Note**
>
> You can set up multiple email accounts on a single desktop in StarOffice. Leaving the password field blank in each one provides security without affecting performance—you will be asked for the password as needed.

Now that we have an object to handle the incoming mail, we need one to handle the outgoing mail. You can create an outbox in much the same way—right-click the `mail` folder in Explorer and choose New, Outbox from the context menu (or you may be prompted to create the outbox immediately after you create the inbox). Use the various tabs to complete the outbox setup.

> **Tip**
>
> Customization of email reading is easy. The Rules tab contains entries to allow you to set up your favorite filters, and the View tab allows you to choose what messages you want to view.

To check your mail, simply choose Start, Mail.

FTP

Setting up frequently-accessed FTP sites for quick access from StarOffice is fairly easy. Using the Update and Synchronize function makes it a simple matter to quickly check an FTP site for any changes since your last visit.

First you must create a folder for storing your FTP site information. Right-click the Explorer entry and choose New, Folder from the context menu. Name it **FTPS**. Now, right-click the new `FTPS` folder and choose New, FTP Account from the context menu. Under the first tab, fill in the server name, username, and password (as with email, if the password entry is left blank, you will be prompted for it as needed).

As an example, let's set up the Caldera Systems FTP site so it's easy to check for updates in the future.

In the server field, type `ftp.calderasystems.com`, click the General tab, and type `Caldera` in the single field—this will be the name the object has in the `FTPS` folder. Enable the Log In As "Anonymous" option by checking that box. Rules and View can be left at the default settings, though these can be changed to suit your needs.

Now whenever you want to check for updates on Caldera's site, simply double-click the Caldera entry under the FTPS folder. The updates can be found in the `/pub/OpenLinux/updates` directory.

Summary

A stable, reliable operating system still requires good software to be useful to the average user. The productivity packages included in Caldera OpenLinux 2.3 are excellent bases from which to begin. Necessary documents can be quickly and easily created to provide a productive, efficient work environment, whether for a home user or business workstation.

CHAPTER 26

MySQL Essentials

IN THIS CHAPTER

- What Is MySQL?   *594*
- Installing MySQL   *595*
- MySQL Administration   *600*
- Managing Databases with MySQL   *606*

Computers were, from the very beginning, invented to make life easier for us. One of the more serious uses for computers is database management, that is, storing large volumes of data.

I think that the earth would probably split into two halves if for one day we didn't have our beloved databases. Although you probably don't think about it, many times every day, such as when you make a payment with your credit card, one or more databases are most likely searched to find needed information. Today, databases are something we can't live without.

Therefore, there's a wide demand for secure and stable database servers all around the planet. MySQL is one of the most popular—probably because it offers both high security and stability, but also because its performance beats all other database systems on the market. (No, this is not a MySQL commercial. I'm just telling the simple truth.)

Whether you're running a worldwide business corporation with thousands of employees or you're just another devoted computer enthusiast sitting at home wanting to learn more about databases, MySQL is probably the best choice you can make.

This chapter will give you a good introduction to the MySQL server software. MySQL is a great help for storing customer information, your CD-ROM collection, information about your Web site, or whatever you want it to store.

What Is MySQL?

MySQL is a multiuser and multithreaded database server. It uses the world's most popular database language, Structured Query Language (SQL), to build and manage databases.

Like many other Linux applications, MySQL is a client/server implementation. The MySQL server daemon, mysqld, takes care of the database connections, which can be made from one of the many existing client programs available. In this way, you can easily connect to your MySQL server through Telnet from any computer in the world and get access to your data.

As I mentioned, SQL is the database language used in MySQL. It is a standardized language that is used by many other database servers as well, such as Essentia (http://www.inter-soft.com/products/essentia/). If you want to store customer information for your Web site, you can do it in no time with SQL.

The MySQL developers say the main goal with MySQL is to provide a database server that is fast, robust, and easy to use. I must say that they have succeeded.

Installing MySQL

Installing MySQL is quite easy, although you need to compile the source yourself. In some cases this can be difficult, but that is absolutely not the case with MySQL.

Getting MySQL

To install MySQL, you will need to download the source distribution. It can be found on a number of archives around the world. Some of them are shown in Table 26.1.

TABLE 26.1 MySQL Mirrors

Country	URL
Australia	http://mirror.aarnet.edu.au/mysql
Austria	http://gd.tuwien.ac.at/db/mysql/
Canada	http://web.tryc.on.ca/mysql/
Chile	http://mysql.vision.cl/
Denmark	http://mysql.ake.dk
France	http://www.minet.net/devel/mysql/
Finland	http://mysql.eunet.fi/
Germany	http://www.wipol.uni-bonn.de/MySQL/
Italy	http://www.teta.it/mysql/
Japan	http://www.softagency.co.jp/MySQL
Korea	http://linux.kreonet.re.kr/mysql/
Portugal	http://mysql.leirianet.pt
Russia	http://mysql.directnet.ru
South Africa	http://www.mysql.mweb.co.za
Sweden	http://ftp.sunet.se/pub/unix/databases/relational/mysql/
Switzerland	http://sunsite.cnlab-switch.ch/ftp/mirror/mysql/
UK	http://mysql.omnipotent.net/
USA (New York)	http://www.buoy.com/mysql/
USA (Los Angeles)	http://mysql.pingzero.net/

It is recommended that you choose the mirror geographically closest to you. By doing this, you help both yourself and all other Internet users by taking up less bandwidth.

From your server of choice, download the latest version of MySQL (the one with the highest version number). At the time of this writing, this was 3.23.4.

> **Note**
>
> There is, in fact, a binary rpm version of MySQL available at www.mysql.com. However, this is intended for Red Hat Linux and may not work with Caldera OpenLinux.

> **Caution**
>
> MySQL 3.23.4 is a so-called "alpha" release. This is a release that has many of the features that will be included in the next stable release but can contain bugs and may, in some environments, be unstable. If stability is a great concern for you (you are planning to store important data with MySQL), I recommend that you use the latest stable release. At this time of writing, this was 3.22.26a. However, it's very possible that this has changed. A whole new stable distribution may have been released. Read about this on www.mysql.com.

Installing the Files

When you have downloaded the source distribution, go to the directory containing the distribution file and unpack it:

```
# tar xvfz mysql-3.23.4-alpha.tar.gz
```

You will now see a lot of output from `tar` showing which files are included in the archive. When this is done, `cd` to your new mysql directory (in my case, this was /mysql-3.23.4-alpha).

In the `mysql` distribution directory, you need to run the `configure` script included there. When you run `configure`, all the "Makefiles" and other configuration files are edited automatically to suit your system. You will not be able to compile the source successfully without running `configure` first. I would also add the option `--prefix=/usr/local/mysql` to `configure`. This will make MySQL install to `/usr/local/mysql` instead of `/usr/local`. I think this gives a better overview of the distribution, and I recommend that you do this, although it's not required for the installation to work.

```
# ./configure —prefix=/usr/local/mysql
```

> **Note**
>
> Note that to make your shell (most likely `bash`) find the `configure` script, you must to tell it exactly where it is located. Because `configure` is located in your current directory, add `./` to the command.

> **Note**
>
> If you get an error message while the `configure` script is running that looks something like:
>
> `configure: error: No curses/termcap library found`
>
> make sure you have the curses library installed.
>
> If you get error messages about other missing packages during the installation of MySQL, try to find out which package(s) is missing and then install it from your Caldera OpenLinux distribution CD.

When `configure` is finished, you're ready to start the actual compilation. Do this by issuing the `make` command in the MySQL source distribution directory (your current directory):

```
# make
```

This time, `./` is not needed because you are executing a command located in your search path.

The compilation starts and you see a lot of cryptic text scrolling down the screen. This is information on what is currently compiled and how it is compiled. The compilation process takes a while, especially on older computers without much memory. However, `make` will finish sooner or later, and then it's time to install MySQL. This is done with the `make` program as well, though you add the string `install` to the command:

```
# make install
```

`make` will now install MySQL under `/usr/local/mysql`. It's quite a few files, so this can take a while.

If this is the first time you're installing MySQL (which I assume it is), you also need to install the grant tables that are used to administer the MySQL server. Do this by using the `mysql_install_db` script, located in the `/scripts` directory of the source distribution.

```
# cd scripts
# ./mysql_install_db
```

Your MySQL installation is now very close to complete. However, I assume you also want the MySQL server to be started at system bootup. For this, you need to make some changes to your `/etc/rc.d` hierarchy. First, as root, copy the file `support-files/mysql.server` (located in your MySQL distribution directory) to your `/etc/rc.d/init.d` directory. Then, make a symbolic link in `/etc/rc.d/rc5.d` to `/etc/rc.d/init.d/mysql.server`:

```
# cd /etc/rc.d/rc5.d
# ln -s ../init.d/mysql.server S99mysqld
```

> **Note**
>
> If your system doesn't start X automatically upon system startup, this means that your system is not configured to start at runlevel 5. You should not make the symbolic link from `/etc/rc.d/rc5.d` but from `/etc/rc.d/rc3.d`.

Now, you can either restart your Linux system, or you can start the server manually:

```
# /etc/rc.d/init.d/mysql.server start
```

> **Tip**
>
> If you get a Permission Denied message when trying to execute the `mysql.server` script, you need to make sure you have permission to do this. `cd` to the `/etc/rc.d/init.d` directory (as root) and issue the following command:
>
> ```
> # chmod 755 mysql.server
> ```
>
> This should solve the problem.

> **Tip**
>
> The MySQL server can also be easily stopped by executing the `mysql.server` script with the `stop` argument instead of `start`:
>
> ```
> # /etc/rc.d/init.d/mysql.server stop
> ```

If all went well, you now have a working MySQL server running on your Caldera OpenLinux system.

Testing the Installation

To make sure that MySQL is correctly installed on your system, you can run a simple test command. Go to the `/usr/local/mysql/bin` directory (as root) and execute `mysql` as follows:

```
# ./mysql -e "select host,db,user from db" mysql
```

If everything is okay, you should get the following output:

```
+------+--------+------+
| host | db     | user |
+------+--------+------+
| %    | test   |      |
| %    | test\_% |      |
+------+--------+------+
```

If you get some kind of error message when doing this, make sure you ran the `mysql_install_db` script.

> **Tip**
>
> To access the binaries that come with MySQL (such as `mysql`) more easily, you can add the `/usr/local/mysql/bin` directory to your system's search path. If you're using `bash` as your shell (if you don't know which shell you're using, you're probably using `bash`), you can change this in your `/etc/profile` file. Search for a string that looks something like the following:
>
> `PATH="/bin:/usr/bin"`
>
> and change it to
>
> `PATH="/bin:/usr/bin:/usr/local/mysql/bin"`
>
> To activate the changes. Run `source`:
>
> `source /etc/profile`
>
> or log out and then log in again. Now you can execute the commands in `/usr/local/mysql/bin` from anywhere on your file system(s).

MySQL Administration

You now have a working installation of MySQL, but to make it really useful, you must set up user accounts and privileges for these users. With MySQL, these tasks are controlled by three tables: user, db, and host. They are all a part of the mysql database. To be able to change these tables, you need to log in to the MySQL server with the root account.

Setting the root Password

The first thing you probably want to do is to set the password for the root account. If you don't set up a password for the root account, anyone can log in to this account by just typing

```
# mysql -u root
```

The MySQL root account works just like the root account on your Linux system, so you probably don't want anyone to have access to this account. You can set a password for it with the mysqladmin tool (of course, without the < and >):

```
mysqladmin password <your password>
```

You can also do this with a single command:

```
mysqladmin -u root password <your password>
```

> **Tip**
>
> Perhaps you feel security isn't the main issue with your new MySQL installation. Maybe your machine isn't even connected to any network. It may be a good idea to wait to set the root password until after you've read this chapter and you're finished with all the testing. In this way, you save some time by not needing to enter a password every time you log in as root (and maybe your keyboard will last a little longer too).

The Privilege System

As I mentioned, administration of the MySQL server is done through the tables user, db, and host. These are often referred to as the *grant tables* or the *privilege tables*. They all reside in the mysql database and can only be accessed by the root user. This administration system is widely known as the *privilege system*. It can feel a bit complicated at first, but is, in fact, quite a simple concept.

By adding, deleting, and changing entries in the user, db, and host tables, you tell the server which users will be able to log in, to which databases they will have access, and from which hosts they can connect. Table 26.2 shows the contents of the three grant tables. The strings inside parentheses after the field name indicate in which of the three privilege tables the particular field is included.

TABLE 26.2 The Privilege Tables

Field	Description
Host (user, db, host)	Determines from which host the user can connect
User (user, db)	Sets the name of the user
Db (db, host)	Determines which database this will affect
Password (user, db)	Sets the password for the user
Select_priv (user, db, host)	Allows the user to select (list) certain rows in the database—can be Y or N
Insert_priv (user, db, host)	Allows the user to insert a row to a database—can be Y or N
Update_priv (user, db, host)	Allows the user to update a existing row—can be Y or N
Delete_priv (user, db, host)	Allows the user to delete a row—can be Y or N
Index_priv (user, db, host)	Allows the user to create or remove indexes–can be Y or N
Alter_priv (user, db, host)	Allows the user to use the ALTER TABLE command—can be Y or N
Create_priv (user, db, host)	Allows the user to create new databases and tables—can be Y or N
Drop_priv (user, db, host)	Allows the user to remove existing databases and tables—can be Y or N
Grant_priv (user, db, host)	Allows the user to give privileges to other users, but only privileges you possess yourself—can be Y or N
Reload_priv (user)	Allows the user to execute the following commands with the mysqladmin program: reload, refresh, flush-privileges, flush-hosts, flush-logs and flush-tables—can be Y or N
Shutdown_priv (user)	Allows the user to execute the shutdown command with mysqladmin—can be Y or N.
Process_priv (user)	Allows the user to execute the processlist and kill commands with mysqladmin—can be Y or N.
File_priv (user)	Allows the user to read and write to any file that can be read and written to by the MySQL server itself—can be Y or N.

When you try to make a connection to your MySQL server (or any other MySQL server), the server determines whether a connection should be accepted or refused by checking the privilege tables. The following is a brief description of how this works:

1. First, the server checks the user table to determine whether you should be able to make a connection at all. If an entry exists in the user table with the username and corresponding password you entered, and the hostname for this entry is the same as the hostname from which you are connecting, a connection is allowed. The user also gets his/her "global" privileges from the user table.

2. When you are logged in, the db and host tables are used to determine whether you are allowed to perform the tasks you try to perform. If no records of the particular user can be found in the db or host tables, the global privileges from the user table are used.

Setting Up Your First MySQL Privileges

Now you are going to use your new knowledge to set up your own privileges. There are two methods of doing this: using GRANT statements or modifying the grant tables directly.

Using GRANT statements to modify the privilege system has a few advantages. It is more understandable for human eyes, and it's also much less error-prone. It's up to you which method to use.

What you have to do first is connect to the MySQL server as the root user, as follows:

```
# mysql -u root -p mysql
Enter password:
Welcome to the MySQL monitor.  Commands end with ; or \g.
Your MySQL connection id is 2 to server version: 3.23.4-alpha-log

Type 'help' for help.

mysql>
```

> **Note**
>
> Note that if you have given a password for the root account, you have to call mysql with the -p parameter. Otherwise, you will get the following message:
> ```
> bash# mysql -u root
> ERROR 1045: Access denied for user: 'root@localhost'
> (Using password: NO)
> ```
> If you don't give the -p parameter, mysql thinks that you don't want to enter any password.

Example 1: A Superuser

Suppose you want to create a user, slackhacker, who will have root privileges—access to everything. slackhacker will be able to connect to the server from any host and wants to use topsecret as his/her password.

To do this by direct modification, enter the following commands:

```
mysql> INSERT INTO user values('localhost','slackhacker'
    ->,PASSWORD('topsecret'),'Y','Y','Y','Y','Y','Y','Y',
    ->'Y','Y','Y','Y','Y','Y','Y');
mysql> INSERT INTO user VALUES('%','slackhacker',PASSWORD('topsecret'),
    -> 'Y','Y','Y','Y','Y','Y','Y','Y','Y','Y','Y','Y','Y','Y');
```

When you are doing direct modification, you must also tell the server to reload the tables:

```
mysql> FLUSH PRIVILEGES;
```

> **Caution**
>
> Note that you enter the password inside the PASSWORD function. This function encodes the password to an unreadable form so other users can't see your password by just entering:
>
> ```
> mysql> SELECT * FROM user WHERE(user="slackhacker");
> ```
>
> You definitely don't want that, do you? So be sure you use the PASSWORD function.

> **Note**
>
> Note that you have to type a semicolon (;) to end a command.

You probably wonder why we entered two separate rows for both slackhacker@localhost and slackhacker@"%" (which means slackhacker at any host). If we don't do this, the anonymous user entry for localhost, created by mysql_install_db, will be used instead. The reason is that the anonymous user entry has a more specific Host field value and therefore it comes earlier in the user table sort order. For more information on this, read the MySQL documentation, which can be found at www.mysql.com.

To add the `slackhacker` user with GRANT tables, you do as follows:

```
mysql> GRANT ALL PRIVILEGES ON *.* TO slackhacker@localhost
    -> IDENTIFIED BY 'topsecret' WITH GRANT OPTION;
mysql> GRANT ALL PRIVILEGES ON *.* TO slackhacker@"%"
    -> IDENTIFIED BY 'topsecret' WITH GRANT OPTION;
```

As you can see, GRANT statements are easier to understand. So it's probably wiser to use those instead of direct modification.

Example 2: Different DB from Different Host

It is very possible that users want to have access to different databases depending on from which host they are connecting. This is easily done with MySQL.

In the following example, we will create the user common. common wants to be able to connect from a total of three hosts, localhost, foreignhost, and anotherhost. From localhost, common wants to have access to the database admin. From foreignhost, he wants access to customers and, from anotherhost, he wants access to economy. He also wants to use the password weakpass.

First, we edit the user database to give common privileges to connect from the three hosts:

```
mysql> INSERT INTO user (Host,User,Password)
    -> VALUES('localhost','common',PASSWORD('weakpass'));
mysql> INSERT INTO user (Host,User,Password)
    -> VALUES('foreignhost','common',PASSWORD('weakpass'));
mysql> INSERT INTO user (Host,User,Password)
    -> VALUES('anotherhost','common',PASSWORD('weakpass'));
mysql> FLUSH PRIVILEGES;
```

These three tables allow common to connect from the three hosts localhost, foreignhost, and anotherhost. We leave the privilege fields (all the Ys) blank so they will default to N. Now, we'll edit the db table to give common access to his databases:

```
mysql> INSERT INTO db
    -> (Host,Db,User,Select_priv,Insert_priv,Update_priv,Delete_priv,
    -> Create_priv,Drop_priv)
    -> VALUES
    -> ('localhost','admin','common','Y','Y','Y','Y','Y','Y');
mysql> INSERT INTO db
    -> (Host,Db,User,Select_priv,Insert_priv,Update_priv,Delete_priv,
    -> Create_priv,Drop_priv)
    -> VALUES
    -> ('foreignhost','customers','common','Y','Y','Y','Y','Y','Y');
mysql> INSERT INTO db
    -> (Host,Db,User,Select_priv,Insert_priv,Update_priv,Delete_priv,
    -> Create_priv,Drop_priv)
    -> VALUES
    -> ('anotherhost','economy','common','Y','Y','Y','Y','Y','Y');
```

common will now be granted access to the database customers if he connects from foreignhost, but he will be denied access to economy. Also, he will be granted access to database economy from anotherhost, but denied access to customers. From localhost, he can access the admin database.

You can also do this with GRANT statements:

```
mysql> GRANT SELECT,INSERT,UPDATE,DELETE,CREATE,DROP
    -> ON admin.*
    -> TO common@localhost
    -> IDENTIFIED BY 'weakpass';
mysql> GRANT SELECT,INSERT,UPDATE,DELETE,CREATE,DROP
    -> ON customers.*
    -> TO common@foreignhost
    -> IDENTIFIED BY 'weakpass';
mysql> GRANT SELECT,INSERT,UPDATE,DELETE,CREATE,DROP
    -> ON economy.*
    -> TO common@anotherhost
    -> IDENTIFIED BY 'weakpass';
```

tables_priv and columns_priv

In the later versions of MySQL, two new tables have been added to the grant tables: tables_priv and columns_priv. With these tables, you can give users very specific privileges, such as giving them access to one single column in a table. tables_priv and columns_priv are only consulted by MySQL if a user tries to access something that he or she is not granted access to in the user, db, or host tables. The fields in tables_priv and columns_priv are shown in Table 26.3. The strings inside parentheses after the field name indicate in which of the tables the particular field is included.

TABLE 26.3 The tables_priv and columns_priv Tables

Field	Description
Host (both)	Determines from which host the user can connect.
Db (both)	Determines which database this will affect.
User (both)	Sets the name of the user.
Table_name (both)	Which table will this affect?
Column_name (columns_priv)	Which column?
Table_priv (tables_priv)	Sets the table-specific privileges.
Column_priv (both)	Sets the column-specific privileges.

The `table_priv` and `column_priv` fields are a bit different from the others. They are so-called SET fields, which can contain only a given set of values. For `table_priv`, these are Select, Insert, Update, Delete, Create, Drop, Grant References, Index, and Alter. For `column_priv`, they are Select, Insert, Update, and References.

If you use GRANT statements for managing your privilege system, the `tables_priv` and `columns_priv` tables are edited automatically when necessary.

There are virtually no limits to how you can set up your user accounts with MySQL. You should now have a basic understanding of how this works and also be able to configure the grant tables for your personal needs. Remember, MySQL server combines all five privilege tables to form a complete description of a user.

For more information, I recommend that you read Chapter 6 of the official MySQL documentation (found at www.mysql.com).

Managing Databases with MySQL

You finally have your MySQL server up and running. It's now time to start doing what you probably wanted to install MySQL for from the very beginning—to create databases. The database language used in MySQL is (of course) SQL (Structured Query Language). SQL is the world's most popular database language, and it gives you (almost) unlimited power when creating your databases.

Of course, you first have to connect to your MySQL server. You do just as you did in the "MySQL Administration" section of this chapter, by using the `mysql -u <user> -p` syntax. Log in as root:

```
# mysql -u root -p
Enter password:
Welcome to the MySQL monitor.  Commands end with ; or \g.
Your MySQL connection id is 3 to server version: 3.23.4-alpha-log

Type 'help' for help.

mysql>
```

You are now logged in and can start entering SQL commands.

MySQL Basics

A SQL command usually consists of a statement followed by a semicolon (;). However, there are a few exceptions (like QUIT). Let's start with a simple command:

```
mysql> SELECT version();
```

This means "print the output from the `version()` function to the screen." If everything is working as it should, MySQL will output something like the following:

```
+------------------+
| version()        |
+------------------+
| 3.23.4-alpha-log |
+------------------+
1 row in set (0.02 sec)
```

and will then bring up another `mysql>` prompt.

MySQL isn't case sensitive with keywords, so `SELECT VERSION()` or `SeleCt veRSiOn()` will also do fine.

You can also enter a command on multiple lines. If you enter the preceding statement without the ending semicolon, MySQL will answer with the following:

```
mysql> select version()
    ->
```

The `->` means you are free to enter more statements. MySQL will continue entering `->` until you tell MySQL that the command is complete by entering a semicolon.

Data Types

Data types are the smallest element in a MySQL database. Each field in a table is declared to store a specific data type. It could, for example, be a string or an integer. When you create a table, you must tell MySQL which type of data should be stored in the columns. Therefore, it's important that you know about the different data types, what they are, and when you should use them.

There are a number of different data types of different forms and sizes. It's what you want to store in a column that decides what data type you should choose. By choosing the right data type at the right place, you increase the performance of the database.

- `CHAR(M)` is used to store strings with a fixed length. It can store 1–255 characters. The `M` indicates the number of characters. The following is an example of a `CHAR` declaration:

    ```
    name CHAR(20);
    ```

- `VARCHAR(M)` stores just the length of the data that is inserted in the field. `CHAR` stores the number of characters that was given when the table was created, no matter how long the data is. The following is an example of a `VARCHAR` declaration:

    ```
    name VARCHAR(20);
    ```

- `INT(M)[unsigned]` is used to store integers ranging from -2147483648 to 2147483648. If it is declared as `unsigned`, it can deal with integers from 0 to 4294967295. The following are some examples of `INT` declarations:

  ```
  years INT;
  many_years INT unsigned;
  ```

- `FLOAT(M,D)` is used to store small decimal numbers. The `M` declares the total number of digits (decimals included) and the `D` the number of decimals:

  ```
  decimal FLOAT(5,3);
  ```

- `DATE` is used to store date-related information. This is done with one of the many date formatting commands provided by MySQL:

  ```
  todays_date DATE;
  ```

- `TEXT` stores strings with a length from 255 to 655535 characters:

  ```
  article TEXT;
  ```

- `BLOB` is the same as `TEXT`, but it is case sensitive:

  ```
  article BLOB;
  ```

- `SET` is a data type that can store a given set of values, up to 64 values. The following

  ```
  cars SET("ford","BMW") NOT NULL;
  ```

  can have four values: `""`, `"ford"`, `"BMW"`, and `"ford,BWM"`.

- `ENUM` is quite similar to `SET`. With `ENUM`, however, only one value can be chosen. For example

  ```
  cars ENUM("ford","BMW") NOT NULL;
  ```

  can hold the values `""`, `"ford"`, and `"BMW"`.

Creating/Removing Databases

There are two ways to create databases in MySQL. You can use the `mysqladmin` tool or use the `CREATE DATABASE` statement when already logged into MySQL.

To create a database with `mysqladmin` and call it `mydb`, enter the following command at the prompt (you should not be logged in to MySQL):

```
# mysqladmin -u root -p create mydb
Enter password:
Database "mydb" created.
```

Or, as I said, you can do this when you're already logged in to MySQL:

```
mysql> CREATE DATABASE mydb;
Query OK, 1 row affected (0.09 sec)
```

Use the SHOW DATABASES statement to list currently existing databases:

```
mysql> SHOW DATABASES;
+----------+
| Database |
+----------+
| mydb     |
| mysql    |
| test     |
+----------+
```

To add tables to your new database, you must tell MySQL that it is the mydb database with which you want to work. There are two ways of doing this too. First, you can select the database when you launch mysql:

```
# mysql -u root -p mydb
```

Or, when you're already logged in to MySQL, choose it with the USE statement:

```
mysql> USE mydb
```

To delete the mydb database, you again use the mysqladmin tool:

```
# mysqladmin -u root -p drop mydb
Enter password:
Dropping the database is potentially a very bad thing to do.
Any data stored in the database will be destroyed.

Do you really want to drop the 'mydb' database [y/N]
y
Database "mydb" dropped
```

Creating/Removing Tables

Now we will look at how to create tables using the data types just discussed. A sample table declaration can look like the following:

```
mysql> CREATE TABLE example(
    -> name VARCHAR(20),
    -> age INT,
    -> phone INT,
    -> ID INT NOT NULL AUTO_INCREMENT,
    -> PRIMARY KEY(ID));
```

This would create the table example in our currently selected database. example would have one VARCHAR column, name, and three INT columns, age, phone, and ID. ID is a special column used to give the row an ID number. ID will be incremented by 1 every time we insert NULL (nothing) into this column. The NOT NULL statement means it can never be NULL (nothing). PRIMARY KEY(ID) means that no two records can hold the same ID value.

We could then easily insert a row into the table

```
mysql> INSERT INTO example VALUES
    -> ("Joe Smith",32,123456789,NULL);
Query OK, 1 row affected (0.00 sec)
```

and to list the table

```
mysql> SELECT * FROM example;
+-----------+------+-----------+----+
| name      | age  | phone     | ID |
+-----------+------+-----------+----+
| Joe Smith |   32 | 123456789 |  1 |
+-----------+------+-----------+----+
1 row in set (0.00 sec)
```

Note that if we insert another row to the table, that row's ID will be 2.

To see what tables are in the database, use the SHOW TABLES statement:

```
mysql> SHOW TABLES;
+----------------+
| Tables_in_mysql|
+----------------+
| columns_priv   |
| db             |
| economy        |
| example        |
| func           |
| host           |
| tables_priv    |
| user           |
+----------------+
```

To delete a table, use the DROP TABLE statement:

```
mysql> DROP TABLE economy;
Query OK, 0 rows affected (0.02 sec)
```

> **Tip**
>
> A "row" is a group of declared data types. A group of rows is called a "table." A group of tables is called a "database"—it's as simple as that.

Useful MySQL Features

MySQL includes a large number of statements and features—an extremely large number. To describe all of them here would be far beyond the scope of this chapter (and this whole book for that matter). However, we will go through some of the most used features so you can do the most needed operations with your tables.

> **Note**
>
> We have already mentioned the most basic MySQL features, and those will not be covered here.

The `DESCRIBE` Statement

The `DESCRIBE` statement shows the names and the types of the columns in a table, for example

```
mysql> DESCRIBE mytable;
+-----------+-------------+------+-----+---------+-------+------------------------------+
| Field     | Type        | Null | Key | Default | Extra | Privileges                   |
+-----------+-------------+------+-----+---------+-------+------------------------------+
| name      | varchar(20) | YES  |     | NULL    |       | select,insert,update,references |
| age       | int(11)     | YES  |     | NULL    |       | select,insert,update,references |
+-----------+-------------+------+-----+---------+-------+------------------------------+
```

Reading Data from Files

When you've created your own table, you will probably soon realize that using the `INSERT` statement for inserting all rows is far too time-consuming. MySQL offers a good solution for this—loading data from a file.

This is very easy to do. Just enter your records to a file, one record per line, with the values separated by tabs. Suppose you want to insert a few records to a table that holds the name and age of some people. You could create a file with the following content:

```
"Joe Smith"      32
"Bill Clayton"   43
"Dan Jones"      27
```

You then can insert these records to the table with the following command:

```
mysql> LOAD DATA LOCAL INFILE "/data.txt" INTO TABLE people;
Query OK, 3 rows affected (0.23 sec)
Records: 3  Deleted: 0  Skipped: 0  Warnings: 0
```

In this example, the table name is `people` and the `data.txt` file is located in the top-level directory (the `root` directory) of the file system. After this, the `people` table has three records:

```
mysql> SELECT * FROM people;
+----------------+------+
| name           | age  |
+----------------+------+
| "Joe Smith"    |   32 |
| "Bill Clayton" |   43 |
| "Dan Jones"    |   27 |
+----------------+------+
```

> **Tip**
>
> NULL is represented by \N when importing from data files. So, enter \N instead of NULL in your files. \N (NULL) is also used if you want to leave a field blank.

Sorting Rows

Until now, we have looked at rows in no particular order with the SELECT statement. You can easily sort the rows by just adding a few new statements. Suppose you want to show the rows in the people table sorted by age. Enter the following command:

```
mysql> SELECT * FROM people ORDER BY age;
+---------------+------+
| name          | age  |
+---------------+------+
| "Dan Jones"   |   27 |
| "Joe Smith"   |   32 |
| "Bill Clayton"|   43 |
+---------------+------+
```

You can also sort in reverse order by adding the DESC statement:

```
mysql> SELECT * from people ORDER BY age DESC;
+---------------+------+
| name          | age  |
+---------------+------+
| "Bill Clayton"|   43 |
| "Joe Smith"   |   32 |
| "Dan Jones"   |   27 |
+---------------+------+
```

Calculations

You can even perform calculations when listing tables in MySQL. The simple example that follows lists the name row in people and multiplies age by 365:

```
mysql> SELECT name, age*365 FROM people;
+---------------+---------+
| name          | age*365 |
+---------------+---------+
| "Joe Smith"   |   11680 |
| "Bill Clayton"|   15695 |
| "Dan Jones"   |    9855 |
+---------------+---------+
```

Pattern Matching

MySQL includes standard pattern matching. % represents an unknown number of characters (including no characters), and _ represents any single character. The following in an example with the people table:

```
mysql> SELECT * FROM people WHERE age LIKE "3_";
+--------------+------+
| name         | age  |
+--------------+------+
| "Joe Smith"  |  32  |
+--------------+------+
```

Here you told MySQL to list all rows where age started with a 3, and you got it.

In the following example, you ask MySQL to find a row where name starts with a D:

```
mysql> SELECT * FROM people WHERE name LIKE "\"D%";
+--------------+------+
| name         | age  |
+--------------+------+
| "Dan Jones"  |  27  |
+--------------+------+
```

> **Note**
>
> Note that we enter the \ to indicate the starting " in "Dan Jones".

We can also list all rows where name is exactly 14 characters long:

```
mysql> SELECT * FROM people WHERE name LIKE "_____";
+----------------+------+
| name           | age  |
+----------------+------+
| "Bill Clayton" |  43  |
+----------------+------+
```

There's an unlimited number of different ways you can use pattern matching to list rows. See the official MySQL documentation (www.mysql.com) for more examples.

Summary

In this chapter, we have looked at the most essential parts of the widely-used database server MySQL. We have by no means covered all aspects of MySQL, but you have at least learned the most basic parts. You can now set up some simple user privileges with the MySQL privilege system as well as create your own databases and tables.

MySQL is a very powerful tool. By learning to use it efficiently, you will discover totally new aspects of using a computer.

Using Image Manipulation Tools

CHAPTER 27

IN THIS CHAPTER

- xv *616*
- Image Magick *624*
- The GIMP *636*

OpenLinux comes with several programs for viewing, manipulating, and creating images and graphics. Some of them have been around for a while and have limited functionality, but others, such as the GIMP, are rather new and very powerful. In this chapter, we will be introducing xv, an older image display and manipulation program; Image Magick, a suite of utility programs for image display, manipulation, and creation; and the GIMP (GNU Image Manipulation Program), an excellent program for image manipulation and creation.

xv is an older program that is no longer being developed, but it is still very useful for certain tasks. Image Magick has been around quite a while as well, but it is still being actively developed and is packed full of features and functionality. The GIMP is the newest of the bunch (only a few years old) and is also being actively developed. The GIMP is an excellent tool for graphics artists and others wanting to create new images or touch up existing images.

We will only scratch the surface of what most of these programs are capable of; don't hesitate to look through the other documentation referenced in each section! You will probably also want to check out the Web sites for Image Magick and the GIMP from time to time to check for new updates, plug-ins, and so on. For example, new plug-ins are written for the GIMP quite frequently.

xv

xv is an interactive image display and manipulation program for use under the X Window system. It can view and manipulate 16 different image formats. It can also generate PostScript files of images, although it can't open and manipulate them. xv is a good program for viewing, resizing, cropping, padding, and adjusting the colors and brightness of an image. One particularly nice feature of xv is the Visual Schnauzer, a browser window that enables you to see thumbnails of all the images in a directory.

> **Note**
>
> If xv was not installed when you installed OpenLinux, you can install it from the RPM file xv-3.10a-8.i386.rpm in the directory Packages/RPMS on the installation CD.

Figure 27.1 shows how xv looks when you start it. You can start xv from the Graphics menu in KDE or by typing **xv** at the command line. If you supply an image name on the command line, xv will displaying that image at startup.

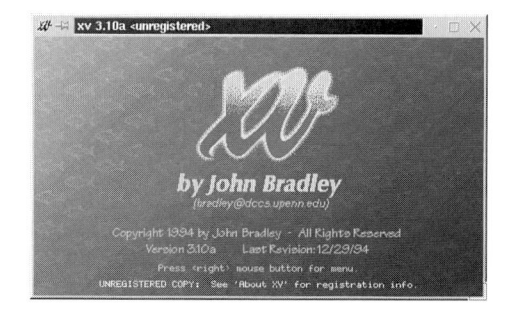

FIGURE 27.1

The main xv window.

When xv starts, it opens only the image display window. Right-clicking anywhere in the window opens the xv controls window. From there, you have access to all of xv's controls. Figure 27.2 shows the xv controls window.

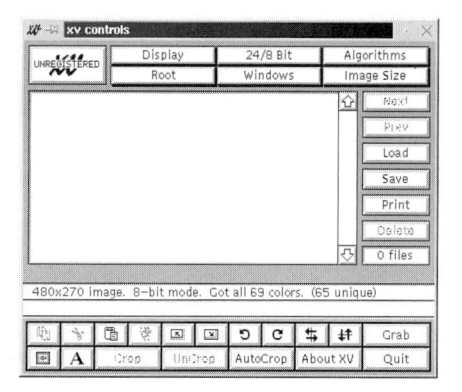

FIGURE 27.2

The xv controls window.

> **Note**
>
> The main application window is the image display window and *not* the xv controls window. If you close the image display window, you will close xv—even if the xv controls window is open.

Using the Menus

The top two rows of buttons in the xv controls window are actually pop-up menus. Clicking one of the buttons will pop up the menu. Releasing the mouse button will close the menu. To select an item in a menu, click the appropriate button, hold the mouse button down, and drag the mouse to the menu item you want. Releasing the mouse button selects that item and executes the appropriate action.

The Display Menu

The Display menu gives you several options about how (not *where*) to display the image. None of these options actually modifies the image. They only affect how the image is displayed on the screen. Table 27.1 describes each of the options in the Display menu.

TABLE 27.1 Options in the Display Menu

Option	Description
Raw	Returns the displayed image to its *raw* state. (That is, the state in which each displayed pixel matches as closely as possible the color of the original pixel in the image.) This option is enabled only after you have issued a Smooth or Dithered command.
Dithered	If you are running on a PseudoColor display and it is unable to allocate color cells for all the colors in an image, this option will dither the colors in the image, using the colors the display was able to allocate. It has no effect if all the needed colors were obtained or if you are running on a TrueColor display.
Smooth	Smoothes out distortion caused by integer round-off when an image is resized. Smooth has a useful effect only when the image has been resized.
Read/Write Colors	Tells xv to use Read/Write color cells, which can help speed up color operations. This option is enabled only when running on a PseudoColor display and the Use Std. Colormap option is not selected.
Normal Colors	This is the default mode when used on PseudoColor displays. In this mode, xv tries to allocate as many colors from the image as it can. If it runs out of colors, xv tries a few other tricks and then maps the remaining colors to the closest allocated colors. This option is disabled when not running on a PseudoColor display.
Perfect Colors	This mode first tries to proceed as in the Normal Colors option, but if it fails to allocated any colors, it frees all the colors it allocated and creates its own private colormap.
Use Own Colormap	This mode causes xv to allocate a private colormap by default.
Use Std. Colormap	This mode causes xv to use a common colormap for all images being displayed, instead of trying to get all the colors for each image individually. Images might not look as nice in this mode, but it allows you to display several different images simultaneously, without running out of colors.

The 24/8 Bit Menu

The 24/8 Bit menu controls the color mode xv operates in: 24-bit color (true color) or 8-bit color (256 colors). When running on an 8-bit (256 color) display, 8-bit mode is the default. When running on a TrueColor display (15-, 16-, 24-, or 32-bit color), 8-bit color is used for image formats such as GIF, in which there can only be up to 256 colors in the image. 24-bit color is used for true color image formats such as JPEG.

One difference between the two modes that can be significant is that in 8-bit mode, xv uses a colormap that can be edited directly. In 24-bit mode, there is no colormap. Also, most of the image editing functions require the image to be in 24-bit mode. If it is not, the image will be converted to 24-bit mode, the editing action will do its work, and then the image will be converted back to 8-bit mode. This can introduce artifacts in the image, so if you plan to use many algorithms, you're probably best off switching xv to 24-bit mode first.

Lock Current Mode keeps xv from changing color modes when a new image is loaded.

The next three options control the method xv will use to convert 24-bit images to 8-bit ones. The fastest one does the worst job of conversion (but it's quick), and the slowest method does the best job. One major difference between the Slow and Best methods is that the Slow method will dither the colors, whereas the Best method will not. The Best method is probably best if you will be enlarging the image much, because the dithering becomes *very* noticeable as the image is enlarged.

The Algorithms Menu

The Algorithms menu contains several algorithms that can be applied to an image or a selection within an image. To put it in more common terms, the algorithms are the same as filters in other programs, such as Photoshop. To apply an algorithm to the entire image, you simply select the desired algorithm. To apply an algorithm to a rectangular selection within the image, first select the desired area with the left mouse button, and then select the desired algorithm. Selecting Undo All will undo all algorithms applied to the image, returning it to its original state.

The Root Menu

The Root menu controls where and how the image is displayed. The two real choices are in a window and in the root window (that is, in the background or on the desktop). If you choose to display the image in the root window, it can be displayed in many different ways. Most of the options simply tile the image in various ways. Root: Centered displays a single copy of the image in the center of the root window. The related warp and brick options act like Root: Centered but also display a warp or brick pattern in the rest of the root window.

The Windows Menu

From the Windows menu, you gain access to the other windows (and associated functions) available in xv. The Visual Schnauzer is like a simple file manager that enables you to work your way around directories and view their contents, but it also displays thumbnails of images in a directory. Figure 27.3 shows the Visual Schnauzer.

FIGURE 27.3
The Visual Schnauzer window.

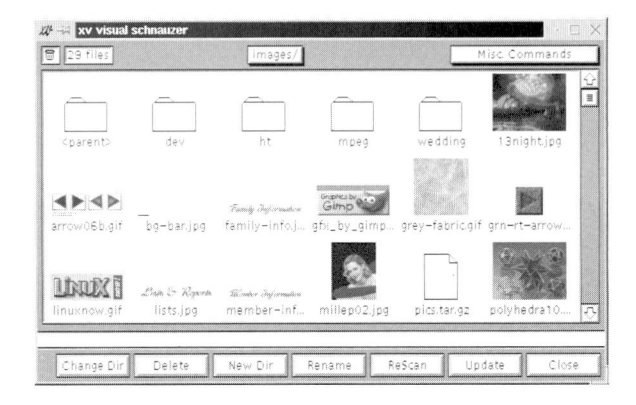

When you first view a directory with the Visual Schnauzer, it will not display thumbnails of any images in the directory until you click the Update button. xv then looks at each file in the directory and, when it finds an image file, xv generates a thumbnail image and saves it in a new file in the hidden directory .xvpics. The next time you view this directory, xv will find the .xvpics directory and use the already-generated thumbnails when displaying the directory contents. If there are new images in the directory, you must click the Update button again to generate thumbnails for them. If you don't have write permission in the directory you are viewing, xv can still generate thumbnails, but they will not be saved. You will have to regenerate them each time you view that directory.

The Color Editor allows you to perform color and brightness operations on the image. With the Color Editor, you can edit the color palette (if in 8-bit mode), change the hue and saturation of the image, and perform gamma correction for all colors at once (intensity) or for the red, green, and blue channels separately. Figure 27.4 shows the Color Editor.

The Image Info window displays information about the image. The Image Comments window enables you to view any comments saved with an image. Comments do not affect the actual image. They are just added to the header section of the image file. The Text Viewer window enables you to view the image file in ASCII or hex format. If you try to open an image that xv doesn't recognize, it will open it in the Text Viewer window. Figure 27.5 shows the Text Viewer window.

FIGURE 27.4
The Color Editor window.

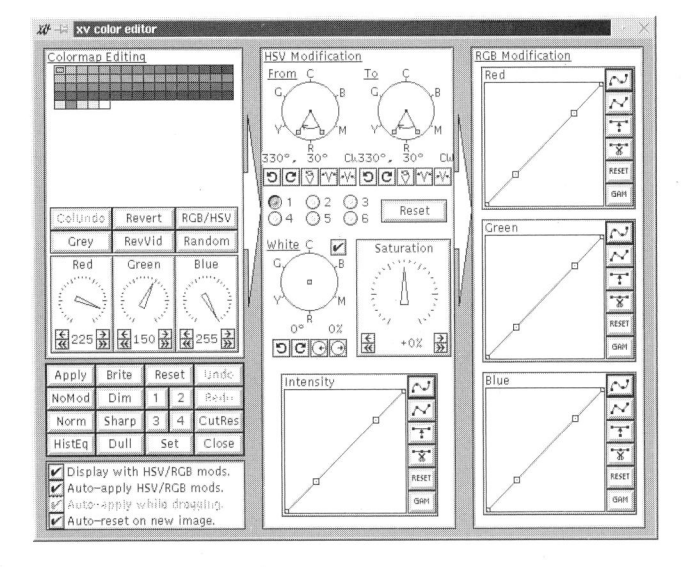

FIGURE 27.5
The Text Viewer window, showing the contents of an image in hex format.

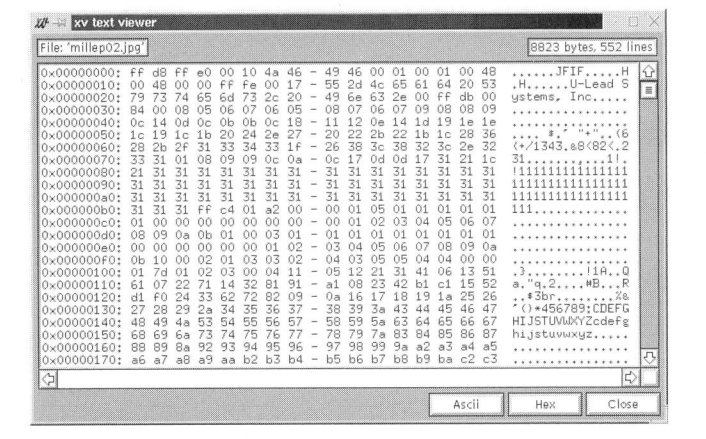

The Image Size Menu

The Image Size menu enables you to manipulate the size of the displayed image. None of the options changes the actual image. The options affect only how the image is displayed on the screen.

Loading an Image File

You can load an image file by clicking on the Load button. This brings up a file dialog similar to the one in Figure 27.6. From there, you can navigate around and select the file you want to open. Selecting a file copies the name of the file to the text field at the bottom of the dialog. You can then click OK or press the Enter key to load the file. Double-clicking a file in the list will also load the file. Rescan rereads the directory and updates the file list. Load All attempts to load all the files in the current directory.

If you want to open several files without bringing up the load dialog repeatedly, you can click the Browse check box just below the file list. This stops the load dialog from closing when a file is loaded. You can then continue selecting and loading files. When you are done, clicking Cancel closes the dialog.

FIGURE 27.6
The xv load dialog for loading image files.

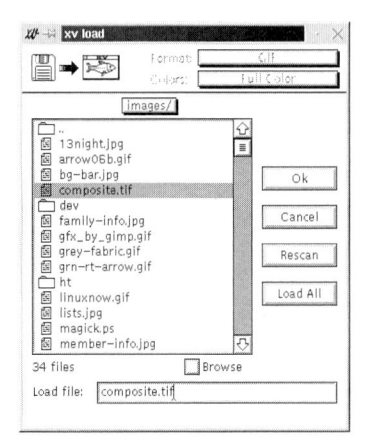

Each file you open will appear in the list in the xv controls window, as shown in Figure 27.7. xv displays only one image at a time, but you can choose which image to display by double-clicking the desired image in the list. You can also move through the images by clicking the Next and Prev buttons, which will show the next or previous image in the list, respectively.

FIGURE 27.7
The xv controls window with loaded files showing in the file list.

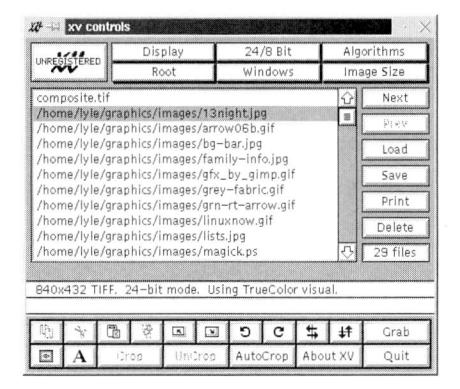

Saving an Image to a File

You can save an image by clicking the Save button, which pops up a save dialog like the one in Figure 27.8. The name of the current image is placed in the text field at the bottom of the dialog. You can change this to save the image to a different file.

FIGURE 27.8

The xv save dialog for saving images to files.

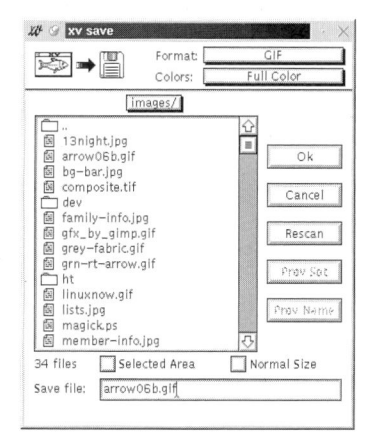

At the top of the dialog are two buttons that pop up menus allowing you to choose the format in which to save the image and the color mode to use. You can convert an image from one format to another simply by opening the image, opening the save dialog, and selecting the image format you want to convert the image to. Upon selection of a different image format, xv automatically changes the filename extension to one appropriate for the chosen format.

The second button enables you to choose what color mode to use. You have four options: Full Color, Greyscale, B/W Dithered, and Reduced Color. Full Color saves the image as you see it on the screen, but with all the colors. If xv was unable to display all the colors and had to dither some colors, the colors in the actual image and not those displayed on the screen will be saved. However, all changes made to the image—such as resizing, cropping, and changes made by algorithms—will be saved. Greyscale acts like Full Color, but it saves the image in greyscale format. B/W Dithered creates a 1-bit-per-pixel, black-and-white dithered image and saves it. Reduced Color saves the image exactly as it appears on the screen, including any dithering that was necessary to display the image.

The Prev Set button restores the format and color settings to the settings used the last time an image was saved. The Prev Name button restores the filename in the text field to the filename that was used the last time an image was saved.

If you have a region of the image selected, clicking the Selected Area check box saves only the selected portion of the image. Also, if you were viewing the image at a size other than its actual size, clicking the Normal Size button saves the image at its actual size. This can be useful if you were viewing an image that was larger than the screen, or if you changed the size of the image while viewing it.

Image Magick

Image Magick is a set of eight command-line and GUI programs for viewing, creating, and manipulating images. The Image Magick utilities recognize and can work with more than 40 different image formats. Perl and C libraries are also available that enable you to use many of Image Magick's features and functions in your own programs. For example, a CGI library exists that enables you to use Image Magick to create on-the-fly graphics for Web pages and other uses.

The eight different utilities are `animate`, `combine`, `convert`, `display`, `identify`, `import`, `mogrify`, and `montage`.

> **Note**
>
> If Image Magick was not installed when you installed OpenLinux, you can install it from the RPM file `ImageMagick-4.2.7-2.i386.rpm` in the directory `Packages/RPMS` on the installation CD.

animate

`animate` allows you to display a sequence of images, like frames of an animation, in rapid succession. The easiest way to load and animate a set of images is to specify them on the command line. For example, if you saved all the frames of an animation as `frame0001.tga`, `frame0002.tga`, and so on, you could load them into animate and view the animation using the following command:

```
$ animate frame*.tga
```

You could also list each of the files you want to animate separately on the command line. The images will be displayed in the order specified on the command line. If you don't specify any files to animate, `animate` will show an empty display window and pop up a file dialog in which you can specify the files you want to animate. You can also use wildcards in the file dialog to specify multiple files.

When all the files are loaded, `animate` starts animating away. If you click anywhere in the display window, a Commands window will pop up that enables you to control the animation in various ways. Figure 27.9 shows the Commands window for `animate`. The buttons with little right arrows on them bring up a submenu. In addition to the menu items, Table 27.2 lists four keyboard accelerators you can use.

FIGURE 27.9
The Commands window for `animate`.

TABLE 27.2 Keyboard Accelerators for `animate`

Key	Description
Space	Displays the next image in the sequence (step)
<	Speeds up the animation (reduces the delay between frames)
>	Slows down the animation (increases the delay between frames)
?	Displays information about the current image

`animate` enables you to specify the delay in milliseconds and seconds between frames of the animation by using the `-delay` option. It has the following syntax:

-delay milliseconds[xseconds]

The first number, *milliseconds*, specifies how much time to wait before advancing to the next frame of the animation. The second number is optional and specifies how long to wait before repeating the animation. For example, `-delay 60x1` would pause 60 milliseconds between frames and then wait for one full second before repeating the animation.

`animate` can also put up a backdrop that covers the entire screen, with the animation playing in the center. This enables you to see the animation without all the other distractions on your desktop. You tell `animate` to do this using the `-backdrop` option. You can specify the background color using the `-background` option. For example, to display your sequence of frames on a black background, you would use the following command:

```
$ animate -backdrop -background black frame*.tga
```

You can find more information about `animate`, including more command-line options, in the `animate` man page (`man animate`).

combine

`combine` combines multiple images to create new images. It is purely a command-line tool. There is no display to enable you to see the results before you commit to them or to experiment. `combine` has the following syntax:

`combine [options] image composite [mask] combined`

So, to combine an image of a cockatoo with a perch, you could use the following command:

`$ combine cockatoo.tif perch.tif composite.tif`

This would actually have the effect of placing the second image (`perch.tif`) on top of the first image (`cockatoo.tif`), replacing each pixel in the first image with one from the second image, starting at the upper-left corner at the coordinates (0,0). This probably isn't what you want, but that's OK because you don't have to do it that way. You can combine images in many different ways. The `-compose` option allows you to specify different types of composite operators. The `-compose` option has one argument, which is the operator to use:

`-compose operator`

Table 27.3 lists the valid arguments for the `-compose` option.

TABLE 27.3 Composite Operations for the `-compose` Option

Operation	Description
over	The composite image will obscure the image below it where they overlap. Black pixels in the composite image will not obscure the image below.
in	The composite image will be cut by the shape of `image`. None of `image`'s data will appear in the result.
out	The composite image will have the shape of `image` cut out.
atop	The same as `over` except that any part of the composite image that is outside of `image`'s shape does not appear in the result.
xor	Only parts of each image that are out of any overlapping regions will appear in the result. The overlapping regions will be blank.
plus	The two images are simply added to each other. Any pixel value that would exceed 255 is simply set to 255.
minus	`image` is subtracted from `composite`. Any pixel value that would be less than zero is set to 0.

Operation	Description
add	The two images are added together, but the resulting value will be (pixel1 + pixel2) mod 256. That is, the color value will wrap around to 0; 256 will change to 0, 257 will change to 1, and so on.
subtract	The two images are subtracted, but negative values will wrap around to 255 (similar to add but the other way around).
difference	composite is subtracted from image, but the resulting pixel value is the absolute value of the difference.
bumpmap	image is shaded by composite.
replace	composite replaces image where they overlap.

There are many more things that combine can do. Take a look at the man page (man combine) or other Image Magick documentation for details.

convert

convert converts an image file from one format to another. Like combine, convert is purely a command-line tool. It has the following syntax:

`convert [options] in-file [file...] out-file`

In many cases, convert can recognize what format you are converting from and to by the filename extension used. For example, if you used the following command:

`$ convert image.tif image.png`

convert would know that you are going from a TIFF image to a PNG image. For other types of images, you might need to help it along a bit by telling it what format you want the image to be in. For example, to convert a TIFF image to a SUN raster file, you might use a command like this:

`$ convert image.tif sun:image.ras`

The sun: before the second image name tells convert what format to convert the image to. There is a complete list of supported image formats along with the tag used to specify them (for example, sun) in the convert man page (man convert). Suffice it to say that the list is *very* long. If convert won't read or write the image format you need, you will probably have a hard time finding a program that does!

An interesting thing about convert is that you can actually use it to draw. You can draw strings (text), lines, points, circles, and more. This can be useful if you want to annotate an image or mark it up in some simple way. For example, to write "Hello World" at the position (100,100) on an image, you could use a command like this one:

```
$ convert -font 12x24 -pen blue -draw "text +100+100 'Hello World'" image.tif
➥newImage.tif
```

This command sets the font to the font 12x24, sets the drawing color to blue, draws the text `Hello World` at the position (100,100) on the image `image.tif`, and writes the new image to `newImage.tif`.

Take a peek at the man page to see what else `convert` can do.

display

`display` is a program similar in spirit to xv, but `display` is much better. You can use it to display images and change them in various ways. You can also load several images at once and display them in sequence like a slideshow. `display` won't animate them as `animate` will, but if you have a bunch of images set up for a slideshow, `display` is an alternative to using something like PowerPoint to display them. The drawback is that `display` doesn't have everything that PowerPoint has to actually make the slideshow. But that's okay, there are still other ways to do it under Linux (the GIMP is a good program for some of that). Also, if you're using an 8-bit (256 color) display, you'll get much better results using `display` than you will with xv.

Similar to `animate`, if you start `display` without specifying an image to display, it opens the display window and pops up a file dialog for you to specify an image to open. If you specify an image on the command line, it will simply display the image. If you specify more than one image or use wildcard characters that match more than one image, `display` will open the first image given. Each time you press the spacebar, `display` will advance to the next image, until it reaches the end.

Also as with `animate`, clicking anywhere in the display window pops up a Commands window with several different menus that enable you to perform different types of actions on the image. Figure 27.10 shows the Commands window for `display`.

> **Note**
>
> Similar to xv, the main application window for `display` is the image display window. Closing that window will exit the application, regardless of what other windows are open.

FIGURE 27.10
The Commands window for display.

Most menu items behave as you would expect. One thing to note, however, is that menu actions act on the entire image by default. It is possible to have them act on only a selected portion of the image, but you can't just select it with the mouse as you can in xv. If you try, you'll see that the Commands window disappears when you click the mouse over the image (click the mouse again to bring it back). To select a rectangular region of the image, choose Region of Interest... from the Image Edit menu. You can then select a rectangular region in the image in the traditional way—click and drag the mouse to draw a rectangle.

You'll notice that the Commands window changes to reflect valid actions and options for the mode you are in or the action you are performing. For example, in the case of selecting a region, after you select Region of Interest..., the Commands window will resize itself and show only two buttons: Help and Dismiss. Clicking the Help button will bring up a little help page about selecting regions, and clicking the Dismiss button will cancel the operation and take you back to the original set of menus.

When you've selected the region you want to operate on, the Commands window changes again to reflect what operations you can perform on the selected region. The selection will remain until you press the Dismiss button. Until then, you can perform as many operations on the selection as you want. Upon pressing the Dismiss button, the selection disappears, and the Commands window returns to its original state. Figures 27.11 and 27.12 show how the Commands window changes during and after the selection of a region of an image.

FIGURE 27.11
The Commands window just after choosing Region of Interest... in the Image Edit menu and before selecting a region. Note that the title has changed to ROI for Region Of Interest.

FIGURE 27.12
The Commands window after selecting a region of the image. Note that the title has changed to Apply, indicating that the selected actions will be applied to the selected region.

Just about anything you can do with xv, you can do with `display`. `display` also has some other nice features, however. It has more filters or algorithms than xv does, and it also enables you to draw on the image (in the same ways that `convert` can draw on an image), place text in the image, and combine images in the same ways as `combine`. For more information, check the `display` man page (`man display`). The online documentation (obtained by clicking the Help button) is also very good.

`identify`

`identify` describes the format and other attributes of one or more image files. It will report a number of facts, including the scene number, the filename, the dimensions in pixels of the image, whether the image has a colormap, the number of colors in the image, the size of the image in bytes, the image format used (GIF, JPEG, and so on), and the number of seconds it took to process the image. `identify` is purely a command-line tool and has the following syntax:

```
identify [options] file [file ...]
```

For example, I get the following output when run on the image `millep02.jpg`:

```
$ identify millep02.jpg
```

```
millep02.jpg 216x267 DirectClass 8823b JPEG 1s
```

This indicates that the image name is `millep02.jpg`, its dimensions are 216 pixels by 267 pixels, it uses a DirectClass colormap (basically meaning there is no colormap), the file size is 8,823 bytes, the image format is JPEG, and it took one second to read and process the image. Actually, the time is rounded up to one second. The image actually processed much faster.

If you specify the `-verbose` option, more output is produced and extra information is given about the image, including any image comment:

```
$ identify -verbose millep02.jpg
```

```
Image: millep02.jpg
  class: DirectClass
  colors: 15066
  matte: False
  runlength packets: 30364 of 57672
  geometry: 216x267
  resolution: 72x72 pixels/inch
  depth: 16
  filesize: 8823b
  interlace: None
  format: JPEG
  comments:
U-Lead Systems, Inc.
```

See the `identify` man page (`man identify`) for more information.

import

`import` takes screen shots of an X server and saves them to a file. You can take a screen shot of a single window, the entire screen, or any rectangular part of the screen. It is purely a command-line program and has the following syntax:

```
import [options] [file]
```

You can use `display` to view the results, make changes, and so on. If you don't specify a file to save to, the output will be saved to the file `magick.ps`.

To capture a window, you can specify it by ID or name or by simply clicking the mouse once anywhere in the desired window. If you click somewhere in the root window (on the desktop), `import` will take a picture of the entire screen. To capture a given rectangular portion of the screen, click and hold the left mouse button and then drag the mouse to form a rectangle around the area you want. `import` will grab the portion of the screen outlined by the rectangle when you release the mouse button.

Table 27.4 lists some useful options for `import`. For more information, see the `import` man page (`man import`).

TABLE 27.4 Useful Options for `import`

Option	Description
`-delay seconds`	Specifies the number of seconds to delay before selecting the target window. This can be used to give you time to get the window ready first.
`-display host: display[.screen]`	Specifies the X server to contact. This allows you to take pictures of a remote screen. Note: You need access permission to the remote X server to get screen shots of or from it.
`-frame`	Tells `import` to include the window manager frame. Otherwise, it leaves the window manager frame off.
`-screen`	Tells `import` that the `GetImage` request used to get the image of the screen should be done on the root window instead of directly on the selected window. This enables you to have pieces of other windows that overlap the specified window included in the image. For example, this would enable you to get pop-up menus in the image, even though they are independent windows that are simply over the specified window.
`-window id`	Tells `import` to grab the window with the given ID or name.

For example, to get a screen shot of the entire screen and save it to the file `screen.tif`, you could use the following command:

```
$ import -window root screen.tif
```

Or, to get a screenshot of the xload window with the window manager frame from the display otherhost:0 and save it as the file `xload.eps`, you could use this command:

```
$ import -window xload -display otherhost:0 -frame xload.eps
```

mogrify

`mogrify` transforms an image or sequence of images. With this command you can scale, rotate, reduce the number of colors in an image, and do many more things. You can do pretty much anything you can do with `display` or `convert` using `mogrify`. In general, the original image will be replaced by the transmogrified one (think of Calvin's transmogrifier from *Calvin and Hobbes*—it doesn't produce a changed *copy* of him, it changes *him*). There are, of course, exceptions. `mogrify` is purely a command-line tool and has the following syntax:

`mogrify [options] file [ [options] file ...]`

`mogrify` can be used in place of `convert` to convert an image from one format to another. It will also enable you to use wildcards to specify multiple images to convert. This is an effective way to do batch processing of images. For example, the following command would convert all TIFF images in the current directory to JPEGs:

`$ mogrify -format JPEG *.tif`

This is one case in which the original image is not overwritten with the modified image. In this case, `mogrify` will convert a TIFF image to JPEG and then save it using the same image name, but with a `.jpeg` extension. The converted image of `picture.tif` will be named `picture.jpeg`.

Table 27.5 lists some of the options that can be used with `mogrify`. For more information and options, see the `mogrify` man page (`man mogrify`).

TABLE 27.5 Options for Use with `mogrify`

Option	Description
-blur factor	Blurs the image. factor is the percentage of enhancement and can be any number from 0.0 to 99.9.
-contrast	Increases the contrast (intensity differences between light and dark colors) of the image.
+contrast	Decreases the contrast of the image.
-despeckle	Reduces speckles in the image.
-edge factor	Detects edges in the image. factor is a percentage value from 0.0 to 99.9.
-emboss	Embosses the image.
-enhance	Enhances the image by applying a digital filter to it.
-equalize	Performs histogram equalization to the image.

continues

TABLE 27.5   continued

Option	Description
-flip	Flips the image vertically.
-flop	Flips the image horizontally.
-format type	Converts the image to the specify format. type is a format recognized by Image Magick.
-gamma value	Performs gamma correction on an image. value is the amount of gamma correction to perform.
-normalize	Transforms the image so that the full range of color values is used. This is a contrast enhancement technique.
-raise <width>x <height>	Shades the edges of the image to produce a 3D effect, making it look as though the image is raised. <width> is the thickness in pixels of the left and right raised edges. <height> is the thickness in pixels of the top and bottom raised edges.
+raise <width>x <height>	The same as -raise but gives the image a "lowered" effect.
-sharpen factor	Sharpens the image. factor is a percentage value from 0.0 to 99.9.

montage

montage creates a new image that is a composite of thumbnails of specified images. The thumbnails are tiled on the new image and can have borders placed around them and have their names appear below them. The composite image can also have a title. You can use wildcards to specify more than one image, or you can list each image individually on the command line. montage is purely a command-line tool and has the following syntax:

`montage [options] file [ [options] file ...] output_file`

Each image on the command line except the last one (`output_file`) is scaled to fit the maximum tile size. By default, this is 120×120. The background color of the composite image is set to the color of the X resource background or to the color given by the -background option. The size of the composite image is determined by the size of the title, the size of the tiles, the number of tiles per row and the number of rows, the border width and height, the image border thickness, and the height of the image labels. By default, there are five tiles per row and up to four rows. If there are fewer images than that, then there may be fewer rows, or if there are fewer than five images, the composite will be wide enough to fit only the given images. If there are more images than can be placed in the maximum number of tiles for the composite (determined by the tiles per row and maximum number of rows), `montage` will create more than one composite image.

For example, to create a montage of your favorite fish and save it to the file `fishes.tif`, you could use a command similar to this:

```
$ montage salmon.tif trout.tif catfish.tif fishes.tif
```

To create a montage of all your fish pictures in the `fish` directory with tiles that are at most 256 by 192 pixels, surrounded by a red border, and separated by 10 pixels of background color, you could use a command similar to this:

```
$ montage -geometry 256x192+10+10 -bordercolor red fish/* fishes.tif
```

Table 27.6 lists some options that can be used with `montage`. See the `montage` manual page (`man montage`) for more information.

TABLE 27.6 Options for Use with `montage`

Option	Description
`-adjoin`	Joins images into a single multi-image file.
`-font name`	Specifies the font to use for the title and image labels.
`-geometry <width>x<height>+<border_width>+<border_height>`	Sets the preferred tile size and border width and height. Note: This is not the same as the image border; this is the spacing between tiles.
`-label name`	Assigns a label to an image.
`-mode type`	Sets the type of montage. Valid modes are `Frame`, `UnFrame`, and `Concatenate`. The default mode is `UnFrame`.
`-pointsize value`	If `montage` is unable to get an X font, a PostScript font is used. This option specifies the point size for the font.
`-shadow`	Adds a shadow beneath a tile.
`-texture file`	Uses the given file as a texture to tile on the background of the composite.
`-tile <cols>x<rows>`	Specifies the number of tiles per row and the maximum number of rows for the composite.

Finding More Information About Image Magick

You can find more information about Image Magick and libraries to go along with it at http://www.wizards.dupont.com/cristy/ImageMagick.html.

The GIMP

The GIMP (GNU Image Manipulation Program) is an excellent program for creating, viewing, and editing images. It was designed to be something of an Adobe Photoshop work-alike. Although it doesn't really work like Photoshop, much of what you can do in Photoshop you can do in the GIMP. The GIMP will also do things that Photoshop won't do. There is a constant debate about which program is better (but we all know that the GIMP *has* to be better, if for no other reason than it runs under Linux, and Photoshop doesn't!).

The GIMP was designed from the outset to be very flexible and easily modified. This was accomplished by implementing much of its functionality through plug-ins. Plug-ins are used for all image filters, importers, and exporters. If you want a certain type of effect that isn't yet part of the GIMP, you can add it by writing a plug-in for it. If you're not a programmer, don't worry; other people are writing plug-ins for the GIMP all the time. You might even be able to talk someone else into writing your plug-in for you, if you can convince that person that your plug-in would be a good thing to have.

The GIMP also has a scripting language called Script-Fu that allows you to automate certain tasks. It comes with quite a few Script-Fu scripts for creating things such as logos, Web page buttons, certain kinds of patterns, and more. Many people have written Script-Fu scripts to perform various types of tasks and have made them publicly available to anyone who would like to use them. You can find a list of some of them at http://www.gimp.org/scripts.html.

The GIMP is also an excellent program for graphics artists. Quite a few people have done extraordinary artwork using the GIMP. There is even a semimonthly contest for the best GIMP-created image. Information about the contest can be found at http://contest.gimp.org/. There is also an image gallery at http://www.gimp.org/gallery.html. By all means, follow the links to the authors' Web sites and take a look at other work they've done. You'll see some amazing things that have been done with the GIMP.

Although the GIMP is an excellent tool for graphics artists, it is not suited to all kinds of artwork. It is purely a pixel-based program and will not do vector graphics. It's more akin to painting than what you can do with a program such as Adobe Illustrator.

> **Note**
>
> If the GIMP was not installed when you installed OpenLinux, you can install it from the RPM files `gimp-1.0.4-1.i386.rpm` and `gimp-data-1.0.0-1.i386.rpm` in the directory `Packages/RPMS` on the installation CD. Both RPMs should be installed.

Running the GIMP for the First Time

You can start the GIMP either from the menu in KDE or from the command line. To start it from the command line, simply type **gimp** at the command prompt. When you run the GIMP for the first time, it will pop up a GIMP Installation dialog like the one in Figure 27.13. This dialog contains some information you should read.

FIGURE 27.13
The GIMP Installation dialog.

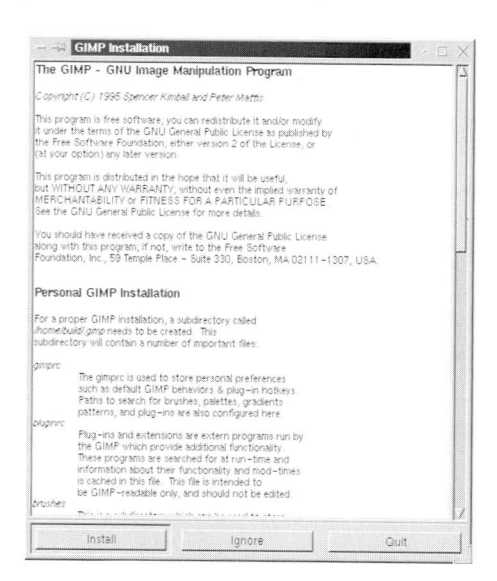

After you've read the information, you should click the Install button. You can click the Ignore button, but then the GIMP will always start up with this dialog, and you will have to keep clicking Ignore or finally give in and allow it to install itself. If you click Install, the GIMP will create a new directory called `.gimp` in your home directory. Within that directory, it will create some other subdirectories and copy a few configuration files. Very little space is required for the GIMP to install itself. Upon successful completion of these tasks, a new dialog window pops up—similar to the one in Figure 27.14—stating that the installation was successful and giving you the option of continuing or quitting. Normally, you want to continue.

FIGURE 27.14
The Installation Log dialog.

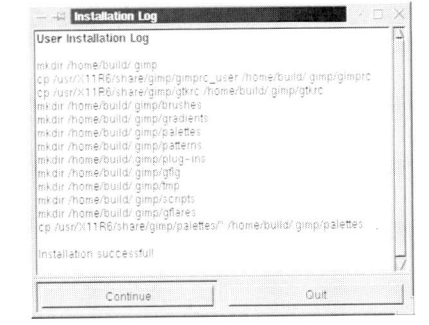

If you continue, a splash screen with a progress bar similar to the one in Figure 27.15 pops up, showing the progress as the GIMP starts up. Each time you start the GIMP after the initial installation, the first thing you will see will be this splash screen. When the GIMP is completely loaded, the splash screen will disappear, and you will be presented with the GIMP toolbar window and the GIMP Tip of the Day window, shown in Figures 27.16 and 27.17, respectively.

FIGURE 27.15
The GIMP startup splash screen.

FIGURE 27.16
The GIMP toolbar window. This is the main application window for the GIMP and the hub of all activity.

FIGURE 27.17
The GIMP Tip of the Day window.

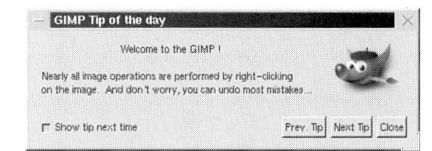

In the GIMP Tip of the Day window, you will see a new tip each time you start the GIMP. You can browse through the different tips using the Prev. Tip and Next Tip buttons. When you're through reading tips, you can close the window by clicking the Close button. If you get tired of reading tips each time the GIMP starts, you can disable them by deselecting the Show Tip Next Time check box in the lower-left corner of the window.

The Toolbar

Unlike xv and `display`, the main application window for the GIMP is the toolbar window. The GIMP will exit only when you close that window or choose Quit from one of the menus.

The toolbar window is the hub of all GIMP activity. The selected tool on the toolbar determines the mode that the GIMP is in. If you hold the mouse over one of the buttons, a ToolTip pops up describing what that particular tool is for. Clicking a tool selects it. Double-clicking a tool brings up an options dialog for that tool.

The currently selected foreground and background colors are displayed at the bottom of the toolbar. Clicking one of them brings up a Color Selection dialog—like the one in Figure 27.18—that allows you to select a color in several different ways. When you have the color you want, clicking Close will change the foreground or background color to the selected color. If you decide you don't want to change the color after all, clicking Revert to Old Color closes the dialog without making any changes to the original foreground and background colors.

FIGURE 27.18
The Color Selection dialog.

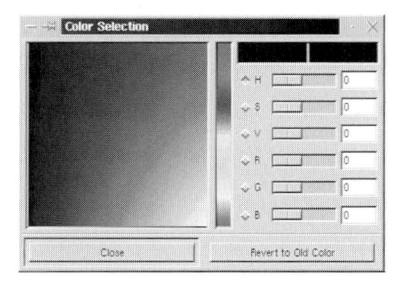

Clicking the two-headed arrow above the background color square on the toolbar will swap the foreground and background colors. Clicking the small black-and-white squares underneath the foreground color square will change the foreground and background colors to black and white, respectively.

The menus above the toolbar are very general and include only items that don't apply to any image that is opened. From them you can do things such as open an image or create a new one, set preferences for the GIMP, gain access to certain dialog windows, take screen shots, and access installed Script-Fu scripts.

Opening an Image File

There are two ways to open an image in the GIMP. One is to supply the filename on the command line when you start it up. The other is to select Open from the File menu in the toolbar window. If you open a file from the File menu, a file dialog like the one in Figure 27.19 pops up.

FIGURE 27.19
The Load Image dialog.

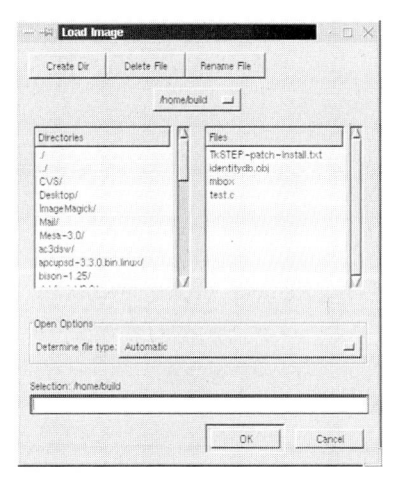

The three buttons at the top of the dialog give you a little file manager functionality by allowing you to create directories and delete and rename files. This can be handy if you want to save an image in a new directory but forgot to create it before you tried to save the image, and so on. You can move around the directory structure by double-clicking the directory you want to change to.

The two special directories ./ and ../ are listed along with the normal directories. ./ represents the current directory, and ../ represents the parent directory. Double-clicking the ../ directory takes you up one directory. If you are at the root directory (/), clicking

../ will have no effect, because you can't go back any farther than the root directory. Double-clicking ./ causes the current directory to be reread. You would want to do this if the directory's contents have changed since you opened the Load Image dialog.

Selecting a file places its name in the text field at the bottom of the dialog. You can then press Enter or click the OK button to open the selected image. Double-clicking the desired file will also open it. When the image is loaded, the file dialog disappears and you will see a new window displaying your image. If the GIMP is unable to open the image for some reason, an error dialog will pop up and the file dialog will stay open, allowing you to try again.

Normally, the GIMP is able to determine the type of image it is opening from the filename's extension or by examining the image file to determine whether it's in a recognizable format. If the GIMP is unable to determine the type of the image for some reason, you can specify it using the drop-down list in the Open Options area of the dialog.

Creating a New Image

If you want to create a new image, select New from the File menu in the toolbar window. This will bring up a New Image dialog like the one in Figure 27.20, allowing you to specify the image's size, whether it will be a grayscale or RGB image, and whether it should have a solid color background or be transparent. You can work with arbitrarily large images, but large images can take up a lot of memory in a hurry, especially if you will have several layers in the image, so don't get too carried away.

Figure 27.20

The New Image dialog.

You start out able to choose only one of two color modes: RGB or grayscale. The GIMP actually supports three modes (RGB, grayscale, and indexed), but it won't let you start out with an indexed color image because it has no way of knowing what colors you want to start out with. In general, it's better to work with an RGB or grayscale image and convert it to an indexed image, if you need to, just before saving it. The GIMP does not currently support the CMYK color model used in printing.

The Fill Type specifies how the image background will be filled. Background means that the image background will be filled using the selected background color (white by default). If you cut or delete part of the image, that space will be filled in using the background color.

White means that the background will be filled in with solid white. Deleting or cutting part of the image always results in the empty space being filled with white, regardless of the selected background color.

Transparent means that the background will not be filled in. Instead, you will see a checkered background, indicating that it is transparent. This is useful for creating transparent GIFs and other types of images that support transparency.

When you have chosen your image options, clicking OK will create the new image. Figure 27.21 shows the image display window with an empty, newly created, transparent, RGB image that is 256 by 256 pixels. Newly created images are named `Untitled-number`, where `number` is replaced with a number. The GIMP has an internal counter that keeps track of how many images have been created or opened since it was started. It uses this counter to determine what number to append to the new name.

The color mode is shown in parentheses in the window title. In this case, it is RGB-alpha. For transparency to exist in an image, there must be an alpha channel. The *alpha* in RGB-alpha simply indicates that there is an alpha channel.

Along the top and left of the image window is a ruler with little arrows indicating what pixel (row and column) the cursor is over. You'll have to look closely to see the little arrows. They move in real time as you move the cursor over the image. The GIMP doesn't currently support the notion of dots per inch (dpi), so you can't change what is displayed on the ruler to represent any unit of measure other than absolute pixel positions. For example, you can't say that the image has a resolution of 300 dpi and then have the ruler display the cursor position in inches. That will likely come in a future version, however.

FIGURE 27.21

The image window displaying a newly created, transparent image.

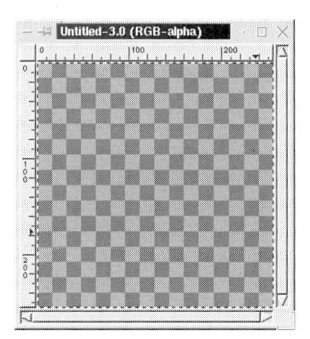

The Pop-up Menus

You'll note that there are no menus in the image display window. How, then, are you supposed to work with the image, if there isn't much that is useful in the toolbar window menus? The answer is that the GIMP designers opted not to add menu bars to the image windows. Instead, they put all the good stuff in pop-up menus that pop up when you click the right mouse button anywhere in the image area. The menus stay up as long as you hold the mouse button down. To select an item, hold the mouse button down while you drag the mouse to the item you want, and then release the mouse button.

In the pop-up menus, you have access to most of what is in the toolbar window menus plus a whole lot more. You have access to file operations such as saving an image and creating or opening a new one. You can do editing operations such as cut, copy, and paste. You can perform various select operations, control how the image is displayed on the screen, perform color operations, change the color mode, apply filters, and perform a whole bunch of other actions on the image. In short, most of what you can do to an image is in the pop-up menus. The key, then, to becoming proficient at using the GIMP is to familiarize yourself with these menus, so you know what's there and how to use it. Figure 27.22 shows some pop-up menus.

FIGURE 27.22
Some of the pop-up menus available in the GIMP.

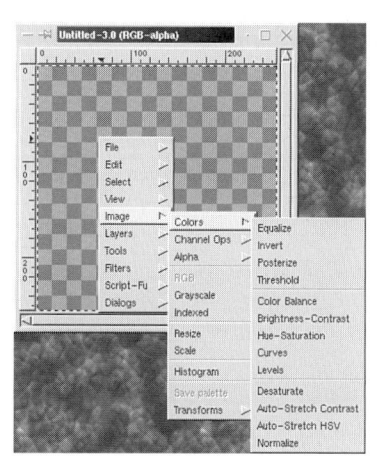

Saving an Image to a File

Now that you know how to open the pop-up menus, you can save an image to a file. To do that, select Save (or Save As if you want to save the image to a different file) from the File menu. If this is the first time you are saving the image, or you selected Save As, a file dialog like the one in Figure 27.23 pops up.

FIGURE 27.23
The Save Image dialog.

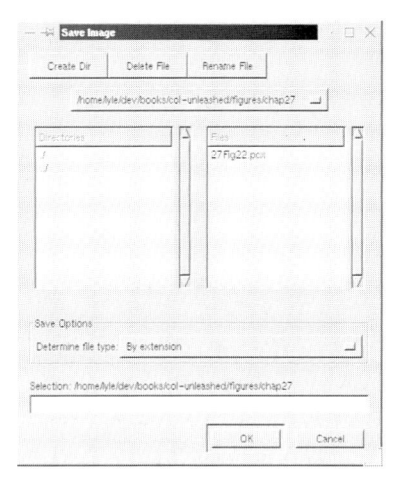

You'll note that this dialog looks suspiciously like the Load Image dialog. As it turns out, it works pretty much the same way. The one thing to note here is the drop-down list in the Save Options area of the dialog. This list enables you to specify an image format to save the image in, or that the GIMP should try to determine the format to use by the filename's extension. For most common formats, this works just fine. For example, if you want to save an image as a JPEG, simply adding .jpg to the image name will be enough to let the GIMP know what format you want.

> **Note**
>
> The GIMP supports many features that most image formats can't handle. For example, it supports multiple layers and layer masks. To save an image with all its layers and other information intact, you need to use the XCF format. This could be considered the native GIMP format.
>
> When working with an image, I recommend that you save the original in XCF format and then make whatever changes are necessary to save it in the final format. For example, when working with different layers, it is wise to save the image first in XCF format with all the layer information intact, and then *flatten* the image (combine all the layers into one) when you are ready to save it in the final format. This allows you to go back and continue working with the individual layers, should you want to change something later.

Using Script-Fu Scripts

Essentially, two categories of Script-Fu scripts are installed: scripts that create a new image and scripts that work with an existing image. The first category is found in the Script-Fu menu under the Xtns menu in the toolbar window. The second category is found in the Script-Fu menu in the image display window's pop-up menus. Among the scripts in the first category are scripts to create logos—for example, for a Web page—buttons, and different patterns. In the second category, you find scripts that enable you to use special effects such as making an image look like an old photo, creating new patterns (replacing the original image) such as a lava pattern, and many other operations.

When you select the script you want to use, a dialog pops up that enable you to customize different aspects of the script's operation. For example, if you decide you want to do a new logo using the 3D Outline script (choose Xtns, Script-Fu, Logos, 3D Outline), a dialog pops up similar to the one in Figure 27.24. Figure 27.25 shows the image produced by the script using the default settings.

FIGURE 27.24
The options dialog for the 3D Outline script.

FIGURE 27.25
The image produced by the 3D Outline script using its default settings.

> **Note**
>
> Most of the logo scripts use fonts that aren't installed on your X server by default. If you try to run a script that uses a font you don't have, you will get an error message and the script will fail. The fonts used by these scripts can be found in the freefonts and sharefonts packages, which can be obtained from the GIMP Web site. You can, however, usually supply a different font name to use.

> **Note**
>
> For any text generated by a text-related Script-Fu script or by the text tool to look nice and smooth around its edge, you must use scalable fonts. Nearly all the fonts that come with OpenLinux are bitmap fonts. A result of this is that the only way the X server can make a font look larger is to essentially magnify it. This results in the text's outline becoming very jagged because the magnification adds a stair-stepped appearance to it. To avoid this, you must install scalable fonts such as the ones that come in the freefonts and sharefonts packages. You can also install other TrueType or Type1 fonts. These types of fonts specify the outlines of the fonts mathematically, allowing the X server to generate a nice, smooth font at nearly any size. Figure 27.26 shows how the Script-Fu logo looks using a bitmapped Times Roman font. More information about fonts that can be used with the GIMP can be found at http://www.gimp.org/fonts.html.

FIGURE 27.26
The Script-Fu logo using a bitmapped Times Roman font.

Installing a New Script-Fu Script

You can install a new Script-Fu script by copying it into the directory `.gimp/scripts` under your home directory. If you want to install the script so that every GIMP user on a particular machine has access to it, you can copy it to the directory `/usr/X11R6/share/gimp/scripts`. You will need to do this as root or the superuser. When you restart the GIMP, you will find the new script in one of the Script-Fu menus.

Installing a New Plug-In

Installing a new plug-in is much like installing a new Script-Fu script. You simply copy it to the directory `.gimp/plug-ins` under your home directory, or the directory `/usr/X11R6/lib/gimp/1.0/plug-ins`, if you want everyone to be able to use it. The plug-in will be available the next time you start the GIMP.

Finding More Information

The GIMP is a program full of wonderful features that can't be discussed here. You don't need to learn about all of them before using the GIMP effectively, however. Many functions are intuitive and easily found in the menus. But for those of you who want to get the most out of the GIMP, there is a lot of documentation available on the Web. The first place to go is `http://www.gimp.org/`. There is an online version of the GIMP Users' Manual (commonly called the GUM) at `http://manual.gimp.org/`. Many other people have also put up their own Web pages dedicated to the GIMP, complete with tutorials, scripts, and plug-ins they've written. You can find many of those simply by searching for "gimp" on many search engines on the Internet. You can also find books written about the GIMP, such as *The Artist's Guide to the GIMP*, by Michael J. Hammel, and *Sams Teach Yourself GIMP in 24 Hours*, by Joshua and Ramona Pruitt.

Summary

In this chapter, you learned how to display, manipulate, and create images and graphics using xv, Image Magick, and the GIMP.

With xv, you learned how to

- Open and save an image
- Display an image in the root window
- Apply algorithms to an entire image or a selected region of an image
- Adjust the hue and saturation of an image
- Apply gamma correction to an image
- Display information about an image

With Image Magick, you learned how to

- Display an image
- Convert an image from one format to another
- Combine two or more images in various ways
- Animate a sequence of images
- Take screen shots of individual windows or the entire screen
- Create a montage of images
- Draw text on an image

With the GIMP, you learned how to

- Open and save an image in various formats
- Create a new image
- Apply filters to an image or to a selected region of an image
- Install and use Script-Fu scripts

Typesetting Documents

IN THIS CHAPTER

- Creating a Typeset Document   *651*
- Typesetting Entry Tools   *654*
- Utilities Used with Typesetting   *662*
- Exotica (or Really Fancy Typesetting)   *669*

This chapter shows you how to do typesetting on your Linux system. As you will see from the extensive number of typesetting routines available in Linux, this was more of a thought than an afterthought for the development project. Typesetting on Linux owes a debt of gratitude to all those students who worked nights using the typesetting capabilities of Linux to generate their camera-ready theses.

Typesetters have an old joke that goes something like "Typesetting—It's not just word processing any more." If you don't have typesetting experience on your resumé, you might not get the joke. The funny part of the joke is that most people think word processing is typesetting if they are using one of the newest word processors.

As you will see in this chapter, that isn't the case. First of all, typesetting predates word processing in both electromechanical and electronic technologies. Second, typesetting is far more than word processing, and the documents produced are usually of a much higher visual quality (although even this can be destroyed by a $16 used dot matrix printer and an old ribbon).

So if you want typeset-quality formatting and printing, Caldera Linux has the tools you need.

Caldera supports a wide variety of typesetting programs and tools. Some are delivered with the installation CD-ROM, and others are available via the Web.

The actual process that does the formatting and font selection for typesetting in almost all UNIX systems is called TeX. There are several implementations of the TeX functionality. Some are quite good, but others are somewhat less so. The TeX implementation that is delivered with Caldera is the Web2c implementation, which was originally written for UNIX. It includes all the standard programs developed by the Stanford TeX project directed by Donald Knuth. In addition, programs such as DVIcopy—written by Peter Breitnelohner and MetaPost—and its utilities (by John Hobby) are included. All in all, Caldera offers the best solution and all the necessary options right out of the box.

This chapter is broken down into three basic parts: typesetting entry tools (editors and the like), typesetting utilities, and typesetting exotica (typesetting foreign languages, mathematical theses, and graphs).

You will definitely want to read the part on the typesetting entry tools and browse the utilities sections. The exotica section is for those who need to produce that type of document, so you will miss nothing if you bypass it.

Creating a Typeset Document

All discussions of typesetting on Linux seem to discuss LaTeX and not TeX. This is probably because TeX is very formal and cryptic, and LaTeX is a simpler set of macros that provides a user-friendly interface to TeX. If TeX is cryptic, LaTeX is complicated. Although it isn't necessary to understand all of LaTeX in order to create beautiful documents, you should be aware that hundreds of macros are available to do almost anything in TeX, and they are all available for the Caldera Linux implementation. There are several definitive texts on LaTeX (some are hundreds of pages long), and you might want to refer to one of those texts after you get your feet wet with LaTeX. However, my purpose is to get you started with typesetting and give you a feel for the possibilities.

LaTeX is a document-preparation system for generating medium or large technical documents. If the document you are planning to make is on the order of five pages, setting it up in LaTeX probably won't be worth the time, but it will work. LaTeX isn't a word processor. It can't even be reasonably used for that. The purpose of LaTeX is to put you, the author, in the driver's seat and leave the details of the formatting to TeX.

To illustrate that point, let's look at the differences in how you would create a document in a word processor and how the same thing would be done in LaTeX.

The Real Economics of Oil

David Schwering

February 1972

Oil is subject to the supply and demand curves in an absolutely linear manner. The more oil that is available at a given time, the lower cost of that oil. The only modification to this absolutely linear supply/demand curve is that which is caused by intervention of a government.

In order to produce this example in most typesetting systems and in a word processor, you would have to do more than type text. First, you would have to decide what layout to use. Second, you would have to pick the typeface for the title—say 14-point Verdana—and then you would have to decide on the typeface for the author's name. Well, you get the point.

This leads to three obvious problems: authors wasting their time designing documents, a lot of poorly designed documents, and wasted tree pulp. LaTeX is an attempt to move the authors away from designing and getting caught up in the details of documents. It is best to leave that to the document designers. This same document in LaTeX would appear as shown in Listing 28.1.

LISTING 28.1 The Real Economics of Oil as It Appears in LaTeX

```
\documentclass{article}
\title{The Real Economics of Oil}
\author{David Schwering}
\date{February 1972}
\begin{document}
    \maketitle
    Oil is subject to the supply and demand curves in an absolutely linear
manner.
The more oil that is available at a given time, the lower cost of that oil.
The only modification to this absolutely linear
supply / demand curve is that which
is caused
by intervention of a government.
\end{document}
```

Now I know what you are going to say. "Gee it seems like a lot of gobbledygook and a lot more work." Well, if you will try it, I am sure that you will find that, even on this small "document," the results are worth it, and you can save time.

What you need to do is the following. Open your favorite editor or word processor. I used vi because I have been using it for 25 years, but WordPerfect or Star Office will produce the same results. Now, enter the text exactly as you see it in the preceding example. Note that *braces* are used around words in lines beginning with the \, *not parentheses*. When you are done, save the file as a text file with the extension .tex. This extension makes everything that follows much easier, but if you want to use any other extension for your own purposes, it will work.

Note that in the example I have interspersed carriage returns at odd places in the sentences. This is to remind you that with LaTeX you concentrate on the content of your document and not the physical formatting.

Now, let's put LaTeX to the test. At the command line, enter the following command:

`#latex [filename]`

Or, use the .tex extension:

`#latex [filename.extension]`

On your terminal screen, you will see information similar to that shown in Figure 28.1.

If you don't have any lines that begin

`! LaTeX Error`

everything is OK (well, maybe not the spelling of the words, but that can be fixed).

FIGURE 28.1

Screen output from LaTeX.

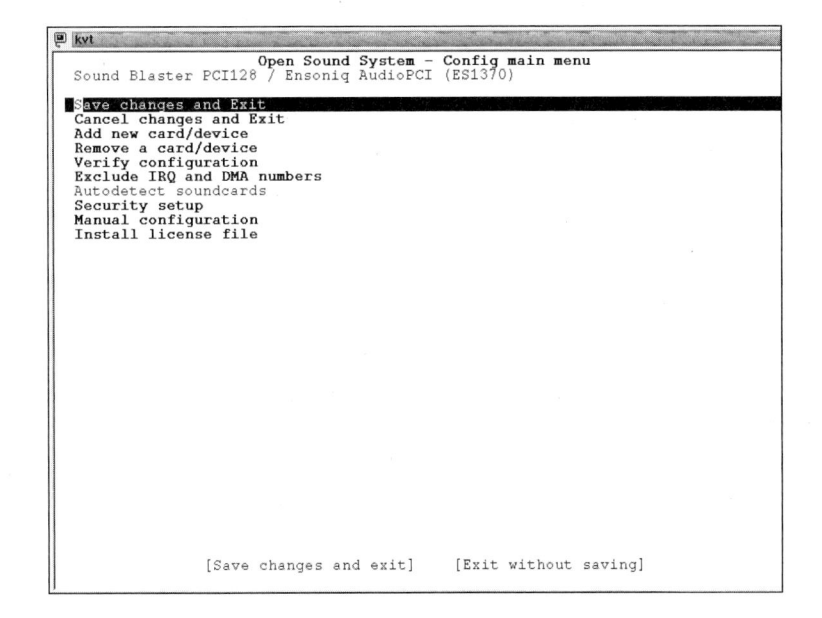

```
Open Sound System - Config main menu
Sound Blaster PCI128 / Ensoniq AudioPCI (ES1370)
Save changes and Exit
Cancel changes and Exit
Add new card/device
Remove a card/device
Verify configuration
Exclude IRQ and DMA numbers
Autodetect soundcards
Security setup
Manual configuration
Install license file




              [Save changes and exit]   [Exit without saving]
```

As you can see from Figure 28.1, LaTeX writes out many files. Some of these are critical to debugging what went wrong on a large document—[filename].log and [filename].aux. However, if you are successful, LaTeX will output a file called [filename].dvi. This is the all-critical device-independent file that we will use in the next step.

The next step is to enter the following command line from a terminal window in X.

`#xdvi [filename]`

Lo and behold, you will see the window shown in Figure 28.2. Nifty, isn't it?

FIGURE 28.2

A screen display of the typeset document.

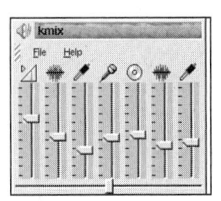

If you want to reduce your document to hard copy, the command is

`#dvips [filename]`

This will produce a typeset copy of your document on your printer if the printer is set up correctly.

All the information necessary to develop this typeset document is contained in the control information provided by TeX information lines beginning with \ and in the document class definition invoked by the \documentclass{article} line in Listing 28.1.

Well that was easy, wasn't it? Unfortunately, the devil is in the details, and there are a lot of details.

Typesetting Entry Tools

Many tools are available for Linux that make the entry of typeset material easier. emacs (which is on the Caldera distribution CD) is a favorite of many UNIX enthusiasts, but LyX, which will assist you in inserting images and graphics into the finished document, is probably a better choice for the other 90 percent of us. Because an excellent version of LyX is included on the Caldera distribution CD, I will concentrate on it here.

Creating a LaTeX Input File

You can create a LaTeX input file using virtually any text processing program. When you become familiar with Caldera OpenLinux, you will probably want to use emacs; but vi, Star Office, and WordPerfect are all acceptable.

The best option, one with a beautiful front end for LaTeX, is LyX (the Caldera distribution version is called KLyX). It combines the comfortable usage of a word processor with the high quality of LaTeX's typesetting, providing an almost WYSIWYG view of the document. Although line and page breaks aren't displayed exactly as they will be in the printed document, most everything else is.

LyX frees you from dealing with low-level formatting such as Large Bold Italic Sans Serif Font and a Little Space Above and Below and allows you to concentrate on the content. The typesetter (that is, LaTeX) has enough information to break your text in a very nice manner, so let it. You can simply choose a layout for each paragraph and leave the driving to the system.

This produces portable documents using a generic mark-up concept. Of course, you can still do low-level formatting, but the usual way is to tell LyX what the text is, not what it should look like. In a sense, LyX gives you WYSIWYM (What You See Is What You Mean) editing.

The LyX organization's Web page can be found at http://www.lyx.org. It contains a number of insights and other helpful information on LyX, as well as hints and current versions of the product.

Caldera's implementation of LyX that is delivered with Caldera is called KLyX. It can be found on the desktop options bar under the K-gear icon, Applications, KLyX, or it can be entered from a terminal running under X with the following command:

```
#klyx
```

By selecting either of these methods, the KLyX opening screen (shown in Figure 28.3) opens on your desktop.

FIGURE 28.3
The KLyX desktop.

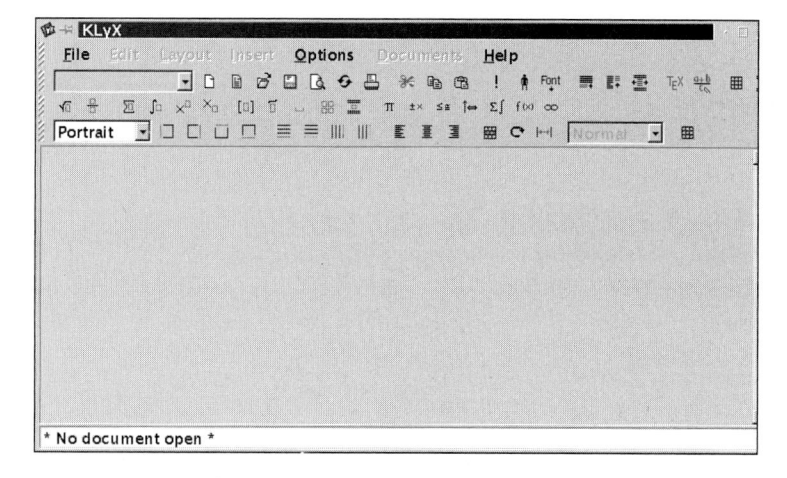

From this point, if you select File, New From Template, you will be given a directory screen. If you follow the directory digression depicted in the location field of Figure 28.4, the default templates available with Caldera will be shown.

FIGURE 28.4
Templates available in KLyX.

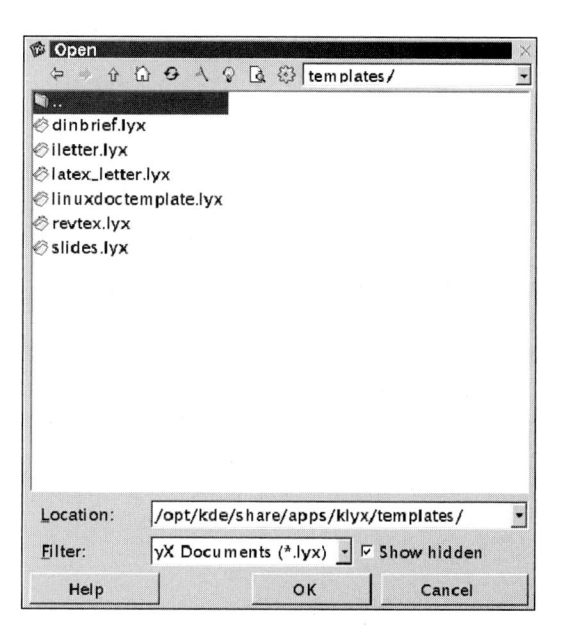

You can expand on these templates and create your own look and feel for your documents. All that is necessary to create a new template is to create a document in KLyX that has your own special look and feel and then save it in the templates directory.

However, you might ask, "How can I create the document from the beginning of this chapter?" All the features are there, and it's simply a matter of locating them. But it's no fun to go over the same ground twice, so why don't we try to start the novel that is in your soul waiting to get out.

To start your novel, go back to the screen depicted in Figure 28.3. To get there, click Cancel to close the templates screen.

Now you need to implement the following steps:

1. Click File.
2. Click New.
3. Enter a filename for your novel.
4. Select and click on Layout on the Menu bar.
5. Select and click on Document.
6. Click on the open select arrow to the right of Class.
7. Browse down and click on Book.
8. Answer Yes to Change Document Class when asked.
9. Click Apply.

    It gets a little tricky the first time. A dialog box is on the upper-left side below the words File and Edit on the selection bar. This box probably says Standard. This is the paragraph environment window.

10. Go to the paragraph environment window and highlight Title.
11. Enter the title of your tome: `My last great novel`.
12. Go back to the paragraph environment window and highlight Author.
13. Go ahead and enter your name; it's your tome.
14. Go back to the paragraph environment window and highlight Date.

    For this I might suggest circa 2000 AD, because, if you're like me, this tome will take a long time to write (a very long time).

15. Go back to the paragraph environment window and select Standard.

    Now comes the real tricky part: the first sentence.

16. You might try something like, "It was neither the best of times nor a dark and stormy night."

Your screen should look similar to Figure 28.5.

FIGURE 28.5
Your novel in the KLyX entry screen.

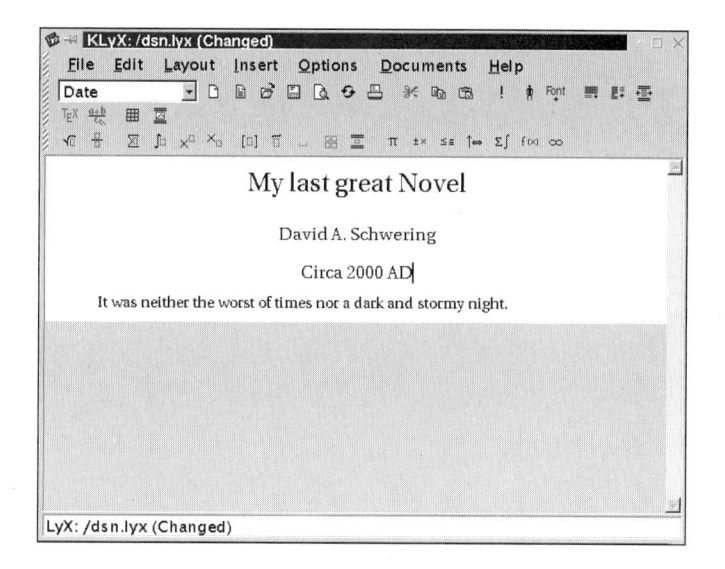

As you can see, KLyX looks and acts a lot like a word processor. And, in fact, with a lot of trouble, you could cause KLyX to act exactly like a word processor. (It's all available in the configuration files.)

However, I'll show you something that your word processor can't do. On this screen, Select File, Preview, View DVI, and you will see your tome taking shape in a device-independent format.

Right before your eyes on the kdvi panel is the first page of your tome (see Figure 28.6). In this case, it is the title page of your document. Document class [book] creates a title page, whereas document class [article] doesn't. If you want to see the first line that you created (it's very important to have a grabber for a first line), click on the right arrow just below "p" in the word Options on the control bar. Now you have been moved to the first page of your tome.

By this time, you have made some mistakes, and that is good. We learn more from our mistakes than our successes. A helpful hint that has come in handy many times is that when Caldera KLyX gets confused or dies (or you confuse it or kill it), it attempts to save your open files as best it can. It will probably save them in the directory that the file would have been saved in normally (that is to say, the directory you were in when it was opened), but to keep you on your toes, it will rename the file [filename].lyx.emergency. All you have to do is rename (I prefer to copy instead—just in case) the file to [filename].lyx so that KLyX can find it, and then you can go back into KlyX and open it the normal way.

FIGURE 28.6
The first page of your novel.

A simple way to find all your emergency files (if you're like me, you'll have several of them eventually) is using the following command:

```
#find / -print | grep emergency
```

The files will be listed, along with the actual directory they are in.

Before we go into the utilities section, there are two more features of KLyX that you have to know about. First is putting figures and pictures in your documents, and the second is putting foreign characters (mathematical characters are foreign to some of us) into the document.

Pictures in KLyX

To attach a picture into your document, on the KLyX panel click on Insert, Figure.

In the dialog box that comes up, select whether you want encapsulated or inline PostScript.

If you select encapsulated, a little box is inserted into your document. Move your mouse over this little box and left-click on it.

This brings up the Edit Figure dialog panel (see Figure 28.7).

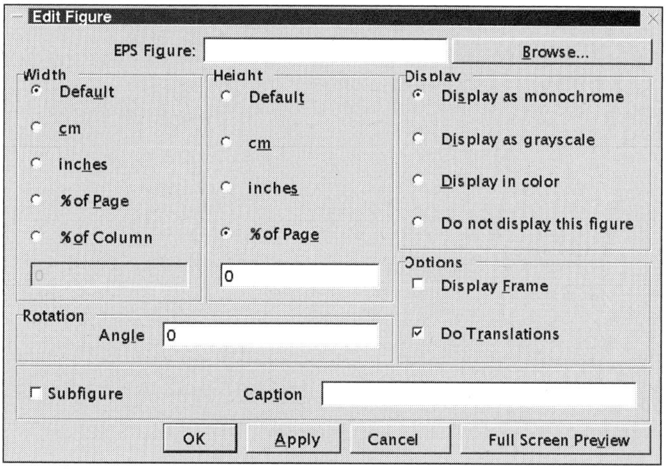

FIGURE 28.7
KLyX's Edit Figure dialog panel.

Click the Browse button on the upper-right and browse over to

/usr/share/ghostscript/5.10/examples/golfer.ps

In the Height section, highlight % of Page and, in the entry box below this button, type **25**. You have added a picture to your document that will occupy 25 percent of this page.

In the lower-right corner of the Edit Figure dialog panel, you can add a caption to the picture. As you can see, you have options to rotate the figure, change the height and width of the figure, display it in color, or even not display it at all.

After you have tweaked the picture to your satisfaction, click on the Apply and OK buttons, and you are back to the KLyX Edit panel.

Tables in KLyX

Another common issue in a document is that of putting data into a table. KLyX has an easy solution to that also.

All you need to do is to click on Insert, Table. Then use the sizing bars to select the number of rows and the number of columns. When you have indicated to KLyX the proper number of rows and columns, click OK, and the table will be inserted into your document.

Well, not exactly. KLyX will put in a table icon with the number of rows and columns that you specified. But not to worry, it works just fine. Move your mouse cursor over any of the small boxes in the table and click; presto, you can start typing. The column or row will grow right before your eyes to the size necessary to hold the text, picture, or graphic that you have inserted.

If you need to insert a mathematical character into your document or for that matter, any foreign character, the procedure is as follows:

First, you need to verify that the options are visible (which is the default, but some people turn it off because it takes up screen space).

On the KLyX main screen, click on Options, Screen Options, Toolbars and verify that Math and Character are both set to Always Visible.

Then, on the main screen, you have a toolbar with math symbols and character selection dialog boxes.

Some of the math symbols are two color, and some of them are only one color. The ones that are two color are symbols that you can enter data into. Why would you want to enter data into a symbol? Well, if the symbol is the square root symbol, you need to take the square root of something, don't you? With KLyX, click on the symbol, and you get one of two options. The first option is that the symbol is inserted into your document, and the second option is that you get a larger block of similar symbols. Try it; click on the square root symbol (the first one on the left of the math bar).

See, you just inserted a square root symbol into your document in the same size and typeface you are using in that paragraph environment. The only remaining task is to enter what you are taking the square root of.

I don't want to get you off track, but if you really want to get transcendental, how about trying this? Click on the square root symbol and, while you are in the blue area under it, move over to the Greek Characters symbol pi on the math bar, and click on it—you will be given a plethora of Greek symbols to use. Because I'm a transcendental type of guy, I actually want the pi symbol (fifth row, fifth character), so I move the mouse over it and click. Presto! I have pi under the square root symbol. Now that's transcendental.

Hundreds of other options are available to the typesetter, but most of them you will never need to use. If you have a question or want to know how to do something, the documentation that can be found by clicking on Help, Reference Manual on the main KLyX panel will be very useful.

Another selection on the main panel help popup is the Known Bugs selection. This can be reached by clicking on Help, Known Bugs.

Here you will find reports of bugs (well, some of them are really preferences and not bugs) that have been reported to the KLyX project from users. It is interesting to note that the tone and content of the reports are cooperative and suggestive. Unlike many operating systems, you don't have to be a certified anything to make a suggestion or report a bug. KLyX, as well as the entire Linux project, is being done by volunteers, and good suggestions are what make the products better. But remember that they are free. So if you have a need for something very special that is very difficult and you will use once, it will probably be a low priority on the list of things to be accomplished by the group supporting the product. If, on the other hand, you find a significant bug, it is easily reproduced, and you convey detailed and meaningful information to the support group, you might find it fixed quickly (sometimes the same day).

Messages concerning bugs should be emailed to lyx@via.ecp.fr. Before you do that, as a courtesy to the time of the volunteer programmers, you should check http://via.ecp.fr/~andre/lyx/archive to verify that the bug hasn't already been brought to their attention.

One final item before we leave KLyX. This is the system level documentation that is available (and delivered with Caldera) for the KLyX and LaTeX programs.

This isn't well documented, but if you try the following, you will be amazed.

```
#cd /opt/teTeX/info
#info web2c
```

You will be presented with the screen shown in Figure 28.8.

FIGURE 28.8

Info documentation for Web2c LyX.

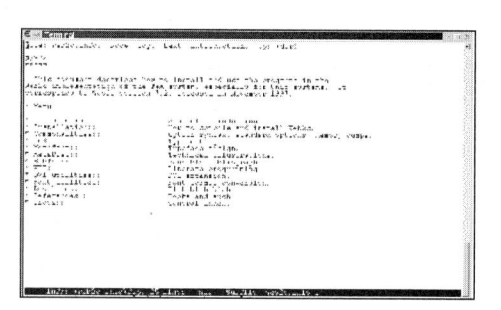

This is the Web2C documentation in info format. If you don't find it in Help, Reference Manual in LyX, you most probably will find it here.

Using info is outside the scope of this chapter, but it's so easy to use that you will be amazed. In fact, you could learn it so quickly that you could be a certified info user in about 10 minutes, if there was such a thing as a CIU.

However, here are some basics.

The cursor keys move around the info file.

When you are on a subject you want more information on, press Enter.

| u (for up) | Takes you back one screen |
| n (for next) | Moves you forward one screen |

d	Takes you to the top of the info tree
q (for quit)	Exits the info process
? (for question mark)	Gives you a Help screen (but gobbles up half of the Info screen)

Here is the real toughie—if you move your cursor into the Help half of the screen, you can get your full Info screen back by typing `control-x 0` (the number zero).

Utilities Used with Typesetting

There are literally several hundred utilities for use with typesetting on Caldera Linux. Many of these are delivered with the release CDs, and others are available over the Web. I like to separate them into three categories for organizational purposes.

- Viewers (utilities that use X)
- Converters
- Exporters (utilities that don't use X)

Viewers consist of programs that use the X-Windowing system to view and modify typeset pages. Converters consist of programs that do conversions of image types as well as utilities that will, for instance, allow you to convert instantly from a typeset page to HTML for Web publishing. Exporters are those utilities that would be used to print a document or perhaps to fax a document, as well as programs that might create dynamic Web page content from typeset originals.

Viewing Utilities for Use with Typesetting

Many utilities are available in Linux to allow you to view the documents you create. Some of these are device independent, and some aren't. Device independence is important when you consider that most typeset files are actually pictures of the typeset page, rather than character representations of the same page. Device independence allows you to print, view, and Web distribute the same image in a very simple manner.

xdvi

xdvi is the semi-standard utility for viewing device-independent graphics files under Linux. Caldera's implementation is linked with most of the graphics packages on its distribution CD.

If you want to view a .dvi file, type the following command on a terminal screen running under X:

```
xdvi    /usr/doc/LDP/network-guide/nag/images.dvi
```

Go ahead and try to type that one perfectly the first time. Remember that you must do this on a terminal under X. If you do this on a console terminal, it will tell you it can't find the display. After a long time, as xdvi finds and loads the supporting files, it will, in fact, display this dvi image.

This image was selected because it's on the distribution CD-ROM from Caldera, not because I was trying to test the nimbleness of your fingers.

When you have done it all correctly, you will see an image similar to Figure 28.9.

FIGURE 28.9
An image displayed with xdvi.

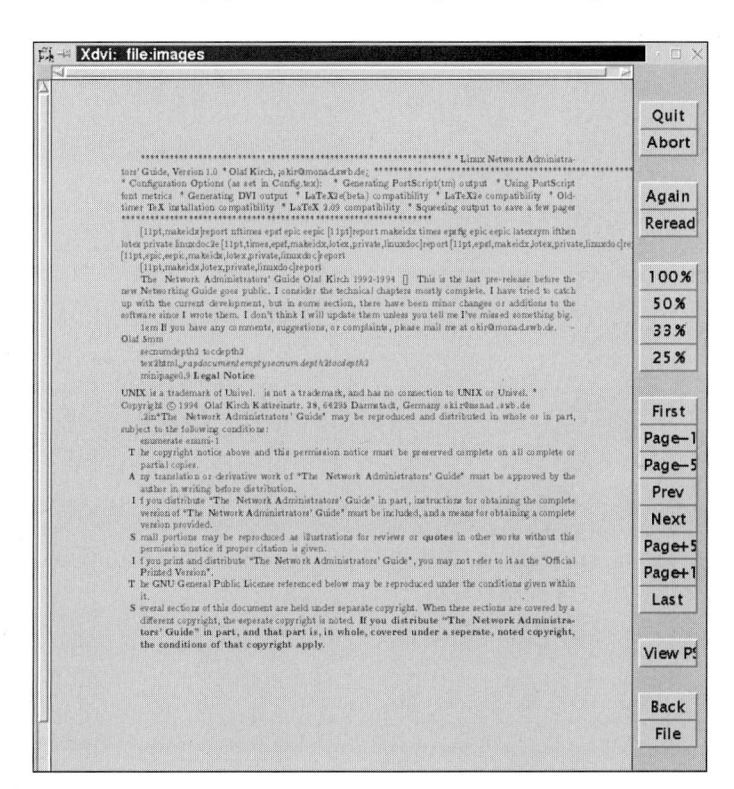

As you can see from the example, xdvi gives you many options. First, you can change the magnification up and down and, second, you can browse through the entire set of pages in the dvi file. Additionally, you can view the image in PostScript. Finally, you can put a single image into a different file with the File command.

A lot of dvi format utilities exist. (Most of them are explained as converting utilities in the following, because usually the image is either OK as it is, in which case xdvi will be entirely adequate, or you want to move it to some other format, and that is a conversion.)

gs (ghostscript)

ghostscript (gs for short) is the Linux implementation of Adobe Systems PostScript and Portable Document Format (PDF) languages. It will read PostScript documents and PDF format documents and display them on virtually any display or printing device.

ghostscript has hundreds of options that allow you to select paper size for display (2.6×3.7 cm through 100×141 cm), and the document or page will be sized correctly, having the correct aspect for the paper size. It allows you to select resolutions and special fonts for each page.

The usual way to invoke gs would be to select K-gear, Graphics, PS Viewer from the desktop, which will bring up ghostscript.

At this point, if you browse over to /usr/share/ghostscript/5.10/examples/golfer.ps, you should see a screen similar to Figure 28.10.

FIGURE 28.10
Using ghostscript to display an image.

On this screen, you have many options, but they are really a user-friendly way to implement only a small portion of the command-line options available with gs.

gv is the general ghostscript viewer, and it comes with a different set of options and utilities. It has some options that are more reminiscent of Microsoft's PowerPoint product than a simple viewer.

XV

Last, but certainly not least, is the xv viewer. You can find it at K-gear, Graphics, XV. It will do just about anything with a graphic image, including the following:

- image format conversions
- screen capture
- dithering
- color map conversions
- color depth conversions (8/24)
- blurring
- edge detection
- embossing
- pixelizing
- despeckling
- cropping

It will load and store in the following formats:

- GIF
- TIFF
- JPEG
- BMP
- Sun Rasterfile
- others too numerous to detail here

If you need to do any image conversion or image improvement as part of your typesetting, there must be at least one tool here that meets your exact need.

Converting Utilities for Use with Typesetting

Hundreds of utilities work with Caldera Linux. Most of them come on the distribution CD, but the rest are easily available over the Net.

I will give you a short tour of some of the most useful ones, the ones you will use in general to create the contents of the document.

dvips

The first of these would have to be `dvips`—the utility that converts dvi documents into PostScript documents. It has a number of features that set it apart from other PostScript drivers for TeX.

`dvips` generates excellent, standard PostScript, which can be included in other documents as figures or printed through a variety of spoolers. The generated PostScript minimizes the use of printer memory, so even very complex documents with many fonts can still be printed on printers with very little memory.

One of `dvips`'s most interesting (and important) features is its capability to create virtual fonts. This capability to handle font remapping in a natural and portable way adds a whole new level of flexibility to the TeX typesetter.

Although it does simple and quick conversions, and those conversions can be output to a file, `dvips` is used more often to take a dvi file and print it to a post script printer. Some of the system options such as Print Only Odd Pages, Collated Copies, or Print Crop Marks make `dvips` irreplaceable in a typesetting environment. They will make your documents look like they were done in a typesetting shop.

`dvilj`

Another variation on the concept of `dvips` is the `dvilj` command. It works exactly like the `dvips` command with the same set of options, but it creates output that is appropriate for a HP LaserJet printer rather than a PostScript printer.

`dvipdfm`

`dvipdfm` is an interesting utility that will convert from dvi format to a variation of Adobe's Acrobat format. It has some limitations in the area of automatic generation of hyperlinks but, at a minimal level, it will save you lots of time. It can be downloaded free off the Net from

```
ftp://ftp.tex.ac.uk/tex-archive/dviware/dvipdfm.tar.gz
```

`dvitomp`

`dvitomp` is a utility that will convert from dvi format to low-level MetaPost commands in an MPX file. Although it is usually called by the `MakeMPX` routine, you can use it on the command line to do a simple conversion in a hurry.

`dmp`

`dmp` converts device-independent troff (ditroff) into low-level MetaPost commands and saves them in an .MPX file.

If you need to accomplish this, `dmp` is a useful utility. Just be aware that when it was written, the author made several assumptions (at the time, all of them were reasonable) that are no longer valid, so much of the output generated will have to be massaged by you before you have a truly professional document.

mpost

`mpost` is a useful utility that will take a series of pictures specified in the MetaPost language and output them in PostScript format.

wp2latex

`wp2latex` is a nifty program available at

http://wuarchive.wust1.edu/mirrors/msdos/tex

This is a PC program written in Turbo Pascal by R. C. Houtepen at Eindhoven University that will take WordPerfect 5 files and convert them to LaTeX format. It is, however, an imperfect program. It stops with WordPerfect 5.0, which means that it doesn't have things like the following: indexes, table of contents, margins, graphics, and the equation formatter.

Although it is a copyrighted program, it is free and comes with Pascal source.

`rtf2TeX` is a program for converting Microsoft's Rich Text Format to TeX format. It is available via anonymous ftp from

ftp://astro.princeton.edu/pub/rtf2TeX.tar.Z

The author and maintainer is Robert Lupton.

A competing (if we can use that word when talking about Linux and free software) implementation is available from

ftp://ftp.vmars.tuwien.ac.at/pub/misc

written by Erwin Wechtl.

WEB—Literate Programming

WEB language allows you to write code once and use it many times. You can create a single source file that is both compilable and provides documentation. The following utilities will allow you to both compile and provide a well-formatted document that will describe the program or system in the finest detail that you provide. Better yet, it is all kept in one place and is where both the typeset documentation and the source code are maintained at the same time.

A considerable amount of information on Literate Programming and the WEB language is available at

http://www.loria.fr/services/tex/english/litte.html

However, some of the highlights are in the following sections.

Tangle

Tangle (which is included with Caldera Linux) creates a Pascal source file from a WEB source file. The output source file might not be pretty (72 characters are packed into one line), but it compiles and, anyway, your real source file is the WEB source file.

Weave

Weave (which is also included with Caldera Linux) creates a TeX document from a WEB source file. It will take care of such details as page layout, indentation, and italicizing identifiers. It also will automatically do an extensive cross reference.

Exporting Utilities for Use with Typesetting

Many utilities will take a LaTeX formatted document and move it to another, more useable format. The most common request for this type of conversion is to go to an HTML format (the old format used by Linux—SGML—is no longer being supported). There are several utilities to assist you in putting your document online, and a small sampling of them is in the following sections.

LaTeX2HTML

This is a program that will convert your LaTeX documents to HTML suitable for use on the Web. The most useful information page for this program is at

http://cbl.leeds.ac.uk/nikos/tex2html/doc/latex2html/latex2html.html

At this site, you will find links to mirror sites all over the world, an overview as well as a manual, and some very informative examples (always most useful).

LTX2X

LTX2X is a more generalized LaTeX-to-HTML (as well as other options) converter. By setting up a table (for instance, for HTML) for the target language/script type, LTX2X will do the conversions for you. This is more of an advanced-to-expert tool, but even the beginner can use some of the canned conversions.

LTX2X is available from

ftp://ftp.dante.de/tex-archive/support/ltx2x.tar.gz

CWEB2HTML

This is a program available from

http://www.cdc.informatik.tu-darmstadt.de/~lippmann/cweb2html/

that will help you solve all those problems you are having documenting your Web page. `CWEB2HTML` will convert a WEB format file into an HTML file for browsers on the Web.

Exotica (or Really Fancy Typesetting)

For those of you who want to do some interesting things with typesetting, the Web has available many tools that work with TeX to provide various functionalities.

Some of the more interesting tools are discussed in the following sections.

Typesetting Music

If you want to typeset either polyphonic or other multiple-stave music, you will want to check out MusicTeX by Daniel Taupin.

It is available from

`ftp://ftp.gmd.de/music/musictex/`

Another alternative (with a very similar name) is MusiXTeX, which is available from

`http://dec2.wi-inf.uni-essen.de/doc/musixtex-T73s-1/`

MusiXTeX supports wide pages as used by most musicians, as well as LaTeX-formatted narrow pages. It will typeset the following: staves, notes, chords, beams, slurs, and ornaments.

It comes with extensive documentation and samples. It is a bit complicated to use, but the output (and the ease of change of the output) will make it worthwhile for most musicians.

Typesetting Plots

The standard for typesetting plots using TeX or LaTeX is DISLIN. It is a high-level library of subroutines and functions that will assist you in displaying plots for inclusion in a LaTeX document.

Most commonly, you will use DISLIN to produce a PostScript plot and include this image in your TeX document. However, the product comes with several other drivers so that you can perfect the plot before you commit it to PostScript for your document.

The major site for information and usage can be found at

`http://www.linmpi.mpg.de/dislin/`

An RPM-installable copy of the software can be found at

`http://linusp.usp.br/rpm2html/contrib/libc5/i386/dislin_vf-7.1-1.i386.html`

Typesetting Feynman Diagrams

Feynman diagrams are interesting things. If you are interested in high-energy physics, you probably use them every day.

They are named for their inventor, Richard Feynman, who was a high-energy physicist when he wasn't playing practical jokes. At Los Alamos, the most heavily guarded military installation in the U.S., Feynman learned to pick locks, and he would often leave safes and filing cabinets open to show that they were no good. He also enjoyed sneaking out of a hole in the fence and then going to the front of the compound and surprising the guards. All in all, he would've loved Linux (he died in 1988).

So if you ever need to typeset a Feynman Diagram, you can use Michael Levine's package to do this, and you can find it at

`ftp://ftp.tex.ac.uk/tex-archive/macros/latex209/contrib/feynman.tar.gz`

So you don't think there is only one of these packages for Feynman Diagrams, you might also check out Thorsten Ohl's contributions at

`ftp://ftp.tex.ac.uk/tex-archive/macros/latex/contrib/supported/feynmf.tar.gz`

which works in combination with MetaFont or MetaPost and will produce a font of images used in Feynman Diagrams or, alternatively, a PostScript image.

Summary

In this chapter, you have been introduced to the typesetting capabilities in native Caldera, as well as functions available via the Web. You have created a typeset document, learned about Literate Programming, and learned how to convert from one form of typeset document to other forms of printed and displayed documents. Finally, you have learned a little bit about typesetting music and graphs and Feynman Diagrams, which are named after a Nobel prize–winning jokester.

CHAPTER 29

Setting Up Sound and Multimedia

IN THIS CHAPTER

- Introduction   *672*
- Getting Sound   *672*
- Linux Kernel Sound   *673*
- OSS—Open Sound System   *679*
- ALSA—The Advanced Linux Sound Architecture   *683*
- Audio Data Manipulation and Conversion   *687*
- Extracting Digital Audio Data   *689*
- MPEG 1 Layer 3 Encoding   *692*
- Lossless Audio Encoding Using Shorten   *695*
- SoundTracker Modules   *697*
- Introduction to MIDI   *700*
- Software MIDI Synthesis   *702*
- Where to Go from Here   *705*

Introduction

When presented with the task of writing a chapter on Linux sound and multimedia, I had a couple of options. I could have chosen to write a broad, shallow treatment of the topic, briefly touching on a wide variety of multimedia technologies without providing much practical information. Or, I could have chosen to provide focused in-depth coverage of the hottest sound and multimedia technologies in the Linux world, packing the chapter to the brim with inside information on how to push Linux multimedia to its limits. Fortunately for you, I picked the latter, figuring that you probably were looking for more than a simple overview of Caldera's multimedia capabilities.

In the second half of this chapter, I focus on cutting-edge Linux sound technologies and applications, such as audio data manipulation and conversion, digital audio extraction, MPEG 1 Layer 3 encoding, lossless audio compression, a review of MIDI technology and an in-depth look at MIDI software synthesis engines. At the very end of the chapter, I provide you with links to online resources that you can use to expand your Linux multimedia knowledge beyond the scope of this book. If you have already mastered the art of configuring your sound card under Linux, you can skip to the "Audio Data Manipulation and Conversion" section.

If you have not yet configured your sound card so that it works properly under Caldera, or you are interested in exploring other sound architectures, read on—I cover the configuration of sound under Linux in depth. In addition to covering standard kernel sound driver setup, we will look into the Open Sound System (a commercial option) and the Advanced Linux Sound Architecture (ALSA), an excellent free alternative. I also provide much-needed information regarding the tricky topic of ISA PnP sound hardware configuration, as well as explore possible sound configuration pitfalls and driver compatibility issues.

Getting Sound

There are several ways to get sound working under Linux, but the basic principle is identical in each case. The trick is to create and install kernel modules that then can be loaded by the kernel. They will provide an interface so that user programs can access your sound hardware safely. If you happen to own an ISA PnP sound card, there is a possible additional step of configuring the PnP resources of your card.

As I mentioned, although the principle is identical, you have several different techniques available to you to actually get sound working. We will explore three in this chapter. The first technique is the use of the standard Linux kernel sound modules, which might be all you need. The second technique is a relatively inexpensive commercial option called OSS, which features sound support for a wider variety of new hardware. Finally, I cover ALSA—the Advanced Linux Sound Architecture. ALSA is a non-commercial effort to provide enhanced support for a wide variety of sound cards, and it is free.

> **Choosing a Sound Card**
>
> Before purchasing a sound card for use with Linux, do a little research and verify that drivers for the card are available in the most recent Linux kernel, in OSS, or in ALSA. Many sound card manufacturers have not yet realized the importance of supplying Linux developers with specifications for their sound cards, or they will release such information only after the developer signs a nondisclosure agreement (NDA), which would violate the terms of the GNU Public License. If at all possible, choose a PCI-based sound card that is supported under Linux. Such a card will offer higher performance and be easier to configure.

Linux Kernel Sound

If you have a PCI-based card or standard ISA (non-PnP) card, setting up sound is quite easy. For PCI-based cards, it's just a matter of loading kernel modules in the right order, starting with a basic sound module called soundcore, and progressing to a hardware-specific module designed for your particular brand of sound card. ISA cards also require you to specify the correct interrupts and memory addresses for the card as command-line arguments when loading the hardware-specific module. ISA PnP sound cards are handled identically, except that before you load the hardware specific kernel module, you need a special set of PnP tools to communicate with the ISA PnP card and configure it to use interrupts and IO addresses that you specify. After the ISA PnP card is configured properly, you can treat it as if it were a standard ISA (non-PnP) card, and load the sound card module with the appropriate parameters. If you're confused, don't worry. I will cover each method step-by-step.

Initial Manual Configuration

First, we are going to attempt to load the sound drivers manually and verify that they are working properly. After we get them working, I will explain how to make changes to your system so that the sound is properly configured on startup.

> **Restarting KDE and Testing Sound**
>
> When you are ready to test your sound card configuration, I recommend that you use the KDE Control Panel to try to play some sample sounds. But before KDE will recognize your new sound configuration, you must restart KDE without completely rebooting the computer. Then, if the settings work, you can configure your system so that it will load the proper sound drivers on boot. To do a quick restart of KDE without rebooting your machine, do the following:
>
> 1. Log out of KDE and restart the system in console mode by clicking Shutdown and selecting Console Mode.
> 2. You might have to press Control+Alt+F1 to switch to a console.
> 3. Log in as root.
> 4. Type init 5 to switch to runlevel 5.
> 5. KDE will now restart and detect your sound card settings.
>
> Now, proceed to the Control Panel. Click the Sound tab, enable sounds, select some sound samples, and press the Test button. You might need to start the Sound Mixer applet (under the Multimedia menu) to adjust your card's output volume so that you can hear the sound. After you have verified that your settings worked, you are ready to make your changes permanent. This tip should help you avoid unnecessary reboots when testing your sound card configuration.

The first step in manually configuring sound is loading the soundcore kernel module. As root, type

```
> insmod soundcore
```

If the preceding process completes successfully, you are presented with a new prompt, and no output. If you want to make sure that the module was inserted correctly, type `lsmod`.

The soundcore module is required for Linux kernel–based as well as ALSA-based sound support, regardless of what sound card you might have. It is used by the hardware-specific module that we will load next. The next step you take depends on what kind of sound card you have. If you have a PCI-based sound card, you will probably have to load only a kernel module corresponding to your particular card, with no extra options. For example, for an es1371-based card, such as an Ensoniq AudioPCI card or a SoundBlaster PCI 64/128, type

```
> insmod es1371
```

> **AudioPCI/SoundBlaster PCI**
>
> If the `es1371` module does not load correctly for your Ensoniq AudioPCI or SoundBlaster PCI 64/128, try the `es1370` module. Creative Labs and Ensoniq have released versions of these sound cards using both the es1370 and es1371 chips. One will work for you.

Now, sound should be functional. If you have a standard ISA (non-PnP) based card, such as the SoundBlaster 16 PnP, you must type in something similar to this:

```
> insmod uart401
> insmod sb irq=5 dma=1 dma16=5 mpu_io=0x300 io=0x220
```

The arguments to the `insmod sb` command specify the hardware settings for your particular card. If you have an ISA (non-PnP) card but don't know your hardware settings, now is the time to find your sound card manual and review the jumper settings on your sound card. Write them down, and enter them on the command line as shown earlier. Here are arguments that are used with SoundBlaster series cards (from the kernel source documentation):

Argument	Description
io	IO address of SoundBlaster chip (`0x220, 0x240, 0x260, 0x280`)
irq	IRQ of the SoundBlaster chip (`5, 7, 9, 10`)
dma	8-bit DMA Channel (`0, 1 ,3`)
dma16	16-bit DMA Channel for SoundBlaster 16 and up (`5, 6, 7`)
mpu_io	IO address of MPU chip if present (`0x300, 0x330`)

If you do not have a SoundBlaster-compatible card and must specify command-line options so that your sound card module will load properly, refer to a recent kernel source archive, and browse the `linux/Documentation/sound` directory. Although I can only touch on a few of the most popular command-line options, the kernel source documentation fully describes every possible configuration parameter. To help you find the appropriate documentation and guide towards the correct hardware-specific module, I have provided a table of sound cards and their corresponding kernel module.

Module	Card(s)
es1370	SoundBlaster PCI128 / some Ensoniq AudioPCI
es1371	SoundBlaster PCI64 / some Ensoniq AudioPCI
sb	SoundBlaster and clones
awe_wave	Extra support for SoundBlaster 32 / AWE 32 / AWE 64 MIDI

Module	Card(s)
`msnd`	Turtle Beach MultiSound
`msnd_classic`	Extra support for Turtle Beach Classic/Monterey/Tahiti
`msnd_pinnacle`	Extra Support for Turtle Beach Pinnacle/Fiji
`wavefront`	Turtle Beach Maui/Tropez/Tropez Plus
`ad1848`	Gravis Ultrasound Family Module 1
`gus`	Gravis Ultrasound Family Module 2

Automatically Loading Modules

After you have identified the modules that must be loaded, along with their proper configuration options (if any), you now need to configure Caldera OpenLinux 2.2 to load these modules automatically on startup. This is simple under KDE—as easy as going to the COAS submenu and choosing Kernel. This will load the COAS Kernel Module configuration program, allowing you to specify the additional modules that must be loaded, along with any necessary command-line parameters. The system will load the appropriate modules as you specify them, as well as remember your changes so that Caldera can automatically set the system up to your liking after a restart.

ISA PnP Cards

If you have an ISA PnP card, you must do a few tricky things before the sound modules can be loaded. To put it as simply as possible, you must first use the `pnpdump` command to query the card to see what possible hardware resources it can be configured to use. Then, you must select hardware resources that do not conflict with any other device in the system, and then use the `isapnp` command to configure the card to use those particular resources (interrupt, I/O port(s), and so on). When this is done, you can then load the kernel sound module, specifying the exact hardware resources that the card is now using. Metaphorically, you are telling the card where to go ("Head over to port 23"), and then telling the kernel sound module where it can find the card ("We sent him over to port 23"). Both `isapnp` and `pnpdump` are included in the `isapnptools` package, which is installed under Caldera OpenLinux by default.

Our first step is to probe the card to see what interrupts and I/O addresses are legal for your particular card, by doing the following as root:

```
> cd /tmp
> pnpdump > mypnp.conf
```

`pnpdump` generates a commented-out `isapnp` configuration file that is specific to your particular ISA PnP hardware. After typing in the preceding commands, a nearly complete configuration file should exist in `/tmp/mypnp.conf`. Your next step is editing that file, selecting the appropriate resources for your sound card from an exhaustive list of possible options, and configuring the card with those resources. If the configuration is successful, you can proceed to loading the sound modules using the PnP settings you selected.

If you look in `mypnp.conf`, you will notice a lot of commented-out lines. This file contains every possible setting for your ISA PnP hardware; it's your job to choose the appropriate settings by "uncommenting" specific lines in this file. The first thing you must do is find the part of the file that refers to your ISA PnP sound card. With my SoundBlaster 16 PnP, this line is

```
(CONFIGURE CTL0024/269330673 (LD 0
```

I know this because the block of comments immediately preceding this line reads as follows:

```
# Card 1: (serial identifier 39 10 0d a8 f1 24 00 8c 0e)
# Vendor Id CTL0024, Serial Number 269330673, checksum 0x39.
# Version 1.0, Vendor version 1.0
# ANSI string -->Creative SB16 PnP<--
#
# Logical device id CTL0031
#
# Edit the entries below to uncomment out the configuration required.
# Note that only the first value of any range is given, this may be changed
# if required. Don't forget to uncomment the activate (ACT Y) when happy
```

For my SoundBlaster 16 PnP, I need to uncomment the INT 0, DMA 0, DMA 1, IO 0, and IO 1 lines in the `config` file to specify the interrupts, DMA channels, and IO addresses for my SoundBlaster to use. I choose to comment out the first block of these options (there are many other possible blocks that have different numeric parameters). You should uncomment only one block at a time rather than picking lines from several different blocks:

```
(CONFIGURE CTL0024/269330673 (LD 0
#       ANSI string -->Audio<--

# Multiple choice time, choose one only !

#       Start dependent functions: priority preferred
#         IRQ 5.
#              High true, edge sensitive interrupt (by default)
 (INT 0 (IRQ 5 (MODE +E)))
#         First DMA channel 1.
#              8 bit DMA only
#              Logical device is a bus master
#              DMA may execute in count by byte mode
```

```
#               DMA may not execute in count by word mode
#               DMA channel speed in compatible mode
 (DMA 0 (CHANNEL 1))
#       Next DMA channel 5.
#               16 bit DMA only
#               Logical device is a bus master
#               DMA may not execute in count by byte mode
#               DMA may execute in count by word mode
#               DMA channel speed in compatible mode
 (DMA 1 (CHANNEL 5))
#       Logical device decodes 16 bit IO address lines
#               Minimum IO base address 0x0220
#               Maximum IO base address 0x0220
#               IO base alignment 1 bytes
#               Number of IO addresses required: 16
 (IO 0 (SIZE 16) (BASE 0x0220))
#       Logical device decodes 16 bit IO address lines
#               Minimum IO base address 0x0330
#               Maximum IO base address 0x0330
#               IO base alignment 1 bytes
#               Number of IO addresses required: 2
 (IO 1 (SIZE 2) (BASE 0x0330))
#       Logical device decodes 16 bit IO address lines
#               Minimum IO base address 0x0388
#               Maximum IO base address 0x0388
#               IO base alignment 1 bytes
#               Number of IO addresses required: 4
 (IO 2 (SIZE 4) (BASE 0x0388))
```

Many other blocks of hardware settings follow, possibly for other hardware devices in your system; you can skip by them. But do not skip the set of lines that look like those that follow. We must make a simple change to these lines so that our hardware settings take effect. Simply uncomment the (ACT Y) line so that it looks something like the following:

```
 (NAME "CTL0024/269330673[0]{Audio                    }")
#       End dependent functions
 (ACT Y)
))
```

We are now ready to test our configuration using `isapnp`, which will take our configuration file and use it to configure our ISA PnP devices. As root, simply type the command

> **isapnp mypnp.conf**

If `isapnp` tells you that a board was configured, you're all set; proceed to the final step. If you get some kind of resource conflict error, repeat the preceding process but uncomment a different block of configuration options in `mypnp.conf`. You probably want to take a look at `/proc/interrupts`, `/proc/ioports`, and `/proc/dma` to get an idea of what hardware resources are currently allocated in your system. This will help you make a good choice for the configuration file. For some, this process is easy; for others, it can be difficult and time-consuming. Much depends on how well your particular hardware conforms to the ISA PnP specification, and how flexible your hardware is when it comes to choosing interrupts, I/O ports, and the like. Take some time to find correct settings for your hardware and be patient.

The Final PnP Step—Making Your PnP Settings Permanent

To configure Caldera OpenLinux 2.2 to configure your ISA PnP card(s) properly at boot time, simply copy `mypnp.conf` to `/etc/isapnp.conf`:

```
cp mypnp.conf /etc/isapnp.conf
```

After you reboot, you will be able to treat your ISA PnP card as if it were a standard ISA (non-PnP) device. Simply use the hardware settings specified in `isapnp.conf` as your hardware settings when loading modules. After the sound hardware is configured properly, refer to the preceding section called "Automatically Loading Modules," and follow those directions so that the modules for your ISA PnP card load automatically when the system is started.

If you haven't been able to get your sound card properly configured by now, you might be interested in trying out the Open Sound System, which is described next. Alternatively, if you are more technically inclined, you might want to try out ALSA—the Advanced Linux Sound Architecture. An introduction to ALSA follows the OSS section.

If your sound card is properly configured and you are ready to give it a try, skip the next two sections and proceed to the "Audio Data Manipulation and Conversion" section.

OSS—Open Sound System

4Front Technologies (http://www.opensound.com) distributes a product called OSS, or Open Sound System, that provides extensive support for a wide variety of sound cards and even supports several digital I/O cards that are suitable for professional or audiophile use. In addition, its product includes a feature called SoftOSS, which provides a software-based 32 voice wavetable engine for MIDI playback. Although many Linux users shy away from commercial drivers, OSS is a high-quality product and normally costs only $20 U.S. for most sound cards. If you have an exotic sound card or have special needs, such as multitrack digital recording, it might be your only option, and a good one at that.

Another reason you might want to consider OSS is that it excels in automatically configuring ISA PnP cards (such as the SoundBlaster 16 PnP). OSS will normally autodetect and configure such cards automatically, without any effort on your part. Therefore, OSS might be a good choice if you are unable to manually configure your card using the isapnptools package. If you're stuck with a SoundBlaster 16 PnP for now, but plan to upgrade to a SoundBlaster PCI128 or PCI64 in the future, OSS will work with them, and it requires minimal time and effort to configure. It might be a good choice if you're not interested in spending much time struggling with your sound card configuration.

If you can't decide whether to order OSS, or you would like to verify that it works properly with your card before purchasing, visit http://www.opensound.com to download a time-limited trial of OSS that you can test on your hardware. You can then use the following instructions to install OSS and determine whether you want to purchase it.

OSS Download and Installation

OSS excels in ease of installation and configuration. I'll walk you through the steps necessary to get OSS running. Note that these steps will work for both the trial and commercial version.

Simply extract the archive to /tmp:

```
> tar xzvf osslinux392o-glibc-2210-UP.tar.gz -C /tmp
```

Note that this is a uniprocessor archive. If you have an SMP machine, you should download an SMP version of the software. Now, run the installer:

```
> /tmp/oss-install
```

Accept all the agreements, and then choose the target directory of your choice. Then OSS will automatically install, autodetect, and properly configure itself for your sound card (see Figure 29.1). Click Save Changes and Exit, and your configuration is saved.

FIGURE 29.1
OSS automatically detected my SoundBlaster PCI128.

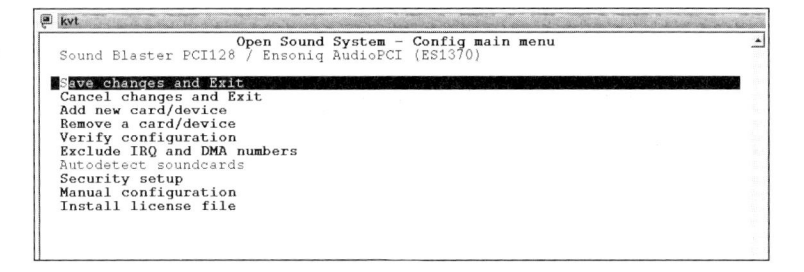

> **Commercial OSS**
>
> If you purchased the commercial version of OSS, you must also install the license file that was emailed to you. To do so, simply select the Install License File option when the OSS Config program is loaded, and direct it to the location of the license file on your hard disk. After reading in this file, your version of OSS should be the full commercial version. You can verify this by noticing what OSS says after typing soundon. If OSS reads the license file correctly, it will say `Licensed to <your name here>`.

To enable OSS, simply type

```
> soundon
```

OSS can be disabled by typing **soundoff**. After the sound is off, it is possible to reconfigure your sound card by typing **soundconf** to load the OSS Config program.

OSS Configuration Tips and Industry News

I wanted to make sure that I covered all the bases relating to the proper functioning of OSS, so I called Dave Mazumdar at 4Front's California office for the low-down on the top three technical support issues, as well as information on support of the new SoundBlaster Live! sound card from Creative Labs. What I found out was both interesting and extremely helpful.

The number-one technical support problem with OSS, according to Dave, is the fact that many kernel hackers recompile their kernel without support for kernel module versioning. OSS requires that this kernel option is enabled for the OSS installation to go smoothly. Kernel versioning allows the OSS module binaries to be inserted smoothly into your kernel without regard to the minor version you are using. When you recompile your kernel, you will find this option under the Loadable Module Support section. For more information on recompiling your kernel, see Chapter 31, "Configuring and Building the Kernel."

The second problem Dave mentioned is the fact that many new laptops with integrated sound chips do not have those chips set to work properly with plug and play, and they cannot be configured in the BIOS. When dealing with these chips, a quick jaunt into Windows 95/98 before installing Linux might be required to determine the type and hardware settings for your integrated sound chip. After you have written these settings down (normally found in the Control Panel), you should be armed with the proper information to get OSS sound working under Linux. Try an autodetect first; if that doesn't work, attempt to get sound working manually.

Dave often gets calls from people asking whether "sound card *X*" works under OSS. Because there are many brands of sound cards available for the PC platform, Dave recommends that you simply try the evaluation version to determine whether your particular brand of sound card is supported. OSS has very good autodetection routines that should pick up almost any kind of compatible sound card.

Dave and I also chatted about OSS's upcoming support for the SoundBlaster Live! series of sound cards. He said that as of the time of the writing of this book, the SoundBlaster Live! drivers are at a standstill because of a lack of cooperation from Creative Labs. He explained that Creative Labs has a financial incentive to keep its hardware specs secret—releasing them to the public would make it fairly easy for a competitor to produce a SoundBlaster Live!–compatible chipset or card. Creative Labs wants to avoid what happened with the SoundBlaster Pro, when the release of hardware specifications allowed for literally hundreds of third-party SoundBlaster Pro–compatible sound cards and chips. By making the hardware specifications for the Live! cards public, Creative Labs also risks losing control over its proprietary EAX Environmental Audio Extensions. This is an unfortunate situation that might hinder the adoption of the SoundBlaster Live! series of cards into the Linux market. Until this situation changes, you might want to avoid purchasing a SoundBlaster Live! sound card unless you have already done so. Creative Labs has started development of a Live! series driver for Linux, but at this time, it is not compatible with a wide range of kernels, and it is somewhat unstable. You might want to visit `http://www.soundblaster.com` to see whether this situation has improved.

Configuring SoftOSS

SoftOSS requires a bit of configuration to get it working properly. The toughest part of this process is to download and install Eric A. Welsh's excellent free patches (instrument samples). This is covered in the MIDI software synthesis section later in this chapter. The only other thing you need to do to get SoftOSS working is to put the following line in your `/etc/profile` file, after installing the EAW patches:

```
export GUSPATCHDIR=<directory to patches>
```

Remember this step; without it, the mplay program included with OSS will not find the patches it needs. For full instructions, see the "Installing Patch Files for TiMidity++ and OSS" section later in this chapter.

ALSA—The Advanced Linux Sound Architecture

The third and most interesting option for sound support under Linux is ALSA, the Advanced Linux Sound Architecture. Planned to eventually replace the OSS/Free-derivative drivers that are currently included with the kernel source, ALSA provides a high-performance, fully modularized sound system that supports a few good cards. To install ALSA, you must download, compile, install, and configure the latest set of three source archives, which are available from the ALSA Project Web site. If your sound card is supported under ALSA (most popular cards are), a little bit of work will pay off by providing a next-generation sound architecture for your Linux box. As an example, using the standard kernel drivers for my SoundBlaster PCI128 gave me choppy audio playback while playing MIDI files using TiMidity++ and browsing the Web at the same time. With ALSA, sound playback was virtually flawless.

The ALSA project began with the goal of replacing the kernel sound for Gravis UltraSound series cards, and eventually turned into a full high-performance sound system. It provides a new improved API for accessing the sound hardware, while offering full OSS compatibility modules for applications that do not yet have native ALSA support. ALSA currently supports the following sound hardware:

- Trident 4D Wave DX/NX
- Gravis UltraSound PnP, Extreme, Classic/ACE, MAX
- Gravis Compatible (Dynasonic 3-D, STD Sound Rage 32, STB UltraSound 32-Pro)
- SoundBlaster, Pro, 16, AWE32, AWE64, PCI64, PCI128
- Ensoniq AudioPCI (ES1370/1371)
- ESS AudioDrive ESx688
- ESS ES18xx (some problems)
- ESS Solo-1 ES1938
- Yamaha OPL3-SA2, OPL3-SA3
- OAK Mozart
- PINE Schubert 32 PCI
- S3 SonicVibes PCI

If ALSA is compatible with your sound card, I encourage you to give it a try. Using ALSA will put you on the cutting edge of Linux sound functionality and provide you with the highest-performance and most advanced Linux sound support currently available.

Installing ALSA

The first step in installing ALSA is to visit the ALSA Project Web site at http://www.alsa-project.org. You must download three source archives: the most recent versions of alsa-driver, alsa-lib, and alsa-utils. Compilation is fairly straightforward. We'll quickly review the process here.

Begin by decompressing alsa-driver to a temporary directory. After entering the alsa-driver directory, type

```
> ./configure --help
```

This will provide you with a list of compilation options for the ALSA driver. The options you will be interested in are (from alsa-driver-0.3.2):

```
--with-debug=level      give the debug level (none,basic,memory,full)
--with-processor=cpu    give the processor type
                        (i386,i486,i586,i686,alpha,ppc,mips,auto)
--with-smp=yes,no,auto  driver will (not) be compiled with SMP support
--with-isapnp=yes,no,auto  driver will (not) be compiled with ISA PnP support
--with-sequencer=yes,no driver will (not) be compiled with sequencer support
--with-oss=no,yes       driver will (not) be compiled with OSS/Lite emulation
--with-cards=<list>     compile driver for cards in <list>.
                        cards may be separated with commas.
                        all compiles all drivers
```

Simply pass the proper arguments to the `configure` script, and the source archive will be configured for building. I suggest using the following options:

```
> ./configure --with-debug=none --with-processor=<yours> --with-sequencer=yes \
--with-oss=yes --with-cards=all
```

Configuration should complete successfully. Now you are ready to compile the drivers. Issue the following command:

```
> make
```

After that, type

```
> make install
```

The drivers will now be installed. You should repeat this process for alsa-lib and alsa-utils, except you will not be required to pass any configuration parameters to the configure script. Running the `configure` script with no options will work just fine. After doing this, run `make` and `make install`; all the correct binaries and libraries will then be installed on your system.

Testing ALSA

ALSA is very modularized; you will notice this if you look in your `/lib/modules/<kvers>/misc` directory after installing alsa-driver! When using ALSA, typically about 10 separate modules are loaded, each providing a specific function, such as interfacing directly with the hardware, sequencing, timing, mixing, playing digital audio streams, and so on. For this reason, we will make heavy use of the `modprobe` binary, which will load the module we want, as well as any modules that the module we are interested in depends on. This makes our lives a lot easier—`modprobe` does the dirty work. To load ALSA, we must type

```
> modprobe <modulename>
```

with the appropriate name for our particular hardware. Take a look at the following table to find the module appropriate for your particular hardware.

Module Name	Cards/Chipsets
snd-audiodrive1688	ESS AudioDrive 1688 and ES-688
snd-audiodrive18xx	ESS AudioDrive 18xx
snd-gusclassic	Gravis UltraSound Classic
snd-gusextreme	Gravis UltraSound Extreme
snd-gusmax	Gravis UltraSound MAX
snd-interwave	Gravis UltraSound PnP, STB Sound Rage & more
snd-interwave-stb	STB UltraSound 32 Pro
snd-sb8	SoundBlaster 1.0, 2.0, Pro
snd-sb16	SoundBlaster 16 (plus PnP)
snd-sbawe	SoundBlaster AWE32, AWE64 (plus PnP)
snd-opl3sa	Yamaha OPL3-SA2/SA3
snd-mozart	OAK Mozart
snd-opti9xx	OPTi 82C9xx
snd-sonicvibes	S3 SonicVibes PCI (PINE Schubert 32 PCI)
snd-audiopci1370	Ensoniq AudioPCI, SoundBlaster PCI 64/128
snd-audiopci1371	Same as above, newer chipset (one will work)
snd-card-ad1848	AD1848/AD1847/CS4248
snd-card-cs4231	CS4231

Module Name	Cards/Chipsets
snd-card-cs4232	CS4232
snd-card-cs4236	CS4235/4236/4236B/4237B/4238B/4239
snd-card-cs461x	PCI sound cards (CS46190/4612/4615/4680)
snd-trid4dwave	Trident 4DWave DX/NX cards
snd-card-fm801	ForteMedia FM801-based PCI

Loading ALSA modules for a typical PCI sound card is as easy as substituting the appropriate module name in the modprobe line shown earlier. For ISA cards, things get a bit trickier, and you must specify hardware settings on the modprobe line. You will find the appropriate parameter names in the alsa-driver directory, in the text file called INSTALL. A line for an ISA card will look something like the following:

```
> modprobe sbawe snd_port=0x220 snd_mpu_port=0x330 snd_irq=5 snd_dma8=1 \
snd_dma16=5 snd_mic_agc=1
```

Certain sound card modules, such as the SoundBlaster 16/AWE32/AWE64, support PnP autoconfiguration by specifying snd_isapnp=1. This tells the module to attempt to configure the sound card automatically. For sound cards that do not support ISA PnP autoconfiguration or do not have the snd_isapnp configuration option, you must follow the ISA PnP configuration instructions as listed previously in the "Linux Kernel Sound" section. After the standard ALSA modules are loaded, full ALSA sound is available, but with no OSS emulation. To get OSS emulation working, the following commands are required:

```
> modprobe snd-pcm1-oss
> modprobe snd-mixer-oss
```

This will load all required modules for OSS PCM emulation. If you try to use a sound-based program at this point, you won't hear anything. That is because the ALSA mixer defaults to no sound until you explicitly enable it. There are a couple of ALSA-specific mixer programs at your disposal: xamixer2 and alsamixer. We're going to ignore them both because the KDE Sound Mixer Panel works just fine for our purposes. Simply load it and adjust the volume to your liking (see Figure 29.2).

FIGURE 29.2
The KDE Sound Mixer Panel.

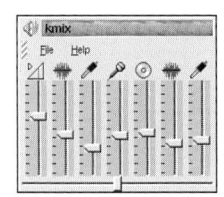

There is a special ALSA-specific program that you should become familiar with, called alsactl. It is primarily useful for setting, storing, and automatically restoring your preferred volume settings. After using a mixer applet or alsactl itself to set your desired volumes, type the following as root:

```
> alsactl store
```

Typing `alsactl restore` will automatically restore these settings. We will use this command to automatically restore our volume settings on system startup.

Making ALSA Load on Startup

Making ALSA load on startup is quite easy. Simply put the following lines at the end of your /etc/rc.d/rc.local file:

```
modprobe snd-<yoursound card>
modprobe snd-pcm1-oss
modprobe snd-mixer-oss
/usr/sbin/alsactl restore
```

Then, on startup, all the necessary modules for ALSA and OSS emulation will be loaded, and your sound card will be set to your preferred volume. You're now ready to have some fun!

Audio Data Manipulation and Conversion

Sox, an essential tool for the manipulation, playback, and conversion of sound samples, is included with your Caldera system. In addition to offering the ability to translate sound samples into a variety of sound sample and instrument formats, sox also allows you to resample sound data, convert stereo to mono, apply echo, reverb, flanger, high-pass and low-pass filters, and more. To introduce you to sox, here's how to use it to play back a WAV file through your sound card:

```
> sox mysound.wav -t ossdsp /dev/dsp
```

Sox accepts two main arguments, consisting of the input and the output file. It also accepts additional options, such as the `-t` option, which specifies the file type for the output stream. Specifying the file type for the input stream is simple:

```
> cat heart.wav | sox -t wav - -t ossdsp /dev/dsp
```

This sample concatenates `heart.wav` to the standard input of the sox program, which is told to interpret the data in WAV format and accept it from `stdin` (`-`). The output type is again set to the OSS dsp device.

Here is a list of supported sox file types, along with the associated names to be used with the `-t` option:

Option	File Type
8svx	Amiga 8SVX instrument
aiff	Amiga IFF Format (also used on Apple IIc/IIgs, SGI, and others)
au	Sun AU files
cdr	Raw CD audio—stereo, unsigned, 44100Hz
cvs	Continuously variable slope delta modulation, to compress speech
dat	Text data
hcom	Macintosh Huffman-compressed audio
maud	Amiga format introduced with Tocatta sound card
ossdsp	OSS audio output
sf	IRCAM sound files (used by CSound and MixView)
smp	Turtle Beach SampleVision
txw	Yamaha TX-16W samples
voc	SoundBlaster VOC
wav	Microsoft WAV
wve	Psion sound files
raw	Raw audio files, must also specify rate, size, sign, and channels
ub	Raw `unsigned byte` data, defaults to 8000Hz and one channel
sb	Raw `signed byte` data, defaults to 8000Hz and one channel
uw	Raw `unsigned word` data, defaults to 8000Hz and one channel
sw	Raw `signed word` data, defaults to 8000Hz and one channel
ul	Raw `ulaw` data, defaults to 8000Hz and one channel
auto	Use this type to have sox try to automatically recognize the input file

When dealing with sound samples that do not have information such as their sample rate, sample size, sign, and number of channels encoded inside the file, things can be a bit tricky. In those situations, a number of extra command-line options might be required to tell sox what to expect from those files. For example, if we convert a CD-quality WAV sound sample to raw `unsigned word` format, we must tell sox the file type, number of channels, sample rate, and sample size when using the file as an input file because this data is no longer stored in the file itself:

```
> sox heart.wav -t uw heart.uw
> sox -t uw -c 2 -r 44100 heart.uw -t ossdsp /dev/dsp
```

Here's a quick listing of the options that you might need to use. Remember that these can be specified for both the input and output files. Any options you put before the first filename are used for the input file, and any options you put after the first filename—but before the second—are used for the output file:

Option	*Description*	*Example*	*Meaning*
-t	Sets file type	-t uw	Raw unsigned word file
-c	Sets number of channels	-c 2	2 channels (stereo)
-r	Specifies rate in Hertz	-r 8000	Set rate to 8000Hz

There are numerous other, less-often used options that are detailed in the sox man page.

Finally, sox has the capability to add special effects and filters to your converted sound samples. To specify a filter, add the effect name and options at the end of the line, after any other options. Here are some examples:

```
> sox heart.wav heart-reverb.wav reverb 0.9 100 50 25 12.5
> sox heart.wav heart-reversed.wav reverse
> sox heart.wav heart-vibrosaw.wav 15
```

There are many other filters and effects, which are detailed in the sox man page.

Extracting Digital Audio Data

The first step in creating an archive of your favorite tunes on your hard disk involves the extraction of digital audio data from your CDs. Although you could simply record the music using your sound card's line input, that would be a big mistake because the audio data would be converted from digital to analog, and then back to digital again, resulting in a loss of sound quality. The best way to save CD audio data to your hard drive is to use a special program that can actually read the digital data from the disc directly, and save it to another disc. We will cover the use of two programs that perform this operation: cdparanoia and dagrab.

But before we begin, it's important to mention that it is entirely possible that your CD-ROM drive is either physically incapable of extracting digital audio data from the CD, or it is very bad at performing this task, and will provide somewhat corrupt digital data, with bit dropouts and other nasty things. In general, SCSI CD-ROMs tend to work the best for CDDA (Compact Disc Digital Audio) extraction. However, you will never know how well your CD-ROM drive will fare until you extract data and give it a listen, so I encourage you to proceed and evaluate the results.

Technical Details

You may wonder why it is so difficult to extract digital audio data when your CD-ROM

> **Plextor CD-ROM Drives**
>
> If you are interested in extracting large amounts of digital audio from your CD collection, you might want to purchase a Plextor CD-ROM drive. Although not as popular as Toshiba or Sony, Plextor is well known in the industry for guaranteeing flawless digital audio extraction. Plextor is certainly not the only brand of drive that can flawlessly extract digital audio, but to the best of my knowledge, it is the only company that guarantees this ability on its entire line of drives. Plextor drives are somewhat more expensive, but they get the job done.

drive functions perfectly while reading data discs. The answer lies in the format of CD audio data itself. Although the CD has been hailed as a random access format, the truth is that only data CDs are truly random access, using about one ninth of the data on the disc for the purposes of tracking and error correction. CD audio data, on the other hand, uses every bit of each audio sector on the disc for music only. This provides no easy way for the digital audio extraction software to detect errors caused by skipping, timing problems, and so on. Regular CD players get around this problem by operating the CD drive at exactly 1X speed, and by using a hardware-based solution to read the data from the disc at very precise timing intervals. Under any modern multitasking operating system such as Linux, conditions are not ideal. There are typically lots of other things going on while the audio extraction process is occurring, which greatly increases the chances of timing-based errors. In addition, when you consider that many CD-ROM drives available today are of relatively low quality and can barely handle data discs, you can see why special extraction tools are needed.

cdparanoia

Enter cdparanoia. cdparanoia is the premiere tool for reliably extracting digital audio from CDs under Linux, and can be downloaded for free from http://www.xiph.org. One of its strengths is cdparanoia's ability to extract digital audio data from less than ideal drives or scratched discs, repairing data (if necessary) during the extraction process. Here is a sample cdparanoia status screen:

```
cdparanoia III alpha prerelease 9.5 (March 24, 1999)
 1999 Monty <xiphmont@mit.edu>

This is PRERELEASE software!  Report bugs to xiphmont@mit.edu
http://www.mit.edu/afs/sipb/user/xiphmont/cdparanoia/index.html

Forcing default to read 16 sectors; ignoring preset and autosense
Forcing search overlap to 8 sectors; ignoring autosense
Ripping from sector   223560 (track 14 [0:00.00])
         to sector   244971 (track 14 [4:45.36])

outputting to cdda.wav

 (== PROGRESS == [!!!!!!!!!>                    | 230242 00 ] == :-P . ==)
```

The exclamation marks in the progress bar (as well as the smiley sticking his tongue out on the right) indicate that cdparanoia is finding and correcting errors in the digital audio that it is extracting from a CD. It's working pretty hard because, unfortunately, my Toshiba IDE drive does not seem quite up to the task of extracting digital audio!

After downloading, compiling, and installing cdparanoia, its use is a snap. Simply place an audio CD in your CD-ROM drive, and enter

> cdparanoia <*tracknumber*>

cdparanoia will then begin the extraction process, displaying a status bar like the one above to keep you updated on its progress. For an explanation of what all the various progress bar symbols mean, type

> cdparanoia 2>&1 | less

You can now scroll the help text, figure out what each symbol means, and determine an appropriate course of action. If you happen to have a not-so-great IDE CD-ROM drive, try using -n 8 -o 4 as options; these options will set the number of sectors read to 8 and the number of overlapping sectors to 4. This will help cdparanoia do a better job at correcting data errors during extraction.

After a song is extracted, you can try playing cdda.wav using your favorite WAV player. After you've played around with your extracted digital audio, we are now ready to encode the data.

MPEG 1 Layer 3 Encoding

MPEG stands for the "Moving Picture Experts Group", an international organization which defines standards for the encoding of both video and audio data. One of its standards is MPEG 1 Layer 3, a lossy compression technique that is specifically designed to efficiently store audio data, allowing for 10:1 compression ratios and beyond. In the digital audio world, *lossy* means that some data is lost in the translation, but in the case of MPEG 1 Layer 3, the encoding algorithm has been designed to throw away as little critical audio data as possible. One of the strengths of MPEG 1 Layer 3 is its ability to efficiently compress audio data at low bitrates (such as 64kbps per channel), a data rate that makes for relatively small files that can easily be transferred over modern networks and even over phone lines via modem. This technical tidbit has had a very big real-world impact on the Internet, where MPEG 1 Layer 3 (or MP3, as it is often called) has provided a nearly ideal way to distribute near CD-quality music for the typical computer user. MP3 technology has spawned an entirely new method of music distribution over the Internet, as well as a new breed of portable music-playing devices. Consider that a typical 5-minute CD audio track occupies approximately 52MB on disk. This is a rather unwieldy amount of data, but after being compressed using MP3 encoding at 64kbps/channel, the resulting file size is under 5MB! That amount of data can be transferred over a 56kbps modem in approximately 15 minutes; although not instantaneous, that transfer rate is at least somewhat practical for a large number of computer users. Suddenly, near CD-quality digital audio can be easily uploaded and downloaded by the average computer owner. Wow!

MP3—Use and Misuse

Because MP3 allows five-minute songs to be compressed to around 5MB, MP3 technology is used by many to pirate copyrighted music. Unfortunately, this common practice gives MP3 encoding a bad reputation among many people in the music industry. As with any technology, MP3 can be used for both legal and illegal purposes. It's important to point out that there is nothing inherently illegal about MPEG compression; in fact, MPEG-based compression is used for digital video satellite transmission as well as for DVD movies! I ask that you do not use MP3 technology for illegal purposes, such as the compression and distribution of copyrighted music. If you are unhappy with retail prices of compact discs, I recommend that you get involved in a solution to this problem rather than using it as an excuse to pirate large quantities of copyrighted music. Fortunately, MP3 does provide several legal alternatives that are now being explored by various artists, such as the use of MP3 as an official music distribution medium to reduce music costs.

MP3 Archiving

That being said, MP3 has many exciting uses that are perfectly legal (and very fun!). Using MP3 compression, you can turn your Linux box into a "music server" for your entire house. When you figure that 22GB hard drives are now available and not unreasonably priced, by using MP3 compression you can store approximately

22000MB / (650MB/11) = ~375 full-length compact discs!

When you take into account that most CDs are not completely full, this number jumps to approximately 500 CDs. Even a spare 3GB hard drive lying around the house can store:

3000MB / (650MB/11) = ~50 full-length compact discs

Again, this number jumps to approximately 60 CDs when you take into account the fact that CDs rarely use the entire capacity of the disc. This means that a Linux box, coupled with a good CD-ROM drive, sound card, and extra hard drive space, can replace the functionality of a 100-disc CD changer that you were thinking of purchasing at the local electronics store.

Others have found even more innovative uses for MP3 technology. Some people have created their own Linux-based car stereo that stores all music in MP3 format. You can see pictures of many of these devices on the Internet, and some are quite impressive.

Of course, MP3 can be used to download music to the new generation of portable music players. Resembling portable CD players, but with no moving parts, they provide anywhere from 40 minutes to several hours of music and will continue playing without interruption even if you happen to be riding a roller coaster!

Sound Quality

Because MP3 compression uses a lossy algorithm that throws away data, many people are concerned about a loss of fidelity from encoding music using MP3. In reality, it is very difficult to notice a difference between the original CD audio data and the MP3 compressed version on a typical stereo—the compression algorithm is that good. You would have to compare the original CD track to the compressed version to notice a difference. Unless your home stereo system happens to consist of several thousand dollars of good audiophile-grade equipment, you will most likely not notice a striking difference in sound quality. You are encouraged to compare the sound quality between the original CD and MP3 on your own stereo and make your own decision. You might find the audio quality totally acceptable, or you might not. If you are an audiophile or have very sensitive hearing, please check out the next section where I cover shorten—a totally lossless audio compression application!

bladeenc

bladeenc is a freely distributable MP3 encoder. The recommended method of tracking down this encoder is to visit `http://freshmeat.net` and search for "bladeenc". Its operation is extremely simple; to covert my `cdda.wav` file to `mysong.mp3`, type

```
> bladeenc cdda.wav mysong.mp3
```

```
BladeEnc 0.81      Tord Jansson        Homepage:
http://www.bladeenc.cjb.net
=========================================================================
BladeEnc is free software, distributed under the Lesser General Public License.
See the file COPYING, BladeEnc's homepage or www.fsf.org for more details.

Files to encode: 1

Encoding:   cdda.wav
Input:      44.1 kHz, 16 bit, stereo.
Output:     128 kBit, stereo.

Status:   27.9% done, ETA 00:04:10        BATCH: 27.9% done, ETA 00:04:10
```

Encoding takes a few minutes, and bladeenc presents a status screen displaying an estimated completion time. After the encoding is complete, notice the remarkable difference in file sizes:

```
-rw-r--r--   1 root     root     50361068 Jul  6 16:11 cdda.wav
-rw-r--r--   1 root     root      4567747 Jul  6 16:20 mysong.mp3
```

Of course, the dramatically reduced file size doesn't mean anything by itself. Try extracting and encoding your own audio data, and then listen to the MP3 data by using the console-based mpg123 (included with Caldera OpenLinux):

```
> mpg123 mysong.mp3
```

If you listen critically on a good stereo system, or using headphones, you might notice some slight differences in the encoded version, such as poorer imaging, a slight loss of clarity, and so on. But for general listening on standard audio equipment, or for use in the car, MP3 is definitely good enough. Let your own ears be the judge—many people can hear no difference at all, and find MP3-encoded music every bit as enjoyable as the original digital data (please excuse the pun!) Enjoy!

Lossless Audio Encoding Using shorten

Let's face it: Although many people will be completely happy with a good lossy audio compressor, there will always be others who will never be satisfied if even so much as a bit of the original data is thrown away. For these people, whether audiophiles, musicians, or sound engineers, MPEG 1 Layer 3 just won't do (at least not for the majority of their needs). Fortunately, those people have a friend at the Cambridge University Engineering Department, Dr. A. J. Robinson. Dr. Robinson has not only written a high-quality lossless waveform compressor called shorten, but he has released the source code under a freely distributable noncommercial license, making his technology available to us. shorten is an excellent compressor, typically able to compress CD-quality audio to between one-half to three-quarters of its original size. We now begin our investigation of a sound compressor that is perfectly acceptable even for perfectionists.

shorten—Where to Get It

To download the Linux version of shorten, visit Tony's Cambridge University Web site, located at `http://svr-www.eng.cam.ac.uk/~ajr`, and click the speech and audio coding link. You will then be able to download the UNIX version of shorten, as well as review an online technical report on the technology. After downloading shorten, perform the following steps to compile it under Linux:

```
> cd /tmp
> tar xzvf /path/to/archive/shorten.tar.gz
> cd shorten-2.3a
> make
```

Then, as root:

```
> make install
```

shorten—How to Use It

Installation is complete, and shorten is now ready to use. But before we begin, let's create a batch file that will help us play back `.shn` compressed files. As root, change directories to `/usr/local/bin`, and create a file called `shnplay` that contains the text in Listing 29.1.

LISTING 29.1 shorten Playback Script

```
#!/bin/bash
for x in "$@"
do
        echo "Playing $x"
        shorten -x $x - | sox -t .wav - -t ossdsp /dev/dsp
done
```

After you're done, type **chmod +x shnplay** to make this script executable. This script now allows you to play back any number of shorten-compressed WAV files, by specifying them as command-line options.

Now, we will create another script, which we will use to easily compress multiple WAV files. One thing that shorten cannot do is accept multiple files to compress at once. Because it would be nice to be able to type **shncomp *.wav** to compress all WAV files in the current directory, the script in Listing 29.2 comes in handy.

LISTING 29.2 shorten Compress Script

```
#!/bin/bash
for x in "$@"
do
        echo "Compressing $x"
        shorten $x
done
```

After making this script executable, we are now ready to attempt to compress some WAV files and take a look at the compression ratio we get. I'm going to take a stab at a directory of sound effects on my hard drive, which contains the following files:

```
total 4842
-rw-r--r--    1 drobbins users     401634 Jun 25  1997 asterisk.wav
-rw-r--r--    1 drobbins users      31854 Aug 31  1998 eglanded.wav
-rw-r--r--    1 drobbins users     141538 Jun 25  1997 error.wav
-rw-r--r--    1 drobbins users     244962 Jun 25  1997 menupop.wav
-rw-r--r--    1 drobbins users     198882 Jun 25  1997 menuselec.wav
-rw-r--r--    1 drobbins users     229602 Jun 25  1997 miniwin.wav
-rw-r--r--    1 drobbins users     198374 Jun 25  1997 question.wav
-rw-r--r--    1 drobbins users    1495266 Jun 25  1997 quitwin.wav
-rw-r--r--    1 drobbins users     229602 Jun 25  1997 restwin.wav
-rw-r--r--    1 drobbins users    1753314 Jun 25  1997 startwin.wav
```

After typing **shncomp *.wav**, my directory now looks like this:

```
total 2456
-rw-r--r--    1 drobbins users     267409 Jun 25  1997 asterisk.wav.shn
-rw-r--r--    1 drobbins users      23313 Aug 31  1998 eglanded.wav.shn
-rw-r--r--    1 drobbins users      52949 Jun 25  1997 error.wav.shn
```

```
-rw-r--r--   1 drobbins users      126653 Jun 25  1997 menupop.wav.shn
-rw-r--r--   1 drobbins users      108473 Jun 25  1997 menuselec.wav.shn
-rw-r--r--   1 drobbins users      108793 Jun 25  1997 miniwin.wav.shn
-rw-r--r--   1 drobbins users      100877 Jun 25  1997 question.wav.shn
-rw-r--r--   1 drobbins users      753609 Jun 25  1997 quitwin.wav.shn
-rw-r--r--   1 drobbins users      108785 Jun 25  1997 restwin.wav.shn
-rw-r--r--   1 drobbins users      842157 Jun 25  1997 startwin.wav.shn
```

Half the size! But have I lost any data in the compressed waveforms? I slip on my headphones, quickly type `shnplay *.shn`, and am immediately relieved. shorten worked as advertised; no data was lost! As you can see, shorten offers truly excellent compression ratios, and the fact that it is free for noncommercial use is great. Note that shorten also supports lossy audio compression, if desired; take a look at shorten's man page for more information.

SoundTracker Modules

SoundTracker modules are a kind of music file that was popularized during the days of the Amiga computer. The primary method of storing music for video games, SoundTracker modules and their derivatives (such as S3M, MED, and many others) are widely available on the Internet. There are a number of module players available for both console and X.

Modules differ from many music files because they store both a musical score and digital sound samples. The module player plays the samples at varying frequencies to emulate different notes of the instrument (a primitive form of wavetable synthesis). The end result is surprisingly good. Modules are an extremely flexible music format. They give the programmer and musician absolute control over the final result of the work because the actual sound samples are transferred verbatim in the module file itself. Contrast this with MIDI files, in which the musician simply provides the musical score and relies on the sound card ROM to provide good-sounding instruments for playback. As you might know, the quality of MIDI instruments varies greatly from sound card to sound card, whereas modules sound virtually identical on nearly all modern sound hardware.

libmikmod

To aid your understanding of module players, we will download a full-featured module and sound player library called libmikmod, and write a simple module player in C. We'll then compile it and use it to play various SoundTracker modules that we download from the Internet. The best way to find libmikmod is to visit http://freshmeat.net and search for "libmikmod". After following the correct links to download libmikmod, you are now ready to compile it. Enter the following:

```
> cd /tmp
> tar xzvf /location/of/file/libmikmod-3.1.7.tar.gz
> cd libmikmod-3.1.7
> ./configure
```

If you are using ALSA, type `./configure --enable-alsa` instead. This tells libmikmod to use ALSA directly instead of going through the OSS compatibility modules. After this step, the source tree is ready to compile, so type

```
> make
```

Now, as root, type

```
> make install
ldconfig
```

Testing libmikmod

libmikmod will now be automatically installed, and your library dependency information will be updated via `ldconfig` so that programs can find libmikmod. Now, create a directory for a special C programming project—we're going to create a simple module player. Listing 29.3 is an almost verbatim copy of a sample program from the libmikmod info documentation; all we added is the ability to specify a module as a command-line argument. Although it's not very many lines of code, it gets the job done, thanks to the power of libmikmod.

LISTING 29.3 libmikmod Sample Module Player

```c
/* MikMod Sound Library example program: a simple module player */
/* A tiny modification by Daniel Robbins, 7/6/99              */

#include <unistd.h>
#include <mikmod.h>

main(int argc, char **argv)
{
        MODULE *module;

        /* register all the drivers */

        MikMod_RegisterAllDrivers();

        /* register all the module loaders */
        MikMod_RegisterAllLoaders();

        /* initialize the library */
        md_mode|=DMODE_SOFT_MUSIC;
```

```
            if(MikMod_Init("")) {
                fprintf(stderr,"Could not initialize sound, reason: %s\n",
                    MikMod_strerror(MikMod_errno));
                return;
            }
            /* load module */
            module = Player_Load(argv[1],64,0);
            if (module) {
                /* start module */
                Player_Start(module);

                while(Player_Active()) {
                    /* we're playing */
                    usleep(10000);
                    MikMod_Update();
                }
                Player_Stop();
                Player_Free(module);
            } else
                fprintf(stderr,"Could not load module, reason: %s\n",
                    MikMod_strerror(MikMod_errno));

            /* give up */
            MikMod_Exit();
}
```

After typing in the preceding program and saving it as `mikplay.c`, it can be compiled by typing the following command:

> `gcc mikplay.c -o mikplay -lmikmod`

This produces a binary file called `mikplay` that can be used to play SoundTracker and SoundTracker-like modules. Simply specify them on the command line as follows:

> `mikplay mymodule.mod`

I encourage you to copy your new binary to `/usr/local/bin` so that it will be in your path and accessible from any directory. Now, before we try our program, we must track down some SoundTracker modules. The easiest way to do this is to head over to `http://www.yahoo.com` and search for "mod files" or browse to the `entertainment > music > computer generated > mod` category. The new player you created can handle `.mod`, `.s3m`, and `.xm` files, as well as others. Download some, give them a listen, and see what you think. One good source of modules is the AmiNet modules archive, at `http://ftp.wustl.edu/~aminet/dirs/tree_mods.html`. Most of these files happen to be lha-compressed—fortunately, Caldera OpenLinux has an lha (de)compression program. After downloading the archive, type the following:

> `lha x myfile.lha`
`mymodule.mod        - Melted`

You can now play the module using your player:

> `mikplay mymodule.mod`

SoundTracker modules provide a simple and easy method to distribute songs that can be played on a variety of hardware. The strength of modules is that they come with their own instruments. We will investigate MIDI, a standard that is instrument-independent and is used for professional and a growing number of PC-based applications.

Introduction to MIDI

MIDI stands for Musical Instrument Digital Interface, and was originally designed in 1982 so that there would be a standard way for music synthesizers to interoperate and share musical information. Since that time, MIDI has become very popular in the PC world. Numerous sound cards have MIDI ports built in, and many also have an advanced MIDI synthesizer built into the sound card itself. But before we delve further into the details of MIDI, it is a good idea to compare MIDI to digitized audio, as well as SoundTracker modules.

Compared to digitized audio, MIDI files are much smaller. Containing only the instructions needed by the MIDI synthesizer to play a particular score of music, and not the digitized sound data itself, allows MIDI files to be incredibly tiny by today's standards, typically 50KB for a five-minute song. When this is contrasted with 50MB for a typical CD-quality song and 5MB for an MPEG 1 Layer 3–encoded song, you can see how tiny MIDI files actually are.

However, this small size comes with some limitations. Because MIDI files contain only instructions for a synthesizer to play particular instruments at particular times, the composer has relatively little control over the final quality of the music. After all, different synthesizers and sound cards use different synthesis techniques to simulate live instruments, and these instruments can vary widely not only in sound quality and character, but in relative sound volume as well. This can lead to a situation in which a MIDI file might sound great when played using one sound card's MIDI synthesis engine, but sounds horrible (or significantly worse) on another. Although modern advances in sound card MIDI wavetable synthesis have greatly improved sound quality overall, it will always be true that no two synthesizers are created equal. So, although MIDI allows for the playback of music on a wide variety of electronic musical devices, it also severely limits the musician's control over the final "sound" of the music. He or she has no idea whether the completed composition will be played back on the electronic equivalent of a grand piano or a kazoo.

Another more obvious limitation in using MIDI is that it is a format specifically designed to represent instrumental music. There is no way to use MIDI to accurately transmit the human voice or intricate and unique sound effects. Using MIDI is somewhat like composing music for an extremely advanced player piano. In effect, that is what a MIDI synthesizer is.

Taking that into consideration, MIDI is an ideal music format for several specific uses. It's ideal for the composition and playback of instrumental music, especially when the music might need to be edited at a later date. Digitized music, such as MPEG 1 Layer 3 and CD audio, is not in a format that can easily be changed. When dealing with MIDI files, a passage of music can easily be changed on a note-by-note basis. It's malleable, whereas digital audio is not. Another ideal use of MIDI is for the playback of instrumental music for multimedia projects, such as games. For background music, MIDI provides an ideal way to compose music that can be heard on nearly any kind of sound hardware. And, of course, if you are a professional musician, MIDI is what you want to be working with. It's the language that electronic instruments speak, and your computer (with the appropriate sound hardware), can speak it too.

General MIDI System

The General MIDI System (GM) was designed to solve an interesting problem that existed among various MIDI devices—selecting the correct instruments for a particular piece of music. Take the example of a MIDI score composed on a particular MIDI system. When played back on another manufacturer's MIDI system, it would not be uncommon for the incorrect instruments to be selected. That is because in a MIDI file, instruments were chosen by number and manufacturers did not have a standard set of numbers that mapped to the same instruments on different pieces of hardware. So, for example, whereas a score might have been composed using a flute, it could play back as a piano on another manufacturer's synthesizer. To resolve this problem, the GM specification defines a standard mapping from number to instrument type, so that a flute is always a flute, and a piano is always a piano. This solves the problem of interchange of MIDI files, and eliminates any kind of tweaking that might be required on the user's end to get a MIDI file to play correctly. Remember General MIDI—you will hear of it often. You'll also know what is happening if you come across a MIDI file that plays back using the wrong instruments.

MIDI Instruments—FM Versus Wavetable Synthesis

We've covered the basics of MIDI, but haven't yet looked in depth at the synthesis stage—how exactly does a MIDI synthesizer represent the digital instrument waveforms that are played back through your speakers? We're going to cover two technologies: FM and wavetable synthesis.

FM synthesis, featured on older sound cards, is a relatively simple way of describing musical instruments. Primarily useful for representing synthesized sounds, FM synthesized instruments take up relatively little storage space in the sound card's ROM. The major drawback of FM synthesis is that is difficult to accurately simulate the sound of real instruments. FM synthesis is easily recognizable because of its "synthy" sound.

Wavetable synthesis, on the other hand, can adequately represent real instruments, and is the preferred instrument format for today's sound cards and synthesizers. In its most basic form, a wavetable consists of samples of particular instruments that can then be played back at different pitches to emulate different notes of a particular instrument. Current wavetable technology, however, is much more sophisticated than this. This sophistication allows for very high-quality results to be achieved using a relatively limited amount of memory. Of course, wavetable sound takes up significantly more storage space than FM, and it is not uncommon for MIDI hobbyists and professionals to sport sound cards with 32MB or more of dedicated onboard RAM for the storage of wavetable samples. Modern wavetable synthesis uses techniques such as pitch shifting, interpolation, and special data compression to push the limits of synthesized sound to new heights.

Software MIDI Synthesis

Traditionally, MIDI playback has been accomplished by using the built-in hardware synthesizer on your sound card, an optional daughter card, or an external MIDI box that is plugged into the sound card's MIDI port. Recently, a new possibility for MIDI synthesis has emerged: software synthesis. Instead of relying on dedicated sound hardware to convert MIDI data into digital audio data, this task can be performed completely in software on modern machines. The software synthesis engine typically uses wavetable instruments to render a MIDI file into a digital bitstream that is then played through the sound driver's digital audio output device. Although you might wonder why anyone would want to do this when dedicated MIDI hardware is readily available, there are a number of good reasons. First, not all people have a sound card that provides MIDI playback. Second, although many cards provide 16-bit sound and MIDI playback, the MIDI hardware might use FM synthesis that does not compare with modern wavetable synthesis in terms of sound quality. Additionally, on a modern Pentium II–class machine, software synthesis requires an almost negligible amount of CPU time, making it an attractive and flexible option, and a required one if your sound card doesn't have any kind of MIDI support.

You might have already used a software-based synthesis engine without even knowing it, under Microsoft Windows. A common practice by sound card manufacturers is to design a card with, let's say, the ability to play 32 simultaneous instruments in hardware, and then advertise the card being able to play 64 instruments simultaneously! The way they get away with this trick is by designing the drivers in such a way to provide software synthesis when the number of simultaneous instruments rises above 32. Commonly, Windows sound card drivers provide an option to turn on or off these extra voices.

SoftOSS

If you are looking for software MIDI synthesis, SoftOSS is one way to go. Implemented as a driver for the Open Sound System, SoftOSS provides a completely software-based synthesizer that appears to OSS-compatible applications as if it were a hardware device. That means it offers the benefit of providing full compatibility with standard Linux MIDI programs. At this time, SoftOSS takes up less CPU power than TiMidity, but does not sound as good.

Kmidi

Kmidi is a KDE-based application that is included with Caldera OpenLinux. It features the ability to play back MIDI files using software synthesis; unfortunately, the version of this program included with Caldera is a beta version and is somewhat unstable. I recommended that you use Kmidi's big brother, TiMidity++, to play back MIDI files.

TiMidity++

TiMidity++ is an excellent MIDI software synthesis engine that fully emulates the Gravis UltraSound series of wavetable sound cards, resulting in truly amazing sound quality. It is available from http://www.goice.co.jp/member/mo/timidity. Although TiMidity++ requires some setting up before it will work, the end result is definitely worth the effort.

The first step in TiMidity installation involves downloading the source code from the TiMidity Web site, compiling the software, and installing the compiled application. Installation goes something like this:

```
> cd /tmp
> tar xzvf TiMidity++-2.1.0.tar.gz
> cd TiMidity++-2.1.0
> ./configure --enable-ncurses

(configuration will begin)

> make

(compilation will begin)
```

After this is done, simply type **make install** as root. The software will be installed into /usr/local, and we will be ready for the next stage of the configuration process—installing the patch files.

Installing Patch Files for TiMidity++ and OSS

Installing the patch files is a tricky and time consuming process, but I'll help you get it done with a minimum of fuss. The first thing you want to do is visit Eric A. Welsh's TiMidity patch site at http://www.stardate.bc.ca/gus_patches.htm. Eric offers a high-quality, freely distributable patch set on his page. Although large, it is definitely worth the effort to download and install. The first step in the installation process is to download an unrar binary. We will use this program to extract the patch file archives. Click on the UNRAR link at the top of his page and download the rarlinux.sfx archive. Move it into its own temporary directory, and type

```
> ./rarlinux.sfx
```

The executable archive will now extract itself into the current directory. Now, as root, copy rar and unrar to /usr/local/bin. We are now ready to begin downloading and installing the patch files. Download all parts of the eawpats patch set, as well as the full drumsfx patch set. These files will end in .rar, .r00, .r01, and so on. After you are done downloading these files, download any updates that are available. We are now ready to install these patches! After TiMidity++ has been installed, simply do the following as root:

```
> cd /usr/local/timidity
> unrar e /path/to/rar/files/eawpats5.rar
> unrar e /path/to/rar/files/drumsfx4.rar
> unrar e /path/to/rar/files/eawp5up1.rar
```

The filenames you use might differ slightly, but they will be somewhat similar to the ones above and end in .rar. After extraction is complete, our final TiMidity step is to edit the /usr/local/lib/timidity/timidity.cfg file, which should contain the following uncommented lines:

```
dir /usr/local/lib/timidity
source gravis.cfg
source gsdrums.cfg
source gssfx.cfg
source xgmap2.cfg
```

After this is done, TiMidity++ should be ready for use. With sound drivers loaded, and the volume set appropriately, the following command should produce music:

```
> timidity myfile.mid
```

For a more impressive sound, try the following command line, which adds some reverb, chorus, antialiases the sound sample, adds 256-voice polyphony, and increases the sampling frequency of the output:

```
> timidity -a -s65000 -EFchorus=1 -EFreverb=1,63 -p 256 -D 10 myfile.mid
```

To get SoftOSS to use the EAW patch set, simply set the `GUSPATCHDIR` environment variable to `/usr/local/lib/timidity` by typing the following command into a shell:

```
export GUSPATCHDIR=/usr/local/lib/timidity
```

Add this line to your `/etc/profile` file if you would like it executed every time your system is started. When this environment variable has been defined, SoftOSS will now work, for example:

```
> /usr/lib/oss/mplay 1 myfile.mid
```

You will need to adjust the path to mplay depending on where you installed OSS. Also note that you might need to use a number other than 1—simply enter **cat /dev/sndstat** and use the number that corresponds with the SoftOSS synth device. Enjoy the world of software synthesis!

Where to Go from Here

I hope that our whirlwind tour of Linux sound and multimedia has given you a taste for the latest and greatest technologies that are available for your system. Because I can't cover everything under the sun in a chapter of this size, I have provided you with pointers to locations on the Web where you can continue your investigation of Linux multimedia technologies. Your first stop should probably be `http://freshmeat.net`, a very popular Linux software news site. You'll be able to browse the most recent releases of Linux applications, as well as take a look at Freshmeat's appendix to browse applications by category. There are a very large number of good multimedia applications contained on freshmeat that I have not touched on.

Secondly, you will want to visit `http://www.real.com` to acquire the most-recent free version of RealPlayer G2. RealPlayer G2 allows you to view industry-standard streaming media files over the Web. Although currently in beta, a full version should be available (or close to available) by the time you read this.

If you are interested in purchasing a set of very high-quality sound samples to use with the MIDI software synthesis engine of your choice, I recommend you head over to Utopia Sound Division's site at `http://utopia.a1.nl`. It has a wonderful patch set that is compatible with the synthesis engines I covered in this chapter.

Even if you are not interested in purchasing OSS, I recommend that you stop by `http://www.opensound.com`, and browse its sound and multimedia applications list, which is quite extensive and will introduce you to new programs that you might not be familiar with.

Also, you should check out an excellent set of sound and multimedia links located at `http://sound.condorow.net`. Between all these sites, you should be well on your way to becominga Linux Multimedia expert!

Programming, Automation, and Kernel Compilation

Part IV

In This Part

30 Shell and Awk Programming Essentials   *709*

31 Configuring and Building the Kernel   *735*

CHAPTER 30

Shell and awk Programming

IN THIS CHAPTER

- Shell Programming with bash *710*
- bash Variables *711*
- Environment Variables *712*
- Shell Scripts *713*
- Conditional Constructs *714*
- Looping Constructs *716*
- Built-In Shell Variables and Positional Parameters *719*
- Functions *720*
- Going Further with Shell Programming *721*
- awk Scripting *722*
- Invoking awk *723*
- Built-in awk Variables *725*
- Arrays *726*
- awk Expressions *728*
- Control Statements *729*
- I/O Statements *731*
- Built-in Functions *732*
- User-defined Functions *733*
- Going Further with awk *734*

The Linux shell is not only a command interpreter, but it also features a powerful built-in programming language. You can write fairly complex shell programs—in fact, early versions of "C News," software that was used to transmit Usenet news postings across the Internet, were written almost entirely as shell scripts.

The shell scripting language, although less powerful than a large language like Perl, is widely used because every UNIX system is guaranteed to have a shell. (Most commercial UNIXes do not include Perl.) Thus, shell scripts are used for programs that must run on any UNIX system without recompilation, making them ideal for installation scripts and configuration programs.

In addition to shell scripting, seasoned UNIX administrators make good use of the awk interpreter. awk (named after its inventors, Aho, Weinberger, and Kernighan) is a scripting language designed for scanning and processing text files. Although Perl has superseded awk for text file processing, awk is still widely used because it, too, is standard across UNIX systems. You can be guaranteed that a POSIX-compliant UNIX system will contain an awk interpreter. If you want to write scripts that are portable, stick to awk rather than Perl.

On Linux, the awk language is interpreted by the GNU awk interpreter gawk. (The command awk is a symbolic link to gawk.) The GNU version of awk includes all the original awk language as well as some powerful GNU-specific extensions.

Because awk is simply a normal UNIX command, you can combine shell scripting and awk programming to create powerful text-processing programs. This chapter describes how to program using the bash shell scripting language and the gawk interpreter. Both of these programs extend the original sh and awk interpreters; I will carefully note which features are bash- and gawk-specific, so you can avoid them if you need to write portable scripts.

Shell Programming with bash

The bash shell is the most commonly-used shell on Linux systems. It is derived from the UNIX Bourne shell that is standard on all UNIX systems. (Bash stands for Bourne Again Shell, continuing the UNIX tradition of bad puns.) The original Bourne shell included a powerful scripting language, but it was inconvenient for interactive use. bash adds many usability features (such as filename completion and command history) as well as features from other shells. It also retains and extends the excellent Bourne shell programming language.

In this chapter, I will concentrate on the bash scripting language. If you want a good overview of other bash features such as its improvements for interactive use, look at the bash info page.

bash Variables

bash allows you to set and use *variables*. A variable is simply a named holder for a string. Setting a variable places a string inside the named holder. Referencing the variable retrieves the string that was last stored there. All programming languages support variables, and bash is no exception. Unlike some languages, however, bash variables have no type—they always hold strings.

To set a variable in bash, simply type:

```
$ var=value
```

For example, the following command sets the value of CITY to Ottawa:

```
$ CITY=Ottawa
```

> **Caution**
>
> Do not leave a space between the variable name and the equals sign. If you type **CITY = Ottawa**, the shell incorrectly assumes that you are trying to execute a command named CITY with the two arguments = and Ottawa. Similarly, if the value has spaces, you must quote it like this: **CITY="Kansas City"**.

Shell variables are conventionally named with all uppercase letters; however, this is tradition and not law. A shell variable that you create should start with a letter and can contain letters, digits, and underscores.

To use the value of a variable, prefix it with a dollar sign. Continuing with the previous example, type the following:

```
$ echo $CITY
Ottawa
```

The shell replaces the word $CITY with the value of the variable, Ottawa. If you reference a nonexistent variable, the shell replaces it with an empty string, as the following example shows:

```
$ echo "My country is $COUNTRY."
My country is .
```

The previous example also reveals that the shell performs variable substitution inside double-quoted strings. The next example shows that single-quotes suppress variable substitution:

```
$ echo 'My country is $COUNTRY.'
My country is $COUNTRY.
```

Environment Variables

Every process in Linux has an area of memory called the environment. In this memory, you can place environment variables. Environment variables are simply strings that look like this:

VAR=value

To look at the contents of your shell's environment, type

```
$ printenv
KDEDIR=/opt/kde
HOME=/home/dfs
SHELL=/bin/bash
DISPLAY=:0.0
HOST=shishi.skoll.ca
...
```

You will see quite a few environment variables. The important thing about the environment is that when a new process is created, it receives a copy of its parent's environment. Many UNIX programs use environment variables for seldom changing configuration hints. For example, X programs use the environment variable DISPLAY to determine which X server to connect to. Because this almost never changes during a session, it would be annoying to have to specify it on the command line each time. Instead, when you start X, it passes the DISPLAY environment variable to clients as they are started.

> **Note**
>
> Child processes get a copy of the environment. That means it is not possible for a child to modify its parent's environment. It can only modify its own environment.

When you create a variable in bash, it is not automatically placed in the environment. The export command places a variable in the environment. For example, to set the environment variable EDITOR to emacs -nw, use the following commands:

```
$ EDITOR="emacs -nw"
$ export EDITOR
```

Many UNIX programs use the EDITOR environment variable to determine your default text editor. You can use the preceding commands to choose your favorite editor.

> **Note**
>
> bash allows you to combine the two commands into one like this: **export EDITOR="emacs -nw"**. However, the standard UNIX Bourne shell does not permit this.

Shell Scripts

A shell script is a text file containing shell commands. You create the file with a normal text editor. Create a sample shell script called `hello` with the following contents:

```
#!/bin/sh
echo "Hello, World!"
exit 0
```

The first line (`#!/bin/sh`) tells the kernel that the program `/bin/sh` should be used to interpret the script. When you try to execute a file and the kernel encounters this "hash-bang" notation, it invokes the program named on the line with the name of the script as its first argument.

> **Note**
>
> Why /bin/sh and not /bin/bash? On most Linux systems, /bin/sh is a symbolic link to /bin/bash. On most commercial UNIX systems, /bin/bash does not exist and /bin/sh is the standard system shell. Using /bin/sh makes it more likely that a script will work on a wide variety of UNIX platforms.

The `exit` command is a built-in shell command. It causes the shell script to terminate immediately with the specified exit value.

In the directory in which you created the file hello, type:

```
$ ./hello
bash: ./hello: Permission denied
```

Before you can execute a script, you have to turn on execute permission. Do this as follows:

```
$ chmod a+x ./hello
$ ./hello
Hello, World!
```

Conditional Constructs

`bash` includes all the usual features of a complete programming language. One basic feature is conditional execution—the ability to choose which pieces of script to execute, based on some condition. The shell scripting language has two conditional constructs: `if` and `case`.

The `if` Statement

The `if` statement looks like the following:

```
if TEST1 ; then
    COMMANDS1 ;
[elif TEST2 ; then
    COMMANDS2 ;]
[else
    COMMANDSn;]
fi
```

The parts in square brackets are optional; don't actually type the square brackets.

The item TEST1 is a list of commands. If the final command in the list exits with a status of zero, the list of commands COMMANDS1 is executed. Otherwise, if the final command in the list TEST2 exits with a status of zero, COMMANDS2 are executed. If all tests fail and an else part is present, COMMANDSn are executed.

Here is a concrete example. Create a file called iftest with the following contents:

```
#!/bin/sh
if [ "$LOGNAME" = "dfs" ] ; then
    echo "Hello, David!"
    FULLNAME=David;
elif [ "$LOGNAME" = "demo" ] ; then
    echo "Hello, Demo User!"
    FULLNAME=demo
else
    echo "Go away, impostor!"
    FULLNAME=unknown
fi
```

Let's examine this script. The part in square brackets after the if statement certainly doesn't look like a list of commands. However, a command called [actually exists on your system. (It is in /usr/bin/[.) This command is executed with four arguments: $LOGNAME, =, dfs and]. In the previous example, if the value of $LOGNAME is dfs, [exits with a status of zero and the commands after the if are executed. Otherwise, [exits with a non-zero status, and the shell skips to the elif clause.

Note that `test` is a synonym for `[`, except that it must not take a final `]` argument. You could rewrite the shell script (in a more traditional form) like the following:

```
#!/bin/sh
if test "$LOGNAME" = "dfs" ; then
    echo "Hello, David!"
    FULLNAME=David;
elif test "$LOGNAME" = "demo" ; then
    echo "Hello, Demo User!"
    FULLNAME=demo
else
    echo "Go away, impostor!"
    FULLNAME=unknown
fi
```

In the previous example, it is clear that a statement follows the `if` keyword.

> **Note**
>
> Most shells, bash included, have built-in implementations of `[` and `test`.

`[` and `test` have many forms—they can check for the existence of files and directories, test for string equality, and more. For more details, see the `test(1)` manual page. Also, under `bash`, type **help test** for information on bash's built-in test command.

Note that I quoted the $LOGNAME environment variable. This ensures that the shell script works even if the variable is not defined. To see what happens if you don't quote the variable name, remove the quotes and type the following:

```
$ LOGNAME=
$ sh ./iftest
./iftest: [: =: unary operator expected
./iftest: [: =: unary operator expected
Go away, impostor!
```

Note that the `[` command is confused by the lack of an argument before the equal sign. Quoting $LOGNAME ensures that the argument is there, even if it is just the empty string.

The case Statement

The case statement looks like the following:

```
case WORD in
    PATTERN1a [| PATTERN1b]...) COMMANDS1 ;;
    PATTERN2a [| PATTERN2b]...) COMAMNDS2 ;;
esac
```

In the case statement, each PATTERN is a shell "glob-style" pattern. If any of the patterns in a list matches WORD, the corresponding COMMANDS are executed. This cries out for a concrete example. Create a file called casetest with the following contents:

```
#!/bin/sh
case "$NAME" in
   dfs | demo) echo "Hello, David or Demo!" ;;
   root) echo "Greetings, O great master!" ;;
   b*) echo "Hello, B-something!" ;;
   *) echo "I don't know who you are, but Hi." ;;
esac
```

Now, test the script:

```
$ NAME=dfs sh ./casetest
Hello, David or Demo!
$ NAME=demo sh ./casetest
Hello, David or Demo!
$ NAME=root sh ./casetest
Greetings, O great master!
$ NAME=bob sh ./casetest
Hello, B-something!
$ NAME=hacker sh ./casetest
I don't know who you are, but Hi.
```

The case statement tries each match in turn until one succeeds. The pattern * matches anything, so you can use it as a default case.

The testing of the script shows off another piece of shell syntax: You can type any number of variable assignments followed by a command. The variable assignments are in effect only during the execution of the command. You can verify that the variable NAME is not set:

```
$ echo "Name is $NAME"
Name is
```

This handy bit of syntax lets you set variables only for commands that require them and not pollute your shell's variable space permanently.

Looping Constructs

The shell has three looping constructs. Two (the while and until statements) repeatedly execute commands until a condition is met, and one (the for statement) executes commands for each word in a list.

The `while` and `until` Statements

The `while` statement looks like the following:

```
while TEST ; do COMMANDS ; done
```

The `until` statement is very similar:

```
until TEST ; do COMMANDS ; done
```

For the `while` statement, the commands in the list TEST are executed. If the last command in the list has a zero exit status, the COMMANDS are executed. This repeats until the last command in TEST exits with a nonzero exit status.

`until` is similar, but it repeats as long as TEST has a nonzero exit status and terminates when TEST has a zero exit status.

Here is an example. Create a file called whiletest with the following contents:

```
#!/bin/sh
ANS='?'

while test "$ANS" != "y" -a "$ANS" != "n" ; do
    echo -n "Please enter 'y' or 'n': "
    read ANS
done

echo "You entered $ANS."
```

Run the following script:

```
$ sh ./whiletest
Please enter 'y' or 'n': foo
Please enter 'y' or 'n': bar
Please enter 'y' or 'n': n
You entered n.
```

In this example, we first initialize the variable ANS to ?. Then, as long as it is not y or n, we prompt the user. The command `read ANS` reads a line of input and assigns it to the variable ANS. The loop continues until the user enters either y or n.

Like C, the shell supports the `break` and `continue` commands. Within a loop, the `break` command causes immediate termination of the loop. The `continue` command starts the next iteration of the loop.

Consider this example: Create a file called addtest with the following contents:

```sh
#!/bin/sh
TOTAL=0
while true ; do
    echo -n "Enter a number or 'q': "
    read NUM
    if test "$NUM" = ""; then
        echo "Blank!"
        continue
    fi
    if test "$NUM" = "q"; then break; fi
    TOTAL=`expr $TOTAL + $NUM`
done

echo "Total is $TOTAL."
```

Run the following script:

```
$ sh ./addtest
Enter a number or 'q': 1
Enter a number or 'q':
Blank!
Enter a number or 'q': 2
Enter a number or 'q': 3
Enter a number or 'q': q
Total is 6.
```

If you enter a blank line, the script echoes `Blank!` and executes continue, which restarts the loop. If you enter q, the break command terminates the loop. Otherwise, the number you entered is added to the running total. (Recall that the back-tick quotes cause the shell to evaluate a command and then substitute the output of that command on the line.)

The expr command is covered in Appendix A, "Useful UNIX Commands."

> **Note**
>
> You were introduced briefly to back-tick quotes in Chapter 3, "Using the Shell." Anything inside back-tick quotes is executed as a shell command. The shell collects the output of the command and replaces the original back-quoted text with the command's output (after converting newlines to spaces.)
>
> For example, the following shell command:
>
> ```
> echo "Today is `date`"
> ```
>
> will produce output that looks something like this:
>
> ```
> Today is Thu Oct  7 12:47:36 EDT 1999
> ```
>
> Note how the output of the date command has been substituted for the original back-quoted text.

The for Statement

The `for` statement looks like the following:

```
for VAR in WORDS ; do COMMANDS ; done
```

Here, `VAR` is the name of a shell variable, and `WORDS` is a list of words. `COMMANDS` is a list of commands.

To see an example of for in action, type the following:

```
$ for X in 1 2 3 4; do echo "I like $X"; done
I like 1
I like 2
I like 3
I like 4
```

You can also make a "poor-man's" `ls` command:

```
$ for X in /etc/* ; do echo "$X"; done
/etc/HOSTNAME
/etc/PHI.conf
/etc/X11
...
```

Built-In Shell Variables and Positional Parameters

The shell has several built-in variables. Some are covered in Chapter 3. Table 30.1 lists some built-in variables useful for shell scripting.

TABLE 30.1   Built-in Shell Variables

Variable	Meaning
PATH	Colon-separated list of directories in which the shell searches for commands.
HOME	Your home directory.
PS1	The shell's primary prompt.
PS2	The shell's secondary prompt (when it is waiting for more input to complete a command.)
RANDOM	Each time this variable is read, a random integer is returned.
*	A list of all positional parameters passed to a shell script. If enclosed in double quotes, it expands to a single parameter.
@	A list of all positional parameters passed to a shell script. If enclosed in double-quotes, expands to a list of double-quoted parameters.

TABLE 30.1 continued

Variable	Meaning
#	The number of positional parameters.
?	The exit status of the most recently executed command.
$	The process-ID of the shell.
0	The name of the shell script.
n	The *n*th positional parameter.

If you invoke a shell script with additional arguments, the extra arguments are called positional parameters. Create a shell script called paramtest with the following contents:

```
#!/bin/sh
echo "My name is $0"
echo "My process-ID is $$"
echo "I have $# positional parameters."
n=0
for PARAM in "$@" ; do
   n=`expr $n + 1`
   echo "Parameter $n: $PARAM"
done
echo "Here is a random number: $RANDOM"
echo "The previous echo command exited with status: $?"
```

Now test the script:

```
$ sh paramtest one "two and a" three
My name is paramtest
My process-ID is 1363
I have 3 positional parameters.
Parameter 1: one
Parameter 2: two and a
Parameter 3: three
Here is a random number: 13011
The previous echo command exited with status: 0
```

Your output will differ slightly; the process-ID and random value should be different.

The previous example illustrates several of the shell's built-in variables and parameters. Consult the bash(1) manual page and the bash info page for more details.

Functions

The shell allows you to define functions, which are lists of shell commands. When you have defined a function, you can call it as if it were a normal shell command. During the execution of a function, the positional parameters take on the values of arguments passed to the function call.

Type the following into a file called functest:

```
max() {
    if test $# = 0 ; then
        echo "??"
        return 1
    fi
    MAX=$1
    for N in "$@" ; do
        if test "$N" -gt "$MAX" ; then MAX=$N; fi
    done
    echo "$MAX"
    return 0
}
```

Now source the file by typing: **source functest**. The source command reads the contents of a file as if you had typed them into the shell. Now test the max function:

```
$ max 1 9 8 4
9
$ max
??
```

As you see, the function behaves just like a built-in command. Note that if you do not supply any parameters, the function prints ?? and returns with a status of 1. (I used return instead of exit to terminate the function. exit would log you out of your shell!)

The back-tick quotes are quite useful with shell functions. This example uses the max function to compute a value to assign the the variable VAL:

```
$ VAL=`max 9 1 8 3 5`
$ echo $VAL
9
```

Going Further with Shell Programming

The previous sections have given you a good introduction to shell programming. To go further, read the excellent bash manual and info pages. You should also examine shell scripts to see how they work. All the programs in /etc/rc.d/init.d are shell scripts; many of the ones in /usr/bin are too. To get a listing of shell scripts in /usr/bin, run this command:

```
$ file /usr/bin/* | grep Bourne
```

Other Bourne-shell derivatives like zsh and ksh are fairly similar to bash. The C shell family (tcsh and csh) have completely different programming syntax, but the concepts are similar. I did not show C shell scripts because there's no point in becoming confused by two sets of syntax. Also, the Bourne shell is available on every UNIX system, whereas some lack the C shell.

If you are interested in learning C shell programming, see the tcsh(1) manual page.

awk Scripting

awk is a language designed to process text files. It is a scanning and pattern-matching language. awk processes text files one line at a time and matches each line against patterns. If a match occurs, an action is taken. The power of awk lies in creating patterns and actions to do exactly the manipulation you need.

The awk language is interpreted by the awk program (on Linux systems, by the gawk program.) I will distinguish between the language and the UNIX command by writing awk for the language and awk for the command.

An awk program consists of a sequence of pattern-action statements:

pattern { action }

awk operates as follows:

- It reads lines from all filenames passed as arguments (or from standard input if no filename arguments were supplied).
- Each time it reads a line, it scans all the patterns. Any pattern that matches cause its associated action to be executed. If more than one pattern matches, the actions are executed in the order in which they appear in the awk program.

awk Patterns

An awk pattern can take one of the following forms:

- BEGIN—Actions associated with BEGIN are executed before any lines are read.
- END—Actions associated with END are executed after all lines have been read.
- /*regexp*/—If the line matches the regular expression *regexp*, the action is executed. (Regular expressions are described in Appendix A in the "Regular Expressions" section.)
- *pattern1* && *pattern2*—Matches if both *pattern1* and *pattern2* match.
- *pattern1* || *pattern2*—Matches if either *pattern1* or *pattern2* matches.

- *pattern1, pattern2*—This is a *range* pattern. Matches all lines starting from the first line that matches *pattern1* and ending with the first line that matches *pattern2*, inclusive.
- *expression*—Matches all lines for which *expression* evaluates to nonzero.

Other forms of patterns exist (see the awk(1) main page), but those shown previously are the most common.

Records and Fields

As each line (called a *record*) is read, awk splits it into fields. Normally, awk splits the line based on whitespace characters. For example, the line *This is a line* would be split into four fields, each corresponding to one of the words. However, you can change the strategy awk uses to split records with the -F command-line option to awk. (I will cover this in more detail when I describe how to invoke awk.)

Each time awk splits a record, it sets certain internal variables. The variable NF is set to the number of fields in the record. The special notation $n (where *n* is an integer) refers to the *n*th field, starting with 1. The notation $0 refers to the entire record.

Invoking awk

The following example is a very simple awk program:

```
$ awk '{print NF ": " $0}' < /etc/issue
0:
2: Caldera OpenLinux(TM)
2: Version 2.3
5: Copyright 1996-1999 Caldera Systems, Inc.
0:
0:
```

The entire program is given on the command line (enclosed in single-quotes to prevent the shell from trying to do variable interpolation).

The program has no pattern part, only an action. In this case, the action is executed for every line read.

The action consists of a single print statement, which (for each input line) prints the number of fields, followed by a colon, followed by the line itself. The program reads from standard input, which I have redirected from the file /etc/issue. As you see, awk splits lines at whitespace characters. Blank lines are considered to have zero fields.

awk programs can get very long and complicated. You certainly don't want to type them on the command line each time. You can place your awk program in a text file and invoke awk with the -f option. It reads its script from the file.

Let's look at a larger awk script. Create a file called vowel.awk with the following contents:

```
#!/usr/bin/awk -f

# Initialize counters
BEGIN {
    na = 0;
    ne = 0;
    ni = 0;
    no = 0;
    nu = 0;
    total = 0;
}

# Count vowels
/[Aa]/ { na = na + 1; }
/[Ee]/ { ne = ne + 1; }
/[Ii]/ { ni = ni + 1; }
/[Oo]/ { no = no + 1; }
/[Uu]/ { nu = nu + 1; }

# Add to total
{ total = total + 1; }

# Summarize results
END {
    print "Out of", total, "lines:"
    print na, "contained the letter 'A'"
    print ne, "contained the letter 'E'"
    print ni, "contained the letter 'I'"
    print no, "contained the letter 'O'"
    print nu, "contained the letter 'U'"
}
```

Note that awk treats lines beginning with # as comments and ignores them. (Most UNIX script interpreters do this; it makes handling the "hash-bang" notation easier.)

Run the following example (it might take a few seconds):

```
$ awk -f vowel.awk < /usr/dict/words
Out of 45402 lines:
23405 contained the letter 'A'
30253 contained the letter 'E'
23873 contained the letter 'I'
17776 contained the letter 'O'
10892 contained the letter 'U'
```

Note the hash-bang line `#!/usr/bin/awk -f`. This lets you run the script as an executable:

```
$ chmod a+x ./vowel.awk
$ ./vowel.awk < /usr/dict/words
Out of 45402 lines:
...
```

Changing the Field Separator

You can change the field separator with the `-F` option. Suppose you want to print the full name field from `/etc/passwd`. This is the fifth field in the file, but fields are delimited with colons. The following awk command will do the trick:

```
$ awk -F: '{ print $5 }' /etc/passwd
```

Assigning Variable Values

You can assign variable values on the command line with the `-v` option. This awk command prints the first field in `/etc/passwd`:

```
$ awk -F: -v COL=1 '{ print $COL }' /etc/passwd
```

whereas this example prints the sixth field:

```
$ awk -F: -v COL=6 '{ print $COL }' /etc/passwd
```

Note that the script is unchanged. The only thing that changed was the assignment to COL. Clearly, for such a small example, there is little benefit to using variable assignment, but for larger awk programs, it might be convenient to assign variables on the command line to tune their behavior.

Built-in awk Variables

awk contains a number of built-in variables that control how it behaves or supplies information to your scripts. Some of the variables are shown in Table 30.2: Consult awk(1) for details about all the built-in variables.

TABLE 30.2 awk Built-in Variables

Variable	Meaning
ARGC	The number of filenames given as command-line arguments.
ARGV	Array of command-line filename arguments indexed from 0 to ARGC-1.
ARGIND	The index into ARGV of the file currently being processed.
FILENAME	The name of the currently processing file. Set to - for standard input and undefined inside a BEGIN block.
FNR	The record number in the current input file. Records usually correspond to lines and are numbered starting from 1. FNR is re-set to 1 when a new file is read.
FS	The input field separator (by default, a space.) If set to a single character, that character is the field separator. If set to a multicharacter string, the string is interpreted as a regular expression and any character that matches the regular expression is treated as a field separator.
NF	The number of fields in the current record.
NR	The total number of records read so far. NR is not re-set when a new file is read.
OFS	The output field separator, a space by default. This string is printed between comma separated arguments of a print command.
ORS	The output record separator, a newline by default. This is printed after every print command.
RS	The input record separator (by default, a newline.) If set to a single character, that character is the record separator. If set to a multicharacter string, the string is interpreted as a regular expression and any character that matches the regular expression is treated as a record separator. If RS is the null string, blank lines separate records.

Arrays

In addition to the simple variables in the previous examples, awk supports array variables. An array is a whole collection of values. A particular value is accessed by its index. In many programming languages, an array index must be an integer. awk, however, supports associative arrays that allow their indexes to be any string.

Let's look at an example. The following script uses a lot of awk constructs I haven't covered yet, but it is a good example of how to use an array. I'll explain each part in detail. Create a file called countwords.awk containing the following:

```
{
    for(i=1; i<=NF; i++) {
        words[$i]++;
    }
}

END {
    for (word in words) {
        printf("%s occurred %d time(s)\n", word, words[word]);
    }
}
```

There is one action, the `for` action. The `for` command is a looping construct similar to C's `for` loop. It works like this:

1. First, the variable `i` is set to 1.
2. Next, `i` is compared to `NF`. If `i` is less than or equal to `NF`, the body of the loop is executed.
3. After the loop body executes, the variable `i` is incremented. (The funny notation VAR++ adds one to VAR.)
4. Go to step 2.

The body of the loop is interesting. The statement `words[$i]++` increments an array variable. The name of the array is `words`; the index is the value of the ith field. Thus, the whole `for` loop goes through each field on the line, incrementing the array element with the field for an index.

Note that I did not initialize the `words` array. If a nonexistent array element is referenced in an expression as I did previously, awk automatically creates the element with an initial value of zero. This is handy because it saves having to test whether the variable exists before manipulating it.

When all the input has been read, the second `for` loop executes. This second loop has a different form:

```
for (VAR in ARRAY) BODY
```

This second form of `for` assigns the variable successive array indexes from the array. Each time it does the assignment, it executes the loop body. In the example, it iterates over all the indexes in `words` and prints each word along with how many times it appeared in the input.

The `printf` statement is similar to C's formatted output statement. It prints its first argument but makes certain substitutions called percent substitution. In this example, printf substitutes the value of `word` as a string for the `%s` and the value of `words[word]` as a decimal number for the `%d`. The final `\n` is converted to a newline character.

Test the script by typing the following:

```
$ awk -f countwords.awk
I like awk and awk likes me
Do I like awk?
^D
awk? occurred 1 time(s)
me occurred 1 time(s)
likes occurred 1 time(s)
and occurred 1 time(s)
I occurred 2 time(s)
awk occurred 2 time(s)
Do occurred 1 time(s)
like occurred 2 time(s)
```

In the previous example, the notation ^D means to enter **Control+D**, your terminal's end-of-file character.

As you see, awk counts the words you enter. Note that it treats awk and awk? as different words. Also note that the words come out in an unpredictable order—the second for loop iterates over the array in an unspecified order. This is because of the low-level implementation details of associative arrays.

awk Expressions

Many awk statements use expressions to control their behavior. For example, the first form of the for statement uses three expressions to control the looping.

An awk expression is similar to a C expression. It consists of a sequence of values and operators. The awk operators in order of decreasing precedence are given in Table 30.3.

TABLE 30.3 awk Operators

Operator	Meaning
(...)	Grouping. Parentheses alter the normal precedence rules.
$	Field reference.
++ and -	Pre- and post-increment and decrement. The pre operators increment or decrement a variable and return the new value; the post operators increment or decrement a variable and return the old value.
^ or **	Exponentiation.
*, /, and %	Multiplication, division, and modulus.
+ and -	Addition and subtraction.
space	String concatenation.

Operator	Meaning
<, <=, > and >=	Relational operators.
== and !=	Comparison operators.
~ and !~	Regular expression match. For example, *expr* ~ *regexp* returns 1 if *regexp* matches *expr*; 0 otherwise.
in	Array membership. *expr* in *array* returns 1 if *array* has an element with index *expr*.
&&	Logical AND. True if both operands are nonzero.
||	Logical OR. True if either operand is nonzero.
?:	C conditional operator. The expression *expr1* ? *expr2* : *expr3* returns *expr2* if *expr1* is nonzero, and *expr3* otherwise. Only one of *expr2* or *expr3* is evaluated.
=	Assignment. The various operator assignments are supported for addition, subtraction, multiplication, division, modulus, and exponentiation. For example, var += val is equivalent to var = var + val, except that var is evaluated only once.

awk expressions might be used as patterns. The following command prints only those lines with one or more fields. It is a simple way to suppress blank lines in a file.

```
$ awk 'NF > 0 { print $0 }' input_file
```

Control Statements

Control statements are built-in awk statements that control program flow or input processing. We've already seen the for statement, which creates loops. The control statements are as follows:

- if (*expr*) *stmt1* [else *stmt2*]
- while (*expr*) statement
- do *statment* while (*expr*)
- for (*expr1*; *expr2*; *expr3*) statement
- for (*var* in *array*) statement
- break
- continue
- delete *array*[*index*]
- delete *array* (GNU gawk only.)

- `exit [expr]`
- `{ statements }` Curly braces introduce a compound statement, which is a grouping of many statements into one.

The `if` Statement

The statement `if (expr) stmt1 [else stmt2]` evaluates the expression *expr*. If it is nonzero, awk executes *stmt1*. Otherwise, if the `else` clause is present, awk executes *stmt2*. Here is an example:

```
{
    if (NF % 2) {
        print $0 ": Odd number of fields"
    } else {
        print $0 ": Even number of fields"
    }
}
```

For each input line, awk echoes the line and prints an indication of whether it contains an even or odd number of fields.

The `while` Statement

The statement `while (expr) statement` performs the following actions:

1. Evaluates *expr*. If the result is zero, it terminates the `while` statement.
2. Executes the loop body *statement*.
3. Goes to step 1.

The `do` Statement

The do statement is similar to the `while` statement, except that the loop body is always executed at least once. The do operation is as follows:

1. Executes the loop body *statement*.
2. Evaluates *expr*. If the result is zero, it terminates the do statement.
3. Otherwise, it goes to step 1.

The `for` Statement

You have already seen the `for` statement in action. Here is a formal description of how it works:

1. Evaluates *expr1* and discards the result.
2. Evaluates *expr2*. If the result is zero, it terminates the `for` loop.

3. Executes the loop body *statement*.
4. Evaluates `expr3` and discards the result.
5. Goes to step 2.

The `break` and `continue` Statements

Within a loop body, `break` causes an immediate termination of the loop. `continue` causes the loop to restart at the next iteration. For `while` loops, awk jumps to step 1 of the algorithm illustrated previously. For `do` loops, it jumps to step 2. For `for` loops, it jumps to step 4 (the evaluation of `expr2`.)

The `delete` Statement

The `delete` statement deletes the specified array element. A GNU extension allows you to delete all the elements of an array by supplying only the array name.

The `exit` Statement

The `exit` statement causes awk to stop processing any further input. If any END actions are present, they are executed. If `exit` appears inside an END block, it causes the program to stop immediately. If an expression is supplied after the keyword `exit`, awk uses that as the operating system exit value when it terminates.

I/O Statements

AWK has a number of statements for performing input and output. These are summarized in Table 30.4.

TABLE 30.4   awk I/O Statements

Statement	Meaning
`close(file)`	Closes a file or pipe.
`getline`	Gets the next input record and sets $0, NF, NR, and FNR.
`getline < file`	Reads the next record from the named file and sets $0 and NF.
`getline var`	Sets *var* to the next input record and sets NR and FNR.
`getline var < file`	Sets *var* to the next input record from the file `file`.
`next`	Stops processing the current record and starts with the next record.

continues

TABLE 30.4 continued

Statement	Meaning
nextfile	Stops processing the current file and moves to the next input file.
print	Prints the current record.
print expr, expr...	Prints the value of each expression. Each printed value is separated by the contents of the variable OFS and the entire list is terminated by ORS.
printf format, expressions	Formatted printing. See the awk(1) manual page for details.
system(cmd)	Executes the UNIX command cmd and returns the exit status.

Here is an example of some of the I/O statements. The following awk script places all odd-numbered input lines into a file called odd and even-numbered lines into a file called even.

```
{
    if (NR % 2) {
        print > "odd"
    } else {
        print > "even"
    }
}
END {
    close("odd")
    close("even")
}
```

This example illustrates how awk handles redirection. The first time an I/O redirection is encountered, the file is opened. Thereafter, if the same filename is encountered, the already opened stream is used to write to the open file.

The END block closes the files. This is not strictly necessary because awk is exiting anyway, but it's tidier to clean up after yourself.

Built-in Functions

awk has a large number of built-in functions that can be used in expressions. These include numeric, string, and time functions. These functions are documented in awk(1); I won't repeat that table here. Instead, I will present some examples as follows:

```
$ awk 'length($0) > 21' < /usr/dict/words
```

```
antidisestablishmentarianism
electroencephalography
```

The length function returns the length in characters of a string. The previous example prints all words in /usr/dict/words longer than 21 characters.

```
$ awk '{print cos(NR/20.0)}'
```

The previous example prints (for each input line) the cosine of the number of records divided by 20. I have no idea why you would want to do this, unless you are writing a book about awk and want to illustrate that it can handle floating-point arithmetic and transcendental math functions.

User-defined Functions

awk allows you to define your own functions. Consider the following awk script:

```
#!/usr/bin/awk -f
function factorial(n) {
    if (n <= 1) {
        return 1
    } else {
        return n * factorial(n-1)
    }
}

{ print $0 " factorial is " factorial($0) }
```

The function factorial is defined that takes a single parameter n. It computes the value of n factorial (the product of all numbers from 1 to *n*). This example illustrates that awk allows recursive function definitions.

A function can have any number of arguments. In a function declaration, separate the argument names with commas. If a function is called with fewer arguments than it has parameters, the remaining arguments default to the empty string. This trick is often used to create local variables—just add local variables to the argument list. When the function is called, the variables will be set to the empty string. Manipulating them will not affect any awk global variables.

To call a function, simply use the function name followed by a parenthesized list of awk expressions. Do not leave a space between the function name and the open parenthesis. When you call a function, arguments are usually passed by value. If the function modifies a particular argument, only its local copy is modified. The value in the function call is unaffected. However, if you pass an array to a function, the array is passed by reference and any changes the function makes to the argument are reflected in the original array. Consider the following script (put it in a file called array.awk):

```
function set(array, idx, value) {
    array[idx] = value
}
BEGIN {
   c[0] = 0
   c[1] = 1
   set(c, 0, "zero")
   printf("c[0] is %s; c[1] is %s\n", c[0], c[1])
}
```

Now test it:

```
$ awk -f array.awk < /dev/null
c[0] is zero; c[1] is 1
```

Note that the function changed c[0].

Going Further with awk

The second part of this chapter has given you an overview of awk's capabilities. awk is amazingly flexible and can perform many text manipulation tasks with ease. The awk(1) manual page is well written and the gawk info page is exceptionally good. See the "Sample Programs" section of the info page for a good look at what awk can accomplish.

Summary

In this chapter, you learned the basics of shell and awk programming. First, you learned about shell variables and their meanings. Next, you learned how to write shell scripts and use the shell's conditional and looping constructs.

You learned about special built-in shell variables and how they control operation of the shell or provide information to shell scripts. Finally, you learned how to write shell function—these combine a series of shell commands into one equivalent command.

In the awk section, you learned about awk's patterns and actions. You learned how awk splits its input into records and fields, and how to access fields from an awk script. You learned how to invoke awk to run an awk program. Next, you learned about awk variables and arrays.

After that, you learned about awk expressions and statements, which form the meat of awk scripts. You learned about built-in awk functions and learned how to write your own user-defined awk functions. Along the way, you saw a lot of examples of awk's power and flexibility.

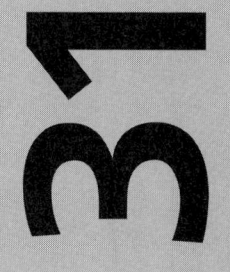

Configuring and Building the Kernel

CHAPTER 31

IN THIS CHAPTER

- Why Rebuild the Kernel? *736*
- Modules Versus Integrated Drivers *736*
- Building a Kernel *737*
- Configuring the Kernel *737*
- Compiling the Kernel *748*

One of the most exciting aspects of Linux is that you can customize the kernel—the core of the operating system. Linux includes full source code, so you can rebuild the kernel from source.

In this chapter, I will cover the reasons why you might want to rebuild the kernel and the steps you must take to build it. You should have good knowledge of your system's hardware before you rebuild a kernel—many of the questions you must answer are hardware-related.

By the end of the chapter, you will be able to build a custom kernel tuned to your hardware and your specific requirements. This can save memory and improve performance and security.

Why Rebuild the Kernel?

In the early days of Linux, it was considered part of the installation procedure to rebuild the kernel. This is because device drivers were linked directly into the kernel. As a result, if you got a new piece of hardware, you had to make a whole new kernel.

Modern versions of Linux support kernel modules, which enable you to load and unload device drivers (and other pieces of the kernel) on-the-fly. Although the Linux kernel is still monolithic—all parts of the kernel run in the same virtual address space—the ability to load and unload modules has all but eliminated the need to compile a new kernel.

However, there are still some reasons to rebuild a kernel:

- If you have a machine with very limited memory, you can save memory by omitting parts of the kernel you do not need.
- For a firewall or other sensitive machine, you might want to compile a kernel without kernel module support. This closes one potential avenue of attack.
- The standard kernel included with your distribution might not include a feature you need. For example, the standard Caldera OpenLinux kernel does not include IP firewalling.
- You might want to write device drivers or use experimental drivers. Or, you might want to apply a security bug-fix to the kernel code without upgrading the kernel.

Modules Versus Integrated Drivers

Nearly all device drivers can be either built-in to the kernel or compiled as loadable modules. Here are some reasons for making drivers loadable modules:

- Drivers can be unloaded when they are not in use, saving memory.
- You can create a standard kernel that can be used on a wide variety of hardware. This is the approach taken by most distributions—they supply a generic kernel and a huge selection of device driver modules.

- If you are writing a device driver, you can unload the driver, modify it, and reload it without rebooting the machine.
- If a bug or security problem is found with a driver, you can change the driver module without rebooting the machine.

On the other hand, there are some reasons for compiling drivers into the kernel:

- Some drivers require large amounts of memory. They might fail when loaded as modules if memory is fragmented. Some drivers might need huge amounts of physically contiguous memory. Current Linux kernels can satisfy this need only at boot time.
- Unless you use an initial RAM disk, the device driver for the device holding the root file system must be compiled directly into the kernel.
- Drivers that are always in use consume less memory when compiled directly into the kernel than when loaded as modules. There is some overhead associated with the machinery to load and unload modules, which can be avoided by compiling drivers into the kernel.
- As mentioned earlier, you might want to disable loadable modules in security-sensitive situations.

Building a Kernel

The Linux kernel sources are located in /usr/src/linux (if you have installed the linux-source-common and linux-source-i386 packages).

To build the kernel, follow these steps:

1. Configure the kernel—This involves answering many configuration questions; I will cover the process in detail in the next section.
2. Compile the kernel—This involves a couple simple UNIX commands.
3. Install the kernel—This consists of copying the compiled kernel to its final location and informing the boot loader how to load it.

Configuring the Kernel

The Linux kernel has a huge number of configuration options. These options control which software is included with the kernel and some aspects of the kernel's behavior.

The configuration options are broken into a number of categories. These categories are

- Code maturity level options—This is actually one option, which simply controls whether or not other options prompt you for experimental or incomplete code and drivers.

- Processor type and features—These options enable you to specify the processor family and any special processor attributes.
- Loadable module support—Whether or not you want loadable module support and some details of how the support works.
- General setup—General options such as whether you want network support, PCI support, and so on.
- Plug and Play support—Whether or not you want the kernel to support ISA Plug and Play devices.
- Block devices—Which block devices should be supported, such as IDE hard drives, PC floppy drives, RAM disks, parallel-port IDE disks, and so on.
- Networking options—Various options related to networking, such as whether to enable firewalling and support for non-IP protocols, such as IPX and AppleTalk DDP.
- QoS and/or fair queuing—Linux includes code for Quality of Service IP networking, which enables you to allocate bandwidth to users based (for example) on how much they pay you. The code is experimental.
- SCSI support—Whether you want SCSI support and some aspects of the SCSI drivers' behavior.
- SCSI low-level drivers—Which SCSI cards to support.
- Network device support—Which network cards to support.
- Amateur radio support—Whether you want support for amateur packet radio modems.
- IrDA subsystem support—Whether you want support for IrDA (infrared) ports. This code is experimental.
- Infrared-port device drivers—Low-level infrared port drivers. This code is experimental.
- ISDN subsystem—Whether you want ISDN support. Note that this is only required for special ISDN adapter cards. If you have an ISDN modem that connects to a serial port, you do not need special ISDN support—the normal networking and serial support works.
- Old CD-ROM drivers—Drivers for old and proprietary CD-ROMs such as old SoundBlaster and Mitsumi CDs.
- Character devices—Character device drivers such as virtual consoles, serial support, multiport serial adapters, parallel printer support, PS/2 mice, and so on.
- Mice—Support for specific nonserial mice such as bus mice, PS/2 mice, and other esoteric pointing hardware.
- Watchdog cards—Support for hardware watchdogs. These reset the computer if it appears to be dead or if cooling fans appear to have seized up. This code is experimental.

- Video for Linux—Support for a number of video capture and overlay cards and FM tuners.
- Joystick support—Support for a number of game controllers.
- Ftape—Support for cheap tape drives that connect to the floppy drive controller.
- Filesystems—Support for various kinds of local file systems.
- Network file systems—Support for various kinds of network file systems, including NFS and Microsoft's SMB.
- Partition types—Support for various partition labeling schemes. Use this only if you dual-boot with an operating system mentioned in the Partition Types dialog.
- Native language support—Support for various languages in the manner used by Microsoft file systems.
- Console drivers—Support for various kinds of console drivers. On an Intel-compatible machine, you usually need only the standard VGA text mode console. Other architectures have more elaborate console drivers.
- Sound—Support for various sound cards.
- Additional low-level sound drivers—Yet more sound configuration questions.
- Universal Serial Bus (USB) —Support for USB ports.
- Kernel hacking—Magic hacks to the kernel that enable you to regain some control over your system even if it crashes during kernel debugging. Details are found in /usr/src/linux/Documentation/sysrq.txt.

As you can see, the kernel is highly configurable with a vast array of options. I'll cover the highlights and important options here, but I will not cover everything. In particular, I will not cover experimental options or all the hardware possibilities. All the options have Help documentation, so it is pointless to repeat it here. In addition, I do not have access to all kinds of hardware and cannot verify the behavior of all the hardware options.

To build a new kernel, you must install the linux-source-common, linux-source-i386, linux-kernel-include, and linux-kernel-doc RPMs. If you did a full installation of Caldera OpenLinux, these RPMs have been installed. Otherwise, go ahead and install them now.

All the examples in this chapter are based on the 2.2.5 kernel included with Caldera OpenLinux 2.2. Newer kernels might have slightly different (or a few additional) options.

The simplest way to configure the kernel is to log in as root with X running. Change directories to /usr/src/linux and type

```
# make xconfig
```

After a while, the dialog in Figure 31.1 appears.

FIGURE 31.1
The Kernel Configuration dialog.

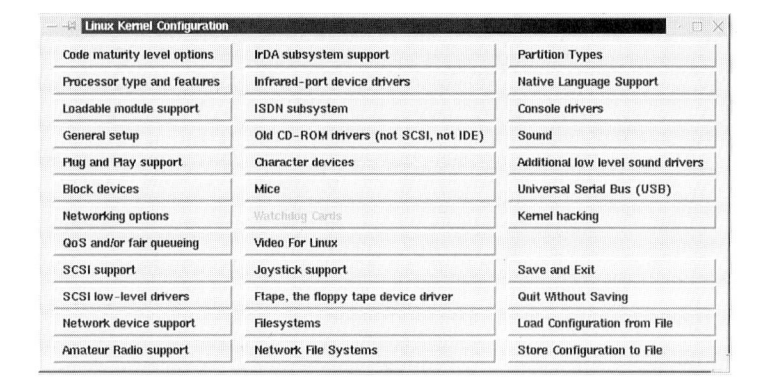

As you see, all the kernel configuration categories are presented. I recommend that you start with the code maturity level options and step through them (by pressing Next on each category's dialog) one at a time.

Each category consists of a number of questions. Most questions have simple yes or no answers. Some require selection of one of a set of choices and others require entries to be filled in. Many device drivers allow three answers: yes (Y), meaning link the driver into the kernel; module (M), meaning compile the driver as a module; and no (N), meaning do not compile the driver at all.

Figure 31.2 shows a dialog for a sample category. Note that most questions have Y, M, and N answers, whereas some have only Y and N. Note also that every question has a Help button. Answering that button (usually) brings up a small help file for the question. I will refer to these help files many times in this chapter.

FIGURE 31.2
A sample configuration category dialog.

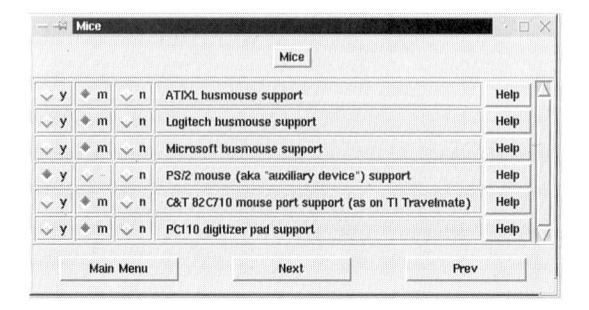

If you are not running X, you can use one of these commands:

```
# make menuconfig
# make config
```

`menuconfig` gives you a character-based menu configuration interface, whereas `config` gives you dumb-terminal questions to which you must type the answers. For the purposes of illustration, I will show `make xconfig` dialogs. However, the questions and answers are the same for any of the configuration methods.

Let's examine the nonexperimental configuration categories.

Code Maturity Level Options

This category has one question: Do you want to be prompted for development or incomplete code? If you want to live on the edge, answer Y. Otherwise, answer N.

Processor Types and Features

There are several questions here related to your processor.

- Processor family—If you answer 386 here, the kernel will work on all Intel-compatible processors. You can specify other options—such as 486, Pentium, or PPro—for kernels that are optimized for specific processors but that might not work on earlier models.

- Math emulation—If you answer Y here, the kernel will include code for emulating a math coprocessor. This might be required for some ancient 386 and 486SX machines. It's usually safe to answer Y.

- MTRR support—Provides access to registers on Intel Pentium Pro and Pentium II processors. You should answer Y here; for more information, see `/usr/src/linux/Documentation/mtrr.txt`.

- Symmetric multiprocessing support—Answer Y if your computer has more than one processor. Otherwise, answer N.

Loadable Module Support

This dialog controls kernel support for loadable modules. The questions are

- Enable loadable module support—Answer Y to enable loadable module support. This should normally be enabled.

- Set version information on all symbols for modules—If you answer Y here, it becomes possible to safely use modules compiled for a different version of the kernel. If you answer Y here, you need the program `/sbin/genksyms`, which is part of the `modutils` RPM.

- Kernel module loader—If you answer Y here, the kernel can automatically load modules when they are needed. See `/usr/src/linux/Documentation/kmod.txt` for details.

General Setup

This category includes all options that didn't fit in any other category. Some of the more important questions are

- Networking support—Always answer Y even if you don't think you need networking support. Even on a standalone machine, X Window (for example) relies on networking support.
- PCI support—Answer Y if you intend to run the kernel on a machine with a PCI bus (practically all modern PCs).
- System V IPC—Answer Y to this to this option. System V IPC is a set of routines for interprocess communication used by many UNIX programs.

For details of the other questions, read their Help files.

Plug and Play Support

This category contains two questions:

- Plug and Play support—If you answer Y, the kernel will configure some plug-and-play devices. If you answer N, you can still use the user-level ISA Plug and Play tools package from the `isapnptools` RPM.
- Auto-probe for parallel devices—Answering Y or M here allows the kernel to automatically identify some parallel port devices.

Block Devices

This category enables you to choose which block devices your kernel will support. The main questions are

- Normal PC floppy disk support—Answer Y or M if you want to access your floppy drive from Linux.
- Enhanced IDE support—Answer Y if you have an EIDE disk, ATAPI CD-ROM, or ATAPI tape drive. You can answer M if your root partition is not on an EIDE disk, but you have (for example) an ATAPI CD-ROM.
- SCSI emulation support—Some types of hardware (notably CD burners) come with both SCSI and ATAPI versions. In some cases, a Linux driver exists for the SCSI version, but not for the ATAPI version. This option enables you to use the SCSI driver with the ATAPI device.

- Loopback device support— Answering Y or M enables the loopback block device. This enables you to use a regular file as a block device. This is useful (for example) for checking the integrity of CD-ROM file system images before burning them. In addition, the loopback device supports encryption, which enables you to create encrypted file systems.

- Multiple devices driver support—Answering Y here enables questions related to RAID. Linux's RAID support enables you to create file systems that span more than one physical disk partition or combine redundant disk drives into a fault-tolerant virtual disk drive.

- RAM disk support—Answering Y or M here enables you to use portions of RAM as a block device.

- Initial RAM disk support—If you said Y to RAM disk support, you can answer Y here to support a root file system on a RAM disk. This enables you to create completely generic kernels that boot up, detect hardware, and load appropriate modules and then continue with the boot process. See `/usr/src/linux/Documentation/initrd.txt` for details.

Networking Options

This category controls the networking features of the Linux kernel. Important questions are

- Network firewalls—Answer Y if you want to use your Linux machine as a firewall. You also have to answer Y to IP: firewalling if you want to firewall IP packets, which you almost certainly do.

- TCP/IP networking—Answer Y if you want support for TCP/IP networking, which you almost certainly do.

- UNIX domain sockets—Answer Y here. Many UNIX programs use this kind of interprocess communication.

- IP: multicasting—Answer Y if you want to support IP multicasting. Unless you want to access multicast information such as audio or video broadcasts, it is safe to answer N.

- IP: always defragment—Answer Y here if you want the kernel to defragment IP packets before firewalling or forwarding them. You should always answer Y to this question for a firewall machine; several attacks based on generating tiny fragments have been reported. Answering Y might add some processing overhead on the firewall machine.

- IP: masquerading—Answer Y if you want support for masquerading. This makes an entire network behind a firewall appear as one IP address to the outside world. The firewall machine masquerades the internal addresses when forwarding packets to the outside world and demasquerades incoming packets.

- IP: aliasing support—If you answer Y here, you will be able to assign more than one IP address to a physical network interface. This can be useful for virtual Web hosting, for example.
- The IPv6 protocol—Answering Y enables the (experimental) IPv6 code. IPv6 is the next-generation Internet protocol.
- The IPX protocol—Answer Y or M to enable support for Novell's IPX protocol.
- Appletalk DDP—Answer Y or M if you want to connect Apple Macintosh clients to a Linux print and file server.

SCSI Support

This category contains general questions related to SCSI support. The questions include:

- SCSI support—Answer Y or M here if you want SCSI support. If you answer N, no SCSI support at all will be included.
- SCSI disk support—Answer Y or M to support SCSI disk drives.
- SCSI tape support—Answer Y or M to support SCSI tape drives.
- SCSI CD-ROM support—Answer Y or M to support SCSI CD-ROM drives.
- SCSI generic support—Answer Y or M to support generic SCSI devices. You'll need this if you have SCSI scanners or other nonstorage SCSI devices.
- Probe all LUNs on each SCSI device—Answer Y if you have a CD jukebox with more than one logical unit number per device.
- Verbose SCSI error reporting—Answer Y if you want more readable SCSI error messages (at the cost of 12KB of memory).

SCSI Low-Level Drivers

This category contains many questions related to specific SCSI hardware. Locate the entries for your SCSI cards and answer Y or M. Some SCSI cards have special features that you can configure from this dialog.

Network Device Support

This category contains an exhaustive (and exhausting) list of network cards supported by Linux. Locate your cards and choose Y or M. One important question is Ethernet (10Mbit or 100Mbit). Answer Y to this question if you want any kind of Ethernet support at all.

Amateur Radio Support

This category contains questions related to amateur radio networking hardware. If you have such hardware, you will know how to answer the questions. Because I do not have any amateur radio hardware, I cannot provide guidance for this category.

IrDA Subsystem Support

If you have an IrDA port (many laptop computers do), you can enable IrDA support. Read the Help files for each question. In particular, note that you need some user-level tools such as irmanager and irattach, which are not included with Caldera OpenLinux. See `/usr/src/linux/Documentation/networking/irda.txt` for details.

Infrared Port Device Drivers

This category lists drivers for specific infrared port hardware. Choose your hardware from the list and answer Y or M.

ISDN Subsystem

This category contains questions related to the ISDN networking subsystem. This is used for special ISDN hardware used mostly in Europe. If you have an ISDN adapter that connects to the serial port, you can ignore this section and use PPP over a normal serial device.

Old CD-ROM Drivers

This section contains questions about old proprietary CD-ROM drives. If you have an old CD-ROM that is not SCSI or ATAPI, select it from the list. It is safe to compile all the drivers as modules and try them all at runtime.

Character Devices

This section contains questions about character devices. Some of the more important questions are

- Virtual terminal—Answer Y if you want virtual consoles. Unless you are building a kernel for an embedded system, you must answer Y here.
- Support for console on virtual terminal—Answer Y here unless you want a headless Linux machine whose console is a serial port.
- Support for console on serial port—Answer Y if you want console messages to be sent to a serial port.
- Standard/generic (dumb) serial support—Answer Y or M to include support for standard PC serial hardware. If you want a serial console, you must answer Y (not M) here.
- Extended dumb serial driver options—Answering Y enables questions about more advanced serial port behavior, such as shared interrupts and support for certain special serial boards.
- Non-standard serial port support—Answer Y here if you want to enable support for some intelligent multiport serial hardware. For example, if you are using your

Linux machine as a dial-in server with a special 32-port serial board, answer Y here.

- Parallel printer support—Answer Y or M if you intend to connect a parallel printer to your Linux machine.
- Mouse support (not serial mice)—Answer Y if you have a bus mouse or PS/2 mouse.

Mice

This category enables you to select options for nonserial mice. The vast majority of such mice are PS/2 mice; answer Y to the PS/2 question. The remaining questions in this category deal with much less common hardware.

Video for Linux

If you have a video overlay card, choose the hardware support from this list. You'll also need user-level tools; see the Help file for the Video for Linux question for details.

Joystick Support

If you have a game controller, select your hardware from the list and choose Y or M.

Ftape

This category includes configuration information for tape drives which attach to the floppy disk controller. If you have such a tape drive, answer Y or M to Ftape support and Zftape, the VFS interface. See also /usr/src/linux/Documentation/ftape.txt.

File Systems

This important category specifies which local file systems your kernel will support. Here are the main questions:

- Quota support—If you answer Y, you will be able to set a per-user limit on disk space usage. This requires additional software that is not included with Caldera OpenLinux. See the Help file for the question for details.
- Kernel automounter support—Answer Y or M if you want support for the kernel-mode automounter. This tool can automatically mount file systems on demand. Read the Help file for the question for more details. Most users do not need the automounter.
- DOS FAT fs support—Answer Y or M if you want to mount MS-DOS FAT filesystems. You should answer Y or M to MS-DOS fs support and VFAT fs support also. This enables you to mount Windows partitions from Linux.
- ISO 9660 CD-ROM filesystem support—Answer Y or M if you want to mount CD-ROM file systems.

- Microsoft Joliet CD-ROM extensions—Answer Y if you want to read Joliet CD-ROMs under Linux.
- NTFS filesystem support—Answer Y or M if you want read-only access to an NTFS partition. NTFS is the file system used by Windows NT.
- /proc filesystem support—Answer Y here or lots of programs will break.
- Second extended fs support—Answer Y here. This is Linux's native file system.

There is support for many other file systems, including the OS/2 HPFS, BSD UFS, Amiga FFS, and Apple Macintosh file system. Select the ones you need.

Network File Systems

Linux can act as a client for a number of network file systems. The important questions in this category are

- Coda filesystem support—Coda is an advanced network filesystem with many useful advantages over NFS. You need additional user-level tools to use Coda; see the Help file for details.
- NFS filesystem support—NFS is the standard Linux network file system; answer Y or M here if you plan to use it.
- Root file system on NFS—Answer Y if you want to set up a diskless workstation that mounts its root directory via NFS. You need to answer Y (not M) to NFS filesystem support.
- SMB filesystem support—Answer Y or M if you want to mount file systems served from a Windows NT or Windows 95/98 machine.
- NCP filesystem support—Answer Y or M to mount Novell NetWare volumes.

Partition Types

This category includes support for different ways of representing disk partition tables. For the vast majority of Linux installations that are on Intel PC's, you should answer N to all the questions. If you are dual-booting Linux and FreeBSD, answer Y to BSD disk table support. See the Help files for details about the other questions.

Native Language Support

Microsoft Windows uses *code pages* to store support for international languages. Unless kernel compilation time is an issue, it's safe to answer M for every question in this category.

Console Drivers

If you are running on standard PC hardware, answer Y to VGA text console and video mode selection support.

Support for frame buffer devices is experimental; this code allows kernel-level control over various graphics cards, with a uniform API for user-level programs. It is not required on standard PC hardware, but might be needed for some architectures.

Sound

Sound configuration used to be extremely painful, but now it's only moderately so. Most sound card drivers can be compiled as modules. Choose M for all the questions (or for your particular hardware). Also, you should read the Sound HOWTO and the files in /usr/src/linux/Documentation/sound as well as Chapter 29, "Setting Up Sound and Multimedia," in this book.

Universal Serial Bus

If you have USB hardware, answer Y or M to these questions. I do not have any USB hardware, so I am unable to experiment with USB support. USB support is experimental, so you are offered this option only if you answered Y to include development/incomplete code in the code maturity level category.

Kernel Hacking

The only question in this category is Magic SysRq key. See the file /usr/src/linux/Documentation/sysrq.txt.

Compiling the Kernel

When you have configured the kernel, you should save the changes by clicking Save and Exit. This saves kernel configuration information in /usr/src/linux/.config. You can also save and restore configurations to and from other files with Store Configuration to File and Load Configuration from File.

To compile the kernel, change to the /usr/src/linux directory and follow these steps:

1. Make dependencies. This ensures that all code that needs to be recompiled is recompiled.
2. Compile the kernel.
3. Compile loadable modules.
4. Install loadable modules.
5. Install the kernel.

These steps are explained in detail in the following sections.

Make Dependencies

To be sure that everything that needs recompiling is compiled, you must build a list of dependencies for the source tree. Do this by typing

`# make dep`

Build the Kernel

To build the kernel, type

`# make bzImage`

You might want to redirect output to a file, like this:

`# make bzImage >& make.log`

> **Background Material**
>
> You can try `make zImage`, but it is useful for small kernel images. If your kernel is too big, use `make bzImage`.

Build Modules

If you answered M to any questions, you need to build all kernel modules. To do this, type

`# make modules`

As before, you might want to redirect output to a file, like this

`# make modules >& make.log.modules`

Install Modules

To install modules, type

`# make modules_install`

This installs modules in `/lib/modules/x.y.z`, where `x.y.z` is the kernel version.

Install the Kernel

The compiled kernel will be in `/usr/src/linux/arch/i386/boot/bzImage` (or `...zImage` if you used `make zImage`).

To install the kernel, copy this file to `/boot`. Do not overwrite your existing kernel (which is likely called `/boot/vmlinuz-2.2.5-modular` or something similar). Keep the original kernel around in case the new one will not boot. Copy the kernel to a new file such as `/boot/vmlinuz-2.2.5-rebuilt`.

Next, you have to install a boot loader that can load the new kernel. Edit the file `/etc/lilo.conf` to do this. The simplest method is to copy the entry for the existing kernel and give it a new label. For example, the `lilo` entry for the old kernel might look something like this:

```
image = /boot/vmlinuz-2.2.5-modular
        label = linux
        root = /dev/hda1
        vga = 274
        read-only
        append = "debug=2"
```

Copy the entry so you end up with two entries like this:

```
#
# default entry
#

image = /boot/vmlinuz-2.2.5-rebuilt
        label = linux
        root = /dev/hda1
        vga = 274
        read-only
        append = "debug=2"


#
# additional entries
#

image = /boot/vmlinuz-2.2.5-modular
        label = Origlinux
        root = /dev/hda1
        vga = 274
        read-only
        append = "debug=2"
```

> **Note**
>
> The `root` and `vga` entries are examples from my system. You should use whatever values the Caldera OpenLinux installation procedure put in your `/etc/lilo.conf` file.

Here, the new entry for `vmlinuz-2.2.5-rebuilt` has been given the label `linux` and the original entry has been moved after the new entry and relabeled `Origlinux`. At the `lilo` boot prompt, you can specify `Origlinux` to boot the original kernel if the new one won't boot.

Finally, to actually install the boot loader, type

`# /sbin/lilo`

Note that `lilo` and the `/etc/lilo.conf` file have many other options and settings; see `lilo(8)` and `lilo.conf(5)` for details.

Summary

In this chapter, you learned why it is desirable (or sometimes necessary) to compile a new kernel. You learned the differences between modules and integrated drivers.

Next, you learned how to configure a kernel and what the various kernel configuration categories are. Finally, you learned how to compile and install a new kernel and its associated kernel modules, and how to set up a boot loader for the new kernel using `lilo`.

Development Environment

PART V

IN THIS PART

32 Perl Programming *755*

33 Introduction to Tcl/Tk *781*

34 Introduction to Python *807*

35 Introduction to C and C++ *857*

36 Using GNU Development Tools *899*

CHAPTER 32

Perl Programming

IN THIS CHAPTER

- A Simple Perl Program   *756*
- Perl Variables and Data Structures   *758*
- Operators   *760*
- Conditional Statements: `if/else` and `unless`   *763*
- Looping   *765*
- Regular Expressions   *767*
- Access to the Shell   *768*
- Switches   *770*
- Modules and CPAN   *772*
- Code Examples   *774*
- Perl-Related Tools   *778*
- For More Information   *778*

Perl (Practical Extraction and Report Language) was developed in the mid 1980s by Larry Wall, who was already responsible for a number of rather important UNIX utilities. Larry claims that Perl really stands for "Pathologically Eclectic Rubbish Lister." With the birth of the World Wide Web in the early 1990s, Perl took off as the language of choice for CGI programming. With the recent burst of interest in the Open Source movement, Perl has gotten almost as much press as Linux.

Perl, according to Larry, is all about "making easy things easy, and hard things possible." So many programming languages make you spend an undue amount of time doing stuff to keep the language happy before you ever get around to making it do what you want it to do. Perl lets you get your work done without worrying about things like memory allocation and variable typing.

Perl contains the best features of C, Basic, and a variety of other programming languages, with a hearty dollop of awk, sed, and shell scripting thrown in. Perl has one advantage over the other UNIX tools—it can process binary files (those without line terminators or that contain binary data). sed and awk cannot do the job.

In Perl, "there is more than one way to do it." This is the unofficial motto of Perl, and it comes up so often that it is usually abbreviated as TIMTOWTDI. If you are familiar with some other programming language, chances are you can write functional Perl code.

A version of Perl comes with most Linux distributions, but it is typically several versions out of date. This makes sense when you consider the time required to produce and actually distribute a distribution. As of this writing, the current production version of Perl is 5.005_03 (which is Perl version 5 point 5, patch level 3). Version 5.005_61 is available as a developer release (generally considered experimental). You can determine what version of Perl you have installed by typing `perl -v` at a shell prompt.

This chapter focuses on version 5. Many of the examples shown will fail if you try them with version 4 of Perl. If you have version 4, you should get one of the newer versions. If you are installing a recent Linux distribution, you should have version 5.

Perl is an interpreted language. The interpreter has been ported to just about every operating system known. For UNIX and UNIX-like (Linux, for example) operating systems, you can just download the code from http://www.perl.com/ and build it yourself.

A Simple Perl Program

To introduce you to the absolute basics of Perl programming, Listing 32.1 illustrates a trivial Perl program.

LISTING 32.1 A Trivial Perl Program

```
#!/usr/bin/perl
print "Look at all the camels!\n";
```

That is the whole program. Type that in, save it to a file called `trivial.pl`, and execute it.

```
$ perl trivial.pl
Look at all the camels!
```

The #! line is technically not part of the Perl code at all (the # character is the comment character in Perl), but is instead a message to the shell, telling it where it should go for the executable to run this program. That is standard practice in shell programming, as is discussed in Chapter 30, "Introduction to Shell and awk Programming."

> **Note**
>
> #! is often pronounced *she-bang*, which is short for *sharp* (the musical name for the # character) and *bang*, which is another name for the exclamation point.
>
> Another pronunciation is *pound-bang* because most people refer to the # character on a telephone keypad as *pound*.
>
> Yet another pronunciation is *hash-bang* (as seen in Chapter 30), which follows the technical word for the # character.

The second line does precisely what you would expect—it prints the text enclosed in quotation marks. \n is the escape sequence for a newline character.

If for some reason Perl is not located at /usr/bin/perl on your system, you can find the correct location of Perl by using the `which` command:

```
which perl
```

If you do not have Perl installed, you might want to skip to "For More Information" in this chapter to find out where you can obtain the Perl interpreter. Because a version of Perl comes with most Linux distributions, this should not be the case.

Perl statements are terminated with a semicolon. A Perl statement can extend over several actual screen lines. Alternatively, you can have Perl statements in one line. Perl is not particularly concerned about whitespace.

The # character is used as the comment character in Perl. That is, there is a comment from the # character until the next newline and it is ignored by the interpreter. Exceptions to this include when the # character is in a quoted string and when it is being used as the delimiter in a regular expression.

A block of code, such as what might appear inside a loop or a branch of a conditional statement, is indicated with curly braces ({ }).

Included with the Perl installation is a document called `perlfunc`, which lists all the available Perl functions and their usage. You can view this document by typing **perldoc perlfunc** at the command line. You can also find this document online at http://www.cpan.org/doc/manual/html/pod/perlfunc.html.

> **Tip**
>
> You can use the `perldoc` and `man` commands to get more information on the version of Perl installed on your system.
>
> To get information on the `perldoc` command, enter the following:
>
> ```
> perldoc perldoc
> ```
>
> To get introductory information on Perl, you have a choice of two different commands:
>
> ```
> perldoc perl
> man perl
> ```
>
> The documentation is extensive and is well organized to help you find what you need.

Perl Variables and Data Structures

Perl is a *weakly typed* language, meaning that it does not require that you specify what datatype will be stored in a particular variable. C, for example, makes you declare that a particular variable is an integer, a character, a pointer, or whatever the case may be. Perl variables are whatever type they need to be and can change type when you need them to.

Perl Variable Types

There are three variable types in Perl—scalars, arrays, and hashes. In an attempt to make each data type visually distinct, a different character is used to signify each variable type.

Scalar Variables

Scalar variables are indicated with the $ character, as in $penguin. Scalars can be numerical and can be strings, and they can change type from one to the other as needed. If you treat a number like a string, it's a string. If you treat a string like a number, it will be translated into a number if it makes sense to do so; otherwise, it will probably evaluate as

0. For example, the string `76trombones` will evaluate as the number 76 if used in a numerical calculation, but the string `polar bear` will evaluate to 0.

Arrays

Arrays are indicated with the `@` character, as in `@fish`. An *array* is a list of values that are referenced by index number, starting with the first element numbered 0, just like C and awk. Each element in the array is a scalar value. Because scalar values are indicated with the `$` character, a single element in an array is also indicated with a `$` character. For example, `$fish[2]` refers to the third element in the `@fish` array. This tends to throw some people off, but it is completely consistent.

Hashes

Hashes are indicated with the `%` character, as in `%employee`. A *hash*, which used to go by the cumbersome name *associative arrays*, is a list of key/value pairs. Individual elements in the hash are referenced by name, rather than by index. Again, because the values are scalars, the `$` character is used for individual elements. For example, `$employee{name}` gives you one value from the hash. Two rather useful functions for dealing with hashes are `keys` and `values`. The `keys` function returns an array containing all the keys of the hash, and `values` returns an array of the values of the hash. The code in Listing 32.2 displays all the values in your environment, much like typing the `env` command.

LISTING 32.2 Displaying the Contents of the env Hash

```
foreach $key (keys %ENV)   {
    print "$key = $ENV{$key}\n";
}
```

Special Variables

Perl has a wide variety of special variables. These usually look like punctuation—such as `$_`, `$!`, and `$]`—and are extremely useful for shorthand code. (`$_` is the default variable, `$!` is the error message returned by the operating system, and `$]` is the Perl version number.)

`$_` is perhaps the most useful of these, and we use it some more within this chapter. `$_` is the Perl default variable, which is used when no argument is specified. For example, the following two statements are equivalent:

```
chomp;
```

```
chomp($_);
```

The following loops are equivalent:

```
for $cow (@cattle) {
        print "$cow says moo.\n";
}
for (@cattle)      {
        print "$_ says moo.\n";
}
```

For a complete listing of these special variables, see the `perlvar` document that comes with your Perl distribution, or jump online at
http://www.cpan.org/doc/manual/html/pod/perlvar.html.

Operators

Perl supports a number of operators to perform various operations. Perl has comparison operators (used, as the name implies, to compare values), compound operators (used to combine operations or multiple comparisons), arithmetic operators (to perform math), and special string constants.

Comparison Operators

The comparison operators used by Perl are similar to those used by C, `awk`, and the various UNIX shells. Most frequently, a comparison operator is used within an `if` statement or loop.

Perl has two categories of comparison operators: relational operators (greater than, less than, and so on) and equality operators (equal, not equal). Both categories include operators for numbers and strings.

Table 32.1 shows the relational operators and their behavior.

TABLE 32.1 Relational Operators in Perl

Numeric	String	Meaning
>	gt	Greater than
>=	ge	Greater than or equal to
<	lt	Less than
<=	le	Less than or equal to

Table 32.2 shows the equality operators and their behaviors.

TABLE 32.2 Equality Operators in Perl

Numeric	String	Meaning
==	eq	Equal to
!=	ne	Not equal to
Û	cmp	Comparison, with signed result

The equal and not-equal operators return 1 for true, and " " for false (the same as relational operators do). The Û and cmp operators return -1 if the left operand is less than the right, 0 if they are equal, and +1 if the left operand is greater than the right.

Compound Operators

The compound operators used by Perl are similar to those used by C, awk, and the various UNIX shells. Compound operators are used to combine other operations into a complex form of logic.

Table 32.3 shows the compound pattern operators and their behavior.

TABLE 32.3 Compound Pattern Operators in Perl

Operator	Meaning
&&	Logical AND
||	Logical OR
!	Logical NOT
( )	Parentheses; used to group compound statements

Arithmetic Operators

Perl supports a wide variety of math operations. Table 32.4 summarizes these operators.

TABLE 32.4 Perl Arithmetic Operators

Operator	Purpose
x**y	Raises x to the y power (same as x^y)
x%y	Calculates the remainder of x/y
x+y	Adds x to y
x-y	Subtracts y from x

continues

TABLE 32.4 continued

Operator	Purpose
x*y	Multiplies x times y
x/y	Divides x by y
-y	Negates y (switches the sign of y); also known as the *unary minus*
++y	Increments y by 1 and uses value (prefix increment)
y++	Uses value of y and then increments by 1 (postfix increment)
--y	Decrements y by 1 and uses value (prefix decrement)
y--	Uses value of y and then decrements by 1 (postfix decrement)
x=y	Assigns value of y to x. Perl also supports operator-assignment operators (+=, -=, *=, /=, %=, **=, and others)

You can also use comparison operators (like == or <) and compound pattern operators (&&, ¦¦, and !) in arithmetic statements. They evaluate to the value 0 for false and 1 for true.

Other Operators

Perl supports a number of operators that do not fit any of the prior categories. Table 32.5 summarizes these operators.

TABLE 32.5 Other Perl Operators

Operator	Purpose
~x	Bitwise not (changes 0 bits to 1 and 1 bits to 0).
x & y	Bitwise and.
x ¦ y	Bitwise or.
x ^ y	Bitwise exclusive or (XOR).
x << y	Bitwise shift left (shift x by y bits).
x >> y	Bitwise shift right (shift x by y bits).
x . y	Concatenate y onto x.
a x b	Repeat string a for b number of times.
x , y	Comma operator—evaluate x and then y.
x ? y : z	Conditional expression—if x is true, then y is evaluated; otherwise, z is evaluated. Provides the capability of an if statement anywhere you want (in the middle of a print, for instance).

Except for the comma operator and conditional expression, these operators can also be used with the assignment operator (similar to the way addition [+] can be combined with assignment [=] giving +=).

Special String Constants

Perl supports string constants that have special meaning or cannot be entered from the keyboard.

Table 32.6 shows most of the constants supported by Perl.

TABLE 32.6 Perl Special String Constants

Expression	Meaning
\\	The means of including a backslash
\a	The alert or bell character
\b	Backspace
\c*C*	Control character (like holding the Control key down and pressing the C character)
\e	Escape
\f	Formfeed
\n	Newline
\r	Carriage return
\t	Tab
\v	Vertical tab
\x*NN*	Indicates that *NN* is a hexadecimal number
\0*NNN*	Indicates that *NNN* is an octal (base 8) number

Conditional Statements: `if/else` and `unless`

Perl offers two conditional statements, `if` and `unless`, which function opposite one another. `if` allows you to execute a block of code only if certain conditions are met, and so to control the flow of logic through your program. Conversely, `unless` performs the statements when certain conditions are not met.

if

The syntax of the Perl `if/else` structure is as follows:

```
if (condition) {
    statement or block of code
    }
elsif (condition) {
    statement or block of code
    }
else {
    statement( or block of code
    }
```

condition can be a statement that returns a true or false value.

> **Note**
>
> Truth is defined in Perl in a way that might be unfamiliar to you, so be careful. Everything in Perl is true except `0` (the digit zero), `"0"` (the string containing the number 0), `""` (the empty string), and an undefined value. Note that even the string `"00"` is a true value because it is not one of those four cases.

The *statement or block of code* is executed if the test condition returns a true value. For example, Listing 32.3 uses the `if/else` structure.

LISTING 32.3 if/elsif/else

```perl
if ($favorite eq "chocolate") {
    print "I like chocolate too.\n";
} elsif ($favorite eq "spinach") {
    print "Oh, I don't like spinach.\n";
} else {
    print "Your favorite food is $favorite.\n";
}
```

> **Note**
>
> Larry is a linguist, and so Perl contains a lot of idiomatic ways of saying things that correspond with spoken English. The `if` statement is one of the good examples. For example, you can say the following:

```perl
if ($name eq "Rich") {
  print "Hello, Rich!\n";
}
```

Alternatively, you can write it as you would more likely say it:

```perl
print "Hello Rich!\n" if $name eq "Rich";
```

Larry designed Perl as a natural language. In this respect, it is different from most other programming languages. The traditional computer science way of doing things is to have a minimal set of keywords from which all other concepts are built. Perl, on the other hand, provides you with more than one way to say the same thing (TIMTOWTDI) like a spoken language would.

Also like spoken language, Perl evolved as it was used. If people saw a need for a particular function or a new syntax, Larry included it in the next version. If nobody used a particular feature, or everyone hated a particular construct, Larry threw it out. As Larry put it, "I picked the feature set of Perl because I thought they were cool features. I left the other ones behind because I thought they sucked."

unless

`unless` works just like `if`, only backward. `unless` performs a statement or block if a condition is false.

```perl
unless ($name eq "Rich")      {
        print "Go away, you're not allowed in here!\n";
}
```

> **Note**
>
> You can restate the preceding example in more natural language, as you did in the `if` example.
>
> ```perl
> print "Go away!\n" unless $name eq "Rich";
> ```
>
> Although it is not a rule, you should try to put the more important part of the statement (think of it as a sentence) on the left, so that it is easier to read.

Looping

A *loop* is a way to do something multiple times. A very simple example is a countdown timer that performs a task (waiting for 1 second) 300 times before telling you that your egg is done boiling.

Looping constructs can either perform a block of code as long as certain conditions apply, or while they step through a list of values, perhaps using that list as arguments.

Perl has four looping constructs: `for`, `foreach`, `while`, and `until`.

for

The `for` construct performs a *statement* (block of code) for a set of conditions defined as follows:

```
for (start condition; end condition; increment function) {
    statement(s)
}
```

The start condition is set at the beginning of the loop. Each time the loop is executed, the increment function is performed until the end condition is achieved. This looks much like the traditional for/next loop. The following code is an example of a `for` loop:

```
for ($i=1; $i<=10; $i++) {
    print "$i\n"
}
```

foreach

The `foreach` construct performs a statement block for each element in a list or array:

```
foreach $name (@names) {
    print "$name\n"
}
```

The loop variable (`$name` in the example) is not merely set to the value of the array elements; it is aliased to that element. This means that if you modify the loop variable, you are actually modifying the array.

If no loop array is specified, as in the following example, the Perl default variable `$_` is used:

```
for (@names)       {
        print "$_ was here\n";
}
```

This syntax can be very convenient, but it can also lead to unreadable code. Give a thought to the poor person who will be maintaining your code. It will probably be you.

> **Note**
>
> `foreach` is frequently abbreviated as `for`.

while

`while` performs a block of statements as long as a particular condition is true:

```perl
while ($x<10) {
    print "$x\n";
    $x++;
}
```

Remember that the condition can be anything that returns a true or false value. For example, it could be a function call:

```perl
while ( InvalidPassword($user, $password) )    {
      print "You've entered an invalid password. Please try again.\n";
      $password = GetPassword;
}
```

until

`until` is the exact opposite of the `while` statement. It performs a block of statements as long as a particular condition is false—or, rather, until it becomes true:

```perl
until (ValidPassword($user, $password))  {
      print "You've entered an invalid password. Please try again.\n";
      $password = GetPassword;
}
```

last and next

You can force Perl to end a loop early by using the `last` statement. `last` is similar to the C `break` command—the loop is exited. If you decide you need to skip the remaining contents of a loop without ending the loop itself, you can use `next`, which is similar to the C `continue` command. Unfortunately, these do not work with `do...while` loops.

do...while and do...until

The `while` and `until` loops evaluate the conditional first. This behavior can be changed by applying a `do` block before the conditional. With the `do` block, the condition is evaluated last, which results in the contents of the block always executing at least once (even if the condition is false). This is similar to the C language `do...while (conditional)` statement.

Regular Expressions

Perl's greatest strength is in text and file manipulation, which are accomplished by using the regular expression (regex) library. Regexes allow complicated pattern matching and replacement to be done efficiently and easily.

For example, the following line of code replaces every occurrence of the string bob or the string mary with fred in a line of text:

$string =~ s/bob|mary/fred/gi;

Without going into too many of the details, Table 32.7 explains what the preceding line says.

TABLE 32.7 Explanation of $string =~ s/bob|mary/fred/gi;

Element	Explanation
$string =~	Performs this pattern match on the text found in the variable called $string.
s	Substitute.
/	Begins the text to be matched.
bob|mary	Matches the text bob or mary. You should remember that it is looking for the text mary, not the word mary; that is, it will also match the text mary in the word maryland.
/	Ends text to be matched; begins text to replace it.
fred	Replaces anything that was matched with the text fred.
/	Ends text to be replaced.
g	Does this substitution globally; that is, replaces the match text wherever in the string you match it (and any number of times).
i	The search text is case-insensitive. It matches bob, Bob, or bOB.
;	Indicates the end of the line of code.

If you are interested in the details, you can get more information using the regex (5) section of the manual.

Although replacing one string with another might seem a rather trivial task, the code required to do the same thing in another language (for example, C) is rather daunting.

Access to the Shell

Perl is useful for administrative functions because it has access to the shell. This means Perl can perform any process you might ordinarily perform by typing commands to the shell. You do this with the `` syntax. For example, the following code in Listing 32.4 prints a directory listing.

LISTING 32.4 Using Backticks to Access the Shell

```perl
$curr_dir = `pwd`;
@listing = `ls -la`;
print "Listing for $curr_dir\n";
foreach $file (@listing) {
    print "$file";
}
```

> **Note**
>
> The `` ` `` notation uses the backtick found above the Tab key (on most keyboards), not the single quotation mark.

You can also use the `Shell` module to access the shell. `Shell` is one of the standard modules that comes with Perl. It gives an even more transparent access to the shell. Look at the following code for an example:

```perl
use Shell qw(cp);
cp ("/home/httpd/logs/access.log", "/tmp/httpd.log");
```

It almost looks as though it is importing the command-line functions directly into Perl. Although that is not really happening, you can pretend that it is and use it accordingly.

A third method of accessing the shell is via the `system` function call:

```perl
$rc = 0xffff & system('cp /home/httpd/logs/access.log /tmp/httpd.log');
if ($rc == 0) {
        print "system cp succeeded \n";
}
else {
        print "system cp failed $rc";
}
```

The system function can also be used with the `or die` clause:

```perl
system('cp /home/httpd/logs/access.log /tmp/httpd.log') == 0
        or die "system cp failed: $?"
```

However, you cannot capture the output of a command executed through the `system` function.

Access to the command line is fairly common in shell scripting languages, but is less common in higher-level programming languages.

Switches

Perl has a variety of command-line options (*switches*) that subtly change Perl's behavior. These switches can appear on the command line or can be placed on the #! line at the beginning of the Perl program.

The following are all the available command-line switches.

> **Note**
>
> Several command-line switches can be stacked together, so that -pie is the same as -p -i -e.

- -0[octnum]   Specifies the input record separator ($/) as an octal number. $/ is usually a newline, so you get one line per record. For example, if you read a file into an array, this gives you one line per array element. The value 00 is a special case and causes Perl to read in your file one paragraph per record. If octnum is omitted, the null character is the separator.
- -a   Turns on Autosplit mode when used with a -n or -p. That means that each line of input is automatically split into the @F array.
- -c   Tells Perl to perform syntax checking on the specified Perl program without executing it. This is invaluable, and the error messages given are informative, are readable, and tell you where to begin looking for the problem, which is a rarity in error messages.
- -d   Runs the script under the Perl debugger. See perldebug for more information.

> **Note**
>
> The Perl documentation is referred to a few times in this section. perldebug, perlrun, perlmod, and perlmodlib, for example, are documents from the Perl documentation. To see these documents, just type **perldoc perlmodlib** at the shell prompt. You can also see all of the Perl documents online at http://www.cpan.org/doc/index.html or on any CPAN site. (CPAN is the Comprehensive Perl Archive Network. See "Modules and CPAN" later in this chapter.)
>
> Perl documentation is written in POD (Plain Old Documentation) format and can be converted into any other format, such as tex, ASCII, or HTML, with the pod2* tools that ship with Perl. For example, to produce HTML documentation on the Fubar module, you would type **pod2html Fubar.pm > Fubar.html**.

- `-d:foo` Runs the script under the control of a debugging or tracing module installed as `Devel::foo`. For example, `-d:Dprof` executes the script using the `Devel::DProf` profiler. See `perldebug` for additional information on the Perl debugger.
- `-Dflags` Sets debugging flags. See `perlrun` for more details.
- `-e commandline` Indicates that what follows is Perl code. This allows you to enter Perl code directly on the command line rather than running code contained in a file.

  `perl -e 'print join " ", keys %ENV;'`
- `-Fpattern` Specifies the pattern to split on if `-a` is also in effect. This is `" "` by default, and `-F` allows you to set it to whatever works for you, such as `','` or `';'`. The pattern may be surrounded by `//`, `""`, or `''`.
- `-h` Typing `perl -h` lists all available command-line switches.
- `-i[extension]` Indicates that files are to be edited in place. If the extension is provided, the original is backed up with that extension. Otherwise, the original file is overwritten.
- `-Idirectory` Directories specified by `-I` are prepended to the search path for modules (`@INC`).
- `-l[octnum]` Enables automatic line-ending processing, which means that end-of-line characters are automatically removed from input and put back onto output. If `octnum` is omitted, this is just the newline character.
- `-m[-]module` or `-M[-]module` Executes use module before running your script. There is a subtle difference between `m` and `M`. See `perlrun` for more details.
- `-n` Causes Perl to loop around your script for each file provided to the command line. Does not print the output. The following example, from `perlrun`, deletes all files older than a week:

  `find . -mtime +7 -print | perl -nle 'unlink;'`
- `-p` This is just like `-n`, except that that each line is printed.
- `-P` Causes script to be run through the C preprocessor before compilation by Perl.
- `-s` Performs some command-line switch parsing and puts the switch into the corresponding variable in the Perl script. For example, the following script prints `'1'` if run with the `-fubar` switch. Your Perl code might look like:

  ```
  #!/usr/bin/perl -s
  print $fubar;
  ```

  When you execute it, you would enter:

  `myperl -fubar`

- `-S` Searches for the script using the `PATH` environment variable.
- `-T` Enables *taint* checking. In this mode, Perl assumes that all user input is tainted, or insecure, until the programmer tells it otherwise. This helps protect you from people trying to exploit security holes in your code and is especially important when writing CGI programs.
- `-u` Tells Perl to dump core after compiling this script. You could presumably, with much time and patience, use this to create an executable file.
- `-U` Allows you to do unsafe things in your Perl program, such as unlinking directories while running as superuser.
- `-v` Prints the version and patchlevel of your Perl executable.
  ```
  % perl -v
  This is perl, version 5.005_03 built for i586-linux

  Copyright 1987-1999, Larry Wall

  Perl may be copied only under the terms of either the
  Artistic License or the GNU General Public License,
  which may be found in the Perl 5.0 source kit.

  Complete documentation for Perl, including FAQ lists,
  should be found on this system using `man perl' or
  `perldoc perl'.  If you have access to the Internet,
  point your browser at http://www.perl.com/, the Perl
  Home Page.
  ```
- `-V` Prints a summary of the major Perl configuration values and the current value of `@INC`.

  `-V:names`

  This parameter prints the value of the names configuration variable to `STDOUT`.
- `-w` Tells Perl to display warning messages about potential problems in the program, such as variables used only once (might be a typo), using = instead of == in a comparison, and the like. This is often used in conjunction with the `-c` flag to do a thorough program check.

  `perl -cw finalassignment.pl`
- `-x directory` Tells Perl that the script is embedded in something larger, such as an email message. Perl throws away everything before a line starting with `#!`, containing the string `'perl'`, and everything after `__END__`. If a directory is specified, Perl changes to the directory before executing the script.

Modules and CPAN

A great strength of the Perl community (and the Linux community) is the fact that it is an Open Source community. Perl expresses this via CPAN (Comprehensive Perl Archive Network), which is a network of mirrors of a repository of code—Perl code, to be more precise.

Most of CPAN is made up of *modules*, which are reusable chunks of code that do useful things, so that you do not have to reinvent the wheel every time you try to build a bicycle.

There are thousands of Perl modules, which do everything from sending email to maintaining your Cisco router access lists to telling you whether a name is masculine or feminine to printing the time in some fancy format. There are modules for CGI programming, modules that access the socket libraries, and modules that post to Usenet for you. If you can think of doing something, chances are pretty good that there is a module to help you. If there is no module that helps, you are encouraged to write one and share it with the rest of the community.

At http://www.perl.com/CPAN/ you will find the CPAN Multiplexor, which attempts to direct you to the CPAN site closest to you.

Perl comes with a set of standard modules installed. Those modules contain much of the function that you will want. You can use the CPAN module (which is one of the standard modules) to download and install other modules onto your system. Typing the following command will put you into an interactive shell that gives you access to CPAN. You can type **help** at the prompt to get more information on how to use the CPAN program.

perl -MCPAN -e shell

After you have installed a module from CPAN (or written one of your own), you can load that module into memory where you can use it with the use function.

use Time::CTime;

use looks in the directories listed in the variable @INC for the module. In this example, use looks for a directory called Time, which contains a file called CTime.pm, which in turn is assumed to contain a package called Time::CTime. The distribution of each module should contain documentation on using that module.

For a list of all the standard Perl modules (those that come with Perl when you install it), see perlmodlib in the Perl documentation. You can read this document by typing **perldoc perlmodlib** at the command prompt.

Code Examples

Over the last few years a lot of people have picked up the notion that Perl is a CGI language, as though it is not good for anything else. Nothing could be farther from the truth. You can use Perl in every aspect of your system administration and as a building block in whatever applications you are planning to run on your shiny new Linux system.

The following sections contain a few examples of things you might want to do with Perl. Perl is versatile enough that you can make it do about anything.

Sending Mail

There are several ways to get Perl to send email. One method that you see frequently is opening a pipe to sendmail and sending data to it (shown in Listing 32.5). Another method uses the Mail::Sendmail module, which uses socket connections directly to send mail (shown in Listing 32.6). The latter method is faster because it does not have to launch an external process.

LISTING 32.5 Sending Mail Using sendmail

```
open (MAIL, "| /usr/sbin/sendmail -t"); # Use -t to protect from users
print MAIL <<EndMail;
To: dpitts\@mk.net
From: rbowen\@mk.net
Subject: Email notification

David,
 Sending email from Perl is easy!
Rich
.
EndMail
close MAIL;
```

> **Note**
>
> Note that the @ sign in the email addresses needs to be escaped so that Perl does not try to evaluate an array of that name.
>
> The syntax used to print the mail message is called a *here document*. The syntax is as follows:
>
> ```
> print <<EndText;
> .....
> EndText
> ```
>
> The EndText value must be identical at the beginning and at the end of the block, including any whitespace.

LISTING 32.6 Sending Mail Using the `Mail::Sendmail` Module

```perl
use Mail::Sendmail;
%mail = ('To'   => 'dpitts@mk.net',
         'From' => 'rbowen@mk.net'
         'Subject' => 'Email notification',
         'Message' => 'Sending email from Perl is easy!',
         );
sendmail(%mail);
```

Perl ignores the comma after the last element in the hash. It is convenient to leave it there; if you want to add items to the hash, you do not need to add the comma. This is purely a style decision.

Note also that the @ sign did not need to be escaped within single quotation marks (' '). Perl does not *interpolate* (evaluate variables) within single quotation marks, but does within double quotation marks and here documents.

Purging Logs

Many programs maintain some variety of logs. Often, much of the information in the logs is redundant or just useless. The program shown in Listing 32.7 removes all lines from a file that contain a particular word or phrase, so that lines you know are not important can be purged. For example, one might want to remove all the lines in the Apache error log that originate with your test client machine because you know that these error messages were produced during testing.

LISTING 32.7 Purging Log Files

```perl
#!/usr/bin/perl
#       Be careful using this program!!
#       This will remove all lines that contain a given word
#       Usage:   remove <word> <file>
$word=@ARGV[0];
$file=@ARGV[1];
if ($file) {
    # Open file for reading
    open (FILE, "$file") or die "Could not open file: $!";     @lines=<FILE>;
    close FILE;
    # Open file for writing
    open (FILE, ">$file") or die "Could not open file for writing: $!";
    for (@lines) {
        print FILE unless /$word/;
    } # End for
    close FILE;
} else {
    print "Usage:   remove <word> <file>\n";
} # End if...else
```

The code uses a few idiomatic Perl expressions to keep the code brief. It reads the file into an array using the `<FILE>` notation; it then writes the lines back out to the file unless they match the pattern given on the command line.

The `die` function kills program operation and displays an error message if the open statements fail. `$!` in the error message, as mentioned in the section on special variables, is the error message returned by the operating system. It will likely be something like `'file not found'` or `'permission denied'`.

Posting to Usenet

If some portion of your job requires periodic postings to Usenet—a FAQ listing, for example—the program shown in Listing 32.8 can automate the process for you. In the sample code, the posted text is read in from a text file, but your input can come from anywhere.

The program shown in Listing 32.8 uses the `Net::NNTP` module, which is a standard part of the Perl distribution. You can find more documentation on the `Net::NNTP` module by typing **perldoc Net::NNTP** at the command line.

LISTING 32.8 Posting an Article to Usenet

```perl
#!/usr/bin/perl
open (POST, "post.file");
@post = <POST>;
close POST;
use Net::NNTP;
$NNTPhost = 'news';
$nntp = Net::NNTP->new($NNTPhost)
        or die "Cannot contact $NNTPhost: $!";
# $nntp->debug(1);
$nntp->post()
   or die "Could not post article: $!";
$nntp->datasend("Newsgroups: news.announce\n");
$nntp->datasend("Subject: FAQ - Frequently Asked Questions\n");
$nntp->datasend("From: ADMIN <root\@rcbowen.com>\n");
$nntp->datasend("\n\n");
for (@post)      {
     $nntp->datasend($_);
} #  End for
$nntp->quit;
```

One-Liners

Perl has the rather undeserved reputation of being unreadable. The fact is that you can write unreadable code in any language. Perl allows for more than one way to do something, and this leads rather naturally to people trying to find the most arcane way to do things.

One medium in which Perl excels is the one-liner. Folks go to great lengths to reduce tasks to a single line of Perl code. Some examples of one-liners that might make your life easier follow.

> **Tip**
>
> Just because you can do something is not a particularly good reason for doing it. I will frequently write somewhat more lengthy pieces of code for something that could be done in just one line, just for the sake of readability—both for myself and for anyone who reads the code later. It is very irritating to go back to a piece of code in which I reduced something to one line for efficiency, or just because I could, and have to spend 30 minutes trying to figure out what it does.

The Schwartzian Transform

Named for Randal Schwartz, the *Schwartzian transform* is a way of sorting an array by something that is not obvious. The `sort` function sorts arrays alphabetically; that's pretty obvious. What if you want to sort an array of strings alphabetically by the third word? Perhaps you want something more useful, such as sorting a list of files by file size? The Schwartzian transform creates a new list that contains the information you want to sort by, referencing the first list. You then sort the new list and use it to figure out the order that the first list should be in. Here's a simple example that sorts a list of strings by length:

```
@sorted_by_length =
  map { $_ => [0] }            # Extract original list
  sort { $a=>[1] <=> $b=>[1] } # Sort by the transformed value
  map { [$_, length($_)] }     # Map to a list of element lengths
  @list;
```

Because each operator acts on the thing immediately to the right of it, it helps to read this from right to left (or bottom to top, the way it is written here).

The first thing that acts on the list is the map operator. It transforms the list into a hash, in which the keys are the list elements and the values are the lengths of each element. This is where you put in your code that does the transformation by which you want to sort.

The next operator is the `sort` function, which sorts the list by the values.

Finally, the hash is transformed back into an array by extracting its keys. The array is now in the desired order.

Command-Line Processing

Perl is great at parsing the output of various programs. This is a task for which many people use tools such as awk and sed. Perl gives you a larger vocabulary for performing these tasks. The following example is very simple, but it illustrates how you might use Perl to chop up some output and do something with it. In the example, Perl is used to list only those files that are larger than 10 KB.

```
ls -la | perl -nae 'print "$F[8] is $F[4]\n" if $F[4] > 10000;'
```

The -n switch indicates that I want the Perl code to run for each line of the output. The -a switch automatically splits the output into the @F array. The -e switch indicates that the Perl code is going to follow on the command line. (See "Switches" earlier in this chapter.)

Perl-Related Tools

A number of tools are related to Perl or are included with the Perl distribution. The most common of these follow:

- perldoc   Displays Perl documentation
- pod2html   Converts Perl documentation to HTML format
- pod2man   Converts Perl documentation to man (nroff/troff) format
- a2p   Converts awk scripts to Perl
- s2p   Converts sed commands to Perl

For More Information

The first place to look for more information is in the Perl documentation and Linux man pages.

Perl, all of its documentation, and millions of lines of Perl programs are all available on the Internet for free. There are also a number of Usenet newsgroups devoted to Perl, as well as shelves of books and a quarterly journal.

Books

Even though your local bookstore may have dozens of titles on Perl, the following books are highly recommended. You might also look at the *Camel Critiques* (Tom Christiansen; http://language.perl.com/critiques/index.html) for reviews of other Perl books that are available.

- *Programming Perl*, Second Edition, by Larry Wall, Randall Schwartz, and Tom Christiansen. O'Reilly & Associates.
- *Effective Perl Programming: Writing Better Programs with Perl*, by Joseph Hall. Addison-Wesley Publishing Company.
- *Mastering Regular Expressions*, by Jeffrey Friedl. O'Reilly & Associates.
- *Perl in a Nutshell: A Desktop Quick Reference*, by Ellen Siever, Stephan Spainhour, and Nathan Patwardhan. O'Reilly & Associates.

Usenet

Check out the following on Usenet:

- `comp.lang.perl.misc`   Discusses various aspects of the Perl programming language. Make sure your questions are Perl-specific, not generic CGI programming questions. The regulars tend to flame folks who do not know the difference.
- `comp.infosystems.www.authoring.cgi`   Discusses authoring of CGI programs; consequently, much of the discussion is Perl-specific. Make sure your questions are related to CGI programming, not just Perl. The regulars are very particular about staying on-topic.

WWW

Check these sites on the World Wide Web:

- `http://www.perl.com/`   The Perl language home page is maintained by Tom Christiansen. This is the place to find all sorts of information about Perl, from its history and culture to helpful tips. This is also the place to download the Perl interpreter for your system.
- `http://www.perl.com/CPAN/`   This is part of the previous site just mentioned, but it merits its own mention. CPAN is the place for you to find modules and programs in Perl. If you end up writing something in Perl that you think is particularly useful, you can make it available to the Perl community here.
- `http://www.perlmonth.com/`   This is a monthly e-zine dedicated to Perl. It is a fairly new venture but already has an impressive line-up of contributors.
- `http://www.hwg.org/`   The HTML Writers Guild is a nonprofit organization dedicated to assisting Web developers. One of their services is a plethora of mailing lists. The hwg-servers mailing list and the hwg-languages mailing list are great places for asking Perl-related questions.
- `http://www.pm.org/`   The Perl Mongers are local Perl users groups. There might be one in your area.

Other

Other valuable resources not falling into any of the preceding categories follow:

- *The Perl Journal* (`http://www.tpj.com/`)

    The Perl Journal is a quarterly publication devoted to the Perl programming language. Orchestrated by Jon Orwant, *TPJ* is always full of excellent, amusing, and informative articles; it is an invaluable resource to new and experienced Perl programmers.

Summary

Perl, in the words of its creator, "combines the best elements of C, `sed`, `awk`, and `sh`," and is also a great language for folks who have no experience with these languages.

Perl's powerful regex (regular expression) library and ease of use have made it one of the preferred scripting languages in use today, particularly in the realm of CGI programming. Many people even think of Perl as exclusively a CGI language, when, in fact, it is capable of so much more.

Perl is often referred to as a glue language for its ability to stick together a variety of disparate applications into something coherent. Perl can make your job as a system administrator easier by taking some of the work off your hands and by making your various applications work together.

Introduction to Tcl/Tk

CHAPTER 33

IN THIS CHAPTER

- A Quick Example *782*
- "Hello, World" in Tk *783*
- Tcl Syntax and Concepts *784*
- Variables *787*
- Expressions *789*
- Lists *791*
- Control Structures *794*
- Procedures *797*
- Tk *799*
- Tcl Extensions *805*
- Going Further *806*

Tcl is an interpreted language developed by John Ousterhout at the University of California at Berkeley. Tcl was originally designed for "gluing" small applications (written in C or another language) together with a scripting language to form larger applications. However, Tcl was so successful that many large applications have been written entirely in Tcl. Tcl is now supported by a company called Scriptics, whose Web site is http://www.scriptics.com.

Along with Tcl, Ousterhout developed the Tk toolkit. Tk is a graphical toolkit and is one of the main reasons for the popularity of Tcl. Using Tcl and the Tk toolkit together, you can create graphical applications very rapidly. Tcl and Tk serve as excellent "wrappers" for command-line programs, turning them into attractive graphical applications.

In addition, Tcl and Tk are *embeddable*. You can link C libraries to your C or C++ programs, making all the capabilities of Tcl and Tk available. Thus, you can write complicated or time-critical portions of your program in C or C++ and tie them together with the Tcl scripting language. You can also develop user-interfaces using Tcl and Tk.

And if that wasn't enough, Tcl/Tk is free software. It is not even licensed under the GPL or LGPL; you can legally embed Tcl/Tk in commercial products without paying any license fees, which is another reason for its popularity. Finally, Tcl/Tk is cross-platform—it works with very minor differences on Linux, practically all UNIX platforms, Windows, and Mac OS. This portability makes Tcl/Tk a very attractive solution for deploying cross-platform applications.

This chapter will give you a brief overview of Tcl/Tk. However, it will not teach you how to program. I assume that you have some familiarity with computer programming and understand concepts like variables, loops, if/then structures and procedures. For a detailed discussion of Tcl/Tk, read *Tcl and the Tk Toolkit* by John Ousterhout (details are in the bibliography.)

Quick Example

Tcl/Tk programs are often called *scripts*. The `tclsh` program interprets Tcl scripts, while the `wish` program interprets Tcl scripts with Tk toolkit extensions.

Start `tclsh` and type **expr 2 + 3**. You should see something like the following:

```
$ tclsh
% expr 2 + 3
5
%
```

The percent sign is `tclsh`'s prompt. The line `expr 2 + 3` is a Tcl command. All Tcl commands consist of words separated by whitespace. In this example, the command has four words, with the first being `expr` and the last being `3`.

The first word of a command is the command name; the remaining words are the arguments. In this respect, Tcl's syntax is very similar to that of the UNIX shell.

Normally, you terminate commands with newlines. However, you can split a long command over several lines by ending each line but the last with a backslash character (\).

When the Tcl interpreter executes a command, the command returns a return value. After interpreting each command, `tclsh` prints the return value. In this case, the return value of `expr 2 + 3` was 5.

To exit from `tclsh`, type **exit**.

"Hello, World" in Tk

Now let's look at some Tk extensions. The `wish` program contains the Tcl language interpreter and the Tk graphical extensions. Start `wish` and enter the following:

```
$ wish
% button .b -text "Hi, There" -command exit
.b
% pack .b
```

You should see a window similar to that shown in Figure 33.1.

FIGURE 33.1
Tk "Hello World."

Let's examine this script. First, notice that each command follows the usual pattern of space-separated words. The first command has six words—the text `Hi, There` is treated as a single word because of the quotes. Although the quotes allow you to put spaces in a word, they are not actually part of the word itself.

The word structure of a Tcl command is very important. Most commands demand either a certain number of words or a specific pattern of words. You must ensure that anything you want treated as a single word really is a single word. Omitting the quotes in this example would make `Hi,` and `There` be treated as separate words, and the command would return an error.

The `button` command creates a widget. A *widget* is simply a window, possibly with some contents and behavior. The two pieces of the command `-text "Hi, There"` and `-command exit` are configuration options. In the case of a button, the `-text` option sets the text to be displayed in the button, and the `-command` option specifies a script to be executed when the button is clicked.

Every widget belongs to a class. There are about a dozen widget classes, such as buttons, scrollbars, scales, frames, radio buttons, and so on. Each widget in a given class has roughly the same behavior and appearance.

Tk organizes widgets hierarchically. The main window (which is always created by `wish`), is called . (a single period.) The button we created, .b, is a descendant of the main window. Widget names, therefore, consist of paths of names starting with and separated by periods. In this respect, they resemble UNIX path names, with the period taking the place of a slash. For reasons we'll discuss later, each component of a widget path should begin with a lowercase letter.

Every widget has a number of configuration options. In our example, we used only the -text and -command options, but options exist to control almost every aspect of a widget, such as its color, font, and so on.

The `pack` command makes the button visible. Widgets are not automatically visible when they are created. Instead, a *geometry manager* puts them into a top-level window. The `pack` command uses a geometry manager called the *packer* to put a widget in another window (in this case, the `pack` command puts .b in its parent window, the main window of the application.)

The packer arranges for .b to fill its parent. Because its parent is larger than necessary, the packer shrinks the main window to just fit around .b.

Tcl Syntax and Concepts

A Tcl script consists of one or more commands. Commands are usually separated by newlines but can be separated by semicolons. For example, the script

```
set a 23
puts $a
```

is identical to the script

```
set a 23; puts $a
```

To execute a script, the Tcl interpreter first parses the script and then evaluates it. During parsing, the interpreter breaks the script into separate words. During evaluation, the interpreter uses the first word in each command to look up a procedure to execute the command. If the interpreter finds such a procedure, it invokes the procedure and passes the remaining words as arguments.

Variable Substitution

Tcl provides several kinds of substitution that affect how words are parsed. The first is variable substitution. Consider the following script:

```
set a Hello_There
set b $a
```

The first command creates a variable a and sets its value to Hello_There.

The second command creates a variable b and sets its value to the value of variable a. In this case, b will also be set to Hello_There. Beginning a word with a dollar sign causes the word to be treated as a variable reference; the value of the variable is substituted for the original word.

Note that variable substitution always yields a single word. For example, if we set a to "Hello there, everyone", $a is substituted with a single word with embedded spaces.

Variable substitution can also occur within a word. Consider the following:

```
set a 123
set b 456
expr $a+$b
```

The second word of the last command becomes 123+456, and the result of the expr is 579.

In the following example:

```
set a feet
set b two$a
```

The value of b is set to twofeet.

Command Substitution

Command substitution replaces part or all of a word with the result of a Tcl script. The Tcl script in question is enclosed in square brackets ([ ]) and may consist of any number of Tcl commands. (The result of a script is the result of the last command executed.)

Consider the following:

```
set hours 2
set minutes [expr $hours * 60]
```

Here, the command expr 2 * 60 is evaluated (remember, $hours is variable-substituted) and returns 120. This converts the second command to set minutes 120.

As with variable substitution, command substitution can appear anywhere in a word and several times within the same word:

```
set woodSize [expr 1+1]_by_[expr 8/2]
```

results in woodSize being set to 2_by_4.

Backslash Substitution

Backslash substitution is used to insert special characters into a word or prevent other kinds of substitution.

For example,

```
set price Price:\n\$4.45\ a\ box.
```

sets *price* to

```
Price:
$4.45 a box.
```

The \n sequence inserts a newline into the word. The backslash before the dollar sign prevents Tcl from interpreting the $4 as a variable substitution. The backslashes before the spaces cause the spaces to be considered as part of the word rather than as word separators.

Tcl understands most of the backslash sequences of ANSI C, as illustrated in Table 33.1.

Table 33.1 Tcl Backslash Substitutions

Backslash Sequence	*Replaced By*
\a	Audible bell
\b	Backspace
\f	Form feed
\n	Newline
\r	Carriage return
\t	Tab
\v	Vertical tab
\ddd	Octal value given by *ddd*
\xhh	Hex value given by *hh*
\newline	A single space

A backslash followed by any character not in Table 33.1 is replaced with the second character. This lets you turn off the special interpretation Tcl normally gives to characters such as $, [, and \.

Quoting

Tcl provides two other ways besides backslash substitution to prevent the parser from giving special meanings to characters, like $.

The first form uses double-quotes. Double-quotes disable word separators. The following is a rewritten form of the backslash substitution example:

```
set price "Price:\n\$4.45 a box."
```

Note that it is no longer necessary to put backslashes before the spaces, but it is still necessary to escape the dollar sign. Inside double-quotes, variable, command, and backslash substitution still occurs.

The second form of quoting is *brace quoting*. Placing text between braces turns off practically all substitution. For example,

```
set price {Price:
$4.45 a box.}
```

In this example, we do not need to backslash-escape anything. Furthermore, to insert a newline, we need a literal newline in the script. The sequence \n inside braces would yield the two characters \n unchanged.

Note that braces nest and that backslash-escaped braces do not count for brace matching. Nevertheless, the backslash will not be removed.

Comments

If the first non-blank character of a line is #, it and all characters following it up to a newline are treated as a comment and discarded. If the # character appears anywhere else in a command (other than the first non-blank character), it is not treated as a comment.

Variables

Variables in Tcl are created automatically when they are assigned. They do not have types; everything in Tcl is treated as a string. You can think of variables as named storage bins that can store a value.

> **Note**
>
> Actually, the latest version of Tcl does not treat everything as a string internally. But, from the point of view of the Tcl programmer, it is convenient to think of everything as being stored as a string.

You can name a variable anything, but it is common to name variables as sequences of letters and digits, starting with a letter.

The `set` command creates variables. The first form takes two arguments (a variable name and a value) and sets the variable to the specified value. The return value of the command is the value to which the variable is set. For example, `set a 5` sets the value of a to 5 and returns 5.

The second form of `set` takes only the variable name and simply returns the value of the variable. For example, `set a` returns the current value of the variable a or results in an error if there is no such variable.

```
% set a 56.555
56.555
% set a
56.555
% set a Frog
Frog
```

The following are some other commands for manipulating variables:

- `append varName ?value?` Appends each of the *value* arguments to the variable *varName*. If *varName* does not exist, it is created with an initially empty value. The return value is the final value of *varName*.

- `incr varName ?increment?` Adds *increment* to *varName*. If *increment* is missing, 1 is assumed. The incremented value is returned.

- `set varName ?value?` If *value* is supplied, sets *varName* to *value* and returns it. Otherwise, returns the value of *varName*.

- `unset varName` Deletes all the named variables and returns the empty string.

Arrays

Arrays in Tcl are collections of elements. The name of an array element has two parts: the base name of the array and the element index. Element indexes can be arbitrary strings and do not have to be numeric. Tcl arrays are associative arrays.

Associative arrays can be used to group sets of related values. For example, if you are keeping track of people's favorite colors, you can create an array whose indexes are people's names and the values are the corresponding favorite colors. This groups the information in a single easy-to-manage place.

To name an array element, follow the array name by the index in parentheses. For example:

```
set favColor(George) Blue
set favColor(Nancy) Green
set person Susan
set favColor($person) Orange
set msg "$person's favorite color: $favColor($person)"
```

You can use an array element anywhere where a simple variable can be used. Note particularly the last example, which shows how an array variable is used in variable substitution.

The `array` command can manipulate arrays. We won't show the command in all its glory, but the following are some examples:

```
% array names favColor
Nacny George Susan
```

The *array* `names` command returns a list of all indexes in the array (in arbitrary order).

Tcl commands have their own manual pages. Unfortunately, the Caldera OpenLinux 2.2 setup is incorrect. To access the Tcl man pages, add the following to your `.bashrc` file:

```
export MANPATH="$MANPATH:/usr/share/tcl-8.0/man:/usr/share/tk-8.0/man"
```

Otherwise, the `man` command will not find the manual pages. Now that you've set up `MANPATH`, you can get more information about `array` from the `array(n)` manual page.

Expressions

Expressions consist of values (operands) and operators. The operators combine operands together to produce new values.

Numbers

Numbers in Tcl can be integers or real numbers. Integers are usually expressed as decimal integers, such as 721 or 33. However, if they begin with a leading zero, they are interpreted in base 8. Thus, the integer `072` is the same as the integer 58. If they begin with `0x`, they are interpreted as hexadecimal. Thus, `072`, `58`, and `0x3A` represent the same integer.

Real numbers are written as in ANSI C. Examples are 12.3, -5.0, 6.23e+33, and 1.0E-9.

Operators

Tcl supports most of the ANSI C operators. They are summarized in Table 33.2. Operators with higher precedence are evaluated before those with lower precedence. Operators with equal precedence are evaluated from left to right. In the table, precedence decreases from top to bottom. Groups of operators within horizontal rules have the same precedence.

Table 33.2 Tcl Operators

Operator	Meaning	Operand Types
-x	Negative of x	Integer, Real
!x	Logical NOT: 1 if x is 0; 0 otherwise	Integer, Real
~x	Bitwise complement of x	Integer
x*y	Product of x and y	Integer, Real
x/y	Quotient of x divided by y	Integer, Real
x%y	Remainder of x divided by y	Integer
x+y	Sum of x and y	Integer, Real
x-y	Difference of x minus y	Integer, Real
x<<y	Left-shift x by y bits	Integer
x>>y	Right-shift x by y bits	Integer
x<y	1 if x is less than y; 0 otherwise	Integer, Real, String
x<=y	1 if x is less than or equal to y; 0 otherwise	Integer, Real, String
x>y	1 if x is greater than y; 0 otherwise	Integer, Real, String
x>=y	1 if x is greater than or equal to y; 0 otherwise	Integer, Real, String
x==y	1 if x equals y; 0 otherwise	Integer, Real, String
x!=y	1 if x does not equal y; 0 otherwise	Integer, Real, String
x&y	Bitwise-AND of x and y	Integer
x^y	Bitwise exclusive-OR of x and y	Integer
x|y	Bitwise-OR of x and y	Integer
x&&y	Logical AND of x and y: 1 if both are non-zero; 0 otherwise	Integer
x||y	Logical OR of x and y: 1 if either is non-zero; 0 otherwise	Integer
x?y:z	Choice: y if x is non-zero; otherwise z	Integer, Real

As in C, the logical operators are short-circuit operators. If the first operand of && is zero, or the first operand of || is non-zero, the second operand is not evaluated.

Within an expression, substitution occurs through the normal parser mechanism. However, the expression evaluator also performs variable substitution. Consider the following example:

```
% set a 5
5
% expr 5+$a
10
% expr {5+$a}
10
```

In the first `expr`, the Tcl parser does the substitution. In the second `expr`, the expression evaluator does the substitution. In the second case, the substituted variable must hold only a simple value. (That is, monkey business like `set a "5+6+7"` won't work. In any case, you should avoid tricks like this.)

Built-in Functions

Tcl has many built-in functions such as `sin`, `exp`, and so on. For details, see `expr(n)` (after fixing your MANPATH).

Lists

Tcl uses lists to represent collections. A *list* is a sequence of elements.

In its simplest form, a list is a space-separated collection of words. For example, the string `Hop Skip Jump` is a list with three elements.

Extracting List Elements

The `lindex` command extracts a particular element from a list. It takes as arguments a list and an index and returns the appropriate element. An index is an integer with 0 corresponding to the first element, 1 to the second, and so on, as shown in the following:

```
% lindex {Hop Skip Jump} 1
Skip
```

When you type a list to the Tcl interpreter, you often enclose the elements in braces to ensure that the list is interpreted as a single word. These braces are not part of the list itself, as the following shows:

```
% set x {Hop Skip Jump}
Hop Skip Jump
% lindex $x 2
Jump
```

Creating Lists

The `concat` command concatenates a number of lists. Consider the following example:

```
% concat {1 2 3} 4 5 {6 7}
1 2 3 4 5 6 7
```

`concat` is given four lists (note that the bare words 4 and 5 are treated as single-element lists) and returns a list consisting of all the elements in the original list.

The `list` command, on the other hand, joins all of its arguments together so that each argument becomes a single element of the resulting list. The following are some examples:

```
% list {1 2 3} 4 5 {6 7}
{1 2 3} 4 5 {6 7}
% list "buzz off" go away
{buzz off} go away
```

Note that `list` adds braces or backslashes as required to ensure that each argument is a proper list element in the final list.

The `llength` command returns the number of elements in a list:

```
% llength {{1 2 3} 4 5 {6 7}}
4
% llength foo
1
% llength {}
0
```

Manipulating Lists

There are several commands for manipulating lists. The following is a brief description here; see the manual pages for details.

- linsert *list index elem ?elem?*   The linsert command forms a new list by inserting all of the *elem* elements in *list*, starting just before the *index*'th element. If *index* is zero, the new elements are placed at the beginning of the list. If it is greater than or equal to the original length of the list, new elements are added to the end of the list. The return value is the new list.

- lreplace *list first last ?elem?*   The lreplace command forms a new list by first deleting all elements whose indexes range from *first* to *last*. It then inserts supplied *elem*s (if any) in place of the deleted elements. The return value is the new list.

- lrange *list first last*   The lrange command returns a list consisting of all elements from index *first* through *last* in the original list. If *last* is the word end, all elements from *first* to the end of the list are returned.

- lsearch *?option? list elem*   The lsearch command returns the index in *list* of the element *elem*. If no such element exists, -1 is returned.

  The *option* controls how *elem* is matched. If it is -exact, *elem* must exactly match a list element. If it is -glob, *elem* is treated as a shell-style wildcard pattern for the purposes of matching. If it is -regexp, *elem* is treated as a regular expression. Tcl has very powerful regular expressions; see regexp(n) for details.

- lsort *list*   The lsort command creates a new list consisting of all the elements in the original list sorted in lexicographic order. lsort has many options to control how sorting is done; see lsort(n) for details.

- laapend *varName elem ?elem?*   The sequence: laapend *varName elem1 elem1* is equivalent to set *var* "$var [list *elem1* elem2]" but is more efficient. lappend is often used to build up large lists a few pieces at a time.

Lists and Commands

A well-formed Tcl list is a sequence of words. Similarly, a Tcl command is a sequence of words. This property is very important: If a Tcl list is evaluated as a script, the parser does not perform any substitutions on the list elements. It simply uses them as-is as words in the command.

Many Tcl and Tk commands take a script as an argument. For example, we saw that the *-command* option of the `button` command expects a script as an argument. You can compose a script by supplying a list:

```
button .b -command {set x 0}
```

The script `set x 0` will be evaluated every time the button is clicked.

Suppose you want to build a script that depends on a variable. The following is a short example:

```
button .b1 -command {set x "A-One"}
button .b2 -command {set x "And a-Two"}
```

You might try something like the following (we'll explain `foreach` later:)

```
foreach {n label} {1 "A-One" 2 "And a-Two"} {
    button .b$n -command {set x $label}
}
```

> **Note**
>
> Obviously, for two buttons, this does not make sense. Consider building 15 buttons and you see the savings in typing yielded by `foreach`.

Note that we use variable substitution to build up the button name. However, this example won't work because the braces suppress variable substitution. The following is a second try:

```
foreach {n label} {1 "A-One" 2 "And a-Two"} {
    button .b$n -command "set x $label"
}
```

Unfortunately, this does not work either. When `.b2` is clicked, the `set x And a-Two` script is executed, which yields an error—there are too many arguments to the `set` command.

The correct way to do it is as follows:

```
foreach {n label} {1 "A-One" 2 "And a-Two"} {
    button .b$n -command [list set x $label]
}
```

The `list` command ensures that we always get a well-formed three-element list, which is therefore guaranteed to be a well-formed script with `set` followed by exactly two arguments.

Control Structures

Tcl has the usual control structures found in modern languages. The implementation of the control structures is unusual in that Tcl control structures are normal commands, some of whose arguments happen to be Tcl scripts.

if

The `if` command looks something like the following:

```
if test1 body1 ?elseif test2 body2...? ?else bodyn?
```

Each *test* is evaluated in turn as an expression. If the result is non-zero, Tcl executes the corresponding *body* and skips the remaining *test*s and *bodies*. If all *test*s are `false` and the `else` clause is present, Tcl executes the final *body*.

The result of an `if` command is the result of whichever body was executed or the empty string if no body was executed.

Consider the following example:

```
if { $a > 0 } {
   set answer Positive
   set b $a
} elseif {$a == 0} {
   set answer Zero
   set b $a
} else {
   set answer Negative
   set b [expr -1 * $a]
}
```

In the example, answer is set to `Positive`, `Zero`, or `Negative`, depending on the value of a. In addition, b is set to the absolute value of a.

while

The `while` command looks like the following:

```
while test body
```

The `while` command evaluates *test* as an expression. If the result is non-zero, the `while` command evaluates *body* as a Tcl script. This repeats until *test* becomes `false`.

```
set i 0
set total 0
```

```
while { $i < 10 } {
    incr i
    incr total $i
}
set total
```

This adds all the numbers from 1 to 10, leaving the result in `total`.

The `while` command returns the empty string.

for

The `for` command looks a bit like its C counterpart:

`for init test update body`

First, Tcl evaluates *init* as a script. Next, Tcl evaluates *test* as an expression. If it returns `true`, Tcl evaluates *body* as a script. After that, Tcl evaluates *update* as a script. The process repeats from the evaluation of *test* until *test* returns `false`.

The following is the previous example written as a `for` loop:

```
for {set i 1; set total 0} {$i <= 10} {incr i} {
    incr total $i
}
set total
```

foreach

The `foreach` command iterates over a list. In its simplest form, it looks like the following:

`foreach var list body`

It assigns *var* successive elements of *list*, executing *body* after each assignment. The following example adds the numbers 22, 75, 41, and 3:

```
set total 0
foreach number { 22 75 41 3 } {
    incr total $number
}
set total
```

You can make the first argument a list of variables. In this case, `foreach` consumes as many elements from the list as there are variables for each iteration, assigning them to matching variables. For example, the following code computes the value of 22*75 + 41*3:

```
set total 0
foreach {x y} { 22 75 41 3} {
    incr total [expr $x * $y]
}
set total
```

Finally, you can supply several lists and variable lists, and they are stepped in parallel. The following example computes 22*75*4 + 41*3*8:

```
set total 0
foreach {x y} { 22 75 41 3} z {4 8} {
    incr total [expr $x * $y * $z]
}
set total
```

See the manual page `foreach(n)` for more details.

break and continue

Within the body of a loop, you can use the `break` and `continue` commands. The `break` command stops execution of the loop body and terminates the loop completely. Execution continues with the command following the loop.

The `continue` statement terminates execution of the loop body and starts a new iteration. For `while` loops, this means that `test` is re-evaluated. For `for` loops, `update` is executed and `test` re-evaluated. For `foreach`, the next loop iteration is performed.

switch

The `switch` command is a more compact way of encoding a series of `if...elseif...` commands.

The following is s an example of `switch`:

```
switch $a {
    1 { incr t1 }
    2 { incr t2 }
    default {incr tx}
}
```

In this example, if a holds the value 1, `t1` is incremented. If it is 2, `t2` is incremented; otherwise, `tx` is incremented.

The `switch` command has other options and capabilities; see `switch(n)` for details. The return value of `switch` is the value of whichever script was executed or the empty string if no script was executed.

source

The `source` command takes a single argument, which is the name of the file. The file is read and evaluated as a Tcl script. The return value is the value of the last-executed Tcl command from the file.

For example, to execute the Tcl commands in `file.tcl`, use

```
source file.tcl
```

eval

The `eval` command concatenates all of its arguments (as if with `concat`) and executes the result as a Tcl script. This is used to build up an execute scripts, or force another round of substitution.

Consider the following example:

```
set a 1
set varName "a"
set b \$$varName
eval set c \$$varName
set c
```

In this example, the arguments to the `eval` command are `set`, `c`, and `$a`. The `eval` command forces another round of parsing, so `c` is set to 1. However, because we didn't use `eval`, `b` is set to the string `"$a"`.

Procedures

While most built-in Tcl commands are executed by C code in the Tcl interpreter, you can write your own commands in Tcl and have them executed just as if they were built-in commands.

proc

The `proc` command defines a procedure:

`proc pname args body`

The *pname* is the name of the procedure. *args* is a list of arguments to the procedure, and *body* is a Tcl script that is the body of the procedure.

When Tcl invokes a procedure, actual arguments are stored in the variables named by *args*. The *body* is executed, and whatever it returns becomes the return value of the procedure.

Consider the following procedure, which returns the sum of the squares of its arguments:

```
proc sos { a b } {
    expr $a*$a + $b*$b
}
```

You can now use `sos` as a Tcl command:

```
% sos 3 4
25
% sos -3 8
73
% sos 7
no value given for parameter "b" to "sos"
```

You can use the `return` command to prematurely end execution of a procedure; the argument of the `return` command is returned as the procedure's value. For example, you can create a recursive procedure to compute the factorial of a number:

```
proc factorial { n } {
   if {$n <= 1} {
      return 1
   }
   expr $n * [factorial [expr $n-1]]
}
```

In this example, if the argument is less than or equal to 1, 1 is returned. Otherwise, the `expr` command is executed and, because it is the last command in the procedure, its return value becomes the return value of the procedure. The following are some sample calls:

```
% factorial 10
3628800
% factorial 0
1
% factorial glup
syntax error in expression "glup-1"
```

Local and Global Variables

All variables created in the body of a procedure, as well as the procedure's formal arguments, are local variables. They are unique to that procedure (in fact, unique to a particular invocation of a procedure).

If you want to access global variables from a procedure body, use the `global` command to declare them as global.

```
set GlobVar 10
proc mult { a } {
   global GlobVar
   expr $a * $GlobVar
}
```

Arguments

The `proc` command has additional syntax for declaring procedures with default values for missing arguments and for procedures that take an arbitrary number of arguments.

If an entry in the procedure's argument list is a two-element list, the first element is the name of the formal argument and the second is the default value:

```
proc mult {a {b 10}} {
   expr $a * $b
}
% mult 5 6
30
```

```
% mult 5
50
```

As the example shows, if the second argument is omitted, it assumes the default value of 10.

You can declare a procedure taking an arbitrary number of arguments by using `args` as the final argument name. In this case, Tcl packs all remaining arguments into a list and assigns this list to `args`. The following procedure takes any number of arguments and returns the sum of their squares:

```
proc sosm { args } {
   set total 0
   foreach num $args {
      incr total [expr $num*$num]
   }
   return $total
}
% sosm 5 6
61
% sosm 1 2 3 4 5
55
% sosm
0
```

In the last case, `args` was assigned the empty list, so the `foreach` command did not iterate at all.

Tk

Let us now look at some Tcl programs using the Tk widget set. You've already seen a simple example; let's write a useful Tcl/Tk program.

The following program creates a very simple color selector dialog box. It presents three sliders that you adjust to select various intensities of red, green, and blue. When you click OK, it prints the color value as a standard X color string on standard output.

> **Note**
>
> The line numbers are for reference; do not actually type them.

```
1  # Main program
2  frame .swatch -height 1i -width 1i
3  scale .red -length 4i -orient horizontal \
4       -from 0 -to 255 -command setcolor -label Red
5  scale .green -length 4i -orient horizontal \
6       -from 0 -to 255 -command setcolor -label Green
7  scale .blue -length 4i -orient horizontal \
```

```
8      -from 0 -to 255 -command setcolor -label Blue
9  button .ok -text OK -command printcolor
10 pack .swatch -expand 0 -fill x
11 pack .red .green .blue .ok

12 # Set the swatch color based on scales
13 proc setcolor { dummy } {
14     set r [.red get]
15     set g [.green get]
16     set b [.blue get]
17     set color [format "#%02x%02x%02x" $r $g $b]
18     .swatch configure -background $color
19 }

20 # Print color and exit
21 proc printcolor {} {
22     set r [.red get]
23     set g [.green get]
24     set b [.blue get]
25     set color [format "#%02x%02x%02x" $r $g $b]
26     puts $color
27     exit 0
28 }
```

Put this in a file called color.tcl and type

```
$ wish color.tcl
```

You should see a window that looks like Figure 33.2.

FIGURE 33.2
Tk color Selector.

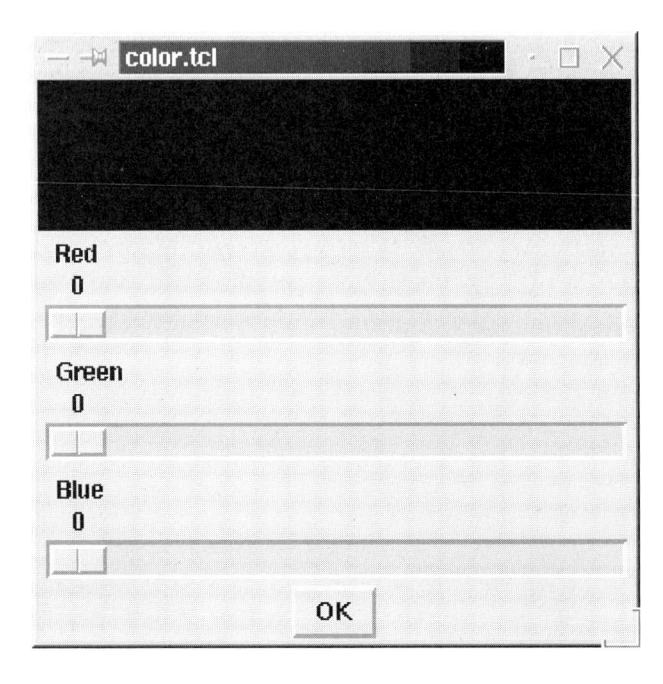

As you slide the scales, the color patch changes color. If you click OK, the color is sent to standard output in X color format. You could use this in a shell script. For example, suppose you want a user to pick a color:

```
echo "Please pick a color."
COLOR='wish color.tcl'
```

Let's look at the color selection program. We'll start with the main program first and then look at the helper procedures.

Line 2 creates a frame called .swatch. A frame is a simple widget that is normally used as a container for other widgets. In this case, we set the height and width to one inch and use the background color of the frame as a color swatch.

Lines 3 and 4 create a scale labeled Red. A scale is a slider for entering numerical values in a certain range. In this case, the range is from 0 to 255. The scale is four inches long with the long direction oriented horizontally.

Every time the scale is moved, Tk calls the script named by the -command option with the current value of the scale appended. Thus, if the red scale were moved from 55 to 56, Tk would execute the script setcolor 56.

Lines 5 through 8 create scales for the green and blue color components.

Line 9 creates a button called .OK. When you press and release the left mouse button with the pointer on the OK button, Tk executes the script printcolor.

Line 10 packs the frame .swatch in its parent. The -expand 0 option causes the frame not to expand if the parent expands. However, if there is extra space left over in the *x* direction, the frame fills it (because of the -fill x option). The frame is packed by default starting at the top of the container window.

Line 11 packs the remaining widgets from the top down, giving the final window arrangement shown in Figure 33.2.

Lines 13 through 19 implement the setcolor command. Recall that when the scale changes, the value of the scale is appended to the script. In this case, the value is passed as an argument to setcolor. Because we are not interested in the value (we retrieve the scale values with other means as shown next), we declare a dummy argument to accept and discard the value.

Lines 14 through 16 retrieve the values on each of the scales. Note that when you create a widget, a similarly-named Tcl command is created. This command lets you query and modify properties of the widget. In this case, we call the widget command get to get the values of the three scales.

Line 17 formats the color values as a six-digit hexadecimal value preceded by #. The Tcl format command is similar to the C printf function (see format(n) for details).

Finally, line 18 calls the `configure` widget command on the `.swatch` widget to set the background color. This causes the swatch to actually change color.

Lines 20 through 28 define the `printcolor` procedure. This is similar to `setcolor`, but it simply prints the color value to standard output and exits rather than setting the swatch color.

Widgets

I can give only a very brief overview of the Tk widgets in this chapter. The best way to get a quick feeling for the widgets available is to run the Tk demo. Unfortunately, the Caldera OpenLinux 2.2 setup is incorrect; you have to run this command as `root` to fix it:

```
# ln -s /usr/share/tk-8.0/Demos /usr/lib/tk8.0/demos
```

Then, run the actual demo as follows:

```
$ wish /usr/lib/tk8.0/demos/widget
```

All widgets have a widget class command that creates the widget. For example, the command `button` creates buttons, `frame` creates frames, and `canvas` creates canvas widgets.

Once a widget is created, the named widget becomes a Tcl command. All widgets have a `configure` widget command, which lets you configure various aspects of the widget such as its color, font, size, and so on. We saw this in use in line 18 of the previous example. Widgets also have a `cget` widget command that retrieves the current value of widget properties.

The following sections discuss the available Tk widgets.

Labels

A label widget is a simple widget that displays a text string or a bitmap. It is used (as its name implies) to label portions of a dialog box and has no built-in behavior.

Buttons

Buttons cause some action to occur when they are clicked. Typical uses of buttons include the OK and Cancel buttons found on many dialog boxes.

Checkbuttons

Checkbuttons allow you to select or deselect items. Each checkbutton can be in the "selected" or "deselected" state. Checkbuttons are independent of one another and are suited for simple Yes/No questions.

Radiobuttons

Radiobuttons allow you to select one from a number of choices. Only one radiobutton in a given group can be selected; selecting another radiobutton automatically deselects all other radiobuttons in the same group.

List Boxes

List boxes contain lists of strings. They allow selection of one (or possibly more) strings. You can use them to provide a choice of one from many possibilities, or to let users choose several files from a list of filenames.

Scrollbars

Scrollbars contain two little arrows and a slider. You usually connect scrollbars to other widgets to cause them to scroll. Scrollbars are often used in conjunction with list boxes, text widgets, and canvases. The Tk demo provides a good illustration of scrollbars.

Entries

Entries are small boxes for entering single lines of text. They are useful as elements in a form for entering information.

Text

The text widget is designed for multiline text displays. However, the text widget can do much more than this. The text widget includes powerful facilities for editing text. It also includes facilities for tagging ranges of text and keeping track of text positions with marks.

Tags can be used to alter text fonts so you can have a mixture of fonts, justification styles, colors, and font sizes within a single widget. You can also have tagged areas of text react to events. This lets you build powerful hypertext widgets and animated text displays.

Finally, you can embed other windows into the flow of text. This lets you embed canvases, pictures, and buttons in a text dialog box, creating very powerful user interfaces.

Figure 33.3 shows the text demonstration included with the Tk demo library.

Canvas

A canvas widget holds canvas items like rectangles, ovals, lines, polygons, images, and other windows. Like the text widget, the canvas widget is extremely powerful. Canvas items can react to mouse and keyboard events, allowing you to create highly-interactive interfaces. Canvas items can be tagged, allowing for grouping. Events can be bound to tags rather than specific items, allowing fine control over which items respond to which events.

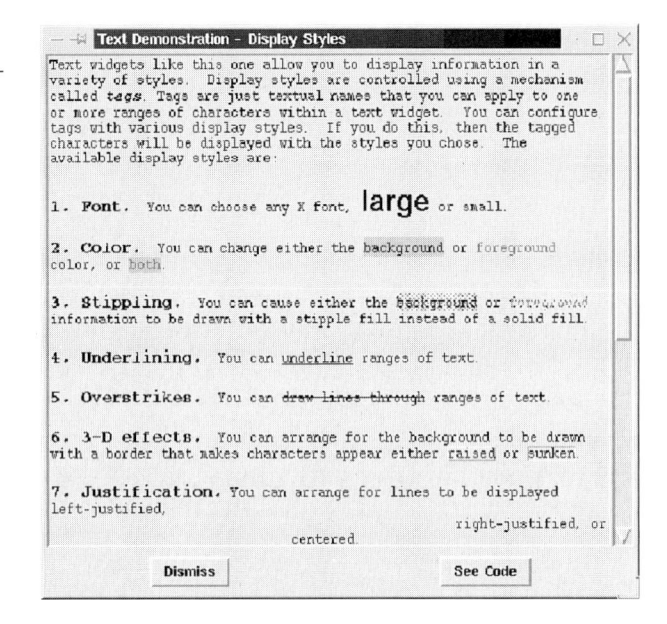

FIGURE 33.3

Tk text demonstration.

Figure 33.4 shows the canvas demonstration included with the Tk demo library.

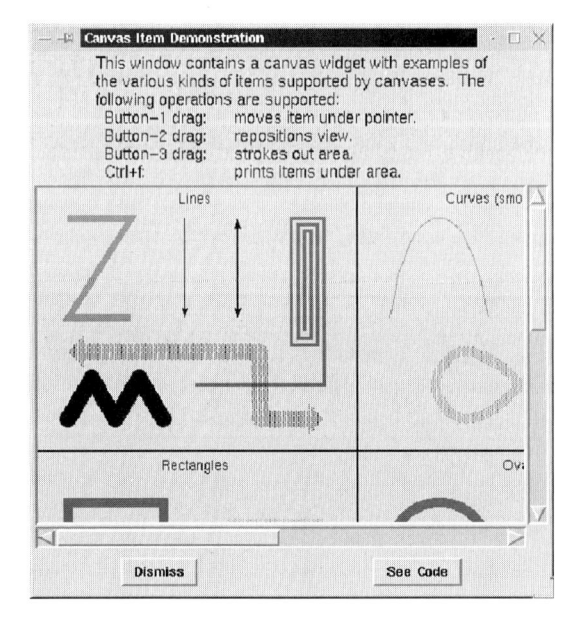

FIGURE 33.4

Tk canvas demonstration.

Scales

Scales provide sliders that allow users to set numerical parameters within a specific range. Configuration options specify the range start and end, the step size, whether and how often to draw ticks, and so on.

Menus

Tk provides built-in support for menu bars along the top of a window as well as pop-up menus. It is very easy to create keyboard accelerators for menu entries. Tk supports cascaded menus, as well as radio buttons, check buttons, and images within menus. You can also create tear-off menus that can be torn off to become top-level windows.

Common Dialog Boxes

Tk provides built-in versions of common dialog boxes like message boxes, file selectors, and color selectors. On UNIX, these are implemented in Tcl, while on Windows and the Macintosh, the native dialog boxes are used.

Tcl Extensions

Tcl is designed in such a way as to make it very easy to add extensions to the basic interpreter. These extensions can be written in C, Tcl, or a combination of the two.

How to write C extensions to Tcl is beyond the scope of this book, but the C API is very clean and understandable. The manual pages in `/usr/share/tcl-8.0/man/man3` and `/usr/share/tk-8.0/man/man3` contain descriptions of all the publicly-accessible C functions.

Some well-known Tcl extensions include [incr Tcl], an object-oriented extension to Tcl; "TclX," an extended version of Tcl that adds access to many UNIX system calls; "BLT" and "TiX" that implement new and useful Tk widgets; and "BWidget," a professional-looking set of widgets implemented entirely in Tcl.

More information about Tcl and its extensions can be found on the Scriptics Web site at `http://www.scriptics.com`.

Going Further

Tcl/Tk has many more features, such as,

- Powerful string manipulation functions.
- Name spaces for organizing library modules in such a way as to avoid name clashes.

- Exception handling for deferring error handling to the appropriate level of abstraction. For example, low-level routines can simply raise exceptions if something goes wrong, leaving error recovery to higher-level routines that have more overall knowledge.
- File and socket I/O for reading and writing files and network connections.
- Variable traces for triggering scripts every time a variable is read or written. This allows user interface widgets to be tied together in intricate ways.
- Safe interpreters for interpreting untrusted Tcl code. Safe interpreters act as a "sandbox" to quarantine unknown code. This gives Tcl a security model similar to Java.
- Send scripts that allow Tk applications to send Tcl scripts to each other. This lets you organize large applications as a set of small tools that interact with each other using scripts.
- A browser plugin that lets you run Tcl/Tk code within a Web browser. The browser plugin uses safe interpreters to assure security.

Summary

Out of necessity, this chapter has been a very brief overview of the Tcl language, and an even more brief overview of Tk and its capabilities.

In this chapter, you learned important concepts about the Tcl language, such as its interpreted and cross-platform nature. You learned that commands in Tcl are simply lists of words. Next, you learned the rules of the Tcl parser, including substitution and quoting.

You learned about Tcl variables, arrays, expressions and lists. You also learned the Tcl control structures: `if`, `while`, `for`, `foreach`, and `switch`.

The chapter showed you how to execute script files with `sourc` and evaluate lists as scripts with `eval`. You learned to define and call procedures and how to access global variables from procedure bodies.

Finally, you had a brief look at the Tk graphical toolkit, how it organizes widgets, and what kinds of widgets it provides.

CHAPTER 34

Introduction to Python

IN THIS CHAPTER

- Introduction *808*
- Fundamentals *811*
- The Power of Python *816*
- More Sequence Types *818*
- Dictionaries *821*
- Comparisons and Looping Constructs *823*
- Functions and Namespaces *828*
- Input and Output *831*
- Exceptions *835*
- The Real World: Example Code *837*
- Object-Oriented Programming *845*
- Standard Modules Overview *849*
- Where to Go from Here *855*

Introduction

Maybe you're wondering why you should even consider reading this chapter. After all, Python appears to be just another obscure language, one of the thousands that is probably safe to simply ignore in favor of the big three: C, C++, and Perl. If you agree with these sentiments, I'd like to show you something that will change your mind. Interested?

pullpush

Let's assume for a moment that you regularly browse the Web and frequently come across files that you want to download. You're a collector of information, and when you find something good, you like to archive it. But unlike regular people, who download files to their local machines, you're currently attending university, and the campus sysadmins have severely restricted the amount of data you can store in your home directory. So, instead of storing files in your campus account, you choose to archive them on a good friend's ftp server, where you have 2 GB of storage set aside for your exclusive use. After a week or two, you begin to get tired of the effort required to manually save HTML documents to your university account, manually uploading all your stuff, and then deleting the original files to clear up space. For the sake of this example, let's say you happen to have a healthy understanding and respect for Python and its abilities and write the program shown in Listing 34.1

LISTING 34.1 pullpush

```python
#!/usr/bin/env python

from urllib import *; from ftplib import FTP; import readline
ftpsite='ftp.friend.net'; ftpdir='/pub/archive/'; user='bob'; passwd='hahehoo'

ftp=FTP(ftpsite); ftp.login(user,passwd)
myurl=raw_input("Get URL http://")
ftp.storbinary("STOR "+ftpdir+raw_input("Save as
ftp://"+ftpsite+ftpdir),urlopen("http://"+myurl),2048)
ftp.quit(); print "OK :)"
```

Running pullpush

To get this script to run, fire up your favorite text editor and type it in. Save it as pullpush. At the shell prompt, type:

> **chmod +x pullpush**

This makes the script executable, so that it can be run by simply typing ./**pullpush** at the shell prompt. Alternatively, you can run the script by typing **python pullpush**. The first option works because of the `#! /usr/bin/env python` line at the beginning of the script; the second option will work whether or not that particular line is present (it will be interpreted as a comment and ignored).

Using only six lines of code, you have created a Python masterpiece. Not only does this program download a file from the Web, but it also uploads this file to your friend's ftp site, all without storing any data in your home directory. When you find a file you want to save, you simply type **pullpush** and press Enter:

```
> pullpush
Get URL http://_
```

Then, you enter the URL of the file you would like to download. After pressing Enter again, you are asked for a filename to create on your friend's ftp server:

```
> pullpush
Get URL http://freshmeat.net
Save as ftp://ftp.friend.net/pub/archive/_
```

A few seconds after entering a filename, you are greeted with a friendly "OK :)" and the transfer is complete. No files were created in your home directory, so there's nothing to clean up, and your data are now safely tucked away in your ftp archive.

I hope this little example has convinced you that Python is a language worth learning. The time you spend reading this chapter is an investment that will pay off in a big way as you start to use Python to get things done faster and better.

What Is Python?

Python is a portable, object-oriented, interpreted programming language. Its many attributes—such as an elegant but powerful syntax, built-in dynamic high-level data structures, and a modular design—lend themselves to rapid application development.

Python runs on a variety of platforms, including Linux, many versions of UNIX, Windows 98/NT, DOS, OS/2, and Amiga. Various Python modules provide interfaces to the underlying operating system, as well as the ability to access the operating system's native GUI.

Finally, Python is freely usable and distributable. It does not use a GPL-style license; instead, it uses a less restrictive one that allows you to use, copy, modify, and distribute Python for any purpose and without fee.

Benefits

One of Python's most exciting benefits is its ability to rapidly create functional programs, often referred to as RAD (Rapid Application Development). Python's elegant syntax and built-in high-level data structures lend themselves to getting the job done, whatever that may be, simply and effectively.

The fact that Python is an interpreted language speeds up development significantly. In practical terms, Python's interpreted nature means that there is no "compile" step in the development process. Programs are simply written and then immediately executed and tested for proper operation. Python can also be run in an "interactive mode," where the user can enter commands and watch them execute in real time. This is a wonderful benefit not only for day-to-day development but also for learning the language quickly and easily. Python can also byte-compile existing programs for enhanced performance.

What makes Python special isn't one feature in particular but rather how these many features combine synergistically to create a fast, fun, and powerful programming environment for both the beginner and the seasoned developer. Python programmers have been known to "fall in love" with the language because of what it has to offer to their development process. Python is arguably one of the best RAD tools available today and is definitely worth becoming familiar with if you do any sort of development or scripting work.

Python can also be used to prototype code that will eventually be written in another language (such as C or C++). This will allow you to play with different algorithms and approaches to the problem at hand without sacrificing a lot of time. After you have worked all the kinks out of your approach, you're ready to start writing your C program. Of course, you will often find that the Python code works great, and no recoding is necessary. However, porting your code over to a lower-level language will sometimes provide a significant speed increase, depending on what you are doing.

Getting Up to Speed

We are now ready to begin a hands-on demonstration of what Python can do. If you have any experience with any kind of structured programming language, you should find Python's syntax familiar because it borrows many standard operators and functions from languages such as C and Pascal. If you have no previous programming experience, you may want to pick up an introductory computer programming textbook. Regardless of the particular language used in the textbook, you will find standard concepts such as operators, procedures, and structured programming directly applicable to Python.

The best way to get started using Python is to start up the interpreter in interactive mode and begin entering commands. To do this, start up a command shell and type:

```
> python
```

You will then be in the Python interpreter in interactive mode. The following text will appear on your screen:

```
Python 1.5.1 (#1, Apr  3 1999, 18:41:12)  [GCC egcs-2.91.60 19981201 (e on
linux-i386
Copyright 1991-1995 Stichting Mathematisch Centrum, Amsterdam
>>>
```

> **If Python Is Not Installed**
>
> Python may or may not be installed, depending on the installation options you chose during the Caldera OpenLinux install. If Python is not installed, first mount your Caldera OpenLinux Installation CD, change to the `Packages/RPMS` directory on the CD, and type the following command:
>
> `> rpm -i python-1.5.1-0a.i386.rpm`
>
> For the purposes of this chapter, you can safely ignore several other Python packages in this directory.

The last line that appears is called the primary prompt, which lets you know that the interpreter is waiting for your input. This is where you get to play around and become familiar with Python's syntax. Try typing the following commands:

```
>>> 100+6
106
>>> a=2100
>>> b=6
>>> c=5
>>> a/b*c
1750
```

The first example is fairly self-explanatory; the expression 100+6 evaluates to a value of 106. In the second example, we create three objects called a, b, and c and assign integer values to them. At the last prompt, we enter an expression using the division and multiplication operators, which evaluates to the numeric value 1750.

This is a good time to mention that because Python is an object-oriented language, we will use the term *object* to refer to entities that you may normally be accustomed to calling variables. In Python, all data are stored in objects.

Fundamentals

Let's look at fundamental operators and functions of the Python language. Operators are special characters that represent a mathematical operation (such as +); they normally appear between numeric objects. Here are a few examples:

Text	Explanation
+	This is an operator.
3+4	This is an expression (two numbers and an operator).
a=3+4	This is a statement (an object, assignment operator, and expression).

Functions are subroutines that accept zero or more arguments and return an optional value. They look like this when used:

`c=myfunction(a,b)`

Here a function called `myfunction` is executed with the arguments a and b and returns a value that is inserted into the object c. All functions have open and close parentheses following the function name, which may (or may not) include arguments. The number of arguments required depends on the particular function being called.

Numeric Objects Overview

Python offers all the numeric types you would expect from a modern language, and then some, including integer, long integer, floating point, and even complex (imaginary) types. It's necessary to know how to represent these types in Python, so let's take a look.

> **Very Long Integers**
>
> If you are familiar with other programming languages, you may have assumed that long integers in Python are 64 bits in length. Not so—Python long integers have an infinite number of available digits, limited only by your computer's available RAM! Standard Python integers, however, can only be 32 bits long on Intel and compatible architectures. Use regular integers if they meet your needs, and if they don't, long integers certainly will.

Type Example	Explanation	How to Type
integer	1	Type literal number
floating point	2.3	Type number followed by decimal points and optional digits
complex	2 + 3j	Type integer +/– imaginary number
octal	023	Type number preceded by one zero
hexadecimal	0xff	Type number preceded by 0x
long integer	3000000L	Type number immediately followed by l or L
imaginary	3j	Type number immediately followed by j

In addition to a wide variety of numeric types, Python provides quite a few built-in arithmetic operators and functions:

Op/Function	Description	Example
`**`	Power operator (exponent)	`2**3`
`+, -, ~`	Unary positive, negative, binary invert	`-2, ~0xfeff`
`*, /, +, -`	Multiply, divide, add, and subtract	`3 - 4 * 6`
`%`	Modulo operator	`13 % 4`
`<<, >>`	Binary left and right shift operators	`1 << 4`
`&, ^, I`	AND, XOR, and OR binary bitwise operators	`0xff ^ 0x10`
`abs(x)`	Absolute value	`abs(-10)`
`cmp(x,y)`	Compare values, returns 0 if equal, –1 if x is smaller, 1 if x is larger	`cmp(20,x)`
`coerce(x,y)`	Converts x and y to common type (if x is an integer and y is floating point, will return a list of both items as floating point)	`coerce(a,b)`
`complex(x,y)`	Creates complex number	`a=complex(4,3)`
`divmod(x,y)`	Returns quotient and remainder of x/y in tuple	`divmod(20,3)`
`float(x)`	Converts strings and numbers to floating point	`float("200")`
`int(x)`	Converts strings of integers and numbers to integer	`int("321")`
`long(x)`	Converts strings and numbers to `long int`	`long("321111")`
`pow(x.y[,z])`	Returns x**y[% z]	`pow(2,16,8)`
`round(x)`	Rounds up (floating point)	`round(3.3)`

String and String Conversion Overview

Now, let's look at another example, this time using integers and strings:

```
>>> name="Daniel"
>>> description='Person'
>>> age=25
>>> name+description
'DanielPerson'
>>> name+description+age
Traceback (innermost last):
  File "<stdin>", line 1, in ?
TypeError: illegal argument type for built-in operation
```

Everything seems to be going well until we type **name+description+age** into the interpreter. Can you figure out what we did wrong? We will go through the lines one by one, and the answer should become apparent. On the first two lines, we define two objects, name and description, which are assigned two different strings. On the first line, we use double quotes to surround the string data, and on the second, we use single quotes. Python doesn't care whether you use single or double quotes, as long as you choose the same character to begin or end a string. We complete our object declarations by defining the object age to be equal to the numeric value 25.

On the next line, we encounter a new kind of expression—we are "adding" two strings together! As you might have guessed by the program output, Python understands that two strings are to be concatenated (joined) when + is used with two string literals or objects.

Our last expression, name+description+age, seems correct, but Python does not like it. The problem is that we are trying to add different types (numeric and string) together. In Python, you can use the + operator either to add numeric values or to concatenate strings, but not to do both at the same time. Here's how to get our desired result:

```
>>> name+description+`age`
'DanielPerson25'
```

It's a simple solution. To turn a numeric value into a string, surround it with reverse quotes. As a string, it can then be concatenated to other strings normally.

It would be nice to separate our three values with a space, and there are several ways to do this. The quickest and dirtiest way is to simply insert *literal spaces*, as in the following example:

```
>>> name+' '+description+' '+`age`
'Daniel Person 25'
```

We will explore the second possibility in the next section.

Writing Python Scripts

It's handy to be able to interact with the Python interpreter in real time, but for most projects, you will want to create Python scripts in a text file. To do this, simply start up your favorite text editor, and on the first line, enter:

```
#! /usr/bin/env python
```

After saving your new script, you need to make the script executable:

```
chmod +x myscript
```

You should now be able to type **./myscript** and Python will load and the script will execute.

As an example, start your favorite text editor and create a new file called `printout.py`. In this file, type the following:

```
#! /usr/bin/env python

# this program prints out some text

a="Hello,"
b="World!"
a+' '+b
```

Before trying to execute this program, remember to type **chmod +x printout.py**. Now, to execute it, type **./printout.py**. Unexpectedly, the famous phrase "Hello World!" is nowhere to be seen! The Python interpreter, when in interactive mode, is extra-friendly and prints out the results of expressions automatically. But when we execute Python commands as part of a script, output needs to be explicitly printed. Fortunately, the fix is easy:

```
#! /usr/bin/env python

# this program prints out some text, for real

a="Hello,"
b="World!"
print a+' '+b
```

The print command explicitly commands the interpreter to print out the result of our expression to standard output. It will now print out the desired result. Note you can use the `print` command in other ways to get the same output:

```
print a,b
```

The `print` command is smart and knows that programmers like us often want to insert a single space between variables; it does this automatically when we separate items to be printed by a comma, rather than concatenating them together. Also note that the command `print a,b` would print *Hello, World!* without a newline at the end of the line. Therefore, the following commands will also produce identical output:

```
print a,
print b
```

How to Add Comments

By the way, the "hash" symbols that appear in the preceding examples are Python's standard way of specifying comments; any text after a # character is a comment and is ignored.

We've reviewed the absolute fundamentals; we're now ready to take a whirlwind tour of the "guts" of Python. In the next section, we will increase the pace and introduce the power that is at your disposal.

The Power of Python

To harness the power of Python, we first need to understand how to separate blocks of code into logical groups. Python uses a simple and elegant method to accomplish this task—indentation:

```
a=1
while a < 10:
        print a
        a = a + 1
print "done!"
```

Here we see an example of a `while` loop. Python understands that the indented lines are part of the `while` loop and that the last print command is not. Not only does this make Python code much easier to read, but it also eliminates a major source of programming errors, incorrectly terminated program blocks. For those who may not be familiar with `while` loops (which are used in most structured programming languages), let's review the code. First, we set the object to an integer value of 1. Then, we enter the `while` loop, which will execute as long as the expression following the "while" evaluates to true (1). Each time the `while` loop evaluates, the following two lines of code are executed (`print a` and `a = a + 1`). When the `while` expression evaluates to false, the loop terminates and the final line is executed.

List Processing Power

Take a look at the following snippet:

```
mylist=["We","are","the","knights","who","say","'Ni!'"]
for x in mylist:
        print x,
print
```

In this example, we see a clear and expressive syntax and formatting that make Python easy to read and understand. Let's take a closer look at the code.

The first thing we do is to create a list consisting of seven strings. A list is an ordered collection of data that can be modified dynamically—think of them as dynamic arrays. The second line is a `for` statement; it iterates through each item in list `mylist` (left to right), each time assigning x to a new value (this is similar to the way the `bash` shell evaluates for loops). The last `print` command completes the line because the `print` command in the loop ends with a comma to suppress the printing of a newline.

Let's explore lists a bit further. Start the Python interpreter in interactive mode and define a `mylist` object exactly as it is typed in the preceding snippet. Try the following commands:

```
>>> mylist
['We', 'are', 'the', 'knights', 'who', 'say', "'Ni!'"]
>>> len(mylist)
7
>>> mylist[0]
'We'
>>> mylist[6]
"'Ni!'"
>>> mylist[2:4]
['the', 'knights']
```

The built-in function `len()` tells us the length of the list. Notice, in the last command, how we can specify ranges of items in lists. Here are a few more advanced list expressions:

```
>>> mylist[1:-1]
['are', 'the', 'knights', 'who', 'say']
>>> mylist[1:100]
['are', 'the', 'knights', 'who', 'say', "'Ni!'"]
>>> mylist[1:1]
[]
>>> mylist[1:2]
['are']
>>> mylist[2:2]
[]
>>> mylist[-3:-2]
['who']
>>> mylist[-2:-3]0
[]
```

In the first line, we specify a list range using a negative offset. When a list index is preceded by a negative sign, it means that the list items are specified from the right-hand side. For example, the -1 element is `'Ni!'`, the -2 element is say, and so on. Now, notice the second command and how we specified a very large range that is out of bounds—Python looks out for us and simply sets the range to the maximum possible "right-side" value, without a fuss. Look at the second to last command and see how we use two negative indexes, which is perfectly legal. This simply evaluates to the slice from the "third from right" (fourth) to the "second from right" (fifth) element. The last element in the slice is not included; this means that `mylist[1:1]` evaluates to a null list. There is an added benefit relating to this, which we will cover later.

List Processing Operators

Here are several additional operators you can perform on lists:

Operator	Description
value (not) in *mylist*	Returns 1 if value exists in *mylist*; otherwise 0
mylist * intvalue	Returns intvalue copies of *mylist*, concatenated
min(*mylist*)	Smallest value in *mylist*, numerically
max(*mylist*)	Greatest value in *mylist*, numerically (min() and max() also work with strings)

Almost all the things you just learned about list indexes and ranges can be applied identically to string values. For example:

```
>>> mystring="I am a string"
>>> mystring
'I am a string'
>>> mystring[-1]
'g'
>>> mystring[1:-1]
' am a strin'
>>> mystring[-3:-1]
'in'
>>> len(mystring)
13
```

Embedding newlines and control characters is also possible. As in many languages, you can use the \ sequence to specify special character sequences. \n\n is a string with two newlines, \n\t contains a newline and a tab, \"\' contains a double and single quote, and "\032\x1f" is a string containing the ASCII character with the octal value 32 and another character with the hexadecimal value 1f.

You are encouraged to fire up the Python interpreter to play around with string and list indexes so that you get a feel for how they work.

More Sequence Types

To put it simply, sequence types are Python data types that are "array-like" in nature and include strings, lists and tuples. We have touched on strings and lists, but before we delve into tuples, it is important to understand a major difference between lists and strings: their mutability.

Mutability of Strings

Strings are not mutable. This means that once a string object has been defined, individual characters cannot be dynamically changed to new values. For example:

```
>>> mytest="Are you mutable?"
>>> mytest[3]="r"
Traceback (innermost last):
  File "<stdin>", line 1, in ?
AttributeError: __setitem__
>>>
```

When we tried to set the third character of the string to a new value, the interpreter got stuck and printed out a stack trace. Note that you can always reassign `mytest` to a new string value but you cannot set individual characters to new values. For practical purposes, immutability means that the actual data in the sequence type is "read-only."

Mutability of Lists

Lists, however, are mutable. Individual list items can be assigned new values at any time in the program. Here are some examples:

```
>>> mylist=["This","is","a","test","of","mutability!"]
>>> mylist[3]="example"
>>> mylist
['This', 'is', 'a', 'example', 'of', 'mutability!']
>>> mylist[2]="an"
>>> mylist
['This', 'is', 'an', 'example', 'of', 'mutability!']
>>> mylist[5:5]=["wacky"]
>>> mylist
['This', 'is', 'an', 'example', 'of', 'wacky', 'mutability!']
>>> del mylist[5]
>>> mylist
['This', 'is', 'an', 'example', 'of', 'mutability!']
>>> mylist.append("The End.")
>>> mylist
['This', 'is', 'an', 'example', 'of', 'mutability!', 'The End.']
```

First, we create a new list called `mylist`. After a few lines, we start acting a bit silly and insert the word "wacky" into the list. Note that we use a range (`[5:5]`) that evaluates to a null list. When we assign a new value to this range, an item is inserted. We then decide we went a bit overboard by inserting such an odd word and delete the `'wacky'` list item using the `del` statement. Finally, we use the `append` method to add a string to the end of the list.

The del Statement

The del statement is an essential tool. With del, we can delete objects and parts of mutable lists that have already been defined. We can use del to "zap" almost anything:

```
>>> mylist
['This', 'is', 'an', 'example', 'of', 'mutability!']
>>> del mylist
>>> mylist
Traceback (innermost last):
  File "<stdin>", line 1, in ?
NameError: mylist
```

As you can see, we have deleted our entire list, and mylist is now undefined.

> **House Cleaning with del**
>
> In a language such as Python where very large objects can be created dynamically, it is very easy to eat up large amounts of memory very quickly. Once you are finished using a large object and will not need it again (such as a list containing several hundred or more items), you are encouraged to del it so that Python can immediately free the memory that is being reserved for that data. By helping Python to "clean some house," your programs will take up a smaller memory footprint and run faster.

The Value None

The special value None can be used to "empty out" an object without redefining it.

```
>>> val=[1,2,3,4,5,6,7]
>>> val
[1, 2, 3, 4, 5, 6, 7]
>>> val=None
>>> val
>>>
```

Notice how val does not contain any data but is still defined. This is handy—we can create a list of two "empty" objects the following way:

```
>>> val=[None,None]
>>> val
[None, None]
```

None is a reserved word and can be used in assignments and comparisons. We can test for whether something equals None in an if statement or use a None value as a terminus in a while statement. A common use of None is to read individual lines from a file:

```
myfile=open("/etc/services","r")
myline=""
while myline!=None
        myline=myfile.readline()
        print myline
```

The preceding code segment works because the `readline()` method returns `None` when it reaches the end of a file.

Sorting Lists

Sorting is easy:

```
>>> mylist=["We","are","the","knights","who","say","'Ni!'"]
>>> mylist.sort()
>>> mylist
["'Ni!'", 'We', 'are', 'knights', 'say', 'the', 'who']
```

The `sort()` method also accepts an optional comparison function which accepts two arguments and returns a `-1`, `0`, or `1` depending on whether the first argument is less than, equal to, or greater than the second.

Tuples

Tuples are very simliar to lists, but they are immutable. You are encouraged to use them when you would like to define lists that will be kept constant for your entire program. Defining a tuple is almost identical to defining a list; the only difference is that square brackets are replaced with parentheses:

```
>>> mytuple=("This","is","tuple-rific!")
>>> mytuple[1]
'is'
>>> mytuple[1]="was"
Traceback (innermost last):
  File "<stdin>", line 1, in ?
AttributeError: __setitem__
```

As you can see, even though you can refer to specific items in a tuple, you cannot set them to new values. In all areas other than their mutability, they are identical to lists.

Dictionaries

Dictionaries are a new object type, called a mapping type. Because they allow us to associate names with arbitrary objects, they could be described as dynamic associative arrays. Behind the scenes, Python uses a technique called hashing to store and retrieve dictionary keys in an efficient manner. Before we get too involved with the technical side of dictionaries, let's look at an example.

Dictionaries create relationships between keys and values. Keys are the same thing as names; we use them as a handle to the value, or "data." Keys can be numbers or strings, and values can be any object, including lists and tuples. We can do a number of things with dictionaries. Here are some examples:

```
>>> favcolor={"Mechanix":"red","Skibum":"blue","RogueMtl":"green"}
>>> favcolor["Mechanix"]
'red'
>>> favcolor["RogueMtl"]
'green'
>>> favcolor.keys()
['Skibum', 'Mechanix', 'RogueMtl']
>>> favcolor={}
>>> favcolor.keys()

[]
>>> favcolor["Mechanix"]="red"
```

In this particular example, we create a dictionary called favcolor, which consists of three items. We first retrieve the item associated with the key "Mechanix" and then the item associated with the key "RogueMtl". After that, we use the keys() method to return a tuple of all the keys in the favcolor dictionary. Finally, we erase all our key/value pairs by assigning an empty dictionary to favcolor. We verify this by using the keys() method to get a list of all the keys in the dictionary (an empty list). Finally, we add an item to our empty dictionary, creating a "Mechanix"/"red" key/value pair.

```
>>> favcolor={"Mechanix":"red","Skibum":"blue","RogueMtl":"green"}
>>> favcolor.keys()
['Skibum', 'Mechanix', 'RogueMtl']
>>> favcolor.has_key("Skibum")
1
>>> favcolor.has_key("drobbins")
0
>>> del favcolor["RogueMtl"]
>>> favcolor
{'Skibum': 'blue', 'Mechanix': 'red'}
>>> favcolor.items()
[('Skibum', 'blue'), ('Mechanix', 'red')]
>>> favcolor.values()
['blue', 'red']
>>> favcolor.get("Skibum")
'blue'
>>> newvals=favcolor.copy()
>>> newvals
{'Skibum': 'blue', 'Mechanix': 'red'}
```

Here's another example; it contains advanced dictionary functionality. In this example, we use the has_key() dictionary method, along with the del statement, which we use to remove the key/value pair associated with `"RogueMtl"`. We then use the `items()` dictionary method, which returns a list of tuples of our key/value pairs. After that, we use the `get()` method, which is another way of getting the value of an item, and we finish by using the dictionary `copy()` method.

> **Copying Lists and Dictionaries**
>
> There is one caveat regarding the assignment of lists and dictionaries to new names. If you just do a simple assignment, such as `"newdict=olddict"` or `"newlist=oldlist"`, the object does not actually get copied; only the reference to the object is copied. This means that both names would now be pointing to the same value in memory, so if you delete an item from the new object, it will also disappear from the old one! To avoid this, type **newdict=olddict.copy()** with dictionaries, and type **newlist=list(oldlist)** when dealing with lists. Then, the old and new objects will be using different memory spaces and will be independent of each other.

Comparisons and Looping Constructs

We have already touched on some comparison and looping constructs, but it's important that we become extremely familiar with all that Python has to offer in this area.

Comparisons

Before we can write an `if...then` statement, we need to know how to properly write a Boolean comparison that can be evaluated. Python supports a variety of standard comparison operations such as: <, <=, >, >=, ==, <>, !=, is, and is not, which in English are "less than," "less than or equal," "greater than," "greater than or equal," "equal," "not equal," "not equal (alternate syntax)," "object identity," and "negated object identity."

Here are some standard comparison operations in action:

```
>>> if 1 < 2:
...     print "yes, it is!"
...
yes, it is!
>>> val=0
>>> if val:
...     print "yes"
```

```
... else:
...     print "no"
...
no
```

We see that an integer value of zero evaluates to false in a Boolean expression, as you would assume. But what you might not expect is that None (see preceding note), any numeric zero, any empty sequence (such as "", (), or []), and any empty dictionary are also considered false. All other values are considered true, and this makes comparisons powerful and flexible.

or...and...not!

In addition, any comparison operation can be negated by inserting the word "not":

```
>>> a="mystring"
>>> if not not a:
...     print a
...
mystring
```

In addition to not, two other Boolean operations are available: and and or. If you use them, I recommend that you use parentheses in your comparison, so that the order of evaluation is clear. Although Python has a specific order of evaluation for operators, using parentheses makes the ordering obvious to the programmer and eliminates the possibility of order of evaluation errors. I encourage you to write **if not ((a < 1) and (b > 2)):** rather than **if not a < 1 and b > 2:** for this reason.

Object Identity

Two comparison operations that we have not yet covered are the object identity is and not object identity operators is not. Before we explore these operators, we need to import our first module. This is accomplished by the following code:

```
>>> from types import *
>>>
```

Python is designed to be modular, and various functions and objects are only available after a module has been imported. Not only are modules a nice organizational tool, but they also allow the programmer to add new abilities to Python in a flexible and powerful way. Python modules can be written in Python itself as well as in C and C++. In the preceding example, the types module defines names for all the object types that are used by Python. The from types import * statement has imported a bunch of names that are now ready to be used, as shown in Listing 34.2.

LISTING 34.2 globals()

```
>>> globals()
{'__doc__': None, '__name__': '__main__', '__builtins__': <module
'__builtin__'>}
>>> from types import *
>>> globals()
{'TracebackType': <type 'traceback'>, 'NoneType': <type 'None'>,
'__doc__': None, 'FunctionType': <type 'function'>, 'LambdaType': <type
'function'>, 'ModuleType': <type 'module'>, 'SliceType': <type 'slice'>,
'TypeType': <type 'type'>, 'BuiltinFunctionType': <type
'builtin_function_or_method'>, 'DictionaryType': <type 'dictionary'>,
'ClassType': <type 'class'>, 'FloatType': <type 'float'>, 'ComplexType':
<type 'complex'>, 'InstanceType': <type 'instance'>, 'LongType': <type
'long int'>, 'StringType': <type 'string'>, 'FrameType': <type 'frame'>,
'UnboundMethodType': <type 'instance method'>, 'TupleType': <type
'tuple'>, '__name__': '__main__', 'ListType': <type 'list'>, 'CodeType':
<type 'code'>, 'EllipsisType': <type 'ellipsis'>, 'BuiltinMethodType':
<type 'builtin_function_or_method'>, 'XRangeType': <type 'xrange'>,
'FileType': <type 'file'>, '__builtins__': <module '__builtin__'>,
'MethodType': <type 'instance method'>, 'IntType': <type 'int'>,
'DictType': <type 'dictionary'>}
>>>
```

In the previous example, we can clearly see how many new names have been imported by our import command. The globals() function returns a dictionary of names that are defined in the global name space. This means that these new names are available globally. We'll cover namespaces in more detail later on.

After we import the type module, we can now use the is comparison operator:

```
>>> myint=3
>>> if type(myint) is IntType:
...     print "It's an integer!"
... else:
...     print "Nope, sorry!"
...
It's an integer!
```

type()

The type() function is very useful; for a full listing of types, see the section entitled "Standard Modules Overview" later in this chapter. When you have lists or tuples that contain objects of varying types, you can write code that can easily differentiate between different types of objects and act accordingly. Let's look at the real-world example in Listing 34.3, which will also provide us with full exposure to if statements.

LISTING 34.3 Example Conditional Statement

```
#! /usr/bin/env python

mylist=[2,"cows","running",["slowly","quickly"]]
from types import *
for x in mylist:
    if type(x) is IntType:
        print "Integer:",`x`
    elif type(x) is StringType:
        print "String:",x
    elif type(x) is ListType:
        print "List:",
        for y in x:
            print y,
        print
    else:
        print "Uh oh!"
```

This script will output the following text:

```
Integer: 2
String: cows
String: running
List: slowly quickly
```

First, we define a list that consists of an integer, two strings, and a list of two strings. It's perfectly legal (even encouraged!) to nest lists and tuples to your heart's content. We determine the appropriate way of outputting x, depending on its type. Let's look at the `if` statement. It can have any number of `elif` sequences, which stand for else if, and an optional `else` at the end. Also note that `if` statements are so compact that there is no `case` statement, as in C. The same thing can be accomplished compactly with an `if` statement and a number of `elif` statements and an `else`.

> **Tip**
>
> If you are having a hard time getting the interpreter to accept your `if` statement, make sure that you are putting a colon immediately after the `if`, `elif`, and `else` statements. It's a common mistake for those unfamiliar with the language. The same thing goes for `while` and `for` statements, which should also end with a colon.

Looping Constructs

A simple way of performing looping in Python is to use a `while` statement. The key to proper `while` loops is to get your indentation right. Here's a more complicated example:

```
x=1
y=0
while x < 10:
        print x,
        x=x+1
        y=x
        while y > 0:
                print "!",
                y=y-1
        print
```

This above code snippet contains two while loops; one is an outer loop, and the other is an inner loop. This means that the inner loop executes repeatedly because it appears in the body of the outer loop. Based on this information, use your mental prowess to figure out what this code does, and then type it into the interpreter, watch it run, and see if you were right!

range()

The important thing to remember about for statements is that they iterate through items in a list, rather than simply incrementing a number. For times where you would like to cycle through a range of numbers, use the range() function to dynamically create a list of sequential numbers:

```
>>> range(0,10)
[0, 1, 2, 3, 4, 5, 6, 7, 8, 9]
>>> range(1,5)
[1, 2, 3, 4]
>>>
for x in range(1,10):
        print x
```

The second to last line is equivalent to for x in [0, 1, 2, 3, 4, 5, 6, 7, 8, 9], and the last two lines will cause the numbers zero through nine to be printed on separate lines.

Two Types of Loops

In the following code, we see that we often have two options in how to perform for loops. The first method is the most efficient:

```
mylist=["Here","is","another","one","of","those","lists!"]

# this prints each item in the list on a separate line
# the variable x is set to each item in the list, one at a time

for x in mylist:
        print x
```

```
# this does too, but uses a different method
# the variable x is set to each list index in the list (zero through six)

for x in range(0,len(mylist)):
        print mylist[x]
```

But the second method is handy when you want to access a numerical list index from within the loop:

```
for x in range(0,len(mylist)):
        print x, mylist[x]
```

Play around with these different methods of iterating through lists in the interpreter or in a shell script.

Loop Control Statements

For all looping constructs, there are three statements that you should know about: `break`, `continue`, and `pass`.

The `pass` statement does absolutely nothing, but it takes up space. Sometimes this is necessary when code is syntactically required, but you want nothing to happen. It can come in handy when creating empty `while` loops. The `continue` statement allows you to jump immediately to the next iteration of the loop, without executing any additional code. The `break` statement immediately aborts the innermost loop and is useful for things like this:

```
f=open("/etc/fstab","r")
while 1:
        a=f.readline()
        if not a:
                break
        else:
                print a
```

The preceding code prints out the contents of your /etc/fstab file, line by line.

Functions and Namespaces

Functions (like their C counterpart) allow you to create logical "bunches" of code that can be passed optional arguments and that can return an optional value. Here's a sample function.

Function Descriptions

```
>>> def foo():
...     "foo prints bar"
...     print "bar"
...
```

```
>>> foo()
bar
>>>
```

It's simple but boring. The only thing to mention here is that it is proper Python etiquette to include a one-line string literal as the first line of the function body, to serve as a description, which does not get printed. Let's consider a more complex example.

Default Arguments

```
def greeting(person="Bob",city="Albuquerque",nickname="Bobster"):
    "My cute little form letter"
    print "Dear",person+":"
    print
    print "Hey",nickname+"!", "How are things in",city+"?"
    print
    print "Sincerely,"
    print
    print "Your friend."
```

The preceding function has default values that will be assumed if not all arguments are specified. This means that all the following function calls are legal:

```
greeting()
greeting("Anthony","Jersey","Big Tony")
greeting(nickname="Robsterino")
greeting("Robert")
```

Return Values

Functions also allow us to return objects, by using the `return` statement. Using the return statement, we can pass back one object as a result. If more than one object needs to be passed back, we can group them into a list or tuple and pass that back to the caller:

```
def squares(mynum):
    if mynum<0:
        # not legal!
        return None
    else:
        myval=[]
        for x in range(0,mynum):
            myval.append(x**2)
        return (myval,"morethings","squirrels",("chicken","pot","pie"))
```

The following statements are legal:

```
print squares(8)
mysquares=squares(100)

for x in squares(10):
    print x
```

Introduction to Namespaces

Python differs from most languages in how it deals with functions that want to access and/or modify global objects. But to understand how this works, we first need to become familiar with namespaces. Practically speaking, a namespace allows Python to find objects by name. Technically speaking, a namespace is a mapping from a name to an object and can be represented as a dictionary.

When a function is called in Python, the interpreter creates a completely new namespace for the function body, called the local namespace. When you refer to an object inside the function, Python searches this local namespace first before looking outside:

```
>>> x=10
>>> def printx():
...     print x
...
>>> printx()
10
```

In the preceding example, when we called `printx()`, it first searched the local namespace, and after not finding the name x, it searched the global namespace. It then found the object and printed it. No surprises here; this is what you probably expected.

Namespace Confusion—`global` to the Rescue

Here comes the interesting part. In Python, creating and modifying global objects from inside a function is done a bit differently. From the following example, you can see how *not* to try to modify a global object:

```
>>> x=10
>>> def setx():
...     x=99999999
...
>>> setx()
>>> x
10
```

What happened? When we created the new object x inside the `setx()` function, Python created a new object in the local namespace. As a rule, when you create a new object or perform an assignment in a code block, Python modifies the *local namespace only*, unless you explicitly tell Python to modify the global namespace. We'll look at an example of how to do this soon, but for now, let's reflect a bit on the ramifications of this design decision. What it means for the programmer is that we can "read" global objects if there is no local object defined with the same name, but we cannot "write" to a global object. From a programming standpoint, this is ideal because it eliminates the possibility of creating unwanted side effects in your code, where global objects are accidentally modified. But what if we want to be able to modify a global object from our function? The following code shows us how:

```
>>> def gxy():
...     global x,y
...     x=999
...     y=999
...
>>> gxy()
>>> x,y
(999, 999)
```

The `global` statement allows us to handpick from the global namespace objects that we would like to be able to modify. After a `global` statement, any following assignment statements modify the global object directly and do not simply create a new object in the local namespace. The decision to design Python this way was a good one. It means that a common kind of programming error—accidentally modify global objects—is eliminated, and code becomes easier to read and understand. Functions are always cleanly encapsulated, unless we explicitly decide that we want to change this behavior.

Input and Output

One of the most common tasks that a program must perform is file IO, so providing an in-depth review of this topic is essential. Python provides many easy-to-use facilities for reading and writing files, and we explore these facilities, along with useful companion functions, in the following two sections.

Input

One of the common things that a program needs to do is to get input from the user, which is accomplished under Python by using the built-in raw_input() function:

```
>>> myinput=raw_input("Gimme some input :) --> ")
Gimme some input :) --->
```

raw_input() accepts an optional argument, which will be used as a prompt.

> **Enhancing Your Interactive Experience with Readline**
>
> The build of Python that comes with Caldera OpenLinux 2.2 does something to make data input less tedious—it uses the GNU readline library for performing input. This means that, rest assured, you will be able to backspace properly, and that all the control sequences you can use for line and word editing are also available at a Python raw_input() prompt. In addition, you can use the up and down arrows at a prompt to scroll through your input history. Isn't GNU readline great?

Handy Type Conversion Functions

Python also offers these useful built-in functions:

Function	Description	Example
oct(x)	Converts integer to octal string	oct(329)
hex(x)	Converts integer to hexadecimal string	hex(10)
chr(x)	Converts integer to character	chr(65)
ord(x)	Converts single-character string to integer	ord("a")
str(x)	Returns object as string, just like interpreter	str(range[0,3])

Opening a File

The built-in `open()` function is used to open a file:

```
newfile=open("/tmp/test.txt","w")
```

The second argument is the mode, which can be r, w, a, r+, w+, or a+ (read, write, append, and update). open() returns a file object. Calling the file object's methods allows you to interact with the file. After you are done, the file is closed by calling `newfile.close()`. If you forget to close a file, don't worry, Python does it for you when the interpreter exits. Still, it's always best to close a file immediately after you are finished with it so that you do not prevent it from being written to or deleted by other processes.

File Methods

When a file is open, a number of method calls return information about the file:

Method	Description
myfile.isatty()	Returns 1 if the file is a tty-like device; otherwise 0
myfile.fileno()	Returns the file descriptor
myfile.tell()	Returns the current file position
myfile.closed	Returns 1 if the file is closed; otherwise 0
myfile.mode	Returns IO mode that the file was opened with
myfile.name	Returns name of file, in case you forgot

To read an arbitrary amount of data from a file object, use `myfile.read(numbytes)`. `myfile.read()` without a numerical value will return the *entire* file as a string—something you may or may not want to do. To read individual lines, use the `myfile.readline()` method, which will return the next line from the file, newline included, and the special value None when EOF is reached.

In the following example, we open your /etc/fstab file for reading, and then get the first line from the file and assign it to the `myline` object. We then print out this line, which contains a trailing newline. After realizing this, we use a slice operation on our `myline` object to return everything but the last character of the string (`[:-1]` will return everything but the last item of any sequence type).

```
>>> myfile=open("/etc/fstab","r")
>>> myline=myfile.readline()
>>> myline
'# /etc/fstab: static file system information.\012'
>>> myline[:-1]
'# /etc/fstab: static file system information.'
```

Notice how easy it is to strip the newline from the end of `readline()` return value. The `myfile.readlines()` method will return a list of every line in the file; use this carefully with large files. The `myfile.seek(offset,opts)` method will seek to a specific point in the file. The `opts` value can be left blank for seeking to an absolute position, set to 1 to seek from the current position, or set to 2 to seek relative to the end of the file.

Output

File output is very similar to file input. After opening a file using a w as the second argument, you can use the `myfile.write(mystring)` method call to write data to a file. Another alternative is to use the `myfile.writelines(mylist)` method call to write out a list of strings. Note that the input to `writelines()` is expected to be similar to the output from `readlines()`; that is, no newlines are appended for you, so you must add your own. This is easily done with the \n newline escape sequence:

```
myfile=open("/tmp/test.txt","w")
mylines=["line1\n","and here is line 2\n"]
myfile.writelines(mylines)
myfile.write("and let's not forget line 3\n and line 4\n")
```

OS Module, Functions, and Methods

That about sums up the built-in file-handling functionality in Python. However, for what Python doesn't have built in, modules that can do the job are normally available. Even though we might be able to read and write to files, it would be nice if we could do such things as test to see if a file exists, get access and modification times on files, test whether a particular path refers to a file or directory, and more. All this is possible with Python's os module. The os module allows us to accomplish almost anything that we would like relating to files and directories. We will learn about the most popular commands in this module. This is not a complete list of all the file-manipulating functions that are available; check out the Python Web site for a complete list (http://www.python.org).

A New Way to Import a Module

Before we start describing the commands in the os module, we must learn a new way to import a module. The last time we imported a module, we used the `from modulename import *` command, which imported the module into our global namespace. This time, we will use the following command:

import os

After this command is typed, the module is imported, but something is very different. The module name os now exists in our global namespace, but none of the things inside the os module exist in our global namespace. You may wonder how we access the os module at all, if this is true. It's easy, type:

```
if os.path.exists("/etc/fstab"):
        print "I've got it!"
```

By typing *modulename.objectname*, we can access the object *objectname* that exists in module *modulename*'s namespace. This keeps everything tidy and also will often make code much more understandable. Before, when we typed **from *modulename* import ***, we actually merged *modulename*'s namespace with our global namespace. This time, everything is organized hierarchically under the name os. We can import the types module again and look at what happens to our global namespace:

```
>>> globals()
{'__doc__': None, '__name__': '__main__', '__builtins__': <module
'__builtin__'>}
>>> import types
>>> globals()
{'types': <module 'types'>, '__doc__': None, '__name__': '__main__',
'__builtins__': <module '__builtin__'>}
```

If you compare this to the output we received the last time we inspected the global namespace after we imported the types module, you will grasp the difference between the two ways of importing modules.

os Module Lowdown

Function	Summary
`os.path.exists("/etc/fstab")`	Returns 1 if file exists; otherwise 0
`os.path.isfile("path")`	Returns 1 if path is a file or a symlink to a file
`os.path.isdir("path")`	Returns 1 if path is a directory
`os.path.islink("path")`	Returns 1 if path is a symbolic link
`os.path.ismount("path")`	Returns 1 if path is a mountpoint

Function	Summary
`os.chmod("/myfile",mode)`	Sets permissions on file to mode
`os.chown("/myfile",uid,gid)`	Sets ownership on file to uid, gid
`os.link("/mysrc","/mydest")`	Creates hard link from dest->src
`os.listdir("/mydir")`	Returns directory list (literally)
`os.mkdir("/mydir",[mode])`	Creates directory, mode defaults to 777
`os.readlink("/mysymlink")`	Returns path to where mysymlink points
`os.unlink("/myf"),os.remove("/myf")`	Two different ways of deleting (unlinking) files
`os.rename("mysrc","mydest")`	Renames `mysrc` to `mydest`
`os.rmdir("mypath")`	Removes directory `mypath`
`os.symlink("mysrc","mydest")`	Creates symbolic link from `dest->src`

Exceptions

Python has extensive abilities to deal with run-time errors, also called exceptions. When a program is executing and some kind of non-syntax-related error is encountered, an exception is raised. If an exception handling functionality isn't in your code, Python will normally print a stack trace and abort execution. Another way to raise an exception is to use the built-in `raise` statement:

```
>>> raise IOError, "Wazzup?"
Traceback (innermost last):
  File "<stdin>", line 1, in ?
IOError: Wazzup?
```

try...except

Notice that exceptions allow an optional second argument that is used to describe the exception. To deal with exceptions that are raised by Python's functions or your own code, we use `try ...except` statements:

This `try...except` statement attempts to convert a string to a float. This illegal conversion raises a ValueError. "We couldn't do that!" is printed, and execution of the program continues. If an IOError or NameError were raised, `Now look what you did!` would appear on the screen:

```
try:
        a=float("23adfadsf")
except ValueError:
```

```
        print "We couldn't do that!"
except (NameError,IOError):
        print "Now look what you did!"
```

The following code snippet prints `Invalid integer :/` if any type of exception is raised. Otherwise, it executes the code following the optional `else` clause and executes normally:

```
try:
        a=atoi(raw_input(" > "))
except:
        print "Invalid integer :/"
else:
        print "Thanks for the int, baby!"
```

> **Be Careful When Handling All Exceptions**
>
> To the untrained eye, this code probably looks perfectly legal, attempting to convert user input to an integer and, on error, printing an error message.
>
> Unfortunately, this code does not work at all, and it could take a lot of time to figure out why because of an empty `except` clause. Empty `except` clauses are perfectly legal, but they handle all possible exceptions that are raised. Although this may seem like a good thing, it isn't. In this example, we call a nonexistent function. (Python uses the `int()` function and does not have an `atoi()` function like C.) If you try this code, it will print `Invalid integer :/` before you even have a chance to enter data! Be careful with unqualified `except` clauses—they can create headaches if you aren't careful!

try...finally

Python provides one other kind of exception-handling mechanism—the `try...finally` statement. Only one `finally` clause is allowed, unlike `except` which allows any number of `except` clauses and an optional `else`:

```
try:
        a=thingee
finally:
        print "Regardless of what happens, I must tell you: You're kewl!"
```

As you might guess from our example, the `finally` clause specifies code that will run no matter what, even if an exception is triggered. This allows your program to finish essential tasks before allowing the interpreter to exit with a stack trace.

Lots of Exceptions

Here is a table of exceptions raised in Python. You can use these names to provide finer-grained exception-handling control. To see how they are used, refer back to our first `try...except` code snippet.

Exception	When It Happens
EOFError	When `raw_input()` returns an EOF character
FloatingPointError	When any floating-point operation fails
IOError	When an IO-related op fails, such as wrong permissions, file does not exist, or disk full
ImportError	When an `import` statement specifies a nonexistent module
IndexError	When specifying an illegal subscript in a list or tuple
KeyError	When specifying a nonexistent dictionary key
KeyboardInterrupt	When execution is interrupted by the user pressing ^C
NameError	When a name is not found in any namespace
ZeroDivisionError	When dividing by zero

There are several other kinds of exceptions. To find out what they are, fire up Python in interactive mode and start writing some bad code!

The Real World: Example Code

We've spent a lot of time using the Python interpreter in interactive mode, which is an incredible learning tool. However, when you need to use Python to write a script, you will almost always want to create a script that can be executed again and again (without your typing it again and again). In this example, we show you several sample Python scripts that perform useful tasks and tie together various concepts covered in this chapter.

Example: Graphical Directory Listing

A seasoned Linux user who is familiar with the `bash` shell may ask, What is the point of using Python for these operations if I can accomplish the same thing with a `bash` shell script? And the user would be making a good point. For small to medium-sized file-oriented tasks, a simple `bash` script may be your best bet. But when you need to perform complex file operations, `bash` cannot touch Python. Sometimes, you simply need the power of Python lists, and `bash` can't do the job cleanly or effectively, as is shown in Listing 34.4.

LISTING 34.4 Graphical Directory Listing

```python
#! /usr/bin/env python

import sys,string,os
from types import *

mydict={}

def dofile(myfile,mylist):
        global mydict
        if os.path.isdir(myfile):
                mylist.append([myfile])
                mylistdir=os.listdir(myfile)
                mydict[myfile]=(`len(mylistdir)`,os.path.islink(myfile))
                if not mydict[myfile][1]:
                        for x in mylistdir:
                                dofile(myfile+"/"+x,mylist[-1])

def drawtree(mylist,depth):
        for x in mylist:
                if type(x) == StringType:
                        if depth==1:
                                myout=x
                        else:
                                myout=string.split(x,"/")[-1]
                        if mydict[x][1]:
                                myout=myout+" (symlink to "+os.readlink(x)+")"
                        print string.rjust(mydict[x][0],7),
                        print (" "*((depth-1)*2))+myout
                else:
                        drawtree(x,depth+1)

def dirtree(mypath):
        if not os.path.isdir(mypath):
                print "Please specify a directory."
                sys.exit(1)
        mydirs=[]
        dofile(mypath,mydirs)
        print "\nHeirarchical Directory List of",mypath
        print "\nNUMOBJS DIRNAME"
        drawtree(mydirs,0)

dirtree(sys.argv[1])
```

Our script scans a particular directory, prints out a hierarchical representation of the directories under it and object counts per directory, and notes all symbolic links. When you are dealing with a task that is at least this complex, Python will most likely be a much better choice than a simple bash shell script, even when dealing with file-related tasks, which is bash's forte. Of course, when it comes to creating a network daemon or client or to designing a graphical user interface, bash doesn't stand a chance. Python really shines when it comes to versatility.

Python Power Tool: Embedded Python

Our next example turns Python into an embedded language. "Embedded" refers to the fact that the language exists in a type of file that is not a Python script, in this case, an HTML text file. This means that the text file appears to be in HTML format, except for special sections that are marked to execute as Python statements. This will allow us to pass the text file to our pytext embedded Python interpreter (see Listing 34.6) and have the Python parts executed and the resultant output inserted into our original text at the correct locations. Listing 34.5 is a simple example of how the embedded Python syntax will work. Let's say that we have a text file that looks like this:

LISTING 34.5   Sample Text File

```
<H1>This is sample HTML code</H1>

<!--code

for x in range(0,10):
        print "This is Python!"

-->

<b>Here is some more HTML</b>
```

After passing this file as an argument to our embedded Python interpreter, the output will be as is shown in Listing 34.6.

LISTING 34.6   pytext Output after Processing Text File

```
<H1>This is sample HTML code</H1>
This is Python!
This is Python!
This is Python!
This is Python!
This is Python!
This is Python!
This is Python!
This is Python!
This is Python!
This is Python!
<b>Here is some more HTML</b>
```

The Many Uses of Embedded Python

A tool like embedded Python is wonderful when creating files that consist of mostly static text but that contain some dynamically generated content. The Python interpreter can execute the dynamic sections, while the rest of the static text is simply printed verbatim. When it comes to working with HTML, embedded Python becomes an invaluable tool, useful for database integration, CGI, or any other kind of use you can think up. Turning Python into an embedded language is very simple with the pytext script. Let's look at Listing 34.7 to see what makes all this possible.

LISTING 34.7 pytext

```
#! /usr/bin/env python

# pytext 2.0 is Copyright 1999 Daniel Robbins
# It is distributed under the GNU Library Public License

import sys

def runfile(myarg):
    "interprets a text file with embedded elements"
    mylocals={}
    try:
        a=open(myarg,'r')
    except IOError:
        sys.stderr.write("Error opening "+myarg+"!\n")
        return
    mylines=a.readlines()
    a.close()
    pos=0
    while pos<len(mylines):
        if mylines[pos][0:8]=="<!--code":
            mycode=""
            pos=pos+1
            while (pos<len(mylines)) and (mylines[pos][0:3]!="-->"):
                mycode=mycode+mylines[pos]
                pos=pos+1
            exec(mycode,globals(),mylocals)
        else:
            sys.stdout.write(mylines[pos])
        pos=pos+1

if len(sys.argv)>1:
    for x in sys.argv[1:]:
        runfile(x)
    sys.exit(0)
else:
    sys.stderr.write("pytext 2.0: Embedded Python Interpreter\n")
```

```
    sys.stderr.write("Copyright 1999 Daniel Robbins\nDistributed under the GNU
➥Library Public License\n\n")
    sys.stderr.write("Usage: "+sys.argv[0]+" file0 [file1]...\n")
    sys.exit(1)
```

Investigating `pytext`

The first thing we do is import the `sys` module, which contains several functions that we need, including the `sys.exit()` function, which exits the script and returns an optional error code. It also contains the `sys.stdout` and `sys.stderr` file objects, which allow us to perform input and output as if we were reading from and writing to a file.

Next, we define a function called `runfile`, which takes one required argument called `myarg`, the filename. As we enter the function, the `mylocals` dictionary is defined, which will be used as the local namespace for the embedded code that appears in the file `myarg`. We try to open a file, and if we get any kind of IO error, we return from the function call rather than continue processing. As you can see, exceptions provide a very natural and easy way to effectively respond to error conditions in your program. If we are able to open the file, all the lines are read in and stored in a list called `mylines`.

Our next task is to scan this list of lines looking for a special sequence of characters that identifies an embedded code block. We chose the special sequence `<!--code` to start an embedded code block. When this sequence of characters is encountered at the beginning of the line, the following lines are executed as Python code until a `-->` sequence is encountered at the beginning of a line. Coincidentally, anything appearing between these two indicators is considered a comment to Web browsers; this isn't essential to the function of our program, but it can come in handy. For example, you can use `xemacs` in HTML mode, and if you have syntax highlighting turned on, your code blocks will show up in an alternate color. But concerning the end result, any special sequence will do, as long as it does not normally appear in the static text itself.

The specifics of our main `while` loop are fairly straightforward. After we encounter our special start sequence `<!--code`, we append each successive line to the string object `mycode` until a `-->` is found at the beginning of a line. At this point, we stop collecting new code. The code we have collected will be executed, and its output will be passed to standard output.

The `exec()` function call, which actually executes our code, is very interesting. Taking a string containing the code, as well as a global and local dictionary to be used as the global and local namespace, the code is executed as if it had appeared all by itself in a script. Notice that even though we are processing the file, we use the same global and local namespace. This makes embedded Python much more fun because it allows us to define objects in one embedded block and still be able to access them in any other blocks that follow. In other words, we can do the following:

```
blah blah blah
blah blah blah
blah blah blah
blah blah blah
<!--code

mycomment="They would have peace in Israel if you weren't such a snootle!"

-->
blah blah blah
blah blah blah
blah blah blah
blah blah blah
<!--code

print mycomment

-->
```

Although not necessary in this example, this functionality can be very useful when dealing with strings that may take a significant time to generate, such as a database query.

> **Other Ways to Execute Code Dynamically**
>
> Python also provides the built-in function that will immediately execute commands that exist in a specified file. Just like exec(), it allows you to specify an optional global and local namespace after the inital filename argument.
>
> Python also has an eval() function that will return the result of an expression passed to it as a string.
>
> ```
> eval(expression[,globals[,locals]])
> ```
>
> These functions are very powerful because they allow you to dynamically create and evaluate Python code, without lauching a separate interpreter.

To finish our function, we simply print any lines exactly as they appear if they are not part of a code block.

The last few lines that appear outside our function definition parse the command-line arguments passed to the script and output any necessary informational messages. To access the arguments passed to our script, we use the object sys.argv, which consists of a list of arguments. The first (zero) element of the list is the name of the script itself, followed by each successive argument. We execute the `runfile()` function for every argument passed to our script, so calling the script in the following manner is legal:

```
pytext file1.txt file2.txt file3.txt
```

This will simply process each file in succession. You may wonder why we write informational messages to `sys.stderr` instead of `sys.stdout`. The reason we do this is so that, when redirecting output from this command, error and/or informational messages do not become part of the data stream. For example, if `file2.txt` does not exist or is not readable, the error message will appear on the terminal instead of being redirected to `outfile`:

```
drobbins> pytext gothrough.txt file2.txt includes-who.txt > /tmp/outdat
Error opening file2.txt!
```

Using Embedded Python to Insert a Timestamp into HTML Code

Now that we've explored the code a bit, it's time for a quick demo. Let's say you would like to insert the current date into your Web page every time it is generated. The text file in Listing 34.8 will do the trick.

LISTING 34.8 Example Embedded Python Text File

```
<!DOCTYPE HTML PUBLIC "-//W3C//DTD HTML 3.2 Final//EN">
<HTML>
<HEAD>
<TITLE>Daniel Robbins</TITLE>
</HEAD>
<BODY>

(some html here)

<!--code
from time import *
mytime=(strftime('%A, %B %d %Y',localtime(time())))
print "Last updated on",mytime
-->

(more html here)

</BODY>
</HTML>
```

If you save this file as `index.ehtml`, the following command will generate `index.html`:

```
pytext index.ehtml > index.html
```

Embedded Python for Power Users

It's important to mention that there are two ways that we can use `pytext`. The first method, which we have already demonstrated, involves executing `pytext` manually from the command prompt:

`pytext file1.txt file2.txt file3.txt > mynewindex.html`

The second method, which is much more interesting, is to use it to execute `pytext` scripts. To do this, copy `pytext` to `/usr/local/bin`, type in the following script, and save it as `mytest`:

```
#!/usr/local/bin/pytext
Hello, There.  I am a big fan of the following number sequence:
<!— code
for x in range(0,10):
        print x
‡
Thank you for your time.
```

After you're done, type **chmod +x mytest** to make our script executable. Now run it and see what happens.

The difference in these two approaches becomes critical when using `pytext` to generate Web pages. For example, for my own personal Web page, I use `pytext` to generate *static* content (that is, pages that are plain text files). Every time I change my pages, I use `pytext` to regenerate them, and then I upload them to my ISP. Using this method, my pages are generated once and then viewed many times. This works well for my particular situation because I use `pytext` mainly for generating complex tables with a simple function call or for inserting the date that the pages were last updated. In these instances, I do not need `pytext` to regenerate the page *every time* someone loads up my Web site in his or her Web browser.

However, you might need to have `pytext` generate a new page every time it is requested if, for instance, you want to have the *current* time display on your home page or you are interested in creating a site with truly dynamic, changing content. To use `pytext` in this capacity, simply copy `pytext` to `/usr/local/bin` on the Web server (make sure that Python is installed!). Then, you can create scripts like the preceding one and put them in your server's `cgi-bin` directory. Every time someone loads this particular page, `pytext` will regenerate the page, allowing you to deliver true dynamic Web content to the world!

You may wonder how `pytext` compares to JavaScript. Now, that's a good question. The major difference is that JavaScript is generally executed on the *client side*; this means that JavaScript is sent as-is to the client's Web browser and interpreted and executed there. The Web server treats the JavaScript no differently than it treats plain text, simply passing it through to the client as it appears in the HTML.

Using the first `pytext` method, where we are generating *static* pages, all processing is done once on the *server side*. This is similar to a C program that is compiled once and the resultant executable is executed many times. The resultant pages are then transmitted directly to the client. For each hit, no `pytext` processing occurs at all. The Web server simply transmits text files that were generated earlier.

When using `pytext` to create dynamic content by using `#! /usr/local/bin/pytext` scripts, all processing is done on the server side, and the page is dynamically regenerated for every page hit. In this case, the Web server is actually executing `pytext` to generate the Web page, and the output is sent back to the client. We hope this helps you to understand the various uses of `pytext`.

With the `pytext` command and a bit of creativity, you can easily automatically generate your own Web page or an entire Web site. You are now encouraged to engage your mind and become the next Internet millionaire!

Object-Oriented Programming

At its heart, Python is an object-oriented language, and by this point, we have used many of Python's object-oriented features in our programs, maybe without your even knowing it. Previously, we have only interacted with the standard objects that Python provides, but now we're going to learn how to create our own objects that are customized to our specific needs. We've worked with Python objects before, but now it's time to learn how to make Python objects work for us.

Intro to OOP—How to Not Get Confused

The biggest mistake you can make in trying to understand object-oriented programming (OOP) is to buy into all of the hype that circulates regarding this technology, calling OOP such things as "the next programming paradigm" and "the wave of the future." Forget it all and remember one thing—although OOP comes with its own terminology and syntax, it is primarily an organizational method designed to make life easier for you, the programmer. It's not some magic formula for "incredible code."

OOP is very good at addressing programming problems that are organizational in nature. It allows you to group functions and related data together into an object, providing a clearer and more compact syntax for our programs. For example, if we have a bunch of functions that operate on a special data structure called a "glorp," it would not be unusual for them to have names like:

. . .

```
glorp_read(myglorp)
glorp_write(myglorp,data)
glorp_initialize(myinitvalue,myflags)
...
```

These functions would probably be used in the following manner:

```
a=glorp_initialize(3,(None,"foo","None",bar))
print glorp_read(a)
glorp_write(raw_input("new data->"))
```

If we had about 50 functions that we used to manipulate `glorp` data, our code would quickly become filled with `glorp_this` and `glorp_that`, all in an attempt to keep our code easy to understand and unambiguous. If we instead used a Python OOP Class (think type) called `glorp`, the code could look more like the following:

```
a=glorp(3,(None,"foo","None",bar))
print a.read()
a.write(raw_input("new data->"))
```

Notice how our function calls, instead of being prefixed with `glorp_` (something we did so that we would know what kind of data they operated on), now have no prefix and are instead called by following the variable with `.function()`. From our perspective, the function is now associated with the data in one logical unit, simplifying our code. Instead of passing a as an argument, we now simply join the two together by typing **data.function()**.

Now here's a quick terminology lesson. On the first line, we created a new instance of a glorp by calling its `init` method and binding it to the name a. On the second line, we called a's `read()` method, and on the third line, we called a's `write()` method. Putting the syntax and terminology together, what once was:

```
dataname_function(mydata,myarg[,myarg]...)
```

becomes:

```
mydata.function(myarg[,myarg]...)
```

or using the new OOP terminology:

```
myobject.methodname(myarg[,myarg]...)
```

The one exception is on the first line, where this:

```
dataname_init(mydata,myarg[,myarg]...)
```

becomes this:

```
myobject(myarg[,myarg]...)
```

This is because when you use the class name as a function by itself, it calls the object's default initializer, which creates a new object and runs some optional initialization code, which you specify.

You may be confused at this point. If you are, just remember that our OOP code does exactly the same thing as our non-OOP code. Nearly identical things are happening "behind the scenes," regardless of whether we are using function calls or OOP methods. Again, this is all just a way of modularly organizing the same old stuff, making it easier for us.

Class Definitions

Before we can create our own individual objects, we need to create a "mold" for them to be created from, and this is what a class definition does for us. After the class has been defined, we are free to create any number of individual objects. These new, dynamically created objects are called instances. Each instance has unique data, but they all share a common set of methods that define how we can interact with the instances. It's time for an example:

```
class myclass:
        def __init__(self):
                self.myvalue=1
        def add(self):
                self.myvalue=self.myvalue+1
        def zap(self)
                self.myvalue=0
        def print(self)
                print self.myvalue

myinstance=myclass()
myinstance.add()
myinstance.add()
myinstance.print()
```

This code would print 3 on the screen. We first defined a class, created a living, breathing instance of that class, and then called some of its methods. In the class definition, we defined what methods are available to us. The __init_848_() method is a special type of method that gets called during instance creation, which happened on the `myinstance=myclass()` line.

Notice how we refer to the `self` object in the class definition. This is how we tell Python that we want to store a particular piece of data in the instance itself. To understand this easily, just realize that a method call:

`myinstance.add()`

will call the add() method with the following argument:

add(myinstance)

Python performs this syntactical switcheroo for us automatically.

Special Method Demo—Talkative Objects

This special example demonstrates two advanced Python OOP features:

```
#! /usr/bin/env python
# talker.py: Talkative objects, in Python

class talker:

    def __init__(self):
        print "Hi. Instance created and initialized!"
        #so that setattr doesn't get called
        self.__dict__["newvalues"]=[]

    def printout(self):
        print "Hi: New objects:",
        for x in self.newvalues:
            print x+"="+`self.__dict__[x]`,
        print

    def __setattr__(self,name,val):
        self.__dict__["newvalues"].append(name)
        print "Hi. New value added to self:",name
        self.__dict__[name]=val

class bigtalker (talker):

    def __call__(self,x=None,y=None,z=None):
        print "Hi. You called with",x,y,z,"?"
```

Enter the code into a Python script and type the following command in the shell:

python -i talker.py

The script will load, but you will remain in interactive mode so that you can play with the code. First, create a bigtalker object by typing

>>> **mything=bigtalker()**

Now, try typing the following instructions:

>>> **mything.newvalue=3**
>>> **mything.anotherone=4**
>>> **mything.blob="blah blah blah"**
>>> **mything.printout()**
>>> **mything("blue","cow","moon")**

This program demonstrates a couple of new things. First of all, it demonstrates the use of inheritance, which is an OOP feature that allows us to create new classes that are similar to already defined classes, without doing a lot of typing. The bigtalker class adds a new method, but it also keeps all the previously defined method from the talker class because of the bigtalker class definition line:

```
class bigtalker (talker):
```

The extra (talker) creates this hierarchical relationship and saves us a lot of typing.

Another thing to note is the bunch of new special method names that allow us to customize our object in special ways. In addition to __init__, we use the __setitem__ method call. This call is automatically triggered when we assign a value to the instance, while either inside or outside a method. Note the use of self.__dict__. This is how we sneakily create a new variable without typing self.variable=value, which would trigger a __getitem__ method call and cause infinite recursion. Also note the special __call__ method, which allows us to create instances that can act as functions! These special methods are great fun and allow us to customize Python objects totally so that they do special things—appear to be functions or even new numeric types! We can't touch on every special method, but you can find out more about them in the online Python Language Reference, Section 3.3.

Standard Modules Overview

This section contains an incomplete outline of standard Python modules, highlighting the specific functions that you will find useful. We don't have space to cover every module so we provide a miscellaneous modules summary at the end of this section. For complete documentation for the standard modules, visit the Python Library Reference, which can be found at http://www.python.org.

sys Module

The sys module contains several functions that allow you to affect how the interpreter behaves. There is no recommended method to import this module.

Function	Description
exit([arg])	Exits immediately from the interpreter, returning an optional error code which defaults to zero.
exitfunc	Setting this value to the name of a parameterless function will cause that function to be automatically executed when the interpreter exits.

Function	Description
stdin, stdout, stderr	These objects point to the interpreter's current standard input, output, and error streams. They are file objects and can be set to new values to affect the default behavior of the interpreter.
__stdin__, __stdout__, __stderr__	These file objects are the default standard input, output, and error streams that are initialized when the interpreter is loaded. Use these to set the interpreter back to normal operation after playing with the sys.stdin, sys.stdout, and sys.stderr objects.

types Module

The types module contains names for different kinds of object types, which can be used in comparisons:

```
from types import *
if type(myintobj) is IntType:
      mystring=`myintobj`+" is now a string"
```

It is convenient and recommended that you import this module into the global namespace directly with the from types import * command.

Name	Description	Example
NoneType	Special value None	None
IntType	Integer types	23
LongType	Long integer types	4000000L
FloatType	Floating-point types	3.25
ComplexType	Complex number types	3 + 4j
StringType	String types	"Hello"
TupleType	Tuple types	(1,2,(3,4))
ListType	List types	[1,2,"fred","*"]
DictType	Dictionary types	{"a":12,"b":6}
FunctionType	Function types	sys.exit
FileType	File types	open ("foo.txt","r")

`string` Module

The `string` module contains useful string constants as well as powerful string manipulation functions. You will most likely make heavy use of this module, so a significant (but not thorough) summary of objects and functions is provided.

Object/Function	*Description*
`digits`	The string `"0123456789"`
`hexdigits`	The string `"0123456789abcdefABCDEF"`
`lowercase`	A string containing all lowercase letters
`uppercase`	A string containing all uppercase letters
`letters`	A string containing all letters
`whitespace`	A string containing characters that are considered whitespace, such as space, tab, and linefeed
`atof(string)`	Converts string to floating point number
`atoi(string[,base])`	Converts string to integer, optional base
`atol(string[,base])`	Converts string to long integer, optional base
`capitalize(word)`	Capitalizes first character of string
`capwords(string)`	Capitalizes all words, replaces whitespace between words with single spaces, removes leading and trailing whitespace
`expandtabs(str[,tabsize])`	Converts tabs to spaces, default `tabsize` is 8
`find(str,substring)`	Returns index of first occurrence of complete string substring, -1 if not found
`rfind(str,substring)`	Returns index of last occurrence of complete string substring, -1 if not found
`count(str,substring)`	Return count of nonoverlapping occurrences of complete string substring
`split(str[,separator])`	Splits string into words, returning list optional separator defaults to any whitespace
`join(mylist[,separator])`	Joins a list or tuple of words, separating each word by separator which defaults to " "
`lstrip(str)`	Strips leading whitespace
`rstrip(str)`	Strips trailing whitespace
`strip(str)`	Strips leading and trailing whitespace
`ljust(str,mywidth)`	Returns `str` left justified in a string of specified width
`rjust(str,mywidth)`	Returns `str` right justified in a string of specified width

Object/Function	Description
center(str,mywidth)	Returns str centered in a string of specified width.
replace(str,old,new)	Replaces all occurrences of old with new in str.

math Module

The math module provides access to standard mathematical functions. All functions accept numerical arguments and return floating-point values. A summary follows.

Object/Function	Description
pi	3.14159...
e	2.71828...
acos(x)	Arc cosine
asin(x)	Arc sine
atan(x)	Arc tangent
atan2(y,x)	Returns atan(y/x).
ceil(x)	Returns x rounded up to next highest integer.
cos(x)	Cosine
exp(x)	e**x
fabs(x)	Returns absolute value of x.
floor(x)	Returns x rounded down to next lowest integer.
fmod(x)	x % y
log(x)	Natural logarithm
log10(x)	Base-10 logarithm
pow(x,y)	x**y
sin(x)	Sine
sqrt(x)	Square root
tan(x)	Tangent

Note

The cmath module provides nearly identical functions that operate on complex numbers.

time Module

The time module provide time querying and printing functions, as well as a handy sleep() function.

Function	Description
sleep(x)	Suspends program for x seconds (can be floating point).
time(x)	Returns the current time expressed as a floating-point number. This value can be used as an argument by the following three functions:

ctime(x)	Accepts a floating-point value and prints the current local date and time. Example usage:
	`from time import *`
	`print ctime(time())`

gmtime(x)	Accepts a floating-point value and returns a tuple representing the current UTC time, which can then be used as the second argument to strftime() to customize output of the date and/or time.
localtime(x)	Similar to gmtime() but returns a tuple that represents the time in the current (local) time zone.
strftime(format,x)	Given the string "format" and a tuple from a gmtime() or localtime() call, strftime() will return a custom-formatted date/time string. In the format string, the following special sequences will be replaced with the corresponding value:

Sequence	Value
%a	Short weekday name
%A	Full weekday name
%b	Short month name
%B	Full month name
%d	Day of month
%H	Hour in 24-hour format
%I	Hour in 12-hour format
%j	Day of year
%m	Month, numeric
%M	Minute
%p	am or pm
%S	Second
%y	Last two digits of year
%Y	Full year
%Z	Time zone
%%	%

`shutil` Module

The `shutil` module contains a bunch of high-level file manipulation commands that are extremely handy. Here are some useful commands from `shutil`:

Commands	Description
`copyfile(source,dest)`	Copies file `source` to `dest`, replacing any existing file and not duplicating permission bits
`copymode(source,dest)`	Copies file permission bits from `source` to `dest`, but not owner and group
`copystat(source,dest)`	Copies file permission bits, `atime` and `mtime`, but not owner and group
`copy(source,dest)`	Copies a file, including permission bits
`copy2(source,dest)`	Copies a file, including permission bits, `atime` and `mtime`

`commands` Module

The `commands` module allows you to execute any executable program from within a Python program and to capture the program's output and/or exit code. This module is useful for occasional access to shell commands. Note that if your entire Python program consists of calls to functions in this module, your needs will be better served by a standard `bash` shell script!

Commands	Description
`getstatusoutput(string)`	Executes command specified in string in a new shell and returns a tuple containing two items: exit status (integer) and output (string). Note that program output includes both standard out (stdout) and standard error (stderr). Consequently, you may get unwanted error messages incorporated into your output data.
`getstatus(string)`	Very similar to `getstatusoutput()`, but simply returns the integer exit status of the command. Use this function when you simply want to verify that the command completed successfully but you are not concerned about the program's text output. Note that an exit status of zero is considered normal and that any integer equal to or greater than one is considered an error condition.

Commands	Description

getoutput(string)	Very similar to getstatusoutput() but returns a string containing the output of the executed command, but no integer exit status. Here is an example:
	``
	>>> import commands
	>>> commands.getstatusoutput('pwd')
	    (0, '/home/drobbins')
	``

Where to Go from Here

This is the end of our Python tutorial, and I hope you've enjoyed the ride. We would like to provide you with instruction regarding further study so that you can continue to develop your Python programming skills.

http://www.python.org

The Python Web site is loaded with excellent documentation. The Library Reference is recommended reading; it contains a complete listing of all standard Python modules and their associated functions. Simply browsing this list will whet your appetite for pushing Python to its limits! To get there, go to http://www.python.org; click on Documentation and then Library Reference. You will notice that the Documentation page contains a complete Language Reference as well as a Tutorial and FAQ. Use this documentation; it is very well written and covers many more topics than we can touch on in this short introductory text.

Download the Docs

Even though http://www.python.org offers a full set of documentation online, if you plan to do any extensive Python development, you are encouraged to download the entire set of HTML documentation that is made available in a .tar.gz archive. By extracting the documentation to your local hard drive, you will be able to browse it faster and take some load off the Python Web site. You can browse the documentation in Netscape or Lynx by specifying a URL like this:

file:///tmp/downloads/python-docs/index.html

You can then browse the Python documentation directly from your hard drive, without setting up a Web server.

Continuing Education

Many of you may like to continue learning more advanced Python topics. One thing we only touched on is the ability to define object-oriented classes—an incredibly powerful and useful tool. We also just touched on Python's flexible exception handling facility. These are covered in Chapters 8 and 9 of the online *Python Tutorial* by Guido van Rossum. Bookmark `http://www.python.org/doc` in your browser; you'll be going there often.

After reading the last two chapters of the online tutorial, you may be interested in playing around with our opening example program, which downloaded a file from the Web while uploading it to an ftp site. For more info on Python's Web and ftp abilities, check out the `urllib` and `ftplib` sections in the online Python Library Reference. The reference is recommended reading, and by this point you should be able to use these modules in your programs. Python offers a large number of modules relating to database integration, socket programming, data compression, graphics, graphical user interfaces, and more. They're worth checking out.

I hope that Python will make a dramatic positive impact in how you approach programming problems. But maybe more important, I hope that Python make programming fun again—the right tool can turn a chore into an adventure!

Summary

Python is an amazingly flexible general-purpose programming and scripting language for Linux and other architectures. Python offers an elegant and flexible syntax, object-oriented design, and list processing features as well as an extensive collection of modules to enhance the functionality of the language. It is arguably the best Rapid Application Development tool available today.

Introduction to C and C++

CHAPTER 35

IN THIS CHAPTER

- A History of C *858*
- "Hello, World" in C *859*
- Data Types *861*
- Declaring Variables *862*
- Statements *866*
- Functions *876*
- Arrays, Structures, and Pointers *877*
- The C Preprocessor *885*
- More C *888*
- C++ *888*
- Classes *890*
- Inheritance *892*
- Operator and Function Overloading *894*
- More C++ *896*

Even though powerful applications can be written in Perl, Tcl/Tk, or Python, most large applications on Linux are written in C or C++ (or a combination of the two). Here are some reasons why C and C++ is favored:

- C and C++ are compiled languages (the others are interpreted). This gives C and C++ significant speed advantages over the other languages.
- C and C++ allow access to low-level parts of the computer. You can access particular bits of memory or even device registers from C. Any program that needs this level of access must be written in C (or assembly language).
- C and C++ are strictly typed. They require a lot of thought about data structures and algorithms. This generally leads to better-organized and more maintainable programs. Although Perl, Python, and Tcl/Tk are great prototyping languages, C and C++ are better for final implementation of complex software projects.
- C and C++ executables can be distributed without distributing source code. This is very important for some commercial software vendors.
- C and C++ are popular. Almost all computer science graduates have had exposure to C and C++; it's easy to find people who know C and C++ (or at least claim to know them).
- The Linux kernel itself is written mostly in C, and C provides the best access to Linux system calls. Any system-level program or application program that makes a lot of system calls should probably be written in C or C++.

In this chapter, we'll cover C first and then look at C++. That said, this chapter cannot teach you to program in C or C++. It will simply give you an overview of the languages and a feeling for what they can do. If you want to program in C or C++, consult a good book on the subject, such as *The C Programming Language* by Brian Kernighan and Dennis Ritchie.

This chapter assumes that you have some familiarity with computer programming concepts. I assume that you understand variables, loop constructs, if/then constructs, procedures and procedure calls, and data types.

A History of C

C was invented by Brian Kernighan and Dennis Ritchie at Bell Laboratories around 1972. It was originally designed as a systems programming language. In fact, the first major use of C was to rewrite UNIX (which was originally in assembler) shortly after UNIX was designed. UNIX and C have since been closely allied. However, C is a general-purpose programming language and is widely used on many operating systems (and even in embedded devices with no operating system to speak of).

C is popular because of a number of factors:

- It features a wide variety of data types, operators, and library functions for dealing with many common programming tasks.
- C is a fairly low-level language and can be translated into very efficient machine code.
- C is standardized (ANSI standard X3.159-1989 and a corresponding ISO standard). This means that if you follow the standard, your C programs are likely to be portable to a wide variety of operating systems and architectures.
- C is a fairly small language. It has only about 32 reserved words and a simple and consistent syntax.

> **Note**
>
> Some would argue about the simplicity of the syntax. Complicated type declarations can, in fact, be quite murderous to disentangle. But mostly C is quite readable.

- There are many implementations of C for a wide variety of machines.

C has had many dialects that lead to the push to standardize C. In my opinion, the ANSI standardization committee has done an excellent job and produced a consistent, understandable language definition. I discuss only ANSI standard C in this chapter; pre-ANSI dialects will not be considered here.

"Hello, World" in C

For some reason, almost all introductions to C present a program that prints "Hello, World" on the terminal. I will continue this strong tradition and present the canonical "Hello, World" C program.

```c
/* Canonical first C program */
#include <stdio.h>

int main()
{
    printf("Hello, World!\n");
    return 0;
}
```

To run this program, you need to enter it into a text file and compile it. Here's how:

1. Create a text file called `hello.c` containing the example program.
2. Type **gcc -o hello hello.c** to compile the program.
3. Type **./hello** to run the program.

Here's what you should see:

```
$ gcc -o hello hello.c
$ ./hello
Hello, World!
```

The program gcc is the GNU C Compiler, the standard C compiler on Linux systems. We told it to compile the file `hello.c` and put the output (the -o option) in a file called `hello`.

> **Note**
>
> If you omit -o, gcc creates a file called a.out. It does this because UNIX C compilers have been doing this for almost 30 years.

The result of the successful compilation was the executable file `hello`.

From now on, when I say "run this C program," I really intend for you to enter this C source code into a text file, compile it with gcc, and then run the resulting executable.

Let's look at the program line by line.

Comments

The first line is a comment. In C, all text from a /* sequence to the first */ sequence is a comment and is ignored. Note that comments do not nest.

Include a Header

The #include line includes a standard header file into the C source code. The header file `stdio.h` is found in /usr/include/stdio.h. The #include directive is a C preprocessor directive that includes the contents of a file in the source code. It's as if you cut and pasted `stdio.h` into the file.

This file is needed because it contains a function declaration for the `printf` function used later. In C, all functions return a specific type of value and take arguments of certain types. A function declaration informs the compiler of this information. It is good practice to declare all functions before using them.

Main Function

The function `main` is always called by the operating system when a C program starts. It is the entry point to the program.

In this example, the line `int main()` declares `main` as returning an integer (int) and taking no arguments. You should always declare `main` as returning an integer; to do otherwise violates the C standard.

> **Note**
>
> In particular, declaring `void main()` is an abomination.

The body of `main` is enclosed in curly braces. It contains two statements. The first statement (`printf...`) calls the `printf` library function. This function prints a string to standard output. (Actually, it is more complicated than this, but we'll get into that later.) It prints the string `"Hello, World!"` followed by a newline (the `\n` escape sequence).

Finally, the `return` statement returns a value of 0 from `main`. When `main` finishes, so does the program, and the shell prompt reappears.

A return value of 0 from `main` traditionally signifies success. Other return values may convey various shades of failure.

> **Note**
>
> When you write C programs, be sure to return a meaningful exit status. This makes your C programs much more useful in shell scripts that test for successful execution.

Data Types

All variables and values in C have a type. C has a number of built-in types, and you can extend this by defining your own types. Here are the C built-in types:

- `int` A signed integer, which is the "natural" size for the processor. Even though `int` is 32 bits under most versions of Linux, you should not count on this. ANSI specifies that `int` must be able to hold values from –32767 to 32767, and that's all you can count on.
- `short int` A signed integer that may be smaller than `int`. A `short int` is 16 bits long under most versions of Linux, but do not count on this. An implementation may very well make `short int` and `int` the same.
- `long int` A signed integer that may be larger than `int`. ANSI specifies that `long int` must be able to hold values from –2147483647 to 2147483647. On many Linux architectures, a `long int` is the same size as an `int`. This is not true for 64-bit architectures.
- `unsigned int` An unsigned integer that is the same size as an `int`. There are analogous unsigned short and unsigned long types. An unsigned type cannot represent negative values but can represent positive numbers about twice as large as the largest value that can be represented by the corresponding signed type.
- `char` A type that can represent a single character. An implementation may treat `char` as signed or unsigned; the standard does not specify which. If you really need one or the other, specify whether it is to be unsigned or signed.
- `float` A type that represents a floating-point number.
- `double` A type that represents a floating-point number, possibly with higher precision than `float`.
- `void` A type that represents nothing. You cannot directly declare a variable of type `void`, but you can use it as the return type of a function that doesn't return anything useful or as the type of a pointer. (We discuss this type in more detail later.)

Declaring Variables

To create a variable of a specified type, you declare the variable. In this simplest case, this is statement consisting of the type and the variable name. Consider this example:

```
int a;
double c, d;
unsigned long foobar;
```

This declares four variables: a of type `int`, c and d of type double, and foobar of type unsigned long.

Variable names in C must begin with a letter or underscore, and can contain letters, underscores, and digits. C is case-sensitive throughout, keywords must be entered in lowercase, and variables are case-sensitive.

> **Warning**
>
> Any name beginning with an underscore is reserved for the C implementation. Do not create any names beginning with an underscore. It is astounding how many programmers violate this rule; don't be one of them.

Variable Scope

A C program consists of variable declarations and function definitions. A variable declaration outside any function definition declares a global variable. This variable is visible from its point of declaration to the end of the source file.

A variable declaration inside a function definition is visible from its point of declaration to the end of the function body.

Variable Storage Class

Variables in C have various storage classes. The storage class controls the lifetime and linkage visibility of the variable.

Automatic variables can be declared only inside functions. They spring into being when the function is called and are destroyed when the function body is executed. Furthermore, each invocation of the function creates a new variable—recursive calls to the function create entirely new variables.

Consider this example:

```
int fibonacci(int n)
{
    int a, b;

    if (n <= 2) return 1;
    a = fibonacci(n-1);
    b = fibonacci(n-2);
    return a+b;
}
```

This is a (highly inefficient!) function for computing the nth Fibonacci number. The variables a and b are automatic variables; they are visible only within the function fibonacci. In addition, the recursive calls do not share variables; they have their own copies of a and b.

> **Note**
>
> The Fibonacci function is highly inefficient. Its running time is exponential in the size of *n*. You'll see many C programs in which the programmer has written cryptic code using convoluted combinations of C operators rather than straightforward C statements. Don't do this. For one thing, code that looks compact may not be faster than straightforward code—the only way to know for sure is to examine the assembly-language output of the compiler. For another, it's far more important to write maintainable code than microoptimized code. And finally, choice of algorithms is more important; even if we wrote the Fibonacci function in hand-tuned assembly language, it would still be slow because it uses a poor exponential-time algorithm.

Static variables can be declared inside or outside functions. Static variables are visible within the source file (or function, if declared in a function body), but they are not exported to the linker.

It is common practice to divide large C programs into several (or many) source files, compile the source files separately, and then link the resulting object files together. (A special program called a *linker* performs this linking step.) Often, most of the contents of a source file are of little interest to other source files; variable names can be hidden by declaring them static. This helps modularize C projects.

Consider this example:

```
static int count;

void up()
{
    count = count + 1;
}

void down()
{
    count = count - 1;
}

int value()
{
    return count;
}
```

The variable count is global in the source file and is visible to the three functions up, down, and value. However, it is not accessible from any function outside the source file.

The three functions up, down, and value are visible outside the source file (because they are not declared static); they therefore provide controlled access to the count variable from outside the file.

Within a function, static variables can be used to hold values that persist between function invocations. Consider this example:

```
int nextSequence()
{
    static int seqno;
    seqno = seqno + 1;
    return seqno;
}
```

In this case, repeated calls to nextSequence return monotonically increasing values. The seqno variable, however, is not visible outside the function.

> **Note**
>
> Static variables are intialized to 0 if no other initialization is given. (To be precise, the memory occupied by static variables is filled with 0 bytes.) Automatic variables are not so initialized; an uninitialized automatic variable contains garbage.

Functions can also be declared static; this makes the function private to the source file in which it is defined.

External variables are like static variables in that they are global and have the same lifetime as the program. However, external variables are visible to other source files—they are accessible to the linker.

By default, any variable declared outside a function definition is external. If we omitted the `static` qualifier from the `static count` declaration a couple of examples ago, the variable count would be accessible from other source files.

The `extern` keyword signifies that a variable is defined in some other source file. Here's an example:

```
/* Someone else defines this... */
extern double fudgeFactor;

double mySin(double x)
{
    return sin(x + fudgeFactor);
}
```

The variable `fudgeFactor` must be defined in some other source file; the linker will resolve the reference to it during linking (or linking will fail).

We could also have written the example like this:

```
double mySin(double x)
{
    /* Someone else defines this... */
    extern double fudgeFactor;

    return sin(x + fudgeFactor);
}
```

The variable fudgeFactor is still external, but the scope of the declaration is limited to the body of mySin.

Statements

A C program consists of a sequence of statements. A statement comes in various flavors:

- Declarations declare functions or variables. We've seen examples of declarations before. Declaration statements are terminated with a semicolon.
- Definitions define functions. The "Hello, World!" program consists of some preprocessing information and a definition of `main`.
- Expression statements evaluate expressions. These are the most common C statements. Expression statements are terminated with a semicolon.
- `if` and `switch` statements control program flow.
- `for`, `do`, and `while` statements create loop structures.
- The `return` statement causes termination of a function.
- The `break` and `continue` statements alter the behavior of a loop statement.
- A compound statement consists of a group of statements enclosed in curly brackets.

Declarations

A variable declaration declares the type of a variable or function. Consider this example:

```
extern double foo;
extern int defenestrate(int window, double force);
```

These statements declare a variable `foo` of type `double`, and a function `defenestrate`, which returns a value of type `int`. The function expects two arguments, the first of type `int` and the second of type `double`. Note that the declarations do not define the function or variable. The definitions presumably appear later in the source file or in another source file.

A function declaration looks almost like a function definition, but the body of the function is omitted and replaced with a semicolon.

Definitions

A variable definition consists of a storage class specifier, a type specifier, and one or more variable names. It may also have an initializer. Here are some examples:

```
int global = 10;
void func()
{
    static int local = 20;
    double temp = 13.0;
}
```

In this example, `global` and `local` are initialized to 10 and 20, respectively, when the program is first run. The variable `temp` is initialized to 13.0 every time `func` is called.

This is important: Initializers for static variables are executed once when the program is first run; initializers for automatic variables are executed every time the flow of control passes through the initializer.

Expression Statements

An expression statement consists of an expression followed by a semicolon. An expression consists of a sequence of operands and operators.

C has a huge variety of operators. They are summarized in Table 35.1.

TABLE 35.1 C Operators

Operator	Meaning
x()	Call function x
x[y]	Index array x
x.y	Access structure element
x->y	Access structure element through pointer
x++	Postincrement x (add 1 to x and return original value)
x--	Postdecrement x (Subtract 1 from x and return original value)
-x	Negative of x
!x	Logical NOT: 1 if x is 0; 0 otherwise

continues

TABLE 35.1 continued

Operator	Meaning
~x	Bitwise complement of x
++x	Preincrement x (add 1 to x and return new value)
--x	Predecrement x (Subtract 1 from x and return new value)
*x	Pointer dereference
&x	Get address of x
(type) x	Cast x to type
sizeof(x)	Get size of x
x*y	Product of x and y
x/y	Quotient of x divided by y
x%y	Remainder of x divided by y
x+y	Sum of x and y
x-y	Difference of x minus y
x<<y	Left-shift x by y bits
x>>y	Right-shift x by y bits
x<y	1 if x is less than y; 0 otherwise
x<=y	1 if x is less than or equal to y; 0 otherwise
x>y	1 if x is greater than y; 0 otherwise
x>=y	1 if x is greater than or equal to y; 0 otherwise
x==y	1 if x equals y; 0 otherwise
x!=y	1 if x does not equal y; 0 otherwise
x&y	Bitwise-AND of x and y
x^y	Bitwise exclusive-OR of x and y
x|y	Bitwise-OR of x and y
x&&y	Logical AND of x and y: 1 if both are nonzero; 0 otherwise
x||y	Logical OR of x and y: 1 if either is nonzero; 0 otherwise
x?y:z	Choice: y if x is nonzero; otherwise z
x=y	Assign y to x
x+=y	Add y to x
x-=y	Subtract y from x
x*=y	Multiply x by y
x/=y	Divide x by y
...	Analogous %=, &=, |=, <<=, and >>= operators
x,y	Evaluate x and then y

Operators between horizontal rules have the same precedence; operators higher in the table have higher precedence than those below them.

All operators are left-associative except for the unary prefix operators (the second group in Table 35.1), the choice operator ?:, the assignment operators, and the comma operator.

Lvalues and Rvalues

An expression is said to be an lvalue if it can appear on the left-hand side of an assignment operator. For example, if a is a variable of type double, it is an lvalue. However, the constant 2.0 is not an lvalue. Expressions that are not lvalues (or are not used as such) are called rvalues.

Right now, the only lvalues we know about are variable names. Later on, we'll encounter some operators that generate lvalues.

Here is an example of some expression statements:

```
void func()
{
   int a;
   double b;
   double c;

   a = 10 * 30;   /* 1 */
   b = a + 1.0;   /* 2 */
   a++;           /* 3 */
   b += 12.5;     /* 4 */
   c = (a > 300) ? b * 2.0 : b / 1.5;   /* 5 */
}
```

In statement 1, a is assigned the value 300, computed by the multiply operator.

In statement 2, b is assigned the value 301.0. Note that the addition operator converts its operands to double if either is double. C has a number of these built-in automatic conversions.

Statement 3 demonstrates the postincrement operator. It almost equivalent to a = a + 1 but is potentially faster.

> **Note**
>
> It is not exactly equivalent because a is evaluated only once, and the return value is the value of a before the increment.

Statement 4 demonstrates a complex assignment operator. It is almost equivalent to b = b + 12.5, but, again, b is evaluated only once.

Statement 5 demonstrates the choice operator. If a is greater than 300, then c is assigned b * 2.0. Otherwise, it is assigned b / 1.5. The choice operator can make if/then constructs quite compact, but don't abuse it. The traditional if statement is usually clearer.

The if Statement

C's if statement looks like this:

if (expr) statement1

or like this:

if (expr) statement1 else statement2

The expr is any expression. If the result is 0, the expression is considered to be false. Otherwise, it is considered to be true. A true expression causes statement1 to be executed. Otherwise, if the else clause is present, statement2 is executed.

Note that statement1 and statement2 may be compound statements.

Here is an example of the if statement:

```
if (balance >= 0) {
    standing = "good";
    printf("You're OK for now.\n");
} else {
    standing = "bad";
    printf("Watch your kneecaps.\n");
}
```

If balance is greater than or equal to zero, then the first two statements are executed. Otherwise, the second two are executed.

Here's another example:

```
if (a >0) printf("positive\n");
else if (a == 0) printf("zero\n");
else printf("negative\n");
```

Note that the final else binds to the closest if. If there is any chance of confusion, use curly braces to make things clear. For example, this is probably wrong:

```
if (temperature < maximum)
    if (pressure < maximum)
        startNuclearStation();
else
    printf("Warning: Temperature too high\n");
```

The else clause binds to if (pressure < maximum); a correct way to do this is

```
if (temperature < maximum) {
    if (pressure < maximum)
        startNuclearStation();
} else
    printf("Warning: Temperature too high\n");[sr]
}
```

In general, I recommend using curly braces any time the body of an if is not on the same line as the if or else keyword. This practice makes things clearer and avoids problems if you later insert lines into the if or else body. So I would write the example like this:

```
if (temperature < maximum) {
    if (pressure < maximum) {
        startNuclearStation();
    }
} else {
    printf("Warning: Temperature too high\n");
}
```

The switch Statement

The switch statement causes a branch depending on the value of an integral expression. The switch statement looks something like this:

```
switch ( expr ) {
case val1: statement_list1
case val2: statement_list2
case val3: statement_list3
default: statement_listN
}
```

Here's an example:

```
switch ( x ) {
    case 1:
        printf("one\n");
        break;
    case 2:
        printf("two\n");
    case 3:
    case 4:
        printf("three or four\n");
        break;
```

```
    default:
        printf("I dunno\n");
}
```

Here's how it works:

- If x is 1, then *one* is printed and the `switch` statement ends because of the `break` statement.
- If x is 2, then *two* is printed. Execution falls through the next cases and three or four is also printed.
- If x is 3, execution falls through to the next case.
- If x is 4, *three* or *four* is printed and the `switch` statement ends.
- Otherwise, *I dunno* is printed.

> **Warning**
>
> If you do not terminate a group of statements in the `switch` body with `break`, execution falls through to the next case. This is occasionally desirable but should be avoided because it is confusing. If you do use fall-through execution, comment that fact prominently. Otherwise, later program maintainers may add cases to the switch body and destroy the fall-through structure.

A `switch` statement should, in general, have a default label. Otherwise, if the expression does not match any of the case labels, execution continues following the `switch` statement without any indication of a problem. The default label lets you catch possibilities that shouldn't happen.

The while Statement

The `while` statement looks like this:

`while ( expr ) statement`

It works like this: *expr* is evaluated as for the `if` statement. If the result is nonzero, the body statement is executed. This repeats until *expr* evaluates to zero.

Within the body, a `continue` statement prematurely terminates the execution of the body and restarts the `while` loop from the testing of *expr*. A `break` statement terminates the body and exits the `while` loop. Execution continues from the statement following the `while` loop.

Here's an example:

```c
int n = 10;
int total = 0;

while ( n ) {
    total += n--;
}
```

This computes the sum of the numbers from 10 down to 1. It's rather tricky; let's examine it.

The `while` statement continues to loop as long as n is nonzero.

The expression statement that is the body of the loop performs the following operations:

- Add the value of n to total.
- Decrement (subtract 1 from) n.

The order of these operations is undefined. However, we are guaranteed that the original value of n is added to `total`.

Eventually, n will be decremented to zero, and the `while` loop will terminate.

Here's another example:

```c
int n = 0;
while ( ++n < 10 ) {
    if ( n == 2 ) continue;
    if ( n == 5 ) break;
    printf("%d\n", n);
}
```

The test function in the `while` loop first increments n and then compares this incremented value to 10. As long as it is less that 10, the body is executed.

In the body, if n is 2, then the `while` loop is restarted by reevaluting the test expression. If n is 5, then the body and the whole loop are terminated. Otherwise, the value of n is printed to standard output. (The special `printf` notation %d means to print the next argument as a decimal integer.)

The output from this code fragment will be:

```
1
3
4
```

Note that the break terminated the loop before the test expression had a chance to evaluate as false.

The do Statement

The do statement is very similar to the `while` statement. It looks like this:

```
do statement while ( expr )
```

First, `statement` is executed. Then, `expr` is evaluated. If it is nonzero, the loop repeats. Otherwise, the loop exits.

do is similar to `while`, but it always executes the loop body at least once. `while` does not execute the loop body at all if `expr` evaluates to false the first time it is evaluated.

Within a do loop, `continue` jumps immediately to the evaluation of `expr`, and `break` terminates the loop body.

Here's an example:

```
do {
   bribePolitician();
} while ( !politicianCooperative() );
```

Here, `bribePolitician()` is always executed at least once, even if the politician is initially quite cooperative.

The for Statement

The for statement is C's do-it-all looping construct. It looks like this:

```
for( expr1 ; expr2 ; expr3 ) statement
```

Here's how it works:

1. The expression `expr1` is evaluated, and the return value is discarded.
2. The expression `expr2` is evaluated. If the result is zero, the loop terminates. Otherwise, `statement` is executed.
3. The expression `expr3` is evaluated, and the return value is discarded.
4. Go to step 2.

In a for loop, `expr1` is usually used to initialize a variable. `expr2` forms some kind of test expression (as in a while loop), and `expr3` is an update expression which updates a particular variable.

Any or all of the expressions may be omitted. A missing `expr2` is treated as 1 (that is, it is always true).

A `continue` statement in the body causes premature termination of the loop body. Execution continues with step 3. A `break` statement in the body terminates the loop.

Here is an example:

```
int i;
int total;
for (i=1, total=0; i<=10; i++) total += i;
```

Look at *expr1*: `i=1, total=0`. We used the comma operator to evaluate two expressions sequentially. This initializes `i` to 1 and `total` to 0.

This example simply adds the numbers from 1 to 10 into `total`. Note how *expr2* forms the test expression and *expr3* (`i++`) forms the update expression.

Here's another example:

```
int i;
int j;
for (i=0; i<10; i++) {
    for (j=0; j<i; j++) {
        printf("*");
    }
    printf("\n");
}
```

This example uses nested `for` loops to create a triangle from lines of asterisks.

There are two canonical ways to write infinite loops in C:

```
while (1) body
```

or

```
for (;;) body
```

> **Note**
>
> Of course, unless you are writing the main program for an embedded controller, the loop body should have some way to terminate the loop, probably with `break` or `return`.

Which of these forms to use is the subject of intense religious debate, much like the "big-endian" versus "little-endian" or vi versus emacs debates.

The return Statement

The `return` statement causes termination of the currently executing function. It looks like this:

```
return expr
```

The value of *expr* is used as the function's return value. If the function is declared as void, you must omit *expr*. Otherwise, you must supply it, and it must be of the correct type.

Here is an example:

```
int sign(double x)
{
    if (x > 0.0) return 1;
    if (x == 0.0) return 0;
    return -1;
}
```

This function returns 1 if its argument is positive, −1 if it is negative, and 0 if it is zero. We don't need to use `else` clauses because the first `return` statement executed will terminate the function.

Functions

A function in C corresponds to a subroutine or procedure in other programming languages. Functions are used to group commonly used code into one place and make it reusable.

A function is defined like this:

ret_type *name* (*arg_list*) *body*

Here, `ret_type` is the return type of the function. A function that returns nothing useful can be declared of type void; this precludes its use in most expressions.

name is the name of the function. `arg_list` is a comma-separated list of formal parameters. These are names that will be used to hold the actual parameters passed in a function call.

body is a compound statement that forms the body of the function.

We've already seen some examples of functions. Here is another:

```
void swap(int x, int y)
{
    int temp = x;
    x = y;
    y = temp;
}
```

Because the function returns `void`, we don't need a `return` statement. An implicit return is executed at the end of the function body.

You might think that calling swap(a, b) would swap the values of a and b. That is not what happens. In C, all function arguments are passed by value. That is, the called function gets a copy of the original arguments. The swap function shown here actually does nothing.

Here is a more useful function:

```
int sum(int from, int to)
{
    int total = 0;
    int i;
    for (i=from; i<=to; i++) {
        total += i;
    }
    return total;
}
```

This function returns the sum of the integers from from to to. For example, if you want to know what the sum from 1 to 10 multiplied by the sum from 30 to 37 is, you could use this expression statement:

```
answer = sum(1, 10) * sum(30, 37);
```

This illustrates how to call a function. Simply use the function name followed by a comma-separated list of actual arguments in parentheses.

All calls to a function should be preceded either by the function definition or a function declaration. The declaration for sum looks like this:

```
int sum(int from, int to);
```

The declaration specifies the return type and argument types. This is enough information for the compiler to generate a correct function call.

Arrays, Structures, and Pointers

Arrays, structures, and pointers are central concepts in C. They are the mechanisms by which complex data structures are built up from the simple C primitive types.

Arrays

An array is simply a homogeneous collection of variables of a specific type. You declare an array like this:

```
float array[100];
```

The variable array is an array of 100 float values. To get at the first value, use `array[0]`. The last value is `array[99]`.

> **Note**
>
> C always uses 0-based array indexes.

> **Warning**
>
> C does not have runtime array bounds checking. If you try accessing `array[300]`, your program will likely crash immediately or fail later in mysterious ways.

C does not directly support multidimensional arrays, but you can simulate them like this:

```c
int matrix[4][5];
```

For example, you can access a particular element like this:

```c
matrix[2][0]
```

Strings

In C, strings are nothing more that arrays of char. By convention, a string is terminated by a zero value. The zero value must be present, but is not considered part of the string.

In fact, string constants in C (such as `"Hello, World!\n"`) are nothing more than arrays of char with a terminating zero byte.

The string `"Hello"` is a six-element array:

```c
char word[6] = "Hello";
/* word[0] == 'H';
   word[1] == 'e';
   word[2] == 'l';
   word[3] == 'l';
   word[4] == 'o';
   word[5] == '\0';
*/
```

As illustrated in the comment, single-character constants are written inside single quotes. The special constant `'\0'` can be used to denote the final zero character in a string.

To reiterate, strings in C are nothing more than zero-terminated arrays of char. C has no higher concept of a string, and all the C string manipulation functions rely on this convention.

Structures

Although an array is a contiguous list of objects of the same type, a structure groups data objects together in a meaningful container. The entries in a structure need not be the same type (and usually are not).

A structure is declared with the `struct` keyword. A structure declaration looks something like this:

```
struct tag {
member_declaration;
...
};
```

The tag is a name identifying the name of the structure. Each `member_declaration` looks just like a variable declaration and specifies the type of the structure member.

Here is an example:

```
struct complex {
    double real;
    double imag;
};
```

This declares a structure called complex with two members: `real` and `imag` of type `double`.

You can declare a variable of type complex like this:

```
struct complex a;
```

To access the real part, use `a.real`. To access the imaginary part, use `a.imag`:

```
struct complex a;
a.real = 0.0;
a.imag = 1.0;
```

Here's another example of a structure:

```
struct student {
    char firstName[32];
    char lastName[32];
    int yearOfBirth;
    double gradePointAverage;
};
```

This structure might be used to keep track of information about a student. It has 32 characters available for the student's first and last names (actually, 31 because of the trailing 0) and keeps his or her year of birth and grade-point average in `int` and `double` members, respectively.

You can declare an array of structures like this:

```
struct student myStudents[200];
```

This creates an array of 200 student structures. You can get the 14th student's grade-point average like this:

```
double bobsGPA = myStudents[13].gradePointAverage;
```

> **Note**
>
> Remember that the "first" student has array index 0.

Structures may contain other structures as elements. For example, in Surrealistic University, students can have complex years of birth. ("I was born in the square root of −1.") Here's how you can do it:

```
struct surrealStudent {
    char firstName[32];
    char lastName[32];
    struct complex yearOfBirth;
};
```

This assumes that the definition of `struct complex` precedes its use by `surrealStudent`. Here's how we access the imaginary part of the 20th student's year of birth in an array:

```
struct surrealStudent kids[200];
double imag = kids[19].yearOfBirth.imag;
```

Just keep stepping along structure elements in the natural way.

> **Note**
>
> Structure element names are in a separate name space from other names. There is no conflict between a variable called imag, a structure element in one structure called imag or even an element in a completely different structure called imag. The compiler can sort out which one is needed based on the context of the name's use.

Pointers

Pointers are a powerful C concept used for creating complex data structures. They are also among the most misunderstood aspects of C.

Conceptually, all the memory in a computer is laid out as an array of bytes. (At least, this is how the C language views it. It may not reflect reality.) Under Linux, a process has a virtual address space of 32 bits. That is, the process "sees" memory as a huge array with 4294967296 (2^{32}) one-byte entries.

> **Note**
>
> This is not strictly true. Processes under Intel Linux have a 2GB virtual address space, and processes under Alpha Linux have around 8TB of virtual address space. But it's close enough for illustrative purposes.

Every data object in C is placed somewhere in memory. For example, if you declare an int variable, it might be placed in memory locations 19387576 through 19387579, assuming that it occupies 4 bytes of memory. In general, you have no control over where objects are placed; the linker and the operating system hand these details. You also almost never need to know the exact numerical value of an object's location in memory.

However, you can obtain the address of a variable at runtime. You can store this address in a pointer. At a later time, you can dereference the pointer to access the original memory locations. And that is all there is to pointers—nothing more.

To take the address of a variable, use the & operator. To dereference a pointer, use the * unary operator. Here is an example:

```
int a = 10;
int *aPtr;

aPtr = &a;
```

Note how we declare a pointer: Use an asterisk just before the variable name in the declaration. The declaration of aPtr should be read: Declare aPtr as pointer to int.

The assignment assigns the address of a to aPtr. Now, the expressions a and *aPtr, which are both lvalues, refer to exactly the same object. For example, consider these statements:

```
int a = 10;
int b;
int *aPtr;
```

```
aPtr = &a;

*aPtr = 31415;
b = a;
```

After the final assignment, b will be assigned the value 31415. That is because *aPtr = 31415 assigned 31415 to the block of memory pointed to by aPtr, which is exactly where a is stored. *aPtr and a are synonyms for the same block of memory.

Pointers and Local Variables

Look at this piece of code:

```
int *uhoh() {
    int a = 10;
    return &a;
}

int main() {
    int *aPtr;
    aPtr = uhoh();
    /* Bug follows! */
    *aPtr = 1000;
}
```

This is a good example of how you can get into trouble with pointers. The function uhoh returns a pointer to int. However, the pointer that it returns points to one of its local variables. This variable ceases to exist after uhoh returns. However, the main program uses the pointer and writes into memory where the local variable a used to be. This could cause all kinds of nasty behavior—anything from a program that works for years until a trivial change is made to one that segmentation faults immediately. The moral of the story is: Make sure your pointers point somewhere valid!

Pointers and Arrays

Pointers and arrays are very closely related in C. In fact, the language plays fast and loose with the definitions, treating them almost equivalently. An array can be considered a pointer to its first element. For example, consider the library function strlen. (It returns the length of a string.) Here's one way to write it:

```
int strlen(char string[])
{
    int len = 0;
    while(string[len]) {
        len++;
    }
    return len;
}
```

The special notation [] denotes an array of indeterminate size; you can use this only for arguments to functions.

> **Note**
>
> Actually, strlen returns size_t (which is a synonym for an unsigned type) and not int; we'll ignore this detail for now.

You are more likely to see it written something like this:

```
int strlen(char *string)
{
    int len = 0;
    while(*string++) {
        len++;
    }
    return len;
}
```

Let's see what happens when we call strlen("Hello");.

We know that "Hello" is a six-element array of char. The compiler conveniently converts it to a pointer to char when we call strlen. The pointer points to the first (i.e, index 0) element of the array.

The curious expression *string++ is seen often in C. The expression dereferences the pointer (returns whatever it is pointing to) and then increments the pointer.

What does it mean to increment a pointer? When a pointer is incremented, it is adjusted to point to the next item in the array. A pointer to char is adjusted to point to the next char. A pointer to int is adjusted to point to the next int. Even though int and char are (probably) different sizes, the compiler knows how much to add to the pointer value because it knows the type of the object pointed to by the pointer.

So, the first time through the loop, the return value of *string++ is 'H' and string is incremented to point to the 'e'. See Figure 35.1 for an illustration of the memory layout.

The grid in Figure 35.1 represents the computer's memory. The pointer string initially points to the 'H'. As it is incremented, it points to successive elements of the array.

FIGURE 35.1
Memory layout for C array.

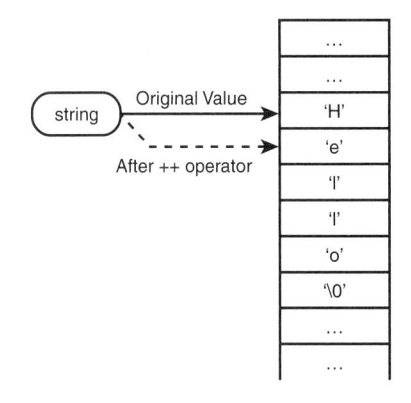

Pointer Arithmetic

Some types of pointer arithmetic make sense. We've already seen how C interprets incrementing a pointer; decrementing a pointer is analogous.

In addition, you can add or subtract integer constants to or from a pointer. Adding n to a pointer corresponds to incrementing it n times. Similarly, subtracting n corresponds to decrementing it n times.

You can also subtract the values of two pointers, yielding a signed integral result. The C standard is a bit wordy, but basically it makes sense to subtract two pointers if you know for sure that they point to objects within the same array or structure (or one past the end of the array.)

> **Note**
>
> This strange qualification appears in the standard primarily because of silly 16-bit architectures and systems like MS-DOS and Windows 3.1 on Intel processors. Pointers under these systems were not the nice array indices they are on modern architectures and systems. If you've ever programmed under these systems, you'll be relieved to know that you can forget about "memory models," "far pointers," "thunks," and other such nonsense under Linux.

Subtracting two pointers yields the number of items between the pointers. For example, if you have a 200-element array a of double, and ptr1 points to a[17] and ptr2 points to a[91], then ptr2 - ptr1 yields 74.

This lets you write `strlen` in yet another way:

```
int strlen(char *string)
{
    char *tmp = string;
    while(*tmp) ++tmp;

    return tmp - string;
}
```

In this case, the `while` loop is simpler—only one variable needs to be incremented—and this may be more efficient than the previous examples.

Note how we save the original value of string and subtract it from the location of the terminating `'\0'` to calculate the length of the string.

Pointers and Structures

Pointers are often used in conjunction with structures. Because of this, it is a very common operation to dereference a pointer and then reference a structure element. The operator `->` is a shortcut. Here's an example:

```
int main()
{
    struct complex c;
    struct complex *p;

    p = &c;
    (*p).imag = 0.0;
    /* Equivalently: p->imag = 0.0; */

    p->real = 0.0;
    /* Equivalently: (*p).real = 0.0; */
}
```

The expressions `(*p).real` and `p->real` are equivalent.

The C Preprocessor

Before a C program is compiled, it is run through the C preprocessor. This is a simple macroprocessor that interpreted preprocessor directives, modifying the source text before it reaches the compiler.

All C preprocessor directives begin with the character #, which must be the first non-blank character on a line. The following are some preprocessor directives.

Include

```
#include filename
```

The `#include` directive inserts the contents of *filename* into the source text. The *filename* is usually called a header file, whose name traditionally ends with .h.

There are two possible forms of #include:

- `#include <filename>`   Searches for the file in some "standard" location before trying the current directory (or other locations specified as options to the compiler.) This form is used for standard and system header files.

- `#include "filename"`   Searches for the file in the current directory or other locations specified as options to the compiler. This form is used for header files you write that are not part of the standard or system header files.

Define

```
#define macro text
```

The `#define` directive defines a macro. Whenever the macro name is encountered in the C source code, it is replaced by its definition. This may trigger another round of macro replacement. Consider this example:

```
#define N 100
#define BIG (N*N)
int a = BIG;
```

> **Note**
>
> Macro names are typically uppercase, but this is tradition, not law.

The line `int a = BIG;` is replaced with `int a = (100*100);`. Macros are not replaced if their names appear inside string literals or comments.

You can also define macros that take arguments. Here's an example:

```
#define SQUARE(x) x*x
int a = SQUARE(5);
```

In this case, `int a = SQUARE(5);` becomes `int a = 5*5;`. You have to be very careful when using macros with arguments, however. Consider this example:

```
#define SQUARE(x) x*x
int a = SQUARE(2+3);
```

This sets a to 2+3*2+3, which is 11. Macros with arguments should be parenthesized liberally. A better way to write the SQUARE macro is like this:

```
#define SQUARE(x) ((x)*(x))
```

Even so, macros can be dangerous. Look at this final example:

```
#define SQUARE(x) ((x)*(x))
int a = SQUARE(i++);
```

If SQUARE were a function call, i would be incremented once. However, because it is a macro that uses its argument twice, i is incremented twice. Be very wary of using macros with arguments that have side effects.

Conditional Compilation

The #if, #ifdef, #ifndef, #else, and #elif directives provide for conditional compilation. That is, at compile time, you can select which pieces of code get compiled. This is useful for porting C programs between operating systems, but take care to not abuse it—code with lots of conditional compilation becomes difficult to follow.

Here's an example of code with conditional compilation:

```
#ifdef __ALPHA__
#define uint32 unsigned int
#else
#define uint32 unsigned long
#endif
```

In this example, if the preprocessor macro __ALPHA__ is defined, then uint32 is defined as unsigned int. Otherwise, it is defined as unsigned long. Here's another example:

```
#ifndef NDEBUG
printf("I'm here!\n";
#endif
```

If the NDEBUG macro is not defined, the printf statement is compiled into the code.

> **Note**
>
> The NDEBUG macro is used in ANSI C to control whether or not the *assert* macro (defined in the header <assert.h>) is effective. You can use it to control debugging code in your programs.

The `#if` directive takes as an argument a constant expression. If it evaluates to nonzero, the code following the `#if` is included. For example:

```
#if VERSION > 2
int x[8];
#else
int x[16];
#endif
```

This selects the size of the array based on the macro `VERSION`, which is presumably defined as some integer constant.

More C

There is much more to C than we can cover in this overview. Here's a sampling of what's available:

- C has a rich standard library of functions. Manual section 3 is devoted to C library functions. Look at the *intro(3)* manual page for an overview, and use a manual browser to look at entries in that section.
- C includes facilities for dynamic memory allocation. These let you allocate and free blocks of memory at runtime. You don't need to (and should not) hard-code limits like array sizes, string lengths, and the like in your program—use dynamic memory allocation to have your program adapt at runtime.
- The C preprocessor has a few other directives, including the `#error` directive for forcing a compilation error, and various operators for concatenating or creating strings out of pieces of text.

C++

C has served (and continues to serve) programmers very well. Unfortunately, it is a fairly low-level language. The modern trend is toward higher levels of abstraction and object-oriented programming techniques. Although it is perfectly feasible to write object-oriented C code, the intricacies of managing the object model often obscure the intent of the code, and you get bogged down in the bookkeeping details.

C++ was invented by Bjarne Stroustrup of Bell Laboratories as a means of adding object-oriented concepts to C. C++ is mostly a superset of C, but adds the following constructs:

- *Classes.* A class is a description of a set of objects. An object can have both data and behavior. By comparison, a C structure (the closest analog to a class) has data, but no behavior. In C++, an object's behavior is implemented with member functions.

- *Operator and function overloading.* Operators and functions can be given different meanings, depending on the types of their operands. For example, if you define a Matrix class, you can overload the multiplication operator to do the natural thing when you multiply two matrices.
- *Inheritance.* Classes can be derived from other classes. This lets you put common behavior in a base class and specific differentiated behavior in derived classes. To some extent, C++ lets you defer implementation of behavior until the derived class is defined.
- *Exception handling.* When an error occurs, a function can raise an exception. This propagates all the way up the call chain until a function prepared to handle the exception does so. This makes error handling much cleaner than in C.
- *Templates.* C++ allows you to define a family of classes or functions whose exact implementation depends on a data type. When you use a particular function or class, you instantiate it for a particular type. This saves on source code (typing), but can produce large executable files if you're not careful.

One of the most important design goals of C++ was that it be link-compatible with C. You can write parts of your program in C++ and parts of it in C, and link them together without any (or too many) difficulties. On the one hand, adhering to this goal has a number of benefits:

- It makes the transition from C to C++ much easier.
- The C++ programmer can still use the huge standard library of C functions.
- It is much easier to set up a C++ development environment on a new operating system because it probably already has a C development environment.

On the other hand, the design decision has (in my opinion) created a number of problems:

- Because C++ is almost a super-set of C, people are tempted to use it as a "better" C compiler. They use syntactic sugar like function and operator overloading but do not write object-oriented programs. Please don't do this. You will lose most of the benefits of C++ if you do.
- C++ is not a pure object-oriented language; it is (of necessity) a hybrid language that includes all C's non-object-oriented concepts. It requires considerably more discipline to write a clean object-oriented program in C++ than in (say) SmallTalk.
- C++ is a very complex language. I believe that this is, in part, due to the desire to maintain compatibility with C. The hybrid nature of the language means that many seemingly strange decisions had to be made. These decisions only make sense when you investigate how the compiler generates code and how it must be link-compatible with C. C++ forces you to understand too many low-level things about the compiler.

In spite of these criticisms, I find C++ an excellent language for program development and a great way to implement object-oriented designs.

Let's look at some C++ features.

Classes

A `class` in C++ is similar to a `struct` in C, except that it can have member functions as well as data members. Consider this example:

```cpp
#include <iostream.h>
class Bus {
private:
    int iPassengers;

public:
    Bus();
    void board();
    void disembark();
    int numPassengers();
};

// Constructor
Bus::Bus()
{
    iPassengers = 0;
}

// A passenger boards
void Bus::board()
{
    iPassengers++;
}

// A passenger gets off
void Bus::disembark()
{
    iPassengers—;
}

// How many passengers?
int Bus::numPassengers()
{
    return iPassengers;
}

int main()
{
    Bus b;
```

```
    cout << "Bus has " << b.numPassengers() << " aboard.\n";

    b.board();
    b.board();
    b.board();
    cout << "Bus has " << b.numPassengers() << " aboard.\n";

    b.disembark();
    b.disembark();
    b.board();
    cout << "Bus has " << b.numPassengers() << " aboard.\n";
    return 0;
}
```

Put this program in a file called bus.cc. Compile and run it like this:

```
$ g++ -o bus bus.cc
$ ./bus
Bus has 0 aboard.
Bus has 3 aboard.
Bus has 2 aboard.
```

Let's look at the program line-by-line.

The #include directive includes the file iostream.h. This header file declares C++'s facilities for I/O. We need it to use cout later on.

> **Note**
>
> C++ is in the process of standardization, and one result may be that the .h suffix for headers will be dropped. For now, the .h forms work (and will probably continue to work for the sake of backward-compatibility).

The class declaration declares a class called Bus. This class has a single instance variable called iPassengers. (I always name my instance variables beginning with i so that I know when I'm referring to an instance variable as opposed to a local variable. You don't have to follow this convention.) The instance variable is private. This means that only member functions of class Bus can access it. It is inaccessible to any other function.

Making instance variables private is generally a very good idea. You should only make functional interfaces visible to the outside world. This lets you change the implementation of your class without breaking external software (as long as you adhere to the functional interface).

The class has four member functions, which are all `public`. These functions can be called by anyone.

The first function has the same name as the class and is called the constructor. It is called any time an object of the class is created.

Following the class declaration are the function definitions. Note how a member function is written `ClassName::functionName`.

The lines beginning with `//` are comments. In addition to normal C-style comments, C++ supports single-line comments beginning with `//`. These are very handy. They are even accepted by some C compilers, but you shouldn't use them in C programs because this behavior is nonstandard.

Member Functions

The constructor for `Bus` simply initializes `iPassengers` to zero.

The function `Bus::board` adds one to the number of passengers, and `Bus::disembark` subtracts one. A more sophisticated version of `Bus::disembark` could flag an error if it is called for an empty bus. Having `iPassengers private` allows you to add access controls like this quite easily.

Finally, `Bus::numPassengers` simply returns the number of passengers on the bus.

Main Program

As with C, C++ programs begin execution in a function called `main`. In this example, a variable `b` of type `Bus` is created. Note that class names, once declared, may be used just like built-in types to declare variables.

The `cout` line prints messages to standard output. Using the `<<` operator, you supply the object you wish printed. C++ knows how to print all the built-in types.

The rest of the program has some `board` and `disembark` calls with periodic messages showing how many passengers are aboard the bus.

Note that to call a member function for a particular object, you use the syntax `object.memberFunction`.

Inheritance

A class can be derived from another class. This is called `inheritance`. A derived class includes all the instance variables and member functions of the base class and may add some of its own. Here's an example:

```
class Shape {
public:
    virtual double area() = 0;
};

class Square : public Shape {
private:
    double iWidth;

public:
    virtual double area() { return iWidth * iWidth; }
};

class Rectangle : public Shape {
private:
    double iWidth;
    double iLength;

public:
    virtual double area() { return iWidth * iLength; }
};
```

In this example, the class Shape is an abstract base class representing shapes. It has a virtual member function called area, which presumably returns the area of the shape. The curious notation = 0; declares a pure virtual function. That is, the function is not defined by Shape but must be defined by derived classes.

The classes Square and Rectangle are derived from Shape and provide implementations of area.

Virtual Functions

In C++, a pointer to a base class can also point to an object of a derived class. No conversion or casting is necessary. This lets you do something like this:

```
int main()
{
    Shape *a = new Square;
    Shape *b = new Rectangle;
}
```

(The new operator allocates memory for an object and calls its constructor.)

Virtual functions differ from normal member functions in the following way:

If you have a pointer to a base class and you use it to call a member function, then:

- If the member function is not virtual, then the member function of the class of the pointer declaration is called. For example, if area were not virtual, then calling a->area() would call Shape::area.

- If the member function is virtual, then the member function of the actual class pointed to by the pointer is called. In this example, calling a->area() calls Square::area, whereas calling b->area() calls Rectangle::area, even though both a and b are pointers to Shape.

Multiple Inheritance

C++ supports multiple inheritance (and a weird form of inheritance called virtual base classes). I would recommend staying away from both. Multiple inheritance is usually confusing and seldom needed. Inheriting a derived class from a base class means that the derived class is a base class (sometimes called the IsA relationship). It's very uncommon for a class to really be two different things; usually there is a strong IsA relationship with one class and a much weaker one with another.

For example, suppose you have classes Vehicle and PaintedThing, representing vehicles and things that are painted, respectively. You can create a class Car, which is both a vehicle and a painted thing. However, a Car is much more importantly a Vehicle than a PaintedThing. Car should be derived from Vehicle. The fact that it is a PaintedThing is likely to be less important and can probably be expressed by adding instance variables to the Car class. (If this example sounds contrived, it is. It is quite difficult to come up with a good object model. The inheritance relationships depend on your application; getting them right is the key to writing clear, maintainable software.)

Furthermore, C++ has complicated rules for resolving name clashes if two classes with identically named member functions are used as base classes for a derived class. In my opinion, it's best to steer clear of the whole multiple inheritance mess.

Operator and Function Overloading

C++ lets you overload functions and member functions. This can be very handy. Consider this modified Bus class:

```
class Bus {
private:
    int iNumPassengers;
public:
    Bus();
    void board();
    void board(int howMany);
    // ... etc.
};
```

In this case, there are two board member functions. The first takes no arguments, and the second takes an integer argument specifying how many passengers have boarded. We can write code like this:

```
int main()
{
    Bus b;
    b.board();
    b.board(10); // Day-care field trip
}
```

The compiler calls the correct function based on its signature. The signature is the number and type of the function's arguments.

> **Note**
>
> C++ has a number of complicated rules for matching signatures if the types don't match exactly. It tires some built-in conversions in an attempt to get the signatures to match.

C++ also lets you overload operators. For example, suppose you want to overload the += operator so that adding a bus to another bus means that all the passengers from the second bus board the first bus. You could write this:

```
class Bus {
    // ... etc.
public:
    Bus & operator+=(Bus &other)
    {
        board(other.numPassengers());
        other.iPassengers = 0;
        return *this;
    }
};

int main()
{
    Bus a;
    Bus b;

    b.board(10);
    a += b;

    cout << a.numPassengers() << " on a and "
         << b.numPassengers() << " on b.\n";
    return 0;
}
```

There are a number of new C++ features here. The & notation in the declaration refers to a reference. This is almost the same as a pointer, but you can use a period (.) rather than -> to access members. (References are widely used in C++; consult a C++ reference manual for details.)

The keyword operator lets you define an operator. In this case, we define the operator +=. Because it is defined in class Bus, it will be called when the first argument is a Bus. The second argument is a reference to Bus because that is how it is declared.

The body of the operator is defined in line. You can define short member functions in line in a class definition; this may produce faster executables. The operator simply transfers the passengers from the other bus to our bus.

The return value of the operator is supposed to be a reference to Bus. All member functions are passed the implicit pointer this, which is a pointer to the object on which the member function is being invoked. To convert a pointer to a reference, dereference it with the * operator. (Yes, the terminology is awful. I'm sorry.)

More C++

C++ has many more features, whicht we are unable to cover because of space limitations. Some of the important ones are

- *Destructors.* Special member functions called when an object is destroyed. You can place clean-up and resource-deallocation code here.
- *Runtime type identification.* Lets you "dynamically" cast pointers and references to different types based on runtime information. You can use it to safely cast a pointer to a base class to a pointer to a derived class.
- *New and Delete operators for memory allocation.* Operators that are more powerful than their C counterparts because they call constructors and destructors where necessary.
- *Standard Template Library (STL).* Library that contains data structures and algorithms for many common data structures such as arrays, strings, and linked lists.

> **Note**
>
> I'm not too crazy about the STL. It does not promote good object-oriented programming techniques, in my opinion.

Summary

In this overview, we briefly reviewed the history of C and C++. We learned the basic structure of a C program, including the main function, comments, declarations, definitions, and function calls.

The chapter provided a description of C's built-in types and described how to declare C variables. We learned the various types of C statements.

The chapter described how to declare and define C functions, and how to use C arrays, structures, and pointers. The final C section described the C preprocessor and its facilities for altering source code before it is presented to the compiler proper.

The C++ overview described some of the facilities offered by C++, including classes, inheritance, function, and operator overloading.

CHAPTER 36

Using GNU Development Tools

In This Chapter

- Terminology 900
- The GNU C Compiler 901
- GNU Make 904
- The GNU Debugger 912

Serious programmers need powerful development environments to write programs. This chapter introduces some of the GNU development tools included with Linux. I discuss the gcc C and C++ compiler, the GNU make program for building projects, and the gdb source-level debugger.

Most large UNIX programs are written in C or C++, and the GNU development tools are perfect for these projects. This chapter introduces the GNU tools so you will know how to start a programming project. It cannot cover them in great depth; fortunately, the GNU tools have excellent info pages. This chapter does, however, give you the background you need to understand the info pages.

For this chapter, I assume you are familiar with C or C++ programming on some platform and understand the basic concepts of editing, compiling, linking, and debugging. This chapter also introduces you to the Linux-specific tools for performing these tasks.

Terminology

I use several programming terms in this chapter. Here is a definition of each term:

- **Source File**—A text file containing C or C++ source code. C source filenames usually end with .c (although headers can end with .h), and C++ source filenames end with .C, .cpp, .cxx or .cc. (My preference is to use .cc.)
- **Executable**—A binary file which that is a complete program. An executable can be run from the shell prompt by typing its pathname.
- **Object File**—A file containing machine code and linker information. Object files cannot be directly executed; they must be linked to form an executable. Object filenames end with .o.
- **Linker**—A program that combines object files into an executable. The linker resolves references to symbols across object files.

> **Note**
>
> Actually, the linker need not produce an executable—it can produce a larger, partially-linked object file. For the purposes of this chapter, the linker will always be used to produce an executable.

- **Library Archive**—A library archive is a collection of object files placed into one file for ease of file maintenance. The linker can extract individual object files from the library archive. Library archive filenames end with .a.

- **Shared Library**—A shared library is a collection of object code that is dynamically linked at runtime. For example, the C standard library is found in a shared library (/lib/libc.so.6.) This code is linked in by the runtime loader when a program that needs it is started.

The great advantages of shared libraries are that executable files are much smaller—the library code does not have to be statically linked into the executable—and multiple programs all share the same library code, saving memory at runtime.

The GNU C Compiler

The GNU C Compiler (gcc) was the first major project of the Free Software Foundation. It was written originally by Richard Stallman, and is now maintained by Cygnus Solutions. gcc exists for practically all major operating systems and processor architectures and is widely used in embedded systems. It is also the native C and C++ compiler on Linux.

gcc conforms to the ANSI C standard and g++ (the C++ compiler) tracks the proposed ANSI C++ standard. Both compilers are documented in the gcc info page.

Invoking gcc

The gcc command, commonly is used to compile a C source files, *gcc* has dozens of options, but in this chapter, I only cover the more common ones.

Let's start with the simplest case—a C program entirely contained in a single C source file. To compile such a file into an executable, invoke gcc like this:

```
$ gcc -o executable_name source_name.c
```

The preceding example compiles source_name.c and links it with the C runtime library to produce the executable file executable_name.

Most non-trivial C programs are split into more than one source file. To create executables from these programs, you need to compile (but not link) each source file separately, and then link the final object files together. To compile a source file into an object file without performing linking, use the -c option:

```
$ gcc -c -o obj_file.o source_file.c
```

Suppose you have two source files, main.c and helper.c. To compile and link them to form an executable, use these commands:

```
$ gcc -c -o main.o main.c
$ gcc -c -o helper.o helper.c
$ gcc -o program main.o helper.o
```

This example generates the object files `main.o` and `helper.o`, and then links them (along with the C runtime library) to form the executable file *program*.

Note that gcc was invoked to perform the linking. Although the actual program that performs linking is called ld, you should generally link object files to form an executable using gcc. This is because gcc adds runtime startup code and the C runtime library to the final executable file.

gcc is a front-end to the actual compiler and linker. It examines the filename suffix to determine what to do for each file. Table 36.1 shows how gcc interprets filename suffixes.

TABLE 36.1 gcc's Interpretation of Filename Suffixes

Suffix	Meaning
.c	C source code which must be pre-processed before compilation.
.i	C source code that has already been pre-processed. It is simply compiled.
.cc, .cxx, .cpp, .C	C++ source file which must be pre-processed before compilation.
.ii	C++ source code that has already been pre-processed.
.h	C header file.
.s	Assembler code.
.S	Assembler code which must be pre-processed.
other	An object file that is passed to the linker.

gcc Compilation Options

gcc has many command-line options; they are well-documented in the gcc info page. Table 36.2 lists some of the most common gcc compilation options.

TABLE 36.2 Common gcc Compilation Options

Option	Meaning
-c	Compile source files, but do not link them. Each source file is compiled into a corresponding object file. By default, this file is named by replacing the suffix of the original source file with .o.
-E	Only perform pre-processing. The C pre-processor is run for each source file and the result sent to standard output.

Option	Meaning
-o filename	Place the result in filename. This applies to whatever kind of output (object file or executable) you have specified.
-v	Be verbose. This prints all the commands executed to run the compilation and linking. (Remember, gcc is a front-end to the compiler and linker proper.)
-ansi	Restrict compiler features to those specified in ANSI C. Use this option to compile ANSI C programs.
-pedantic	Be very strict about issuing warnings, and reject certain GNU extensions to ANSI C.
-Wall	Issue many kinds of warnings. See the gcc info page for the various types of warnings available.
-g	Produce debugging information so your program can be debugged using a source-level debugger.
-pg	Produce extra information to enable your program to be profiled using the gprof analysis tool.
-Olevel	Set optimization level to level. -O2 is the safest and most common optimization level, although -O3 is claimed to be safe for modern versions of gcc. Note that if you turn on optimization, the code may be reordered, making debugging a bit confusing.
-DMACRO=TEXT	Define MACRO as TEXT. If the =TEXT part is missing, MACRO is defined as 1.

For maximum portability and robustness, you should ensure that all your programs compile without warnings or errors with the -ansi, -pedantic and -Wall options enabled.

The -D option is useful for controlling conditional compilation. For example, if you make use of debugging code and want to exclude it from the final executable, you can invoke gcc like this:

```
$ gcc -DNDEBUG ...
```

Using the -DNDEBUG option has the same effect as putting #define NDEBUG in each C or C++ source file.

gcc Path and Linking Options

gcc has another set of options for determining where to locate header files and library files. Table 36.3 lists some of those options.

TABLE 36.3 Common gcc Path and Linking Options

Option	Meaning
-I*path*	Add *path* to the list of directories searched for header files. The #include preprocessor directive searches a predefined list of locations for header files; you can add to this list with the -I option, and you can specify multiple -I options.
-L*path*	Add *path* to the list of directories searched for library files. The linker searches a predefined list of directories for library files; you can add to this list with the -L option. As with -I, you can specify multiple -L options.
-l*lib*	Link against the library *lib*. Libraries are named lib*lib*.a. For example, if you specify -lm to link with the math library, the actual filename used is libm.a (the full path is /usr/lib/libm.a).

Compiling C++ Programs

To compile and link C++ programs, you should invoke the compiler as g++ rather than gcc. This is especially important at link time because it forces the linker to link in certain libraries required by C++ programs.

GNU Make

Any non-trivial C or C++ project has several (probably many) source files and headers. If you edit a source file, you need to rebuild the project. There are several approaches you can take:

- When you change something, you can recompile and relink everything. This is very slow and wasteful.
- When you change something, you can enter the commands needed to compile the parts of the project that need recompilation. This is efficient, but tedious and error-prone.
- You can use make to keep track of dependencies and automatically rebuild those parts of the project which need rebuilding.

Clearly, the make approach is the best.

Makefiles

The make program reads a special file called a Makefile. This file contains a list of targets and dependencies. It also contains rules specifying which commands should be run if a target needs to be rebuilt.

Here is a sample project. Create the following files:

File hello.c:

```
/* hello.c */
#include <stdio.h>
#include "hello.h"
void hello(char *who)
{
    printf("Hello, %s!\n", who);
}
```
File *hello.h*:

```
/* hello.h */
void hello(char *who);
```
File *main.c*:

```
/* main.c */
#include "hello.h"
int main()
{
    hello("World");
    return 0;
}
```

To build the program (call it pro), you need to compile each of the C source files and link them, like this:

```
$ gcc -c -o hello.o hello.c
$ gcc -c -o main.o main.c
$ gcc -o prog main.o hello.o
$ ./prog
Hello, World!
```

Now, suppose you want to change the exclamation mark in the message to a period. You have to edit hello.c to make the change. You must them recompile hello.c, but you do not have to recompile main.c. You only need to perform the final linking step.

Let's create a makefile for this project. Create a file called Makefile (note the capitalization) with the following contents:

```
# Makefile for sample project
# NOTE: Use "tab" for indented lines, NOT spaces!
# Also leave blank lines exactly as shown.

prog: main.o hello.o
        gcc -o prog main.o hello.o

main.o: main.c hello.h
```

```
        gcc -c -o main.o main.c

hello.o: hello.c hello.h
        gcc -c -o hello.o hello.c
```

Remove the `prog` executable and the object (`.o`) files and type:

```
$ make
gcc -c -o main.o main.c
gcc -c -o hello.o hello.c
gcc -o prog main.o hello.o
```

Note how make ran the compilation and linking commands in the correct order. Now let's pretend that `hello.c` has changed. Since make uses the file's modification time to determine whether it has changed, use the touch command to update `hello.c`'s modification time, and rerun make:

```
$ touch hello.c
$ make
gcc -c -o hello.o hello.c
gcc -o prog main.o hello.o
```

Note that make did not recompile `main.c`, it only recompiled `hello.c` and relinked the project. Type make once more:

```
$ make
make: `prog' is up to date.
```

Since nothing has changed, make does nothing.

Let's now examine the Makefile in detail.

The lines beginning with # are comments. make ignores them, but they are helpful for programmers who have to understand Makefiles.

The line `prog: main.o hello.o` specifies a target called prog. It further specifies that the target depends on main.o and `hello.o`. If make determines that the target must be rebuilt, it runs all the tab-indented commands following the target line until the first blank line. In this case, it runs the gcc command given on the next line.

The prog target is an explicit rule. It tells make exactly how to decide whether the target needs rebuilding. If `main.o` or `hello.o` are newer than prog (or if prog does not exist,) the target needs rebuilding. The next line specifies how to rebuild the target: The gcc command should be run.

Let's look at the next rule: `main.o: main.c hello.h`. This causes `main.o` to be built if it does not exist or if it is older than `main.c` or `hello.h`. Since the source file includes `hello.h`, the target really does depend on the header. If the header changes, it likely indicates a major change to the `hello` C function, and `main.c` will need recompiling. It is important to include all the dependencies in a rule; otherwise, make may not correctly rebuild parts of a project that need rebuilding. (There are techniques to automate this for C and C++ source code, which I'll cover shortly.)

The hello.o target is similar to main.o. Now let's look what happens when you invoke make.

First, make reads the Makefile. Since you did not specify which target to build, make builds the first target encountered in the Makefile (in this case, prog.)

make determines that prog depends on main.o and hello.o. It checks to see if these targets have been specified in the Makefile. Since they have, it recursively decides whether to rebuild them. Once make has rebuilt the object files (or determined that they do not need rebuilding), it checks the prog rule. If the (possibly newly-compiled) object files are newer than prog, it executes the rule; otherwise, it does not.

Note that make builds a tree of dependencies and executes rules from the leaves up. This ensures that all compilation and linking steps are performed in the right order. This tree of dependencies is illustrated in Figure 36.1. (Note that computer scientists like to draw their trees with the root at the top and the leaves at the bottom.)

FIGURE 36.1
Make's tree of dependencies.

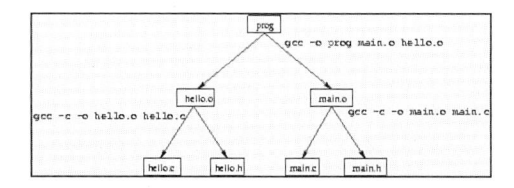

> **Note**
>
> To be precise, make builds a directed *acyclic* graph of dependencies. (Acyclic implies that you cannot have loops in dependencies.) If target1 depends on target2 and target2 depends on target1, make will print this error message:
>
> make: Circular target2 <- target1 dependency dropped.

make Variables

make allows you to define and use variables in Makefiles. It also includes several implicit variables that are set while processing a dependency. Here's another version of the sample Makefile:

```
# Second version of sample Makefile
# Remember to use Tab, not space for indented lines
```

```
SRCS = main.c hello.c
OBJS = $(SRCS:.c=.o)
HDRS = hello.h

prog: $(OBJS)
        gcc -o $@ $^

main.o: main.c $(HDRS)
        gcc -c -o $@ $<

hello.o: hello.c $(HDRS)
        gcc -c -o $@ $<
```

The SRCS line creates a variable called SRCS with a value of main.c hello.c.

The OBJS line is a little bit magic: The notation $(SRCS:.c=.o) means the contents of the SRCS variable, but with each word's .c suffix replaced with .o. In the end, this sets OBJS to the list main.o hello.o.

Finally, we set HDRS to hello.h.

The prog dependency states that prog depends on the contents of OBJS; that is, on main.o and hello.o.

But look at the rule for building prog. It looks totally unrecognizable. Within a rule's command, the variable $@ means the name of the target. In this case, $@ will be replaced with prog. The variable $^ is replaced with all the dependencies, in this case main.o hello.o.

This variable substitution is extremely powerful. Consider what happens if you add a new source file hi.c to your project. You need only add it to the SRCS variable; the OBJS variable and the prog target will automatically be adjusted to include the new object file. To add a new header that is used by all the C source files, you simply adjust HDRS.

The remaining targets are similar to their original counterparts, except you use the $@ variable to put the target name in the command and the new variable $< to put only the first dependency in the command line. Remember, you want to put only the C program name on the compiler command line, not the header filenames.

To check a Makefile, invoke make with the -n option. This causes make to print the commands it would execute, but not actually execute them. Delete the object and executable files and test the new Makefile:

```
$ rm main.o hello.o prog
$ make -n
gcc -c -o main.o main.c
gcc -c -o hello.o hello.c
gcc -o prog main.o hello.o
```

Implicit Rules

Earlier, I wrote that adding a new C source file like `hi.c` to the project involves adjusting SRCS. As the Makefile was written, that is not quite true—you have to explicitly add a rule to build `hi.o`. Let's look at the third version of the Makefile, which corrects this deficiency:

```
# Third version of sample Makefile
# Remember to use Tab, not space for indented lines
SRCS = main.c hello.c hi.c
OBJS = $(SRCS:.c=.o)
HDRS = hello.h

prog: $(OBJS)
        gcc -o $@ $^

%.o: %.c
        gcc -c -o $@ $<
```

The new rule `%.o: %.c` is a pattern rule. It tells make how to build a .o file from a .c file. Test the new Makefile with `make -n`; it should print the same commands as before.

Pattern rules are very powerful. As you have seen, they greatly simplify maintenance of Makefiles. GNU make has a number of built-in rules; see the make info page for details.

Still, there is one tiny problem with this last Makefile: We've lost the fact that the object files depend on the header file as well as the C source files. Here is the fourth and final Makefile. (For now, remove `hi.c` from the project so you can test the Makefile.)

```
# Fourth version of sample Makefile
# Remember to use Tab, not space for indented lines
SRCS = main.c hello.c
OBJS = $(SRCS:.c=.o)

prog: $(OBJS)
        gcc -o $@ $^

%.o: %.c
        gcc -c -o $@ $<

depend:
        gcc -MM $(SRCS) > .depend

.phony: depend

-include .depend
```

This Makefile has a number of curious additions. The `depend` target invokes gcc with the `-MM` option. This causes gcc to generate a Makefile-like dependency list of all header files used by the source files on the command line. This list is sent to standard output; we direct it to the file `.depend`.

The `.phony` line states that the `depend` target will not generate a real file. It's just a housekeeping target.

Finally, the `-include` line includes the file `.depend` if it exists. If `.depend` does not exist, no error is issued.

Here's how you use the Makefile:

```
$ make depend
gcc -MM main.c hello.c > .depend
$ make
gcc -c -o main.o main.c
gcc -c -o hello.o hello.c
gcc -o prog main.o hello.o hi.o
```

Take a look at the `.depend` file:

```
$ cat .depend
main.o: main.c hello.h
hello.o: hello.c hello.h
```

Note how gcc generated the correct dependencies.

This fourth version of the Makefile is completely generic; you can add source files to the project by adjusting `SRCS` and re-running `make depend`.

Common make Command-Line Options

Like any good GNU program, `make` has many command-line options. Table 36.4 lists some of the most common ones.

TABLE 36.4 make Command-Line Options

Option	Meaning
-f *file*	Uses *file* as the Makefile (rather than Makefile.)
-n	Prints commands which would be executed, but do not actually execute them.
-k	as many commands as possible in the face of errors.

Option	Meaning
	Normally, make stops building a project if any rule fails. The -k option causes make to build as many targets as possible. This allows it to build targets that are not affected by the failed rule.
-C dir	Changes to directory dir before doing anything else.
-h	Prints help and exit.
-i	Ignores all errors in executed commands.

When you invoke make, you can specify a list of targets to build and vary assignments. For example, consider this command:

```
$ make -i depend all DEBUG=1 ZUB=0
```

This is equivalent to placing DEBUG=1 and ZUB=0 in the Makefile and building the target depend followed by all. The -i option causes make to ignore errors in executed commands.

Building Third-Party Packages

There is a vast array of free software available for Linux and UNIX systems. While many of these packages are available in precompiled RPM (or source RPM form), the vast majority are distributed as compressed tar files containing source code. You need to compile them for your system.

If a package is distributed as package.tar.gz or package.tgz, you can unpack it with the tar command as follows:

```
$ tar -xvfz package.tar.gz
```

Inside the unpacked archive, there is likely to be a README file and a Makefile. Modern packages come with a configure shell script. If the package has a configure shell script, building it is usually simple:

```
$ ./configure
$ make
```

The configure shell script examines your system and creates a Makefile from another file called Makefile.in. configure looks for needed libraries, header files, and so on. In fact, configure is the distillation of hundreds of programmers' accumulated experience on dozens of different UNIX systems. It helps ensure that software will compile and run on virtually every UNIX and Linux system.

> **Note**
>
> The `configure` script is not usually hand-generated. It is created with the autoconf suite. This suite includes the autoscan program, which aids in cross-UNIX porting by examining your code and looking for portability problems. The autoconf tool itself generates a `configure` script based on input from autoscan and other input that you provide. The autoconf suite is the best solution for cross-UNIX portability. If you are writing programs that you want to run on many UNIX systems, see the autoconf info page.

Going Further with `make`

GNU `make` is a very powerful program with many sophisticated directives and options. Read the `make` info pages for details.

Although `make` is usually used to compile programming projects, you can use it in many other situations. For example, I am writing this book with the LaTeX typesetting program, and I am using xfig to generate the figures. I have a Makefile that performs all the necessary conversion and PostScript generation required to typeset the book. If, for example, I update a figure, the Makefile notices that, regenerates the PostScript version of the figure, and invokes LaTeX to re-typeset the book.

Sams (my publisher) requires my material in HTML format. I have another `make` target that converts the text to HTML and the figures to TIFF format for the use of the publisher. I don't have to remember (or retype) the dozen or so commands needed to arrange the material for publication.

Any time you have to perform a series of steps to build a target from a group of dependencies, you should investigate whether make can assist you.

The GNU Debugger

What you have learned so far will enable you to compile and link programs. Almost certainly, the first few versions of your programs will contain bugs. (Probably the released versions will have bugs, too.) Since it is very hard to debug a program if you can't see exactly what it is doing, you need a *debugger* to assist with tracking down and fixing bugs.

The GNU debugger (gdb) is a powerful source-level debugger. It lets you step through your compiled C and C++ programs while watching what is going on at the source code level. To experiment with the GNU debugger, you need a program with bugs in it. Here is such a program; put the following text into the file bad.c. (This program, even if bug-free, wouldn't do very much. It's intended to crash so I can illustrate some gdb features.)

```c
/* bad.c */
#include <stdio.h>
#include <string.h>

void hello(char *str)
{
    int len = (int) strlen(str);
    printf("Hello, %s, you %d-character string.\n", str, len);
}

int main()
{
    char *world = NULL;
    hello(world);
    return 0;
}
```

Compile and run bad.c:

```
$ gcc -o bad bad.c
$ ./bad
Segmentation fault (core dumped)
```

Oops. That looks bad. Recompile the program with the debugging switch and run gdb:

```
$ gcc -g -o bad bad.c
$ gdb ./bad
(gdb)
```

The (gdb) prompt is the GNU debugger prompt. Let's set a breakpoint at the main function. When the program encounters a breakpoint, it stops running and returns control to the debugger.

```
(gdb) break main
Breakpoint 1 at 0x80485d2: file bad.c, line 13.
```

Now run the program with the run command:

```
(gdb) run
Starting program: /home/dfs/Proj/./bad
Breakpoint 1, main () at bad.c:13
13      char *world = NULL;
```

Note that the program stopped when it reached the breakpoint. gdb prints the filename and line number (bad.c:13) of the breakpoint and lists the source line that is about to be executed.

Go to the next line with the `next` command:

```
(gdb) next
14 hello(world);
```

Here you have to be careful. The `next` command causes gdb to execute the line being displayed. If the line is a function call, the entire function call is executed. In this case, you want to step into the function. Use the `step` command:

```
(gdb) step
hello (str=0x0) at bad.c:7
7 int len = (int) strlen(str);
```

gdb tells you that the program has entered the function `hello` with the argument `str` having a value of `0`. This should alert you to the source of the bug; `str` is set to `NULL`.

The current line involves a function call to `strlen`, but there is little to be gained by stepping into `strlen`. The function is part of the C runtime library and does not have debugging information. Use the `next` command:

```
(gdb) next
Program received signal SIGSEGV, Segmentation fault.
0x40078314 in strlen ()
```

You see that at a certain location in `strlen`, the program received a segmentation fault. This happened when `strlen` dereferenced the `NULL` pointer.

Type `quit` to exit from gdb.

Post-Mortem Debugging

Many times, you'll run a program that core-dumps. It is often annoying to have to fire up the debugger and re-create the bug, but you don't have to. You can run a post-mortem debugging session. Rerun the bad program from the shell prompt to generate a core dump.

> **Note**
>
> A *core dump* is a file containing the complete contents of all a process's virtual memory. It is a snapshot of the process's state when it terminated. You can use a core dump (as described in the next section) to debug a program even after it has crashed and terminated.
>
> If you do not get a core dump, you may have turned off production of core dumps. To enable them in bash, type:
>
> `$ ulimit -c unlimited`
>
> If you are using tcsh, type:
>
> `% limit core unlimited`

Invoke gdb as follows:

```
$ gdb ./bad core
Core was generated by `./bad'.
Program terminated with signal 11, Segmentation fault.
Reading symbols from /lib/libc.so.6...done.
Reading symbols from /lib/ld-linux.so.2...done.
#0  0x40078314 in strlen ()
```

As you see, the `core` file contains a complete memory image of the program at the moment it crashed. It also contains all the values in the processor registers at the time of the crash. Look at the call chain of the dead program:

```
(gdb) where
#0  0x40078314 in strlen ()
#1  0x80485af in hello (str=0x0) at bad.c:7
#2  0x80485e2 in main () at bad.c:14
#3  0x40031b0f in __libc_start_main ()
```

The `where` command prints a complete stack trace of function invocations. You can see that the program crashed in `strlen` after it had been called from `hello` that in turn had been called by `main`.

> **Note**
>
> When a C program calls a function, a *stack frame* is created. A stack frame is a block of memory that holds the return address of the function call, as well as automatic variables, temporary variables, and arguments used by the called function. A special processor register called the stack pointer keeps track of stack frames.

Move up the stack one frame to the `hello` stack frame:

```
(gdb) up
#1  0x80485af in hello (str=0x0) at bad.c:7
```

Take a look at the value of `str`:

```
(gdb) print str
$1 = 0x0
```

You can examine the contents of local variables and function arguments with `print`. Look at the value of `len`:

```
(gdb) print len
$2 = 134522096
```

Because `len` is an uninitialized automatic variable, it contains garbage.

> **Note**
>
> Post-mortem debugging is powerful. If you distribute a program, you can have clients send you the core file if it crashes, allowing you to pinpoint why it crashed. (Since core files tend to be huge, it's best to distribute them via ftp rather than email.)

Attaching to a Running Process

As powerful as post-mortem debugging is, sometimes you need to debug a process that is already running. To illustrate this, I will create a program which, rather than crashing, sits in an endless loop. While this is a simplistic example, real-world programs might require complex setup before they fall into an endless loop. It would be tedious and time-consuming to have to restart the program and re-create the bug; it's better to be able to attach to an already-running process.

To experiment with the attachment feature of the GNU debugger, create this file called `loop.c`:

```c
/* loop.c */
#include <stdio.h>
int main()
{
    char *str = "Hello, World!";
    int len;
    while (*str) {
        ++len;
    }

    printf("Length of %s is %d\n", str, len);
    return 0;
}
```

Compile it and run it in the background:

```
$ gcc -o loop -g loop.c
$ ./loop &
[1] 1494
```

(Of course, the process ID printed by your shell might be different.) `loop` seems to be taking awfully long to do anything. Perhaps there is a bug somewhere. Attach to the running process as follows:

```
$ gdb ./loop 1494
/home/dfs/Proj/1494: No such file or directory.
Attaching to program `/home/dfs/Proj/loop', Pid 1494
Reading symbols from /lib/libc.so.6...done.
Reading symbols from /lib/ld-linux.so.2...done.
main () at loop.c:9
9 }
(gdb)
```

> **Note**
>
> Replace the 1494 with the process-ID of your running loop program.

Note that gdb first looks for a file called 1494, and failing that, attaches to the process 1494. This halts the running process and places it under the control of gdb. The process happened to halt at line 9; it may halt at another line for you.

You can step and print as usual. Here are some debugging commands:

```
(gdb) next
8       ++len;
(gdb) print str
$1 = 0x8049434 "Hello, World!"
(gdb) next
9 }
(gdb) next
8       ++len;
(gdb) print str
$1 = 0x8049434 "Hello, World!"
(gdb) next
9 }
```

As you see, the program is bouncing around between lines 8 and 9, incrementing `len` but never altering `str`. The `while` condition will never be false. Quit from gdb. This causes the program to resume execution. To kill it, kill the process.

```
(gdb) quit
The program is running. Quit anyway (and detach it)? (y or n) y
Detaching from program: /home/dfs/Proj/loop Pid 1494
$ kill 1494
```

gdb has many more commands and options. Some nice facilities offered by gdb are listed here. See the gdb info page for details about these and other gdb commands.

- Watchpoints let you interrupt the program when a memory location is written. This lets you look for code that is modifying a variable without knowing exactly which code is responsible for modifying the variable.
- Exception handling lets gdb intercept exceptions in languages that support them (for example, C++.)
- gdb supports programs that use multiple threads, and it lets you specify breakpoints that are active only for particular threads.
- gdb supports sophisticated data examination commands that let you examine and print the contents of memory in various formats.
- gdb supports many programming languages, including C, C++, assembler, FORTRAN, Java, Modula-2, and Scheme. gdb understands expressions written in these various languages.

The Data Display Debugger

The Data Display Debugger (ddd) is an amazing graphical front-end to gdb. While gdb is powerful, its user-interface is a bit primitive. ddd remedies this by building a powerful graphical user interface on top of gdb.

Invoke ddd on the bad example:

```
$ ddd bad
```

You should see a window similar to that in Figure 36.2.

FIGURE 36.2
The ddd main window.

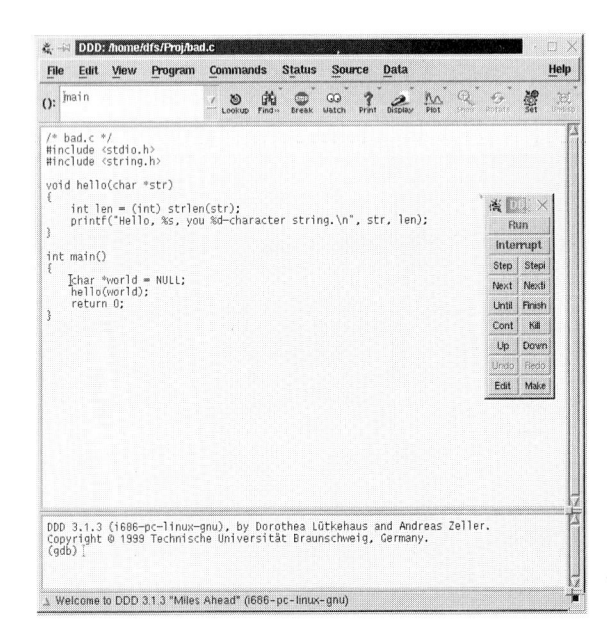

To set a breakpoint in main, right-click on the curly bracket following main and select Set Breakpoint. You should see a little stop sign on the line (see Figure 36.3)

FIGURE 36.3
DDD Breakpoint.

The small window with the Run button makes many gdb commands available at the click of a mouse. Click Run to run the program.

The small pane at the bottom of the main window is the gdb window. You can type gdb commands in it. Also, gdb sends its output to that pane.

After you click Run, a small green arrow appears near the stop sign. The green arrow is the current line. Click Next until the arrow is on the `hello(world)` line. Then click Step to step into the `hello` function. Note how ddd makes it easy to visualize the flow of program execution.

Move the mouse pointer over the word `str` in the `hello` function call. Let the pointer linger a while. A little yellow window containing the string 0´0 pops up. If you let the mouse pointer linger over a local variable name, ddd displays the variable's value. (It is also displayed in the status line at the bottom of the main window.) Try looking at the value of `len`.

Going Further with ddd

ddd has many useful facilities that are too numerous to cover here. I'll give you an overview of some of the nicer features. For more details, consult the excellent ddd help facility using the Help pull-down menu. Not only does ddd include a reference manual for itself, but it also includes a reference manual for gdb, the underlying debugger.

As promised, here is an overview of some nice ddd features:

- ddd features a graphical data display. This lets you display data structures in graphical format. Pointers link objects with arrows. This graphical display is updated as you step through the program. You can actually watch your data structures in action.
- ddd features facilities to plot array and variable values. This requires the gnuplot program (which, unfortunately, is not included with Caldera OpenLinux 2.3).
- ddd gives you fine control over window placement and appearance and gdb options and behavior. Use the Edit, Preferences and Edit, GDB Settings to explore the possibilities.

- You can attach to processes using File, Attach to Process and perform post-mortem debugging with File, Open Core Dump.
- ddd includes a graphical stack trace dialog in Status, Backtrace. You can use this dialog to jump around the stack frame during debugging.

While you can do all your debugging with plain gdb, ddd makes it much easier and more fun. It's so much fun that you may be tempted to add bugs to your programs so you can play with ddd.

Summary

In this chapter, you learned how to invoke the GNU C compiler. You also learned how to create object files from source files and how to link object files to form an executable file. You learned how to use GNU make to automate project maintenance. And you learned how make keeps track of dependencies and automatically determines what steps are needed to keep a project up-to-date. Finally, you learned how to use the GNU debugger (gdb) to debug a C program at the source-code level. You also learned how to do post-mortem debugging using core files and how to attach gdb to a running process. Finally, you learned how to use the graphical ddd front-end to make debugging faster and more fun.

Appendixes

PART VI

IN THIS PART

A Useful Linux Commands *923*

B Installing Caldera Openlinux 2.2 *965*

C Bibliography *1001*

D RPM *1005*

APPENDIX A

Useful Linux Commands

by David F. Skoll

IN THIS APPENIDX

- Online Documentation *924*
- Managing Files *929*
- Examining Files *937*
- Regular Expressions *941*
- Text Manipulation *944*
- Compressing and Archiving Files *950*
- Informational Commands *954*
- Disk Space *957*
- Process Management *959*
- Starting and Stopping the System *961*
- Miscellaneous Commands *963*

This appendix describes a whole collection of useful Linux commands. Linux and UNIX are built around small software tools. Once you've "filled your tool box" with these tools, you'll find them surprisingly versatile and be able to use them in powerful and creative ways. Many of the commands are quite simple, but mastering them is essential if you want to administer a Linux system.

Online Documentation

Let us begin by looking at the commands for getting help. One thing Linux demands (as you've probably discovered) is the willingness to read. There is a huge amount of documentation on the system. The documentation is very accurate, but is also very detailed, and packs a lot of information into a small amount of prose.

We'll cover the following sources of documentation: the traditional UNIX manual pages, the GNU "info" system, and the informal set of documentation in the /usr/doc directory.

man and apropos

By now, you should be very familiar with man, introduced in Chapter 2, "Essential Linux Concepts." The simplest ways to invoke man are

```
$ man item
$ man section item
```

which look up the manual page for *item* or (in the case of the second example) the page for *item* in a specific section. However, man has a number of additional options:

- man -k *string* looks for matching strings in the "Name" section of manual pages. You can also type apropos *string* to get the same effect. For example:

  ```
  $ man -k calendar
  ```

  will display the "Name" sections of all manual pages having something to do with calendar.

  The command

  ```
  $ apropos calendar
  ```

  does the same thing.

- man -f *keyword* looks for matching keywords in the "Name" section of manual pages. You can also type whatis *keyword* to get the same effect. This is similar to apropos, but whatis only looks for complete words, whereas apropos looks for strings anywhere in the section, even if they are part of larger words.

whatis is useful to determine what mysteriously named programs do. For example, Caldera OpenLinux comes with a program called ldd (in /usr/bin):

```
$ whatis ldd
ldd (1) - print shared library dependencies
```

Note that you can type `man 1 ldd` for more information.

> **Background Material**
>
> whatis is not likely to work for KDE programs, unfortunately. KDE has its own HTML-based help system and does not include man pages for most applications. In my opinion, this is regrettable.

- `man -a item` searches all manual pages for *item*. As you may recall, some items are both commands and system calls (for example, chown(1) and chown(2)). If you don't specify a section, man just displays the first manual page it finds. To see all the manual pages for chown, use

  ```
  $ man -a chown
  ```

  After you finish reading chown(1), man shows the pages for chown(2).

- `man -K keyword` looks for *keyword* in the body of all each system man pages. This process is very slow and likely to produce huge amounts of useless information. But if you're desperate, you can try it.

Of course, man has many more options. To read more about these option, type the following:

```
$ man man
```

This will take to the man page for man.

info

As the GNU project developed, its leaders invented a new documentation system called Texinfo. For its time, the system was powerful and innovative. With a single source file, Texinfo authors could generate both high-quality typeset documentation (using Donald Knuth's TeX program) and hyper-linked online documentation. The online viewer is (traditionally) character-based, making Texinfo seem rather archaic compared to modern HTML-based help systems. Still, Texinfo is very powerful and most of the GNU utilities are documented using it.

The online copies of Texinfo documentation are called *info pages*. You can view them with the info viewer embedded in `emacs(1)` or use the standalone `info` program. On Caldera OpenLinux, you can also view man pages with `info`, so you can type

```
$ info ldd
```

This displays the `ldd(1)` man page.

To start `info`, simply type **info**. You are presented with a large amount of help about `info` itself and what documents you can view.

> **Background Material**
>
> GNU system documentation is notoriously thorough and pedantic. It's also quite intimidating at first.

Just press H to see a short tutorial on `info`. Although the tutorial urges you to press the spacebar to move forward and Delete to move backwards, you can use Page Up and Page Down, too. You can also use the arrow keys to move the cursor around.

The `info` system is organized as a series of nodes. (A *node* is a page of information about a single topic.) Each node contains documentation and possibly links to other nodes. Some links are lists of menu items, each preceded by an asterisk. Other links are cross-references, each preceded by `*note`.

To read the documentation, just page around. To follow a menu item, move the cursor to the item and press M. Press Enter to confirm the menu item.

Unfortunately, this does not work for a cross-references that requires a different keystroke. To follow a cross-reference, press F. (This, of course, will not work for a menu item.)

`info` pages are organized hierarchically, so a master node will have sections and subsections. Table A.1 lists some handy navigation keys.

TABLE A.1 info Navigation Keys

Pressed Key	Function
N	Move to the next section in the same level of hierarchy as the current page.
P	Move to the next section.
U	Move up one level.
Lowercase L	Move to the last page you were viewing. This key works like the Back button in a Web browser. Unfortunately, there is no equivalent for Forward.

To get help, press ?. An info page listing over more than 100 possible keystrokes and actions appears below the page currently displayed.

> **Background Material**
>
> The standalone info program shares a lot of keystrokes and notation with emacs(1). If you like emacs, you'll like info.

The /usr/doc Hierarchy

The /usr/doc directory contains many useful documentation files. Many packages create subdirectories under /usr/doc and deposit documentation files there. The documentation tends to be less formal than man or info pages; it usually consists of README files and other miscellaneous documentation that comes with source packages but isn't an essential part of an installed package.

There is no consistent organization for files in /usr/doc. Most are plain text files; some are PostScript or HTML files. Some are in their original format and some are compressed.

Two of the most useful directories under /usr/doc are /usr/doc/HOWTO and /usr/doc/LDP.

/usr/doc/HOWTO

The /usr/doc/HOWTO directory contains the Linux HOWTO documents. These documents address specific issues and tell you how to achieve something in Linux. For example, the Modem-HOWTO advertises that it offers "help with selecting, connecting, configuring, trouble-shooting, and understanding modems for a PC."

The HOWTOs in /usr/doc/HOWTO are compressed with the gzip program (which we'll cover later); for now, if you want to read a HOWTO, type

```
$ gunzip -c Name-HOWTO.gz | less
```

The gunzip -c uncompresses Name-HOWTO.gz to standard output, which is then piped into less so you can read it comfortably.

Table A.2 lists some important subdirectories under /usr/doc/HOWTO.

TABLE A.2 Subdirectories of /usr/doc/HOWTO

Subdirectory	Contents
/usr/doc/HOWTO/mini	Contains "mini-HOWTOs." These are shorter than regular HOWTOs and may be less structured. (For example, they might lack a table of contents.)
/usr/doc/HOWTO/other-formats/html	Contains HTML versions of some HOWTOs. You can view these conveniently with a Web browser.
/usr/doc/HOWTO/translations	Contains HOWTOs in other languages, such as German, Spanish, and French.
/usr/doc/HOWTO/unmaintained	Contains obsolete or unmaintained HOWTOs.

To read an index of HOWTOs, type the following:

```
$ gunzip -c /usr/doc/HOWTO/INDEX.gz | less
```

/usr/doc/LDP

The /usr/doc/LDP directory contains documents from the Linux Documentation Project. These documents are written using the LaTeX typesetting system. The document directories may can include compressed PostScript files (for printing) and HTML versions (for online viewing). The following important documents are found in /usr/doc/LDP:

- /usr/doc/LDP/install-guide is the excellent *Linux Installation and Getting Started* guide. The most convenient way to view it is to type

    ```
    $ cd /usr/doc/LDP/install-guide
    $ netscape install-guide-3.2.html/index.html &
    ```

> **Note**
>
> If you don't have X working, you can use `lynx` instead of `netscape`.

- /usr/doc/LDP/linux-kernel contains a description of the Linux kernel internal principles. It is most conveniently viewed by opening the /usr/doc/LDP/linux-kernel/tlk-0.8-3.html/tlk.html file with netscape. Unfortunately, the document describes kernels in the 2.0 series rather than the 2.2 used by Caldera OpenLinux 2.2 and 2.3. However, there is still much a lot of accurate and interesting information, especially about the PC hardware architecture.

- `/usr/doc/LDP/network-guide` contains Olaf Kirch's *Network Administrator's Guide*, viewable by opening `/usr/doc/LDP/network-guide/nag/index.html` with `netscape`.
- `/usr/doc/LDP/system-admin-guide` contains Lars Wirzenius's *System Administration Guide*. To view it, open `/usr/doc/LDP/system-admin-guide/sag-0.6-html/index.html`.
- `/usr/doc/LDP/users-guide` contains Larry Greenfield's *Linux System Users' Guide*. The guide is incomplete and a bit out of date, but may might contain useful information. Unfortunately, Caldera OpenLinux does not come with an HTML version of the book; you can look at the compressed PostScript version of the book with the gv PostScript previewer:

  ```
  $ gv /usr/doc/LDP/users-guide/user-beta-1.ps.gz
  ```

Managing Files

Chapter 2 introduced some commands for managing files, such as `ls` for listing directories, `rm` for removing files, and `mv` for renaming files. This section describes some more advanced commands.

Copying Files: cp

Although you can copy a file with `cat`, the `cp` command is the usual way to copy files in Linux. `cp` lets you do things you can't do with `cat`, such as copy groups of files at once. `cp` has many options that let you control the semantics of copying:

- To copy a file, type:

  ```
  $ cp oldfile newfile
  ```

- To copy a file from one directory into another, keeping the same filename, type:

  ```
  $ cp file /path/to/new/directory
  ```

cp supports a number of options:

- `-I` Prompts before overwriting an existing file. Normally, if you copy a file to an existing name, the destination is overwritten. The `-i` option makes `cp` prompt you before overwriting.
- `-R` Recursively copies an entire directory structure. Thus,

  ```
  $ cp -R oldDir newDir
  ```

  copies the entire directory tree *oldDir* to *newDir*.

> **Warning**
>
> cp also has a `-r` option that does almost the same thing as `-R`; do not use it. The `-R` option copies special files, such as device files, correctly; the `-r` option assumes than all non-directory files are normal files and tries to read them as normal files. This could cause serious problems if the hierarchy you are copying contains device files.

- `-p` Preserves the original files' owner, group, permissions, and modification and access times. (The owner and group cant only be preserved if you run cp as root.)
- `-d` Does not follow symbolic links. Normally, cp treats symbolic links as normal files and copies the files to which they point. The `-d` option causes it to copy only the link itself. This option is not standardized by POSIX; it is available only with GNU cp.
- `-a` Preserves as much of the original structure and attributes of the original tree as possible. The `-a` option is equivalent to `-dpR`.

cp has many more options for such things as making symbolic links instead of actual copies and making versioned backups of destination files. Consult cp(1) for details.

Finding Files: `find`

The find command is one of the most powerful and useful commands in UNIX. It's also fairly hard to master.

Essentially, find does the following:

- Starts from an initial path (or set of paths)
- Finds files that meet certain criteria
- Does something with the filenames

Thus, you supply three pieces of information to find:

- The starting path
- The criteria for files you're interested in
- The action to be taken when an interesting file is found

Let's look at an example before diving into the syntax:

```
$ find /usr/doc -name '*mail*' -print
/usr/doc/fetchmail-4.7.7
/usr/doc/fetchmail-4.7.7/fetchmail-FAQ.html
...
```

The three pieces of information for the example are

- The initial path: /usr/doc.
- The criteria: -name '*mail*'. In this case, this is a single criterion saying "Match all files or directories whose names contain mail." (The *mail* part is quoted to prevent the shell from expanding it.)
- The action: -print. This tells find to print the names of matching files.

The following is another example:

```
$ find /usr/doc -type f -name '*mail*' -print
/usr/doc/fetchmail-4.7.7/fetchmail-FAQ.html[sr]
/usr/doc/fetchmail-4.7.7/fetchmail.lsm[sr]
...
```

This example added an additional criterion: -type f. This tells find to accept only plain files, not directories (or device files). If there are several criteria on the command line, as in the example, all must be met for the action to be triggered. Thus, the example prints the names of all ordinary files under /usr/doc whose names contain "mail".

find Syntax

The overall syntax of find is

find [path...] [expression]

If the *path*s are omitted, the path list defaults to the current directory. If *expression* is omitted, it defaults to -print.

> **Note**
>
> Thus, a bare find will print the entire directory hierarchy rooted at the current directory.

The *expression* contains four types of terms that return true or false:

- *Options*—Affect the overall operation rather than the processing of a particular file. Options always return true.
- *Tests*—Return true or false.
- *Actions*—Have side effects and can return true or false.
- *Operators*—Alter the results of a test or combine two tests together.

Normally, the *expression* is evaluated from left to right for each file. As soon as any term returns `false`, `find` moves to the next file. Otherwise, if the end of the expression is reached and no action has been taken, `find` invokes the `-print` action.

Options

Options always take effect rather than being processed only as `find` moves through the expression. For clarity, you should place options at the beginning of the expression. Table A.3 lists and describes some important options.

TABLE A.3 Options

Option	Description
`-depth`	Process the contents of a directory before the directory itself. This causes `find` to move through a hierarchy in a depth-first manner.
`-follow`	Follow symbolic links. Normally, they are not followed.
`-maxdepth` *levels*	Descend at most *levels* (a non-negative integer) levels of directories below the paths supplied on the command line.
`-mindepth` *levels*	Descend at least *levels* (a non-negative integer) levels of directories below the paths supplied on the command line before applying any tests or performing any actions.
`-mount` or `-xdev`	Do not descend into directories on other file systems.

For example, to find and list all files larger than 100KB but only in the current directory (not in any subdirectories), use

```
$ find . -maxdepth 1 -size +100k -ls
```

Tests

Many tests take a numeric argument. This argument can be specified in one of three ways:

+*n*	Greater than *n*.
-*n*	Less than *n*.
n	Exactly *n*.

The following are some useful tests:

- `-atime` *n* true if the file was last accessed *n* days ago. For example, to find all files that haven't been accessed in seven days or more, use

    ```
    $ find path -atime +6 -print
    ```

To find files that have been accessed in the last day, use

```
$ find path -atime -2 -print
```

- `-ctime n`:   true if the file's status was changed *n* days ago.
- `-empty`   true if the file is a plain file or directory and is empty.
- `-fstype type`   true if the file system containing the file is of type *type*. Common values for *type* are `ext2` for normal Linux file systems, `proc` for the /proc pseudo-file system, and `iso9660` for CD-ROM file systems.
- `-gid n`   true if the file's numeric group ID is *n*.
- `-group gname`   true if the file's group is *gname*.
- `-name pattern`   true if the file's base name (with leading directories removed) matches the shell pattern *pattern*.
- `-iname pattern`   Like `-name`, but matching is case-insensitive.
- `-mtime n`   true if the file's contents were last modified *n* days ago.
- `-newer otherFile`   true if the file was modified more recently than *otherFile*.
- `-perm mode`   true if the file's permission bits are exactly *mode*.
- `-perm -mode`   true if all the bits set in *mode* are set for the file.
- `-perm +mode`   true if any of the bits set in *mode* are set for the file.
- `-size n[bckw]`   true if the file uses *n* units of space. A "unit" is 512 bytes, unless a letter follows *n*. In this case, `c` makes a unit one byte, `k` makes a unit one kilobyte, `b` makes a unit 512 bytes, and `w` makes a unit two bytes.

  For example, to find all files under your home directory that are larger than one megabyte, use

  ```
  $ find $HOME -size +1024k -print
  ```

- `-type x`   true if the file is of type *x*, where *x* is one of the following:
    - `b`   A block device
    - `c`   A character device
    - `d`   A directory
    - `f`   A regular file
    - `l`   A symbolic link
    - `p`   A named pipe (FIFO)
    - `s`   A socket

> **Note**
>
> I have not yet discussed named pipes or sockets yet. They are two special kinds of files used for inter-process communication (IPC).

- -uid *n*   true if the file's numeric user ID is *n*.
- -user *uname*   true if the file is owned by user *uname*.

Actions

An action term in an expression can appear anywhere a test does. It can return true or false, but has side effects. The following are some useful actions:

- -exec *command*   Executes *command*. Returns true if the command executes without errors. All the arguments following -exec are taken as part of the command until an argument consisting of a semicolon is found. The string {} is replaced by the filename being processed.

> **Warning**
>
> You must escape the semicolon so it is not interpreted by the shell.

For example, let's say you have a text editor that makes backup files named filename.bak and you want to delete all such files from your home directory. Use

```
$ find $HOME -name '*.bak' -print -exec rm '{}' \;
```

Let's dissect this command:

1. The command starts looking for files in your home directory ($HOME).
2. It looks for files named '*.bak'. Note how the shell pattern was quoted to prevent the shell from expanding it.
3. As it finds each matching file, it prints the name.
4. It also removes the file by executing the command rm *filename*. Note how the curly braces ({}) are replaced by the filename. Note also how the terminating semicolon was escaped with a backslash.

- -ok *command*   Similar to -exec, but prompts for confirmation before executing the command.
- -print   Prints the name of the file on standard output followed by a newline. Always returns true.

- **-prune** If -depth was not used, returns `true` and does not descend into the current directory. If -depth was used, returns `false`.
- **-ls** Lists the current file in `"ls -dils"` format to standard output. Returns `true`.

Operators

Finally, you can combine the results of terms and actions with operators:

- **(*expr*)** Forces precedence of evaluation. The parentheses need to be escaped.
- **-not *expr*** `true` if *expr* is `false`.
- ***expr1 expr2*** `true` if both expressions are `true`; *expr2* is not evaluated if *expr1* is `false`.
- ***expr1* -a *expr2*** `true` if both expressions are `true`; *expr2* is not evaluated if *expr1* is `false`.
- ***expr1* -o *expr2*** `true` if either expression is `true`; *expr2* is not evaluated if *expr1* is `true`.

There are other options, tests, actions, and operators; See `find(1)` for details. For now, let's look at some of them in action.

The following command finds all files under the current directory whose names end in `.cc` or `.h` and are older than seven days, and prints them:

```
$ find . \( -name '*.cc' -o -name '*.h' \) -mtime +7
```

The next command will finds all files in the entire directory hierarchy that have `set-uid` or `set-gid` bits turned on:

```
# find / -perm +6000 --ls
```

> **Note**
>
> You should run the previous example as `root` because regular users are denied access to some files and directories.

The next example does the same search, but only for local files. It will not look at CD-ROMs, the `/proc` file system, or remotely mounted volumes:

```
# find / \( -not -fstype ext2 -prune \) -o -perm +6000 -ls
```

Note how the first part of the expression is grouped with parentheses. If the file system is not of type `ext2`, you "prune" the search. This makes `find` not descend into the directory. Otherwise (the `-o` operator), you perform the permission test, and if that passes, the filename is listed.

`find` is the system administrator's friend; study `find(1)` and look for other examples of `find` in shell scripts and other books. You can accomplish many routine system administrative chores with a `find` command.

Making Links: `ln`

You've seen the `ln` command in action in Chapter 2. In that chapter, you always used the `-s` option to make a symbolic link. The following is a review of how to use `ln -s`:

- `ln -s` *path linkName* creates a symbolic link called *linkName* pointing to the file or directory *path*. If *path* is a relative pathname, it is interpreted relative to the directory containing *linkName*. If *linkName* already exists, the command fails. If you supply the `-f` option, *linkName* is overwritten if it exists. The `-i` option makes `ln` query whether or not it should overwrite existing files.

- `ln -s` *path1 path2... dirName* creates symbolic links called *path1*, *path2...*, and so on inside the (already-existing) directory *dirName*.

There are several more options that control the behavior of `ln -s`; See `ln(1)` for details.

Note that if you remove a symbolic link with `rm`, the link itself is removed, not the file to which it refers.

Hard Links

Linux supports another kind of link called a hard link. To understand how hard links work, you need a bit of background about the internals of the Linux file system.

Under Linux (and UNIX), a special block on the disk called the *inode* contains all the information about a file's contents. That is, the inode records the date and time of modification of the file, the size of the file, and all the bookkeeping information necessary for the file system to find the file's contents. Inodes are numbered on each file system. An inode is uniquely identified by specifying the file system it resides on and its inode number.

A directory entry stores exactly two pieces of information: a filename and an inode number. It is quite possible for two different directory entries to contain the same inode number. Each entry is called a *hard link* to the file. The inode records the number of hard links pointing to it and, only when the last link is removed, are the file contents actually removed.

> **Note**
>
> Even then, UNIX may defer removing the file contents if a process has the file open.

Let's look at an example of a hard link. Type the following commands:

```
$ echo This is a test > file
$ ln file hlink
$ ls -l file hlink
-rw-rw-r- 2 dfs dfs 15 Jun 28 09:34 file
-rw-rw-r- 2 dfs dfs 15 Jun 28 09:34 hlink
```

Now, append some information to `file`:

```
$ echo More stuff >> file
$ ls -l file hlink
-rw-rw-r- 2 dfs dfs 26 Jun 28 09:36 file
-rw-rw-r- 2 dfs dfs 26 Jun 28 09:36 hlink
```

Notice how both `file` and `hlink` grew and had their modification times changed. That's because they are links to the same file. If you remove `file` with `rm`, the contents are undisturbed. If you then remove `hlink`, the contents will be removed.

You can look at the inode numbers of files with `ls -i`:

```
$ ls -i file hlink
45145 file 45145 hlink
```

Note that both files have the same inode number.

You'll seldom have the need to create hard links, but it is useful to understand how they work. Programs such as `mv`, for example, rename a file by creating a new hard link and deleting the existing hard link (where possible). Some UNIX manual pages refer to links and inodes, and understanding them makes life easier.

Examining Files

For the most part, `cat`, `more`, and `less` are all you'll need to look at files. Sometimes, however, a few other commands are useful.

Identifying a File: `file`

The `file` command makes an educated guess about the contents of a file. It looks at the filename, the first few hundred bytes of the file, and the file permissions, and tries to deduce what is in the file.

```
$ file /usr/bin/locate
/usr/bin/locate: ELF 32-bit LSB executable, Intel 80386, version 1,[sr]
➥ dynamically linked (uses shared libs), stripped
```

This tells you that `/usr/bin/locate` is an `ELF 32-bit LSB executable`. This is a long-winded way of saying that it's an executable program. It runs on the Intel 80386 family of processors and follows version 1 of the ELF standard.

> **Background Material**
>
> ELF (Executable and Link Format) is a file format for executable files. It is widely used in the UNIX world.

You also discover that /usr/bin/locate is dynamically linked, and that it contains no symbol table or debugging information—it is stripped.

The following is another example:

```
$ file /opt/kde/share/wallpapers/parrots.jpg
/opt/kde/share/wallpapers/parrots.jpg: JPEG image data, JFIF standard
```

file makes surprisingly good guesses about most file types. If it cannot identify a file type, it simply prints ASCII text or data.

file has built-in algorithms for some types of files, but it also makes use of two files for user-supplied hints. /usr/share/misc/magic and /etc/magic contain hints in a special format that file can use to identify files. You can find out how they work by reading the manual pages find(1) and magic(5).

Looking at Part of a File: head and tail

head and tail are very simple commands. They send the first or last few lines of a file to standard output. The following explains how to use them:

- head *-n file* sends the first *n* lines of *file* to standard output. If *-n* is omitted, 10 lines are outputted. If *file* is omitted, *head* sends the first *n* lines of its standard input to standard output.

- tail *-n file* sends the last *n* lines of *file* to standard output. If *-n* is omitted, 10 lines are outputted. If *file* is omitted, standard input is used.

- tail *+n file* sends the last lines of *file* starting with line *n* to standard output. For example, to see all but the first line of a file, use

    ```
    $ tail +2 file
    ```

- tail *-f file* causes tail to loop forever, waiting for the file to grow. If the file grows, the additional lines are sent to standard output. This is useful if you have a process writing to a file and you want to monitor the progress of the file.

Both head and tail can take more than one *file* argument; in that case, they print a one-line header before the file contents to identify which file is being viewed.

GNU `head` and `tail` have many more options. These are sparsely documented in the `man` pages `head(1)` and `tail(1)`, and they are well documented in the `info` pages `head` and `tail`.

Comparing Files: `cmp` and `diff`

The `cmp` command is useful for seeing if two (possibly binary) files differ. The simplest way to invoke it is

```
$ cmp file1 file2
```

If the files differ, `cmp` prints *file1 file2* differ: char *n*, line *m* and exits with a status of 1; otherwise, it prints nothing and exits with a status of 0.

If you use the `-l` option, `cmp` will prints the offsets and byte values of all differing bytes. The `-i` *n* option causes `cmp` to ignore the first *n* bytes of each file when reporting differences.

Unfortunately, `cmp` doesn't have either a manual page or an `info` page on Caldera OpenLinux. Type **cmp -help** for a brief outline of how to use `cmp`.

The `diff` command is useful mostly for comparing text files. `diff` has many options and modes of operation. Consider the following two files:

file1	file2
Here is some text.	Here is some text. Ouch.
Here is a line.	Here is a line.
Here is another line.	Yet another line.
Yet another line.	fooo bar.

The following is the output from `diff`:

```
$ diff file1 file2
1c1
< Here is some text.
---
> Here is some text. Ouch.
3d2
< Here is another line.
4a4
> fooo bar.
```

The first four lines indicate that one line was changed (`1c1`). The original changed line or lines are preceded by <. A line of three dashes follows, and then the new line or lines, preceded by >.

The `3d2` indicates that line 3 of the original file should be deleted. The deleted line is shown preceded by <.

The `4a4` indicates that a line should be added after line 4, and the new line is shown preceded by >.

You can produce a more readable format by using the `-c` option. The following produces a so-called context `diff`:

```
$ diff -c file1 file2

***file1      Mon Jun 28 10:09:49 1999
--- file2      Mon Jun 28 10:09:46 1999
***************
***1,4****
! Here is some text.
  Here is a line.
- Here is another line.
  Yet another line.
--- 1,4 ----
! Here is some text.  Ouch.
  Here is a line.
  Yet another line.
+ fooo bar.
```

A context `diff` has the following format:

- Three asterisks followed by the first filename and its date of modification.
- Three dashes followed by the second filename and its date of modification.
- A line of 15 asterisks.
- Blocks of changes.

Each block of changes has the following format:

- Three asterisks, followed by the starting and ending line of the block in the first file, followed by four asterisks.
- Lines from the first file. Changed lines are flagged with !; deleted lines are flagged with -, and unchanged lines are not flagged.
- Three dashes, followed by the starting and ending line of the block in the second file, followed by four dashes.
- Lines from the second file. Changed lines are flagged with !; additional lines are flagged with +, and unchanged lines are not flagged.

`diff` has a number of useful options. Table A.4 lists some of these.

TABLE A.4 diff Options

Option	Explanation
-b	Causes diff to ignore changes in the amount of whitespace.
-c	Produces the "context diff" format.
-I	Causes diff to ignore differences in case—upper- and lowercase letters are treated the same.
-q	Causes diff only to report whether or not files differ; it does not print details of the differences.
-r	Causes diff to recursively compare subdirectory trees. Files in one tree are compared against the corresponding files in the other tree.
-y	Causes diff to print the differences in a "side-by-side" format. You need a large terminal window for this format to be easy to read.

diff has many more options and features; consult diff(1) for more details.

If you want to compare English text, the wdiff program may produce easier-to-read output. It compares the words in two files. The following is an example:

```
$ wdiff file1 file2

Here is some text.  {+Ouch.+}
Here is a line.
[-Here is another line.-]
Yet another line.
{+fooo bar.+}
```

New text is surrounded by {+...+} and deleted text by [-....-]. For more details, see wdiff(1).

> **Background Material**
>
> diff is a standard UNIX program; wdiff is a GNU-specific program.

Regular Expressions

Regular expressions are special patterns that match pieces of text. Regular expressions are pervasive in UNIX; many text-processing commands use regular expression matching, and they are an important part of scripting languages, such as Perl and Tcl. Regular expressions are widely used for powerful text searching and processing. You can quickly perform many otherwise tedious text transformations using regular expressions.

Unfortunately, there are several flavors of regular expressions. You have to remember which programs support which variant. This section describes the "extended" version recognized by the `egrep` command. Where appropriate, I will indicate sections that do not apply to "basic" regular expressions.

Atoms

An atom is a regular expression that matches a single character of text. Most characters, including letters and digits, are atoms that match themselves. Special atoms are

- . (period)   Matches any single character.
- [*chars*]   Matches any single character in the list *chars*. If the first character of the list is ^ (caret), the atom matches any single character not in the list. For example, [0123456789] matches a digit. You can give a range of characters by separating the first and last characters with a hyphen. For example, [A-Z] matches an uppercase letter, and [^A-Za-z0-9] matches any character that is not a letter or digit.
- *char*   Matches exactly the single character *char*. You can use this to "escape" special characters. For example, whereas . matches any single character, \\. matches only a period.

Table A.5 lists some sample atoms.

TABLE A.5   Sample Atoms

Atom	Matches
A	The letter "a"
[a-z]	Any lowercase letter
.	Any single character
\\.	The character "." (period)

Quantifiers

An atom can be followed by a quantifier:

- ?   The preceding atom is optional and is matched at most once.
- *   The preceding atom is matched if it occurs zero or more times.
- +   The preceding atom is matched if it occurs one or more times.
- {*n*}   The preceding atom is matched exactly *n* times.
- {*n*,}   The preceding atom is matched at least *n* times.

- {,*m*}   The preceding atom is optional and matched at most *m* times.
- {*n*,*m*}   The preceding atom is matched at least *n* times and at most *m* times.

> **Note**
>
> The last four quantifiers are supported by extended regular expressions only.

Table A.6 lists sample uses of quantifiers.

TABLE A.6   Sample Quantifiers

Pattern	Matches
a?	Matches an "a" or the empty string
b+	Matches one or more "b"s
c{2,3}	Matches "cc" or "ccc"

Concatenation

Two concatenated regular expressions match concatenated strings that would be individually matched by each regular expression. For example, a.b matches any three-character string starting with a and ending with b.

Alternation

The pipe character (|) causes a regular expression to match if either the left part or the right part matches. For example, a.b|cd matches either a three-character string starting with a and ending with b, or the two-character string cd. Alternation is not supported by basic regular expressions.

Meta-Characters

If the caret (^) is the first character of a regular expression, the remainder of the expression must match starting at the beginning of the line. For example, whereas a.b matches both afbzz and fooatbg1, ^a.b matches only afbzz.

If the dollar sign ($) is the last character of a regular expression, the expression must match to the end of the line. For example, a.b matches both afbzz and g9a7b, but a.b$ would match only g9a7b.

Grouping

A regular expression enclosed in parentheses becomes an atom. Consider the regular expression ^(a.b)+$. The following are some strings it would match:

- acb   One repetition
- acbadb   Two repetitions
- aababbacbadbaeb   Five repetitions

The following are some strings ^(a.b)+$ would not match:

- accb   More than one character between a and b
- foobar   Doesn't match at all
- 123acbaeb   Doesn't match at the beginning of the line

> **Warning**
>
> Regular expressions are not the same as shell expansion patterns. Although they share some special characters, these characters have different meanings. Regular expressions are far more powerful than shell patterns.

To finish this section, study the following examples of regular expressions:

- ^[0-9]+$ Matches lines consisting only of a single decimal number.
- [A-Za-z_][A-Za-z0-9_]*   Matches C language identifiers. These start with a letter or underscore, and can have letters, digits, or underscores following the first character.
- fou?r(ty)?   Matches for, four, forty, or fourty.
- four¦forty   Matches four or forty.

Text Manipulation

UNIX was originally designed to support text processing. Linux follows the UNIX tradition and includes several powerful commands for manipulating text files.

Search for Text in a File: grep

The grep command searches for lines of text matching a regular expression.

The simplest way to use grep is

```
$ grep regular_expression file
```

Any lines in *file* matching *regular_expression* are sent to standard output. If *file* is omitted, grep reads from standard input. For example,

```
$ ls -1 /usr/bin | grep zz
pizza
pizzadoc
ppmtopuzz
```

grep reads the output of ls and prints lines containing zz.

You can also use grep to cheat on crossword puzzles. The file /usr/dict/words contains a list of English words. Suppose you need an eight-letter word starting with t, ending with h, and having the letters "oro" as the third through fifth letters. Use

```
$ grep '^t.oro..h$' /usr/dict/words
thorough
```

How about a word of at least nine letters ending in "ength"?

```
$ grep '^.....*ength$' /usr/dict/words
wavelength
```

Examine the last example carefully. The first four dots match any four characters. The fifth dot is followed by an asterisk, so it matches zero or more characters.

You can give grep any number of filename arguments. If you give grep more than one, it precedes matching lines with the name of the file:

```
$ grep Global /etc/*rc

/etc/wgetrc:## Global settings ...
/etc/zshrc:# Global aliases ...
```

This shows that the pattern Global was found in /etc/wgetrc and /etc/zshrc.

grep has the following useful options:

- -c   Do not print matching lines; instead, print a count of matched lines for each input file.
- -e *pattern*   Use *pattern* as the regular expression. Useful if *pattern* begins with a dash.
- -h   Do not print filenames when multiple files are searched.
- -i   Perform case-insensitive matching. Upper- and lowercase letters are considered identical.
- -l   Do not print matching lines; instead, print a list of filenames that contain at least one matching line.

  For example,

```
$ grep -l Global /etc/*rc
/etc/wgetrc
/etc/zshrc
```

The `-l` option is handy for using `grep` inside shell back-tick expansions. To use Emacs to edit files named `/etc/*rc` that contain the string `Global`, use

```
$ emacs `grep -l Global /etc/*rc`
```

- `-n` Prefix each line of output with the line number.
- `-v` Invert the sense of matching. Lines that do not match will be output. For the `-l` option, files that have no matching lines will have their names output.
- `-w` Match only whole words. A "word" is considered to be a sequence of letters, digits, and underscores. The word must be at the beginning of a line or preceded by a non-word character and at the end of a line or followed by a non-word character.
- `-E` Use extended regular expressions. Normally, the pattern is interpreted as a basic regular expression. Alternatively, you can invoke the command as `egrep` instead of `grep`.
- `-F` Interpret the pattern as a fixed string, not a regular expression at all. Alternatively, invoke the command as `fgrep`.

`grep` has many more options; consult `grep(1)` for details. This `man` page also has a good description of regular expressions.

Altering Text Streams: sed

The `sed` command (Stream EDitor) reads lines of text, alters them according to a `sed` program, and writes the altered lines to standard output.

`sed` is invoked as shown in the following:

```
$ sed options [input_file...]
```

options controls the operation of `sed`. *input_file*s specifies the input sources for `sed`. If more than one filename is provided, `sed` reads the files in sequence. If no filenames are provided, `sed` reads from standard input.

`sed` makes a single pass over the input stream. Thus, it is able to edit lines of text in a pipeline. The following are some `sed` command-line options:

- `-e` *script* Add the commands in *script* to the program to run. You can give any number of these options to build a up complex multi-command program.
- `-f` *script_file* Add the contents of *script_file* to the program to run.

- `-n` By default, `sed` prints each line after it has been processed by the commands in the program. The `-n` option suppresses this automatic printing; the program must explicitly ask for a line to be printed. (You'll see how to do this soon.)

sed Programs

A `sed` program consists of one or more `sed` commands. Each `sed` command consists of an optional address range followed by a one-character command name and any command-specific arguments.

Addresses

An address in `sed` can take one of the following forms:

- *n* Matches only line *n* (where *n* is a positive integer) in the input. Line numbers are counted cumulatively across all input files. The first line is numbered 1.
- `$` Matches the last line of input.
- `/regexp/` Matches any line matching the regular expression *regexp*.

You specify an address range by listing two addresses separated by a comma. An address range matches lines starting from when the first address matches and continuing until the second address matches, inclusively. For example, the address `10,20` matches lines 10 through 20 of the input, inclusive.

Appending a `!` to the end of an address or address range negates the sense of the match. Only lines not matching the address or address range will be selected.

sed Commands

The following are some useful `sed` commands:

- `#` Lines beginning with `#` are comments. They are ignored.
- `s/regexp/replacement/flags` This command replaces *regexp* with *replacement*. The *flags* are optional; some useful flags are
    - `g` Apply *replacement* to all matches of *regexp*. Normally, `sed` only replaces the first match.
    - `p` If the regular expression matches, print the altered line.

For example, suppose you'd like to change the American spelling "neighbor" to the British "neighbour" when looking at `/usr/dict/words`. Look at the following commands:

```
$ grep neigh /usr/dict/words
neigh
neighbor
```

```
neighborhood
neighborhoods
neighboring
neighborly
neighbors
$ grep neigh /usr/dict/words | sed -e 's/bor/bour/'
neigh
neighbour
neighbourhood
neighbourhoods
neighbouring
neighbourly
neighbours
```

> **Note**
>
> Only the output was changed. The original /usr/dict/words is untouched.

If you only want to change the second through fourth lines (for whatever reason), the following is an address range in action:

```
$ grep neigh /usr/dict/words | sed -e '2,4s/bor/bour/'
neigh
neighbour
neighbourhood
neighbourhoods
neighboring
neighborly
neighbors
```

Note that the address range limits the scope of the command.

- q   This command exits sed immediately. Usually, you use this command in conjunction with an address. For example, the following commands have identical behavior:

```
$ sed -e '10q' /usr/dict/words
$ head -10 /usr/dict/words
```

- d   Do not print the current line, and do not process any more commands in the program; start the cycle with the next input line.

- p   Print the current line to standard output. You should use this only in conjunction with the -n option.

For example, the following commands have identical behavior:

```
$ sed -n -e '/a.be/p' /usr/dict/words
$ grep 'a.be' /usr/dict/words
```

> **Note**
>
> For some reason, the grep is much faster.

sed has many more commands. See the sed info page for details. This page classifies sed commands as *often used*, *less frequently used*, and *for die-hard sed programmers*. The info page also details exactly how sed manages its work space, which may be of interest if you are trying to do something more complex, such as reorder lines of text.

You can use sed to great advantage in shell scripts. For example, suppose you have a few hundred files whose names end in .tiff, and you want to rename each one to end in .tif. The following bash script will do the trick:

```
$ for i in *.tiff; do
j=`echo $i | sed -e 's/.tiff$/.tif/'`
mv $i $j
done
```

Note how you use sed to form the new name from the old.

> **Note**
>
> Actually, the example is not quite correct. See if you can spot the mistake. (Hint: What will happen to a file named motiff?) How can you correct this?

Update a File: patch

patch takes the output of diff and applies it to a file, producing the modified file that was the other argument to diff.

patch is very versatile. Usually, you feed it a context diff (produced by diff -c), but it can process most types of diff output. patch tries to skip leading and trailing garbage, so you should be able to give patch a whole Usenet article containing a difference listing, for example, and have it do the right thing.

Updates to software packages are often distributed as diff listings. For example, let's say you have version 1.0 of a package, and version 1.1 is released. Often, the difference listing between 1.0 and 1.1 is much smaller than the entire 1.1 package. If you have the 1.0 version, you need only obtain the difference listing and feed it to patch. This reconstructs the 1.1 version.

patch is usually invoked as

```
$ patch < patchfile
```

patch simply reads standard input and deduces the names of the files to patch from the diff listing.

For example, consider the following sequence of commands:

```
$ diff -c file1 file2 > diffs
$ patch < diffs
patching file '`file1'
```

The first command makes a context diff called diffs. This contains instructions for deriving file2 from file1.

The second command patches file1. That is, it alters it according to the context diff. Afterward, file1 is identical to the original file2. You can verify this with diff:

```
$ diff -s file1 file2
Files file1 and file2 are identical
```

patch has many command-line options and modes of behavior; see patch(1) for details.

Compressing and Archiving Files

Linux contains a few commands for dealing with compressed files and for archiving entire directory trees into a single archive file.

In the MS-DOS and Windows world, the zip utilities perform both compression and archiving. For example, Zip places a number of files in a .zip file, compressing them as it goes.

Under UNIX, archiving and compression are considered two different things, and they are performed by different programs.

Compressing and Uncompressing Files

The gzip command compresses a file. To use it, type the following:

```
$ gzip filename
```

This example compresses *filename*, replacing it with *filename*.gz. You can supply any number of filenames; files are compressed one after the other.

gzip accepts a number of command-line options:

- -c   Write the compressed data to standard output rather than replacing the file with *filename*.gz. You can also achieve this by invoking the command as zcat.

- `-d` Decompress rather than compress. You can also achieve this by invoking the command as `gunzip`.
- `-f` Force compression or decompression even if the compressed `filename.gz` already exists.
- `-l` List statistics about the compressed files.
- `-r` Recurse through directories, compressing (or decompressing) files found in the directory tree.
- `-v` Verbose. Display the name and reduction ratio for each file compressed.
- `-n`, where *n* is a digit   Compress using different compression strengths, where 1 is the fastest method (least compression) and 9 is the slowest method (best compression). The default is 6.

See the `gzip info` page for more details.

> **Background Material**
>
> Traditional UNIX systems use the `compress` command to compress files. Unfortunately, the compression method is patented and cannot be used by GNU tools. Fortunately, the decompression method is not patented, so `gunzip` is able to decompress files compressed with `compress`. Also, `gzip` generally achieves better compression ratios than `compress`, so even commercial UNIX users often install `gzip`.

gzip-Related Programs

The following handy programs are available:

- `gunzip filename.gz`   Equivalent to `gzip -d filename.gz`
- `zcat filename.gz`   Equivalent to `gzip -c filename.gz`
- `zmore filename.gz`   Equivalent to `gzip -c filename.gz | more`

Archiving Files: tar

The `tar` command (Tape ARchiver) archives several files into one file (called a tar file). Tar files are the canonical UNIX method for distributing collections of files.

`tar` has many options and modes of behavior; we will discuss only how to create archives, extract files from archives, and list the contents of archives. The `tar info` page and `man` page `tar(1)` contain full information about `tar`.

tar is invoked as shown in the following:

```
$ tar mode options filename...
```

mode is one of the following:

- `-c` Create an archive.
- `-l` List the contents of an archive.
- `-x` Extract files from an archive.

options include the following possibilities:

- `-f filename` Read (for `-l` and `-x`) or write (for `-c`) the archive *filename*. If you do not supply a filename (or supply it as `-`), tar reads from standard input and writes to standard output.

> **Warning**
>
> Most UNIX tar programs do not behave like this—if you omit the option, they use the tape special file `/dev/rmt0`. If you want to use standard input or output, supply the `-f` option with an argument of `-`.

- `-h` Dereference symbolic links. Normally, tar archives a symbolic link as a link. If you supply `-h`, tar archives the file to which the link points instead.
- `-k` Keep existing files. When extracting from an archive, do not overwrite existing files.
- `-p` Try to preserve file permissions when creating the archive or extracting from the archive.
- `-v` Verbose. List files processed verbosely.
- `-z` Filter the archive through gzip when archiving and gunzip when extracting.

All of the filename arguments are added to the archive (in `-c` mode) or extracted (in `-x` mode). If a filename names a directory, the entire tree rooted at that directory is processed.

For example, suppose you have a directory called foo that contains the three files bar, baz, and blech. The following example creates a tar file called foo.tar, which contains all of foo:

```
$ tar -cvf foo.tar foo
foo/
foo/bar
foo/baz
foo/blech
```

You can list the file as shown in the following:

```
$ tar -tf foo.tar
foo/
foo/bar
foo/baz
foo/blech
```

You can extract it as shown in the following (let's change to another directory first, just for fun):

```
$ mkdir glup
$ cd glup
$ tar -xvf ../foo.tar
foo/
foo/bar
foo/baz
foo/blech
```

Note how `tar` recreates the entire directory.

`tar` is the "canonical" method for copying entire directory trees. For example, suppose you run out of disk space and need to move someone's home directory—let's say you need to move /home/joe to /home2/joe. The following command (as `root`) makes the copy:

```
# (cd /home; tar cfp - joe) | (cd /home2; tar xvfp -)
```

The first `tar` packages the directory to standard output, and the second `tar` unpacks it in its new home.

Linux software is often distributed as compressed `tar` files, named *.tgz or *.tar.gz. To unpack such files, simply supply the -z option:

```
$ tar xvfz package.tar.gz
```

It's probably a good idea to list the package first with `tar tvfz` to see exactly how the files will unpack. Polite `tar` file creators make everything unpack into a subdirectory; rude ones scatter files all over the current working directory.

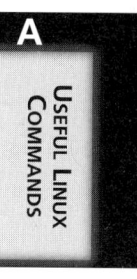

Informational Commands

These commands display information about your system or its users.

The Name of the Computer

The `hostname` command displays the name of the computer. The following are examples run on my machine, shishi.skoll.ca:

```
$ hostname
shishi.skoll.ca
$ hostname -a #(Aliases)
shishi
$ hostname -f #(Full name)
shishi.skoll.ca
$ hostname -i #(IP address)
192.168.2.3
$ hostname -s #(Short name)
shishi
$ hostname -d #(Domain Name)
skoll.ca
# hostname newname #(set name - root only)
```

`hostname` has a few more options; see `hostname(1)` for details.

uname displays information about your computer. The following shows uname in action:

```
$ uname #(Operating system name)
Linux
$ uname -m #(Machine type)
i686
$ uname -n #(Node name)
shishi.skoll.ca
$ uname -r #(Operating system release)
2.2.5
$ uname -s #(Operating system name)
Linux
$ uname -p #(Host processor type)
unknown
$ uname -v #(Operating system version)
#1 Sat Apr 3 21:49:22 MST 1999
$ uname -a #(Everything)
Linux shishi.skoll.ca 2.2.5 #1 Sat Apr 3 21:49:22 MST 1999 i686 unknown
```

Who Am I?

A number of commands tell you who you are

```
$ logname #(What's my login name?)
dfs
```

```
$ id #(What are my user and group ID's?)
uid=500(dfs) gid=500(dfs) groups=500(dfs),17(postgres)
$ whoami (What's my effective user-ID?)
dfs
$ who am i #(Who am I)
shishi.skoll.ca!dfs ttyp0 Jun 28 09:09 (:0.0)
```

Note the last example, `who am i`. It displays who you are as shown in the following:

```
machine!user terminal login_time login_location
```

How Long Since the Last Reboot?

The command `uptime` gives information about the system up time:

```
$ uptime
3:31pm up 6:23, 2 users, load average: 0.11, 0.20, 0.13
```

The `uptime` command tells you that the current time is 3:31 p.m. and the computer was last rebooted 6 hours and 23 minutes ago. There are two users. The system load averages for the past 1, 5, and 15 minutes were 0.11, 0.20, and 0.13, respectively. (The load average is the average number of runnable processes at any given instant.)

Who Is Logged On?

The following command tells you who is logged on:

```
$ w #(Who is logged on and what are they doing?)

3:32pm up 6:24, 2 users, load average: 0.11, 0.20, 0.13
USER TTY   FROM  LOGIN@ IDLE  JCPU  PCPU  WHAT
dfs  ttyp0 :0.0  9:09am 0.00s 7:49  0.01s w
dfs  ttyp3 shevy 3:36pm 5.00s 0.04s 0.00s -bash
```

The first line of output is the same as for `uptime`. The next line is a header. For each person logged in on a terminal, a line of output is produced. The line contains the following fields:

- USER The name of the user.
- TTY The terminal device the user is logged on to.
- FROM The remote system the user is logged on from. In the first line, this is shown as `:0.0` because the terminal is an xterm in the display `:0.0`. The second line shows that `dfs` is remotely logged in from the machine `shevy`.
- LOGIN@ The time of login.
- IDLE How long the user has been idle.
- JCPU The cumulative CPU time of all jobs on the user's terminal.

- PCPU   The CPU time of the currently running job.
- WHAT   The foreground job (the currently running job) on the user's terminal.

who gives somewhat less information:

```
$ who     #(Who is logged on?)

dfs       :0       Jun 28 09:09
dfs       ttyp3    Jun 28 15:36 (shevy.skoll.ca)
```

Here, the fields are USER, TTY, LOGIN@, and FROM (if not from the local machine).

The command last shows the last time someone logged on. It's syntax is

```
$ last [-n] [user]
```

For example, last dfs shows the login history for user dfs. The following example shows the last four logins for dfs:

```
$ last -4 dfs

dfs ttyp3 shevy Mon Jun 28 15:36 still logged in
dfs :0           Mon Jun 28 09:09 still logged in
dfs :0           Sun Jun 27 12:23 - 22:43 (10:19)
dfs :0           Sun Jun 27 11:22 - 12:05 (00:43)
```

The fields are USER, TTY, FROM (if not the local machine), login time, logout time, and total time spent logged in.

last has several options; consult last(1) for details.

Free Memory

The free command displays statistics about memory usage:

```
$ free
              total      used    free   shared  buffers  cached
Mem:         128220    100168   28052    59756     4624   55472
-/+ buffers/cache:      40072   88148
Swap:        377516       388  377128
```

The total column shows the total amount of available memory in kilobytes. This computer has 128MB of physical memory and about 368MB of swap space.

The used column shows how much memory is used, and the free column shows how much is free. shared shows how much memory is shared by more than one process. buffers and cached show how much memory is used by file system buffers and caches.

Linux caches disk files in memory, but this memory can be claimed by running processes—they take priority. The line -/+ buffers/cache shows how much memory is really available for processes. The memory used by the disk cache is subtracted from the used memory.

`free` is Linux-specific; it is not found on other UNIXes. For more details, see the `man` page `free(1)`.

You can also look at memory statistics by typing `cat /proc/meminfo`. This produces a similar output to `free`, but gives memory statistics to the byte level.

Disk Space

Linux has two commands for determining the amount of free disk space and the amount of disk space used by files and directories.

Free Space

The `df` command tells how much disk space you have:

```
$ df

Filesystem 1k-blocks     Used Available Use% Mounted on
/dev/hda1    1554262    73090   1400849   5% /
/dev/hda2    3106103  1131281   1814172  38% /usr
/dev/hda3    4655757   220433   4194349   5% /home
```

The fields have the following meanings:

- `Filesystem` The block special file corresponding to the file system.
- `1k-blocks` The total number of 1KB blocks on the file system.
- `Used` The number of used blocks.
- `Available` The number of available blocks. Note that `Used` and `Available` add up to less than `1k-blocks` because some blocks are reserved for use by `root` only.
- `Use%` The percentage of available blocks that are used.
- `Mounted on` The mount point of the file system.

`df` has a number of options; consult `df(1)` for details. My favorite is the `-h` option, which results in human-readable output:

```
$ df -h

Filesystem Size  Used Avail Use% Mounted on
/dev/hda1  1.5G   71M  1.3G   5% /
/dev/hda2  3.0G  1.1G  1.7G  38% /usr
/dev/hda3  4.4G  215M  4.0G   5% /home
```

Used Space

The du command computes how much disk space is used by files and directories.

du is invoked as shown in the following:

```
$ du [options] [pathname...]
```

For each *pathname*, du computes the disk space used by the file or directory. If no pathnames are supplied, the current directory is assumed.

du recurses into directories given as arguments and displays the space used by all subtrees as well as the directory given as an argument. For example,

```
$ du DFClass

4       DFClass/CVS
4       DFClass/src/CVS
182     DFClass/src
4       DFClass/tests/CVS
346     DFClass/tests
3       DFClass/include/CVS
4       DFClass/include/df/CVS
33      DFClass/include/df
37      DFClass/include
614     DFClass
```

The disk usage for each subtree is shown. On the last line, you see that the total disk space used by the DFClass directory and all of its descendants is 614KB.

du has a number of options:

- -s Summarize disk space. du prints disk space only for items explicitly named on the command line. For example,

    ```
    $ du -s DFClass Bilge

    614     DFClass
    3855    Bilge
    ```

    Details are not shown. The -s switch is useful for finding out who is hogging the disk:

    ```
    # du -s /home/* > /DISKHOGS
    ```

- -a Show all details, even for ordinary files. This produces large amounts of output.
- -x Only count space on the same file system as the argument given. This prevents du from recursing into a different file system.

du has many more options; consult du(1) for details.

Process Management

Each running Linux program is called a *process*. We discussed the `ps` command in Chapter 2. `ps` lets you look at running processes and determine their process IDs (pids).

Signaling Processes: `kill`

The `kill` command lets you send a signal to a process. By default, `kill` sends the `TERM` signal, which (usually) terminates a process. You can type `kill -l` to list all the possible signals:

```
 1) SIGHUP      2) SIGINT     3) SIGQUIT    4) SIGILL
 5) SIGTRAP     6) SIGIOT     7) SIGBUS     8) SIGFPE
 9) SIGKILL    10) SIGUSR1   11) SIGSEGV   12) SIGUSR2
13) SIGPIPE    14) SIGALRM   15) SIGTERM   17) SIGCHLD
18) SIGCONT    19) SIGSTOP   20) SIGTSTP   21) SIGTTIN
22) SIGTTOU    23) SIGURG    24) SIGXCPU   25) SIGXFSZ
26) SIGVTALRM  27) SIGPROF   28) SIGWINCH  29) SIGIO
30) SIGPWR
```

You can send a process any signal by using `kill -NAME pid`, where `NAME` is the signal name without the leading `SIG`. For example, to send a `SIGKILL` to process number 34567, use

```
$ kill -KILL 34567
```

or equivalently:

```
kill -9 34567
```

You can send signals only to processes you own. `root` can send signals to any process.

Most signals are of interest only to programmers; some, however, are useful to everyone:

- `SIGHUP` The "hangup" signal. `SIGHUP` is sent to all processes running on a terminal if you hang up the phone line or the connection is otherwise broken. Some system programs use `SIGHUP` as a signal to re-read configuration files.
- `SIGINT` The "interrupt" signal. `SIGINT` usually terminates the process. It can be generated with the interrupt key, usually Ctrl+C.
- `SIGQUIT` The "quit" signal. `SIGQUIT` usually terminates the process and produces a core dump. It can be generated with the quit key, usually Ctrl+\ (backslash).

  A core dump is a dump of the entire memory image of the process. It is created as a file named `core` in the process's current directory. Core dumps are immensely useful to programmers trying to debug a program—they provide for post-mortem analysis—and are immensely annoying to everyone else.

- SIGILL   The "illegal instruction" signal. You don't usually send SIGILL to a process; the kernel sends it if the process executes an illegal instruction (that is, the program is buggy).
- SIGIOT   The "I/O trap" signal. SIGIOT causes a core dump and program termination. The Standard C function abort sends a process with this signal.
- SIGBUS   The "bus error" signal, causing core dump and termination. Symptomatic of a buggy program.
- SIGFPE   The "floating-point exception" signal, causing core dump and termination. Symptomatic of a buggy program.
- SIGSEGV   The "segmentation fault" signal, sent when a process tries to access memory in an illegal manner. Causes a core dump and termination.
- SIGKILL   The "kill" signal. SIGKILL is the nuclear bomb of UNIX. Although most other signals can be intercepted by a process, the KILL signal cannot. SIGKILL is the most drastic (but reliable) way to terminate a process.
- SIGSTOP   The "stop" signal. SIGSTOP stops (but does not terminate) a process. You can achieve much the same thing for a running process by typing the stop key, usually Ctrl+Z.
- SIGCONT   The "continue" signal. SIGCONT resumes a stopped process.

For more details about kill, see kill(1). Note that if you are using bash or tcsh, kill is actually built into the shell. However, it operates similarly to the non–built-in kill program (found in /bin/kill).

Monitoring Processes: top

The top command shows a snapshot of the running processes on the system, updated every few seconds. Once top is running, you can use the following keys:

- Spacebar—Update the display.
- F—Add or remove columns from the display. You can display 26 pieces of information for each process; this screen lets you choose which pieces of information you want to see.
- I—Toggle the display of idle processes. Normally, idle processes are displayed (unless you start top with the -i option).
- S—Set the delay in seconds between updates. You can also use the command-line option -d *n* where *n* is the delay.
- Q—Quit.

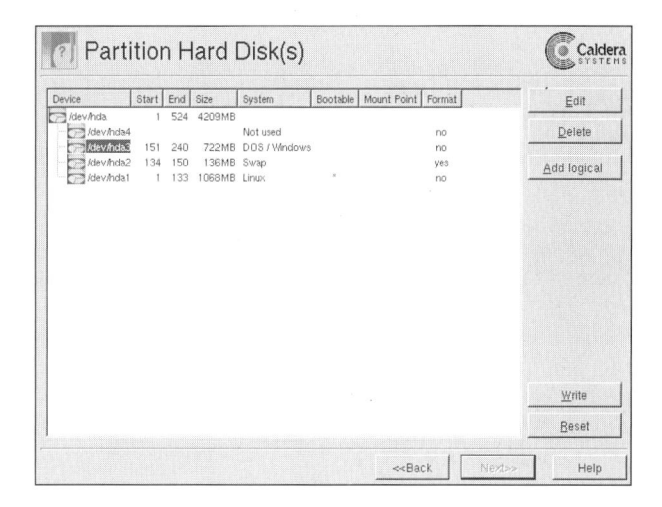

- ?—Display a list of available keystrokes. There are many more than the six keys described here.

Figure A.1 shows an example of a `top` command.

FIGURE A.1
The top *command.*

For more information on `top`, see top(1).

Starting and Stopping the System

If you are using KDE, the KDE login manager has an option for shutting down the system.

> **Warning**
> Never shut down a Linux system by turning off the power or pressing the reset button. You could corrupt the file system.

If you are not using KDE, you can shut down the system in a number of ways. You do need `root` privileges, however.

Shut Down with Warning: `shutdown`

The `shutdown` command shuts down the system after a specified time interval. When the shutdown time approaches, it writes warnings to the terminals of all logged-in users. This is a polite way to shut down a system with many remotely logged-in users.

To use `shutdown`, type

```
# shutdown time [message]
```

Here, `time` is when to shut down. It can be an absolute time in 24-hour format, such as `11:30` or `22:15`, or a number preceded by a plus sign, such as `+10` or `+60`. The second form specifies how many minutes from now to shut down. The special time `now` is equivalent to `+0`.

The optional `message` is sent to users advising them of the shutdown. If you don't supply a message, `shutdown` uses a default message.

If you start a `shutdown` process, but later realize you want to cancel it, use

```
# shutdown -c
```

`shutdown` has a few more options; see `shutdown(8)` for details.

Halt or Reboot Now

You must run `halt` and `reboot` as `root`. Use `halt` when you're ready to switch off your computer, or `reboot` if you want to reboot it (for example, to start another operating system).

To halt the system, use

```
# halt
```

To reboot the system, use

```
# reboot
```

Three-Fingered Salute

Most Linux installations allow you to cleanly shut down the system with the famous Ctrl+Alt+Delete "three-fingered salute."

Any user can do this, not just `root`. If this is not what you want, create a text file called `/etc/shutdown.allow` and place the login names of users you want to be able to use the three-fingered salute, one per line. This file is documented in `shutdown(8)`.

Miscellaneous Commands

Finally, here are a few commands that didn't fit into any other category.

Printing a Calendar

Try the following commands:

```
$ cal
$ cal 2000
$ cal 11 2022
$ cal 9 1752
```

`cal` displays a little calendar for a month or a year. If the output for the last example puzzles you, see `cal(1)`.

Getting or Setting the System Date

The command `date` gets or sets the system date. To display the date, use

```
$ date
Tue Jun 29 22:14:45 EDT 1999
```

You can set the date by supplying a date on the command line in the form *MMDDhhmm[[CC]YY][.ss]* That is, to set the date to 6 January, 2000, at 2:45.13 p.m., use

```
# date 010614452000.13
```

Only `root` can set the system date. The `date` command changes only Linux's understanding of the date; it does not change the hardware clock in your computer. To transfer the Linux system date to the hardware clock, use

```
# hwclock -systohc
```

For more information on these commands, see `date(1)` and `hwclock(8)`. (`date` in particular has many more options and capabilities.)

APPENDIX B

Installing Caldera OpenLinux

IN THIS APPENDIX

- Introduction   966
- Installing Caldera OpenLinux   966
- Installing Caldera OpenLinux Using LIZARD   966
- Installing Caldera OpenLinux Using LISA   973
- Introduction to Partitions   978
- Getting Up to Speed with Partitions   980
- Advanced Partitioning—Solutions for Optimal Performance   983
- Partitioning Tutorial 1—Moving Home   986
- Partitioning Tutorial 2—Using Symlinks   989
- Linux Software RAID   990
- Implementing Software RAID   992
- Configuring a RAID 0 Volume   994
- Configuring a Linear Volume   996
- Configuring a RAID 1 Volume   997

Introduction

This appendix contains a potpourri of installation-related information, with sections geared toward beginners as well as advanced users. For the beginners, we walk through the LIZARD installation process, as well as the older text-based LISA installation process. For intermediate and advanced readers, we investigate how to set up partitions for maximum efficiency, provide two examples of how to move partitions on a running Linux system, and finish up with some valuable documentation explaining how to enable software RAID on your Caldera system. There should be something for everyone in this chapter, so pick a spot and dig in!

Installing Caldera OpenLinux

Caldera has created something really special, which is included with OpenLinux, called LIZARD. Unlike other text-based installers, LIZARD runs in VGA mode and is an incredibly well-designed installation program. In fact, you will probably find that LIZARD-based installation is not only easier than installing Windows, but that it is also a more professional and enjoyable experience.

We also cover Caldera's older installation method, called LISA. LISA offers more options during the installation process, but we can only recommend it if you want to set up your system without X or KDE. LISA currently has problems setting up the X Window System correctly. If possible, use LIZARD.

Installing Caldera OpenLinux Using LIZARD

LIZARD, Caldera's graphical installation process, is the preferred way to install OpenLinux. If you haven't heard of or seen LIZARD yet, you are in for a treat. It makes installing OpenLinux incredibly easy and pleasant. But before we begin our overview of the installation process, make sure that you have the correct disks ready. If you purchased the boxed version of Caldera OpenLinux, you have a boot/install disk that automatically starts LIZARD. However, this might not be enough; there's a good chance you will need to create a Modules disk, which will enable LIZARD to detect and configure a much greater variety of hardware. For example, LIZARD would not detect my BusLogic SCSI card using only the Boot/Install disk, but with the supplemental Modules disk, installation went like a charm! It's a good idea to create one, just in case. So track down a blank disk, and follow these instructions to create a Modules disk (we've included directions for DOS, Linux and Windows):

Here's how create a Modules disk from DOS, assuming that your CD-ROM drive letter is D. First, insert the disk and Caldera CD-ROM, and type:

```
> CD D:
> CD \COL\LAUNCH\FLOPPY
> MODULES.BAT
```

This batch script will create the Modules disk for you.

Under Linux, the process is similarly simple. After inserting the Caldera CD and the blank disk, do the following:

```
> mount /mnt/cdrom
> cd /mnt/cdrom/col/launch/floppy
> dd if=modules.144 of=/dev/fd0
```

After a minute or two, you'll have yourself a Modules disk!

Under Windows, the process is also easy. After installing the Caldera OpenLinux Tools under Windows, go to Start, Programs, OpenLinux, Create Module Diskette.

Now that you're armed with your Modules disk, you are ready to begin the installation process.

Starting the LIZARD Install Process

There are actually two ways to begin the LIZARD installation process; you can boot using the Boot/Install disk, or boot directly from the CD-ROM. We recommend booting from the Boot/Install disk if at all possible. Although slower, it is easier to do and works more consistently across a wide variety of machines. If you truly are interested in booting from the CD-ROM, insert it in your drive and restart your computer. Otherwise, insert the Boot/Install disk and restart your machine.

On restart, you'll be greeted by a very nice looking installation screen that says "boot:" on it. You can either wait a few seconds for installation to begin, or press Enter to proceed.

This next part is tricky. LIZARD will start loading the kernel, and then it will begin booting the kernel. As soon it begins booting the kernel, remove the Boot/Install disk from the drive and insert the Modules disk. Immediately after booting the kernel, LIZARD will look for this disk. If you are booting from the CD-ROM drive you can simply insert the Modules disk into your empty floppy as soon as you reboot.

LIZARD should then say "Mounting Modules Floppy...ok". If it says this, great! If not, you should repeat the earlier steps and swap the disks out faster; LIZARD doesn't give you much time to insert the Modules floppy, so this step can be tricky. However, from this point on, everything should be smooth sailing. Caldera will begin its Automatic

Appendixes

PART VI

Hardware Detection process, detecting any supported PCMCIA, SCSI, and other miscellaneous devices in your computer. It will then try to locate the Caldera OpenLinux CD, and the real fun will begin! After witnessing a groovy demo animation, you will be presented with the screen shown in Figure B.1.

FIGURE B.1
LIZARD Language Select Screen.

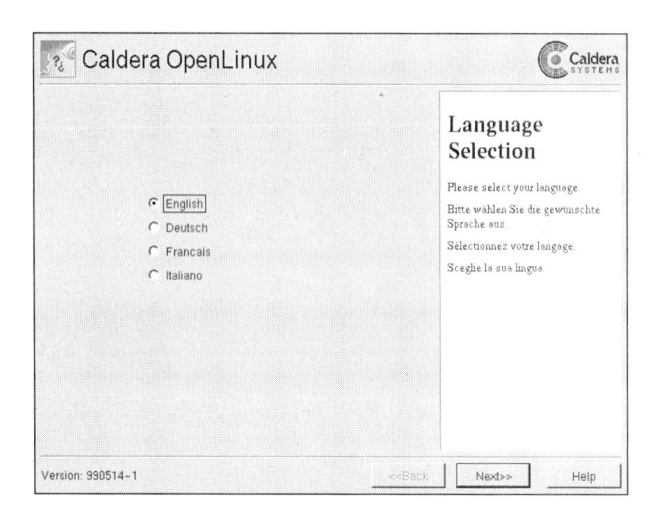

Try moving your mouse; this should cause your mouse to be automatically detected and enabled. Now, select your native language (if listed) and proceed to the next step by clicking the Next button.

The next screen allows you to configure your mouse. LIZARD is so easy to use that you probably won't need any explanation for this screen, except a bit of encouragement to test your mouse settings in the gray area, making sure that every mouse button works and is configured properly. Click Next to continue. Now you are ready to select an installation target, as shown in Figure B.2.

You'll be able to choose whether to use an entire hard drive, partitions prepared using PartitionMagic, or a custom configuration. For this example, we are going to choose Custom; it's the trickiest method and we want to make sure you can get through it with flying colors. If you select another installation target, you can skip ahead to the part where you select a set of packages for installation. Assuming you selected Custom, you will be presented with the screen shown in Figure B.3.

You will be presented with a graphical display of all the hard drives in your system, along with a hierarchical display of all partitions on your hard drives. If you have any extended partitions, they will be indented under the logical area that contains them. This is where you get to create and delete partitions, and you are encouraged to be careful. Never delete a partition if you are not sure what is on it. If you want to delete a partition, select the partition on the left and click Delete. To create a new primary partition in free space, select the free space on the left and click Edit; if you are creating a logical partition, click the Add Logical button instead. If you do click the Edit button, you will be able to change various parameters for the partition, such as its size and intended use (Linux, Swap, or DOS/Windows). Check the Bootable box on the partition you plan to use for your root partition if you want your machine to boot Caldera immediately when the machine is turned on. You can also create multiple Linux partitions and select a mount point for each one. This allows you to create partitions for specific parts of your file system, so that your /usr tree can reside on a separate partition if desired, for example. We cover some partition optimization strategies later in the chapter, so if you're interested in doing this but are not quite sure how, we encourage you to mark this page and skip ahead a few pages to the "Getting Up To Speed With Partitions" section. We'll still be here when you get back!

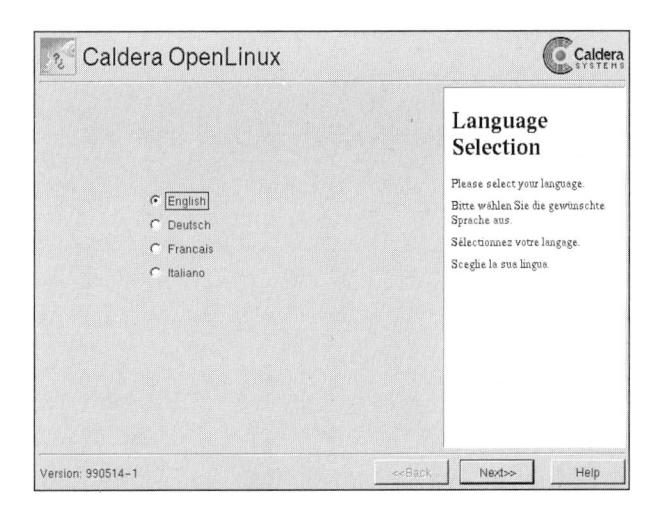

FIGURE B.2
LIZARD Installation Target Selection.

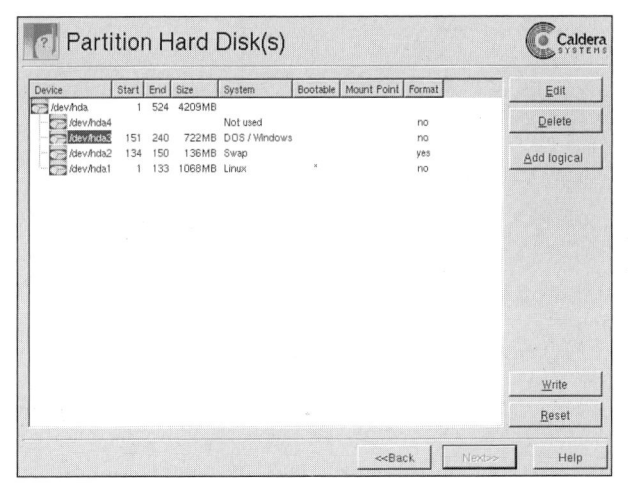

FIGURE B.3
LIZARD Partition Hard Disks Screen.

After you have completed your modifications, press the Write button to make your changes permanent, or the Reset button to not apply your changes to your hard drives. When you're finished, click Next.

The next step is to select a root partition. This is easy and doesn't require much explanation. On the next screen, you will have the option of formatting selected partitions. LIZARD automatically scans your drive for valid swap partitions, and it might pick the wrong one. If so, make sure the right one is checked and click Format Chosen Partitions. The process shouldn't take more than a minute, even on large drives, and when completed, the Format Chosen Partitions button will gray out and the Next button will become active.(See Figure B.4.)

FIGURE B.4
LIZARD Select Installation Screen.

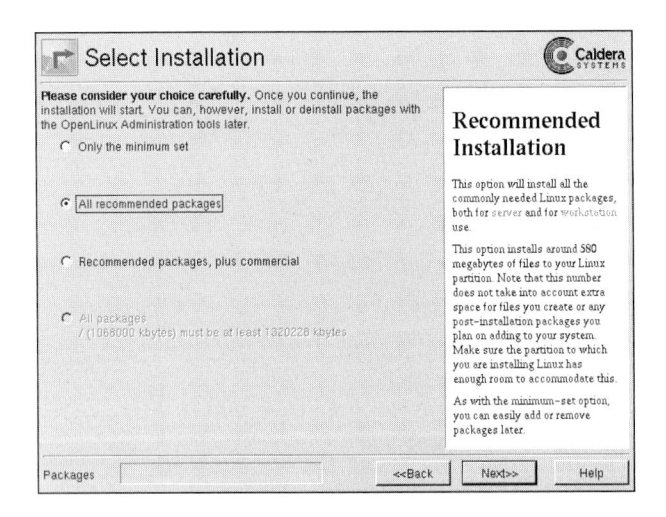

The next stage of the process involves selecting what set of packages to install. On the Select Installation screen, you are presented with several options. If you are a "lean and mean" Linux user, you should select the first option, Only the Minimum Set. This install takes less than 200MB and includes X and KDE. You can then manually add the packages you need from the CD, as you need them, saving (sometimes) precious hard drive space. If you really don't have a preference, select All Recommended Packages or All Recommended Packages, Plus Commercial. If you have over 2GB set aside for Caldera, you can go ahead and select All Packages if you want. But remember, you can always install packages later, when you need them. After you've made your selection, click Next, and package installation will begin. However, you will still be able to configure Caldera while package installation is in process, thanks to LIZARD!

The next screen is fairly self-explanatory and allows you to select a keyboard type. Pick the right one and click Next. The following Select Video Card screen, shown in Figure B.5, is a bit more complicated so we'll cover it in more detail.

FIGURE B.5
LIZARD Select Video Card Screen.

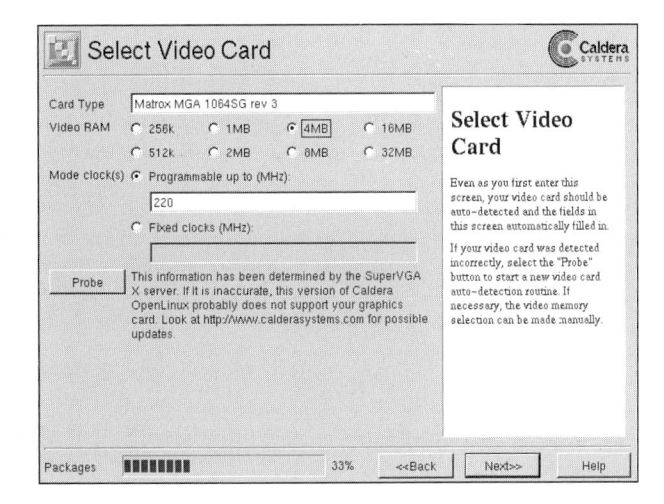

The first thing you should do is click the Probe button, so that Caldera can detect your video card. After detection is complete, verify the settings that were autodetected, and make any corrections if necessary. Autoprobing normally gets the video card type and the mode clocks detected correctly, but will sometimes not detect the Video RAM setting correctly. Verify this, and when you're finished, click Next to proceed to the Select Monitor screen, shown in Figure B.6.

FIGURE B.6
LIZARD Select Monitor Screen.

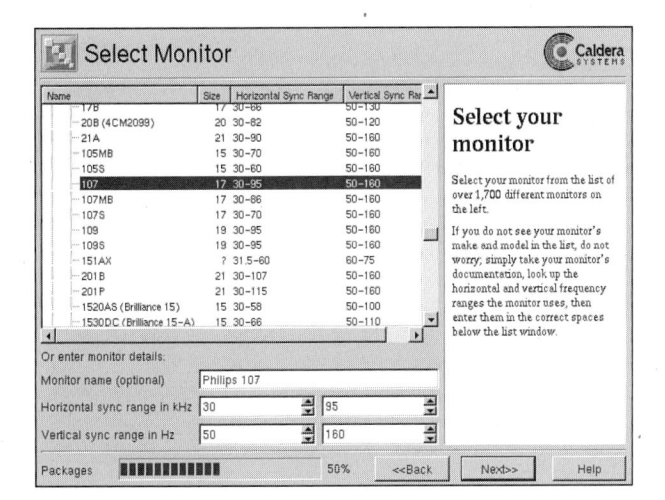

This next screen is truly incredible. Taking the sting out of configuring your screen mode under X, LIZARD presents a very up-to-date monitor database, so that X can be configured optimally for your monitor. Try to find your exact monitor in the list; if you can't, choose one of the generic options, or choose a monitor that is similar to yours, and click Next to proceed to the Select Video Mode screen.

On the Select Video Mode screen, pick a resolution and a color depth, and click Test This Mode. After finding your favorite resolution and color depth, click Next. You have now provided LIZARD with all the information it needs to configure X optimally for your system, and you're now in the final stretches of the installation process.

On the next screen, set a root password for your system that you will remember. Write it down if necessary, and proceed to the next screen, shown in Figure B.7.

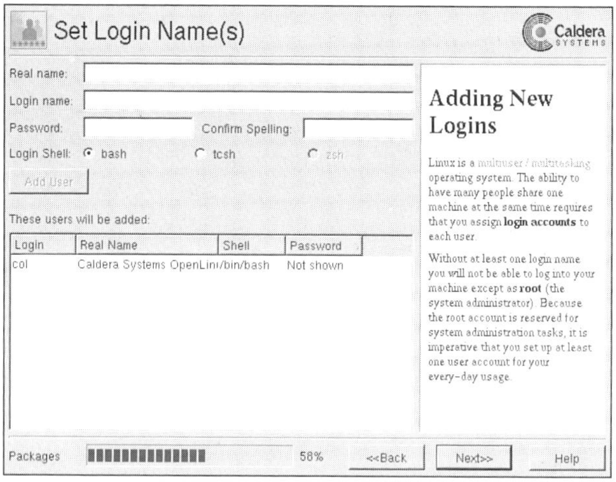

FIGURE B.7
LIZARD Set Login Name(s) Screen.

On the Set Login Name(s) screen, you should create at least one normal user that you can use as your primary account. To do this, type your real name, your login name, and your password and click Add User. All the other default settings are correct. Now you can set up networking.

On the Set Up Networking screen, you will be able to configure any Ethernet devices in your system, as well as set your proper hostname. If this is all Greek to you, ask your system administrator what your settings should be. And if you don't have an Ethernet card in your machine, simply select No Ethernet and click Next to continue.

The next screen, shown in Figure B.8, is really neat, allowing you to set your time zone by clicking on what appears to be a satellite image of the earth. You can get to additional selections not on the map by using the drop-down box below the map. After you're finished making a selection, remember to choose whether your hardware clock runs in GMT or local time. If you don't know exactly what this means, select local time, and click Next. Now, you're given the option to play a block-stacking game until installation completes. Wow! LIZARD is pretty amazing, isn't it?

FIGURE B.8
LIZARD Time Zone Selection Screen.

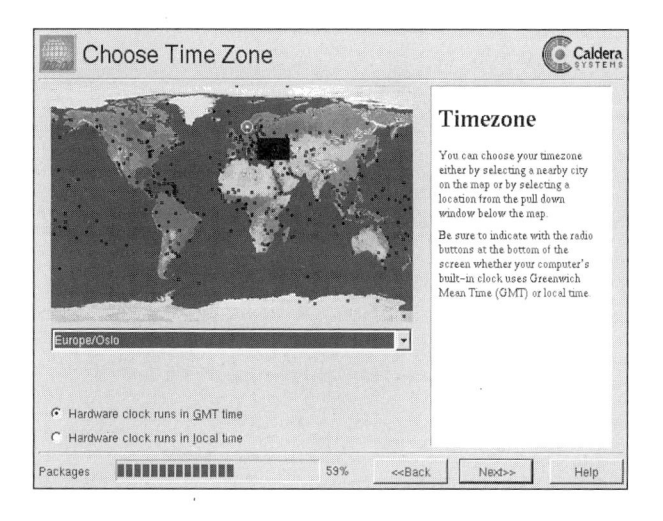

After installation is finished, your system will immediately start, without a reboot. Ta da! The Caldera installation is complete!

Installing Caldera OpenLinux Using LISA

Although the standard graphical install of Caldera usually suffices for most people, there are circumstances where LISA is the preferred method. Generally this is true if you want to install a "bare bones" version of Caldera, with no X, because the graphical install does not provide this option. For such situations, Caldera provides a text-based installation package called LISA, which provides much more control over the installation process. For some, the graphical Caldera installer simply won't work (or it crashes!) and LISA is your only option.

Creating Disks for LISA

You can create disks for LISA under DOS, Windows, or Linux. Under Linux, mount your Caldera CD-ROM, and change directories to /mnt/cdrom/col/launch/lisa/floppy.

After finding two blank 1.44MB floppy disks and inserting one in the drive, type the following as root:

```
> dd if=install.144 of=/dev/fd0
```

After the drive has finished writing, remove the disk and label it "LISA". Then, stick the next disk in the drive and type this:

```
> dd if=modules.144 of=/dev/fd0
```

Remove it from the drive and label this one "Modules". The Modules disk contains kernel modules that will allow you to install and configure your hardware correctly. The standard install disk only contains drivers for a typical PC; the modules disk contains additional support for nearly every hardware device that is supported under Linux.

Creating LISA and Modules disks is also possible from DOS. To do this, change directories to your CD-ROM drive, which in this example is D:

```
> CD D:
> CD COL\LAUNCH\LISA\FLOPPY
```

You will now need to create a LISA install disk, along with a Modules disk by using the following commands:

```
> INSTALL.BAT
> MODULES.BAT
```

Have two blank 1.44MB disks ready.

Creating LISA and Modules disks under Windows 95 is similarly straightforward. After installing OpenLinux Tools (from the CD) under Windows, put a blank disk in your floppy drive, and select Start, Programs, OpenLinux, Create LISA Install Diskette. After the disk is created, put another blank disk in the drive and select Start, Programs, OpenLinux, Create LISA Module Diskette. You'll now have the disks you need to start up the LISA text-based configuration program.

Using LISA

To use LISA, simply insert the LISA disk in the drive and reboot your machine. You'll want to place the Caldera OpenLinux 2.2 CD-ROM in the drive as soon as your system begins booting. A prompt will be displayed that looks like this:

```
boot:
```

Simply press Enter, and the installation process will begin. You should be presented with a series of blue text-based menus that allow you to configure your new installation to your liking. The first ones you will encounter are fairly straightforward, allowing you to select your language and keyboard map. You'll then be asked whether you want to use a previously saved configuration. Choose No. LISA allows you to save your install configuration so that this process can be automated at a later date, if necessary. After this screen, you will be presented with a Change LISA Setup dialog. You can normally just select Call to proceed, without changing any of the defaults, although you might want to turn on Disable Plug and Play Cards if you have at least one in your system that you suspect of locking up the LISA installation process.

> **Going Back in LISA**
>
> If you change your mind, you can easily return to a previous dialog in LISA by pressing Escape.

Now the hardware configuration process begins. LISA should give you a summary of the devices it has found in your system. For many people, it will have detected all your hard drives and network cards. But for many, some things will be missing, especially if you have a SCSI controller that happens to be connected to a SCSI drive that you want to install Caldera on. For this reason, we will get into the gritty details of getting your hardware configured properly for Caldera installation. If everything has been detected perfectly, you can skip this part.

Configuring Extra Hardware in LISA

When LISA asks you whether "all hard disks, CD-ROM drives, and network cards on your system" have been correctly detected, choose No. You'll then have a chance to tell LISA to do "cautious autoprobing" of your system, in the attempt to try to discover additional hardware. In this first stage of autoprobing, LISA will only attempt to discover a limited set of additional hardware, limited to a base set of modules that are included on the LISA install disk. Try the autoprobe first, but if your hardware is still not detected, don't despair; we'll have a chance to do the autoprobe again, using the modules disk (which contains many more additional drivers). After the autoprobe is complete, determine whether all your CD-ROM drives, hard disks, and network cards have been detected by browsing the list. If not, elect to start the Kernel Module Manager, where we will be able to do additional probing.

The LISA Kernel Module Manager

When you are in the Kernel Module Manager, select option three, "Load Kernel Modules". You will be able to select from several categories of modules to load. Selecting a particular category will allow you to browse modules for specific hardware devices. You can elect to load the appropriate modules directly, or select the Autoprobe option, which will autoprobe using these new modules. You will need to insert the Modules disk when prompted to do so. Hopefully, all your hardware has been configured, and you can proceed to the disk partitioning stage.

Partitioning Under LISA

Partitioning under LISA is accomplished using the antiquated Linux `fdisk` utility. Although it's not a lot of fun to use, it does get the job done and will allow you to get your partitions set up the way you want them. You can choose to partition any or all of the disks that have been detected by the installation program. When you're in `fdisk`, be careful—it's possible to severely mess up or destroy the existing data on your hard drive if you do not know what you are doing! There are several things you need to know to use `fdisk` correctly. First, your changes will not be saved unless you type **w** to write the new partition table information to disk. If you type **q** without typing **w** first, your changes will not be applied to your hard drive. Second, it is very important that you set the proper partition type for each partition you plan to use for your OpenLinux installation. Remember, use number 83 on ext2 partitions-to-be and 82 on swap partitions, and use the `t` command to set this information. This allows LISA to detect these partitions later; otherwise, you will not be allowed to install onto the partitions you have created, and you will have to escape back and (gasp!) be forced to use `fdisk` again!

Selecting LISA Install Method

After your partitions are properly configured, it's time to install Caldera. You will now need to select the installation method. We'll only cover CD-ROM based installation here, but Caldera can also be installed from a local hard disk, or from the network. After selecting the CD-ROM method, you will need to pick your CD-ROM device. If you have no idea which device is your CD-ROM, first try selecting the default highlighted value. For IDE CD-ROM drives, try these in order: hdc, hdd, hdb, hda. For SCSI CD-ROM drives, try sda through d. If you have a proprietary CD-ROM controller, you'll need to chose a specific option from the list.

When you're finished doing this, LISA will ask you the following question: "Do you want to include additional partitions within the root partition for the installation?". LISA is asking you whether you would like to specify an additional partition that will be mounted at a specific place on your root partition, and will be used to hold files. For example, if you choose Yes and type /**home**, the new partition you select will be dedicated to storing everything in /home.

> **Warning**
>
> If you are a current Linux user, you might be tempted to use this functionality to mount your existing /home partition from your other distribution under Caldera. *Do not do this!* Wait until after installation. If you do it now, Caldera could possibly mess up the file permissions on your /home partition. You are encouraged not to use this functionality to add currently existing ext2 file systems and just use it to add new ones that you have just created.

You will be asked whether you want to format the partition you have selected. Select No unless you are absolutely sure that you have selected a new, empty partition that you just created; otherwise, you might lose data! Remember, you can always press Escape to go back a menu without exiting LISA, to check partition configuration.

Installing Packages Under LISA

You are now in the final stretch and are ready to select the packages to be installed on your new Caldera system. In the Software Package Pre-Selection dialog, you can pick a standard package selection, or hand-pick your own individual packages. This dialog offers significantly more control than the current graphical installation, so you can get as specific as you like.

After you select an appropriate X server (although we don't recommend that you use LISA to install X, because it doesn't configure it correctly), package installation begins. It'll take several minutes for the installation and post-installation to complete, so sit back and relax.

After package installation, you will be able to set your machine's hostname, and configure any network cards. After configuring your time zone, your mouse, and your printer, and setting the root password for your system, you now have the option to install LILO, the Linux boot loader, either onto your hard drive or a boot floppy. It's important that you get this option right, so we'll talk about each option a bit.

If you want to boot directly into Caldera OpenLinux when your machine is turned on, you should choose options 1 or 2, First IDE/SCSI Disk, depending on whether your system first boots from IDE or SCSI. If you have another operating system installed and would like to boot directly into this operating system rather than having Caldera automatically start, or if you have a boot manager of some kind (like System Commander), select option 3, Linux Root Partition. This makes the Linux partition bootable, so that boot managers can start Linux easily. If you are unsure which option to choose or you do not want to modify your existing boot configuration, select option 4, Diskette Drive, after inserting a blank disk in the floppy drive. You will then be able to boot Caldera OpenLinux by rebooting your machine with this disk in the drive (after installation is complete, that is).

Enabling/Disabling Services in LISA

Now, LISA will present you with the ability to enable or disable services that start when your Caldera system boots. Nearly all these services start additional programs that run in the background, so you should disable any that you do not plan to use. We offer a few suggestions of some that you might like to disable:

Service	Disable If...
Auto Mount Daemon	...you don't know what this is
Web Server	...you won't be using a Web server
Int. Packet Exch. (IPX)	...you don't know what this is (it's optional)
Print Server	...you don't have a printer
Mail Transfer Agent	...you don't plan to use email
NFS Server	...you don't know what this is

Of course, enable any additional services that you know you will need. If you don't know what a particular thing does, keep it enabled if it is already enabled (unless it is in the list earlier). Being selective here will free up some RAM for your Caldera system. You can also always disable these services later by deleting the appropriate symlinks in the /etc/rc.d/rc5.d directory.

LISA installation should now be complete!

Introduction to Partitions

About a decade ago, many people got along just fine with a single hard drive, which contained a single operating system (most likely DOS). At that time, hard drives stored a relatively tiny amount of data, and because there weren't many choices when it came to operating systems, the entire drive would normally be dedicated to one use. As technology advanced and hard drive storage capacity grew and grew, there was a need to break a single physical hard drive into several linear sections, or partitions, so that several "virtual" hard drives could be created. This allowed users to do two things: First, they could partition their drives so that multiple virtual hard drives were available under their operating system of choice. For example, under DOS, users could have a C and D drive. Another possibility was the ability to install multiple operating systems on a single hard drive. Under Linux, the use of multiple partitions is normal and usually encouraged. In addition to allowing you to continue to keep other operating systems on your machine, they serve as an excellent organizational tool and can even dramatically enhance system performance and stability if planned properly.

Primary Partitions

Primary partitions were the original kind of partition that was available for the PC. Over the years, as hard drives have expanded in size, primary partitions have remained as the most popular means of splitting up a drive for multiple uses. You are allowed to have up to four primary partitions per drive. Each partition has a single-byte "type" associated with it that specifies the type of data contained on the partition. For example, a Windows 95 FAT32 partition has a hex partition type value of "0b"; a Linux ext2 partition has a hex type of "83"; and a BeOS file system partition has a type of "eb". These partition types not only help partitioning software properly display a representation of your hard drive on the screen, they also often allow install programs (such as the Caldera installation programs) identify which partitions are available on a particular drive for a specific use. For example, when the Caldera installer wants to present a list of possible swap partitions for you to select from, it scans your hard drives for partitions of type "82", which corresponds to Linux swap. If you have created a swap partition but did not set its type correctly, Linux will still be able to use it, but it is likely that the Caldera installer won't. So always label your partitions correctly.

Another thing that should be mentioned about primary partitions is that they have a "bootable" flag that can be set or unset. If this flag is set, the partition will be considered in an attempt to boot the system. This doesn't actually mean that the boot process will happen successfully, but it means that by default, your computer will attempt to boot from this bootable partition.

Extended Partitions

Extended (or logical) partitions were created to work around the original limitations of the primary partitioning scheme. Using extended partitions, it is possible to have more than four partitions per drive, which allows for much greater flexibility. Linux can use and even boot from extended partitions, so you are encouraged to use them if at all possible. Extended partitions do have limitations, however. Although Linux can boot from an extended partition, your BIOS (the firmware that initially starts up your computer) cannot. This means that you will normally want to have an initial, bootable primary partition on your hard drive. Besides this, extended partitions are incredibly useful. You can think of an extended partition as a primary partition that can hold other partitions. So, if you have three primary partitions, you can have only one additional logical partition; however, this logical partition can contain several smaller partitions of any configuration, allowing for significant flexibility. Just remember, you are limited to four partitions, either primary or logical, but the logical partitions can be further subdivided into other partitions. Additional information on partitions can be found in Chapter 8, "Setting Up File Systems."

> **Tip**
>
> There are many reasons to partition. One obvious one is that sometimes you simply need to, for example, run Windows 98 and Linux on the same machine. Even when using a single operating system, partitioning can be great, and is often safer than not partitioning at all. If anything goes wrong with a particular file system, damage will be limited to a single partition. This turns potential big messes into smaller messes and small messes into barely any mess at all.

Getting Up to Speed with Partitions

There might be times when you will need to add or delete partitions on an already-installed Linux system. This can happen if you purchase a new hard drive for extra storage, or if you decide to delete a partition that contains an operating system that you no longer use. Although there are a couple of relatively easy-to-use tools for Linux that can perform this task, it is important to note that partition creation and deletion is a dangerous process, and you should know what you are doing. Of course, you often can't learn everything without trying. If you are repartitioning for the first time, it is critical that you back up your data first! You have been warned!

Before you can delete a partition, you need to make sure the partition is not mounted. You can unmount a partition like so:

```
> umount /dev/hdc1
```

Don't expect to be able to unmount / or /var on a running system. But if you have a partition or two that just stores personal data irrelevant to proper system operation, unmounting should work, as long as you have no files or shells open in a directory on that partition when you try to unmount it.

Say you have a lot of junk on /dev/hdc1 and you want to reformat the partition and start from scratch. How would you do it? After unmounting, you'd type:

```
> mkfs.ext2 /dev/hdc1
```

This would erase all data on the partition and create a fresh file system that could be mounted again with the following command:

```
> mount /dev/hdc1 /attach/this/file system/here
```

It's quite simple. If you need to create a new swap partition, you would use the command `mkswap` instead of `mkfs.ext2`:

```
> mkswap /dev/hdc1
```

After you have the partitions created, it's a good thing to create a standard place for them to be mounted on startup. This is done by adding entries to the /etc/fstab file, as follows:

```
<file system>    <mount point>    <type>    <options>    <dump>  <pass>
/dev/sda1        /                ext2      defaults     1       1
```

A root file system, such as the one earlier, should be mounted with default options and dump and pass numbers of 1. Here's a standard partition that should be mounted automatically the next time you boot:

```
/dev/sda2        /home            ext2      defaults     0       2
```

The /home partition uses default options, which means that it will get automatically mounted on boot. Note that all non-root standard ext2 partitions should have dump and pass numbers of 0 and 2. How would you specify that a particular partition should not be mounted automatically on boot, such as an infrequently used "junk" partition?

```
/dev/sda3        /mnt/junk        ext2      noauto       0       2
```

You might wonder why you would want to add partitions to your `fstab` if you do not want the system mounting them automatically on startup. One answer is that it's an organizational tool and will help you keep track of your partitions and how they are organized. In addition, it will make life easier for you from the command line:

```
> mount /dev/sda3 /mnt/junk
```

can be replaced with:

```
> mount /dev/sda3
```

or

```
> mount /mnt/junk
```

For unmount, you can also use either the device name or the mount point to refer to the partition. Pretty nice, eh? It's especially useful with CD-ROM drives:

```
/dev/hdb         /mnt/cdrom       iso9660   noauto,ro    0       0
```

Now, the cumbersome mount command previously required:

```
> mount /dev/hdb /mnt/cdrom -t iso9660 -o noauto,ro
```

becomes either:

```
> mount /dev/hdb
```

or:

```
> mount /mnt/cdrom
```

Because these options aren't going to change often, if ever, it makes sense to add a line to the `fstab`. It'll make things easier for you. Also worth pointing out in the example earlier is the fact that all non-ext2fs partitions should have dump and pass numbers of 0.

So far, we've been covering fairly basic operations that you might already be familiar with, but here is something that you probably do not know—a hidden gem within the Linux kernel. It is possible to set up multiple swap spaces, each one on a separate disk, and have them all active at once. Furthermore, if you set them to the same priority in /etc/fstab, they will operate in *parallel*, dramatically increasing swap file performance in most instances. How does it work? Say that you have two swap partitions that you want to use in parallel, one on /dev/hda1 and another on /dev/hdb1. The following two lines in /etc/fstab would do the trick:

```
/dev/hda1       none        swap        sw,pri=1        0       0
/dev/hdb1       none        swap        sw,pri=1        0       0
```

If you want to expand your swap space by using partitions on the same hard drive, you do not want to run your swap in parallel, because this will cause your hard drives to thrash and dramatically reduce swap performance. In this case, put something such as the following in /etc/fstab:

```
/dev/hda1       none        swap        sw,pri=10       0       0
/dev/hda6       none        swap        sw,pri=1        0       0
```

This will cause hda1 to be used as swap first, and after it is filled up, hda6 will be used. The priority is a number between 0 and 32767, so there's great (possibly too much) flexibility when it comes to laying out swap storage. Here's a complex example:

```
/dev/sda1       none        swap        sw,pri=10       0       0
/dev/sda2       none        swap        sw,pri=10       0       0
/dev/sda3       none        swap        sw,pri=10       0       0
/dev/hda4       none        swap        sw,pri=1        0       0
```

In this example, the kernel first uses the swap space on my three blazingly fast SCSI drives (in parallel, increasing performance even further!) until space is exhausted. Then, the kernel will begin using swap space on the slower (but still appreciated) IDE drive. As you can see, you have many options when it comes to swap file performance. If you are planning to use your Caldera system as a high-performance file or Web server, you might want to get a bit creative with your swap arrangement!

> **Tip**
>
> Some people who have large hard drives initially set up a huge array of partitions, in anticipation of every possible need. Although this is definitely possible, you might want to actually *not* partition all your hard drive space, leaving some at the end of your drive as free space. Your computer will still work wonderfully, and you will then be able to easily create a partition of the exact size you need when the need arises, instead of guessing at the size you might need in the future. If you have a brand new shiny 22GB drive but only have a use for 10GB, resist the urge to divvy up the additional 12GB of unused space at the end of the drive. Don't worry, it'll still be there when you need it.

Advanced Partitioning—Solutions for Optimal Performance

For the average home user, partitioning is not something to spend a lot of time thinking about. An ext2 partition of suitable size, as well as a decent swap partition is all that is required. However, Caldera OpenLinux is a versatile operating system, and you might not be an average user. If you aren't, we encourage you to study this section. In it, we will investigate various methods to partition hard disks for maximum performance, and will even explore Software RAID arrays as possible configuration options. *RAID (Redundant Array of Inexpensive Disks)* is a nickname for a handful of technologies that can be used to dramatically increase disk performance or availability.

Organizing to Reduce Fragmentation

Fragmentation happens when files are written to and deleted from the disk over time. Several months worth of frequent deletions and writes (especially on nearly full disks) can create a condition that is referred to as fragmentation. Simply, this means that a good number of the files on the disk are not stored in a single contiguous block but are instead chopped up into several file fragments scattered various places on the disk. This can (sometimes significantly) affect IO speed. These problems are normally caused when there is only a small amount of contiguous free space on the partition and a large file is created. Although the ext2 file system has been designed to minimize fragmentation, the problem can still occur, and you should be aware of what causes the problem and how to avoid it.

Well, what does cause fragmentation? We mentioned writes and deletes, but how does one avoid writing and deleting files, because that happens normally as you use your computer? In a sense, fragmentation can't be eliminated, but it can be isolated and controlled, and in a well-designed file system, fragmentation can remain dramatically low, with the right planning.

The best technique to deal with fragmentation is to isolate files and parts of the file system tree that you expect will be modified often and put them on a separate partition. Things that you should consider isolating are files that have a short life span (those that are created and deleted frequently), such as files that are created in /tmp. Also worthy of consideration are files in /var, especially log files, which gradually grow over time and are modified frequently. Another part of your file system which might experience a good amount of fragmentation is your /home tree. Areas where you will probably not have problems with fragmentation are in /usr, /bin, /lib, and /opt. These parts of your file system are mainly used to store binary data that does not change often; because these files rarely get modified, fragmentation is rarely a problem. By separating files with short lifetimes from those with long lifetimes, you can dramatically reduce fragmentation over time on the partitions that have few changes.

Organizing to Facilitate Backups

Another important thing to consider when expertly creating partitions and laying out your file system is how you plan on backing up files. If, for example, you have a 4GB tape drive which you plan to use to back up your home directories, it might be a good idea to keep the size of the partition you use for /home to 4GB. This will eliminate the possibility that your tape will not be able to back up all the files in /home, which might be a good thing if you plan to have heavy usage of your machine and your backups are automated. Think about it, and plan wisely.

Organizing for Performance

If you have Caldera installed on a machine with a single hard drive, you have limited options available to optimize your partitions for performance. If, however, you have more than one hard drive in your system, you have numerous possibilities to speed up disk reads and writes. The key concept to remember here is that a disk can only read from or write to one physical place on the hard drive at a time. So that if you are reading from two files, or reading and writing on the same hard drive, the hard drive's heads must quickly jump between two locations on the drive so that both file operations can occur at (almost) the same time. This will drastically reduce performance. But what happens if you have two hard drives, and you are reading from one and writing to the other, or reading a file from each drive at the same time? In this case, performance is still at near

100%, because each drive can focus on reading or writing a specific file, instead of trying to skip between two things at once. It might help you to think of your hard drive as a record player; the needle can only be at one position at once, and you want to avoid situations where the needle has to jump back and forth between two locations to attempt to satisfy two simultaneous requests.

> **Extreme Performance with Multiple Drives**
>
> For extreme performance with multiple drives and partitions, do your best to make sure that the various hard drives in your system are using separate controllers. For example, all modern motherboards have at least two IDE interfaces. If you have two hard drives daisy-chained on the same interface, and you are performing simultaneous read/write operations on the drives, performance can suffer. But, if you physically reconfigure your drives so that they are on separate cables and interfaces, reads and writes on both drives can happen in parallel. SCSI drives do not suffer as much from this problem, and are better able to share cable bandwidth among multiple devices on the same cable.

Another interesting option that can dramatically boost performance is the use of software RAID-0 striping. Simply put, RAID-0 allows you to configure two or more partitions (on separate drives) that will be used to form a single "virtual partition". Reads and writes will happen to all drives in parallel. So, if you create a 3MB file on a RAID-0 virtual partition, about 1.5MB of data will exist on each drive. When it comes time to read the data, each drive can operate in parallel, reading half the amount of data that it would if you were using a normal partition. What this means is that read and write performance multiplies depending on the number of drives that you use for striping—with two drives, IO performance nearly doubles, and with 4 drives, IO performance is nearly quadrupled! A well-designed RAID-0 partition can offer a tremendous performance boost! The downside is that as you add more drives, the odds of corrupted data due to hard drive failure increase linearly with the number of drives used for the RAID-0 volume. However, RAID-0 is still perfectly fine for non-critical situations, such as implementing very fast /tmp storage. Additionally, you can set up multiple swap spaces under Linux, with no additional kernel modules, that operate similar to RAID-0 stripes. This support is in the kernel automatically, and we'll explain how to take advantage of this as well.

Optimizing for Reliability

When you are looking for high reliability, you want to consider the Linux kernel's software RAID levels 1, 4, and 5. RAID is incredibly helpful in reducing the possibility of data loss due to hard drive failure by providing several techniques to redundantly store data so that no data is lost, even if one drive fails. By stacking logical RAID volumes on top of each other, even more redundancy is possible, allowing for recoveries from three and more simultaneous disk failures! Before we describe the various kinds of redundant storage, it's important to emphasize that RAID can only protect against hard drive failure—it does not "back up" your data, and it does not prevent the data itself from being accidentally deleted or modified. It keeps a real-time, redundant store of your data. Compare RAID to an airplane with multiple engines—if one fails, the remaining ones will provide enough lift to allow it to make an emergency landing at an airport. In a similar way, RAID allows the system to continue to function for a period of time after a hard drive failure. Then, the administrator can schedule a time to take the system temporarily offline to replace the defective drive.

Partitioning Tutorial 1— Moving Home

Sometimes, you'll have a fully installed and customized Linux system set up just the way you like it, and suddenly you notice that you're running out of hard drive space. Using `cfdisk` to view your partition information, you notice that you have 12GB of unused space sitting at the end of your hard drive, that you left alone for a time such as this. After spending a few minutes using the `du` command to find out which part of the file system tree is eating up all your space, you narrow down the culprit. A user on your machine (who we will call "hog"), has over 1GB of files stored in his home directory. Even worse, after a little more research, you discover who this hog is: yourself! To avoid the embarrassment of bringing your own Linux box to a screeching halt, you need to start using that extra 12GB of space, and quickly. Here's how to do it.

Do the following:

1. Enter single user mode.
2. Create an extended partition in the free space.
3. Subpartition the 12GB into a 6GB partition and 6GB free space.
4. Create an ext2 file system on the new 6GB partition.
5. Mount the new partition.
6. Copy the contents of /home to the new partition.
7. Temporarily mount the new partition at /home, do some testing, and make sure that all files were transferred successfully.
8. After verification, unmount the new partition and delete all the old data in the original /home.

9. Remount /home and modify /etc/fstab appropriately.
10. Verify directory permissions on /home.
11. Bring the system back up into multiuser mode.

The first step, entering single-user mode, is easy. Going into single-user mode will kick all other users off your machine, and zap most unnecessary running processes, so make sure you have quit out of all programs (including X and KDE), and that nothing important is happening on your machine. Then, as root, type:

```
> init 1
```

The system will now start killing processes and getting your machine ready for some maintenance. After this process is complete, you will be prompted to either press Ctrl+D to bring the system back up again or type the root password for maintenance. Go ahead and type the root password. Now you're ready to get your hands dirty.

The second thing you need to do is create a partition in the 12GB of free space at the end of the drive. Fire up `cfdisk`:

```
> cfdisk
```

If you need to run `cfdisk` on a drive other than the one it defaults to, type **cfdisk /dev/sda**, or something similar. Now that you're in `cfdisk`, you'll notice that there is a row marked "free space" at the end of the drive. Eager to tap into that space, you down-arrow until that line is highlighted, and then right-arrow over until new is highlighted. You then select that a logical partition should be created, type **6000** to create a 6GB partition, and select for this partition to be created at the beginning of the free space. With the partition still highlighted, you right-arrow over to type, press Enter, and type **83** to set the partition's type to Linux. With your task complete, you right-arrow over to write, and press Enter to write your changes to disk. Knowing you did the right thing, you type **yes**, and your changes are saved to disk. After the partition table is saved, `cfdisk` informs you that it could not reread the new partition table from disk, and that a reboot is required to update the table. Not being a fool, you heed `cfdisk`'s advice (you should!) by rebooting your machine. After reboot, log in as root, go back into single user mode, and continue to the next step.

You're now ready to put a file system on your new partition. Because the partition you created is associated (in this particular case) with the device /dev/hda4, type:

```
> mkfs.ext2 /dev/hda4
```

Within a matter of seconds, the new file system is created and is ready for use. You create a new mount point, and mount the file system.

```
> mkdir /mnt/new
> mount /dev/hda4 /mnt/new
```

The partition has been created, the file system is mounted, and now you are ready to copy over huge gobs of data to the new partition. Wanting to store everything in /home on the new partition, you do the following:

```
> cd /home
> cp -ax * /mnt/new
```

(This command would not work if you had any files or directories that began with a ., but /home contains none of these so you're fine.)

Before you're ready to delete the old data, you should give this new partition a test run to ensure that the all the files have been copied successfully. So, you type:

```
> umount /mnt/new
> mount /dev/hda4 /home
```

The new 6GB partition is now acting as an in-place replacement for your original subdirectory. Although you can't currently get to your old home directory, the files have not been deleted and will "reappear" when /dev/hda4 is unmounted. You want to be sure your copy was successful, so you use your machine for a couple of days, and find all your files in the right places. Now you're ready to get rid of your original data, so you do the following:

```
> umount /home
> cd /home
> rm -rf *
```

Now that the old data is deleted, you temporarily remount your new home directory:

```
> mount /dev/hda4 /home
```

Everything is working great, and you're ready to modify your /etc/fstab so that your new /home partition gets attached to file root file system at boot. You fire up /etc/fstab in your favorite editor and add the following line:

```
/dev/hda4       /home    ext2    defaults    0    2
```

After saving your changes, you're almost home free. With /dev/hda4 mounted, you check the permissions on /home, and finding that they are incorrect, set them to the correct values:

```
> cd /
> chmod 755 home
```

Ta da! Your /home data has been moved! You'll want to return back to multiuser mode. To do this, type **exit** in the root shell. The system will be back the way you left it in a few seconds.

Partitioning Tutorial 2— Using Symlinks

You can use symbolic links to do lots of neat things in combination with partitions. For those who don't know, symbolic links are special objects on the file system that point to another directory or file. Opening the symlink will open the file it points to, and changing directories into a symlink will change directories into the directory it points to. Symbolic links have the advantage of working properly across file systems, and this opens up a lot of possibilities for you. We've put together a second tutorial to familiarize you with the proper use of symlinks in combination with partitions.

Now continue where you left off in Partitioning Tutorial 1, after you created the new 6GB /home partition. Say that you have now started using /tmp frequently as temporary storage space to compile the latest programs that you have been downloading from the Internet. Having read the section about fragmentation in this appendix, you are concerned that your rapid creation and deletion of large amounts of data in /tmp might eventually lead to a fragmentation problem. You'd be right in thinking this; because /tmp is on your root file system, it is on the same partition as many of your infrequently changing files, such as your system binaries and libraries. Generally, you want to isolate your short life-span files from your long life-span files to minimize fragmentation. So, armed with this knowledge, you survey your hard drive and look for a solution. You have a free 6GB of unpartitioned space at the end of the drive, but you would rather save all this space for a future use. After poking around a bit, you notice that you are using only 3GB of the 6GB of available space on your new /home partition, leaving plenty of extra room for temporary files. However, you're not sure how you can possibly use your already in-use /home space for temporary files. After all, /tmp cannot appear in /home/tmp; it must be located at /tmp to be found by programs. Fortunately, you are not stumped for long, as you remember how you can use symbolic links to make connections between disparate pieces of your file system. You devise a plan to move /tmp, which consists of:

1. Entering single-user mode
2. Creating a /home/tmp directory
3. Setting correct permissions on /home/tmp
4. Creating a symbolic link at /tmp pointing to /home/tmp
5. Exiting single-user mode
6. Testing it out!

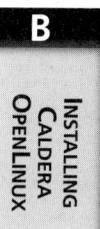

After reviewing the plan, you decide to proceed. Again, you enter single-user mode by typing the following as root:

```
> init 1
```

When prompted, you enter the root password to perform system maintenance. Now, you do the following:

```
> cd /home
> mkdir tmp
> chmod 777 tmp
```

A /home/tmp directory has been created, and permissions have been set so that any user can create files in /home/tmp. Because this is public temporary space, this is a good idea. All that is left is to create a symbolic link from /tmp, pointing to /home/tmp. But first, look in /tmp to make sure that you don't have any important files lurking around. Fortunately, because this is temporary storage, you don't need to back anything up before /tmp gets zapped. You now do the following:

```
> cd /
> rm -rf /tmp
> ln -sf /home/tmp /tmp
```

Now, any references to /tmp will transparently use /home/tmp instead. You've successfully moved /tmp to a different partitions, without irritating programs that expect to find it at /tmp! You can verify that the symlink is in place by typing:

```
> cd /
> ls -l
```

and reading the output.

Linux Software RAID

Linux Software RAID is a really neat technology that is worth looking into. Unfortunately, there is little good up-to-date documentation on the subject, so we've compiled a detailed overview of how to create your own modern Linux RAID system. Implementing software RAID is a process suitable for intermediate to advanced Linux users; if you are one, please read on!

The first kind of software RAID we'll look at is called RAID 1. RAID 1 is also called mirroring, and is the most robust form of software RAID under Linux. When you have a RAID 1 volume consisting of N partitions, each partition contains identical data. When you save a file to the RAID 1 partition, data is written to all N disks at the same time. When data is read from disk, reads are scattered across all N disks to increase performance. Using N disks, N-1/N of the space is wasted. So, if you have a 2-drive mirror, you are wasting 50% of your storage space, and with a 3-drive mirror, you are duplicating 66% of your storage space. But although RAID 1 is quite inefficient in how it uses your disk, it has a number of advantages. Unlike other RAID levels, in level 1, each partition that makes up a RAID 1 volume is a valid file system by itself. This makes recovery much easier than in a RAID 4 and 5 situation, where "reconstruction" is required. This means that if your computer crashes hard, and not even the RAID recovery software will work, you can still mount one of the RAID 1 partitions normally in an attempt to recover data. That's what makes RAID 1 so robust.

Advantages of RAID 1

Most Robust Software RAID under Linux

- Each mirror partition contains a valid file system
- Read Performance is enhanced
- Easy to Recover From Errors, even if RAID tools fail

Disadvantages of RAID 1

- Wastes at least 50% of storage space for mirror
- Data gets written to all partitions, slightly degrading write performance

RAID 4 and 5 are also available, with RAID 5 being the most popular of the two. With RAID 4, at least three separate partitions on separate disks are required. One of the partitions is used to store special parity information, which allows the data on the other disks to be reconstructed, even if one disk fails. People tend to avoid RAID 4 in favor of RAID 5, because with RAID 5, the parity information is spread over all the disks, resulting in a more evenly balanced IO load on all the disks, and avoiding an IO bottleneck on the RAID 4 parity disk. One of the nice things about RAID 4 and 5 is that they are significantly more efficient than RAID 1. Using N equally sized disks, only 1/N of the storage space is wasted. This is a boon for large RAID 4 and 5 volumes—for example, a 5 drive RAID 5 volume only stores 20% redundant data, but can still recover from a single drive failure. One drawback of RAID 4 and 5 is that you are dependent on the RAID tools to recover from a disk failure, as the partitions that make up a RAID 4 or 5 volume do not contain a valid file system by themselves. For this reason, you are encouraged to try out RAID 4 or 5 only after doing a good amount of your own research or testing. If you are interested in these RAID levels, you will need to get familiar with the RAID tools so that you know the proper way to recover in the case of an emergency. Remember, if you don't know the steps to recover from a single-disk failure, the fact that you have a fancy RAID 5 volume won't help very much!

Advantages of RAID 4, 5

- Wastes significantly less space than RAID 1
- Uses space more efficiently as number of partitions increase
- Reads/Writes occur in parallel, speeding IO performance
- Ideal for volumes consisting of a large number of drives

Disadvantages of RAID 4, 5

- You depend on the RAID tools to recover from disasters
- Additional Disadvantages of RAID 4
- Single parity disk creates IO bottleneck

Implementing Software RAID

Software RAID can be implemented on any combination of hard drives and controllers. For example, you can create a RAID 0 stripe that uses a partition on an IDE drive, along with a partition on a SCSI drive. Linux Software RAID gives us this flexibility, allowing any type of file storage to be used. Although high-speed SCSI drives normally provide the highest performance, IDE drives can also work well. I set up a Software RAID 0 stripe which uses a partition on my IDE drive, as well as one on my significantly faster SCSI drive, and still noticed a significant speed improvement, around a 50% and 100% performance increase! Doing this also took some load off my main SCSI drive (I don't hear it "thrash" as much anymore.) For those who are curious, I use this RAID 0 stripe as my /tmp partition; because I decompress and compile many source tarballs, /tmp file IO speed becomes critical, and the RAID 0 stripe has helped immensely!

> **Patch Might Not Be Needed with 2.2.11 and Up**
>
> If you are using kernel 2.2.11 or greater, the kernel patch might not be required. You will still need to recompile a kernel with RAID support, but probably will not need the RAID patches. Only install them if you find that the kernel isn't able to recognize your RAID partitions. You *will* need to install RAIDtools, however.

Software RAID support is added using a kernel patch, along with the installation of various Software RAID utility programs. It's important to patch your kernel sources, even if you have the most recent kernel, because the RAID support included in the kernel is usually somewhat incompatible with the current RAIDtools that are available from the net. Make a mental note that your kernel *will* need to be patched. If not, the RAIDtools won't work, and you'll get stuck.

Installation begins with a trip to your favorite kernel source mirror, such as `ftp://ftp.us.kernel.org`. If you are looking in the /pub/linux/daemons/raid directory, you'll be heading in the right direction. It's a bit tricky to find exactly the right files; I normally look in the alpha directory, because it contains the most recent versions of the files you need. You will need the following things:

```
raid0145-<date>-<kernelversion>.bz2
raidtools-<date>-0.90.tar.bz2
```

The first file consists of the most recent Software RAID patches for a particular kernel version—make sure the version number you download matches the current version of your kernel sources, and download the files with the most recent date strings possible. By the time you read this, RAIDtools and the raid patches might have later numbers than 0.90 and 0145; simply download the most recent version and follow these directions to install.

Patching the Kernel

To patch the kernel sources, do the following as root:

```
> cd /usr/src
> cat raid-0145-19990713-2.2.10.bz2 | bzip2 -d | patch -p0
```

Kernel files will then be patched. If you have a gzipped file, replace `bzip2 -d` with `gzip -d`. After the kernel sources have been patched, it's important to do the following if you have ever built a kernel using these sources (this cleans up any old object files lying around in the source tree):

Note that this will erase your current kernel configuration settings! To save these, copy /usr/src/linux/.config to a temporary directory, and copy it back after the following process.

```
> cd linux
> make mrproper
```

Now, you should reconfigure your kernel using your favorite method, such as `make xconfig` or `make menuconfig`. We will need to change some settings to enable Software RAID. We'll go through them one by one:

First, set Multiple Devices Driver Support to Yes. Multiple Devices (or `md`) refers to a class of services supported by the kernel which includes Software RAID. You will also want to turn on Autodetect RAID Partitions. This option will allow the kernel to automatically "discover" and start RAID partitions when you refer to them by their RAID volume name and is especially handy when you have a RAID volume that needs to get mounted on boot. What you enable beyond this point depends on what kind of RAID system you would like to set up. I recommend that you select Y or N and do not use modules, as this will make it very difficult to have the kernel automatically mount your RAID volumes on startup. After you have made the appropriate selections, save your changes. You are now ready to recompile your kernel and should refer to Chapter 31, "Configuring and Building the Kernel," if you need any more help getting the system set up. If you went against my advice and decided to build modules, you will also need to build and install modules so that RAID support will be available.

After the kernel has been "RAIDified", and you have rebooted using your new kernel, you are ready to compile and install RAIDtools, which provides special commands that we can use to create and work with RAID volumes.

Installing RAIDTools

Compiling and installing RAIDTools isn't too hard. As root, do the following:

```
> cd /tmp
> tar xzvf /path/to/raidtools/raidtools-<date>-0.90.tar.gz
```

If you have a .tar.bz2 file, use the following command:

```
cat raidtools-<date>-0.90.tar.bz2 | bzip2 -d | tar xvf - )
```

```
> cd raidtools-0.90
> ./configure
```

Configuration text will follow:

```
> make
> make install
```

After you've finished this, you are ready to set up RAID partitions. Type **cat /proc/mdstat**. You should be presented with RAID-related kernel information. After you have created and started a RAID volume, this information will update and list your new RAID configuration.

Configuring a RAID 0 Volume

Follow these steps if you would like to configure a RAID 0 (striped) volume. First, create several partitions on multiple disks of approximately the same size, and set their partition type to FD. This will allow the kernel RAID autodetection to work. After saving your changes (and possibly rebooting if cfdisk informed you that it could not reread the new partition table and you'll need to reboot), you are ready to associate all these partitions into one RAID 0 volume, so that you can mount your conglomeration, format, and read and write to it like any standard Linux partition. To do this, create a file called /etc/raidtab, with the following contents:

```
# raidtab configuration for RAID 0 volume

raiddev /dev/md0
        raid-level              0
        nr-raid-disks           2
        persistent-superblock   1
        chunk-size              4

        device                  /dev/yourfirstpartition
        raid-disk               0
        device                  /dev/yoursecondpartition
        raid-disk               1
```

Now review these settings so you know what you are doing. `raid-level 0` selects, of course, RAID 0. `nr-raid-disks` specifies the total number of partitions that constitute the RAID volume. `persistent superblock` should always be 1 and means that extra data is written to each partition to help the kernel mount your RAID system automatically. Chunk size specifies the size of the parts, in kilobytes, that a file should be broken into as it is written in parallel to multiple devices. This value should be in the range of 4 to 128 and must be a power of 2. With a chunk size of 4, a 40KB file will be split into 10 separate chunks, and an average of 5 chunks will be stored on each disk defined earlier (in a 2-drive RAID 0 volume). Devices are specified by pointing to the partitions that you created, something like /dev/hda2 or /dev/sdb4. Be careful to type the right partitions here, as a mistake in this section could cause the RAIDtools to fry your data if it points to the wrong partition! The `raid-disk` command sets the most recently defined device as member "x" in the RAID array.

To create this RAID setup, type the following as root:

```
> mkraid /dev/md0
```

`mkraid` is a one-time step to initialize the partitions to be used for RAID. You might need to use the `--force` or the `--really-force` option here. After you have used `mkraid`, the md0 volume should be automatically enabled; `cat /proc/mdstat` to see. You can disable the RAID 0 volume temporarily by typing **raidstop /dev/md0** and can start it again by typing **raidstart /dev/md0**. If you set the partition type of all the RAID 0 partitions to FD, you should be able to have a line in /etc/fstab that mounts /dev/md0 during startup. Linux will use the FD identifier to track down all your RAID partitions. After you have verified that your RAID 0 volume is active, you'll probably want to format it:

```
> mkfs.ext2 /dev/md0
```

Now you can mount it:

```
> mount /dev/md0 /mnt/test
```

Go ahead and try out the RAID partition, and see how fast it is!

Configuring a Linear Volume

One of the "multiple device" types that we haven't talked about yet is called Linear. What this means is that several partitions are logically concatenated together, creating one larger virtual partition. For example, if you have two 250MB partitions on two separate drives, sda1 and hda3, the first 250MB of the disk will reside on sda1, and the second half of the disk will reside on hda3. Read and write performance is no different from what you would expect from a standard partition, although performance will vary across the partition if you are using partitions on drives with widely varying performance.

A RAID 0 volume is usually preferred over a Linear volume, because a RAID 0 volume will increase overall file IO bandwidth, whereas a Linear volume will not. But you still might be interested in using Linear mode in special circumstances. It can be useful to logically group noncontiguous partitions on the same hard drive, forming a single virtual partition out of several smaller ones. Linear mode is ideal in this specific situation, unlike all the RAID modes, which should never be used this way. This is because Linear mode does not parallelize reads or writes between its constituent partitions; in general, you are reading from or writing to one partition in particular. This means that a Linear volume created on the same disk will not "thrash" your drives when used—you can expect near-100% performance.

Here's an example of a situation where someone might use linear mode. Say that you are a speed freak and want your swap space to operate at the maximum possible speed. You have heard that it's best to have the swap space located in the center of the drive, so that the average seek time to reach the swap space is at its minimum. So, you create three partitions on your 3GB drive: a single partition of 1.45GB, followed by a 100MB partition and then followed by another 1.45GB partition:

```
/dev/hda1      1.45Gb
/dev/hda2      0.10Gb
/dev/hda3      1.45Gb
```

The 100MB partition will be used for swap, and the two other partitions will be combined to form one Linear volume using Software RAID. This means that your swap space will be physically located in the most optimal place on the drive, yet you can still set up your system using only one partition, your preferred method. Here's the /etc/raidtab that allows you to have your cake and eat it too:

```
# raidtab configuration for linear volume

raiddev /dev/md0
        raid-level              linear
        nr-raid-disks           2
        persistent-superblock   1
        chunk-size              4
```

```
device                  /dev/hda1
raid-disk               0
device                  /dev/hda3
raid-disk               1
```

After starting up RAID (identically to the RAID 0 method), you will have a virtual /dev/md0 device that can be used to install your operating system.

Configuring a RAID 1 Volume

To create a RAID 1 volume, create several partitions on separate disks, of similar sizes. Setup is very similar to RAID 0, with a few exceptions. Here's a sample `raidtab`:

```
# raidtab configuration for RAID 1 volume

raiddev /dev/md0
        raid-level              1
        nr-raid-disks           2
        nr-spare-disks          0
        persistent-superblock   1
        chunk-size              4

        device                  /dev/yourfirstpartition
        raid-disk               0
        device                  /dev/yoursecondpartition
        raid-disk               1
```

The first thing to notice is a new option, `nr-spare-disks`. If you have any partitions you would like to use as standbys, you can add them to the drive list as follows:

```
device                  /dev/anotherpartition
spare-disk              0
```

Then, update the `nr-spare-disks` value to the appropriate number. If a mirror disk reports failure to the kernel, your spare disk will be commandeered into service, and the kernel will begin reconstructing the mirror data on the disk. Remember that because data gets written to both disks redundantly, when a spare drive is swapped into a mirror, a copying process is required to synchronize the spare drive to the other mirrors. Fortunately, the mirror is still usable while this is in progress, but it runs slightly slower until it is complete.

The command-line method to start a RAID 1 volume is identical to that of setting up a RAID 0. But there's one thing you should observe; after you type **mkraid /dev/md0**, the array will begin synchronizing their data. You can watch the progress by typing **cat /proc/mdstat**:

```
Personalities : [linear] [raid0] [raid1]
read_ahead 1024 sectors
```

```
md1 : active raid1 sda6[1] hda5[0] 256896 blocks [2/2] [UU] resync=89%
finish=0.0min
unused devices: <none>
```

As you can see, a resync is in progress, and should be finished any second. After the resync is complete, catting /proc/mdstat will display something like this:

```
Personalities : [linear] [raid0] [raid1]
read_ahead 1024 sectors
md1 : active raid1 sda6[1] hda5[0] 256896 blocks [2/2] [UU]
unused devices: <none>
```

The mirror is now sync'd up. Note that it's perfectly safe to start using a mirror even when the syncing process is underway; drive IO will be slightly slower, but not significantly slow, as the kernel paces itself during the resync process so that mirror IO performance does not suffer. Now that you have your RAID 1 volume created, mount it and play around with it. Notice that writes are slightly slower and reads are slightly faster.

The Software RAID 1 implementation under Linux is incredibly flexible and robust. One major benefit of using RAID 1 is that it is easy to turn off in an emergency situation. For example, say that one of the hard drives in your mirror fails, and it is past warranty. You're broke, and you don't have any money to purchase a replacement drive. Turning off a RAID 1 mirror is as easy as:

```
> umount /mnt/raid
> raidstop /dev/md0
```

Then, assuming that /dev/hda3 is the RAID 1 partition that is on your working drive, change all references to /dev/md0 to /dev/hda3 in your /etc/fstab. Because each mirror contains a valid ext2 file system in its own right, you can continue normal operation of your machine in non-mirrored mode:

```
> mount /dev/hda3 /dev/raid
```

The system can now be powered down and the defective drive can be thrown away! This trick only works with RAID 1; it will not work with RAID 0, 4, 5 or Linear mode.

You should now have a good overview of the Linux kernel's flexible Software RAID abilities. If you are interested in setting up a RAID 4 or 5 volume or a Linear volume, look at the following man pages:

```
> man mkraid
> man raidtab
```

They should give you all the information you need. Unfortunately, most of the Web-based information (including the Software-RAID HOWTO) is seriously out-of-date, and differ from the steps required to get a modern Software RAID setup working under Linux. Keeping this in mind, you might want to look at http://www.linas.org/linux/raid.html, which contains a complete listing of all the RAID resources that are currently available for Linux. Software RAID is an incredible tool for enhancing system reliability and performance; I know that it has made a huge positive impact on the performance of my machine!

Summary

Caldera OpenLinux 2.2 features an innovative graphical installation process called LIZARD, which provides a near-ideal "out of box" experience for the Linux user. In addition, Caldera offers their earlier text-based installer, LISA. Although less advanced, LISA offers more control over the installation process.

Although many users choose to install Caldera in one partition, there are several other partitioning options worth considering. When a partitioning scheme is chosen to complement the intended use of the system, disk performance can often be dramatically enhanced. In addition, Linux Software RAID can be used to increase the integrity and availability of critical data, as well as to further boost disk IO performance.

Appendix C

Bibliography

Costales, Bryan, and Eric Allman. *sendmail, Second Edition.* O'Reilly and Associates, Inc., 1997. ISBN 1-56592-222-0. This imposing and intimidating book tells you everything you ever wanted to know about configuring *sendmail*. Impressively cross-indexed and complete, this book reads like a GNU info page on steroids.

Garfinkel, Simson, and Gene Spafford. *Practical UNIX & Internet Security, Second Edition.* O'Reilly and Associates, Inc., 1996. ISBN 1-56592-148-8. This book is the bible of UNIX and network security. If you are even contemplating putting your Linux machine on the Internet, you must read this book.

Harbison, Samuel P., and Guy L. Steele, Jr. *C: A Reference Manual, Fourth Edition.* Prentice Hall, 1995. ISBN 0-13-326224-3. This is a detailed C reference manual covering both ANSI C and common pre-ANSI C dialects.

Harrison, Mark, and Michael McLennan, *Effective Tcl/Tk Programming: Writing Better Programs with Tcl and Tk.* Addison-Wesley Publishing Company, 1998. ISBN 0-201-63474-0. This book assumes a basic knowledge of Tcl/Tk. It describes advanced features and great programming tricks. It comes with a library of freely reusable Tcl routines. The authors have a deep appreciation for Tcl/Tk and their sample programs are clear and elegant.

Lamport, Leslie. *LaTeX: A Document Preparation System, Second Edition.* Addison-Wesley Publishing Company, 1996. ISBN 0-201-52983-1. This book, by the author of LaTeX, describes the typesetting system with clarity and humor. Highly recommended if you want to learn LaTeX.

Ousterhout, John K. *Tcl and the Tk Toolkit.* Addison-Wesley Publishing Company, 1994. ISBN 0-201-63337-X. This book by the author of Tcl and Tk explains how to use the language and toolkit. It is somewhat dated, but still mostly accurate. It is also the clearest Tcl and Tk tutorial I have ever read.

Plauger, P. J. *The Standard C Library.* Prentice Hall, 1992, ISBN 0-13-131509-9. This book gives painstaking description of the C standard library by one of the members of the C standardization committee. This book also contains complete source code for a full implementation of the standard C library.

Rubini, Alessandro. *Linux Device Drivers.* O'Reilly and Associates, Inc., 1998. ISBN 1-56592-292-1. This book describes the Linux kernel internals from the point of view of device drivers. Given the rapid pace of Linux development, such a book quickly becomes outdated. Nevertheless, the book is a great starting point before you plunge into reading the Linux kernel code.

Schneier, Bruce. *Applied Cryptography: Protocols, Algorithms, and Source Code in C, Second Edition.* John Wiley and Sons, Inc., 1996. ISBN 0-471-11709-9. This book is an encyclopedic reference for cryptographic protocols and algorithms. As a bonus, it's fun to read. If you are tempted to invent your own cryptographic algorithm, read this book to find out why it's a bad idea.

Stevens, W. Richard. *Advanced Programming in the UNIX Environment.* Addison-Wesley Publishing Company, 1993. ISBN 0-201-56317-7. A wonderful reference that describes the UNIX API and advanced UNIX programming techniques. This is the preeminent UNIX programming reference text.

———. *TCP/IP Illustrated, Volume 1: The Protocols.* Addison-Wesley Publishing Company, 1994. ISBN 0-201-63346-9. This book describes the IP, TCP, UDP and ICMP protocols in detail. Stevens illustrates hundreds of test cases using the *tcpdump* tool so that the abstract protocol descriptions are illustrated with concrete and understandable examples.

———. *UNIX Network Programming, Volume 1, Second Edition: Networking APIs: Sockets and XTI.* Prentice Hall, 1998. ISBN 0-13-490012-X. This book describes the Sockets API (used by Linux) in great detail. If you wish to write client-server software under UNIX, read this book.

APPENDIX D

RPM Listing

All of the examples in this book have assumed a full installation of Caldera OpenLinux. If you have not performed a full installation, some software may be missing. The following table lists all executables in /bin, /sbin, /usr/sbin *and* /usr/bin along with the RPM from which they are derived. Note that the RPM version numbers may change as Caldera OpenLinux is updated. The base name of the RPM should remain the same, however.

Some files do not belong to any packages. For example, /bin/csh is listed as not belonging to a package. These files are all symbolic links which are set up during installation. To find the package which creates them, run `rpm -q -f real_file`, where *real_file* is the file to which the symbolic link refers.

TABLE D.1 OpenLinux Executables and Their Source RPMs

Executable	Directory	RPM
activate	/sbin	lilo-0.21-6
addtosmbpass	/usr/sbin	samba-2.0.5-1
adduser	/usr/sbin	adduser-1.2-1
amd	/etc/rc.d/init.d	am-utils-6.0-4
amd	/usr/sbin	am-utils-6.0-4
arch	/bin	util-linux-2.9s-4
arp	/sbin	net-tools-1.52-4
atd	/etc/rc.d/init.d	at-3.1.7-1
atd	/usr/sbin	at-3.1.7-1
avmcapictrl	/sbin	isdn4k-utils-3.0beta2-4
badblocks	/sbin	ext2fs-1.14-2
bash	/bin	bash-1.14.7-9
bash2	/bin	bash2-2.03-1
bigfs	/etc/rc.d/init.d	SysVinit-scripts-1.05-5
booter	/sbin	SysVinit-scripts-1.05-5
booterd	/sbin	SysVinit-scripts-1.05-5
box	/bin	lisa-4.0-7
bru	/bin	BRU-15.0P-11
build_menu	/bin	lisa-4.0-7
bunzip2	/bin	bzip2-0.9.0b-1
bzcat	/bin	bzip2-0.9.0b-1
bzip2	/bin	bzip2-0.9.0b-1

Executable	Directory	RPM
bzip2recover	/bin	bzip2-0.9.0b-1
cat	/bin	textutils-1.22-3
cfdisk	/sbin	util-linux-2.9s-4
chat	/usr/sbin	ppp-2.3.8-1
checkpc	/usr/sbin	LPRng-lpd-3.5.3-1
chgrp	/bin	fileutils-4.0-1
chmod	/bin	fileutils-4.0-1
chown	/bin	fileutils-4.0-1
chpasswd	/usr/sbin	shadow-misc-1.1-3
chroot	/usr/sbin	sh-utils-1.16-7
cleandir	/usr/sbin	cleandir-1.0-1
convert_smbpasswd	/usr/sbin	samba-2.0.5-1
convertsmbpasswd	/usr/sbin	samba-2.0.5-1
cp	/bin	fileutils-4.0-1
cpio	/bin	cpio-2.4.2-3
cron	/etc/rc.d/init.d	vixie-cron-3.0.1-18
cron	/usr/sbin	vixie-cron-3.0.1-18
cronloop	/usr/sbin	crontabs-1.12-1
ctags	/bin	vim-5.3-4
ctrlaltdel	/sbin	util-linux-2.9s-4
date	/bin	sh-utils-1.16-7
db_printf	/bin	lisa-4.0-7
dd	/bin	fileutils-4.0-1
debugfs	/sbin	ext2fs-1.14-2
depmod	/sbin	modutils-2.1.121-9b
df	/bin	fileutils-4.0-1
dhcpcd	/sbin	dhcpcd-1.3.17p4-0
dhcpd	/etc/rc.d/init.d	dhcpd-1.0pl2-3
dhcpd	/usr/sbin	dhcpd-1.0pl2-3
diald	/usr/sbin	diald-0.16-1
dip	/usr/sbin	dip-3.3.7o-9
diplogin	/usr/sbin	dip-3.3.7o-9

continues

TABLE D.1 continued

Executable	Directory	RPM
dmesg	/bin	util-linux-2.9s-4
dnsdomainname	/bin	net-tools-1.52-4
do_calc	/bin	lisa-4.0-7
do_echo	/bin	lisa-4.0-7
do_netcalc	/bin	lisa-4.0-7
do_quote	/bin	lisa-4.0-7
domainname	/bin	nis-client-2.0-8
dpasswd	/usr/sbin	shadow-misc-1.1-3
dump	/sbin	dump-0.4b4-2
dumpe2fs	/sbin	ext2fs-1.14-2
dumpreg	/usr/sbin	svgalib-1.3.1-2
e2fsck	/sbin	ext2fs-1.14-2
e2label	/sbin	ext2fs-1.14-2
echo	/bin	sh-utils-1.16-7
ed	/bin	ed-0.2-5
end_use	/bin	lisa-4.0-7
ex	/bin	vim-5.3-4
false	/bin	bool-2.0-1
faxrunqd	/usr/sbin	mgetty-1.1.20_Jan17-0
fdformat	/usr/sbin	util-linux-2.9s-4
fdisk	/sbin	util-linux-2.9s-4
filesize	/bin	lisa-4.0-7
find-scanner	/usr/sbin	sane-1.00-1
findsmb	/usr/sbin	samba-2.0.5-1
freeramdisk	/bin	lisa-4.0-7
fsck.ext2	/sbin	ext2fs-1.14-2
fsck.minix	/sbin	util-linux-2.9s-4
fsck	/sbin	ext2fs-1.14-2
fsinfo	/usr/sbin	am-utils-6.0-4
functions	/etc/rc.d/init.d	SysVinit-scripts-1.05-5
fuser	/bin	psmisc-18-1

Executable	Directory	RPM
genksyms	/sbin	modutils-2.1.121-9b
get_info	/bin	lisa-4.0-7
get_key	/bin	lisa-4.0-7
get_val	/bin	lisa-4.0-7
getty	/sbin	cgetty-1.0-1
gpm	/etc/rc.d/init.d	gpm-1.17.8-2
groupadd	/usr/sbin	lisa-4.0-7
groupdel	/usr/sbin	lisa-4.0-7
groupmod	/usr/sbin	shadow-misc-1.1-3
grpck	/usr/sbin	shadow-misc-1.1-3
grpconv	/usr/sbin	shadow-misc-1.1-3
grpunconv	/usr/sbin	shadow-misc-1.1-3
gunzip	/bin	gzip-1.2.4-9
gzip	/bin	gzip-1.2.4-9
h2n	/usr/sbin	bind-utils-8.1.1-6
halt	/etc/rc.d/init.d	SysVinit-scripts-1.05-5
halt	/sbin	SysVinit-2.76.3-2
hdparm	/sbin	hdparm-3.5-1
hilfe	/bin	lisa-4.0-7
hisaxctrl	/sbin	isdn4k-utils-3.0beta2-4
hostname	/bin	net-tools-1.52-4
httpd.apache	/usr/sbin	apache-1.3.4-3
httpd	/etc/rc.d/init.d	apache-1.3.4-3
hwclock	/sbin	util-linux-2.9s-4
hwinfo	/bin	lisa-4.0-7
hwprobe	/sbin	hwprobe-990806-1
icnctrl	/sbin	isdn4k-utils-3.0beta2-4
ifconfig	/sbin	net-tools-1.52-4
ifdown	/sbin	SysVinit-scripts-1.05-5
ifup	/sbin	SysVinit-scripts-1.05-5
imapd	/usr/sbin	imap-4.6.BETA-1
imon	/sbin	isdn4k-utils-3.0beta2-4

continues

TABLE D.1 continued

Executable	Directory	RPM
imontty	/sbin	isdn4k-utils-3.0beta2-4
in.comsat	/usr/sbin	biff+comsat-0.10-2
in.fingerd	/usr/sbin	bsd-finger-0.10-4
in.ftpd	/usr/sbin	wu-ftpd-2.5.0-1
in.identd	/usr/sbin	pidentd-3.0b1-2
in.ntalkd	/usr/sbin	netkit-ntalk-0.11-1
in.rexecd	/usr/sbin	netkit-rsh-0.10-8
in.rlogind	/usr/sbin	netkit-rsh-0.10-8
in.rshd	/usr/sbin	netkit-rsh-0.10-8
in.saned	/usr/sbin	sane-1.00-1
in.talkd	/usr/sbin	netkit-ntalk-0.11-1
in.telnetd	/usr/sbin	netkit-telnet-0.12-2
inet	/etc/rc.d/init.d	SysVinit-scripts-1.05-5
inetd	/usr/sbin	netkit-base-0.11-6
init	/sbin	SysVinit-2.76.3-2
innd	/usr/sbin	inn-2.2-3
inndstart	/usr/sbin	inn-2.2-3
insmod	/sbin	modutils-2.1.121-9b
ipchains-restore	/sbin	ipchains-1.3.8-1
ipchains-save	/sbin	ipchains-1.3.8-1
ipchains	/sbin	ipchains-1.3.8-1
ipfwadm-wrapper	/sbin	ipchains-1.3.8-1
ipfwadm	/sbin	ipchains-1.3.8-1
ipmaddr	/sbin	net-tools-1.52-4
ipop2d	/usr/sbin	imap-4.6.BETA-1
ipop3d	/usr/sbin	imap-4.6.BETA-1
ipppd	/sbin	isdn4k-utils-3.0beta2-4
ipppstats	/sbin	isdn4k-utils-3.0beta2-4
iprofd	/sbin	isdn4k-utils-3.0beta2-4
iptunnel	/sbin	net-tools-1.52-4
ipx	/etc/rc.d/init.d	ipx-1.0-13

Executable	Directory	RPM
ipx_configure	/sbin	ipx-1.0-13
ipx_interface	/sbin	ipx-1.0-13
ipx_internal_net	/sbin	ipx-1.0-13
ipx_route	/sbin	ipx-1.0-13
ipxd	/usr/sbin	ipxripd-0.7-6
ipxripd	/etc/rc.d/init.d	ipxripd-0.7-6
isapnp	/sbin	isapnptools-1.18-1
isdnctrl	/sbin	isdn4k-utils-3.0beta2-4
isdnlog	/sbin	isdn4k-utils-3.0beta2-4
kbdrate	/sbin	util-linux-2.9s-4
kerneld	/sbin	modutils-2.1.121-9b
keytable	/etc/rc.d/init.d	kbd-0.99-1
kill	/bin	util-linux-2.9s-4
killall5	/sbin	SysVinit-2.76.3-2
klogd	/usr/sbin	sysklogd-1.3.31-1
ksyms	/sbin	modutils-2.1.121-9b
ktzset	/sbin	ktzset-2.1-4
ldconfig	/sbin	ld.so-1.9.11-1
lilo	/sbin	lilo-0.21-6
lisa	/bin	lisa-4.0-7
ln	/bin	fileutils-4.0-1
local	/etc/rc.d/init.d	SysVinit-scripts-1.05-5
login	/bin	util-linux-2.9s-4
logoutd	/etc/rc.d/init.d	shadow-misc-1.1-3
logoutd	/usr/sbin	shadow-misc-1.1-3
logrotate	/usr/sbin	logrotate-3.3-2
loopctrl	/sbin	isdn4k-utils-3.0beta2-4
losetup	/sbin	util-linux-2.9s-4
lpc	/usr/sbin	LPRng-3.5.3-2
lpd	/etc/rc.d/init.d	LPRng-lpd-3.5.3-1
lpd	/usr/sbin	LPRng-lpd-3.5.3-1
lpraccnt	/usr/sbin	LPRng-3.5.3-2

continues

TABLE D.1 continued

Executable	Directory	RPM
ls	/bin	fileutils-4.0-1
lsmod	/sbin	modutils-2.1.121-9b
lsof	/usr/sbin	lsof-4.44-1
lspci	/sbin	pciutils-2.0-1
mail	/bin	mailx-8.1.1-6
make_smbcodepage	/usr/sbin	samba-2.0.5-1
makedev	/sbin	DEV-3.4-1
makewhatis.cs	/usr/sbin	man-pages-cs-0.12-1
makewhatis.es	/usr/sbin	man-pages-es-0.7a-1
makewhatis	/usr/sbin	man-1.5f-5
mgetty	/usr/sbin	mgetty-1.1.20_Jan17-0
mk-amd-map	/usr/sbin	am-utils-6.0-4
mkdir	/bin	fileutils-4.0-1
mke2fs	/sbin	ext2fs-1.14-2
mkfs.ext2	/sbin	ext2fs-1.14-2
mkfs.minix	/sbin	util-linux-2.9s-4
mkfs	/sbin	util-linux-2.9s-4
mklizard	/bin	lisa-4.0-7
mklost+found	/usr/sbin	ext2fs-1.14-2
mknod	/bin	fileutils-4.0-1
mksmbcodepage	/usr/sbin	samba-2.0.5-1
mksmbpasswd	/usr/sbin	samba-2.0.5-1
mksmbprinterdef	/usr/sbin	samba-2.0.5-1
mkswap	/sbin	util-linux-2.9s-4
mktemp	/bin	mktemp-1.4-2
mode3	/usr/sbin	svgalib-1.3.1-2
modinfo	/sbin	modutils-2.1.121-9b
modprobe	/sbin	modutils-2.1.121-9b
more	/bin	util-linux-2.9s-4
mount	/bin	util-linux-2.9s-4
mt	/bin	mt-st-0.4-4

Executable	Directory	RPM
mta-switch	/usr/sbin	mtabase-1.0-7
mta	/etc/rc.d/init.d	mtabase-1.0-7
mv	/bin	fileutils-4.0-1
named-bootconf	/usr/sbin	bind-8.1.2-1
named-xfer	/usr/sbin	bind-8.1.2-1
named	/etc/rc.d/init.d	bind-8.1.2-1
named	/usr/sbin	bind-8.1.2-1
ndc	/usr/sbin	bind-8.1.2-1
netmount	/etc/rc.d/init.d	SysVinit-scripts-1.05-5
netstat	/bin	net-tools-1.52-4
network	/etc/rc.d/init.d	SysVinit-scripts-1.05-5
news	/etc/rc.d/init.d	inn-2.2-3
newusers	/usr/sbin	shadow-misc-1.1-3
nfs	/etc/rc.d/init.d	nfs-server-2.2beta44-3
nis-client	/etc/rc.d/init.d	nis-client-2.0-8
nis-server	/etc/rc.d/init.d	nis-server-2.0-4
nisdomainname	/bin	nis-client-2.0-8
nmbd	/usr/sbin	samba-2.0.5-1
nnrpd	/usr/sbin	inn-2.2-3
ntp	/etc/rc.d/init.d	xntp-3.5.93e-4
ntpdate	/usr/sbin	xntp-3.5.93e-4
pam_conv1	/sbin	libpam-0.66-3
pcbitctl	/sbin	isdn4k-utils-3.0beta2-4
pidof	/bin	SysVinit-2.76.3-2
ping	/bin	netkit-base-0.11-6
plipconfig	/sbin	net-tools-1.52-4
pmap_dump	/usr/sbin	portmap-5beta-3
pmap_set	/usr/sbin	portmap-5beta-3
pnpdump	/sbin	isapnptools-1.18-1
poweroff	/sbin	SysVinit-2.76.3-2
pppd	/usr/sbin	ppp-2.3.8-1
ppplogin	/usr/sbin	ppp-2.3.8-1

continues

TABLE D.1 continued

Executable	Directory	RPM
pppstats	/usr/sbin	ppp-2.3.8-1
prep_use	/bin	lisa-4.0-7
ps	/bin	procps-2.0.2-1
pwck	/usr/sbin	shadow-misc-1.1-3
pwconv	/usr/sbin	shadow-misc-1.1-3
pwd	/bin	sh-utils-1.16-7
pwunconv	/usr/sbin	shadow-misc-1.1-3
ramsize	/usr/sbin	util-linux-2.9s-4
rarp	/sbin	net-tools-1.52-4
rcapid	/sbin	isdn4k-utils-3.0beta2-4
rdev	/usr/sbin	util-linux-2.9s-4
rdump	/sbin	dump-0.4b4-2
readprofile	/usr/sbin	util-linux-2.9s-4
reboot	/etc/rc.d/init.d	SysVinit-scripts-1.05-5
reboot	/sbin	SysVinit-2.76.3-2
red	/bin	ed-0.2-5
request-route	/sbin	modutils-2.1.121-9b
restore	/sbin	dump-0.4b4-2
restorefont	/usr/sbin	svgalib-1.3.1-2
restorepalette	/usr/sbin	svgalib-1.3.1-2
restoretextmode	/usr/sbin	svgalib-1.3.1-2
rm	/bin	fileutils-4.0-1
rmdir	/bin	fileutils-4.0-1
rmmod	/sbin	modutils-2.1.121-9b
rmnologin	/etc/rc.d/init.d	SysVinit-scripts-1.05-5
rmt	/sbin	dump-0.4b4-2
rootflags	/usr/sbin	util-linux-2.9s-4
route	/sbin	net-tools-1.52-4
rpc.mountd	/usr/sbin	nfs-server-2.2beta44-3
rpc.nfsd	/usr/sbin	nfs-server-2.2beta44-3
rpc.portmap	/usr/sbin	portmap-5beta-3

Executable	Directory	RPM
rpc.rstatd	/usr/sbin	rstatd-3.03-1
rpc.rusersd	/usr/sbin	netkit-rusers-0.11-2
rpc.rwalld	/usr/sbin	netkit-rwall-0.10-6
rpm	/bin	rpm-2.5.5-2
rpmextr	/bin	rpm-2.5.5-2
rpminst	/bin	rpm-2.5.5-2
rpmshow	/bin	rpm-2.5.5-2
rrestore	/sbin	dump-0.4b4-2
rstatd	/etc/rc.d/init.d	rstatd-3.03-1
runlevel	/sbin	SysVinit-2.76.3-2
rusersd	/etc/rc.d/init.d	netkit-rusers-0.11-2
rview	/bin	vim-5.3-4
rvim	/bin	vim-5.3-4
rwalld	/etc/rc.d/init.d	netkit-rwall-0.10-6
rwhod	/etc/rc.d/init.d	netkit-rwho-0.12-1
rwhod	/usr/sbin	netkit-rwho-0.12-1
safe_finger	/usr/sbin	tcp_wrappers-7.6-4
samba	/etc/rc.d/init.d	samba-2.0.5-1
samba	/usr/sbin	samba-2.0.5-1
savetextmode	/usr/sbin	svgalib-1.3.1-2
sed	/bin	sed-3.02-1
sendfax	/usr/sbin	mgetty-1.1.20_Jan17-0
sendmail	/usr/sbin	mtabase-1.0-7
set_val	/bin	lisa-4.0-7
setfdprm	/usr/sbin	util-linux-2.9s-4
setpci	/sbin	pciutils-2.0-1
setserial	/sbin	setserial-2.15-1
sfdisk	/sbin	util-linux-2.9s-4
sh	/bin	bash-1.14.7-9
showmount	/usr/sbin	nfs-2.2beta44-3
shutdown	/sbin	SysVinit-2.76.3-2
single	/etc/rc.d/init.d	SysVinit-scripts-1.05-5

continues

TABLE D.1 continued

Executable	Directory	RPM
skeleton	/etc/rc.d/init.d	SysVinit-scripts-1.05-5
skipped	/etc/rc.d/init.d	SysVinit-scripts-1.05-5
slattach	/sbin	net-tools-1.52-4
sleep	/bin	sh-utils-1.16-7
sliplogin	/usr/sbin	sliplogin-2.1.2-5
sln	/sbin	util-linux-2.9s-4
smbadduser	/usr/sbin	samba-2.0.5-1
smbd	/usr/sbin	samba-2.0.5-1
ssd	/sbin	SysVinit-scripts-1.05-5
start-stop-daemon	/sbin	SysVinit-scripts-1.05-5
stty	/bin	sh-utils-1.16-7
su	/bin	sh-utils-1.16-7
sulogin	/sbin	SysVinit-2.76.3-2
svgakeymap	/usr/sbin	svgalib-1.3.1-2
swapdev	/usr/sbin	util-linux-2.9s-4
swapoff	/sbin	util-linux-2.9s-4
swapon	/sbin	util-linux-2.9s-4
swat	/usr/sbin	swat-2.0.5-1
sync	/bin	fileutils-4.0-1
sysinfo	/bin	lisa-4.0-7
syslog	/etc/rc.d/init.d	sysklogd-1.3.31-1
syslogd	/usr/sbin	sysklogd-1.3.31-1
tar	/bin	tar-1.12-3
tcpd	/usr/sbin	tcp_wrappers-7.6-4
tcpdchk	/usr/sbin	tcp_wrappers-7.6-4
tcpdmatch	/usr/sbin	tcp_wrappers-7.6-4
tcpdump	/usr/sbin	tcpdump-3.4-5
tcsh	/bin	tcsh-6.08.00-2
telesctrl	/sbin	isdn4k-utils-3.0beta2-4
telinit	/sbin	SysVinit-2.76.3-2
textmode	/usr/sbin	svgalib-1.3.1-2
tickadj	/usr/sbin	xntp-3.5.93e-4

Executable	Directory	RPM
traceroute	/usr/sbin	traceroute-1.4a5-5
true	/bin	bool-2.0-1
try-from	/usr/sbin	tcp_wrappers-7.6-4
tune2fs	/sbin	ext2fs-1.14-2
tunelp	/usr/sbin	util-linux-2.9s-4
udosctl	/sbin	umsdosfs-0.9-0
umount	/bin	util-linux-2.9s-4
umssetup	/sbin	umsdosfs-0.9-0
umssync	/sbin	umsdosfs-0.9-0
uname	/bin	sh-utils-1.16-7
update	/sbin	bdflush-1.6.2-1
updatesmbpasswd	/usr/sbin	samba-2.0.5-1
urandom	/etc/rc.d/init.d	SysVinit-scripts-1.05-5
useradd	/usr/sbin	lisa-4.0-7
userdel	/usr/sbin	lisa-4.0-7
usermod	/usr/sbin	shadow-misc-1.1-3
usleep	/bin	SysVinit-scripts-1.05-5
utempter	/usr/sbin	utempter-0.5-3
uuchk	/usr/sbin	uucp-1.06.1-10
uucico	/usr/sbin	uucp-1.06.1-10
uuconv	/usr/sbin	uucp-1.06.1-10
uusched	/usr/sbin	uucp-1.06.1-10
uuxqt	/usr/sbin	uucp-1.06.1-10
vboxd	/sbin	isdn4k-utils-3.0beta2-4
vboxgetty	/sbin	isdn4k-utils-3.0beta2-4
vgetty	/usr/sbin	mgetty-1.1.20_Jan17-0
vi	/bin	vim-5.3-4
vidmode	/usr/sbin	util-linux-2.9s-4
view	/bin	vim-5.3-4
vigr	/usr/sbin	util-linux-2.9s-4
vim	/bin	vim-5.3-4
vipw	/usr/sbin	util-linux-2.9s-4

continues

TABLE D.1 continued

Executable	Directory	RPM
wire-test	/usr/sbin	am-utils-6.0-4
xferstats	/usr/sbin	wu-ftpd-2.5.0-1
xntpd	/usr/sbin	xntp-3.5.93e-4
xxd	/bin	vim-5.3-4
ypbind	/usr/sbin	nis-client-2.0-8
yppoll	/usr/sbin	nis-client-2.0-8
yppush	/usr/sbin	nis-server-2.0-4
ypset	/usr/sbin	nis-client-2.0-8
zap	/etc/rc.d/init.d	SysVinit-scripts-1.05-5
zcat	/bin	gzip-1.2.4-9
zdump	/usr/sbin	zoneinfo-1999d-1
zic	/usr/sbin	zoneinfo-1999d-1
zsh	/bin	zsh-3.1.5-1

What's on the Disc

The companion CD-ROM contains Caldera's OpenLinux 2.3.

Installation Instructions

If your computer supports booting directly from a CD-ROM, follow the instructions below for a CD-ROM boot install. Otherwise, you should follow the instructions for a floppy boot install.

CD-ROM Boot Install

1. Insert the Caldera OpenLinux 2.3 CD-ROM in your CD drive.
2. If you want to use Caldera's Windows setup software, launch the setup program by double-clicking on the CD drive, WINSETUP, and SETUP.EXE. Select Install Products and then select Launch Linux Install. Follow the setup instructions. Otherwise, you may proceed to step 3.
3. Restart your computer.
4. You may need to change your BIOS settings to boot from the CD-ROM. Typically, you enter your BIOS setup program with the F2 or DEL key.
5. Make your changes (if any) and exit the BIOS setup utility.
6. When your computer restarts, you will boot into the Caldera OpenLinux setup program.
7. Follow the onscreen prompts to complete the installation.

Floppy Boot Install

If you are using Windows 95 and Windows 98:

1. Insert the Caldera OpenLinux 2.3 CD-ROM in your CD drive.
2. If you want to use Caldera's Windows setup software, launch the setup program by double-clicking on the CD drive, WINSETUP, and SETUP.EXE. Select Install Products, and select Create Floppy Install Disks.
3. When you are finished with the boot disk preparation, restart your computer with the boot disk inserted in your floppy drive.
4. You may need to change your BIOS settings to boot from the floppy drive. Typically, you enter your BIOS setup program with the F2 or DEL key.

5. Make your changes (if any) and exit the BIOS setup utility.
6. When your computer restarts, you will boot into the Caldera OpenLinux setup program.
7. Follow the onscreen prompts to complete the installation.

If you are using DOS

1. Navigate to your CD drive and go to the directory \COL\LAUNCH\FLOPPY.
2. Prepare two 1.44MB floppies by formatting them.
3. Type INSTALL and press <ENTER>. This will prepare your boot floppy and a modules disk, if needed.
4. When you are finished with the boot disk preparation, restart your computer with the boot disk inserted in your floppy drive.
5. You may need to change your BIOS settings to boot from the floppy drive. Typically, you enter your BIOS setup program with the F2 or DEL key.
6. Make your changes (if any) and exit the BIOS setup utility.
7. When your computer restarts, you will boot into the Caldera OpenLinux setup program.
8. Follow the onscreen prompts to complete the installation.

INDEX

SYMBOLS

! (exclamation point), vi commands, 140
" (double quotes)
    bash syntax, 64
    Tcl/Tk, 786
 # (pound sign)
    comments in Tcl/Tk, 787
    Python comments, 815
 # (root prompt), 193
$ (dollar sign), text searches, 148
$ command (vi), 143
% (percent sign), Perl variables, 759
& (ampersand), background processes, 62
' (single quotes), bash syntax, 64
(command (vi), 144
) command (vi), 144
* (asterisk)
    bash wildcard character, 67
    wildcard character, 148
: (colon), vi commands, 140
+ command (vi), 143
- command (vi), 143
...(ellipsis), bash wildcard character, 67
. (period), wildcard character, 148
/ (slash)
    comments in C programming language, 860
    pathnames, 27
? (question mark), bash wildcard character, 67
@ (at sign), Perl arrays, 759
24/8 Bit menu (xv), 619

A

a command (vi), 149
A-type records, 296
absolute paths, 27
ACCEPT target (firewall chain), 481
access rights, UNIX security model, 553
accounts, 256-257
    files, 239
    passwords, 258-259
activating NetWare client, 371
addresses
    IP, 269-270
    DNS (domain name system), 272, 287, 294, 296-305
    fixed, 292
    masquerading, 502-504
    network protection, 499-501
    PPP, 314
    private, 270
    routes, 272, 274, 279-283
    sed command, 947
administration
    COAS (Caldera Open Administration), 247
    COAStool, 247
    menu, 248-249
    console, 238
    user management, 238-241
    kernel, /proc, 244-246
    MySQL, 600
        privilege system, 600, 602, 604-606
        setting root password, 600
    NDS, 383-385, 387-391
    NetWare servers, 377-379, 381
Advanced Linux Sound Architecture. *See* ALSA, 683
Algorithms menu (xv), 619
alias command, 72
aliases (email), 454
aliases file, 454
alignment. *See also* justification. WordPerfect documents, 584
ALSA (Advanced Linux Sound Architecture), 683-684
    downloading, 684
    hardware modules, 685
    hardware supported, 683
    installing, 684-685
    loading on startup, 687
    testing, 685-687
alternation, atom expression, 943
amateur radio, kernel configuration, 744
AmiNet modules archive Web site, 699
ampersand (&), background processes, 62
animate command (Image Magick), 624-625
Apache, 17, 396-397
    configuration, 398
        AllowOverrides directives, 403-404
        htaccess, 402
        httpd.conf, 399-401
        options directives, 402-403
        runtime, 398-399

installation, 397-398
logging, 406-407
starting, 413-415, 417
stopping, 413-415, 417
virtual hosting, 404
    address-based virtual hosts, 404
    name-based virtual hosts, 405
Web site, 396
application proxies, 510-511
Application Starter (kwm), 117-118
applications
at, 243-244
crontab, 243-244
DVIcopy, 650
gzip command, 951
LaTeX, 651-654
    creating input file, 654-662
    LyX, 654, 656-662
linkers, 900
LyX, 654, 656-658
    pictures, 658-659
    tables, 659-662
printers, 226, 228
sed command, 947
StarOffice, 585
    Beamer, 588
    creating documents, 589
    creating templates, 589
    customizing workspace, 588
    desktop, 586-587
    documents, 589
    email, 590-591
    events, 589-590
    Explorer, 588
    file management, 588
    FTP, 591
    installation, 586
    opening documents, 589
TeX, 650
user management, 239-241
/usr/bin/chfn, 240-241
/usr/bin/passwd, 240
/usr/sbin/userdel, 240
/usr/sbin/usermod, 240
WordPerfect, 578
    bulleted lists, 585
    configurations, 585
    creating documents, 579
    file management, 579-580
    formatting documents, 580-584
    graphics, 584
    installation, 578
    opening files, 579
    opening windows, 579
    outlines, 585
    saving files, 579-580
    shortcut keys, 579
applications category (KDE Control Center), 125
appointments (StarOffice), 590
apropos command, 924-925
archives
library, 900
tar command, 951-953
archiving MP3s, 693
arguments
SoundBlaster sound cards, 675
Tcl/Tk procedures, 798-799
arithmetic operators
Perl, 761
Python, 813
arrays
awk scripting, 726-728
C programming language, 877-878
    pointers, 882
    strings, 878
Perl, 759
    Schwartzian transform, 777
Tcl/Tk, 788-789
asm mode (XEmacs), 164
assigning values in lists (Python), 819
asterisk (*)
bash wildcard character, 67
wildcard character, 148
at, 243-244
at sign (@)
Perl arrays, 759
atom expression, 942
alternation, 943
concatenation, 943
grouping, 944
meta-characters, 943
quantifiers, 942-943
attributes, NetWare client administration, 388
authentication
PPP, 314-315
    CHAPsecrets file, 316
    PAPsecrets file, 315-316
public key cryptography, 571
auto fill mode (XEmacs), 165
auto mount option, 196
auto save mode (XEmacs), 165

autocorrect variable
(tcsh), 76
automatic functions
(C programming
language), 863
automounting, NFS,
347-348
Autopilot command
(AutoPilot File menu),
589
awk scripting, 722
arrays, 726-728
built-in variables, 725-726
expressions, 728-729
field separators, 725
fields, 723
functions
built-in, 732-733
user-defined, 733-734
invoking, 723-725
patterns, 722-723
records, 723
statements, 729
break, 731
continue, 731
delete, 731
do, 730
exit, 731
for, 730
I/O, 731-732
if, 730
while, 730
variable assignments, 725

B

B command (vi), 143
background processes,
62-63
backslash (\), bash syntax,
64

backslash substitution
(Tcl/Tk), 786
backticks, accessing shell
from Perl, 768-769
Backup command (BRU-
2000)
File menu, 544
Options menu, 545
backups, 530-532
BRU-2000, 542-544
definitions, 545
file selection, 544-545
options, 545-546
running, 546
scheduling definitions,
546-547
compressed, 541
computer security, 552
full, 535-539
incremental, 535-536, 538
partitions, 984
selecting tools for, 533-534
selecting type of, 532-533
SMB shares, 362
strategy scheme, 535-537
tapes, 539
bars. *See* toolbars
base 8 numbers (numeric
permissions), 202
bash, 35, 56
background processes,
62-63
command history, 57-59
comparing to tcsh, 72
configuration files, 49,
70-71
filename completion,
65-66
syntax, 63, 65
variables, 68-69
wildcards, 66-67

bash shell, 710
case statement, 715-716
environment, 712
for statement, 719
functions, 720-721
if statement, 714-715
positional parameters,
719-720
scripts, 713
shell variables, 719-720
until statement, 717-718
variables, 711
while statement, 717-718
batch files
.shn compressed files,
playing, 695
wav file compression, 696
Beamer (StarOffice), 588
bell volume, adjusting,
108
bg command, 72
/bin directory, 33, 232-233
binaries, accessing, 599
bindery servers
file systems, 381-383
NetWare administration,
377-379, 381
quotas, 381-383
bindkey command, 72
Bladeenc MP3 encoder,
694
blink paren mode
(XEmacs), 165
block devices, 186
kernel configuration,
742-743
Boolean expressions
(Python), 823-824
/boot directory, 33
Bourne Shell, 35, 56
brace quoting (Tcl/Tk),
787

braces ({}), Tcl/Tk, 787
branching statements (C programming language), 871-872
break command (Tcl/Tk), 796
break statement
  awk scripting, 731
  Python, 828
broadcast packets, 268
BRU-2000
  backups, 542-544
    definitions, 545
    file selection, 544-545
    options, 545-546
    running backups, 546
    scheduling definitions, 546-547
  restoring data, 547-548
BSD model, 241
buffer overrun (computer security), 555
buffers (XEmacs), 156
  editing, 161-162
  updating, 161
bugs. *See* Debugger
built-in functions (awk scripting), 732-733
bulleted lists (WordPerfect), 585
button widget (Tcl/Tk), 802
ButtonPress event (X Windows), 85
ButtonRelease event (X Windows), 85
byte counters, firewall chains, 487

C

C programming language
  comments, 860
  data types, 861-862
    arrays, 877-878
    naming, 863
    pointers, 880-883, 885
    storage classes, 863-864, 866
    strings, 878
    structures, 878, 880
    variable scope, 863
  Fibonacci function, 864
  functions, 876-877
  header files, 860
  Hello World program, 859-860
  history of, 858-859
  operators, 867-868
  preprocessor
    conditional compilation, 887-888
    define directive, 886-887
    include directive, 886
  statements
    declarations, 866
    definitions, 867
    do, 873
    expressions, 867, 869
    for, 874-875
    if, 870-871
    return, 875
    switch, 871-872
    while, 872-873
  variables, declaring, 862
c mode (XEmacs), 164
c$ command (vi), 150
c) command (vi), 150

C++ programming language
  classes, 890, 892
    inheritance, 892-894
  compiling programs, 904
  features of, 888, 890
  functions, 892
    overloading, 894, 896
    virtual functions, 893-894
  main function, 892
c++ mode (XEmacs), 164
cache hint files (DNS), 303-304
calculations, MySQL, 612
calculators, 106
Caldera Open Administration System. *See* COAS
Caldera OpenLinux, 13, 18. *See also* Linux
  hardware requirements, 20-21
  installation, 966
    LISA, 973-978
    LIZARD, 966-972
  logging into, 24-25
  logging out, 25
calendars, printing, 963
canvas widget (Tcl/Tk), 803
caret (^), text searches, 148
case sensitivity (vi), 145
case statement, bash shell, 715-716
cat command, 36, 41-42
cd command, 38
  tcsh, 72
CD-ROM drivers, kernel configuration, 745

cdparanoia, 691
CDs, digital audio data extraction, 689-690
centering pages (WordPerfect), 584
cfdisk, 189d, 987
   setting hard disk geometry, 191
CGI, 408-409, 411
chains (firewalls), 480-481, 483
   appending rules to chain ends, 488
   configuring with ip chains, 483-490, 492-499
   creating, 486-487
   deleting, 485-486
   handling packet fragments, 493-494
   inserting into chains, 489
   interfaces, specifying, 492
   protocols, specifying, 492
   resetting counters, 487
   rules
      deleting, 489
      listing in, 484-485
      replacing, 489
      side effects of, 495-496
      specifying, 489-491
   setting policy, 487-488
   SYNpackets, specifying, 492-493
   targets, 481
      specifying, 494-495
changing
   directories, 38
   passwords, 25
CHAP (Challenge Handshake Authentication Protocol), 315
   secrets file, 316, 318

char data type (C programming language), 862
character devices, 186
   kernel configuration, 745
chat, PPP, 312, 314
checkbutton widget (Tcl/Tk), 802
checking file systems, 197-198
chgrp command, 204
chmod command, 199, 202
chown command, 204
chr( ) function (Python), 832
circuit-level proxies, 510-511
class definitions (Python), 847-848
class names (X Windows components), 86
classes
   C++ programming language, 890, 892
      inheritance, 892-894
   zones, 298
client/server
   NFS, 340-341
   X Windows, 80-81
clients
   DHCP, 290
   mail hub configuration, 455-456
   NetWare, 368
      activating, 371
      administration, 383-385, 387-391
      configuring, 370-371
      installing, 368-370
      login, 372-373
      printing, 375-377

NFS, configuring, 344-345
NIS, 326
   setting up, 331-332
   tools, 335-337
   proxies, 510
   SMB coient program, 361-362
   X Windows, 102
      options, 102
      xcalc, 106
      xclock, 105
      xload, 105
      xterm, 103-104
clocks, 105
closing XEmacs files (without saving), 161
cmd command, 411
cmp command, 939-941
CNAME record, 302
CNAME-type records, 296
CNews, 462
COAS (Caldera Open Administration System), 220, 222, 247, 424
   COAStool, 247
   mail hub client configuration, 456
   menu, 248-249
   sendmail.cf file, rebuilding, 424
   Sendmail configuration, 453-454
code maturity level options, kernel configuration, 741
colon (:), vi commands, 140
colors
   X Windows, specifying, 97-98
   xv (image manipulation program), 619

columns priv, 605-606
combine command (Image Magick), 626-627
command history
  bash, 57-59
  tcsh, 73-74
command mode (vi), 138
command-line options
  Makefiles, 910-911
  mkfs command
    -c ext2, 193
    -q, 193
    -t ext2, 193
    -v, 193
  mount options
    auto, 196
    noauto, 196
    nodev, 196
    noexec, 197
    nosuid, 197
    ro, 196
    user, 196
  Perl, 770-773
  rpm
    -a, 181
    -c, 183
    -d, 183
    -f, 182
    -i, 182
    -l, 183
    -p, 182
    nodeps, 174
    -R, 184
    replacefiles, 177
    replacepkgs, 176
  -test, 177
commands. *See also* **command-line options**
  apropos, 924-925
  break
    Tcl/Tk, 796
  cat, 36, 41-42

cd, 38
cfdisk, 987
chgrp, 204
chmod, 199, 202
chown, 204
cmd, 411
cmp, 939-941
config, 409
continue, Tcl/Tk, 796
cp, 929-930
cpio, 533-534, 539
  restoring data, 540-541
Ctrl+Alt+Delete, 962
date, 963
DATEGMT, 411
DATELOCA, 411
dd, 205
del (Python), 820
df, 957
diff, 939-941
DOCUMENTNAME, 411
DOCUMENTURL, 411
du, 958
echo, 411
errmsg, 409
eval (Tcl/Tk), 797
ex editor, 140
exec, 411
expressions. 941
file, 937
File menu (BRU-2000), Backup, 544
File menu (StarOffice)
  Autopilot, 589
  New, 589
  Open, 589
File menu (WordPerfect)
  New, 579
  Open, 579
  Save, 579
  Save As, 580

find, 538, 930-936
flastmod, 411
for (Tcl/Tk), 795
foreach (Tcl/Tk), 795
Format menu (WordPerfect)
  Justification, 581
  Line, 581
  Make It Fit, 582
  Margins, 580
  Page, 580, 584
  Typesetting, 583
free, 956-957
fsck, 197-198
fsize, 411
grep, 944, 946
groff, 226
gzip, 950-951
  programs, 951
  uncompressing files, 950-951
halt, 962
hard links, 936-937
head, 938-939
hostname, 954
if (Tcl/Tk), 794
ifconfig, 275-279
import (Python), 834
include, 412
info, 925-927
ipchains, 483-490, 492-499
job control commands, 62
kill, 51, 959-960
LASTMODIFIED, 411
ln, 936
logon identification, 955-956
ls, 29, 38
man, 924-925
mkdir, 28, 40
mkfs, 193
mkswap, 206

more, 42
mount, 194
mv, 38
MySQL, 606
nwadsttrs, 387
nwbprm, 379
nwlogin, 372-373
nwlogout, 374
nwpasswd, 375
online help commands, 924-926
Options menu (BRU-2000)
    Backup, 545
    Restore, 548
parameters, NDSadministration, 385-388
patch, 949-950
pnpdump, 676
pppd, running, 310-312
print (Python), 815
printenv, 412
printer, 217-219
printing calendars, 963
proc (Tcl/Tk), 797-799
ps, 50, 959
    KDETask Manager, 130-131
reboot, 962
rm, 39-40
rmdir, 28, 40
route, 279
RPC, 328
sed, 946-949
    addresses, 947
    programs, 947
set, 412
showmount (NFS), 347
shutdown, 962
Sizefmt, 410
smbstatus, 363-364
source (Tcl/Tk), 796

Start menu (StarOffice), Mail, 591
stderr, 61
stdin, 61
stdout, 60
switch (Tcl/Tk), 796
tail, 938-939
tar, 533-534, 537-539, 951-953
    GNU version, 537
    restoring data, 540
Tcl/Tk
    backslash substitution, 786
    command substitution, 785
    lists, 793-794
tcsh shell, 72
Timefmt, 410
top, 960-961
troff, 226
uptime, 955
vi
    $, 143
    (, 144
    ), 144
    +, 143
    -, 143
    ^, 143
    {, 144
    }, 144
    /pattern, 147
    0, 143
    3cw, 150
    3dl, 153
    3dw, 153
    4dd, 154
    6x, 154
    :n (**italicize n), 144
    :q, 140
    :q!, 140
    :w, 140

:w!, 140
:wq, 140
A, 149
b, 143
c$, 150
c), 150
Ctrl+B, 144
Ctrl+D, 144
Ctrl+E, 144
Ctrl+F, 144
Ctrl+U, 144
Ctrl+Y, 144
cw, 150
c^, 150
c}, 150
D, 154
d$, 153
d0, 153
dd, 154
dw, 153
e, 143
Enter key, 143
h, 143-144
i, 149
j, 143, 155
k, 143
l, 143-144
M, 144
nG, 144
nH, 144
nL, 144
O, 149
r, 150, 155
u, 155
w, 143
x, 154
y, 154-155
y$, 155
y), 155
y0, 154
yank, 154
yw, 154

yy, 155
y}, 155
ZZ, 140
virtual, 411
while (Tcl/Tk), 794
Who AmI?, 954-955
X Windows
  xbiff, 106
  xeyes, 107
  xman, 107
  xset, 108-110
  xvidtune, 108
XEmacs
  Ctrl+x 0, 165
  Ctrl+x 1, 166
  Ctrl+x 2, 166
  Ctrl+x 3, 166
xrdb, 86, 88
ypcat, 336
ypmatch, 336
yppasswd, 337
ypwich, 336
ypxfr, 335
commands module (Python), 854
comments
  C programming language, 860
  Python, 815
  Tcl/Tk, 787
commercial domains, 294
Common Gateway Interface. *See also* **CGI**
comparison operators
  Perl, 760
  Python, 823-824
compilation options (gcc), 902-903
compiling
  C++ programs, 904
  kernel, 748-749, 751

components (X Windows), 86
compound operators (Perl), 761
compressed backups, 541
compressing files
  gzip command, 950-951
  WAV files, 696
computer security, 550
  attack techniques
    buffer overrun, 555
    denial of service, 557
    network sniffing, 556
    passwords, 557
    social engineering, 556
  backups, 552
  daemons, 565
    TCP Wrappers, 565-567
  employee computer crime, 551
  encryption
    GNU Privacy Guard, 571
    PGP (Pretty Good Privacy), 570
    public key cryptography, 571
    virtual private networks, 571
  file modification
    detecting, 563-564
    preventing, 562
  firewalls, 558-560
  hackers, 550
  network security, 552
  physical security, 551
  port-scanning, 569
    Crack, 569
    nmap, 569
    open security solutions Web page, 570

  SAINT, 569
  Trinux, 569
  privacy, 570
  repair, 564
  risk assessment, 551
  system logs, 561
  UNIX security model
    access rights, 553
    device files, 555
    root account, 553
    SUID program, 554-555, 560
concatenation
  atom expression, 943
  lists (Tcl/Tk), 791-792
config command, 409
configuration
  Apache server, 398
    AllowOverrides directives, 403-404
    htaccess, 402
    httpd.conf, 399-401
    options directives, 402-403
    runtime, 398-399
  DHCP, 291-292
  DNS, 297
    options, 297
    zones, 298-300
  firewalls, ipchain, 483-490, 492-499
  hardware, LISAinstall, 975-976
  INN, 473-475
  ISA PnP cards at boot time, 679
  kernel, 737, 739-740
    amateur radio support, 744
    block devices, 742-743
    CD-ROMdrivers, 745
    character devices, 745

configuration

code maturity level options, 741
console drivers, 747
file system support, 746-747
infrared ports, 745
IrDA subsystem support, 745
ISDN networking, 745
joystick support, 746
loadable modules, 741
mouse, 746
native language support, 747
network device support, 744
network file system support, 747
networking options, 743-744
partition types, 747
plug and play support, 742
processor type and features, 741
SCSI support, 744
sound, 748
tape drives, 746
universal serial bus, 748
video for Linux, 746
mail hub clients, 455-456
mail hub DNS, 456-457
mail hubs, 455, 457
mgetty, 317-318
NetWare client, 370
environment variables, 370-371
network interface, 284-285
NFS clients, 344-345
NFS servers, 342-343
OSS, 681-682
PPP serial port, 309
RAID 0 volumes, 994-995
RAID 1 volumes, 997-999
RAID linear volumes, 996-997
resolver, 288
Samba, 351
encrypted passwords, 353
file shares, 354-356
global options, 351, 353
PDF(Portable Document Format), 357-359
printer shares, 356-357
Web-based, 364-365
Sendmail, 423
COAS, 453-454
m4 macros, 452
SoftOSS, 682
TCP/IPnetworking, 275
ifconfig, 275-279
TIS, 519-521
tin, 476
WordPerfect, 585
XFree86, 88
configuration file, 93-97
graphics cards, 96
graphics modes, 91
keyboard, 90, 94
monitors, 91
montiors, 95
mouse, 90, 95
server behavior, 92
video card, 90-91
video hardware, identifying, 89
xf86config, 92-93
XF86Setup program, 89

configuration files
/etc, 233-235
bash, 49, 70-71
listing, 183
Sendmail, 425-427, 429-450
sendmail.cf printout example, 426-450
tcsh, 50, 76, 78
configure script, 912
console administration, 238
user management, 238-241
console drivers, kernel configuration, 747
continue command (Tcl/Tk), 796
continue statement
awk scripting, 731
Python, 828
Control Center (KDE)
applications category, 125
desktop category, 126-127
information category, 127
input devices category, 127
keys category, 127
network category, 127
sound category, 128
windows category, 128
control statements, awk scripting, 729
break, 731
continue, 731
delete, 731
do, 730
exit, 731
for, 730
if, 730
convert command (Image Magick), 627-628

converters
  dmp, 666
  dvilj, 666
  dvipdfm, 666
  dvips, 665-666
  dvitomp, 666
  mpost, 667
  Wp2latex, 667
convertng sound, 687-689
copy( ) method (Python), 823
copying
  dictionaries (Python), 823
  files, cp command, 929-930
  lists (Python), 823
  text
    vi, 154-155
    XEmacs, 162
  X Windows, 84
cp command, 929-930
cpio command, 533-534, 539
  restoring data, 540-541
Crack (port scanner), 569
crackers, 550
creating
  appointments (StarOffice), 590
  databases (MySQL), 608-609
  disks (LISAinstall), 973-974
  documents
    StarOffice, 589
    WordPerfect, 579
  files
    vi, 138-139
    XEmacs, 160
  firewall chains, 486-487
  links (ln command), 936

NetWare properties, 378-379
swap partitions, 981
tables (MySQL), 609-610
templates (StarOffice), 589
typeset documents, 651
  LaTeX, 651-662
crontab, 243-244
cryptography, public key, 571
csh, 35
customizing
  panel (kwm), 118-119
  StarOffice workspace, 588
cutting text
  vi, 154-155
  XEmacs, 162
cw command (vi), 150
CWEB2HTML, 668-669
cylinders (hard disks), 189

D

D command (vi), 154
d$ command (vi), 153
d0 command (vi), 153
daemons, 241, 243, 259
  controls, 242
  security, 565
    TCP Wrappers, 565
  tcpd, 566-567
data backups. *See* **backups**
Data Display Debugger (ddd), 918-920
data types. *See also* **variables**
  C programming language, 861-862
    arrays, 877-878
    declaring in, 862

  naming in, 863
  pointers, 880-883, 885
  strings, 878
  structures, 878, 880
  variable scope, 863
  MySQL, 607-608
  Tcl/Tk, 787
    arrays, 788-789
database files, DNS, 299
database servers (MySQL), 594
  accessing binaries, 599
  administration, 600, 602, 604-606
  calculations, 612
  database management, 606-610
  DESCRIBEstatement, 611
  INSERTstatement, 611
  installing, 595-597, 599
  pattern matching, 612-613
  reading data from files, 611
  security, 600
  SELECTstatement, 612
  sorting rows, 612
  stopping, 598
databases
  domain name system. *See* DNS
  MySQL, 606-607
    creating databases, 608-609
    creating tables, 609-610
    data types, 607-608
    removing, 608-609
    removing tables, 609-610
  NISmaps, 326-327
    building, 330-331
    setting up sources, 329

datagrams, 268
date command, 963
DATEGMT command, 411
DATELOCALcommand, 411
dd command, 205
    vi, 154
ddd (Data Display Debugger), 918-920
deactivating. *See* activating, 371
Debian Linux, 13
Debugger (GNU C), 912-914
    Data Display Debugger, 918-920
    post-mortem debugging, 914-916
    running processes, 916-918
debugging (Samba), 360-361
declarations (C programming language), 866
    structures, 878, 880
    variables, 862
default routes, 281-282
define directive (C programming language), 886-887
defining
    procedures (Tcl/Tk), 797-798
    strings (Python), 819
definitions
    backups, scheduling, 546-547
    C programming language, 867
del command (Python), 820

delete statement (awk scripting), 731
deleting
    files, 39-40
    firewall chains, 485-486
    NetWare properties, 379, 381
    Python objects, 820
    rules (firewall chains), 489
    text
        vi, 153-154
        XEmacs, 161
denial of service security attach, 557
DENY target (firewall chain), 481
dependencies
    compiling kernel, 749
    files/packages, 174-175
        uninstalling packages, 178-179
DESCRIBE statement (MySQL), 611
description section (man pages), 46
desktop
    kfm, 123
    StarOffice, 586-587
        Beamer, 588
        Explorer, 588
        toolbars, 586
        windows, 587
desktop category (KDE Control Center), 126-127
desktop menu (kwm), 120
/dev directory, 34
development packages, 178
device drivers, loadable modules in kernel, 736-737

device files. *See also* devices
    computer security, 555
    /etc/fstab file, 195
    printers, 210-211
Device section (/etc/XF86Config file), 96
devices, 186
    block, 186
    character, 186
    identifying, 187-188
    names, 186-187
    networks, 274
        names, 274-275, 279
    permissions, 188
df command, 957
DHCP, 290
    client setup, 290
    server setup, 290
        configuration, 291-292
diagnostics programs
    ping, 288
    traceroute, 289-290
dial-in servers (PPP), 317
    mgetty, 317-318
    per-port options, 318-319
    secrets file, 318
diald, 321-323
    monitoring, 323-324
dialog box widget (Tcl/Tk), 805
dialog boxes
    Edit Figure (LyX), 658
    Edit Preferences, 257
    Edit User, 257
    File System, 259-260
    File Systems Options, 261
    GPMMouse Configuration, 252
    Kernel Modules, 263
    Mail Relay Host, 456

Mount File System, 260
Name Resolver Setup, 250
Password Expiration, 258
Printer Configuration, 222, 253
Software Package Pre-Selection, 977
Software Selection, 264
Source Selection, 265
System Hostname, 261
System Load Average, 262
System Module Configuration, 264
System Resource, 261-262
System Services, 259
System Time, 263
User Accounts, 256-257
Visible Domain, 456

dictionaries (Python), 821-822
  copying, 823
diff command, 939-941
digital audio data, extracting, 689-691
directories
  /bin, 33, 232-233
  /boot, 33
  changing, 38
  creating, 28, 40
  /dev, 34
  /etc, 33
    configuration files, 233-235
  /etc/rc.d, 415, 417
  /etc/rc.d/init.d/, 242
  /etc/rc.d/rc2.d/ directory, 242
  /home, 33, 235
  /lib, 33
  /lib/modules, 33
  listing, 29-30, 38
  /mnt, 235

mount points, 32
naming, 38
/opt, 34
permissions, 30-31
/proc, 33
  kernel administration, 244-246
removing, 28, 40
root directory, 33
/sbin, 33, 232-233
ScriptAlias, 408
/tmp, 33, 236-237
/usr, 34, 237-238
/usr/doc, documentation files, 927
/usr/doc/HOWTO, documentation files, 927-928
/usr/doc/LDP, documentation files, 928-929
/usr/sbin, 241
/var, 236-237
working directory, 27

directory option, DNS configuration, 297
DirectoryIndex setting (Apache), 401
disabling
  encrypted passwords (Samba), 353
  services (LISA), 978
  swap space, 208
discarding output, 37
disk quotas, 198
disks
  creating, LISA install, 973-974
  inode, 936
  quotas (NDS), 391-392
  space
    df command, 957
    du command, 958

display command (Image Magick), 628-630
Display menu (xv), 618
Display Power Management System (DPMS), X Windows, 109
displays (X Windows), 81-82
Dithered command (xv Display menu), 618
dmp utility (typesetting), 666
DNS (domain name system), 272, 287, 294, 296-305
  cache hint files, 303-304
  CNAMErecord, 302
  configuration, 297
    options, 297
    zones, 298-300
  database files, 299
  domains, 294
  host names, 294
  mail hub configuration, 456-457
  MXrecord, 302
  nslookup, 304, 306
  NSrecord, 301-302
  queries, 295
  records, 296
  reverse lookup files, 302-303
  root servers, 294
  SOArecord, 300-301
do statement
  awk scripting, 730
  C programming language, 873
do, while loop (Perl), 767
documentation, online
  commands, 924-926
  /usr/doc files, 927

/usr/doc/HOWTO, 927-928
/usr/doc/LDP, 928-929
documentation files, listing, 183
DOCUMENTNAMEcommand, 411
DocumentRoot setting (Apache), 401
documents
  StarOffice, 589
    creating, 589
    opening, 589
  typesetting, 651
    LaTeX, 651-662
  WordPerfect
    creating, 579
    formatting, 580-584
DOCUMENTURL command, 411
dollar sign ($), text searches, 148
domain name system. *See* **DNS**
domains, 294
  NIS, 326
  naming, 329
double data type (C programming language), 862
double quotes ("")
  bash syntax, 64
  Tcl/Tk, 786
downloading
  ALSA, 684
  cdparanoia, 691
  libmikmod module player, 697
  newsgroups, 461-463
    INN, 464-469, 471-475
  OSS, 680-681
  shorten, 695

DPMS (Display Power Management System), X Windows, 109
dragging and dropping files (kfm), 124
drivers, loadable modules in kernel, 736-737
du command, 958
dump field (/etc/fstab file), 196
DVIcopy, 650
dvilj utility (typesetting), 666
dvipdfm utility (typesetting), 666
dvips utility (typesetting), 665-666
dvitomp utility (typesetting), 666
dw command (vi), 153
Dynamic Host Configuration Protocols. *See* **DHCP**

E

E command (vi), 143
echo command, 411
echo function, 68
echo line (XEmacs), 158
Edit Figure dialog box (LyX), 658
Edit Preferences dialog box, 257
Edit User dialog box, 257
editing
  appointments
    StarOffice, 590
  buffers (XEmacs), 161-162

/etc/XF86Config file
  Device section, 96
  Files section, 93-94
  Keyboard section, 94
  Module section, 94
  Monitor section, 95
  Pointer section, 95
  Screen section, 96-97
  ServerFlags section, 94
files, vi
  changing text, 150-151
  copying text, 154-155
  cutting text, 154-155
  deleting text, 153-154
  inserting text, 149-150
  joining lines, 155
  pasting text, 154-155
  replacing text, 150-151
  substituting text, 151-153
files, XEmacs, 161-162
  copying text, 162
  cutting text, 162
  deleting text, 161
  pasting text, 162
source files, GNU C, 904-912
editors (text). *See* **vi; XEmacs**
educational domains, 294
elif directive (C programming language), 887
ellipsis (...), bash wildcard character, 67
else directive (C programming language), 887
email
  aliases, 454
  mail hubs, 454
    client configuration, 455-456
    configuring, 455, 457
    DNS configuration, 456-457

MDA (Mail Delivery Agent), 420-421
message format, 422-423
monitoring, xbiff command, 106
MTA (Mail Transport Agent), 420-421
MUA (Mail User Agent), 420-421
overview, 420
Perl, 774
Sendmail. *See* Sendmail
SMTP (Simple Mail Transfer Protocol), 421-422
StarOffice, 590-591
embedded Python, 839
pytext script, 841, 843-845
timestamps, inserting in code, 843
uses, 840
employee computer crime, 551
enabling
services (LISA), 978
swap space, 207
encryption
GNU Privacy Guard, 571
PGP (Pretty Good Privacy), 570
Samba passwords, disabling, 353
public key cryptography, 571
virtual private networks, 571
Ensoniq Audio PCI sound card, 675
Enter event (X Windows), 85
Enter key command (vi), 143

environment section (man pages), 46
environment variables
bash shell, 712
NetWare client, 370-371
EOFError exception (Python), 837
errmsg command, 409
/etc directory, 33
configuration files, 233-235
/etc/ exports file (NFS), 343
/etc/fstab, NFS volumes, 346
/etc/fstab file, 195-196
/etc/inittab file, 242
/etc/news/control.ctl, 466
/etc/nsswitch.conf file, 332-333
/etc/rc.d directory, 415, 417
/etc/rc.d/init.d/ directory, 242
/etc/rc.d/init.d/network script, 285
/etc/rc.d/init.d/news, 468
/etc/rc.d/rc2.d/ directory, 242
/etc/samba.d/smb.conf, 351
global options, 351, 353
/etc/XF86Config file, 93-97
Device section, 96
Files section, 93-94
Keyboard section, 94
Module section, 94
Monitor section, 95
Pointer section, 95
Screen section, 96-97
ServerFlags section, 94

Ethernet interface, 275, 279
eval command (Tcl/Tk), 797
events
StarOffice, 589-590
creating appointments, 590
editing appointments, 590
X Windows, 85
ex editor, 140
exceptions (Python), 835-837
exclamation point (!), vi commands, 140
exec command, 411
Exec() function (Python), 842
executable files, 900
execute permissions (files), 199
exit command (tcsh), 72
exit statement (awk scripting), 731
exiting
vi, 140-142
XEmacs, 160
Explorer (StarOffice), 588
exporters
CWEB2HTML, 668-669
laTeX2HTML, 668
LTX2X, 668
expression statements (C programming language), 867
expressions, 941
atom, 942
alternation, 943
concatenation, 943
grouping, 944
meta-characters, 943
quantifiers, 942-943

expressions

awk scripting, 728-729
C programming language, 869
Tcl/Tk, 789
ext2 file system, 192
extended partitions, 979-980. *See also* **logical partitions**
extracting
    digital audio data, 689-691
    elements from lists (Tcl/Tk), 791

F

fdisk, 189
Feynman diagrams, typesetting, 670
fg command, 72
Fibonacci function (C), 864
fields (awk), 723
figures. *See* **pictures**
file command, 937
file manager (kfm), 121
    Desktop, 123
    drag-and-drop capability, 124
    files, selecting, 122
    mime types, 124
    views, 122
    Web browser, 123
file managment (StarOffice), 588
File menu commands
    BRU-2000, Backup, 544
    StarOffice
        Autopilot, 589
        New, 589
        Open, 589

    WordPerfect
        New, 579
        Open, 579
        Save, 579
        Save As, 580
file names, zones, 298
file ownership, changing, 204
file permissions, 198-199
    device files, 555
    sgid bit, 201
    sticky bit, 201
    suid bit, 200
file system, 26, 191-192, 259-260
    bindery servers, 381-383
    checking, 197-198
    creating, 193
    directories
        /bin, 33
        /boot, 33
        changing, 38
        creating, 28, 40
        /dev, 34
        /home, 33
        /lib, 33
        /lib/modules, 33
        listing, 29-30, 38
        mount points, 32
        naming, 38
        /opt, 34
        /proc, 33
        removing, 28, 40
        root directory, 33
        /sbin, 33
        /tmp, 33
        /usr, 34
    ext2, 192
    FSSTND, 232
        /bin directory, 232-233
        configuration files in /etc, 233-235

        /home, 235
        /mnt, 235
        /sbin directory, 232-233
        /tmp, 236-237
        /usr, 237-238
        /var, 236-237
    ISO 9660, 192
    kernel configuration, 746-747
    Linux Filesystem Standard, 32, 34
    mounting, 193-194
        automatically, 195-196
        manually, 194-195
        options, 196-197
    NFS (Network File System), 340
        automounting, 347-348
        client-server communications, 340-341
        configuring clients, 344-345
        configuring servers, 342-343
        /etc/ exports file, 343
        mount options, 345-346
        mounting volumes, 341
        permissions, 342
        security, 344
        showmount command, 347
        starting servers, 344
    pathnames, 27
    permissions, 30-31
    root, mounting, 193
    symbolic links, 31-32
    universal serial bus, 748
    vfat, 192
    working directory, 27
File System dialog box, 259-260

File System Options dialog box, 261
filename completion
    bash, 65-66
    tcsh, 75-76
filename length, 63
filenames, 580
    packages, 172
files
    accounts, 239
    aliases, 454
    archives, tar command, 951-953
    batch
        .shn compressed files, playing, 695
        WAV file compression, 696
    CHAP secrets, 316, 318
    compressing, gzip command, 950-951
    configuration
        bash, 49, 70-71
        /etc, 233-235
        listing, 183
        tcsh, 50, 76, 78
    copying, cp command, 929-930
    /dev/null, 37
    device. *See also* devices
        printers, 210-211
    DNS
        cache hint, 303-304
        database, 299
        reverse lookup, 302-303
    documentation, listing, 183
    /etc/fstab, 195-196
    /etc/inittab file, 242
    /etc/news/control.ctl, 466
    /etc/nsswitch.conf, 332-333
    /etc/rc.d/init.d/news, 468

    /etc/samba.d/smb.conf, 351
        global options, 351, 353
    /etc/XF86Config, 93-97
        Device section, 96
        Files section, 93-94
        Keyboard section, 94
        Module section, 94
        Monitor section, 95
        Pointer section, 95
        Screen section, 96-97
        ServerFlags section, 94
    executable, 900
    finding, 930-936
    htaccess (Apache), 402
    INN, startup, 468-469, 471-472
    LaTeX, input, 654-662
    listing, 38
    logins, 239
    management (WordPerfect), 579-580
    moving, 38
    MySQL, installing, 596-597, 599
    names, 580
        gcc, 902
    NFS
        /etc/fstab, 346
        security, 340
    numbering lines, 41
    object, 900
    opening
        GIMP, 640-641
        kfm, 121
        WordPerfect, 579
    PAP secrets, 315-316
    password, NIS servers, 329
    patch
        SoftOSS MIDI synthesis, 704-705
        TiMidity++, 704-705

    removing, 39-40
    saving (WordPerfect), 579-580
    Sendmail
        configuration files, 425-427, 429-450
        m4 configuration file (sendmail.mc), 450-452
        storing, 423, 425
    shares (Samba), 354-356
    .shn compressed, 695
    source, 900
        GNU C, 904-912
    Sox supported, 688
    swap, 205-206
    uncompressing, gzip command, 950-951
    updating, patch command, 949-950
    /usr/libexec/inn/bin/rc.news, 470-472
    vi
        creating, 138-139
        navigating, 142-148
        saving, 140-142
    viewing contents, 41-42
        more command, 42
    WAV, compressing, 696
    XEmacs
        closing (without saving), 161
        creating, 160
        navigating, 156
        opening, 158-159
        saving, 160
        selecting, 158
    XFree86, specifying location, 93-94
Files section (/etc/XF86Config file), 93-94

filtering packets, 479
   IPfilters, 479-481, 483
find command, 538, 930-936
finding. *See also* **searching**
   files, find command, 930-936
   text in files, grep command, 944, 946
firewalls, 478-479, 509, 558-560
   chains, 480-481, 483
      appending rules to chain ends, 488
      configuring with ipchains, 483-490, 492-499
      creating, 486-487
      deleting, 485-486
      deleting rules, 489
      handling packet fragments, 493-494
      inserting rules into, 489
      listing rules in, 484-485
      replacing rules, 489
      resetting counters, 487
      setting policy, 487-488
      side effects of rules, 495-496
      specifying interfaces, 492
      specifying protocols, 492
      specifying rules, 489-491
      specifying SYN packets, 492-493
      targets, 481, 494-495
   IP masquerading, 502-504
   restoring, 504
   saving, 504
   testing, 496

fixed IP addresses, 292
flastmod command, 411
float data type (C programming language), 862
FloatingPointError exception (Python), 837
flooding (Usenet newsgroups), 462
FM synthesis (MIDI), 702
focus, 85
font lock mode (XEmacs), 165
font path, changing, 109-110
fonts
   WordPerfect documents, 582-583
   X Windows, 98
      descriptions, 99-100
      scalable, 101
      viewing, 100
   xterm, 103
for command (Tcl/Tk), 795
for loop (Perl), 766
for statement
   awk scripting, 730
   bash shell, 719
   C programming language, 874-875
foreach command (Tcl/Tk), 795
foreach loop (Perl), 766
Format menu commands (WordPerfect)
   Justification, 581
   Line, 581
   Make It Fit, 582
   Margins, 580
   Page, 580, 584
   Typesetting, 583

formatted printing, 225-226
formatting
   documents (WordPerfect), 580-584
   email messages, 422-423
   swap space, 206
fortran mode (XEmacs), 164
forwarders option (DNS configuration), 297
fragmentation
   packets, 493-494
   partitions, 983-984
frames (XEmacs), 156
free command, 956-957
FreeS/WAN, 572
Freshmeat Web site, 694, 705
frozen terminal, 53
fsck command, 197-198
fsck field (/etc/fstab file), 196
fsize command, 411
FSSTND, 232
   /bin directory, 232-233
   configuration files in /etc, 233-235
   /home, 235
   /mnt, 235
   /sbin directory, 232-233
   /tmp, 236-237
   /usr, 237-238
   /var, 236-237
FTP
   StarOffice site, 591
   URLs, 173-174
full backups, 535-539
function bars, StarOffice, 587

functions
  awk scripting
    built-in functions, 732-733
    user-defined functions, 733-734
  bash shell, 720-721
  C programming language, 876-877
  C++ programming language, 892
    main function, 892
    overloading functions, 894, 896
    virtual functions, 893-894
  echo, 68
  Fibonacci function (C), 864
  Python
    default arguments, 829
    exec( ) (Python), 842
    globals( ) (Python), 825
    namespaces, 830-831
    open( ) (Python), 832
    range( ), 827
    raw_input( ), 831
    return statement, 829
    type( ), 825
    type conversion functions, 832
  Tcl/Tk, 791
fundamental mode (XEmacs), 164

G

gcc (GNU C Compiler), 901
  compilation options, 902-903
  Debugger, 912-914
    Data Display Debugger, 918-920
    post-mortem debugging, 914-916
    running processes, 916-918
  editing source files, 904
  Makefile, 904-912
  filename suffixes, 902
  invoking, 901
  linking options, 903-904
  path options, 903-904
General MIDI System (GM), 701
geometry of hard disks
  setting, 191
  viewing, 190
get( ) method (Python), 823
ghostscript utility (typesetting), 664
GIMP, 636
  files, opening, 640-641
  images, creating, 641-642
  images, saving to file, 643-644
  installation, 637, 639
  plug-ins, installing, 646
  pop-up menus, 643
  Script-Fu, 645-646
    installing scripts, 646
  toolbar, 639-640
  Web resource, 636, 646
global variables (Tcl/Tk), 798
globals() function (Python), 825
GM (General MIDI System), 701

GNU C Compiler (gcc), 901
  compilation options, 902-903
  Debugger, 912-914
    Data Display Debugger, 918-920
    post-mortem debugging, 914-916
    running processes, 916-918
  editing source files, 904
  Makefile, 904-912
  filename suffixes, 902
  invoking, 901
  linking options, 903-904
  path options, 903-904
GNU General Public License, 14
GNU Privacy Guard, 571
GNU tar command, 537
government domains, 294
GPMMouse Configuration dialog box, 252
Grant Taylor's Linux Printing HOWTO, 229
graphics
  GIMP, 636
    files, opening, 640-641
    images, creating, 641-642
    images, saving to file, 643-644
    installation, 637, 639
    plug-ins, installing, 646
    pop-up menus, 643
    Script-Fu, 645-646
    Script-Fu, installing scripts, 646
    toolbar, 639-640
    Web resource, 636, 646

graphics

Image Magick, 624
   animate command, 624-625
   combine command, 626-627
   convert command, 627-628
   display command, 628-630
   identify command, 630-631
   import command, 631-632
   mogrify command, 633-634
   montage command, 634-635
   Web resource, 636
LyX, 658-659
WordPerfect, 584
xv, 616
   24/8 Bit menu, 619
   Algorithms menu, 619
   Display menu, 618
   image files, loading, 621
   Image Size menu, 621
   images, saving to file, 623-624
   Root menu, 619
   Windows menu, 620
graphics cards, configuring (X Windows), 96
graphics modes, configuring (X Windows), 91
grep command, 944, 946
groff command, 226
group permissions (files), 198
Group setting (Apache), 400

grouping, atom expression, 944
gs (ghostscript), 664
gzip command, 950-951
   programs, 951
   uncompressing files, 950-951

H

h command (vi), 143-144
hackers, 550
halt command, 962
hard disks
   cylinders, 189
   geometry, setting, 191
   geometry, viewing, 190
   heads, 189
   partitions, 188
      creating, 190-191
      deleting, 190
      logical, 189
      primary, 189
      space, 986-988
      types, 191
   platters, 189
   sectors, 189
   tracks, 189
hard links, 936-937
hardware
   ALSA modules, 685
   ALSA supported, 683
   configuration (LISAinstall), 975-976
   INN, 464-465
   keyboards (NIS), 251
   mouse (NIS), 252-253
   partitions. *See* partitions
   PPP serial port configuration, 309-310
   printers. *See* printers

hardware requirements, 20-21
hashes (Perl), 759
HDLC (High-Level Datalink Control), 308
head command, 938-939
header fields, email messages, 422
header files (C programming language), 860
heads (hard disks), 189
Hello World program
   C programming language, 859-860
   Tcl/Tk, 783-784
help, online, 924-926
hex( ) function (Python), 832
High-Level Datalink Control. *See* **HDLC**
hint zones, 298
histfile variable (tcsh), 76
history
   bash command history, 57-59
   tcsh command history, 73-74
history command, 72
history variable (tcsh), 76
home directory, 27, 33, 235
Homes share (Samba), 354
home variable (tcsh), 76
host names, 294
hostname command, 954
hosts, 268
   protecting, 497-499
htaccess file (Apache), 402
httpd.conf, 399-401

I

I command (vi), 149
ICMP (Internet Control Message Protocol), 269
identify command (Image Magick), 630-631
identifying devices, 187-188
identity operators (Python), 824
if command (Tcl/Tk), 794
if directive (C programming language), 887
if statement
  awk scripting, 730
  bash shell, 714-715
  C programming language, 870-871
if/else statement (Perl), 764
ifconfig command, 275-279
ifdef directive (C programming language), 887
ifndef directive (C programming language), 887
ihave/sendme protocol, 463
Image Magick, 624
  animate command, 624-625
  combine command, 626-627
  convert command, 627-628
  display command, 628-630
  identify command, 630-631
  import command, 631-632
  mogrify command, 633-634
  montage command, 634-635
  Web resource, 636
Image Size menu (xv), 621
images. *See also* graphics; pictures
  KDE image viewer, 131, 133
implicit rules (Makefiles), 909-910
import command
  Image Magick, 631-632
  Python, 834
ImportError exception (Python), 837
importing modules (Python), 834
include command, 412
include directive (C programming language), 886
incremental backups, 535-536, 538
IndexError exception (Python), 837
info command, 925-927
information category (KDE Control Center), 127
infrared ports, kernel configuration, 745
inheritance
  C++ programming language, 892-894
  Python, 849
INN (InterNETNews), 462, 466-467
  configuration, 473-475
  hardware requirements, 464-465
  installing, 467-468
  software requirements, 464-465
  startup files, 468-469, 471-472
inode disk, 936
input, stdin command, 61
input devices category (KDE Control Center), 127
input file (LaTeX), 654-662
input mode (vi), 138
INSERT statement (MySQL), 611
inserting text (vi), 149-150
installation. *See also* uninstalling
  ALSA, 684-685
  Apache server, 397-398
  Caldera, 966
    LISA, 973-978
    LIZARD, 966-972
  GIMP, 637, 639
  INN, 467-468
    startup files, 468-469, 471-472
  kernel, 749, 751
  libmikmod module player, 698
  modules, 749
  MySQL, 595
    files, 596-597, 599
    testing, 599
  NetWare client, 368
    NDS tree, 369-370
  OSS, 680-681
  packages, 172-173
    checking for conflicts, 177
    conflicts, 176
    dependencies, 174-175
    FTP, 173-174

plug-ins (the GIMP), 646
RAIDTools, 994
rebuilding kernel, 736-737
Script-Fu scripts (the GIMP), 646
shorten, 695
StarOffice, 586
TiMidity++, 703
tin, 476
TIS, 519-521
xv, 616
WordPerfect, 578
instance names (X Windows components), 86
int data type (C programming language), 862
interfaces, 268
   network
      adding, 285-286
      configuration, 284-285
   networks
      Ethernet, 275, 279
      loopback, 274
      PPP, 275
   specifying, firewalls, 492
   vi, 136
   X Windows, 82-83
   XEmacs, 157
Internet, 268
Internet Control Message Protocol. *See* **ICMP**
InterNet News. *See* **INN**
Internet Protocol. *See* **IP**
internets, 268
Internetwork Packet Exchange (IPX), 368
I/O redirection, 36-37, 60-61
   pipe character, 62
I/O statements (awk scripting), 731-732
IOError exception (Python), 837

IP (Internet Protocol), 269
   addresses, 269-270
      DNS(domain name system), 272, 287, 294, 296-305
      fixed, 292
      masquerading, 502-504
      network protection, 499-501
      private, 270
      routes, 272, 274, 279-283
   filters, 479-481, 483
   firewall chains, 480-481, 483
      appending rules to chains ends, 488
      configuring with ipchains, 483-490, 492-499
      creating, 486-487
      deleting, 485-486
      deleting rules, 489
      inserting rules into, 489
      listing rules in, 484-485
      replacing rules, 489
      resetting counters, 487
      setting policy, 487-488
      side effects of rules, 495-496
      specifying rules, 489-491
      targets, 481
   specifying, 494-495
IP addresses, 314
ipchains command, 483-490, 492-499
IPX (Internetwork Packet Exchange), 368
IrDA subsystem support, kernel configuration, 745

is not operator (Python), 824
is operator (Python), 824
ISA PnP sound cards, 676-679
   configuring at boot time, 679
ISDN networking, kernel configuration, 745
ISO 9660 file system, 192
ISPs, connecting to, 316-317

J

j command (vi), 143, 155
job control commands, 62
joining lines of text (vi), 155
Joy, Bill, 138
joystick, kernel configuration, 746
justification. *See also* **alignment, 584**
   WordPerfect documents, 581
Justification command (WordPerfect Format menu), 581

K

k command (vi), 143
KDE (K Desktop Environment), 112-113
   Control Center
      applications category, 125
      desktop category, 126-127

information category, 127
input devices category, 127
keys category, 127
network category, 127
sound category, 128
windows category, 128
file manager (kfm), 121
   Desktop, 123
   drag-and-drop capability, 124
   files, selecting, 122
   mime types, 124
   views, 122
   Web browser, 123
image viewer, 131, 133
Kmidi, 703
kwm window manager, 84
logging into, 24
logging out, 25
package manager, 128-129
Task Manager, 130-131
twn window manager, 84
window manager (kwm), 113-114
   Application Starter, 117-118
   buttons, 114-115
   desktop menu, 120
   panel, 116, 118-119
   resizing windows, 116
   title bars, 115
   virtual desktops, 120

kernel, 263-264. See also Linux Kernel
administration, /proc, 244-246
compiling, 748-749, 751
configuring, 737, 739-740
   amateur radio support, 744
   block devices, 742-743

   CD-ROM drivers, 745
   character devices, 745
   code maturity level optoins, 741
   console drivers, 747
   file system support, 746-747
   infrared ports, 745
   IrDA subsystem support, 745
   ISBN networking, 745
   joystick support, 746
   loadable modules, 741
   mouse, 746
   native language support, 747
   network device support, 744
   network file system support, 747
   networking options, 743-744
   partition types, 747
   plug and play support, 742
   processor type and features, 741
   SCSI support, 744
   sound, 748
   tape drives, 746
   universal serial bus, 748
   video for Linux, 746
installing, 749, 751
loadable modules, 736-737
patching, 993-994
rebuilding, 736-737

Kernel Module Configuration dialog box, 264
Kernel Module Manager (LISA install), 975-976

Kernel Modules dialog box, 263
key click, enabling/disabling, 109
keyboard
configuring (X Windows), 90, 94
focus, 85
Keyboard section (/etc/XF86Config file), 94
KeyboardInterrupt exception (Python), 837
keyboards (NIS), 251
KeyError exception (Python), 837
KeyPress event (X Windows), 85
KeyRelease event (X Windows), 85
keys, Python dictionaries, 822
keys category (KDE Control Center), 127
keywords (MySQL), 607
kfm (KDE file manager), 121
Desktop, 123
drag-and-drop capability, 124
files, selecting, 122
mime types, 124
views, 122
Web browser, 123
   bookmarks, 123
kill command, 51, 959-960
tcsh, 73
killing processes, 51
KLyX. See LyX
Kmidi, 703
Kppp, 324

kwm (KDE window manager), 84, 113-114
    Application Starter, 117-118
    buttons, 114-115
    desktop menu, 120
    panel, 116
        customizing, 118-119
    resizing windows, 116
    title bars, 115
    virtual desktops, 120

L

l command (vi), 143-144
L option, 484-485
label widget (Tcl/Tk), 802
laser printers, 212
LASTMODIFIED command, 411
LaTeX, 651-654
    creating input file, 654-658
    LyX, 654, 656-658
        pictures, 658-659
        tables, 659-662
laTeX2HTML, 668
launching. See starting, 101
LCP (LinkControl Protocol), 308
LDP (Linux Documentation Project), 19
Leave event (X Windows), 85
len( ) function (Python), 817
/lib directory, 33
/lib/moduels directory, 33

libmikmod module player, 697-698, 700
    downloading, 697
    installing, 698
    testing, 698-700
libraries
    shared, 901
    versions, package installations, 175-176
library archives, 900
Line command (WordPerfect Format menu), 581
line number mode (XEmacs), 165
linear RAID volumes, configuring, 996-997
lines, spacing in WordPerfect documents, 582
Link Control Protocol, 308
linkers, 900
linking options (gcc), 903-904
links
    creating, ln command, 936
    hard links, 936-937
    pppd automation, 320
        diald, 321-324
    routing (PPP), 319-320
    symlinks, partitions, 989-990
Linux. See also Caldera OpenLinux
    advantages of, 14-15
    Caldera, 13, 18
    compatibility with UNIX, 15
    Debian, 13
    features of, 16-17

file system, 26
    directories, 33
    directories, creating, 28
    directories, listing, 29-30
    directories, removing, 28
    file permissions, 30-31
    Linux Filesystem Standard, 32-33
    mount points, 32
    pathnames, 27
    symbolic links, 31-32
    working directory, 27
GNU General Public License, 14
hardware requirements, 20-21
history, 8-11
interoperability with Windows and Macintosh, 17
open standards, 15
philosophy of UNIX, 11
Red Hat, 13
resources, 19
shells, 35
Linux Documentation Project (LDP), 19
Linux Ext2 partitions, 191
Linux Kernel
    sound
        automatically configuring, 676
        ISA PnP cards, 676-679
    configuring at boot time, 679
        manual configuration, 673-676
    sound, 673

sound card modules, 675
soundcore module, 674
Linux native partitions, 191
Linux swap partitions, 191
LISA
  installing Caldera, 973-975
    disk creation, 973-974
    enabling/disabling services, 978
    hardware configuration, 975-976
    method selection, 976
    package creation, 977-978
  troubleshooting printing problems, 213-214, 216
lisp mode (XEmacs), 164
Lisp programming language, 155
list box widget (Tcl/Tk), 803
listing
  directories, 29-30, 38
  processes, 50-51
listings
  conditional statements, 826
  embedded Python, 843
  globals() function, 825
  graphical directory listing, 838
  if/elsif/else (Perl), 764
  libmikmod sample module player, 698-699
  Perl program, 757
  posting to Usenet (Perl), 776
  purging log files (Perl), 775
  pytext script, 840

sendmail (Perl), 774
shorten Compress script, 696
shorten playback script, 695
lists
  bulleted (WordPerfect), 585
  Python, 816-817
    assigning values, 819
    copying, 823
    processing operators, 818
    sorting, 821
    tuples, 821
  Tcl/Tk, 791
    commands, 793-794
    creating, 791-792
    extracting elements, 791
    manipulating, 792
LIZARD, installing Caldera, 966-972
ln command, 936
loadable modules in kernel, 736-737
  configuration, 741
loading
  ALSA on startup, 687
  image files (xv), 621
  sound drivers
    automatically, 676
    manually, 673-676
local routes, 281
local variables
  C programming language, 882
  Tcl/Tk, 798
log analysis, 561
LogFormat statement (Apache), variables, 407

logging
  Apache, 406-407
  KDE, 24
  Linux, 25
  packets, 496
logging out
  KDE, 25
  NetWare servers, 374
logical font descriptions (X Windows), 99-100
logical partitions, 189
logins
  files, 239
  NDS, 372-373
  NetWare client for Linux, 372-373
  NetWare servers, 374-375
logout command, 73
logs, purging (Perl), 775
long int data type (C programming language), 862
loopback interface, 274
loopback routes, 280-281
looping constructs
  C programming language
    do, 873
    for, 874-875
    while, 872-873
  Perl
    do, while, 767
    for, 766
    foreach, 766
    until, 767
    while, 767
  Python, 823-824, 826-827
    control statements, 828
lossless audio encoding. See shorten, 695
lossy, 692
ls command, 29, 38
LTX2X, 668

lvalues (C programming language), 869
LyX, 654, 656-658
    pictures, 658-659
    tables, 659-662

M

M command (vi), 144
m4 configuration file (sendmail.mc), 450-452
m4 macros, Sendmail configuration, 452
Macintosh, interoperability with Linux, 17
Mail command (Start menu):StarOffice, 591
Mail Delivery Agent (MDA), 420-421
mail hubs, 454
    client configuration, 455-456
    configuring, 455, 457
    DNS configuration, 456-457
Mail Relay Host dialog box, 456
Mail Transport Agent (MTA), 420-421
Mail User Agent (MUA), 420-421
main function (C++ programming language), 892
make file system (mkfs) command, 193
Make It Fit command (WordPerfect Format menu), 582

Makefiles
    command-line options, 910-911
    editing source files, 904-907, 912
    implicit rules, 909-910
    variables, 907-908
man command, 924-925
man pages
    descript section, 46
    environment section, 46
    name section, 45
    sections, 43
    structure, 43
    synopsis section, 45
    xman command, 107
management
    StarOffice files, 588
    WordPerfect files, 579-580
manipulating sound, 687-689
maps (NIS), 326-327
    building databases, 330-331
    setting up sources, 329
margins (WordPerfect), 580
Margins command (WordPerfect Format menu), 580
MASQ target (firewall chain), 481
masquerading (IP), 502-504
master zones, 298-300
math module (Python), 852
md5sum program (file modification detection), 563
MDA (Mail Delivery Agent), 420-421

memory
    free command, 956-957
    swap space, 204
        enabling, 207-208
        formatting, 206
        swap files, 205-206
        swap partitions, 205
    virtual memory, 16
memory protection, 16
menu bars (StarOffice), 586
menus, 256
    COAS, 248-249
menus widget (Tcl/Tk), 805
messages (email), format, 422-423
meta-characters, atom expression, 943
methods (Python)
    copy( ), 823
    get( ), 823
mgetty, 317
    configuring, 317-318
MIDI (Musical Instrument Digital Interface), 700-701
    FM synthesis, 702
    GM (General MIDI System), 701
    software synthesis, 702-703
        Kmidi, 703
        SoftOSS, 703-705
        TiMidity++, 703-705
    Wavetable synthesis, 702
military institutional domains, 294
mime types, kfm, 124
mkdir command, 28, 40
mkfs command, 193
mkswap command, 206

/mnt directory, 235
mode line (XEmacs), 158
modifying. *See* editing
Module section
  (/etc/XF86Config file), 94
modules
  ALSA hardware, 685
  building, 749
  installing, 749
  Python
    commands, 854
    importing, 834
    math, 852
    os, 834
    shutil, 854
    string, 851
    sys, 849
    time, 852
    types, 850
  sound cards, 675
  soundcore, 674
  SoundTracker modules, 697
    libmikmod player, 697-698, 700
mogrify command (Image Magick), 633-634
Monitor section
  (/etc/XF86Config file), 95
monitoring diald, 323-324
monitors, configuring
  (X Windows), 91, 95
montage command
  (Image Magick), 634-635
more command, 42
Motion event
  (X Windows), 85
mount command, 194
Mount File System dialog box, 260
mount options, 196-197

mount points (directories, 32
mounting
  file systems, 193-194
    automatically, 195-196
    manually, 194-195
    options, 196-197
    root system, 193
  NFS volumes, 341
    mount options, 345-346
  SMB shares, 362-363
mount_point field
  (/etc/fstab file), 195
mouse
  acceleration, changing, 110
  configuring (X Windows), 90, 95
  kernel configuration, 746
  NIS, 252-253
  selecting files (XEmacs), 158
moving files, 38
moving through files
  vi, 142-143
    commands, 143-144
    line-by-line, 145-146
    moving to specific lines, 146
    paragraph-by-paragraph, 146
    scrolling, 147
    sentence-by-sentence, 146
    space-by-space, 145
    text searches, 147-148
    word-by-word, 145
  XEmacs, 156
MP3s (MPEG 1 Layer 3), 692
  archiving, 693
  bladeenc encoder, 694
  legality, 692
  quality, 693

mpag, 229
mpost utility (typesetting), 667
MTA (Mail Transport Agent), 420-421
MUA (Mail User Agent), 420-421
multicast packets, 268
multiple inheritance (C++ programming language), 894
music, typesetting, 669
Musical Instrumetn Digital Interface. *See* MIDI
MusicTeX, 669
mv command, 38
MX records, 296, 302, 456-457
MySQL, 594
  accessing binaries, 599
  administration, 600
    privilege system, 600, 602, 604-606
    setting root password, 600
  calculations, 612
  commands, 606
  databases, 606-607
    creating databases, 608-609
    creating tables, 609-610
    data types, 607-608
    removing, 608-609
    removing tables, 609-610
  DESCRIBE statement, 611
  INSERT statement, 611
  installing, 595
    files, 596-597, 599
    testing install, 599

keywords, 607
pattern matching, 612-613
reading data from files, 611
security, 600
SELECTstatement, 612
sorting rows, 612
stopping, 598
Mysql.server.script, 598

N

Name Resolver Setup dialog box, 250
name section (man pages), 45
name service switch (NIS), 332, 334
 actions, 334
NameError exception (Python), 837
names
 computers, hostname command, 954
 files, 580
  gcc, 902
 network devices, 274
  Ethernet interface, 275, 279
  loopback interface, 274
  PPP interface, 275
 zones, 298
namespaces (Python), 830-831
naming
 devices, 186-187
 directories, 38
 files, 38
 NIS domains, 329
 packages, 172
 partitions, 187

native language support, kernel configuration, 747
navigation
 vi, 142-143
  commands, 143-144
  line-by-line, 145-146
  moving around screens, 146
  moving to specific lines, 146
  paragraph-by-paragraph, 146
  scrolling, 147
  sentence-by-sentence, 146
  space-by-space, 145
  text searces, 147-148
  word-by-word, 145
 XEmacs, 156
NDS (Novel Directory Service), 369
 administration, 383-385, 387-391
 disk quotas, 391-392
 listing directory trees with nwwhoami utlity, 374-375
 login, 372-373
 servers, 392
 tree, 369-370
NetWare client, 368
 activating, 371
 configuring, 370
  environment variables, 370-371
 installing, 368
  NDS tree, 369-370
 login, 372-373
 NDS
  administration, 383-385, 387-391
  login, 372-373

printing, 375-377
NetWare servers, 373-374
 administration, 377-379, 381
 logging out, 374
 login information changes, 374-375
network category (KDE Control Center), 127
Network File System. *See* **NFS**
Network Information Service. *See* **NIS**
Network News Transfer Protocol (NNTP), 460
network security, 552
 daemons, 565
  TCP Wrappers, 565-567
 denial of service attacks, 557
 encryption
  GNU Privacy Guard, 571
  PGP (Pretty Good Privacy), 570
  public key cryptography, 571
  virtual private networks, 571
 file modification
  detecting, 563-564
  preventing, 562
 firewalls, 558-560
 network sniffing, 556
 passwords, 557
 port-scanning, 569
  Crack, 569
  nmap, 569
  open security solutions Web page, 570
  SAINT, 569
  Trinux, 569

privacy, 570
repair, 564
system logs, 561
   log analysis, 561
   signs of attack, 561
networks. *See also* **NIS**
  devices, 274
    names, 274-275, 279
  diagnostics programs
    ping, 288
    traceroute, 289-290
  firewalls. *See* firewalls
  interface, 268
    adding, 285-286
    configuration, 284-285
  IPaddress protection, 499-501
  kernel configuration, 743-744
  packages. *See* packages
  packets. *See* packets
  printing, 224
  protocols. *See* protocols
  resolver configuration, 288
  routing, 272, 274, 279
    adding routes, 282-283
    default routes, 281-282
    deleting routes, 283
    local routes, 281
    loopback routes, 280-281
  starting, 285
  stopping, 285
  TCP/IP configuration, 275
    ifconfig, 275-279
  TCP/IP networking, 17
  variable assignments, 283
New command (File menu)
  StarOffice, 589
  WordPerfect, 579
newsfeeds, 462-463

newsgroups, 19, 460-461
  downloading, 461-463
    INN, 464-469, 471-475
  newsfeeds, 462-463
  NNTP, 460
  preventing duplicate postings, 463
  pushing, 463
  TCP/IP, 460
  tin newsreader, 475
    configuring, 476
    installing, 476
newsreaders, tin, 475
  configuring, 476
  installing, 476
NFS (Network File System), 340
  automounting, 347-348
  client-server communications, 340-341
  configuring clients, 344-345
  configuring servers, 342-343
  /etc/exports file, 343
  /etc/fstab, 346
  mount options, 345-346
  mounting volumes, 341
  permissions, 342
  security, 340, 344
  showmount command, 347
  starting servers, 344
nG command (vi), 144
nH command (vi), 144
NIS (Network Information System), 249-250
  client tools, 335-337
  clients, 326
    setting up, 331-332
  domains, 326
    naming, 329

  maps, 326-327
    building databases, 330-331
    setting up sources, 329
  name service switch, 332, 334
    actions, 334
  peripherals
    keyboard, 251
    mouse, 252-253
    printer, 253-256
  Resolver, 250-251
  security, 331
  servers, 326
    password files, 329
    slave, 334-335
    starting, 331
  shadow passwords, 329
NIS servers, setting up, 329
NIS+, 327
nL command (vi), 144
nmap (port scanner), 569
NNTP (Network News Transfer Protocol), 460
NNTPCache, 462
noauto mount option, 196
nodeps option (rpm), 174
nodev mount option, 196
noexec mount option, 197
noncommercial organizations, 294
None values (Python), 820
Normal Colors command (xv Display menu), 618
nosuid mount option, 197
Novel Directory Service. *See* **NDS**
nroff mode (XEmacs), 164
NS record, 301-302

NS-type records, 296
nslookup, DNS setup, 304, 306
numbering
   lines in files, 41
   pages (WordPerfect documents), 583-584
numeric permissions, 202-203
numeric types (Python), 812
nwbprm command, 379
nwdsattrs command, 387
nwlogin command, 372-373
nwlogout command, 374
nwpasswd command, 375
nwwhomi uitlity, 374-375

O

o command (vi), 149
object files, 900
objects (Python)
   dictionaries, 821-822
   namespaces, 830-831
oct( ) function (Python), 832
octal digits (numeric permissions), 202
online documentation
   commands, 924-926
   /usr/doc files, 927
   /usr/doc/HOWTO, 927-928
   /usr/doc/LDP, 928-929
OOP (object-oriented programming), Python, 845, 847
   class definitions, 847-848
   inheritance, 849

Open command (File menu)
   StarOffice, 589
   WordPerfect, 579
open security solutions Web page, 570
Open Sound System. *See* OSS
open standards, 15
open( ) function (Python), 832
opening
   files
      kfm, 121
      WordPerfect, 579
      XEmacs, 158-159
   StarOffice documents, 589
   windows (WordPerfect), 579
OpenLinux. *See* Caldera OpenLinux
operators. *See also* arithmetic operators
   C programming language, 867-868
   comparison operators, 760
   find command, 935-936
   Tcl/Tk, 789, 791
/opt directory, 34
optimization, 985. *See also* performance
   partitions, 985-986
Options menu commands (BRU-2000)
   Backup, 545
   Restore, 548
options. *See* command-line options, 177
opts field (/etc/fstab file), 195
ord( ) function (Python), 832
os module (Python), 834

OSS (Open Sound System), 679-680
   commercial version, 681
   configuration news, 681-682
   downloading, 680-681
   industry news, 681-682
   installing, 680-681
   SoftOSS
      configuring, 682
      MIDI synthesis, 703-705
   SoundBlaster Live! support, 682
   Web site, 679
ouput, discarding, 37
outline mode (XEmacs), 164
outlines (WordPerfect), 585
output, stdout command, 60
overloading functions (C++), 894, 896
overwrite mode (XEmacs), 165
owner permissions (files), 198
ownership, changing in files, 204

P

package manager (KDE), 128-129
packages, 268. *See also* RPMs; software
   development, 178
   installing, 172-173
      checking for conflicts, 177
      conflicts, 176

dependencies, 174-175
FTP, 173-174
LISA, 977-978
listing files in, 183
names, 172
third-party, 911
uninstalling, 177-178
dependencies, 178-179
upgrading, 179-180
viewing information on, 180-181
information selection options, 182, 184
package selection options, 181-182
packets
broadcasts, 268
filtering, 479
IP packets, 479-481, 483
fragmentation, 493-494
logging, 496
multicast, 268
SYN, specifying, 492-493
Page command (WordPerfect Format menu), 580, 584
page numbering (WordPerfect documents), 583-584
page setup (WordPerfect documents), 580
panel, kwm (KDE window manager), 116
customzing, 118-119
PAP (Password Authentication Protocol), 314
secrets file, 315-316
parameters
bash shell, 719-720
commands, 385-388

partition tables, 189
partitions, 188, 978
adding to fstab, 981, 983
backups, 984
creating, 189-191
swap partitions, 981
deleting, 190
extended, 979-980
fragmentation, 983-984
hard drive space, 986-988
kernel configuration, 747
LISA install, 976
logical, 189
mount points, 32
naming, 187
optimizing for reliability, 985-986
performance, 984-985
primary, 189, 979
RAID, 983, 990, 992
configuring linear volumes, 996-997
configuring RAID 1 volumes, 997-999
configuring RAID 0 volumes, 994-995
implementing, 992-993
installing RAID Tools, 994
patching kernel, 993-994
swap, 205, 983
symlinks, 989-990
types, 191
unmounting, 980
pass statement (Python), 828
Password Authentication Protocol (PAP), 314
secrets file, 315-316

Password Expiration dialog box, 258
password files, NIS servers, 329
passwords
accounts, 258-259
changing, 25
computer security, 557
encrypted (Samba), 353
root, setting, 600
shadow, NIS, 329
pasting
text
vi, 154-155
XEmacs, 162
X Windows, 84
patch command, 949-950
patch files
SoftOSS MIDI synthesis, 704-705
TiMidity++, 704-705
path options (gcc), 903-904
path variable (tcsh), 76
pathnames, 27
pattern matching (MySQL), 612-613
patterns (awk), 722-723
PDF (Portable Document Format) printers, Samba configuration, 357-359
per-port options, PPP dial-in servers, 318-319
percent sign (%), Perl variables, 759
Perfect Colors command (xv Display menu), 618
performance. *See also* **optimization**
partitions, 984-985
period (.), wildcard character, 148

peripherals (NIS)
  keyboard, 251
  mouse, 252-253
  printer, 253-256
Perl
  accessing shell with backticks, 768-769
  arithmetic operators, 761
  comparison operators, 760
  compound operators, 761
  conditional statements
    if/else, 764
    unless, 765
  email, 774
  looping constructs
    do, while, 767
    for, 766
    foreach, 766
    until, 767
    while, 767
  posting to Usenet, 776
  purging logs, 775
  regexes, 767
  resources, 778-779
  sample program, 756-757
  Schwartzian transform, 777
  string constants, 763
  switches (command-line options), 770-773
  variables
    $_, 759
    arrays, 759
    hashes, 759
    scalar variables, 758
permissions, 30-31
  changing
    chmod command, 199
    symbolic permissions, 199-200
  device files, 555
  devices, 188

file, 198-199
  sgid bit, 201
  sticky bit, 201
  suid bit, 200
NFS, 342
numeric, 202-203
symbolic, 199-200
umask values, 203-204
PGP (Pretty Good Privacy), 570
pictures. See also graphics; images, LyX, 658-659
ping, 288
pipe character (|), 62
platters (hard disks), 189
Plextor CD-ROM drives, 690
plots, typesetting, 669-670
plug and play, kernel configuration, 742
plug-ins (GIMP), installing, 646
pnpdump command, 676
Point-to-Point Protocol. See PPP
Pointer section (/etc/XF86Config file), 95
pointers
  C programming language, 880-883, 885
  X Windows, 84
PopTop, 572
port numbers, RPC, 327
Port setting (Apache), 400
port-scanning, 569
  Crack, 569
  nmap, 569
  open security solutions Web page, 570

SAINT, 569
Trinux, 569
positional parameters, bash shell, 719-720
posting to Usenet
  Perl, 776
  preventing duplicates, 463
pound sign (#)
  comments in Tcl/Tk, 787
  Python comments, 815
PPP (Point-to-Point Protocol), 308
  authentication, 314-315
    CHAPsecrets file, 316
    PAPsecrets file, 315-316
  chat, 312, 314
  connecting to ISPs, 316-317
  dial-in servers, 317
    mgetty, 317-318
    per-port options, 318-319
    secrets file, 318
  interface, 275
  IPconfiguration options, 314
  kppp, 324
  pppd automation of links, 320
    diald, 321-324
  routing through links, 319-320
  running pppd, 310-312
  serial port configuration, 309
    hardware, 309-310
pppd, link automation, 320
  diald, 321-324
pppd command, running, 310-312

preprocessor (C programming language)
 conditional compilation, 887-888
 define directive, 886-887
 include directive, 886
Pretty Good Privacy (PGP), 570
primary partitions, 189, 979
print command (Python), 815
printenv command, 412
Printer Configuration dialog box, 222, 253
printer shares (Samba), 356-357
printers
 applications, 226, 228
 COAS (The Caldera Open Adminisration System), 220, 222
 commands, 217-219
 device files, 210-211
 laser, 212
 NIS, 253-256
 PDF (Portable Document Format), Samba configuration, 357-359
 port verification, 212
 remote, 222, 224
 selecting, 211
printing, 210-211
 calendars, 963
 device files, 211
 formatted, 225-226
 mpag, 229
 NetWare client, 375-377
 on networks, 224
 process, 219-220
 tools, 216, 229
 troubleshooting, 211-214, 216

private IPaddresses, 270
privilege system, MySQL, 600, 602, 604-605
 tables priv, 605-606
privilege tables (MySQL), 600, 602, 604-605
 columns priv, 605-606
 tables priv, 605-606
proc command (Tcl/Tk), 797-799
/proc directory, 33
 kernel administration, 244-246
processes
 background processes, 62-63
 KDETask Manager, 130-131
 kill command, 959-960
 listing, 50
 ps command, 959
 suspending, 63
 top command, 960-961
processing
 killing, 51
 listing, 51
processors, kernel configuration, 741
programming languages. *See* **C; C++; Perl;Tcl/Tk**
programs. *See* **applications**
prompt variable (tcsh), 76
prompt2 variable (tcsh), 76
prompt3 variable (tcsh), 76
properties (NetWare)
 creating, 378-379
 deleting, 379, 381

protocols, 268
 Challenge Handshake Authentication Protocol. *See* CHAP
 DHCP, 290
  client setup, 290
  server setup, 290-292
 ICMP (Internet Control Message), 269
 ihave/sendme, 463
 IP (Internet Protocol), 269
  addresses. *See* IP, addresses
 LCP (Link Control Protocol), 308
 NDS administration, 389-391
 NNTP (Network News Transfer Protocol), 460
 Password Authentication Protocol. *See* PAP
 PPP (Point-to-Point Protocol), 308
  authentication, 314-316
  chat, 312, 314
  connecting to ISPs, 316-317
  dial-in servers, 317-319
  IP configuration options, 314
  kppp, 324
  pppd automation of links, 320-324
  routing through links, 319-320
  running pppd, 310-312
  serial port configuration, 309-310
 SMB (Server Message Block), 350-351, 361-362

SMTP (Simple Mail
Transfer Protocol),
421-422
specifying, firewalls, 492
TCP (Transmission
Control Protocol), 269,
271-272
SYNpackets, 492-493
TCP/IP, 268-269
configuration, 275-279
*Usenet newsgroups,
460*
UDP (User Datagram
Protocol), 269, 272
proxies, 508-509, 511
application, 510-511
circuit-level, 510-511
clients, 510
firewalls, 509
routing, 509
servers, 510
*SOCKS, 511-512, 514,
517-518*
*Squid, 513, 521-523,
525-526*
TIS, 512, 518-521
ps command, 50, 959
KDE Task Manager,
130-131
PTR-type records, 296
**public key cryptography,
571**
pulling newsgroup postings, 463
purging logs (Perl), 775
pushing newsgroup postings, 463
**pytext script, 840-841,
843-845**

Python, 808-809
arithmetic operators, 813
benefits of, 809-810
code indentation, 816
commands
del, 820
print, 815
comments, 815
comparison operators,
823-824
object identity, 824
dictionaries, 821-822
copying, 823
embedded Python, 839
*pytext script, 841,
843-845*
*timestamps, inserting in
code, 843*
uses, 840
exceptions, 837
*try, except statement,
835*
*try, finally statement,
836*
functions
default arguments, 829
exec( ), 842
globals( ), 825
namespaces, 830-831
open( ), 832
range( ), 827
raw_input( ), 831
return statement, 829
type conversion functions, 832
type( ), 825
lists, 816-817
assigning values, 819
copying, 823
*processing operators,
818*
sorting, 821

looping constructs,
823-824, 826-828
methods
copy( ), 823
get( ), 823
modules
commands, 854
importing, 834
math, 852
os, 834
shutil, 854
string, 851
sys, 849
time, 852
types, 850
None values, 820
numeric types, 812
objects, deleting, 820
OOP, 845, 847
*class definitions,
847-848*
inheritance, 849
RAD (Rapid Application
Development), 809-810
scripts, 814
statements
break, 828
continue, 828
pass, 828
return, 829
while, 826
strings, 813-814
defining, 819
tuples, 821
Web site, 833, 855

Q

quantifiers, atom expression, 942-943
queries
    DNS, 295
    packages, 180-181
        information selection options, 182, 184
        package selection options, 181-182
question mark (?), bash wildcard character, 67
quitting. *See* exiting
quotas
    bindery servers, 381-383
    disk, 198
    NDS, 391-392

R

r command (vi), 150, 155
R option (Sox), 689
RAD (Rapid Application Development), Python, 809-810
radiobutton widget (Tcl/Tk), 803
RAID (Redundant Array of Inexpensive Disks, 990, 992
    configuring linear volumes, 996-997
    configuring RAID 1 volumes, 997-999
    configuring RAID0 volumes, 994-995
    implementing, 992-993
    patching kernel, 993-994
    RAIDTools, installing, 994

range( ) function (Python), 827
Raw command (xv Display menu), 618
raw_input( ) function (Python), 831
read permissions (files), 199
Read/Write Colors command (xv Display menu), 618
reading data from files (MySQL), 611
Real.com, 705
reboot command, 962
rebuilding
    kernel, 736-737
    sendmail.cf file, 424
records
    awk, 723
    CNAME (DNS), 302
    DNS, 296
    MX (DNS), 302
    NS (DNS), 301-302
    SOA (DNS), 300-301
recursion option, DNS configuration, 297
Red Hat Linux, 13
Red Hat Package Manager. *See* rpm
REDIRECT target (firewall chain), 481
redirecting I/O, 60-61
    pipe character, 62
redoing changes (vi), 155
Redundant Array of Inexpensive Disks. *See* RAID
regexes (Perl), 767
regular expressions, 941
    atom, 942
        alternation, 943
        concatenation, 943

        grouping, 944
        meta-characters, 943
        quantifiers, 942-943
REJECT target (firewall chain), 481
relative paths, 27
reliability, partitions, 985-986
remote printers, 222, 224
Remote Procedure Call. *See* RPC
removing
    databases (MySQL), 608-609
    directories, 28, 40
    files, 39-40
    tables (MySQL), 609-610
renaming. *See* naming
replacefiles option (rpm), 177
replacepkgs option (rpm), 176
replacing
    rules (firewall chains), 489
    text
        vi, 150-151
        XEmacs, 163
resizing windows (kwm), 116
Resolver, 250-251
    configuration, 288
resources (X Windows), 85-86, 88
    components, 86
    examples, 87
    listing, 86
    setting, 88
    values, 86
Resources utility, 261
Restore command (BRU-2000 Options menu), 548

restoring
  data, 530-531
    BRU-2000, 547-548
    cpio command, 540-541
    tar command, 540
  firewalls, 504
return statement
  C programming language, 875
  Python, 829
RETURN target (firewall chain), 481
reverse lookup files (DNS), 302-303
risk assessment (security), 551
rm command, 39-40
rmdir command, 28, 40
ro mount option, 196
root account, 24, 553
root directory, 33
root file system, mounting, 193
Root menu (xv), 619
root passwords, setting, 600
root prompt (#), 193
root servers, 294
route command, 279
routers, 268
routing, 272, 274, 279
  adding routes, 282-283
  default routes, 281-282
  deleting routes, 283
  local routes, 281
  loopback routes, 280-281
  proxies, 509
RPC (Remote Procedure Call), 327-328
  port numbers, 327
  servers, listing, 328

rpcinfo command, 328
rpm (Red Hat Package Manager), 172
  command-line options
    -a, 181
    -c, 183
    -d, 183
    -f, 182
    -i, 182
    -l, 183
    -p, 182
    -R, 184
    nodeps, 174
    replacefiles, 177
    replacepkgs, 176
  install mode, 172
  installing packages, 172-173
    checking for conflicts, 177
    conflicts, 176
    dependencies, 174-175
  query mode, 181
  uninstall mode, 178
  uninstalling packages, 177-178
    dependencies, 178-179
  upgrade mode, 180
  upgrading packages, 179-180
  viewing package information, 180-181
    information selection options, 182, 184
    package selection options, 181-182
RPM, 172
  KDE package manager, 128-129

rules
  firewall chains
    appending to end of chains, 488
    deleting, 489
    inserting, 489
    listing, 484-485
    replacing, 489
    side effects, 495-496
    specifying, 489-491
  implicit, Makefiles, 909-910
runlevels, 241-242
running Samba, 360
runtime server configurations (Apache), 398-399
rvalues (C programming language), 869

S

SAINT (port scanner), 569
Samba
  configuration, 351
    encrypted passwords, 353
    file shares, 354-356
    global options, 351, 353
    PDF (Portable Document Format) printer, 357-359
    printer shares, 356-357
    Web-based, 364-365
  debugging, 360
    configuration file, 360-361
  encrypted passwords, 353
    disabling, 353
  printing, 224
  running, 360

SMB, 350-351
  (Server Message Block), 350
  backup shares, 362
  client program, 361-362
  mounting shares, 362-363
  status, 363-364
Save As command (WordPerfect File menu), 579-580
savehist variable (tcsh), 76
saving
  files
    vi, 140-142
    WordPerfect, 579-580
    XEmacs, 160
  firewalls, 504
  images to file, GIMP, 643-644
  images to file (xv), 623-624
/sbin directory, 33, 232-233
scalable fonts (X Windows), 101
scalar variables (Perl), 758
scales widget (Tcl/Tk), 805
scheduling
  definitions (backups), 546-547
  tasks, 243-244
Schwartzian transform (Perl), 777
Screen section (/etc/XF86Config file), 96-97
screens (vi), navigating, 146

Script-Fu, 636, 645-646
  installing scripts, 646
ScriptAlias directory, 408
scripts
  awk, 722
    arrays, 726-728
    built-in functions, 732-733
    built-in variables, 725-726
    expressions, 728-729
    field separators, 725
    fields, 723
    invoking, 723-725
    patterns, 722-723
    records, 723
    statements, 729-732
    user-defined functions, 733-734
    variable assignments, 725
  configure, 912
  /etc/rc.d/init.d/network, 285
  mysql.server.script, 598
  Python, 814
  shell, 713
scrollbar widget (Tcl/Tk), 803
scrolling (vi), 147
SCSI devices, kernel configuration, 744
searching. *See also* **substituting**
  for text
    vi, 147-148
    XEmacs, 162
  grep command, 944, 946
secondary partitions. *See* **logical partitions**
sectors (hard disks), 189

security, 550
  attack techniques
    buffer overrun, 555
    denial of service, 557
    network sniffing, 556
    passwords, 557
    social engineering, 556
  backups, 552
  daemons, 565
    TCP Wrappers, 565-567
  employee computer crime, 551
  encryption
    GNU Privacy Guard, 571
    PGP (Pretty Good Privacy), 570
    public key cryptography, 571
    virtual private networks, 571
  file modification
    detecting, 563-564
    preventing, 562
  firewalls, 479, 509, 558-560
  hackers, 550
  MySQL, 600
  network security, 552
  NFS (Network File System), 340, 344
  NIS, 331
  permissions
    file, 198-199
    umask values, 203-204
  physical security, 551
  port-scanning, 569
    Crack, 569
    nmap, 569
    open security solutions Web page, 570

SAINT, 569
Trinux, 569
PPP, authentication, 314-316
privacy, *570*
repair, *564*
risk assessment, *551*
shadow passwords (NIS), *329*
system logs, *561*
log analysis, 561
signs of attack, 561
UNIX security model
access rights, 553
device files, 555
root account, 553
SUID program, 554-555, 560
sed commands, 946-949
addresses, *947*
programs, *947*
SELECT statement (MySQL), 612
selecting
files (XEmacs), *158*
printers, *211*
selections (X Windows), 84
Sendmail, 421
configuration files, *425-427, 429-450*
sendmail.cf example printout, 426-450
configuring, *423*
COAS, 453-454
m4 macros, 452
file locations, *423, 425*
m4 configuration file (sendmail.mc), *450-452*

Sendmail
Perl, *774*
SMTP (Simple Mail Transfer Protocol), *421-422*
sendmail.cf file
printout example, *426-450*
rebuilding, *424*
sendmail.mc file, 450-452
serial ports (PPP), configuration, 309-310
Server Side Includes. *See* SSI
ServerAdmin setting (Apache), 400
ServerFlags section (/etc/XF86Config file), 94
ServerName setting (Apache), 401
ServerRoot setting (Apache), 399
servers
Apache
logging, 406-407
name-based hosting, 405
starting, 413-415, 417
stopping, 413-415, 417
virtual hosting, 404
behavior, configuring (X Windows), *92*
bindery
file systems, 381-383
NetWare servers, 377-379, 381
quotas, 381-383
DHCP, *290*
configuration, 291-292
InterNet News. *See* INN
MySQL, *594*
accessing binaries, 599
administration, 600, 602, 604-606

calculations, 612
database management, 606-610
DESCRIBE statement, 611
INSERT statement, 611
installing, 595-597, 599
pattern matching, 612-613
reading data from files, 611
SELECT statement, 612
sorting rows, 612
stopping, 598
NDS, *392*
NetWare, *373-374*
administration, 377-379, 381
logging out, 374
login information changes, 374-375
NFS
configuring, 342-343
starting, 344
NIS (Network Information Service), *249, 326*
password files, 329
setting up, 329
slave, 334-335
starting, 331
proxies, *510*
firewalls, 509
SOCKS, 511-512, 514, 517-518
Squid, 513, 521-523, 525-526
TIS, 512, 518-521
root, *294*
RPC, listing, *328*
Samba. *See* Samba
X Windows, *81. See also* XFree86

ServerType setting (Apache), 399
services, 241-243
   LISA, enabling/disabling, 978
   NIS (Network Information Service), 249-250
      peripherals, 251-256
      Resolver, 250-251
set command, 412
set group id bit (file permissions), 201
set user id bit (file permissions), 200
setting resources (X Windows), 88
sgid bit (file permissions), 201
SGID program, computer security, 554-555, 560
shadow passwords (NIS), 329
shared libraries, 901
shares
   Samba
      files, 354-356
      printer, 356-357
   SMB
      backups, 362
      mounting, 362-363
shell prompt, 25
shell scripts, 713
shells, 35
   bash, 56, 710
      background processes, 62-63
      case statement, 715-716
      command history, 57-59
      comparing to tcsh, 72
      configuration files, 70-71
      environment, 712
      filename completion, 65-66
      for statement, 719
      functions, 720-721
      if statement, 714-715
      positional parameters, 719-720
      scripts, 713
      shell variables, 719-720
      syntax, 63, 65
      until statement, 717-718
      variables, 68-69, 711
      while statement, 717-718
      wildcards, 66-67
   tcsh
      command history, 73-74
      commands, 72
      comparing to bash, 72
      configuration files, 76, 78
      filename completion, 75-76
      variables, 76
.shn compressed files, playing, 695
short int data type (C programming language), 862
shortcut keys (WordPerfect), 579
Shorten, 695, 697
   downloading, 695
   installing, 695
showmount command (NFS), 347
shutdown command, 962
shutil module (Python), 854
Simple Mail Transfer Protocol. See SMTP
single quotes ('), bash syntax, 64
sites (Web)
   AmiNet modules archive, 699
   Apache, 396
   cdparanoia download, 691
   Crack, 569
   FreeS/WAN, 572
   Freshmeat, 694, 705
   GIMP, 636, 646
   GNU Privacy Guard, 571
   Image Magick, 636
   Linux Documentation Project (LDP), 19
   nmap, 569
   open security solutions, 570
   OSS, 679
   Perl, 779
   PGP (Pretty Good Privacy), 570
   PopToP, 572
   portal sites, 19
   Python, 833, 855
   real.com, 705
   SAINT, 569
   SoundBlaster, 682
   TiMidity++, 703
   Tony's Cambridge University, 695
   Trinux, 569
   Tripwire Security, 563
   Utopia Sound Division, 705
   XEmacs, 166
Sizefmt command, 410

sizing windows (kwm), 116
slash (/)
  comments in C programming language, 860
  pathnames, 27
slave servers (NIS), 334-335
slave zones, 298
Smooth command (xv Display menu), 618
SMB (Server Message Block), 350-351
  client program, 361-362
  shares
    backups, 362
    mounting, 362-363
Smbclient, 361-362
Smbstatus command, 363-364
Smbtestparm, 360-361
SMTP (Simple Mail Transfer Protocol), 421-422
SOA record, 300-301
SOCKS, 511-512, 514, 517-518
SoftOSS
  configuring, 682
  MIDI synthesis, 703
  patch files, 704-705
software, 264. *See also* **packages**
  Caldera OpenLinux, 18
  GNU General Public License, 14
  INN, 464-465
  proxy
    SOCKS, 511-512, 514, 517-518
    Squid, 513, 521-523, 525-526
    TIS, 512, 518-521

software MIDI synthesis, 702-703
  Kmidi, 703
  SoftOSS, 703
    patch files, 704-705
  TiMidity++, 703
    installing, 703
    patch files, 704-705
Software Package Pre-Selection dialog box, 977
Software Selection dialog box, 264
sorting
  lists (Python), 821
  rows (MySQL), 612
sound, 672
  ALSA (Advanced Linux Sound Architecture), 683-684
    downloading, 684
    hardware modules, 685
    hardware supported, 683
    installing, 684-685
    loading on startup, 687
    testing, 685-687
  configuring, 682
  converting, 687-689
  digital audio data, extracting, 689-691
  kernel configuration, 748
  Linux Kernel sound, 673
    automatically configuring, 676
    ISA PnP cards, 676-679
    manual configuration, 673-676
  lossless audio encoding. *See* shorten
  manipulating, 687-689

MIDI (Musical Instrument Digital Interface), 700-701
  FM synthesis, 702
  GM (General MIDI System), 701
  software synthesis, 702-705
  Wavetable synthesis, 702
MP3s (MPEG 1 Layer 3), 692
  archiving, 693
  bladeenc encoder, 694
  legality, 692
  quality, 693
OSS (Open Sound System), 679-680
  commercial version, 681
  configuration news, 681-682
  downloading, 680-681
  industry news, 681-682
  installing, 680-681
SoftOSS
shorten, 695, 697
  downloading, 695
  installing, 695
SoftOSS, MIDI synthesis, 703-705
SoundTracker modules, 697
  libmikmod player, 697-698, 700
testing, 674
sound cards, 673
  Ensoniq Audio PCi, 675
  ISA PnP cards, 676-679
    configuring at boot time, 679
  kernel modules, 675

SoundBlaster, 675
SoundBlaster Live!, OSS support, 682
SoundBlaster PCI 64/128, 675
sound category (KDEControl Center), 128
sound drivers
  loading
    automatically, 676
    manually, 673-676
SoundBlaster Live!, OSS support, 682
SoundBlaster PCI 64/128 sound card, 675
SoundBlaster sound cards, 675
SoundBlaster Web site, 682
soundcore module, 674
SoundTracker modules, 697
  libmikmod player, 697-698, 700
    downloading, 697
    installing, 698
    testing, 698-700
source command, 73
  Tcl/Tk, 796
source files, 900
  GNU C, editing, 904-912
Source Selection dialog box, 265
Sox, 687-689
  file types supported, 688
space
  disks
    df command, 957
    du command, 958
  hard drives, partitions, 986-988

spacing lines in WordPerfect documents, 582
Squid, 513, 521-523, 525-526
SSI (Server Side Includes), 408
  directives, 409-412
  flow control, 412-413
StarOffice, 585
  creating templates, 589
  customizing workspace, 588
  desktop, 586-587
    Beamer, 588
    Explorer, 588
    toolbars, 586
    windows, 587
  documents, 589
    creating, 589
    opening, 589
  email, 590-591
  events, 589-590
    creating appointments, 590
    editing appointments, 590
  file management, 588
  FTP, 591
  installation, 586
Start menu commands (StarOffice), Mail, 591
startup, loading ALSA, 687
startup files (INN), 468-469, 471-472
starting
  Apache, 413-415, 417
  networking, 285
  NFS servers, 344
  NIS servers, 331

vi, 138-139
X Windows, 101-102
XEmacs, 157-158
statements
  awk scripting, 729
    break, 731
    continue, 731
    delete, 731
    do, 730
    exit, 731
    for, 730
    I/O, 731-732
    if, 730
    while, 730
  bash shell
    case, 715-716
    for, 719
    if, 714-715
    until, 717-718
    while, 717-718
  break (Python), 828
  C programming language, 866
    declarations, 866
    definitions, 867
    do, 873
    expressions, 867, 869
    for, 874-875
    if, 870-871
    return, 875
    switch, 871-872
    while, 872-873
  if/else (Perl), 764
  MySQL
    DESCRIBE, 611
    INSERT, 611
    SELECT, 612
  Python
    continue, 828
    pass, 828
    try, except, 835

statements

try, finally, 836
return, 829
while, 826
unless (Perl), 765
static variables (C programming language), 864
stderr command, 61
stdin command, 61
stdout command, 60
sticky bits (file permissions), 201
stopping
    Apache, 413-415, 417
    MySQL, 598
    networking, 285
storage classes (variables)
    C programming language, 863-864
    statements, 866
storing files (Sendmail), 423, 425
str( ) function (Python), 832
string (Perl constants), 763
string module (Python), 851
strings
    C programming language, 878
    Python, 813-814
        defining, 819
structures
    C programming language, 878, 880
        pointers, 885
stub zone, 298
substituting text (vi), 151-153
suid bit (file permissions), 200

SUID program, computer security, 554-555, 560
SuperProbe program, 89
superuser, root account, 24
suspending processes, 63
swap partitions, 983
    creating, 981
swap space, 204
    disabling, 208
    enabling, 207
    formatting, 206
    swap files, 205-206
    swap partitions, 205
SWAT, 364
switch command (Tcl/Tk), 796
switch statement (C programming language), 871-872
switches (Perl), 770-773
switching directories, 38
symbolic links, 31-32
symbolic permissions, 199-200
symlinks, partitions, 989-990
SYN packets, specifying, 492-493
synopsis section (man pages), 45
syntax
    bash, 63, 65
    find command, 931-936
sys module (Python), 849
System Hostname dialog box, 261
System Load Average dialog box, 262
system logs, 561
    log analysis, 561
    signs of attack, 561

System Resource Information dialog box, 261-262
System Services dialog box, 259
System Time dialog box, 263
system up time, 955
System V model, 241

T

t option (Sox), 688-689
tables
    loopback routes, 280-281
    LyX, 659-662
    MySQL, sorting rows, 612
    privilege (MySQL), 600, 602, 604-606
tables priv, 605-606
tabs (WordPerfect documents), 581-582
tail command, 938-939
Tangle, 668
tape backups, 539
tape drives, kernel configuration, 746
tar command, 533-534, 537-539, 951-953
    GNU version, 537
    restoring data, 540
targets
    firewall chains, 481
    specifying, 494-495
task bars (StarOffice), 587
Task Manager (KDE), 130-131
tasks, scheduling, 243-244
Tcl/Tk, 782
    " (double quotes), 786
    backslash substitution, 786

brace quoting, 787
command substitution, 785
commands
   break, 796
   continue, 796
   eval, 797
   for, 795
   foreach, 795
   if, 794
   proc, 797-799
   source, 796
   switch, 796
   while, 794
comments, 787
expressions, 789
extensions, 783-784
functions, 791
lists, 791
   commands, 793-794
   creating, 791-792
   extracting elements, 791
   manipulating, 792
operators, 789, 791
Tcl extensions, 805
Tk widget set, 799, 801-803
variables, 784-785, 787, 798
   arrays, 788-789

TCP (Transmission Control Protocol), 271-272
specifying SYNpackets, 492-493

TCP Wrappers, 565
tcpd, 566-567

TCP/IP, 268-269
configuration, 275
   ifconfig, 275-279
Usenet newsgroups, 460

TCP/IP networking, 17

tcpd, 565-567

tcsh, 35
command history, 73-74
commands, 72
comparing to bash, 72
configuration files, 50, 76, 78
filename completion, 75-76
variables, 76

templates (StarOffice), creating, 589

terminal emulators
xterm, 103-104
   fonts, 103
   main options, 104
   scrollbar navigation, 104
   VT options, 103

testing
ALSA, 685-687
libmikmod module player, 698-700
MySQLinstall, 599
sound, 674

tests, find command, 932-934

TeX, 650

tex mode (XEmacs), 164

text
changing (vi), 150-151
copying
   vi, 154-155
   XEmacs, 162
cutting
   vi, 154-155
   XEmacs, 162
deleting
   vi, 153-154
   XEmacs, 161
finding in files, grep command, 944, 946

inserting (vi), 149-150
joining lines (vi), 155
pasting
   vi, 154-155
   XEmacs, 162
replacing
   vi, 150-151
   XEmacs, 163
searching for
   vi, 147-148
   XEmacs, 162
streams, sed command, 946-947
substituting (vi), 151-153

text editors.
See vi: XEmacs

text widget (Tcl/Tk), 803

third-party packages, 911

time, 263

time module (Python), 852

Timefmt command, 410

TiMidity++, 703
installing, 703
patch files, 704-705

TiMidity++ Web site, 703

tin, 475
configuring, 476
installing, 476

TIS (Trusted Information System), 512, 518-519
configuration, 519-521
installing, 519-521

title bar
KDE window manager, 115
StarOffice, 586

Tk. *See* Tcl/Tk/tmp directory, 33, 236-237

Tony's Cambridge University Web site, 695

toolbars
  GIMP, 639-640
  StarOffice, 586
top command, 960-961
traceroute, 289-290
tracks (hard disks), 189
Transmission Control Protocol. *See* **TCP**
Trinux (port scanner), 569
Tripwire package(file modification detection), 563
troff command, 226
troubleshooting, 53
  printing, 211-214, 216
  Samba, 360
    configuration file, 360-361
Trusted Information Systems. *See* **TIS**
try, except statement (Python), 835
try, finally statement (Python), 836
tuples (Python), 821
twm (window manager), 84
type conversion functions (Python), 832
type field (/etc/fstab file), 195
type( ) function (Python), 825
types module (Python), 850
typesetting, 650
  creating documents, 651
    LaTeX, 651-662
  DVIcopy, 650
  Feynman diagrams, 670

  LaTeX, 651-654
    creating input file, 654-662
    LyX, 654, 656-662
  music, 669
  plots, 669-670
  TeX, 650
  utilities, 662, 667
    CWEB2HTML, 668-669
    dmp, 666
    dvilj, 666
    dvipdfm, 666
    dvips, 665-666
    dvitomp, 666
    ghostsript, 664
    laTeX2HTML, 668
    LTX2X, 668
    mpost, 667
    Tangle, 668
    Weave, 668
    Wp2latex, 667
    xdvi, 662-663
    XV, 664-665
Typesetting command (WordPerfect Format menu), 583

U

U command (vi), 155
UDP (User Datagram Protocol), 269, 272
umask values, 203-204
unalias command, 73
uncompressing files, gzip command, 950-951
undoing changes (vi), 155
uninstalling packages, 177-179. *See also* **installing**

UNIX
  compatibility with Linux, 15
  history, 8, 10-11
  man pages, structure, 43
  philosophy of, 11
  Sendmail, 421
    configuration files, 425-427, 429-450
    configuration files, example printout, 426-450
    configuring, 423
    configuring with COAS, 453-454
    configuring with m4 macros, 452
    file locations, 423, 425
    m4 configuration file (sendmail.mc), 450-452
    SMTP (Simple mail Transfer Protocol), 421-422
UNIX security model
  access rights, 553
  device files, 555
  root account, 553
  SUID program, 554-555, 560
unless statement (Perl), 765
unmounting partitions, 980
unsigned int data type (C programming language), 862
until loop (Perl), 767
until statement (bash shell), 717-718

updating
  buffers (XEmacs), 161
  files, patch command, 949-950
upgrading packages, 179-180
uptime command, 955
URLs (FTP), 173-174
Use Own Colormap command (xv Display menu), 618
Use Std. Colormap command (xv Display menu), 618
Usenet
  downloading, 461-463
    INN, 464-469, 471-475
  newsfeeds, 462-463
  NNTP, 460
  posting to (Perl), 776
  preventing duplicate postings, 463
  pushing, 463
  TCP/IP, 460
  tin newsreader, 475
    configuring, 476
    installing, 476
User Accounts dialog box, 256-257
User Datagram Protocol. *See* UDP
user mount option, 196
User setting (Apache), 400
user-defined functions (awk scripting), 733-734
UserDir setting (Apache), 401
users, management, 238-239

/usr directory, 237-238
  Linux Filesystem Standard, 34
/usr/bin/chfn, 240-241
/usr/bin/passwd, 240
/usr/doc directory, documentation files, 927
/usr/doc/HOWTO, documentation files, 927-928
/usr/doc/LDP, documentation files, 928-929
/usr/libexec/inn/bin/rc.news, 470-472
/usr/sbin directory, 241
/usr/sbin/useradd, 239
/usr/sbin/userdel, 240
/usr/sbin/usermod, 240
utilities
  typesetting, 662, 667
    CWEB2HTML, 668-669
    dmp, 666
    dvilj, 666
    dvipdfm, 666
    dvips, 665-666
    dvitomp, 666
    ghostscript, 664
    laTeX2HTML, 668
    LTX2X, 668
    mpost, 667
    Tangle, 668
    Weave, 668
    Wp2latex, 667
    XV, 664-665
    xvi, 662-663
Utopia Sound Division Web site, 705

V

values (X Windows resources), 86
/var directory, 236-237
variables
  assignments, 283
  awk scripting
    assigning, 725
    built-in, 725-726
  bash shell, 711
    shell, 719-720
  C programming language, 861-862
    arrays, 877-878
    declaring in, 862
    naming in, 863
    pointers, 880-883, 885
    storage classes, 863-864, 866
    strings, 878
    structures, 878, 880
    variable scope, 863
  environment (NetWare client), 370-371
  LogFormat statement (Apache), 407
  Makefiles, 907-908
  Perl
    $_, 759
    arrays, 759
    hashes, 759
    scalar variables, 758
    Schwartzian transform, 777
  shell, 68-69
  Tcl/Tk, 784-785, 787, 798
    arrays, 788-789
  tcsh, 76
vfat file system, 192

vi, 136-137
  command mode, 138
  commands
    /pattern, 147
    3cw, 150
    3dl, 153
    3dw, 153
    4dd, 154
    6x, 154
    :q, 140
    :q!, 140
    :w, 140
    :w!, 140
    :wq, 140
    a, 149
    c$, 150
    c), 150
    cw, 150
    c^, 150
    c}, 150
    D, 154
    d$, 153
    d0, 153
    dd, 154
    dw, 153
    i, 149
    J, 155
    movement, 143-144
    o, 149
    R, 150, 155
    u, 155
    x, 154
    y, 154-155
    y$, 155
    y), 155
    y0, 154
    yank, 154
    yw, 154
    yy, 155
    y}, 155
    ZZ, 140
  exiting, 140-142
  files
    creating, 138-139
    saving, 140-142
  history, 137
  input mode, 138
  interface, 136
  navigation, 142-143
    commands, 143-144
    line-by-line, 145-146
    moving around screens, 146
    moving to specific lines, 146
    paragraph-by-paragraph, 146
    scrolling, 147
    sentence-by-sentence, 146
    space-by-space, 145
    text searches, 147-148
    word-by-word, 145
  running, 138-139
  text
    changing, 150-151
    copying, 154-155
    cutting, 154-155
    deleting, 153-154
    inserting, 149-150
    joining lines, 155
    pasting, 154-155
    replacing, 150-151
    substituting, 151-153
video card, configuring (X Windows), 90-91
video for Linux, kernel configuration, 746
video hardware, identifying (XFree86), 89
video mode, tuning, 108
View menu (kfm), 122
viewers
  ghostscript, 664
  xdvi, 662-663
  XV, 664-665
viewing
  file contents, 41-42
    more command, 42
  fonts (X Windows), 100
virtual command, 411
virtual consoles, 46
virtual desktops (kwm), 120
virtual functions (C++ programming language), 893-894
virtual hosting, 404
  address-based virtual hosts, 404
  name-based virtual hosts, 405
virtual memory, 16
virtual private networks, 571
Visible Domain dialog box, 456
Visual Schnauzer, 620
void data type (C programming language), 862
VT options, 103

W

W command (vi), 143
watch variable (tcsh), 76
WAV files, compressing, 696
Wavetable synthesis (MIDI), 702
Weave, 668
Web browser (kfm), 123

WEB languages, 667
　Tangle, 668
　Weave, 668
Web servers, Apache, 17, 396-397
　configuration, 398-404
　installation, 397-398
Web sites
　AmiNet modules archive, 699
　Apache, 396
　cdparanoia download, 691
　Crack, 569
　FreeS/WAN, 572
　Freshmeat, 694, 705
　GIMP, 636, 646
　GNU Privacy Guard, 571
　Image Magick, 636
　Linux Documentation Project (LDP), 19
　nmap, 569
　open security solutions, 570
　OSS, 679
　Perl, 779
　PGP (Pretty Good Privacy), 570
　PopToP, 572
　portal sites, 19
　Python, 833, 855
　real.com, 705
　SAINT, 569
　SoundBlaster, 682
　TiMidity++, 703
　Tony's Cambridge University, 695
　Trinux, 569
　Tripwire Security, 563
　Utopia Sound Division, 705
　XEmacs, 166
Web-based Samba configuration, 364-365

while command (Tcl/Tk), 794
while loop (Perl), 767
while statement
　awk scripting, 730
　bash shell, 717-718
　C programming language, 872-873
　Python, 826
Who Am I? commands, 954-955
widgets (Tcl/Tk), 799, 801-803
wildcards
　bash, 66-67
　text searches
　　vi, 147-148
window manager (kwm), 113-114
　Application Starter, 117-118
　buttons, 114-115
　desktop menu, 120
　panel, 116
　　customizing, 118-119
　resising windows, 116
　title bars, 115
　virtual desktops, 120
window managers (X Windows), 82, 84
Windows, interoperability with Linux, 17
windows
　focus, 85
　opening, WordPerfect, 579
　resizing in kwm, 116
　StarOffice, 587
　XEmacs, 156
　　multiple, 165
windows category (KDE Control Center), 128

Windows menu (xv), 620
word processing applications
　StarOffice. *See* StarOffice
　WordPerfect. *See* WordPerfect
WordPerfect, 578
　bulleted lists, 585
　configurations, 585
　creating documents, 579
　file management, 579-580
　formatting documents, 580
　　centering pages, 584
　　fonts, 582-583
　　justification, 581
　　line spacing, 582
　　page numbering, 583-584
　　page setup, 580
　　tabs, 581-582
　graphics, 584
　installation, 578
　opening files, 579
　opening windows, 579
　outlines, 585
　saving files, 579-580
　shortcut keys, 579
working directory, 27
Wp2latex utility (typesetting), 667
write permissions (files), 199

X

x command (vi), 154
X terminals, 81
X Windows. *See also* **XFree86**
　architecture, 82
　client/server relationship, 80-81

X WINDOWS

clients, 102
  options, 102
  xcalc, 106
  xclock, 105
  xload, 105
  xterm, 103-104
colors, specifying, 97-98
commands
  xbiff, 106
  xeyes, 107
  xman, 107
  xset, 108-110
  xvidtune, 108
displays, 81-82
events, 85
focus, 85
fonts, 98
  descriptions, 99-100
  scalable, 101
  viewing, 100
history, 80
interface, 82-83
mechanism versus policy, 82
pointer, 84
resources, 85-86, 88
  components, 86
  examples, 87
  listing, 86
  setting, 88
  values, 86
selections, 84
server, 81
starting, 101-102
terminals, 81
window managers, 82, 84
xbiff command, 106
xcalc, 106
xclock, 105
xdvi utility (typesetting), 662-663

XEmacs, 155-156
buffer
  editing, 161-162
  updating, 161
buffers, 156
commands
  Ctrl+x 0, 165
  Ctrl+x 1, 166
  Ctrl+x 2, 166
  Ctrl+x 3, 166
echo line, 158
exiting, 160
files
  closing (without saving), 161
  creating, 160
  opening, 158-159
  saving, 160
  selecting, 158
frames, 156
interface, 157
mode line, 158
modes, 161, 163
  asm, 164
  auto fill, 165
  auto save, 165
  blink parenl, 165
  c, 164
  c++, 164
  font lock, 165
  fortran, 164
  fundamental, 164
  line number, 165
  lisp, 164
  nroff, 164
  outline, 164
  overwrite, 165
  tex, 164
navigation, 156
starting, 157-158

text
  copying, 162
  cutting, 162
  deleting, 161
  pasting, 162
  replacing, 163
  searching for, 162
user manuals, 166
Web site, 166
windows, 156
  multiple, 165
xeyes command, 107
xf86config program, 92-93
XF86Setup program, 89
XFree86
configuring, 88
  configuration file, 93-97
  graphics modes, 91
  keyboard, 90
  monitors, 91
  mouse, 90
  server behavior, 92
  video card, 90-91
  video hardware, identifying, 89
  xf86config, 92-93
  XF86Setup program, 89
files, specifyinig location, 93-94
xload, 105
xman command, 107
xrdb command, 86, 88
xset command
bell volume, 108
DPMS, 109
font path, 109-110
key click, 109
mouse acceleration, 110

xterm terminal emulator, 103-104
   fonts, 103
   main options, 104
   scrollbar navigation, 104
   VT options, 103

xv (image manipulation program), 616
   24/8 Bit menu, 619
   Algorithms menu, 619
   Display menu, 618
   image files, loading, 621
   Image Size menu, 621
   images, saving to file, 623-624
   Root menu, 619
   Windows menu, 620

XV utility (typesetting), 664-665

xvidtune command, 108

Y

y command (vi), 154-155
y$ command (vi), 155
y) command (vi), 155
y0 command (vi), 154
yank command (vi), 154
Yellow Pages (YP). *See* NIS
ypbind program, 331
ypcat command, 336
ypmatch command, 336
yppasswd command, 337
yppasswdd program, 331
ypserv program, 331
ypwhich command, 336
ypxfr command, 335
yw command (vi), 154
yy command (vi), 155
y} command (vi), 155

Z

ZeroDivisionError exception (Python), 837

zones
   DNS configuration, 298-300
   hint, 298
   master, 298-300
   slave, 298
   stub, 298

ZZ command (vi), 140